FOURTH EDITION

The Handbook of

Mortgage Backed Securities

❖

Frank J. Fabozzi

EDITOR

McGraw-Hill

New York San Francisco Washington, D.C. Auckland Bogatá
Caracas Lisbon London Madrid Mexico City Milan
Montreal New Delhi San Juan Singapore
Sydney Tokyo Toronto

McGraw-Hill

A Division of The **McGraw·Hill** *Companies*

ISBN 1-55738-576-9

Printed in the United States of America

BB

3 4 5 6 7 8 9 0

AR

Contents

Preface

The Handbook of Mortgage-Backed Securities, Fourth Edition, is designed to provide not only the fundamentals of these securities and the investment characteristics that make them attractive to a broad range of investors, but also extensive coverage on the state-of-the-art strategies for capitalizing on the opportunities in this market. The book is intended for both the individual investor and the professional manager.

To be effective, a book of this nature should offer a broad perspective. The experience of a wide range of experts is more informative than that of a single expert, particularly because of the diversity of opinion on some issues. I have chosen some of the best known practitioners to contribute to this book. Most have been actively involved in the evolution of the mortgage-backed securities market.

DIFFERENCES BETWEEN THE THIRD AND FOURTH EDITIONS

Money managers must justify their management and transaction costs to clients. Consequently, all money managers eventually must demonstrate to their clients how much *value* they've added to portfolio performance above and beyond what could have been achieved by employing a lower-cost, buy-and-hold strategy. As the editior of *The Handbook of Mortgage-Backed Securities,* I am effectively the portfolio manager of the assets of this book—the chapters. The fourth edition must justify to my current clients (those who purchased the third edition of the *Handbook*) why they should not follow a buy-and-hold strategy of simply continuing to use the third edition and reduce advisory fees and transaction costs (i.e., the cost of this book). In short: What value has been added to the third edition?

The differences between the third and fourth editions are summarized below. The number of chapters has been reduced from 41 chapters to 39 chapters. However, 27 of the chapters are either new or have been substantially revised. Consequently, this book can be characterized as a new book, reflective of the dynamic changes that have occurred in this market in terms of new product development and advances in technologies since the publication of the third edition in 1992. There is much more detailed coverage on the following topics: prepayment behavior and modeling, whole-loan CMOs, commercial mortgage-backed securities, and option-adjusted spread analysis.

SUMMARY OF DIFFERENCES BETWEEN THIRD AND FOURTH EDITIONS

The third edition has 41 chapters and an appendix, divided into the following seven sections:

    I.   Mortgage Products
   II.   Pass-Through Securities
  III.   Prepayment Forecasting
  IV.   Collateralized Mortgage Obligations and Stripped MBS
   V.   Valuation Techniques
  VI.   Portfolio Strategies
 VII.   Accounting, Tax and Operational Considerations

The fourth edition has 39 chapters and an appendix, divided into the following eight sections:

    I.   Mortgages and Pass-Through Securities
   II.   Prepayment Behavior and Forecasting
  III.   Stripped Mortgage-Backed Securities
  IV.   Collateralized Mortgage Obligations
   V.   Commercial Mortgage-Backed Securities
  VI.   Valuation Techniques and Risk Measurement
 VII.   Hedging Strategies
VIII.   Accounting and Tax Considerations

The following 27 of the 39 chapters in the fourth edition are new or substantially revised:

  2. Mortgages
  3. Mortgage Pass-Through Securities
  4. Agency Adjustable-Rate Mortgage Securities
  5. Trading, Settlement, and Clearing Procedures for Agency MBS
  6. Collateralized Borrowing via Dollar Rolls
  7. Multifamily Project Securities

ACKNOWLEDGEMENTS

I would like to express my appreciation to the contributors and their organizations. Special thanks to Michael Ferri of George Mason University for reviewing the entire manuscript and assisting in various ways. The following individuals assisted in various ways: Scott Amero (BlackRock Financial Management), Keith Anderson (BlackRock Financial Management), Cliff Asness (Goldman Sachs Asset Management), Charles Basner (TIPS), David Canuel (Aletus Investment Management), Andrew S. Carron (First Boston), Jeff Detwiller (RFC Corporation), M. Song Jo (Alex. Brown & Sons), Frank J. Jones (Guardian Life Insurance), Matt Mancuso (Bear Stearns), Jan Mayle (TIPS), Ed Murphy (Merchants Mutual Insurance Company), Scott Pinkus (Goldman Sachs), Frank Ramirez (Alex. Brown & Sons), Chuck Ramsey (Alex. Brown & Sons), Nicholas Wentworth (Investment Advisors, Inc.), and David Yuen (Alex. Brown & Sons).

Frank J. Fabozzi

Contributing Authors

Chris Ames
Director
Mortgage Strategies Group
Lehman Brothers International (Europe)

William A. Barr
Vice President
Fuji Securities Inc.

William Batts, Jr.
Director, Multifamily Credit Risk
Federal National Mortgage Association

Anand K. Bhattacharya, Ph.D.
Managing Director of
 Financial Strategies Group
Mortgage and Asset Finance Group
Prudential Securities Inc.

Jeffrey Biby
Vice President
Mortgage Strategies Group
Lehman Brothers

Douglas T. Breeden, Ph.D.
President and Chairman of the Board
Smith Breeden Associates, Inc. and
Research Professor of Finance
Fuqua School of Business, Duke University

Vernon H. Budinger, C.F.A.
Director
Financial Strategies Group
Global Advanced Technology

Steven J. Carlson
Managing Director
Emerging Markets
Lehman Brothers

Patrick J. Corcoran, Ph.D.
Vice President
Nomura Securities International, Inc.

Ed Daingerfield
Managing Director
Bear Stearns & Co., Inc.

Andrew S. Davidson
President
Andrew Davidson & Co., Inc.

Nancy DeLiban
Managing Director
Bear Stearns & Co., Inc.

Kimbell R. Duncan
Mortgage Securities Product Manager
Nomura International PLC (NIP)

Lynn M. Edens
Vice President
Goldman, Sachs & Co.

Frank Fabozzi, Ph.D., C.F.A.
Editor, *Journal of Portfoilo Management*
Adjunct Professor of Finance
School of Management, Yale University

Yizhong Fan, Ph.D.
Consultant
Financial Strategies Group
Global Advanced Technology

Evan B. Firestone
Director
Mortgage Products Group
CS First Boston Corporation

Jacqueline Galdieri
Senior Associate of the Primary Marketing Group
Market Group
Prudential Securities Inc.

Sean Gallop
Vice President
Nomura Securities International, Inc.

Michael J. Giarla
Chief Operating Officer
Smith Breeden Associates, Inc.
President, Smith Breeden Family of Mutual Funds

Bennett W. Golub, Ph.D.
Partner
BlackRock Financial Management

Mark N. Gordon
Senior Vice President
Mortgage Research
Kidder, Peabody & Co., Inc.

Lakhbir S. Hayre, DPhil
Director of Mortgage Research
Salomon Brothers

Michael D. Herskovitz
Morgan Stanley

Joseph C. Hu, Ph.D.
Senior Vice President
Director of Mortgage Research
Oppenheimer & Co., Inc.

David P. Jacob
Managing Director and Director of Research
Nomura Securities International, Inc.

Duen-Li Kao
Director
General Motors Investment
    Management Corporation

Adrian Katz
Director
Prudential Securities Inc.

Robert W. Kopprasch, Ph.D., C.F.A.
Senior Vice President
Alliance Capital Management, L.P. New York

Robert Kulason
Salomon Brothers

Brian P. Lancaster
Managing Director
Bear Stearns & Co., Inc.

Michael Levine
Vice President
Mortgage Trading
Bear Stearns & Co., Inc.

Linda Lowell
First Vice President
Mortgage Strategies
PaineWebber, Inc.

Bruce Mahood
Vice President
Merrill Lynch Capital Markets

Cyrus Mohebbi, Ph.D.
Managing Director
Market Group
Prudential Securities Inc.

Patrick Moore

Errol Mustafa, Ph.D.

David Z. Nirenberg
Counsel
Weil, Gotshal & Manges

Gregg N. Patruno
Mortgage Securities Research
Goldman, Sachs & Co.

James M. Peaslee
Partner
Cleary, Gottlieb, Steen & Hamilton

Lisa Pendergast
Director of Fixed-Income Strategies
Financial Strategies Group
Prudential Securities Inc.

Vincent Pica
Managing Director
Prudential Securities Inc.

Shaiy Pilpel, Ph.D.
Managing Director
Canadian Imperial Bank of Commerce

Scott F. Richard, D.B.A.
Portfolio Manager
Miller, Anderson & Sherrerd

R. Blaine Roberts, Ph.D.
Senior Managing Director
Financial Analytics and
   Structured Transactions Group
Bear Stearns & Co., Inc.

Charles Schorin
Vice President
Mortgage Research
Morgan Stanley & Co., Inc.

Dan Spina
Managing Director
Financial Analytics and
   Structured Transactions Group
Bear Stearns & Co., Inc.

Ken Spindel
Managing Director
Bear Stearns & Co., Inc.

David Sykes, Ph.D.
Principal Director of Taxable Fixed-Income
   Research
Alex. Brown & Sons, Inc.

Carol Sze
Director of Fixed-Income Strategies
Financial Strategies Group
Prudential Securities Inc.

Andrew J. Taddei
Managing Director
Bear Stearns & Co., Inc.

John F. Tierney, C.F.A.
Senior Vice President
Mortgage Strategies Group
Lehman Brothers

Hendrik Van Schieveen, Ph.D.

Rick Villaume
Vice President
Prudential Securities Inc.

Karen Auld Wagner, C.F.A.
Vice President
Fixed Income Research
CS First Boston Corporation

Michael L. Winchell
Senior Managing Director
Risk Management Group
Bear Stearns & Co., Inc.

CHAPTER 1

Overview

Frank J. Fabozzi, Ph.D., C.F.A.
Editor, Journal of Portfolio Management
and Adjunct Professor of Finance
School of Management, Yale University

Innovation and growth have characterized the mortgage market in the past 25 years. In the 1970s and early 1980s, the focus of innovations was in the design of new mortgage loans such as adjustable-rate mortgages, and the pooling of mortgage loans to create mortgage pass-through securities. New mortgage designs attempted to overcome the unappealing features of the traditional fixed-rate, level payment mortgage from the perspective of both borrowers and lenders/investors, thereby broadening the institutional base of potential investors.

The pooling of the traditional fixed-rate, level payment mortgages to create pass-through securities in February 1970 with the issuance of Ginnie Mae Pool #1 made investing in the mortgage market more palatable to an even greater institutional investor base, which had found the investment characteristics of owning individual mortgage loans unappealing. As issuers of pass-through securities became more comfortable with the securitization process, other types of mortgage designs were securitized.

Until 1977, all pass-through securities carried the full faith and credit of the U.S. government or a government-sponsored enterprise. In 1977, the private-label pass-through security was first publicly introduced by Bank of America. Since then, techniques for enhancing the credit quality of private-label pass-through securities have increased the appeal of these securities to investors willing to accept credit risk.

Aside from credit risk, the key characteristic that distinguishes Treasury securities, corporates, municipals, and mortgage pass-through securities from each other is the degree of uncertainty associated with the cash flow (*i.e.,* principal repayment and interest). In the case of Treasuries, with the exception of some outstanding callable Treasury bonds, the amount and

timing of the cash flow are known with certainty. Since most long-term corporates and municipals are callable by the issuer prior to maturity, the cash
flow of these securities is not known with certainty. Typically, however, the
issue may not be called or refunded until a specified number of years after
issuance. Generally, the bondholder can expect that the issuer will not "irra-
tionally" exercise the call option; that is, the bondholder can expect that the
issuer will not call the issue when the coupon rate is less than the current
market interest rate.

Mortgage loans also have uncertainty about the cash flow, mainly
because the investor has effectively granted the borrower/homeowner the
option to prepay (call) part or all of the mortgage at any time. Any payment
that is made in excess of the regularly scheduled principal repayment (*i.e.,*
amortization) is called a *prepayment.* While the prevailing borrowing rate may
be an important determinant affecting the homeowner's decision whether or
not to exercise the option to prepay, other unique factors may dominate,
resulting in unscheduled principal repayments when the prevailing mortgage rate is greater than the loan rate. These individual circumstances facing
the borrower may affect the cash-flow timing, making its uncertainty greater
than that for callable corporates and municipals, which solely depend on the
prevailing borrowing rate relative to the bond's coupon rate. Investors in
mortgage-backed securities face this uncertainty about prepayments, referred
to as *prepayment risk,* and wish to be compensated for accepting unscheduled
principal repayments.

An investor in a pass-through security is exposed to the total prepayment risk associated with the underlying pool of mortgage loans. The total
prepayment risk can be divided into two components: *contraction risk* and
extension risk. The former is the risk that prepayments will occur when interest rates have declined, forcing the investor to reinvest the cash flow at an
interest rate lower than the coupon rate on the security. Extension risk
results from the slow down of prepayments when interest rates have
increased, forcing the investor to realize less cash flow that can be reinvested
at an interest rate greater than the coupon rate on the security.

In 1983, a new security structure was introduced by Freddie Mac called
the *collateralized mortgage obligation* (CMO). In this structure, backed by mortgage pass-through securities and whole loans, the total prepayment risk was
divided amongst classes of bonds (or tranches). Instead of distributing the
monthly cash flow on a pro-rata basis, as in the case of a pass-through security, the distribution of the principal repayment (both scheduled and prepayments) was done on a prioritized basis so as to redistribute prepayment risk
among the various bond classes in the CMO structure.

In the first generation of CMOs, the priority was such that only one
class of bonds would receive principal repayment until it was completely paid

off. Then, another class of bonds would begin receiving principal repayment until it too was completely paid off. Such structures are known as *sequential-pay* or *plain vanilla* CMOs. Then, to further reduce prepayment risk for some classes of bonds, tranches with a specified principal repayment schedule were introduced; the repayment schedule of such bonds is assured if the actual speed of prepayments is within a designated range. These classes of bonds are known as *planned amortization class* (PAC) bonds, and provide protection against both contraction and extension risks. They were particularly attractive to institutional investors who sought to reduce their exposure to the corporate bond sector resulting from an increase in event risk. PACs provided a structure similar to the sinking-fund provision in corporate bond indentures.

The creation of PAC bonds with their greater prepayment protection meant that bond classes with greater prepayment risk had to be created. These bonds are called *support* or *companion* bonds, and they exhibit greater prepayment risk than the collateral from which the PAC bonds are created.

Whereas some institutional investors want protection against both contraction and extension risks, some desire only protection from one of these risks. For example, there are institutional investors who wish to be protected against contraction risk but are willing to accept extension risk. For them, a bond class known as a *targeted amortization class* (TAC) was created. The *reverse TAC* was created for institutional investors who are willing to accept contraction risk, but desire protection again extension risk. Very accurately determined maturity (VADM) bonds also provide protection against extension risk.

CMOs can be backed by pools of agency pass-through securities or by whole loans. The former are issued by Fannie Mae, Freddie Mac, and Ginnie Mae (which recently began issuing CMOs) and are referred to as agency CMOs. Issuance of whole-loan CMOs is on the rise. In these CMO structures, both prepayment risk and default risk must be carefully analyzed.

The various types of CMO structures will be discussed throughout this book. The key to the success of the CMO innovation is that the principal distribution can be structured so as to satisfy the asset/liability needs of institutional investors. It must be clearly understood, however, that the creation of a CMO does not eliminate the total prepayment risk associated with the underlying collateral; it can only redistribute it.

An important development in the CMO market is a key provision introduced into the tax law. An entity that issues a mortgage-backed security simply acts as a conduit in passing interest payments received from homeowners through to the security holders, and thus it wants to make sure that any legal structure created to distribute those payments is not taxed. Tax laws provide that the issuer is not treated as a taxable entity if the pass-through is issued through a legal structure known as a *grantor trust*, which is the arrangement used by issuers of pass-throughs. There is one major disadvantage of the grantor trust arrangement: if there is more than one class of bonds (*i.e.*, a multiclass pass-through such as a CMO), the trust does not qualify as a non-taxable entity. The Tax Reform Act of 1986 created a new trust vehicle called the *Real Estate Mortgage Investment Conduit* (REMIC) allowing the issuance of mortgage-backed securities with multiple bondholder classes without adverse tax consequences. While it is common to hear market participants refer to a CMO as a REMIC, not all CMOs are REMICs.

In July 1986, another type of derivative mortgage-backed security was introduced by Fannie Mae, the *stripped mortgage-backed security*. The principal and interest were divided unequally between two classes of bonds, not on a pro-rata basis as with pass-through securities, and not on a prioritized basis as with CMOs. As a result of this unequal distribution, the two bond classes had different synthetic coupon rates and performed differently from the underlying collateral when interest rates changed. In the second generation of stripped mortgage-backed securities, all of the interest was distributed to one bond class (called the *interest-only* or *IO* class) and all of the principal distributed to the other class (called the *principal-only* or *PO* class). The investment features of stripped mortgage-backed securities allowed institutional investors to create synthetic securities with risk/return characteristics previously unavailable in the market and, more importantly, provided institutional investors with instruments that could be used to more effectively hedge a portfolio of pass-through securities or servicing rights than exchange-traded, interest rate risk-control contracts could.

The growth of the market has brought with it techniques for valuing mortgage-backed securities and strategies for capitalizing on mispricing. The three basic approaches are the static cash-flow yield approach, the option modeling approach, and the option-adjusted spread approach. All of these techniques can be incorporated into a total return framework suitable for use for asset/liability management.

Once past the pricing problem created by the uncertain class flow, the investor's next step is to measure the interest-rate risk associated with a mortgage-backed security. The usual measure of interest-rate risk used by investors is Macaulay (or modified) duration. This measure is, however, inappropriate for not only mortgage-backed securities, but also for current coupon and premium callable corporate and municipal bonds. In particular, as market yields decline, call risk increases. This results in price compression (popularly referred to as "negative convexity") because investors become unwilling to pay a premium far above the call price (par in the case of mortgage-backed securities) as the market rate falls below the coupon rate. Several approaches discussed in this book have been suggested for use in measuring the interest-rate sensitivity of a mortgage-backed security.

ORGANIZATION OF THE BOOK

I have divided the book into eight sections. Section I describes the various mortgage and mortgage pass-through security products. Section II focuses on prepayment behavior and modeling. Sections III and IV cover derivative mortgage-backed securities. Section III discusses stripped mortgage-backed securities and Section IV covers the wide range of collateralized mortgage obligation products, including PACs, TACs, accrual (Z) bonds, floaters, inverse floaters, support bonds, support bonds with schedules, and residuals. Commercial mortgage-backed securities are covered in Section V.

Valuation techniques are reviewed in Section VI. Section VII covers hedging strategies. Section VIII covers financial accounting and federal income taxation for mortgage-backed securities. The appendix to this book provides a review of mortgage mathematics.

SECTION I

MORTGAGES AND
PASS-THROUGH SECURITIES

CHAPTER 2

Mortgages

Frank J. Fabozzi, Ph.D., C.F.A.
Editor, Journal of Portfolio Management
and Adjunct Professor of Finance
School of Management, Yale University

Lynn M. Edens
Vice President
Goldman, Sachs & Co.

A mortgage loan is a loan secured by the collateral of some specified real estate property, which obliges the borrower to make a predetermined series of payments. The mortgage gives the lender (the *mortgagee*) the right of foreclosure on the loan, if the borrower (the *mortgagor*) defaults. That is, if the borrower fails to make the contracted payments, the lender can seize the property in order to ensure that the debt is paid off.

The types of real estate properties that can be mortgaged are divided into two broad categories: residential properties and nonresidential properties. The former category includes houses, condominiums, cooperatives, and apartments. Residential real estate can be subdivided into single-family (one-to-four-family) structures and multifamily structures (apartment buildings in which more than four families reside). Nonresidential property includes commercial and farm properties.

The market where these funds are borrowed is called the *mortgage market.* This sector of the debt market is by far the largest in the world. The mortgage market has undergone significant structural changes since the 1980s. Innovations have occurred in terms of the design of new mortgage instruments and the development of products that use pools of mortgages as collateral for the issuance of a security. Such securities are called *mortgage-backed securities.*

Reprinted from the *Handbook of Fixed Income Securities,* Fourth Edition, edited by Frank J. Fabozzi and T. Dessa Fabozzi (Burr Ridge, IL: Irwin), 1995. Reprinted with permission.

The focus of this chapter is the structure of the mortgage market, the risks associated with investing in mortgages, and the different types of mortgage design. Only residential mortgages are discussed.

PARTICIPANTS IN THE MORTGAGE MARKET

In addition to the ultimate investor of funds, there are three groups involved in the market: mortgage originators, mortgage servicers, and mortgage insurers.

Mortgage Originators

The original lender is called the *mortgage originator*. Mortgage originators include commercial banks, thrifts, mortgage bankers, life insurance companies, and pension funds. The three largest originators for all types of residential mortgages are commercial banks, thrifts, and mortgage bankers, originating more than 95% of annual mortgage originations. Before 1990, thrifts were the largest originators, followed by commercial banks. In 1990, thrift origination declined; with an increase in commercial bank origination, the share of thrift origination dropped below that of commercial banks. In 1990 mortgage bankers' share of origination was the largest.

Originators may generate income for themselves in one or more ways. First, they typically charge an *origination fee*. This fee is expressed in terms of points, where each point represents 1% of the borrowed funds. For example, an origination fee of two points on a $100,000 mortgage represents $2,000. Originators also charge application fees and certain processing fees.

The second source of revenue is the profit that might be generated from selling a mortgage at a higher price than it originally cost. This profit is called *secondary marketing profit*. Of course, if mortgage rates rise, an originator will realize a loss when the mortgages are sold in the secondary market. Finally, the mortgage originator may hold the mortgage in its investment portfolio.

A potential homeowner who wants to borrow funds to purchase a home will apply for a loan from a mortgage originator. Upon completion of the application form (which provides financial information about the applicant) and payment of an application fee, the mortgage originator will perform a credit evaluation of the applicant. The two primary factors in determining whether the funds will be lent are the *payment-to-income* (PTI) ratio and the *loan-to-value* (LTV) ratio.

The PTI, the ratio of monthly payments (both mortgage and real estate tax payments) to monthly income, is a measure of the ability of the applicant to make monthly payments. The lower this ratio, the greater is the likelihood that the applicant will be able to meet the required payments.

The difference between the purchase price of the property and the amount borrowed is the borrower's down payment. The LTV is the ratio of the amount of the loan to the market (or appraised) value of the property. The lower this ratio, the more protection the lender has if the applicant defaults and the property must be repossessed and sold.

After a mortgage loan is closed, a mortgage originator can either (1) hold the mortgage in its portfolio, (2) sell the mortgage to an investor who wishes to hold the mortgage or who will place the mortgage in a pool of mortgages to be used as collateral for the issuance of a mortgage-backed security, or (3) use the mortgage as collateral for the issuance of a mortgage-backed security. When a mortgage is used as collateral for the issuance of a security, the mortgage is said to be *securitized.*

When a mortgage originator intends to sell the mortgage, it will obtain a commitment from the potential investor (buyer). Two federally sponsored credit agencies and several private companies buy mortgages. As these agencies and private companies pool these mortgages and sell them to investors, they are called *conduits.* The two agencies, the Federal Home Loan Mortgage Corporation and the Federal National Mortgage Association (examined further below), purchase only *conforming mortgages.* A conforming mortgage is one that meets the underwriting standards established by these agencies for being in a pool of mortgages underlying a security that they guarantee. Three underwriting standards established by these agencies in order to qualify as a conforming mortgage are (1) a maximum PTI, (2) a maximum LTV, and (3) a maximum loan amount. If an applicant does not satisfy the underwriting standards, the mortgage is called a *nonconforming mortgage.* Loans that exceed the maximum loan amount are called *jumbo mortgages.*

Mortgages acquired by the agency may be held as investments in their portfolio or securitized. Two examples of private conduits are the Residential Funding Corporation (a subsidiary of General Motors Acceptance Corporation) and Chase Manhattan Mortgage Corporation. Private conduits typically will securitize the mortgages purchased rather than hold them as an investment. Both conforming and nonconforming mortgages are purchased.

Mortgage Servicers

Every mortgage loan must be serviced. Servicing of a mortgage loan involves collecting monthly payments and forwarding proceeds to owners of the loan; sending payment notices to mortgagors; reminding mortgagors when payments are overdue; maintaining records of principal balances; administering an escrow balance for real estate taxes and insurance purposes; initiating foreclosure proceedings if necessary; and furnishing tax information to mortgagors when applicable.

Servicers include bank-related entities, thrift-related entities, and mortgage bankers. There are five sources of revenue from mortgage servicing. The primary source is the servicing fee. This fee is a fixed percentage of the outstanding mortgage balance. Consequently, the revenue from servicing declines over time as the mortgage balance amortizes. The second source of servicing income arises from the interest that can be earned by the servicer from the escrow balance that the borrower often maintains with the servicer. The third source of revenue is the float earned on the monthly mortgage payment. This opportunity arises because of the delay permitted between the time the servicer receives the payment and the time that the payment must be sent to the investor. Fourth, there are several sources of ancillary income: (1) a late fee is charged by the servicer if the payment is not made on time; (2) many servicers receive commissions from cross-selling their borrowers for credit life and other insurance products; and (3) fees can also be generated from selling mailing lists.

Finally, there are other benefits of servicing rights for servicers who are also lenders. Their portfolio of borrowers is a potential source for other loans such as second mortgages, automobile loans, and credit cards.

Mortgage Insurers

When the lender makes the loan based on the credit of the borrower and on the collateral for the mortgage, the mortgage is said to be a *conventional mortgage*. The lender may require the borrower to obtain mortgage insurance to insure against default by the borrower. It is usually required by lenders on loans with loan-to-value (LTV) ratios greater than 80%. The amount insured will be some percentage of the loan and may decline as the LTV ratio declines. Although the insurance is required by the lender, its cost is borne by the borrower, usually through a higher contract rate.

There are two forms of this insurance: insurance provided by a government agency and private mortgage insurance. The federal agencies that provide this insurance to qualified borrowers are the Federal Housing Administration (FHA), the Veterans Administration (VA), and the Farmers Home Administration (FmHA). Private mortgage insurance can be obtained from a mortgage insurance company such as Mortgage Guaranty Insurance Company and PMI Mortgage Insurance Company.

Another form of insurance may be required for mortgages on property that is located in geographical areas where the occurrence of natural disasters such as floods and earthquakes is higher than usual. This type of insurance is called *hazard insurance*.

When mortgages are pooled by a private conduit and a security issued, additional insurance for the pool is typically obtained to enhance the credit of the security. This occurs because the major commercial rating agencies of such securities require external credit enhancement for the issuer to obtain a particular investment-grade rating. Factors that the commercial rating agencies assess to judge the credit quality of a pool of mortgages, in addition to the credit quality of the individual mortgages, are the credit rating of the mortgage insurer, the underwriting standards and procedures of the originator, and the quality of the operations of the servicer.

PREPAYMENT RISK

The investor in a mortgage grants the homeowner the option to prepay the mortgage in whole or in part at any time. No penalty is imposed on the homeowner for prepaying the mortgage. That is, the loan is repaid at par value at any time. Because of the prepayment option granted to the homeowner, an investor in a mortgage cannot be certain of the cash flow. A 30-year mortgage could turn out to have a maturity of a year or a maturity of 30 years. The uncertainty about the cash flow due to the prepayment option granted the homeowner is called *prepayment risk*.

An investor is exposed to prepayment risk for an individual mortgage and for a pool of mortgages. Consequently, any security backed by a pool of mortgages exposes an investor to prepayment risk.

Prepayments occur for one of several reasons. First, homeowners prepay the entire mortgage when they sell their home. The sale of a home can result from (1) a change of employment that necessitates moving, (2) the purchase of a more expensive home ("trading up"), or (3) a divorce in which the settlement requires sale of the marital residence, among other reasons. Second, in the case of homeowners who cannot meet their mortgage obligations, the property is repossessed and sold. The proceeds from the sale are used to pay off the mortgage in the case of a conventional mortgage. For an insured mortgage, the insurer will pay off the mortgage balance. Third, if property is destroyed by fire, or if another insured catastrophe occurs, the insurance proceeds are used to pay off the mortgage. Finally, the borrower will have an incentive to refinance the mortgage when the current mortgage rate falls by a sufficient amount below the contract rate after taking into account refinancing costs.

The key in analyzing an individual mortgage or a pool of mortgages is the projection of prepayments. All primary dealers and several vendors have developed prepayment models. While a discussion of these models is beyond the scope of this chapter, it is sufficient to say that there is not one prepayment model for all of the mortgage designs that we review in the next section. Although a good deal of data on the prepayment activity of certain types of mortgage designs is available, the same cannot be said of some of the newer mortgage designs.

Prepayment risk also has implications for the performance of a mortgage. The performance is similar to that of a callable bond, a fact that should not be surprising given that a mortgage is nothing more than a callable security. Specifically, the investor in a mortgage is exposed to negative convexity when interest rates decline below the loan's contract rate. In addition, the investor is exposed to reinvestment risk.

ALTERNATIVE MORTGAGE INSTRUMENTS

Both the design of mortgages and the origin of the funds that finance them have, since the Great Depression, undergone revolutionary changes and have been affected by spectacular innovations. Until that time, mortgages were not fully amortized, but were balloon loans in which the principal was not amortized, or only partially amortized at maturity, leaving the debtor with the problem of refinancing the balance. Sometimes the bank could even ask for repayment of the outstanding balance on demand or upon relatively short notice, even if the mortgagor was fulfilling his or her obligation.

This system of mortgage financing proved disastrous during the Great Depression and contributed to both its depth and personal distress, as banks, afflicted by losses on their loans and by depositors' withdrawals, found it necessary to liquidate their mortgage loans at a time when debtors found it impossible to refinance.

This experience led, in the middle of the 1930s, to the widespread adoption of a superior instrument called the fixed-rate, level-payment, fully amortized mortgage (for short, *level-payment mortgage*). This adoption was encouraged by the newly created Federal Housing Administration (FHA), whose assignments include providing for an affordable insurance to protect the lender's claim against default by the borrower. The FHA specified what kind of mortgages it was prepared to insure, and one of its requirements was that it had to be a level-payment mortgage.

The level-payment mortgage was initially a great success. It contributed to the recovery of housing after the Great Depression, and it continued to perform a valuable role in financing residential real estate in the first two decades of the post-World War II period until the inception of the era of high inflation, just before the mid-1970s.

The level-payment mortgage suffers from two basic and very serious shortcomings. These may be labeled the *mismatch* problem and the *tilt* problem. The mismatch problem arose in the United States during most of the post-World War II period, because mortgages—a very long-term asset—were largely financed by savings and loan associations and banks, institutions that obtained their funds through deposits primarily, if not entirely, of a short-term nature. These institutions were engaging in the highly speculative activity of borrowing short and lending very long. Speculation on the term structure of interest rates is a losing proposition if interest rates rise, as is bound to happen in the presence of significant inflation. The mismatch problem made these mortgages unattractive to investors during times of significant inflation and led to the development of the variable-rate mortgage, or as it is more popularly known, the adjustable-rate mortgage design.

The tilt problem refers to what happens to the real burden of mortgage payments over the life of the mortgage as a result of inflation. If the general price level rises, the real value of the mortgage payments will decline over time. If a homeowner's real income rises over time, this rise coupled with a decline in the real value of the mortgage payments will mean that the burden of the mortgage payments will decline over time. Thus, the homeowner's mortgage obligation places a greater burden in real terms in the initial years. In other words, the real burden is "tilted" to the initial years. As a result, this precludes individuals from purchasing a home because of the greater real burden of the mortgage payments in the initial years of the mortgage's life. The tilt problem is behind the development of other types of mortgage instruments that we describe below.

Since 1989, lenders have offered a number of new mortgage loan structures to single-family mortgage borrowers. Other structures, which are not new but were not previously popular, have also gained significant primary market share. These products include tiered payment mortgages, balloon mortgages, "two-step" mortgages, and fixed/adjustable mortgage hybrids. Such rapid innovation was last seen in the early 1980s, when extremely high mortgage rates forced lenders to create loan structures that offered lower initial monthly mortgage payments in an attempt to alleviate the tilt problem. As we discuss shortly, current innovations are motivated by important, and probably enduring, changes in the market for mortgage originations.

Today, many of these new products are finding their way into the secondary market, where they present investors with both opportunities and challenges. The opportunities include the chance to invest in new securities that may provide a better portfolio fit than other mortgage products have to date. Some of these loan types are likely to become permanent features of both the primary and the secondary mortgage market; others are likely to disappear, such as one of the mortgage designs discussed below, the graduated payment mortgage.

In the past, the secondary mortgage market has provided originators with an incentive to produce mortgage loans that have short durations and are relatively insensitive to prepayments, a risk associated with mortgages that was mentioned in the previous section. In fact, the use of collateralized mortgage obligations to create mortgage-backed securities with these characteristics helped expand the breadth of the mortgage investor base substantially over the past several years. Adjustable-rate mortgages (ARMs) were another response to this phenomenon. The declining competitiveness of ARMs with what are referred to as teaser rates (which occurred both because of the flat or inverted yield curve in the late 1980s and early 1990s, and because of the decision by thrifts to price ARMs less aggressively) has created room for new, short-duration mortgage products to flourish.

Other, more recent market developments also favor new mortgage products. Accompanying (and, in some cases, precipitating) the decline in the origination role of thrifts is a dramatic increase in the mortgage activity of banks, both as originators and portfolio lenders. Risk-based capital requirements for banks, which favor residential mortgages, particularly in securitized form, as well as a lack of appealing opportunities in their traditional lending sectors, will continue to drive the trend toward an origination market dominated by banks. Interest-rate risk-management concerns will focus the lending activity of banks on shorter-duration mortgage products, as we have seen already. Because many banks will experience a demand for mortgage securities beyond their origination capacity (if any), and because many other mortgage investors also prefer shorter-duration mortgage-backed securities, these new mortgage loan structures can offer very competitive rates to borrowers. Other mortgage bankers are also actively marketing these loan types.

These new mortgage products are likely to continue to provide a lower rate to the borrower, and thus a marketing advantage to the originator, only if they enjoy a viable secondary market. A few of these new products are likely to become permanent and substantial elements of the securitized market. Others, with more complicated (and therefore harder to price) structures or less obvious portfolio applications, may well disappear.

Level-Payment, Fixed-Rate Mortgage

The basic idea behind the design of the level-payment mortgage is that the borrower pays interest and repays principal in equal installments over an agreed-upon period of time, called the *maturity* or *term* of the mortgage. Thus, at the end of the term the loan has been fully amortized. Each monthly mortgage payment for a level-payment mortgage is due on the first of each month and consists of:

1. Interest of $1/12$ of the fixed annual interest rate times the amount of the outstanding mortgage balance at the beginning of the previous month.

2. A repayment of a portion of the outstanding mortgage balance (principal).

The difference between the monthly mortgage payment and the portion of the payment that represents interest equals the amount that is applied to reduce the outstanding mortgage balance. The monthly mortgage payment is designed so that after the last scheduled monthly payment of the loan is made, the amount of the outstanding mortgage balance is zero (i.e., the mortgage is fully repaid).

To illustrate a level-payment mortgage, consider a 30-year (360-month), $100,000 mortgage with a 9.5% mortgage rate. The monthly mortgage payment would be $840.85.[1] Exhibit 1 shows how each monthly mortgage payment is divided between interest and repayment of principal. At the beginning of month 1, the mortgage balance is $100,000, the amount of the original loan. The mortgage payment for month 1 includes interest on the $100,000 borrowed for the month. The interest rate is 9.5%, so the monthly interest rate is 0.0079167 (.095 divided by 12). Interest for month 1 is therefore $791.67 ($100,000 times 0.0079167). The $49.18 difference between the monthly mortgage payment of $840.85 and the interest of $791.67 is the portion of the monthly mortgage payment that represents repayment of principal. This $49.18 in month 1 reduces the mortgage balance.

The mortgage balance at the end of month 1 (beginning of month 2) is then $99,950.81 ($100,000 minus $49.19). The interest for the second monthly mortgage payment is $791.28, the monthly interest rate (0.0079167) times the mortgage balance at the beginning of month 2 ($99,950.81). The difference between the $840.85 monthly mortgage payment and the $791.28 interest is $49.57, representing the amount of the mortgage balance paid off with that monthly mortgage payment. Notice in Exhibit 1 that the last monthly mortgage payment is sufficient to pay off the remaining mortgage balance. When a loan repayment schedule is structured in this way, so that the payments made by the borrower will completely pay off the interest and principal, the loan is said to be *fully amortizing*. Exhibit 1 is then referred to as an *amortization schedule*.

---

1 The formula for obtaining the monthly mortgage payment is

$$MP = MB_0 \frac{[i(1 + i)^n]}{[(1 + i)^n - 1]}$$

where

MP = monthly mortgage payment ($);
n = number of months;
MB_0 = original mortgage balance ($);
i = simple monthly interest rate (annual interest rate/12).

For our hypothetical mortgage:

$$n = 360; \quad MB_0 = \$100,000; \quad i = 0.0079167 \ (= 0.095/12).$$

$$MP = \$100,000 \frac{[0.0079167(1.0079167)^{360}]}{[(1.0079167)^{360} - 1]} = \$840.85$$

Exhibit 1. Amortization Schedule for a Level-Payment, Fixed-Rate Mortgage (Mortgage Loan: $100,000; Mortgage Rate: 9.5%; Monthly Payment: $840.85; Term of Loan: 30 Years [360 Months])

Month	Beginning Mortgage Balance	Monthly Mortgage Payment	Interest for Month	Principal Repayment	Ending Mortgage Balance
1	$100,000.00	$840.85	$791.67	$ 49.19	$99,950.81
2	99,950.81	840.85	791.28	49.58	99,901.24
3	99,901.24	840.85	790.88	49.97	99,851.27
4	99,851.27	840.85	790.49	50.37	99,800.90
5	99,800.90	840.85	790.09	50.76	99,750.14
6	99,750.14	840.85	789.69	51.17	99,698.97
7	99,698.97	840.85	789.28	51.57	99,647.40
8	99,647.40	840.85	788.88	51.98	99,595.42
9	99,595.42	840.85	788.46	52.39	99,543.03
10	99,543.03	840.85	788.05	52.81	99,490.23
...	...	...	...	...	...
...	...	...	...	...	...
...	...	...	...	...	...
98	92,862.54	840.85	735.16	105.69	92,756.85
99	92,756.85	840.85	734.33	106.53	92,650.32
100	92,650.32	840.85	733.48	107.37	92,542.95
101	92,542.95	840.85	732.63	108.22	92,434.72
102	92,434.72	840.85	731.77	109.08	92,325.64
103	92,325.64	840.85	730.91	109.94	92,215.70
104	92,215.70	840.85	730.04	110.81	92,104.89
105	92,104.89	840.85	729.16	111.69	91,993.20
106	91,993.20	840.85	728.28	112.57	91,880.62
...	...	...	...	...	...
...	...	...	...	...	...
...	...	...	...	...	...
209	74,177.40	840.85	587.24	253.62	73,923.78
210	73,923.78	840.85	585.23	255.62	73,668.16
211	73,668.16	840.85	583.21	257.65	73,410.51
212	73,410.51	840.85	581.17	259.69	73,150.82
...	...	...	...	...	...
...	...	...	...	...	...
...	...	...	...	...	...
354	5,703.93	840.85	45.16	795.70	4,908.23
355	4,908.23	840.85	38.86	802.00	4,106.24
356	4,106.24	840.85	32.51	808.35	3,297.89
357	3,297.89	840.85	26.11	814.75	2,483.14
358	2,483.14	840.85	19.66	821.20	1,661.95
359	1,661.95	840.85	13.16	827.70	834.25
360	834.25	840.85	6.60	834.25	0.00

As Exhibit 1 clearly shows, *the portion of the monthly mortgage payment applied to interest declines each month, and the portion applied to reducing the mortgage balance increases.*

The reason for this is that as the mortgage balance is reduced with each monthly mortgage payment, the interest on the mortgage balance declines. Because the monthly mortgage payment is fixed, a larger part of the monthly payment is applied to reduce the principal in each subsequent month.

What was ignored in the amortization is the portion of the cash flow that must be paid to the servicer of the mortgage. The servicing fee is a specified portion of the mortgage rate. The monthly cash flow from a mortgage loan, regardless of the mortgage design, can therefore be decomposed into three parts:

1. The servicing fee.

2. The interest payment net of the servicing fee.

3. The scheduled principal repayment.

For example, consider once again the $100,000 30-year level-payment mortgage with a rate of 9.5%. Suppose the servicing fee is 0.5% per year. Exhibit 2 shows the cash flow for the mortgage with this servicing fee. The monthly mortgage payment is unchanged. The amount of the principal repayment is the same as in Exhibit 1. The difference is that the interest is reduced by the amount of the servicing fee. The amount of the servicing fee, just like the amount of interest, declines each month because the mortgage balance declines.

Graduated-Payment Mortgage

The graduated-payment mortgage (GPM) was designed to alleviate the tilt problem. With this mortgage design, both the interest rate and the term of the mortgage are fixed, as they are with a level-payment mortgage. However, the monthly mortgage payment for a GPM is smaller in the initial years than for a level-payment mortgage with the same contract rate, but larger in the remaining years of the mortgage term.

The terms of a GPM plan include (1) the mortgage rate, (2) the term of the mortgage, (3) the number of years over which the monthly mortgage payment will increase (and when the level payments will begin), and (4) the annual percentage increase in the mortgage payments.

The monthly mortgage payments in the earlier years of a GPM are generally not sufficient to pay the entire interest due on the outstanding mortgage balance. The difference between the monthly mortgage payment and the accumulated interest (based on the outstanding mortgage balance) is

Exhibit 2. Cash Flow for a Mortgage with Servicing Fee
(Mortgage Loan: $100,000; Mortgage Rate: 9.5%; Servicing Fee: 0.5%;
Monthly Payment: $840.85; Term of Loan: 30 Years [360 Months])

Month	Beginning Mortgage Balance	Monthly Mortgage Payment	Net Interest for Month	Servicing Fee	Principal Repayment	Ending Mortgage Balance
1	$100,000.00	$840.85	$750.00	$41.67	$ 49.19	$99,950.81
2	99,950.81	840.85	749.63	41.65	49.58	99,901.24
3	99,901.24	840.85	749.26	41.63	49.97	99,851.27
4	99,851.27	840.85	748.88	41.60	50.37	99,800.90
5	99,800.90	840.85	748.51	41.58	50.76	99,750.14
6	99,750.14	840.85	748.13	41.56	51.17	99,698.97
7	99,698.97	840.85	747.74	41.54	51.57	99,647.40
8	99,647.40	840.85	747.36	41.52	51.98	99,595.42
9	99,595.42	840.85	746.97	41.50	52.39	99,543.03
10	99,543.03	840.85	746.57	41.48	52.81	99,490.23
...	...	...	...	...	...	...
...	...	...	...	...	...	...
...	...	...	...	...	...	...
98	99,862.54	840.85	696.47	38.69	105.69	92,756.85
99	92,756.85	840.85	695.68	38.65	106.53	93,650.32
100	92,650.32	840.85	694.88	38.60	107.37	92,542.95
101	92,542.95	840.85	694.07	38.56	108.22	92,434.72
102	92,434.72	840.85	693.26	38.51	109.08	92,325.64
103	92,325.64	840.85	692.44	38.47	109.94	92,215.70
104	92,215.70	840.85	691.62	38.42	110.81	92,104.89
105	92,104.89	840.85	690.79	38.38	111.69	91,993.20
106	91,993.20	840.85	689.95	38.33	112.57	91,880.62
...	...	...	...	...	...	...
...	...	...	...	...	...	...
...	...	...	...	...	...	...
209	74,177.40	840.85	556.33	30.91	253.62	73,923.78
210	73,923.78	840.85	554.43	30.80	255.62	73,668.16
211	73,668.16	840.85	552.51	30.70	257.65	73,410.51
212	73,410.51	840.85	550.58	30.59	259.69	73,150.82
...	...	...	...	...	...	...
...	...	...	...	...	...	...
...	...	...	...	...	...	...
354	5,703.93	840.85	42.78	2.38	795.70	4,908.23
355	4,908.23	840.85	36.81	2.05	802.00	4,106.24
356	4,106.24	840.85	30.80	1.71	808.35	3,297.89
357	3,297.89	840.85	24.73	1.37	814.75	2,483.14
358	2,483.14	840.85	18.62	1.03	821.20	1,661.95
359	1,661.95	840.85	12.46	0.69	827.70	834.25

added to the outstanding mortgage balance, so that in the earlier years of a GPM there is *negative amortization.* The higher-level mortgage payments in the later years of the GPM are designed to fully amortize the outstanding mortgage balance, which is, by then, greater than the original amount borrowed.

The Federal Housing Administration introduced GPMs in late 1979. GPMs became eligible for pooling in certain types of mortgage-backed securities in 1979. Origination of GPMs has faded in popularity in recent years with the growing popularity of the other mortgage instruments discussed in this section.

Growing-Equity Mortgage

A growing-equity mortgage (GEM) is a fixed-rate mortgage whose monthly mortgage payments increase over time. Unlike a GPM there is no negative amortization. The initial monthly mortgage payment is the same as for a level-payment mortgage. The higher monthly mortgage payments are applied to paying off the principal. As a result, the principal of a GEM is repaid faster. For example, a 30-year, $100,000 GEM loan with a contract rate of 9.5% might call for an initial monthly payment of $840.85 (the same as a level-payment, 9.5%, 30-year mortgage loan). However, the GEM payment would gradually increase, and the GEM might be fully paid in only 15 years. Pools of GEMs have been securitized.

Adjustable-Rate Mortgage

An adjustable-rate mortgage (ARM) is a loan in which the contract rate is reset periodically in accordance with some appropriately chosen reference rate.

Outstanding ARMs call for resetting the contract rate either every month, six months, year, two years, three years, or five years. In recent years ARMs typically have had reset periods of six months, one year, or five years. The contract rate at the reset date is equal to a reference rate plus a spread. The spread is typically between 200 and 300 basis points, reflecting market conditions, the features of the ARM, and the increased cost of servicing an ARM compared to a fixed-rate mortgage.

Reference Rate

Two categories of reference rates have been used in ARMs: (1) market-determined rates and (2) calculated rates based on the cost of funds for thrifts. The most popular market-determined rates are Treasury-based rates. The reference rate will have an important impact on the performance of an ARM and how it is priced.

Indexes for the cost of funds for thrifts are calculated based on the monthly weighted average interest cost for liabilities of thrifts. The two most popular are the Eleventh Federal Home Loan Bank Board District Cost of Funds Index (COFI) and the National Cost of Funds Index, the former being the most popular.

The Eleventh District includes the states of California, Arizona, and Nevada. The cost of funds is calculated by first computing the monthly interest expenses for all thrifts included in the Eleventh District. The interest expenses are summed and then divided by the average of the beginning and ending monthly balance. The index value is reported with a one-month lag. For example, June's Eleventh District COFI is reported in July. The contract rate for a mortgage based on the Eleventh District COFI is usually reset based on the previous month's reported index rate. For example, if the reset date is August, the index rate reported in July will be used to set the contract rate. Consequently, there is a two-month lag by the time the average cost of funds is reflected in the contract rate. This obviously is an advantage to the borrower and a disadvantage to the investor when interest rates are rising. The opposite is true when interest rates are falling.

The National Cost of Funds Index is calculated based on all federally insured S&Ls. A median cost of funds is calculated rather than an average. This index is reported with about a 1.5-month delay. The contract rate is typically reset based on the most recently reported index value.

Features of Adjustable-Rate Mortgages

To encourage borrowers to accept ARMs rather than fixed-rate mortgages, mortgage originators generally offer an initial contract rate that is less than the prevailing market mortgage rate. This below-market initial contract rate, set by the mortgage originator based on competitive market conditions, is commonly referred to as a *tea* one-year ARMs are typically offering a 100-basis-point spread over the reference rate. Suppose also that the reference rate is 6.5%, so that the initial contract rate should be 7.5%. The mortgage originator might set an initial contract rate of 6.75%, a rate 75 basis points below the current value of the reference rate plus the spread.

A pure ARM is one that resets periodically and has no other terms that affect the monthly mortgage payment. However, the monthly mortgage payment, and hence the investor's cash flow, are affected by other terms. These are due to (1) periodic caps and (2) lifetime rate caps and floors. Rate caps limit the amount that the contract rate may increase or decrease at the reset date. A lifetime cap sets the maximum contract rate over the term of the loan.

Fixed-Rate Tiered-Payment Mortgage

Fixed-rate tiered-payment mortgages (TPMs) are a successful new mortgage loan structure, incorporating a variety of features that give the mortgage appeal in both the primary and the secondary markets.

As with most new mortgage structures that have evolved over the past decade, TPMs were designed to provide originators with an advantage in the single most important competitive criterion: the ability to offer borrowers a low initial payment, which gives borrowers greater purchasing power than they would have under a standard 30-year or 15-year fixed-rate mortgage lending program (i.e., to alleviate the tilt problem). This innovation trend was first stimulated by the high interest rates of the early 1980s, when buydown and graduated payment mortgage lending programs flourished. In more recent years, adjustable-rate mortgages originated with a teaser rate have largely fulfilled the demand for low initial payments.

The contractual features designed to permit low initial payments on these types of mortgages have varied. Buydown origination programs carried market accrual rates and subsidized the payments in the early years with payments from a separate account typically established by the builder or owner of the property. Graduated payment mortgages also carried near-market accrual rates and allowed the mortgage to experience negative amortization in the early years of its life. On the other hand, most adjustable-rate mortgages relied on low initial accrual rates and subsequent limitations to interest rate increases to create low initial payment requirements; other adjustable-rate structures carried low initial rates, employed payment caps, and allowed the mortgage to negatively amortize to maintain a low payment schedule for some time into the future.

Tiered-payment mortgages provide the payment advantage in a unique way. The mortgage carries a market accrual rate and a 15-year or, less commonly, 30-year final maturity, but the payment is calculated based on an interest rate as much as 300 to 500 basis points lower than the actual interest rate on the loan (even lower for some 30-year loans). The structure does not allow negative amortization. Therefore, it stipulates that if the payment is less than the amount required to pay the interest due on the loan based on the actual interest rate, then the difference between the borrower's payment and the amount required to pay the entire interest accrued must be made up from a subsidy account established by the borrower, seller, builder, or other party. The payments are adjusted annually and allowed to increase by a maximum of 7.5% per year until the payment fully amortizes the loan over its remaining term.

The primary way TPMs differ from GPMs is that TPMs do not experience negative amortization and typically carry a 15-year maturity. TPMs differ from buydowns because any initial subsidy to the borrower's payment (from the interest shortfall account) is typically much smaller than that required by a buydown loan and is also frequently funded by the borrower.

TPMs have unique comparative advantages to attract borrowers in the primary market. Unlike ARMs, TPMs have a certain payment schedule with relatively moderate annual payment increases. They also carry a fixed rate, and they typically offer a 15-year final maturity attractive to many borrowers. Unlike some ARMs and graduated-payment mortgages, they do not experience negative amortization. The interest-only nature of the earliest total cash flows on the mortgage (including any necessary subsidies) also allows the payment to be set based on an extremely low accrual rate, much lower than can be profitably offered on most ARMs.

Balloon Mortgages

Most single-family balloon mortgages originated today carry a fixed rate and a 30-year amortization schedule. They typically require a balloon repayment of the principal outstanding on the loan at the end of five or, more commonly, seven years. Other balloon dates are possible and may become common. Balloon mortgages are attractive to borrowers because they offer mortgage rates that are significantly lower than generic 30-year mortgages in a steep-yield-curve environment. In turn, the short final maturity of balloon mortgage pools offers investors substantial performance stability.

Today, many balloon mortgage contracts are actually hybrids that contain certain provisions allowing the borrower to take out a new mortgage from the current lender to finance the balloon repayment with minimal requalification requirements. In order for the new loan to qualify for a Fannie Mae pool, for instance, the borrower receiving the new loan to finance a balloon payment must not have been delinquent on payments at any time during the preceding 12 months, must still be using the property as a primary residence, and must have incurred no new liens on the property. In addition, the interest rate on the new loan must be no more than 500 basis points greater than the rate on the balloon loan. If these conditions are met, Fannie Mae requires no additional requalification of the borrower taking out a new mortgage to meet a balloon payment, and will accept the resulting mortgage in a generic Fannie Mae pool.

Whether or not investors need concern themselves with the refinancing option offered to the borrower in conjunction with issuance of the balloon loan depends primarily on what form the balloon investment takes. Investors who own agency balloon mortgages can ignore the refinancing options offered to borrowers because, if the borrower fails to make the required balloon principal payment to the lender, the agency ultimately supports the balloon repayment to the investor. Investors in balloon mortgages with credit support provided in another manner should carefully assess the sufficiency of that support to meet borrower shortfalls at the balloon date, as the rating agencies do when assigning credit ratings to mortgage-backed securities backed by pools of such loans. It is possible, of course, that the nature of the refinancing option may influence borrower prepayment behavior before the balloon date, affecting both agency and nonagency balloon mortgage holdings.

Balloon mortgages have been a successful secondary market product and there is growing liquidity of the balloon product. Each agency also has a five-year balloon pool issuance program in its budding stage.

Ordinarily, any discussion of a new mortgage product would dwell extensively on the likely prepayment behavior of the underlying borrowers. There are at least two schools of thought on the likely prepayment behavior of balloon borrowers. One theory suggests that conforming balloon borrowers have selected this type of mortgage because they believe they are likely to move before the balloon date, and thus pools backed by these mortgages will prepay faster than otherwise similar pools backed by generic fixed-rate loans. A second theory suggests that the lower rate offered to balloon borrowers will tend to attract a wide range of borrowers, including the marginal borrowers who are less able to afford their housing purchase. This theory suggests that the balloon pools would prepay similarly to or perhaps more slowly than generic 30-year pools. In fact, prepayment rates on balloon securities have in general been faster than those of other mortgage products with similar refinancing incentives, suggesting that balloon borrowers tend to be a self-selected group with a shorter-than-average borrowing horizon.

"Two-Step" Mortgage Loans

Akin to the idea of a balloon loan with a refinancing option for the borrower is a fixed-rate loan with a single rate reset at some point before maturity. Unlike a refinancing option, this rate reset occurs without specific action on the part of the borrower.

One example of this structure is the so-called two-step loan structure, in which a loan carries a fixed rate for some period, usually seven years, and then resets once. The rate reset can be based on any rate; currently Fannie Mae's two-step mortgage purchase program specifies that the new rate be calculated by adding 250 basis points to a weekly average of the 10-year constant-maturity Treasury yield. Fannie Mae also limits any increase in the mortgage rate to no more than 600 basis points over the initial mortgage rate; other cap levels may become popular as well. Unlike balloon mortgages, the rate reset on the two-step does not consist of a repayment of the initial loan and the origination of a new one; thus, a pool backed by two-step loans has a 30-year final maturity rather than the shorter final maturity of a balloon pool. Essentially, the two-step mortgage is an adjustable-rate mortgage with a single reset. The borrower is compensated for assuming the rate reset risk by an initial mortgage rate that is lower than the generic 30-year fixed rate, the difference depending on the steepness of the yield curve.

In effect, the lender or investor who holds the two-step mortgage has extended an additional option to the borrower—the option to extend the loan when the available market rate at the reset date is more than 250 basis points above the 10-year Treasury rate. If the available mortgage rate from other lenders is less than 250 basis points above that of the 10-year Treasury, the borrower can prepay the two-step loan and achieve financing at a lower rate. In a rational world without transaction costs, this two-step loan would have to trade at wider levels than a balloon loan with a maturity equal to the reset date of the two-step loan, because the two-step is short one additional option that has some positive value.

However, because borrowers will not always prepay rationally and there are transaction costs associated with refinancing a loan, the reset may actually have some positive value to investors. For instance, it is likely that at the reset date there will be some borrowers in the pool who are unable to prepay their two-step loans, even if the new rate is higher than currently available fixed rates, because they are unable to qualify for the new loan. They may be unemployed, for instance, or the value of the property may have declined, requiring an additional down payment.[2] Also, the difference between the new rate on the two-step and the current mortgage rate may not be large enough to compensate borrowers for the costs of arranging a new loan.

For example, a two-step mortgage that resets at 250 basis points over the 10-year Treasury when generic mortgage rates were 200 basis points over the 10-year may not experience significant prepayments, but it would offer enhanced value to investors. Because of the points typically charged for the origination of a mortgage, the borrowers' choice would also probably be a function of how long they expected to remain in their home. A borrower with a relatively short horizon over which to amortize the points on a new loan is more likely to accept the reset even if it means paying a relatively high mortgage rate versus the prevailing market rate.

The additional value offered by these types of borrower behavior may also be a function of the form of the investors' two-step mortgage holdings. Take, for instance, a nonagency pool where only the weakest borrower credits remained after a rate rest that was significantly above prevailing market rates. Such a pool could suffer an impairment in value as a result.

Fixed/Adjustable-Rate Mortgage Hybrids

Another type of mortgage loan structure that has experienced growing popularity is the *fixed/adjustable-rate mortgage hybrid*. Typically, these mortgages are originated with fixed rates for their first 5, 7, or 10 years, after which the interest rate on the loan begins floating with contractual characteristics similar to those of current ARM structures. For instance, one popular hybrid structure

---

2 This process of adverse selection also occurs in premium 30-year mortgage pools, of course, and explains why some borrowers never prepay their high-rate mortgages.

carries a fixed rate for five years, and thereafter has a floating rate that resets every six months at a margin over the six-month CD index. Like many other ARMs, the coupon is subject to both periodic and lifetime limitations on the rate change. Other fixed/ARM hybrids turn into one-year Treasury ARMs, or monthly Eleventh District COFI ARMs after their fixed period. In many cases, the first coupon reset is not subject to any periodic caps that may apply to later coupon resets, and instead is subject only to the lifetime cap.

Although this mortgage structure is a combination of two types of products with which the market is very familiar, the combination presents some unique valuation challenges. The first involves a choice of prepayment model. Will the borrowers of this product prepay like fixed-rate borrowers or like ARM borrowers? Historically, these two borrower groups have responded differently to similar refinancing incentives.

CHAPTER 3

Mortgage Pass-Through Securities

Linda Lowell
First Vice President
Mortgage Strategies
PaineWebber Inc.

The pass-through market received its major impetus in the 1980s, growing from $11 billion at the end of 1980 to $914 billion at the end of 1989. At the end of 1993, that total leapt to $1.5 trillion.[1] Only the U.S. Treasury market, with about $3.4 trillion outstanding, is larger. The bulk of that production has been fostered by the U.S. government through government or government-sponsored housing agencies whose missions include promoting a secondary market for home mortgage debt.

Burgeoning investor interest has been a key factor spurring this tremendous growth. The primary impetus for this growth has been the fact that agency mortgage-backed securities represent the highest credit quality while providing excess expected yield compared to comparable Treasury and corporate securities. Specific forces have accelerated this interest. Chief among these is the growth of the collateralized mortgage obligation (CMO) market, permitting investors to buy mortgage cash flows across a spectrum of maturity sectors and to partition the prepayment risks. In addition, risk-based capital requirements established for banks and thrifts in 1989 assigned low risk weightings to agency pass-throughs and CMOs. In the current market environment, several developments are encouraging a dramatic shift in focus from CMOs back to pass-throughs on the part of many fixed-income investors. Perhaps the most sweeping and enduring of these is the growing practice of evaluating portfolio managers' performance against a bond market index. Mortgage-backed securities are represented in the common

---

1 *The Mortgage Market Statistical Annual* for 1994, Inside Mortgage Finance Publications, Inc. Of that, outstanding ARM securities amounted to $43 billion at the end of 1989, and $187 billion at the end of 1993.

indices by the outstanding agency pass-through market. As a consequence, an expanding number of portfolio managers find it difficult not to hold some portion of their portfolios in the pass-through market.

This chapter is intended to provide an overview of the variety of pass-through types and an introduction to the general structure and analysis of fixed-rate level payment pass-throughs, the largest and most frequently traded form of MBSs. The discussion then focuses on the cash flows and other features of pass-throughs that distinguish them from noncallable corporate or Treasury debt instruments and that give them their market properties. The chapter concludes with a discussion of the economic or total rate of return performance of pass-throughs in various interest-rate scenarios and the relative value analysis of these securities. Methodologies for analyzing pass-through securities are discussed in greater detail in later chapters.

WHAT IS A MORTGAGE PASS-THROUGH SECURITY?

Pass-through securities are created when mortgages are pooled together and undivided interests or participations in the pool are sold. Normally, the mortgages backing a pass-through security have the same loan type (fully-amortizing level payment, adjustable-rate, *etc.*) and are similar enough with respect to maturity and loan interest rate to permit cash flows to be projected as if the pool were a single mortgage. The originator (or another institution which purchases this right) continues to service the mortgages, collecting payments and "passing through" the principal and interest, less the servicing, guarantee, and other fees, to the security holders. The security holders receive pro-rata shares of the resultant cash flows. A portion of the outstanding principal is paid each month according to the amortization schedule established for the individual mortgages. In addition, and this is a critical feature of mortgage pass-through securities, the principal on individual mortgages in the pool can be prepaid without penalty in whole or in part at any time before the stated maturity of the security. This characteristic has important implications for the cash flow and market performance of the security, as will be explored in detail later.

Mortgage originators (savings and loans, commercial banks, and mortgage bankers) actively pool mortgages and issue pass-throughs. In most cases, the originator obtains the guarantee of one of three federally sponsored agencies: the Government National Mortgage Association (GNMA), or "Ginnie Mae"; the Federal National Mortgage Association (FNMA), or "Fannie Mae"; and the Federal Home Loan Mortgage Corporation (FHLMC), or "Freddie Mac." A significant volume of mortgages is directly purchased, pooled, and securitized by the agencies as well. A smaller amount of mortgages is securitized directly by private issuers.

The pass-through structure has proved to be an excellent vehicle for securitizing many different types of mortgage instruments available to home buyers. As a result, in addition to the standard level payment fixed-rate mortgage, large amounts of balloon, adjustable-rate mortgages, and graduated-payment mortgages have been securitized.

AGENCY PASS-THROUGH SECURITIES

The vast majority of regularly traded pass-throughs are issued and/or guaranteed by federally sponsored agencies. Differences between the agencies—the nature of their ties to the U.S. government, their stated role in national housing policy, and so forth—can affect the characteristics and relative value and performance of their pass-throughs. In addition, considerable diversity exists within each agency's pass-through programs and differences exist between programs which also influence the investment characteristics of the securities. For this reason, the agencies and their major programs are discussed in some detail.

The market generally classifies agency pass-throughs into two groups: those guaranteed by GNMA and those guaranteed by FHLMC and FNMA. The distinction reflects two issues: a perceived difference in credit quality and the nature of the underlying loans. Since GNMA is part of the Department of Housing and Urban Development, it is an arm of the U.S. government. As such, a GNMA guarantee carries the full faith and credit of the U.S. government. FHLMC and FNMA are not government agencies; they are government-sponsored entities (GSEs) which exist pursuant to government housing policy. FHLMC and FNMA are for-profit corporations (and their stock is exchange-traded) regulated by the federal government. As such, their guarantee does not carry the full faith and credit of the U.S. government. However, the rating agencies consider FNMA and FHLMC securities eligible collateral for triple-A securities "due to their close ties with the U.S. government." The market generally trades FNMAs and FHLMCs as if they were virtual triple-A or government agency issues.

The market perceives a difference in credit quality between GNMA and FHMLC/FNMA, and, as a consequence, demands a risk premium for the pass-throughs guaranteed by the latter. All other factors being equal, this would translate into a higher yield for the GSE-guaranteed issues. However, supply and demand forces typically obscure the existence of this spread premium. The most significant of these forces is the CMO bid. The vigorous participation of FNMA and FHLMC in the CMOs and strip markets has helped to bid up the price of these securities relative to GNMAs, largely obscuring the credit premium. CMOs are backed by GNMA pass-throughs as well; GNMA now has its own REMIC[2] program and the conventional agencies will issue GNMA-backed CMOs as well. However, GNMAs are typically more expensive to repackage as CMOs than are conventional pass-throughs, in part owing to their very different prepayment sensitivity in high-interest-rate environments. As a result, a larger amount of GNMAs are still available to trade in most coupon classes.[3] Given their greater liquidity, premium GNMAs are subject to strong demand by investors seeking defensive instruments in bear markets, while the longer seasoning required by assumable mortgages with below market rates gives discount coupon GNMAs long durations, reducing their attractions in a bear market. These forces also obscure the credit differential.

The market also differentiates between conventional pass-throughs and GNMAs because the underlying loans prepay very differently in low-interest-rate environments. Conventional loans are due on sale, in contrast to FHA and VA loans, which can be assumed by the buyer (hence the distinction between FNMA and FHLMC, as the "conventional" agencies, and GNMA as well as the usage "conventional" pass-throughs). Another important difference between conventional and FHA/VA mortgages is the fact that the FHA insurance and the VA guarantee provide implicit housing subsidies to people with moderate incomes and to veterans. For instance, the government loan programs permit borrowers to make very low down payments and to finance many closing costs. Similarly, the ceiling on VA and FHA loans is lower than that on the conventional loans pooled in FHLMCs and FNMAs.[4] As a result, borrowers tend to be first time and moderate income buyers.

Government National Mortgage Association Pass-Through Securities

The largest and best-known group of pass-through securities is guaranteed by GNMA. The mortgage pools underlying GNMA pass-through securities are made up of FHA-insured or VA-guaranteed mortgage loans. GNMA pass-throughs are backed by the full faith and credit of the U.S. government.

---

2 REMIC—Real Estate Mortgage Investment Conduit—is the term coined by Congress in the Tax Reform Act of 1986 for the tax treatment created in the Act for CMOs. Many market participants use CMO and REMIC interchangeably when referring to multiclass bond issues collateralized by pass-throughs or a single package of mortgage loans.

3 As of November 1, 1994, 8.5s (the current production coupon at the time) were the only 30-year conventional coupon class in which less than 50% of the outstanding principal amount had not been pledged to CMOs or strips (so that over 50% of the current face amount was available to trade). By contrast, at most 50% of principal outstanding in GNMA 6s to 10s had been pledged, and in most cases less than 25% had been pledged.

4 The current maximum VA loan amount is $184,000; the FHA maximum loan amount is $151,725. The maximum applies in high-cost areas such as New York. The FNMA and FHLMC ceiling is $203,150; loan limits are higher in high-cost areas.

Furthermore, the GNMA pass-through security is what is known as a *fully modified* pass-through security, which means that regardless of whether the mortgage payment is made, the holder of the security will receive full and timely payment of principal and interest. Among MBSs, GNMA is considered to be of the best credit quality since it is backed directly by the U.S. government.

GNMA administers two primary pass-through programs, the original GNMA program (GNMA I), in existence since 1970, and GNMA II, established in 1983. The GNMA I and II programs are further divided into pool types depending on the type of mortgages and other characteristics of the pool. For many years the most commonly held and traded of all pass-throughs securities was a 30-year maturity, fixed-rate GNMA backed by level payment mortgages on single-family residential homes (SF). The GNMA SF pool type is created in both the GNMA I and GNMA II programs. Single-family mortgages with original maturities of 15 years are part of the same SF pool type; the pools are called GNMA "Midgets" and differ from the 30-year securities only in stated maturity. GNMA pool types are based on other types of single-family mortgages as well, including adjustable-rate (ARM) loans as well as less commonly originated graduated-payment (GPM), growing-equity (GEM), and buydown (BD) loans. Markets for GNMA II SF, 15-year SF, GPM, GEM, and BD pools are smaller and less liquid than for the 30-year GNMA SFs. Mobile home loans (MH) and project loans (PL) are also securitized. Project loan securities are normally backed by a single FHA-insured loan for multifamily housing, hospitals, and similar public benefit housing-related projects. Construction loans for projects are also securitized as CL pool types.

Among the various agency and private pass-through programs, GNMA I pools are the most homogeneous. All mortgages in a pool must be of the same type and be less than 12 months old. Ninety percent of the pooled mortgages backing 30-year pass-throughs must have original maturities of 20 or more years. The mortgage interest rates of GNMA I pools must all be the same and the mortgages must be issued by the same lender. GNMA I payments have a stated 14-day delay (payment made on the 15th day). Minimum pool size for GNMA I pools is $1 million.

GNMA recently announced a program allowing investors to recombine smaller pools into a new, single pool in amounts of $10 million and up. Below a certain remaining principal amount, pools become harder to trade.[5] For a fee investors can recombine smaller GNMA I pools only into a single Platinum pool.

---

5 "Good delivery" on a TBA trade, requirements are three pools per million for coupons below 11% and five pools per million for coupons of 11% or higher. See footnote 10 below on TBA and generic pass-through trades.

The changes introduced with GNMA II include the ability to assemble multiple issuer pools, thereby allowing for larger and more geographically dispersed pools, as well as securitization of smaller portfolios. Also, a wider range of coupons is permitted in a GNMA II pool (the excess coupon income over the lowest rate is retained by the issuer or servicer as servicing income and is not passed through). Issuers are permitted to take greater servicing fees, ranging from 50 to 150 basis points. GNMA Is and IIs also differ in permitted payment delay; GNMA I payments are received with a 15-day delay, while GNMA IIs have an additional 5-day delay passing through principal and interest payments because issuer payments are consolidated by a central paying agent. The minimum pool size for GNMA IIs is $250,000 for multi-lender pools, $1,000,000 for single-lender pools. Despite these changes, issuance of GNMA II pools has been fairly small (as of November 1, 1994, the current face amount of liquid coupon classes in the 30-year GNMA I SF program was almost nine times as great as that of comparable 30-year GNMA II SF securities).

Federal National Mortgage Association Mortgage-Backed Securities

The Federal National Mortgage Association is the oldest of the three agencies, but the latest agency player to enter the pass-through market. FNMA was created in 1938 to provide liquidity to housing lenders. In 1968, the agency was split into GNMA and the private corporation FNMA, which was charged with the mission of promoting a secondary market for conventional mortgages on mid-priced housing and seasoned FHA/VA single- and multi-family mortgages. The first FNMA MBSs were issued in 1981. FNMA is, in effect, a quasi-private corporation. While a number of federal constraints on its activities exist, it does not receive a government subsidy or appropriation, its stock is traded on the New York Stock Exchange, and it is taxed at the full corporate rate. In addition to holding loans purchased from originators in its portfolio, FNMA also may securitize and sell the mortgages. FNMA pools mortgages from its purchase programs and issues MBSs to originators in exchange for pooled mortgages. Like GNMA, FNMA guarantees the timely payment of principal and interest for all securities it issues. Similarly, its securities are not rated by the rating agencies.

The 30-year conventional security, pool type CL, is backed by level payment mortgages fully amortizing in 16 to 30 years. FNMA also issues securities under pool type CI backed by conventional mortgages amortizing in 8 to 15 years, FNMA CIs. Seven-year balloon mortgages are securitized under the pool type CX. The agency also has played a significant role in issuing adjustable- and variable-rate mortgage pass-throughs. In addition, it administers programs to securitize FHA and VA 30-year loans and FHA-insured project loans under pool type GL.

Pool size starts at $1 million and more than one originator may join together to form pools. FNMA pools may contain aged mortgages, and underlying mortgage rates may range from 0 to 200 basis points above the pass-through coupon rate. For a fee, FNMA also permits investors to exchange small, older pools with the same coupon for a single MEGA Certificate in amounts of $10 million and up.

Federal Home Loan Mortgage Corporation Participation Certificates

FHLMC was created in 1970 to promote an active national secondary market for conventional residential mortgages, and has been issuing mortgage-backed securities since 1971. At its creation, FHLMC was governed as an entity within the Federal Home Loan Bank System, with stock held by member thrift institutions. The 1989 Financial Institutions Reform, Recovery, and Enforcement Act (FIRREA) restructured FHLMC to give it a market-oriented corporate structure similar to that of FNMA under the regulatory control of the Department of Housing and Urban Development (HUD).

The agency pools a wide variety of fixed- and adjustable-rate mortgages under its Gold Participation Certficate (PC) program. Standard fixed-rate PC programs include 30-, 20-, and 15-year mortgages. The Non-Standard conventional loans PCs include 5- and 7-year balloon mortgages, biweekly mortgages (paid every two-weeks), mortgages on cooperative shares, extended buydown mortgages, newly originated assumable mortgages, relocation loans (made to relocating employees under special lending arrangements established between large employers and mortgage bankers) and second mortgage loans. In addition, FHLMC will pool FHA/VA loans under its Gold program. Pooling criteria for Gold PCs have evolved over the years: currently the interest rates on the underlying mortgage may range as much as 250 basis points above the pool coupon rate. Loans may be any age. Twenty-year loans may be pooled separately or included in Standard or Non-Standard PC pools containing 30-year mortgages. Up to 10% of the conventional mortgages in a standard PC pool (by original principal balance) may be a Non-Standard mortgage other than second, biweekly, or balloon mortgages, so long as the combination of these types does not exceed 15% of the original principal balance. The minimum pool size for fixed-rate Gold PCs is $1,000,000 (fixed-rate Mini-PCs, containing Standard and some Non-Standard mortgage types, are pooled with a minimum pool size of $250,000). FHLMC also allows investors to repackage small, older pools in a single GIANT pool.

Prior to October 10, 1994, FHLMC distinguished between Gold securities issued in swap transactions with mortgage originators (Guarantor pools) and those backed by mortgages purchased in cash transactions with mortgage originators (Cash pools).[6] The Cash program allowed the underlying mortgage rates to vary from 25 and 75 basis points above the pool coupon (after October 1, 1993; before that the range between highest and lowest could not exceed 100 basis points, with the highest no more than 200 basis points above the pool coupon). Minimum pool size for Cash pools was $50 million. The Guarantor program was originally established in the 1980s to provide liquidity to the thrift industry by allowing originators to swap pooled mortgages for PCs backed by those same pools (hence they were called swap PCs). This program quickly became popular with mortgage bankers and grew to account for the bulk of FHLMC pass-through production.

The Gold guarantee provides for timely payment of interest and scheduled principal and ultimate payment of all principal without offset or deduction. Gold PCs have a stated payment delay of 14 days. Prior to June 1990, most FHLMC pass-throughs were issued with "modified" guarantees and they all had 44-day payment delays. A modified guarantee provides timely payment of interest and eventual payment of principal. These securities are now referred to as the 75-day-delay PCs since the payment was made on the 45th day and mortgage payments are made 30 days in arrears (due on the first day of the next month), the total delay on those securities was 75 days. The 75-day-delay securities may be exchanged for Gold PCs.

Private Pass-Through Securities

Mortgage pass-throughs have also been issued by private entities such as commercial banks, thrifts, homebuilders, and private conduits. These issues are referred to as conventional pass-throughs, private label, or "double-A" pass-throughs. These securities are not guaranteed or insured by a government agency or GSE. Instead, their credit is normally enhanced by pool insurance, letters of credit, guarantees, or subordinated interests. The great majority of private pass-throughs issued have received a rating of "AA" or better. The pass-through structure was more popular in the 1980s; with the advent of the REMIC tax rules, multi-class CMO-type structures and various levels of subordinated credit tranches (rated mezzanine classes and an unrated first lost piece) have become far more popular.

---

6 Since October 10, 1994, FHLMC distinguishes between programs by attaching the following prefixes to pool numbers: 30-year A0-A9, C0-C8, D0-D8, G0; 15-year B0-B1, E0-E9, G1; 20-year C9, D9, F8, G3; 5-year balloons L7, L9, M0-M1, M9, G5; and 7-year balloons L8, M8, N8-N9, G4. These prefixes map complexly back to a complex system for numbering Gold pools. The agency has readily available documentation for investors with questions about pool prefixes.

Private issuers of pass-throughs and CMOs provide a secondary market for conventional loans that do not qualify for FHLMC and FNMA programs. Normally, it is more profitable for originators of conforming loans (i.e., loans that do qualify for an agency security) to use the agency programs. There are a number of reasons why conventional mortgage loans may not qualify, but the chief one is that the principal balance exceeds the maximum allowed by the government (these are called "jumbo" loans in the market).

MORTGAGE AND PASS-THROUGH CASH FLOWS

The investment characteristics and performance of pass-throughs cannot be evaluated without a thorough understanding of what cash flows are received by the investor. Analysis of the cash flow pattern begins with the simplest case, the payment stream of a single mortgage, assuming a fixed mortgage rate, level payments, and no prepayment of principal. Following that, the effects of servicing fees (the amount retained by a servicer reduces the cash flow to pass-through holders) and, most important, prepayments are incorporated into the analysis.

Standard residential fixed-rate mortgages are repaid in equal monthly installments of principal and interest (hence, the term *level payment*).The payment amount is determined such that, for a given interest rate, principal payments retire the loan as of the final payment date. In the early years, most of the monthly installment consists of interest. Over time, the interest portion of each payment declines as the principal balance declines until, near maturity, almost all of each payment is principal.

Under the assumption that all of the mortgages have the same interest rates and maturities, a "scheduled" cash-flow pattern can be projected for the pool. In other words, the pool is treated as if it were an individual mortgage. Exhibit 1 shows the scheduled cash-flow pattern for a $1 million pool of 10%, 30-year mortgages, assuming no prepayments or servicing fees. Note that the proportion of the payment that is interest declines as the proportion of principal increases over time. It is important to understand that, even without considering prepayments, the projected cash flows calculated by this procedure are *estimates*. The alternative to assuming all loans have the same interest rate and maturity would be to calculate the payments for each loan individually and then aggregate them. This is far too inefficient an approach and the loan level data are not provided by agencies or servicers. Instead, the scheduled cash flows from a pool are estimated using the weighted average of loan interest rates, or coupons (WAC) as the pool's mortgage rate and the weighted average of loan maturities (WAM) as the pool's maturity.[7] It is possible to

---

7 The WAC and WAM are computed using as weights the principal amount outstanding. Sometimes the WAC is referred to as the pool's "Gross WAC" and the pool coupon rate as the "Net WAC."

project the payments with reasonable accuracy when pools are fairly homogeneous, as GNMA pools are. (The discrepancy arises from the fact that amortization is not a "linear" function. Individual loans will be paying principal and interest at different rates depending on the age and term of the loan.[8]) The accuracy of projected amortization schedules using WAC and WAM statistics is reduced somewhat when a wide range of coupons, maturities, and seasonings is permitted in a pool.

The cash flow from a pass-through certificate is similar but not identical to the cash flow from the underlying pool of mortgages. The differences arise from the deduction of servicing fees (and a servicing delay in the receipt of payments, discussed below) so that the scheduled total monthly cash flow from the mortgage pool is level, while the cash flow from the corresponding pass-through is not. The servicing fee is defined as a percentage of the outstanding principal, and is subtracted from the interest paid on the underlying mortgages. The remaining interest income is passed through to the security holder as coupon income. (In other words, servicing is equal to the WAC less the coupon.) Thus the dollar amount of servicing fee decreases as principal declines. As a consequence, the total cash flows to pass-through owners increase slightly over the term. The cash flows from a pass-through certificate with a 9.5% coupon (the difference between the 10% WAC and a 0.5% servicing fee) are depicted in Exhibit 2. The graph shows that the decline in servicing fees leads to slightly increasing cash flow over time.

The possibility individual loans will prepay is the critical issue for investors evaluating mortgage securities. Individual loans can be paid off prior to pool maturity because the borrower sells the property or refinances. *The*

---

8 Actually, assuming an original principal amount of $1, three parameters are needed to calculate scheduled interest and principal: term, coupon, and age. The term and the coupon are used to calculate a full series of monthly P&I payments (180, 240, or 360 payments) and the age is used to roll off payments already estimated to have been made. The term WAM is normally used to indicate the remaining maturity of pools, so that WAM equals the pool term minus the age. This usage is accurate if all loans in a pool have the same terms. For example, the average age of underlying loans in a 30-year pool (term 360 months) with a WAM of 359 months (WAM + AGE = TERM) is 1 month. This assumption works less well when, as in conventional pools, loans of different ages and different original terms (20-year with 30-year) can be pooled together. For instance, a 30-year pool can have an original (at issue) WAM of 352. If all the loans are 30-year loans, then the average loan age is 8 months. If an uncertain number of loans have 20-year terms, then 8 months is only an estimate of the pool's age, impounding additional uncertainty in the projected cash flows. The agencies provide different statistics to help the market resolve some of this uncertainty. The agencies now update their WAM statistics for pools monthly to capture the changing contents of the pool. In addition, FHLMC and GNMA provide an actual weighted average loan age, updated monthly (WALA).

**Exhibit 1. Scheduled Mortgage Pool Cash Flows ($1 Million Pool of 10%
30-Year Mortgages)**

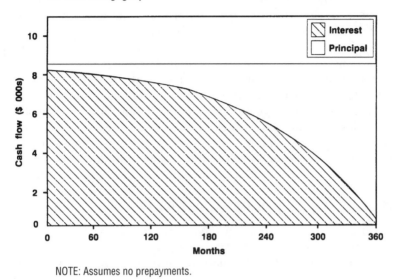

NOTE: Assumes no prepayments.

**Exhibit 2. Scheduled Mortgage-Backed Security Cash Flows ($1 Million Pool of 10%,
30-Year Mortgages and a 9.5% Pass-Through Certificate)**

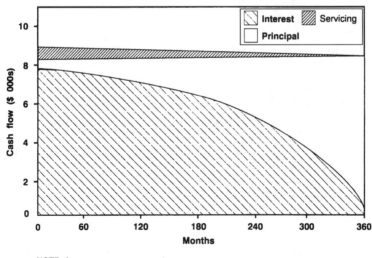

NOTE: Assumes no prepayments.

possibility of prepayments means that cash flows cannot be predicted with certainty. Assumptions concerning the likely prepayment pattern must be made in order to estimate the cash flows.

Exhibit 3 depicts the cash flow patterns for the 9.5%, 30-year pass-through in the previous example when a prepayment assumption is introduced. The cash flow pattern shown in the diagram is based on the assumption that a constant fraction of the remaining principal is prepaid each month (in this case, at a constant prepayment rate of 0.5% per month). The cash flow is no longer level in each month over the period. Instead, it declines each month as both prepayments and scheduled principal payments reduce the remaining principal balance of the pool. The reader should note that prepayments lower the total amount of interest paid over the life of the pass-through in addition to accelerating the return of principal.

DETERMINANTS OF PREPAYMENT RATES

The chief determinant of a pass-through's investment performance is the effect of prepayments on cash flows actually received. For this reason, MBS investors devote considerable attention to the underlying causes of prepayments and to projecting prepayments over the investment horizon. The

---

Exhibit 3. Scheduled and Unscheduled Mortgage-Backed Security Cash Flows ($1 Million Pool of 10%, 30-Year Mortgages, and a 9.5% Pass-Through Certificate)

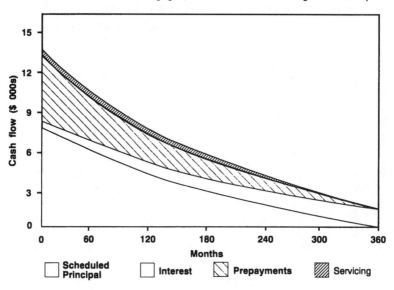

causes of prepayments generally fall under two categories—refinancing and mobility. Homeowners tend to refinance when the current market mortgage rate is far enough below the rate on their existing mortgage to lower their monthly payment significantly.[9] The difference in payments must be at least great enough to permit the homeowner to recover the loan fees and other costs of refinancing over some reasonable period of time. In the 1980s, a common rule of thumb put this lower mortgage rate at 200 basis points below the existing mortgage's rate. Aggressive marketing by mortgage banking firms, the leading originators of loans securitized in GNMA and conventional agency securities, have resulted in no-point and even no-fee loan terms. In such a lending environment, borrowers may consider an interest-rate cut as small as 50 basis points sufficient inducement to refinance.

Since the future level of interest rates is very difficult to anticipate, the resulting prepayments are also difficult to predict. Refinancings are a negative event for pass-through investors since they are triggered by a fall in market rates and the principal returned must be reinvested at lower yields. Investors who purchase their high-coupon pass-throughs at a premium may experience additional losses, since the principal is repaid at par and must remain outstanding to earn interest sufficient to recover the future value of the premium paid over par.

Mobility refers to the fact that at any time, in any mortgage rate environment, homeowners sell their homes and move. Mobility is also linked to the level of interest rates. Higher interest rates act as a disincentive to buy a new home while lower interest rates favor housing turnover. The due-on-sale clause, now enforceable by federal law, ensures this kind of prepayment of conventional loans. By contrast, GNMA pools, made up of assumable government-insured mortgages, experience this form of prepayment at a lower rate. An assumable loan is less likely to prepay when it has a below-market interest rate.

The chief indicator of a pass-through's prepayment risk is the average underlying mortgage rate—the pool WAC. The farther below current mortgage rates a pool's WAC is, the slower the pool is expected to prepay. Likewise, prepayments are faster for pools with above-market-rate WACs. It follows that securities with higher pass-through coupons are expected to pay faster than those with lower coupons, but investors must not lose sight of the fact that the pass-through coupon is less than the underlying mortgage rates

---

9 Actually, prepayments can arise from a third source, cash-out refinancings. In this case, homeowners refinance in order to realize paid-in equity or increases in appraised home value. Homeowners may be more likely to refinance for this purpose when they can pay the same or a lower rate of interest, but in many situations the need to do so (home improvement or expansion, illness or education expenses, *etc.*) is not interest-rate sensitive.

by the amount of servicing and guarantee fees. In the case of GNMA I securities, the coupon precisely indicates the underlying mortgage rate, since every mortgage in the pool must have the same rate and 50 basis points are stripped off. However, with conventional agency (and private issue) pools, there is considerable room for variation in underlying mortgage rates above the coupon. For example, we know GNMA SF 8s have a WAC of 8.50%. By contrast, as of November 1, 1994, in aggregate, FNMA CL 8s (18,304 pools with a current principal balance of $45.9 billion) had a WAC of 8.554%, while FHLMC Gold 8s (10,230 pools, $56.6 billion) had a WAC of 8.594%.

Nonetheless, because the WAC is indicated by the coupon of a GNMA I security and can be assumed on average for a conventional pass-through, the market uses the coupon as a short-hand indication of prepayment risk and trades pass-throughs accordingly. The most fundamental relative value distinctions among pass-throughs are made on the basis of prepayment risk: between GNMAs and conventionals and among discount, current, and premium coupon securities. To satisfy investor preference, the vast majority of pass-throughs pools are issued with a whole or half coupon (8, 8.5, 9, *etc.*) and securities with quarter, eighth, or other coupon groups are illiquid. The current coupon is usually defined as the pass-through with a whole or half coupon priced closest to but below par. Under normal market conditions this is also the coupon class where most new supply is entering the market.

The age or *seasoning* of a pool is another key determinant of prepayment behavior and, accordingly, of relative value within and across coupon classes. Normally, some months or years elapse after a mortgage is closed before the borrower is willing or able to go to the effort and expense of moving or refinancing. As a result, prepayment rates increase from a very low level during the early years of a pass-through's life to level off sometime after 12 to 60 months (depending on program and coupon). As a result, newly issued pass-throughs will demonstrate low prepayment rates, but significant rates of increase from month to month. Likewise, the prepayment rates of fully seasoned securities will be relatively stable. ("Seasoned" means that the pass-through has been outstanding long enough for this process to have occurred and prepayments to have reached a steady state approrpriate for the interest-rate environment. When the loans are unrefinanceable, the steady state is characterized by a pronounced seasonal prepayment pattern, reflecting the fact that housing turnover is highly seasonal. When a security is refinanceable, the steady state is indicated by a slowing of the rate at which prepayments accelerate from month to month. In general, lower coupons season more slowly than higher coupons. Historically, GNMAs have seasoned more slowly than conventionals because the loans are assumable.

Depending on the characteristics of current tradable supply and the prevailing interest-rate environment, some degree of price tiering can exist in coupons or coupons groups. For example, investors will pay a premium for seasoned discounts over new pools, on the assumption that principal will be returned more quickly. Similarly, very seasoned premium coupons are valued in sustained rally environments because they tend to be less responsive to refinancing opportunities. One of the explanations for this effect is that, as years pass, the interest portion of the monthly payment declines, lowering the total savings a cut in rate would produce. Another is that when pools are exposed to repeated refinancing opportunities over time, the borrowers remaining in the pool are somewhat less likely to respond to the next opportunity. This effect is often termed "burnout."

Considerable attention has been given to identifying the factors underlying prepayment activity in mortgage pass-throughs and specifying them in econometric models which can be used to project prepayments. These factors include the economic incentive, the weighted average age of the pool, burnout, and seasonality. More recent models have attempted to capture other influences on borrower behavior such as price appreciation (depreciation) and macroeconomic factors. Prepayment modeling is discussed in greater detail in Chapters 9 and 10.

The unique securitization and cash flow characteristics of mortgage pass-throughs give rise to important differences from Treasury and corporate securities. These are summarized in Exhibit 4.

Measuring Prepayments

In order to facilitate the evaluation and trading of mortgage-backed securities, the market has evolved a variety of conventions for quantifying prepayments. The oldest and simplest of these was the prepaid life assumption employed by secondary market traders of whole loan mortgages. At that time the 12-year prepaid life assumption was the industry standard for quoting mortgage yields. Under this convention, a 30-year pass-through is treated like a single mortgage prepaying in the twelfth year of its life (or, no loans prepay until the twelfth year, when they all prepay). Other prepaid life assumptions were used, such as 7-year prepaid life, but the 12-year assumption was the standard. During the 1970s and mid-1980s, however, interest rates and, in turn, prepayments became far more volatile. Prepaid life assumptions could not be adjusted for actual prepayment experience or the differences in coupon, maturity, seasoning, and other security characteristics which began to appear as the pass-through market evolved.

Recognizing the problems with the prepaid life assumptions, traders and investors began using the termination experience collected on FHA-insured mortgages issued since 1970 to model expected prepayments. These data are published periodically by HUD in the form of a table of 30 numbers indicating the probability of survival of a mortgage at any given year up to

Exhibit 4.   Features of Pass-Through, Government, and Corporate Securities Compared

	Pass-Throughs	Treasuries
Credit Risk	Generally high grade; range from government guaranteed to A (private pass-throughs)	Government guaranteed
Liquidity	Good for agency issued/guaranteed pass-through	Excellent
Range of Coupons (Discount to Premium)	Full range	Full range
Range of Maturities	Medium- and long-term (fast-paying and seasoned pools can provide shorter maturities than stated)	Full range
Call Protection	Complex prepayment pattern; investor can limit through selection variables such as coupon, seasoning, and program	Noncallable (except certain 30-year bonds)
Frequency of Payment	Monthly payments of principal and interest	Semiannual interest payment
Average Life	Lower than for bullets of comparable maturity; can only be estimated due to prepayment risk	Estimate only for small number of callable issues; otherwise, known with certainty
Duration/Interest-Rate Risk	Function of prepayment risk; can only be estimated; can be negative when prepayment risk is high	Unless callable, a simple function of yield, coupon, and maturity; is known with certainty
Basis for Yield Quotes	Cash-flow yield based on monthly payments and a constant CPR assumption	Based on semiannual coupon payments and 365-day year
Settlement	Once a month	Any business day

maturity. Prepayment rates (the percentage or fraction of principal prepaying in a year) are implicit in these survivorship rates. An example of an FHA series converted to prepayment rates is graphed in Exhibit 5. Its advantage was that it linked prepayments to age; prepayments rise rapidly in the first 30 months and then level off (the staircase pattern in the last years was an interpolation provided by FHA actuaries). Given a pool's age, prepayments over the remaining months to maturity could be projected based on the FHA

Exhibit 4. *Continued*

	Corporates	**Stripped Treasuries**
Credit Risk	High grade to speculative	Backed by government guarantees
Liquidity	Generally limited	Fair
Range of Coupons (Discount to Premium)	Full range for a few issuers	Zero coupon (discount securities)
Range of Maturities	Full range	Full range
Call Protection	Generally callable after initial limited period of five to ten years	Noncallable
Frequency of Payment	Semiannual interest (except Eurobonds, which pay interest annually)	No payments until maturity
Average Life	Minimum average life known, otherwise a function of call risk	Known with certainty
Duration/Interest-Rate Risk	Function of call risk; can be negative when call risk is high	Known with certainty; no interest-rate risk if held to maturity
Basis for Yield Quotes	Based on semiannual coupon payments and 360-day year of twelve 30-day months	Bond equivalent yield based on either 360- or 365-day year, depending on sponsor
Settlement	Any business day	Any business day

series of annual rates. Faster or slower prepayment speeds were expressed as a multiple of the base table. For instance, "0% of FHA" means no prepayments, "100% of FHA" refers to the average rate, and "200% of FHA" means twice the FHA rate.

The FHA experience was welcomed in the early years of the mortgage market before huge databases of actual prepayment experience were accumulated which allowed the market to link prepayment behavior to other factors besides age. As the market's empirical understanding of prepayment behavior grew, the shortcomings of the FHA series became more problematic. For one, the underlying data are from assumable FHA mortgages and can be misleading when applied to conventional pass-throughs. Moreover, FHA experience did not provide a consistent standard because a new series is published each year or so, often based on different statistical manipulations

Exhibit 5. PSA vs. FHA CPR Series

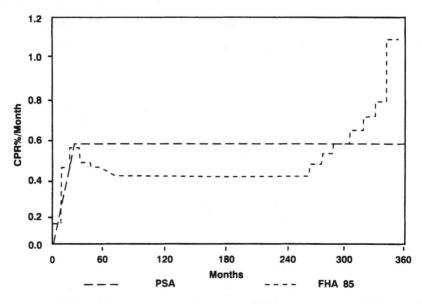

of the underlying data. For instance, prior to FHA 83, all mortgages back to 1957 were included; subsequently all mortgages prior to 1970 were excluded. Extrapolation was used to a greater degree to derive experience for years not covered by actual data. Similarly, through 1981, each year's data were equally weighted; starting in 1982, mortgages issued in the 1980s were given additional weight. For instance, in 1986, investors could conceivably be pricing MBSs based on 1981, 1983, 1984, or 1985 FHA statistics.

Conditional Prepayment Rates. As the market expanded during the mid-1980s, large Wall Street firms making markets in pass-throughs developed the capability to report historical prepayments on individual pools as well as specific coupons within programs and, within coupons, groups of pools with various degrees of seasoning. These reports allowed investors and traders to form empirical views on prepayment behavior and to base projections of future prepayments on the aggregate response of generic pass-throughs to actual interest-rate environments. The fundamental measure employed in these reports was the conditional prepayment rate (CPR) or single monthly mortality (SMM). This measure has become the principal means traders and investors employ to quantify prepayment activity in pass-throughs. The CPR measures prepayments as a fraction or percentage of the remaining principal balance at the beginning of the measurement period (hence, "conditional" on the principal balance). Thus it can be employed to express an average or compound rate over many periods, or a single-period rate. The resulting rate sometimes is expressed as an annualized percentage. (In recent years CPR has increasingly come to refer to an annualized prepayment rate, SMM to the monthly rate.) This simple quantification is intuitive and easy to incorporate into pricing and yield formulas. In calculating yields, investors may employ a single or "constant" CPR assumption across the term of the investment to project the cash flows. The use of a constant CPR is the most common (hence it is sometimes thought that CPR stands for "constant prepayment assumption"). Some analytic tools allow investors to project pass-through cash flows using a series (sometimes called a "vector") of varying CPR assumptions reflecting historical experience or projections from formal prepayment forecast models.

The PSA Prepayment Standard. The Public Securities Association (PSA) introduced a Standard Prepayment Model for the purpose of valuing CMOs. The intention was to to replace with a single standard the proliferation of FHA experience tables being used to project cash flows on the underlying collateral when CMO issues were structured and priced. It is not really a model; more correctly, it is a measurement standard or yardstick, expressed as a series of 360 monthly prepayment rates expressed as annual CPRs. It begins at 0.2% in the first month and increases by 0.2% in each successive month until month 30, when the series levels out at 6% per year until maturity. Prepayments are measured as simple linear multiples of this schedule. For instance, 200% PSA is 0.4% per year in the first month, 0.8% per year in the second month, and 12% per year after month 30. Market participants often speak of the first 30 months of the series as the "ramp" and speak of securities seasoned 30 months as "off the ramp." Exhibit 5 compares the PSA standard to the 1985 FHA series.

One advantage of the PSA CPR series is that it does reflect the normal increase in CPRs that occurs as the pool ages. (Since a CMO issue effectively "carves up" the cash flow from pass-through collateral among a series of bond classes with short, intermediate, and long average lives, it is important to be as realistic as possible when projecting the amount of cash available in the early years to pay off the bonds with the shortest expected average lives.) This effect is also captured by the FHA series, but the PSA series of CPRs do not display the fluctuation in prepayment rates found in the FHA series. After month 30, using the PSA is equivalent to applying a constant CPR over the remaining life of the pool. The PSA standard was intended to simplify the comparison and analysis of CMOs, but has increasingly been used to express prepayment speeds in the fixed-rate pass-through market (ARM speeds are expressed in CPR terms). This practice can be confusing and even misleading. For instance, for very new securities, a relatively small CPR can be reported as a very large PSA because the divisors are so small on the "foot of the ramp." A similar sort of illusion is created when the monthly prepayment rates on new securities go up, but not as fast as suggested by the PSA ramp. In this case it will appear as if reported speeds, in PSA terms, are going down, when in fact the CPRs are going up. Thirty months is much too long a seasoning period for conventional securities and is too long for GNMAs if they become refinanceable. Furthermore, differences in prepayments between fast-paying and slow-paying pools are not proportional over the lives of the pools. Relying on a PSA prepayment assumption, without considering the CPRs and hence the actual magnitudes of the cash flows which it expresses, can result in mistaken security valuations and investment decisions. Finally, the PSA standard should not be used with securities backed by loans making balloon payments at maturity.

EVALUATING PASS-THROUGH SECURITIES YIELD, AVERAGE LIFE, AND DURATION

The price of a pass-through is the present value of the projected cash flows discounted at the current yield required by the market, given the specific interest rate and prepayment risks of the security in question. Generic[10] agency pass-throughs trade on price, subject to supply and demand forces. That means the required yield and the prepayment assumption may both have to be imputed from the price. Increasingly the market has gravitated toward using econometric models (or a median of Street firms' prepayment models) to fix the prepayment assumption given the current level of interest rates. It is then an easy matter to find the yield. Investors use the yield-to-maturity on the projected cash flows (given the prepayment assumption) at a given market price as the basis for determining if the anticipated investment return is a good value relative to other investment alternatives.

Yield is useful for determining relative value but it is a poor predictor of future performance. Yield-to-maturity is a poor predictor of any bond's performance because it assumes that (1) all cash flows are reinvested at an interest rate equal to the yield, and (2) the security is held to maturity. Further, there is the implication that the market values cash flows of different maturities at the same average yield.

Deviations from the first assumption are particularly significant for pass-throughs owing to their monthly coupon and principal payments, since

---

10 The most generic of pass-throughs is a coupon class of a specific agency program with a whole or half coupon. This security trades "TBA" or "to be announced," meaning that the seller may deliver at settlement a pool or pools of any age that meet the description (subject to good delivery guidelines established by the PSA). A year class within a coupon class may be stipulated (based on WAM). In most circumstances it would trade at a premium to the "TBA" price.

interest on these payments compounds monthly in the yield calculation instead of semiannually on coupon payments only, as with Treasury and corporate bonds. Exhibit 6 demonstrates how much the realized return or internal rate of return on the cash flows can vary when reinvestment rates different from the yield-to-maturity are used to project the total cash flows to be received from a pass-through. The second assumption is as unrealistic for MBS as it is for Treasury and corporate bonds. If an investment is not held to maturity, the realized yield will be affected by any capital gain or loss on the remaining cash flows, as market yields and prices are likely to have changed since the initial investment was made.

More importantly, the yield anticipated on a pass-through can vary significantly depending on the prepayment rate used to project the cash flows. If the pass-through is priced at par, changes in prepayment speeds do not affect the yield calculation. (Actually, the yield does not change if the security was purchased at its *parity price* (slightly less than 100), which adjusts par for the payment delay. The delay lowers yield at a given price by moving the cash flows further out into the future.) No matter when the principal is returned, the security will continue to yield its coupon rate on the remaining principal. At faster speeds, the earlier receipt of principal offsets the loss of coupon income, and at slower speeds, additional coupon income offsets the additional delay in return of principal. However, if the security is purchased at a premium, faster than expected prepayments will reduce the yield: prepayments shorten the amount of time principal remains outstanding to earn above-market coupon payments, thereby lowering the total cash flows. In a similar fashion, the yield of a discount security increases with faster

---

Exhibit 6. Effect of Reinvestment Rate on Realized Yield from Monthly Payments on a 9.5% Pass-Through Priced at 99 8/32 to Yield 9.54%

Reinvestment Rate%	Realized Cash- Flow Yield(%)	Change from Expected Yield (%)
4	5.93	-37.84
6	7.16	-24.95
8	8.48	-11.11
10	9.87	3.46
12	11.33	18.76
14	12.84	34.59
16	14.41	51.05

NOTE: Assumes 0.50% service fee and no prepayments.

prepayments as the time required to earn the discount is shortened. Principal purchased at, say, 90% of its value, is returned at 100%. The effect of prepayments on yield for securities purchased close to, above, or below par is shown in Exhibit 7.

Two additional issues requiring brief discussion arise from the differences between the cash-flow characteristics of mortgage securities and those of Treasury or corporate bonds. First, the difference in payment timing between pass-throughs and bonds with semiannual coupons and bullet principal payments means their yields are not directly comparable. The greater frequency of payments increases the value of a pass-through of a given coupon compared to traditional corporate or government debt. Interest compounds monthly. This monthly compounding gives pass-through securities a yield advantage over other securities of the same coupon. Quoted cash-flow yields, however, do not reflect the advantage. For instance, a 10.00% cash-flow yield is equivalent to a 10.21% bond yield. In order to compare pass-through yields to yields on other securities, it is necessary to adjust the mortgage yield upward to its bond equivalent yield (BEY). Basically, the monthly coupons are treated as if they are collected and reinvested at the cash-flow yield rate until the end of each semiannual or other period. The accumulated (compounded) amount is larger than the sum of the face amount of six monthly coupons.

The second, the payment delay, does not alter the level of payments, but it does affect their timing. In effect, it pushes the stream of payments further out in time and effectively lowers the current value of the payment stream. There are two sources of payment delay in pass-throughs. Mortgage

Exhibit 7. Effect of Different Prepayment Rates on the Cash-Flow Yield of Discount, Current, and Premium Coupon Pass-Throughs*

CPR	Price		
(%/yr)	89 20/32	99 28/32	105 4/32
2	8.78	9.57	10.67
4	8.97	8.58	10.57
6	9.18	9.58	10.46
8	9.39	9.59	10.35
10	9.62	9.60	10.23
12	9.85	9.62	10.11
18	10.58	9.65	9.74
24	11.37	9.68	9.33

*7.5%, 9.5%, and 11.5% coupons, respectively.

payments are made in arrears; that is, interest accrues during the month (on a 30-day basis) and is payable, along with a scheduled principal amount, on the first day of the second month. Second, there is a further delay as the servicer collects payments due (a 15-day grace period is typical) before the holder of the corresponding pass-through receives the payment. An investor in a GNMA single-family pass-through, for example, does not receive payment until the fifteenth day of the second month (a 14-day actual delay plus 30 days for the accrual period plus 1 amounts to a 45-day stated delay). FNMA securities have a stated delay of 55 days, which means the first payment takes place on the twenty-fifth day of the second month. Older FHLMC securities have a 75-day delay, while newer Gold PCs have 45-day delays.

Delay decreases the current value of the stream of payments: the greater the delay, the lower the price for a given cash-flow yield. Similarly, for a given yield and payment stream, yield declines as delay increases. Yield and cash flows held equal, GNMA securities with lower delays will trade at higher prices than FNMAs or FHLMCs, and FNMAs will trade higher than FHLMCs. The effect of varying the delay on the yield, price held constant, and the price, yield held constant, for a 9.5% coupon pass-through is indicated in Exhibit 8. For instance, assuming the security has a price of 99:08 points, adding 15 days to a stated delay of 30 days lowers the yield to 9.54% from 9.59%. In price terms, the table indicates that the difference in delay between otherwise comparable Gold and FNMA 9.5s is worth about 8+/32 point.

The interest rate and age of a mortgage (or WAC and WAM of the underlying loans in a mortgage pool), as we have noted, determine the rate at which scheduled principal is expected to be paid to the investor. In general, for the same principal amount and term, the higher the mortgage rate is, the greater the interest payments, and, accordingly, the lower the principal payments in the early years of the mortgage are. A look at any of the cash-flow figures should make apparent the effect of age on cash flows. All other

Exhibit 8. The Effect of Payment Delay on Pass-Through Yield and Price

Stated Delay	Yield	Change	Price	Change (%)
30	9.59		99 8/32	
45	9.54	-0.05	98 27/32+	-0.39
50	9.53	-0.06	98 23/32+	-0.52
55	9.51	-0.08	98 19/32	-0.66
75	9.45	-0.14	98 2/32	-1.20

NOTE: Assumes 9.5 coupon, 99 8/32 price, 9.59 yield, and no prepayments.

things being equal, age affects the cash flow by establishing the amount of principal included in a given monthly payment and the number of payments remaining. As the security ages, a greater proportion of the payments will be principal. For pass-throughs purchased at a given discount price, older pass-throughs will have higher yields—more principal is returned sooner at par. Age has the opposite impact on premium securities; at the same price and coupon older pass-throughs have lower yields, since less principal is outstanding for shorter periods of time to earn high coupon income while principal is coming back to the investor at par. In either case, the further the price of the security is from par, the greater the impact of seasoning on the yield. The yields for securities that are near par are not significantly affected.

The natural variability of expected cash flows from a pass-through investment makes it difficult as well to determine the degree of risk undertaken. A fundamental measure of the risk in any investment is its term, or longevity. Because the principal is returned throughout the pass-through's life, maturity is not a good measure of the longevity of this form of debt. The likelihood of prepayments amplifies this deficiency. For these reasons, a preferred measure for mortgage-backed securities, including pass-throughs, is the average elapsed time until the principal is returned. *Average life* is calculated as the weighted average time to principal repayment, with the amount of the principal paydowns (both scheduled and prepaid) as the weights. Average life expresses the average number of years that each principal dollar will be outstanding. Clearly, the higher the prepayment rate, the sooner the principal is returned and hence the shorter the average life. It should also be apparent from the definition that average life declines as a security ages.

Determining a pass-through's interest-rate risk, or duration, with certainty is also impossible. Modified, or cash-flow, duration[11] is as sensitive to the prepayment assumption used to project a pass-through's cash flows as are its yield and average life. As a result, a duration can significantly misestimate the actual price change of pass-throughs when interest rates decline and the market changes its estimates of prepayment risk. More importantly, a pass-through's duration changes as the expected prepayment rates used to calculate it change in response to changes in the general level of interest rates. Pass-through duration lengthens in a bear market and shortens in a bull market. As a result, a pass-through's price can decline more quickly than a Trea-

---

11 Macaulay duration is defined as the weighted average time to receipt of the present value of both principal and interest cash flows. With a routine adjustment, this expression is equivalent to the first derivative of price with respect to yield. That is, *modified duration* expresses the percentage change in price that would occur for a small change in yield, assuming cash flows are fixed. Since prepayments are also interest-rate sensitive, this assumption is violated. Duration shrinks or grows with interest-rate shifts and it drifts with time.

sury with the same duration at the outset when interest rates rise. Similarly, pass-through prices increase more slowly for successive declines in the general level of interest rates. This characteristic of a pass-through's price behavior is generally referred to as "negative convexity." It is also observed in the phenomenon called "coupon compression." This term refers to the fact that price spreads between coupons shrink as the coupon—and the prepayment expectation—increases. In other words, the market might price GNMA 7s 3:06 points above GNMA 6.5s and GNMA 8.5s only 2:24 points above GNMA 8s.

Modified duration, then, is not a good prospective measure of a pass-through's price risk because it reflects a static prepayment assumption. Approaches taken by the market to adjust for this shortcoming include effective duration, empirical duration, and option-adjusted duration. Effective durations are measured by calculating the relative change in price that would result, assuming a large enough shift in rates (for example, 25, 50, or 100 basis points up and down) to generate a change in the prepayment assumption. The new prepayment rates are used to calculate a new price given the shifted yields; solving for the percentage price change per one basis point of yield shift produces the effective duration. Empirical durations are determined by a statistical analysis of actual price changes for observed changes in market yields, so that an empirical duration captures the duration implied by actual trading behavior. Option-adjusted duration is computed similarly to an effective duration using option pricing models, discussed below. Which measure of price risk an investor uses depends on the horizon, the strategy, and the mortgage instrument. For instance, a short-term hedge may work best when constructed using an empirical measure of price behavior, while an effective or OA duration may be a better indicator of interest-rate risk over a longer investment horizon.

The cash flows from pass-throughs, particularly as they reflect monthly amortization, delays, and the likelihood of prepayments, give rise to the major differences between pass-throughs on the one hand and Treasury and corporate bonds on the other. The differences among these instruments are summarized in Exhibit 9.

Relative Value Analysis

The chief objective of any investment evaluation technique is to identify the securities which provide the highest return for a given level of risk. Yield-to-maturity or the internal rate of return on a bond's cash flows is traditionally used to order investment opportunities in fixed-income instruments. For securities of comparable risk, the highest yielding security would be the cheapest and most attractive. With mortgage pass-throughs the difficulty is determining the degree of risk. Credit risk is normally assumed away, but the

Exhibit 9.   One-Year Return (%)

Total Rates of Return on Selected Conventional Pass-Throughs

Interest Rate Shift (Basis Points)	FNMA 6.5	FNMA 8.5	FNMA 10
-250	22.00	18.15	15.37
-200	20.55	17.20	13.81
-150	17.88	15.88	12.42
-100	15.09	14.13	11.16
-50	12.30	12.07	9.99
0	9.57	9.78	8.87
50	6.95	7.32	7.76
100	4.44	4.80	6.60
150	2.03	2.31	5.38
200	-0.29	-0.12	4.13
250	-2.51	-2.46	2.86

interest-rate risk and the yield of a mortgage pass-through are uncertain at the time the investment decision is made. Nonetheless, the mortgage market has adapted traditional techniques of bond analysis in order to make relative value comparisons to other fixed-income sectors and across sectors of the pass-through and CMO markets.

The first comparison made between pass-throughs and other instruments is to Treasury instruments, typically the on-the-run Treasury with the maturity closest to the pass-through's average life. Average life is not the best basis on which to compare a monthly-pay mortgage security to a bullet Treasury, but it approximates maturity. (The better comparison would be between securities of comparable price sensitivity, or duration). Given the widespread acceptance of prepayment models, most participants now use a median of dealer prepayment projections (such as published on Bloomberg Capital Markets screens or by the PSA on Telerate) as the consensus of market prepayment expectations. For instance, as of October 26, 1994, the market price for GNMA 8s was 98:08,[12] and the median of dealer prepayment projections, assuming interest rates are unchanged, was 135% PSA to yield 8.92 (assuming a WAM of 349, representative of the coupon class). At that speed the pass-through has an average life of 9.6 years and provides a yield spread to the 10-year of 106 basis points. That is, the pass-through would provide 106 basis points additional yield to a comparable Treasury benchmark if interest rates are unchanged and the prepayment assumption is on target.

---

12 Source: Bloomberg L.P.

This spread to a Treasury benchmark[13] can be used to make rudimentary relative value distinctions between pass-throughs. (Is an FNMA or FHLMC pool of FHA/VA loans cheap to a GNMA with the same coupon? Or, is an FHLMC 6.5 rich compared to a GNMA 8?) It fails to account for the much greater uncertainty in the pass-though than in the Treasury cash flows. That is, the pass-through is cheap to the Treasury only in the very unlikely case that interest rates are unchanged and the median of Street firms' prepayment projections is correct. In other scenarios the 106 basis points of base case yield may not compensate an investor for holding the pass-through instead of the Treasury. For instance, if interest rates fall sharply, the pass-through investor must reinvest monthly principal and interest in lower yielding securities while the Treasury investor has locked in a higher coupon on the entire principal until the maturity date. Worse, falling interest rates accelerate prepayments. As an example of how badly the pass-through yield can be reduced by reinvesting rapid prepayments at a lower rate, assume yields drop 200 basis points instantaneously. If interest cash flows, now returned at 350% PSA, are reinvested at a yield 200 basis points less than the original pass-through yield, or in the case of the Treasury alternative, at the Treasury yield less 200 basis points, the GNMA 8.5 would yield 7.18%, the Treasury 7.32% (the expected yield was 7.86%). That is, instead of yielding 106 basis points more than the 10-year, as anticipated at the time of purchase, the GNMA 8.5 yields 14 basis points less than the Treasury. Altogether, the GNMA 8.5 provides 120 basis points less yield than anticipated at the time of purchase.

The prepayment uncertainty in mortgage cash flows, then, makes it difficult to make a relative value determination between a pass-through and a Treasury. Many market participants adjust by looking at the pass-through's yield across a range of prepayment/interest-rate scenarios (using a model or a Street consensus projection). The yield in each scenario can be compared to the yield of the Treasury security with a maturity closest to the pass-through's average life (or to capture the slope of the yield curve, an interpolated Treasury). The most attractive MBS would be the one that provides the widest spread to Treasuries across the scenarios deemed most likely.

Traditional yield-to-maturity techniques can be adjusted for the greater complexity of pass-through cash flows, but they are ultimately arbitrary and even misleading. To overcome many of the shortcomings of static cash-flow analysis, many market participants have adopted option-adjusted spread (OAS) simulation models. In brief, their objective is to evaluate explicitly the

---

13 For premium pass-throughs with rapid prepayment expectations and consequently short average lives, the yield-to-the-average-life, or to the curve, is preferable because it picks up the value of the curve when the curve is upwardly sloped. It is found by interpolating between the on-the-run Treasury yields at the expected average life of the pass-through.

option to prepay given the current yield environment, a process for modeling likely changes in interest rates for realistic levels of interest-rate volatility, and a prepayment model that links prepayment activity to interest-rate levels. Different analytic techniques may be used to arrive at such models, but the basic outputs will include measures of yield and yield spread over Treasuries that are adjusted for the average exercise of the prepayment option over a wide range of interest-rate paths. Other outputs include option-adjusted measures of price sensitivity or duration. Rich-cheap analysis is conducted using these measures in the same way as with older techniques: investments with similar risk characteristics are compared to identify superior value. The difference is that the investor has the advantage of being able to compare a theoretical value to the actual market spread to make a better informed investment decision.

Total Return Analysis

Yield is not commonly used to describe the historical investment performance of a pass-through. Instead, the total rate of return is used. The actual or economic return received by an investor is the sum of interest and principal payments as well as any reinvestment income received over a holding or measurement period, plus any capital gain or loss if the bond is sold at the end of the period. If the bond is not sold, the total return calculation takes into account any appreciation or depreciation in market price as of the end of the period.

Total returns can also be projected to support trading and investment decisions. Such analysis, if performed with adequate care, overcomes many of the shortcomings of yield. For one thing, assumptions about interest-rate and prepayment scenarios can be used to project principal and interest payments and reinvestment income over the period, as well as market prices at the end of the measurement horizon. The results, however, are highly dependent on the terminal prices. Many investors perform total rate of return analysis in a static cash-flow calculator by using a prepayment model and assuming that the current spread curve for pass-throughs holds at the end of the horizon. That is, the remaining cash flows are projected for the specific interest-rate scenario and, given their resultant average life, priced at the required spread currently observed for a pass-through of the same average life. This approach is rough, but can help build intuition regarding the perfomance of pass-throughs in different scenarios. A better approach is OAS-based. It prices the remaining cash flows at the same option-adjusted spread to Treasuries as demonstrated by the security at the beginning of the period. This approach has the advantage of incorporating a mathematical expectation rather than a point estimate of the required spread.

Projected returns for new discount and current coupon FNMA pass-throughs and for a seasoned premium coupon FNMA securities (as of late October 1994) are depicted in Exhibit 9. These were calculated on the PaineWebber SuperBond system, holding OAS constant to determine the terminal pricing. Readers should note the differences in projected total return performance between pass-throughs from different coupon sectors of the market. The current coupon 8.5 outperforms in the base-case, owing to its higher base case yield. As interest rates rise, the discount extends somewhat, underperforming the current and premium. At the same time prepayments slow on the current coupon 8.5, extending its duration and hurting its performance in rising-rate scenarios. By contrast, the seasoned premium has a shorter duration and yield at the outset of the horizon—and consequently underperforms in the base case. However its short duration is more stable owing to the seasoned prepayment pattern, limiting price declines somewhat as rates rise. The 10% premium coupon helps to buffer price declines as well. In the rally scenarios the long duration of the discount gives it the superior performance, although rising prepayment risk begins to limit price gains in the most. The current coupon 8.5 performs less well as its duration shortens more rapidly. The shorter duration of the seasoned premium results in smaller price appreciation; this effect is accentuated in the increasingly bullish scenarios as its prepayments accelerate and its duration shortens sharply.

Total return projections are typically used in making relative value assessments. In this context, the investor would prefer the securities offering the greatest return advantage over comparable Treasuries in the anticipated interest-rate scenarios.

SUMMARY

In this chapter, the investment characteristics of mortgage pass-through securities and the various types of securities are explained. In the next chapter, agency adjustable-rate mortgage securities are discussed. While the basic factors that influence prepayments are reviewed, a more detailed discussion of prepayment modeling is provided in Chapters 8 and 9. Cash-flow yield and duration are parameters often used to describe the investment characteristics of these securities. Later chapters discuss the limitations of these measures in greater detail and suggest better methodologies for valuing pass-throughs and estimating their price volatility.

CHAPTER 4

Agency Adjustable-Rate Mortgage Securities

Jeffrey Biby
Vice President
Mortgage Strategies Group
Lehman Brothers

Adjustable-rate mortgage (ARM) securities have become an increasingly important sector of the mortgage-backed securities market. ARM securities have coupons that adjust based on changes in an underlying index rate, subject to periodic and lifetime interest rate caps. Traditional holders of ARM securities have been financial institutions, which find ARMs attractive to match against floating-rate liabilities. More recently, however, money managers have become active buyers of ARMs as a high-yielding alternative to other short duration securities.

This chapter describes the features of ARM pass-through securities and the ARM securities programs of GNMA, FNMA, and FHLMC. The first section reviews the growth and current composition of the ARM market. The second section describes the structural features of ARM securities, and the third section reviews the agency ARM programs. The last section describes net effective margin (NEM), option-adjusted spread (OAS), and duration, the most common measures of relative value in the ARM market.

THE ARM MARKET

Adjustable-rate mortgages have coupons that periodically adjust based on an index of market rates. These mortgages were first originated in significant volume in the early 1980s. ARMs were attractive to thrift institutions during this period because their cost of funds rose more rapidly than yields on their fixed-rate mortgage portfolios. ARMs allowed them to reduce their asset/liability mismatch.

Through the 1980s, borrowers came to accept ARMs as an alternative to traditional fixed-rate mortgage financing. Since 1982, the ARM share of total mortgage originations has ranged from a high of 69% in December 1987 to a low of 15% in February 1992. The ARM share of total mortgage originations is largely dependent on three variables: the spread between fixed and adjustable mortgage rates, the absolute levels of fixed mortgage rates, and the variety of other financing opportunities. Throughout the 1980s, a strong correlation existed between the share of ARMs originated and the spread between 30-year fixed and adjustable mortgage rates (see Exhibit 1). ARM share increased as this spread widened and decreased as the spread tightened. However, since 1991, the fixed to ARM spread has widened without a corresponding increase in the ARM share. This breakdown reflects the impact of low mortgage rates and the introduction of balloon mortgages. Since January 1991, the 30-year fixed mortgage rate has been below 10% (see Exhibit 2). Even as the spread between fixed and ARM rates widened, risk averse mortgagors chose single-digit, fixed-rate mortgages. Adding to the decrease in ARM share in the 1990s has been the introduction of alternative forms of short maturity mortgage financing, principally 5- and 7-year balloon mortgages. With a steep yield curve, balloons allow borrowers to combine the advantages of both: the low risk of a fixed rate and a lower coupon than traditional 15- or 30-year fixed-rate mortgages due to the shorter final maturity.

The Federal National Mortgage Association (FNMA) and the Government National Mortgage Association (GNMA) began issuing ARM passthrough securities in 1984, and the Federal Home Loan Mortgage Corporation (FHLMC) followed in 1986. Nonagency ARMs, rated AAA and AA, have

Exhibit 1. ARM Share of Total Mortgage Originations and the Spread between 30-Year Fixed and Adjustable Mortgage Rates (January 1983–January 1994)

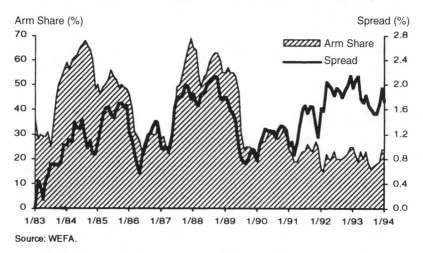

Source: WEFA.

become an increasingly important part of the ARM market due in part to the introduction of credit enhancement structures in late 1986. Today there is approximately $170 billion outstanding in agency, AAA, and AA ARM pass-throughs (see Exhibit 3).

FEATURES OF ARM SECURITIES

A primary difference between ARM and fixed-rate mortgage pass-throughs in the secondary market is the diversity of ARM features. Because of their structural diversity, most ARM securities are bought and sold on a pool-specific basis. In contrast, most agency fixed-rate mortgage pass-throughs are bought and sold on a generic or to be announced (TBA) basis. In a TBA trade, the seller and buyer agree to the type of security (*i.e.*, agency, program, coupon, face value, price, and settlement date) at the time of the trade, but they do not specify the actual pools to be traded. Because ARM securities have many structural features that differ, TBA trading is not possible except for some FNMA monthly ARMs indexed to the 11th District Cost of Funds Index (COFI-11) and new issue GNMA ARMs. However, demand from investors in the secondary market has led to increasing homogeneity, which adds to market liquidity. Although ARMs still offer diverse structures, in general they can be characterized by several well defined features.

The coupon of an ARM security resets periodically according to its *rate reset frequency*, at a spread (*net margin*) over the security's *index* rate, subject to

Exhibit 2. ARM Share of Total Mortgage Originations and the 30-Year Fixed Mortgage Rate (January 1983–1994)

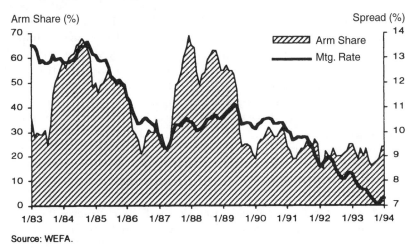

Source: WEFA.

Exhibit 3.   Outstanding ARM Securities As of December 1993

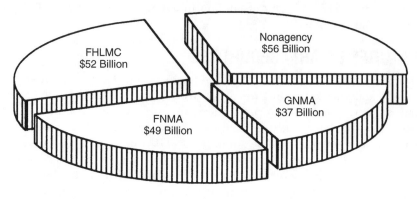

Source: GNMA, FNMA, FHLMC, and *Inside Mortgage Securities.*

periodic and *lifetime caps and floors* that specify the maximum and minimum amount by which the security's coupon can adjust on any rate reset date and over the life of the security, respectively. Other characteristics are based primarily on differences in the underlying collateral backing the securities. This chapter deals with structural features of agency pass-through ARM securities. Nonagency ARM pass-throughs may have additional features arising from the structure and credit enhancement of the securities.

The Index

One of the key features of an ARM security is its underlying index. The index level is the basis over which the coupon on the ARM periodically resets. Therefore, understanding the behavior of the underlying index is important to understanding the investment characteristics of the ARM security. There are two primary index types: Treasury indexes based on U.S. Treasury security yields of various maturities, and indexes based on the cost of funds at thrift institutions. Other indexes that are becoming common are the London interbank offered rate (LIBOR) and the secondary market certificate of deposit (CD) rate.

The most common Treasury-based index is the 1-year constant maturity Treasury (CMT). Over 60% of agency ARM securities outstanding is indexed to the 1-year CMT. Constant maturity Treasury yields are calculated by the U.S. Treasury Department as its estimate of borrowing costs at various maturities. These yields are calculated based on the Federal Reserve Bank of New York's daily yield curve, constructed from closing market bid yields on actively traded Treasury securities submitted by five leading U.S. government securities dealers. The 1-year CMT is based on the average yield of a range of Treasury securities adjusted to a constant maturity of one year. The weekly average of the one-year CMT is published weekly in the Federal Reserve's Statistical Release H.15.

Other Treasury-based indexes used for ARMs are the 3- and 5-year CMT and the 6-month Treasury bill rate. Each of these indexes is also published weekly in Statistical Release H.15. The 3- and 5-year CMT indexes are calculated the same way as the 1-year CMT but adjust for 3- and 5-year constant maturities, respectively. The 6-month Treasury bill index is the average rate for the Treasury's weekly auction of 6-month Treasury bills weighted by the amount sold at various rates. It is reported on a bond equivalent yield (BEY) and discount basis.

The most common cost of funds index (COFI) is the 11th District Cost of Funds Index. COFI-11 measures the average cost of funds for member institutions in the Federal Home Loan Bank's 11th District, which consists of California, Nevada, and Arizona. It is computed by dividing the total monthly interest expense of member thrifts by the average principal amount of liabilities outstanding during the month. It is then adjusted for the number of days in the month and annualized. The index is released by the FHLB of San Francisco on the last business day of each month and pertains to the previous month.

Because COFI-11 is the weighted average cost of all thrift liabilities, including intermediate and long-term liabilities, only a small percentage of total liabilities matures and reprices in any given month. Therefore, movements in COFI-11 lag movements in short-term market rates (see Exhibit 4). COFI-11 is less volatile than market rates, like the 1-year CMT and 6-month LIBOR, in both month-to-month changes and absolute high and lows.

Exhibit 4. Selected ARM Index Levels

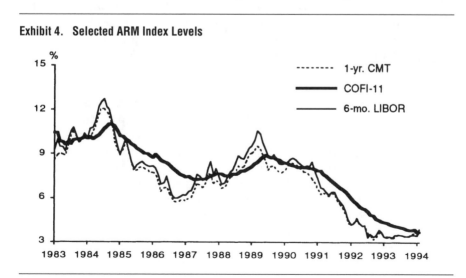

Another popular cost of funds index is the National Median Cost of Funds Index (COFI-NM) for federal savings and loan institutions. It is calculated like COFI-11 except it is the median cost of funds for all thrifts regulated by the Office of Thrift Supervision (OTS). This index generally moves with COFI-11, though it is slightly less volatile and has a more pronounced lag.

Two other indexes that have become increasingly popular for ARM securities are 6-month LIBOR and 6-month secondary market CD rate. Although both are small compared to 1-year CMT and COFI-11 in total amount issued and outstanding, each is growing rapidly on a percentage basis. Six-month LIBOR ARMs have been issued largely in the form of AAA/AA nonagency pass-throughs rather than as agency ARMs.

Net Margin

The margin on an ARM is the spread added to the underlying index rate to determine the new ARM coupon and is expressed in basis points (bp). *Gross margin* refers to the spread on the underlying mortgage loans while *net margin* refers to the spread on the ARM security; the difference is servicing and guarantee fees. All else being equal, the higher the net margin, the more valuable the ARM security because it will pay a higher coupon over the life of the security.

Adjustment Frequency

The adjustment frequency is the time between coupon and/or payment changes. For most ARMs the coupon and payment adjustment frequencies are the same and correspond to the maturity of the underlying index. For instance, the coupon and payment of 1-year CMT ARMs typically reset annually, and 6-month CD and LIBOR ARMs reset semiannually. However, the majority of COFI ARMs have coupons that reset monthly and payments that reset annually. Because of this mismatch, the mortgage may experience accelerated or decelerated amortization[1] between payment reset dates. In a rising interest-rate environment, the loan will experience decelerated amortization. The portion of the borrower's monthly payment going to payment of interest increases, and the portion going to amortization of principal declines. If interest rates rise rapidly, the loan balance may actually increase if the monthly payment is not sufficient to cover the total interest due. This is referred to as negative amortization, which will be discussed in greater detail. During periods of falling interest rates, the loan experiences accelerated amortization.

---

1 The monthly payment of a typical mortgage loan in the United States goes partly toward interest and partly toward principal. Amortization refers to the scheduled monthly repayment of principal on a loan.

Caps

Most ARMs are subject to caps that place limits on coupon and/or payment changes. Coupon caps limit the amount the coupon can adjust on coupon reset dates, or over the life of the loan. Payment caps limit the amount the mortgagor's payment can change on payment reset dates.

Coupon Caps

The most common caps on ARM securities are coupon caps, both periodic and lifetime. Periodic caps limit the amount the coupon can adjust on each coupon reset date and are symmetric, meaning they limit both upward (cap) and downward (floor) adjustments. ARMs that reset annually generally have 2% periodic caps, while those that reset semiannually have 1% periodic caps. However, GNMA ARMs reset annually and they have periodic caps of 1%.

The mechanics of periodic caps are best illustrated with an example. Assume a conventional 1-year CMT ARM has a current coupon rate of 5.5%, a net margin of 200 bp, a periodic cap of 2%, and is based on a CMT index rate of 3.5%. If the index rises to 6.0% on the next reset date, the fully adjusted coupon will be 8.0% (6% index plus the 200-bp margin). But because the security has a 200-bp periodic cap, the coupon can only adjust upward to 7.5% (5.5% current coupon plus the 200-bp periodic cap). Exhibit 5 illustrates the coupon pattern of three 1-year CMT ARMs over the past six years: one has a 1% periodic cap, another has a 2% periodic cap, and the third has no periodic cap. In each case the ARM has an initial coupon of 8%, a 200-bp net margin, and six months to the next reset. In no instance

Exhibit 5. Coupon Pattern for 1-Year CMT ARM with Various Periodic Caps (8% initial coupon, +200 margin, six months to first reset)

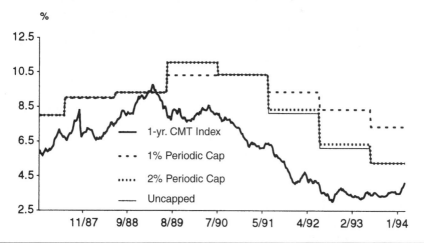

did the 2% periodic cap limit the full upward adjustment of the coupon, and on the last two reset dates the 2% periodic floor only marginally limited the full downward adjustment of the coupon. However, the 1% periodic cap/floor was much more restrictive.

Life Caps

These caps define the maximum level of the coupon over the life of the loan and are typically 500 bp or 600 bp above the original coupon. For newly originated securities, the life cap is often expressed in basis points over the original coupon, but once the security has reset, the life cap is quoted as an absolute level. The life cap is the maximum coupon rate, not the maximum index rate at which the coupon is capped. For instance, two 1-year CMT securities with life caps of 11% may be capped at different levels of the index. One security may have a 150-bp margin and therefore be capped when the index reaches 9.5% (index 9.5% + margin of 150 bp = maximum coupon of 11%). The second security may have a 250-bp margin and therefore be capped when the index reaches only 8.5%.

Payment Caps

Payment caps limit the amount the mortgagor's monthly payment can change on each payment adjustment date. These caps are prevalent on ARMs where the coupon and payment resets do not match. The most common example is monthly COFI ARMs that have a monthly coupon reset frequency, an annual payment reset frequency, and no periodic coupon caps. Annual payment changes are often limited to 7.5%.

Negative Amortization

Negative amortization occurs when a mortgage loan balance increases rather than decreases through regularly scheduled amortization. The most common type of ARM with this feature is the monthly COFI ARM. During periods of rapidly rising interest rates, negative amortization can occur in two ways: if there is a mismatch in the frequency of coupon and payment adjustments, or if the mortgage has a payment cap. These typically occur in tandem.

If the mortgage coupon increases before a scheduled payment adjustment, then the portion of the mortgagor's payment going toward interest increases and the portion going toward amortization of principal decreases. If there is a substantial increase in interest rates, the monthly payment may not be enough to cover the interest due and the loan will begin to experience negative amortization. The portion of interest that the payment does not cover is deferred and added to the outstanding loan balance.

Payment caps are the second cause of negative amortization. If on a payment reset date the payment cap prohibits the monthly payment from increasing enough to cover the monthly interest due on the loan, it will be subject to negative amortization.

When negative amortization is allowed, restrictions are imposed to ensure that the loan will be fully amortized over its original term. Two types of restrictions are common: negative amortization caps and payment recast dates. Negative amortization caps limit the amount the original balance can increase, typically to 110% or 125% of the original loan balance. If a negative amortization cap is reached, the mortgagor's monthly payment is adjusted to an amount that will fully amortize the balance over the remaining life of the loan. The second type of limit usually occurs on five-year anniversaries of the loan. On these recast dates, cap and floor restrictions are waived and the mortgagor's monthly payment is recast, based on the current rate, to a level that will fully amortize the loan over its remaining term.

Lookback

A security's *lookback* determines the index level at which the adjusted coupon will be based on each reset date. ARMs have lookbacks because homeowners are given notification of the mortgage rate change prior to the reset date. Lookbacks are typically one to three months prior to the reset date. For instance, the lookback on a FNMA 1-year CMT ARM is usually 45 days. If the coupon resets on March 1, the index rate used is the most recently published 1-year CMT rate prior to January 15. Any change in the index after the lookback date will not be reflected in the adjusted coupon until the following reset date.

Teaser Rate

The sum of the index plus net margin is the security's *fully indexed* rate. However, most ARMs have an initial coupon rate below the fully indexed rate referred to as a *teaser rate*. Lenders offer below market or teaser rates to attract borrowers to an adjustable rather than a fixed-rate mortgage. These teaser rates last until the first rate reset date, usually 6 to 18 months, and typically range from 50 bp to 200 bp below the fully indexed rate. Teasers are important in evaluating ARMs because of the low initial coupon: the life cap of an ARM is usually based on its initial coupon; therefore, the lower the initial coupon, the lower the life cap. In a rising interest-rate environment, a low teaser rate increases the likelihood that the periodic cap will keep the coupon from adjusting fully on its initial reset date.

Convertible

Some ARMs are convertible in that the borrower has the option to convert the adjustable-rate mortgage to a fixed-rate mortgage. The conversion option is normally available for a specified time period, called the *conversion period*, that is usually four years and typically begins and ends on reset dates corresponding to the first and fifth anniversaries of the mortgage. The conversion option for conforming loans is usually based on either the FNMA or FHLMC fixed commitment rate for 60-day mandatory delivery plus a fixed spread of 3/8 - 5/8 point. For the ARM security holder, a mortgage conversion results in a full prepayment of the converted loan.

Stratified Reset

A security backed by loans that all have the same reset date is commonly referred to as a single reset or bullet pool. However, some pools diversify reset risk by combining loans with different reset dates. This diversification of coupon reset dates is referred to as stratification; the security is said to have a *stratified reset*. Exhibit 6 displays the coupon pattern for a single reset 1-year CMT pool and a stratified pool with 1/12 resetting each month. The stratified reset security is more responsive to current changes in the index because the coupon changes more frequently.

AGENCY ARM PROGRAMS

Although ARMs represent a significant share of primary mortgage originations, fewer have been securitized and sold in the secondary market than corresponding fixed-rate mortgages, mostly because bank and thrift institutions prefer to retain the majority of their adjustable-rate mortgages for their own portfolios.

Exhibit 6. Coupon Pattern for 1-Year CMT ARM with Bullet and Stratified Resets (8% initial coupon, +200 margin, six months to first reset)

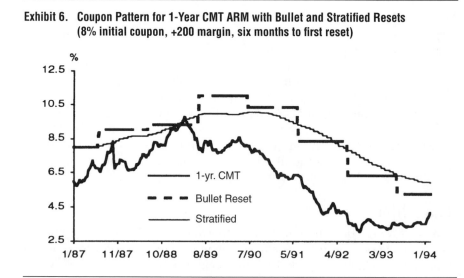

Each of the mortgage agencies has an ARM securities program. FNMA and FHLMC securitize conventional mortgages and GNMA securitizes only FHA mortgages. GNMAs are guaranteed for full and timely payment of both interest and principal and are backed by the full faith and credit of the U.S. Government. FNMA guarantees full and timely payment of both interest and principal and FHLMC guarantees full and timely payment of interest and eventual recovery of principal when collected.

FNMA has led the other agencies in single-family ARM issuance and accounts for approximately 49% of the total. A more recent trend shows a dramatic increase in GNMA ARM issuance. In 1992, GNMA issued $11.2 billion in ARMs, more than the combined total of $9.7 billion in all prior years (see Exhibit 7).

There are ARM securities based on more than 15 different indexes in the agency market, but over 86% are indexed to 1-year CMT and COFI-11 (Exhibit 8). COFI-11 has historically been the largest sector of the agency ARM market, but light issuance in the 1990s and fast prepayments have caused it to decline compared to the conventional and GNMA 1-year CMT sectors (Exhibit 9). Exhibit 10 highlights the major features of the most common agency ARMs for each of the agency programs.

GNMA ARM Program

GNMA securitizes only FHA-insured mortgages under its GNMA II multiple issuer ARM program. Standard pooling requirements give GNMA ARMs homogeneous features. The combination of the multiple issuer program,

Exhibit 7. Annual Single-Family Agency ARM Issuance ($ billion)

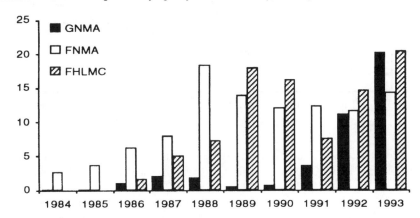

Source: GNMA, FNMA, and FHLMC

Exhibit 8.   Agency Single-Family ARMs Outstanding by Index as of December 1993

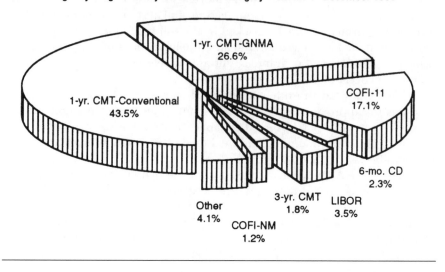

Exhibit 9.   Changes in Outstanding Balances (July 1991–December 1993, $ billion)

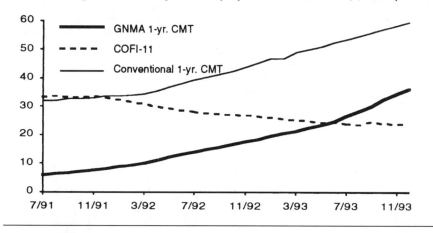

which allows GNMA to combine loans from different issuers, and strict pooling
requirements make GNMA pools larger than typical FNMA or FHLMC pools.
GNMA ARMs are all indexed to the 1-year CMT and approximately 97% have
a 150-bp net margin. GNMA ARMs are all single reset pools that reset annually
on one of four specified dates: January 1, April 1, July 1, or October 1. The
reset date depends on the security's issue date. For instance, all GNMA ARMs

Exhibit 10.   Most Common Characteristics of Agency ARM Programs

Index			11th District	3-year	National	Six-month
	1-year CMT		COFI	CMT	Median COFI	CD
Agency	GNMA	FNMA/FHLMC	FNMA/FHLMC	FNMA/FHLMC	FNMA	FNMA
Coupon Reset	Annual	Annual	Monthly	3 years	Monthly	Semiannual
Payment Reset	Annual	Annual	Annual	3 years	Annual	Semiannual
Periodic Caps						
Coupon Caps	1%	2%	None	1%, 2%, or 3%	None	1%
Payment Caps	None	None	7.50%	None	7.50%	None
Life Caps	5%	5%-6%	5%-6%	5%-6%	5%-6%	6%
Net Margin bp	150 bp	150 - 225 bp	125 bp	150 - 225 bp	125 bp	100 - 175
Negative Amortization	None	None	Allowed	None	Allowed	None
Teaser Period	1 year	1 year	6 mos.	30 - 42 mos.	6 mos.	6 mos.
Convertible	No	Yes/No	No	Yes/No	No	Yes/No
Payment Delay	50 days	55 days/75 days	55 days/75 days	55 days/75 days	55 days	55 days
Total Issuance* ($ billion)	$41.1	$38.2/$61.1	$39.6/$19.8	$3.6/$2.2	$3.0	$3.8
Current Outstanding* ($ billion)	$36.5	$23.2/$36.4	$14.7/$8.8	$1.7/$0.7	$1.5	$3.1

*Through December 1993.
Source: GNMA, FNMA, and FHLMC.

issued in the first quarter of the year reset on April 1 and so on. Unlike the majority of conventional 1-year CMT ARMs with 2% periodic caps, FHA-insured ARM loans backing GNMA ARMs all have 1% periodic caps. The lifetime caps and floors on GNMA ARMs are 500 bp above and below the initial coupon. The stated payment delay for GNMA ARMs is 50 days.

Conventional ARM Programs

FNMA and FHLMC both securitize conventional ARM loans covering diverse collateral and index types. Both agencies securitize ARMs indexed to COFI-11 and the 1-year CMT, although FNMA has been the predominant issuer of COFI-11 ARMs and FHLMC has dominated in 1-year CMT ARMs. FNMA and FHLMC have similar ARM programs. The stated payment delay for FNMA and FHLMC securities is 55 days and 75 days, respectively.

FNMA monthly COFI-11s are the only conventional ARM securities that can be traded on a TBA basis. To meet good delivery requirements, securities must have the following characteristics: a monthly coupon reset frequency, a net margin of 125 bp, and a life cap of at least 13%. All other conventional ARMs trade on a pool-specific basis.

FNMA and FHLMC both offer single and stratified reset pools. FNMA offers stratified reset pools in its Flex ARM program and FHLMC offers them in its weighted average coupon (WAC) ARM program.

Both FNMA and FHLMC have created ARM programs to increase the size and liquidity of specific securities. FNMA Megapools and FHLMC Giants are created by combining pools with similar characteristics into larger, more liquid pools. In addition to their increased size and liquidity, Megapools and Giants offer greater loan diversification, more stable prepayments, and reduced accounting requirements. The Megapool and Giant concept also creates securities with stratified resets by combining pools with varying reset dates into a single pool.

ARM EVALUATION

The three most common measures of relative value for ARM securities are net effective margin, option-adjusted spread, and duration. Each method has its benefits and limitations.

Net Effective Margin

NEM is the most commonly used method of ARM evaluation and the simplest to calculate and understand. NEM measures the yield spread over the security's current index rate that is required to discount all future cash flows back to the original price in a static interest-rate environment. It is expressed on a BEY basis. NEM takes into account the security's price premium/discount as well as the upward adjustment of coupons lower than the fully indexed rate (teasers) and the downward adjustment of coupons higher than the fully indexed rate. The NEM can be viewed as the expected spread over the index rate that a buy and hold investor would receive if interest rates and prepayments remained unchanged.

The examples below will show how NEM is calculated for a teaser rate and a more than fully indexed ARM. The initial 4% coupon on the teaser ARM will adjust to 5.3% (3.2% index + 210 bp net margin = 5.3%) in 12 months and remain at that level (Exhibit 11). Assuming an 18% constant prepayment rate (CPR) and an initial price of 101-01, cash-flow yield on a BEY basis is 4.7% and the NEM is 150 bp (4.7% BEY – 3.2% index value = 150 NEM). Similarly, for the fully indexed security, the NEM is 85 bp assuming an 18% CPR. In this case the initial coupon of 6.3% resets to 5.3% in six months and remains constant (Exhibit 12).

Another performance measure, discount margin (DM), is similar to NEM in that it represents the security's yield spread over the underlying

Exhibit 11. Net Effective Margin for Teaser ARM (FNMA 4%, index 1-yr. CMT +210 bp; caps: 2% periodic, 10% life)

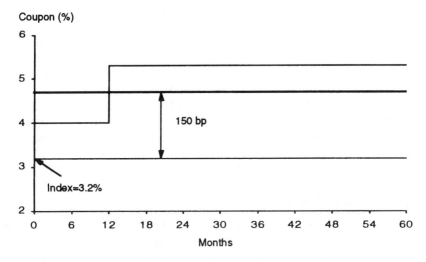

NEM = 150 bp; reset: 12 months; price = 101-01; 18% CPR.

Exhibit 12. Net Effective Margin for Fully Adjusted ARM (FNMA 6.25%, index 1-yr. CMT +210 bp; caps 2% periodic, 13% life)

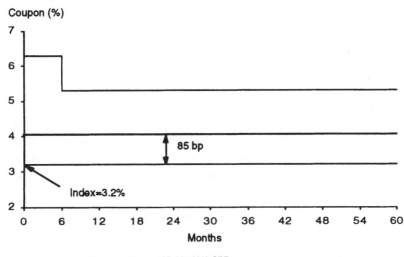

NEM = 85 bp; reset: 6 months; price = 105-03; 18% CPR.

index, except that it assumes monthly equivalent yield (MEY) compounding rather than semiannual yield or BEY compounding. It is most frequently quoted for LIBOR CMO floaters. LIBOR floaters are often match-funded with monthly LIBOR liabilities; therefore, the DM more accurately captures the realized spread over funding.

Although NEM is an easily calculated and understood method of evaluating ARMs, it assumes that interest rates remain constant over the life of the security and does not reflect the cost of the embedded options in ARMs. In addition to the prepayment option inherent in all mortgage securities, ARMs are subject to periodic and lifetime caps and floors. Investors should expect that with interest-rate volatility, these caps and floors may cause actual monthly cash flows to deviate from expected cash flows in a stable rate environment. A more comprehensive approach that incorporates the value of these embedded options is OAS analysis.

Option-Adjusted Spread[2]

OAS measures the average spread over the Treasury yield curve that an investor can expect to receive over the life of a security under many different interest-rate scenarios. OAS analysis incorporates an interest-rate model that generates a large number of possible interest-rate scenarios. The model generates projections for both the index rate underlying the ARM security and the monthly discount rate that represents the future path of short-term Treasury rates. Each scenario represents one possible path of future interest rates. The security's monthly cash flow is then generated for each scenario, taking into account all of the security's structural features, including the limiting effects of caps and floors. The large number of scenarios makes it possible to calculate the cost of the security's embedded options. In each scenario, a price is calculated by discounting the security's monthly cash flows at the monthly discount rate plus a fixed spread.

The OAS model uses an iterative process to solve for the constant spread over the monthly discount rates, across all scenarios, such that the average of the discounted prices in each scenario equals the initial price. The OAS represents the return an investor could expect to receive above the return on a strategy of buying and continually rolling a position of short Treasury securities.[3] In most cases the OAS will be less than the NEM calculated in a static interest-rate environment due to the security's option costs.

---

2 Option-adjusted spread analysis is described in more detail in Chapters 28–30

3 Assumptions inherent in the OAS model will affect the absolute OAS value. Therefore, investors should concentrate more on the relative ranking of securities than on individual OAS levels. For instance, changing the interest rate volatility assumption will change individual OAS levels, but the relative ranking of securities remains stable..

An example will illustrate the value of OAS in relation to NEM for ARM securities. We compare two fully adjusted FNMA 1-year CMT ARMs with the same characteristics except that bond A has a 1% periodic cap and bond B has a 2% periodic cap (see Exhibit 13). At a dollar price of 103-00, each security has an NEM of 98 bp. If NEM were the only measure of relative value, the two securities would appear equally attractive. However, it is unlikely that interest rates will remain constant over the life of the securities. OAS methodology allows evaluation of the different periodic caps of the two securities and determination of an OAS to the Treasury curve, assuming interest-rate volatility. In this case, bond A with the 1% periodic cap has an OAS of 64 bp and bond B with the 2% periodic cap has an OAS of 89 bp. Therefore, bond B is more valuable than bond A.

Duration

Duration is a measure of a security's price sensitivity to changes in interest rates. Because the coupon of an ARM security periodically adjusts to current market rates, its duration is generally less than comparable average-life, fixed-rate mortgage securities. However, the duration of an ARM security is largely dependent on the structural features of the security, such as the time to next reset and how restrictive the periodic and lifetime caps are. Duration for ARM securities is calculated with an OAS model to capture their interest-sensitive cash flows and implied cost of caps in changing interest-rate environments. The calculation is done by shifting the current Treasury yield curve up and down by a small amount, generating new interest rate paths and security cash flows, and then holding the initial OAS constant, recalculating new prices. The duration can then be calculated as the percentage change in price divided by the change in Treasury yields.

The duration of ARM securities ranges from approximately 0.5 to 4.0 years depending on the structural characteristics of the security; the majority have durations of less than two years. Conventional, fully adjusted 1-year CMT,

Exhibit 13. Effect of Reset on OAS of Two FNMA 1-Year CMT ARMs

	Bond A	Bond B
Initial Coupon	5.00%	5.00%
Net Margin	200 bp	200 bp
Periodic Cap	1%	2%
Life Cap	11%	11%
Next Reset	12 mo.	2 mo.
Price	103-00	103-00
NEM	98 bp	98 bp
OAS	64 bp	89 bp

6-month LIBOR, and 6-month CD ARMs have the shortest durations, generally less than 1 year. The 1% periodic cap on GNMA 1-year CMT ARMs causes them to have longer durations than comparable coupon conventional 1-year CMT ARMs with 2% periodic caps. COFI ARMs have longer durations than conventional 1-year CMT ARMs due to the lagging nature of cost of funds indexes. Exhibit 14 shows guidelines for the effect of individual ARM features on duration. We have isolated the impact of each variable, with all else assumed to be equal. Generally speaking, the more restrictive a security's caps, the longer its duration, because restrictive caps place greater limits on the coupon's ability to adjust to changing interest rates. Time to next reset is also an important determinant of duration: since the coupon will reset to new market rates on the next reset date, subject to caps and floors, the shorter the time to next reset, the shorter the duration. This means that the duration of a 1-year CMT ARM will shorten as the next reset date approaches and then lengthen after resetting. Newly issued teaser rate securities have longer durations than similar, fully indexed securities. A teaser's below-market coupon rate increases the likelihood that the periodic cap will limit the next coupon adjustment. The examples given so far are applicable to all ARM securities. For COFI ARMs, an additional factor is the lagging nature of the index in relation to changes in other short market rates. For instance, a 50-bp change in short Treasury rates is expected to result in a gradual change in the COFI index. The lagging nature of the index increases the duration of COFI ARMs compared to the duration of ARMs based on a market rate such as the 1-year CMT index.

CONCLUSION

This chapter provides an introduction to ARM securities. It is intended as a means of familiarizing investors with the fundamental features of ARMs, the

Exhibit 14.   Impact of Individual Security Features on ARM Duration

Change*	Effect	Cause
Longer reset frequency	Increase	Longer time until coupon changes to new market rates
Lower coupon (teaser rate)	Increase	More likely to hit periodic cap on first reset
Higher periodic cap	Decrease	Less likely that periodic cap will restrict coupon adjustment
Higher life cap	Decrease	Less likely to hit life cap
Faster prepayments	Decrease	Shorter average life/reduced time that the investor is short the caps
Decline in interest rates	Decrease	Reduces likelihood of hitting caps
Increase in interest rates	Increase	Increases likelihood of hitting caps

*Holding all else equal.

agency ARM programs, and the terminology used in the ARM market. It also provides a primary understanding of the relative value measures for ARMs. With market growth and increased liquidity, an ever-increasing investor base has been attracted to the ARM market. This trend will continue as more investors become familiar with the performance characteristics of ARM securities in relation to other short-duration investment alternatives.

APPENDIX
GLOSSARY
Adjustable-Rate Mortgage

A fully amortizing mortgage characterized by a coupon rate that adjusts periodically based on changes in an underlying index rate. The coupon rate adjusts to the index rate plus a constant adjustment margin or spread, subject to interest-rate caps and floors that may restrict the mortgage rate change at each adjustment date.

Adjustment Frequency

The time period between the coupon and/or payment adjustment dates. The adjustment frequency for an adjustable-rate mortgage-backed security is determined when the security is originated. The frequency generally remains constant over the life of the security, although the time to the first adjustment date may vary by a few months. For most ARMs, the coupon and payment adjustment frequencies are the same. The principal exception is COFI ARMs, which typically have a monthly coupon reset frequency and an annual payment reset frequency.

Convertible

An option offered to some borrowers to convert an adjustable-rate mortgage into a fixed-rate mortgage. The conversion option is normally available for a specified time period, called the conversion period or conversion window. The conversion period is usually four years long and typically begins and ends on reset dates that correspond to the first and fifth anniversaries of the mortgage.

Fully Indexed Rate

The coupon rate equal to the current index rate plus the net margin.

Lookback

The feature that determines which index rate will be used to adjust a security's coupon on reset dates. The lookback period is typically 1 to 3 months prior to the reset date. A 45-day lookback specifies that the index rate used to adjust the coupon will be the most recently published index rate 45 days prior to the coupon reset date.

Net Margin

The constant spread added to the index rate at each adjustment date to determine the new coupon of the adjustable-rate security. Gross margin is the constant spread on the underlying mortgage loans. The difference between the gross and net margin is servicing and guarantee fees.

Interest-Rate Caps

These caps establish limits on the allowable change in the security coupon rate at each adjustment date. There are two types of interest-rate caps: periodic and life.

Periodic Cap

A cap that defines the maximum amount the coupon rate can change on each adjustment date. Periodic caps are symmetric, meaning that the security rate cannot increase or decrease by more than the amount of the cap. They are expressed in terms of absolute percentage changes, not as a percent of the current rate.

Life Cap

A cap that defines the bounds on the allowable coupon rate over the security's life. It may be expressed in absolute terms (*e.g.*, a maximum rate of 11.0%) or as a spread in relation to the initial coupon rate (*e.g.*, five percentage points). The life cap may be either symmetric or asymmetric. For the GNMA adjustable-rate MBS program, the life cap is symmetric; thus, the mortgage rate cannot go above or below a specified level. Securities issued through the Freddie Mac and Fannie Mae adjustable-rate MBS programs may or may not be symmetric.

Index

The market interest-rate series that is used as the basis for adjusting the new ARM security coupon rate at each adjustment date. There are two primary index types: Treasury indexes based on U.S. Treasury security yields of various maturities, and indexes based on the cost of funds of thrift institutions. The most common Treasury-based index is the one-year constant maturity Treasury (CMT), and the most common cost of funds index is the 11th District Cost of Funds (COFI-11). Two other indexes that are becoming increasingly popular are the London interbank offered rate (LIBOR) and the secondary market certificate of deposit (CD) rate.

Negative Amortization

Growth in the mortgage balance that occurs when the monthly payment on a mortgage is not sufficient to cover the interest expense due. The interest shortfall is added to the principal balance, causing the mortgage balance to grow. Typically, mortgages that allow negative amortization also specify a maximum allowable principal balance, such as 125% of the original balance. If the mortgage balance reaches this limit, the payment is reset to a fully amortizing payment over the remaining term. ARMs that allow negative amortization are generally those with different coupon and payment reset frequencies; the most common are COFI ARMs.

Payment Cap

Limits the amount that the mortgage payment can increase at each adjustment date; however, payment caps do not limit the coupon (or accrual) rate. If the fully amortizing payment based on the mortgage rate exceeds the capped payment, the difference is added to the principal balance as negative amortization. Payment-capped ARMs typically limit the payment adjustment each period to 7.5%, and restrict negative amortization to a maximum of 125% percent of the original principal balance. Payment caps were introduced to protect borrowers from large increases in monthly payments if interest rates rose sharply between adjustment dates. Payment caps generally apply to securities with different coupon and payment adjustment frequencies; a common type is COFI ARMs.

Stratified Reset

An ARM security with underlying loans that do not all reset on the same date.

Teaser Rate

An initial coupon rate that is below the fully indexed rate. Lenders offer below-market or teaser rates to attract borrowers to an adjustable rather than a fixed-rate mortgage. Teaser rates last until the first reset date and usually range from 50 bp to 200 bp below the fully indexed rate. The initial coupon rate is important because it is the basis for interest-rate caps.

CHAPTER 5

Trading, Settlement, and Clearing Procedures for Agency MBS

John F. Tierney, C.F.A.
Senior Vice President
Mortgage Strategies Group
Lehman Brothers

*Patrick Moore**

INTRODUCTION

Agency mortgage-backed securities (MBS) offer return and risk characteristics that are unlike other fixed-income investments. These differences arise because MBS are collateralized by residential mortgages and because the homeowner has the option to prepay at any time.

These features of agency MBS have led to specialized trading practices and back office procedures unlike those in the government and corporate bond markets. These procedures have evolved to ensure smooth-running and liquid markets, although they may seem somewhat arbitrary to investors new to the MBS market. This chapter focuses on the basics of how agency pass-throughs trade, settle, and clear—and why.

TBA TRADING: TURNING POOL-SPECIFIC SECURITIES INTO GENERIC SECURITIES

Every agency pass-through pool is unique, distinguished by features such as size, prepayment characteristics, and geographic concentration or dispersion. However, most agency pass-through securities trade on a generic or to-be-announced (TBA) basis. In a TBA trade, the seller and buyer agree to the type of security (*i.e.*, agency, program), coupon, face value, price, and settlement

---

* Patrick Moore was employed by Lehman Brothers as an associate when this chapter was written.

date at the time of the trade, but they do not specify the actual pools to be traded. Two days before settlement, the seller identifies or announces the specific pools to be delivered to satisfy the commitment. (Later in this chapter we show how a typical MBS transaction unfolds from the trade date to receipt of the first monthly payment.)

TBA trading was established to improve the liquidity of pass-through mortgage pools by making them fungible.[1] In effect, agency MBS trade as though their primary characteristics—weighted average coupon (WAC), weighted average maturity (WAM), and prepayment history—are equal to the average of all similar pools outstanding, even though each pool is unique. Generally speaking, this is a reasonable assumption. Since most TBA trades are composed (at a minimum) of securities from several pools, their distinct characteristics tend to blend together into a close approximation of generic securities.

Investors can specify particular pool characteristics at the time of the trade. These requests may be fairly general (*e.g.*, current coupon Fannie Maes composed of newly issued pools) or quite specific (*e.g.*, Fannie Mae 8s with a WAC between 8.60% and 8.65%). The major mortgage securities dealers use sophisticated computer systems to process allocations, allowing dealers to fulfill particular investor specifications at minimal cost.

Other market participants that benefit from TBA trading are the mortgage bankers, commercial banks, and thrifts that originate residential mortgages and sell them into the secondary mortgage market in securitized form. Most mortgage application processes allow a borrower to lock in a mortgage rate at some point prior to closing. After this rate-lock, the mortgage originator is exposed to interest rate risk—the risk that the value of the mortgage may change as market rates change before the mortgage is sold. Actual MBS pools can be formed only after mortgages close; while they are in the pipeline, pool characteristics may shift if applicants withdraw their applications or postpone closing, fail to meet underwriting standards, or change loan amounts. Originators frequently hedge their pipelines of rate-locked mortgages by selling them into the forward market as mortgage securities for TBA delivery one to three months (or more) in the future.[2] TBA trading allows originators to sell prospective mortgage securities before they know the specific collateral characteristics of the pools. Without the TBA mechanism, mortgage pools could not be sold until they had been formed, and origina-

---

1 By fungible it is meant that one security can be used in place of another to satisfy an obligation.

2 Selling forward is the most common hedging strategy for mortgage originators. The originator determines when a pool of mortgages will be deliverable as a pass-through. It then contracts with a dealer to set a price that will be paid for the pass-through at the agreed upon future delivery date.

tors would have to hedge their pipelines using Treasury futures or Treasury or MBS options. Using TBA forward sales to hedge pipelines is more efficient and has probably resulted in lower mortgage rates for borrowers.

SETTLEMENT PROCEDURES FOR AGENCY PASS-THROUGHS

TBA trades of agency pass-throughs generally settle according to a monthly schedule established by the Public Securities Association (PSA), the trade association for primary dealers in U.S. Government and municipal securities. PSA releases a schedule for the upcoming six months on a quarterly basis: it divides all agency pass-through programs into six groups, each group settling on a different day of the month. Two business days before settlement (known as the pool notification or call-out date), sellers must provide buyers with pool information by 3:00 P.M. Eastern Standard Time (EST). Exhibit 1 shows the PSA schedule for January through June 1994. Exhibit 2

Exhibit 1. PSA Call-Out and Settlement Schedule

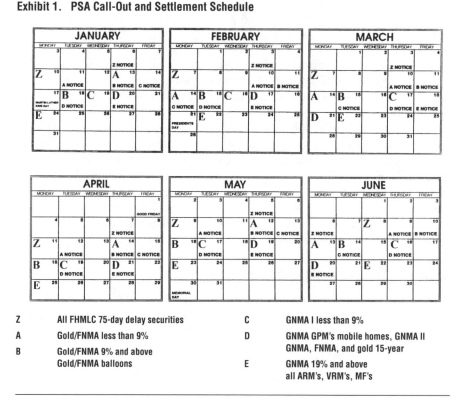

Z	All FHMLC 75-day delay securities	C	GNMA I less than 9%
A	Gold/FNMA less than 9%	D	GNMA GPM's mobile homes, GNMA II
B	Gold/FNMA 9% and above		GNMA, FNMA, and gold 15-year
	Gold/FNMA balloons	E	GNMA 19% and above
			all ARM's, VRM's, MF's

Exhibit 2. Sample Pool Information for $1 Million Trade

Customer Name	Orig. Contract	Coupon	Price
ABC Management	$1,000,000.00	8.5%	102 47/64

Trade Date	Settlement Date	Sec'ty Des.	Trade Specs
6/18/92	7/13/92	FNMA 30-year	None

Pool# Issue Date	Coupon Rate Maturity Date	Original Face Factor	Current Face Delivery Date	Principal Accrued Int. Total Due
#1 7/1/92	8.5% 7/1/22	$525,149.00 1.00000000	$525,149.00 7/13/92	$539,508.54 $1,487.92 $540,996.46
#2 6/1/92	8.5% 6/1/22	$455,150.29 0.99934464	$454,852.00 7/13/92	$467,289.36 $1,288.75 $468,578.11
			Total Principal	$1,006,797.90
	Total Original Face	$980,299.29	Total Accr. Interest	$2,776.67
	Total Current Face	$980,001.00	Total Due	$1,009,574.57

shows typical pool information provided on the call-out date. PSA scheduling is designed to distribute settlement activity as evenly as possible over a series of days. As market trends affect the distribution of activity, PSA modifies its schedules.

The monthly schedule was established for two main reasons. Dealers must await pool factors released near the beginning of the month before security trades can be settled.[3] The factor is used to determine the current face value of securities. In addition, dealers can more easily create tradable blocks if all pools for a month of trading are specified on the same day; the larger the inventory of pools, the easier it is to meet the requirements of each buyer. Thus, the monthly settlement schedule is the key to ensuring liquidity in the agency MBS market.

PSA GOOD DELIVERY GUIDELINES

To qualify for delivery on the settlement date, the seller must provide the buyer with pool information by 3:00 P.M. EST two days prior to settlement (this is known as the 48-hour rule). The seller must also indicate the face

---

3 A factor is the outstanding principal balance of a security divided by its original principal balance.

value of securities to be delivered. International investors are subject to these requirements and should pay close attention to time differences.

Variance is the amount by which the face value at delivery can vary from the amount specified at the time of the trade, expressed as a percentage of the initial face value requested. The face value to be settled must be within 2% of the value agreed upon at the time of the trade. For example, for a $1 million trade, a seller can deliver any face amount greater than or equal to $980,000 or less than or equal to $1,020,000.

Each million dollars traded can be settled by delivering up to three pools (or 5 pools if the coupon is 11% or higher), but pools cannot be added once a combination of one or two pools falls within the variance range. For example, if pool #1 is $500,000, pool #2 is $490,000, and pool #3 is $25,000, then pool #3 is ineligible, *i.e.*, the sum of pools #1 and #2 ($990,000) already falls within the variance. An investor buying a $10 million security could receive as few as 1 pool and as many as 30 pools, or 3 pools per million. This is known as the combo rule.

In the event of early notification, the seller can modify any of the pool information, such as substituting pools or providing a different face amount, as long as the pools have not been delivered. However, the seller must notify the buyer of any changes by 12:15 P.M. EST (instead of 3:00 P.M.) in order to deliver the pools two business days later.

Occasionally, sellers cannot provide pool information by the notification date or cannot deliver pools on the settlement date. Sometimes an originator must delay a delivery date with a dealer, or a dealer may not be able to cover a short position in TBAs. In these cases, a fail occurs.

All sellers have a strong economic incentive to deliver pools as soon as possible because buyers pay only the amount agreed to plus accrued interest through the original settlement date, and they do not pay until the securities are delivered. In the meantime the buyer can invest the funds at short-term rates. A seller that delivers pools after the record date must also advance monthly payments to buyers.[4] Buyers who are particularly averse to fails sometimes request settlement after the official settlement date. By giving the dealer more time to assemble appropriate pools, the buyer further minimizes the possibility of a fail.

These good delivery guidelines were established because of certain unique characteristics of the mortgage market. In part, they help mortgage originators manage their mortgage pipelines (the inventory of potential mortgage securities from the time of mortgage application to securitization and sale of the loans). Mortgage originators often hedge their pipelines of

---

4 Record date is the date on which the recipient of a security's next payment is determined. The record date for agency pass-throughs is the last calendar day of the month.

mortgage applications and closed mortgages by selling securities into the forward market. In essence, they sell securities that do not yet exist, based on expectations that loans in their current pipeline will become securities by the settlement date. But originators face some uncertainty about actual delivery due to fall-out risk (the possibility that some applicants will not close on approved loans), and due to amortization and prepayments on mortgages and securities that have been sold but not yet delivered. The variance rule provides some flexibility in dealing with these issues.

These guidelines also help facilitate trading activity in the secondary market. The variance rule helps investors deal with amortization and prepayment activity between the trade date and settlement date. In addition, ongoing amortization and prepayment of mortgage pools mean that securities will rarely have current face values in convenient multiples of $1,000, making the good combo rule essential both for combining awkward pools or securities and for ensuring that buyers are not forced to accept delivery of a large number of splintered pools. The notification rule gives the parties to a trade time to prepare for settlement and ensure that the trade goes smoothly.

While most TBA trades conform to the PSA guidelines, trades can be negotiated to settle in whatever fashion is satisfactory to both the buyer and seller. For example, two parties may agree to trade a TBA security on any day of the month. They could also agree to change the amount of variance or allow no variance at all.

TRADING AND SETTLEMENT PROCEDURES FOR OTHER MBS PRODUCTS

Non-agency MBS and REMICs (backed by both agency and non-agency collateral) are composed of specified pools and do not trade on a TBA basis. New issues settle on the date provided in the prospectus. In the secondary market, these securities trade on an issue-specific basis and generally settle on a corporate basis (five business days after the trade). Unlike TBA securities, they have nothing to gain from a monthly settlement schedule in which pools are pieced together to create more generic totals.

Clearing Procedures for MBS

There are currently two methods for clearing MBS (that is, settling trades): physical delivery and electronic book-entry transfer. Physical delivery is still used for only a small portion of non-agency securities. All agency and most non-agency MBS trades are cleared through the electronic book-entry transfer systems of Fedwire, the Depository Trust Company (DTC), or the Participant Trust Company (PTC). Fedwire, a system maintained by the Federal Reserve System, handles Freddie Mac and Fannie Mae securities. PTC and

Exhibit 3. MBS Classified by Clearinghouse

Clearinghouse	Securities Cleared
Fedwire	FHLMC/FNMA
Participant Trust Company	GNMA
Depository Trust Company	Most non-agency REMICs and pass-throughs
Physical Delivery	Some non-agency REMICs and pass-throughs

DTC, established and owned by consortia of securities dealers and institutional investors, clear Ginnie Mae and nonagency securities, respectively. (See Exhibit 3).

Electronic book-entry systems are also used to transfer principal (amortization and prepayments) and interest payments to investors. On the record date (the last day of the month for MBS and various dates for derivative securities), each system identifies the current holders of each MBS. These holders receive the next monthly payment.[5] Each investor also receives a monthly report from the clearinghouse indicating the securities owned and interest and principal received.

To invest in MBS cleared through book-entry transfer, buyers have some options. Securities can be removed from the book-entry systems and physically delivered, but the cost of removal is substantial. Alternatively, investors can hold an account with a bank that is a member of the appropriate clearing systems. Or investors can have a dealer hold the securities on their behalf and send monthly payments at no expense. This option is attractive to many investors because it considerably reduces their paperwork.

WHAT HAPPENS WHEN AN INVESTOR BUYS A MORTGAGE-BACKED SECURITY?

We now follow a sample trade through the settlement and clearing procedures for agency pass-throughs. Exhibit 4 provides a timeline from the date of the trade to receipt of the first monthly payment. Exhibit 5 shows the calculation of principal and interest components of the purchase price and the first monthly payment. Procedural details vary depending on the dealer, customer, and security purchased.

On June 18, 1992, Joe Investor of ABC Management calls a dealer to buy a mortgage backed-security. After some discussion about the advantages

---

5 Each agency has established a *payment delay* that gives it time to process monthly payments received from mortgage originators and distribute them to the appropriate investors. The actual payment delays are 14, 19, 24, 44, and 14 days for Ginnie Mae I, Ginnie Mae II, Fannie Mae, Freddie Mac, Freddie Mac Guarantor, and Freddie Mac Gold PC, respectively.

Exhibit 4.   Trade, Settlement, and Clearance Timeline
             For a Sample 30-Year Fannie Mae Security

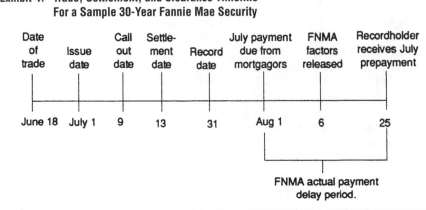

and relative value of various securities, Joe decides to buy a 30-year Fannie Mae pass-through with $1 million face value and a coupon of 8 1/2%. He agrees to pay a price of 102 47/64 and he does not specify any pool characteristics. The dealer tells Joe that ABC will receive pool information on Thursday July 9 (the call-out date), and the security two business days later on Monday, July 13. On June 22, ABC receives a confirmation letter by mail verifying the terms of the trade.

Sometime before 3:00 P.M. EST on July 9, ABC receives a fax indicating that in two days it will receive two pools (though the guidelines allow from one to three) with the characteristics shown in Exhibit 2. One of the pools is new; it was issued on July 1 and has a 1.00 factor. The other has just begun to pay principal; it was issued on June 1 and has a factor slightly less than 1.00. ABC will receive 98% of the face value requested, as allowed by the two percent variance rule. On the settlement date, ABC must pay the premium agreed to plus accrued interest from July 1 to July 12, a total of $1,009,574.57.

On the July 13 settlement date, ABC receives notification that Fedwire has credited its securities account and debited its reserve account in accordance with the terms of the transaction.

On the last day of July (the record date), Fedwire takes a snapshot of the location of all MBSs in its system and registers ABC as the new holder of record for the security purchased. Coupon payments are delayed until the release of pool factors. On the fourth business day of the month (August 6), Fannie Mae pool factors for July are released; Fannie Mae pass-throughs pay coupons on the 25th of the month to the holder as of the last record date. Therefore, on August 25 ABC receives notification that Fannie Mae has transferred a principal (amortization and prepayments) and interest payment to

Exhibit 5.   Purchase Price and First Monthly Payment for ABC's Purchase of 30-year Fannie Mae

Trade date: June 18 (Thursday)

Face Value:	$1,000,000.00
Coupon:	8.5%
Price:	102 47/64 (102.73%)

Call-out date: July 9 (Thursday)

	Pool #1	Pool #2	Total
Orig. Face Value:	$525,149.00	$455,150.29	$980,299.29
Factor:	1.00000000	0.99934464	
Curr. Face Value:	$525,149.00	$454,852.00	$980,001.00

Settlement date: July 13, (Monday)

	Pool #1	Pool #2	Total
Principal:	$525,149•102.73%•1.00	$455,150.29•102.73%•0.99934464	$1,006,797.90
Accrued interest:	$525,149•8.5%•(12/360)•1.00	$455,150.29•8.5%•(12/360)•0.99934464	$2,776.67
Total due for purchase:			$1,009,574.57

FNMA releases July pool factors: August 6 (Thursday)

	Pool #1	Pool #2
Factor:	0.99942414	0.99872234

Monthly payment date: August 25 (Tuesday)

	Pool #1	Pool #2	Total
Principal:[a]	$525,149•(1.00-0.99942414)	$455,150.29•(0.99934464-0.99872234)	$585.65
Interest:[b]	$525,149•8.5%(30/360)•1.00	$455,150•8.5%•(30/360)•0.99934464	$6,941.67
Total payment received:			$7,527.32

a Principal payment is based on the difference between previous and current factor. It includes scheduled amortization and prepayments.
b Interest payment is based on previous month's factor.

its account via Fedwire based on July factor information. ABC will continue receiving monthly payments until it sells the pools.

A fail can occur on either of the call-out or settlement dates. PSA guidelines prohibit delivery of securities until two business days after pool information has been provided; if the dealer does not give ABC the pool information until July 14, settlement cannot occur until July 16. If the dealer fails to deliver the pools on time, it will make every effort to deliver them as soon as possible. If it cannot deliver the pools identified on the call-out date it can substitute other pools, but it cannot deliver them until two business days after notifying ABC of the change. Meanwhile, ABC can use the money set aside for purchase of the security to generate short-term interest; the dealer must bear the cost of fail for each day it fails to deliver the security.

If the dealer delivers the security after the record date, it will receive the payment for July. If the dealer delivers the security after the record date and before the payment date, it must send a due bill indicating it will advance the monthly payment to ABC. If delivery occurs after both the record and payment dates, then the dealer must send the payment along with the security. Thus, in any fail scenario, ABC can earn short-term interest on the cash for purchase of the security at the expense of the dealer, and ABC earns monthly payments. In the rare instances of a fail, the buyer always comes out ahead.

SUMMARY

The trading, settlement, and clearing procedures for mortgage-backed securities differ from those for government and corporate securities. These differences arise due to the intrinsic features of agency MBS and the needs of mortgage originators who sell new securities into the secondary market.

Although each agency pass-through pool is unique, most trade on a generic or to-be-announced (TBA) basis. In a TBA trade, investors receive specific pool information two days before settlement. TBA trading is essential to market liquidity because it makes agency pools fungible (interchangeable). However, TBA trading is not obligatory; investors can request specific pools or characteristics.

Trading in agency pass-throughs may take place on any business day, but TBA securities usually settle on one specific date each month. The Public Securities Association (PSA) releases a monthly schedule that divides all agency pass-throughs into six groups, each settling on a different day. PSA has also established good delivery guidelines to ensure that settlement procedures are fair and efficient. While most TBA trades conform to the PSA schedule and guidelines, trades can be negotiated to settle in whatever fashion is satisfactory to the buyer and seller.

Like most government and corporate securities, agency pass-throughs generally clear through electronic book-entry systems. While physical delivery is possible, the cost of removing mortgage securities from book-entry systems is substantial. The Participant Trust Company (PTC) controls GNMA products, and Fedwire handles FNMA and FHLMC securities. These systems also transfer monthly payments to investors.

CHAPTER 6

Collateralized Borrowing via Dollar Rolls

Steven J. Carlson
Managing Director
Emerging Markets
Lehman Brothers

John F. Tierney, C.F.A.
Senior Vice President
Mortgage Strategies Group
Lehman Brothers

The mortgage securities market offers investors a specialized form of reverse repurchase agreement known as a *dollar roll.* A dollar roll is a collateralized short-term financing, where the collateral is mortgage securities. These transactions provide security dealers with a liquid and flexible tool for managing temporary supply/demand imbalances in the market. An investor initiates a dollar roll by delivering securities to a dealer and agreeing to repurchase similar securities on a future date at a predetermined price. The investor assumes some delivery risk at the end of the roll period, for unlike a normal reverse repurchase agreement, the dealer is not obligated to return the identical securities to the investor. In return for this privilege, the dealer extends a favorable borrowing rate to the investor that may be anywhere from a few basis points to several points below current repo market rates.

This chapter first introduces collateralized borrowing via the dollar roll transaction. Second, it describes a methodology for calculating the cost of funds using an example of a typical transaction. Third, it describes the risks to the calculated cost of funds due to prepayments, the delivery option, and adverse selection. Fourth, it takes a snapshot view of the dollar roll market

---

The authors would like to thank Andreas Christopoulos for his assistance in preparing this chapter.

for 30-year agency securities using breakeven analysis. Finally, it displays dollar roll prices (drops) and their associated borrowing costs for GNMA securities for the 12-month period from January 1993 to December 1993, offering some insights into TBA (to be announced) GNMA trading.

DOLLAR ROLL DEFINED

A dollar roll can be thought of as a collateralized borrowing, where an institution pledges mortgage pass-throughs to a dealer to obtain cash. The dealer is said to "roll in" the securities. In contrast to standard reverse repurchase agreements, the dealer is not obliged to return securities that are identical to the originally pledged collateral. Instead the dealer is required to return collateral which is "substantially identical." In the case of mortgage pass-throughs, this means that the coupon and security type, i.e., issuing agency and mortgage collateral, must match. As long as certain criteria are met, dollar rolls may be accounted for as financing transactions (rather than sales/purchases) for financial accounting purposes. According to the American Institute of Certified Public Accountants, the securities used in a dollar roll must meet the following conditions to satisfy the substantially identical standard.[1] The securities must:

1. Be collateralized by similar mortgages, e.g., 1- to 4-family residential mortgages;

2. Be issued by the same agency and be a part of the same program;

3. Have the same original stated maturity;

4. Have identical coupon rates;

5. Be priced to have similar market yields; and

6. Satisfy "good delivery" requirements, i.e., the aggregate principal amounts of the securities delivered and received back must be within 2.5% of the initial amount delivered.

The flexibility in returning collateral has value for a dealer because it provides a convenient avenue for covering a short position. That is, a trader may require a particular security for delivery this month, and by entering

---

1 For a detailed discussion of "substantially identical," see "Definition of the Term *Substantially the Same* for Holders of Debt Instruments, as Used in Certain Audit Guides and a Statement of Position," The American Institute of Certified Public Accountants, Statement of Position 90-3, February 13, 1990. Investors considering dollar rolls should discuss these issues with an accountant to ensure the transaction receives the desired accounting treatment.

into a dollar roll agreement can effectively extend a delivery obligation to next month. If a dealer were required to return the identical security sold, as in the case of a standard repurchase agreement, the dealer would be unable to cover a short position. Dollar rolls offer dealers a convenient way to obtain promised mortgage securities, avoiding much of the cost of failing to make timely delivery. In theory, the dealer (the short coverer) will be willing to pay up to the cost of failure to deliver for the short-term opportunity to borrow or purchase securities required to meet a delivery commitment. For this reason most dollar rolls are transacted close to the monthly settlement date for mortgage-backed securities. Dollar rolls also allow dealers to even out the supply and demand for mortgage securities in the current settlement month and "back" months. Primary market mortgage originators frequently sell anticipated new mortgage security production in the forward market, for delivery 1 to 3 months (or more) in the future. This expected supply provides liquidity to the dollar roll market, by ensuring that dealers will have the securities required to close out dollar roll transactions.

In return for this service, dealers often offer dollar roll financing at extremely cheap rates and on flexible terms. Unlike most collateralized borrowings, there is no haircut, or requirement for over-collateralization. The investor gets 100% of the full market price, not a four to six point haircut as in a one- to three- month reverse repo. Dollar roll transactions are generally opened or closed as of the settlement date of each month, with the terms set some time prior to settlement. They typically cover the one-month period between consecutive settlement dates, but they may also extend over multiple months, for up to 11 months. The dollar roll market also allows investors to negotiate more flexible borrowing windows. For example, terms can be arranged for 34, 44, or 89 days (reverse repos tend to centralize around 30-, 60-, or 90-day intervals) thus enabling the investor to exploit short-term investment opportunities, such as certificates of deposit or banker's acceptances.

DOLLAR ROLL: COST OF FUNDS EVALUATION

In calculating the actual cost of funds obtained through a dollar roll there are several key considerations:

1. Price of securities sold versus price of securities repurchased. In a positive carry (or a positively sloped yield curve) environment, the repurchase price will be lower than the original purchase price. The drop (dollar roll price) is the difference between the initial and ending prices plus the difference between the dealer's bid/ask prices.

2. Size of coupon payments.

3. Size of principal payments, both prepayments and scheduled amortization.

4. Collateral attributes of securities rolled in and securities rolled out.

5. Delivery tolerances. Both parties can over- or under-deliver. Most dollar roll agreements allow for the delivery of plus or minus 2.5% of the face amount.

6. Timing. The position of settlement dates within the months of the transaction impacts the accrued interest (paid to the seller at each end of the transaction). The days between settlements is the length of the borrowing period.

Each of these factors can influence the effective cost of funds implied by the dollar roll. For illustrative purposes, the calculations for a typical roll are described in the following section.

Dollar Roll Transaction Example

On January 7, 1994, a dealer and a mortgage security investor enter into a one-month dollar roll agreement as described in Exhibit 1. The dealer agrees to purchase $1,000,000 of recent production GNMA 7s at 102 and 22/32nds on January 19, 1994, and the investor agrees to repurchase $1,000,000 of face value GNMA 7s at 102 and 12/32nds on February 16, 1994. (The value of the drop is therefore 10/32nds of a point in price.) Good delivery is the delivery of anywhere from $975,000 to $1,025,000 of unpaid principal amount, since the investor and the dealer have the option of delivering plus or minus 2.5% of the original amount agreed upon. For the moment, let us assume that both parties deliver the notional quantity of securities, $1,000,000 of face value. On the first settlement date, January 19, the investor delivers the GNMA 7s and receives $1,030,375 in cash. Twenty-eight days later, on February 16, the investor will purchase GNMA 7s from the dealer and pay $1,026,667. This amounts to a bonus to the investor of $3,708 resulting from the drop.

During the twenty-eight days of the agreement, the dealer receives both coupon payments and principal payments from the security sold by the investor. As a result, the investor forgoes the coupon income due in February, equal to $5,833 ($7\%/12 \times \$1,000,000$). The principal payments from the security will also be paid to the dealer. Because all payments of principal are made at par value, whoever owns a premium security loses the premium on the principal paid down (through normal amortization and prepayments). This month, it will be the dealer. The payment of principal to the dealer represents an opportunity gain to the investor equal to the premium times the February principal payment. Had this transaction been done with a pass-through security selling at a discount to its par value, principal payments to the dealer would be viewed as an opportunity loss from the investor's perspective.

Exhibit 1.   Sample Cost of Funds Calculation for Dollar Roll

Dollar Roll Transaction Amount:	$1,000,000	
GNMA:	7.00%	
Servicing	0.50%	
Remaining Months to Maturity	350	
Prepayment Assumption (CPR)	2.00%	
Trade Date:	1/7/94	
Days of Accrual to 1st Settlement (1/19/94)	18	
Days of Accrual to 2nd Settlement (2/16/94)	15	
Days Between Settlement Dates	28	
Roll in Price	102–22	
Drop:	10/32	
Roll Out Price	102–12	
Principal Payments		
Scheduled Amortization	$796	
Prepayments	$1,681	
Cash Rolled in (Borrowed)	$1,030,375	(7%/12 x 18/30 x $1,000,000) +
		($1,000,000 x $102 22/32/100)
Cash Rolled Out	$1,026,667	(7%/12 x 15/30 x $1,000,000) +
		($1,000,000 x $102 12/32/100)
Price Spread (Dollar Roll)	$3,708	($1,030,375 - $1,026,667)
Interest Payment Foregone	($5,833)	(7%/12 x $1,000,000)
Principal Paydown Premium Gain:		
Due to Prepayment	$45	($1,681 x $2 22/32/100)
Due to Scheduled Amortization	$21	($796 x $2 22/32/100)
Total Financing Cost	($2,058)	($3,713 - $5,833 + $45 + $21)
Effective Annual Financing	2.57%	($2,053/$1,030,380 x 360/28)

The exact size of the investor's opportunity gain in this example depends on prepayments for January. Since these figures are not available until early February, a projection must be made. A good indicator of the next month's prepayments is the prior month's prepayment rate for comparable maturity securities. The last one-month annualized constant prepayment rate (CPR) for new production GNMA 7s with a weighted average maturity of 350 months is 2%. If we assume this annual constant prepayment rate, the investor's opportunity gain is $66 ($45 for prepayments + $21 for scheduled amortization). In this scenario, the investor effectively borrows $1,030,375 for 28 days at a cost of $2,058, giving an effective annual cost of 2.57%. This figure compares favorably with other cost of funds as of January 7, 1994, particularly the one-month GNMA repo rate of 3.15%.

RISKS

The cost calculation presented above is subject to risk arising from three sources. The first is prepayment uncertainty. If GNMAs trade close to par, then this risk is minimal; dollar rolls of coupons that trade away from par involve increased risk of prepayment. The second type of risk arises because the effective cost of funds can be influenced by the quantity of loans actually delivered. Since both parties have delivery tolerances, each has an option that is implicitly written by the other party. The third source of risk is the problem of adverse selection; investors are likely to be returned pools that exhibit less desirable characteristics. The impact of each of these risks is described below.

Prepayment Risk

In the cost of funds example, we assumed a CPR of 2.0%, but a faster prepayment rate reduces the effective borrowing cost. The investor gains because he avoids receiving the principal payments at par. If the security actually pays down at a 16% CPR, the effective cost of borrowing is reduced to 2.15%, a savings of 42 basis points over the expected borrowing cost of 2.57% (see Exhibit 2).

Exhibit 2 extends the example by presenting a sensitivity analysis of the effective cost of borrowing under various prepayment rate assumptions. Different prepayment rates can significantly change the effective cost of funds for GNMA 7s. This fact makes the dollar roll a useful tool for institutions that anticipate faster prepayments over a given period than the rest of the market participants do (the reverse is true for discounts). For dollar roll transactions

Exhibit 2. Dollar Roll Sensitivity Analysis
(Breakeven Financing Rates for Security Used in Exhibit 1)

	Annual Prepayment Rates (% CPR)								
Drop	0	2	4	6	8	10	12	14	16
0–14	1.07	1.01	0.96	0.90	0.85	0.79	0.73	0.67	0.61
0–13	1.46	1.40	1.35	1.29	1.24	1.12	1.12	1.06	0.99
0–12	1.85	1.79	1.74	1.68	1.62	1.56	1.50	1.44	1.38
0–11	2.24	2.18	2.13	2.07	2.01	1.95	1.89	1.83	1.75
0–10	2.63	2.57	2.51	2.46	2.40	2.34	2.27	2.21	2.15
0–09	3.02	2.96	2.90	2.84	2.78	2.72	2.66	2.60	2.53
0–08	3.41	3.35	3.29	3.23	3.17	3.11	3.05	2.98	2.92
0–07	3.80	3.74	3.68	3.62	3.56	3.50	3.43	3.37	3.30
0–06	4.19	4.13	4.07	4.01	3.94	3.88	3.82	3.75	3.68

with securities priced at or near par, prepayments become less important. Exhibit 2 also shows the effective cost of borrowing at various dollar roll prices. As the drop increases, the cost of funds decreases because the borrower repurchases the securities at a lower price.

Delivery Risk

The preceding example was based on the assumption that both parties to the dollar roll return exactly the notional amount of the transaction and deliver a substantially identical security that will bring the same price. In reality, both parties have delivery tolerances because they can under- or over-deliver by 2.5%. The delivery tolerance theoretically gives both parties put options: that is, the option but not the obligation to sell securities to each other. If the market price of the security to be rolled rises/falls between the contract date of the roll and the initial settlement, the investor will have an incentive to under/over deliver securities. For example, if the market price has risen before the roll is executed, the investor would deliver less securities at the lower roll price (i.e., would not exercise the put option on the balance of the acceptable amount of securities). Likewise, if at the end of the roll transaction, the market price of the underlying security is higher/lower than the repurchase price of the roll agreement, the dealer will have an incentive to under/over deliver securities. The effective cost of funds will be lower/ higher than projected if the dealer under/over delivers relative to what the investor initially delivered. The investor's option has an exercise date as of the first settlement date and an "at-the-money" strike price equal to the roll-in price. The dealer's exercise date is the final settlement date, and the strike price is lower by the amount of the drop, or slightly "out-of-the-money".

In practice, neither party can fine tune deliveries to exploit fully the ex-post value to their delivery options. Fine tuning the delivery for either the dealer or investor becomes difficult when the delivery tolerance is only plus or minus 2.5%. These options exist in a notional sense, in most cases.[2]

Adverse Selection Risk

Because the dealer is not obliged to return the identical collateral, the dealer and the investor both have a clear incentive not to deliver collateral with attractive specified attributes, i.e., short WAM and fast prepay pools in the case of discounts or long WAM and slow prepay pools in the case of premiums. As a

---

2 This has been the case since April 11, 1987, when the PSA reduced delivery tolerance from [plus/minus]5% to [plus/minus]2.5%. The value of the delivery option is determined by the maturity of the roll agreement (the longer the roll maturity, the greater the dealer's delivery option) and by the price volatility of the coupon rolled (the greater the volatility, the greater the value of the dealer's option).

consequence, the parties would be ill-advised to roll in pools with above average attributes that could command a higher price. As a result, both parties usually transact the dollar roll with pools that are average or less attractive than the universe of deliverable securities. As long as both parties recognize this, there is little chance that one party or the other will be affected negatively.

Investors who wish to use high quality, specified securities for dollar rolls can stipulate that the securities returned must be of similar quality and/or that the drop be increased in recognition of the securities' more attractive attributes. As long as the lender and the borrower recognize that dollar rolls, like all TBA transactions, trade to the lowest common denominator, both parties will benefit from the transaction.

BREAKEVEN ANALYSIS

As has been demonstrated above, an assessment of the relative value of dollar rolls should include the alternative financing costs (that is, the one-month repo rate), the size of the drop, and the expected prepayment rate of the pass-through. These three factors are interrelated. For example, the size of the drop and the expected prepayment rate determines an implied repo rate for the dollar roll transactions. If the market rate is above this level, dollar rolls make sense, barring any outside considerations. Or combining a target short-term financing rate with the expected prepayment rate can help the borrower find a breakeven level for the drop. If the offered drop is larger than the breakeven level, again a dollar roll makes sense. Since the characteristics of the pass-throughs involved in a dollar roll are not fixed, breakeven analysis must be used judiciously. Prepayment sensitivity plays an important roll in the analysis. Dollar rolls on current coupons have little sensitivity to prepayments, while rolls on discounts and premiums are quite sensitive. A small increase in CPR on a premium security will drive the implied financing rate down, while the opposite will occur for a discount security. Because prepayment opportunity gain/loss is an important factor in dollar roll valuation, investors must keep prepayment sensitivity in mind when doing a breakeven analysis. An example of a breakeven/sensitivity analysis for actually traded pass-throughs appears in Exhibit 3.

To illustrate the use of the breakeven analysis, we offer the following example. Suppose an investor is evaluating a dollar roll on a GNMA 7. He receives a quote of 10/32nds for a one-month roll. Using the previous month's CPR, he calculates the implied financing rate to be 2.58%, 57 basis points below the current GNMA repo rate of 3.15%. On review of his breakeven levels, he sees that prepayments could slow to near 0% CPR and the implied financing rate would remain below 3.15%, and that the breakeven drop is 8+/32nds. From this analysis, the investor knows that, finan-

Exhibit 3.   Dollar Roll Breakeven and Sensitivity Market Analysis for Selected 30-Year Coupons (January 7, 1994) (Target Financing Rate Is the GNMA Repo Rate: 3.15%)

						Breakeven Values (Target Fin. Rate: 3.15%)		Sensitivity Analysis Change in Fin. Rate	
Type	Coupon	Age	Price	Drop (32nds)	1 mo. CPR	Implied Fin. Rate	CPR	Drop (32nds)	Drop falls of 1/32 (bp)	Change of 1% CPR (bp)
GNMA	6.00%	1	97–09	9	0.5	2.27	2.6	7	+41	3.0
GNMA	6.50%	1	100–05	9	0.5	2.64	NA	8+	+40	0.0
GNMA	7.00%	2	102–22	10	1.6	2.58	NA	8+	+40	3.0
GNMA	7.50%	3	104–18	9	8.0	3.02	5.3	8+	+38	5.0
GNMA	8.00%	10	105–24	4	19.5	4.42	35.2	7+	+37	8.0
GNMA	8.50%	10	106–06	-2	43.2	4.74	55.9	2+	+36	11.2
FNMA	6.00%	2	92–12	9	1.2	2.28	27.7	7	+41	3.0
FNMA	6.50%	2	100–05	10	1.4	2.23	NA	7+	+40	0.2
FNMA	7.00%	2	102–15	11	2.5	2.18	NA	8+	+39	2.6
FNMA	7.50%	2	104–03	10	8.6	2.66	NA	8+	+38	4.6
FNMA	8.00%	15	105–08	7	30	2.66	23.2	5+	+37	7.6
FNMA	8.50%	35	105–22	0	52	3.27	53.0	0+	+35	11.9
FHLMC	6.00%	1	97–16	9	0.8	2.27	28.0	6+	+41	NA
FHLMC	6.50%	1	100–08	10	1.5	2.23	NA	7+	+40	0.2
FHLMC	7.00%	3	102–17	10	2.8	2.56	NA	8+	+39	2.7
FHLMC	7.50%	3	104–01	8	10.8	3.34	14.8	8+	+38	4.7
FHLMC	8.00%	15	104–28	5	32.5	3.4	35.8	5+	+37	7.4
FHLMC	8.50%	30	105–11	1	62.5	1.93	52.9	3+	+35	14.1

cially, the trade is priced in his favor. He then considers the risk factors discussed earlier and makes his decision.

As mentioned, dollar roll deliveries are made on a TBA basis. As a general rule, a borrower will not use a security for a dollar roll that investors are willing to pay a premium for in the "specified pool" market. This is true because the borrower is likely to end the dollar roll with a security that trades in the TBA market (with a lower price). Against this background, the breakeven analysis should be based only on those securities likely to be traded in the TBA market.

To offer a longer term perspective, Exhibit 4 shows the one-month dollar roll prices (drops) along with the computed effective annual financing rates (using actual prepayments for TBA type loans), the one-month GNMA repo rate, and the benchmark GNMA coupon. This analysis of the bids on

Exhibit 4.   GNMA Dollar Roll Prices, Dollar Roll Implied Repo Rates, and GNMA Repo Rates for 12-Month Period (January-93 through December-93)

Date	Jan-93	Feb-93	Mar-93	Apr-93	May-93	Jun-93	Jul-93	Aug-93	Sep-93	Oct-93	Nov-93	Dec-93
1 mo. GNMA Repo Rate	3.20%	3.20%	3.25%	3.15%	3.15%	3.25%	3.18%	3.18%	3.25%	3.18%	3.10%	3.35%
Benchmark GNMA	7.00%	7.00%	7.00%	7.00%	7.00%	6.50%	6.50%	6.50%	6.00%	6.00%	6.00%	6.50%
Roll Drops												
6.00	NA	NA	NA	NA	NA	NA	NA	NA	11	11	11	11
6.50	NA	NA	15	15	13	13	13	10	10	9	8	9
7.00	11	14	11	12	12	10	10	11	9	9	10	10
7.50	13	13	12	10	12	10	10	12	9	9	8	8
8.00	13	14	12	12	13	10	9	12	8	10	4	4
8.50	12	13	9	8	5	6	6	5	3	-2	-2	-2
9.00	11	12	9	3	1	4	4	10	0	0	-2	-2
9.50	5	9	4	4	2	2	2	1	0	0	0	-3
10.00	7	7	7	4	4	4	2	2	2	2	0	0
Implied Repo Rate												
6.00	NA	NA	NA	NA	NA	NA	NA	NA	1.55	1.77	2.57	1.47
6.50	NA	NA	0.72	0.49	2.15	1.23	1.42	3.02	2.35	2.96	3.21	2.68
7.00	2.96	2.13	2.71	2.09	2.90	2.79	2.92	3.09	3.12	3.34	3.41	2.65
7.50	2.55	2.85	2.72	3.22	3.27	3.14	3.26	3.15	3.47	3.64	4.29	3.59
8.00	2.87	2.87	3.03	2.68	3.06	3.13	3.53	3.11	3.58	2.71	4.76	3.78
8.50	3.48	3.47	4.33	3.97	5.16	3.88	3.87	5.01	5.10	6.92	6.69	6.15
9.00	3.44	3.48	3.68	4.37	3.16	0.12	0.25	0.37	2.77	2.99	4.47	2.12
9.50	2.90	2.73	4.40	3.19	1.75	1.54	0.35	3.26	2.48	2.90	3.43	2.78
10.00	2.08	3.24	3.49	3.58	2.30	2.34	1.41	3.71	2.19	2.90	4.11	2.43

GNMA dollar rolls shows some interesting aspects of TBA trading activity, as well as highlighting some attractive financing opportunities that were available in 1993. The savings in finance costs can be seen by observing the difference between the dollar roll implied repo rate and the actual GNMA repo rate. Dollar rolls with coupons near current production tend to offer the lowest financing opportunities. This is mostly due to large forward sales of these coupons by mortgage originators wishing to hedge their origination pipelines. Heavy activity of this type tends to depress forward prices, thus increasing the drop. This translates into attractive financing opportunities for borrowers who hold pools with these coupons.

Dollar roll drops on premiums varied widely throughout 1993, largely due to changing prepayment expectations. Early in the year, drops for

GNMA 9s and 9.5s were 9/32nd to 12/32nds and implied financing rates were roughly in the 3%–4% range. During June and July, drops on GNMA 9s and 9.5s collapsed to 4/32nds and 2/32nds, respectively, but the implied financing rates were only 25 bp and 35 bp. These implied financing rates were calculated based on prepayment rates for the prior month, which were far more rapid than market expectations, and projections by prepayment models. Later in the year, roll drops fell to or below zero as the market revised its prepayment expectations upward and in line with reality, and implied financing rates rose to near 3%.

SUMMARY

Dollar rolls often offer an attractive means of borrowing at low cost primarily because they allow dealers to cover their short positions. We have focused our discussion of dollar rolls on GNMA fixed rate pass-throughs but it should be noted that there are also very active markets for dollar rolls in conventional fixed-rate and ARM pass-throughs, and that similar cost of funds savings can be found in these transactions. This chapter has demonstrated a methodology for calculating the effective cost of funds obtained through dollar rolls, and outlined the primary risks associated with the cost of funds calculation.

CHAPTER 7

Multifamily Project Securities

Ed Daingerfield
Managing Director
Bear Stearns and Co., Inc.

INTRODUCTION

Projects are mortgages on multifamily homes that are insured by the Federal Housing Administration (FHA) under various federal programs created by the National Housing Act of 1934, as amended. For more than 60 years, one of the primary goals the government has set for the FHA is to enhance the nation's supply of multifamily housing. Several FHA programs have evolved to insure the construction financing and permanent mortgage financing on several types of multifamily residences (including rental apartments, condominiums, and cooperatives), on nursing homes, residential facilities for the elderly and on healthcare units. In addition, the FHA has long-established insurance programs used to refinance the mortgages on these types of properties.

Many investors are unfamiliar with the specific details of project securities and so do not take advantage of the value this sector of the market offers. This chapter provides an introduction to projects and highlights the most relevant features of the project market.

FHA AND GNMA PROJECTS: TWO PRIMARY STRUCTURES OF PROJECTS

Projects most commonly trade in two forms: either as FHA-insured pass-through certificates or as Ginnie Mae securities. Regardless of form, all projects are government guaranteed by the U.S. Department of Housing and Urban Development (HUD) through one of the FHA insurance funds. Projects may only be originated by mortgage lenders in good standing with the FHA and HUD, and all projects are first created as *FHA-insured whole loans*. However, the secondary market for projects in whole-loan form is relatively small. More common are *FHA pass-through certificates (PCs) or FHA pools.* FHA PCs are created whenever an FHA-insured project loan originated by an approved mortgage banker is used to collateralize a pass-through certificate. FHA pools are simply an aggregate of FHA-insured projects.

GNMA project pass-through securities are created when a mortgage banker originates an FHA-insured project but then selects the additional guarantee and standardization provided by GNMA securities. This is analogous to the single-family market, where the FHA or VA insures mortgages that are then issued as GNMA pass-throughs. The credit backing of all FHA and GNMA projects derives from the FHA insurance fund, and so projects issued in both GNMA and FHA form enjoy the credit backing of the U.S. government.

Differences Between FHA and GNMA Projects

There are several important differences between projects issued in FHA-insured form and projects issued as GNMA securities, and as a result GNMA project securities command a price premium over FHA projects. Like single-family GNMA securities, GNMA projects pay principal and interest with a 44-day delay, while FHA projects pay on a 54-day delay. In the event of default, GNMA project pass-through securities incorporate the same standardized procedures as single-family GNMA pass-throughs: full and timely reimbursement of principal and interest is guaranteed in the event of default, and claims are paid out in cash, generally in a timely manner.

In contrast, in the event of default, procedures are not standardized with FHA projects: investors may have to rely on specific information written into the servicing agreement to determine the exact default proceedings. Also, although FHA projects do insure full payment of principal and interest, the FHA takes a 1% administrative fee when a project defaults and is assigned to HUD, and so the investor receives only 99 cents on the dollar. In addition, the FHA does not guarantee timely payment of principal and interest. Investors may have to wait many months in the event an FHA-insured project defaults, although interest does continue to accrue during this time (with the exception of a one-month grace period for which no interest is paid, although no interest is lost on a GNMA project). Finally, although all projects issued in GNMA form pay cash in the event of default, claims on some FHA project defaults are paid in cash, while others are paid in FHA debentures, which are federal agency debt issues of the FHA. Many FHA projects are designated either "cash pay" or "debenture pay" at origination, while others are designated cash or debenture pay at the time of default at the option of either the mortgagee or of HUD. FHA projects designated "cash pay" pay default claims in cash, while those designated "debenture pay" may pay default claims either in FHA debentures with a 20-year maturity or in cash, at the option of HUD. Given all these differences it is no surprise that FHA projects trade cheaper than GNMA projects, or that the spread differential between GNMA and FHA projects does widen or tighten in response to market factors.

Exhibit 1 summarizes the key differences between FHA and GNMA projects.

FHA and GNMA Trends in Originations

Whether projects are issued in FHA form or in GNMA form is a function of the rates at which either can be sold in the secondary market, as well as the costs to issue and insure either form of project. GNMA projects are more expensive to issue than FHAs, although the cost difference has varied widely in recent years. Consequently, at various points in time new issuance in projects shifts back and forth from predominately FHA to predominately GNMA new issuance. Prior to 1981, the majority of all projects were issued as FHA pass-through certificates or in FHA pools. With the advent of the coinsurance program (see below) in 1983, issuance shifted and most projects were issued as GNMA coinsured securities through 1990, when the coinsurance program was terminated. After coinsurance, issuance shifted back to favor FHA projects, which dominated new originations from 1990 through early 1993. In March of 1993, GNMA lowered its guarantee fee, which reduced the cost of issuing GNMA projects, and so at present most new projects are being issued as GNMAs.

PREPAYMENTS

Most project pools consist of one mortgage loan, unlike single-family pools which are backed by numerous mortgages. Consequently, projects do not trade to estimates of prepayment speeds like single-family mortgage-backed

---

Exhibit 1. Primary Differences between GNMA and FHA Projects

GNMA	FHA
If Default:	If Default:
- 100% of principal paid upon default	- 99% of principal upon default
- Full & timely payment of P & I	- Ultimate payment of P & I less one month interest
44-day payment delay	54-day payment delay
Securities wired through depository denominations of $\geq$ 100,000	Physical delivery of certificates Standard piece limit: three per pool
Delivery of GNMA prospectus supplement available	Delivery of supporting documents is recommended
Pool data on Bloomberg	Pool data not on any central data base

securities. Rather, prepayments on projects are driven by the definite incentives most mortgagors have to prepay their mortgages. The likelihood that a project will prepay is based largely on the economics of the underlying building and the characteristics of the mortgagor, as well as on the specific prepayment restrictions and penalties of each project. A key determinant of prepayment likelihood in projects is whether the borrower is a profit-motivated private enterprise or a not-for-profit group. As a general rule, profit-motivated developers prepay project mortgages as early as is economically feasible, while non-profit developers rarely prepay.

Prepayments Unlikely on Projects Owned by Non-Profit Groups

Most non-profit groups that operate projects are state or local housing authorities, church or community groups. As non-profit entities, these groups are not concerned with prepaying a mortgage to access built-up equity or with refinancing to generate increased tax benefits. Also, non-profit organizations are not likely to convert a rental project to a cooperative or sell out to another developer for a profit, and such groups often receive government and/or private subsidies that effectively limit default risk. As a result, prepayments on not-for-profit projects are rare. These projects provide more reliable call protection, and since their cash flows are consistent, most non-profit projects trade to their final maturity rather than to any assumed prepayment date.

Prepayments Unlikely on Projects with Section 8

One feature that provides call protection to investors exists when a project has a Section 8 rent subsidy contract between the project owner and HUD. Under a Section 8 Housing Assistance Payment (HAP) contract, HUD agrees to pay the difference between what a tenant can afford to pay for rent (based on tenant income) and the prevailing market rate for a similar apartment in the same area. Typically, tenants pay 30% of their monthly income for rent and Section 8 subsidies cover the balance. To be eligible for Section 8 payments, tenants must be low-income families whose incomes do not exceed 50% of the median income for the area; over 3 $1/2$ million families are currently served by some form of Section 8 subsidy. Subsidy payments are made directly to the owner of the project, which assures a reliable cash flow from the project and makes prepayments from default less likely. Section 8 subsidy payments also provide additional call protection since it is generally uneconomical for the project owner to prepay the mortgage while the HAP contract is in force (most HAP contracts are for 20 years and are renewable). Section 8 contracts cannot be transferred nor terminated, and remain with the project under a change of ownership.

Section 8 HAP contracts may cover fewer than 100% of the rental apartments in a given project; obviously, projects with higher percentages of Section 8 provide the greatest call protection. Finally, those Section 8 projects covered by the Low Income Housing Preservation Act are expressly prohibited from prepaying. If the developers of such projects wish to refinance for any reason, they must take out a Section 241 (see below) second mortgage rather than prepay the first Section 8 mortgage.

Prepayments Likely on For-Profit Projects

Private-sector, profit-motivated borrowers may refinance projects if interest rates decline, but they also have powerful incentives to refinance loans at current or even higher rates. While higher rates increase the expenses of project owners, the higher debt service can often be offset by rent increases. For existing properties that have increased in value, selling the property or refinancing at a higher loan-to-value ratio enables developers to take equity out of a project. The economics of a profit-motivated developer's business often dictates that private-sector project borrowers refinance to capitalize available equity. Refinancing a for-profit project may also be driven by a need for the mortgagor to raise money to refurbish or rehabilitate a property without putting up scarce equity. This is very common since most developers maximize profits by gradually increasing rents over time as leases expire and tenants move. The ability to increase rents is obviously dependent on the physical condition of the property. As projects age, developers frequently refinance the mortgage to generate money for refurbishing the building, which in turn protects their long-term investment and encourages higher rents.

As for-profit projects age and the mortgage is paid down, the probabilities increase that private developers will prepay the mortgage to rehabilitate the project or to take out equity. The likelihood and timing of prepayments on profit-motivated projects depends on several factors, including the loan-to-value ratio of the project, the type and location of the project, the physical condition of the property, and the type of borrower. Borrowers are more likely to prepay projects with lower loan-to-value ratios, since this permits them to access a substantial amount of equity quickly. Also, projects built for upper- and middle-income rather than low-income tenants are generally more likely to refinance, since they typically have more amenities that require upkeep (pools, dishwashers, microwave ovens, *etc.*) and are generally in better neighborhoods, and so are more likely to increase in value or be converted to condominiums. Under FHA regulations, if a project does not continue to serve the same use it must be prepaid. Thus, before a mortgagor on a rental project could convert the property to a cooperative or condominium, the mortgage must be prepaid. Moderate and higher income projects also tend to prepay faster since, as the physical plant ages and amenities deteriorate, developers often need to refinance to access equity to refurbish and maintain the project to protect their investment. Projects in high-growth areas and other favorable locations more frequently increase in value and so tend to prepay faster. Exhibit 2 illustrates that even assuming a conservative 1% annual increase in value, equity in a project increases by roughly one third after 10–12 years.

Tax considerations provide motivation for many limited partnerships and private investors to refinance projects. The Tax Reform Act of 1986 curtailed accelerated depreciation, which had provided significant incentives to refinance older projects. Projects originated since 1986 must be depreciated over 27 1/2 years, using a straight-line method. However, tax factors remain a consideration in refinancing decisions. The tax shelter provided by mortgage interest payments, coupled with the tax advantages that remain under the current depreciation rules, begin to abate in years 10–12 as the project mortgage amortizes. Exhibit 3 shows that typically, by year 10 passive tax losses in a project partnership dissipate and begin to generate taxable income by years 10–12. This encourages partnerships to refinance project mortgages to reset the passive tax losses that are vital to many limited partners.

Taken together, Exhibits 2 and 3 illustrate how profit-motivated projects often refinance in 10–12 years for two complementary reasons: 1) owners

Exhibit 2. Project Equity Accrues over Time

**Percent
Equity**

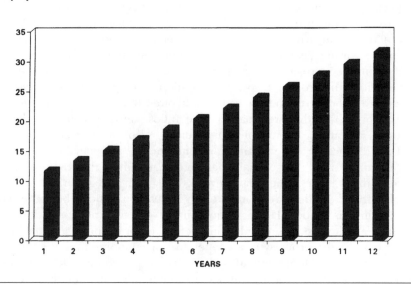

Exhibit 3.   Project Tax Advantages Erode over Time

Taxable
Income

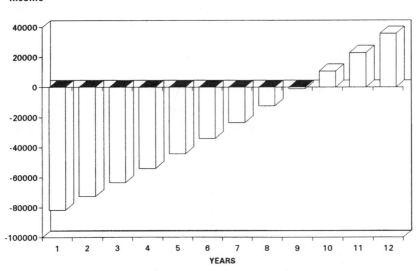

access equity for rehabilitation, to pay off limited partners, and to purchase other projects; and 2) refinancing or sale of the property is a common exit strategy for owners interested in the tax-shelter advantages of projects.

PREPAYMENTS, CALL PROTECTION, LOCKOUTS AND PENALTIES

FHA/HUD does not prohibit profit-motivated developers from prepaying or refinancing project mortgages, although prepayments on non-profit projects are generally restricted. Non-profit projects built under several programs may not be prepaid, while under other programs prepayments on non-profit projects are permitted only if the mortgagor is able to secure HUD's approval. In addition, prepayments on projects with Section 8 are restricted, some by formal HUD regulations and others by economic forces (see above).

Most project pass-throughs are whole pools backed by one building, and so a full prepayment effectively generates a call at par on the security. As a result, prepayment restrictions and penalties are written into the documentation that governs project trades. HUD has approved three basic types of prepayment restrictions and penalties (see HUD mortgagee letter 87-9): 1) prepayment lockout restrictions that extend to a maximum of 10 years plus the stated construction period, 2) prepayment penalties of 1% or less, 10 years after the stated construction period, and 3) some combination of prepayment lockout and penalties with a lockout less than 10 years and a premium no more than 1% 10 years after the stated construction period. At present, the three most common forms of call protection are 10-year lockouts; five-year lockouts with prepayments then permitted in year 6 at a 105% of par, declining to 101% in year 10; and five-year lockouts alone, with no prepayment penalties.

PREPAYMENTS AND DEFAULT: BACKGROUND

Default generates an unanticipated prepayment, received in cash at par for GNMA projects and at 99 in cash or debentures (depending on program) for FHA projects. Defaults on HUD-insured projects have primarily occurred in two programs: 1) the older 221(d)3 Below Market Interest Rate or BMIR program, which insured low-income projects in an effort to ameliorate poverty and provide inner-city housing (although construction design, planning, location, and underwriting later proved to be flawed); and 2) the coinsured program of the 1980s. The structural failures of HUD's GNMA coinsurance program are now widely acknowledged (see coinsurance, below). Accurate numbers are difficult to obtain from HUD, but default rates on BMIRs and coinsured projects are generally assumed to exceed 40% (that's over 40% in each program). For investors, the economic consequences or return characteristics of default depend purely on interest rates. Many investors have reaped windfalls when discount BMIRs defaulted, although other investors have suffered when premium coinsured GNMAs defaulted.

HUD was hit hard by the overleverage and subsequent drop in multi-family real estate values from the mid-1980s through early 1990s, when many HUD insured projects defaulted. When a project goes into delinquency, the servicer assigns it to HUD, and HUD's inventory of projects has tripled over the past seven years and now stands at about 2,400 projects. Cumbersome federal regulations have prevented HUD from foreclosing on many troubled properties and resolving these problems, and budget constraints have left HUD ill-equipped to manage problem properties. Together, these factors have left HUD with over $6 billion of defaulted projects in inventory. By early 1993, Congress required the agency to increase its loss reserves from $5.5 billion to $11.9 billion to cover anticipated multifamily losses.

Recently, HUD announced its intention to sell the projects that have been assigned to the agency. Not all the troubled projects assigned to HUD have defaulted, and even the defaulted real estate varies tremendously in quality. While some of the properties are seriously troubled, others are performing, while still other loans have been helped by recovering real estate values and lower interest rates. As HUD begins to liquidate this portfolio, investors can expect to see HUD-insured mortgage pools as well as senior/subordinate structures similar to the RTC's multifamily real estate mortgage sales.

COINSURANCE

For most of its existence, HUD has been a thinly staffed and lightly funded federal agency. Also, as the nation's largest insurer/provider of multifamily rental housing, HUD has frequently been subject to political pressures at the city, state, and particularly the national levels. Significant political pressures were brought to bear on HUD with the advent of the Reagan administration in the early 1980s, when the agency suffered substantial reductions in staffing. HUD loan underwriters and auditors bore the brunt of these cutbacks, and this vitiated the agency's ability to implement strict underwriting standards. In response, in 1983, HUD introduced the coinsurance program.

Under this coinsurance program, private GNMA mortgage originators took on the role of HUD staffers and were responsible not just for originating loans, but also for all due diligence and underwriting for project loans. In an attempt to preserve credit standards, HUD required mortgage originators to reimburse the agency for 20% of any insurance claims the agency paid out on projects that defaulted. This 20% liability was intended to keep mortgage bankers in the coinsurance program honest. At that time, the feeling was that the government could minimize risk to the FHA insurance fund by enabling private-sector lenders to risk their own capital on a project in return for greater origination fees. Predictably, the program ran into problems. By the late 1980s, it became clear that underwriting standards had generally received a lower priority than mortgage lenders' desire for the lucrative fee income generated by originating new projects. HUD also lacked the systems needed to monitor the thinly capitalized coinsurers. In addition, cases of outright fraud were well publicized; after many defaults, HUD canceled the coinsurance program in 1990.

A significant number of coinsured GNMA project securities remain in circulation and trade regularly in the secondary market. Since these outstanding projects are in GNMA form, investors are shielded from credit risk by the U.S. Government guarantee of GNMA. However, given the decline in interest rates from the 1980s to the early 1990s, almost all coinsured GNMAs trade at significant premiums. Investors should use caution in evaluating premium projects underwritten with co-insurance; to the degree that weak underwriting leads to a default (par call), the return characteristics of coinsured GNMAs can shift dramatically.

CLC/PLCs

Under multifamily insurance programs, the government insures the construction financing of projects as well as the permanent mortgages on the completed structures, unlike single-family mortgage pass-throughs in which the government only insures mortgages on completed homes. Investors purchase new projects by committing to fund construction costs on a monthly basis until the project is built. When construction is completed, the investor's cumulative monthly construction financing payments are rolled into a permanent mortgage on the building. The construction financing portion of a project trades in the secondary market as insured *Construction Loan Certificates (CLCs)*, in either FHA-insured or GNMA form. CLCs operate as follows: each month during a predetermined construction period (typically 16 - 20 months), the contractor completes a specified portion of the construction and then submits a bill for the work to the local FHA office. The FHA then sends an inspector to the job site, and if the work meets specifications the FHA issues an insured CLC for that month's work. The investor funds the work by fulfilling a commitment to purchase each insured CLC. When the project is completed, the investor exchanges all the monthly CLCs for an insured *Permanent Loan Certificate (PLC)*. The PLC is simply a fully funded project, an insured pass-through security backed by the final mortgage on the completed property. There are vastly more fully funded projects (PLCs) than CLCs in the market, owing to the long economic lives of project structures, and while CLCs are generally held by one investor over a relatively short construction period, PLCs trade frequently in the secondary market.

SPECIFIC PROJECT PROGRAMS

The FHA has established numerous multifamily insurance programs since its creation under the National Housing Act of 1934. Each program serves a specific purpose, and is referred to by the section of the National Housing Act under which it was created. Specific characteristics vary from program to program, since the types of projects, their purposes, allowable mortgage limits, prepayment features, and other criteria often differ. As discussed above, regardless of which program a project is insured under, securities backed by mortgages insured under any HUD program may exist in either GNMA form or as FHA pass-throughs. Below is a brief discussion of several of the most common multifamily insurance programs. Exhibit 4 provides a quick reference chart on these programs. Exhibit 5 shows the relative size of each program within the project market.

Exhibit 4.   Project Quick Reference Chart

SECTION 202

Type of Program: Direct loans for housing the elderly or handicapped

Type of Borrower: Private, non-profit sponsors (including non-profit cooperatives)

Maximum Loan Amount: The lesser of: 95% of anticipated net project income or 100% of the project's development costs

Maximum Term: 50 years by statute, but HUD has limited loans to 40 years

Date Program Enacted: 1959 (amended 1974)

Additional Features: Older loans fixed-rate; newer loans adjust annually at a HUD-determined margin over Treasuries. All projects under 202 have 100% Section 8 HAP contracts (see Section 8, pgs. 6-7)

Program Status: Active

Insurance in Force: $8.7 billion

SECTION 207

Type of Program: Construction or rehabilitation of rental housing

Type of Borrower: Primarily profit-motivated sponsors

Date Program Enacted: 1934

Prepayment Restrictions: Negotiable

Program Status: Authorized but not used; multifamily rental projects now issued under Sections 221(d)3 and (4)

Insurance in Force: $3.4 billion

SECTION 213

Type of Program: New construction, rehabilitation, acquisition, conversion, or repair of cooperative housing projects

Type of Borrower: Profit-motivated co-op sponsors as well as non-profit corporations or trusts

Date Program Enacted: 1950

Prepayment Restrictions: Negotiable

Program Status: Authorized but not used; cooperative projects now issued under Sections 221(d)3 and 221(d) 4

Insurance in Force: $878 million

SECTION 220

Type of Program: New construction or rehabilitation of projects in designated Urban Renewal Areas

Type of Borrower: Profit-motivated and non-profit sponsors

Date Program Enacted: 1949 (expanded 1980)

Prepayment Restrictions: Negotiable

Program Status: Active but infrequently used; Urban Renewal projects are being eliminated

Insurance in Force: $1.5 billion

Exhibit 4. *Continued*

SECTIONS 221(d)3 and 221(d)4

   Type of Programs: Construction or rehabilitation of multifamily rental or cooperative housing for low- or moderate-income tenants

   Type of Borrower: For-profit corporations or partnerships (developers, builders, investors); also no-profit public or community groups

   Maximum Loan Amount: 221(d)4: 90% of FHA-estimated replacement cost (maximum can be higher only with explicit FHA approval)

   221(d)3: 100% of FHA-estimated replacement cost

   Maximum Term: 40 years from origination

   Date Programs Enacted: 221(d)3: 1954; **221(d)4:** 1959

   Additional Features: FHA pass-throughs auctioned before 1/1/84 have an option that permits investor to put the mortgage to HUD in its 20th year

   Prepayment Restrictions: Negotiable between mortgagor and mortgagee unless project has a Section 8 HAP contract

   Program Status: Active

   Insurance in Force: 221(d)4: $23 billion; 221(d)3: $3.9 billion

SECTION 223(f)

   Type of Program: Purchase or refinancing of existing multifamily projects

   Type of Borrower: Primarily profit-motivated sponsors (HUD as well as conventional borrowers)

   Maximum Loan Amount: 85% of HUD-estimated value (may be raised to 90% for cooperative apartments)

   Maximum Term: 35 years from origination

   Date Program Enacted: 1974

   Prepayment Restrictions: Negotiable

   Program Status: Active

   Insurance in Force: $13.6 billion

SECTION 223(a)7

   Type of Program: Refinancing of existing multifamily projects (HUD only) designed by HUD for faster down-in-coupon refinancings

   Type of Borrower: Existing HUD borrowers only

   Maximum Loan Amount: Limited to the lesser of 1) the original amount of the existing mortgage; or 2) the unpaid balance of the existing mortgage

   Maximum Term: 40 years from origination, although most take on the maturity of the original, seasoned HUD mortgage

   Date Program Enacted: 1993

   Prepayment Restrictions: Negotiable

   Program Status: Active

   Insurance in Force: Program reactivated in 1993

SECTION 231

   Type of Program: Rental housing for the elderly or handicapped

   Type of Borrower: Profit-motivated and non-profit sponsors

Exhibit 4. *Continued*

Maximum Loan Amount: 90% (for-profit project) 100% (non-profit project) of the FHA-estimated replacement cost
Maximum Term: 40 years, or 75% of the project's estimated economic life
Date Program Enacted: 1959
Prepayment Restrictions: Negotiable
Program Status: Active
Insurance in Force: $780 million

SECTION 232

Type of Program: Construction or rehabilitation of nursing homes, intermediate care facilities, and board and care homes
Type of Borrower: Profit-motivated and non-profit sponsors
Maximum Loan Amount: 90% of FHA-estimated value of property (includes the value of equipment used to operate the facility)
Maximum Term: 40 years from origination
Date Program Enacted: 1959
Prepayment Restrictions: Negotiable
Program Status: Active
Insurance in Force: $4.4 billion

SECTION 236

Type of Program: Interest-rate subsidies for low- to moderate-income families and elderly individuals
Type of Borrower: Profit-motivated and non-profit sponsors
Maximum Loan Amount: 90% of FHA-estimated replacement cost (100% or higher permissible for non-profit sponsors)
Date Program Enacted: 1968
Prepayment Restrictions: Negotiable
Program Status: Inactive
Insurance in Force: $6.5 billion

SECTION 241

Type of Program: Equity take-out (2d mortgage), qualified low-income housing
Type of Borrower: Owners of eligible low-income housing who have filed a plan of action under HUD's prepayment programs
Maximum Loan Amount: 90% of estimated replacement cost on entire project, including first mortgage, or 95% of preservation equity
Maximum Term: 40 years from origination,
Date Program Enacted: 1968, although not frequently used by HUD until 1993

SECTION 242

Type of Program: Construction or rehabilitation of public or private hospitals (includes major movable equipment)
Type of Borrower: Profit-motivated or non-profit sponsors
Maximum Loan Amount: 90% of FHA-estimated replacement cost

Exhibit 4. *Continued*

Maximum Term: 25 years from origination
Date Program Enacted: 1968
Prepayment Restrictions: Negotiable; non-profit sponsors may only make prepayments
with HUD's written consent
Program Status: Active
Insurance in Force: $4.5 billion

Exhibit 5. Relative Size of the Various Programs That Constitute the $72 Billion Project
Securities Outstanding as of 9/1/94 (HUD Data)

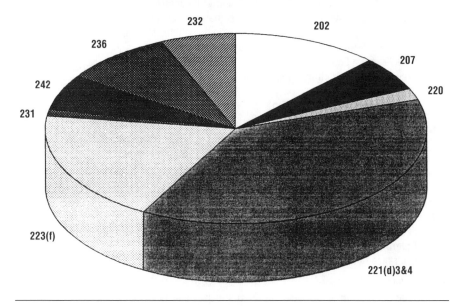

Multifamily Housing

Section 221(d)4: Rental Housing for Low- to Moderate-Income Families: The
221(d)4 program is the largest project program, with just over $28 billion in
cumulative insurance issued on 7,957 projects and $23 billion insurance
remaining in force since the program began in 1959.[1] This program insures
mortgages made by private lenders to finance construction or substantial

---

1 All data reported in this chapter are from the U.S. Department of Housing and Urban
Development, as of September 1, 1994.

rehabilitation of multifamily rental or cooperative housing for low- to moderate-income or displaced families. Projects insured under Section 221(d)4 must have five or more units, and may consist of detached, semi-detached, row, walk-up, or elevator structures.

Section 221(d)4 projects may be owned by either non-profit or profit-motivated developers and may be insured for up to 90% of their FHA-determined replacement cost. While 100% of the funds invested in project securities is insured, the mortgagor only borrows 90% or less of replacement cost; the balance represents owner equity. The majority of loans insured under Section 221(d)4, and most new production, are unsubsidized, market-rate projects. That is, project owners set the rental rates at whatever the market will bear (subject to HUD underwriting), and there are no income restrictions on tenants. Over the last several years, sophisticated developers have elected HUD financing as the most cost-efficient way to finance new apartment construction, and the majority of recent projects insured under Section 221(d)4 have been suburban garden apartments and other higher-end real estate. Non-market rate projects may also be insured under Section 221(d)4, and most Section 8 subsidized projects are financed through the 221(d)4 program; only these Section 8 projects have restrictions on monthly rents and tenant income.

The maximum term of mortgages insured under Section 221(d)4 is either 40 years or 75% of the FHA-estimated remaining economic life of the project, whichever is less. The majority of these projects carry 40-year terms. FHA/HUD does not restrict prepayments between the mortgagee and mortgagor. HUD may allow mortgagors to prepay up to 15% of a mortgage per year, unless documents which record the transaction specify in the lockout that the bonds are non-callable in whole or in part for a specified period of time. However, even if documents do not prohibit prepayments, the 15% prepayment option is not exercised often, since U.S. Government backing makes project financing much less expensive for developers than private financing alternatives.

Section 221(d)3: Rental and Cooperative Housing for Low- to Moderate-Income Families: The 221(d)3 program has two components. The first was an older, below-market interest-rate program (BMIR) that provided financing to sponsors of lower-income housing projects. The default rate on BMIRs has been high, roughly 50% as discussed above, and so the BMIR program was closed in 1972 (of the $2.87 billion BMIRs originally insured, only $1.3 billion remain outstanding).

The second component of Section 221(d)3, the market-rate program has been virtually replaced by the 221(d)4 program. The market-rate 221(d)3 program remains in force, with $3.2 billion in cumulative insurance issued on 2,069 projects and $2.6 billion insurance remaining in force since the program began in 1954. The primary difference between the 221(d)3 and the 221(d)4 program is that Section 221(d)3 provides developers with more leverage for public, non-profit groups and cooperatives, since HUD may insure up to 100% of a project's FHA-determined replacement cost under this program, versus only 90% under Section 221(d)4. The majority of market-rate projects insured under Section 221(d)3 do have Section 8 rental subsidies. Finally, during the first 20 years of a mortgage insured under Section 221(d)3, borrowers must obtain HUD's permission before making any prepayments on the mortgage. Aside from these differences, the 221(d)3 market-rate program closely resembles the 221(d)4 program. The program may also be used for new construction or substantial rehabilitation of various types of buildings.

7.43 Putable Projects: Older FHA Projects Insured Under Sections 221(d)3 and 221(d)4: FHA projects insured under Section 221(d)3 and 221(d)4 prior to 1984 included a 20-year put feature. This put option gives the FHA pass-through holder the right to assign, or put, the mortgage to HUD for a 1-year period 20 years after the original mortgage was endorsed by HUD/FHA. When investors put the securities, they receive FHA series MM (Mutual Mortgage) debentures with a 10-year maturity; these debentures are obligations of the FHA, and as such are unconditionally guaranteed by the U.S Government as to payment of interest and principal. The debentures' face value will equal the unpaid principal balance of the mortgage plus accrued interest. The servicers of most project loan pools automatically exercise this put option and then liquidate the debentures for investors, unless bondholders who represent a controlling interest in the pool object. The investors then receive the proceeds as a cash distribution from the project pool.

Prior to December 1983, many FHA projects were auctioned by GNMA. The majority of these projects were purchased by servicers as 7.50% loans and issued as FHA pass-through securities with 7.43 coupons. They are commonly referred to as 7.43s since the issuers often retained 7 basis points of servicing. The vast majority of 7.43s were auctioned between 1979 and 1983; consequently, most 7.43s are putable between 1999 and 2003 and trade at a spread over the Treasury curve. Many of the projects underlying 7.43s carry Section 8 contracts (see above), which provide the investor with a defined cash flow and also limit prepayments. This cash-flow certainty coupled with the put feature make putable 7.43s very convex securities.

The exact value of the FHA debentures definitely affects the value of the put option. To compensate for the additional market risk and record-keeping associated with debentures, investors have typically valued FHA debentures at 96-to-98 cents on the dollar. However, a 1990 Federal budget resolution changed the put process on 7.43s in order to reduce the budget deficit. At present, investors in 7.43s putable 1995 or earlier can elect to receive cash in lieu of debentures when the bonds are put, and investors who valued the put option assuming they would receive debentures worth 96 can now receive cash, or par. As a result, the put option is now worth much more than most investors assumed upon purchase. Further, the shift from debenture pay to cash pay shaved the Federal budget deficit substantially, and many observers think it very likely that future budget laws will extend the change from debenture pay to cash pay to reduce future budget deficits. Thus, a case can be made that the put option on 7.43s is worth more than a 96–98 assumption implies.

Section 223(f): Purchase or Refinancing of Existing Multifamily Projects: The 223(f) program was created to insure the purchase or refinancing of existing rental apartment projects, to refinance existing cooperatives, or to purchase and convert existing rental projects to cooperative housing. Section 223(f) was added to the National Housing Act by the Housing and Community Development Act in 1974 in order to help preserve an adequate supply of affordable housing. Rental projects already insured by HUD, as well as private, non-insured rental projects, can be refinanced by using Section 223(f). Since 1974, 3,150 projects have been originated under Section 223(f), representing $16 billion of insurance written with $13.6 billion remaining in force.

Section 223(f) is a market-rate, unsubsidized program created primarily to improve the financing flexibility for profit-motivated project developers by making it easier for owners to refinance, convert a project to a co-op, and buy or sell an existing building. To qualify for insurance under Section 223(f), a project must be at least three years old, must contain five or more units, and must have sufficient occupancy to pay operating expenses, annual debt service, and maintain a reserve fund for replacement requirements. A mortgage insured under Section 223(f) cannot exceed 85% of the HUD/ FHA-estimated value of the project, although this requirement can be raised to 90% for cooperatives and those projects located in Target Preservation Areas as designated by HUD.

The maximum term for mortgages insured under Section 223(f) is either 35 years or 75% of the FHA-estimated remaining economic life of the project, whichever is less. Most 223(f) projects carry 35-year terms. As with other programs, HUD/FHA permits prepayments on mortgages insured under Section 223(f), although prepayment lockouts and penalties are usually negotiated between the mortgagee and mortgagor.

Section 223(a)7: Streamlined Refinancing of HUD-Insured Multifamily Projects: The 223(a)7 program was revamped in April of 1993 and now enables developers to refinance a project that is already HUD-insured in a quick and efficient manner. The new program minimizes HUD procedures and requirements to reduce the processing time needed to refinance a mortgage. Although mortgages insured under Section 223(a)7 can have a maximum term of 40 years, many 223(a)7 loans run only to the maturity of the first mortgage. Consequently, 223(a)7 loans generally have the shortest maturities of newly originated project securities. Mortgages insured under 223(a)7 can be processed faster than refinancings under section 223(f), since HUD does not reunderwrite projects that are refinanced under 223(a)7. HUD reasons that the (a)7 mortgages are already in its insured portfolio, and that reducing their interest rates can only strengthen the financial condition of the projects. Unlike the 223(f) program, HUD does not permit developers to take equity out of a project under a Section 223(a)7 refinancing; the program is used only to reduce the loan's interest rate, and this increases debt service coverage. Consequently, the lack of a new underwriting should probably not concern investors. Equity in the project continues to compound as the 223(a)7 seasons, and this initial equity compounds significantly by year 10 of the a(7) mortgage. Thus, the net effect the 223(a)7 program has on project investors is to increase the likelihood that project securities will be called after their lockouts expire, as a result of an early refinancing of the underlying real estate.

Section 207: Section 207 was enacted in 1934 as the first program used by the FHA to finance construction or rehabilitation of multifamily housing projects. Section 207 projects are primarily moderate-income projects sponsored by for-profit developers. The 207 program is rarely used today, as multifamily projects are now originated under Sections 221(d)3 and 221(d)4. However, seasoned Section 207 projects continue to trade in the secondary market. Total cumulative insurance issued under Section 207 was $4.2 billion, with $3.4 billion insurance remaining in force.

Section 213: The Section 213 program was enacted in 1950 to provide mortgage insurance on cooperative projects. Section 213 insurance can be used for new construction, rehabilitation, acquisition, conversion, or repair of existing housing in several types of cooperative projects that consist of five or more units. The program is available for both non-profit cooperative corporations as well as for profit-motivated developers who build or rehabilitate a project and sell it to a cooperative corporation. Total cumulative insurance written under Section 213 is $1.6 billion on 2,043 projects, with $852 million insurance now in force.

Section 220: The Section 220 program was created to insure mortgages and home improvement loans on multifamily projects in urban renewal areas. Before 1980, Section 220 insurance was available in urban renewal areas in which federally assisted slum clearance and urban redevelopment projects were being undertaken. In 1980, the Housing and Community Development Act expanded the scope of the Section 220 program to include those areas in which housing, development, and public service activities will be carried out by local neighborhood improvement, conservation, or preservation groups. The main focus of Section 220 is to insure mortgages on new or rehabilitated multifamily structures located within designated urban renewal areas. Over 540 projects have been insured under Section 220, which represents $3.1 billion in total cumulative insurance with $1.5 billion remaining in force.

Section 241: Section 241 was reactivated early in 1993 to address the refinancing of low-income housing that receives Section 8 rent subsidies (see above). Section 8 projects are rarely refinanced (see above), and under the Low Income Housing Preservation Acts of 1987 (Title I) and 1990 (Title II), low-income preservation Section 8 projects can not be refinanced at all. As of 1993, however, owners whose low-income properties have increased in value can access that equity with a second mortgage loan insured under Section 241 without refinancing the project's underlying first mortgage. Under 241, HUD reunderwrites the entire project to a maximum of 90% loan-to-value, subtracts the remaining balance on the first mortgage, and then insures a 241 loan for the balance. The 241 loan is fully insured by HUD; there is no credit difference between the original mortgage and the 241. Obviously, given the use of the 241 program, securities backed by first mortgages with Section 8 subsidies provide significant call protection to investors. In addition, many observers feel that securities backed by 241 loans are also well call protected, given the economics and legal housing preservation aspects of the underlying properties.

Healthcare

Section 231: Rental Housing for the Elderly or Handicapped: In 1959, Congress enacted Section 231 of the National Housing Act to provide insurance for the construction or rehabilitation of rental housing for the elderly and/or handicapped. Section 231 was expanded to include housing for the handicapped in 1964. Residents of projects for the elderly must be at least 62 years old, while residents in projects for the handicapped must be people with a long-term physical impairment that substantially impedes an independent living arrangement, but who could live independently in suitable housing.

    Projects must have 8 or more units to qualify for insurance under Section 231, and the maximum term for mortgages insured under Section 231 is 40 years or 75% of the project's estimated economic life. In addition, HUD may insure up to 100% of the estimated replacement cost for projects originated by non-profit and public borrowers, but only up to 90% of replacement cost for profit-motivated mortgagors. Section 231 is no longer used for new loans; elderly housing is now financed under the Section 221(d)4 program. Total cumulative insurance issued under Section 231 is $1.2 billion, with $780 million insurance remaining in force.

Section 232: Nursing Homes, Intermediate Care Facilities, and Board and Care Homes: Under Section 232, HUD insures mortgages to finance new construction or rehabilitation of nursing homes for patients who require skilled nursing care and related medical services, as well as intermediate care facilities and board and care homes for patients who need minimum but continuous care provided by licensed or trained people. Section 232 insures mortgages on any of these facilities; also, nursing homes, intermediate care, and board and care homes may be combined within the same facility and insured under Section 232. Board and care homes must have a minimum of 5 1-bedroom or efficiency units, while nursing homes and intermediate care facilities must have 20 or more patients who are unable to live independently but are not in need of acute care. Mortgage insurance under Section 232 may also cover the purchase of major equipment needed to operate the facility. Also, Section 232 may be used to purchase, rehabilitate, and/or refinance existing healthcare projects already insured by HUD.

Legislation establishing this program was enacted in 1959. Borrowers may include private non-profit associations or corporations or for-profit investors or developers. To qualify for insurance under Section 232, sponsors must first qualify for licensing in the state of the facility and must comply with all relevant State regulations. Total cumulative insurance issued under Section 232 is $4.8 billion on 1,936 projects; total insurance remaining in force is $4.4 billion.

Section 236: Interest-Rate Subsidies for Low-to Moderate-Income Families and Elderly Individuals: Section 236 was added to the National Housing Act in 1968, but was suspended during the subsidized housing moratorium of 1973 and has never been revived. The 236 program combined governmental mortgage insurance on projects with subsidized payments to reduce the project owners' monthly debt service payments. These reduced interest payments, in turn, are passed on to tenants of the project in the form of lower rents. To qualify for rental assistance under Section 236, tenants' annual income must be less than 80% of the median income of the area. The program serves both elderly individuals and low-income families.

The maximum mortgage amount for limited-dividend sponsors is 90% of replacement cost; for non-profit sponsors, the maximum mortgage amount can be 100%. In certain, defined, high-cost areas, maximums may be increased up to an additional 75%. The maximum term under this program is 40 years, and prepayments are prohibited for at least 20 years without prior approval from HUD. Total cumulative insurance issued under Section 236 was $8.0 billion on over 4,200 projects; $6.5 billion insurance remains in force.

Section 242: Mortgage Insurance for Hospitals: In 1968, Congress enacted Section 242 of the National Housing Act to provide insurance for the construction or rehabilitation of hospitals. Major equipment used in the hospital may also be included in an insured mortgage under Section 242. Hospitals built or rehabilitated under Section 242 must have appropriate licenses, must meet the regulatory requirements of the State in which they are located, and must be approved by the U.S. Department of Health and Human Services. A Section 242 mortgage may not exceed 90% of the FHA-estimated replacement cost, and the maximum term for these mortgages is 25 years.

Borrowers under Section 242 may be either profit-motivated or not-for-profit hospitals. HUD permits full or partial prepayments on profit-motivated Section 242 projects, subject to prepayment restrictions and penalties negotiated between the mortgagor and mortgagee, but prepayments by non-profit mortgagors are permitted only with the written consent of HUD. Total cumulative insurance issued under Section 242 is $6.6 billion on 262 projects, with $4.5 billion insurance remaining in force.

SECTION II

PREPAYMENT BEHAVIOR AND FORECASTING

CHAPTER 8

Mortgage Prepayment Modeling: I

Charles Schorin
Vice President
Mortgage Research
Morgan Stanley & Co., Inc.

Mark N. Gordon
Senior Vice President
Mortgage Research
Kidder, Peabody & Co., Inc.

INTRODUCTION

Prepayments are fundamental to mortgage-backed securities. Were it not for the right of mortgagors to prepay their mortgages without penalty, a mortgage security would be similar to an ordinary, non-callable corporate or Treasury bond; but from the option of mortgagors to prepay and their inefficient exercise of this option, the risk characteristics of mortgage-backed securities are derived and they differ dramatically from those of ordinary bonds. As important as prepayments are to the risk and return pattern of mortgage pass-throughs, they are especially crucial to the performance of derivative mortgage products, such as interest-only/principal-only strips (IOs/POs) and collateralized mortgage obligation (CMOs), particularly the companion tranches.

With prepayments playing such an important role in the performance of mortgage securities, it is imperative that market participants have a means of estimating prepayments. Ideally, these prepayment estimates will be derived from a formal mathematical model that has been estimated statistically using historical data. A model of this type can be used to evaluate prepayments on mortgage pass-throughs, and therefore to price both pass-throughs and more complicated derivative mortgage instruments and structured products.

A prepayment model needs to consider four basic determinants of prepayment behavior: seasonality, burnout, seasoning, and interest rates. When analysts were building prepayment models in the mid-1980s, the interest rate and seasonal components were by that time pretty well understood; the more vexing parts of the problem were understanding prepayment burnout, which was just beginning to be experienced, and the extent to which the actual seasoning pattern of a mortgage security deviates from the assumption of the PSA Standard Benchmark. Now that the market has accumulated more data and experienced more interest rate environments, there is pretty widespread agreement on the importance of burnout and seasonality and an understanding that actual seasoning may differ from the pattern of the PSA Curve. What ironically now deserves renewed attention is the modelling of the response of prepayment behavior to interest rates.

The four prepayment surges from late 1991 to early 1994 were the strongest bursts of refinancing and prepayment activity since 1986–87. Similar to the 1986–87 cycle, the 1991–94 cycle caught many market participants off guard. There were aspects of the latter environment—such as the availability of relatively short maturity mortgages priced off of the short end of an historically steep yield curve—that made it different from the previous prepayment wave, but what is remarkable is how similar prepayment behavior was in the two periods. When the differences in the environments are controlled for by modelling them explicitly, the similarities between the two periods actually is reassuring!

One aspect that needs to be modelled explicitly is the slope of the yield curve and the importance of shorter maturity mortgages. Even though adjustable-rate mortgages (ARMs) and 15-year mortgages priced off the short end of the yield curve were available in the 1986–87 refinancing surge, the recent addition to the mortgage menu of balloon mortgages enhanced the move to shorter maturity mortgages, allowing borrowers who could not qualify for 15-year mortgages the advantage of a 30-year amortization schedule, as well as removing the interest-rate risk faced by an ARM borrower at each reset. Borrowers who expect to move before reaching the 5- or 7-year balloon period also avoid having to worry about the interest-rate risk of refinancing into a new mortgage. In addition to the introduction of balloons, the use of 15-year mortgages became more popular.

The latest prepayment surge also saw the widespread use of low- and no-point refinancing. The often used rule of thumb that an interest-rate differential between a mortgage security and the prevailing 30-year mortgage rate of 150 to 200 basis points is required to make refinancing financially attractive (so as to amortize the expenses) must be set aside if borrowers can refinance into 30-year mortgages for little (or no) points or refinance into shorter maturity mortgages with much lower interest rates than those on 30-year mortgages. Low-point refinancing also allowed borrowers to refinance several times as interest rates fell fairly steadily over a 3-year period.

These developments in the mortgage origination business also have implications for prepayment burnout. The availability of low- or no-cost refinancing has slowed the burnout process, so that even coupons that have had literally four years of refinancing opportunities still are prepaying very quickly by historical standards.

The model described here is the Kidder Peabody Prepayment Model, used by Kidder to evaluate mortgage pass-throughs and CMOs. It explicitly captures the importance of the slope of the yield curve and the availability of short maturity mortgages. It also includes the observed phenomenon that while prepayments increase when interest rates decline, they surge when interest rates increase following a decline, as borrowers attempt to catch the bottom in rates, but do not realize it has occurred until it has passed. The explicit modelling of these features enables this model to capture these aspects of behavior that other models might miss.

This chapter begins with a discussion of the seasonal pattern of prepayments and then moves to a discussion of prepayment burnout. The seasoning (or aging) pattern of prepayment rates is next explored. The chapter then turns to look at the importance of interest rates, expanding upon the ideas presented in this introduction. The conclusion discusses some implications of incorporating all of these features into the model.

SEASONALITY

Mortgage prepayments display a tendency toward a seasonal pattern, with prepayments rising in the spring and summer (reaching a peak in the late summer) and declining in the autumn and winter (reaching a trough in the late winter), all else being equal. The pattern derives from the timing of homeowner mobility in the primary market. Homeowners prefer to move in the spring and summer, owing to the weather and school year.

It is important to note the term "all else being equal" in the above paragraph. This refers primarily to interest rates. Prepayments have a seasonal tendency, but it is only a tendency, and it can be swamped by swings in refinancing activity. Note that in the prepayment cycle of late 1991 to early 1992, prepayments soared in the autumn and winter of 1991 and reached a peak in March 1992, which typically is one of the slowest months for prepayments. Prepayments surged as homeowners engaged heavily in refinancing, overwhelming the tendency for slower prepayments due to seasonal patterns in homeowner mobility.

A graph of the seasonal pattern for FNMAs from the prepayment model is displayed in Exhibit 1. The slowest month of the year, all else being equal, is February, with August being the fastest month. The pattern for GNMAs is broadly similar, although the actual values differ from those for FNMA. The FHLMC pattern also is similar, but tends to lag the FNMA

Exhibit 1. FNMA Seasonal Factors

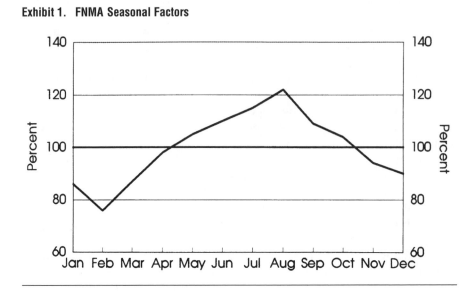

pattern by one month because of different reporting periods between FNMA and FHLMC.[1]

BURNOUT

The term "burnout" means that prepayment rates depend not only upon the interest-rate differential between the mortgage security and prevailing primary market mortgage rates, but also upon the path taken by mortgage rates to arrive at this level. This is referred to as the "path dependence" of prepayments. This behavior occurs because when faced with a refinancing opportunity, the most aware borrowers will react and prepay their mortgages, but after a while, given the same refinancing incentive, a decreasing share of the remaining borrowers will respond. Those remaining in the pool either are unaware of the refinancing opportunity or cannot qualify for a new mortgage.

Exhibit 2 shows the prepayment path of FNMA 12 $1/2$s and the current coupon yield. Prepayments on the FNMA 12 $1/2$s spiked sharply to almost 1200% PSA in 1986, when they first became refinanceable. As interest rates con-

---

1 The reported prepayment rate for say, July, for FNMA and GNMA reflects prepayment behavior at the primary market level resulting in closed mortgages essentially over the month of July, while for FHLMC, July prepayments report new mortgages originated from June 16th through July 15th.

Exhibit 2.   Premium Prepayment Spike and Burnout

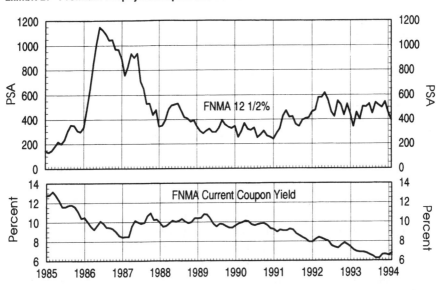

tinued to decline through early 1987, prepayments still trended downward and continued to do so even after current coupon conventional yields stabilized at about the 10% level (still providing a refinancing incentive of about 250 basis points) for most of the period from mid-1987 through late 1990. Interest rates declined again in 1991 to levels below those of the mid-1980s, but prepayments reached only about half of the peak level of 1986 (despite about 450 basis points of refinancing incentive). Interest rates fell further throughout 1993, but prepayments on FNMA 12 1/2s stabilized at about 500% PSA.

Prepayment burnout has been modified dramatically by developments in the mortgage origination industry. The early 1990s saw tremendous consolidation among mortgage originators, with strong investment by originators in computer systems that allow them to target borrowers to alert them to refinancing opportunities. At the same time, originators offered borrowers menus of interest rates/points combinations, allowing many borrowers to profitably refinance multiple times as interest rates steadily fell. These developments slowed the burnout process, so that coupons that had been refinanceable for three or four years continued to prepay at historically fast levels (albeit slower than when they first became refinanceable). The net result of these developments is that the fully burned out prepayment rate is perhaps as much as twice what it used to be. The challenge of incorporating this changing burnout behavior into the prepayment model is not trivial.

SEASONING (AGING)

Prepayment rates on mortgage securities generally are low shortly after the securities are issued and gradually increase over time. The reason is that it is unlikely that family or employment circumstances would have changed significantly shortly after purchasing a new home or that interest rates would have moved enough to make refinancing attractive so soon after taking out a new mortgage. Furthermore, there are costs involved in originating a new mortgage and homeowners would not want to pay another set of origination fees so soon after taking out a mortgage unless it either was necessary to move or interest rates had fallen so dramatically that it made sense to refinance. That prepayment rates begin at low levels and gradually increase until reaching a stable, or "seasoned," level is the notion behind the PSA Standard Model.

The PSA Model, however, is not really a model *per se*, but rather a yardstick or benchmark with which to measure prepayments. While actual prepayment rates increase gradually over time until reaching their peak or "seasoned" level, the point at which a security becomes fully seasoned depends upon whether it is a GNMA or conventional and whether it is a current coupon, discount, or premium. Conventional securities reach their peak faster than GNMAs, and premiums season faster than current coupons, which in turn season faster than discounts. Premiums respond to refinancing incentives, while discounts are dissuaded from moving.

Exhibit 3 compares prepayment rates on FNMA 8s, 9s, and 10s to the shape and level of the PSA curve and its multiples for April 1992. For each of FNMA 8s, 9s, and 10s, the CPR plotted on the vertical axis belongs to the origination year aggregate with mortgages having an average age given on the horizontal axis. The sequence for FNMA 8s is missing some points (there was a period of almost two years with none issued), but connecting the points would suggest that the 8s would be seasoned at about 50 months. The 9s plateau at about 45 months, and the 10s just beyond 20 months. The seasoned or plateau prepayment level in Exhibit 3, however, is further to the right than it would have been if we were to project the seasoning paths of hypothetical newly issued 8s, 9s, and 10s in the market environment of mid-1992. This is because in April 1992, the 9s, for example, were premium securities backed by mortgages that had prepayment opportunities, whereas for much of the previous few years they were the current coupon. As current coupons, the mortgages did not have significant refinancing opportunities, which slowed the seasoning process.

To examine this further, Exhibit 4 shows the path generated by the prepayment model of hypothetical newly issued FNMA 7s, 8s, 9 $1/2$s, and 10s in an environment with the 7- and 10-year Treasuries yielding 6.36% and 6.88%, respectively, and the 12-month and 2-year at 3.48% and 4.21%. FHLMC's

Exhibit 3.   Seasoning Relative to PSA Curve: April 1992

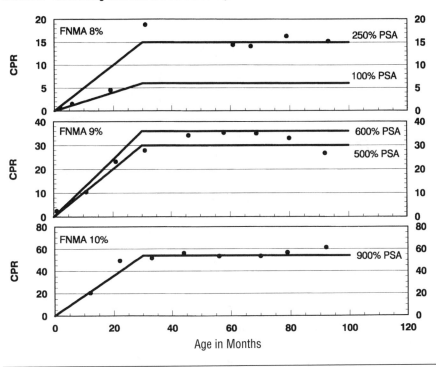

index of primary market commitment rates on 30-year mortgages was 8.09% with 1.6 points, while the 15-year commitment rate was 7.63% with 1.5 points. The monthly seasonal pattern was suppressed in Exhibit 4 so as to concentrate on the seasoning process.

We refer to the securities in Exhibit 4 as "hypothetical" because 10% securities, backed by mortgages with coupons about 60 basis points higher, would not be issued in the interest-rate environment described in the previous paragraph. Nonetheless, Exhibit 4 is useful to see how the model would depict seasoning paths of securities with various relations to the current coupon, because one of the most common uses of a prepayment model is to project prepayment behavior under various, instantaneously shifted yield curve scenarios.[2] Exhibit 4 can be thought of as showing prepayment

---

2   Indeed, depository institutions subject to Federal Financial Institutions Examination Council (FFIEC) guidelines are required to examine their securities under instantaneous parallel upward and downward shifts of the yield curve of 100, 200, and 300 basis points, in addition to stable rates.

Exhibit 4. Seasoning Paths of Hypothetical New FNMA MBSs

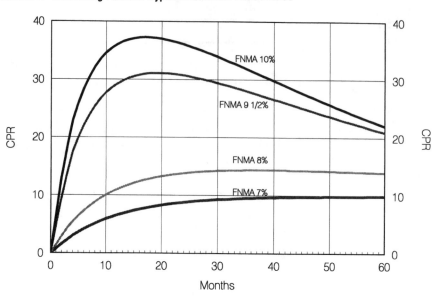

behavior of new securities under sudden interest rate shifts (say, newly issued FNMA 10s with an instantaneous downward shift in the yield curve of 250 basis points). As described above, the seasoning pattern of FNMA securities differs from that of the PSA curve, with the extent of the difference depending upon whether the security is a discount, current coupon, or premium. Exhibit 4 also depicts the prepayment model's version of the burnout pattern of higher coupon securities that remain in-the-money for a long period of time.

INTEREST RATES

The interest-rate component of prepayment models has always been the most important in terms of explaining prepayments. Previous generations of prepayment models had used a measure of 30-year fixed-rate mortgage rates to proxy the primary market mortgage rate as the alternative to the borrower of remaining in his present mortgage. Lower primary market rates provide an incentive to refinance, while higher rates not only remove the incentive to refinance, but impart a disincentive to mobility, as moving would require taking on the burden of higher mortgage payments. A model must also incorporate a lag structure between a change in interest rates and prepayment behavior, allowing for both a lag between interest rates and borrowers' recognition, decision, and application, as well as the pipeline lag between application and closing of the new mortgage.

While the 30-year primary market mortgage rate certainly is an important determinant of prepayment behavior, the experience over the past 3 years has demonstrated that mortgages that mature in less than 30 years and that are priced off the short end of the yield curve also are an important determinant of prepayment behavior. This particularly is the case with lower coupon mortgages that are out-of-the-money (or, not profitably refinanceable) relative to 30-year mortgage rates, but which can be refinanced into shorter maturity mortgages. This means that the often stated rule of thumb that an interest-rate differential of 150 to 200 basis points is required to make refinancing attractive is clearly inappropriate. With the yield curve at historically steep levels in 1992–93, mortgages priced off of the short end availed the homeowner of significantly lower interest rates than 30-year mortgages.

Borrowers took advantage of the shorter maturity mortgages. Exhibit 5 shows the increase in production of 15-year and balloon mortgage securities from the fourth quarter of 1991 to the second quarter of 1992 and compares that to the increase in production of 30-year mortgages. Fifteen-year MBS issuance almost tripled for FNMA and FHLMC and more than tripled for GNMA, while balloon production doubled; this compares to 30-year MBS increases of about 35% for conventionals and 25% for GNMA.

Exhibit 5. Production of Short Maturity Mortgages Surged When the Yield Curve Steepened

	MBS Issuance (in Millions)		
15-Year	1994 Q4	1992 Q2	%Change
GNMA	$ 410.9	$1,390.5	238%
FNMA	6,471.3	18,681.0	189
FHLMC	5,469.8	15,584.2	185
Balloon			
FNMA	$1,879.4	$3,970.5	111%
FHLMC	2,625.4	5,426.9	107
30-Year			
GNMA	$11,298.9	$13,910.4	23%
FNMA	22,478.4	30,017.4	34
FHLMC	15,385.9	20,638.1	34

In addition to the greater popularity of shorter maturity mortgages, there has been an increase in the origination of mortgages with low or no points, as mortgage originators have been aggressively trying to entice borrowers to refinance. More than before, originators are offering borrowers a wider menu of interest rates/points combinations. The steepness of the yield curve allows this type of price differentiation and discrimination.

This prepayment model captures the importance of the slope of the yield curve and shorter maturity mortgages for influencing prepayment behavior. To illustrate the importance of the yield curve, Exhibit 6 shows the prepayment history of seasoned FNMA 8s in the top panel, with the current coupon yield and yield curve slope in the two lower panels to provide perspective. Note that in 1986 and 1987, when prepayment rates on seasoned 8s reached their previous peak, the current coupon yield was about 8.5% and the yield spread between the 1- and 7-year Treasuries was about 100 basis points. Prepayment rates trended downward from their 1986–87 peaks until 1991, when yields began to decline and the curve steepened. In 1992, with mortgage yields only about 100 basis points lower than the trough of 1987 but the yield curve about three times as steep between the 1- and 7-year areas, prepayment rates reached a level that was more than 75% (175% PSA)

Exhibit 6. FNMA 8% PSAs vs. Current Coupon Yield and Yield Curve Slope

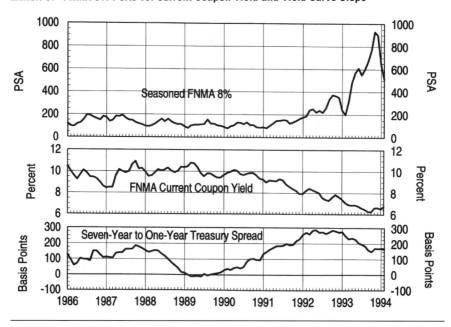

greater than the peak speeds attained in the 1986–87 period. This is especially noteworthy in that the 1986–87 top speeds of about 200% PSA were achieved in the summer months in a strong economy with a healthy housing market, while the speed of 375% PSA attained in 1992 occurred during the autumn in a weak economy with a moribund housing market. Ultimately, interest rates declined so much from late 1992 through the end of 1993 that the importance of the slope of the curve was overwhelmed by the low absolute level of interest rates, and prepayments soared in late 1993 to almost five times their peak level of 1986–87.

To further drive home the importance of the slope of the yield curve, consider Exhibit 7. Whereas Exhibit 6 displayed the prepayment behavior of seasoned FNMA 8s, Exhibit 7 shows the recent prepayment experience of whatever FNMA security was 100 basis points in-the-money relative to 30-year primary market mortgage rates for the given month. This corrects for changes in the overall level of mortgage rates while focusing on the slope of the curve—the 100-basis-point differential relative to 30-year mortgage rates means that the mortgages are not being refinanced into 30-year mortgages with points because 100 basis points does not provide enough of a refinancing incentive. Prepayments in Exhibit 7 increased briefly in the spring of

Exhibit 7.   PSAs of Seasoned FNMAs 100 bp In-the-Money vs. Yield Curve Slope

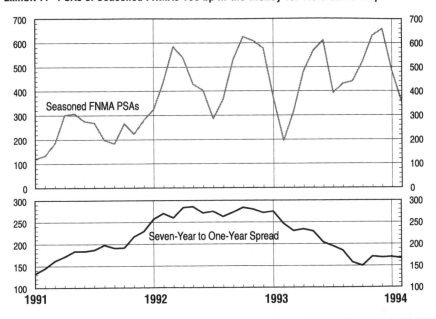

1991, but really began to take off late in the year when the yield curve steepened to almost 250 basis points. Speeds remained fast in 1992 as the steepness hovered at about 275 basis points and began to slow late in 1993 after the curve flattened by about 100 basis points. Because we are controlling for the level of interest rates by looking at whatever security is 100 basis points in-the-money relative to the 30-year mortgage rate, the prepayment behavior depicted in Exhibit 7 clearly is related to the slope of the yield curve.

Another aspect of prepayment behavior that the model incorporates is the phenomenon that prepayment rates not only increase when interest rates decline, but they then spike when interest rates increase suddenly following a decline. When interest rates fall, some borrowers (those with mortgages the furthest in-the-money) act to refinance, while others wait for interest rates to fall still lower, hoping to catch the bottom in rates. If interest rates then spike, homeowners perceive that the bottom in rates has just been realized and that they had better refinance now before mortgage rates go any higher. This activity of crowding through a rapidly closing refinancing window tends to cause a spike in prepayment rates, followed by a decline.

This behavior is shown in Exhibit 8, which compares the 1991–92 refinancing wave with that of 1986–87. (Some market participants had said that the 1991–92 prepayment cycle was unique; in fact, Exhibit 8 shows just how similar 1991–92 was to the previous refinancing wave.) Exhibit 8 displays prepayment behavior (top panel) and interest rates (bottom panel) for both the 1986–87 (solid line) and 1991–92 (dashed line) refinancing booms. Rather than using the actual dates on the horizontal axis, the graph is scaled to display the number of months since the trough in interest rates; therefore, the date corresponding to "0 months since rate trough" is March 1987 for the 1986–87 refinancing period and January 1992 for the 1991–92 refinancing wave—the month in the cycle in which interest rates were at their lowest point. (In 1992, interest rates eventually moved lower, but when interest rates increased in January, and for the five months thereafter, it appeared—and borrowers behaved—as if January 1992 was the low point in interest rates.) The area to the right of the "0 months" point pertains to the months after the trough, while the left of "0 months" refers to the period prior to the trough. The extension of the dashed line for 1991–92 represents projected prepayments in an unchanged interest rate scenario as of July 1992.

Exhibit 8 shows the prepayment behavior of the FNMA security that is 250 basis points in-the-money relative to the lowest point in interest rates: for 1986–87, this would be the FNMA 11s, while for 1991–92, it would be the FNMA 10s.

The key feature is that in both prepayment cycles, prepayments are fast going into the trough in interest rates, but when interest rates increase suddenly, prepayment rates in the top panel spike and reach their respective

Exhibit 8.   Seasoned FNMAs 250 bp In-the-Money 1991-92 vs. 1986-87

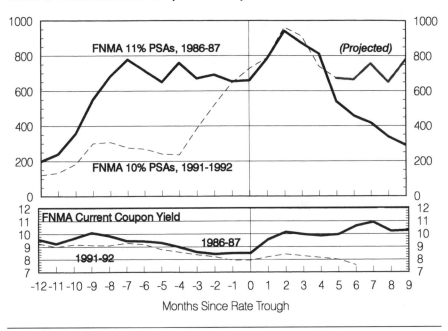

peaks two months later, and then decline from there. Prepayment rates of the FNMA 11s before the interest-rate trough in 1986–87 were much faster than those of FNMA 10s prior to the bottom in rates in 1991–92 because the mid-1980s were characterized by a much more vigorous housing market and economy than the early 1990s. Coming out of the rate trough, prepayments in 1992 were projected to be much faster than in 1987 because the interest-rate differential between the mortgage security and market rates in the later period was about 100 basis points greater than in the earlier. The prepayment behavior around the trough in interest rates, however, is remarkably similar, with both securities in both time periods reacting in a similar manner to the spike in interest rates: prepayments jumped up and then declined when interest rates increased suddenly following a long decline in mortgage rates. Borrowers were bottom fishing, hoping to catch mortgage rates at their lowest point, but the low was only realized, of course, after it had occurred.

OTHER CANDIDATE VARIABLES

Various macroeconomic variables were considered for inclusion in the model. The only macro variable that consistently was statistically significant and of proper sign was sales of existing homes, but this really introduces no information that is not already incorporated within prepayment data. That macroeconomic variables do not add significantly to prepayment equations suggests that either virtually all relevant macro information is incorporated within the prevailing mortgage market interest rate in the expression for the interest-rate differential, or the prepayment data do not embody enough cycles of the economy and housing market to determine statistically a relationship between macroeconomic variables and prepayment behavior.

There is a practical problem with including macroeconomic variables in a prepayment model of this kind. This is that the projection of prepayments would then depend heavily upon the ability to project the macro variables. In pricing mortgages and CMOs, a prepayment model is invoked by an OAS model as it moves through 30 years of randomly generated interest-rate paths. To include a macro variable in the model would require making 360 macroeconomic forecasts contingent on the interest rate path. Although a very tight relationship has been established between relative interest rates and prepayment rates, there is not enough information to establish a similarly tight long-range relationship between other macro variables and prepayment rates.

CONCLUSION

Prepayment models should incorporate the main determinants of prepayment behavior: seasonality, burnout, seasoning, and interest rates. Unlike previous generations of prepayment models, models today should explicitly embody both long- and short-term interest rates and the slope of the yield curve in their projections of prepayment rates. Shorter maturity mortgages as alternatives to traditional 30-year mortgages played an important role in the 1991–94 refinancing booms. Models should also incorporate a lag structure such that prepayment rates increase when interest rates decline, and receive an additional fillip when interest rates increase following the decline as homeowners, trying to time the market to achieve the lowest possible mortgage rate, sense the trough in rates only after interest rates have started back up.

A model also should explicitly incorporate shorter maturity alternatives to 30-year mortgages. This may make lower coupon mortgages in-the-money, whereas they may be out-of-the money relative to 30-year mortgage rates. When projecting prepayments during 1992–93, when the yield curve was at historically steep levels, a model of this type would have made stable rate projections on lower coupon mortgages that were fast relative to then-historical levels of prepayments on these coupons. As it turned out, prepayments on these coupons came in at levels much faster than previously experienced, so that a model that incorporates the slope of the curve would have performed very well by encompassing both short and long refinancing alternatives.

Models that do not include the slope of the yield curve and the presence of shorter maturity mortgages nonetheless are implicitly embodying in their coefficients and structure the long-term average yield curve relationship. Since this model explicitly incorporates the yield curve, we can more directly capture its effects. "Fast" projections in 1992–93 would have been slower if, instead of assuming stable rates, we had assumed a flatter yield curve with stable long rates but higher short rates.

Prepayment models ultimately are used to evaluate mortgage passthroughs and CMOs, including derivative mortgage securities, as part of a broader analytics system. The prepayment analytics should be incorporated within an option-pricing framework, allowing analysis of all of a mortgage security's embedded options. The better the model does at projecting prepayments, the more realistic will be the effective durations produced by the option model. This was an especially important consideration in early 1994, when the fixed-income market experienced a dramatic sell off, causing many mortgage securities (especially derivative CMOs) to have large price declines. Market participants who were armed with accurate prepayment models had the best likelihood of getting appropriate assessments of their securities and the best chances of successfully negotiating the sudden turns in the market.

CHAPTER 9

Mortgage Prepayment Modeling: II

Gregg N. Patruno
Mortgage Securities Research
Goldman, Sachs & Co.

INTRODUCTION

Over the last several years, the U.S. mortgage securities market has endured a dramatic range of prepayment experiences, frustratingly few of which were adequately predicted by existing prepayment models. Today, the market has both the motive and, for the first time, the opportunity to seek a superior approach to prepayment prediction.

Why mortgage investors need new prepayment models is clear: previous models have tended to provide seriously inaccurate predictions whenever the conditions influencing borrowers' prepayment decisions have changed to any significant degree. However, this very range of conditions provides the opportunity to substantially improve our quantitative understanding of prepayment behavior. We now have a wealth of data on the impact of changing interest rates and yield curve shapes, differences in loan size and transaction costs, varying housing market conditions, evolving regulations, and mortgage product innovation. Subtleties in seasoning patterns and the important distinctions among different vintages of mortgages have now become much clearer. Finally, the extended market rally that drove mortgage rates to successive lows provides the researcher with a perfect laboratory for examining refinancing behavior and, particularly, changes in the refinancing efficiency and composition of a mortgage pool over time.

* The author wishes to thank the following individuals for their many contributions: Gary Nan Tie, Jeremy Primer, Jesse Goodman, Carlo Romero, Jeff Davis, Rich Wertz, Giles Nugent, Peter Niculescu, Ed Bergman, Dave Chako, Homer Cheng, Marissa Padilla, Sean Suh, Mark Buono, Philip Kearns, Erica Adelberg, Alan Brazil, Howard Chin, Kelly LaRosa, Ron Krieger, Vinitha Panjabi, Terri Mullan, Larry Weiss, Fischer Black, Scott Pinkus, Bob Litterman, Lynn Edens, Bob Gerber, and Evan Firestone.

This chapter was originally published by Goldman, Sachs & Co. in June 1994 under the title "Mortgage Prepayments: A New Model for a New Era," copyright June 1994 by Goldman, Sachs & Co.

Goldman Sachs has taken advantage of this opportunity to develop an entirely new generation of prepayment models, based on data from the early 1970s to the present and spanning all the major fixed-rate, single family mortgage sectors—level-pay and balloon, agency and non-agency. This family of models, which we collectively designate the *new Goldman Sachs prepayment model,* is not an update of existing specifications, but represents a complete rethinking of how prepayment modeling should be done. Indeed, we believe it will establish a new market standard for prepayment research.

The new approach departs from previous models in many respects, two of which are particularly important: we model the individual homeowner's decision criteria more realistically and comprehensively than ever before, and we explicitly estimate the detailed composition of a mortgage pool in terms of its refinanceability. The focus throughout is directly on borrower behavior and decision-making, and we model these in a dynamic and path-dependent way that overcomes many of the problems that have plagued prepayment models in the past. The new model also provides three new measures of prepayment risk, along with substantially improved measures of duration and convexity, that offer significant insights into the valuation and hedging of prepayment-sensitive securities.

In thinking about mortgage prepayment models, investors should keep in mind three basic questions. First, what does it truly take to model prepayments realistically? Second, how well can a prepayment model—any prepayment model—actually work as the conditions affecting prepayment rates continue to change? And finally, what tangible benefits can more accurate prepayment modeling provide? In this chapter, we take up each of these three central questions in turn.

MODELING PREPAYMENTS REALISTICALLY— WHAT DOES IT TAKE?

In constructing our new prepayment model, we have used major advances in *data, estimation,* and *structure* to full advantage. In the pages that follow, we sketch the data and estimation aspects briefly and concentrate primarily on the structural properties of the new model.

Modeling prepayments realistically depends heavily on the availability of accurate and comprehensive data, including not just prepayment rates themselves but also the many variables that influence them. Both the quantity and quality of data relevant to prepayment modeling have grown enormously over the past few years, from both agency and non-agency sources. These now encompass a rich variety of mortgages and economic environments, to the point where today we have the ability to quantify a great many features of prepayment behavior.

Our new prepayment model distinguishes data by *mortgage characteristics* such as loan type, coupon, vintage, and dollar balance, as well as by *environmental variables* including interest rates and origination points for the entire term structure of mortgage alternatives (level pay, balloon, and adjustable rate), housing values, income tax rates, and relevant government regulations—every significant element affecting the prepayment decision. The abundance and diversity of data, built up over more than 20 years of MBS prepayment history, have enabled us to analyze the effects of each of these variables with a good degree of reliability; all of these are explicitly incorporated into the Goldman Sachs prepayment model.

Realistic modeling of prepayments also requires careful attention to a number of thorny statistical issues regarding the estimation of model coefficients. To guard against inconsistency and bias and to ensure the overall stability and robustness of the results, the modeler must properly address difficulties concerning the highly nonlinear relationships and interactions among the variables, the aggregation and relative weighting of various historical observations, the appropriate treatment of outliers, and the critical distinction between historical fit and predictive power.

At least as crucial as these data and estimation issues, however, is the conceptual structure of the analysis, which is what makes or breaks the ability of a statistical model to extrapolate past relationships into the future. We find that prepayment behavior reveals the greatest consistency over time when analyzed in terms of the true fundamental mechanisms and incentives underlying *homeowner decisions*. Once we "get inside the heads" of homeowners and their bankers, we can reflect these fundamentals as closely as possible in the mathematical structure of the prepayment model, to the full extent permitted by the data.

Despite all the revolutionary changes that have occurred in the mortgage market since the first MBS prepayment data of the early 1970s, and even though the prepayment behavior of U.S. homeowners is not theoretically "rational" by a long stretch, such behavior has been *extremely consistent* in key respects when viewed in terms of the real dollar incentives that homeowners actually consider in reaching their decisions. The consistent decision-making behavior of millions of homeowners, over long time periods spanning a wide range of circumstances, is what gives well-structured statistical prepayment models their potential for success.

Mortgage prepayment rates can be broken down into four primary structural components; accordingly, our prepayment model actually comprises separate "sub-models" of these four distinct mortgagor decisions:

$$\frac{\text{Total}}{\text{Prepayments}} = \frac{(1)}{\text{Relocations}} - \frac{(2)}{\text{Assumptions}} + \frac{(3)}{\text{Curtailments}} + \frac{(4)}{\text{Refinancings}}$$

All four of these components need to be analyzed separately, using the appropriate set of variables and dynamics for each, for a prepayment model to perform realistically across the full range of possible securities and scenarios. When this is done properly, the result is greater consistency with historical prepayment behavior, less *ad hoc* curve-fitting, better out-of-sample performance, more reliable interpretation of prepayment trends as they occur, and a more robust framework for incorporating new developments as required. Indeed, we firmly believe that a prepayment model *needs* to work this way to have any hope of capturing the relevant complexities of actual prepayment patterns in a mature market.

Relocation

Relocation prepayments (whose definition we broaden slightly to include defaults, cash paydowns, and certain equity-takeout refinancings) are affected by a number of *economic considerations,* notably home equity levels, mortgage rates, and tax deductibility. Together, these influence the affordability of "trading up" to a larger home, and relocating homeowners tend to be very well informed about these variables. Relocations are also influenced by *noneconomic considerations,* such as the age of the loan, the yearly seasonal cycle, and the multiyear housing cycle. The new Goldman Sachs prepayment model distills the economic elements of the homeowner's relocation decision into a dollar measure of "relocation incentive," which then scales up or down the normal "demographic" or cyclical pace of relocations that would prevail in the absence of economic concerns.

Exhibit 1 shows 10 years of monthly prepayment rates on seasoned FNMA 8s (late 1970s originations), beginning with the issuance of the first pools in mid-1982. During most of this period, these 8s were discount mortgages, so their prepayment rates can reliably be taken as representing predominantly relocations.

In fact, during the early 1980s, relocation rates were substantially *faster* than the indicated prepayment rates, because in many cases the buyer of the home was able to assume the seller's conventional mortgage, and record market interest rates frequently made this an attractive option. However, the assumability of conventional mortgages was phased out as enforcement of the due-on-sale provision was standardized from 1982 to 1985. Since then, full repayment of any conventional mortgage has been legally required upon sale of the home. As a result, baseline prepayment rates for these securities today are substantially higher than what might be suggested by the early years of data.

As the subsequent prepayment history of the seasoned FNMA 8s shows, the pace of homeowner relocations is somewhat variable. During 1986–87, a period of strong housing activity and rising home prices, prepayment rates

Exhibit 1.   The Relocation Baseline: Rate/Equity/Tax Incentives
(Plus Demographic Seasoning, Housing Cycle, Seasonal Cycle)

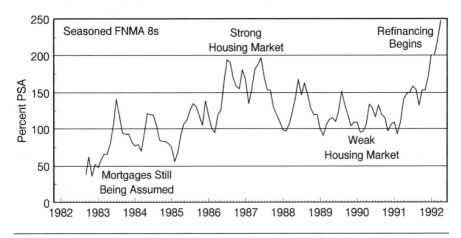

averaged more than 150% PSA. Around 1989–90, however, a severe downturn in the national housing market slowed relocation activity considerably,
as reflected in average prepayment rates closer to 115% PSA. Seasonal patterns add a further degree of variability to short-term relocation rates, and
different rates of home appreciation and equity buildup for different segments of the national housing market add some variability over the intermediate term.

But while these normal cyclical fluctuations will cause relocation prepayments to fall above and below long-term average rates for short periods, it
seems clear that neither fast nor slow relocation rates are sustainable for
more than brief episodes. (Interest-rate adjustments along the economic
cycle tend to act as automatic stabilizers.) Certainly, 100% PSA is an exces-
sively slow long-term prepayment scenario for most non-assumable 30-year
mortgages; realistic projections for even deep discounts should generally be
in the range of 120–150% PSA with normal buildup of homeowner equity.

It is worth recalling here how the standard PSA seasoning pattern,
intended to approximate the increasing likelihood of relocation over time
for 30-year current coupon mortgages, differs somewhat from the more realistic seasoning patterns actually observed for these and other mortgage types.
Exhibit 2 is a schematic illustration of the relocation component of the Goldman Sachs prepayment model for 30-year conventional mortgages (with
cyclical elements omitted for simplicity). In the top panel, the upper smooth
curve represents our empirical estimate for the relocation rate, as a function
of mortgage age, for a hypothetical mortgage pool with maximum economic

Exhibit 2.   Relocation "Sub-Model" for 30-Year Conventionals

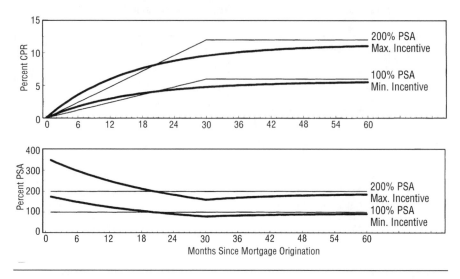

incentive (full equity and relatively low current mortgage rates). The lower smooth curve corresponds to a case of minimum economic incentive (negative equity and high current mortgage rates). On average, the smooth curves tend to outpace the simple PSA "ramp" profile in the early months after mortgage origination, and experience a relative shortfall concentrated at two to four years of age.

The lower panel of Exhibit 2 displays the same four seasoning profiles on the PSA scale rather than the CPR scale. It shows how demographic relocation patterns generally translate into a downward-trending sequence of PSAs through month 30, with a slight upward bias beyond that point (again, holding economic incentives constant). This effect is most pronounced for balloon mortgages, whose particular appeal to short-tenure homeowners results in a much higher rate of early relocations than called for by the PSA scale. In all cases, using the actual month-to-month sequence of prepayment rates projected by the Goldman Sachs model should result in more faithful timing of MBS cash flows than any single PSA speed.

Assumption

Upon sale of a home, under appropriate conditions, an existing FHA/VA mortgage may be assumed by the buyer rather than prepaid. Assuming the existing mortgage, though not a widely familiar procedure, in fact is often easier than qualifying for a new loan, entails minimal transaction costs, and requires essentially no judgment on interest-rate timing. It appears to be the most rational prepayment decision of all, and in fact it is a very straight-forward decision for a homebuyer to make.

When the interest rate of an assumable mortgage is low compared with current market rates *and* the LTV ratio is high enough to finance the buyer's purchase of the home (perhaps in combination with a small second mort-gage at market rates), then the buyer's economic incentive to assume the mortgage can be compelling, and prepayment rates can fall substantially below the baseline relocation rate for sustained periods.

We can find extreme examples during the years of record high mort-gage rates in the early 1980s. At one point, six-year-old GNMA 7.5s registered an astonishingly low 12-month speed of 8% PSA. A less extreme but more recent example is that of GNMA 7.5s and 8s originated at the bottom of the interest-rate cycle in 1987.

As Exhibit 3 shows, these 7.5s held below 40% PSA, and the 8s below 70% PSA, for four years after origination, a period when 9.5s and 10s were the cur-rent coupons. Analogously, we can now expect very slow speeds for recently originated GNMA 6s and 6.5s in today's market. Conventional discounts are no longer legal to assume, and seasoned, low-balance GNMA loans are no longer economic to assume (given today's home price levels), so the prepayment dis-parity between all of these and unseasoned GNMA discounts can be quite dra-matic. Once again, quantifying the relevant dollar incentives at the homeowner level allows the Goldman Sachs prepayment model to track these patterns real-istically and consistently across different mortgages and time periods.

Exhibit 3. Mortgage Assumability: Strong Effect on New, Large GNMA Loans

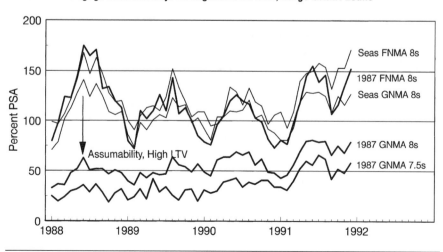

Curtailment

Although curtailments (partial prepayments of mortgages) generally account for less than 1% of total prepayment dollars at the beginning of the life of a mortgage pool, they can have a substantial *cumulative* impact on reported prepayment rates (and actual cash flows) as a mortgage pool seasons. An extra month's payment at the beginning of a 30-year mortgage can save a homeowner about an extra year of payments at the end, and the accelerated amortization in these future months is almost never fully captured by the weighted average maturity (WAM) of the pool. Instead, a portion of the accelerated amortization registers as "unscheduled" principal payments, raising the apparent prepayment rate of the pool. This effect is especially evident as the pool approaches maturity, when the scheduled principal amounts are large relative to the remaining mortgage balance. The effect is further exaggerated if the pool had a wide variety of mortgage maturity dates to begin with.

Exhibit 4 shows the consequences of curtailment for seasoned GNMA 5.5s, with an exponential acceleration pattern that recalls the old "FHA Experience" prepayment curves, and that clearly cannot be attributed to an acceleration in relocations or refinancings. The Goldman Sachs prepayment model captures the cash-flow effect of curtailment by projecting an appropriate increment to monthly prepayment rates to mimic mathematically the cash flows of a suitably accelerated pool amortization schedule.

Exhibit 4. Curtailment's Consequences: WAM Dispersion Effects

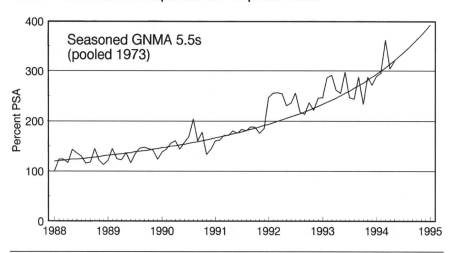

Refinancing

The most complicated type of prepayment from a modeling point of view, and the one that dominates valuation in most circumstances, is, of course, interest-rate-related refinancing. Fortunately, recent experience—the last three years in particular—has provided a treasure-trove of data with which to analyze refinancing patterns, and the new Goldman Sachs prepayment model makes great strides in sorting out their complexity. In a very real sense, we believe that for the first time ever, this volume of data now permits the estimation of a properly structured mortgage refinancing model.

Unlike the other three major components of mortgage prepayments, refinancing is greatly complicated by the property of *path dependency*. To forecast refinancing activity, it is not enough to know the current level of mortgage rates; we need to consider the whole historical path of mortgage rates that brought the homeowners to this point, to know whether they are experiencing a new level of refinancing incentive or just getting another look at an incentive level they already passed up in the past.

Once refinancing episodes have occurred, they can result in remnants of a mortgage pool with dramatically different prepayment behavior from that of the original pool before the episodes occurred. In particular, history teaches us that progressively lower lows in mortgage rates are usually required for reviving significant refinancing activity. As Exhibit 5 shows (using only 30-year fixed mortgage yields for simplicity), today's interest-rate levels are prompting virtually no mortgage refinancing activity (applications are

Exhibit 5.   Path Dependency in Refinancing: Activity Surges Once Rates Set New Lows

being filed at the slowest pace since 1990), whereas we experienced an unprecedented surge in refinancings when rates first declined to similar levels two years ago. This path-dependent behavior pattern has profound implications for valuing and hedging the prepayment option embedded in mortgage securities—and it so happens that the 1991–93 market rally, with mortgage rates notching down 50 bp to new lows every six months or so, provides a nearly perfect laboratory for analyzing this behavior in depth.

One of the most widely discussed refinancing patterns, the phenomenon referred to as "burnout," is also one of the most widely misunderstood—probably owing to overly casual use of the term. Burnout does *not* mean that refinancing speeds on a mortgage pool can be expected to decline continually over time; rather, speeds will generally exhibit sizable short-term fluctuations around a *gradual declining trend*, once a full-strength refinancing episode has begun.

Exhibit 6, showing monthly prepayment rates for a range of coupons that refinanced heavily during the two-year rally, illustrates the true nature of refinancing burnout. Note how, by late 1993, each coupon starting from 8.5% ended up faster than the next-higher coupon—a pattern that can be explained only by the more extensive prior refinancing of the higher premiums. Observe also that conventional 10s were the fastest-prepaying coupon when they first became fully refinanceable in early 1992, and that although they reaccelerated substantially each time mortgage rates dropped to new lows, each crest was lower than the last. On average, their speeds followed a declining trend of roughly 10% CPR per year—even with mortgage rates

Exhibit 6. Refinancing and Burnout Occur "Layer by Layer"

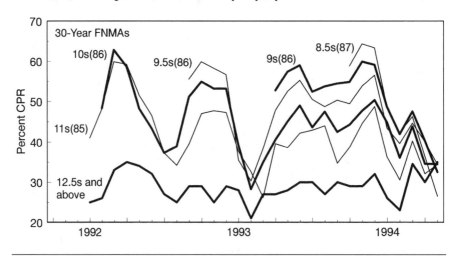

sinking at the rate of 100 bp per year—and monthly speeds declined much *more* abruptly each time mortgage rates firmed up and stopped setting new lows. Nevertheless, it is clear that each stage of the rally brought new "layers" of people into the refinancing process, and this is the behavior we need to focus on.

As we can see, even FNMA 11s experienced an acceleration in prepayments as the current coupon fell from 7% to 6% during 1993, demonstrating that some homeowners were actually willing to refinance for 500 bp of savings who weren't willing for 400 bp. There may not have been *many* such homeowners, but that tier of interest-rate sensitivity clearly exists within the premium mortgage sector. This relentless refinancing by new layers of homeowners every time rates set new lows—up through *very* high premiums—is what makes it so difficult for premium pass-throughs ever to rally very far, and is thus what keeps their effective durations down.

All these observations make sense in the context of the refinancing histories of various coupons, but until now it has been extremely difficult for a prepayment model to capture this behavior with any degree of realism. In fact, one of the *most* severe and widespread shortcomings of traditional prepayment models is the chronic underestimation of the interest-rate sensitivity of partially burned-out premium mortgages, and therefore the chronic overestimation of their option-adjusted spreads and durations.

To overcome these problems, we have to begin with the basics: the essence of refinancing burnout is *the change in composition of a mortgage pool over time* as the most rate-sensitive homeowners exit the pool. Therefore, the refinancing component of the Goldman Sachs prepayment model explicitly attempts to estimate these changes in pool composition. It does this across three different dimensions, modeling the refinanceability of a mortgage pool in terms of the fractions of homeowners who are "Ready, Willing, and Able" to refinance.

Homeowners are *Willing* to refinance if the financial incentive is high enough to meet their requirements. We use the measure of refinancing incentive actually considered by typical homeowners and their bankers: *not* an abstract interest-rate differential or *ad hoc* statistical artifact, but the real dollar savings expected on an after-tax basis, taking into account an appropriate mix of available mortgage rates and points. There is a *continuous spectrum of homeowners* in terms of incentive requirements, ranging from those willing to refinance for just marginal savings to those willing to refinance only at extremely high incentives. In a significant departure from previous modeling practice, we estimate and keep track of this entire distribution within each mortgage pool. Then, with each passing month, the levels of current mortgage rates and transaction costs determine what fraction of the homeowners in the distribution should be considered Willing to refinance that month.

Raise the refinancing incentive with a 100 bp rate decline, and another segment of the distribution becomes Willing. Lower the refinancing incentive with a 100 bp sell-off, and many Willing prospects become Unwilling.

Whether a homeowner is *Able* to refinance is a different question—possibly a question of credit situation (unemployment or over-indebtedness), of resources (shortage of cash, income, equity, or time), of moving soon (always a sizable fraction of U.S. homeowners), or sometimes just of temperament. These are all *non-interest-rate elements* in the refinancing decision. And for individual homeowners, this Able or Unable classification can change over time; so burned-out mortgage pools can and do "recharge" if they have the opportunity to season without refinancing for a period, gradually replenishing the supply of Able refinancers. We model this with a slow, continual flow of homeowners between the Able and Unable categories as their preferences and circumstances change and the mortgages season.

Finally, of those mortgagors who are Willing and Able to refinance, only a small fraction are actually *Ready* to prepay in any given month (no more than about an eighth of any sizable mortgage pool). This can be thought of as a question of *timing*: indecision over interest rates, procrastination, holidays, pipeline lags, and so forth. It is not necessarily a matter of homeowner sophistication; very often it just takes several months for individuals to respond to financial opportunities.

What our refinancing sub-model attempts to do is track the entire distribution of homeowners in a mortgage pool as it evolves over time, across all three dimensions of the Ready, Willing, and Able framework. This compositional analysis can be viewed as the MBS equivalent of "card counting" in blackjack: if you know what's in the deck when you start and you can keep track of what gets pulled out along the way, then you gain substantial insight into what's left as the deck winnows down—except that in the case of a mortgage refinancing model, we have to figure out first "what's in the original deck" and then "how to read the cards." Neither the initial distribution of homeowner refinancing characteristics nor the way that they evolve over time is directly measurable; they have to be inferred from empirical prepayment rates, quantified so as to be thoroughly consistent with the data. (Not surprisingly, this is the most challenging part of the statistical estimation.) Once this is done, however, highly realistic path-dependent spike-and-burnout prepayment patterns, option-adjusted spreads, and interest-rate sensitivities (durations and convexities) all emerge naturally from the way the various categories of Ready, Willing, and Able refinancers are depleted and replenished over time, over a wide range of market conditions.

This "compartmental" model structure is self-reinforcing: as incremental prepayment data for specific securities arrive each month, this increased information flows back into continually updating our estimates of the prepayment characteristics of the underlying mortgagors. Various market participants and academic researchers[1] have taken steps toward this methodology in the past, but generally with oversimplified model structures and insufficient data. We believe that the Goldman Sachs model is the first of its kind to actually succeed with the problem.

Exhibit 7 shows a simplified schematic representation of 1991 FNMA 9s as tracked by the refinancing sub-model. In the lower panel, the horizontal dimension represents the continuum of homeowner refinancing thresholds, and the vertical dimension indicates what percentage of the original pool we believe has a Willingness threshold in each range of dollar values. The outermost bell curve depicts the Willingness distribution of the pool at origination; the shaded area depicts what we consider to be the distribution of the pool today, now that successive waves of refinancing have chipped away large segments of the original composition of the pool. By now, we find that only a

Exhibit 7.   The Refinancing Decision: Distribution of Homeowner Incentive Requirements

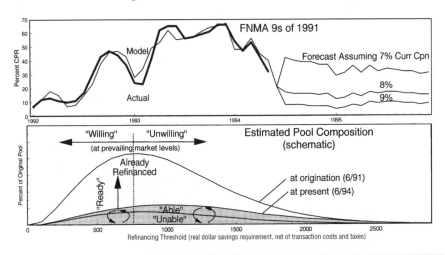

1 Dunn, K.B. and J. J. McConnell, 1981, Valuation of GNMA mortgage-backed securities, *Journal of Finance* 36, 599–617. Dunn, K.B. and C.S. Spatt, 1986, The effect of refinancing costs and market imperfections on the optimal call strategy and the pricing of debt contracts, Working paper, Carnegie-Mellon University. Johnston, E.T. and L.D. Van Drunen, 1988, Pricing mortgage pools with heterogeneous mortgagors: empirical evidence, Working paper, University of Utah. Richard, S.F. and R. Roll, 1989, Prepayments on fixed rate mortgage-backed securities, *Journal of Portfolio Management* 15, 73–82. Stanton, R., 1995, Rational prepayment and the valuation of mortgage-backed securities, *Review of Financial Studies* (forthcoming).

small fraction of the pool is left, retaining a disproportionate fraction of Unable refinancers, and with most of the remaining Able refinancers Willing to refinance only under conditions providing significantly higher incentive levels than today's.

In the upper panel, we show the actual prepayment implications of this analysis for the FNMA 9s. The left portion shows how the model has tracked the pool's considerable fluctuations in prepayment speeds over its two years of refinancing, and the right portion goes on to show the monthly prepayment speeds we would project for three different levels of interest rates. Note in particular that even a 100 bp rally should bring prepayment rates on these securities only about halfway back to their former peak, since so many of the more Willing and Able refinancers have left the pool over the last two years.

In fact, since the start of 1994, the premium mortgage market has gone from one extreme of interest-rate sensitivity to the other (extremely treacherous to surprisingly tame). In January 1994, a 50 bp rally would have brought us yet another new low in mortgage rates and sent the whole country racing to refinance yet again. In June 1994, a 50 bp rally would have merely returned premium mortgagors to refinancing incentives they had already been passing up for the previous two years. Thus, we strongly believe that prepayment speeds for the rest of 1994 will be much slower and more stable than for comparably priced premiums in 1992–93, and hence that the negative convexity of the mortgage sector has been greatly alleviated.

Exhibit 8 portrays some further interesting conclusions from this line of analysis. Coupons originated with a low percentage of *experienced refinancers* (such as 10s and above, virtually all of which were home purchase mortgages) start out with a high percentage of "inefficient" homeowners in the Willingness distribution—many who would be Willing to refinance for only marginal savings as well as many who would be Willing to refinance only for extremely high savings. Visually, the original distribution of FNMA 10% homeowners by refinancing threshold is thicker in both tails, compared with the original distribution of FNMA 9% homeowners.

Conversely, coupons originated with a high percentage of previous refinancers (such as 8s and below, either from 1987 or from 1992–93) appear to start out with a lower percentage of inefficient homeowners on both extremes and proportionally more homeowners who, from experience, "know when" to refinance most advantageously. We would conclude from this analysis that 1994 7.5s and 8s, which contain very few refi originations, should be substantially less efficient about refinancing in a future rally than the 7.5s and 8s of 1987 or 1992–93, which include a much heavier concentration of refi originations. This distinction could make for some interesting vintage effects in the market going forward.

In Exhibit 9, we see another significant example of pool composition effects, in this case a highly unusual comparison between the refinancing patterns of the 1985 and 1989 vintages of FNMA 11s. When this coupon became refinanceable in early 1991, the older vintage started out with the

Exhibit 8. Previous Refinancers Behave More "Efficiently"

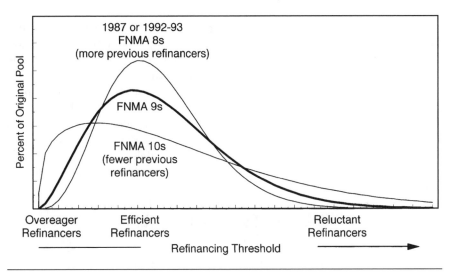

Exhibit 9. "Ability" to Refinance: A Critical Ingredient

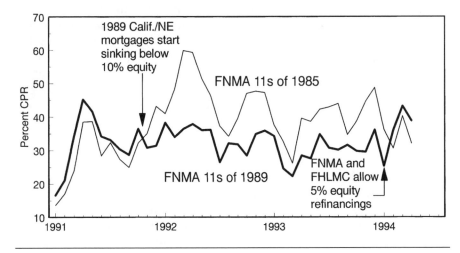

slower speeds, as we would expect given its burnout from the 1986–87 refinancing wave, and given the smaller dollar refinancing incentives resulting from its smaller loan balances. However, by late 1991, the California and Northeast real estate downturns had gone far enough to drop many of the 1989 mortgages *below 10% equity* (the level that was required for refinancing at the time), and prepayment rates on the 1989 pools were greatly restrained relative to the 1985 pools. In our analysis, the 1989 mortgagors were every bit as Willing to refinance; they simply were not as Able.

This situation persisted for another two years, until in December 1993, both FNMA and FHLMC relaxed their underwriting guidelines to permit just 5% equity for refinancings. Suddenly the home appraisal *stopped* screening out such a large percentage of the 1989 refinancing applicants, with the result that these 1989 11s were among the very few mortgage issues to have prepaid *faster* in 1994 than in late 1993. Even with a nearly 200 bp backup in mortgage rates, prepayment rates for these 11s accelerated to three-year highs, once so many pent-up refinancings were released by making Unable refinancers Able again. The usual prepayment models, along with any price- or coupon-based rules of thumb for prepayment patterns, would miss out on such developments entirely.

MODELING PREPAYMENTS REALISTICALLY— HOW WELL CAN IT WORK?

However plausible the methodology one chooses to pursue for modeling prepayments, at the end of the day the actual results are what matter. And since the mortgage agencies do not distinguish the four building blocks of prepayments in their reported data (much less the distribution of savings requirements of those who refinance), the entire Goldman Sachs prepayment model has to be estimated indirectly, through its consistency with historical aggregate prepayment rates. To gauge the success of such an undertaking, we propose three key properties of model performance to analyze: the tracking of prepayment *levels* (absolute prepayment rates), the tracking of prepayment *differences* (relative prepayment rates), and the tracking of prepayment *outliers* (aberrant prepayment rates). A model consistent with these three aspects of empirical prepayments is one that will have strong prospects for success in the marketplace.

Prepayment Levels

To illustrate, we start by examining (in Exhibit 10) the manner in which the four components of the Goldman Sachs model combine to track the prepayment history of a particular pass-through issue, 1980 GNMA 10.5%—not because this is an especially important coupon, but because it demonstrates

Exhibit 10.   Tracking Prepayment Levels: Putting the Sub-Models Together

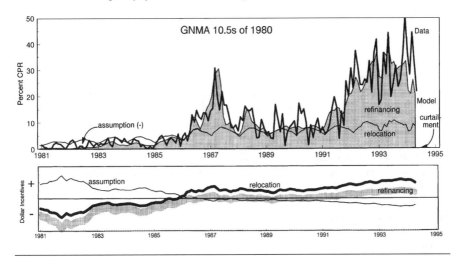

an unusual variety of historical prepayment experience. In the first years of its life, as mortgage rates soared, the dominant prepayment-related incentive was that of mortgage assumability. Refinancings were out of the question; even relocations were quite difficult to afford at the time with mortgage rates so high, and most relocations that did occur resulted in mortgage assumptions rather than prepayments.

These forces combined to produce the extremely slow prepayment rates of 1981–82. By 1985, easing mortgage rates and modest appreciation in home values had gradually eroded the assumability incentive, so even without a significant increase in housing turnover, the prepayment level began creeping higher. By 1986, these interest-rate and home-price trends had progressed far enough so that (1) the 10.5s were no longer economically assumable at all, and (2) relocation became an affordable option for the first time. Relocation prepayment rates appear to have jumped a notch higher, and at about the same time, the first refinancers in the pool swung into action.

Refinancing fluctuated around a borderline incentive level from mid-1987 through late 1991, and by 1992 a combination of lower mortgage rate levels (particularly those in the 15-year and adjustable-rate GNMA sectors) and lower transaction costs (from reductions in both origination points and FHA fees) had left virtually the entire pool with positive refinancing incentives, soon to surpass those experienced in 1987. Prepayment rates surged, and month-to-month variation became more pronounced as the outstanding number of loans in the issue, never large to begin with, continued to fall.

Likewise, the current slowdown, expected to continue in this coupon through at least the summer of 1994, is accompanied by a heavy dose of statistical noise. Curtailment is only now beginning to make a meaningful contribution to the prepayment mix.

The patterns traced by our four structural sub-models clearly do make intuitive sense for this coupon, and they track the total prepayment level consistently well (especially given the growing uncertainty inherent in a dwindling sample of loans). These are the kinds of verifications performed in developing and testing the Goldman Sachs prepayment model, not just "on average," but for the full range of individual issues—all relevant sectors, time periods, coupons, vintages, and loan sizes (including several tiers of jumbo whole loans). These validate the ability of a stable model of homeowner behavior to track the tremendous variation that exists in historical prepayment levels.

Prepayment Differences

Another, even more strenuous, test for a prepayment model is its ability to track relative prepayment rates, achieving suitably consistent results *across mortgage types, coupons, and vintages*. Exhibit 11 illustrates the ability of the Goldman Sachs model to reproduce the complex prepayment differences among four varieties of FNMA 8.5s (three major 30-year vintages and a 15-year counterpart). Here again, our approach of quantifying the fundamental homeowner incentives pays off.

Exhibit 11. Tracking Prepayment Differences

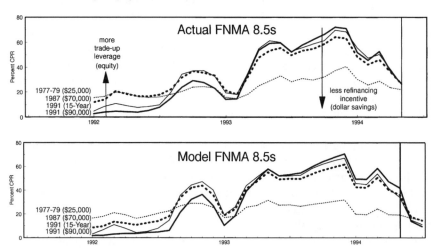

At the start of 1992, prepayments on these coupons were predominantly relocations, and the borrowers with the *smallest loan balances* (greatest home equity) had the most favorable economics for trading up to larger homes. The relative prepayment rates of the three 30-year issues reflected that relationship. Once the mortgages became high premiums for the first time, however, the *largest loan balances* provided the most favorable economics for refinancing, and so in 1993 the relative prepayment rates reversed their previous ordering. (This pattern extended to jumbo mortgages as well, where larger loan balances automatically resulted in even stronger refinancing incentives, faster premium prepayment speeds, and greater interest-rate sensitivity.) Because of these economic incentives, seasoned pass-throughs boast both superior extension protection (fast speeds as discounts) and superior call protection (slow speeds as premiums), significantly enhancing their stability, their convexity, and their value to investors.

We believe the extent to which our new model captures the prepayment comparisons among securities such as these—and therefore the *value* comparisons among securities such as these—provides a level of realism an order of magnitude beyond previous models. In particular, quantifying homeowner prepayment incentives in real dollar terms is key to our understanding of many of these comparisons.

Prepayment Outliers

The third key aspect of model performance concerns the tracking of prepayment outliers. Once we venture beyond the market for generic "TBA" pass-throughs, some mortgage securities simply prepay consistently faster or slower than one would expect, given the fundamental characteristics reported for the pools. One example of this is FNMA Strip Trust 23, which for many years prepaid significantly more slowly than generic FNMA 10s with the same basic characteristics, whether as a discount or as a premium, as shown in Exhibit 12. The underlying influences behind such exceptional cases may never be fully discernible from the available data. Has a servicer been unusually inefficient? Has an originator catered to an unusually slow-prepaying segment of the population? Have the mortgagors been subject to a permanent local tax disincentive? Or have the prepayments instead been pent-up by a temporary equity shortfall, with the situation now starting to reverse? The truth in this case may well be a mixture of all these causes.

But even if we can't definitively identify the "reason" for the aberration, we should still take the aberration into account in analyzing the security (to the extent possible). We can do this by automatically testing the prepayment history of the specific set of mortgages in question (be they from a specific CMO, a certain pass-through coupon or vintage, or even a particular issuer

Exhibit 12.   Tracking Prepayment Outliers

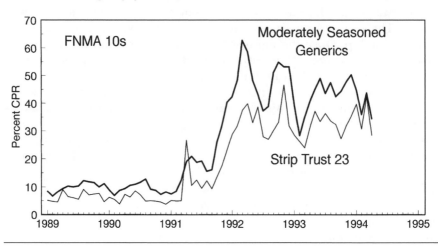

or geographic region) for systematic, *statistically significant deviations* from average prepayment behavior.

When, after we account for all the fundamental influences already built into the prepayment model, the deviations are large enough, consistent enough, persistent enough, and based on a large enough sample of loans, then we start to adjust our projections systematically with reference to those historical discrepancies. The more evidence there is that the specific mortgages are different from average, the more weight we give to their own history in choosing statistically appropriate forecasting coefficients for each separate component of the model—*not* the usual catchall "multipliers" that need to change every time interest rates move. The Goldman Sachs prepayment model's provisions for "custom alterations" are especially valuable for derivatives, but in fact they are useful for any mortgage security whose prepayment behavior consistently differs from normal patterns.

MODELING PREPAYMENTS REALISTICALLY— WHAT DOES IT GET YOU?

Improved prepayment modeling provides a much better qualitative understanding of general prepayment trends. It allows us to predict short-term prepayment movements with a high degree of accuracy and to anticipate reactions to significant changes in mortgage rates or other environmental influences. If we are sufficiently attuned to market expectations, this improved predictive accuracy can help us judge, in general terms, how the market will change security pricing in response to new releases of prepayment data.

Even more important, though, modeling provides us with a much better quantitative understanding of how prepayments affect specific securities. There are several major ways in which this shows up. Most obviously, models allow us to improve our *predictions of cash flows* in different market scenarios. This will always be the key to mortgage security valuation; without it, no other approach is likely to succeed.

Modeling also allows us to provide direct *relative value comparisons* across securities. By capturing the appropriate cash-flow distinctions among securities backed by mortgages of different type, coupon, vintage, loan size, refinancing efficiency, or prepayment history, we are able to provide richer and more reliable relative value comparisons across the MBS universe than we could otherwise obtain.

Also, with improved prepayment models, *hedging strategies* become more accurate and robust to different market conditions. Traditional mortgage models suffer from two serious problems with respect to their handling of risk. First, many models are unable to keep up with changes in market level, and the "model durations" they produce diverge substantially from the "empirical durations" with which the market trades the securities. Significant and persistent divergences of this type usually point to a fundamental misspecification of the interest-rate sensitivity of the prepayment model. Second, changing regulations and market innovations, such as periodic adjustments to the FHA insurance program and the advent of balloon mortgages, are difficult, if not impossible, to predict. Nonetheless, they can have substantial impacts on prepayment rates and security valuation. Until this time, it has been hard to quantify prepayment risk accurately. We now have three new and much better measures available to quantify prepayment risk, which we discuss in detail in a later section.

Finally, improved prepayment modeling allows us to approach a better fundamental valuation of mortgage securities. Prepayment risk is not necessarily diversifiable or hedgeable across all securities. But it is significant, and at times the market appears to demand incremental expected returns for securities that are significantly exposed to various aspects of undiversifiable prepayment risk. The standard measure of mortgage relative value, option-adjusted spread (OAS), does not account for the complete nature of prepayment risk. Rather, it adjusts for the optionality due to interest-rate fluctuations under the presumption that prepayment rates are a known, permanent function of interest rates.

As we improve our understanding of *intrinsic prepayment risk,* however, we can start to make better sense of OASs for securities with different prepayment risk profiles. For example, OASs for IOs have shown the ability to persist above 500 bp for extended time periods. In a real sense, we do expect that a high OAS is suggestive of high expected return (relative to an equivalent position in Treasuries and options). But in the case of IOs, the reason for the high expected return may be that it is compensation for very significant prepayment risks that not even POs can fully hedge. Our new prepayment sensitivity measures allow a more precise quantification of those risks, thus enabling OASs to be viewed more meaningfully in the context of the prepayment risks that investors are taking.

Valuation Results

To indicate some of the model's functionality in tracking dynamic market changes, we show in Exhibit 13 two analytical snapshots of the conventional mortgage pass-through sector: first from June 15, 1994, and then compared with September 30, 1993, near the peak of the market. Being able to handle a change of the magnitude of this nine-month period, both in market level and in refinanceability, is a reasonably significant test.

The extension of *durations* in the mortgage market has by now been well publicized and understood. It shows up with equal drama in the model results: durations for 8.5s, for example, extended from 0.7 to 4.1 years. In September 1993, as the onset of new lows in rates resulted in extreme levels of interest-rate sensitivity, many market participants felt that premium pass-throughs were virtually unhedgeable and traded as cash. The model results confirm that empirical wisdom. As the durations extended, the long-term prepayment projections for 8.5s fell from 47% CPR to 9% CPR, while the 12-month prepayment projections declined even more dramatically, from 57% CPR to 7% CPR.

The move from extreme cuspiness to much more tameness in refinanceability can also be seen from the changes in *convexities*. The most negatively convex securities in September 1993 were 7.5s (experienced refinancers on the verge of their first repeat opportunity) with a convexity gain of -1.16% for a 100 bp market move. By June 1994, the worst convexity number was for 9s (a seasoned, heavily burned-out coupon) and was only -0.60%.

Finally, we note that the greater stability of CPR and duration estimates at June 1994 market levels was also mirrored in the greater consistency of pass-through pricing and *OASs*. The market of September 1993 experienced considerable pricing disarray coupon-to-coupon but, reassuringly, neither then nor in the middle of 1994 did our valuation model display any systematic bias toward higher or lower coupons.

All these changes between the two market snapshots seem reasonable given the magnitudes of the differences in mortgage rates and the makeup of the underlying pools, but capturing them is difficult for any model to do accurately. Now for the first time, with an appropriate framework for incorporating interest-rate sensitivity, our prepayment model goes a long way toward making OASs and durations the useful market indicators they were meant to be.

Exhibit 13.   Conventional Pass-Through Valuation Summary

FNMA Coupon	6/15/94 Price	Static Yield	Static Spread	Avg Life	12mo CPR	LT CPR	LT PSA	OA Sprd	OA Dur	Gain Cnvx	Prepay Sensitivities		
											Relo	Cusp	Refi
6.0	88-14	7.98	74	9.8	3	7	125	50	6.2	0.22	0.52	0.05	-0.01
6.5	91-18	7.96	72	9.8	3	7	131	47	6.0	0.13	0.41	-0.01	-0.02
7.0	94-18	7.96	74	9.6	3	7	140	45	5.7	0.02	0.31	-0.08	-0.03
7.5	97-10	8.00	78	9.6	3	7	144	43	5.4	-0.06	0.22	-0.12	-0.06
8.0	99-22	8.10	89	9.3	3	8	151	43	4.9	-0.28	0.15	-0.20	-0.09
8.5	101-28	8.17	101	8.2	7	9	159	50	4.1	-0.50	0.07	-0.31	-0.10
9.0	103-30	8.01	99	6.0	17	14	240	44	3.3	-0.60	-0.01	-0.37	-0.14
9.5	105-26	7.88	92	5.3	20	17	277	51	3.2	-0.46	-0.09	-0.33	-0.18
10.0	107-17	7.66	78	4.6	23	19	322	48	2.9	-0.36	-0.14	-0.33	-0.24

OAS (bp)

Duration (yrs)

Gain From Convexity (% per 100 bp)

——— 6/15/94   ·········· 9/30/93

Prepayment Risk Measures

Despite the empirical fit of the Goldman Sachs prepayment model, investors may wish to analyze mortgage-backed security valuation using custom variations of the prepayment model, or they may wish to quantify the impact of an unanticipated change in the behavior of the underlying borrowers or their refinancing opportunities relative to our model. Although the salient features of prepayment behavior will remain the same—mortgage rate declines will always be associated with accelerations in prepayments—the magnitudes of the relationships can change. Recognizing that views may differ, and acknowledging the risks of relying on any single set of long-term assumptions, we have developed three economically independent measures of the price sensitivity of a security to key prepayment model parameters: the "relocation, cusp, and refinancing sensitivities." As with multifactor models of interest-rate risk, these prepayment risk measures can be used both as indicators of the relative sensitivity of a security to possible market changes and as hedging tools.

The *relocation sensitivity* measures the percentage impact on price of a 10% increase in the monthly relocation rates for each path of the OAS simulation. If an investor believes that relocation-driven prepayments in the future will be 10% faster than the model projects, the relocation sensitivity shows the percentage benefit in price if this view is true. Prepayment changes stemming from the underlying rate of economic activity or housing market patterns might show up here first.

Similarly, the *refinancing sensitivity* measures the percentage impact on price of a 10% increase in the monthly refinancings for each path. A future change in underwriting standards for refinancing, for example, could have an impact on the prepayment rates of high coupons and would best be hedged by using this variable. (Note that refinancing sensitivity will almost always be negative for mortgage pass-throughs—even those currently trading at discounts—since rate-related refinancing occurs only in scenarios where the pass-through is a premium and prepayments tend to reduce its value.)

The *cusp sensitivity* measures the impact of a shift of 25 bp in the prepayment function itself. This would capture the future impact of the introduction of a lower coupon mortgage program, such as balloons, or the impact of mortgage bankers lowering the cost of refinancing. Exhibit 14 sketches these three principal changes to the prepayment function.

In Exhibit 15, we show the output from our OAS model, including the prepayment sensitivities, for a selection of mortgage securities. The results for pass-throughs and strips are fairly straightforward. Refi and cusp sensitivities are magnified for the higher coupons (up to a point), and are significantly positive only for POs. Relo sensitivity is positive for POs and dis-

Exhibit 14. Quantitative Risk Measures

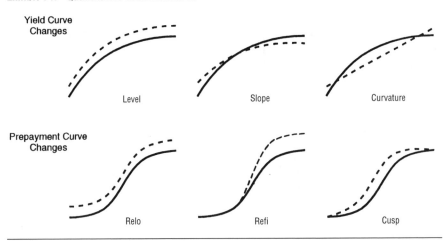

count pass-throughs, and negative for IOs and most premium pass-throughs. These results would probably accord with most investors' intuition, although the absolute levels may not.

The prepayment sensitivities can offer special insight into structured products, in particular. These measures can be used as an adjunct to traditional interest-rate risk measures to determine the true risk characteristics of a CMO class. The questions of "When is a PAC like a sequential?" or "When is a type II like a companion?" can be answered by comparing their prepayment sensitivity measures. As shown in Exhibit 15, the main difference among PACs, sequentials, and collateral at the moment is extension risk, and this is captured by their relocation sensitivities. Type II PACs, for example, generally have very high relocation sensitivities. Ranking these securities on the basis of OAS for relative value can then be weighed against their respective degrees of risk relative to the prepayment model.

Investors can also use these measures to hedge mortgages against changes in prepayment behavior. Hedging an IO—for example, with a Treasury using option-adjusted duration—will leave the position exposed to an unanticipated increase in the refinancing efficiency of borrowers, as occurred in 1993 for GNMAs as the result of a late-1992 FHA rule change. Investors can partly offset such risks by adding POs to the hedge, using the prepayment sensitivities to gauge how much of a particular PO strip to add. This leaves Treasuries hedging the interest-rate risk and POs hedging the prepayment risk.

Exhibit 15. Prepayment Risk Analysis (Pricing Date 6/15/94)

Security	Type	Collateral	OA Sprd	OA Dur	Prepay Sensitivities		
					Relo	Cusp	Refi
FN 6.5	PT	—	47	6.0	0.41	−0.01	−0.02
FN 8.0	PT	—	43	4.9	0.15	−0.20	−0.09
FN 9.5	PT	—	51	3.2	−0.09	−0.33	−0.18
GN 6.5	PT	—	35	7.2	0.26	0.14	−0.01
GN 8.0	PT	—	37	5.9	0.08	−0.17	−0.10
GN 9.5	PT	—	52	3.5	−0.07	−0.44	−0.21
FN T249 IO	IO	FN 6.5	211	1.2	−2.95	−1.33	−0.13
FN T203 S2	IO	FN 8.0	446	−5.1	−2.95	−2.88	−0.49
FN T4 IO	IO	FN 9.5	698	−7.8	−3.35	−3.25	−1.29
FN T249 PO	PO	FN 6.5	−31	9.2	2.81	0.99	0.06
FN T203 S1	PO	FN 8.0	−166	10.7	2.23	1.55	0.20
FN T4 PO	PO	FN 9.5	−195	8.4	1.55	1.27	0.40
FN 9475 G	PAC I	FN 7.0	61	5.7	0.05	−0.09	−0.02
FH 1720 PG	PAC I	FH 7.5	68	5.7	0.06	−0.07	−0.01
FN 9475 M	PAC II	FN 7.0	38	5.7	1.74	0.27	−0.00
FH 1720 A	PAC II	FH 7.5	56	5.4	1.02	0.03	−0.02
FN 9479 A	Seq	FN 7.0	58	3.2	0.22	−0.03	−0.01
FN 9479 B	Seq	FN 7.0	40	6.4	0.55	−0.09	−0.02

CONCLUSION

A good prepayment model in a mature market has to be complex and comprehensive in looking at all aspects of homeowners' decisions. Because those decisions themselves are influenced by a considerable variety of circumstances, prepayment modeling must be detailed and sophisticated; it cannot be oversimplified if it is still to perform well. But it must also make solid, intuitive sense in the way it models the homeowner's decision dynamics. Anything less will result in a framework that is not sufficiently stable over time or sufficiently realistic over the "stress" scenarios that determine the value of mortgage securities. We have been guided by these two primary considerations of comprehensiveness and plausibility in developing the new Goldman Sachs prepayment model, and we believe the valuation and risk management results are likely to be significantly more accurate and robust than any previously available.

CHAPTER 10

Modifying the PSA Curve for Newly Issued Mortgage Pass-Throughs

Joseph C. Hu, Ph.D.
Senior Vice President
Director of Mortgage Research
Oppenheimer & Co., Inc.

The rampant refinancing in 1992 and 1993 replaced voluminous higher-coupon pass-throughs with newly issued ones that carry a 6.5% to 8% coupon rate. On average, at least 50% of the mortgage pools backing these new pass-throughs are "refinancing mortgages"—those that are originated to facilitate refinancing. This phenomenon raises the need to modify the ramp of the PSA curve as a yardstick for measuring prepayment speeds of new pass-throughs. The PSA curve implicitly assumes that new pass-throughs are backed exclusively by "housing-mortgages"—those that are originated to facilitate housing transactions. Because of this assumption, the PSA curve has a 30-month "ramp period" allowing a gradual increase in prepayments as the new pass-throughs age.

But this assumption is no longer valid. By taking into consideration that new pass-throughs are backed by a significant amount of refinancing mortgages, the ramp of the PSA curve should be modified to have a much flatter slope. The time period of the ramp, however, remains unchanged.

In this chapter, we point out three issues relating to the ramp of the current PSA curve. First, when new pass-throughs trade at a discount, their cash-flow yields are underestimated. Second, in an environment of a positively sloped yield curve, the short REMIC tranches backed by newly issued discount-coupon collateral are underpriced because their average lives are overestimated. Third, for new pass-throughs backed by refinancing-mortgage dominated pools, their prepayments during the ramp period are exaggerated in terms of PSA speeds.

REFINANCING VERSUS HOUSING MORTGAGES

In 1993, newly issued fixed-rate pass-throughs amounted to $590 billion. Of this record volume, $366 billion, or 62%, were estimated to be backed by refinancing-mortgages.[1] Refinancing mortgagors are by definition homeowners who were already occupants of the houses on which the mortgages were originated. They may well be "seasoned" homeowners and, in that case, much more likely to prepay their "new" mortgages early on by selling their houses than housing-originated mortgagors.[2] Judging by the level of mortgage rates that prevailed from 1991 to 1993, refinancing mortgagors are likely to have been homeowners for at least one year when they refinanced. By contrast, housing mortgagors are brand new occupants of the houses on which mortgages are originated. They are unlikely to move within the first few years of occupancy.

THE RAMP OF THE PSA CURVE

The ramp of the PSA curve allows prepayments of new pass-throughs to rise while aging during the first 30 months (the ramp period) of the securities. If the prepayment pattern of a pass-through conforms to 100% of the PSA curve, then its first-month prepayment rate will be 0.2% CPR. As the pass-through ages, its prepayment rate will rise incrementally by 0.2% CPR per month for 30 months. By the 30th month, it will reach 6.0% CPR. From that point on, the pass-through is said to have aged to a "seasoned" stage, and its prepayment rate will then remain constant at 6% CPR for the remaining life.

The ramp of the PSA curve implicitly assumes that all new mortgages backing newly issued pass-throughs are originated to facilitate housing transactions. This assumption was realistic prior to the huge refinancing waves of 1992 and 1993. But it may no longer be valid for newly issued pass-throughs

---

1 Prepayments of all coupons of fixed-rate pass-throughs amounted to $490 billion in 1993. Given the 3.7 million sales of existing homes in 1993, the housing turnover rate for the year was around 9%. This rate is based on a specified single-family owner-occupied housing stock of 48 million in 1993, adjusted for the existing home sales of the previous two years. The adjustment assumes that homes that were sold in the past two years are unlikely to be sold again. This turnover rate, coupled with the normal defaults and other miscellaneous disastrous events such as fire and earthquake, raises the total non-refinancing related prepayment rate to roughly 10%. Applying this 10% rate to the $1,240 billion outstanding fixed-rate pass-throughs, non-refinancing prepayments in 1993 amounted to an estimated $124 billion. By subtracting this amount from the total fixed-rate prepayments, refinancing is estimated at $366 billion.

2 This is especially true in recent years, as there have been an increasing number of mortgages originated with no points (origination fees). The refinancing cost therefore has become modest. It no longer requires homeowners to occupy the houses for a minimum period of time to recoup the expenses of refinancing.

during the past two years. In terms of the PSA curve, refinancing-originated mortgages are already far along on the ramp when the new pass-throughs are issued. Without aging, they are already seasoned mortgages. The slope of the PSA ramp should therefore be much flatter. That is, the initial prepayment rate of a new pass-through should be much higher than the 0.2% CPR assumed by the current PSA curve.

A MODIFIED RAMP

Assuming homeowners who refinanced their mortgages had already occupied their houses for at least 30 months, the ramp of the PSA curve can be easily modified to measure prepayments of newly issued pass-throughs in 1993. Based on the relative volume of refinancing and housing mortgages in 1993 (62% versus 38%), Exhibits 1 and 2 show a new PSA curve with a modified ramp to account for the overwhelming presence of refinancing mortgages in the pool of a newly issued pass-through.

The modified ramp is much flatter than that of the current PSA curve. Because 62% of the underlying mortgages are refinancing related, their prepayment rate is expected to be always 6% CPR at a 100% PSA. The weighted prepayment rate for the first month of the pass-through is therefore 3.80%

Exhibit 1. Structuring a Modified PSA Ramp of a Newly Issued Mortgage Pass-Through

Age (months)	New Mortgage CPR (%)	Refinancing Mortgage CPR (%)	Modified Ramp CPR (%)	Age (months)	New Mortgage CPR (%)	Refinancing Mortgage CPR (%)	Modified Ramp CPR (%)
1	0.2	6.0	3.80	16	3.2	6.0	4.94
2	0.4	6.0	3.87	17	3.4	6.0	5.01
3	0.6	6.0	3.95	18	3.6	6.0	5.09
4	0.8	6.0	4.02	19	3.8	6.0	5.16
5	1.0	6.0	4.10	20	4.0	6.0	5.24
6	1.2	6.0	4.18	21	4.2	6.0	5.32
7	1.4	6.0	4.25	22	4.4	6.0	5.39
8	1.6	6.0	4.33	23	4.6	6.0	5.47
9	1.8	6.0	4.40	24	4.8	6.0	5.54
10	2.0	6.0	4.48	25	5.0	6.0	5.62
11	2.2	6.0	4.56	26	5.2	6.0	5.70
12	2.4	6.0	4.63	27	5.4	6.0	5.77
13	2.6	6.0	4.71	28	5.6	6.0	5.85
14	2.8	6.0	4.78	29	5.8	6.0	5.92
15	3.0	6.0	4.86	30	6.0	6.0	6.00

Note: The modified ramp is the sum of 0.32 × (new mortgage CPR) + 0.68 × (refinancing mortgage CPR).

Exhibit 2. Current vs. Modified PSA Ramps

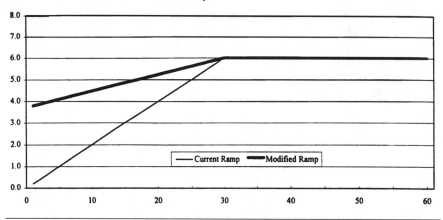

CPR. (That is the sum of 62% of 6% CPR and 38% of 0.2% CPR.) As the pass-through ages, its prepayment rate will rise gradually, following the current PSA pattern to allow for the aging of the 38% of the pass-through that is still backed by housing mortgages. But the monthly increase in the prepayment rate will be much more moderate—only 38% of the 0.2% CPR, or 0.075% CPR. By the 30th month, however, the prepayment rate still reaches 6% CPR.

To test whether the modified ramp resembles reality, we compare the current PSA ramp with the prepayment patterns of eight randomly selected REMICs that are backed by newly issued 30-year FNMA and FHLMC 7s. The original face of collateral of these deals totals $7.5 billion. As shown in Exhibit 3, newly issued pass-throughs have been prepaying much faster during the ramp period than suggested by the current PSA curve. The difference is particularly noticeable when the WAM shortens to below 355 months. This suggests that refinancing mortgagors may have already occupied their houses for over 20 months. Between 344 and 354 months of WAM, the prepayment rates of the new collateral were generally two to four times faster than the current PSA ramp.

UNDERESTIMATION OF CASH-FLOW YIELDS OF DISCOUNT COUPONS

Based on the modified ramp, the bond-equivalent cash-flow yield of discount coupons is markedly higher than that calculated on the current PSA ramp. This outcome is expected because for given prices of discount coupons faster prepayments always raise yields. For example, as shown in Exhibit 4, a new

Exhibit 3. Prepayments of Collateral of Randomly Selected REMICs versus the PSA Ramp

WAM (month)	PSA Ramp CPR (%)	Prepayments in CPR (%)							
		FNR 93-70	FNR 93-112	FNR 93-116	FNR 93-195	FHR 1541	FHR 1593	FHR 1603	FHR 1663
359	0.2								
358	0.4								
357	0.6	0.7	0.6	0.8					
356	0.8	1.8	1.9		6.4	0.8		5.2	
355	1.0			1.6	10.4	3.3		12.9	
354	1.2	2.2	3.3	2.9		5.7	6.3		
353	1.4	4.2	5.5	4.0	6.1		13.5	8.8	4.4
352	1.6	9.2	7.9		4.1	10.2	11.7	5.9	
351	1.8	12.0		9.7	4.4	13.4		6.8	5.3
350	2.0		6.1	7.4		9.8	7.5		5.3
349	2.2	14.4	3.6	3.3	5.6		10.3	5.7	5.1
348	2.4	10.9	4.9	2.6		6.7		5.0	
347	2.6	4.9	4.6			7.3	7.1		
346	2.8			4.1		6.1	5.6		
345	3.0	5.6				5.7			
344	3.2	7.1							

Note: The first four REMICs are backed by 30-year FNMA 7s; the next four, 30-year FHLMC Gold 7s.

Exhibit 4. Bond-Equivalent Cash-Flow Yield Differential Based on Current and Modified PSA Ramps of 30-Year FNMA 7s with a WAM of 360 months

Price	Current PSA Yield (%)	Modified PSA Yield (%)	Modified minus Current (bp)	Price	Current PSA Yield (%)	Modified PSA Yield (%)	Modified minus Current (bp)
90	8.89	9.02	13	100	7.02	7.01	-1
91	8.68	8.80	12	101	6.85	6.84	-1
92	8.48	8.58	10	102	6.69	6.66	-3
93	8.29	8.37	8	103	6.52	6.49	-3
94	8.10	8.17	7	104	6.36	6.32	-4
95	7.91	7.97	6	105	6.21	6.15	-6
96	7.73	7.77	4	106	6.05	5.99	-6
97	7.54	7.57	3	107	5.90	5.82	-8
98	7.37	7.38	1	108	5.75	5.67	-8
99	7.19	7.20	1	109	5.60	5.51	-9

30-year FNMA 7% pass-through with a WAM of 360 months at a price of 92 on a "160% modified PSA" yields 8.58% on a bond-equivalent basis. This "modified yield" is 10 basis points higher than the bond-equivalent cash-flow yield calculated on a "160% current PSA." As the new pass-through ages (WAM shortens), this yield differential decreases because the gap between the modified and the current PSA ramps becomes increasingly smaller. When the WAM shortens to 330 months, the gap reduces to zero and the yield differential no longer exists.

AVERAGE-LIFE OVERESTIMATION AND UNDERPRICING OF SHORT REMICS

The modified ramp has important implications for new pass-through backed REMICs, especially those with short average lives. Short REMICs are structured with the collateral's early principal cash flow. Since the current PSA curve underestimates this cash flow early on, their expected average lives are overestimated. For example, a three-year average-life PAC based on the current PSA curve may have only an expected average life of two years with a much shorter window based on the modified PSA curve.

The average-life overestimation has the impact of underpricing securities. The underpricing could be substantial if the slope of the Treasury yield curve is steep. In 1993, the three-year Treasury on average yielded 40 basis points more than the two-year Treasury. For a two-year average-life PAC to provide a three-year average-life yield, its price has to be lowered by roughly $3/4$ point.

EXAGGERATING SPEEDS OF NEW PASS-THROUGHS ISSUED IN 1992 AND 1993

Given that a realistic ramp of the PSA curve is much flatter than the current one, prepayments in 1992 and 1993 were exaggerated in terms of PSA speeds for newly issued pass-throughs. These were mostly 6.5% to 8% pass-throughs backed by mortgages originated in 1992 and 1993 carrying a mortgage rate of 7% to 8.5%. About 50% to 62% of the underlying mortgages backing these new pass-throughs were refinancing mortgages.[3]

To measure the overestimation of prepayment speeds, consider for example 1992 production of 30-year FNMA 7s. In November 1993, this pass-through had a WAM of 353 months and a prepayment rate of 9.5% CPR.

---

3 The volume of refinancing mortgages in 1993 is estimated in footnote 1. The 1992 figure is estimated on the basis of $480 billion issuance of new, fixed-rate pass-throughs in 1992. Prepayments of fixed-rate pass-throughs were estimated to be $340 billion, of which $240 billion were the result of refinancing.

Measured by the current PSA ramp, its speed was 679% PSA ($9.5/1.4 \times 100$). But in terms of the modified ramp for new pass-throughs issued in 1993, this speed would have been 224% "modified PSA" ($9.5/4.25 \times 100$), a whopping 455 basis points slower than the speed measured by the current PSA curve.

CONCLUDING REMARKS

From the 1992-93 experience of rampant refinancing, we have learned that the prepayment pattern of new pass-throughs can be markedly changed if their underlying mortgage pools are dominated by refinancing mortgages. In the future, whenever interest rates decline, investors should be aware of the potentially different prepayment pattern of newly issued pass-throughs. It is particularly critical when the new pass-throughs trade at a discount. In an environment where the shape of the yield curve is positively sloped, short average-life REMICs have a tendency of being underpriced when they are backed by new pass-throughs whose pools are dominated by refinancing mortgages. During the first 30 months of new pass-throughs, investors should make certain price adjustments to recognize the flatter ramp of the PSA curve.

CHAPTER 11

Homeowner Mobility and Mortgage Prepayment Forecasting

Karen Auld Wagner, C.F.A.
Vice President, Fixed Income Research
CS First Boston Corporation

Evan B. Firestone
Director, Mortgage Products Group
CS First Boston Corporation

INTRODUCTION

In 1993, in the midst of a 2½ year rally, the watchword for the mortgage market was call risk. By late 1994 rates had backed up 200 basis points (b.p.), most mortgages were discounts, and the market concern shifted to extension risk. The market reaction was to revert to a prepayment assumption of 100% PSA on discount mortgage collateral. We believe that 100% PSA long term is unrealistic for conventional mortgages, based on historical homeowner mobility.

WHAT IS 100% PSA?

Some investors have assumed that 100% PSA was designed to represent housing turnover on current coupon conventional agency mortgages. This is not the case. The long-term prepayment rate of 6% CPR implied by 100% PSA was chosen as a reference point only.

Two examples of historical prepayment behavior for agency securities are shown in Exhibit 1. From 1988 to 1990, mortgage rates averaged 10.5% (resulting in an FNMA current coupon of 9.75%). That 10.5% average mortgage rate was more than 150 b.p. higher than mortgage rates at the beginning of 1987. The FNMA 6.5% security contained mortgages at a deep discount to market rates (–325 b.p. on average from 1988–90) which were seasoned 16 years. As shown in the exhibit, the prepayment rate for these securities was close to 120% PSA over this timeframe.

Exhibit 1.   Historical Prepayment Activity on Discount FNMAs

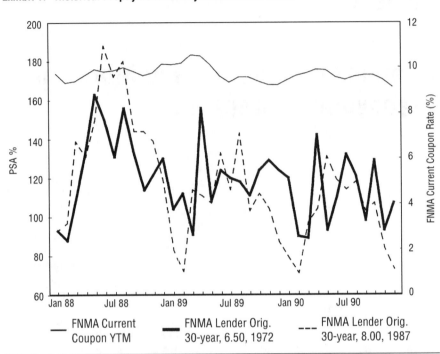

The FNMA 8% securities were originated at the end of the last bond market rally in 1987, and were *unseasoned* discount mortgages (–175 b.p. relative coupon) over the timeframe shown. As such, the FNMA 8s are very similar to the 7% gross WAC securities issued in late 1993 before interest rates rose dramatically in 1994. Although prepayment rates for the FNMA 8s dipped below 100% PSA during the winter months, the average PSA for the whole time period is also close to 120% PSA.

The data support our contention that 100% PSA long-term understates normal housing turnover, even for deep-discount agency collateral.

PSA SPEEDS AND HOUSING TURNOVER

Housing turnover is a cause of mortgage prepayments because most conventional mortgages (*i.e.*, not government guaranteed) contain "due-on-sale" provisions, whereby the borrower is required to pay off the mortgage if the home is sold. By contrast, GNMAs contain FHA and VA mortgages, which are assumable by a new buyer. If an investor considers it unlikely that interest rates will move sufficiently to cause the discount mortgages to be refinanceable (either ever or over the investor's time horizon), the primary driver of prepayment forecasts will be mobility.

In making assumptions about the likely rate of future prepayment activity, it is helpful to examine what various PSA assumptions imply about housing turnover, and then to look at historical data on housing turnover to evaluate the appropriateness of one's PSA assumptions.

In Exhibit 2 we show the "average time to move" implied by various PSA assumptions. Because of the impact of seasoning on the PSA curve, the implied average time to move varies slightly with the age of the collateral, and so we've shown the analysis for collateral of various ages. The results are not the traditional average-life calculation, but rather a weighted average time to recovery of principal assuming only prepayments and *ignoring amortization*. The purpose of the chart is to demonstrate how a given PSA equates to an average length of tenure for a homeowner, in order to assess the "reasonableness" of a given PSA assumption.

As Exhibit 2 shows, 100% PSA implies that borrowers prepay, on average, after 17.4 years. Because no refinancing opportunities are assumed, the speed represents housing turnover only. As such, 100% PSA would suggest that people move about as often as locusts (which appear every 17 years). Alternatively, if one believes the correct assumption is that people move every 7 years, for example, the correct PSA assumption would be approximately 250% PSA (for new collateral).

CALCULATING IMPLIED AVERAGE TIME TO MOVE

The methodology for translating a PSA assumption into the "implied average time to move" is relatively straightforward.

At a given PSA assumption monthly prepayment cash flows are generated. For each month, the prepayment cash flow (not scheduled principal or interest cash flows) is expressed as a percentage of the *original* principal balance. That percentage is then multiplied by the month in which it occurs. The summation of each such monthly statistic equals the implied average

---

Exhibit 2.   Average Time to Move Implied by PSA (Years)

Mortgage Age (mos.)	PSA									
	75%	100%	125%	150%	175%	200%	225%	250%	275%	300%
0	22.9	**17.4**	14.1	11.8	10.3	9.1	8.1	7.4	6.8	6.3
6	22.5	17.0	13.6	11.4	9.8	8.6	7.7	7.0	6.4	5.8
12	22.2	16.6	13.3	11.1	9.5	8.3	7.4	6.6	6.0	5.5
24	21.8	16.2	12.9	10.7	9.1	7.9	7.0	6.2	5.6	5.1

time to move. Because the PSA model calculates prepayments as a percentage of the outstanding principal balance, a long tail of prepayment flows is created in the absence of amortization, especially at low PSA rates.

Long Term vs. Short Term

Assume that one believed homeowners were likely to move, on average, every 12 years. Using Exhibit 2, and assuming the collateral is new, we see that 150% PSA is implied. However, even if our mobility estimate (every 12 years) were correct, it is highly likely that prepayments would be below 150% PSA in the short term. In the short term (particularly under 5 years), mobility factors may play less of a role. That is, we do not have enough data to know whether the pattern of mobility does in fact fit the PSA curve. So while a 12-year turnover assumption equates to 150% PSA in the long run, short-run differences can be material.

HOUSING TURNOVER MOTIVATIONS

What motivates housing turnover? A recent survey of California home sellers details their reasons for selling. Given the significance and size of the California market, it is probably an acceptable proxy for examining housing turnover motivations in the United States generally. Exhibit 3 compares seller motivations in 1993 (the depth of the recession in California) and 1990 (as the California economy peaked).

The most important source of housing turnover, "Change in Family Structure," is fairly stable over time. Moves related to job changes were understandably lower as the economy worsened. The impact of housing prices versus interest rates in motivating move-up buying ("Desired Better Location" and "Desired A Larger Home") appears mixed. However, the comparatively large decline from 1990 to 1993 in the "Desired Larger Home" category would indicate that high actual or expected real estate appreciation (as in 1990) is more important than low interest rates (as in 1993) in move-up buying.

Exhibit 3. Housing Turnover Motivations: Survey of California Homeowners

Reasons for Selling	1990	1993	Difference
Change in Family Structure	21.2%	23.0%	+ 1.8%
Changed Job	14.6	12.1	- 2.5
Desired Better Location	10.8	13.5	+ 2.7
Desired Larger Home	20.6	12.7	- 7.9
Desired Smaller Home	6.2	4.9	- 1.3
Financial Difficulty	N/A*	9.8	N/A
Investment/Tax Considerations	11.0	6.5	- 4.5

*Not a category in 1990. Source: California Association of Realtors

INTEREST RATE CORRELATIONS

Forecasting mortgage prepayments on deep-discount collateral where mobility is the key assumption is less precarious than forecasting prepayments on current coupon mortgages which may become refinanceable. The range of outcomes is likely to be narrower—for example, 125% PSA to 175% PSA—while a current coupon deal could prepay as rapidly as 50% and 60% CPR in a modest rally or as slowly as 125% PSA in a back-up.

Further, prepayment forecasts based on mobility entail estimation error that is *not necessarily strongly correlated* with interest-rate risk. It is true that, all else being equal, homeowners are increasingly less likely to move as current mortgage rates rise versus their existing mortgage rate. However, homeowners' primary motivations to move—change in job and change in family structure—are not correlated with interest rates. Therefore we believe that, while relative coupons (the difference between a homeowner's existing mortgage rate and the current mortgage rate available) will influence homeowners on the margin, a great deal of housing turnover occurs without regard to interest-rate levels.

The attraction for investors is that the cash flow variability on mortgage collateral where prepayment activity is due to housing turnover is arguably less onerous than cash flow variability correlated with interest rate changes.

MOBILITY DATA

Our opinion is that long-term PSA speeds on conventional mortgages—absent any subsequent refinancing opportunity—are likely to be in the 125% PSA to 150% PSA range. As Exhibit 2 shows, this would imply 12-14 years on average until a homeowner moves.

According to the journal *American Demographics*, "...various studies have shown that the average American moves every 5, 6, 7, or even 11 years." The reason for these different estimates is that there are different definitions of "moving." In some studies, the number of people moving is analyzed, while other studies analyze the number of households moving, and still other studies look at the number of *homeowners*. The journal goes on to say that middle-aged homeowners (age 45 to 54), for example, have a median tenure in their home of 8 years.

According to the Census Bureau's most recent population report, *Geographical Mobility: March 1991 to March 1992*, an estimated 17.3% of Americans moved in the period studied. As one might expect, the mobility rate[1] is highest among young people (age 20 to 24), higher for the lowest income

---

1 The mobility rate is the percentage of a given group of households that changes residence over the annual period indicated. An annual mobility rate is similar to an annual prepayment rate, which is expressed as a CPR. Thus, a mobility rate of 10%, for example, is analogous to 10% CPR.

households, and higher for renters than homeowners. Even so, the data generally does not indicate that any group moves as infrequently as implied by 100% PSA. Highlights of the report are presented in Exhibit 4.

MOBILITY DATA AND PREPAYMENT FORECASTING

As shown in Exhibit 4, the overall mobility rate for homeowners in '91-'92 was 8.1%. This mobility rate equates directly to an 8.1% CPR. On seasoned collateral, an 8.1% CPR for life equates to a PSA of 135%. Therefore, simply on the basis of housing turnover one might expect non-refinanceable collateral to prepay at 135% PSA.

Some adjustments may be appropriate. For example, 1991 and 1992 were recessionary years, and recession suppresses housing turnover. Therefore we might expect higher mobility as the United States continues to come out of recession. For example, if overall mobility rose from the 17.3% '91-'92 experience to the '84-'85 level of 20.2% (an emergence from recession), we might expect prepayments to be 17% higher (17.3% vs. 20.2%). This would raise our assumption from 8.1% CPR to 9.5% CPR or from 135% PSA to 158% PSA.

A further adjustment might be made based upon geographical distribution. For example, after developing the 9.5% CPR forecast above, suppose we determined that the mortgage collateral we were evaluating contained one-third Northeast loans and two-thirds Southern loans. We might then revise our mobility-based prepayment forecast as follows:

1. Nationwide Homeowner Mobility Assumption   9.5%
2. Adjustment for Southern Mobility

$$\frac{2}{3} \times \left[\left(1 - \frac{18.8}{17.3} \right) \times 9.5\% \right]$$
        +0.5%

3. Adjustment for Northeastern Mobility

$$\frac{1}{3} \times \left[\left(1 - \frac{11.9}{17.3} \right) \times 9.5\% \right]$$
        <u>-1.0%</u>
        9.0%

The more loan level detail is available, the more adjustments can be made using census demographic mobility data. For example, in the case of non-agency mortgages, mobility data by income can be used to forecast mobility for jumbo borrowers.

HOUSING TURNOVER AND APPRECIATION

Housing turnover is heavily influenced by housing price trends. In strong housing markets, turnover will be more rapid. Again we look to California data to illustrate this point. According to the California Association of Realtors, in 1993 the average time a seller had lived in the home was 7 years (see Exhibit 5). Seven years is the longest seller tenure since the survey began, and reflects poor market conditions in the depressed California market.

Exhibit 4.   Highlights of Geographic Mobility:[1] March 1991 to March 1992

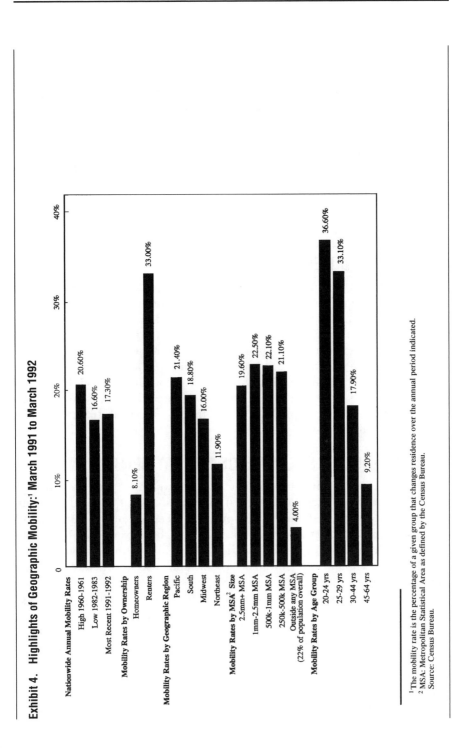

[1] The mobility rate is the percentage of a given group that changes residence over the annual period indicated.
[2] MSA: Metropolitan Statistical Area as defined by the Census Bureau.
Source: Census Bureau.

Exhibit 5.   California Association of Realtors Housing Finance Survey

Year	Median Number of Years Seller Owned Home	Equivalent Homeowner Mobility Rate
1986	6 years	16.6%
1987	6	16.6
1988	6	16.6
1989	4	25.0
1990	5	20.0
1991	5	20.0
1992	6	16.6
1993	7	14.3

MOBILITY AND REFINANCINGS

An important point to note in using mobility to forecast prepayments is that new mortgages do not necessarily represent new homeowners. In 1993 and early 1994, new mortgage originations contained 65% to 75% refinancings. With the lowest rates available in some 20 years, many homeowners who refinanced had already been in their homes for some time. Therefore the average time to move in Exhibit 2 is actually understated for borrowers who are refinancing, and have already been in the home for some period. If a homeowner refinanced in 1993 after being in the home 3 years, for example, then a PSA of 250% would imply an average time to move of 10 years (using Exhibit 2, 7.4 years + 3 years = 10.4 years).

MISCELLANEOUS SOURCES OF PREPAYMENTS

There are other minor, miscellaneous factors which impact prepayments (including casualty losses, for example). After refinancing opportunities and mobility, the third most important source of prepayments is curtailments (*i.e.*, partial prepayments). While it is likely that borrowers would be more apt to curtail their mortgages when they are premiums than when they are discounts, curtailments are still likely as consumers seek to deleverage their personal finances.

Evidence of borrowers' eagerness to deleverage is in the popularity of 15-year mortgages. In late 1993, borrowers had the opportunity of borrowing 30-year, fixed-rate money at rates as low as 6.00% and 6.50%, tax deductible. As long as one believed it was possible to earn more than 6.50% over the 30-year horizon, the best strategy would have been to borrow as much as possible (a high LTV) for as long as possible (30 years) and invest the cash available from the lower down payment and lower monthly mortgage payments. The increased extent to which people refinanced at 65% LTV, using 15-year product, indicates that borrowers are interested in a more conservative approach to their finances. For this reason we expect some borrowers to continue to use discretionary income to pay down their mortgages regardless of their mortgage rate.

MOBILITY MYTHS

It has often been assumed that we are a more mobile society today than in the past. Anecdotally many people can find evidence to support this. Interestingly, though, Census Bureau data does *not* support the contention that the U.S. population has become increasingly mobile in past decades.

For example, Exhibit 6 shows annual nationwide mobility rates for selected periods. This data is shown for *all* groups, as it is not available for homeowners only.

The 1960-61 year experienced the highest mobility, at 20.6%, versus 16.6% in 1982-83. Mobility in the 1980s averaged 17.9%, actually *lower* than

Exhibit 6.   Selected Annual Nationwide Mobility Rates*

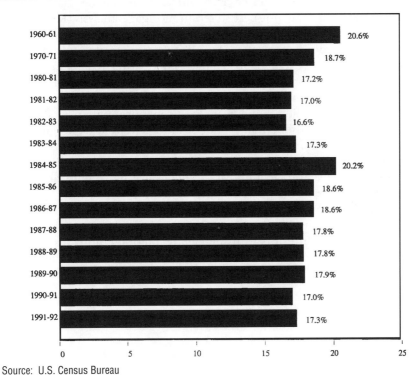

* Source: U.S. Census Bureau

the '60s and '70s. Thus, three patterns emerge: 1) the data do not indicate that the mobility of the population has increased over time; 2) mobility rates are not terribly volatile; and 3) recession inhibits mobility. In 1982 and 1983, for example, mobility reached its low point due to the twin effects of recession and extraordinarily high mortgage rates.

What could explain the surprising conclusion that mobility rates have not risen in the past several decades? One explanation is that as the percentage of people who own homes has risen, overall mobility has declined. Homeowners may move more today than homeowners did in the past (creating the impression of higher mobility overall), but still move far less frequently than renters.

INVESTMENT IMPLICATIONS AND CONCLUSION

Most investors find it fairly easy to reject the notion that average homeowners move every 17.4 years. The investment implications are numerous, especially in an environment where much of the market is deep-discount and securities are widely priced at very slow speeds.

A few caveats are in order. First, the Census Bureau data measures mobility in a narrow way not best suited to mortgage analysis. For example, we know of no census data that contains information about the distribution of observations around an average. Even if homeowners do move, for example, every 10 years on average, do the moves occur over years 3 to 15 or 7 to 12? This information would have an obvious impact on collateral cash flows and hence security valuation.

As we've said earlier, mobility analysis is inappropriate over short horizons. It is certainly possible that a pool of mortgages that experiences long-term PSAs of 150%, for example, may follow a pattern where PSAs are 100% (or even lower) for several years, then rising above 150% in later years. Investors in shorter average-life CMO tranches are unlikely to be aided by the long-term forecasts that mobility analysis provides.

Perhaps the most valuable aspect of this study is simply to help illustrate, in simplest terms, how extreme a 100% PSA-for-life assumption may be. This insight can aid investors with sufficiently long time horizons in finding value when the market overreacts to extension fears and prices to extreme assumptions.

CHAPTER 12

An Unbiased Method of Applying Historical Prepayment Speeds to Project Future Cash Flows

Dan Spina
Managing Director
Financial Analytics
and Structured Transactions Group
Bear Stearns & Co., Inc.

David Sykes, Ph.D.
Principal Director
of Taxable Fixed-Income Research
Alex. Brown & Sons, Inc.

Hendrik Van Schieveen, Ph.D.

There are several methods of applying historical prepayment numbers to project the future cash flows of mortgage products backed by a collection of mortgage pools such as an interest-only—principal-only (IO-PO) trust. The usual approaches of aggregating either the historical prepayments of the individual pools or their WACs/WAMs or both are shown to be biased estimates of future paydowns. However, given the mathematical form of the biases, a linear combination of the usual approaches can be devised that is not biased: this is our BLUE (best linear unbiased estimator) projection of future prepayments. The degree of bias depends on the degree of prepayment dispersion in conjunction with WAC/WAM dispersion. To

The authors would like to thank Frank Ramirez and Sung Jo for providing the impetus for this study, and Blaine Roberts and Peter Cherasia for helpful comments and discussion. Mr. Sykes was Managing Director and Mr. Van Schieveen was Associate Director of the Financial Analytics and Structural Transactions Group at Bear Stearns & Co., Inc. when this chapter was written.

measure this we introduce two indices, a prepayment dispersion index and a WAC/WAM dispersion index.

THE ALTERNATIVE METHODS

There are at least three possible methods to apply historical prepayment speeds to a collection of mortgage pools.

1. Calculate a single speed based on aggregate balances and apply this speed to amortize the entire trust as if it were a single mortgage with a maturity and coupon equal to the average WAC and WAM of the pools in the trust. Although this method of amortizing may be an acceptable approximation in simple cases, it will produce incorrect cash flows if there is dispersion in the WACs and WAMs of the underlying pools. Nevertheless, this method is often used in practice.

2. Incorporate all available pool information into the valuation process by using the aggregate prepayment speed to amortize each pool individually. The resulting cash flows are then totaled for stripping, slicing, or dicing, according to the issue's structure.

   The use of a single aggregate speed suggests itself because of the relatively homogeneous character of the pools that comprise most trusts. To the extent that the pools are similar, prepayment dispersion across pools is largely noise. Hence, in the long run, each pool is expected to prepay at pretty much the same average speed. Thus the *aggregate* "model" for applying historical speeds to project future cash flows regards a weighted average speed at a given point in time as representative of the lifetime average speed expected of all the pools in the trust.

3. A further step in using pool level data involves not only amortizing each pool individually, but also applying prepayment speeds on a pool-by-pool basis. The intuition is that this *individual* method may be more appropriate when a trust is comprised of pools that are fundamentally different in respects that affect their prepayment speeds; that is, when there is some basis for expecting slow pools to continue to prepay relatively slowly, and similarly faster-paying pools to remain relatively faster.

   The difference between methods (1) and (2) is one of amortization techniques. To calculate the cash flows that a given prepayment speed will produce, one has to amortize pools separately if there is WAC and/or WAM differences among the pools. However, when the prepayment speed being applied is regarded as a reasonably accurate approximation of prepayments to come, the imprecision arising from treating the pools as one large pool can often be regarded as negligible. A more interesting difference, and the one we focus on here, is in the individual method vis-à-vis the aggregate method of applying historical prepayment speeds to project future cash flows.

ANALYSIS OF THE INDIVIDUAL AND AGGREGATE METHODS

There are two levels of analysis. The first concerns the effect of the two approaches on the projected rate of paydown/amortization, independent of any statistical properties. The second level of analysis deals with the question of the statistical soundness of the alternative methods.

Implications for Relative Rate of Projected Paydown

The relative rate of amortization/paydown between the two approaches depends on the degree of prepayment dispersion across the pools in the trust, and on the amount of WAM/WAC dispersion. These two properties of a collection of mortgage pools can be quantified by a Prepayment Dispersion Index (PDI), and a WAM/WAC Dispersion Index (WDI). The PDI is on a scale of 0 to 1, with 0 indicating no dispersion and increasing values as prepayment dispersions increase. Most actual deals have PDI values under 0.60. The PDIs for a number of FNMA Strip Trusts are shown in column 6 of Exhibit 1. If a Trust consists of only a single pool, then of course the PDI is 0.0, as is the case for Trust 25 and 26.

The WDI is on a scale of -1 to +1, with negative values indicating the extent to which shorter WAMs are associated with faster speeds, and positive values indicating the extent to which shorter WAMs are associated with slower speeds. Intuitively, if a trust contains some relatively older shorter WAM pools, then one might expect these "burned-out" pools to be associated with relatively slower stable speeds. Hence the WDI would be positive. However, virtually all existing trusts are comprised of relatively new pools, where, because of the seasoning process, shorter WAMs tend to be associated with faster speeds. See column 7 of Exhibit 1 for the WDIs on FNMA Strips.

The influence of the WAC/WAM dispersion on cash flow projections depends on the prepayment dispersion. For example, in the extreme case where there is no prepayment dispersion, all pools are paying at the same speed, and, consequently, there would be no effective difference between the aggregate and individual method. This is reflected in the construction of the PDI and WDI, in that a PDI of zero will result in a WDI of zero. More generally, the WDI will tend to be larger the greater the PDI.

Together, the PDI and WDI interact to determine the relative rate of paydown that will be projected under the individual versus the aggregate method. Specifically, the net of the two indices, the Collateral Dispersion

Exhibit 1.   Percent Balance Reduction Using Different CPP Projections (One Year)

(1) FINSTRI	(2) AGG	(3) BLUE	(4) IND	(5) CDI	(6) PDI	(7) WDI
2	11.0624	10.7117	10.4468	.55278	.55163	-.00115
22	11.1922	10.9377	10.7360	.40900	.40884	-.00016
16	10.4328	10.2055	9.9958	.39545	.39579	.00033
13	15.0467	14.8060	14.6175	.38885	.38520	-.00365
17	10.6018	10.4342	10.2524	.31541	.31466	-.00076
10	11.3177	11.1339	10.9768	.30513	.30484	-.00029
21	8.8023	8.5976	8.4640	.31130	.31107	-.00023
11	9.4591	9.2942	9.1598	.27384	.27350	-.00034
15	14.1567	14.0013	13.8718	.26065	.25803	-.00263
24	7.6916	7.5399	7.4099	.26285	.26275	-.00010
19	9.1445	9.0023	8.8846	.23842	.23790	-.00052
1	8.2802	8.1421	8.0330	.22920	.22903	-.00017
23	8.2022	8.0744	7.9598	.22437	.22379	-.00057
20	9.7545	9.6564	9.6187	.12365	.12359	-.00006
14	8.9659	8.9360	8.9041	.05674	.05688	-.00013
18	8.6625	8.6414	8.6179	.04115	.04095	-.00020
25	11.2493	11.2493	11.2493	.00000	.00000	.00000
26	8.6557	8.6557	8.6557	.00000	.00000	.00000

Index (CDI = PDI - WDI), determines the difference that will occur in the projected balances under the two methods as follows:

$$\mathrm{Bal}^{\mathrm{IND}}\,(12) - \mathrm{Bal}^{\mathrm{AGG}}\,(12) = \mathrm{Bal}^{\mathrm{S}}\,(0) \times \mathrm{CDI}/100$$

where Bals (0) is the current aggregate balance before prepayments (*i.e.*, the current scheduled balance), and Bal (12) refers to the balance projected twelve months forward. Thus the individual method is slower whenever the CDI is positive, and conversely the aggregate method will be slower whenever the CDI is negative.

Practically speaking, the individual method will always pay down more slowly than the aggregate method. This follows partly from the fact that most pools are deliberately constructed with relatively low WAC/WAM dispersions. Thus, in practice the PDI tends to overwhelm the WDI. Moreover, as previously discussed and as shown in Exhibit 1, the WDI is almost always negative, which reinforces a positive CDI.

The reverse result, where the aggregate method projects slower paydowns than the individual method, requires a relatively high positive WAC/WAM dispersion. For example, a two-pool example that produces this result is presented in Exhibit 2. The negative CDI indicates that the aggregate method would project a larger balance one year from now than the individual method.

Exhibits 1 and 3 present the results of a dispersion analysis for a series of actual FNMA Strip Trusts. They are ranked in terms of greatest dispersion to lowest. Columns 2 and 4 of Exhibit 1 show the percent reduction in the balance

Exhibit 2. High Positive WAC/WAM Dispersion

		Pool 1		*Pool 2*
WAC		10%		10%
WAM		30 years		6 years
CPP		10%		9.5%
	PDI		.0057	
	-WDI		-.1634	
	CDI		-.157	

Exhibit 3. Percent Balance Reduction Using Different CPP Projections

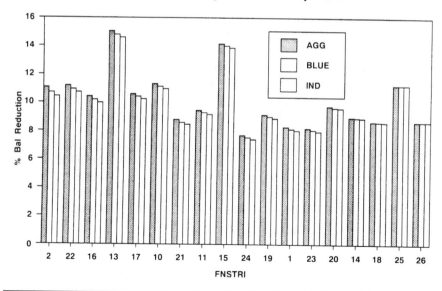

projected by the aggregate and individual method, respectively. The aggregate method projects a greater balance reduction in all cases, with the difference in projected reductions being greater, the greater the CDI. This correlation of the size of the balance difference with the CDI is illustrated in Exhibit 3.

Thus, different methods of applying the same historical data can clearly affect value. This is especially true for securities like strips, whose values are quite sensitive to the rate of paydown.

Analyzing Statistical Properties and the BLUE Projection

To evaluate the relative merits of the different methods, we considered a simple statistical model with the prepayment rates normally distributed about a constant long-term speed. In this framework, both the individual and aggregate method of predicting prepayments are biased. To say a particular method is biased means that the balance (or prepayment) predicted by the method will be, on average, different than the actual value expected. This model thus provides a basis for determining which method "makes more sense"; the better method of the two is the one with the smaller bias.

As discussed earlier, the individual method seems intuitively more appealing if a trust can be identified as containing distinctly slow- and fast-paying pools, perhaps due to some fundamental characteristic such as geographic origin. This intuition is found to be valid within our statistical framework under the following condition: in addition to having significantly different average speeds, the pools in the trust also pay with relatively low variability about their average speeds. In this case, the bias of the individual method is distinctly smaller than the bias of the aggregate method.

The significance of the variability can be conveyed by considering the following case. A trust is comprised of pools that have distinctly different average speeds. However, certain pools that are on-average slow, sometimes pay faster than pools that are on-average fast; and, vice versa, some of the pools that are typically fast, occasionally have periods where paydowns are slower than the "slow" pools. Even though pools can be categorized as on-average distinctly slow, medium, fast, and so on, the variation from period to period "smears" the distinctive prepayment character of the individual pools. In this case, it is not intuitive that the historic prepayment speeds of the individual pools necessarily provide a better method of projecting future prepayments. This intuition is also borne out in our statistical framework: when pools have distinct average speeds but with high variability, then the bias of the individual and the aggregate are more or less equal.

In general, the bias of the individual method is primarily a function of the variability of the individual pools' prepayments: the more stable the pools' prepayments are, the smaller the bias in the individual method. The bias of the aggregate method depends primarily on the CDI: the greater the prepayment and WAM/WAC dispersion, the greater the bias of the aggregate method. Thus, a third case, where the pools in a trust all have close to the same average speed and thus a low CDI, would always favor the aggregate method.

Estimates of the biases for all of the trusts listed in Exhibit 1 were calculated. In all cases, the biases were in opposite directions and of more or less equal amounts, indicating no cases where the pools have both distinct average speeds and low variability about these averages. One implication of the size and direction of the two biases is that the individual method will always be more accurate during down trends in prepayment rates, whereas the aggregate method will always be more accurate during up trends.

Based on the above findings, we conclude that if one is to use a single static scenario cash flow projection to price a mortgage product, a hybrid of the aggregate and individual method that eliminates the bias should be used. We have devised such a prediction procedure, based on a linear combination of the balances that would be projected under the two methods, and with weights such that the predicted balance is unbiased. This procedure is our BLUE (Best Linear Unbiased Estimate) prepayment projection.

A comparison of the results of the BLUE projection can be seen in Exhibits 1 and 3. As designed, the BLUE estimator will project a balance twelve months forward about halfway between the projections of the aggregate and individual projections. Exhibit 4 illustrates the significance of the different methods in terms of yield. The BLUE yields tend to be closer to the aggregate speed, because although it is based on both methods, it is ultimately a single speed being projected over the life of the security. Thus, unlike the pure individual method where the "average" rate of paydown slows down as faster pools pay off, leaving only the slower pools, the BLUE paydown maintains a constant rate throughout the securities' projected life. This feature brings out the fact that the BLUE projection is a value based on a one-year time frame, using the most recent data available on a given trust. As the character of the trust changes over time, so will the BLUE projection.

Exhibit 4.   Yield Impact of Different CPP Projections

(1) FINSTRI	(2) AGG	(3) BLUE	(4) IND	(5) CDI	(6) PDI	(7) WDI
2	12.595	13.002	15.043	.55278	.55163	-.00115
16	11.973	12.234	13.841	.39545	.39579	.00033
22	12.454	12.751	14.283	.40900	.40884	-.00016
17	11.799	11.992	13.366	.31541	.31466	-.00076
21	11.078	11.309	12.576	.31130	.31107	-.00023
10	12.309	12.523	13.700	.30513	.30484	-.00029
13	12.496	12.784	13.827	.38885	.38520	-.00365
11	11.708	11.896	12.991	.27384	.27350	-.00034
24	12.419	12.589	13.656	.26285	.26275	-.00010
19	13.483	13.646	14.604	.23842	.23790	-.00052
1	12.485	12.641	13.599	.22920	.22903	-.00017
23	12.978	13.123	13.895	.22437	.22379	-.00057
15	11.579	11.762	12.480	.26065	.25803	-.00263
20	12.878	12.991	13.385	.12352	.12346	-.00006
14	12.337	12.371	12.660	.05674	.05688	.00013
18	12.657	12.681	12.917	.04115	.04095	-.00020
25	13.237	13.250	13.250	.00000	.00000	.00000
12	11.331	11.343	11.343	.00000	.00000	.00000

CHAPTER 13

RFC Whole Loan Prepayment Behavior

Vernon H. Budinger, C.F.A.
Director, Financial Strategies Group
Global Advanced Technology

Yizhong Fan, Ph.D.
Consultant, Financial Strategies Group
Global Advanced Technology

In a joint effort, Residential Funding Corporation (RFC) and Global Advanced Technology (GAT) have developed a prepayment model using the extensive loan records maintained by RFC. This study had two objectives: 1) to understand the factors that affect a mortgagee's incentive to prepay, and 2) to develop a model that predicts prepayments on whole loan CMOs. This study differs from previous works because it started with loan-level data and utilized this additional information to enhance the model's explanatory power.

Most whole loan prepayment studies with which we are familiar use deal-level prepayment data to estimate the prepayment model. The database for this study is built from loan data aggregated into cohorts of loans with similar characteristics. This distinction is important because issuers can use diverse collateral in whole-loan CMOs. The range of mortgage rates on the collateral loans can exceed 400 basis points in a given CMO deal. For example, RFC 87-S4 collateral had a minimum coupon of 9.625% and a maximum of 13.75%. Similarly, the collateral weighted average remaining maturities (WARMs) can range from 200 to 355 months (RFC 93-S45). Such ranges in

The authors would like to thank Miles Hutton, Hanya Kim, Michael Lee, Robert Matthews, David Brown, Val Emerson, Warren Loken, Chris Nordeen, Susan Cirillo and Basil Rabinowitz for their assistance in the study reported in this chapter.

loan characteristics reduce the predictability of prepayment models estimated from deal-level data.

This study has yielded a unique understanding of the variables motivating prepayments on whole-loan CMOs. We distinguished between two distinct prepayment incentives: refinancing/relocation and curtailments, or partial prepayments. We are able to add several variables available only in whole-loan collateral such as LTV, documentation, loan size, geography, and loan purpose (purchase or refinance).

We found that prepayments on non-conforming loans respond dramatically to small changes in interest rates and the response is very efficient. There seems to be very low refinancing costs for non-conforming loan holders, since prepayment speeds pick up immediately when refinancing rates fall below the gross WAC of the loans. As compared to agency data with similar coupons, whole-loan prepayments drop to the same level when the mortgage coupon is lower than the refinancing rate, but exhibit much higher prepayment rates when the mortgage coupon is equal to or higher than the refinancing rate. Non-conforming loans also follow different seasoning behavior than agency mortgages. The differences cause some concern about the popular use of accelerated agency prepayment models to simulate whole loan prepayment behavior.

CHARACTERISTICS OF WHOLE LOAN COLLATERAL

The data consisted of the complete monthly mortgage records for loans held by the RFC since inception in 1986. The loans in the RFC database are, for the most part, "jumbo" mortgage loans that are not eligible for sale to FNMA or FHLMC, or to be originated into GNMA pools (the "agencies"). They have no federal insurance or guarantee associated with them. These are loans which have been used as collateral for securities issued by RFC or otherwise sold on the secondary market. RFC has retained master servicing responsibilities, namely the collection of loan payments from the primary servicers of the loans and disbursement of the same to the ultimate investors.

The 30-year fixed-rate loans, which are the focus of this study, are usually packaged into the highly structured mortgage-backed securities, such as collateralized mortgage obligations (CMOs). Unlike the loans for agency CMOs that are accumulated into pass-through securities before they are securitized, RFC loans are placed directly into the structure. Thus, RFC, and other non-agency CMOs, are frequently referred to as "whole loan" CMOs.

We first screened the data in order to manage it more effectively. We started by excluding loans with balances under $25,000 and current factors greater than 1. This initial data set contained monthly records for 60,801 loans. Each loan record had multiple observations, *i.e.*, a loan that was outstanding for 120 months would have 120 prepayment observations. We had to aggregate the data because of the large number of records. Aggregating the data into homogenous cohorts and calculating average single monthly mortality (SMM) for each cohort maximized use of the loan-level information and permitted the RFC/GAT prepayment model to be used on a loan-by-loan basis when making predictions for prepayments on CMOs.

The data were rescreened and reaggregated until the database accurately represented the characteristics of the loan population. In the final database, observations were aggregated into cohorts using eight criteria: coupon, original loan size, geography (California, non-California), age, factor, loan purpose (purchase, rate and term refinancing, equity refinancing, and other), documentation code (full documentation or limited documentation), and month (time). (Appendix A provides the aggregation rules.) When the aggregation was complete each cohort included all the loans that could be characterized by an eight-tuple (C, S, G, A, P, D, F, T) matrix. The list and description of loan variables are in Exhibit 1.

After aggregation, we had 115,530 observations (since one loan will generally appear in many observations, one for each month of prepayment history until it dies). Each cohort contains at least one loan; the largest cohort contains 1,584 loans. On average, a cohort contains 12 loans. The statistics on the final data set reveal that the data are sparse and heterogeneous. The data are sparse because cohorts with low coupons, high coupons, and older mortgages tend to have less than 12 observations. The data are heterogeneous because the cohorts in the center of the coupon distribution have significantly more loans than surrounding cohorts. (See Exhibit 2 for more details.) Exhibit 3 shows the problems with predicting prepayments for noisy data. RFC 91-S12 has a weighted average coupon (WAC) of 10.29 and a WARM of 317, while RFC 91-S15 has a WAC of 10.27 and a WARM of 327. The actual prepayments from the two deals can vary signficantly. The prepayment model would produce similar prepayment estimates for the two deals. One could reduce some of these problems by enlarging the buckets; however, that reduces the value of loan-level data. Instead, we use statistical approaches to redefine the measures for prepayment predictions and then use maximum likelihood (ML) to handle sparseness and heterogeneity.

REVIEW OF PREPAYMENT MEASUREMENTS

Although prepayments are traditionally measured by the dollar amount leaving a loan, a pool, or a deal, they are more reasonably modeled by measuring the number of loans leaving a pool or a deal. When a borrower refinances or relocates, the individual dollars are not independent if they belong to the

---

Exhibit 1.   Loan Variables for the Prepayment Model

VARIABLES KEPT
Variables Used in Aggregation

C = Coupon	Coupon rate on the loan, 9 classes.
S = Loan size range	Average size of the loans in each cohort, 3 classes.
G = Geography	Non-California and California.
A = Age range	Months that the loan has been outstanding, 7 classes.
P = Loan purpose	This category was split into loans for purchase and loans for refinancing. Refinancing further subdivided into rate-term refinancing and equity reducing refinancing (3 classes).
D = Documentation	Full documentation and limited documentation.
F = Factor range	Ratio between the original loan balance and the current loan balance, 8 classes.
T = Month	Monthly index, starting on January 1987 and ending April 1993.

Other Loan Variables in Model (not used in aggregation)

WARM	Weighted average remaining life
LTV	Loan-to-value ratio at origination multiplied by the factor.

Market Variables

Refinancing Rate	The 60-day RFC refinancing rate.
Yield curve	We used the implied spot curve derived from the Treasury yields and divided the curve into two segments; the difference between the 5-year and 2-year rate, and the difference between the10-year and 5-year rate.

VARIABLES REJECTED

Number of units	Number of units in the structure.
	Single units accounted for 98.9% of the observations.
Property Type	Single-family or planned unit development.
	Planned unit development comprised only 13% of the data.
Owner Occupied	Owner-occupied versus other categories.
	Owner-occupied dwellings account for 99.2% of the data.

---

same loan, *i.e.*, they must stay or leave together. This distinction is not important in agency data because the law of large numbers guarantees that the two concepts are equivalent. However, individual loans are completely independent regardless of the statistical characteristics of the data. Restating prepayment measures is the fundamental consideration in the RFC/GAT prepayment model. Because mortgage data are based on monthly records, the mortgage industry developed SMM to measure prepayments. SMM is given by the following equation:

$$SMM = 100 \times \frac{(\text{Scheduled Balance} - \text{Actual Balance})}{\text{Scheduled Balance}}$$

where

Exhibit 2. Loan Count* by Age and Ratio**

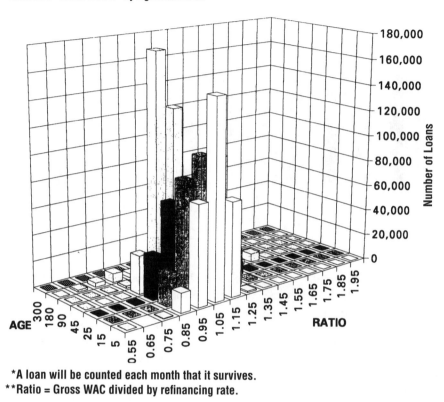

*A loan will be counted each month that it survives.
**Ratio = Gross WAC divided by refinancing rate.

Scheduled Balance = The expected balance given the amortization schedule, last month's balance, and no prepayments.

Actual Balance = The remaining balance after the scheduled balance is adjusted for prepayments.

The Constant Prepayment Rate (CPR), which expresses SMM as an annual rate taking into account the effect of compounding, is more commonly used when discussing prepayment rates. Thus, one often refers to a CPR for a given month, meaning the annualized rate that would occur if the SMM for that month were repeated each month for a full year. This relationship is expressed as follows:

$$CPR = \left[1 - \frac{(1 - SMM)^{12}}{100}\right] \times 100$$

Exhibit 3.   Monthly Prepayment History

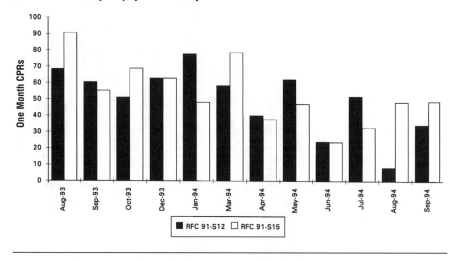

Since agency data are based on pool-level statistics, prepayments must be lumped together and the SMM measures the percent of the pool that pays down. We can only guess at which loans left the pool and their size. Luckily, the large amount of loans in agency pools and the homogeneity of the loans make the SMM approach equivalent to the loan-counting approach. RFC loan-level data permits us to use either measure. However, the relatively small number of loans, the sparseness, and the heterogeneity of the RFC data suggest that we use the loan-counting approach. For an individual loan, there are four possible outcomes for prepayments:

SMM = 0   the borrower pays according to schedule;

SMM = 100   the borrower completely prepays because of refinancing, relocation, or default (agency);

0<SMM<100   the borrower partially prepays (curtailment); or

Default

SMM = (Refinance + Relocation) + Curtailment + Default

Our model takes advantage of the loan-level data by separating the first three outcomes into groups, *i.e.*, no prepays, relocation, refinancing, and curtailments. This solved two problems. We were able to devise an efficient method for measuring curtailments and refinancing/relocation separately. By combining statistical methods with the loan-count measure of prepayments, we reduced the bias from sparseness and heterogeneity. The fourth outcome represents the amount that is recovered upon liquidation of a defaulted loan. For the purpose of this study, we did not differentiate voluntary prepayments from involuntary prepayments occurring through default.

MODEL DEVELOPMENT

We reviewed several models for this project.[1] We found that the best approach is the logistic function (see Exhibit 4). The logistic function is a natural choice for prepayment modeling because its range is bounded by zero and one. Prepayments are also bounded by this range. In addition, the logistic function has the general shape observed in prepayment data.

Defining the Dependent Variables

Since a mortgagee's motivation for partially prepaying and refinancing is quite different, we can also hypothesize that curtailments and refinancing/relocation should be modeled separately. We used a least squares (LS)

Exhibit 4. Refinancing Function: Logistic Function

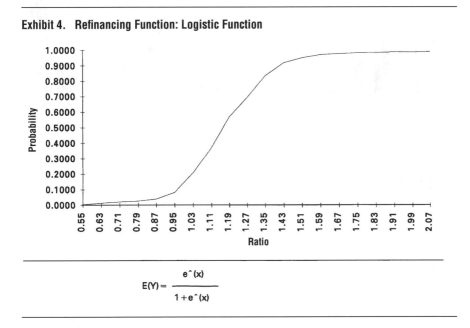

$$E(Y) = \frac{e^{\wedge}(x)}{1 + e^{\wedge}(x)}$$

---

1 We first considered non-linearly fitting the data using a straightforward fit of the logistic curve. However, this approach proved to be intractable; it was difficult to evaluate and the data caused it to be very sensitive to changes in the initial parameters. Since the data are largely binary, we also evaluated distributions and statistical techniques designed for discrete data.

model to fit curtailments, and a maximum likelihood model to fit refinancing/relocation prepayments. In Exhibits 5 and 6, we can see the plots of prepayments due to curtailments plotted versus refinancing incentive and WARM. Exhibits 7 and 8 show the same plots for refinancing activity. The plots confirm that there is little relationship between the two activities. The rate at which borrowers partially prepay increases as the loan seasons. Further, the curtailment sensitivity to interest-rate levels also increases as

Exhibit 5. Curtailment CPR Versus Ratio
Average over all Categories

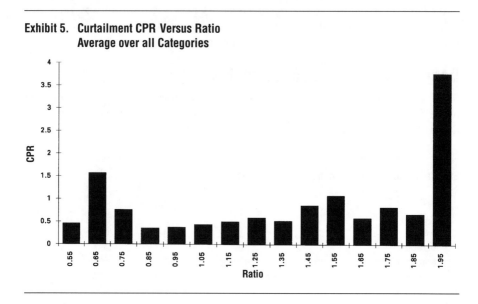

Exhibit 6. RFC 30-Year Curtailment Versus WARM

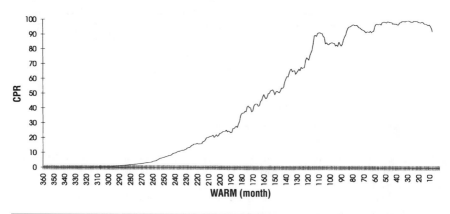

the loans age. Separating curtailments from prepayments has other advantages. First, we can develop better models because we avoid fitting two different patterns with one set of parameters. Second, we can use more

Exhibit 7. Refinance CPR Versus Ratio

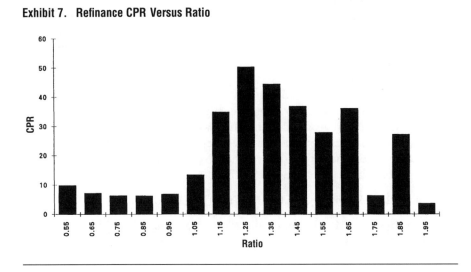

Exhibit 8. RFC 30-Year Refinancing Prepayment Versus Age

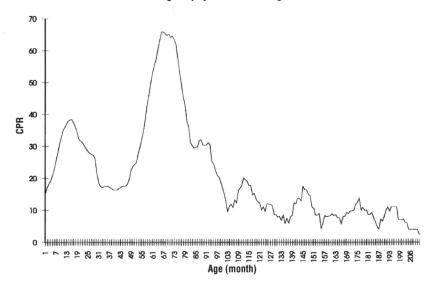

sophisticated statistical procedures in order to fit the refinancing prepayment data better.

As discussed previously, we used the statistical relationship between the number of loans refinancing out of the cohort and total number of loans in the cohort as the dependent variable in place of the SMM derived by PSA standards. Although this approach loses information about the loan sizes, it gains more from the ability of logistic maximum likelihood to take the number of loans in each cohort into account. It can be proven that differing loan size does not change the expectation for prepayment results, although it does change the variance.

We calculated the curtailment SMM according to PSA convention. To calculate the dependent variable, we transformed the SMM using the approach outlined in Appendix B. When we predict prepayments, we estimate two probabilities from each model. Because these two probabilities are independent and mutually exclusive, the surviving dollar amount should follow the probability multiplication principle,

$$\text{prob (loan surviving)} = [1 - \text{prob (refi)}] \times [1 - \text{prob(curt)}],$$

where prob(x)=SMM/100. Since the total SMM equals the probability of a loan dying, it equals one minus the probability of a loan surviving.

Model Fitting

Since we did not use least square procedures to estimate the refinancing model parameters, we could not use R^2 to evaluate the validity of the model. Because of violations of certain statistical assumptions, we also could not use the chi-square approximation to estimate the goodness of fit. Instead, we relied on backtesting to evaluate the validity of the model. We did use chi-square statistics to determine the statistical significance of the different variables in the maximum likelihood function. The chi-square statistics for important variables are significant. More importantly, the signs on the coefficient for each variable are logical. Additional tests show that there is no heteroskedasticity in the errors between predictions and actual observations.

PREPAYMENT MODEL DESCRIPTION
Refinancing—Factors Shared with Agency Models

We focused most of our effort on developing this component of the model because refinancing/relocation is by far the most important and most volatile component of prepayments. Exhibit 9 compares the average refinancing response from RFC loans to the same data from FNMA 30-year pools. When the

Exhibit 9.   RFC 30-Year Versus FNMA 30-Year—Average Prepayments by Ratio

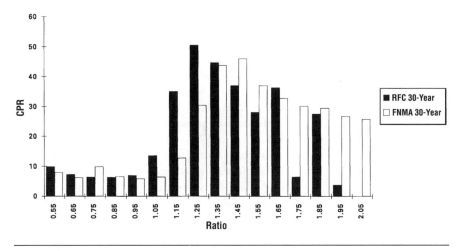

gross WAC (GWAC) of a loan is relatively low, prepayments on RFC loans settle down in the 7 CPR area. This is about the same area as predicted for agency pools. Prepayments respond dramatically to changes when the ratio is between 0.95 and 1.05. Given a 7.5% refinancing rate, the ratio for a 9.5% loan is 1.27. This is generally considered an at-the-money loan, *i.e.*, 200 basis points over the refinancing rate. Exhibit 9 shows that RFC loans are not only well into the refinancing surge at that ratio, but have in fact reached a ceiling at about 50 to 60 CPR.

In addition, prepayments on RFC loans respond to changes in rates more quickly than agency data. While we found that a two-month delay between the refinancing incentive and prepayments fit the RFC data the best, our studies of agency pools suggest it usually takes about three months before prepayments begin to respond to changes in interest rates.

Seasoning: Seasoning means that the loan's propensity to prepay changes as the loan ages. Indexing the prepayment data by age buckets permitted seasoning to be modeled as two separate components. First, the model measures the effect of aging on expected prepayment levels if rates were to remain constant. Second, it measures the effect of aging on the loan's sensitivity to changes in interest rates. Prepayments on mortgage loans vary even if rates do not change. Mortgagees rarely prepay in the first few months after the mortgage is originated, they are unlikely to default during the first few months, and they rarely refinance after they have just moved in (refinancing incentive is being held constant). This propensity to prepay grows during the first few months of the loan's life.

The seasoning for RFC data is more erratic than the agency data. Exhibit 10 compares the prepayment predictions for RFC and FNMA 30-year collateral over the life of the mortgage. Prepayments for both sets of data first peak at 20 to 30 months. However, the RFC prepayments peak at 15 CPR, while the FNMA prepayments peak at 12 CPR. Both data sets maintain this level until about 100 months, when RFC prepayments hit a much higher peak of 33 CPR, while FNMA data increase only slightly. Homeowners tend to move after an average of 8 to 10 years, which indicates that the surge at 100 months is probably a result of relocation. The large difference between the agency and RFC prepayments at this age is probably the result of higher mobility among RFC borrowers.

We created a survival table to get another perspective on seasoning behavior (see Exhibit 11). This table was produced with data from January 1987 to April 1993. The second column is the number of loans that died during this period. This gives the average lifetime of a non-conforming mortgage. The fourth column ("Number of Loans Alive") shows the loans that had survived as of April 1993. It provides an age distribution for that date. We can draw several interesting conclusions from this table. As of April 1993, all of these loans are relatively young. The proportion of loans older than 120 months was 0.8%. Furthermore, all of the cohorts with an age greater than 120 months are relatively empty and any statistical inference

Exhibit 10. Comparison of Prepayments between RFC30 and FN30

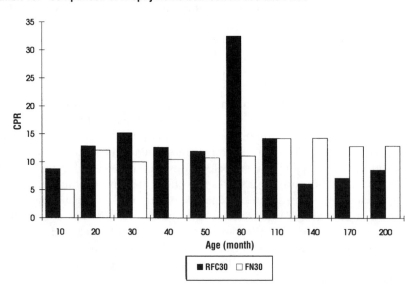

Exhibit 11. Survival Table

	Median Age	Number of Loans Died	Contribution to Avg. Life	Number of Loans Alive	Contribution to Avg. Age	Latest Issue	Earliest Issue
1-30 Months	15.5	13,726	7.504	25,693	12.273	3/31/94	11/12/91
31-60 Months	45.5	7,731	12.407	2,948	4.134	10/13/91	5/26/89
61-120 Months	90.5	6,755	21.562	3,563	9.937	4/26/89	6/21/84
121-240 Months	180.5	134	0.853	230	1.279	5/22/84	8/13/74
241-360 Months	300.5	6	0.064	15	0.139	7/14/74	10/4/64
TOTAL/AVERAGE		28,352	42.390	32,449	27.762		

about this region is qualitative. The average probability of a loan surviving over 120 months during the entire period was 0.5%. In April 1993, more than 79% of the loans were younger than 30 months. Over this period, approximately 76% of these mortgages did not live longer than 60 months.

The second component of seasoning measures borrowers' decreasing sensitivity to changes in interest rates as the mortgage grows older. As the loan is paid down, the borrower has to refinance at progressively lower rates in order to maintain the same level of savings. Also, financially sophisticated borrowers can be more mobile. As these borrowers leave the pool, the remaining mortgagees have lower sensitivity to refinancing savings.

RFC loans are very sensitive to refinancing incentive, especially during the first 100 months. This sensitivity changes dramatically over the life of the mortgage (see Exhibit 12). Very small changes in RFC's refinancing rate causes dramatic changes in prepayments. New mortgages are especially sensitive to increases in the refinancing incentive. After the mortgage reaches an age of 15 months its refinancing sensitivity stays in a narrow range until the mortgage reaches an age of 120 months.

Seasonality: Seasonality measures the cyclical changes in prepayments during the year. As is clear from Exhibit 13, most of the housing activity— home sales, building, and relocation—occurs in the summer or early fall. As a result, prepayments are higher during the summer and the fall. The fitting procedure used a dummy variable (zero or one) to identify the month during which the prepayment occurred. The coefficients for these variables provide us with the predicted monthly increase or decrease.

Exhibit 12. Refinancing Sensitivity

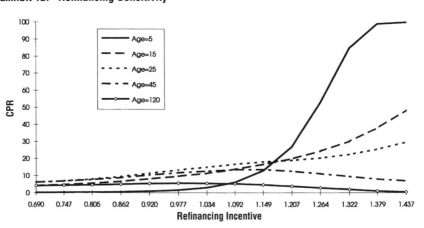

Exhibit 13.   RFC 30-Year Seasonality

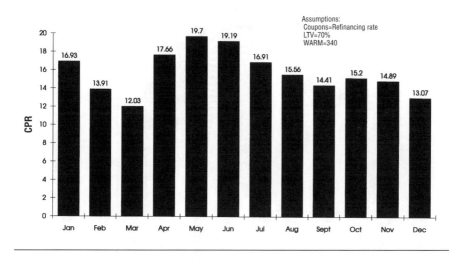

Burnout: Burnout is the tendency for loan prepayments to be less sensitive to changes in interest rates after they have been exposed to a relatively low interest-rate period. Burnout in a CMO deal is caused by the changes in the composition of a mortgage pool as mortgagees prepay as interest rates fall. Mortgagees with higher propensity to prepay will do so first, leaving mortgagees who are not as sensitive to changes in interest rates or whose refinancing costs are higher. As a result, the deal becomes "burned out" and is less sensitive to changes in interest rates. The reduction in prepayment sensitivity from burnout adds to the reduction in sensitivity from seasoning. The RFC/GAT prepayment model measures burnout by tracking interest rates from the date each loan was originated and measuring the difference between the refinancing rate and the gross WAC of a loan each month. The burnout calculation keeps a cumulative total of the positive differences derived from subtracting the gross WAC from the refinancing rate. Exhibit 14 shows how burnout would be measured for a 10% mortgage issued in 1987. The burnout is represented by the bars at the bottom of the graph.

We did not observe much difference between the burnout coefficients for the RFC/GAT prepayment model and the GAT agency prepayment model. The coefficient for the RFC/GAT model was significant. However, RFC loans prepay so quickly that burnout would not contribute significantly to total prepayment predictions. Given the few remaining loans available after 120 months, we could make a case that the RFC loans tend to burn

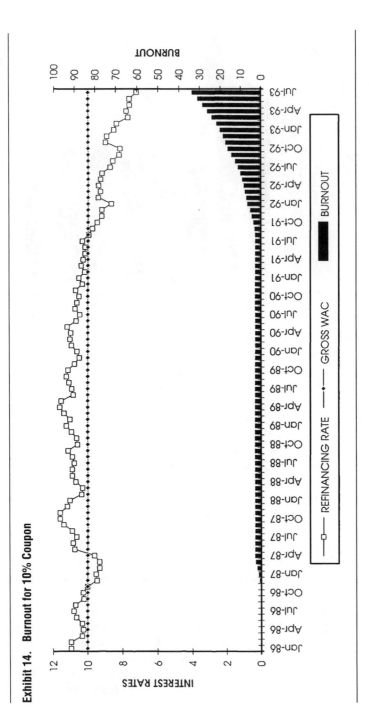

Exhibit 14.   Burnout for 10% Coupon

completely and that the rest of the loans have little sensitivity to refinancing. Once the loans reach this age, curtailments play a large role in the prepayment speed. This will be covered in the next section.

Yield Curve: The steepness of the yield curve affects prepayments by providing financing alternatives to the mortgagee, especially those holding 30-year mortgages. As the curve steepens, loans prepay faster as borrowers have the opportunity to refinance at lower rates on 15-year or balloon mortgages. This incentive is especially strong in moderately seasoned pools. During 1992 and 1993, the homeowner could often refinance into a shorter maturity mortgage and still make lower payments because the rates charged on the new loans were so low. The coefficient for the 2- to 5-year spread was especially strong and positive, while the coefficient for the 5- to 10-year spread was insignificant.

Refinancing—Whole-Loan-Specific Factors

Exhibit 15 contains a hypothetical loan that we constructed that provides examples of the effect of collateral-specific factors on the prepayment expectations. We set up a loan with the generic characteristics listed under default assumptions. We then calculate a new prepayment prediction after

---

Exhibit 15.   Generic Characteristics of Hypothetical Loan

Default assumptions
WAC = Refinancing Rate
California Loan
Loan used to purchase home (not refinance)
Loan Size = $300,000
LTV = 80%
Age = 25
CPR = 12
Factor = .95

Changes to assumptions:*

Non-California Loan before 1992	9.51
Non-California Loan 1992 and after	12.00
Rate/Term Refinance	9.24
Equity Refinance	7.69
$200,000 Original Loan Size	11.97
90% LTV	9.92
70% LTV	14.47
50% LTV	20.83

---

changing one characteristic of the loan. For instance, the hypothetical loan is a California loan with an LTV of 80%, an age of 25 months, a ratio of 1, and a CPR of 12. When we then assume the LTV to be 70%, the CPR increases to 14.47%. Documentation and loan size did not have a significant effect on the loans prepayment predictions even though they had statistically significant coefficients.

Loan-to-Value (LTV): The largest factor in prepayments outside of aging is the LTV. Loans with under 70% LTV experience significantly higher prepayments than loans with 80% LTV. When there is more security for the loan, lenders will provide more financing and better rates for the applicant. In addition, borrowers will have more refinancing options and possibly lower costs.

Geography: Investors generally believe that mortgages originated in California prepay at substantially faster rates than mortgages originated in other states. However, Exhibit 16 shows this belief is no longer valid. During early 1992, the systematic difference in prepayment rates between California loans and non-California loans dissipated. Our model also fits the out of sample data better when we removed the distinction between California and other states after 1992 (see Exhibit 15).

Exhibit 16. SMM (California versus Non-California)

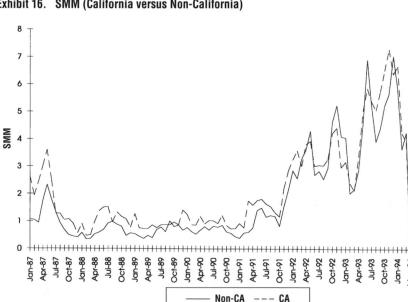

Purpose: The results also showed that mortgagees that originally borrowed to purchase the house were more likely to refinance than borrowers who had borrowed to refinance a previous mortgage. In addition, borrowers who refinanced and took out equity are less likely to refinance than those that take out rate/term refinancing.

Curtailment Model

Mortgage investors have long disputed the effects of curtailments on prepayments. In general, partial prepayments account for a very small portion of total prepayments. However, curtailments can be a very important component of prepayments on seasoned mortgages. Curtailments increase dramatically and become more sensitive to interest-rate levels as the WARM declines. This section will examine the most important factors affecting curtailments.

Seasoning: The WARM is an important factor in determining the probability and size of a partial prepayment on a loan. Curtailment rates remain low in the early months of a loan life, and pick up dramatically as the WARM approaches 200 months (see Exhibit 17). One interesting finding is that the relationship between the time from issue (age) and curtailments is very weak. When we used age as a regression variable we found that R^2 dropped from 76% to 32%. This happens because the WARM is adjusted by curtailments, while the age is not. As a result, two loans could have the same age, but significantly different WARMs.

Loan-to-Value: LTV also played a very large part in curtailments, but the sign goes in the opposite direction from the coefficient for refinancing. The higher the LTV, the more the borrower pays curtailments. This probably reflects the reduced access to refinancing opportunities that forces the borrower to prepay by increasing the payment size.

Average Loan Size: While average loan size contributes almost nothing to refinancing, this variable has a positive and large coefficient in the curtailment model. Larger loans probably experience higher curtailments than smaller loans because wealthier borrowers have more disposable income and have more to gain from prepaying their mortgage.

Seasonality: Curtailments exhibit very different seasonal behavior. They are quite low in August through November, then begin to pick up again in December. They continue to climb into the spring and reach their peak in March and April. This corresponds to typical consumer spending habits. Consumers generally get tax refunds in the spring and incur the highest drain on their budgets in the late summer and early fall as the school year starts and the holiday season approaches.

Interest-Rate Savings: It is apparent that interest-rate incentive provides little motivation for partial prepayments during most of the life of a mortgage.

Exhibit 17.   Curtailments by WARM and Ratio

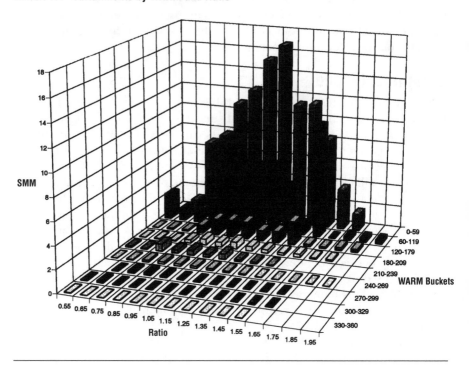

However, partial prepayments become more sensitive to interest rates as the mortgage ages (see Exhibit 17).

Other Factors: Some of the other factors provided interesting insight into prepayment behavior. Limited documentation mortgages tended to pay more in curtailments, probably reflecting the difficulties that these borrowers have in finding refinancing. Borrowers outside of California tend to pay more curtailments than borrowers in California.

BACK-TESTING

The first test of the model simulated prepayment predictions for the historical data which we used to fit the model. Exhibit 18 provides the fit across all coupons. In Exhibits 19, 20, and 21, we broke up the predictions into coupon ranges of 8% to 10%, 10% to 12%, and greater than 12%. The linear regression of predicted monthly prepayments versus real prepayment produces a R^2 of 89%. The slope is 0.91, indicating that the model tends to

Exhibit 18.   RFC 30-Year Prepayment: Back-Testing for All Coupons

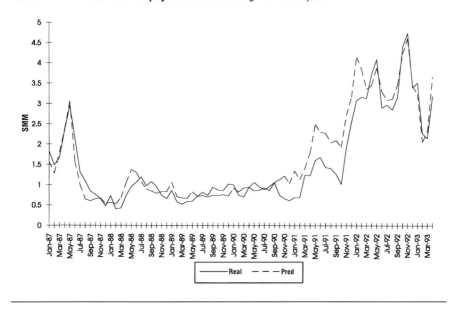

Exhibit 19.   RFC 30-Year Prepayment: Back-Testing for 8-10% Coupons

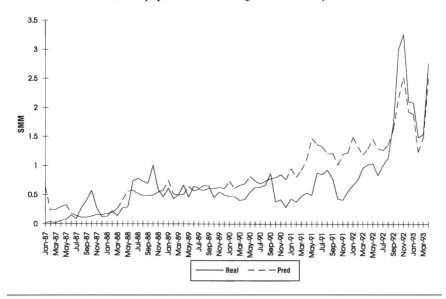

Exhibit 20. RFC 30-Year Prepayment: Back-Testing for 10-12% Coupons

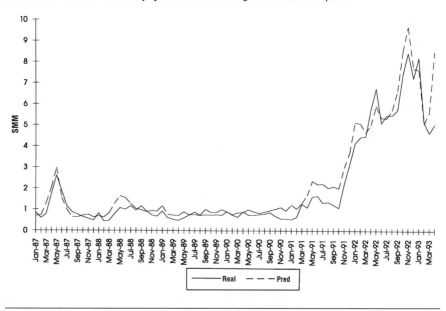

Exhibit 21. RFC 30-Year Prepayment: Back-Testing for >12% Coupons

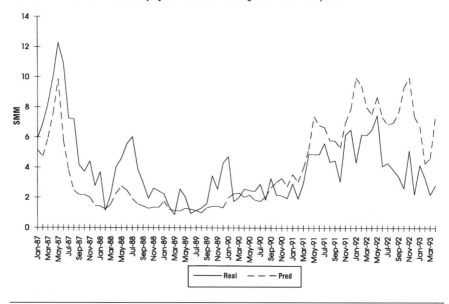

slightly underpredict prepayments. The predictions for the 10% to 12% coupon range gives the best results for back-testing because that range contains the most observations.

CONCLUSION

The results show that there is clearly a distinction between prepayment behavior of conforming and non-conforming loans. Surprisingly, the differences do not appear to be significantly related to the size of the loan. Other demographic characteristics of the loan or the borrower do have a very large impact on the probability that the borrower prepays.

While RFC borrowers prepay about 50% faster on average than agency borrowers, the results clearly show that multiplying the results of an agency prepayment model by 1.5 would not provide an accurate model for RFC prepayments. RFC borrowers with low coupon loans (10% lower than the current refinancing rate) refinance or relocate at about the same rate as borrowers in agency pools. However, current coupon and premium RFC collateral prepays significantly faster than agency collateral, even after taking the higher RFC refinancing rate into account. This relationship is so non-linear that a multiplier applied to an agency model would not capture it.

The seasoning behavior of RFC loans parallels the behavior of the agency collateral, but some significant differences do exist. First, the RFC borrowers appear to have a much higher probability of relocating after about 8 to 10 years. Second, the higher refinancing/relocation rate for RFC means that very few loans survive past 120 months in age. This holds true even for lower coupon RFC loans; relatively few loans migrate to the 240-month cohorts. Agency pools, on the other hand, start thinning out when the age is greater than 240 months.

Curtailments do not play a big part in prepayments until the loans have reached a WARM of 100 to 150 months. When a loan reaches this stage, curtailments pick up dramatically and become sensitive to changes in interest rates. Otherwise, curtailments are a very small part of the total prepayment forecast and are very insensitive to changes in interest rates.

Other characteristics about a loan also affect the probability that a loan refinances. The most important of these factors is the adjusted LTV. As we described earlier, we adjusted the LTV to estimate the effect of prior amortization. However, LTV was also important when we kept it constant from the time of origination. Loans with lower LTVs prepay at much higher rates. A deal could be exposed to very high prepay potential if its demographic characteristics are concentrated in low LTV loans meant for purchasing homes.

While this study and the model lend important insights into prepayments on all loans, there is still significant work that needs to be done to understand whole loan prepayment behavior.

APPENDIX A

Aggregation Rules

Factor Buckets 1.00 to 0.95
0.95 to 0.90
0.90 to 0.85
0.85 to 0.80
0.80 to 0.70
0.70 to 0.50
0.50 to 0.30
0.30 to 0.00
For example, if the loan's factor was 0.97, then that loan should be grouped with all other loans between 1 and 0.95.

Geographic California versus non-California

Age Buckets   0-10
(Months)   11-20
21-30
31-60
61-120
121-240
241-360

Mortgage Size $200,000 and smaller
$200,001 to $400,000
$400,001 and larger

Purpose Owner Purchase
Rate-term
Equity refinancing and other

Quality Code Full documentation
Limited documentation

WAC Buckets 7.5% and lower
7.5%-8.5%
8.5%-9.0%
9.0%-9.5%
9.5%-10%
10%-11%

11%-12%
12%-13%
14% and higher

WAC Range   5% - 15%

APPENDIX B

The Logistic Function

The decision to prepay a mortgage when the mortgage rates fall can be modeled using detection theory. The Neyman-Pearson Lemma is a well-known result from detection theory that states that the optimum decision statistic for determining the presence or absence of the condition is the likelihood ratio, the ratio of the probability of an event occurring divided by the probability that the condition is absent:

$$p/(1-p)$$

Since SMM is the probability that one dollar will leave a pool, the prepayment function, and especially the incentive to refinance, can be specified in terms of the Neyman-Pearson Lemma. For example, as the refinancing incentive increases we would expect the probability of a loan leaving the pool to go up.

However, this function is extremely non-linear. Since the logarithm is a monotonically increasing function, we can transform the likelihood ratio into a linear function. If we assume that the function has a linear form depending on an underlying variable X (ratio between the WAC and the current refinancing rate), then we have:

$$aX + b = \ln(p/(1-p))$$

$$\exp(aX + b) = p/(1-p)$$

$$p = \exp(aX + b)/[1+\exp(aX + b)]$$

Where p = SMM/100 = probability that \$1.00 will leave the pool;

$$1 / \text{Variance} = N(p)(1-p) = (\text{amount outstanding}) \, p \, (1-p)$$

SECTION III

STRIPPED MORTGAGE-BACKED SECURITIES

CHAPTER 14

Stripped Mortgage-Backed Securities

Lakhbir S. Hayre, DPhil
Director of Mortgage Research
Salomon Brothers

Errol Mustafa, Ph.D.

Vincent Pica
Managing Director
Prudential Securities Inc.

INTRODUCTION

As the mortgage pass-through market has matured, a number of derivative mortgage products have been introduced to appeal to different investors of the fixed-income market. In 1983, FHLMC launched the Collateralized Mortgage Obligation (CMO) structure that enabled issuers to tailor-make mortgage securities according to investor coupon, maturity, and prepayment-risk specifications.[1] In July 1986, FNMA introduced a new addition to the mortgage security product line—Stripped Mortgage-Backed Securities (SMBSs). By redistributing portions of the interest and/or principal cash flows from a pool of mortgage loans to two or more SMBSs, FNMA developed a new class of mortgage securities that enabled investors to take strong market positions on expected movements in prepayment and interest rates.

SMBSs are highly sensitive to changes in prevailing interest and prepayment rates and tend to display asymmetric returns. SMBS certificates that are allocated large proportions or all of the underlying principal cash flows tend to display very attractive *bullish* return profiles. As market rates drop and

---

Dr. Hayre was Director of Mortgage Research in the Financial Strategies Group at Prudential Securities Inc. when this chapter was written. Dr. Mustafa was Vice President in the Financial Strategies Group at Prudential Securities Inc. when this chapter was written.

1 CMOs are discussed in Section IV of this book.

prepayments on the underlying collateral increase, the return of these SMBSs will be greatly enhanced since principal cash flows will be returned earlier than expected. Conversely, SMBSs that are entitled to a large percentage or all of the interest cash flows have very appealing *bearish* return characteristics since greater amounts of interest cash flows are generated when prepayments of principal decrease (typically when market rates increase).

This chapter is divided into three sections: The first section provides an overview of the SMBS market and discusses the various types of SMBSs. The second section examines the investment characteristics of SMBSs. A review of the fundamentals of mortgage cash flows is first presented, followed by an investigation of the price, OAS, effective duration, and convexity characteristics of SMBSs. The third section describes various SMBS applications and the use of SMBSs in portfolio hedging strategies.

OVERVIEW OF THE STRIPPED MORTGAGE-BACKED SECURITIES (SMBS) MARKET
Size of the SMBS Market

The SMBS market has grown substantially since the introduction of the first SMBS in July 1986 (see Exhibit 1). In total, an estimated $81.1 billion SMBSs in 306 issues have come to market as of March 1993. FNMA has been the predominant issuer of SMBSs. The remainder of new SMBSs have been issued by private concerns and FHLMC.

Types of SMBSs

Strip securities exist in various forms. The first and earliest type of mortgage strip securities are called *synthetic-coupon pass-through securities.* Synthetic-coupon pass-throughs receive fixed proportions of the principal and interest cash flow from a pool of underlying mortgage loans. Synthetic-coupon pass-throughs were introduced by FNMA in mid-1986 through its "Alphabet" Strip Program. IOs and POs, the second and most common type of strip security, were introduced by FNMA in January 1987. *IOs* and *POs* received, respectively, only the interest or only the principal cash flow from the underlying mortgage collateral. More recently, a third type of strip security, the *CMO strip,* has become popular among issuers and investors. As implied by their name, CMO strips are tranches within a CMO issue that receive only principal cash flows or have synthetically high coupon rates.

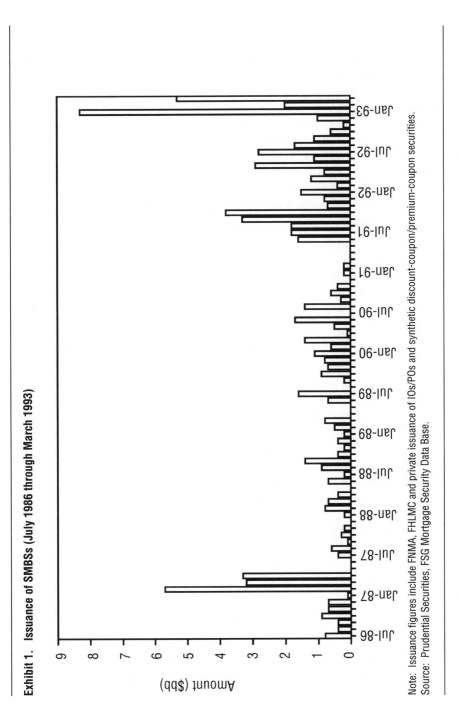

Exhibit 1. Issuance of SMBSs (July 1986 through March 1993)

Note: Issuance figures include FNMA, FHLMC and private issuance of IOs/POs and synthetic discount-coupon/premium-coupon securities.
Source: Prudential Securities, FSG Mortgage Security Data Base.

Development of the SMBS Market

The first mortgage strips—FNMA SMBS "alphabet" strip securities. FNMA pioneered the first stripped mortgage security in July 1986 through its newly created SMBS Program. For each issue of SMBS Series A through L, FNMA pooled existing FHA/VA and GPM mortgage loans that had been held in its portfolio and issued two SMBS pass-through certificates representing ownership interests in proportions of the interest and principal cash flows from the underlying mortgage loan pool. Alphabet strips were subsequently called synthetic discount- and premium-coupon securities since the coupon rate of the alphabet strip was quoted as a percentage of the total principal balance of the issue.[2] In total, 12 alphabet strip deals were issued by FNMA in 1986 totaling $2.9 billion.

The FNMA SMBS trust program and IOs and POs. The successive and current FNMA strip program, the SMBS Trust Program begun in 1987, provides a vehicle through which deal managers (e.g., investment banks) can swap FNMA pass-throughs for FNMA SMBS Trust certificates. In the swapping process, eligible FNMA pass-through securities submitted by the deal manager are consolidated by FNMA into one FNMA Megapool Trust. In return, FNMA distributes to the deal manager two similarly denominated SMBS certificates evidencing ownership in the requested proportions of that FNMA Megapool Trust's principal and interest cash flows.[3]

To date, the majority of FNMA SMBS Trusts have contained IO and PO securities. IOs and POs represent the most leveraged means of capturing the asymmetric performance characteristics of the two cash-flow components of mortgage securities. Recently, however, the SMBS market has witnessed a resurgence in synthetic-coupon security issuance (see FNMA Trust 66, 68, and 72). Although IOs and POs can be combined in different ratios to create synthetic-coupon securities, some investors have shown a preference for one-certificate synthetic securities due to their bookkeeping ease.

To promote liquidity in the SMBS Market, all FNMA SMBS certificates (except FNMA SMBS Series L) have a unique conversion feature that enables like-denominations of both classes of a FNMA SMBS issue or Trust

---

2 For example, a strip that receives 75% interest and 50% principal of the cash flow from a FNMA 10% would be a synthetic 15% coupon security since the 7.50% coupon is expressed as 100% of principal (i.e., 7.50% coupon/50% principal = 15.00% coupon/100% principal). By the same logic, a strip security from a FNMA 10% that receives 50% interest and 1% principal would be a 5,000% coupon security.

3 FNMA tightly restricts the type of collateral that can be placed in Trust. For example, all mortgage securities must have the same prefix (be of the same loan type) and be within certain WAC and WAM ranges to correspond with preliminary pricing. Moreover, the minimum initial principal balance of each SMBS Trust must be $200 million.

to be exchanged on the book-entry system of the Federal Reserve Banks for like-denominations of FNMA MBS certificates or Megapool certificates. The Federal Reserve generally charges an administration fee for this service. Any converted FNMA MBS certificate or Megapool certificate is subsequently *not* exchangeable for SMBS certificates. Because of the potential for profitable arbitrages, the aggregate price of the two classes of any same FNMA issue or Trust tend to be slightly higher than the price of a comparable-coupon and remaining-term FNMA pass-through certificate.

All FNMA SMBS pass-throughs (alphabets and Trusts) have the same payment structure, payment delays, and FNMA guarantee as regular FNMA pass-throughs. Payment histories and other relevant information can be obtained by referencing the pool number of the Megapool Trust. As of March 1993, 205 FNMA SMBS Trust deals have come to market, totaling approximately $54.6 billion.

Private issuance. Investment firms began to issue private-label SMBSs in late 1986. To date, it is estimated that 34 private-label SMBS issues totaling approximately $6.9 billion have been brought to market. Many of these private-label SMBSs were issued through REMIC structures. Since one class of a REMIC issue must be designated the residual interest, the super-premium coupon class of many of these private-label SMBSs is often the residual interest of the REMIC deal. Unlike investing in FNMA SMBSs, investors who purchase these residual securities are responsible for the tax consequences of the entire REMIC issue.

Recent Developments in the SMBS Market

A number of recent developments have occurred in the SMBS market that should further enhance its depth and efficiency. Among them are:

PO-collateralized CMOs. Profitable arbitrage opportunities have led to the recent introduction of CMO securities collateralized by POs. PO-collateralized CMOs allocate the cash flow from underlying PO securities between several CMO tranches with different maturities and payment patterns. The potential for profitable arbitrages with PO securities has enhanced the efficiency of the SMBS market by effectively placing a floor on the price potential of POs and a price ceiling on corresponding IOs in a given market environment. To date, 124 PO-collateralized CMOs totaling approximately $50.8 billion have been issued by FNMA and private issuers.

CMO strip securities. Strip securities are increasingly included in CMO issues as regular-interest (non-residual) CMO tranches. CMO strip securities that pay only principal or large proportions of interest cash flows (relative to principal cash flows) over the underlying mortgage collateral's life are termed PO securities and "high-interest" securities,[4] respectively, and tend to have performance characteristics similar to FNMA SMBSs. Other types of CMO strip securities receive initial and on-going collateral principal or interest cash flows after other classes in the CMO issue are retired or have been paid. These types of strip CMO securities are structured as PO or "high-interest" PACs, TACs, or Super-POs and perform differently from FNMA SMBSs.[5]

FHLMC stripped giant program. FHLMC has also become a participant in the SMBS market. In October 1989, FHLMC announced its Stripped Giant Mortgage Participation Certificate Program. As of March 1993, FHLMC had issued 34 FHLMC Giant PO and IO PCs totaling approximately $10.1 billion.

FHLMC's Stripped Giant Program is similar to FNMA's swap SMBS Trust Program. Deal managers submit FHLMC PCs to FHLMC; FHLMC, in turn, aggregates these PCs into Giant pools and issues Strip Giant PCs representing desired proportions of principal and interest to the deal manager. All FHLMC Strip PCs have the same payment structure, payment delays and payment guarantee as regular FHLMC PCs. Like FNMA SMBSs, FHLMC Giant Strip IOs and POs have a conversion feature that allows them to be exchanged for similarly denominated FHLMC PCs. Characteristics of each FHLMC Giant Strip issue can be referenced by their pool number. 30-year and 15-year FHLMC IO securities are identified by the FHLMC prefix 90 and 92, respectively, while 30-year and 15-year PO or synthetic securities have 80 and 82 prefixes, respectively.

FHLMC Gold MACs Program

GNMA collateral for FNMA SMBSs. In 1990 FNMA began to issue SMBSs collateralized by GNMA pass-through certificates. Since the beginning of 1990, FNMA has issued 50 trusts that have had underlying GNMA collateral. The increased availability of GNMA SMBSs has further broadened the investor base of SMBSs, enhance the liquidity of the SMBS market and increase the number of hedging alternatives available to GNMA investors.

Buyers of SMBSs

The asymmetric returns of SMBSs appeal to a broad variety of investors. SMBSs can be used effectively to hedge interest-rate and prepayment exposure of other types of mortgage securities, such as CMO residuals and

---

4 Since regular interests of a CMO issue currently must have a notional principal balance to qualify for REMIC tax status, true IO CMO securities do not exist. Typically, 99.5% of the initial value of a high-interest security is comprised of interest cash flows and .5% is comprised of principal.

5 For a description of CMO security types, please see Chapter 16.

premium-coupon mortgage pass-through securities. SMBSs also can be combined with other fixed-income securities such as U.S. Treasuries and mortgage securities to enhance the total return of the portfolio in varying interest-rate scenarios. Insurance companies and pension funds with conservative duration-matching needs frequently use SMBSs as a method of tailoring their investment portfolio to meet the duration of liabilities and thus minimize interest-rate risk.

SMBSs are used by various types of investors to accomplish their investment objectives. Insurance companies, pension funds, money-managers and other total rate-of-return accounts use SMBSs to improve the return of their fixed-income portfolios. PO securities, which tend to have long durations, enable pension funds to more effectively manage the duration of their portfolios. Thrift institutions and mortgage bankers often use PO securities to hedge their servicing portfolios or use IO securities as a substitute for servicing income.[6]

INVESTMENT CHARACTERISTICS

SMBSs enable investors to capture the performance characteristics of the principal or interest components of the cash flows of mortgage pass-through securities. These individual components display contrasting responses to changes in market rates and prepayment rates. Principal-only (PO) SMBSs are bullish instruments, outperforming mortgage pass-throughs in declining interest-rate environments. Interest-only (IO) SMBSs are bearish investments that can be used as a hedge against rising interest rates.

Variation of Interest and Principal Components with Prepayments

The cash flows that an MBS investor receives each month consist of principal and interest payments from a large group of home owners. The proportion of principal and interest in the total payment varies depending on the prepayment level of the mortgage pool. Exhibit 2 illustrates these cash flows for a $1 million 30-year FNMA current coupon pass-through security at various PSA prepayment speeds.

The top portion of Exhibit 2 shows the interest component and the lower portion shows the principal component of the monthly cash flows. Since the interest is proportional to the outstanding balance, the top part of

---

6 According to the applicable risk-based capital guidelines, strip securities that are backed by agency (FNMA, FHLMC and GNMA) pass-through securities (agency-issue or private-label issue) are in the 100% risk-based category for thrift institutions and commercial banks.

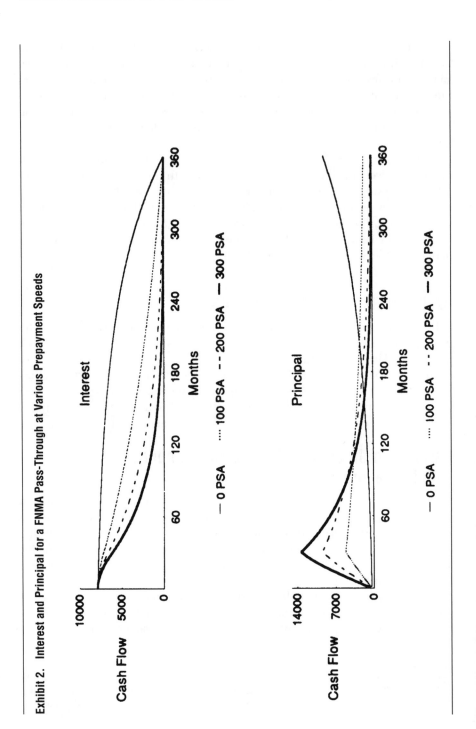

Exhibit 2. Interest and Principal for a FNMA Pass-Through at Various Prepayment Speeds

Exhibit 2 also can be viewed as showing the decline in the mortgage balance at the various prepayment speeds.

At a zero prepayment level, the interest and principal cash flows in Exhibit 2 compose a normal amortization schedule. In the earlier months of the security's life, the cash flows primarily contain interest payments. This occurs because interest payments are calculated based on the outstanding principal balance remaining on the mortgage loans at the beginning of each month. As the mortgage loans amortize, the cash flows increasingly reflect the payment of principal. Towards the end of the security's life, principal payments make up the bulk of the cash flows.

Prepayments of principal significantly alter the principal and interest cash flows received by the mortgage pass-through investor. Home owners who prepay all or part of their mortgage loans return more principal to the investor in the earlier years of the mortgage security. All else being equal, an increase in prepayments has two effects:

1. The time remaining until return of principal is reduced as shown in Exhibit 2. At 100% PSA, the average life of the principal cash flows is 12.4 years while at faster speeds of 200% PSA and 300% PSA, principal is returned in average time periods of 8.2 years and 6 years, respectively.

2. The total amount of interest cash flows is reduced, which also is illustrated in Exhibit 2. This occurs because interest payments are calculated based on the amount of principal outstanding at the beginning of each month and higher prepayment levels reduce the amount of principal outstanding.

Effect of prepayment changes on value. A mortgage pass-through represents the combined value of the interest and principal cash flows. The effects of prepayments on the present value of each of these components tend to offset each other. Increases in prepayments reduce the time remaining until repayment of principal. The sooner the principal is repaid, the higher the present value of the principal. Conversely, since increasing levels of prepayments reduce interest cash flows, the value of the interest decreases.

Thus, the interest and principal cash flows individually are much more sensitive to prepayment changes than the combined mortgage pass-through. This is illustrated in Exhibit 3, which shows the present values of the principal and interest components of a FNMA current coupon pass-through at various prepayment levels.

The greater sensitivity of IOs and POs to prepayment changes is further illustrated in Exhibit 4, which shows the realized yields to maturity (or internal rates of return) for a typical IO and PO and for the underlying collateral for given purchase prices.

The IO and PO reflect sharply contrasting responses to prepayment changes; the IO's yield falls sharply as prepayments increase, while the PO's yield falls sharply as prepayments decrease. The yield of the underlying collateral is, on the other hand, relatively stable since it is assumed to be priced close to par.

Price performance of SMBSs. The discussion above indicates that prepayment speeds are by far the most important determinant of the value of an SMBS. Since the price response of an SMBS to interest-rate changes is deter-

Exhibit 3. Present Values of Principal and Interest Components of Cash Flows at Various Prepayment Speeds

Exhibit 4. Realized Yields to Maturity for a Current Coupon IO and PO and the underlying Collateral at Various Prepayment Speeds

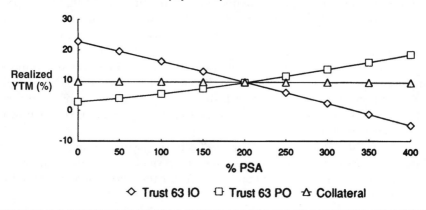

mined, to a large extent, by how the collateral's prepayment speed is affected by the interest-rate changes, we will start with a discussion of mortgage-prepayment behavior.

The prepayment S-curve. The prepayment speed of an MBS is a function of the security's characteristics (such as coupon and age), interest rates, and other economic and demographic variables.[7] While detailed prepayment projections generally require an econometric model, the investor can obtain some insight into the likely behavior of an SMBS by examining the spread between the collateral's gross coupon and current mortgage rates.

This spread is generally the most important variable in determining prepayment speeds. With respect to this spread, prepayment speeds have an "S" shape; speeds are fairly flat for discount coupons (when the spread is negative and prepayments are caused mainly by housing turnover), start increasing when the spread becomes positive, surge rapidly until the spread is several hundred basis points and then level off when the security is a high premium. At this point, there is already substantial economic incentive for mortgage holders to refinance and further increases in the spread lead to only marginal increases in refinancing activity. This S-curve is illustrated in Exhibit 5, which shows projected long-term prepayments for current coupon collateral for specified changes in mortgage rates.

In the remainder of this section, we make repeated references to Exhibit 5, as the performance of an SMBS can be explained to a large extent by the position of its collateral on the prepayment S-curve.[8]

---

7 Prepayment modeling is discussed in Section II of this book.

8 However, the investor should note that not all aspects of prepayment behavior are explained by the spread between the coupon and the mortgage rate.

The projected prepayments shown in Exhibit 5 are long-term averages. Month-to-month prepayment rates vary (for example, due to seasonality) even if mortgage rates do not change.

If a substantial and sustained decline in mortgage rates occurs, then mortgage holders exposed to refinancing incentives for the first time initially exhibit a sharp increase in prepayments. This gradually decreases as the homeowners most anxious and able to refinance do so. This non-interest rate-related decline in the prepayment speeds of premium coupons usually is referred to as "burnout." The projected speeds shown in the declining-rate scenarios are the averages of the high early speeds and lower later speeds.

For seasoned coupons that have experienced a heavy refinancing period, burnout implies that prepayments may be less responsive to declines in interest rates. This applies to the majority of premium coupons currently outstanding.

The age effect on prepayments is well known. Prepayment speeds are low for new mortgages and increase gradually until the mortgages are two to three years old, after which the age is less important. This means that, other things being equal, an IO is worth more if it is collateralized by new FNMA 9s, for example, than by seasoned FNMA 9s.

Projected price behavior. Exhibit 6 gives projected price paths for a current coupon IO and PO for parallel interest-rate shifts.[9]

The projected price behavior of the SMBSs as interest rates change can be explained largely by the prepayment S-curve in Exhibit 5.

- As rates drop from current levels, the collateral begins to experience sharp increases in prepayments. Compounded by lower discount rates,

Exhibit 5. Projected Prepayments for Curent Coupon FNMA Collateral

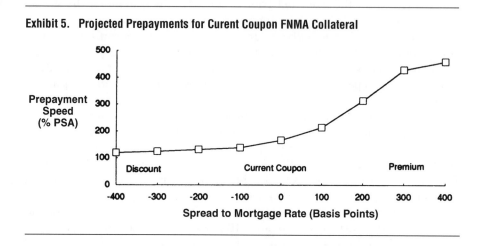

Exhibit 6. Projected Prices for a Current Coupon FNMA IO and PO

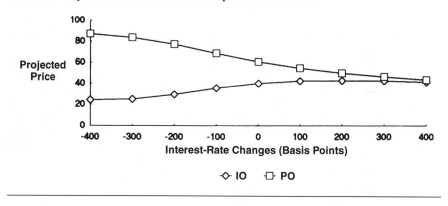

---

9 The prices are calculated to give an option-adjusted spread (OAS) of 100 basis points in all cases. A discussion of OAS analysis is given in the next section. Note that if it is also priced at an OAS of 100 basis points, the collateral price is just the sum of the IO and PO prices.

this causes substantial price appreciation for the PO. For the IO, however, the higher prepayments outweigh the lower discount rates and the net result is a price decline.

- If rates drop by several hundred basis points, the collateral becomes a high-premium coupon and prepayments plateau. The rates of price appreciation of the PO and price depreciation of the IO both decrease. Eventually the IO's price starts to increase, as the effect of lower discount rates start to outweigh the effect of marginal increases in prepayments.

- If rates rise, the slower prepayments and higher discount rates combine to cause a steep drop in the price of the PO. The IO is aided initially by the slower prepayments, giving the IO negative duration, but eventually prepayments plateau on the lower side of the prepayment S-curve and the IO's price begins to decrease.

Effective duration and convexity. Exhibit 6 indicates that for current or low-premium collateral, POs tend to have large, positive effective durations while IOs have large, negative effective durations.[10]

The effective durations in Exhibit 7 reflect the price paths in Exhibit 6:

- For the PO, as rates decline, the effective duration initially increases, reflecting its rapid price appreciation as prepayments surge. Note that this is in complete contrast to traditional measures such as Macaulay or modified duration, which, reflecting the shortening maturity of the PO,

---

10 Effective duration is a measure of the proportional price change if interest rates change by a small amount. Let $PRICE(0)$ be the current price of a security. Let $PRICE(\Delta)$ be the price if interest rates increase by a small amount Δ and $PRICE(-\Delta)$ be the price if interest rates decrease by a small amount Δ. Then

$$\text{Effective Duration} = \frac{\text{Price}(-\Delta) - \text{Price}(\Delta)}{PRICE(0) \times 2\Delta} \times 100$$

This formula is straightforward; we take the total price change (the difference in the new prices), divide by the interest-rate change (2Δ), and, since we want a proportional price change, divide by the initial price (the 100 is a scaling factor).

To obtain the projected prices and durations, we have, for simplicity, assumed parallel shifts in interest rates. In practice, of course, rates do not move in parallel (typically, short-term rates tend to be more volatile than long rates). However, using nonparallel yield-curve shifts raises questions which, while interesting, are best left for another book. For example, suppose the yield curve shifts such that short rates move twice as much as long rates, and we compute the corresponding price change. The effective duration will be twice as large if we compare the price change against the change in short rates (*i.e.*, Δ = change in short rates) as opposed to comparing the price change against the change in long rates (*i.e.*, Δ = change in long rates).

would actually decrease. As rates continue to drop, the PO's effective duration levels off and then decreases, reflecting both a leveling off of prepayments and the fact that, to calculate the effective duration, we are dividing by an increasing price. If rates increase, the PO's duration decreases but remains positive.

- For the IO, the effective duration is initially negative and decreases rapidly as rates drop, before eventually increasing and becoming positive after prepayments plateau. If rates increase, the duration increases and eventually becomes positive.

Convexity measures the rate of change of duration and is useful in indicating whether the trend in price change is likely to accelerate or decelerate. It is calculated by comparing the price change if interest rates decrease with the price change if rates increase.[11] Exhibit 8 shows the convexities obtained using the projected prices in Exhibit 6.

Comparing Exhibit 8 with Exhibits 6 and 7 shows that the convexity indicates how the duration is changing. When the duration is increasing (as

Exhibit 7. Effective Durations of a Current Coupon FNMA IO and PO

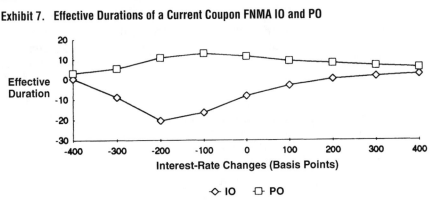

---

11 Convexity is calculated by comparing the price changes if rates move up or down by small amounts. Let

$\Delta P^+ = \text{PRICE}(0) - \text{PRICE}(\Delta)$

$\Delta P^- = \text{PRICE}(-\Delta) - \text{PRICE}(0)$

where ΔP^+ and ΔP^- are the price changes if rates increase or decrease by Δ, respectively. Then

$$\text{Convexity} = \frac{\Delta P^- - \Delta P^+}{\text{PRICE}(0) \times \Delta \times \Delta} \times 100$$

in the case of the PO when rates begin to decline from the initial value), the convexity is positive, and when the duration is decreasing, the convexity is negative. For example, the IO's convexity is initially negative but begins to increase after rates fall by more than 100 basis points; although the duration is still negative at –200 basis points, the positive convexity indicates that the duration is increasing. The peak in the convexity of the IO at a change of –300 basis points indicates that the *rate* of increase in its duration is greatest at this point, as shown in Exhibit 7; the slope of the IO's duration curve is higher from –200 to –300 than from –300 to –400.

In summary, the prepayment S-Curve implies that for SMBSs collateralized by:

- Current or discount pass-throughs, the PO has substantial upside potential and little downside risk, while the converse is true for IOs;

- Low premiums, there is somewhat comparable upside potential and downside risk;

- High premiums (including the majority of SMBSs issued to date), the PO has little upside potential and significant downside risk while the reverse is true for IOs.

Pricing of SMBSs and Option-Adjusted Spreads

The strong dependence of SMBS cash flows on future prepayment rates, combined with the typically asymmetric response of prepayments to interest-rate changes, make traditional measures of return such as yield to maturity of limited usefulness in analyzing or pricing SMBSs. The most common method

Exhibit 8. Convexities of a Current Coupon IO and PO

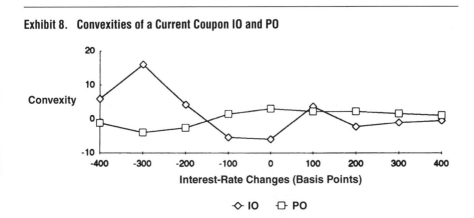

of pricing SMBSs is with OASs. OAS analysis uses probabilistic methods to evaluate the security over the full range of interest-rate paths that may occur over its term. The impact of prepayment variations on the security's cash flows is factored into the analysis. The OAS is the resulting average spread over Treasuries provided by the security.[12] It gives a long-term average value of the security assuming a market-neutral viewpoint on interest rates.

Exhibit 9 shows the use of OAS analysis for FNMA Trust 215 and FNMA Trust 6 and the underlying pass-through collateral. In each case, the price is chosen to give an OAS of 100 basis points at a 15% annual volatility of short-term interest rates. Also shown are the yields to maturity and standard spreads over the WAL Treasury at these prices using a projected prepayment speed.

The OAS at a 0% volatility when mortgage rates stay at current levels, is typically close to the standard Treasury spread in a flat yield curve environment. The difference between the OASs at 0% and 15% volatilities, which we label the *option cost*, is a measure of the impact of prepayment variations on a security for the given level of interest-rate volatility. The option cost, to a large extent, does not depend on the pricing level or the absolute

Exhibit 9. OAS Analysis of SMBSs

		Price	YTM	WAL	SPD/Tsy.	OAS @ Vol. 0%	OAS @ Vol. 15%	Opt. Cost
FNMA Trust 215	PO	61-30+	6.25	9.0	35	30	100	−70
FN 7% Coll.	IO	38-11	8.39	9.0	248	280	100	180
WAM 29-09 Years	PT	100-10	6.70	9.0	108	114	100	14
Proj. PAS: 156%								
FNMA Trust 6	PO	82-18+	6.29	3.4	182	138	100	38
FN 9% Coll.	IO	24-05	7.05	3.4	257	72	100	28
WAM 22-04 Years	PT	108-21	6.50	3.4	201	120	100	20
Proj. PSA: 413%								

Note: PT stands for pass-through; projected prepayment speeds are obtained from the Prudential Securities Prepayment Model; and the option cost is the difference in OASs at short-rate volatilities of 0% and 15% per annum. Analysis based on yield curve from close on March 30, 1993.

12 More detailed descriptions of the OAS and how it is calculated is presented in Section VI of this book and the following sources: Lakhbir S. Hayre, *An OAS Primer*, Financial Strategies Group, Prudential Securities Inc., July 1989, and Lakhbir S. Hayre and Kenneth Lauterbach, "Option-Adjusted Spread Analysis," Chapter 29 in Frank J. Fabozzi and T. Dessa Fabozzi (eds.), *The Handbook of Fixed Income Securities* (Burr Ridge, IL: Irwin Professional Publishing, 1995).

level of prepayment projections (although it does depend on the slope, or response, of prepayment projections to interest-rate changes). Hence, the option cost is a measure of the intrinsic effect of likely interest-rate changes on an SMBS.

Before discussing the option costs in Exhibit 9, note that, in general, interest-rate and prepayment variations have two effects on an MBS:

1. For any callable security, being called in a low interest-rate environment typically has an adverse effect, since a dollar of principal of the security in general would be worth more than the price at which it is being returned. (An exception is a mortgage prepayment resulting from housing turnover, when the call could be uneconomic from the call-holder's point of view.) To put it another way, the principal that is being returned typically has to be reinvested at yields lower than that provided by the existing security.

2. For MBSs priced at a discount or a premium, changes in prepayments result in the discount or premium being received sooner or later than anticipated. This may mitigate or reinforce the call effect discussed in (1).

In general, the first effect is much more important than the second; however, for certain deep-discount securities, such as POs, the second effect may at times outweigh the first. The net result of the two effects depends on the position of the collateral on the prepayment curve shown in Exhibit 5.

- FNMA Trust 215, shown in Exhibit 9, illustrates the characteristics typical of SMBSs collateralized by current or discount coupons. For discount or current-coupon collateral, prepayments are unlikely to fall significantly but could increase dramatically if there is a substantial decrease in interest rates. This asymmetry means that the PO is, on average, likely to gain significantly from variations in prepayment speeds. The option cost for the PO is usually negative, *i.e.*, the PO *gains* from interest-rate volatility indicating that the benefits of faster return of principal outweigh the generic negative effects of being called in low interest-rate environments. On the other hand, the underlying collateral tends to have a positive (but usually small in the case of discount collateral) option cost; the negative effects of being called when rates are low outweigh the benefits of faster return of principal. Finally, the IO typically has a large positive option cost; the asymmetric nature of likely prepayment changes, discussed above, means that the IO gains little if interest rates increase (since prepayments will not decrease significantly), while a substantial decline in rates is likely to lead to a surge in prepayments and a drop in interest cash flows.

- FNMA Trust 6 is representative of most outstanding SMBSs, which currently have premium collateral. For *premium* collateral, there is, generally speaking, potential for both increases and decreases in prepayments, and the net effect of prepayment variations will depend on the particular coupon and prevailing mortgage rates. Seasoned premiums, for example, will not have potential for substantial increases in speeds and, hence, FNMA Trust 6 PO has a positive option cost. The collateral has a positive option cost for the same reasons. The IO has a negative option indicating that the beneficial effect of prepayment variations outweighs call effects for this security.

The importance of likely variations in prepayments makes the standard yield to maturity of very little relevance in pricing SMBSs and therefore, they tend to be priced (as in Exhibit 9) on an OAS basis.

HEDGING APPLICATIONS
Hedging Prepayment Risk and Interest-Rate Risk

The much higher price sensitivity and yield sensitivity of IOs and POs to changes in interest rates and prepayments compared with non-stripped mortgage pass-throughs have been discussed in the preceding section. It is natural, therefore, to consider whether a portfolio of several mortgage pass-through securities can be hedged adequately for short-term holding periods against changes in prepayments or interest rates with a small but highly price-sensitive position in either IOs or POs. Before discussing details of how such a hedge works in practice, it is important to consider the relationship between prepayment risk and interest-rate risk.

Prepayment risk for a security is defined as the price sensitivity of the security to changes in the rate at which unscheduled principal is prepaid. All other factors that may affect price, in particular interest-rate movements, are held constant in order to isolate prepayment risk. The much greater price sensitivities of IOs and POs to changes in prepayments compared with mortgage pass-throughs were discussed in the previous section and illustrated in Exhibit 3.

A second component of price sensitivity, referred to as interest-rate risk, arises from changes in interest rates over a given holding period. Shifts in prevailing interest rates have a direct impact on the present values of a security's cash flows and, hence, its price. In addition, changes in interest rates affect projected prepayment rates (see Investment Characteristics section) which, in turn, have a bearing on the security price. Thus, shifts in interest rates affect price both directly and indirectly (via changes in prepayments).

Mechanics of a Hedge

In the previous section, two risks that are relevant to hedging MBSs—changes in interest rates and prepayments—were described. In this section, the issue of quantifying the degree of hedging is addressed.

In hedging a portfolio of securities against a particular risk, the investor must be willing to sacrifice some portion of his potential profit (in favorable market environments) in order to reduce the variation in portfolio performance across a wide range of market environments. The investor also must consider how long the portfolio will be held before either closing out or rehedging the position. This holding period could vary from one day for an interest-rate-sensitive portfolio in a volatile market to perhaps a month or two in a more stable environment. For short holding periods, the market value of the hedge position at the end of the period is the measure of portfolio performance used in this section. An investor who wishes to evaluate a hedge on this basis must then decide:

1. The range of interest-rate (or prepayment) changes to hedge against. For example, for a one-month holding period, the investor may wish to hedge the market value of the portfolio only against gradual interest-rate moves of between +200 basis points and –200 basis points in the yield on six-month Treasuries.[13] In general, a greater variance in market value is implied by a wider range of interest-rate or prepayment changes.

2. The spread in market value of the portfolio that is considered to be acceptable. The extreme case is to hedge so that there is no change in market value across the range chosen in (1). In practice, a small variation of a few percent in market value may be acceptable.

The calculation of the market value of a hedged portfolio is done using an "average" OAS for each security in the portfolio, as described in the Investment Characteristics section earlier. Two specific examples that illustrate the unique hedging characteristics of SMBSs are discussed later.

Hedging Characteristics of IOs and POs

One reason for the attractiveness of IOs and POs as instruments for hedging MBS portfolios is that they have much higher (absolute) effective durations

---

13 Assuming a normal distribution for relative interest-rate changes, an initial interest rate of 8% and a volatility of 15%, there is a probability of approximately two-thirds that interest rates will change by no more than 35 basis points over the course of a month. Although unlikely, interest-rate moves of up to 200 basis points within a short period have occurred in recent years, e.g., following October 19, 1987.

than mortgage pass-throughs (see Exhibit 7, for example). This implies a much greater price sensitivity to changes in interest rates. An investor who wishes to reduce the price sensitivity of a portfolio to changes in interest rates can achieve this by establishing a small position in the appropriate SMBS. (The market value of the SMBS need only be a small fraction of the market value of the portfolio.) The large negative durations of IOs make these securities appropriate for hedging portfolios with an overall positive duration; POs may be used for hedging portfolios with an overall negative duration. In each case, the hedged portfolio exhibits a lower (absolute) effective duration than the unhedged portfolio. Exhibit 10 illustrates the effect of an IO and a PO on reducing the effective duration of two MBS portfolios.

The first portfolio matches the large negative duration of the Trust 215 IO with the positive duration of a GNMA 7% pass-through. A combination of approximately $41 million market value of the IO with $59 million market value of the GNMA pass-through has an overall effective duration of close to zero, and should show little price sensitivity to small changes in interest rates. The second portfolio combines the Trust 215 PO with a servicing portfolio of FNMA 8% pass-throughs as collateral (from which the servicer receives a gross coupon of 75 basis points). The servicing portfolio exhibits the features of an IO, e.g., large negative effective duration for low-premium collateral and as such is a bearish security. The combination of $35 million market value of the servicing portfolio with $65 million of the PO has an overall effective duration of close to zero. For both portfolios in Exhibit 10, variations in the mixture of the appropriate SMBS results in a synthetic security that exhibits either bullish, bearish or neutral price characteristics (as measured by overall effective duration).

Exhibit 10.   Matching Effective Duration with SMBSs

Portfolio 1*: GNMA 7 and FNMA Trust 215 IO

IO Market Value ($mm)	0	10	20	30	41	60	80	100
GNMA 8 Market Value ($mm)	100	90	80	70	59	40	20	0
Effective Duration of Portfolio	7.0	5.3	3.6	1.9	0.0	−3.2	−6.6	−10.0

Portfolio 2*: FNMA 8 Servicing Portfolio and FNMA Trust 215 PO

PO Market Value ($mm)	0	10	20	40	50	65	80	100
Servicing portfolio Market Value ($mm)	100	90	80	60	50	35	20	0
Effective Duration of Portfolio	−28.6	−24.2	−19.8	−11.0	−6.7	−0.1	6.5	15.3

*Total market value of portfolio is $100 mm.

Note: The servicing portfolio of FNMA 8% pass-through collateral receives a gross coupon of 75 basis points.

Additional points in favor of using SMBSs for hedging include:

- The market for SMBSs has become increasingly liquid as more investors take advantage of the characteristics offered by these securities. Increased liquidity facilitates the use of SMBSs for particular hedging purposes, since the appropriate SMBS or combination of SMBSs is more easily assembled in a liquid market. In a less liquid market, the limited availability of certain SMBSs would restrict the type of portfolio that can be hedged. One particular concern in an illiquid environment would be a mismatch between some of the factors affecting prepayment characteristics of the portfolio under consideration and those of the available SMBSs.[14]

- Prepayment risk for mortgage pass-throughs is best hedged with mortgage instruments such as SMBSs since Treasuries, by their very nature, have no prepayment sensitivity.

Hedging Portfolio Market Value

Exhibits 11 and 12 illustrate the sensitivity of the market value of the Trust 215 IO/GNMA 7 synthetic security and the Trust 215 PO/FNMA Servicing Portfolio synthetic security to sudden parallel shifts in the yield curve. The holding period is one month in each case and the initial market value of each portfolio is $100 million.

The total market value of each portfolio is shown for various interest-rate scenarios and for different proportions of the hedging security (SMBS). The least variation in total market value, *i.e.*, the flattest profile, for interest-rate shifts of –200 basis points to +200 basis points is obtained when approximately $20 million of the GNMA/IO combination is invested in the Trust 215 IO and $60 million of the FNMA Servicing Portfolio/PO combination is invested in the Trust 215 PO. These amounts result in a low or zero overall effective duration for each of these portfolios in the NC case (see Exhibit 10). This is hardly surprising, since a portfolio with a zero effective duration (and small convexity) in the NC base case should have a flat-market value profile for small (*i.e.*, local) changes in interest rates.

Summary

POs and IOs offer the investor the opportunity to hedge a portfolio of MBSs against interest-rate and prepayment risk for short-term holding periods. In addition, an investor can choose to adjust the proportion of the SMBS hedge in the portfolio according to his perception of market direction. The resulting customized portfolio would then offer optimal performance in a market environment that adheres to investor expectations.

---

14 One such factor is the geographical origin of the mortgages underlying the security.

Exhibit 11. Market Value of FNMA Trust 215 IO/GNMA 7 Synthetic Security

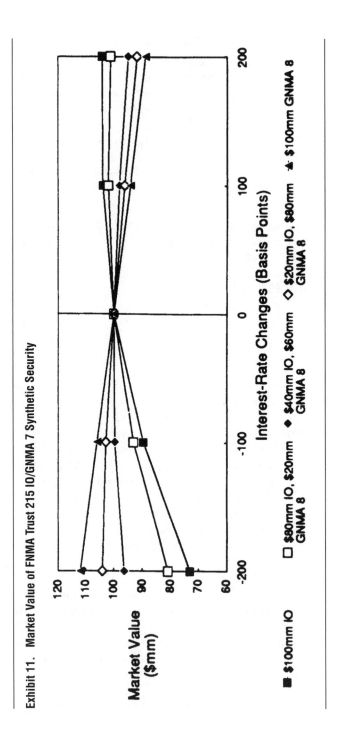

Exhibit 12. Market Value of FNMA Trust 215 PO/FNMA 8 Servicing Portfolio Synthetic Security

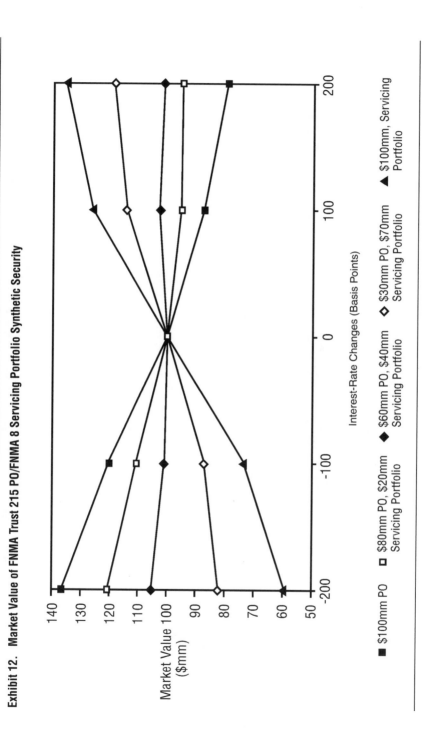

CHAPTER 15

Synthetic Mortgage-Backed Securities

Anand K. Bhattacharya, Ph.D.
Managing Director of Financial Strategies Group
Mortgage and Asset Finance Group
Prudential Securities Inc.

Carol Sze
Director of Fixed-Income Strategies
Financial Strategies Group
Prudential Securities Inc.

The structured mortgage-backed securities (MBS) market, whereby mortgage pass-through securities are used to collateralize assets spanning a wide maturity and risk-propensity spectrum, is one of the fastest growing segments of the fixed-income market.[1] Growth in the MBS market has produced a virtual alphabet soup of different types of "exotic" MBS structures—PACs, TACs, POs, PAC POs, TAC POs, super POs, IOs, PAC IOs, IO-ettes, vanilla Z-bonds, PAC Zs, companion Zs, jump Zs, floaters, inverse floaters, and the like.

These securities have appealing risk/return profiles and cash-flow characteristics in certain markets. The market-dependent features of such securities can be exploited to obtain even higher-yielding synthetic securities by combining them with other securities with opposite but equally attractive cash-flow characteristics. Moreover, the yield profile of such synthetic securities can be customized to attain a desired duration in response to a particular bullish or bearish market sentiment. However, due to the nature of these more exotic bonds, they are fairly sensitive to market changes. Investors should exercise the utmost caution when employing synthetic strategies as part of their management program.

---

1 According to Inside Mortgage Finance Publications, Inc., the approximate outstanding amount of structured MBS, as of first-quarter 1994, was $710 billion.

This chapter explores issues in the creation of synthetic securities using various types of structured MBSs.

SYNTHETIC COMBINATIONS USING SMBSs

In the creation of stripped mortgage-backed securities (SMBSs), the cash flows associated with the underlying collateral are diverted to create an interest-only (IO) security that receives 100% of the coupon cash flow and a principal-only (PO) security that receives 100% of the principal cash flow.[2] As a general rule, IOs are bearish and POs are bullish securities.

The value of these securities is mostly determined by the prepayment behavior of the underlying collateral. While the prepayment propensity of mortgages is determined by a variety of factors, such as demographics, seasonal influences, and the assumability of the underlying loans, the single largest determinant of prepayments is interest rates.

As interest rates decline, causing a resultant increase in prepayments, PO cash flows are returned faster; as the PO is usually priced at a deep discount and cash flows are returned at par, the value of the PO increases as prepayment speeds increase. On the other hand, the IO (which is a pure premium) decreases in value when prepayments speed up since its cash flow is dependent on the outstanding balance of principal, which depletes quickly in this case. As interest rates increase, causing prepayments to slow down, PO cash flows are returned at par more slowly, hence causing the value of the PO to decrease. As for the IO, the value increases since its cash flow increases due to the slower depletion of principal.

---

2 The earliest form of SMBS was issued by the Federal National Mortgage Association in the form of synthetic-coupon securities. They assumed the characterization "alphabet" strips because of the alphabetic shorthand of referring to the issuing trusts. The securities involved the partial stripping of the underlying collateral to produce two classes of securities with synthetic coupons different from that of the underlying collateral. For instance, FNMA Series B, collateralized by FNMA 9s, involved the creation of two classes in which Class 1 received 33.33% of the interest and 50% of the principal while Class 2 received 66.67% of the interest and 50% of the principal. Since Class 1 received 33.33% of the interest from 50% of the principal, the security effectively received 66.66% of the interest income. Therefore, the synthetic coupon of the security is determined as 66.66% of 9% (pass-through rate) = 6%. Similarly, since Class 2 received 66.67% of the interest from 50% of the principal, the security received 133.34% of the interest income. The synthetic coupon of this security was determined as 133.34% of 9% = 12%. Note that despite the fact that the synthetic coupons differ from the pass-through coupon, the prepayment propensity of the two classes of synthetic securities remained unchanged. Using stripping technology, a premium coupon (12%) was created with slower prepayment characteristics and a discount coupon (6%) was created with faster prepayment characteristics. Recognition of the unique risk/return characteristics of such securities led to the creation of securities that involve the complete separation of principal and interest to create IOs and POs, which has remained the structure of choice since the emergence of the SMBS market in 1986. However, in recent years, there has been a resurgence of SMBS structures with synthetic coupons.

Exhibit 1. Bullish and Bearish Synthetic Combinations

	——Immediate Interest-Rate Shifts (Basis Points) ——						
	-300	-200	-100	NC	+100	+200	+300
PSA (%)	549	437	262	151	129	126	123
				Yields (%)			
T257 PO	21.25	13.04	7.35	6.60	6.50	6.40	6.33
T257 IO	-15.25	-0.26	9.30	10.58	10.75	10.92	10.25
1:1 Ratio PO:IO	9.00	8.42	8.02	7.97	7.96	7.96	7.95
2:1 Ratio PO:IO	13.84	10.23	7.76	7.42	7.38	7.34	7.31
1:2 Ratio PO:IO	3.01	6.20	8.35	8.64	8.68	8.74	8.75

The prepayment effect on SMBSs is critically dependent on whether the underlying collateral is a discount, current, or premium coupon.[3] Note that the current coupon is usually the "cuspy coupon" (*i.e.*, it resides on the inflected part of the prepayment curve) and will react the most as interest rates change. As interest rates decline, prepayment pick-up should be greater for discount and current coupons than for premiums, since premiums should already be prepaying at faster speeds relative to discount and current coupons. This implies that POs backed by discount and current coupons will exhibit a greater increase in value than those backed by premium coupons.

As interest rates rise, IOs backed by premium and current coupons should perform better than those backed by lower coupons. Prepayment speeds on premium coupons will exhibit a sharp decline resulting in a significant loss in the value of the PO and increased value of the IO. As for discount coupons, prepayments will not slow down significantly when rates rise as such coupons should already be exhibiting slow prepayments.

Consider an example combining various amounts of current-coupon (at the time of this publication) IOs and POs to create a synthetic MBS. Exhibit 1 presents the yield profiles of several bullish and bearish synthetic combinations created using FNMA SMBS Trust 257 IO and PO, which is backed by FNMA 30-year 7.0%, which is currently a cuspy coupon. As a general rule, in order to create an x% synthetic rate from an SMBS with an underlying collateral coupon of y%, the x% synthetic combines x units of the IO class with y units of the PO class.

---

3 "Current coupon" refers to a mortgage pass-through security trading slightly below par. Using this benchmark, discount (premium) coupons are defined as securities priced at below (above) par.

For instance, in order to create a 6% synthetic coupon from FNMA SMBS Trust 257, collateralized by FNMA 7%, the synthetic would require six units of the IO and seven units of the PO. Assuming the price of the IO is 36:15 and the price of the PO is 58:3, the effective price of the 6% synthetic would be given as:

$$[(x/y) \times \text{Price of IO}] + [\text{Price of PO}] = [(6/7) \times 36{:}15] + (58{:}03)$$
$$= 89{:}11$$

Generally, in rising-rate scenarios, synthetic combinations, created by using premium collateral, outperform similar combinations using discount and current-coupon collateral because of the superior hedge value of the premium IO. In falling-rate scenarios, synthetic combinations using discount collateral outperform similar combinations using current or premium coupons because of the higher value of the discount PO. This is a reflection of the characteristics of discount, current, and premium coupons discussed earlier in this chapter.

Using the prepayment propensity and characteristics of the underlying collateral, a wide range of yield profiles can be generated by combining SMBSs. This is the premise of FHLMC's introduction of its GOLD MACS deal in January 1993.

REPLICATING SMBSs USING OPTIONS AND FUTURES

If price performance of the SMBS is affected by the prepayment propensity of the underlying collateral, so are duration and convexity. As a general rule, SMBSs collateralized by deep-discount and super-premium coupon pass-throughs exhibit interest-rate sensitivity patterns similar to those of other fixed-rate securities. The main reason for this similarity stems from the fact that prepayments of deep-discount and super-premium collateral react minimally to interest-rate changes.

For the current or slight-premium coupons, prepayments become more sensitive to interest-rate moves. Because the cash flow received by the IO and PO depends directly on the prepayment behavior of the underlying collateral, IOs backed by this coupon range take on different duration characteristics than other fixed-income securities. In other words, contrary to fixed-income securities that normally have positive durations, these IOs would have negative durations, which means that the value of the IO increases (decreases) as interest rates increase (decrease).

With respect to convexity patterns, discount and slight-premium coupon POs exhibit positive convexity. Prepayments on these coupons are likely to increase substantially as rates fall, but not decrease as dramatically when rates rise. Hence, PO prices are likely to rise at a faster rate in market rallies and decrease at a slower rate in market declines. It is for the same reason, *i.e.*, the prepayment behavior of the underlying collateral, that IO prices are likely to fall at a higher rate as rates fall and increase at a slower rate as rates rise, indicating that IOs have negative convexity.

For SMBSs collateralized by high-premium pass-throughs that are already prepaying at high rates, the convexity patterns are reversed. With the high prepayment rate of the underlying collateral, the prices of premium IOs are likely to be relatively low, while those for premium POs are likely to be relatively high. At such levels, with prepayments not expected to change substantially, premium PO prices are not likely to rise much higher in the face of a market rally. There is, however, a greater likelihood that PO prices could fall at a faster rate in the event of a market decline. In view of this consideration, such POs are likely to be negatively convex in terms of price movement. At the same time, premium IO prices could rise much higher in the event that interest rates rise, but would not fall much below existing low levels in the face of a market rally, causing the price behavior to be positively convex.

Given these results regarding the duration and convexity patterns of SMBSs, it is possible to characterize the SMBS position as an equivalent position in non-amortizing bonds and options. This description is similar to the analytical decomposition of MBSs as representing a long position in a bond and a short position in a series of call options representing the homeowners' right to prepay their loans at any time. By establishing such analytical analogues between SMBSs and equivalent positions in Treasury bonds and either OTC options or options on futures, one can exploit arbitrage opportunities between the SMBSs and the Treasury/derivatives market or create synthetic strategies that use SMBS to replicate OTC futures options positions.

With respect to options, duration and convexity characteristics of SMBSs can be replicated. There are two strategies that add convexity to a portfolio, both of which incorporate buying options; in which case, the only downside is the cost of the premium:

- *Long call options.* Long call options are positively convex because of their limited downside and virtually unlimited upside in a market rally.

- *Long put options.* With long put options, there is virtually unlimited upside in a market decline.

By the same token, the convexity of a portfolio can be decreased by incorporating opposite strategies (*i.e.*, either writing call or writing put options). The only upside in writing options is the premium received:

- Writing call options can incur potentially unlimited losses in a market rally, to the extent that market rates go to zero.

- Writing put options can incur potentially unlimited losses when the market declines, to the extent that the price goes to zero.

Given the duration and convexity patterns of SMBSs, Treasury bond- and option-equivalent positions with duration and convexity profiles similar to those of SMBSs are presented in Exhibit 2. Note that a short position in a non-amortizing bond reduces the duration of the portfolio.

Theoretically, while it is possible to create these synthetic positions, they are likely to be fraught with mortgage-to-Treasury basis risk and yield-curve risk because the Treasury and mortgage markets are affected by different fundamental factors. In the event that options on futures are used, there is the additional element of futures-to-cash basis risk.

STRUCTURED POs

As the ingenuity of financial-engineering techniques has risen in recent years, SMBSs have been included in REMIC structures as either collateral or as regular interest tranches. For instance, POs have been included in REMIC structures in which the underlying bullish features of the collateral are either dampened or emphasized to satisfy the various risk-management and yield-enhancement preferences of investors.

A typical PO-backed REMIC structure may include level I PO PACs, level II PO PACs, PO TACs, and a super PO (whose counterpart in interest bearing REMICs is the companion tranche). The principal cash-flow behavior of struc-

Exhibit 2. Treasury Bond- and Option-Equivalent Positions of SMBSs

	Collateral Type	Duration	Convexity
POs:	Current Coupon and Slight Premium	Positive	Positive
	High Premium	Positive	Negative
IOs:	Current Coupon and Slight Premium	Negative	Negative
	High Premium	Negative	Positive

	SMBS Option Equivalent Positions		
	Collateral Type	Bond	Option
POs:	Current Coupon and Slight Premium	Long	Long Call
	High Premium	Long	Short Put*
IOs:	Current Coupon and Slight Premium	Short	Short Call*
	High Premium	Short	Long Put

* To the extent that the premium is pocketed when the option is not exercised.

tured PO tranches is similar to that of interest bearing REMIC structures, except that the structured PO tranches are deep, deep discounts, and hence they are much more bullish than their interest bearing counterparts.

Consider FNMA 1994-35, which is backed by the PO side of FNMA Trust 257 SMBS. The underlying collateral is FNMA 30-year 7% with a WAC of 7.467% and a WAM of 352 months. Exhibit 3 describes each class and its sensitivities to changes in interest rates. The PO PACs (35A and 35B) have the highest priority of cash flow and pay sequentially. After the PACs are paid their scheduled principal, the PO TAC is paid its targeted principal and the

Exhibit 3.   FNMA 1994-35

Security	FNMA 94-35
Collateral	FNMA Trust 257 SMBS
Net/GWAC (%)	7/7.467
WAM (Mos.)	352
Size ($)	162,500,000
Pricing PSA (%)	250

Class	Price (32nds)	Pricing Band (% PSA)	Effective Band (% PSA)	Description
35A	92-06+	95-951	94-935	PO PAC
35B	79-22	95-611	96-606	PO PAC
35C	55-20	250-250	250-250	PO TAC
35D	42-00	NA	NA	Super PO

Yield Sensitivity (%)							
———— Immediate Interest-Rate Shifts (Basis Points) ————							
	-300	-200	-100	NC	+100	+200	+300
PSA (%)	549	311	150	128	125	122	120
35A	6.30	6.30	6.30	6.30	6.30	6.30	6.30
35B	7.39	7.39	7.39	7.39	7.39	7.39	7.39
35C	17.03	12.87	8.17	7.14	7.00	6.87	6.77
35D	123.11	16.26	4.21	3.92	3.88	3.85	3.82

Average-Life Sensitivity (Yrs.)							
———— Immediate Interest-Rate Shifts (Basis Points) ————							
	-300	-200	-100	NC	+100	+200	+300
PSA (%)	549	311	150	128	125	122	120
35A	1.32	1.32	1.32	1.32	1.32	1.32	1.32
35B	3.14	3.14	3.14	3.14	3.14	3.14	3.14
35C	4.07	5.23	7.92	8.97	9.14	9.30	9.42
35D	1.01	8.77	21.12	22.57	22.77	22.96	23.09

balance is directed to the super PO. Hence, the TAC and the super PO pay down concurrently and lend support to the PACs. Exhibit 3 shows the yield and average-life sensitivities of each tranche under various interest rate scenarios.[4]

As Exhibit 3 shows, the PO PACs are virtually unaffected by prepayment variations due to their wide PAC bands. Based on our analysis, any shortening or lengthening due to PSAs outside the bands is minimal. The super PO shows the greatest pickup in yield in a falling interest-rate environment due to its deep discounted price and the fact that the average life shortens tremendously. The super PO and (eventually) the TAC are support classes for the PACs; hence, they are more sensitive to prepayment fluctuations than the PACs.

When market conditions allow, synthetic combinations of structured POs and IOs may be created to outperform collateral or interest-bearing REMIC tranches. Or IOs can be added as a yield hedge/enhancement for an anticipated slow down in prepayments. To avoid the basis risk of prepayment mismatch, it is ideal to combine structured POs and IOs that are backed by similar collateral (*i.e.*, same coupon and term).

Exhibit 4 shows synthetic combinations of each of the tranches in FNMA 94–35 with FNMA Trust 257 IO priced at 36–15 using a current principal ratio of 1:1. Remember that the PO from Trust 257 is collateral for FNMA 94–35. As cheap sectors are recognized, synthetic combinations of securities backed by different collateral may be attractive enough to relieve any basis-risk concerns. For example, if FNMA Trust 257 IO is priced higher,

---

Exhibit 4. Synthetic Combinations of Tranches in FNMA 94–35 Immediate Interest-Rate Shifts (Basis Points)

	─── Immediate Interest-Rate Shifts (Basis Points) ───						
	-300	-200	-100	NC	+100	+200	+300
PSA (%)	549	311	150	128	215	122	120
	─────────── Yield (%) ───────────						
FNMA 7%	8.74	8.25	7.90	7.85	7.85	7.84	7.83
T257 IO	-15.25	-0.26	9.30	10.58	10.75	10.92	10.25
35A + IO	-3.45	2.69	8.13	8.94	9.05	9.16	9.24
35B + IO	1.55	4.70	8.21	8.79	8.87	8.95	9.01
35C + IO	7.99	8.66	8.54	8.25	8.21	8.17	8.14
35D + IO	43.49	9.74	5.29	5.38	5.40	5.41	5.43

---

4 Note that the prepayment assumptions are based on Prudential Securities' Prepayment Model.

thus making the combination less attractive, a more effective IO can be used, be it higher or lower coupon collateral than FNMA 7s.

The analysis in Exhibit 4 shows that the addition of the IO to the PAC classes enhances yields to the extent that the combination outperforms collateral in all scenarios except in a market rally of 200 to 300 basis points. When combined with the TAC, the yield profiles flatten dramatically but outperform collateral in all scenarios analyzed. The super PO, due to its high leverage, maintains a very bullish profile. Each of the combinations above can be altered by merely changing the ratio of the IO to the PO classes or by substituting the IO with a higher or lower coupon IO.

SYNTHETIC COMBINATIONS USING OTHER REMIC TRANCHES

Over the past year or two, as the REMIC market grew in sophistication, more exotic bonds were created with very unique features in terms of their reactions to changes in the marketplace. Structured IOs (e.g., PAC IOs, TAC IOs, IO-ettes); structured accrual or Z bonds (e.g., sticky/non-sticky jump Zs, PAC Zs, companion Zs); indexed amortizing bonds; floaters; inverse floaters; and inverse IOs are just some of the examples of these new exotic securities.

These bonds have personalities of their own and caution is advised when using them to create an ideal synthetic. With the direction of interest rates and the prepayment option being the two major factors that affect MBSs, the task of analyzing these bonds is far from simple. When considering a synthetic combination, there must be some comfort level in terms of the assumptions made on the volatility of these bonds. Many investors have a standard battery of tests that the synthetic must pass to be even considered as a sound investment. However, as long as the assumptions are extremely conservative and bonds are analyzed to the hilt, then and only then should it be considered for investment.

With such a variety of bonds in the marketplace, there are almost always opportunities to create cheap synthetic securities. The premise remains that two cheap bonds will create a cheap synthetic and that opposite characteristics work best together.

HOW IS THE PRINCIPAL RATIO DETERMINED FOR A SYNTHETIC COMBINATION?

In determining the optimal ratio of the components in a synthetic combination, it is necessary to first determine the objective of the synthetic. Is the purpose to outperform an alternative security? Is it to have a desired yield profile that is not available elsewhere in the marketplace? Is it to have a duration profile (but higher yielding than an alternative security)? Is it to have a desired total-return profile not available in the marketplace? These questions and others like them need to be addressed first in order to best determine the proper components and the appropriate ratios to create the optimal synthetic.

The synthetic combinations that this chapter has explored so far have focused only on yield combinations. However, if total rate of return (TRR) or duration are the targets, then the ratios must be altered.

Take, for example, combining various bonds to outperform collateral on a TRR basis. For the sake of consistency, we will again use the securities in our yield combination analysis. Exhibit 5 shows the one-year TRR sensitivity of collateral, as well as the TRR for Trust 257 IO and structured POs from FNMA 94–35. Note that the TRRs are based on keeping the current option-adjusted spread (OAS) constant at the horizon (one-year from settlement) for each of the scenarios. In Exhibit 5, we use an optimization routine to select a combination that outperforms collateral; the constraints are such that the minimal TRR is that of the collateral and the cost of synthetic is not to exceed $1 million.

As the analysis shows, the combination of a PAC PO and a super PO from this particular REMIC can outperform the collateral on a TRR basis at a very comfortable margin, indicating that this particular sector is cheap. This

Exhibit 5. One-Year Total Rate of Return Sensitivity of Collateral

Synthetic Security	Current Face Value ($ Thousands)	Price	Market Value ($ Thousands)
FNMA 94-35-B PAC PO	1,222.42	79-22	974.12
FNMA 94-35-D Super PO	61.62	42-00	25.88

	Immediate Interest-Rate Shifts (Basis Points)						
	-300	-200	-100	NC	+100	+200	+300
FNMA 7%	15.25	13.31	9.84	5.20	0.32	-4.56	-9.40
T257 IO	-47.01	-25.27	2.37	9.81	10.51	9.39	7.93
35A	6.97	6.66	6.35	6.04	5.72	5.40	5.03
35B	14.95	12.47	10.27	8.11	5.97	3.76	1.19
35C	48.82	36.29	22.20	7.87	-2.69	-12.31	-21.96
35D	108.88	94.74	34.58	3.10	-21.67	-42.88	-61.18
Synthetic Security	17.89	14.99	10.93	7.98	5.30	2.70	-0.18
Adv. vs. Coll.	+264	+168	+109	+278	+498	+726	+922

process of determining optimal combinations can have different feasible solutions depending on the type of constraints specified.

Concluding Comments

Due to the increasingly complex needs of the investment community, the revolution in financial structuring technology is unlikely to come to a halt. In certain instances, "designer" securities with unique investment characteristics may be successful in meeting particular investment or risk-management objectives.

In other instances, the cash flows from such securities may have to be combined with other securities either to exploit profitable arbitrage opportunities or to accomplish stated investment objectives.

In any case, as newer securities are developed, combinations of such securities exhibiting opposite characteristics are likely to be an integral part of any asset management program. Investors are reminded that these more exotic bonds are fairly sensitive to market changes and, due to the sensitive nature of these bonds, investors should exercise the utmost caution when employing synthetic strategies as part of their management program.

SECTION IV

COLLATERALIZED MORTGAGE OBLIGATIONS

CHAPTER 16

Introduction to Collateralized Mortgage Obligations

Chris Ames
Director
Mortgage Strategies Group
Lehman Brothers International (Europe)

INTRODUCTION

The U.S. mortgage-backed securities (MBS) market has grown significantly in the last ten years. At the end of 1980, approximately $111 billion MBS were outstanding; by the end of 1993, the amount had grown more than 12-fold to $1.4 trillion. Much of this growth has come in the form of collateralized mortgage obligations (CMOs) and real estate mortgage investment conduits (REMICs),[1] structures that significantly broadened the investor base for mortgage-backed securities by offering near-U.S. Treasury credit quality, customized performance characteristics, attractive yields across a range of maturities, and a variety of risk and return profiles to fit investors' needs. CMOs currently account for 53% of all fixed-rate mortgage-backed securities outstanding.

Throughout the 1970s and early 1980s, most mortgage-backed securities were issued in pass-through form. Pass-throughs, which are participations in the cash flows from pools of individual home mortgages, have long final maturities and the potential for early partial repayment of principal. These securities primarily appeal to investors willing to accept long and uncertain investment horizons in exchange for relatively high yields and credit quality.

The author thanks Patrick Moore for his research and technical assistance on this chapter.

1 Although CMOs and REMICs have different tax and regulatory characteristics for issuers, there is little difference between them for the investor. In practice, the market uses the terms interchangeably and the term CMO is used generically in this chapter. A detailed discussion of the differences between the two is described later in this chapter.

In 1983, a dramatic fall in mortgage rates and a surging housing market caused mortgage orginations to double. Much of this production was sold in the capital markets; pass-through issuance jumped from $53 billion in 1982 to $84 billion. To accommodate this surge in supply, financial innovators designed a security that would broaden the existing MBS investor base. In mid-1983 the Federal Home Loan Mortgage Corporation (Freddie Mac or FHLMC) issued the first CMO, a $1 billion, three-class structure that offered short-, intermediate-, and long-term securities produced from the cash flows of a pool of mortgages. This instrument allowed more investors to become active in the MBS market. For instance, banks could participate in the market more efficiently by buying short-term mortgage securities to match their short-term liabilities (deposits).

The CMO market evolved rapidly, growing in size and complexity. Annual issuance of agency CMOs has risen steadily, from $5 billion in 1983 to $316 billion in 1993. Exhibit 1 shows CMO issuance from 1983 to 1992. Currently over 70% of all 30-year FHLMC and Federal National Mortgage Association (Fannie Mae or FNMA) pass-throughs are pledged as collateral for CMOs. More recently, CMOs backed by individual mortgages and issued by nonagency entities (known as whole-loan or private label CMOs) have become a significant market in their own right: 1992 issuance was $89.5 billion (81% higher than 1991's $48 billion), and today the balance of whole-loan CMOs outstanding is approximately $137 billion.[2]

Exhibit 1.   CMO Issuance ($ billion)

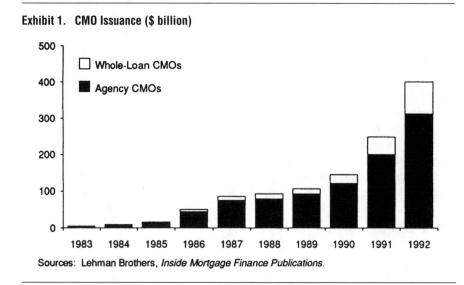

Sources: Lehman Brothers, *Inside Mortgage Finance Publications.*

---

2 *Inside Mortgage Securities,* 1993:27, p. 2.

The thrust in the CMO market has been the development of innovative structures to meet the needs of institutional investors and broaden the investor base for mortgage-backed securities. For example, demand from traditional corporate bond investors for CMO bonds with insulation from prepayment volatility led to the creation of planned amortization classes (PACs) and targeted amortization classes (TACs). Regulatory pressures on banks and thrifts led to the creation of very accurately defined maturity (VADM) bonds that were guaranteed not to extend past a given date. Growing interest from overseas investors gave rise to floating-rate bonds indexed to the London interbank offered rate (LIBOR). Increased investor sophistication and technological breakthroughs have created a large market for derivative securities: interest- and principal-only bonds (IOs, POs), inverse floaters, and others. A broad range of products is now available to suit almost any investor preference (see Exhibit 2).

This chapter explains how CMOs are structured, and defines the major types of securities available. It also describes the evolving CMO regulatory environment, PAC band drift, the pricing relationship between CMOs and collateral, some valuation techniques employed by CMO investors, and trading conventions.

PASS-THROUGHS AND WHOLE LOANS: THE BUILDING BLOCKS OF CMOs

In order to develop realistic expectations about the performance of a CMO bond, an investor must first evaluate the underlying collateral, since its

Exhibit 2. Agency CMOs Outstanding by Class ($ billion, as of 6/93)

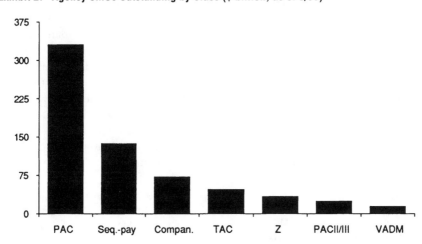

performance will determine the timing and size of the cash flows reallocated by the CMO structure. Agency and whole-loan CMOs have distinct collateral, credit, and prepayment characteristics.

Collateral

Individual home mortgages are the underlying collateral and source of cash flow for CMOs. In the case of agency CMOs, these mortgages are already pooled and securitized in pass-through form. The mortgages backing an agency pass-through are of similar size, age, and underwriting quality and have similar rates. All principal and interest cash flows generated by the underlying mortgages, including any prepayments, are channeled to investors, net of a servicing spread (a small portion of each month's interest payment paid to the institution that collects and distributes the mortgage payments). Pass-through investors share in the cash flows on a pro rata basis.

Whole-loan CMO issuers do not take the interim step of creating a pass-through security from a pool of individual mortgages; instead, they create a structure directly based on the cash flows of a group of mortgages. Whole-loan pools, like agency pass-throughs, usually contain mortgages of similar underwriting quality, age, and rate (the range of ages and rates is often somewhat wider for whole-loan pools than for agency pass-throughs). The most common distinguishing characteristic of whole loans is their size. The agencies accept only mortgages below a certain size (currently $203,150 for FNMA and FHLMC and $151,725 for GNMA); larger loans, known as jumbo loans, make up the primary collateral for whole-loan CMOs.

Credit

GNMA is a U.S. government agency and FHLMC and FNMA are government-sponsored enterprises. All three entities guarantee the full and timely[3] payment of all principal and interest due from pass-throughs issued under their names. GNMA securities, like U.S. Treasury securities, are backed by the full faith and credit of the U.S. government. FNMA and FHLMC, although not government agencies, are federally chartered corporations and the market assumes an implicit U.S. government guarantee backing the agency guarantee. Securities issued by all three entities are called agency securities.

Although whole loans do not carry agency guarantees against default, they generally adhere to agency underwriting standards for types of documentation required, loan-to-value ratios, and income ratios. The strength of

---

3 Early FHLMC pass-throughs, known as 75-day delay pass-throughs, carry a guarantee of full and timely payment of interest and eventual payment of principal (after disposal of the foreclosed property). FHLMC CMOs backed by these securities carry the same guarantee as the underlying pass-throughs.

the collateral is evident in the historical loss data on whole-loan CMOs. At the end of 1992, for pools of 30-year mortgages backing CMOs rated by Moody's Investors Service, Inc., cumulative losses were only 0.29% for CMOs originated in 1987–1989, the first years of significant production. Losses of this size are easily absorbed by the credit enhancements[4] added to whole-loan CMOs; to date, no investor in any senior whole-loan CMO class has ever experienced a loss from default.

Prepayments

Expected prepayment behavior is a critical factor in evaluating CMO collateral. Three collateral characteristics are necessary for evaluating collateral from a prepayment perspective: issuer/guarantor, gross weighted average coupon (WAC), and weighted average loan age (WALA) or weighted average maturity (WAM). The issuer/guarantor is important because of the details known about borrowers within different programs. For example, GNMAs are backed by loans insured by the Federal Housing Administration (FHA) or guaranteed by the Veterans Administration (VA). Borrowers under these programs tend to be less mobile than non-FHA/VA (conventional[5]) borrowers and therefore GNMA prepayments have been slower and more stable than conventional prepayments. Whole loans, on the other hand, tend to be larger and therefore represent more wealthy or sophisticated borrowers: they have prepaid approximately 1.5–2 times faster than comparable coupon conventionals.

Gross WAC is the average of the interest rates of the mortgages backing a structure. Since the actual mortgage rate determines a borrower's refinancing incentive, gross WAC is a better indicator of prepayment potential than the net coupon of the collateral. Finally, loan age is important in determining short-term prepayments. The best measure of age is WALA, which tracks the age of the underlying mortgages. If WALA is not available, then taking the original term of the mortgages and subtracting the WAM will give an approximation.

CMO STRUCTURES

In a CMO, cash flows from one or more mortgage pass-throughs or a pool of mortgages are reallocated to multiple classes with different priority claims. The CMO is self-supporting, with the cash flows from the collateral always

---

4 Common whole-loan CMO credit enhancements are senior/subordinated structures and third-party pool insurance. These are described in Chapter 23.

5 A conventional mortgage is any mortgage not FHA-insured or VA-guaranteed. In practice, the market uses the term *conventional* to group loans eligible for securitization under FHLMC and FNMA programs, since securities from these agencies are usually backed by non-FHA/VA mortgages.

able to meet the cash-flow requirements of the CMO classes under any possible prepayment scenario. The CMO creation process is a dynamic one. This chapter describes the most common types of CMO classes, but dealers will frequently tailor bonds to fit investors' specific needs.

The following general points are important for any discussion of CMO structures:

- CMOs issued by FNMA and FHLMC (known collectively as conventional CMOs) carry the same guarantee as conventional pass-throughs and CMOs issued by GNMA carry the same guarantee as GNMA pass-throughs. Both FNMA and FHLMC are authorized to issue CMOs with GNMA pass-throughs as collateral. The guarantee for a FNMA- or FHLMC-issued CMO backed by GNMA collateral is the same as that for a conventional CMO. Since credit risk is not an issue for agency CMOs, there is no need for credit enhancements in the structures.

- Whole-loan CMOs do not carry government default guarantees and are therefore usually rated by the bond rating agencies. A variety of credit enhancement techniques is employed so that most or all bonds in a structure receive a AAA rating. The most common technique today is the senior/subordinated structure, with senior bonds generally rated AAA and layers of subordinated bonds receiving lower investment- or non-investment grade ratings.

- Most CMO classes pay interest monthly, based on the current face amount of the class, even if it is not currently paying down principal.

- Most CMO classes have a principal lockout period during which only interest payments are received. The payment window is the period during which principal payments are received. In most cases, the lockout period and the payment window are not absolute but are affected by prepayments on the underlying collateral.

- CMO classes are structured with specific cash-flow profiles and investment terms based on an assumed prepayment rate. This assumed rate, which represents the market's current expectation of future prepayments on the collateral, is known as the pricing speed.

- CMOs can be structured from collateral of any maturity. The examples that follow focus on 30-year collateral, but in the last few years CMOs have been backed by 20- and 15-year fixed-rate and 5- and 7-year balloon collateral, depending on the supply and cost of the collateral and the demand for CMOs with the particular characteristics imparted by the collateral.

CMO structures are of two major types: one provides for the redirection of principal payments only, and the other for redirection of interest as well as principal. Sequential-pay, PAC/companion, and TAC/companion structures redirect principal and are the starting point for all CMOs.

Sequential-Pay Classes

The primary purpose of the first CMOs was to bring a broader range of maturity choices to the MBS market. These CMOs—called sequential-pay, plain vanilla, or clean structures—reallocate collateral principal payments sequentially to a series of bonds. All initial principal amortization and prepayments from the collateral are paid to the shortest maturity class, or tranche, until it is fully retired; then principal payments are redirected to the next shortest class. This process continues until all classes are paid down. Exhibit 3 demonstrates how the principal flows of a $1 million pool of FNMA 7.5s would be distributed in a sequential-pay structure if the collateral prepaid consistently at 185% PSA. In this example, owners of the first class, identified as a 3-year class due to its weighted average life of 3.0 years, receive all principal flows from month 1 until month 64, when their principal balance is $0. Investors who own the second class (the 7-year) receive principal flows from month 65 to month 107. Owners of the 10-year class receive principal from month 108 to month 134, and investors in the final class receive the

Exhibit 3. Principal Flows from a Four-Tranche Sequential-Pay Structure
($1 million 7.5% pool at 185% PSA)

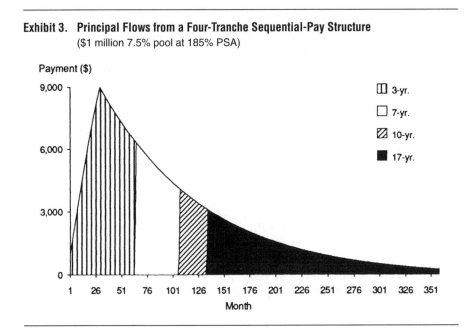

remaining principal flows. The amount of time that each class is outstanding, as well as the months that principal payments begin and end, vary as actual prepayment experience varies from the assumed prepayment rate.

With the creation of the sequential-pay structure, capital market participants with short investment horizons were able to enter the MBS market because they could buy bonds that more closely matched their desired terms. Investors with long-term horizons also benefited because they were insulated from prepayments during the early years of a pool's life.

Planned Amortization Classes

In 1986, after a period of substantial interest-rate declines and the resulting surge of mortgage refinancing activity and prepayments, issuers began producing prepayment-protected bonds called planned amortization classes (PACs). These structures offered substantial protection from the reinvestment risk and weighted average-life volatility associated with prepayments.

PACs have a principal payment schedule (similar to a sinking fund mechanism) that can be maintained over a range of prepayment rates. This schedule is based on the minimum amount of principal cash flow produced by the collateral at two prepayment rates known as the PAC bands. For example, if the PAC bands were 95% PSA and 240% PSA, a PAC principal payment schedule could be constructed equal to the shaded area in Exhibit 4. The minimum amount of principal produced in the early months follows the principal payment path of the lower band (95% PSA), and after 116 months (where the two lines on the graph intersect), the schedule is constrained by the upper band (240% PSA) because principal has paid off more quickly under this scenario. The total principal flow available under the PAC schedule determines the original amount of PACs in a structure (in this example, PACs represent 70% of the structure). If wider bands are chosen, the derived PAC schedule will be smaller—i.e., there will be fewer PACs in the structure.

The PAC schedule is maintained by redirecting cash-flow uncertainty to classes called companions. In times of fast prepayments, companions support PACs by absorbing principal payments in excess of the PAC schedule. In times of slow prepayments, amortization of the companions is delayed if there is not enough principal for the currently paying PAC. As a result of this support mechanism, faster than expected prepayments cause companions to pay off sooner, or contract in weighted average life. Conversely, slower than expected prepayments cause companions to remain outstanding longer, or extend. Exhibit 5 shows how the companions support the PACs at both ends of the protected prepayment range.

Total PAC and companion principal flows can be divided sequentially, much like a sequential-pay structure. Exhibit 6 illustrates a possible PAC/companion structure. Exhibit 7 shows the WALs of the PACs and companions

Exhibit 4. Determining the PAC Schedule
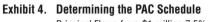
Principal Flows from $1 million 7.5% Pool

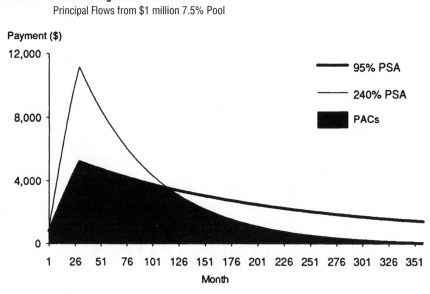

Exhibit 5. PAC/Companion Profile at PAC Band Limits
Principal Flows from $1 million 7.5% Pool

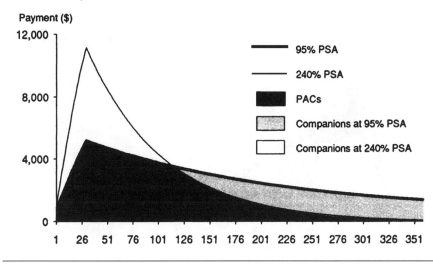

compared to a sample sequential-pay structure and to the collateral across a range of prepayment rates. In relation to the sequential-pay bonds, the PACs are completely stable at prepayment rates within the bands and less volatile when prepayments fall outside the bands because the companions continue to provide stability. As a result, PACs are generally priced at tighter spreads to the Treasury curve, and companion bonds at wider spreads, than sequential-pay bonds with the same average lives.

Effective PAC bands are important in evaluating PACs. These bands define the actual range of collateral prepayment rates over which a particular PAC class can remain on its payment schedule. An example of this distinction can be seen in the first class of the sample PAC structure. Even though the structure was constructed with bands of 95%–240% PSA, this class is actually protected from WAL changes over a broader range of prepayment rates: the effective PAC bands are 95%–288% PSA. All the companions in a structure must be paid off before the WAL of a PAC will shorten, so the earlier PACs in a structure generally have higher upper effective bands than the later PACs since there are more companions outstanding. The effective bands of a PAC will change over time, depending on the prepayment experience of the collateral. As discussed later, most of the time, this change (drift) is small and gradual.

Exhibit 6. PAC/Companion Structure at 185% PSA
Principal Flows from $1 million 7.5% Pool

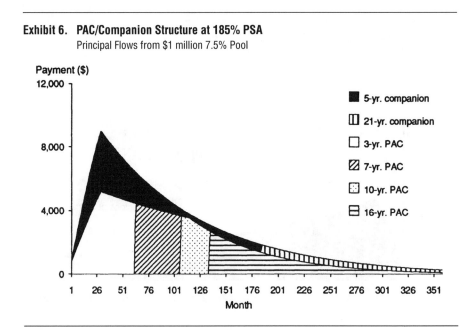

**Exhibit 7.   Weighted Average Lives of Alternative CMO
Structures Under Selected Prepayment Assumptions**
Backed by 30-year 7.5% pass-throughs
Pricing speed: 185% PSA
PAC bands: 95%–240% PSA

PSA:	50%	95%	185%	240%	300%
Pass-through	15.4	12.2	8.3	6.9	5.9
Sequential-pay					
A	6.6	4.5	3.0	2.6	2.3
B	16.0	11.3	7.0	5.7	4.8
C	20.9	15.9	10.0	8.1	6.7
D	26.3	23.3	17.1	14.2	11.9
PAC/Companion					
PAC A	4.3	3.0	3.0	3.0	2.9
PAC B	10.4	7.0	7.0	7.0	6.1
PAC C	14.4	10.0	10.0	10.0	8.3
PAC D	19.1	16.2	16.2	16.2	13.6
Companion E	24.6	19.2	5.0	2.8	2.2
Companion F	29.2	28.2	21.5	6.6	4.2

PACs have been structured with varying protection levels and yield trade-offs. The most common variants are Type II/Type III PACs and super/subordinate PACs.

Type II and Type III PACs

As the CMO marketplace grew more sophisticated, investors sought bonds that would offer some prepayment protection and earn higher cash-flow yields than generic PACs. The resulting innovation was the Type II PAC, structured from companion cash flows in a PAC/companion structure. These bonds have narrower prepayment protection bands than standard PACs, but as long as prepayments stay within the bands, they pay down according to a schedule, much like regular PACs. Because Type II PACs are second in priority to PACs, the remaining companion bonds provide support even if prepayments are outside the bands. If extended periods of high pre-payments cause the companions in a structure to be paid off, the remaining Type II PACs become companions to the PACs, with the potential WAL volatility of companion bonds.

Exhibit 8a shows the addition of Type II PACs (125%–220% PSA bands) to the PAC/companion structure illustrated in Exhibit 5. The PAC principal flow has not changed, and the Type II PACs are layered on top of the PACs.

Exhibit 8. PAC/Companion Structure
Principal Flows from $1 million 7.5% Pool

a. With Type II PACs

Payment ($)

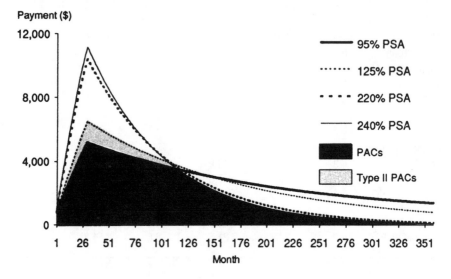

b. With Super and Sub-PACs

Payment ($)

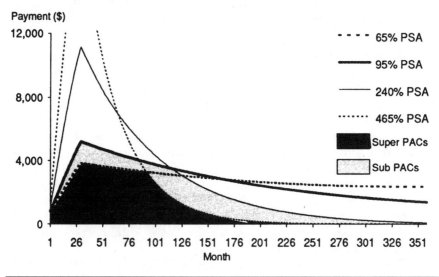

Another layer of PACs, with narrower bands, is sometimes created as well. These securities, known as Type III PACs, act as support for PACs and Type II PACs in a structure but retain some stability because of the companions that remain.

Super/Subordinate PACs

The prepayment experience of 1992–1993 caused many investors to view MBSs as more callable than they had previously thought and to demand significantly higher levels of prepayment protection. In early 1993 Lehman Brothers responded by issuing the first super/subordinated PAC structure. In this structure, standard PACs are divided into super and subordinate (sub-) PACs. By rearranging the cash-flow priorities within the total PAC class, the super PACs receive additional prepayment stability from the sub-PACs and therefore have much wider protection bands.

Since both super- and sub-PAC classes are created from the total PAC cash flows and generally have all the structure's companions available to support them, sub-PACs offer more protection from average-life volatility than similar average-life Type II or Type III PACs in the same structure. This relationship can be seen in FHLMC 1499, which has 3-year super, sub-, and Type III PACs. The effective bands are 70%–625% PSA on the super PAC, 100%–250% PSA on the sub-PAC, and 140%–220% PSA on the Type III PAC. Sub-PACs trade at higher yields than PACs because they can have more average-life volatility at prepayment rates outside their protection bands.

Exhibit 8b shows super and sub-PACs in the example PAC/companion structure. The combined principal flows of the super and sub-PACs are equivalent to the original PAC principal flows.

Targeted Amortization Classes

Targeted amortization classes (TACs) were introduced to offer investors a prepayment-protected class at wider spreads than PACs. Like PACs, TACs repay principal according to a schedule as long as prepayments remain within a range. If the principal cash flow from the collateral exceeds the TAC schedule, the excess is allocated to TAC companion classes. Unlike PACs, TACs do not provide protection against WAL extension if prepayments fall below the speed necessary to maintain the TAC schedule. Therefore, the typical TAC can be viewed as a PAC with a lower band equal to the CMO pricing speed and an upper band similar to that of PACs backed by comparable collateral. In falling/low interest-rate environments, investors are primarily concerned that increasing prepayments will shorten average life due to increasing prepayments. Many investors are willing to forego the protection against extension offered by PACs in exchange for the higher yields of TACs.

Companions

Companion is a general term in the CMO market for a class that provides pre-payment protection for another class. In evaluating companions (also known as *support classes*), it is important to review the rest of the CMO structure; the behavior of a particular companion class is influenced by the class(es) it supports. For instance, if the companion is supporting a TAC, it will have less extension risk than a PAC companion because the TAC is not protected from extension. In addition, other bonds in the structure may affect the companion's potential performance. For example, the presence of Type II PACs in a structure indicates that part of the original companions is being traded in a more stable form, leaving the remaining companions more volatile. Another important consideration for companions is the collateral backing the CMO. If the pass-throughs have a shorter maturity than 30 years, such as 15-year or balloon MBSs, the PACs in the structure will require less extension protection. Therefore, there will be fewer companions in the structure than in a 30-year structure with the same PAC bands, and the companions will have less extension risk. Finally, a class's sensitivity to prepayments should be viewed in a yield or total return context. Because prepayments are paid at par, faster-than-expected prepayments will have a positive effect on a discount bond's yield, and slower-than-expected prepayments will have a positive effect on a premium bond's yield. On a total return basis (see "Evaluating CMOs" below for details on total return calculation), these generalizations will usually apply as well, although the interaction between prepayments, average life, and reinvestment rate may offset the effects of being repaid at par.

The CMO classes that have been reviewed (sequential-pay, PAC, TAC, and companion) are structures that provide for the redirection of principal payments. The classes that follow address the redirection of interest payments as well. These classes usually rely on one of the above structures to reallocate principal payments.

Z-Bonds

The Z-bond is a CMO class with a period of principal and interest lockout. It typically takes the place of a coupon-bearing class at or near the end of a CMO structure. When the CMO is originally issued, the Z-bond has a face amount significantly lower than it would have if it were an interest-bearing class. Each month that the Z is outstanding, it generates coupon cash flows, like any other bond in the structure; however, as long as the Z class is not paying out principal, this coupon flow is used to pay down other classes. The Z gets credit for the foregone interest payments through increases to its principal balance, known as accretion. Once the classes preceding the Z-bond are fully paid down, it begins to receive principal and interest.

The Z-bond in Exhibit 9 begins with a face amount of $118,000. The coupon in the first month ($118,000 × 7.5%/12 = $737.50) is paid as a prepayment to the first class in the structure, and the Z-bond accretes that amount. The accretion amounts increase as the principal amount (on which coupon cash flows are calculated) grows. In month 133, the final sequential-pay class receives its last principal payment, which includes $1,678.57 from the Z coupon. The collateral has produced an additional $47.44 in principal cash flows that month, and since the Z is the only outstanding class, it receives the principal payment. The Z-bond balance has grown to $270,203. Since the Z is the only remaining class from month 134 on, it receives all principal and interest payments generated by the collateral.

In a simple sequential-pay/Z-bond structure, the Z accelerates the principal repayments of the sequential-pay bonds. As a result, restructuring a sequential-pay bond as a Z allows for larger sequential-pay classes with the same WALs as the original classes. Since a portion of the principal payments of these sequential-pay bonds is coming from the Z coupon flows (which do not vary until the Z begins amortizing), average-life volatility is decreased in the sequential-pay classes. In fact, in the sample structure all bonds including the Z have less average-life volatility when the Z is introduced to the structure (see Exhibit 10). The Z's impact is clearest in the scenario where prepayments fall from 185% PSA to 95% PSA: the change in average life is 10%–23% lower for all bonds than in the basic sequential-pay structure.

Although the Z structure appears to have reduced uncertainty across the board, it is important to look at the effective durations of the bonds as

Exhibit 9. Sample Z-Bond Cash Flows
In sequential-pay/Z-bond structure
backed by 30-year 7.5% pass-throughs($)

Month	Beginning Balance	Coupon Accretion	Coupon Cash Flow	Amortiz./ Prepay.	Ending Balance	Total Cash Flows
1	118,000.00	737.50	0.00	0.00	118,737.50	0
2	118,737.50	742.11	0.00	0.00	119,479.61	0
3	119,479.61	746.75	0.00	0.00	120,226.36	0
.	.	.	.	.	.	0
.	.	.	.	.	.	0
131	265,245.57	1,657.78	0.00	0.00	266,903.35	0
132	266,903.35	1,668.15	0.00	0.00	268,571.50	0
133	268,571.50	1,678.57	0.00	47.44	270,202.63	47.44
134	270,202.63	0.00	1,688.77	3,131.55	267,071.08	4,820.31
135	267,071.08	0.00	1,669.19	3,099.51	263,971.57	4,768.70

**Exhibit 10.   Weighted Average Lives of Alternative Sequential-Pay
Structures Under Selected Prepayment Assumptions**
Backed by 30-year 7.5% pass-throughs
Pricing Speed: 185% PSA

PSA:	95%	185%	240%
Sequential-pay			
A	4.5	3.0	2.6
B	11.3	7.0	5.7
C	15.9	10.0	8.1
D	23.3	17.1	14.2
Sequential-pay/Z			
A	4.2	3.0	2.6
B	10.1	7.0	5.9
C	13.5	9.9	8.5
Z	21.5	17.0	14.8

well. Exhibit 11 shows that the durations of the first three sequential-pay
bonds do not change substantially when the last class is replaced with a Z.
The Z-bond, on the other hand, has almost twice the effective duration of
the sequential-pay bond that it replaced, moving from 10.2 years to 18.5
years. The price of the Z is highly sensitive to interest-rate movements and
the resulting changes in prepayment rates because its ultimate principal balance depends on total accretions credited by the time it begins to pay down.
Although WAL volatility has decreased, the price sensitivity of the last class is
increased dramatically by making it a Z.

Z-bonds offer much of the appeal of zero coupon Treasury strips: there
is no reinvestment risk during the accretion phase. In addition, Z-bonds offer
higher yields than comparable WAL Treasury zeros.

Accretion-Directed Classes

In the falling interest-rate environment that has characterized most of the CMO
era, many structures have been developed to protect investors from higher-
than-anticipated prepayments. *Accretion-directed* (AD) bonds are designed to
protect against extension in average life if rates rise and prepayments are lower
than expected. These bonds, also known as *very accurately defined maturity*
(VADM) bonds, derive all their cash flows from the interest accretions of a Z
class. Because there is no deviation in Z accretions until the Z-bond begins to
pay down, VADMs do not extend, even if there are no prepayments. VADMs
are also protected from prepayment increases because the Z-bonds that support them tend to be the last classes to begin repaying principal.

Exhibit 11.   Effective Durations of Alternative Sequential-Pay Structures
Backed by 30-year 7.5% pass-throughs

Class	Sequential-pay	Sequential-pay with Z
A	1.53 years	1.69 years
B	6.80	6.47
C	8.58	8.16
D/Z	10.19	18.47

Floaters and Inverse Floaters

The first floating-rate CMO class was issued by Shearson Lehman Brothers in 1986. These classes are created by dividing a fixed-rate class into a floater and an inverse floater. The bonds take their principal paydown rules from the underlying fixed-rate class. A floater/inverse combination can be produced from a sequential-pay class, PAC, TAC, companion, or other coupon-bearing class. The coupon of the floater is reset periodically (usually monthly) at a specified spread, or margin, over an index. Typical indices include LIBOR, the Federal Home Loan Bank 11th District Cost of Funds Index (COFI), and various maturities of the constant maturity Treasury (CMT) series. The coupon of the inverse floater moves inversely with the index. Floaters and inverses have caps and floors that set the maximum and minimum coupons allowable on the bonds. These caps and floors may be explicit (*e.g.*, a floater cap of 10%) or implicit (a floater's floor would equal the floater's margin if the underlying index fell to 0%), and may either be constant throughout the life of the bond or change according to a predetermined schedule.

Floaters are usually designed to be sold at par; their caps and margins are dictated by the option and swap markets and by expectations about the performance of the underlying fixed-rate CMO class. Floaters have many natural buyers, such as banks, which prefer the limited interest-rate risk that an adjustable-rate security provides. Since inverse floater coupons move in the opposite direction from their index, investors generally require higher yields for inverses than for floaters or the underlying fixed-rate classes. To increase the yield, cap, and initial coupon, inverses are often structured with multipliers in the coupon formulas that magnify movements in the underlying index.

Exhibit 12 shows how a floater and an inverse can be created from a fixed-rate bond. Both floater and inverse have coupon formulas tied to COFI; the floater coupon adjusts at COFI + 65 bp with a 10% interest-rate cap, and the inverse coupon, which has a multiplier of 2, adjusts at $21.20 - 2 \times$ COFI with a 2.50% floor. In this example, the floater class is twice the size of

Exhibit 12. Creating a Floater and Inverse

$120MM 5-year 7.5% companion becomes...
$80MM 5-year companion COFI floater (coupon = COFI + 65 bp, 10% cap)
$40MM 5-year companion COFI inverse (coupon = 21.20% - 2 x COFI,
2.50% floor)

| COFI Index | Coupon | | Wt. Avg. Coupon |
	Floater	Inverse	
0.00%	0.65%	21.20%	7.50%
2.00	2.65	17.20	7.50
4.00	4.65	13.20	7.50
6.00	6.65	9.20	7.50
8.00	8.65	5.20	7.50
9.35	10.00	2.50	7.50
10.00	10.00	2.50	7.50
12.00	10.00	2.50	7.50

the inverse floater. When a multiplier greater than 1 is used to set the inverse floater's coupon, the face amount of the inverse must be smaller than the floater to keep the weighted average of the two coupons equal to the fixed-rate bond coupon.

Interest- and Principal-Only Strips

Any pool of coupon-bearing collateral can be stripped into interest-only (IO) and principal-only (PO) segments and sold separately. Exhibit 13a illustrates the interest cash flows for 7.5% collateral at various prepayment rates. The total amount of interest flow varies depending on the prepayment rate. Since interest cash flows exist only if principal remains outstanding, IOs benefit from slowing prepayments. POs represent a stream of principal payments purchased at a discount. If prepayments rise, discounted principal flows are received at par earlier than expected, improving the security's performance. Exhibit 13b illustrates principal cash flows from the collateral. Here the total flows will always equal the face amount of the collateral, but the prepayment rate affects the timing and value of the flows. IOs are bearish securities and usually have negative durations (their prices rise as rates rise); POs are bullish securities with long positive durations.

The same principles for stripping pools of collateral can be applied to individual CMO classes or to blocks of classes within a single structure. CMO strips may represent 100% of the interest or principal flows or, more commonly, only a portion of the interest may be stripped, resulting in an IO and a reduced-coupon fixed-rate bond. For example, if a dealer is structuring a PAC class with a 7.5% coupon but investors are more willing to buy the class if it has

Exhibit 13a.   Interest Flows from $1 Million 7.5% Pool

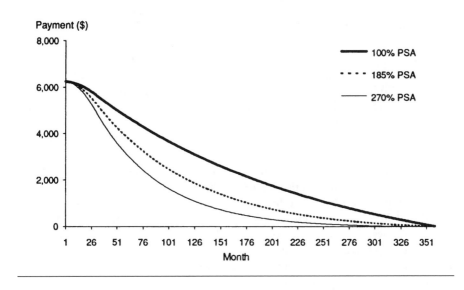

Exhibit 13b.   Principal Flows from $1 Million 7.5% Pool

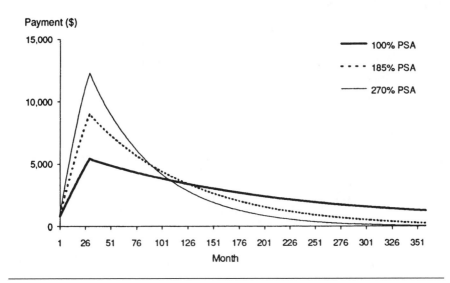

a 7% coupon, a 50-bp PAC IO can be stripped from the class and sold separately.[6] Structurers may also strip part of the coupon flows from the entire block of collateral before dividing it into classes. This method produces an IO-ette security and is employed to lower the coupons on all bonds in a structure.

Strips made from CMO bonds require more analysis than regular IOs and POs. In the above example, since the IO has been stripped from a PAC class, it will be insulated from cash-flow changes as long as prepayments remain within the PAC bands. Only if the PAC begins to pay down principal early will the holder of the PAC IO experience the negative effects of prepayments. An investor should look to the underlying class that defines the rules for principal paydown. Since prepayments are the primary consideration in evaluating stripped securities, the behavior of the underlying class plays a significant role in the overall analysis.

Another type of strip results from the creation of whole-loan CMOs. For agency CMOs, the coupon of the collateral (the pass-throughs) is fixed; for whole-loan CMOs, the collateral coupon is a weighted average of all the individual mortgage coupons (which may vary by 100 bp or more). As loans prepay, the weighted-average coupon (WAC) of the collateral can change. To be sure that all fixed-rate bonds in a structure receive their allotted coupons, issuers often split off part of the principal or interest cash flow from individual mortgages in a pool, leaving a block of collateral with a stable WAC. These strips of principal or interest are combined into WAC POs or WAC IOs and trade much like Trust POs and IOs.

PAC BAND DRIFT

Effective PAC bands change (drift) over time, even if prepayments remain within the initial bands. Band drift results from the interaction of actual prepayments and the current PAC bands, and the resulting changes in collateral balance and relative PAC and companion balances. The band drift of a par-

---

6 Until recently, all REMIC IO classes had to be sold with some small amount of principal, called a nominal balance. To generate the cash flows for bonds with this structure, the nominal balance is amortized and prepaid according to the type of bond. Since the balance is small, the coupon is extremely large. IOs sold this way tend to have multiple-digit coupons (*e.g.*, 1183%) and high dollar prices (*e.g.*, 3626-12). Alternatively, IOs may be based on a notional balance. Here, the IO tranche has no principal balance and its coupon flows are calculated on the declining balance of the underlying principal-bearing tranche. No principal cash flows are paid to the IO holder. This procedure results in MBS-like coupons (7.5%, 8%, *etc.*) or in basis-point coupons (*e.g.*, 100 bp) and below-par prices. These two techniques result in equivalent investment amounts and cash flows. The difference in prices (3626-12 versus 18-02, for example) does not denote any relative value difference between IOs priced with one method or the other.

ticular PAC can be viewed under three scenarios: when prepayments are within the current effective bands, when prepayments are above the current upper band, and when prepayments are below the current lower band.

If prepayments are within the bands, the currently paying PAC will pay on schedule. Any additional prepayments will go to the currently paying companion. Over time, both upper and lower bands will drift up. This happens because any prepayment within the bands is also lower than the upper band and higher than the lower band. From the point of view of the upper band, prepayments have been slower than expected and more companions are available to absorb high prepayments in the future. Thus, the upper band rises. From the point of view of the lower band, prepayments have been faster than expected and less collateral is outstanding to produce principal flows. If prepayments slow to the original lower band, there may not be enough principal coming in to pay the PACs on schedule and they will extend. Thus, the lower band rises as well. For most prepayment rates within the bands, the upper band will rise at a faster rate than the lower, so prepayments within the bands tend to cause the bands to widen over time.

If prepayments are above the current upper band, the PAC will continue to pay on schedule until all companions are retired. If the fast prepayments are only temporary, there will probably be little impact on the bands. If prepayments remain above the upper band, however, the upper and lower bands will begin to converge. This happens because there are fewer companions available to absorb fast prepayments and less collateral outstanding to generate principal cash flows if prepayments slow. The bands will converge once all companions have been retired and the PAC will pay like a sequential-pay class from that point.

If prepayments are below the current lower band, the currently paying PAC will not be able to pay according to its schedule, since there will be no other principal flows coming into the structure that can be redirected to the PAC. This is typically a temporary situation because the lower band is usually substantially lower than the base prepayment rate expected from simple housing turnover and because most PACs have priority over all subsequent cash flows until they are back on schedule. Prepayments below the current lower band cause the upper band to rise (more companions are available to absorb faster prepayments in the future) and may cause the lower band to rise slightly (since most PACs have catch-up features, a higher future prepayment rate is necessary to put the PAC back on schedule).

Most band drift is small and gradual. Large changes to PAC bands will occur only if prepayments are significantly outside the bands, or if they remain near either of the bands for a long period of time. Effective bands represent the range of prepayment rates that the collateral can experience for its remaining life and still maintain the payment schedule for a specific

PAC. Temporary movements outside the bands will not affect PAC cash flows as long as companion cash flows and principal balances are available to support them.

CMO STRUCTURING EXAMPLE

In this section, we follow a structurer through the process of creating a multiclass CMO. Diagrams (not drawn to scale) are included to illustrate the structures.

The structurer begins with a block of collateral—in this case FNMA 7.5s (Exhibit 14a). If the market expects interest rates and prepayments to be stable, the structurer may construct a sequential-pay CMO (Exhibit 14b). If investors are concerned about rates rising and prepayments slowing (*e.g.*, extension risk), the structurer may produce the last class as a Z-bond (Exhibit 14c). This allows him to apply the Z coupon flows as principal payments to the early sequential-pay classes, or to create VADMs that offer the strongest extension protection (Exhibit 14d). If the collateral is priced at a premium, the structurer may strip some interest cash flows before creating the rest of the classes. This allows the creation of discount or par bonds. Figure 14e shows the FNMA 7.5s after a 50-bp IO-ette is stripped and sold separately. The remaining collateral now has a 7% coupon and can be structured in any way that the original 7.5s could have been.

If the market expects high interest-rate and prepayment volatility, then the structurer will likely create PAC/companion or TAC/companion CMOs. Exhibit 14f illustrates the initial allocation of cash flows to PACs and companions. Once the amount of principal that can be attributed to PACs or companions is identified, these classes go through the sequential-pay structuring process to create PACs and companions of various average lives (Exhibit 14g). Individual classes from any of these structures can be further divided. If a foreign bank wants to purchase a LIBOR-based floater with a relatively high margin and a 5-year average life, for example, the structurer can produce a bond with the desired characteristics from the 5-year companion class (Exhibit 14h) that will offer a higher yield than non-companion tranches. At the same time, he will look at the inverse floater market to determine yield and coupon (set by adjusting the multiplier) for the resulting LIBOR inverse floater. On the PAC side, there may be an investor who wants to purchase a 7-year PAC with a 6% coupon (and therefore a lower price) as protection from the risk of high prepayments on premium-priced bonds. If so, the structurer can split the 7-year PAC into a 150-bp PAC IO and a 6% PAC (Exhibit 14i). These are a few examples of the flexibility in the structuring process. The customizable nature of many CMO classes is a key to the popularity of these bonds.

Exhibit 14. CMO Sructuring Example
FNMA 7.5% Collateral

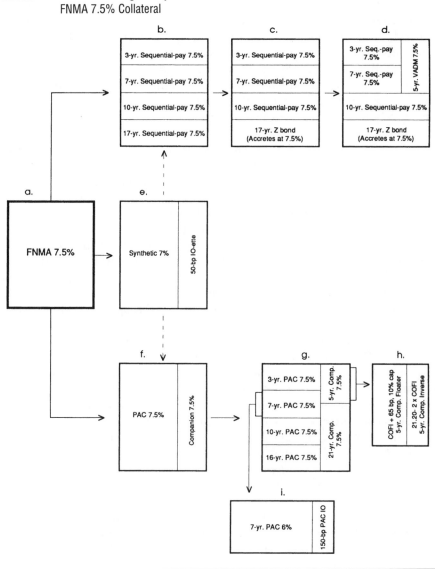

REGULATORY DEVELOPMENTS AFFECTING CMOs*

When FHLMC issued the first CMO in 1983, multiclass mortgage securities were subject to various regulatory constraints. For example, federal tax law treated payments from a multiclass trust as equity dividends, and unlike debt payments, dividend payments are not tax deductible. Therefore, the issuer who established a multiclass trust was unable to claim a tax deduction for interest paid to security holders to offset taxes on interest received from the underlying collateral. The resulting double taxation—interest income was taxed at both the trust and investor level—made the transaction economically impractical.

The CMO avoided this problem because it was an offering of collateralized debt. Therefore, tax deductions for interest paid to certificate holders offset the tax liability on interest received from the underlying collateral. However, CMOs were subject to other constraints to ensure that they were treated as debt instead of equity for tax purposes. Issuers had to maintain a portion of residual interests, record CMOs as liabilities in their financial statements, and satisfy minimum capital requirements. Issuers also had to include a call provision, forcing them to price longer maturity bonds at a wider spread to the Treasury curve. In addition, issuers had to structure a mismatch between receipts on the underlying mortgages and payments to the CMO bondholders; generally they passed monthly collateral payments through to bondholders on a quarterly basis. These constraints made it difficult to issue CMOs efficiently.

Toward the end of 1985, issuers overcame some of these obstacles by issuing CMOs through an owner's trust. This mechanism allowed issuers to sell their residual interests and remove the debt from their books. The owner's trust, however, was not conducive to a liquid market because residual buyers became personally liable for the CMO: if the cash flow from the collateral was insufficient to pay regular interest holders, residual owners had to cover the shortage. As a result, issuers could sell residual interests only to investors capable of meeting ongoing net worth tests. Although these tests were different for each transaction, all effectively limited potential buyers to institutional investors with adequate net worth.

The 1986 Tax Reform Act addressed these problems by defining a new issuance vehicle, the real estate mortgage investment conduit (REMIC). To qualify for REMIC status, a multiclass offering can have multiple classes of regular interests but only one class of residual interest. The legislation defines a regular interest as a fixed principal amount with periodic interest payments or accruals on the outstanding principal balance. Buyers of regular interests are taxed as holders of debt obligations. A residual interest consists entirely of

---

* This section is contributed by Patrick Moore.

pro rata payments (if any). Buyers of residual interests are taxed based on the taxable income of the REMIC. Taxable income is the excess collateral and reinvestment income over REMIC regular interest and servicing expenses.

REMIC legislation was a milestone in the development of multiclass mortgage securities because it allowed issuers to adopt whatever structure best exploited particular economic, financial, or accounting considerations. For tax purposes, all conduits qualifying for REMIC status are treated equally whether they structure a multiclass mortgage transaction as a borrowing collateralized by mortgages or as a sale of the underlying mortgages. In either case, only the investors and residual holders are subject to tax, not the conduit itself. REMIC legislation also allows issuers to sell the entire residual class, and since 1987 it has permitted issuers to sell floating-rate classes. This flexibility has allowed issuers to develop new products, particularly since repeated interest-rate declines since 1982 have led investors to seek products with either improved call protection or higher risk/reward opportunities.

Following a five-year phase-out of all previous structures that ended in 1991, all issuers of multiclass mortgage securities must now use REMICs. However, from the investor's perspective, there is little difference between CMO and REMIC products; in either case the investor is buying multiclass mortgage securities. Consequently, the terms CMO and REMIC are often used interchangeably, even though they are crucially different tax vehicles from the issuer's perspective.

Until 1988, private issuers (primarily investment bankers and home builders) accounted for almost the entire supply of multiclass mortgage securities. These issuers generally used agency collateral to obtain the highest ratings from the nationally recognized rating agencies. However, the credit quality of the issuer was important insofar as cash flows from the underlying collateral might be insufficient to cover obligations to all bondholders. Therefore issuers had to take extra measures, such as overcollateralizing the bonds or buying insurance, to obtain investment-grade credit ratings.

In 1988, FHLMC and FNMA gained full authorization to issue REMICs. Their REMICs automatically obtained government agency status, regardless of the underlying collateral. Therefore FHLMC and FNMA were not subject to the credit-enhancing constraints imposed on private issuers, giving them a crucial market advantage. Agency CMOs jumped from only 2% of total CMO issuance in 1987 to 33% in 1988 and 83% in 1989. In 1992, agencies issued 85% of CMOs.

By 1988, regulatory and market developments had stimulated demand for multiclass mortgage securities. In July 1988, the Basle Committee on Banking Regulations and Supervisory Practices set forth risk-based capital guidelines to ensure the fiscal stability of the international banking infrastructure by requiring minimum capital levels as a percentage of assets—

loans made and securities purchased—weighted according to risk classification. Since agency-issued REMICs offer high yields in relation to their 20% risk weighting, they became increasingly popular with banks and thrifts. Less volatile REMIC products, such as floaters and short and intermediate maturity PACs and TACs, were most appropriate since banks and thrifts needed to match assets with liabilities of similar maturities.

Since about 1988, insurance companies have looked to the REMIC market for assets to offset intermediate to long-term liabilities. Given the poor performance of real estate holdings and commercial mortgages, insurance companies needed to diversify their portfolios, and REMICs offered an attractive alternative because of their credit quality and spread levels. At year end 1993, life insurance companies implemented their own risk-based capital requirements, which provided an additional incentive to hold mortgages in securitized form.

EVALUATING CMOs

The most common way to communicate the value and performance expectations of a CMO bond is the yield table, showing cash-flow yields under a series of prepayment rate assumptions. Computer models that produce yield tables take price(s) and prepayment rates as inputs (and index levels, in the case of floaters and inverse floaters), and calculate yields and spreads, average lives, durations, and payment windows for each prepayment assumption. With this information, the investor can determine the level of prepayment protection offered by the bond, the average life volatility for given changes in collateral prepayment rates, the impact of prepayments on yields, and the time over which principal is likely to be received. Exhibits 15 and 16 are yield tables for the 3-year sequential-pay and PAC bonds in the earlier examples. The yield changes for the sequential-pay bond under each prepayment scenario, but the PAC yield is stable from 95% PSA to 285% PSA. The average life and duration of the PAC are more stable at prepayment rates outside the PAC bands as well. The payment windows show when the bonds will begin to pay principal and when the final payment will occur under each prepayment scenario. Finally, a comparison of the two tables shows that in the base case the sequential-pay bond is being offered at nearly double the spread of the PAC to compensate investors for its additional average-life volatility.

Total return scenario analysis may also be used to evaluate CMOs. It addresses two drawbacks of the cash-flow yield approach: many investors do not expect to hold their securities to maturity, and the reinvestment assumption in the cash-flow yield analysis—that all cash flows are reinvested at the security's yield—is usually unrealistic. Total return calculations cover a specific investment period and make an assumption about the bond's price at the end of the period (the horizon). They further assume a reinvestment rate and prepayment rate for the period to generate cash flows. Total return is the change in market value of the bond (reflecting price changes and principal paydown) plus the cumulative value of all cash flows and reinvestment proceeds as of the horizon date, divided by the initial market value. Although total return scenario analysis involves several assumptions, it is often a desirable addition to the yield tables, especially if the investment period is expected to be relatively short.

Option-adjusted spread (OAS) analysis is another relative value measurement tool used by fixed-income market participants. Based on multiple interest-rate simulations and the resulting prepayments predicted by a prepayment model, the cash flows of a callable bond are analyzed to calculate the average spread to the Treasury spot curve implied by the security's current price. Since this process nets out the impact of prepayments (partial calls) of MBSs, OAS allows direct comparisons among MBSs and other callable and noncallable fixed-income securities. Using current OAS to calculate the horizon price of a CMO is a common method in total return analysis. This allows the investor to avoid making a direct horizon price assumption and incorporates more information (such as the shape of the yield curve) into the analysis.

Exhibit 15. Yield Table for 3-Year Sequential-Pay Class (Price – 104-04)

PSA	35%	95%	135%	Base Case 185%	200%	240%	285%	335%
Yield(%)/Spread(bp)	6.79/105	6.37/111	6.13/127	5.86/140	5.79/133	5.61/114	5.42/143	5.24/125
Avg. Life (yr.)	7.85	4.54	3.64	3.00	2.86	2.57	2.33	2.13
Mod. Dur. (yr.)	5.54	3.67	3.06	2.60	2.49	2.27	2.08	1.92
Windows (yr.)	0.1-14.7	0.1-8.6	0.1-6.7	0.1-5.3	0.1-5.1	0.1-4.4	0.1-3.9	0.1-3.5
Benchmark Tsy.	7-yr.	5-yr.	4-yr.	3-yr.	3-yr.	3-yr.	2-yr.	2-yr.

Exhibit 16. Yield Table for 3-Year PAC (Price – 106-04)

PSA	35%	95%	135%	Base Case 185%	200%	240%	285%	335%
Yield(%)/Spread (bp)	6.04/78	5.31/85	5.18/72	5.18/72	5.18/72	5.18/72	5.18/72	5.13/67
Avg. Life (yr.)	5.07	3.00	3.00	3.00	3.00	3.00	3.00	2.92
Mod. Dur. (yr.)	4.04	2.62	2.62	2.62	2.62	2.62	2.62	2.56
Windows (yr.)	0.1-9.3	0.1-5.2	0.1-5.2	0.1-5.2	0.1-5.2	0.1-5.2	0.1-5.2	0.1-4.7
Benchmark Tsy.	5-yr.	3-yr.	3-yr.	3-yr.	3-yr.	3-yr.	3-yr.	3-yr.

THE CMO/COLLATERAL PRICING RELATIONSHIP

Because of strong investor demand for CMOs, a large percentage of newly issued pass-throughs and jumbo mortgages has gone into CMO structures in recent years. Investor preference for structured mortgage securities has led to a highly efficient pricing relationship between the CMO and collateral sectors.

The source of the CMO/collateral pricing relationship is the interplay between the yield curve and spreads on collateral and CMOs. Exhibit 17 shows the projected yields and payment windows of each bond in a four-class, sequential-pay CMO and the yield of the collateral. Each bond's yield is quoted as a spread to the on-the-run Treasury with a maturity closest to the bond's average life. In this example, the 3-year CMO class has a lower yield than the collateral. The 7-year yield is about equal to, and the 10- and 17-year yields are higher than, the yield of the collateral. When the yield curve is positively sloped, earlier classes are generally offered at lower yields than later classes. Assuming that spreads remain constant, a steepening of the yield curve results in a greater difference between the yields of shorter and longer classes.

By definition, the price of an individual CMO bond represents the present value of the bond's projected cash flows, using the bond's yield as the discount rate. Therefore, the cash flows of any class with a lower yield than the collateral will be priced using a lower discount rate than the single discount rate used to price all the collateral cash flows. This means that this por-

Exhibit 17.   Yields on Collateral and Sequential-Pay CMO Tranches

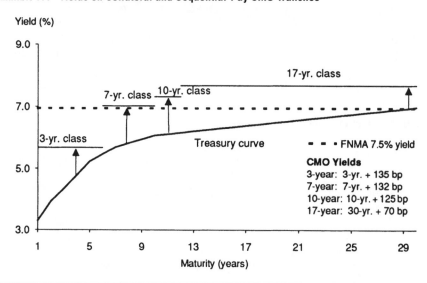

tion of the pass-through's cash flows will have a higher value when structured as part of a CMO. Likewise, the cash flows of bonds with yields higher than the collateral yield will be priced with a higher discount rate than the collateral, leading to lower valuations in relation to collateral cash flows.

Over time, as CMOs are created using a particular collateral type and coupon, supply and demand forces cause the collateral spread to tighten and/or the spreads of the CMO classes to widen until there is no profit in issuing the CMO. If collateral is too expensive (rich) to make the creation of CMO bonds economic, then CMO issuance will slow until pass-through spreads widen and/or CMO spreads tighten. Because of temporary changes in market preference for structured products, collateral can trade at levels too rich to create CMOs. However, in equilibrium it is rare for CMOs to trade rich to collateral, since collateral spreads will quickly tighten as more CMOs are issued.

CMO TRADING AND CLEARING

Generally, CMO bonds are offered on the basis of a yield (more accurately, a spread over the yield of a benchmark Treasury) and a prepayment assumption. A price is calculated from this information and is agreed upon by both parties to the trade. The CMO market convention is corporate settlement (five business days after the trade date), unless the CMO is a new issue. In the case of a new issue, the settlement date for all the CMO classes is usually 1–3 months after the CMO is initially offered for sale. This period allows dealers to accumulate the collateral that will back the CMO. Whether the CMO bond is a new offering or a previously traded security, interest begins accruing on the first day of the settlement month. An exception to this rule is that most floating-rate CMO bonds begin accruing interest on the previous month's payment date, so that they more closely resemble floating-rate notes.

Because of their credit quality, most CMOs can be used in repurchase and reverse repurchase agreements.

Most agency CMO trades are cleared through electronic book-entry transfers via Fedwire, a clearing system maintained by the Federal Reserve. This system also handles monthly principal and interest payments, which are paid to the investor who holds the security on the record date (generally the last calendar day of the month). Whole loan CMO trades are cleared through physical delivery or electronic book entry, depending on the issuer. Most MBS pay with a delay—the cash flows earned during one month are paid out a fixed number of days after the end of the month to give mortgage servicers time to collect payments. Exhibit 18 identifies payment delays for the various combinations of CMO issuers and collateral types.

CONCLUSION

A consistent theme in the CMO market throughout the past decade has been innovation in response to investor needs. As the CMO market has grown more liquid, larger structures have become feasible, providing the flexibility to develop new products. These products have refined the distribution of prepayment uncertainty and risk/reward opportunities to meet the increasingly specialized needs and objectives of investors. The range of options in the CMO market will continue to grow as both originators and investors adapt to a continually changing marketplace.

Exhibit 18. Payment Delays for CMO Issuers and Collateral Types

CMO Issuer	Collateral Type	Payment Delay
FHLMC	FHLMC 75-day	45 days after the record date*
FHLMC	FHLMC Gold	15 days after the record date
FHLMC	GNMA	25 days after the record date
FNMA	FNMA	25 days after the record date
FNMA	GNMA	25 days after the record date
Nonagency	Whole loans	25 days after the record date**

 *Record date is the last calendar day of each month.
**May vary by issuer.

CHAPTER 17

Prospects of Derivative Mortgage Securities

Joseph C. Hu, Ph.D.
Senior Vice President
Director of Mortgage Research
Oppenheimer & Co., Inc.

The derivative mortgage securities market in 1994 underwent a major correction. Interest rates rose sharply early in the year and prices of most mortgage derivatives dropped precipitously—particularly those of more exotic nature such as inverse floaters and support classes. Issuance volume of REMICs plummeted. Many underwriters and investors in mortgage derivatives incurred heavy losses. Liquidation of derivative mortgage portfolios has been widespread. While rising interest rates precipitated the price decline of mortgage derivatives, four factors intensified its severity: heightened volatility, average-life extension, leveraged investment, and lack of liquidity.

The turmoil in mortgage derivatives raises the following questions that we will address in this chapter. Will the REMIC market recover? How large can annual issuance be in the coming years? What types of derivative securities will be issued? Who will be the investors? Will yield spreads of derivative securities widen further or begin to tighten?

THE GROWTH OF THE REMIC MARKET

Since the creation of the Real Estate Mortgage Investment Conduit (REMIC) by the Tax Reform Act of 1986, annual issuance of multiclass mortgage securities electing the REMIC status has grown at a recordbreaking pace.[1]

---

[1] Prior to 1986, multiclass mortgage securities were issued as collateralized mortgage obligations (CMOs). Created in 1983, CMOs were debt instruments: they were booked as borrowing by the issuer. By contrast, REMICs are pass-throughs. They are treated as asset sales by the issuer. From the structural point of view, however, there is no cash-flow difference between CMOs and REMICs. Nowadays, REMICs are still habitually referred to as CMOs.

Issuance of REMICs expanded from $48 billion in 1986 to $195 billion in 1991 (Exhibit 1). In the two years that followed, the expansion was even more phenomenal: $280 billion in 1992 and $323 billion in 1993. During this two-year period, monthly issuance averaged $25 billion. For 1994, however, the issuance dropped to an estimated $130 billion. The precipitous drop actually occurred in the second half of the year, when issuance totaled a meager $30 billion—an average of $5 billion per month.

In addition to strong demand for structured mortgage securities, two factors facilitated the rapid growth of the REMIC market: voluminous originations of fixed-rate, single-family mortgages and active securitization of these originations into pass-throughs as collateral for REMICs. Both activities were exceedingly strong during the 1992-93 period, when 30-year mortgage rates ranged between 9% and a 25-year low of 6.75%. Low mortgage rates elevated housing activity and refinancing to record high levels. As a result, originations surged more than $330 billion to $894 billion in 1992 and ballooned to $1.01 trillion in 1993 (Exhibit 2).[2]

The historically low mortgage rates enabled fixed-rate mortgages to reclaim their dominance in the housing finance market. They accounted for 80% of originations in the last two years. By contrast, in 1988, when fixed

Exhibit 1.   Annual Issuance of Agency-Guaranteed Fixed-Rate Pass-Throughs and REMICs, 1986 to 1994*

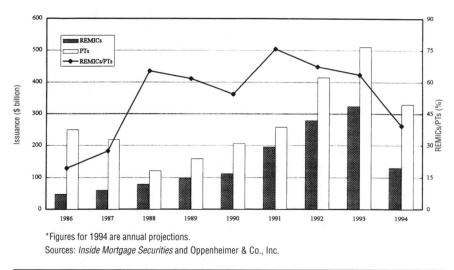

*Figures for 1994 are annual projections.
Sources: *Inside Mortgage Securities* and Oppenheimer & Co., Inc.

---

2 For a detailed discussion, see "Originations, Mortgage Credit Demand, and Yield Spreads," *Mortgage Research,* Oppenheimer & Co., Inc., May 25, 1994.

Exhibit 2.   Annual Originations of Single-Family Mortgages and Issuance of Agency-Guaranteed Fixed-Rate Pass-Throughs, 1986 to 1994*

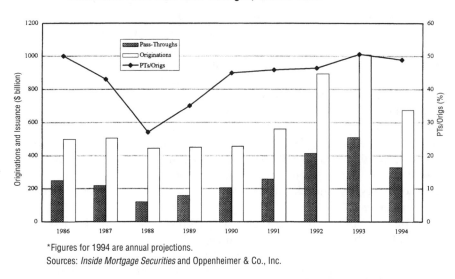

*Figures for 1994 are annual projections.
Sources: *Inside Mortgage Securities* and Oppenheimer & Co., Inc.

mortgage rates averaged 10.3%, adjustable-rate mortgages represented 58% of single-family originations. Securitization of fixed-rate mortgages has been active. Since 1990, over 45% of newly originated mortgages were pooled for agency-guaranteed, fixed-rate pass-throughs. Issuance of these pass-throughs amounted to $415 billion in 1992 and $511 billion in 1993. More than 60% of these pass-throughs were collateralized for the issuance of REMICs.

INCREASED VARIETY OF REMIC CLASSES

As the volume of REMIC issuance expanded rapidly between 1986 and 1993, the variety of REMIC classes also proliferated. In addition to the traditional, fixed-rate sequential classes (sequentials), they include: floaters and inverse floaters, PACs and support classes (supports), IOs and POs, and VADMs (very accurately defined maturity bonds) and Z-bonds.

Floaters made their capital-market debut in September 1986. Indexed to LIBOR, they were issued to meet the demand of commercial banks and foreign investors that had LIBOR-based liabilities. Initially, floaters were offered (with floating-rate residuals) without the pairing of inverse floaters. However, technology and marketing quickly developed to pair floaters with inverse floaters. The variety of indexes of floaters also expanded to include the Eleventh District Cost of Funds Index (COFI), various constant-maturity Treasuries (CMTs), yields on certificates of deposits (CDs), and the prime rate.

Floaters were an instant success at debut. They accounted for 36% of 1987's total REMIC issuance (see Exhibit 3). As LIBOR escalated almost 400 basis points in the following two years to over 10%, the issuance of floaters plunged. But over the next three years, floaters flourished again, representing between 15% and 25% of newly issued REMICs. In the early years, floaters were basically sequentials or PACs in terms of principal paydown. Recently, their structures extended to include a significant amount of supports.

PACs were introduced around the same time as floaters. They were also warmly received by investors. Insurance companies, which needed mortgage securities with more stable average lives than sequentials, purchased the bulk of PACs. Since their inception, PACs have been refined to include Tier-I and Tier-II PACs (PAC Is and PAC IIs), TACs, and VADMs. (A VADM constitutes a very small portion of a REMIC because it uses the accrued interest from the Z-bond to "accurately" retire its principal on schedule.) As Exhibit 3 shows, these securities together accounted for at least 55% of new REMICs in the past three years.

The concept of stripping mortgage pass-throughs was developed in the early 1980s, although the actual issuance of IOs and POs first occurred in 1986. The idea of stripping pass-throughs came from the trading of servicing cash flows, which consisted of a strand of roughly 40 to 70 basis points of interest from the underlying mortgages. Unlike regular fixed-income securities, the value of servicing cash flows depreciated with declining interest rates *but appreciated with rising interest rates*. They were an ideal hedging vehicle

---

Exhibit 3. Dollar Amount of Issuance and Share of REMICs of Various REMIC Classes and IOs/POs, Selected Years, 1987 to 1993

	1987		1989		1991		1992		1993	
	$ Bil	Share	$ Bil	Share	$ Bil	Share	$ Bil	Share	$ Bil	Share
PACs	5.1	7.8	60.3	57.9	112.3	55.9	172.0	61.0	185.8	59.0
Supports	4.3	6.6	22.1	21.2	12.5	6.2	11.3	4.0	5.9	1.9
Floaters	23.9	36.4	2.4	2.3	24.6	12.2	56.4	20.0	67.6	21.5
Inverse Fl.	NA	NA	NA	NA	5.5	2.7	8.8	3.1	17.7	5.6
Sequentials	27.8	42.3	10.3	9.9	36.6	18.2	21.4	7.6	17.8	5.7
Z-Bonds	1.9	2.9	4.9	4.7	6.6	3.3	6.3	2.2	6.0	1.9
All Others	2.7	4.0	4.1	4	2.8	1.5	5.9	2.1	14	4.4
TOTAL	65.7	100%	104.1	100%	200.9	100%	282.1	100%	314.8	100%
IOs/POs	8.5		6.0		14.1		18.3		55.2	

Note: From 1991 on, PACs include PAC Is, PAC IIs, TACs, and VDAMs.

Sources: For REMICs, Bear Stearns as reported by *Inside Mortgage Securities;* IOs/POs, Bloomberg

against rising interest rates. To magnify their effectiveness as a hedge, servicing cash flows were modified and expanded to cover the entire coupon, or interest-only (IO), of pass-throughs. Issuance of IOs (and their companion POs) grew quickly from $2.9 billion in 1986 to $55.2 billion in 1993 (see Exhibit 3). In addition, there were also several billion dollar's worth of IO-ettes (a strip of a fraction of coupon from the underlying collateral), PAC IOs and PAC POs (interest-only and principal-only portion of PACs) issued as REMIC classes.

THE GREAT PRICE DEPRESSION

The phenomenal growth of REMICs came to an abrupt end in April 1994 after interest rates surged 150 basis points during the prior four months. Not only did the primary-market issuance dwindle, but secondary-market prices of certain REMIC classes plummeted. As of May 1994, the prices of exotic derivatives such as inverse floaters and supports had since January already plunged anywhere between 15% and 40%. In comparison, during this period, the price of 30-year GNMA 7s retreated just under 12%, from 103 to 91. While rising interest rates caused this great price depression, four factors intensified its severity: heightened volatility, average-life extension, leveraged investment, and lack of liquidity.

The prices of mortgage securities are known to be sensitive to interest-rate volatility because they are callable at par. In essence, the price of a mortgage security can be approximated by subtracting the value of the embedded call option from the price of a non-callable security of similar maturity and credit. Since the value of the option is a positive function of volatility, the mortgage security price is negatively affected by volatility. During the first five months of 1994, interest-rate volatility heightened due to three major events: four rounds of short-term interest rate hikes by the Federal Reserve, the weakening of the dollar, and investors' overriding concern regarding future inflation. Mortgage derivatives such as supports, which are structured to absorb the prepayment fluctuation of PACs, are embedded with tremendous call options. In a volatile and bearish market, they experienced much greater price declines than pass-throughs. In fact, support inverse floaters fared the worst in this environment. In addition to the prepayment risk, they also assumed the risk of short-term rates rising steadily.

Supports and POs also suffered great price declines due to substantial extensions in their expected average lives. For example, prepayments of FNMA or FHLMC 7s collapsed from 680% PSA in October 1993 to 180% PSA in May 1994. This sharp drop further reduced market expectations of future prepayments. For a two-year, average-life support inverse floater (backed by the 7% pass-through at a speed of 200% PSA) offered in late 1993, its expected average life quickly extended to more than 19 years in recent months under a 130% PSA. In the midst of a 150 basis point rise in interest rates, the average-life extension alone can push the price down by 10% to 15%.

Leveraged investments in mortgage derivatives by a few hedge funds worsened the demise of the REMIC market. In theory, these funds were to boost returns from mortgage derivatives by leveraging and self-hedging. For instance, by combining a certain mixture of IOs and POs in a leveraged manner, the fund manager can structure a zero-duration portfolio that earns a return markedly above that of money-market instruments. But this strategy overlooks the potential threat of margin calls when the market value of leveraged derivative securities falls significantly below their purchase prices. This actually happened in 1994. Margin calls forced these funds to liquidate, and the liquidation precipitated further price declines. This vicious cycle continued until some of the funds became insolvent. Meanwhile, the market of mortgage derivatives suffered a greater price collapse.

Secondary-market liquidity for mortgage derivatives, measured by the difference between their bids and offers, was never a critical issue when the market was bullish. During most of 1994, however, the bearish sentiment put the liquidity issue to the test. As dealers experienced huge mark-to-market losses, they substantially lowered their bids for derivative securities. Meanwhile, there was widespread liquidation of mortgage derivatives. Realizing the risk of quickly disappearing liquidity, investors became even more reluctant to make purchases—despite the fire-sale prices of these securities. All these factors furthered the price depression.

FUTURE ISSUANCE OF REMICs

We believe the primary market of REMICs will recover strongly. For the balance of this decade, annual issuance of REMICs will rebound to at least $200 billion, comparable to that of 1991 but far less than 1992-93. There are two fundamental reasons for this belief.

First, the brief history of the development of a variety of REMIC classes suggests that there are investors for mortgage securities with specifically structured cash flows. The technology of structuring mortgage cash flows out of single-class mortgage pass-through collateral has been well developed. Investors, who have grown accustomed to "tailor-made" mortgage securities, will continue to demand these securities. For example, the large number of floater investors has been well established. They will not disappear, although for various reasons they were temporarily out of the market in 1994. When they return, the issuance of floating-rate REMIC classes will resume.

Similarly, for regulatory and accounting reasons, banks and thrifts need to invest in assets such as short average-life PACs to match roughly their short-term liabilities. For the same reason, insurance companies need to purchase intermediate or long average-life PACs. Pension funds have a special appetite for the longest average-life assets, such as Z-bonds. In order to satisfy their demands, PACs and Z-bonds will have to be issued. Also, to hedge against rising interest rates, there will be demand for IOs. As long as all these demands exist, REMICs will be issued.

Second, the demand for mortgage credit will remain enormous and the financing of this demand dictates the continued large issuance of REMICs. For the balance of the 1990s, originations of single-family mortgages to facilitate housing starts and existing home sales are likely to be around $500 billion annually.[3] This amount, plus originations for refinancing and other miscellaneous purposes (e.g., taking a second mortgage to pay for children's college education) will put annual originations in the neighborhood of $675 billion annually. Based on a historical 45% ratio of pass-throughs to originations, annual issuance of agency-guaranteed, fixed-rate pass-throughs will amount to $300 billion.[4] Again, between 1988 and 1993, about 65% of pass-throughs have been collateralized for REMICs. This will produce just about $200 billion in new REMICs annually.

Since the successful mortgage securities programs at federal agencies in the early 1980s, fixed-rate originations have been funded primarily in capital markets in the form of pass-throughs. This type of funding has become increasingly efficient in recent years, as different types of cash flows from pass-throughs have been "tailor-made" in REMIC classes for different investors. The increased efficiency in funding has lowered the relative cost of mortgage credit. Yield spreads between mortgages and Treasuries have tightened. Time will not roll back. Mortgage credit demand will continue to be funded in the capital markets in the most efficient manner through the technology of REMICs.

The market correction in 1994 has interrupted the funding efficiency of mortgage originations. A large amount of newly issued pass-throughs have not been further processed into REMICs. Some investors, who were disappointed in the performance of REMICs, have been purchasing only pass-throughs. It will take time before they return to REMICs.

---

3 Currently, the average price is around $150,000 for new, single-family homes and $140,000 for existing homes. Single-family housing starts and existing home sales for the balance of this decade are projected to be around 1 million and 3.7 million, respectively. Assuming a 75% loan-to-value ratio, originations for these two types of housing activities will amount to $500 billion annually. See also "Originations, Mortgage Credit Demand, and Yield Spreads."

4 Implicitly, this ratio of 45% assumes that fixed-rate mortgages account for 60% of total mortgage originations.

FUTURE YIELD SPREADS AND STRUCTURES OF REMIC CLASSES

While we expect the REMIC market to rebound, we believe individual REMIC classes will be offered at much different yield spreads. Given the price of the collateral, yield spreads will tighten for floaters and PACs. Correspondingly, yield spreads for inverse floaters and supports will widen. More conservatively structured PACs with narrower prepayment protection bands will be offered. For a given REMIC, a smaller amount of floaters will be created. Corrections in the prices of IOs and POs will be less pronounced because of the constant arbitrage between IOs/POs and the collateral.

Yield spreads of newly offered PACs will have to tighten. The substantial cheapening of supports in 1994 suggests that investors have not been adequately compensated for all the risk associated with the securities. Supports are exceedingly risky not only in terms of average-life variation but also in secondary-market liquidity. While large yield spreads of supports are primarily the reward for absorbing the prepayment fluctuation of PACs, in the future they will have to compensate for the liquidity risk as well. To do so, the greater yield spreads of supports will necessitate tighter yield spreads for PACs.

Additionally, future PACs will be offered with more conservative prepayment bands. Structurally, aggressive PACs with wide bands and great prepayment protection can only be produced with supports of substantial average-life fluctuation. But supports have experienced the most price depreciation during the derivative market debacle in 1994. To the extent that investors are unwilling to assume the greater prepayment risk of supports for greater yield spreads, PACs of conservatively structured bands will be offered.

For the same reason, discount margins of floaters will have to tighten in order to enhance yields of inverse floaters. Also, for a given size REMIC, a floater of a smaller principal amount will be offered. Structurally, the size of a floater is proportional to the multiplier of its companion inverse floater. To offer a large floater, the multiplier of the inverse floater increases correspondingly. Again, in the disarrayed secondary market in 1994, the price of high-multiplier inverse floaters suffered most severely. This experience suggests that few highly leveraged inverse floaters will be offered in the future.

CHAPTER 18

The Effect of PAC Bond Features on Performance

Linda Lowell
First Vice President
Mortgage Strategies
PaineWebber, Inc.

Planned amortization classes or PAC bonds represent one of the largest sectors of the CMO market. Among the factors expanding the market for these bonds were widespread defections from the corporate market by investors who were attracted by the high yields and triple-A credit quality and discouraged in their natural habitat by limited supply and tight spreads, as well as by event risk.

With the increased size of the market and an expanding investor base came greater standardization of certain PAC features and improved liquidity. While typical PAC buyers still tend to be life insurance companies and commercial banks, the PAC market appeals as well to investors with active bond management strategies. These investors may have, for instance, opinions about the direction of mortgage-Treasury spreads or mortgage-corporate spreads, they may wish to execute barbell or other strategies designed to take advantage of expectations regarding the shape or direction of the yield curve, or they may be seeking value advantages, either between the PAC and other CMO sectors, or within the PAC sector, among PACs with different features.

The main attraction of PAC bonds lies in the fact that they provide a defined schedule of principal payments (or, similarly, target balances), which is guaranteed so long as prepayment rates remain within a specified range. (Hence the name, planned amortization.) Holders are insulated to a significant degree from the uncertainty regarding the cash flows of most MBS, which arises from the right of mortgage borrowers to prepay their loans at any time. The fact that the prepayment process is interest-rate sensitive—that the tendency of homeowners to move or refinance is inversely related to the direction of interest rates[1]—has a material impact on the average life, duration, and performance of mortgage securities. MBS shorten in rising markets and extend in declining markets. To compensate investors for taking this risk, pass-throughs and other MBS are priced at higher yields than other, noncallable bonds of similar credit quality (such as agency debt). PAC bonds partake of the incremental yield available in the MBS market while at the same time providing more certain cash flows. In addition to providing guaranteed payments within a range of prepayment behavior, PAC bonds can be further refined to concentrate payments over a shorter period of time or "window." PACs with narrow windows are perceived to be better substitutes for corporate and Treasury bonds with bullet principal payments, and therefore typically trade at tighter spreads than PACs with wider windows.

This chapter is intended to serve both classes of investors—the buy-and-hold PAC buyer, who wants to partake of the high yields in the mortgage market but whose liabilities or actuarial requirements necessitate more stable cash flows than either pass-throughs or standard CMOs can provide, and the active portfolio manager. The chapter examines the different features of PAC bonds, and their effect on market value and investment performance. Where it is possible to isolate a specific characteristic, an attempt is made to model and examine its impact on the average life and yield behavior of the bond, as well as on its theoretical or option-adjusted value.

THE TERM STRUCTURE OF CMO YIELDS

The yields that investors require for occupying different average life sectors of the PAC market are determined by the same factors that influence other fixed-income investors: portfolio objectives and constraints, the current and anticipated shape of the yield curve, expectations regarding the underlying monetary and economic determinants of interest rates, and so forth. In addition, PAC buyers require additional yield as they extend the maturity of their investments to compensate them for the increased risk that the prepayment collars may be broken, as well as the greater average life volatility of the later tranches in a transaction when the prepayment collars are broken. An indication of the average life volatility of PAC tranches of different nominal average lives is provided by Exhibit 1. The graph depicts the average lives of a series of PACs from a single CMO issue[2] at two prepayment speeds extreme enough to break both the upper and lower collars of all the PAC bonds. The range between the average lives at the extremes gradually widens for longer expected average lives to its widest point among the intermediate-term PACs.

---

1 See Chapters 8 and 9 for a discussion of prepayments.
2 This example assumes a structure in which PACs have priority to excess principal payments in the order of their scheduled maturities after the companions have been retired.

As a result of investors' demand for greater compensation for holding longer-term PACs, the generic CMO yield curves are more steeply sloped than the Treasury yield curve. Generic yields for current coupon PACs backed by current coupon conventional collateral and for on-the-run Treasuries are depicted in Exhibit 2. Although a satisfying discussion of the issue is beyond the scope of this chapter, it should be noted that CMO spreads are also influenced by the same factors that affect pass-through spreads—volatility of market yields, prepayment expectations, supply of new product, and so forth. Normally CMO spreads track pass-through spreads, with the relationship enforced by the existence of CMO arbitrage opportunities. When pass-throughs cheapen relative to CMOs, new transactions are marketed, increasing the supply of CMOs and ultimately allowing CMOs to cheapen relative to pass-throughs, thereby reducing the arbitrage opportunity.

Other features of the structure, such as the collateral coupon, the PAC's coupon, the collars, and the window result in additional adjustments to the required yields. In addition, the cash flow performance of the bond outside the collars is affected by other characteristics, such as whether its schedule is supported by accrual from a longer-term Z-bond later in the structure, and its priority for receiving excess cash flow. These characteristics determine how

Exhibit 1. Extension and Shortening of PAC Bond Average Lives as Prepayments Vary between 0% PSA and 600% PSA

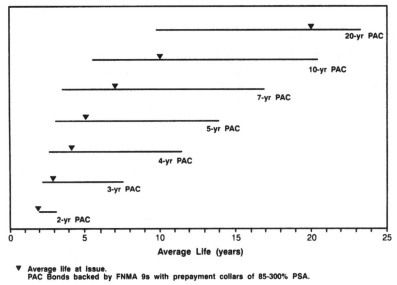

▼ Average life at issue.
PAC Bonds backed by FNMA 9s with prepayment collars of 85-300% PSA.

Exhibit 2. Treasury and PAC Yield Curves

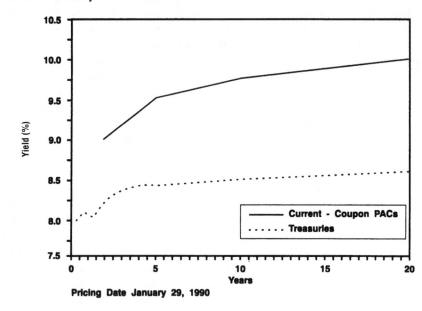

Pricing Date January 29, 1990

volatile its average life and returns are outside the collars, and so also affect the marketability of a PAC bond.

COLLARS AND COLLATERAL

The strength of the collars—whether they will be broken by actual prepayment experience—should be investors' primary concern. The strength is only nominally indicated in the differential between the top and bottom collar speeds. This range must be related to the specific collateral to gauge the strength of the protection provided. The type of collateral—the agency, the differential between current mortgage rates and the mortgage rates on the underlying loans, seasoning of the loans, and the degree to which the pools have prepaid in the past—determines how quickly or slowly the collateral will prepay in different interest rate scenarios. The collars simply define a range of prepayment speeds over which the PAC payments will not vary. When prepayments fall outside the collars, payments to the PAC holders may be either delayed or accelerated (the collars could be broken temporarily without affecting the payment schedule). A given set of PAC collars will provide stronger or weaker protection, depending on the collateral. For example, a top collar of 300% PSA provides greater call protection should interest rates decline if the collateral is a current coupon than if it is a premium coupon.

Similarly, a bottom collar of 100% PSA provides better protection from extension if the collateral is a conventional pass-through than if it is a GNMA.

All else being equal, PAC bonds backed by premium coupon collateral do exhibit greater average life variability than PACs backed by current coupon collateral. This is illustrated by the comparison in Exhibit 3, which displays the average lives at different prepayment speeds of two series of PACs, one backed by FNMA 9s (9.77% weighted average coupon [WAC], 349-month weighted average remaining term [WART]) and scheduled at 85% to 300% PSA, the other backed by FNMA 10 $^1/_2$s (11.13% WAC and 347-month WART) and scheduled at 95% to 350% PSA.[3] (Similar comparisons could be made in the case of discount and current coupon collateral, but are omitted from this discussion for the sake of brevity.)

Investors recognize the stability lent by discount collateral and will accept a tighter spread for structures backed by discounts when they anticipate prepayments will accelerate. Similarly, bearish investors require wider spreads for PACs backed by premium collateral than if backed by current coupon collateral. In markets characterized by bearish sentiment, the relative values can be reversed and investors will pay up for premium coupons and premium coupon collateral while demanding a concession for discount collateral.

INTERACTION OF COLLARS AND COLLATERAL

Before further examining the contribution of the collar to the PAC's value, it is useful to review the mechanics of defining a collar and creating a payment schedule. Visualizing the cash flows is also helpful in seeking to understand the behavior of the structure in different scenarios. The PAC schedule is defined by projecting the paydowns from the given collateral at a high and a low constant prepayment speed. Those payment amounts that can be satisfied by both sets of projected principal payments (that is, the smaller of the two amounts generated for each date) make up the schedule. This is depicted graphically in Exhibit 4. The example depicted was structured from $500 million FNMA 9s with a 9.77% WAC and a 349-month WART[4] on the underlying mortgages, assuming collars of 85 to 300% PSA and a two-year lockout (the period before the first scheduled principal payment).

The faster speed results in a cash flow pattern with the bulk of the principal thrown off during the first five to seven years of the issue's life. The slower speed produces a more level set of smaller cash flows extending to the final maturity of the collateral. The intersection of these two sets of payments

---

3 These examples were created in January 1990, when 9% coupon pass-throughs were priced below but closest to par, and permitted the creation of tranches with coupons at current market yields across the PAC CMO yield curve.

4 The scheduled amortization for the collateral is determined by the WAC and WART.

Exhibit 3. Impact of Collateral Coupon on the Average Life Variability of PAC Bonds

Average Life (years)

Payment Speed (% PSA)	FNMA 9% Collateral (85-300% PSA Collars)							FNMA 10.5% Collateral (95-350% PSA Collars)						
	2-yr.	3-yr.	4-yr.	5-yr.	7-yr.	10-yr.	20-yr.	2-yr.	3-yr.	4-yr.	5-yr.	7-yr.	10-yr.	20-yr.
0	3.20	7.70	11.44	13.74	16.97	20.50	22.75	3.63	8.81	12.78	15.06	18.11	21.01	22.61
50	2.23	3.61	5.25	6.67	9.37	13.49	19.24	2.27	3.79	5.60	7.16	10.06	13.82	19.07
85	2.14	3.05	4.16	5.16	7.13	11.22	19.23	2.16	3.15	4.37	5.45	7.57	11.33	19.07
95	2.14	3.05	4.16	5.16	7.13	11.22	19.23	2.14	3.05	4.16	5.16	7.13	11.22	19.07
300	2.14	3.05	4.16	5.16	7.13	11.22	19.23	2.14	3.05	4.16	5.16	7.13	11.22	19.07
350	2.14	3.05	4.16	4.99	6.29	9.69	17.06	2.14	2.05	4.16	5.16	7.13	11.22	19.07
400	2.14	3.05	3.93	4.40	5.51	8.48	15.09	2.14	3.05	4.16	4.88	6.28	9.81	19.03
450	2.14	2.98	3.52	3.93	4.90	7.52	13.43	2.14	3.04	3.83	4.33	5.56	8.67	15.17
600	2.10	2.38	2.67	2.97	3.67	5.54	9.86	2.14	2.51	2.86	3.22	4.10	6.32	11.11

Exhibit 4.   Principal Cash Flows at 300% and 85% PSA—FNMA 9% Collateral

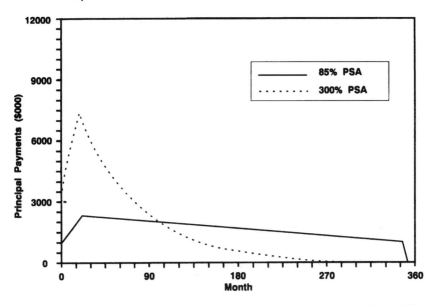

forms the schedule. In the example, the bottom collar determines the payment amounts during the first 100 or so months of the schedule, and the top collar the amounts in the remaining months.

The graph of *any speed between* those of the top and bottom collars also would contain the area of the schedule below it. The graph of any speed *faster* than the top collar would bunch more principal in the first years and truncate the tail of the schedule in front of the point where the top and bottom collars intersect. Similarly, the graph of any speeds *slower* than the bottom collar would reduce the size of paydowns in the front years. At very slow speeds, most of the principal payments are pushed into the back years.

Once the scheduled principal payments are defined at given collars, the PAC schedule may be further divided into classes with different average lives. The example in Exhibit 5 is split into seven tranches. Some of the earlier bonds in the structure have higher *effective top* collars. An effective collar is the highest (or lowest) constant prepayment speed that would satisfy the entire tranche's payments. For instance, many speeds faster than 300% PSA will contain the first tranche in this example. The fastest speed containing all of the first tranche is that bond's effective upper collar. Effective top collars are shown in Exhibit 5 for the third and fourth tranches. These effective collars are approximately 370% and 330% PSA, respectively. It should be apparent as well that earlier tranches have still higher effective collars.

Exhibit 5. Effective Top PAC Prepayment Collars—FNMA 9% Collateral

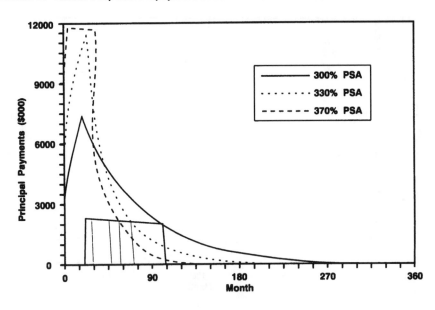

Likewise, the lower collars used to structure the PACs in Exhibits 4 and 5 do not fully indicate the degree of extension protection the longer average life bonds, tranches 6 and 7, actually possess. Speeds below 85% PSA throw off principal too slowly to satisfy the scheduled payments in the early PAC tranches, but they provide more cash than needed to meet payments after about month 100, where the upper collar binds the schedule. For example, the effective bottom collar on tranche 7 is 55% PSA. Since tranche 6 begins to pay at the point where the top and bottom collars intersect, its effective collar is the same as the structuring collar.

When PACs first became popular, a wide variety of collar ranges and levels were used to generate the schedules, and even as late as the first quarter of 1989, it was not uncommon still to see some variety in collars on new CMO issues backed by similar collateral. However, the smorgasbord of prepayment collars largely has given way to increasing standardization of the speeds at which PAC schedules are created. This standardization was in part the result of demand for liquidity on the part of the growing PAC clientele.

The standard speeds used to create PAC schedules may represent the market's aggregate opinion of what constitutes a "good" collar; however, investors should translate the PSA collars into interest-rate collars by using an econometric prepayment model to determine how much interest rates must shift to break the collars. Once the collar speeds are explicitly linked to interest-rate shifts, investors can determine if the collar does deliver "good" protection over the scenarios appropriate to the investor's outlook and portfolio.

New-issue PACs may be marketed either at the collars used to create the schedule or at their effective collars, although since 1990 the trend has been to advertise effective collars. Unless the effective collar is known, the extent of the PAC's protection against shifts in interest rates cannot be determined. Investors, therefore, should insist on this information, as well as analysis of the bond's performance outside the effective collars.[5] By the same token, investors cannot assume that a new issue, short-term average-life PAC with a very high effective collar is better than a comparable average-life PAC from a series with only the structuring collars indicated.[6]

With greater standardization of structuring speeds, the PAC market has developed a two-tiered structure, with standard PACs in the first tier and PACs with weaker collars in the second, trading significantly cheaper than "good" PACs. In mid-1989, issuers began to issue both types of PACs from the same transaction by layering a second set of PACs with narrower collars over the first. These two-layered PACs are, in essence, companion bonds with schedules. They are discussed at length in Chapter 20.

In the 1991-94 rally, the practice of carving "SuperPACs" out of the first priority PAC schedule became widespread. The PACs which had second priority to the SuperPACs still had standard new-issue PAC collars, but they were subject to much greater average-life variability outside the collar speeds. As a result, they tended to trade behind standard PACs. As the "prepayment emergency" continued, collars became less important to astute investors who instead scrutinized bond performance across a spectrum of prepayment scenarios.

PAC COLLAR DRIFT

Many investors do not understand that the PAC collars are not fixed for the life of the tranche, but instead change over time with the actual prepayment experience of the collateral. This is evident from the number of investors who seek to evaluate trades in the secondary PAC market by looking at the collars advertised at issue (which could be either structuring or effective

---

5 The top collar may provide little protection in a bull market, when prepayments speeds are sustained at 100% PSA or higher. In that environment, the bond's value will derive from its stability outside the top collar.

6 If effective collars are indicated, it is usually easy enough to deduce the schedule speeds if information on all the tranches is available. Early PACs in the series will have the same bottom collar—the structuring collar—and varying effective top collars. One or more intermediate PACs will have the structuring collars. Later PACs will show the structuring collar as their top collar and varying effective collars for the bottom. Doing so permits first-cut comparisons with PACs offered with their structuring collars stated.

collars). Instead, off-the-run PACs should be evaluated by looking at the current effective collars. In most cases, they can be determined by the security dealers or third-party data services that have modeled the structure and know the current bond and collateral balances.

The effective collars simply express the highest and lowest constant prepayment speeds at which the given collateral can continue to meet the scheduled prepayments. Unless the collateral prepays at precisely the collar speed (and then it can match only one, the upper or the lower collar speed), it will have a different balance than was projected when the schedule was defined. Likewise, the amount of companions (and proportion of companions to PACs) will be different. Prepayment rates below the top collar cause the collar to shift upward over time (as there is a greater amount outstanding than anticipated), while the collar is lowered if prepayments are higher. Likewise, prepayments above the bottom collar cause it to rise. Short- and intermediate-term PACs are affected differently by speeds below the collar than are long-term PACs at the end or tail of the schedule. Very slow speeds cause the collar to drift up in the earlier tranches, while speeds below the bottom collar can improve the extension protection of long PACs. Prepayment rates somewhere between the top and bottom collars—historically, the common occurrence—cause the effective prepayment protection to widen as the top collar changes more quickly than the bottom collar (unless prepayments are very near the top collar).

WHEN THE PAC BREAKS

Breaking a PAC's schedule and causing it to be partially called or extended are not necessarily negative events for the bond's economic performance. The bond's coupon relative to market yields (or the bond's price relative to parity[7]) determines the effect prepayments outside the collar have on the realized yield or total return. A PAC with a discount coupon may benefit if the upper collar is broken, returning principal at par earlier than anticipated at pricing. Similarly, the extension caused by breaking the lower collar adversely affects the performance of a discount coupon PAC. In the case of a premium coupon PAC, it benefits performance when the bottom collar is broken, since the principal remains outstanding longer than anticipated, earning additional coupon interest. And of course, the higher the coupon, the worse the effect of breaking the top collar.

The shape of the yield curve is also a consideration. Extension can be costly in a steep yield curve; discounting a bond's cash flows at a sharply

---

7 The delay in passing payments through to investors from the mortgage borrowers lowers the yield slightly for any given price because the cash flows are pushed out into the future. Different prepayment speeds do not change the yield if a bond is purchased at the parity price (slightly below 100), which adjusts par for the payment delay.

higher yield can offset any value additional coupon income might have. Likewise, the capital gain from rolling down a steep curve can offset the loss of coupon income.

WINDOWS

A PAC "window" is the interval over which scheduled principal payments are made to the bondholder. As long as prepayment speeds remain at a constant speed within the upper and lower protection bands, or PAC collars, the dates of the first and last principal payments (and equivalently, the length of the repayment period) are certain. PAC buyers in general prefer tighter windows. To some extent, this preference reflects the practicalities of managing their portfolios. The match between a single liability and a single asset is easier to conceptualize when payments are concentrated over a short period. They also are easier to convert to floating-rate assets with swaps. A shorter window also means fewer and larger repayments. Tighter windows producing a more bullet-like paydown are, conceptually, better substitutes for corporates. The chief benefit of a tight window, however, is the superior roll down the yield curve it provides as it ages. Ideally the average life declines by a year for every year the bond is outstanding (assuming a stable yield and prepayment scenario).

Generally, a tighter window is a greater consideration on the longer the average life of the bond. Shorter-term PACs inherently have shorter windows, while the desire for tight windows in the twenty-year sector is difficult to satisfy, owing to the "tailish" nature of the cash flows in the later years of the transaction. That is, the principal payments scheduled for the later years are relatively small in any month. This is easily confirmed by glancing at Exhibit 4. Carving the "tail" into shorter windows would result in more classes with odd, less marketable average lives.

A "good" window in the three- and four-year sectors is 12 to 15 months long. Five- and seven-year buyers prefer a window of 18 to 24 months. Ten-year buyers prefer paydowns over a 24 to 30 month period.

Some investors claim to prefer tight windows because they expect superior average-life stability. For example, they may believe a tighter window has less average life variability when prepayments are outside the PAC collars. This hunch is disproved by experimenting with different window lengths in otherwise identical PACs (same collateral, same average lives). Exhibit 6 shows two such experiments manipulating the windows of the five- and ten-year PACs in a structure containing a complete series of PACs with average lives from two to twenty years, backed by $500 million FNMA 9s (9.77% WAC, 349-month WART) and protected between 85% and 300% PSA. Even at fairly extreme prepayment speeds (0% and 600% PSA, for instance), there is little difference in the average lives of otherwise comparable PACs with

Exhibit 6. Impact of Window Size on the Average Life Variability of PAC Bonds

Payment Speed (% PSA)	Average Life (years)					
	5-Year PAC			10-Year PAC		
	0.5 yr. Window	2.2 yr. Window	4.4 yr. Window	3.2 yr. Window	5.0 yr. Window	7.3 yr. Window
0	13.78	13.69	13.38	20.68	20.61	20.50
50	6.68	6.67	6.65	13.70	13.62	13.49
75	5.49	5.48	5.48	11.42	11.47	11.50
100	5.16	5.16	5.16	11.22	11.22	11.22
300	5.16	5.16	5.16	11.22	11.22	11.22
350	5.01	4.96	4.87	9.68	9.69	9.69
400	4.40	4.41	4.41	8.47	8.48	8.48
450	3.93	3.94	3.96	7.51	7.51	7.52
600	2.97	2.98	3.00	5.53	5.53	5.54

Note: All structures are backed by $500MM FNMA 9s, 9.77 WAC, 349 WAM and have 85% to 300% PSA collars.

different windows. *All else equal, as a result of their slightly wider spreads, PACs with average or wide windows should outperform those with tight windows.* This result suggests that investors who do not require a bullet-like repayment of their investment, but rather can accommodate greater payment dispersion, should not discriminate between window sizes, particularly in a flatter yield curve environment. Investors who can adapt to a longer paydown period by such means as modifying their cash management procedures, adopting more sophisticated techniques for modeling and managing their asset-liability positions, or other procedural changes, would also be able to take advantage of the relative cheapness of wide windows.

Tighter windows may improve performance when the PAC is a current pay bond. In this case, a shorter window reduces the likelihood that prepayments can accelerate or decelerate to levels outside the bands before it is fully retired according to schedule.

LOCKOUT

A lockout is properly a feature of the companion rather than the PAC bonds in a CMO structure. A portion of the PAC schedule at the very front is added to the companion classes; PAC bonds are "locked out" for the period over which those principal payments are made instead to companions. Lockouts typically occur over the first twelve to 24 months of the issue's life. The desired effect of the lockout is to stabilize the early companion class. This is achieved by acquiring for the companions the principal cash flows that in effect have the highest effective collars (that is, they will be realized across a very wide range of prepays). These cash flows, which have a high degree of certainty, are used during the lockout to pay the companions. Some market participants, however, speak of the lockout as a PAC bond characteristic or feature; they may be viewing the lockout as a device for narrowing the PAC window. Others may perceive the lockout as somehow detrimental to the PACs in the structure, perhaps assuming that the PACs are somehow hurt to the extent the companions are helped.

Whether any of these assumptions are valid should be apparent from the example in Exhibit 7. The table contrasts the volatilities of three-, seven-, and ten-year average-life bonds from a structure without any lockout with those from one with a two-year lockout. Both structures are backed by the same collateral, FNMA 9s, with a 9.77% WAC and 349-month WART, and use the maximum PAC schedule consistent with collars of 85% to 300% PSA, and, as appropriate, a lockout. The sizes of the bonds compared have been adjusted to match their average lives within two decimal places. (The twenty-year bonds are not included in the comparison because their average lives were too different after matching the earlier bonds.)

The lockout, according to the exhibit, benefits the PAC bonds by reducing both call and extension risk. Earlier bonds benefit more than later bonds, with the

Exhibit 7. Impact of Lockout Feature on the Average Life Variability of PAC Bonds

Payment	Average Life (years)					
(Speed	No Lockout			2-Year Lockout		
(% PSA)	3-yr.	7-yr.	10-yr.	3-yr.	7-yr.	10-yr.
0	11.14	18.98	21.96	7.46	16.57	20.72
50	4.41	10.22	14.36	3.60	9.23	13.75
85	3.05	7.10	11.22	3.05	7.10	11.22
300	3.05	7.10	11.22	3.05	7.10	11.22
355	3.01	6.26	9.70	3.05	6.34	9.68
400	2.84	5.49	8.49	3.02	5.58	8.47
450	2.66	4.89	7.53	2.89	4.96	7.51
600	2.17	3.66	5.55	2.37	3.71	5.53

Note: Both structures are backed by $500MM FNMA 9s, 9.77 WAC, 349 WAM and have 85% to 300% PSA collars.

ten-year classes displaying only marginal reductions in average life volatility. Two effects are at work here. First, the lockout reduces the size of the schedule by removing all payments in the first two years. This results automatically in a smaller amount of PAC bonds relative to the companions; conversely, more companions protect the remaining PAC schedule. Since they contain those cash flows from the collateral with the lowest degree of call risk, the companions are much less vulnerable to call risk, and even at very high prepayment speeds a larger proportion of companion bonds remain outstanding to shelter the PAC bonds than would otherwise have been the case. At the same time, these principal amounts are no longer bound to a schedule, meaning that later scheduled payments have a better likelihood of being paid on schedule in event of speeds below the bottom collar.

IS THERE A Z IN THE DEAL?

A Z- or accrual bond ("Z" standing for zero coupon) is a type of CMO bond structure that pays no interest until it begins to pay principal. Until that time, the interest payments are accrued at the coupon rate and added to the principal amount outstanding. A Z-bond is most typically included in a CMO structure as the last bond class to be retired. Of course, the underlying collateral continues to pay coupon interest; the portion that would have gone to the Z-bond holders, had it been structured as a coupon-paying bond, is used instead to retire the earlier classes. In effect, then, the presence of a Z-bond permits CMO structurers to increase the size of the earlier classes, since the "accrual" amounts are additional to the projected principal payments from the collateral. More pertinently, the "accrual" helps to stabilize the earlier bonds, since a portion of the cash flow used to retire them is not directly determined by the level of prepayments.

The interaction of Z-bonds with earlier classes is discussed in detail in Chapter 19. Readers who are unfamiliar with the Z-bond structure, or are interested in more complex manifestations of the Z-structure, should refer to that chapter. The objective of this discussion is to examine the value, if any, that a long-term Z-bond contributes to PACs. A related issue also is explored, namely the possibility that accrual from the Z-bond is used to stabilize earlier companion bonds and not the PAC bonds, or equivalently, to pay down stated-maturity-type bonds. Such a mechanism might not be explicitly disclosed when the bonds from the structure are traded, and may only be indicated in the prospectus or by careful review of the entire issue.

Two CMO structures were modeled to examine more closely the impact of a Z-bond on their performance and relative value, again backed by the same FNMA 9% collateral, and containing the maximum principal amount of PACs given collars of 85% to 300% PSA and the relevant accrual mechanism. The schedule has been divided into a series of bonds with nominal average lives of two, three, four, five, seven, ten, and twenty years, the average lives of all but the twenty-year matching to within two decimal places (as in the lockout example, because the schedules differ significantly in amount, the twenty-year bonds are not comparable).

Both structures contain twenty-year Z-bonds. The first passes accrual to PAC and earlier companion bonds alike, the second to earlier companions only. The average lives of the two PAC series at various prepayment rates are displayed in Exhibit 8.

Investors should note the difference in average life performance between the PACs supported by a Z-bond and the PACs whose companions alone are supported by the Z-bond. The *Z-bond stabilizes the PAC bonds when prepayments break the lower collar.* This makes sense—accrual cash flow is generated as long as the Z-bond is outstanding. On the other hand, *PAC bonds shorten more sharply* in the structure with the Z-bond when the upper collar is broken, because a smaller proportion of companion bonds is outstanding at any time to cushion PACs from high rates of prepayments. In fact, the faster the prepayments, the smaller the principal balance of the Z-bond when it begins to absorb excess cash, and the quicker it can be extinguished. This example should warn investors not to assume, however, that because a Z-bond is present in the structure, that the PACs will have less extension risk. There is no rule in the marketplace requiring issuers to pay accrual to PAC bonds. In some market environments, diverting accrual to the companions can make them more marketable, and a CMO arbitrage more viable. If this is the case, then issuers will structure their CMOs accordingly. The moral of the story: ask for the priorities in detail and read the prospectus.

Readers also may have noticed that the average life profile of the PACs that receive no accrual in this example is identical to that of the PACs backed by the same collateral in a structure with no Z-bond. (See Exhibit 3.) In other words, for PAC buyers, diverting accrual to the companions is the same as not including a Z-bond in the structure at all. This makes sense—the same aggregate amount of companion bonds is available to support the PAC bonds, with the only difference being that the weight of companion principal payments is shifted forward in time since the payments to the non-Z companions consist in part of interest accrued by the Z-bond.

EFFECT OF JUMP-Zs AND VADMs ON PAC BONDS

During 1990, structurers began to create a special bond class from the accrual thrown off by a Z-bond. Variously called thrift liquidity bonds, VADMs (Very Accurately Determined Maturity), or SMAT (Stated Maturity), these bonds first appealed to savings and loan institutions, who are required by regulation to maintain a portion of their assets in very high-quality, short-term investments, and who, accordingly, are willing to pay a premium for

Exhibit 8.   Impact of Z-Bond Accrual on the Average Life Variability of PAC Bonds

Prepayment Speed (% PSA)	Average Life (years)											
	Accrual to PACs and Companions						Accrual to Companions Only					
	2-yr.	3-yr.	4-yr.	5-yr.	7-yr.	10-yr.	2-yr.	3-yr.	4-yr.	5-yr.	7-yr.	10-yr.
0	2.74	6.03	9.05	11.04	14.01	17.11	3.20	7.70	11.44	13.74	16.97	20.50
50	2.21	3.53	5.07	6.40	8.85	12.24	2.23	3.61	5.25	6.67	9.37	13.49
85	2.13	3.05	4.16	5.16	7.13	11.23	2.13	3.05	4.16	5.16	7.13	11.22
300	2.13	3.05	4.16	5.16	7.13	11.23	2.13	3.05	4.16	5.16	7.13	11.22
350	2.13	3.00	4.13	4.76	6.19	9.68	2.13	3.05	4.16	4.99	6.29	9.69
400	2.13	2.82	3.68	4.19	5.93	8.47	2.13	3.05	3.93	4.40	5.51	8.48
450	2.13	2.21	3.30	3.74	4.83	7.51	2.13	2.95	3.52	3.93	4.90	7.52
600	1.97	1.82	2.52	2.84	3.62	5.53	2.10	2.38	2.67	2.97	3.67	5.54

Note: Both structures are backed by $500MM FNMA 9s, 9.77 WAC, 349 WAM and have 85% to 300% PSA collars.

instruments that qualify *and* offer yields more attractive than those of, for example, government issues. These bonds appeal to investors such as commercial banks, who are sensitive to the extension risk associated with rising yield environments, so that VADMs with final maturities greater than two years have been issued in growing amounts. The size of a VADM class is determined by the amount of accrual (or accrual and principal) thrown off at a zero prepayment rate up to the desired final maturity; obviously, faster prepayments will shorten the maturity, but no event can lengthen it. The presence of a VADM has the same effect on the PAC performance as diverting the accrual to the companion classes has in the preceding example.

In a handful of issues, structurers designed the companion Z-bonds to convert to a "payer" early, changing their priority among companions for principal from last to current. There are a variety of ways to make a Z "jump"; the chief ones are described in Chapter 19. Once the Z-bond converts to the current pay bond and begins to pay coupon interest, its support is no longer available to the PAC classes. The effect on PAC performance is generally the same as in the basic example above. However, the degree to which the PACs lose extension protection is moderated by the amount of time it takes to trigger the conversion, and by whether the jump is a temporary response to some condition (such as a specified prepayment threshold) or permanent (a "sticky" Z). This structuring strategy was more common in the late 1980s and is never seen in the current environment.

PRIORITY TO RECEIVE EXCESS CASH FLOWS

The PAC schedule is protected by the existence of companion classes. The mechanism is simple—in any period the companions absorb all principal in excess of the scheduled payments, and any current-paying PACs have first claim on all principal received. This protection ceases when all the companion classes have been fully retired, an event that occurs if the collateral consistently pays at speeds above the top collar. Once the companions are retired, any principal is distributed to the outstanding PACs, according to priorities defined for the particular CMO issue. Frequently, these priorities pay excess principal to the outstanding PACs in order of final maturity, but this is not always the case. A wholesale examination of CMO prospectuses will unearth numerous examples of structures that paid excess in the reverse of maturity order or otherwise insulated some classes at the expense of others. The impact of such schemes has, as would be expected, a significant effect on the average life volatility of the various PACs.

A simple example contrasting two priority schemes is shown in Exhibit 9. This exhibit compares the average lives of two sets of PACs at various prepayment speeds—one receiving excess principal in the maturity order,

Exhibit 9.   Impact of Excess Payment Order on the Average Life Variability of PAC Bonds

Average Life (years)

Speed (% PSA)	Excess in Order of Maturity							Excess in Reverse Maturity Order						
	2-yr.	3-yr.	4-yr.	5-yr.	7-yr.	10-yr.	20-yr.	2-yr.	3-yr.	4-yr.	5-yr.	7-yr.	10-yr.	20-yr.
0	3.20	7.70	11.44	13.74	16.97	20.50	22.75	3.20	7.70	11.44	13.74	16.97	20.50	22.75
50	2.73	3.61	5.75	6.67	9.37	13.49	19.24	2.73	3.61	5.75	6.67	9.37	13.49	19.24
85	2.14	3.05	4.16	5.16	7.13	11.22	19.23	2.14	3.05	4.16	5.16	7.13	11.22	19.23
300	2.14	3.05	4.16	5.16	7.13	11.22	19.23	2.14	3.05	4.16	5.16	7.13	11.22	19.23
350	2.14	3.05	4.16	4.99	6.29	9.69	17.06	2.14	2.05	4.16	5.16	7.14	11.95	5.42
400	2.14	3.05	3.93	4.40	5.51	8.48	15.09	2.14	3.05	4.16	5.16	7.17	9.65	4.07
450	2.14	2.95	3.52	3.93	4.90	7.52	13.43	2.14	3.04	4.16	5.16	7.26	7.56	3.35
600	2.10	2.38	2.67	2.97	3.67	5.54	9.86	2.14	2.51	4.16	5.16	7.24	3.09	2.27

Note: Both structures are backed by $500 MM FNMA 9s, 9.77 WAC, 349 WAM and have 85% to 300% PSA collars.

the other in the reverse maturity order. As the exhibit indicates, reversing the order in which PACs are subjected to prepayments above the top collar drastically alters the average life performance of the PACs, if prepayments are outside the collars. As would be expected, shorter PACs benefit at the expense of the longer. When the excess is paid in reverse, the short- and intermediate-term PACs are more significantly stable; when prepayments increase, longer PACs, with ten- and twenty-year average lives, shorten up much more significantly.

THE OPTION COSTS OF PAC FEATURES

Most participants in the PAC market evaluate individual bonds by examining their average life and yield over various constant prepayment scenarios outside the collars, a technique similar to the one used in this chapter to ana-lyze the various PAC features. The procedure has recognized disadvantages, some of which can be reduced to the complaint that they use a constant pre-payment assumption. Using such tools, investors can devise investment crite-ria for PACs such as "I will buy ten-year PACs with four-year windows at 120 off if they don't shorten to less than eight years average life given an instanta-neous 200 basis point drop in yields." Implicitly, they are using these tools to measure and value the prepayment options embedded in their PAC bonds. However savvy and tough-minded the criteria sound, they are at bottom purely subjective guesses about how much the random exercise of those options will impair or help investment results.

It is possible to measure the impact of prepayment risk on the yields earned by PACs by employing the option pricing models. These models gen-erate spreads, durations (price sensitivity), and convexities (the sensitivity of duration to yield changes) that are explicitly adjusted to account for expected prepayments on a large sample of possible interest-rate paths over the life of the PAC. In particular, these models derive an average cost of the prepayment options in the PAC, and determine the expected reduction in total spread caused by interest-rate volatility.[8] The model, in simple terms,

---

8 The model employed in this discussion, like many other OAS models, used Monte Carlo simulation and an econometric prepayment model. A minimum of 200 paths was generated in the analysis. The total spread computed is a total spread to the entire Treasury yield curve (precisely, the forward rates implied by current Treasury yields), as opposed to a sin-gle benchmark. It roughly approximates the spread to a particular Treasury quoted in the market, but differs more or less depending on the slope of the yield curve. The total spread is the spread over Treasuries the security would earn given its current market price if there were zero volatility. The option-adjusted spread (OAS) is the average spread earned across a large sample of interest-rate scenarios given the market price. The option cost is measured as the difference between total and option-adjusted spread, and captures the reduction in total spread caused by interest-rate volatility.

summarizes hundreds more scenarios than investors can digest looking at price/yield tables. The scenarios, moreover, are more realistic in that they permit interest rates to move randomly at each point along the path.

Option-adjusted spreads (OASs) vary with market conditions. For this reason, a discussion of current OASs is inappropriate here. However, the option costs derived from the analysis are not very sensitive to current market yield levels (although they will vary somewhat with changes in the level of implied volatility), and can be discussed here without becoming hopelessly stale with the next rally or correction in fixed-income markets.

As expected, PACs demonstrate very low option costs. *Option costs in the current-coupon-backed structures discussed in this chapter generally ranged from zero to twenty basis points for bonds with three- to twenty-year average lives.* By comparison, the collateral (FNMA 9s) had thirty-five basis points of option cost. The PAC bonds backed by premium collateral (FNMA 10 ½s) had demonstrably higher option costs, ranging from 3 to over 40 basis points. The collateral had an option cost of 68 basis points.

The general pattern revealed by the option-pricing model is illustrated in Exhibit 10. The option costs are calculated for the series, described in earlier sections, of two-, three-, four-, five-, seven-, and twenty-year average-life-PACs backed by FNMA 9s. (See Exhibit 3 for the average-life profile of these bonds.) The patterns displayed by option costs for premium-backed PACs are shown in

Exhibit 10. Sensitivity of Option Costs in PACs to Interest-Rate Shifts (Current-Coupon Conventional Collateral)

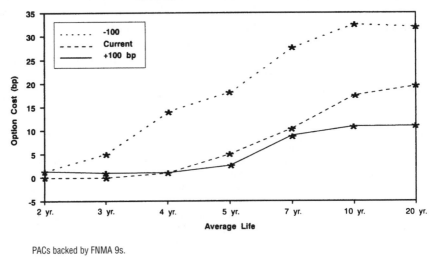

PACs backed by FNMA 9s.
Instantaneous interest-rate shifts assumed.

Exhibit 11. The option costs for these series are analyzed in three scenarios: assuming the interest-rate environment (of January 23, 1990) remains constant and assuming instantaneous parallel shifts in interest rates of up and down 100 basis points. Assuming a constant option-adjusted spread, the shifts in the up and down cases are typically large enough to give the tranches, which currently are priced close to par, a discount or premium price. In this way it is possible to draw some conclusions about the sensitivity of the structure to interest-rate shocks. Ranging from three to over thirty basis points, the option costs demonstrated by the current-coupon-backed PACs in the bullish scenario are consistent, as well, with the general magnitude of option costs observed in premium-coupon-backed PACs.

As expected, the option costs rise with the average life of the PAC. This result is expected if only because the probability an option will be exercised is greater the later its expiration date. Comparing the current and bearish cases, the increase in extension risk as interest rates rise results in a slightly higher option cost for two- and three-year PACs. Of greater interest is the fact that, going from the ten-year PAC to the twenty-year, option costs either decline or increase at a slower rate in every interest-rate case. This result holds for the option costs in a similar set of PACs depicted in Exhibit 11, backed in this

Exhibit 11.   Sensitivity of Option Costs in PACs to Interest-Rate Shifts (Premium-Coupon Conventional Collateral)

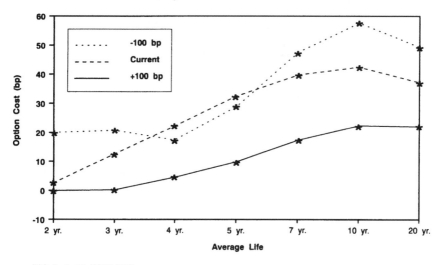

PACs backed by FNMA 10 1/2s.
Instantaneous interest-rate shifts assumed.

instance by premium coupon collateral (the average life profile is in Exhibit 3). *The fact that option costs tend to peak with ten-year PACs rather than twenty-year PACs* should take some market participants by surprise, and suggest to others that the typical incremental spread required by twenty-year PAC buyers over 10-year PACs represents extra value. The result is intuitively appealing as well. The twenty-year PAC consists of the tail of the PAC schedule, and the low, widely dispersed payment amounts lend stability. Moreover, the prepayment model used to project prepayments over various interest-rate paths correctly reflects the tendency of mortgage pools to "burn out" following sustained periods of fast prepayment rates. As a result, prepayments tend to slow down in the later years of the pool's life. In addition, as long as the PACs have sequential priority to excess cash flow, the last PAC in the series is protected by the earlier PACs.

When the effect of a lockout was examined using average-life profiles (Exhibit 7), the benefits to the PACs were more pronounced the earlier the bond came in the series. By explicitly valuing the option costs for the same example, a similar effect is observed, as is shown in Exhibit 12. However, the seven- and ten-year tranches receive no benefit from the lockout on an option-cost basis, whereas their average lives are observed to lengthen less sharply in

Exhibit 12. Sensitivity of Option Costs in PACs to Interest-Rate Shifts in Structures With and Without a Lockout

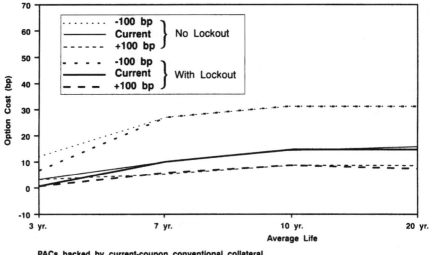

PACs backed by current-coupon conventional collateral.
Instantaneous interest-rate shifts assumed.

extremely slow prepayment rate environments. The exhibit also indicates a benefit to the twenty-year PAC, except when interest rates drop and the collateral becomes a premium security and subject to faster prepayments. The twenty-year PACs were not compared in Exhibit 6 since, given a different amount in the schedules, it was not possible to match the average lives of all four bonds (the twenty-year in the lockout structure had an average life close to sixteen years). This difference also may account for the lower option cost imputed to the twenty-year in the lockout structure.

The impact of various window lengths on five- and ten-year PACs also was examined, with no increase or diminution of option costs observed, except for the five-year bonds in the bullish case. Even then, only slight differences, at best three basis points, were manifested. This reiterates the conclusion, stated earlier, that the length of the window does not significantly affect the average-life stability of the bond outside the collars.

Some security analysts and investors resist this result. They believe, for instance, that a tight window lowers the likelihood of breaking the collars during the paydown period. Therefore, they reason, the prepayment options that they effectively hold should be less costly. The time value of the options, however, includes the period prior to the first payment, because the protection implicit in the collars can be damaged or enhanced by prepayment experience in earlier months or years of the structure's life. More than one full interest-rate and housing industry *cycle* can occur before a single principal payment is made to a five- or seven-year PAC, with periods of slower prepayments tending to improve a PAC's call protection and faster prepayments tending to erode it. If prepayments violate the lower collar when earlier PACs are paying, both the call and extension protection of the later PACs can actually improve! When many such possibilities are simulated, the net effect should be small or negligible.[9]

The option costs for two series of PACs in Z-bond structures, one funded by the Z-bond and one not, are displayed in Exhibit 13. The fact that the Z-bond helps to reduce the extension risk in the PACs but exposes them to additional call risk is illustrated. The PACs paid down with accrual tend to have higher option costs, except in the bearish case, where prepayments are less likely to retire the Z-bond before the PACs have been paid. (The relationship appears to weaken for twenty-year bonds, but this most likely reflects the fact that the twenty-year bonds have very different average lives as a result of matching the earlier bonds. The twenty-year PAC paid by accrual actually has an average life of over twenty-six years.)

---

9 The first PAC, then, should benefit the most from a tight window. A two- or three-year PAC, however, already tends to have a short window and very low option costs, for reasons previously explained.

Exhibit 13. Sensitivity of Option Costs in PACs to Interest-Rate Shifts When Z-Bond Funds Companions Only and When Z-Bond Funds PACs and Companions

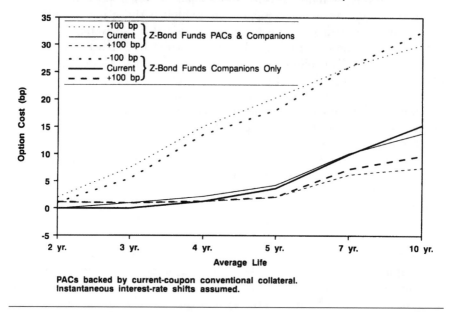

PACs backed by current-coupon conventional collateral.
Instantaneous interest-rate shifts assumed.

Reversing the priorities when the top collar is broken, so that the last PAC in the schedule is the first to receive excess principal after the companions are retired, has a very large effect on the option costs in the seven-, ten-, and twenty-year PACs. This effect is apparent in Exhibit 14. The higher the priority, the greater the call risk and the higher the option costs. The impact is, as expected, accentuated as declining yields elevate the risk of prepayment. By contrast, shifting the call risk to the later tranches strips most of the already low option costs from the earlier tranches.

CONCLUSION

The scheduled payments of PACs, protected over a wide range of possible prepayment speeds, appeal primarily to insurance companies and other buy-and-hold investors who are matching specific liabilities. The liquidity, yields, and wide diversity of features in the market also attract growing numbers of active bond managers. Misconceptions about the value of certain PAC features can create a number of opportunities for investors in both groups. Most notably, many premium-coupon-backed PACs may be undervalued when their current effective collars are taken into account; the length of the PAC window does not contribute to economic value; lockouts benefit short-

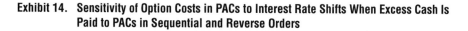

Exhibit 14.   Sensitivity of Option Costs in PACs to Interest Rate Shifts When Excess Cash Is Paid to PACs in Sequential and Reverse Orders

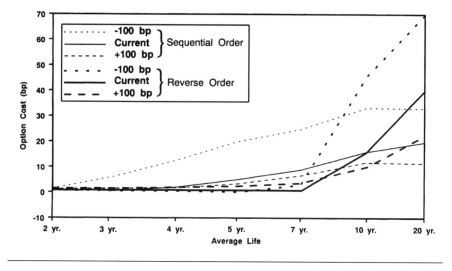

term average life PACs as well as companions; and Z-bonds can protect earlier PAC bonds from extension risk.

The considerable standardization of the PAC market achieved since 1988 should not distract investors from the need to carefully examine the performance of every bond outside the stated collars. Investors who fail to stress-test PAC investments may overlook the fact that effective collars are significantly different from those stated at issue. Any kink or deviation from sequential order in the prioritization of excess cash flow to the PACs after companion classes are retired must be detected, as it could drastically affect the performance of the longer-term PACs. Although the impact on value is less dramatic, investors should also determine whether a long-term Z-bond pays companions or PACs in the structure.

PACs are normally evaluated by examining the yields and average lives of PAC investments over a variety of prepayment scenarios. Such analyses must be carried a step further and linked to possible interest-rate scenarios. The soundest way to do this is to employ a prepayment model that explicitly recognizes the determinants of prepayment behavior. Such an analysis can be supplemented and its insights extended by employing option-based pricing methods. The results of explicitly measuring the option costs associated with a variety of PAC features have been summarized in this chapter, and confirm the general results derived from a price-yield-average-life evaluation of the same series of PAC bonds. In some instances, the option-pricing approach differentiated more strongly between the contribution or subtraction to value made by different PAC features. For example, it was observed that option costs decline or are little higher for twenty-year PACs than for ten-year PACs, whereas the required spreads for twenty-year PACs are substantially higher than those of ten-years. This finding suggests valuable opportunities in the twenty-year sector.

CHAPTER 19

Z-Bonds

Linda Lowell
First Vice President
Mortgage Strategies
PaineWebber, Inc.

Bruce Mahood
Vice President
Merrill Lynch Capital Markets

Traditional accrual CMO bonds are long-term bonds structured so that they pay no coupon interest until they begin to pay principal. Instead, the principal balance of an accrual bond is increased by the stated coupon amount on each payment date. Once the earlier classes in the CMO structure have been retired, the accrual bond stops accruing and pays principal and interest as a standard CMO bond. Accrual bonds are commonly called Z-bonds because they are zero coupon bonds during their accrual phase. Bonds created in this way provide investors with long durations, very attractive yields, and protection from reinvestment risk throughout the accrual period. The cash flow pattern produced is suited to matching long-term liabilities, and, as a result, the bonds are sought after by pension fund managers, life insurance companies, and other investors seeking to lengthen the duration of their portfolios and reduce reinvestment risk.

Z-bonds have been a staple product of the CMO market since its earliest days. The bulk of the Z-bonds currently outstanding are from traditional, sequential-pay CMOs, but the generic structure has adapted well to the PAC-based CMOs favored by the market since the late 1980s, and the inclusion of an accrual bond in the last class continues to be a common practice. At the same time, the Z-bond was the focus of innovation in the CMO market, as issuers created a significant amount of intermediate average-life Z-bonds, a growing number of bonds of various average lives that accrue and pay according to a PAC schedule, and bonds that use various conditions or events to turn the accrual mechanism on or off. These innovations expanded the traditional market for Z buyers by improving the stability of Z-bonds' cash flows, issuing Z-bonds in a wider range of average lives, or by creating bonds that perform well in rallies and preserve their high yields better in declines.

The chapter discusses this important sector of the CMO market. We begin with an examination of the mechanics of the traditional Z-bond as well as Z-bonds issued with PACs, and focus on the behavior of these structures in different prepayment scenarios. We also consider the effect Z-bonds have on the other bonds in a CMO, and the relationship between the basic characteristics of the Z-bond and its market properties and economic performance. A discussion then follows of the characteristics of more complex Z-bond structures, such as serial Z-bonds, Z-PACs, and Jump-Zs.

THE BASIC ACCRUAL STRUCTURE

Most Z-bonds have been issued from traditional, sequential pay CMO structures. Typically, they were the last in a four-class bond issue, and had nominal average lives of twenty years. The principal and interest cash flows for a

Exhibit 1.   Total Principal and Interest Payments of a Traditional Sequential-Pay CMO with a Z-Bond

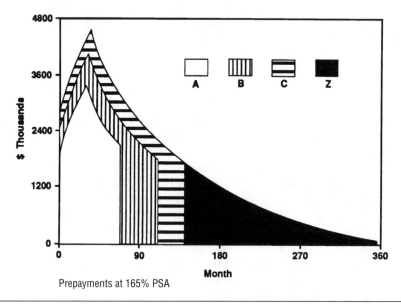

Prepayments at 165% PSA

traditional, sequential-pay CMO containing a Z are diagrammed in Exhibit 1. As the graph indicates, the first class pays principal and interest until it is retired, at which time the second class begins to pay down. The coupon-paying bonds, Classes A, B, and C, receive payments of interest at their stated coupon rates on their original principal balances. The Z-bond, Class Z, however, receives no payments of interest until the preceding classes are fully retired. Instead, its principal balance increases at a compound rate, in effect guaranteeing the bondholder a reinvestment rate equal to the coupon rate during the accrual period, and insulating the investment from reinvestment risk as long as the earlier classes remain outstanding. The principal balance can triple or quadruple in amount over the accrual period projected at issue. This is graphically depicted in Exhibit 2, which indicates the growth of the principal balance of the Z-bond in Exhibit 1 over its expected life at an assumed constant prepayment speed of 165% PSA. The principal balance of the tranche at issue is $25 million, and grows to a maximum level of $79.5 million by about the 150th month. From that point, coinciding with the last payment to the preceding tranche, the balance begins to decline as scheduled amortization and prepayments from the collateral are paid to the bondholders.

Exhibit 2. Principal Balance of a Z-Bond Over Time—$25 Million Beginning Balance

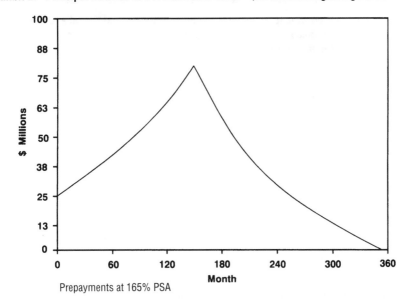

Prepayments at 165% PSA

If actual prepayments occur at a faster rate than 165% PSA, the principal balance of the Z-class at the end of the accrual period will be smaller than the $79.5 million shown in the diagram. Since the earlier tranches pay down sooner, the Z-bonds accrue over a shorter period of time, and the total amount of accrued interest is less. Conversely, slower prepayments allow the Z-bond to accrue for a longer period, resulting in a larger principal balance at the time when the Z-bond begins to generate cash for the bondholders. Principal balances at the end of the accrual period are shown for various constant prepayment speeds in Exhibit 3. At the pricing speed of 165% PSA, the balance in this example reaches an amount more than three times the size of the original face amount at issue. At a faster speed of 350% PSA, the original face amount doubles, and at a slower speed, 100% PSA, it quadruples. Likewise, faster prepayments accelerate the receipt of the first payment of principal and interest. In the example, the first payment jumps from halfway into the twelfth year at 165% PSA to the beginning of the ninth year at 350% PSA. If prepayments slow to a constant rate of 100% PSA, the first payment to the Z-bond is not made until the beginning of the sixteenth year after issue.

The effect of faster or slower prepayments on the average life and yield of this same example is shown in Exhibit 4, under the heading "Z-Bond in a Traditional Sequential-Pay CMO." The average life of the Z-bond at the pric-

Exhibit 3. Effect of Prepayment Speed on the Length for the Accrual Period and the Principal Balance at the End of the Accrual Period of a $25 Million, 20-Year Aveage-Life Z-Bond Class*

Payment Speed (% PSA)	Principal Balance Outstanding ($MM)	Months From Issue
75	115.4	194
100	102.1	180
125	91.8	166
165	79.5	150
200	71.4	135
250	63.4	119
300	57.2	106
350	52.9	96
425	46.6	80
600	41.1	64

* Total issue $300 million sequential-pay CMO backed by FNMA 9 1/2s.

Exhibit 4. Yield and Average Life at Various Prepayment Speeds of Comparable CMO and 20-Year Average Life-Bonds in Structures with and Without Z-Bonds (Pricing Assumption: 165% PSA)

Payment Speed (% PSA)	Coupon-Paying Bond in a Traditional Sequential-Pay CMO Yield* (%)	Average Life (Years)	Z-Bond in a Traditional Sequential-Pay CMO Yield** (%)	Average Life (Years)	Z-Bond in a PAC Structure Yield*** (%)	Average Life (Years)
75	9.97	25.01	9.82	22.91	10.17	22.91
100	9.98	23.25	9.83	21.71	10.20	21.71
125	9.94	21.40	9.83	20.47	10.24	20.47
165	10.00	18.55	9.85	18.55	10.30	18.55
200	10.02	16.41	9.86	17.02	10.35	17.02
250	10.05	13.88	9.89	15.02	10.44	15.02
300	10.08	11.92	9.91	13.37	10.52	13.54
350	10.11	10.38	9.93	11.96	10.69	12.48
425	10.15	8.66	9.98	9.80	11.18	8.38
600	10.27	6.18	10.06	7.61	13.02	3.05

  * Price: 96:28
 ** Price: 96:29
*** Price: 90:10

ing assumption of 165% PSA is about 18.5 years; traditional Zs typically have average lives at pricing of 18 to 22 years (and expected accrual periods of 8 to 10 years). If prepayments occur at a constant rate of 100% PSA, the bond lengthens modestly, to an average life of about twenty-two years. Like other last tranches, the Z has more room to shorten. In this example, the Z shortens to an average life of about twelve years at 350% PSA, and down to about 7.5 years at 600% PSA.[1]

---

1 Average-life calculations are intended to measure the weighted average time until receipt of principal payments. Some measures of expected life may include the accrued interest as a cash flow. These increases in the principal balance can enter the calculation as negative weights applied to the elapsed time to early payment dates, and the actual principal payments as positive weights applied to the elapsed time to later payment dates. By placing negative weights on small numbers and positive weights on large numbers, the results can be larger than the remaining term of the underlying collateral (for example, a number of years greater than thirty). To avoid this unrealistic result, the convention in the CMO market is to exclude from the calculation all increases in the factor or balance, with the understanding that this method can substantially understate the true interest rate sensitivity of a security.

The yield received on a Z-bond is less sensitive to differences in prepayment speeds the closer to par it is priced. At deeper discounts, Z-bonds, like other discount mortgage-backed securities, will benefit as their average lives shorten, since principal is returned at par earlier than assumed at pricing. The deeper the discount, the sharper the boost in yield at faster prepayment speeds. Conversely, the yield declines as a function of a slowdown in prepayments and the original discount. Traditional twenty-year average-life Zs have been issued at original prices as low as thirty, but prices above eighty-five currently are more common. In general, issuers can lower the coupon, achieving a more attractive price, by using discount collateral or by stripping interest into another class.

HOW THE Z INTERACTS WITH OTHER BONDS IN THE STRUCTURE

The interaction of the Z-bond with earlier bonds in the CMO structure is a key determinant both of its own behavior and that of the other bonds. By including an accrual bond in the CMO structure, issuers accomplish two purposes: (1) a higher proportion of the total issue can consist of tranches with earlier final maturities than if there were no Z-bond in the structure, and (2) the earlier classes have more stable cash flows and average lives across a range of prepayment rates than in a comparable structure without a Z-bond. Furthermore, since the timing of cash flows from the Z-bond depends on when the earlier tranches are retired, the Z-bond itself also is more stable.

An accrual bond supports a larger proportion of early classes because the coupon interest that would have been paid on the outstanding balance of the Z-bond is added to the principal payments from the collateral and used to retire the earlier classes. At the same time, the principal amount of Z-bonds is increased by the dollar amount of interest diverted. Although at first glance this may look like sleight of hand, the accrual procedure maintains a simple algebraic relationship in which the sum of the principal balances of the outstanding bonds always equals the outstanding principal balance of the collateral. The simple numerical example in Exhibit 5 illustrates this relationship. In the example, the collateral pays a 10% coupon and a $100 principal balance in ten equal payments. Both Class A and Class Z have stated coupons of 10%, so that the sum of the interest paid to Class A and either accrued or paid to Class Z is always equal to the interest paid by the collateral. (In an actual CMO, there can be a differential between interest on the collateral and the interest paid to the bondholders, which is then payable to the residual holders.) Notice that Class A is paid down more quickly than it would be if the Z were a coupon-paying bond.

Exhibit 5. How a Z-Bond Accrues and Pays: A Simplified Example

Collateral:	$100 10% loan amortizing in 10 annual payments	CMO:	Class A $50 paying 10% coupon Class Z $50 Z with 10% coupon

| | Collateral | | | Class A | | | Class Z | | |
| | Payments | | | Payments | | | Payments | | |
Payment	Interest ($)	Principal ($)	Balance ($)	Interest ($)	Principal ($)	Balance ($)	Interest ($)	Principal* ($)	Balance ($)
0	0.00	0.00	100.00	0.00	0.00	50.00	0.00	0.00	50.00
1	10.00	10.00	90.00	5.00	15.00	35.00	0.00	(5.00)	55.00
2	9.00	10.00	80.00	3.50	15.50	19.50	0.00	(5.50)	60.50
3	8.00	10.00	70.00	1.95	16.05	3.45	0.00	(6.05)	66.55
4	7.00	10.00	60.00	0.34	3.45	0.00	6.66	6.65**	60.00***
5	6.00	10.00	50.00	0.00			6.00	10.00	50.00
6	5.00	10.00	40.00	0.00			5.00	10.00	40.00
7	4.00	10.00	30.00	0.00			4.00	10.00	30.00
8	3.00	10.00	20.00	0.00			3.00	10.00	20.00
9	2.00	10.00	10.00	0.00			2.00	10.00	10.00
10	1.00	10.00	0.00	0.00			1.00	10.00	0.00

* Amounts in parentheses are not cash flows but upward adjustments of principal balance.
** $6.65 = Principal Remaining After Class A Retired
*** $60 = Previous Balance – Principal Paid = $66.55 – $6.65

Exhibit 6. Total Principal Payments of a Traditional Sequential-Pay CMO with a Z-Bond

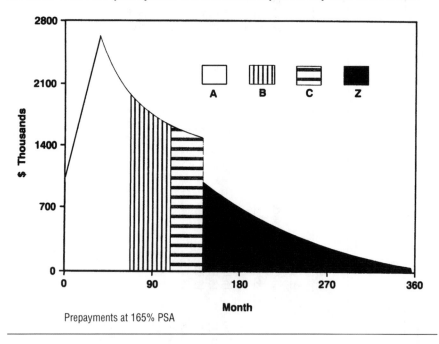

Prepayments at 165% PSA

The accrual structure permits issuers to create larger classes with short- and intermediate-term average lives. The effect of an accrual bond on the size of the earlier classes is graphically illustrated in Exhibit 6, a diagram of the principal payments only from the CMO in Exhibit 1. The discontinuity between the size of principal payments to the Z and those to the earlier tranches reflects the fact that the Z-bond's pro rata share of coupon interest is treated as principal in order to pay down larger earlier tranches (if the last payment to the fourth would be much smaller). This strategy is attractive to issuers when the CMO arbitrage depends primarily on the shape of the yield curve, and larger profits can be made the larger the amount of bonds that can be priced off the front end of the yield curve. In periods when the yield curve is flat or inverted, this strategy helps issuers minimize the proportion of longer average-life bonds in the issue. This works because interest payments from the collateral, which would have been paid to holders of the last tranche, are used to support the first tranche. Just how much of an effect an accrual class can have on the allocation of principal to the earlier classes is shown in Exhibit 7. The exhibit compares two four-tranche sequential pay CMOs backed by the same collateral, one with a Z and one without. The four tranches in each issue have the same average lives, roughly three, seven, ten, and twenty years. (The fourth tranches from these examples, all nominally twenty-year bonds, are included as well in Exhibit 4.) The two structures differ in the way the collateral's principal is distributed among the classes. For example, in the Z-bond structure, a $25 million Z-bond class supports a $136 million three-year first tranche. The structure without a Z-bond has $120 million three-year bonds in the first class and $79 million twenty-year bonds in the fourth tranche.

The accrual mechanism imparts greater stability to all the bonds in a typical structure. This is readily apparent in Exhibit 8. Each column compares the average life at different prepayment speeds of the different tranches from the sample structures. In each case, the average lives of the tranches are less variable across all scenarios for the structure containing a Z-bond than in the structure without.

CMOs WITH PACs AND A Z-BOND

The Z-bond has a similar effect on earlier bonds in a typical PAC structure. For a given collateral and pricing assumption, accrual from the Z can be used to support a larger amount of PAC and companion bonds in the earlier tranches. The principal and interest payments for a structure containing three- and seven-year PACs, a seven-year companion, and a twenty-year Z are shown in Exhibit 9. The yield and average life at various prepayment levels of the Z-bond from this structure are included in Exhibit 4, and the size and average life of the various classes are shown in Exhibit 7. (In fact, the average life of the Z-bond is 18.6 years, matching, for the sake of discussion, the average lives of the Z and regular coupon-paying tranches in the other examples.) Funding the earlier classes from the Z-bond's accrual generally creates a much larger portion of available principal, for a given pricing speed, from which to carve PACs, allowing issuers to increase the size of the PAC classes.

Since companion bonds absorb the prepayment volatility from which the PACs are shielded, the proportion of PACs to companions is an important parameter in determining the degree to which the average lives of the companions will vary over various prepayment scenarios. The presence of a Z-bond increases the total amount of principal available at the pricing speed to pay both the PACs and the companions. This means that, all other factors being equal, more PACs may be issued with less negative effect on the stability of the companion bonds. In turn, the length of the accrual period is more stable. Nonetheless, the Z-bonds created to support PAC tranches are necessarily more volatile than Z-bonds in the traditional CMO issues. The truth of this can be seen by comparing the average life at various prepayment speeds of a Z from a PAC structure to those of a Z from a traditional CMO, as was

Exhibit 7. Comparison of Various CMO Structures Created With and Without Z-Bonds

	Traditional CMO Without Z		Traditional CMO With Z		PAC CMO with Z	
	Original Balance	Average Life	Original Balance	Average Life	Original Balance	Average Life
Class A	$120,000,000	3.0 Years	$136,000,000	3.0 Years	$ 80,000,000	2.8 Years
Class B	66,200,000	7.4	84,000,000	7.4	70,000,000	7.0
Class C	34,500,000	10.9	55,000,000	10.9	125,000,000	7.3
Class D	79,300,000	18.6				
Class Z			25,000,000	18.6	25,000,000	18.6
Total	$300,000,000		$300,000,000		$300,000,000	

Collateral: FNMA 9 1/2s
Structured at 165% PSA

Exhibit 8. Effect of a Z-Bond on the Average Life Variability of the Various Classes in a Traditional, Sequential-Pay CMO

	Average Life in Years							
	3-Year Tranche		7-Year Tranche		10-Year Tranche		20-Year Tranche	
Prepayment Speed	No Z-Bond	With Z-Bond	No Z-Bond	With Z-Bond	No Z-Bond	With Z-Bond	Coupon Bond	Z-Bond
75% PSA	5.2	4.7	13.2	11.1	18.4	14.9	25.0	22.9
165% PSA	3.0	3.0	7.4	7.4	10.9	10.9	18.6	18.6
425% PSA	1.6	1.7	3.4	3.8	4.8	5.9	8.7	10.3

Collateral: FNMA 9.5s

Exhibit 9.   Total Principal and Interest Payments of a CMO with PACs and a Z-Bond

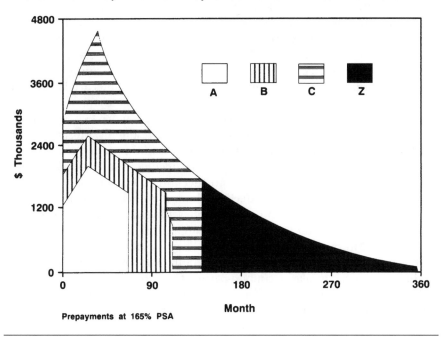

Prepayments at 165% PSA

shown in Exhibit 4. As is the case with the fourth tranches in the sample traditional deals, this Z also has an average life of 18.6 years at 165% PSA. As the exhibit indicates, the average life of the Z from a PAC structure would extend more significantly as well, since slow prepayment rates will delay the retirement of the companion bonds, further extending the accrual period for the Zs. (This effect is obscured by over simplification of the example.)

If the companion tranche(s) in front of a Z are TACs, the Z may be more volatile than if structured with standard companions. When the priorities enforcing the structure require that principal in excess of the TAC (and PAC) payments be paid to the Z, then the Z may begin to receive payments before the companion TAC is retired. This kind of structure produces a Z that is much more volatile in bull markets than a traditional or companion Z-bond. Prepayment speeds fast enough to shorten a traditional twenty-year Z to a ten-year can shorten this bond to a one-year. When they carry a low coupon, these bonds are priced to produce generous returns from accelerating prepayments. Indeed, this is one way to create the bullish Z-bond known as a "Jump-Z." The Jump-Z is discussed in greater detail later in this chapter.

PERFORMANCE OF Z-BONDS

The variability in the yield of a Z-bond over a range of prepayment rates gives at best an imperfect indication of the Z's expected price, and hence, economic performance in different interest rate scenarios. A major drawback of using yield as a measure of a Z-bond's, or for that matter, any mortgage-backed security's expected performance is that the calculation of yield-to-maturity presumes that the amount and timing of cash flows are known with certainty and are reinvested over the life of the investment at a rate equal to the yield. In actuality, mortgage-backed securities are more exposed to reinvestment risk than other common fixed-income investments. Most CMOs pay both principal and interest monthly. More importantly, prepayments of principal normally accelerate when market rates decline, just as the yields available on reinvestment opportunities are declining. The opposite occurs as market yields rise; prepayments decline, slowing the receipt of principal just as more attractive reinvestment opportunities appear. Z-bonds are protected somewhat from this later source of reinvestment risk, since the reinvestment rate is locked in over the accrual period. They are not fully protected, however. The accrual period is of uncertain length, and when it ends the bonds begin to pay exactly like a coupon-paying CMO bond. For these reasons, yield does not capture the difference in the Z-bond's performance relative to a security with lower reinvestment risk, such as a Treasury bond that pays only coupons until maturity, or one with a fixed accrual period, such as a Treasury zero.

Prepayment risk also exposes investors to call and extension risk, and these have additional consequences for market value. For mortgage-backed securities purchased at prices above par, the early return of principal at par is a negative event, since less interest is earned over the investment horizon. Reflecting the market's perception of these risks, the prices of premium coupon CMOs, including Z-bonds, rise more slowly the steeper the decline in interest rates. Investors also are exposed to possible declines in market value when the bond's average life extends and it shifts outward on a positively sloped yield curve. When a bond lengthens in an upwardly sloping yield curve environment, the discount rate applied to the expected cash flow rises, resulting in a lower market value.

Another characteristic that yield calculations cannot reflect is the call provisions established for CMOs. These tend to be more important in the case of older, non-REMIC CMOs, but many REMICs also have significant call provisions. The bonds issued before 1987 used call provisions to insulate the transaction from a more onerous sale tax treatment; some REMIC CMOs have significant call provisions to permit residual holders favorable accounting treatment. Newer issues tend to have minimal clean-up call provisions, designed to pay off the bonds when the remaining balance falls below a certain low level. The market considers as fairly favorable terms that permit the bonds to be called at par, ten or fifteen years after issue, when the outstanding balance of the tranche has declined by 10 to 20% of its original amount. These also are the most common. Less favorable terms stipulate a higher remaining balance, a shorter period, or both. A handful of Z-bonds currently outstanding could have been called as early as 1990, and a significant number become callable after 1994. Investors are advised to carefully examine the call provisions of Z-bonds before trading them.

Z-bonds have considerably longer expected durations than coupon payers with similar average lives because the principal balance grows over time. This can be seen by comparing a Z to a coupon payer with the same principal structure (sequential, companion, ets.) and similar average life at the same pricing speed. For example, FHLMC 1727 Z, a companion Z, and FNMA 93-204 J, a companion payer, are both 20-year bonds at 125% PSA (on November 28, 1994) backed by 6.5s. FHLMC 1727 Z has an average life of 20.4 years at 125% PSA, FNMA 93-204 J an average life of 21.5 years. At this speed, the Z-bond has a modified duration of 15.4 while the payer has a modified duration of 9.8. At slower prepayment speeds the divergence is even greater: at 90% PSA the Z-bond has an average life of 23.4 but a duration of 16.7, the payer an average life of 24.0 and duration of 10.3. Only at speeds which significantly shorten the average lives of these companion structures does the Z-bond's duration converge to that of the comparable payer. At 250% PSA, the Z-bond shortens to an average life of 6.1 years, with a modified duration of 3.6 and the payer to an average life of 6.2 years with a duration of 3.5. An option-adjusted analysis produces a similar result: the Z has an expected duration of 15.9, the payer 10.0. Given this pattern of price sensitivity, investors should expect Z-bonds on a total return basis to under perform CMO payers and Treasuries with comparable average lives and maturities in bearish scenarios. However, as a result of the accrual mechanism, Z-bonds tend to outperform comparable Treasury zeroes in rising rate scenarios. In bullish scenarios, the long duration of the Z-bond produces high rates of return, although the Z-bond loses its advantage over comparable securities as it shortens dramatically in more sharply declining yield interest rate scenarios.

MORE FUN WITH ACCRUAL BONDS

Some of the CMOs issued since the beginning of 1989 make more creative use of the basic accrual mechanism. The variations on the accrual theme include Z-PACs and structures containing an intermediate- as well as long-term Z-bond or a series of Z-bonds of various average lives. Other structures turn the accrual mechanism on and off depending on the amount of excess principal available after scheduled payments are met. As complex and exotic as these structures may appear at first glance, the same basic principles at work in traditional Z-bonds continue to apply. And in most cases, any additional complexity is accompanied by considerable additional value for investors with particular objectives and investment criteria.

Z-PACs

Z-PACs combine the cash flow characteristics of a standard Z-bond with the greater certainty of a PAC regarding the amount and timing of actual payments. When prepayments occur within the range defined by the PAC collars, the Z-PAC will accrue to a scheduled principal balance over a fixed period and make scheduled payments thereafter. As with more familiar, coupon-paying PACs, any excess cash flow is absorbed by companions as long as they are outstanding. Similarly, the coupon interest earned on the Z-PAC's outstanding balance during the accrual period is used to support earlier classes in the structure, and the balance of the Z-PAC is increased by an equal amount. For prepayment levels within the PAC collars, the structure eliminates reinvestment risk over a defined accrual period, and then provides predictable payments until maturity. This structure is particularly well suited to matching liabilities. The fact that Z-PACs are issued in a range of average lives (typically five, seven, ten, or twenty years) increases their applicability. Furthermore, the call and extension protection provided by the planned payment schedule means that the duration of the investment is less likely to increase as interest rates rise (or decrease as interest rates decline) than is the duration of a standard or companion Z. That is to say, the Z-PACs are less negatively convex than standard or companion Zs. For this reason, active portfolio managers should consider using the Z-PAC to lengthen the duration of their portfolios in anticipation of market upswings.

STRUCTURES WITH MORE THAN ONE Z-BOND

Although the practice of issuing two or more Zs from a single structure is not new, more of these structures have been created since 1989 than previously. Considerable variety is possible in structuring deals with multiple classes of Z-bonds, but two common strategies have been to issue a sequential series of Zs with a range of average lives (five, seven, ten, and twenty years, or seven, ten, fifteen, and twenty years, for example), or a pair of Z-bonds having intermediate- and long-term average lives (five- and twenty-year bonds or ten- and twenty-year bonds are common examples). In the case of an intermediate- and long-term average life pair, the bonds do not necessarily pay in sequence, but more typically pay down before and after intervening coupon-

Exhibit 10. Total Principal and Interest Payments of a Sequential-Pay CMO with a Series of Z-Bonds

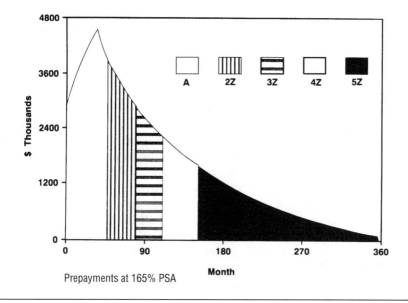

Prepayments at 165% PSA   Month

Exhibit 11. Average Lives at Various Prepayment Speeds of the Bonds in a Sequential-Pay CMO with a Series of Z-Bonds

	\multicolumn{5}{c}{Average Life (years)}				
	A	2Z	3Z	4Z	5Z
75% PSA	2.5	6.6	10.1	14.0	22.9
165% PSA	2.0	5.0	7.6	10.5	18.6
425% PSA	1.4	3.1	4.5	6.0	10.3

paying classes. Both strategies have been employed in traditional CMOs as well as in structures containing PAC bonds.

In general, multiple accrual classes in a CMO interact with the rest of the structure in the same way a single traditional Z-bond does, supporting the repayment of earlier classes, which themselves may either pay current coupon interest or accrue it. In a series of Zs, the longer Zs lend stability to the shorter Zs, just as they would to coupon-paying bonds with earlier final maturities. Accrual from the later Zs can be used to retire earlier Zs when they become current paying bonds, just as if they were coupon-paying bonds.

The cash flows from a sequential-pay CMO containing a series of five-, seven-, ten-, and twenty-year Zs preceded by a two-year coupon-paying tranche are shown in Exhibit 10. This example was constructed using the same collateral and pricing speed as in the previous examples containing a single Z. The last tranche, 5Z, is the same size as in the previous example as well, and for this reason has the same average life at various prepayment speeds. For the sake of discussion, the first tranche is also the same size as the first tranche in the traditional CMO with a Z-bond, $136 million. As indicated in Exhibit 11, the large amount of accrual bonds in the structure has the effect of shortening the average life of this bond from three years at 165% PSA in the single Z example, to two years in this. (Readers will note that this example is not necessarily realistic. Structurers would be concerned to issue larger amounts of short-term average life bonds that can be sold at lower yields for greater arbitrage profits, manipulating the coupon and offer price, and so forth.) Exhibit 11 lists the average lives of the first five classes at various prepayment speeds. In general, intermediate-term Zs demonstrate considerable stability. This is more evident when the seven- and ten-year Zs are compared to the seven- and ten-year coupon-paying bonds from earlier examples in Exhibit 8. The ten-year is supported by a twenty-year Z, and is noticeably less variable than one in a CMO without a Z. As would be expected, given the larger amount of accrual being passed to successively shorter bonds in the current example, the five-year Z-bond is considerably more stable than a comparable five-year standard payer supported by a single Z. The general result is that the shorter Zs in a series of Zs are "cleaner," that is, they have progressively less average life variability than otherwise comparable coupon-paying bonds. Intermediate-term average life Zs interspersed among coupon-paying classes in a structure supported by a twenty-year Z (the other common strategy) will benefit similarly. They will be more stable than otherwise, and the degree of stability will depend on the size of the Z-bond supporting them.

The consequences of multiple-Z strategies are that they produce bonds possessing relatively stable cash flow patterns—not as stable as PACs with decent collars, but more stable than traditional sequential-pay bonds. These stable bonds also possess the partial shield against reinvestment risk that is a chief attraction of traditional Z-bonds, and they make it available in any array of expected lives, broadening the appeal of Z-bonds to investors with intermediate- rather than long-term horizons.

Tricky Zs

Other innovative approaches to Z-bonds appeared in the late 1980s. The common theme of these "trick" Zs involves turning the accrual mechanism on or off under certain conditions. One such condition might be a date; for example, the rule of allocating cash flows between classes might be "accrue until such and such a date" instead of the traditional "accrue until A, B, and C tranches are retired." Or, the decision to accrue the Z-bond might depend on the amount of principal available to make payments to the nonaccrual bonds currently paying. The use of such rules results in bonds with performance characteristics that can be very different from the Z-bonds discussed above.

CMO issuers have tinkered with the accrual mechanism of Z-bonds to create CMO classes that alternate between paying interest and accruing interest. These special-purpose classes are structured with a set of rules that turn their accrual mechanism on or off according to certain cash flow conditions. These accrual rules are often designed to help preceding classes meet their cash flow schedules and/or expected maturity dates. Beginning in 1988, issuers included these variable-accrual bonds in CMO structures to help earlier classes meet the five-year maturity requirement for inclusion in thrift liquidity portfolios. These benevolent Zs pay as follows: when cash flows from the mortgage collateral are insufficiently large enough to retire the liquidity bonds according to schedule, their accrual mechanisms are turned on and corresponding coupon from the collateral is applied to the earlier classes; when cash flows are sufficient to retire the liquidity bonds on schedule, their accrual mechanisms are turned off and the bonds act like standard coupon payers. Incorporating a conditional accrual rule into a bond class is an effective way to reduce extension risk on earlier classes. Of course, the extension risk is not eliminated but is instead largely transferred to the benevolent Z and other, later bond classes.

Another wrinkle is to permanently transform Z-bonds into coupon-paying bonds when certain cash flow levels are met. An early example of this Z-bond structure was issued as the last of nine classes in FNMA 89-15. This bond was not marketed with any distinguishing label. The other bonds in the structure were a series of PACs and TACs followed by a companion dubbed an "S" bond. The Z-bond pays as follows: any excess above the scheduled PAC and TAC payments is distributed to the Z-bond as an interest payment; if the amount is less than the amount that was accrued, the shortfall is accrued; if the amount is greater, the excess is distributed as principal; beginning in the month following the first payment of a complete interest payment, the so-called Z-class distributes interest each month. One month of exceptional prepayment experience can trigger the conversion to coupon bond. Thereafter, the average life will be shorter than it would otherwise have been, owing to the fact that a portion of its cash flows is dispersed over what would have been the accrual period. Any protection against reinvestment risk offered by this "chameleon" bond is ephemeral at best. Once converted, the bond behaves like any other companion bond.

Even Z-PACs have been subjected to genetic alteration. The first Z-PAC issued, the fifth tranche in Ryland Acceptance Corporation Four, Series 88, accrues only until the date of its first scheduled payment or until non-PAC classes in the deal have been retired. Until that date, the Z-PAC is the first PAC in line for excess cash flows should the companions be paid down, and after that date it is last in line. This means it has greater call risk during the accrual period. As a result, its average life is only stable at or below the pricing speed (90% PSA for this deal backed by GNMA 8s). The resultant average life volatility is more typical of a reverse TAC, which does not extend but has considerable call risk.

Jump-Zs

Another Z-bond innovation, the notorious Jump-Z, made its debut in the CMO market during the summer of 1989. Generically, the Jump-Z is a bullish companion Z-bond that is designed to convert to a current payer and to receive excess principal when prepayments accelerate. Under bullish scenarios, this bond "jumps" ahead of other bond classes in the order of priority for receiving principal payments. Once triggered, a Jump-Z typically receives all excess principal (above scheduled PAC payments) until it is retired. Conceivably, holders of the Jump-Z could receive these payments early in the expected accrual period. This acceleration of principal can shorten the bond's average life significantly—a Z-bond issued with a twenty-year average life might shorten to less than one year. Since these bonds typically have low coupons and are issued at significant discounts to par (in the eighties), Jump-Z holders realized high returns in the 1991-94 rally. In general, a Jump-Z priced at a deeper discount traded at a tighter spread, because investors assigned more value to the jump feature. Many investors purchased Jump-Zs to offset the negative convexity of their other mortgage securities and to enhance the performance of their MBS portfolios in bullish scenarios. Few of these bonds remain outstanding after the 1991-94 rally, characterized as it was by very high prepayment rates. As the rally continued, the inverse floater became a more popular vehicle for bullish investors and few new Jump-Zs were issued. However, as the current bearish sentiment grows, the Jump-Z could make a reappearance.

Jump-Z bonds were issued with an extremely diverse set of jump rules. Although apparently lacking uniformity or standardization, these rules have the common objective of increasing the bonds' performance in bullish economic environments. Jumps are typically activated by an event associated with a market rally: rising prepayment rates, declining interest rates, or increased cash flow. However, most Jump-Zs were structured with prepayment triggers—the bonds shortened when prepayment rates on the underlying mortgage collateral rose above a CMO's pricing speed or some other predefined prepayment level. Generally, prepayments above the pricing speed shortened the average life of the Jump-Z considerably. In structures containing TAC bonds, Jump-Zs were often designed to shorten when prepayments exceed the speed that defines the TAC schedule. In addition to prepayment triggers, CMO issuers also structured Jump-Zs with interest rate triggers that were activated when Treasury yields fall below some threshold level. Interest rate triggers eliminated the need for investors accurately to forecast prepayment rates, and ensured that Jump-Z holders would benefit even in a market rally that was not accompanied by rising prepayments. In general, the closer the jump trigger is to actual prepayment speeds or current interest rates, the more valuable the Jump-Z.

Jump-Z bonds can be classified as "cumulative" or "noncumulative," as well as "sticky" or "nonsticky." A cumulative trigger is activated when since-issuance prepayment rates, or other cumulative measures of prepayment experience, exceed some threshold value. In contrast, a noncumulative trigger only requires prepayments to satisfy the jump condition during a single period. Holders generally prefer noncumulative triggers, since a single month of abnormally high prepayments could force early retirement of their discount security. The adjectives "stick" and "nonstick" indicate whether a Jump-Z bond will revert back to its original priority in the CMO structure if jump conditions are no longer met. Once triggered, a sticky-Z will continue to receive principal payments, even if prepayments subsequently decline below the threshold value. On the other hand, a nonstick-Z can revert back to an accrual bond once its jump rules are no longer satisfied. Holders generally assign the greatest value to Jump-Zs with noncumulative sticky triggers, because a single increase in monthly prepayment rates could force early retirement of the entire bond class. For Jump-Zs backed by unseasoned mortgage collateral, a tiny increase in prepayments could trigger a jump—a small increase in CPR can translate into a large PSA spike when prepayments are benchmarked off the early part of the PSA ramp.

The other common approach for creating a Jump-Z bond—preceding it with a TAC and other companion bonds in a PAC structure—was described earlier. The Jump-Z acts like a traditional companion bond and absorbs volatility from both PACs and TACs. Preceded by a TAC, the Jump-Z receives principal when principal payments from the underlying collateral and Z-accrual exceed the amount required to meet the PAC and TAC schedules. The degree to which the bond's average life will shorten depends on its jump rules and the overall deal structure. Jump rules control whether the bond jumps in front of the TAC class when payments break the TAC schedule (sticky-Z) or receives only excess payments above the PAC and TAC schedules (nonsticky-Z). All else being equal, the average life of a sticky-Z is likely to shorten more than a comparable nonsticky-Z. Preceded by PACs, TACs, and other support bonds, these Jump-Zs have a negligible amount of extension risk since they are typically structured as the last companion class in the CMO. In addition to their jump rules, the average life variability of Jump-Zs is also affected by the features of their preceding PAC bonds. For example, PAC lockouts, typically one to two years in length, can accentuate the shortening of Jump-Z average lives. Since no scheduled principal payments are made during a lockout, there is a much larger amount of cash flow available to pay down a Jump-Z in the event it is triggered.

This simple form of Jump-Z (simple to visualize and analyze) does not involve any modification of the standard accrual mechanism—the Z's share of interest is added to principal payments used to pay down earlier bonds according to the schedules and order of priorities established for the deal. Many of the Jump-Zs issued during 1990 and 1991, however, have modified accrual mechanisms that impose conditions under which accrual is turned on or off. These rules can control how coupon interest is paid both before and after the bonds have jumped. Perhaps the most common example of accrual manipulation occurs with Jump-Zs that pay only a portion of their coupon interest and accrue the shortfall. The exact amount of interest that a Jump-Z will pay, after being triggered, often depends on the number and size of the companion classes that the bond jumped over. For example, when preceded by both Level I and II PACs, the amount of coupon interest paid to a Jump-Z bond will depend on whether it jumps over the secondary PACs. If the Jump-Z remains subordinate to the Level II PACs, then part of the Jump-Z's coupon interest can be used to support the second-tier PACs.

CONCLUSION

Z-bonds offer investors some of the longest durations and highest yields available in the derivative MBS market, as well as a cash flow pattern well suited to matching long-term liabilities. They also are one of the most liquid varieties of CMO bonds traded in the secondary market. The favorable economics of issuing these bonds will help ensure that a steady supply continues to be produced. Recent innovations have introduced accrual bonds with new and valuable characteristics, including greater stability or accelerated return of principal in rallies, and have widened the availability of intermediate-term Zs. Given the large number of Z-bonds outstanding, and the wide familiarity they already enjoy, this trend should continue, creating bonds that meet distinct investor requirements.

CHAPTER 20

Companions with Schedules

Linda Lowell
First Vice President
Mortgage Strategies
PaineWebber, Inc.

INTRODUCTION

Collateralized mortgage obligations (CMOs) were first devised to meet two general objectives. The first was to make a better match between a wide range of investors' maturity requirements and the expected cash flows from a pool of mortgages. The second was to redistribute prepayment risk to different classes at levels that many more investors would accept. The initial solution to the problem simply split the returning principal among a series of sequential-pay bonds. Subsequently, this structure has evolved into an array of reduced-risk CMO bond structures, the most heavily issued of which is the planned amortization class (PAC). PACs provide investors with payments scheduled as to payment date and amount, occurring within a defined paydown period (window), and protected over a range of likely prepayment scenarios.

Companion bonds are the natural by-product of creating PAC bonds.[1] In order to protect the schedules of PAC bonds in a CMO issue, a sufficient amount of bond classes must be created to absorb excess principal paydowns and to provide a buffer from which scheduled payments can be made when prepayments are slow. Because companion classes accept additional prepayment volatility, their payments are necessarily more uncertain than either PACs or traditional CMO bonds. As a result, the actual yields or economic returns realized from an investment in companion bonds can vary widely

---

1 Other structural devices intended to reduce or transform prepayment risk for some classes in a CMO issue also create support classes. The discussion here should not be presumed to apply to them. Unless clearly indicated, the term "companion" when used in this chapter means PAC companion.

from those projected at the time of investment. Investors recognize this risk and demand yields that compensate them accordingly.

Issuers and underwriters also have developed a variety of devices that serve either to reduce the risk of a portion of the companion classes or to create more volatile instruments that reward holders when interest rates (and presumably prepayment rates) move strongly in a particular direction. Lockouts[2] are among the first group, while Super POs and Jump-Zs are typical of the second. Another very common strategy is to create companions with floating and inverse floating rate coupons. One of the oldest and most extensively employed strategies, however, is to give schedules to a portion of the companion cash flows and to provide those schedules with more limited prepayment protection than the primary PAC series receive. This family of reduced-risk companions is the subject of this chapter.

Companions having schedules partake either of the properties of targeted amortization classes (TACs)—so that they are protected against either call or extension risk (a reverse TAC) but not both—or of PAC bonds, so that they have call and extension protection over a range of prepayment scenarios (a "Level II" PAC). The largest class of these bonds, companion TACs, has been issued since 1988, and is now one of the most liquid of generic CMO classes. Reverse TACs were introduced more in the middle of 1988, but have been marketed explicitly as reverse TACs only since the beginning of 1989. These are more scarce. The concept of Level II PACs took hold during the third quarter of 1989. During the 1990-94 rally it became common to create several levels of PACs with successively narrower bands of prepayment protection, so that a single transaction could contain PAC Is, IIs and IIIs. In addition, the practice of carving a "Super PAC" schedule out of a primary PAC schedule became popular.

The following discussion explains how companion PAC and TAC bonds are structured, and how their structures affect their performance in different prepayment scenarios. The effect of adding a TAC, reverse TAC, or Level II PAC on the behavior of the remaining companion bonds is also explored.

COMPANION BASICS

Companion classes are created from the principal payments remaining after the PAC schedules are defined. In general, companion classes have second claim on excess principal paid down from the collateral after the PAC sched-

---

2 A lockout shifts to a companion bond principal payments that otherwise might be used in a PAC schedule. The effect of a lockout is to push forward the beginning of the first PAC window to a specified date and to stabilize the companion. Lockouts are normally applied to the first PAC for a period of two or three years, lending stability to the earliest companion class.

ules, and pay sequentially until all the companions are retired. At the pricing prepayment assumption, companion classes pay simultaneously with the PACs. At very slow constant prepayment rates, they must wait to receive principal until the PACs have been retired. At very high speeds, they pay simultaneously with the short-term average-life PACs and are quickly retired, after which the PACs themselves must absorb excess paydowns and are retired ahead of schedule.

A simplified example of a standard PAC/companion structure is depicted in Exhibit 1. The large unshaded area paying from the first to about the 300th month contains *all* the scheduled payments that would be available to construct PAC bonds assuming collars of 85% and 300% PSA, and FNMA 9% collateral with a WAC of 9.76% and a WAM of 339 months.[3] Normally, structurers would divide this PAC region into a number of PACs with varying average lives. The actual number of PACs created would depend on the demand for particular maturities and windows (the time elapsed between first and last principal payments to the PAC bondholders). For ease of exposition, the PAC region in this and subsequent examples is not divided. The

Exhibit 1. PAC with Standard Companion Bonds, 165% PSA

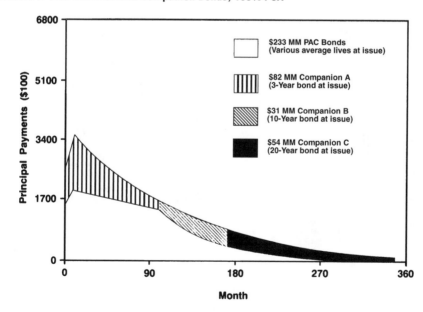

---

3 This is the largest PAC region that could be accommodated by this collateral for the collar given.

companion bonds are not influenced by the partitioning of a single PAC region into individual bond classes; they are affected, instead, by the size of the entire region in relation to the total size of the companion classes. (In general, the larger the PAC class, given a fixed amount of collateral, the more volatile the companion class is.) The principal payments left over after the PAC region is defined constitute the companion classes. In Exhibit 1, these are depicted by the shaded areas. At a pricing prepayment assumption of 165% PSA, the companions pay sequentially over the entire remaining life of the collateral. In this example the companion paydowns at 165% PSA have been divided into three classes with average lives of 3.1, 11.5, and 20.3 years (nominally a series of 3-, 10- and 20-year bonds).

The impact of actual prepayment experience on the size and timing of principal payments to the companion classes is graphically depicted in Exhibits 2 and 3. When prepayments occur at a constant speed of 300% PSA (the upper PAC collar), as shown in Exhibit 2, the PAC schedule is not disturbed, but the companions shorten dramatically and are all fully retired by the eighth year. By contrast, when prepayments slow to 85% PSA (the lower PAC collar), the first companion does not begin to pay until about the eighth year, as Exhibit 3 indicates. The resultant average-life volatility is very signi-

Exhibit 2. PAC with Standard Companion Bonds, 300% PSA

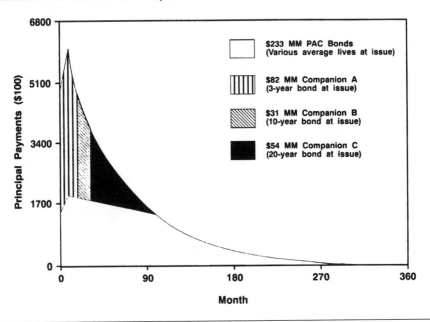

ficant. Bonds with average lives at pricing of 3, 10, and 20 years shorten to
1.0, 2.5, and 5.8 years, respectively, at 300% PSA, and at 85% PSA, the bonds
have average lives of 15.0, 21.1, and 25.6 years, respectively.

The average-life variability of a companion bond is generally a function
of the size of the PAC region relative to the entire issue, the size of the companion relative to the remaining companions, and its average life at the pricing prepayment assumption. A detailed examination of how these characteristics interact to produce the actual behavior of companion bonds in
different prepayment scenarios is beyond the scope of this chapter. Still, it is
worth outlining the basic relationships between companion structure and
behavior because they apply as well to the more complex, schedule-based
structures which are the subject of this chapter.

The order in which a companion is scheduled to receive excess cash
flows also can profoundly affect its average life behavior. It is normally
assumed that companions will be retired in the order of their average lives at
issue and that this order of priority does not change over the term of the
transaction (indeed, that assumption is made throughout this discussion).
This assumption, however, could be altered, generating results that are
entirely specific to the transaction in question. Rather than assume that a

Exhibit 3. PAC with Standard Companion Bonds, 85% PSA

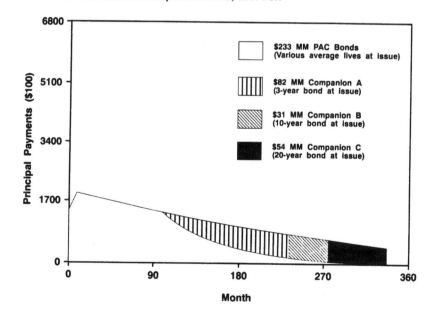

certain order of priorities is standard, investors should assure themselves that they understand the priorities and other rules on which the structure is based, as well as the conditions under which they may be switched on or off.

There are basically three different ways to vary the relative size of the companions. Lockouts, already mentioned above, are typically employed to improve the stability of payments to the earliest companion class in the issue. Moreover, with two or three years of schedulable paydowns added to its size, the first companion can provide a larger buffer against call and extension for subsequent companions. A similar technique is to pay the later years or "tail" of the PAC schedule to the companions projected to be paying at the same time. Intermediate- or long-term companions can benefit from this technique. The third, tightening the collars, can increase the size of the companions.

Raising the bottom collar increases the principal available for companion classes in the early years (generally the first quarter to first third of the remaining term of the collateral) and lowering the top collar increases principal in later years.

It also should be apparent that the smaller the scheduled PAC payments, the more principal will be available to make payments to companions at any given prepayment speed. This means that extension risk is reduced; call risk is also reduced. The smaller the PAC region, the larger the projected paydowns to the companion in any one period and the smaller the excess principal as a proportion of the projected companion principal payment will be. In other words, excess principal has a proportionally smaller impact on the dollar weights used to compute the companion's average life.

For similar algebraic reasons, changing the proportion of PACs, while holding the average lives about the same, has a bigger impact on the volatility of companions constructed from cash flows at the tail, because smaller dollar weights are applied to later dates. The absolute magnitude of the average life at issue of a companion also determines how much it can lengthen or shorten. This is also very intuitive: the longer the average life at issue, the less room to lengthen and the more room to shorten. Similarly, short-term bonds have less room to shorten, more to lengthen.

The shortening of a CMO bond's average life in a bull market, or, conversely, its lengthening in a bear market generally are negative events from the investor's point of view. Two effects are of particular concern. For one, the additional cash flow accelerates or decelerates at the wrong time. As a consequence of the interest-rate sensitivity of the prepayment process, reinvestment opportunities are most likely to have declining yields when prepayments are increasing, and rising yields when prepayments are drying up. Second, as average life varies, so too does the bond's duration or price sensitivity. In a bull market, the bond's price appreciates more slowly as market yields decline, generating a lower economic return than a bond of like but stable average life. In a bull market, the companion's value depreciates more quickly as yields rise.[4]

Since companion bonds absorb additional volatility from the protected bonds, changes in expected average life resulting from changes in prepayment experience in the collateral are of heightened concern to investors who hold them. As crucial as an accurate model of the prepayment process is for anticipating the performance of other mortgage-related products in various interest-rate scenarios, it is even more valuable in the evaluation of companion bonds. Without appropriate prepayment projections, such as can be derived from an econometric prepayment model, it is not possible to link changes in interest-rate levels to meaningful estimates of the yield or total rate of return of a companion.

COMPANION TACs

Since their introduction in the third quarter of 1988, companion TAC bonds have proven to be a highly marketable innovation. Indeed, since the first TACs were issued, the market has evolved away from TAC-only structures to prefer companion TACs. Clean TAC bonds (from structures without PACs) now are offered less frequently.

A TAC schedule is created by projecting the principal cash flows for the collateral at a single constant prepayment speed. This speed is typically the prepayment speed at which the bonds are priced. In the case of a clean TAC, the projected principal payments define the schedule. In the case of the companion TAC, projected principal remaining after scheduled PAC payments are made defines the schedule. The TACs have first priority after the PACs to principal payments, and their schedules are protected from call risk by the existence of other companion classes that absorb any principal paydowns that exceed both the scheduled PAC and TAC payments in any period. The larger these "support" classes are in relation to the companion TAC, the greater the protection provided to the TAC schedule.

Compared to a clean TAC with similar (in the example they are the same) average life and underlying collateral, the companion TAC necessarily receives less protection, because a larger proportion of the total collateral has already been allocated to high priority PAC bonds, and a much smaller proportion of principal remains to be allocated to lower priority support tranches. For this discussion, a simplified example of a companion TAC was created from the three-year companion in Exhibit 1. This was done simply by

---

4 Structurers can improve the appeal of volatile securities to some investors by manipulating the coupon so that they are priced as deep discounts to benefit from fast prepayment speeds or as high premiums to benefit from slow prepayments.

defining a schedule as the principal payments to the three-year companion assuming a constant prepayment speed of 165% PSA. Since it is identical at 165% PSA to the PAC/standard companion example, readers should refer to the cash-flow diagram in Exhibit 1 to understand this structure. The impact of faster prepayments on this PAC/TAC structure is shown in Exhibit 4. At 300% PSA, the higher priority given the TAC schedule forces the 10- and 20-year companions to pay down simultaneously with the TAC (instead of sequentially as in the first example). Readers will note that the shape of the companion TAC at 300% PSA is almost but not entirely identical to its shape at 165%, indicating that the schedule is still well protected at this speed. The size and timing of later payments has been altered slightly at the higher prepayment speed for reasons discussed below.

Companion TACs generally have the same properties as clean TACs: they provide a degree of call protection and little extension protection. Many structures actually will first extend, when prepayments slightly exceed the TAC speed, before shortening at higher speeds. The important difference is that companion TACs have significantly less call protection since they must absorb excess principal once the remaining unscheduled companions are retired. This can be seen by examining Exhibit 5, in which the average lives

Exhibit 4. PAC with Standard Companion TAC, 300% PSA

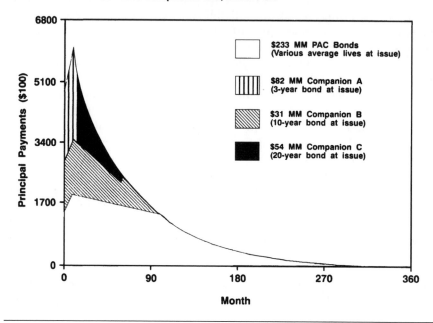

Legend:
- $233 MM PAC Bonds (Various average lives at issue)
- $82 MM Companion A (3-year bond at issue)
- $31 MM Companion B (10-year bond at issue)
- $54 MM Companion C (20-year bond at issue)

Y-axis: Principal Payments ($100)

X-axis: Month

Exhibit 5. Average Lives at Various Prepayment Speeds of Different Three-Year PAC Companion Structures (Pricing Assumption 165% PSA)

Prepayment Speed (% PSA)	Average Life (Years)			
	Clean TAC	PAC Companion	Companion TAC	Level II PAC
0	16.7	24.7	24.7	23.3
50	8.0	19.9	19.9	16.8
85	6.0	14.9	14.9	9.5
90	5.2	13.7	13.7	3.1
125	4.0	7.2	7.2	3.1
165	3.1	3.1	3.1	3.1
225	3.1	1.6	3.1	3.1
275	3.1	1.2	3.1	2.7
300	3.1	1.0	3.2	2.5
475	3.1	0.6	1.6	1.5
600	3.1	0.5	1.2	1.1

of various three-year CMO bonds at various prepayment speeds are compared. For comparison, a clean TAC with a 3.1-year average life has been constructed from the same collateral used to create the PAC/standard companion and PAC/TAC examples. The clean TAC has unnaturally exceptional call protection (it is protected by $360 million of companion bonds, which comprise the remainder of the structure). The smaller size of the clean TAC also results in its having a lower average life at very low prepayment speeds than the companion TAC does (the clean TAC is small enough for even small paydowns at low speeds to reduce its principal balance significantly in the early years).

The more important comparison, since so few clean TACs are issued at present, is with the three-year companion from Exhibit 1. The companion TAC clearly provides meaningful call protection, requiring speeds in excess of 600% PSA before it shortens as much as the standard companion does at 300% PSA. The two bonds extend identically. This happens because they both have the same priority after the PACs to receive principal paydowns and no companions in front of them (the TAC would have priority over an earlier companion, which would protect it to a degree from extending, whereas the standard companion would wait until earlier companions were retired, which would cause it to extend).

Notice that at 300% PSA, the companion TAC's average life is about a month longer than at the pricing speed (rounding exaggerates the difference

—at several more places of significance the difference is really about 0.08 year). This phenomenon occurs at relatively high speeds, as principal payments become more bunched in the early months and trail off more sharply in later months. Exhibit 4, as mentioned above, gives some indication of what is happening at this speed to the principal cash flows thrown off by the collateral. The paydowns become more "tailish" toward the end of the companion's schedule, forcing it to wait as excess payments are, going into the tail, not large enough to meet the schedule.

The other great difference between PAC/TAC structures and both clean TAC and PAC/standard companion structures is how much more volatile the unscheduled companions can be. The presence of additional risk-reduced structures forces the remaining companions to absorb more prepayment volatility. This is demonstrated in Exhibit 6, where various 20-year companion structures are compared. At prepayment speeds above 225% PSA, the companion in the PAC/TAC structure begins to shorten much more quickly than the standard companion.

REVERSE TACs

Payment rules and priorities also can be devised that protect a companion bond from extension risk while leaving it more exposed to call risk. These

Exhibit 6. Average Lives at Various Prepayment Speeds of 20-Year Companions from Different CMO Structures (Pricing Assumption 165% PSA)

Prepayment Speed (% PSA)	Average Life (years)		
	PAC Structure	PAC/TAC Structure	Layered PAC Structure
0	27.7	27.7	27.8
50	26.8	26.8	27.0
90	25.3	25.3	25.6
125	23.3	23.4	23.3
165	**20.3**	**20.3**	**18.2**
190	18.0	18.0	12.5
225	13.6	13.1	5.1
250	10.4	9.2	3.8
275	7.4	5.7	3.1
300	4.8	2.6	2.6
475	2.0	1.0	1.3
600	1.5	0.7	1.0

structures fittingly are termed "reverse TACs." Significant amounts of reverse TACs have been issued since the beginning of 1989, stimulated in part by the bearish sentiment prevalent during much of the first half of the year. These structures typically are created as twenty-year companion classes. Their long lives make them natural candidates for this treatment, as they have not, in any case, more than six or maybe eight years to extend. Additionally, these structures are priced at significant discounts from par in order to benefit from increases in prepayments.

An example of a reverse TAC was created for this discussion by defining a payment schedule for the fourth tranche of the PAC/companion structure depicted in Exhibits 1, 2, and 3. A cash-flow diagram for prepayments at 85% PSA is included in Exhibit 7. (At 165% PSA and faster speeds, the PAC/ reverse TAC structure, as will be explained below, pays exactly like the PAC/standard companion, which is depicted at 165% PSA in Exhibit 1 and 300% PSA in Exhibit 3.) The schedule was run at 165% PSA, the pricing speed in all of these examples, and has priority after the scheduled PAC payments are made. The reverse TAC receives excess cash flow only after the three- and ten-year companions are retired. These arrangements preserve

Exhibit 7. PAC with Reverse TAC Bond, 85% PSA

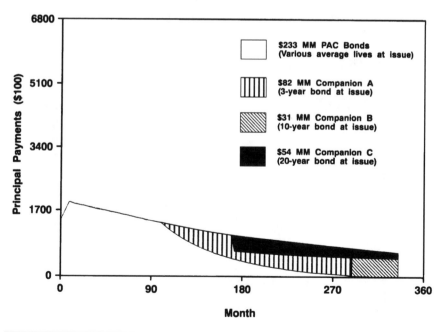

the schedule at prepayment speeds slower than those used to generate the schedule, but not at faster speeds. The reverse TAC does not begin to extend until prepayments fall below a constant rate of about 70% PSA.

The average life volatility of the reverse TAC is compared to that of other 20-year companion structures in Exhibit 8. The reverse TAC in the example has an average life of 20.3 years; in the worst case, that of no prepayments, the bond's average life only extends to 24.5 years. By comparison, the last tranche of the simple structure extends to 27.7 years. The cash-flow diagrams in Exhibits 3 and 7 make it clear why this is so. In the simple PAC/companion structure (Exhibit 3), at a speed equal to the upper collar, the companions pay down sequentially after the PAC bonds are retired. In the structure with the reverse TAC (Exhibit 7), the three- and ten-year companions extend to permit the scheduled reverse TAC payments to be met. At 85% PSA, the lower PAC collar, the short- and intermediate-term companions pay simultaneously with the reverse TAC. At slower prepayment speeds, the average lives of both companions exceed that of the reverse TAC.

The reverse TAC imparts considerably more volatility to the other companions when prepayments slow, but it does not cause them to be more volatile in faster prepayment scenarios. This effect can also be seen by comparing the average lives of three-year companions from both structures listed

Exhibit 8. Average Lives at Various Prepayment Speeds of 20-Year PAC Structures (Pricing Assumption 165% PSA)

Prepayment	Average Life (years)		
Speed (% PSA)	PAC Companion	Reverse TAC	Level II PAC
0	27.7	24.5	24.6
50	26.8	20.7	20.3
85	25.6	20.3	18.1
125	23.3	20.3	18.1
165	20.3	20.3	18.1
190	18.0	18.0	18.1
225	13.6	13.6	18.1
250	10.4	10.4	14.7
275	7.4	7.4	
300	4.8	4.8	5.8
350	3.3	3.3	3.7
475	2.0	2.0	2.2
600	1.5	1.5	1.6

in Exhibit 9. This is a natural consequence of the one-sided protection afforded by targeted amortization structures.

Schedules can also be applied to intermediate-term companion bonds to protect their average lives from extending in slow prepayment scenarios. At the same time, the structure is "protected" from call risk in moderately fast prepayment scenarios by taking advantage of the natural tendency of TACs to extend slightly as prepayments exceed the pricing speed. The resulting average life profile can be reasonably stable across a significant range of prepayment speeds (for example, extending no more than two or three years across a range from 50% or 75% PSA to 225% or 250% PSA, assuming a schedule run at 165% PSA). In effect, an intermediate-term companion TAC can be constructed to provide PAC-like stability. A number of such bonds have indeed been issued, some of them with monikers indicating that the payments are stabilized or controlled.

LAYERED PACs

The value of companion classes also can be enhanced by establishing secondary PAC schedules for a portion of the principal remaining after the primary PAC payments are met. A cash-flow diagram for an example of a

---

Exhibit 9. Average Lives at Various Prepayment Speeds of Three-Year Companions from Different CMO PAC Structures (Pricing Assumption 165% PSA)

	Average Life (years)		
Prepayment Speed (% PSA)	PAC Structure	PAC/ Reverse TAC Structure	Layered PAC Structure
0	24.7	26.3	26.1
50	19.9	22.7	22.7
85	14.9	16.5	18.3
90	13.7	15.0	17.4
100	11.5	12.4	14.5
125	7.2	7.2	8.7
165	3.1	3.1	3.1
225	1.6	1.6	1.5
275	1.2	1.2	1.1
300	1.0	1.0	1.0
475	0.6	0.9	0.6
600	0.5	0.6	0.5

two-tiered PAC structure, run at a pricing speed of 165% PSA, is shown in Exhibit 10. This example uses the same collateral as the previous examples. The same collars—85% to 300% PSA—were used to create the same amount of primary or Level I PACs—$233.0 million of a total original balance of $400 million CMO bonds. Collars for the second tier of PACs were set at 90% to 225% PSA. The second-tier PAC region was further divided into a series of nominally 10- and 20-year bonds, the companions into 3- and 20-year bonds. (In order to match the 3.1 year average lives in the previous examples, it was necessary to let the long-term bonds in the layered PAC example have average lives closer to 18 than to 20 years. This does not vitiate the comparison.) The Level II PACs appear in the figure as a narrow band between the PAC region and the companions: at 165% PSA they pay down simultaneously with the primary PACs in the deal. The size of the second tier of PACs is a function of the collars—the tighter the protection band the larger the amount of PACs that can be created. In this example, protecting the Level II schedule up to 225% PSA limits the amount of 3-year Level II PACs that can be created to $5.6 million. In total, the second layer of PACs only amount to about 11% of the transaction (58.25% of the transaction is standard, Level I PACs).

Exhibit 10. Layered PAC Structure, 165% PSA

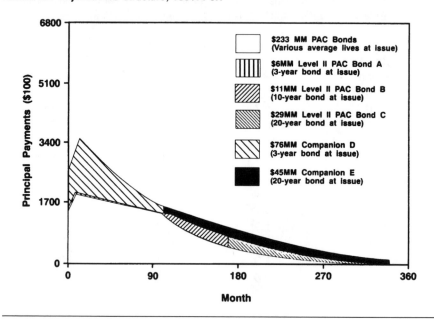

The Level II PAC schedule remains intact until prepayment speeds break the primary PAC collars. For example, Exhibit 11 shows the principal payments at 300% PSA. At this speed, the primary PAC schedule is not violated, but payments to the Level II PACs are significantly accelerated, shortening to average lives of 2.5, 3.9, and 5.8 years, respectively. Similarly, when prepayments slow to a constant speed of 85% PSA, primary PAC payments are made on schedule, but the payments to Level II PACs are delayed. At 85% PSA, as shown in Exhibit 12, the companion PACs have average lives of 9.5, 11.3, and 18.1 years, respectively. As would be expected, the longer Level II PACs are more volatile on the upside, when prepayments accelerate, and the shorter PACs are more volatile on the downside, when prepayments decelerate. The 3- and 20-year bonds receive no principal until the Level II PACs are paid, extending their average lives to 18.3 years and 25.8 years, respectively.

The average-life volatility of Level II PACs is compared to that of companion TACs and 3-year standard companions in Exhibit 8. Although not as well protected as primary PACs, Level II PACs do provide modest call protection and decent extension protection. Moreover, these examples demonstrate that they can shorten and extend less vigorously than their TAC and

Exhibit 11. Layered PAC Structure, 300% PSA

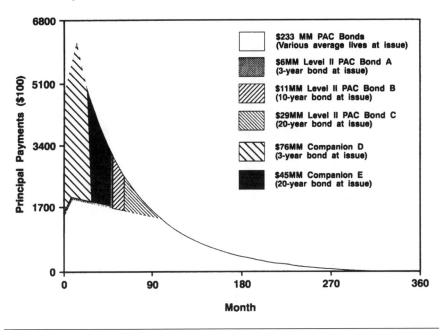

Exhibit 12. Layered PAC Structure, 85% PSA

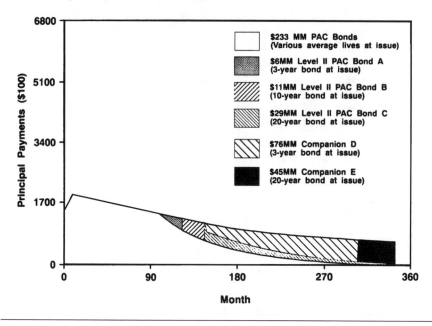

reverse TAC counterparts when prepayments move outside the appropriate protective boundary. The companions of layered PACs are somewhat more volatile over moderate prepayment shifts. As the comparison in Exhibit 6 with a 20-year standard PAC companion and a reverse TAC suggests, the 20-year layered PAC companion shortens faster between 165% and about 250% PSA than either of its counterparts. Similarly, Exhibit 9 indicates that the 3-year layered PAC companion lengthens more abruptly than its counterparts at prepayment speeds between 165% and 50% PSA.[5]

CONCLUSION

The average life volatilities of the 3-year companion structures discussed in this chapter are summarized in Exhibit 13, as are those of the 20-year com-

---

5 Readers are reminded that all these examples are highly simplified and furnish a basic understanding of how the structures behave. Actual CMO issues frequently are more complex, containing other structures or variations on those discussed in this chapter. Additional complexity could result in behavior valuably different from that of these examples.

Exhibit 13. Different Three-Year CMO Companion Structures (Average Lives over a Range of Constant Prepayment Speeds)

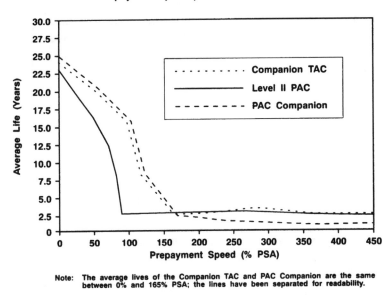

Note: The average lives of the Companion TAC and PAC Companion are the same between 0% and 165% PSA; the lines have been separated for readability.

panions in Exhibit 14. The graphs make plain the differences in call and extension protection that can be provided by furnishing companion classes with TAC or PAC schedules. The Level II PACs have stable average life patterns between the upper and lower collar speeds. (A Level I PAC would have a similar pattern, only it would be stable over a wider range, say 75% to 300% PSA, and owing to the presence of the companions, would shorten or lengthen more moderately outside that range.) By comparison, the standard companions demonstrate steep and continuous changes in average life over the same ranges for which the Level II PACs are protected. The TACs, as would be expected, provide call protection, but no extension protection, while the reverse TACs are stable at slower speeds, but shorten abruptly when prepayments occur at faster constant rates than the prepayment assumption.

Exhibit 14. Different Twenty-Year CMO Companion Structures (Average Lives over a Range of Constant Prepayment Speeds)

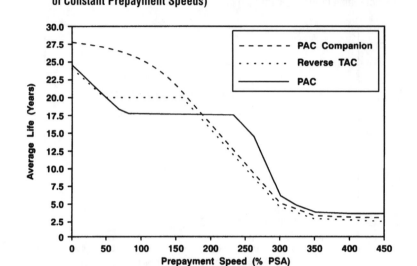

Note: The average lives of the PAC Companion and Reverse TAC are the same at
         prepayment speeds above 165% PSAs. The lines are separated for readability.

CHAPTER 21

Inverse Floaters and Inverse IOs

Shaiy Pilpel, Ph.D.
Managing Director
Canadian Imperial Bank of Commerce

INTRODUCTION

Investors in the fixed-income markets, accustomed to the simple structure of government and corporate bonds, view collateralized mortgage obligations (CMO) as bizarre bonds. This is a valid perception because even the simplest CMO bonds are complex derivative structures; nevermind the more esoteric bonds. This chapter is devoted to the most complex CMO substructures currently existing, namely, inverse floaters and inverse IOs.

The complexity of inverse bonds comes from the fact that their cash flows, and hence their characteristics, are determined by more than one factor. While the cash flows of most mortgage bonds are affected, through the collateral's prepayment behavior, by the long-term interest rate, inverse structures are affected by both long- and short-term interest rates. To complicate things even further, these rates affect the bond's cash flows in opposing directions.

Inverse bonds are floating-rate obligations, with payments inversely related to some index. A bond that pays 9% – LIBOR is an example of an inverse bond. Old structures in this family included three generic types of bonds: *inverse floaters, inverse IOettes,* and *inverse IOs.* Recently, a new generic bond structure has gained popularity—*notional inverse IOs.* We shall define and analyze these structures throughout the chapter.

The most popular index used in inverse structures is the *London Interbank Offered Rate,* known as *LIBOR.* When LIBOR is used as the index, the cash flows of the inverse bonds depend on both ends of the yield curve spectrum. The long-term rate affects the bonds' prepayments, while the short-term rate determines their monthly payments via the coupon formulas.

This chapter describes inverse floaters and inverse IOs from several perspectives:

- Legal: legal requirements and limitations on REMIC derivatives.

- Economical rationale: the economic reasons for creating complex inverse bonds.

- Structure: classification of inverse bonds according to their main characteristics.

- Investment: investment considerations of inverse bonds.

- Analysis: analyzing, pricing, and hedging inverse bonds.

The methodologies and ideas that are discussed throughout this chapter should be regarded as generic tools. These tools can be used in the process of analyzing and understanding each specific structure.

LEGAL

Inverse bonds owe their popularity to changes in regulations governing Real Estate Mortgage Investment Conduit (REMIC) structures. Modern financial engineering allows the creation of an almost unlimited number of derivative structures. Cash flows, either fixed or contingent, can be combined in any imaginable way to generate almost any desired characteristics.

Prior to 1986, multi-class mortgage securities were issued as Collateralized mortgage obligations (CMO). Legally, these were debt instruments and were treated as borrowing by the issuer. REMIC regulations allow these pass-throughs to be treated as asset sales by the issuer. There is no cash-flow difference between CMOs and REMICs, and we refer to both structures as CMOs.

Regulations, by limiting the definitions governing allowable REMIC status, limit the variety of structures that can be *bonded*. In other words, regulators and not structurers eventually determine which of the possible cash-flow combinations can be defined as eligible for REMIC status.

REMIC regulations were overhauled at the end of 1991. Major changes were made, reflecting the development of financial engineering and the CMO market. The greatest effect of the changes is on inverse bonds. The new regulations permit the creation of IO strip classes from almost all classes of a REMIC structure. Previously, only one pure strip had been allowed, based on the collateral and a limited number of IOettes (strips with principal). The new regulations also allow conditional option-like cash flows to be packed into bonded cash flows.

The changes allow, among other things, the creation of derivative bonds based on any other bond or combination of bonds in the structure. The only limitation is that the options' conditions or their indexes be based on interest-rate instruments. Equity-related options based, for example, on the S&P index do not qualify as REMICs, and therefore can carry complex tax consequences. As a result, new REMICs can include, as bonds, pure cash flows that have no intrinsic principal. These are *notional bonds*, based on the principal amount of another bond, the notional principal, to which they have no claim.

The new regulations enhance the set of allowable CMO bonds beyond simple floating-rate bonds to include almost any combination of interest rate cash flows. Before 1991, only simple floaters could be structured as bonds. All other contingent cash flows were treated as equity and had to be siphoned into only one class, the *residual* class. Every REMIC CMO still needs a residual class for legal and tax purposes. Residuals, however, have lost most of their economic worth, which is now captured by a new set of "cleaner" derivative bonds such as IOs, super-POs, and various inverse floating-rate classes.

ECONOMIC RATIONALE

With all due respect to Wall Street and the talented people employed by the brokerage houses and investment banks, the success or failure of any financial instrument still depends on whether it has economic justification. Derivative instruments, as sophisticated, smart, or elegant as they may be, still need *bona fide* investors to use them. Financial instruments that are good only for trading sooner or later find themselves on the rubbish heap of obsolete inventions.

There is room nevertheless (and some need) for a specific class of financial instruments that may have no intrinsic economic justification *per se*. The exception covers instruments that are the by-products of the process that creates economically needed instruments. In other words, there are instruments that possess no direct economic value; yet their existence allows us to create desirable financial instruments. The new breed of inverse bonds belongs to this class.

Investors in mortgage-backed securities are motivated by one reason: *yield*. For their complexity, mortgage products offer improved yield characteristics at less default risk than alternative investments. Whole-loan products offer even better yields than "classic" agency-backed products without compromising the credit quality of the investment. The senior tranches in whole-loan CMOs are practically comparable to agency-guaranteed mortgages with surplus yield. All this makes whole-loan bonds an attractive investment vehicle for even the most conservative institutions.

Investors, in general, are averse to changes which entail "the risk of the unknown." Therefore, even when new investment vehicles are considered, investors would prefer to meet familiar structures. This is the reason that one meets corporate-like structures in regular CMOs and in whole-loan CMOs. Investors are ready to pay back a fraction of the excess yield generated by the collateral if the cash flow it generates can be packed into desired structures.

THE SUPPLY ANGLE

Financial institutions, especially those whose liabilities depend on the prevailing short-term interest rate, prefer securities that offer the same type of return as their liabilities. Floating-rate bonds that offer a "good" spread to LIBOR or COFI (Eleventh District Cost of Funds Index) are, therefore, in high demand among such investors. Banks and other depository institutions increase the demand for floating-rate notes backed by whole-loans (as compared to agency-backed bonds) because of the different treatment of such bonds for capital adequacy purposes.

To facilitate investors' demands, the brokerage houses employ legions of mathematicians and structurers. Armed with the most sophisticated analytical tools, they can slice the collateral's cash flow in almost any desired way. But even this brain power cannot defy the first rule of mortgage-backed bonds: *The collateral should always generate enough cash to pay off the obligations.*

Newton's first law of physics, which states that action equals reaction, can be adapted as the first law of modern finance. Each derivative cash flow has its "counter cash flow," defined as:

Counter cash flow = Collateral cash flow − Desired cash flow

Applying these rules to floating-rate bonds shows that each floater must come with a corresponding inverse floater. In other words, there is no way to create a CMO structure containing even a single floating-rate bond without creating a corresponding inverse bond.

Under the old regulations, all inverse cash flows could be siphoned into only the residual class. The new REMIC rules let the CMO structurers mold those cash flows into almost any form. They can attach the cash flows to any existing class or create a new class of pure cash flows.

The object of this semi-philosophical introduction is to emphasize the economic legitimacy of inverse bonds. While investors in these securities may treat them as abstract cash flows, it is important to understand the logic behind the creation of such bonds. This understanding facilitates better selection of bonds as well as improved handling of their hedging. Moreover, it allows the pricing of inverse floaters, using arbitrage arguments and calculating their implied creation value.

STRUCTURES OF INVERSE BONDS

We explore the characteristics of the most common types of inverse bonds by identifying and tracking the source of their cash flows. This is done by first looking at the mechanics of creating CMO floating-rate tranches and then dealing with the possible packaging alternatives of the residual cash flows.

FLOATING-RATE BONDS

To structure a floating-rate bond with given time characteristics, a schematic algorithm is usually applied.

Step 1. Determine an appropriate cap. The *first law* prohibits uncapped liabilities. Mortgages that are used to collateralize CMOs are either fixed-rate or capped ARMs. Both types cannot support uncapped liabilities. Therefore, all floaters must carry a cap. (Note that the cap can be higher than the collateral's coupon, but it always exists.)

Step 2. Structure a fixed-rate bond with the desired maturity and cash-flow properties. This bond may be a PAC, TAC, sequential, or any other bond. The coupon of the bond equals or is less than the collateral's coupon.

Step 3. Change this bond into a (temporary) fixed-rate bond having the previous properties but with a coupon that equals the desired cap. The new bond may be smaller (in its principal amount) than the original one. If this happens, another bond is also created, absorbing the principal differences.

There are many ways to create bonds bearing the targeted coupon, each resulting in a different size for the bond as well as different types of support bonds that are created through the process. The examples highlight two of the many alternatives.

Example 1

Original bond: $30MM tranche.
Original coupon: 7%. Desired coupon: 9%.

Bonds created:
   Bond A: $15MM, coupon: 9%.
   Bond B: $15MM, coupon: 5%.

Example 2

Original bond: $30MM tranche.
Original coupon: 7%.
Desired coupon: 9%.

An alternative solution:
   Bond C: $20MM, coupon: 9%.
   Bond D: $10MM, coupon: 3%.

Note that because "slicing" the original bond takes place in tandem (along the time axis), each bond resulting keeps the same properties as the original one: sequential, PAC, TAC, and so on.

Step 4. From the new bond (with the coupon set at the cap's rate), create a floating-rate bond and its residual cash flow.

Example 3

From bond C in example 2 create:

Bond E: $20MM floater paying LIBOR + 0.5% with a cap of 9%.
Bond F: Pure cash flow of 8.5% – LIBOR.
Bond F has no principal. The remaining principal of bond E is used as the notional amount to calculate the coupon.

The four steps in the algorithm demonstrate a method of creating a simple (capped) floating-rate bond. Structuring more complex bonds such as super-floaters, bonds with floors, or two-tiered bonds is basically the same but with appropriate modifications. Note that this process creates some other bonds and cash flows. These bonds are an integral part of any structuring algorithm. The first law states that there is no way to eliminate them from the CMO structure.

The new REMIC regulations permit blending almost any imaginable combination of bonds and cash flows into "legal" CMO bonds. Different blends of bonds create inverse structures with totally different characteristics. Inverse bonds may be short or long, robust or volatile, bullish or bearish. This way, the CMO designers, after satisfying the requests of the floating-rate notes buyers, still have the versatility to fulfill different requests coming from investors in the inverse bond community.

TYPES OF INVERSE BONDS

The distinction between different structures of inverse securities is based on the source of cash flow of each bond. Using this method, the investment characteristics of the various bonds become relatively clear.

Pure Cash-Flow: Known also as *notional bonds*, pure cash-flow bonds have no principal of their own, and their cash flows come from the differences between the caps and the floating-rate obligations of other bonds. In example 3, bond F is a notional inverse floater. The owner of that bond receives a notional coupon of 8.5% – LIBOR based on the principal amount of bond E.

Notional bonds have no principal. The convention is to use the notional principal of the reference bond for quoting prices of notional inverses, determining their factors, and so on. The prices of notional bonds are, in most cases, a fraction (*e.g.*, 10% or 2%) of the par value of the reference bond. Do not be misled by the fact that such levels usually indicate discount prices; in fact, *notional bonds are pure premium bonds*. This quote convention magnifies the importance of each 1/32nd of the bond's price, because, compared to the notional price, which may be 5 or 10, it is comparable to almost one point of the price of a regular par bond.

Being pure premium bonds, notional inverses react negatively to a decrease in interest rates because this speeds up prepayments, which, in turn, erode the bond's premium. The response is different, however, when one considers the cash-flow stream as a function of LIBOR. An inverse bond's cash flows increase, *ceteris paribus*, when LIBOR decreases. The weighted reaction to a shift in the yield curve depends on factors such as the specific structure of each bond or its average life.

The price of a notional inverse bond is the price of the premium. Thus, the inverse cash flow pays the bond's principal as well as its expected return as a function of this premium. Therefore, unlike regular floating-rate bonds in which the coupon covers only the interest payments, small changes in the short-term rate can have a tremendous effect on the bond's yield.

Inverse IOs: Sometimes, investors must have real principal instead of notional, usually to satisfy regulations written before the notional idea was introduced. If this is desired, a small principal stripped out of the notional bond can be attached to the pure cash flow, thus creating the familiar IOettes. IO- and inverse IO-type bonds are quoted based on their real principal rather than their reference.

Example 4

Using the data from example 3, strip away $100,000 principal from bond E (the floater), and add it to bond F (the notional), creating two new bonds:

Bond G: $19,900,000 floater, paying LIBOR + 0.5% with a cap of 9%.
Bond H: $100,000 principal, with a coupon formula
1,700.5% – 199 x LIBOR and a floor of 0%.

The coupon formula of bond H results from expressing the residual cash flow of bond G in terms of the $100,000 principal of bond F rather than the original $20 million. Mathematically,

$$\text{New coupon} = 9\% + \left(\frac{20,000,000 - 100,000}{100,000} \right) \times (8.5\% - \text{LIBOR})$$

$$= 1,700.5\% - 199 \times \text{LIBOR}$$

The owner of bond H is entitled, in addition to its coupon, to the principal payments of the $100,000 as scheduled.

Note that the previous formula is correct for LIBOR if under 8.5%. If LIBOR exceeds 8.5%, bond H has a floor of 9%. Since the floor is relatively low compared to the 1,700% cap, we shall neglect this edge effect in one discussion.

The investment characteristics of notional inverses and inverse IOs are practically identical. Since in really high premiums the principal amount is almost negligible, notional inverses and IO inverses should be treated as the same type of bond.

Combination Bonds: Sometimes, a few cash flows are combined to form a new, complex bond. No theoretical reason prohibits packaging together any combination of cash flows. In practice, three combinations are most commonly observed:

1. A notional inverse and a fixed notional IO strip.

2. A weighted combination of two or more pure notional inverses.

3. A notional inverse and a matched fixed-coupon bond.

1. A notional inverse and a fixed notional IO strip. Since notional inverses rely heavily on LIBOR, they have high *gearing*. A relatively small change in LIBOR changes the cash-flow yield by a large amount. For example, a change of 1% in LIBOR may change the bond's yield by 15%, *i.e.*, a gearing of 15. Extreme cases of gearing above 100 have also been observed. In order to dampen the gearing effect, a fixed strip of 0.5% or 1% is sometimes added to the notional bond's cash flow. This strip is taken out of some (real) reference bond.

Example 5

Using examples 2 and 3, a 1% coupon can be stripped away from the $10 million of bond D and added to the cash flow of bond F. This generates a 0.5% notional strip for this $20 million notional bond.

Bond K: $20MM notional inverse bond with a coupon formula of 9% − LIBOR and a floor of 0.5%.

The importance of the added pure cash flow is not in creating the floor (which is touched only when LIBOR exceeds 8.5%) but in changing the notional cash flow from 8.5% − LIBOR to 9% − LIBOR, thus reducing the degree of dependence on LIBOR.

2. A weighted combination of two or more pure notional inverses. If the generating floating-rate bond is short-termed, it creates an extremely volatile notional inverse. Volatile bonds trade very cheaply and are difficult to hedge and sell. To reduce the volatility of the cash flow it is sometimes combined with a longer-term notional bond. This way, the short-term bond contributes more to the cash flow in the early phases of the bond's life, and is replaced by the long-term bond in the later stages of the combined bond's life.

The original notional size of such a bond is the sum of its components. The monthly factors refer to that size, but the contributions of the different bonds vary disproportionately and they depend on the deal and the specific notional tranches. The investment characteristics of a combination bond may change drastically with the passage of time.

3. A notional inverse and a matched fixed-coupon bond. This is a regular, not a premium, inverse floater bond (discussed below).

Inverse Floater Bonds

An inverse floater bond is generated by attaching the notional cash flow to a real regular bond instead of a small strip.

Example 6

Using examples 2 and 3, define a combination bond:

Bond L: Combine the cash flows (and principal) of bond D and those of F. The result is a bond with a principal of $20 million and a coupon formula

$$3\% + 2 \times (8.5\% - \text{LIBOR}) = 20\% - 2 \times \text{LIBOR}.$$

The multiplier (2 in example 6) arises because the coefficients of the $20 million coupon of 8.5% – LIBOR are described in reference to a $10 million principal bond. The inverse floater in example 6 has a cap of 20% and a floor of 3%.

The bond's sizes in example 6 are chosen arbitrarily. In order to maximize the size of the floating-rate bond that can be generated from a given tranche and a cap, other ratios should be used. Example 7 outlines the efficient solution.

Example 7

Using the original tranche from example 1 ($30MM principal, 7% coupon), and targeting a cap of 9%, the following bonds can be created:

Bond M: $23,333,333 principal amount, paying LIBOR + 0.5% with a cap of 9%.

Bond N: $6,666,666 principal amount, paying

$$(7/2) \times (8.5\% - \text{LIBOR}) = 29.75\% - 3.5 \times \text{LIBOR}.$$

Bond N has a cap of 29.75% and a floor of 0%.

Most inverse floaters have the form of bond N, with various multipliers, rather than the form of bond L. Yet, even though bond N is structured differently from bond L, it can still be viewed as the sum of two hypothetical bonds of the same kind of bond L's components: a pure $6,666,666 PO and an equi-sized notional inverse bond paying 29.75% – LIBOR.

The investment characteristics of inverse floater bonds are different from those of the pure premium or high premium IOs. The reason is that, in most cases, when the inverse bond is dissected into its components, the regular bond carries a low coupon and is generally a zero-coupon bond. This means that for the bulk of the investment PO-like characteristics dominate the characteristics of the inverse floater.

"Kitchen-Sink Bonds"

Kitchen-sink bonds are a very new breed of CMO structures. The name refers to CMO deals that use as collateral a combination of tranches from previous deals. Note the difference between a combination bond and a kitchen-sink deal. In the former, the combination is very specific, affecting only that particular bond, while in the latter, the combination takes place at the collateral level, affecting the entire CMO.

Dealers stuck with a large inventory of bonds that they cannot sell occasionally pool the cash flows of those bonds, reslice them, and more importantly, rename them to create a new deal. Such REMICs receive, and rightly so, the pejorative name *kitchen-sink deals*. The behavior of even a simple bond backed by a combination collateral may be very erratic, reflecting the nature of the complex collateral. The characteristics of a complex combination bond of a kitchen-sink deal are difficult to imagine.

Kitchen-sink deals are created to camouflage some very risky bonds. Investors should not only examine the collateral of their bond by its WAC and WAM but also make sure that it is "pure collateral." The extra yield offered in the primary market for kitchen-sink bonds does not usually justify the excess risk hidden in such deals.

INVESTMENT CLASSIFICATION OF INVERSE BONDS

Inverse bonds are fixed-income derivative products. Therefore, their classification follows, like all other interest-rate instruments, the classification of their yield profile.

Many things can happen to mortgage-backed bonds during their lifetimes: PAC bands can be broken, support tranches may pay down, Z-bonds can jump ahead of schedule, or floating-rate bonds might hit their caps or floors, to name a few. Inverse bonds that are affected by other bonds in a CMO issue have, therefore, not only structure-dependent characteristics but path-dependent ones as well. They may completely alter their yield profile during their life cycle and be classified differently at different times.

Primary Classification

The primary classification of inverse bonds matches that of all other mortgage-backed bonds: bearish or bullish instruments. The derivative nature of CMO inverses adds a new category—bonds that do not respond directionally to changes in interest rates. Such bonds are called "*humped*."

The prevailing interest-rate environment affects the cash flows of inverse bonds in many ways, but most importantly in coupon payments, principal prepayments, and call features.

Coupon Payments. By definition, lower interest rates translate to higher coupon payments to the inverse bond. Symmetrically, when interest rates are higher, the inverse coupon is lower.

Prepayments. Refinancing activity depends on the relationship between the old mortgage rate and the current interest rates. When the prevailing rates are lower than the collateral's rate, refinancing increases. While refinancing is just one component of prepayment, it may dominate the prepayment rate, especially if the current interest rate is much lower than that of the collateral. High prepayment rates considerably shorten the life of the bonds.

Another contributor to fast prepayment that is also affected by interest rates is *curtailment (i.e.,* increased payments). If the market's alternative investments offer low yields, homeowners may choose to invest in their mortgage by lowering their debt. Curtailment is influenced more by the shape of the yield curve than by absolute interest-rate levels. The current tax structure, which provides for tax deductibility of mortgage interest, benefits competing investments implicitly by the tax rate. If this changes, curtailment activity will increase considerably.

There are not many models that describe the prepayment patterns of whole-loan collaterals. Most of the existing ones are nothing more than slight modifications to the regular prepayment models of agency-backed collaterals. The study of the prepayment behavior of non-conforming and jumbo mortgages is still in its infancy. We expect to gain a better understanding of the nature of such prepayments in the next few years.

The falling interest-rate environment in 1992 and 1993 showed that whole-loan collateral responds more drastically to refinancing incentives than agency collateral with the same coupon. Many pools prepaid at 70, 80, and even 90 CPR.

Call Features. Most call features are defined in terms of a given percentage of the outstanding collateral to the original size of the deal. For example, a deal can be called when the outstanding amount is less than 20% of the original size of that deal. In such cases, high prepayment rates advance the call date, while low prepayment rates delay it. Moreover, the interest-rate environment at the time the call is exercised determines the value of the collateral and hence that of the call. The owners of the "right to call," usually the owners of the residual tranche, will exercise their right only if the call value is positive.

Call features may increase or decrease the bond's value, depending on whether the bond is a premium or discount. Agency deals have usually 1%–3% cleanup calls. Private label or whole-loan deals have usually a meaningful cleanup call clause (at least 10%). Investors, especially in the longer tranches, should check the effect of such a call on their bond's cash flows.

Yield Profile

Refinancing activity, through its dependence on interest rates, is a major factor in determining an inverse bond's cash flow and therefore its characteristics and value. Even though the classification of inverse bonds uses their interest-rate profile, changes in interest rates affect them not only through their direct influence on the coupon payments but also via their influence on refinancing.

For each interest rate R, assume that neither R nor its corresponding prepayment rate are changed throughout the life of the inverse bond. The expected return of the inverse bond can then be calculated. The interest-rate profile of an inverse bond is the graph of its theoretical yield plotted as a function of the (fixed) interest rate R. Since the inverse bond's returns and hence its profile depend on its price, we assume a "normal" price when plotting the yield profile.

It is unrealistic to believe that the values drawn in the yield profile represent the actual expected returns, because interest rates are practically "guaranteed" to change throughout the life of the inverse bond. The shape of the curve, however, determines the inverse bond's response to changes in the interest rate. Do the bond owners gain from interest rates going up, or do they benefit from them going down?

The terminology used to classify inverse bonds follows that used for other interest-rate instruments in terms of the shape of the interest-rate profile:

Upsloping curve—*bearish* bond
Downsloping curve—*bullish* bond
Oscillating curve—*humped* bond

Humped Inverse Bonds. Humped inverse structures respond differently to small changes in interest rates than to major shifts of the yield curve. This usually happens in a relatively small dynamic range of the interest-rate scale. Outside this range the bonds are either bullish or bearish.

The peculiarity of such a bond is due to the fact that the total cash flow of an inverse bond is the sum of two sources: the floater's coupon spread and the time "window" over which it contributes. These sources have opposing scales. Low interest rates increase the first component but shorten the bond's time window. When the prevailing interest rate is high, prepayment slows down, yet the inverse cash flow is smaller. Therefore, as an inverse floater, such a bond has a bullish exposure, while as a premium bond it has a bearish exposure. The exact weight of each component depends on the specific structure of the CMO and the bond under consideration.

In a rising interest-rate environment, the interest spread source of the inverse bond's cash flow declines (due to its inverse nature), while prepayment slowdown lengthens the life of the bond. In a declining interest-rate

Exhibit 1.   Yield Profiles of Humped Inverse Bonds

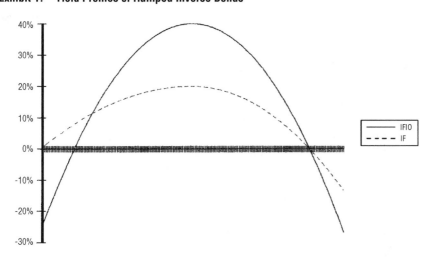

environment, the spread contributes more, while the premium (or the collateral supporting that bond and hence the spread) erodes faster.

The interplay between the short- and the long-term effects generates a dynamic range in which the inverse bond's profile may be humped. In extreme cases, when interest rates shift by several hundred basis points, one component usually predominates. Exhibit 1 pictures the yield profiles of humped inverse bonds.

The base price of the graph shown in Exhibit 1 is at its center yield. As one can see, if interest rates drop, the inverse floater loses its small premium, or gains its small discount rapidly, to register low yield. If interest rates rise, the bond extends, and the investor will recognize a loss. The notional inverse bond loses its premium in either extreme case: if its coupon becomes zero (increasing interest rate) or if its notional principal vanishes (decreasing interest rate).

There are two different interest rates that control the cash flow of inverse floating-rate bonds: (1) long-term rates, which define the market's mortgage rates and therefore the prepayment speed; and (2) short-term rates, usually LIBOR or COFI, which contribute to the spread. The yield profile, which is a single parameter classification, assumes unidirectional, parallel shifts of the yield curve.

The characteristics of inverse bonds may vary with time due to the relative effect of the different components of their cash flows. A front-loaded bearish bond may become bullish after the paydown of the CMO's support bonds. The complete history of the CMO issue and the historical interest-rate and prepayment paths are also important in predicting the inverse bond's behavior. A burnt-out collateral responds differently to changes in interest-rate than does a "brand-new" collateral for which every change is new.

Option-Adjusted Classification

We have observed that it is unreasonable to assume that interest rates will remain fixed during the entire life of an inverse bond. Modern option pricing models attempt to address this issue by providing a dynamic expression that is more realistic in a varying interest-rate environment. In this technique, the inverse bond's pattern is analyzed along a large sample of futuristic interest rate scenarios. Possible interest-rate paths are generated, and the bond's cash flow is studied along each path. The results are then weighted according to the statistical parameters of the model's stochastic process governing the interest rates and the yield curve. The spread between the yield measured this way and the comparable Treasury yield is called *option-adjusted spread* (OAS).

The drawback of this method is that it relies heavily on auxiliary and ever-changing parameters as well as prepayment models. Most prepayment models are far from accurate and are constantly rebuilt and updated with new data. Nevertheless, this stochastic methodology is a powerful technique for pricing and hedging inverse bonds.

UNDERSTANDING INVERSE BONDS

Inverse bonds are financial instruments generating cash flows that are contingent on a number of auxiliary variables from the very first payment. The main difficulty in structuring a general framework to analyze inverse bonds arises from the fact that each bond's cash flow depends first of all on its CMO structure. Every CMO deal is unique, and there is no way to parameterize structures. In other words, there is no "generic" inverse bond from which all inverse bonds can be derived using a small set of parameters.

Except for very simple CMO structures, it is impossible to picture the inverse bond's alternative cash flows intuitively and measure how different market conditions will affect them. The only way to get a bond's cash flow is through simulation. Using simulators to generate cash flows is a fairly recent idea, seen mainly in financial derivative products. While computers have been used before to perform complex financial calculations, their tasks have been limited to solving equations and performing other mathematical operations on cash flows derived from other sources. In the present case, however, the computer's role is not limited to solving the price-yield equations of given cash flows; it generates the cash flows themselves.

This reliance on computer simulation to generate cash flows is unique to all mortgage-backed securities, especially to the more esoteric bonds such as notional bonds, inverse floaters, and residuals. These simulators work with a set of parameters (prepayment, index, *etc.*) and are deterministic, given these parameters. That means that under the same assumptions (*i.e.*, parameters) all simulators will generate the same cash flow. The investor's role is therefore to determine the correct set of parameters "predicting" the future.

CMO deals are pass-through securities. Principal paid by the mortgage holder is immediately passed to the bond owners according to each CMO's structure. That means that, for a given deal, the monthly payments of each bond are uniquely determined by two factors: (1) the monthly collateral payments, and (2) the index for floating-rate bonds.

Collateral payments are the sum of two types of payments: scheduled and unscheduled. For a given collateral (*i.e.*, coupon, age) the scheduled payment is determined according to a simple formula. Unscheduled payments, on the other hand, consist of money coming from mortgage owners exercising their option to prepay all or part of their remaining debt. If this contribution is known for a given month, the total collateral's contribution is also known.

In structures containing floating-rate bonds, the coupon payments of the floaters or inverse floaters are determined by the index. Since in most cases this index is one-month LIBOR, we shall refer to LIBOR throughout the discussion.

Given prepayment and LIBOR assumptions, the computer can simulate the bond's cash flow and solve its corresponding price-yield equation. Note that each parameterization is good for a specific deal; there is no known method to parameterize the deals themselves.

Investors should be warned against blind reliance on simulators. Before running any simulated analysis it is important to understand the nature of the inverse bond's cash flow and how exactly it is generated. In other words, what is the exact time and importance of each of the bond's sources of cash flow?

Because modern CMO deals include many tranches, sometimes more than 40, it is impossible to picture and isolate the contribution of each bond. The investor has, therefore, to follow the logic of the CMO designer, who also cannot grasp the interrelationship of different tranches in such complex structures. Most deals are structured in major blocks, e.g., PAC-I, PAC-II, and their support bonds. Breaking the deal into a small number of building blocks makes it easier to identify and concentrate on the specific bonds that contribute to the inverse bond's cash flow.

An important rule that investors should obey is never to purchase a bond without fully understanding the CMO's structure. The precise yield numbers are a matter of calculation, but the investor should be aware of the risk/reward trade-off associated with each scenario. Poor structuring can hide enormous risks for premium or discount buyers, especially in complex derivatives.

INVESTMENT CONSIDERATIONS

Portfolio managers use derivative instruments such as inverse floaters or inverse IOs to achieve certain investment objectives. They may have an opinion on the long-term interest rate, LIBOR, COFI, or the shape of the entire yield curve, and wish to set up a profitable trade based on that opinion, or they can use mortgage-backed derivatives to capture higher yield.

Inverse bonds, because of their dependence on both extremes of the yield curve and the internal leverage that most of them have, may be a perfect tool to implement yield curve strategies. Yet in building any portfolio using inverse bonds, the investor should keep in mind three considerations.

Risk versus Reward. What are the expected returns if the investor is right compared to the losses if the investor is wrong?

Risk measurement and risk control are crucial (and, unfortunately, usually neglected) issues that should be addressing any portfolio that includes derivatives. Risking a loss of $100 to make a $10 profit is not such a great idea even if the probabilities are biased.

Inverse bonds may offer excellent risk/reward characteristics for implementing some strategies. At the same time, their risk may be too high when other investment goals are considered.

Alternative Investments: The return of each inverse bond should be compared to investment in simpler securities that can achieve the targeted goal.

If, for example, an investor has an opinion on the levels of LIBOR in the next few years, there are two strategies possible: (1) buying or selling Eurodollar futures contracts, or (2) buying an inverse bond. The use of the second alternative is recommended only if the risk/reward parameters of a specific whole-loan candidate dominate those of the Eurodollar futures position.

Liquidity. The secondary market for inverse bonds, especially for the more esoteric whole-loan products, is very thin. This means that the investor should not overlook the possibility that the bonds may be owned until their maturity. Strategies that assume dynamic positioning of such bonds should be avoided.

Liquidity affects pricing. The prices of inverse bonds should reflect the bonds' illiquidity.

We raise these issues not to scare away potential investors. On the contrary, in many cases inverse bonds offer exceptional risk/reward features compared to direct investments. Investors should be aware of the added risks and complications of these securities and demand proper yield compensation. The market offers this supplementary yield to sophisticated investors.

THE CHARACTERISTICS OF INVERSE BONDS

Inverse bonds have just one appeal for investors—their high yield. The yields offered by inverse bonds may be hundreds of basis points over the market's yields. This excess yield compensates the owner for the higher risk attached to inverse bonds. The two major components of this risk are premium risk and negative convexity.

Most inverse bonds are either high premium or discount bonds. Trading around par should be viewed as only a temporary phenomenon. These are risky investments, and buyers should fully understand the nature of the creature before investing a single penny in these securities.

Depending on its structure, each inverse bond usually contains a dominant IO or PO factor. While most premium factors (the IO component) are visible, as in the case of inverse IOs or inverse notional bonds, the discount factor (the PO component) is sometimes well hidden.

Inverse floaters can be viewed as a combination of a notional inverse and a PO. The market capitalization of these components, however, is weighted heavily toward the PO part, which in most cases overwhelms that of the notional. Therefore, if the interest rate rises, the bond may extend dramatically, losing a large percentage of its value.

Example 8

Bond N of example 7 is a typical inverse floater with a multiplier of 3.5. The notional inverse component of bond N contributes 15 to 25 points to its value, while the PO component adds 80 to 90 points, depending on the original bond's average life. In other words, the market capitalization of the PO component is about four to five times larger than the premium's. For bonds with lower multipliers (e.g., 8.5% – LIBOR), this ratio may be 1:8 or even higher.

This phenomenon is most noticeable in structures where the collateral is slightly in-the-money or in a declining interest-rate environment. Investors who pay par or a small premium are those who may lose the most. Even a small change in interest rates will make it uneconomical to refinance, bringing prepayments to a grinding halt. At the beginning of 1994, many investors saw the average life of their bonds extend from about 2 years to more than 20 years. The losses on the PO components dwarfed the gains (if any) on the notional components.

Convexity

Convexity is one of the most commonly used, yet misunderstood, terms in modern finance. Mathematically speaking, convexity is the second derivative of the price of a security to changes in the variable to which it relates. For mortgage-backed securities, the underlying variable is the interest rate (assuming there is just one applicable interest rate).

Another, more intuitive way to view convexity is by measuring and comparing the corresponding gains and losses of a security price following symmetric shifts in interest rate. If, for example, a bond gains 5 points in price following a drop of 50 basis points in the interest rate, while losing only 4.5 points following a 50-basis point increase, then this bond has positive convexity. If it is the other way around, then the bond has negative convexity.

In the options theory framework, where models assume continuous random shifts in interest rates, convexity measures the option component of a given security or an entire portfolio. Positive convexity means that the bond's owner benefits from frequent, random changes in interest rates (high volatility); the opposite is true for negative convexity. Convexity is thus related to the option's gamma.

Strip IOs are considered to have negative convexity. This is usually true, since the price of an IO is affected by two factors: yield (interest rate) and prepayment rate. Careful measuring of the speedup or slowdown of prepayment rates shows that they increase faster when interest rates drop than they decrease when interest rates go up. Since prepayments affect the IO's price more than yield, strip IOs have negative convexity.

It is said that, "pornography is a matter of geography." This quip, dressed in a mathematical suit, fits the application of convexity. The classic attribution of negative and positive convexities to strip IOs and POs does not automatically translate itself to CMO tranches. Tranche paydown schedules may have different characteristics from those of IO or PO strips because of complex principal assignment structures.

More important, our discussion of the convexity of IOs implicitly assumes that it refers to current-collateral bonds. When the deal's collateral is much higher than the current collateral, prepayment rates are so high that they will not increase meaningfully when interest rates drop further—they can only slow down. This means that in such situations IOs have high positive convexity, while POs, which can only extend, have negative convexity.

A mathematically detailed discussion of the convexity of mortgage-backed securities is beyond the scope of this chapter. We will try instead to explain in words what it means to own a negatively convex security.

Prepayment can be viewed as an American option held by the mortgage-takers. It allows them to refinance their debt any time they want. The implicit writers of this option are the owners of securities based on the refinanceable collateral. Refinancing occurs when interest rates are low, and homeowners can take a new mortgage at a lower interest rate. Investors, upon receiving their cash, can reinvest it only in lower-yielding instruments (such as lending at lower rates). When interest rates are high, and investors are eager to purchase securities offering the market's high yields, refinancing activity drops.

The buyers of mortgage-backed securities are at an even higher risk, since refinancing erodes their premium. Such buyers should be aware of the fact that they are writing an option. There is nothing wrong with writing options as long as the price reflects this. In other words, the yield spread is not a gift. It results from the price of an option being added to the bond's price.

The mirror image of this argument applies to owning extendible low-coupon securities. The discount compensates investors for the for low coupon. The bond's yield is derived assuming a certain prepayment rate. If refinancing retards the assumed prepayment rate, the bond extends, causing a large drop in yield (given the original price). Therefore, price has to drop in order to get back the original yield.

In other words, the loss of a premium is the same as the loss resulting from the price of a security dropping from small discount to deep discount. For example, an investor loses more than 30% of the investment whether a pure IO that cost 3,000 is worth only 2,000 or if a notional inverse which was 9 is worth only 6. Someone who paid 90 for a PO suffers the same loss if the value of the PO is now only 60.

This fact has dearly cost many investors who purchased inverse floaters paying par or slight premiums. During the refinancing saga of 1992 and 1993, inverse floaters were considered "safe" compared to the risky inverse IOs or the notional inverses. When refinancing came to an end, inverse floater investors registered heavy losses due to the extension of their zero- or low-coupon bonds.

Our discussion of the convexity of inverse bonds is intended to clarify that because in most cases their excess yield is just a form of paying for some options implicitly sold by the owners. Convexity is one way of measuring the theoretical price of those options.

Another factor that investors should consider is that it is almost impossible to hedge complex inverse bonds effectively. Hedging these bonds would rely on complex and inaccurate models and would be, at best, partial. This means that the price of the embedded option cannot be estimated using regular option pricing models. Investors should, therefore, be compensated, in yield, for taking the unhedgeable risk.

EVALUATING INVERSE BONDS

The methods used in analyzing floating-rate mortgage-backed securities fall into one of three categories:

- Two-dimensional analysis.

- Vector analysis.

- Option-adjusted spread (OAS).

Two-Dimensional Analysis

We have observed that the major drawback of the yield profile is its reliance on a specific, simple prepayment model that relates a fixed, static interest rate to refinancing speed. In order to analyze an inverse bond, it makes more sense to study first the direct effect of each of the components identified before in controlling the bond's cash flow rather than viewing it through an intermediary.

Two-dimensional analysis refers to the studying of the inverse bond's cash flow as a two-dimensional function of the two parameters, prepayment rate and interest rate. A set of, say, nine possible prepayment speeds is chosen together with another set of nine possible short-term rates. (The most common index default set is choosing current LIBOR as the center index, increased or decreased by 100 basis points each time. This creates a 900-basis point LIBOR window centered at the current rate.) These two sets serve as the coordinates of a two-dimensional matrix.

The simulator is now run 81 (9 x 9) times, each time fixing prepayment rate and LIBOR to any pair of prepayment and LIBOR combinations of the coordinates' value. For each run, the appropriate cash flow is generated and (assuming a price for the bond) measures such as the corresponding yield, average life, and modified duration are calculated.

The results are summarized in a 9-by-9 table as shown in Exhibit 2. This is the yield matrix of an actual notional inverse IO. The high gearing of 30 is typical of short-term bonds.

For a given prepayment speed, look at the swap rate corresponding to the average life of the bond. Then, look at the matrix entry whose coordinates are the previous prepayment rate and swap rate. This specific matrix shows that the investor will make a handsome profit if prepayments stay below 600 PSA. A burst of refinancing would cause heavy losses.

Exhibit 2. Yield Matrix for RFMSI 93-S7 A4

LIBOR	PSA 100	200	300	400	500	600	700
3.5%	153.32	136.00	116.58	95.19	72.30	48.53	24.53
4.5%	119.58	102.68	83.49	62.37	39.97	17.02	-5.82
5.5%	87.22	70.43	51.14	30.08	8.07	-14.07	-35.69
6.5%	55.90	38.73	18.91	-2.34	-24.02	-45.30	-69.57
7.5%	24.71	6.33	-14.61	-36.31	-57.67	-77.89	-96.47
Average Life	3.53	2.38	1.76	1.39	1.14	0.97	0.84
		1 Yr.	2 Yr.	3 Yr	4 Yr	5 Yr	10 Yr
Treasury Curve		5.24	5.90	6.23	6.53	6.72	7.14

Yields or annualized returns *per se* do not tell the entire story. Even high return rates do not generate large sums of money if they last for a short period of time. For example, if an investor earns $1,000 for one day on a $1 million investment, the annualized return is 44%. Clearly, this is an insignificant profit if it lasts only one day. On the other hand, small negative returns translate into a real loss if they continue for a prolonged period of time.

In Exhibit 2, if LIBOR shifts to 5.5% and prepayment rates are at 600 PSA, the bond's return is -14.07%. This negative return, however, lasts for less than a year, *i.e.*, the investor risks losing only about 14% of capital. If LIBOR shifts to 7.5% and prepayment rates slow to 100 PSA, the expected return is 24% for more than three and a half years, which doubles the investor's capital. (Again, this assumes smooth behavior of the bond's cash flows under the various prepayment scenarios.)

Exhibit 3 is a typical matrix of a par inverse floater. The gearing is much smaller, usually 3 to 5, compared to the high gearing of the pure premium bonds.

Since, priced at par, there is no premium, the static matrix shows no loss under any scenario. Yet this is a misleading observation. It is like saying that one cannot lose by investing in 30-year Treasury bonds. In fact, everything can yet go wrong with this bond.

If interest rates go up, all three factors that determine the bond's value (COFI rate, discount rate, and longer maturity) work together to reduce the bond's value. In such a scenario, the price of the bond can drop drastically. If things go well and interest rates move down, the gain is for a relatively short period (1.27 years versus 14.63 years for the pessimistic scenario).

The major difference between this matrix and the yield profile is that the matrix numbers are uniquely determined. They are a deterministic function of only these parameters and involve no further suppositions. Instead of relying on some broker's mysterious prepayment model that predicts the relationship between future prepayment rates and interest rates, the investor can study the influence of interest rates and prepayment rates on the inverse bond's yield and average life directly.

The table shown in Exhibit 3 provides no magical powers; it does not answer the investor's most important question—What will future prepayment rates and LIBOR be? Yet it allows a detailed analysis of the structure of cash flows and their sensitivity to changes in prepayments.

It is now the investor's dilemma to decide whether the results in the table are satisfactory or not. The matrix shows the yields under a set of definite hypothetical scenarios, which, unfortunately, are simple and inaccurate. The chosen set of prepayment rates should be large enough to represent a wide variety of possibilities. If the cash flow's average life is short, the

Exhibit 3. Yield Matrix for RFMSI 92-S16 A9

COFI	100	200	300	400	500	600	PSA 700
3.75%	34.35	24.25	24.09	23.87	23.66	23.43	23.19
4.75%	19.36	19.28	19.16	18.99	18.83	18.65	18.47
5.75%	14.44	14.38	14.29	14.17	14.06	13.94	13.82
6.75%	9.57	9.54	9.49	9.42	9.36	9.29	9.22
7.75%	4.77	4.77	4.76	4.74	4.72	4.71	4.69
Average Life	14.63	7.91	4.38	2.62	1.95	1.55	1.27

floating-rate parameters should be concentrated around the forward yield curve, allowing good estimation of hedging costs.

The parameters of the matrix may (and should) describe extreme conditions. Inverse bonds, being complex, non-linear structures, do not necessarily respond smoothly to changes in these parameters. Therefore, the numbers in the matrix may show a tremendous variance of possible returns. Since short- and long-term rates change, usually, in the same direction, in order to get a more realistic view of the possible returns the investor should concentrate first on the matrix's diagonal.

For example, it is logical to assume that if LIBOR goes up by 300 basis points, long-term rates will also be shifted by close to that amount, and as a consequence, prepayment rates will be very low. The opposite is true if LIBOR drops.

Determining the right combination of LIBOR and prepayment parameters to get a representative diagonal is more art than science. Prepayment models, such as those used in charting the inverse bond's profile, can be used in order to determine prepayment rate coordinates corresponding to interest rate coordinates.

Investors are not feeling in the dark when they view the 9-by-9 matrix. Futures contracts and swaps offer the best estimate of the market as to where LIBOR levels will be in the next years. These estimates are neither theoretical predictions nor abstract numbers. They represent the real market's level, and market participants are ready to take each side of the trade at those levels. By entering into a swap contract, investors can practically eliminate their LIBOR exposure, replacing it by the market's predicted levels.

Therefore, the matrix should be tested not only at the current LIBOR but also at its appropriate level as indicated by the swap market. Note that, for most mortgage-backed securities, this is only a theoretical level since the pay down of principal prevents the investor from completely hedging the bond's exposure using a swap contract. Finer, more powerful, analytical tools (discussed later) allow investors to determine explicitly the timely LIBOR rates as indicated by the Eurodollar futures contracts.

Even though the analysis concentrates on the forward curve or the diagonal, the other entries are of no less importance. They *stress-test* the CMO structure and that of the inverse bond, telling the investor what the margin for error is.

A word of caution. Matrix representation, which is provided by vendor services, includes in many cases not only yields but also the average life and modified duration. Since inverse bonds are derivatives, the use of modified duration to approximate to the cash flow's life, as in the case of straight bonds, does not work.

Modified duration measures the price elasticity of the bond. It is used only to calculate the effect of small changes in yield on the inverse bond's price and vice versa. It does not treat LIBOR changes. Investors may find bonds with high duration combined with short average life if, for example, the bond is callable.

Average life may be even more misleading. The average life of a mortgage security is the time needed to pay its principal. This definition is used also for notional inverses where the definition refers to the notional principal. This is different from the bond's cash flow's average life.

In order to use the correct swap level (*i.e.*, accurate timeframe), it is important to determine the distribution of payments and the cash flow's average life. An example will highlight the difference between the notional bond's average life and the cash flow's average life.

Example 9
Split a 5-year 8% Treasury bond into components as follows:
   - A zero-coupon bond maturing in 5 years.
   - A sequence of ten 4% semi-annual coupons.
The average life of the zero-coupon bond is 5 years, while the second bond's (notional IO) average life is only $2^1/_2$ years.

The average life of a swap contract, for fixed LIBOR, is one-half of its length. Therefore, in the case of a notional inverse bond one can approximate the maturity of the needed swap by using the average life of the bond. Investors should, however, keep in mind that these approximations are valid only for bonds whose cash flows behave smoothly.

The bottom line of the analysis is summarized, eventually, in a single number—the inverse bond's price. The final number the investor chooses, *i.e.*, a specific set of yields under the 81 scenarios, is a matter of taste and opinion. Risk plays a major role in the final decision. A robust structure fetches a higher price (lower yield) than a structure that has a probability of large losses. *There is no algorithm* that does the investor's job and derives a specific price from the matrix.

Price (or value) by itself does not fully describe the characteristics of a given inverse bond. The matrix method, with its simplicity, grants a look into the complex profile of an inverse bond's returns. A portfolio manager may decide that the bond's yield volatility is too high, or that its worst-case scenario returns do not fit a portfolio's needs, and it need not be purchased at any price.

Another advantage of the matrix is that it allows investors to analyze portfolios of mortgage-backed securities. Such an analysis is most representative if all securities have the same collateral. The computer can combine the cash flow of an entire portfolio together with other hedging tools such as swaps, options, and futures contracts, or other interest-rate securities.

The matrix method, even though it uses very simple assumptions, is a most powerful tool. It gives the best "first impression" of any mortgage-backed security. The bond's matrix should be examined prior to using any advanced method such as scenario analysis.

Vector Analysis

The major disadvantage of the matrix picture is that it assumes constant and unchanged parameters throughout the life of the inverse bond. Each entry represents the yield outcome of an *immediate shift* in the prepayment rate and LIBOR parameters to the corresponding coordinates' parameters, assuming that these rates will not change further. The impact of a yield shift scenario that takes a year or two cannot be measured using this method.

Moreover, even if the investor has an estimate for the average long-term prepayment rate, the inverse floater's responses to short-term, extreme scenarios should still be stress-tested. Such tests are beyond the power of the matrix method, which allows only a single prepayment rate and a single LIBOR in each test.

The vector analysis method offers a delicate tool to test a wide variety of definite scenarios. *Each vector is the time representation of prepayment rates and LIBOR* assumed throughout the life of the bond. Theoretically, a vector can consist of up to 360 pairs, representing all monthly changes throughout the life of the collateral. In practice, however, a vector is broken into 3 or 4 scenarios, such as 600 PSA for the first 5 months, a gradual decrease to 250 PSA over a period of 2 years, and steady 250 PSA thereafter.

The investor can prepare a large set of generic vectors and test the inverse bond under all of them to determine its robustness and weak points. Such a task is somewhat similar to what is done in medical imaging. From a set of line integrals, *i.e.*, indirect measurements, one can picture the internal body structures. In practice, vector tests are run only if an investor likes the initial "look" of the yields in the 9-by-9 matrix.

The forward LIBOR curve and the swaps market determine the base case for vector analysis. Initial tests should concentrate on scenarios in which

LIBOR is determined by the forward curve. The corresponding prepayment rates are determined using a prepayment model as a function of these rates.

The vector method can be used to test an entire portfolio that may include more than one bond. Moreover, the positions may include hedges in the form of futures contracts, swap contracts, and offsetting bonds, or a combination of them.

An advanced version of vector analysis looks at the actual cash-flow stream generated for each scenario vector, not only at the calculated yield. This allows investors actually to see what they get. It pinpoints "break points" in the structure in which drastic changes in the inverse bond's cash flow can occur. Such cases warrant further analysis.

There is no substitute to direct cash-flow analysis, at least for some sample cases. Without viewing concrete cash flows, the investor can rely only on aggregate parameters such as yield or duration. The only way to detect peculiarities in a bond's behavior is by viewing its possible cash flows.

Option-Adjusted Spread (OAS)

The availability of computer simulation allows further refinement of the analysis. So far we have observed the development from the coarse grid used in matrix analysis through the finer sieve of the vector analysis, which is still limited to a fairly small number of scenarios. The next logical step is to let the computer analyze not only human-generated scenarios but self-(computer)-generated scenarios as well.

Methodologies of analysis patterns gradually shift from human-controlled to computer-controlled and from deterministic simulations to stochastic simulations. This is summarized in Exhibit 4.

Letting the computer both generate and analyze cash flows is the idea behind the OAS method. Technically speaking, the computer generates random sequences (according to a given distribution) of monthly LIBOR and prepayment rates, 360 samples for each path. Given a specific path, the CMO simulator then generates the inverse bond's cash flow, which is a deterministic sequence under the path's assumptions, and calculates the yield and average

Exhibit 4. Methodologies of Analysis

	Scenarios	Parameters	Control	Type
Matrix	Single	Fixed	Human	Deterministic
Vector	Single	Changing	Human	Deterministic
	Multiple	Changing	Human	Deterministic
OAS	Multiple	Changing	Computer	Stochastic

life of this sequence. Analyzing thousands or millions of random paths gives an adequate approximation to the yield and average life of the inverse bond.

Key in the OAS method is choosing the right stochastic process that drives the random selection. At each month, which distribution should be used to generate next month's samples of prepayment rate and LIBOR?

Most simulators do it in two phases. In the first phase, a stochastic model generates the prevailing interest rates. Interest-rate stochastic models are heavily used by derivative traders to price long-term, esoteric, over-the-counter options. There are a few classical models based on various assumptions that are in common use. In the second phase, a prepayment model, depending on interest rates, generates the required prepayment rates.

Reliance on these two models (futuristic interest rate and prepayment) is the "Achilles heel" of the OAS method. The results are model-dependent; they are only as good as the models representing the statistical characteristics of the forces that drive interest rates and prepayments. Nowadays people use almost identical prepayment models for whole loans and agency-qualified loans. These models do not take into account the different levels of economic sophistication of people or the different incentives (even within the whole-loan group) that people may have to refinance their mortgage as a function of the size of their loan. The investor must have full faith in the capabilities of this black box. Sometimes, using different models results in completely different numbers—which only adds to the confusion.

Classical OAS produces only one result—yield, which is the weighted average of the paths' yields. The same computer programs can, with minor modifications, generate the yield distribution as well. Studying the histogram of the results allows the investor to estimate the variance of the possible yields and decide if the risk/reward parameters fit the portfolio's constraints.

Callable Deals

In many private label and whole-loan deals, the residual holders can call the bonds if the outstanding balance of the CMO falls below a given percentage of the original issue's size. This is a valuable option to the residual holder, as many of these deals have high-coupon collateral. While a 10% call feature may be far away for a newly issued CMO, it is a much more meaningful percentage once the collateral pays down.

A call feature, especially when it is "in sight," alters the characteristics of the inverse bond. Exercising the call stops payments for a premium bond or accelerates them for a discount one. Both call date, through its dependence on prepayment rate, and the decision to exercise the call are affected positively by lower interest rates. Investors should beware of deals having at-the-money collateral, because those show tremendous average life volatility.

The methodologies we have discussed apply, with only minor modifications, to callable CMOs. The simulation utilities, matrix, vector analysis, or OAS should include provisions for handling the call.

SUMMARY

Inverse bonds are one of the most interesting investment vehicles. In return for structural complexity and risk, inverse bonds offer extremely lucrative pro-forma returns.

Investors can find a wide spectrum of opportunities in inverse structures that offer superior risk/reward performance compared to other securities. Mortgage derivatives suit only the most sophisticated investors, who are equipped with the knowledge and technology needed to analyze such securities. The yield offered by inverse bonds, however, more than justifies the intellectual investment and the risks taken.

CHAPTER 22

CMO Residuals

Adrian Katz
Director
Prudential Securities Inc.

Vincent Pica
Managing Director
Prudential Securities Inc.

Rick Villaume
Vice President
Prudential Securities Inc.

Residuals can be extremely complex instruments. A thorough comprehension of the cash flow dynamics allows the investor to use a residual either for the purpose of hedging or to build a stable portfolio of securities. Whatever the application, there is no doubt that a complete understanding of residuals is a definite advantage to the investor.

In this chapter, we intend to address the following issues—where do residuals come from? what types of residuals are available? and what affects their value? In addition, we will discuss hedging considerations, risk-based capital requirements, accounting issues, and phantom-income and phantom-loss implications.

WHAT IS A RESIDUAL?

The word "residual" aptly describes the investment as it is comprised of the remaining cash flows from the underlying mortgages after all other cash flows are securitized into either a bond or a pass-through security. In essence, a residual's cash flow is comprised of the difference between the cash flows of the collateralizing assets and the collateralized obligations. For certain residuals, reinvestment income and servicing fees are also components of the cash flows. Residuals can take the form of scheduled principal and interest-bearing securities or of cash flows with neither a defined coupon nor any principal. The amount of cash flow can vary tremendously, from very small to even being the largest component of an issue. The legal characteristics of the offering can be as simple as a government agency security with a REMIC (Real Estate Mortgage Investment Conduit) tax election, or as complex as an Owner Trust equity private placement. Residual cash flow features can span the entire performance spectrum; they can be either bullish or bearish in nature or can act as either a long or short straddle. The multitude of available performance characteristics is a function of client-requested design, economic realities (*i.e.*, the shape of the yield curve), and changes in the tax, accounting, and regulatory environment.

History of the Residual Market

The first CMO was issued in 1983 by FHLMC as a debt obligation collateralized by a designated pool of FHLMC mortgage pass-through certificates. The collateral remained an asset on FHLMC's balance sheet, while the fully cash flow-supported bond obligations remained a liability. A necessary outgrowth of this structure was the equity component (otherwise known as the residual). The tax treatment of residuals as equity implied that, in a rather illiquid manner, the only method for investing in residuals was through the creation or purchase of an issuing vehicle. For tax benefits, many of the earlier issuers were builder conduits, with only a few precocious investors creating arbitrage subsidiaries. These conduits or subsidiaries required up-front capital investments for such expenses as legal, accounting, and SEC filing fees. Since residuals were integral components of the issues, the awkward and expensive legal treatment significantly impaired the early growth of CMO issuance and residual liquidity.

In 1985, Wall Street, in conjunction with legal counsel, created a "better mousetrap" with the introduction of the Owner Trust residual structure. This structure allowed for the sale of equity partnerships in a residual. The immediate effect was the proliferation of Wall Street subsidiaries establishing registration shelves with the SEC to become CMO issuers. The innovation permitted the investor in a residual to be decoupled from the bond-issuance business. Further, the residual could now be purchased in percentages deemed small enough to eliminate accounting concerns over on-balance-sheet recognition. Typically, the ownership percentage was understood to be less than 50%, in order to maintain the off-balance-sheet treatment. The residual investor base was now expanded to include investors with no special knowledge of bond origination and investors who required the off-balance-sheet treatment.

Probably the most significant development in the cash flow engineering of residuals occurred in 1986 with the introduction of the floating-rate bond class. Up until 1986, the residual cash flows were comprised of either fixed-coupon spread or principal (invariably in the form of overcollateralization). The residual's investment dynamics therefore were either bullish or bearish, with the dominant influence being the prepayment rate on the underlying mortgages securing the deal. The introduction of the floating-rate class and the natural leftover effect of inverse floating-rate cash flows allowed the residual characteristics to vary with more subtlety. It was now possible to design a residual with characteristics previously external to the mortgage product securing the issue, such as the inclusion of LIBOR as an index for some of an issue's coupons. Furthermore, the effects of prepayments (usually influenced by long rates) now could be combined with the effects of coupon adjustments (usually influenced by short rates).

The enactment of the REMIC tax law in 1986 significantly improved the previously clumsy legal structures by removing many of the potential economic disadvantages associated with prior regulations. Essentially, REMIC allowed for the creation of fast-pay/slow-pay, multiclass pass-throughs whose mortgage cash flows would be passed through to investors with no equity retained by the issuer. Thus, in most cases, the transaction would be accounted for by the issuer as a sale of assets for tax purposes, and taxed at the investor level. For financial accounting purposes, the issuer can treat the transaction as either a sale of assets or as a financing. In sum, REMICs reduce inefficiencies, increase flexibility, and enable more issuers to enjoy the economic benefits of off-balance-sheet, multiclass mortgage financing.

Under REMIC, residuals can be structured so that they are sold as rated, SEC-registered bonds with no restrictions on transferability, financial statement consolidation concerns, or contingent liability for expenses. There would be numerous enhancements to and simplifications of the REMIC laws through subsequent Technical Corrections Bills, providing further flexibility to issuers and investors. The more flexible and efficient treatment of residuals under REMIC helped to increase the investor base significantly—and in turn helped to create a more liquid and more active residual market. The tax implications associated with residuals are discussed later in this chapter.

In 1986, another significant cash flow engineering development occurred with the introduction of PAC (Planned Amortization Class) bonds. This method of cash flow separation allowed for classes to be designed with more or less prepayment stability, and this flexibility implied the ability to design long-straddle or short-straddle investments. Not only could residuals now be influenced by long and short interest rates, but also could react with substantial variation with respect to anticipated changes in interest rate volatility.

The inversion of the Treasury yield curve in 1988 and the economic reality that accompanied it provided the stimuli for more stable performing residuals. As floating-rate classes became too expensive to include in issues, residuals were less able to offer inverse-floater characteristics. Even bearish, fixed-coupon spread was not easily created, as a flat yield curve suggested that all classes of deals include the same coupon, which was typically the same as the underlying collateral coupon. By 1989, this trend had in fact stimulated the formation of residuals with insignificant cash flow value, sometimes called *de minimus* residuals.

Residual Investment Characteristics

By now we have indicated that a kaleidoscope of residuals exists. Here, the various types of residuals currently available are categorized and explained. Specific hedging techniques as they apply to different residual types are explained in the next section.

Bear Residuals. The first residuals consisted primarily of coupon spread, that is, the differential between the higher coupon on the underlying mortgage collateral and the lower coupon on the outstanding obligation. For example, if mortgages with a net coupon of 10% secured a single-class obligation with a coupon of 9%, the cash flow difference available to be passed through to the residual would be 1%. Since the balance on which the amount of interest due varies with prepayments, some discussion of the prepayments is appropriate.[1]

Home owners are less inclined to prepay their mortgages if the prevailing interest rate environment is higher than the rate on their obligation. Conversely, in a lower-rate environment, a home owner is more likely to prepay a mortgage in order to refinance at a lower cost. This suggests that in a higher-rate environment the effect of slower prepayments would cause more cash to be paid to the residual holder, since the coupon is based on a higher outstanding principal balance. Conversely, when rates are falling, the probability is that the outstanding principal balance will decline more rapidly due to an increase in prepayments, hence generating less coupon payments and inherently less cash flow to the residual investor.

Investments that perform well in rising-rate environments are considered to be bearish. The degree of bearishness is determined by the coupon on the underlying collateral relative to current market rates and the structure. The most bearish investments typically are those with anticipated short

---

1 For a discussion of prepayments, see Chapter 10. Also see Lakhbir Hayre, Kenneth Lauterbach, and Cyrus Mohebbi, "Mortgage Pass-Through Securities," in Frank J. Fabozzi (ed.) *Advances and Innovations in the Bond and Mortgage Markets* (Chicago, IL: Probus Publishing, 1989), and Lakhbir Hayre and Cyrus Mohebbi, *Prepayment Behavior of 15-Year Pass-Through Securities*, (New York, N.Y.: Financial Strategies Group, Prudential Securities Incorporated, May 1989).

durations. Short-duration investments have the potential to extend the most, ultimately creating higher returns as more cash flow is returned to the investor over a longer period of time. Coupon cash flows from companion classes, volatile bonds themselves, tend to increase the bearish behavior of a residual. Conversely, coupon cash flows from PAC classes naturally tend to stabilize the performance. In addition, residuals from higher-coupon under-lying cash flows tend to be more volatile as a function of more volatile pre-payment behavior. This in turn causes the bearish residuals from such collat-eral to be even more accentuated. Bearish residuals can act as excellent hedging tools for a fixed-income portfolio, or for a balance sheet whose com-bined assets have a longer duration than its liabilities (see Exhibit 1).

Bull Residuals. Since interest spread is what leads to the creation of bearish residuals, it is not surprising that a residual comprised only of principal cash flows is considered to be bullish. As the principal of a mortgage is returned in full (at par), the issue most affecting a bullish residual consisting only of principal is the timing of the return of the principal. Therefore, higher pre-payment rates, which are experienced in declining interest rate environ-ments, positively influence the performance of bullish residuals. Conversely, an increase in rates causes underperformance (see Exhibit 2). Residual "principal" can be created by overcollateralization over time. This "principal" is typically returned once the bonds have matured.

Bullish investments can be more or less leveraged based on the struc-ture from which they are carved and the coupon on the underlying collat-eral. Generally speaking, longer-duration principal cash flows are more volatile, as they are purchased at a greater discount price to par, and thus have the greatest upside potential when they are returned at par sooner than anticipated. Further, principal cash flows that are derived from companion

Exhibit 1. Typical Bearish Residual Return Profile

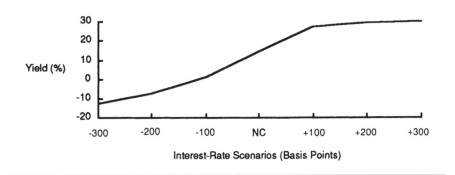

Exhibit 2. Typical Bullish Residual Return Profile

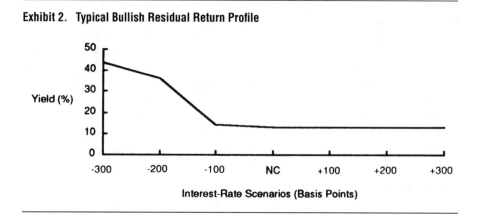

bonds within structures containing PAC bonds tend to be more bullish. This effect can be attributed to the added volatility implicit in these structures, which increases the possibility of tremendous upswings in value in the event of increased prepayments. By contrast, PAC principal cash flows stabilize the residual fluctuations. The uses of bullish residuals in fixed-income portfolio management range from lengthening the effective duration of a portfolio that is inadequately positioned for a rally, to providing a hedge to a mortgage servicer.[2]

Humped Residuals (Short Straddles). Residuals derived from structures that contain floating-rate classes may vary significantly due to such factors as the coupon on the underlying collateral, the size of the floating-rate component as a percentage of the deal, the position of the floater in the deal, the floating-rate index, and the absolute level of the floating-rate cap relative to the current coupon. In most cases, there is a common cash flow characteristic, which is evident when scenario analysis reveals that the residual tends to underperform when interest rates vary from the initial environment. This behavior is a function of the combined effect of changes in prepayments and the coupon adjustments.

In a rising interest rate environment, the amount of interest rate spread declines while, at the same time, prepayments decline. Therefore, the remaining spread is outstanding for a longer period of time. These influences may be offsetting. As rates rise sufficiently for the floating-rate class(es) to approach its (their) coupon cap, the residual cash flow typically is curtailed,

2 For details on hedging mortgage servicing, see Adrian Katz, Vincent Pica, and Michael Sternberg, *Strategies for Mortgage Bankers in a Bullish Environment,* Financial Strategies Group, Prudential Securities Incorporated, May 29, 1989 and Adrian Katz, Vincent Pica, and Michael Sternberg, *Strategies for Traders and Investors in a Bullish Environment,* Financial Strategies Group, Prudential Securities Incorporated, June 14, 1989.

and hence the residual's performance is undermined. When interest rates decline, the coupon spread increases and prepayments accelerate; thus the amount of time during which the spread is outstanding is abbreviated. If rates decline sufficiently for prepayments to be almost instantaneous, the residual cash flow becomes insignificant, and the residual will underperform. These so-called "humped" residuals (so named because of their return profiles in declining and rising rate scenarios; see Exhibit 3) are therefore not well suited for an investor anticipating a volatile environment. In contrast, investors who foresee a market stall will be well rewarded by the higher base-case yields associated with humped residuals.

A further subtlety relating to the shape of the yield curve should be noted here. Yield-curve movements seldom occur in parallel, and the implications of a steepening or inverting yield curve for these humped residuals are critical. First, keep in mind that floating-rate coupons are indexed off a short interest rate, and that prepayments typically are triggered by changes in long interest rates. In an environment in which long rates are increasing and short rates are declining, humped residuals experience an increase in available coupon spread and a longer time period over which the spread is received. Hence, the steepening is doubly beneficial.

However, the opposite holds true when the yield curve is inverted, and, in fact, the effect is doubly disadvantageous. Any serious attempt to hedge this type of short-straddle residual should not only address the question of volatility but also the potential fluctuations in the shape of the yield curve. Due to these implied vulnerabilities and the range of cash flow fluctuations, these residuals are the most volatile generically. (The coupling of very high base-case yields and sharp declines in value outside the base case should come as no surprise to the reader.) The majority of residuals being offered by the thrift industry through liquidations fall into the humped residual category.

Exhibit 3. Typical Humped Residual Return Profile

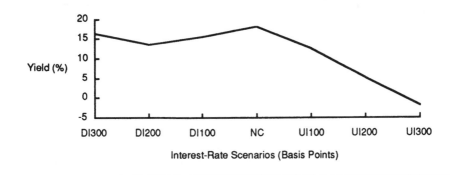

Smile Bonds (Long Straddles). Mortgage securities, by their nature, are "buy/writes" consisting of a long-bond component (scheduled payments by the home owner) and a short-call component (the prepayment option held by the home owner). Therefore, with mortgage securities as the collateral for CMO structures with multiple classes and a residual, it is fairly difficult to design a long-straddle residual, and very few exist. Residuals with superior performance in highly volatile environments invariably consist of short-duration interest spread and long-duration principal. The compromise for the smile bond residual investor is that the anticipated yield for the base-case scenario (no interest rate change) tends to be below Treasuries.[3] See Exhibit 4 for a typical smile bond return profile.

Stable Residuals. There is no rule that requires residuals to be complex or volatile. Indeed, when a residual consists of PAC cash flows, the residual is more stable than the underlying collateral, and actually could be designated the most stable class in the entire issue (see Exhibit 5). In many structures, the residual is a class carved from a regular PAC component, and may even pay in parallel with such a PAC. Not surprisingly, stable residual investments of this type offer purchasing opportunities to a very broad spectrum of investors.

***De Minimus* Residuals.** As shown later in this chapter, the residual class of a REMIC bears the tax liability of the entire REMIC. Noneconomic, or *de minimus* residuals, receive little or no cash flow. Given minimal (or no) economic value, these instruments then become a tax strategy unto themselves. An investor can use these instruments to create or modify an existing tax strategy.

Exhibit 4. Typical Smile Bond Return Profile

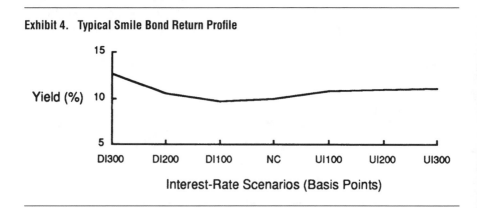

Interest-Rate Scenarios (Basis Points)

3 For details on smile bonds, see Howard Chin, Alan Galishoff, and Vincent Pica, *Structured Portfolio Trades: Unruliness Begets Opportunity*, Financial Strategies Group, Prudential Securities Incorporated, October 25, 1989.

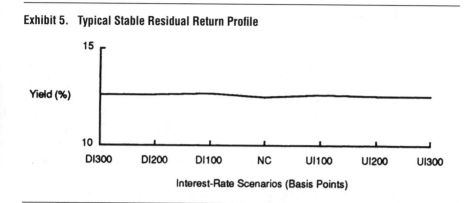

Exhibit 5. Typical Stable Residual Return Profile

This type of residual is typically sold with a zero or "negative" price (*i.e.*, the investor receives cash at settlement). The investor then reinvests this money in securities that, on an after-tax basis, generate enough cash to pay the tax liabilities of the REMIC (recalling that all taxable income from a *de minimus* residual is nonshelterable). After the "income period" of the REMIC, the investor can then use the losses created by the REMIC to offset other sources of income. In short, the investor is "buying" these tax losses in the future.

THOUGHTS ON HEDGING RESIDUALS

As could be inferred from our above comments, residuals can be divided into two basic groups—those that allow the investor to take a position on the direction of future interest rates, and those that allow the investor to take a position on interest rate volatility. Bearish and bullish residuals essentially take a position on the direction of rates. Humped (short-straddle) residuals appeal to investors who expect interest rates to remain generally the same (*i.e.*, low volatility). Long straddles and stable residuals typically appeal to investors who expect at least some degree of interest rate volatility. Hedging against adverse interest rate moves is fairly straightforward—take the opposite position for the amount of expected risk (*i.e.*, the chance of rates reversing). Hedging residuals based on a volatility position is more complex.[4]

---

4 The analyses for all securities/hedges discussed in this section were generated using the Prudential Securities Structured Portfolio/Synthetic Security (SP/SS) System. All results were stated on a pre-tax basis. SP/SS total returns are the "all-in" percent return on an investment, assuming complete reinvestment of all interim cash flows at the assumed reinvestment rate. In all cases, the analysis was done based on immediate parallel shifts of the yield curve by the appropriate amount.

Bearish Residuals

As mentioned in the previous section, bearish residuals tend to perform better in rising rate environments. The obvious hedge for this type of residual is a bullish security with similar underlying prepayment characteristics. For those wishing to add to their residual portfolio, bullish residuals of similar collateral are an obvious hedge. For the investor concerned about using additional residuals to hedge a current position, leveraged PO classes provide good protection. With the large variety of PAC structures being created, there are numerous opportunities to obtain Companion or Targeted Amortization Class (TAC) POs that are custom-designed to provide the necessary cash flow "kick" in declining interest rate environments without the tax implications of some bullish residuals. The investor who purchases a bearish residual as an investment rather than as a hedging instrument has implicitly taken a position on the direction of future rates. Duration-matched hedges in this scenario do not make economic sense. Instead, the investor should use expectation-weighted matching; for example, if the investor believes that there is a 20% chance of rates reversing and the total exposure is $10 million, then approximately $2 million in bullish securities should be added to the portfolio (all other things, such as leverage and yield sensitivity, being equal). See Exhibit 6 for a return profile of this hedge.

Bullish Residuals

Since bullish residuals tend to perform better in declining rate environments, the obvious hedge is a bearish security using similar underlying collateral. A typical nonresidual hedge for this type of residual is a TAC IO, generally purchased at a very low yield, that has some call protection but little, if any, extension protection. The lengthening of the TAC IO's duration in rising rate environments provides for a yield pick-up, making the TAC IO a good hedge for bullish residuals. See Exhibit 7 for a return profile of this

---

Exhibit 6. Performance Characteristics of a Bearish Residual and a Super PO Hedge

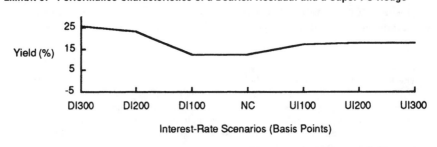

Interest-Rate Scenarios (Basis Points)

hedge. The purchase of a bullish residual for investment purposes indicates that the investor has an opinion on the direction of future interest rates. Again, investors must consider the probability of interest rates reversing direction before any hedging program is established.

Humped Residuals (Short Straddles)

Humped residuals are volatility plays—the investor believes that there will be little or no interest rate change and no prepayment change from current levels. These residuals are effectively short positions on both short-term and long-term rates. Decreases in short-term rates (and the floating-rate coupons based on these rates) typically are offset by increases in prepayments (assuming parallel shifts in the yield curve). Decreases in prepayment speeds are usually offset by increases in short-term rates (again, using parallel shifts for example purposes). When factors such as nonparallel shifts and inversions in the yield curve are added to the equation, you have an instrument that is a challenge to hedge.

At any point in time, the holder of a humped residual is at the no-interest-rate-change point in Exhibit 8. The curve may slope differently in different

Exhibit 7. Performance Characteristics of a Bullish Residual and an IO Hedge

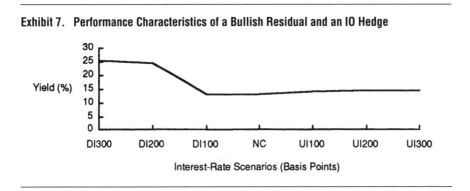

Interest-Rate Scenarios (Basis Points)

Exhibit 8. Performance Characteristics of a Humped Residual

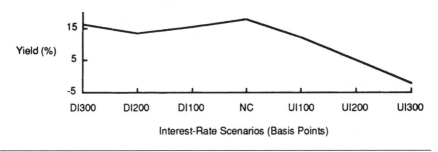

Interest-Rate Scenarios (Basis Points)

rate environments (and may even turn bullish or bearish), but generally has the characteristic hump shape. While the investor may believe that interest rates will remain close to where they are now (*i.e.*, low/no volatility), he probably has an opinion as to the most likely direction of future rates.

If short-term rates rise and the corresponding decrease in coupon spread causes a less negative effect than changes in prepayments (in parallel shifts, one would expect a benefit), then there is little benefit in hedging against prepayment risk since the additional cost of hedging would result in little or no gain. Conversely, if the holder expects long-term rates to decrease (prepayments to increase) and the residual is more sensitive to increases in prepayments than decreases in short-term rates, then there is little benefit in hedging short-term-rate risk. In brief, the investor must consider the following three questions:

- Which rate, long or short, is expected to move the most (or cause the most harm)?

- In which direction is the rate expected to move?

- How long is this rate change expected to affect the residual?

When these questions are answered, a hedging program that fits the investor's expectations can be established.

Working Through an Example

To answer the questions above, assume that short rates will rise, while long rates will remain more or less stable. In addition, assume that the change will last for two months (similar to year-end changes in LIBOR). The dollar amount of the floating-rate classes in the underlying CMO is the amount of short-term rate exposure that must be hedged; for example, a $300 million CMO with $150 million in floating-rate class(es) has $150 million in short-term rate exposure. To hedge the entire amount of exposure, LIBOR caps must be purchased, with an expiration date approximating the expected time period to be hedged. As the floating-rate classes prepay, the hedge needs to be rolled off on a 1:1 basis, *e.g.*, if, in month one, $5 million in the floating-rate classes pays off, then $5 million of the hedge needs to be rolled off. Ideally, the gain (loss) on the hedge should approximate the loss (gain) in cash flows on the residual. See Exhibit 9 for a return profile of this 1:1 hedge.

This strategy of matching hedging to expected changes in interest rates requires constant monitoring of the residual and hedge instruments. A month-by-month adjustment in hedge positions must be undertaken, as well as a constant review of short-term and long-term interest rate expectations.

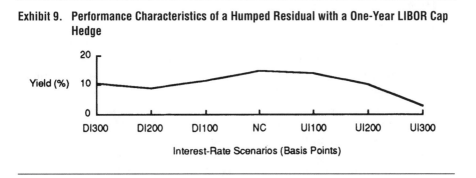

Exhibit 9. Performance Characteristics of a Humped Residual with a One-Year LIBOR Cap Hedge

This example illustrates the hedging of short-term expected cash flows. For longer-term hedging, the investor should use something closer to duration matching. Smile bonds or stable residuals with durations similar to that of the humped residual can be used.

Stable Residuals and Smile Bonds (Long-Straddles)

Stable residuals and smile bonds are also volatility plays—they presume that there will be high levels of interest rate volatility, but that its direction will not be easy to discern. These residuals, by their nature, tend to sell at lower yields than other types. Since stable/long-straddle residuals have flat (stable) to smile-shaped (long-straddle) return profiles, hedging them against interest rate movement is not beneficial; they are a hedge themselves. The primary use of these residuals is to pick up yield outside the base case, which makes them a good match for humped residuals. For both bearish and bullish residuals, stable residuals and smile bonds provide some protection by lessening declines in adverse rate environments.

RISK-BASED CAPITAL CONSIDERATIONS
Banks

Residuals fall within the 100% risk weight basket for banks under their risk-based capital standards. In meeting its risk-based capital requirements, a bank must hold capital equal to 8% times 100% of the residual value. Relative to other securities, this is five times the amount required for an equivalent amount of FNMA and FHLMC pass-throughs (20% risk weight), and the same as for an equivalent amount of IO/PO strips (100% risk weight).

Thrifts

Residuals fall within the 100% risk weight basket for thrifts under their risk-based capital standards. Thrifts must hold 8% of 100% of the residual value in capital. The Office of Thrift Supervision has indicated that residuals may be moved to a lower risk weight category when an interest rate risk component of capital is introduced. Thus, the interest rate risk calculation will be used to determine the capital required based on the interest rate-related volatility separately from capital required for credit risk. Residuals that reduce the overall volatility of a thrift's market value of portfolio equity (the present value of all asset cash flows less the present value of all liability cash flows plus the present value of all off-balance-sheet cash inflows less outflows) could potentially lower the capital required for interest rate risk. If the reduction of capital for interest rate risk exceeded the marginal capital required for residual credit risk, the overall risk-based capital required could be reduced.

Both banks and thrifts can benefit by maximizing the return on capital generated by the assets they hold. In purchasing assets, they should consider the spread-to-funding generated given the capital allocation. This will continue to be a consideration particularly for capital-constrained institutions in light of their other existing investment criteria.

GAAP AND TAX ACCOUNTING FOR RESIDUALS

GAAP income for REMIC residuals may be calculated according to the Statement of Financial Accounting Standards No. 91 (SFAS 91) method.

The Emerging Issued Task Force (EITF) of the Financial Accounting Standards Board (FASB) discussed a method of accounting for nonequity CMO investments on December 14, 1989. It was determined during these discussions that CMOs that were carried as long-term investments would be considered to be nonequity if the investor had little or no control of the cash distribution for the CMO structure. Securitized residuals (*i.e.*, bond form) are considered to fall into this category.

SFAS 91 details the appropriate method for income recognition. Specifically, SFAS 91 states that income should be calculated by applying the "interest method," using a yield that is recalculated for every period in which the remaining projected cash distributions will differ from those previously projected. This will occur whenever the prepayment assumptions for future cash flows are changed or the current distribution differs from that last projected. The original yield is calculated by using the purchase price and the residual cash flow at the pricing speed. When a distribution occurs that is other than that projected, a new yield is calculated by using the actual distributions to date, the new projected distributions, and the original purchase price. The yield is then used to compute a new carrying value of the residual by discounting the new set of future cash flows at this rate to the current accounting date. When the carrying value of the residual is changed, a corresponding adjustment should be made to income from that period. If this new yield is less than zero, the investment is subject to an *impairment test.*

If the residual is an equity interest in an Owner Trust, the appropriate accounting method is determined by the percentage owned. Ownership of greater than 50% of the residual may require full consolidation of assets and liabilities, with adjustments made for minority residual interests. Investors with ownership of less than 50% but greater than 20% may be able to use the equity method, or SFAS 91. With the equity method, an investor reports the pro-rata share of GAAP earnings, reported by the issuer, corresponding to the percentage owned. Investors with ownership of less than 20% in an Owner Trust may not use the equity method. The EITF is considering a proposal that would recommend the use of the SFAS 91 method for all residuals that are considered to be nonequity CMO investments. This would include all securitized residuals and equity interests of less than 50% in Owner trusts.

Taxable income on residuals is computed under a different method than SFAS 91. Taxable income is computed by taking the excess collateral and reinvestment income over the REMIC regular interest deductions, expenses, and ongoing fees. If the regular interest expense relative to the outstanding bond principal amount increases over time, there will be less relative expense at the beginning, with greater relative expense toward the end. This increase will occur if shorter-maturity regular interests have lower yields than longer-maturity ones. This is typically the case in a normal yield-curve environment. This results in phantom income followed by phantom losses. The excess taxable income over economic income is referred to as phantom income. The sum of all phantom income and phantom losses will equal zero, and the total taxable income will be equal to the total GAAP income over the life of the residual.

Phantom Income and Phantom Losses of Residuals

What is phantom income? Simply stated, phantom income is created when taxable income exceeds economic income (GAAP income). How is this phantom income created? From the standpoint of the Trust that owns the collateral supporting a REMIC transaction, the collateral is an asset and the payments received are income. Conversely, the bonds outstanding are liabilities and the payments due to the bondholders are expenses. In a positive yield-curve environment, phantom income is created when these deductible weight-average expenses are deferred through the tranching of the collateral into bonds with different yields and maturities. The creation of phantom income is increased if the collateral going into the Trust is "bought-in" below par. The IRS treats this market discount as if it were an Original-Issue Discount, and thus it must be accreted into income. In addition, certain types of bonds, such as Z bonds, also increase phantom income due to the accrual feature. Usually, however, the majority of phantom income/loss is created through timing and yield mismatches between the assets and the liabilities of the Trust. In the later years, when earlier tranches have been retired, the relationship between the assets and the liabilities flip-flops such that phantom losses are created when economic income exceeds taxable income. (For many investors, phantom losses are desirable since they shelter cash flow that otherwise would be taxed.) These phantom amounts always net out to zero at maturity, or, in other words, taxes are due only on the *true* economic income of the residual over the entire life of the residual.

Of additional interest, and of perhaps dominating import given the volatility extant in the fixed-income marketplace, the actual accounting for phantom income and phantom losses is dominated by *prepayments*. Specifically, if the entire issue pays down because of prepayments accelerating through the pricing speed (thus retiring early tranches very quickly and long tranches commensurately early), the amount of phantom income/phantom losses will be dramatically lower than projected at pricing. This is due to the foreshortening of the timing disparities between the assets (the collateral) and the liabilities (the bonds). In the case of a powerful rally after pricing, the difference between the *projected* phantom income and the *actual* phantom income can be dramatically in favor of the residual holder. In contrast, if there is a dramatic market decline, this will cause the timing disparities between the assets and the liabilities to be outstanding longer. This results in actual phantom income exceeding the pricing projections. It is a function of the nature of mortgages, however, that this is not a symmetrical relationship. Mortgage collateral that is going into a REMIC issue generally has a weighted-average maturity that is not *dramatically* shorter than its original maturity. Thus, it cannot get that much longer. This is why not as much additional phantom income is created in a market decline as is destroyed in a rally. In short, a mortgage can get prepaid tomorrow, but there isn't any chance that homeowners will pay one more month than they are required to!

Excess Inclusions/Unrelated Business Taxable Income

While not by any means an exhaustive discussion of the causes of phantom income, the above text does present an accurate picture of the major components of phantom income. Of more interest to sophisticated investors would be the economic effect of phantom income on the yield of a residual held in portfolio. The economic effect is the reduction of the effective after-tax yield during the early years of the CMO, caused by the present value of the taxes being paid on phantom income exceeding the present value of the tax savings due to phantom losses.

With very limited but important exceptions, all residual income, including phantom income, is always subject to tax, because such income is treated as an excess-inclusion item. The "excess-inclusion amount" is the amount of interest income generated by the residual that is greater than 120% of the *Federal Long-Term Rate.*[5] If the residual is held by a tax-exempt entity such as a pension plan or any entity that is only taxed on its Unrelated Business Taxable Income (UBTI), phantom income will be treated as UBTI.

As far as exceptions go, there are few, and what follows is a general, not detailed, description of them.

1. If a residual does not have significant value, all income from a residual is treated as excess inclusion. Significant value generally is regarded as being at least 2% of the value of the REMIC. Thus, ultrasmall residuals are always part of the excess-inclusion base.

2. Thrift institutions are exempt from the rule that prohibits excess inclusions from being offset by unrelated losses. In addition, qualified subsidiaries[6] of the thrift can be consolidated for tax purposes with respect to offsetting losses of the thrift against excess inclusions realized by the qualified subsidiary.

3. Real Estate Investment Trusts (REITs) and Registered Investment Companies (RICs) can offset excess-inclusion income with a dividends-paid deduction. The excess-inclusion taxation issue is passed along to the shareholders.

SUMMARY

At this time, there exists an incredible variety of residuals; it is hoped the above abbreviated history of their issuance will help the investor understand the breadth of choices available and the inherent complexities. Of course, we anticipate that the future of the residual market is likely to be an improvement on the past with respect to flexibility, creativity, and liquidity.

---

5 By statute, the Federal Long-Term Rate is defined as the average of the current yields on U.S. Treasury obligations that have a remaining term to maturity of greater than nine years. The IRS computes this figure and publishes it monthly.

6 A qualified subsidiary is one whose stock and substantially all of its indebtedness is owned by the thrift. The qualified subsidiary also must be operated and organized for the express and exclusive purpose of operating one or more REMICs.

CHAPTER 23

Whole-Loan CMOs

Anand K. Bhattacharya, Ph.D.
Managing Director of Financial Strategies Group
Mortgage and Asset Finance Group
Prudential Securities Inc.

Jacqueline Galdieri
Senior Associate of the Primary Marketing Group
Market Group
Prudential Securities Inc.

Cyrus Mohebbi, Ph.D.
Managing Director
Market Group
Prudential Securities Inc.

Lisa Pendergast
Director of Fixed-Income Strategies
Financial Strategies Group
Prudential Securities Inc.

INTRODUCTION

In recent years, demand for non-agency mortgage-backed securities (MBSs) in all of their varied shapes and sizes has risen consistently, making this market one of the fastest growing fixed-income sectors. While the term *non-agency CMO* is used most often in this chapter, these securities are commonly referred to as *whole-loan CMOs*.

While issuance levels of non-agency MBSs increased at a respectable pace during the mid- to late-1980s, issuance exploded at the outset of the new decade (as shown in Exhibit 1), with $54 billion in non-agency MBSs issued in 1990, $109 billion in 1992, and $114 billion in 1993. In the first-quarter 1994, new production of non-agency MBSs hit a record level of just over $35 billion, representing the largest quarter on record, outpacing the

Exhibit 1. Non-Agency MBS Issuance (1983-1994*)

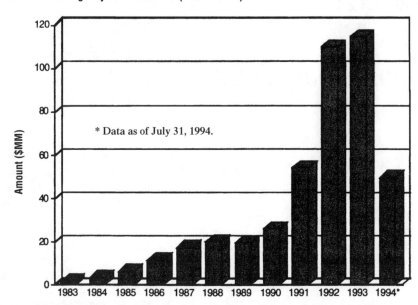

Source: *The Mortgage Market Statistical Annual for 1994.* Inside Mortgage Finance
Publications, Inc.

fourth-quarter 1993's historical levels.[1] In the second-quarter 1994, non-agency MBS issuance fell to approximately $16 billion and as of early September, only $8.2 billion had been issued. Despite this recent development, the growth of the whole-loan market and its relative value in the fixed-income arena over the past decade are certainly worth investigating.

WHY THE SURGE IN GROWTH?

The growth of the non-agency MBS sector since the 1980s is attributable to several key factors: (1) growing investor sophistication; (2) technology; (3) increased supply; and (4) the role of the Resolution Trust Corporation (RTC).

Growing Investor Sophistication

The growing sophistication of investors and their increased comfort level with the workings of the MBS marketplace have led to an ever-increasing

---

1 See "Conduits, Senior/Sub Structure and Fixed-Rate Collateral Dominate Private-Label MBS Market in Early 1994," *Inside Mortgage Securities* (April 29, 1994).

level of participation in this sector of the mortgage market. Moreover, the yield pick-up available in this sector has been responsible for attracting first-time investors; this was particularly true for most of 1991, 1992 and 1993, during which yields of fixed-income securities fell to historical lows.

Technology

The massive strides in technology, combined with more thorough and improved standardization of whole-loan reporting, now allow issuers, underwriters, rating agencies, and investors to make decisions based on more accurate and timely information. Standardized remittance reports that contain current information on collateral balances, bond factors (principal and interest), resets on adjustable-rate coupons, delinquencies and foreclosures, prepayments, WAC, WAM, and, in some cases, credit-enhancement details, are now made available by the trustees. Moreover, independent services have emerged and are providing the marketplace with more complete and standardized information on both collateral and bond structure.

A key advancement that served to enhance trading activity within the whole-loan CMO market has been the introduction of Bloomberg into the analytical environment. Bloomberg is an on-line service that is offered to various participants within the financial community—dealers, brokers, investors, *etc.* Bloomberg is a mainstream enterprise that provides users with details on issuers, collateral, and ratings of CMOs. Most notably, its analytic capabilities were the keys necessary to open the whole-loan CMO market to a large number of investors, allowing them to make timely decisions on investment opportunities in the whole-loan CMO marketplace based on sophisticated analytics.

Typically, access to Bloomberg and remittance reports gives the investor information to evaluate structures and keep abreast of developments within any particular deal on a month-to-month basis.

In terms of the collateral backing non-agency CMOs, the Mortgage Information Corporation (MIC) sells a database/software package that gives investors, issuers, servicers, and dealers independent information on the loans backing non-agency CMOs in the form of computer tapes or hard-copy reports. Moreover, underwriters have increased their willingness to make details of given structures more readily available to competing underwriters in order for them to reverse engineer each other's deals. Consequently, non-agency CMO liquidity in the secondary market is enhanced.

The advent of such analytical capabilities, combined with the development of whole-loan specific prepayment models, has further propelled the growth of the non-agency MBS sector. A whole-loan prepayment model differs from an agency model in a number of ways. The whole-loan model accounts for the greater propensity of non-agency mortgages to refinance when presented with the opportunity, resulting in faster prepayment rates for premium-coupon whole loans. It also factors in the steeper refinance-aging curve and the weaker burnout factor associated with whole-loan mortgages, as well as the greater inclination for such mortgagors to move more frequently than agency mortgagors. Of note, a whole-loan model should also include a facility for addressing deal-specific issues, such as the tendency for geographic concentrations in whole-loan mortgage pools, their prepayment variance from the national average, and the ability to address the diversity of mortgage-loan types within pools.

Increased Supply

The overall increase in whole-loan originations that resulted from the historically low mortgage rates that prevailed in the early 1990s served as one of the main catalysts behind the growth of the non-agency MBS structured market (see Exhibit 2). In addition, much of the growth can be attributed to the emergence and expanded role of private mortgage conduits.

During the first three months of 1994, private conduits accounted for 46% of all non-agency MBS production.[2] At the same time, mortgage companies' share of the non-agency CMO market fell to 29% in the first-quarter 1994 from 34% in the fourth-quarter 1993. Exhibit 3 clearly illustrates the emerging dominance of the private mortgage conduit.

Exhibit 2. Growth in Whole-Loan Originations

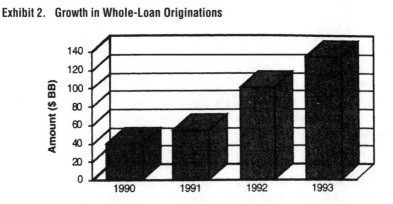

Source: *The Mortgage Market Statistical Annual for 1994.* Inside Mortgage Finance Publications, Inc.

---

2 *Inside Mortgage Securities,* Issue 1994:17 (April 29, 1994).

Exhibit 3.   Non-Agency MBS Issuance by Issuer (1992 and 1993)

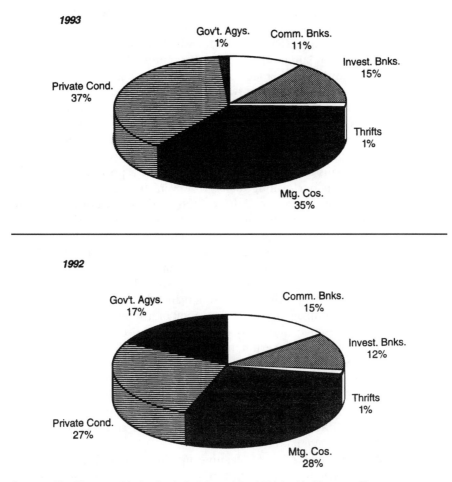

1993

Gov't. Agys.
1%

Comm. Bnks.
11%

Invest. Bnks.
15%

Private Cond.
37%

Thrifts
1%

Mtg. Cos.
35%

1992

Gov't. Agys.
17%

Comm. Bnks.
15%

Invest. Bnks.
12%

Thrifts
1%

Private Cond.
27%

Mtg. Cos.
28%

Source: *The Mortgage Market Statistical Annual for 1994.* Inside Mortgage Finance
Publications, Inc.

Role of the Resolution Trust Corporation (RTC)

The arrival of the Resolution Trust Corporation (RTC)[3] onto the non-agency
MBS landscape in 1991 proved to be another strong stimulus in the growth
of this sector.

---

3 See Nancy Olson, Thomas Pluta, and Stuart Silpe, *An Introduction to RTC Mortgage Securities*,
  Mortgage and Asset-backed Capital Group, Prudential Securities Incorporated, February
  1993.

The RTC was established on August 9, 1989, with enactment of the Financial Institutions Reform, Recovery & Enforcement Act (FIRREA) as an instrumentality of the U.S. Government. It was charged with managing and resolving failed savings associations formerly insured by the Federal Savings and Loan Insurance Corp. (FSLIC) and for which a conservator or receiver was appointed between January 1, 1989 and September 30, 1993.

Under its mandate to manage and resolve failed savings associations, the RTC was given the power as a conservator to take actions necessary to preserve the business of an institution and to bring it to a sound and solvent condition, and as receiver, to liquidate an institution and its assets.

One of the most effective ways for the RTC to maximize the net present value of the portfolio of single-family mortgage loans under its management was to sell those loans in securitized form, including a portion of its delinquent loans as well as performing loans. However, the non-standard nature of the single-family mortgage portfolio complicated its Congressional mandate. The tremendous size and uneven quality of the RTC's single-family mortgage loan portfolio posed securitization challenges to the RTC, rating agencies, investment banks, mortgage servicers, and due-diligence firms.

To help deal with its problems, the RTC launched its private-label mortgage-backed securities program in June 1991. Despite the challenges it faced, the RTC was one of the top private MBS issuers in 1991 and 1992, with 44 single-family residential non-agency MBSs for a total of just under $27 billion.

The RTC's presence increased investor awareness in the non-agency sector and, as a result of its government backing, attracted first-time investors into the market. Most investors learned that, with or without the RTC's backing, the non-agency CMO marketplace differed little in terms of structure from the agency CMO sector. While the RTC's involvement did indeed lend credibility to the market, investors soon realized that even non-RTC issues carried a high credit rating as a result of some level of credit enhancement dictated by the rating agencies.

Notably, as the RTC's job of cleaning up the thrift industry began to wind down, its non-agency single-family MBS issuance has diminished. While the RTC ranked first and second in issuance levels in 1991 and 1992, respectively, it dropped considerably in 1993 to place seventeenth in non-agency MBS ranking with just under $1.2 billion in new issuance.

The RTC will cease to exist on January 1, 1997. The FDIC will succeed the RTC as conservator or receiver of any institutions still held in those capacities. All assets and liabilities of the RTC will be transferred to the FSLIC resolution fund, which is managed by the FDIC and includes all assets and liabilities of the now defunct FSLIC.

WHOLE LOANS AND NON-AGENCY CMOs

A non-conforming mortgage loan is one that does not conform to GNMA, FNMA, or FHLMC mortgage-loan pooling requirements, and thus timely principal and interest payments are not guaranteed. Nonconforming loans are pooled by a private entity that in turn issues an MBS, using a specific type and level of credit enhancement(s) to achieve a particular credit rating. Just as in the agency MBS sector, non-agency MBSs can take many forms; they can be sold either as whole loans (un-rated and non-securitized) or as structured pass-throughs and CMOs (which carry a credit rating from one or more industry accepted rating agencies).

RELATIVE VALUE OF NON-AGENCY MBSs

Non-agency MBSs provide attractive yields relative to agency MBSs. Moreover, when compared to corporate bonds, non-agency MBSs that are credit enhanced via some form of subordination tend to be perceived as higher credits as they are not (albeit arguably) subject to downgrade.

Agency CMO investors are natural candidates for whole-loan CMO investment as, structurally, there is little difference between a non-agency PAC and an agency one. Obviously, from a credit standpoint, the agency PAC is guaranteed by the issuing agency and carries an implicit triple-A rating, whereas the whole-loan backed CMO must either—structurally or via a third-party—provide additional credit enhancements up to the amount stipulated by the major rating agencies in order to achieve a triple-A rating.

So we know that non-agency CMOs offer more yield than is available from agency CMOs. Thus the main questions become: how much more, and what is the risk of the higher reward? Over the years, the key determinants of just how much incremental yield is provided have been (1) the degree to which investors have become comfortable with the product and (2) the amount of whole-loan supply currently available for securitization (see Exhibit 4).

For example, in 1992, the RTC, as the largest private-label issuer of MBSs, brought almost $21.8 billion to market; far exceeding the second-place runner, Prudential Home Mortgage, which brought only $16.9 billion to market.[4]

As a result of the RTC's injection of new supply into the market, supply far outpaced demand and spreads widened to unprecedented levels. However, the RTC is currently much less of a presence than it was in 1992. This, combined with the fact that mortgage originations in general declined significantly in the second-quarter 1994, caused spreads on these securities to tighten and trade more directionally and in line with agency CMO spreads.

---

4 *The Mortgage Market Statistical Annual For 1994,* Inside Mortgage Finance Publications, Inc.

Exhibit 4. Spread Levels (BPs) for Fixed-Income Triple-A Credit Quality Securities

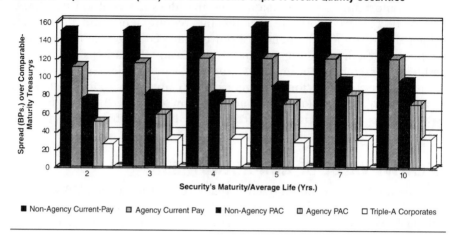

While the CMO market in general has been beset by fears of extension risk in 1994's rising-rate environment, there are a number of positive factors currently in place in the non-agency CMO sector. These factors include: (1) reduced amount of supply; (2) the positive effect an expansionary business cycle will have on defaults, foreclosures and home prices in general; and (3) the overall better-educated consumer (in this case, traditional agency CMO buyers).

Non-agency MBSs provide attractive yields relative to Treasurys and other MBSs and have excellent credit quality (speaking predominantly of senior/subordinated structures) in comparison to corporate bonds, which are subject to event risk. When evaluating the viability of an investment in triple-A rated non-agency CMOs, investors should consider: (1) issue structure (cash-flow profile); (2) credit enhancement utilized; (3) issuer of the security; (4) servicer of the loans; and (5) quality of the collateral.

Issue Structure. As in the agency CMO market, the way in which cash flows are allocated among individual classes is a key determinant of value. For example, if an investor is evaluating a non-agency PAC bond, he or she would focus on the PAC bands and the types of support bonds in the issue.

Credit Enhancement. Focusing for the moment only on triple-A rated issues, it is important to evaluate the type of credit enhancement used to bring the issue to that particular rating level. Knowing and understanding the credit enhancement used for a given transaction helps to determine the types and quantities of risk from which the investor is protected. Considerations such as event risk in third-party credit enhancements or the amount of subordination used in a senior/subordinated structure must be determined and investigated. However, it is important to remember that, in rated non-agency CMOs, one or more of the major rating agencies perform thorough analyses of the collateral and quantify the amount of credit enhancement necessary to achieve the desired rating.

Strong Credits as Issuers. Most investors prefer non-agency CMOs that have been issued by well known and highly rated issuers. Familiarity with the issuer's underwriting procedures and overall integrity is an important consideration for many investors.

Efficiency of Servicer. The quality of the mortgage servicer is vital to the safety of the transaction. The servicer is responsible for billing and collecting and is contractually obligated to collect on delinquent accounts, to foreclose on properties, and to liquidate those properties in order to maximize value to the creditors through reasonable efforts. In some cases, servicers are required to advance principal and interest on missed payments, which they then recover from later collections. The value of the underlying mortgages could be adversely affected if the servicer fails to perform as expected.

Collateral Review. As previously mentioned, credit-rating agencies review in detail the collateral for rated non-agency CMOs. In effect, this allows investors in such securities to take comfort in the fact that the collateral has been properly reviewed and that its value has been determined in such a way as to quantify the appropriate credit-enhancement level required to achieve the desired credit rating. Nevertheless, investors still may want to review the characteristics of the collateral as such an analysis will shed light on the prepayment levels of the issue going forward. The characteristics of the underlying collateral (*e.g.*, fixed-rate or adjustable-rate, geographic dispersion, LTVs, relocation loans) not only provide insight into default and delinquency expectations, but also affect prepayment expectations.

REGULATORY ENVIRONMENT BRINGS TIGHTENING PRESSURE TO BEAR

In 1993, new FASB accounting regulations required that banks and insurance companies mark to market many debt securities. Any asset held in an available-for-sale or held-for-trading account will be marked to market, with unrealized losses arising from the held-for-trading category to be fully reflected in company earnings, while unrealized losses for available-for-sale investments will affect only shareholders' equity.

These regulations made it prohibitively expensive for institutions to hold mortgage securities on their balance sheets. The practice of selling non-conforming mortgages (known as whole loans) in the marketplace became a more attractive option for investors (namely banks and thrifts) who found themselves restricted to some extent in their security purchases.

Importantly for the whole-loan MBS marketplace, the new rule covered the treatment of securities only, as opposed to all assets, thus making the non-securitized whole-loan market an extremely attractive one to investors subject to the FASB regulation. Thus as banks and thrifts clamored for whole-loan MBSs, thereby reducing the supply of collateral needed to create whole-loan CMOs, spreads in the whole-loan CMO market began to tighten for scarcity value reasons.

NON-AGENCY MORTGAGE LOAN COLLATERAL

As stated earlier, a non-conforming mortgage loan is one that does not conform to GNMA, FNMA, or FHLMC mortgage loan pooling requirements, and thus the timely payments of principal and interest are not guaranteed to the same degree as those of conforming securities.

The agency programs are designed to assist first-time home buyers and those with modest incomes. Therefore, acceptable loans have limits on the original balance of the mortgages. Mortgages with an original balance of over $203,150 are ineligible for the FNMA and FHLMC programs, while mortgages over $151,725 are ineligible for the FHA program, and mortgages of more than $184,000 are ineligible for the VA program. Typically, the underlying mortgage loans collateralizing a non-agency MBS are larger (so-called jumbo) than the GNMA, FNMA, and FHLMC maximum conforming loan sizes.

Three of the main underwriting standards established by these agencies for qualification as a conforming mortgage are: (1) a maximum payment-to-income ratio; (2) a maximum loan-to-value ratio; and (3) a maximum loan amount.

There are a few other "checks" mandated by the agencies that render a mortgage loan conforming or non-conforming.

Non-conforming loans are pooled by a private entity that uses a specific type and level of credit enhancement(s) to achieve a particular credit rating and issues an MBS. Just as in the agency MBS sector, non-agency MBSs can take many forms: they can be sold either as whole loans (unrated and non-securitized) or as structured pass-throughs and CMOs (which carry a credit rating from one or more industry accepted rating agencies).

The most important factor for an investor in highly rated, non-conforming MBSs to remember is that the structure and cash flows for a non-conforming issue are exactly the same as for a conforming one. The main exception is that if the mortgage pool backing the issue experiences severe losses, timely payments of interest and principal will not be assured by a government agency, causing the investor to rely on the structure's credit enhancement.

EVALUATING THE CREDIT QUALITY OF UNDERLYING MORTGAGES

Before we can understand the types of credit enhancements required for non-agency CMOs, we need to familiarize ourselves with the standard characteristics of whole loans from a number of perspectives, mainly: (1) type of mortgage/mortgagor; (2) mortgage-loan LTVs; (3) underwriting standards; (4) geography; and (5) mortgage originator and servicer.

Type of Mortgage: Key to the evaluation of the underlying collateral's credit quality is the type of mortgage loans that make up a pool. There are many characteristics of a mortgage loan that cause it to be valued in different ways. For example, the different amortization schedules by which mortgage loans are originated can affect their appeal to investors. The mortgage-loan characteristics most often evaluated are:

Property types (single-family detached, condominium, cooperative, multifamily, commercial). An evaluation of the property types backing the mortgages in a pool would include how an economic downturn would affect demand for the properties and how much the market value would decline. Most credit rating agencies view the single-family detached unit as the safest type of property.

Payment characteristics (fixed-rate or adjustable-rate, balloon, graduated-payment). Defaults on level-payment loans tend to occur less frequently than defaults on loans with payments that increase over time according to some predetermined formula. When a mortgage pool includes adjustable-rate mortgages (ARMs), the evaluation must include a determination of the frequency of rate increases, the amount of potential rate increases allowable per period and over the life of the mortgage, whether negative amortization is allowed, and the volatility of the ARM's index.

Mortgage rates and terms. Mortgage loans that are shorter than the standard 30-year traditional mortgages are looked upon more kindly as they amortize more quickly, allowing equity to build up faster. The mortgage rate is also important as it will shed light as to the potential prepayment characteristics of the mortgages. If the rates of the mortgages in a given pool are higher than existing rates by, say, 100 basis points or more, then it is likely that the pool will see an up-tick in prepayments.

Mortgage-Loan Loan-to-Value (LTV) Ratios: The most compelling argument in favor of the credit quality of mortgages lies in the borrowers' equity in their homes—the greater the equity in the home, the more the mortgagor will do to avoid foreclosure. This is the obvious reason that loan-to-value (LTV) ratios of a given collateral pool are key indicators of the pool's credit quality. The lower the LTV, the more market value can fall before mortgagors' equity in their homes becomes negative.

Loans with LTV ratios in excess of 80% usually are required to have primary mortgage insurance (PMI). PMI usually covers the claim amount down to a 75% LTV. As all pool insurers require claim settlement from PMI insurers before honoring a claim, the rating of an issue with loans requiring PMI depends on the rating of the PMI company insuring the loans.

If the rating on the claims-paying ability of a PMI company insuring the loans in a pool securing an issue falls below the issue's rating, the rating agencies will review the situation on a case-by-case basis. Rather than uniformly lowering the rating of the bonds in such cases, the rating agencies increase the loss-severity assumption for the affected loans. Specifically, assumptions are made depending on the creditworthiness of the particular PMI company about how much of the promised coverage actually will be paid.

Underwriting Standards: A prime-quality loan has what is commonly referred to as "full" documentation. This means that the originator has obtained a credit report on the borrower and verified the mortgagor's income (VOI), the mortgagor's employment (VOE), and the source of the down payment (VOD) securing the contract of sale. The presence of all these items clearly serves to reduce the originator's risk.

As a standard practice, originators use the mortgagor's tax returns for the previous two years as a means of verifying income. The mortgagor's employment typically is verified by obtaining a written statement from the employer. Verification of the source of the mortgagor's deposit is generally obtained by examining bank account statements and credit card statements. Credit reports are obtained from national credit bureaus such as TRW.

In recent years, originators have made efforts to hasten the approval process by using different forms of documentation. For instance, a lender may use W-2s or pay stubs for VOI and VOE. Such programs usually are referred to as "alternative" documentation, although many lenders dub them with other names for marketing purposes. Investors should seek a full understanding of any documentation program that is unclear.

In establishing an aggressive lending policy, a lender may dispense with any or all of the four documentation items, but their absence increases the riskiness of the loans. Indeed, the more items that are missing, the more loss coverage required by the rating agencies. Of course, the riskiest of all documentation programs is the "no-doc" program in which the lender does not obtain a VOI, VOE or VOD. Perhaps the most important of all of these items is the verification of the down-payment source, since without VOD, the possibility that the mortgagor has borrowed some or all of the down payment is raised. The real risk in such situations is due to the effective reduction of LTV. If the entire down payment is borrowed, the home owner's equity in the property may be illusory and there may be nothing monetary for the mortgagor to lose in the event of foreclosure.

In addition to the above factors, there are typically three due-diligence reviews of the whole-loan pools conducted prior to securitization: (1) the loan originator completes a credit review at origination; (2) the underwriter of any securitization is likely to review the loan package; and (3) if there is any third-party insurer, the insurer also would review the loans.

Geography: Due to regional variations in housing costs, larger (or jumbo) loans often tend to be concentrated in certain areas, notably California and the Northeast. Therefore, both the geographic location and the geographic dispersion of the underlying mortgages in the pool are key determinants as to the likely behavior of the mortgages. Generally speaking, a pool of mortgage loans that is not well diversified will be deemed more risky by the credit-rating agencies and thus require a higher degree of loss coverage.

In particular, non-agency MBSs with heavy concentrations of California loans require special consideration. In dollar terms, California accounts for about 30% of mortgage originations each year in the U.S. More importantly, California mortgage loans make up an even larger share of the collateral in non-agency CMOs because the cost of housing in the state is well above the national average. This places many California-originated mortgages above the agency limits and forces mortgagors to take out jumbo loans.

Since Californians tend to move more frequently than mortgagors from other states, prepayment speeds on pools of mortgage loans originated in California are perceived as being faster. There is also some concern as to the amount of risk caused by natural disasters in pools of mortgages in which California concentrations are high. For example, in 1993, California was afflicted by two major earthquakes and, in years past, there have been instances of widespread fires.

In the past few years, the Californian economy in general and the housing market in particular have suffered major downturns, causing the prices of some homes to fall dramatically and thus increase concerns of mortgage-loan defaults and foreclosures. This situation caused spreads on non-agency MBSs with a high concentration of California mortgages backing the issue to widen as investors shunned those particular securities or swapped out of those positions into securities backed by collateral that had not come under pressure. However, more recently, as the Californian economy has begun to show signs of improving, this situation has receded as an issue of concern for non-agency MBS investors.

Quality of the Servicing

The quality of the entity responsible for servicing the pool of mortgages underlying an issue of non-agency MBSs also is very important to its security. The servicer is responsible for billing the mortgagors and making collections on a regular basis. In addition, the servicer generally is contractually obligated to make reasonable efforts to collect on delinquent accounts, to foreclose on properties as soon as is practicable, and to liquidate those properties in such a manner as to maximize value to the creditors. Most importantly, many issues are structured so that the servicer is required to advance interest and scheduled principal on any missed payments as long as the servicer deems such advances to be recoverable from later collections. When this is the case, the servicer's financial ability to make such advances becomes vital. This motivates the servicer to make its best efforts in the collection process since the advances have a zero rate of return. Thus a servicer who fails to perform will have an adverse effect on the value of the mortgages serviced. Regardless, if a servicer does fail to fulfill its contractual obligations, it must be replaced.

EFFECTS OF DEFAULTS AND FORECLOSURES

In order to assure the investor that timely payments of principal and interest will occur, liquidity must be provided for covering temporary shortfalls (due to delinquencies and the time required for the foreclosure and liquidation of properties) and losses. Losses generally are divided into five categories:

1. Normal credit losses due to delinquencies and defaults (caused, for example, by loss of employment) that cannot be absorbed by the underlying equity in the home due to market depreciation.

2. Losses caused by uninsured physical damage due to special hazards such as earthquakes and floods.

3. Losses caused by fraud in the origination process.

4. Losses caused by modification of the terms of a mortgage note by a bankruptcy judge.

5. Losses caused by normal hazards such as fire, lightning, windstorm, and hail.

Security analysis always involves determining the presence of risk factors, their effect on expected losses, and the amount and quality of the credit enhancement provided to cover those losses. Consequently, any investment decision concerning non-agency MBSs also requires consideration of the credit quality of the underlying collateral.

Because the credit quality of mortgages lies in the mortgagors' equity in their homes, and the greater the equity, the more the mortgagor will do to avoid foreclosure, the LTV ratio of a given pool is a key indicator of its credit quality. The lower the LTVs, the more market value can fall before mortgagors' equity in their homes becomes negative.

Determining Loss Coverage for Normal Credit Losses: Rating agencies quantify the amount of credit support that is needed (to protect against losses) in order for an issue to obtain a particular credit rating. To quantify the risk associated with foreclosures, an estimate must be made of the largest amount of losses that can be attributed to normal credit losses. This estimate must be based on two critical assumptions:

Foreclosure frequency. Percentage of a mortgage pool that is assumed to default and go into foreclosure.

Loss severity. Average loss assumed to be realized on such foreclosures.

The amount of loss coverage required to achieve a particular rating is the product of these two assumptions. In some cases, more consideration is given to the expected timing of the losses and to how the timing will affect overall expected losses. Rather than being based on current economic conditions, these estimates are based on assumptions of worst-case scenarios. Both the Great Depression and early-1980s Texas, with their associated high unemployment and sharply falling real-estate prices, provide historical bases for these estimates.

Exhibit 5 shows Standard & Poor's (S&P's) loss assumptions for a prime-quality pool of mortgages under a worst-case scenario and the levels of credit enhancement required to achieve three different ratings. In addition, Exhibit 6 defines the properties of a prime-quality mortgage pool.

STRUCTURE AND CREDIT ENHANCEMENTS OF NON-AGENCY MBSs

When evaluating non-agency MBSs, investors must understand the more complex credit issues of the pass-through or structured transaction in comparison to agency CMOs, which carry a government or quasi-government guarantee as to the timely payment of interest and principal. One component of a non-agency transaction that issuers in the whole-loan market must employ when addressing investor concerns is the form of credit enhancement that will be used to bring the rating of the issue to the desired level. From the investor's

---

Exhibit 5. Standard & Poor's Loss Assumptions

Rating	Foreclosure Frequency (%)	Loss Severity (%)	Required Loss Coverage (%)
AAA	15	43	6.50
AA	10	40	4.00
A	8	35	2.80

Source: *Standard & Poor's Credit Week*, October 25, 1993.
*Loss coverage = foreclosure × loss severity. Foreclosure costs assume a 12% mortgage rate.

Exhibit 6. Characteristics of a Prime-Quality Mortgage Pool

Mortgage Securities	First liens on single-family, one-unit, detached properties
Mortgage Payments	Fixed rate, level-payment, fully amortizing loans
Morgagor Status	Mortgagor's primary residence
Location	Well dispersed geographically throughout an area having a strong economic base
Mortgage Size	Less than $300,000
Loan-to-Value Ratio	80% or less
Number of Loans	300 or more
Mortgage Documentation	Must conform to FHLMC/FNMA guidelines

Source: *Standard & Poor's Credit Week*, October 25, 1993.

---

perspective, the type of credit enhancement, as well as its amount and quality, are structural features that determine the types and quantities of risk from which the investor is protected.

Importantly, non-agency MBSs are much less susceptible to downgrades than other comparable types of investments. Most downgrades experienced in the non-agency MBS sector have not been the result of a deterioration in the underlying collateral's performance, but rather due to the downgrade of the issuer or the guarantor. Such types of downgrades could be the result of: (1) a number of different issues not given proper attention by the issuer or guarantor; (2) the inability of the issue to meet certain regulations; or (3) the deterioration of the creditworthiness of the third-party guarantor.

The decision to downgrade a given non-agency issue is based on a ratings approach that balances the assessment of the expected timing and size of losses on the underlying mortgage pool and the assessment of the amount and quality of third-party guarantees. Notably, for those cases in which a non-agency MBS is downgraded due to reasons other than the performance of the underlying mortgage collateral, bondholders are still assured of receiving timely payments of principal and interest as long as the collateral continues to perform.

There are several forms of credit enhancement that are available to provide non-agency MBS investors protection against losses due to foreclosure. They include:

- Senior/subordination

- Super-senior structures

- Pool insurance

- Financial guarantees

- Letters of credit (LOCs)

- Corporate guarantees

Generally speaking, these five types of credit enhancement can be broken down into two categories: (1) self-enhancing (senior/subordination and super-senior structures), and (2) third-party credit enhancements (pool insurance, financial guarantees, letters of credit, and corporate guarantees).

In 1992 and 1993, the senior/subordinated structure and the variations that have sprung from it have become the dominant method of enhancing non-agency CMOs, as shown in Exhibit 7. Thus, while we do discuss the third-party credit-enhancement methodologies at the end of this chapter, the lion's share of our discussion is focused on the senior/subordinated methodology.

SENIOR/SUBORDINATION

A form of credit enhancement that does not rely on a third-party guarantor is a subordinated structure. MBSs using subordination for credit enhancement are not subject to the same kind of event risk as MBSs that use pool insurance,

Exhibit 7. Evolution of Credit-Enhancement Tools 1991-93

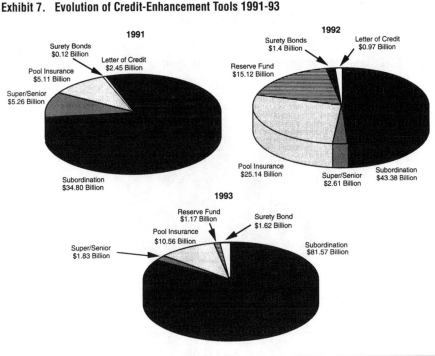

corporate guarantees, financial guarantees, or LOCs. While issuers and underwriters did use a variety of these types of third-party credit enhancements in the past, as previously stated, the senior/subordinated structure has become the predominant form of credit enhancement for non-agency issues within the past few years.

In the first quarter of 1994, the senior/subordinated structure was undoubtedly the most prevalent form of credit enhancement, accounting for 97% of all of the non-agency MBS issues underwritten. This percentage represents an increase from all of 1993, when the percentage was 81%. Pool insurance was used in only 2% of the non-agency issues in the first-quarter 1994, down from 11% in all of 1993.[5] (See Exhibit 8.)

Subordination is a form of credit enhancement in which a senior class of certificates is given priority over one or more subordinate classes for principal and interest payments. Any shortfalls of scheduled principal and interest payments caused by losses on the underlying mortgage collateral are absorbed by the subordinated-certificate holders. When this occurs, the principal balance of the subordinate securities is reduced by the amount of realized losses.

Determining Subordination Amount: The factors involved in determining the size of the subordinated piece are no different from those used to determine the credit support required in a traditional pass-through structure utilizing an alternative credit-enhancement vehicle. The credit support for a

Exhibit 8.   Private-Label Issuance by Credit Enhancement for 1993

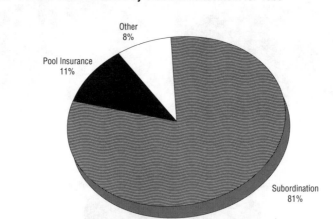

Source: *The Mortgage Market Statistical Annual for 1994.* Inside Mortgage Finance
Publications, Inc.

---

5 *Inside Mortgage Securities,* Issue 1994:17 (April 29, 1994).

senior/subordinated structure is determined by adjusting pre-established credit support guidelines for a representative sample of prime loans, labeled as benchmark pools for the attributes of the specific pools under consideration, in order to account for the relative risk of the asset being rated.

While there are a variety of ways in which the amount of subordination is determined, the credit risk of a pool of non-conforming mortgages is assessed by comparing the characteristics of the pool under consideration to that of a standard pool. A standard or *benchmark* pool is usually one that consists of 30-year, geographically diverse, fixed-rate, owner-occupied, fully documented, newly originated, purchase-money mortgages on single-family, average-value properties. The credit support for each benchmark pool is a function of the forecasted foreclosure frequency and the expected severity of loss percentage.

The foreclosure frequency refers to the probability of default of the mortgages in the pool. As a general rule, the prime determinant of default for a mortgagor is the amount of equity accumulated in the property. The greater the amount of price appreciation, the faster the rate of loan amortization and principal repayment, the greater the rate of equity accumulation and the lower the incidence of default. In view of this consideration, benchmark pools for various LTV ratios are used in the assessment of credit risk for pools of non-conforming mortgages. The severity of loss measures the extent of the loss in the event of default as a function of factors such as specific loan attributes, mainly age, coupon rate, seasoning, LTV, adequacy of PMI, and costs associated with delinquency and foreclosure.

Deviations from the attributes of a prime pool in the characteristics of the pool under consideration are expressed in terms of *risk weights* or multiples of prime-pool credit support. For an individual mortgage with multiple deviations from the characteristics of the benchmark pool, the aggregate risk is determined as the product of the various risk weights and then averaged across individual mortgages to obtain a credit support level for the overall pool.

On the micro level, contractual features of the mortgage, along with the characteristics of the property, are considered in assessing the relative riskiness of the pool. This micro assessment of the mortgage loans is combined with a macro evaluation of features such as diversification of the pool, geographical concentration, and structural features of securities in the determination of the overall credit-support level.

While the credit protection provided by the subordinated piece may be considered adequate, it is not a perfect substitute for other credit-enhancement devices in terms of immediate coverage in the event of mortgagor delinquency and default. The ability of the subordinated cash flows to meet shortfalls in the senior class' cash flow is limited by the balance in any fund created specifically for the purpose of such contingencies and any current cash flow due to the subordinated holders. In order to guard against such occurrences, liquidity safeguards in the form of either a reserve fund or a shifting-interest mechanism are used in senior-subordinated structures.

Reserve Fund: A reserve fund typically is used in conjunction with another credit-enhancement mechanism, predominantly senior/subordinated structures. When a reserve fund is used, cash flows from principal payments that otherwise would be distributed to the subordinated certificate holders are maintained in a reserve fund.

The combination of the reserve fund and the subordinated class principal allocation provide the credit support for the senior class. While a cash performance bond or guarantor could be used to provide delinquency coverage, in most instances such coverage is provided in the form of an initial deposit by the issuer into the reserve fund under the aegis of self insurance. The issuer may retain the right to recover the initial deposit and subrogate the rights of the subordinated holders to receive cash flows over these funds.

Senior/Subordinated Shifting-Interest Structures: Structures using subordination often have a shifting-interest feature in which interest and scheduled payments of principal are distributed on a pro-rata basis to the senior and subordinate classes; however, for an initial period (typically 5 years for fixed-rate mortgages and 10 years for adjustable-rate mortgages), 100% of the prepayments on the mortgage pools are allocated to the senior class (or classes, in the event of tranching). Over time, a smaller percentage of the pro-rata share of the subordinate classes' prepayments are paid to the senior class, reducing the shifting prepayment percentage to zero. As shown in Exhibit 9, the step-down structure usually looks like this: 100% of the prepayments are allocated to the senior class during the period from issuance until the first step-down, 70% during the second, 60% during the third, 40% during the fourth, and 20% in the last. After the last step-down, both classes receive their full pro-rata share of prepayments.

This initial allocation of prepayments to the senior class shortens the average life of the senior class and lengthens the average life of the subordinate classes. If the underlying collateral does not prepay at all, the relative ownership interests of the senior and subordinate classes remain constant; however, to the extent that the underlying collateral prepays, the ownership interest of the senior class will fall and that of the subordinate class will rise.

The allocation of additional prepayments to the senior class is the greatest at the beginning, when the default or loss risk of the underlying loans is usually the highest. Also, keep in mind that prepayments come from borrowers who have the financial means to make them; the borrowers whose mortgages remain in the pool may or may not have the required resources to prepay. During the early period, which is usually the first five years, the

Exhibit 9.   Detailed Look at Shifting-Interest Senior/Subordinated Structure

The shifting-interest structure allocates certain portions of the subordinate certificates' unscheduled principal payments to the senior certificates. Due to the shifting of such payments to the senior certificates, the subordination level increases as a percentage of outstanding certificates during the first 10 years. For an initial period of 5 years, 100% of the unscheduled principal payments allocated to the subordinate certificates are redirected to the senior certificates. After this initial 5-year period, the senior certificates will receive the following percentage of the subordinate's share of unscheduled principal payments:

Year 6 - 70%
Year 7 - 60%
Year 8 - 40%
Year 9 - 20%
Year 10 - 0%

Unscheduled principal payments are allocated among the senior and subordinate certificates pro-rata in year 10 and thereafter. The cash-flow diagram illustrates a typical super/senior subordinated shifting-interest structure with a 10% triple-A mezzanine tranche and a 6.5% subordinate piece that was not tranched, but retained by the issuer as one bond.

The "A" classes (A1, A2, A3, *etc.*) represents the senior bonds, which are sequentially paying, with the exception of the A2 class, which pays pro-rata with the A3, A4, and A5 because the coupons of these bonds were stripped to synthetically create a premium bond out of the A2. As you can see from the cash-flow diagram, the triple-A mezzanine bond and the subordinate bond are outstanding for the life of the deal, assuming a no-loss scenario.

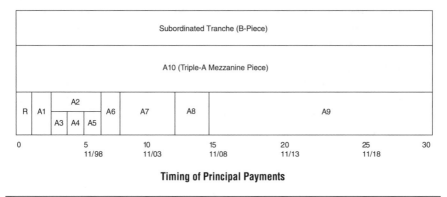

Timing of Principal Payments

senior class receives the most support from the subordinate class, thereby paying down the senior class' outstanding balance, increasing the ratio of the subordinate- to the senior-class balance and improving the relative credit-enhancement level.

Unlike MBSs that use corporate guarantees, pool insurance, or LOCs, subordination does not specifically cover losses due to special hazard, fraud, or bankruptcy. These risks are sometimes covered in limited amounts by separate policies as described earlier. However, subordination may be used to cover losses due to these causes in amounts less than the total amount of subordination. For example, an issue may have 10% subordination and a 3% *carve out* for special-hazard losses. Once the coverage for any or all of these risks is exhausted, losses will be borne by both the senior- and subordinate- certificate holders in accordance with their relative ownership interests at the time such loss is incurred.

The ratings of MBSs using subordination for credit enhancement do not depend on any third party and are therefore not subject to associated event risk. Consequently, the other types of credit enhancement shift some or all of the risk of losses to a third-party guarantor; if the guarantor encounters financial stress and is downgraded, there is a good chance that the MBSs that are covered by that guarantor also will be downgraded (albeit the severity of the downgrade may be less for the MBS than the guarantor). As a result, senior certificates in a subordinated structure are usually priced at a premium over MBSs utilizing other forms of credit enhancement, all other things being equal.

Upgrades/Downgrades to Senior/Subordinated Structures: Keep in mind that MBSs using subordination are still subject to downgrades. If the underlying collateral fails to perform, the amount of subordination may fall, causing the senior class to be downgraded. Usually, investors are still very well protected from losses because, in many cases when the underlying collateral is not performing as expected, the overall subordination percentage has not decreased below its original level. Conversely, senior certificates can be upgraded if their original rating was not already triple-A. This can occur if:

- Prepayments during the initial step-down period are paid to the senior certificates in such vast amounts that the amount of subordination relative to the pool has grown. Once the amount of subordination has reached the level required for a higher credit rating, the rating agencies will upgrade the issue; or if

- The credit quality of the collateral pool has improved after it has reached a certain age.

As historical data have shown, 80% to 90% of all defaults have occurred during years five through seven of the life of a mortgage. Rating agencies do not require as much loss coverage for older pools and this is why rating upgrades become more likely as collateral pools age.

THIRD-PARTY CREDIT ENHANCEMENTS

Third-party credit enhancements include pool insurance, corporate guarantee, financial guarantee, and LOC.

Pool Insurance: To achieve a particular rating, a pool-insurance policy must be obtained in an amount equal to the loss coverage required for that rating. While pool insurance protects bondholders from losses due to default, additional coverage is required for protection from losses due to mortgagor bankruptcy, fraud, and special hazard. The amount of coverage originally provided by the pool-insurance policy can be reduced as the underlying mortgage pool ages (typically when the collateral is five years seasoned), provided that such a reduction does not adversely affect the rating of the securities. Pool-insurance claims can be made only on the basis of certain conditions, as described in the offering documents on an issue-by-issue basis.

The pool insurer generally has the option to either: (1) purchase the property securing the defaulted mortgage loan for a price equal to the unpaid principal balance plus all unpaid accrued interest and certain expenses incurred by the trustee and servicer; or (2) pay the amount by which the aforementioned price exceeds the net proceeds derived from the sale of the property.

In rating an issue that uses pool insurance for credit enhancement, the rating agencies analyze (1) the assessment of the expected timing and size of the losses on the underlying mortgage pool; and (2) the assessment of the amount and quality of protection provided by the pool insurer.

A rating upgrade or downgrade can be caused by a change in the assessment of the claims paying ability of the insurer, a change in the performance of the collateral or both. The claims-paying ability of the insurer is noteworthy in that it shows that pool-insured MBSs are subject to event risk since an issue's rating can change even when the underlying collateral is performing well.

Corporate Guarantee: Another form of credit support used to protect the bondholder against losses due to default is the corporate guarantee. Unlike other credit enhancements, the corporate guarantee provides bondholders with protection from losses due to default, bankruptcy, fraud, and standard and special hazards, giving bondholders full recourse to the guarantor. The corporate guarantee may provide coverage for the entire issue or for only that class required by the rating agencies to give the class a desired rating. In the case of such a limited guarantee, the amount of the guarantee will be reduced by any losses incurred by the guarantor; however, with structures utilizing a letter of credit, the guarantor is often protected from losses by a pledge of excess servicing to a spread account or a subordinate bond, either of which must be fully exhausted before the amount of the guarantee is reduced.

Since the rating of an issue utilizing a corporate guarantee depends on the claims-paying ability of the guarantor, the rating of any issue supported by such a guarantee is likely to be upgraded or downgraded along with the rated claims-paying ability of the guarantor.

Financial Guarantee: When a financial guarantee is used as credit enhancement for a non-agency MBS, a financial guarantee company such as the Financial Guaranty Insurance Corporation (FGIC), Financial Security Assurance (FSA), or Capital Markets Assurance Corporation (CAPMAC) issues an insurance policy that provides for the timely payment of principal and interest on the bonds.

Non-agency MBSs credit-enhanced by financial guarantees have the same risks as issues backed by corporate guarantees. Like the corporate guarantee, a financial guarantee protects the bondholders without limitation from all risks associated with the underlying mortgage pool, including credit losses, standard and special hazards, fraud, and bankruptcy. MBSs backed by financial or corporate guarantees are subject to event risk since the rating of the MBS is dependent on the claims-paying ability of the insurer, as well as the performance of the underlying loans. When determining market prices of MBSs backed by a financial guarantee, a direct influential factor is the market's perception of the credit quality of the insurer.

Letters of Credit: Credit enhancement also can be obtained by securing the issue with a letter of credit (LOC) from a financial institution. A LOC is an obligation by a financial institution to reimburse losses up to a specified amount. The LOC can be used as credit support for an entire transaction or to cover a specific type of risk.

In many structures that utilize a LOC, losses are first absorbed by either a subordinate bond or a spread account, which usually is funded initially with a cash deposit at closing and enlarged through periodic deposits of excess servicing. When such a subordinate bond or spread account is in a first-loss position, it must be exhausted in its entirety before the amount of the LOC coverage is reduced. Like a pool-insured deal, separate insurance may be provided to protect the bondholders from loss due to special hazard, fraud, and/or bankruptcy.

STRUCTURAL INNOVATION IN NON-AGENCY MBSs

In addition to an ordinary senior/subordinated structure in which an issue consists strictly of "A" and "B" classes, there have been a number of innovative developments in the structuring of senior/subordinated non-agency MBSs that make them even more desirable.

A key innovation in the senior/subordinated MBS marketplace over the past two years or so has been the development and growth of multiclass senior/subordinated structures with varying levels of subordination. Multiclass subordinated structures have either been structured with classes in which losses are absorbed sequentially, or with sequential-pay classes wherein the loss allocation is distributed over all outstanding classes.

For instance, an example of the first type of multiclass security may be a three-class structure with a senior class (investment-grade rating), a rated subordinate class (non-investment-grade rating) and an un-rated subordinate class, which is essentially "carved" out of the total subordinate class. This simple structure also can be used as a template for structures with more than three classes and with each class subordinated to the class below it, creating a super-senior, semi-senior, super-subordinate, and subordinate class.

As a general rule, assuming the level of subordination is constant, the larger the size of the class, the smaller the severity of loss and, consequently, the higher the rating. Additionally, in such structures, the loss positions for each class are inversely related to the seniority of the class in the structure. For instance, in a four-class subordinated mezzanine class structure, the super-senior bonds will have the fourth-loss position in the structure, and hence the credit risk for such bonds would be minimal.

As for other types of structures that use a design of sequential allocation of principal cash flows combined with a proportional allocation of credit losses, the losses can be determined either as a function of the original or current balance of the bond classes. The use of the current balance penalizes the longer dated classes in a sequential-pay structure, while the use of the original balance appears more equitable. However, this method cannot equitably account for the allocation of losses that occur after a particular class has been paid off.

Super/Senior Structure

One key innovation was the introduction of the super/senior structure. The super/senior structure affords an added degree of credit protection in that a portion of the senior class is divided in such a way that it acts as a credit support class to the balance of the senior class. This credit-support class is referred to as a *senior support class*. An attractive feature of the senior support class is that it is still considered to be a senior class and therefore carries the same rating as the senior class.

A simple example of how the super/senior structure works in a triple-A pool-insurance issue is as follows. Pool insurance is obtained in an amount equal to the loss coverage required for a particular rating. However, in addition to pool insurance, a percentage of the senior piece is set aside to absorb any losses if the pool insurance coverage is exhausted. Since this class of the senior piece is covered by pool insurance, it maintains its triple-A rating. The result is that the senior class receives significantly more credit enhancement than that which the rating agencies would normally require for a triple-A rating.

Senior/Subordinated Structures with Triple-A Mezzanine Classes

Another alternative to the typical senior/subordinated structure is the inclusion of a triple-A mezzanine class (known as a *triple-A "mezz"*). The triple-A mezz class acts similarly to the senior support class in its credit characteristics, but it bears the characteristic of a subordinate bond in its prepayment-lockout feature. Interest and scheduled payments of principal are distributed on a pro-rata basis to the senior (including the triple-A mezz) and subordinate classes; however, for an initial period (typically 5 years for fixed-rate mortgages and 10 years for adjustable-rate mortgages), 100% of the prepayments on the mortgage pools are allocated to the senior class or classes in the event of tranching, but not to the triple-A mezz. Over time, a smaller percentage of the pro-rata share of the subordinate classes' and triple-A mezz's prepayments are paid to the senior class, reducing the shifted prepayment percentage to zero. After the particular step-down structure of each deal (typically 100% until the first step-down, 70% during the second, 60% during the third, 40% during the fourth, and 20% in the last), both classes receive their full pro-rata share of prepayments.

Innovative Tranching to Suit the Rate Environment

As mentioned earlier, almost all non-agency MBS issuers are now utilizing the senior/subordinate structure or some variation of it. They are doing so not only to reduce the event risk associated with third-party credit enhancements, but also because the senior/subordinate structure typically allows them to sell their product at higher dollar prices because of the increased stability of the collateral underlying the issue.

For these reasons, underwriters are developing senior bonds within the senior/subordinate structure that have behavioral patterns that are very attractive to investors in certain interest-rate environments and different market conditions. In order to stir interest among MBS investors, underwriters can no longer expect to sell "plain-vanilla" sequential paying structures or typical planned amortization class (PAC)/companion structures.

Multi-Tiered PAC Classes: In the fourth-quarter 1993, investors were concerned greatly with the rapidly increasing prepayment speeds that resulted from a historically low interest-rate environment in which homeowners were prompted to refinance their higher rate mortgages. Prudential Securities was faced with the challenge of creating bonds that afforded investors tremendous call protection; in other words, investors wanted bonds whose cash-flow structures would protect them from the high level of prepayments and the resultant shortening of average lives from those projected at issuance.

One solution developed by Prudential Securities is referred to as a *multi-tier PAC* structure. An example of this structure was the General Electric Capital Mortgage Services, Inc., 1994-10 issue. The structure consisted of five tiers of PAC bonds and two companion classes. Each tier of the PACs had different PAC bands and different priorities for "catchup" and "overflow" cash flows. When prepayment speeds rose above the upper PAC band and the companion bonds had been paid down in full, the first-tier PAC would receive the overflow of principal before the second tier, the second tier before the third tier, and so on down the line.

Due to the nature in which the "catchup" and "overflow" priorities were structured for this issue, each PAC bond has more stability than it would have if it had been within a typical PAC structure. If prepayments came in slower than the pricing speed such that they even fell below the speed on the lower PAC band, the first tier of PACs would take priority for receiving principal over the second tier, the second tier over the third tier, and so on down the line.

Non-Extendable Companion Classes: Beginning in the first-quarter of 1994, interest rates began a steep trek upward, causing prepayment speeds to decline precipitously. The result was that investors became concerned with extension risk, *i.e.*, rising interest rates slowed refinancings and caused issues to prepay slower than estimated at issue origination. Thus Wall Street was faced with the challenge of creating bonds whose cash-flow structures prevented their average lives from extending.

Companion bonds in a PAC/companion structure are usually most susceptible to extension risk because the PACs, which are supported by the companion's bonds, take priority in receiving any principal pay-downs if principal comes in so slowly that the PAC schedules are not met. The result is that the average lives of the companion bonds extend.

To alleviate the extension concern, Prudential Securities is now in the process of developing non-extendable companion tranches. A few different variations of this theme are beginning to be marketed as of this writing.

The first is a PAC/companion structure in which all of the PACs, including the short-term PAC, are locked out from all cash flows during a predetermined period of time. The result is that the companion is insured cash flow at least from the time of origination up until the period in which the PACs begin to receive principal. This provides the companion classes with a certain degree of extension protection. The second structure combines a portion of the short-term PAC cash flows with some companion cash flows, again in order to stabilize the extension risk of the companion bond.

For those situations in which principal cash flows come in at slower speeds than the lower PAC band, a third structure allots principal cash flows to both the PACs and the companions in the issue on a pro-rata basis, thus minimizing the amount of extension risk to which the companion bond is exposed.

THE GROWING MARKETPLACE FOR SUBORDINATED MBSs

Along with the development of multiclass senior-subordinated structures, there have been parallel developments in cultivating investor interest in subordinated classes. The surge of interest in subordinated MBSs coincided with the slowdown in the development of the high-yield market, which forced traditional junk bond investors to pursue other, higher yielding alternatives.

As prudent investments in high-yield bonds involve extensive credit analysis, as well as an understanding of the fundamental factors affecting the economy, subordinated classes are considered to be a viable alternative as their evaluation focuses on similar credit analyses. Moreover, the historically low interest-rate environment that prevailed for much of the early 1990s caused investors to explore alternative markets in order to gain incremental yield. The subordinated MBS marketplace proved to be a popular alternative.

What Is a Subordinated Certificate?

Generally speaking, a subordinated MBS is a class of security within a structured transaction that is junior to other classes of the same transaction. In effect, this means that the subordinated security absorbs cash-flow shortfalls caused by default-related losses with respect to each loan in the collateral pool.

In the earlier stages of its development, the subordinated portion of the senior/subordinated structure consisted of just one class, which was usually retained by the issuer. However, since about 1992, it has become common to credit tranche the subordinated class so that each class is assigned a rating from investment grade to non-investment grade to no rating at all (see Exhibit 10). Each subordinated class is protected from credit losses by homeowner equity and lower rated certificates, with the exception of the first-loss piece. The credit ratings of the various subordinated tranches are based solely on the credit quality of the collateral and the structure of the issue (mainly the size of the various classes and the order in which they absorb losses). The higher rated of these subordinated classes (or mezzanine classes) have ratings to triple-A. The remaining, intermediate classes have ratings from double-A to triple-B. These intermediate classes absorb losses when the first-loss class is exhausted.

Many bank and thrift issuers of early senior/subordinated transactions sold the senior classes and retained the subordinated classes. However, with the advent of risk-based capital guidelines, which require reserves against the entire issue if the junior class is retained, it became prudent for depository

Exhibit 10.   Detailed Look at Shifting-Interest Senior/Subordinated Structure When Subordinated Piece Is Credit Tranched

The diagram below illustrates a senior-subordinated shifting-interest structure with a 6.0% subordinate piece that was tranched into various credit ratings. The "A" classes (A1, A2, A3 *etc.)* represent the senior bonds and pay sequentially. As you can see from the cash-flow diagram, the subordinate bonds are outstanding for the life of the deal, assuming a no-loss scenario.

Allocation of Losses

Realized losses will be allocated:

- First to the 0.45% first-loss piece until its principal balance is reduced to zero.

- Thereafter, losses will be allocated to Class B5 until its principal balance is reduced to zero.

- Then to Class B4 until its principal balance is reduced to zero and so on up the credit-rating curve until Class B1's principal balance is reduced to zero.

- Only then would the senior class' (the triple-A rated piece) principal decline due to losses.

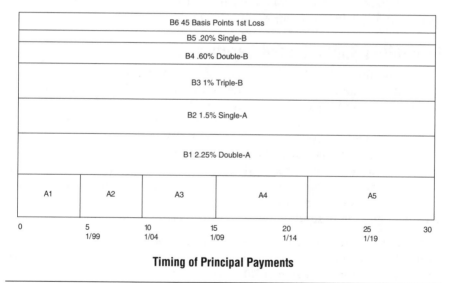

Timing of Principal Payments

institutions to sell the subordinated class as well as the senior class. This development has greatly expanded the market for subordinated CMO classes.

As the subordinated class or classes act as a form of loss protection to the senior classes, it is said to be an asset with leveraged credit risk. Investors are attracted to subordinated securities because of their potential for higher returns as compensation for the associated higher credit risk. Depending on the structure of individual transactions, a subordinated bond will be assigned either a public or private rating.

Subordinated classes are said to "de-lever" themselves through seasoning, inflation and principal payment, with seasoning and inflation leading to greater homeowner equity. The additional equity reduces both the probability and severity of any default that may occur. The principal prepayment component serves to decrease the ownership interest of the senior class, causing the subordinated class' ownership to rise due to the shifting-interest structure. Subordinated securities allow investors in search of added yield a method of fine tuning the degree of risk they wish to assume. Each type of subordinated security has its own risk/return profile. The factors that determine a subordinated security's profile include:

- Its placement within the senior/subordinated structure.

- The type of protection it provides the more senior classes.

- The characteristics of the collateral backing the issue.

While all of these factors are integral to subordinated security performance, perhaps the most important is the underlying collateral.

Evaluating Subordinated Certificates

In the subordinated MBS marketplace, sophisticated investors should evaluate closely the collateral backing the issue as it is the subordinated bond that carries the weight of prepayments, defaults, and foreclosures. When evaluating a subordinated security, there are a number of data sources that must be included in one's analysis. On the loan level, these include statistics on delinquency and foreclosure rates, the percentage of real estate owned (REO) and the level of losses experienced to date, as well as the current seasoning of the portfolio, which will provide the needed information to create an expected default and loss curve for the portfolio. Another important consideration is the dollar amount of funds advanced by the servicer on delinquent loans.

Types and Coverage of Loan-Level Credit Enhancements: Regardless of the form of credit enhancement used in securitization, the underlying mortgages are covered by a standard-hazard policy before they are securitized. Coverage for mortgagor bankruptcy, special hazard and fraud may or may not be required depending on the type of credit enhancement used in the structure of the issue. Should it be determined that these added credit enhancements are needed in order to securitize the mortgage pool (and assuming that the individual mortgages in the pool are not already so covered), either the mortgage originator or the issuer of the security may in fact provide complete pool coverage. These types of coverage can take the form of additional insurance, letters of credit, surety bonds, or cash reserves.

1. Standard-Hazard Insurance. Mortgage originators generally require mortgagors to maintain a standard-hazard insurance policy that usually covers damage or destruction due to fire, lightning, explosion, smoke, windstorm, hail, riot, strike, and civil commotion. Claims are subject to certain conditions and exclusions stipulated in each policy. Most standard-hazard policies do not provide coverage for damage resulting from floods and earthquakes, as well as a number of other hazards.

2. Homeowner's Insurance. Many mortgagors also carry homeowner's insurance policies, which, in addition to standard-hazard insurance, provide coverage for certain other risks. Mortgage originators generally require the homeowner to carry insurance of a specific percentage (usually 80% to 90%) of the full replacement value of the improvements on the property in order to fully recover on any partial loss. It should be pointed out that when insurers refer to "improvements" on the property, the property is defined as "the house." There are different percentages that the coverage can and cannot decline to, and different amounts of liabilities that the insurer potentially can be responsible for; however, these vary from policy to policy.

3. Bankruptcy Insurance. In order to avoid bankruptcy risk, which could take place when, under certain personal bankruptcy filings, a judge orders a modification of the mortgage loan's interest rate or a reduction in its principal amount, an amount of bankruptcy coverage is required. Usually a bond is set aside by the issuer in an amount that is derived from the mortgage-pool characteristics.

Under the Bankruptcy Code of 1978, as amended, individuals filing for Chapter 13 bankruptcy are protected from unsecured creditors. However, the Code specifically exempts claims secured by the primary residence of the borrower. Unless the form of credit enhancement protects investors from mortgagor bankruptcy, S&P's, for example, will require a non-restorable bankruptcy bond in the amount of $100,000 to cover delays in receipt of payment from borrowers who have filed under Chapter 13. This amount applies to pools with only first-lien mortgages on single-family primary residences. Pools with vacation homes, two-to-four family homes, or property held for investment, which are considered to be more risky, require additional coverage (usually the greater of 1% of the unpaid principal balance of all non-primary residential loans or the amount of the largest such loan) since these properties are not primary residences and are therefore not exempt under the Code.

4. Special-Hazard Insurance. A separate special-hazard insurance policy is required when the form of credit enhancement does not protect the investor from the risk of loss due to physical damage that is not sufficiently mitigated by standard-hazard insurance. Special-hazard insurance usually covers loss due to earthquakes, mud slides, and floods, as well as the application of coinsurance by the standard-hazard insurer. Usually, the amount of special-hazard insurance coverage is equal to 1% of the balance of the loans in the pool, but it may be higher if loan balances are large or the loans are concentrated geographically. The amount of coverage will be reduced by the losses experienced by the special-hazard insurer.

5. Fraud Coverage. When the form of credit enhancement does not protect the investor from losses due to suspected fraud or misrepresentation in preparation of the loan application, separate fraud coverage must be obtained. Rating agencies assume that fraud risk is highest at the time of the loan origination through year five of the mortgage seasoning. Mechanisms that the issuer can provide to ensure payment stability in the event of fraud are advanced claims endorsements to the pool policy, cash reserves, or performance bonds, which are calculated by taking one-third the calculated foreclosure frequency and multiplying it by the monthly mortgage constant times 18 months.

Impact of Mortgage Defaults on Subordinated Securities: When collateral pools experience high levels of defaults and predominantly full recoveries on liquidated properties, the average lives of the subordinated securities will contract. As subordinated securities are purchased at a discount, the shortened average life will serve to improve yield performance. However, if defaults are high and recovery is poor, the subordinated MBSs will experience yield declines. Of note, the issuer/servicer has the right to enact a clean-up call on the transaction if the remaining balance of the mortgage portfolio is less than 10% of the portfolio's original balance. Such a call will shorten the average life of the subordinated bonds.

Average-Life Stability

A less obvious advantage of the subordinated security is its potential for more stable average lives. As noted earlier, one of the better used credit enhancements is the senior/subordinated shifting-interest structure. In this structure, 100% of the prepayments on the mortgage pool are used to pay down the senior classes for a stated time period (usually 5 years for fixed-rate collateral and 10 years for adjustable-rate collateral). After the initial prepayment lockout, a smaller percentage of the pro-rata share of the subordinated class' prepayments is paid to the senior class. Each issue has its own step-down schedule, which eventually reduces the prepayment percentage to pro-rata.

In effect, the prepayment lockout feature prevents the subordinated class from receiving any principal payments other than its pro-rata share of scheduled principal payments. In fact, the principal cash flow of the subordi-nated security stays almost exactly the same regardless of the prepayment speed on the underlying mortgage pool during this period, assuming no defaults and that the senior class has not been retired.

Thus, while subordinated certificates are initially subject to a high level of credit risk, they are shielded from prepayment risk for a time. The acceler-ated principal pay-down on the senior certificates tends to increase the aver-age-life volatility of the subordinated certificates in terms of credit risk, but decreases the amount of senior certificates enhanced by the subordinated cer-tificates. Stated another way, as the mortgage portfolio amortizes and the sub-ordinated certificate balance remains constant (except for scheduled distribu-tions), the subordinated certificates are enhancing a decreasing principal amount of senior certificates. The decrease in the credit-enhancement lever-age should be viewed positively by subordinate certificate holders when the amount of expected losses that may occur in the future due to lower expected loss amounts is considered.

Prepayment Interest Shortfall

Investors should determine whether or not provisions are made for prepay-ment interest shortfall when purchasing a subordinated certificate. When a mortgagor prepays a mortgage in full, the principal amount may be accom-panied by less than the full 30 days of interest. In some cases, the servicer may offer its monthly servicing fee in an attempt to subsidize the prepayment interest shortfall; if the servicing fee is less than the prepayment interest shortfall, the shortfall will be distributed pro-rata among both the senior and subordinated classes.

Relative Value of Subordinated Certificates

As the structured non-agency market has grown, so has the subordinated securities market. When spreads on rated subordinated classes are compared to similarly rated corporate bonds, the yield pickup is substantial (see Exhibit 11). Since 1993, investors have shown an increased willingness to extend fur-ther down the rating curve. While the single-A and triple-B subordinated classes have always enjoyed sound sponsorship, it was just recently that new players began to focus on the double- and single-B classes.

Since 1992, a number of methodologies have been introduced to better analyze the value of credit-sensitive securities such as subordinated classes. The Public Securities Association (PSA) adopted a Standard Default Assump-tion (SDA) for use in analyzing (among other securities) subordinated MBS classes. The SDA attempts to standardize market assumptions about the pat-tern of mortgage-loan defaults, with defaults assumed to occur at some

Exhibit 11. Comparative Analysis: 10-Year Corporate vs. Subordinated MBS

Rating	Subordinated MBS Spreads (BPs.)	Corporate Bond (30-Yr. Indust.) Spreads (BPs.)
AA	+150	+53
A	+175	+62
BBB	+220	+94
BB	+425	9.5% Yield
B	+550	10.5% Yield
Unrated	$25-$30	11-13% Yield

Source: Prudential Securities' IMPACT database as of July 29, 1994.

chosen multiple of the path established by a standard default curve.[6] This concept is not unlike the PSA seasoning curve for prepayments. The idea is that combining the projections of the SDA and PSA curves, using a multiple of SDA together with a multiple of PSA, will convey to investors the exact default and prepayment assumptions that are being used to analyze a credit-sensitive MBS.

Armed with improved default information, several Wall Street firms have developed methodologies for evaluating yields and OASs on these securities from a credit-adjusted standpoint.[7] The upshot is that investors now have a much broader arsenal of tools for evaluating these securities, a fact that has led to growth in this market. Moreover, in terms of relative value versus the corporate sector, these tools allow for a more "apples-to-apples" comparison.

Generally speaking, investors in subordinated classes assume more credit risk than most whole-loan mortgage participants due to the fact that any losses that result from the underlying collateral are concentrated in the subordinated securities. However, for this added risk, investors in these securities are treated to discount prices.

While the universe of investors in subordinated classes has grown within the last few years, the current, heightened regulatory and capital environment has dampened the appetite of some of the more traditional in-

---

6 Nancy Olson, *PSA Releases a Standard Default Assumption Curve: An Effort To Standardize Analysis of Credit-Sensitive MBSs,* Financial Strategies Group, Prudential Securities Incorporated, May 25, 1993.

7 Nancy Olson and Warren Xia, *Evaluation of Credit-Sensitive Mortgage Securities: Credit Adjusted Yields and OASs,* Financial Strategies Group, Prudential Securities Incorporated, September 1993.

vestors in this product. Moreover, many buyers of structured securities are constrained by regulatory or capital requirements and are restricted to buying triple-A or double-A rated paper only. Subordinated certificates are non-ERISA eligible and thus the non-investment-grade classes are frequently offered as a private placement under section 144-A; investment-grade classes are allowed to be offered publicly.

Traditional investors in the subordinated MBS marketplace include insurance companies and pension funds (longer-duration, credit-oriented investment), mutual funds (due to their current yield focus and need to outperform specified indices), money managers (due to their growing liquidity), yield-oriented buyers, and speculators who believe spreads are likely to tighten as the supply of mortgage collateral drops off from the heady levels seen in 1992 and 1993.

While the insurance industry once represented the subordinated MBS market's largest investor base, continued insurance industry capital constraints have curtailed insurance industry participation to some extent. In the place of the insurance companies have come the non-capital-constrained investors, such as money managers and high-yield funds, which have reaped the benefits of the current regulatory environment and purchased some of these securities at extremely attractive yield spreads. Of note, many buyers of subordinated certificates believe that the rating agencies overestimate the amount of subordinated protection that is needed to support a triple-A rating, thus leaving valuable cash flows on the table.

Creativity in Subordinated Classes

The creation of structuring alternatives that enhance investor comfort in obtaining cash flows from subordinated interests has served to expand the investor base for such classes. Since about 1992, underwriters have become more creative with the way they tranche the subordinate structure. Typically, the subordinated classes in a senior/subordinated structure are pro-rata paying bonds with various credit ratings. Generally speaking and depending on the overall issue size and the amounts of each class that can be economically created, the subordinated piece is carved into several tranches that carry the following ratings (S&P's and Fitch): AA, A, BBB, BB, and B; in addition, there is usually an unrated first-loss piece.

Scheduled principal is applied to the bonds in a pro-rata manner and losses are applied starting from the first-loss piece and working their way from the lower rated bonds up. Often times, the class sizes are so small that they are referred to as "odd lots," which can be difficult for trading desks to market and sell. The main reason for this is the way these odd lots behave under loss scenarios: because of their size, losses cause their cash flows to shorten dramatically and thus provide the investor with a much lower yield. To counteract this, the cash flows of two different-rated tranches are often combined bearing the lower credit rating of the two.

Let's look at an example of such a combination. Assume that Fitch required a subordination level of 5% on a $100 million REMIC issue. The subordinated class would be tranched in the following manner: a 2% double-A piece, a 1% single-A piece, a 1% triple-B piece, a 40-basis-point double-B piece, a 50-basis-point double-B piece, a 10-basis-point single-B piece, and a 50-basis-point first-loss piece. However, difficulty may arise in trying to sell a $100,000 single-B rated bond. Thus, the cash flows of the 40-basis-point double-B piece would be combined with the 10-basis-point single-B piece in order to create a 50-basis-point bond that would carry a single-B rating.

CHAPTER 24

Understanding and Valuing Mortgage Security Credit

Nancy DeLiban
Managing Director
Bear Stearns & Co., Inc.

Brian P. Lancaster
Managing Director
Bear Stearns & Co., Inc.

INTRODUCTION

In the 1980s and continuing into the 1990s, securitization replaced traditional borrowings and in many cases became the chief funding mechanism for many financial institutions. By securitizing and selling assets a financial institution decreases capital requirements, raises money, and reduces credit and interest-rate risk.

Of all asset classes, mortgage debt has been the most frequently securitized. Total U.S. mortgage debt outstanding at the end of 1993 totaled in excess of $4.2 trillion, about $1.7 trillion of which has been securitized. By contrast, at the end of March $800 billion of consumer installment debt was outstanding, $116 billion of which was securitized.

To date, most mortgage-backed securities have been insured by a government agency or an affiliated government agency (about $1.3 trillion) such as GNMA, FHLMC, and FNMA. In order to become eligible for inclusion into an agency securitization program, the underlying mortgage assets must meet certain guidelines, such as a maximum current balance limit (currently $203,150), delinquency rates (no delinquencies in the last 12 months), and documentation standards (full and complete). Underlying mortgages passing these tests are referred to as "conforming mortgages." However, house price inflation during the 1980s, the creation of a plethora of mortgages by originators jockeying for market share, and the Resolution Trust

Corporation's (RTC) need to quickly securitize the unusual mortgage assets of bankrupt thrifts led to massive growth in the non-conforming or non-agency market and the creation of credit-enhancement techniques. The purpose of this chapter is to explain mortgage security credit and how to value it. Although we focus on the techniques used in the single-family market, most are also used in the burgeoning commercial and multifamily markets.

EVOLUTION OF CREDIT ENHANCEMENT TECHNIQUES

Credit-enhancement techniques in the non-agency mortgage security market have evolved along with the growth in the market's size and sophistication. Prior to 1991, the amount of non-conforming or whole-loan mortgages securitized was moderate. Lacking a government agency guarantee, most whole-loan MBSs, were credit-enhanced by corporate guarantees, letters of credit (LOCs), surety bonds, pool insurance, spread accounts, and/or reserve funds instead of the subordinate classes which are common today. After its introduction in 1986, the senior/subordinate transaction gained a small share of the market. However, under then prevailing familiarity and regulations, it was difficult for investors, outside of banks and insurance companies, to purchase the credit risk associated with subordinate tranches. More importantly, the lack of performance information, liquidity, familiarization, and ratings made the purchase of subordinates unappealing for most investors, thereby forcing issuers to retain the first-loss position or obtain some form of insurance. In addition, because most transactions were sold privately during the 1970s and early 1980s, revealing and accurate long-term performance information has become available only recently.

BASIC TYPES OF CREDIT ENHANCEMENT
Corporate Guarantees

A corporate guarantee is an obligation of a third party to cover mortgage losses. It may cover all losses of an entire issue without limit or just a portion. Corporate guarantees are often written to cover all losses regardless of whether they are from fraud, bankruptcy, or special hazards. The security generally assumes the rating of the corporation, and as such changes in the credit rating of the guarantor are likely to affect the issue's rating. A buffer of credit protection in the form of a spread account or subordinated bond usually absorbs losses before the corporate guarantee is activated.

Letter of Credit (LOC)

An LOC is written by a financial institution which may be drawn upon, as agreed upon, by the trustee. The security generally assumes the rating of the LOC provider. Another party is responsible to pay the financial institution for any draws on the LOC. An LOC may be used to credit-enhance an entire deal or to cover a particular type of risk. However, additional insurance must be obtained to cover losses due to bankruptcy, fraud, and special hazards which are usually not covered by LOCs.

The major credit-rating agencies on average require a 6.5% LOC for fixed-rate collateral and a 12% LOC for ARMs. This may vary considerably depending on the underlying credit quality of the collateral. The issuer of the LOC must have a rating at least as high or higher than that of the security. If the issuer is downgraded, the rating of the security may be placed in jeopardy. The security could be put on credit watch until the rating agencies can review the defaults and performance of the collateral of the security to determine if the security should be downgraded or its rating maintained. If the agency decides that the rating should be downgraded, it may be restored through a new LOC or a cash injection by the original issuer of the LOC.

Pool Policies

A pool policy is simply an insurance policy. The mortgages must be under-written in accordance with the provider's guidelines. The policy covers losses by reason of default in an amount specified, not covered by primary mort-gage insurance. The master servicer presents claims to the pool insurer, who upon satisfaction of certain conditions will cover the claim. The pool gener-ally assumes the rating of the insurer.

Mortgage pool insurers typically do not cover losses arising from mort-gagor bankruptcy, special hazards, or fraud. Additional coverage for these risks is required. Pool insurance is usually relatively easy to understand as the credit risk and ratings of the securities are derived from the insurer. How-ever, the extent to which potential downgradings of the insurer will impact the securities also depends on the collateral of the security.

Surety Bonds

A surety bond is a 100% guarantee on all scheduled payments of principal and interest. It differs from other types of insurance because there is no loss limit.

Reserve Funds

Reserve funds, spread accounts, and senior/subordinate structures differ from insured deals in that they actually have cash to protect the bonds. Reserve funds may be funded with an initial deposit and/or ongoing depos-its as required by the rating agencies. They are often funded over time by excess interest on the collateral. Excess interest, or excess spread, is the interest generated by a loan that is greater than the pass-through rate, servicing fees, and any fees of a structured transaction that are paid out of interest.[1] If a reserve fund is funded exclusively by excess interest, it is typically called a spread account.

Spread Accounts

Spread accounts became increasingly popular following passage of the Financial Institutions Reform, Recovery, and Enforcement Act (FIRREA) of 1989. Issuers of whole-loan securities had historically held the subordinated piece of a senior/subordinated structure; however, the FIRREA significantly raised the amount of capital banks would have to hold. In response, banks began to sell the subordinated pieces using excess servicing to credit-enhance these junior bonds. Since the credit enhancement is coming from a strip of excess servicing, the amount available depends on the prepayment speed of the underlying collateral.

Spread accounts are often used in conjunction with other forms of credit enhancement, such as LOCs, to enhance an entire deal or a specific risk. If the spread account is in a first-loss position, losses flow to it until it is exhausted and only then to the LOC or other form of enhancement.

Senior/Subordinate Structures

Senior/subordinate structures are designed to protect the senior bonds at the expense of the subordinates. Each structure is divided into two pieces, a senior tranche and a subordinate one. The amount of each tranche is determined by the rating agencies. Losses are first allocated to the subordinates. In addition, the cash due the subordinates is often used to maintain the liquidity of the seniors.

The most common form of senior/subordinate structure is a senior/subordinate structure with shifting of prepayments (also called a shifting-interest structure). Shifting of prepayments occurs from taking the pro-rata share of prepayments due the subordinates and applying them to accelerate the amortization of the seniors. The prepayment lockouts to the subordinates follow a schedule derived by the rating agency, dependent on the size of subordination and the credit quality of the collateral. The typical schedule for a fixed-rate, single-family mortgage is a 100% prepayment lockout to the subordinates for 5 years, then declining to 70%, 60%, 40%, and 20%, respectively for each year thereafter for 1 year (see Exhibit 1). Because of the greater credit risk of adjustable-rate mortgages, prepayments are typically locked out 100% for 10 years or until the original percent doubles, only shifting to the subordinate investors according to the slower schedule. The prepayment lock-

---

1 "Spread Account Criteria for Mortgage Pass-throughs," *Standard and Poor's Creditweek*, February 1991.

Exhibit 1. Typical Prepayment Lockout Schedule

Fixed-Rate Mortgages		Adjustable-Rate Mortgages	
% of Prepayments Locked Out	Number of Years	% of Prepayments Locked Out	Number of Years
100%	5 years	100%	10 years
70%	1 year	80%	1 year
60%	1 year	60%	1 year
40%	1 year	40%	1 year
20%	1 year	20%	1 year
0%	maturity	0%	maturity

outs may be affected by delinquencies and/or losses. After this, the prepayment lockout diminishes and the subordinates receive their pro-rata share of prepayments. By shifting prepayments in this manner the ratio of the subordinate piece to the senior bonds increases, initially corresponding to the early typical rise in losses and delinquencies as mortgage collateral seasons. However, as time passes and loss levels begin to stabilize, the subordinate tranches can begin to be paid down. Thus the shifting of prepayments technique requires less up-front subordination, making the deal more economically efficient while at the same time protecting the investor in the senior bonds.

Other Risks

Besides credit risks, there are other risks associated with mortgages that are typically insured against or sold within a bond. These include special hazard, bankruptcy, and fraud. Special hazard policies protect the bonds from loss by reason of special hazards, which may include such hazards as earthquakes, vandalism of unoccupied homes, mud slides, volcanic activity, and to a lesser extent, tidal waves and floods (in non-federally-designated flood areas) not covered by standard hazard insurance or flood insurance. Bankruptcy covers losses resulting from proceedings under the federal bankruptcy code whereby a federal court reduces schedule loan payments, interest, and/or principal due on the mortgage. Fraud/mortgage repurchase covers fraud or negligence in origination and servicing of the mortgage, including misrepresentation and breach of warranties by mortgagor or originator.

Representations and warranties are an obligation of the originator or servicer to repurchase any such loan. The insurance covers losses on loans the seller will not repurchase. Using insurance for non-credit-related risk is common, although many deals have included special hazard bonds or subordinate bonds which cover all types of risk.

In the current environment, the subordinates' liability is usually limited to some specified amount, the *carve-out*. Carve-outs often exist for special hazards, bankruptcy, and fraud. Losses in excess of carve-outs are applied pro-rata either among the subordinates alone or among the senior and subordinate tranches.

EARLY PROBLEMS HINDERING GROWTH OF THE MARKET

These early credit-enhancement structures faced many problems, most of which resulted from the cost of achieving a AAA or AA rating and the risk associated with a potential downgrading. At the time, there were not many corporations, financial institutions, or insurers with a AAA rating. As a result, the elite few could charge high premiums, and therefore most deals were structured with only a AA rating, limiting the potential investor base for whole-loan-backed securities. In addition, the market for senior/subordinate securities was not yet developed, so the cost of selling the subordinate tranches could be quite expensive, thereby raising the all-in cost of the transaction. Securities enhanced by reserve funds and spread accounts also faced problems. Reserve funds require that cash flows be reinvested at low rates similar to fed funds while still covering the cost of a higher-yielding bond, resulting in a high cost of carry. The rating agencies did not (and still do not) give much credit for spread accounts, making them very expensive. As a result, issuers retained either some portion or all of the subordinates that they thought were undervalued by the market, found an insurance company to buy some or all of the subordinate bonds, usually as a private placement, or paid up for an insurance policy.

BURGEONING OF THE MARKET

By 1991, the continual bull market and the active solicitation of refinancings by highly competitive mortgage bankers led to an explosion in prepayments and issuance. Non-agency mortgage securitization hit new highs in 1991 and continued at a record pace through 1993 (see Exhibit 2).

It was not until 1991 that the market saw a dramatic increase in the economic and structural efficiency of credit-enhanced transactions. At that time, the majority of deals used either General Electric Mortgage Insurance Corp. (GEMICO) pool insurance or a senior/subordinate structure, since the price execution of these alternatives was very close.

THE RISE OF THE SUPER SENIOR STRUCTURE

As with most developing markets, as the structural efficiency of the transactions increased, so did the popularity of senior/subordinated structures.

Exhibit 2.   Burgeoning of the Whole-Loan Market

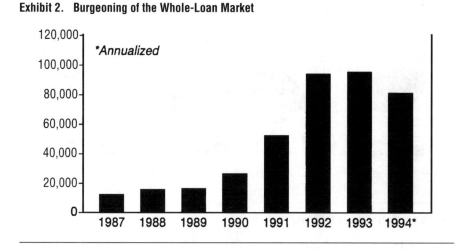

However, in 1991, there were still many investors who did not feel comfortable with the credit risk of non-agency mortgage securities and believed the rating agency requirements might be insufficient. This gave rise to the super senior structure, whereby an additional credit layer was stripped from the senior tranches and used as subordination (see Exhibit 3). Since the remaining, regular AAA senior bonds retained the original subordination behind them, they generally maintained the same rating. Clearly, a case can be made that these mezzanine bonds were more risky than the original seniors, since if subordination levels were inaccurate, additional losses could be concentrated in a small sector. To address this concern, a "credit wrap" by the Financial Security Assurance Holdings Co. Ltd. (FSA) was placed around the AAA-rated regular seniors or AA-rated mezzanines in super senior structures (see Exhibit 4). Although the FSA wrap acted much like a pool policy, the guarantee was on a specified bond(s) rather than the entire pool of mortgages (compare with Exhibit 10).

In addition to addressing investor concerns regarding subordination levels, the super senior structure also became popular as a defensive mechanism to protect senior-rated bonds against the downgrading of a third-party credit enhancer. The added value of this approach became apparent in 1992 when Primary Mortgage Insurance Co. (PMI) was temporarily downgraded after the hurricane in Florida.

Super senior tranches may also prove their worth in periods where prepayments are slow. With a shifting-interest structure, the faster the prepayment rate, the quicker the ratio of the subordinate tranche increases relative to that of the senior tranche, thus improving the credit enhancement of the

Exhibit 3.   Growth of the Senior/Subordinated Structure

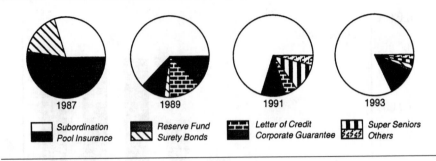

Exhibit 4.   Super Senior Structure

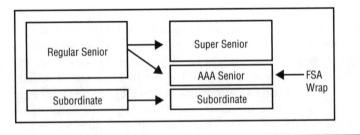

senior tranche. For example, in 1993, 63 MBS were upgraded by Moody's.[2] The upgrades stemmed from increased protection levels resulting from fast prepayments which were allocated almost exclusively to the senior tranches. As prepayments slow, the opposite effect will occur (see Exhibit 5). A period of fast prepayments followed by slow prepayments also tends to reduce the credit quality of the remaining collateral as homeowners in better financial situations tend to prepay before others.[3] Super seniors are designed not only to have increased protection against losses but also to provide protection against a downgrading. Downgrading can be very expensive even if losses do not occur. For example, a AA-rated security generally trades 15–30 basis points wider than a comparable AAA-rated one.

---

2 Moody's also downgraded 62 structures primarily because of declining collateral credit quality.
3 Higher incomes, lower loan-to-value (LTV) ratios.

Exhibit 5.   Impact of Prepayments on Percent Subordination Level

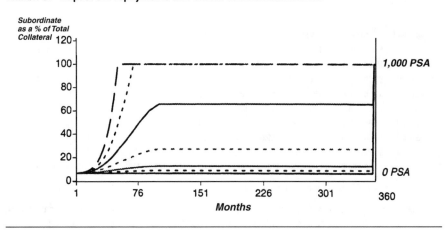

DOMINANCE OF THE SENIOR/SUBORDINATE STRUCTURE

The market witnessed a relatively large increase in the cost of pool insurance in the beginning of 1992, primarily a result of general loss experience in California and several other states. Also in 1992, new SEC regulations allowing subordinates rated BBB and above to be included as publicly traded securities contributed to increased liquidity of the subordinates. As a result, the market began to further credit tranche the subordinates with the percentage of senior/sub deals increasing to 83% (see Exhibit 6). The total subordinate tranche was typically divided into a small, unrated bond, followed by B-rated, BB-rated, BBB-rated, A-rated, and AA-rated securities.

These changes, along with reduced loss expectations in the higher-rated subordinates and better analytics, assisted in attracting new buyers. This new acceptance and confidence in the evaluation of credit risk was most evident in the BBB-rated sector and above. Investor participation in the non-agency mortgage sector was further spurred on as the bull market caused many investors to consider alternative investments to increase yield and provide prepayment protection. Mortgage funds, hedge funds, and foreign investors began to join insurance companies in buying the credit risk embedded in the subordinates. Confidence was further increased when in 1993 S&P dramatically reduced the amount of subordination necessary to achieve a AAA-rating. Given the new investors, increased volume, more extensive historical data, and lower interest rates, total execution on subordinate tranches increased substantially (by about 10 percentage points for new origination current coupon securities) from the levels achieved three years earlier.

Exhibit 6. Private-Label MBS Production by Enhancement

Credit Enhancement	1987		1988		1989		1990		1991		1992**		1993	
Subordination	$3.30	30%	$12.87	79%	$8.89	62%	$12.09	49%	$38.40	70%	$43.38	48%	$81.57	83%
Pool Insurance	$0.00	0%	$0.63	4%	$1.44	10%	$5.68	23%	$5.11	10%	$25.14	28%	$10.56	11%
Reserve Fund	$0.00	0%	$0.00	0%	$0.00	0%	$0.00	0%	$0.00	0%	$15.12	17%	$1.17	1%
Surety Bonds	$1.95	18%	$0.64	4%	$0.31	2%	$1.10	4%	$0.12	0%	$1.40	2%	$1.62	2%
Letter of Credit	$0.00	0%	$0.00	0%	$1.89	13%	$3.76	15%	$2.45	5%	$0.97	1%	$0.00	0%
Corp. Guaranty	$5.85	53%	$2.11	13%	$1.71	12%	$0.64	3%	$0.15	0%	$0.00	0%	$0.00	0%
Super-Senior*	$0.00	0%	$0.00	0%	$0.00	0%	$0.00	0%	$5.26	11%	$2.61	3%	$1.83	2%
Other	$0.00	0%	$0.00	0%	$0.00	0%	$1.17	5%	$1.81	4%	$0.86	1%	$1.76	2%
Totals	**$11.10**	**100%**	**$15.85**	**100%**	**$14.24**	**100%**	**$24.43**	**100%**	**$49.71**	**100%**	**$89.47**	**100%**	**$98.49**	**100%**

* Securities enhanced by pool insurance and subordination are included, causing those categories to be understated.

** In 1992, many Resolution Trust Corp. (RTC) deals were credit-enhanced by both reserve funds and subordination or pool insurance. These deals are classified under the reserve fund and pool insurance category.

SUPERIOR CONVEXITY CHARACTERISTICS OF SUBORDINATES

In a market plagued by rapid prepayments, the extra call protection offered by subordinates in a shifting-interest structure was also a key factor in their growth and their lower all-in transaction costs. As a result, AA-rated mezzanine tranches often traded tighter than a AAA-rated plain vanilla tranche of equal average life. This is because the shifting-interest structure reduced their prepayment risk. Shifting-interest structures work by directing all collateral prepayments to the senior bonds without paying down a pro-rata amount of the subordinates for a period of time (typically 5 years for fixed-rate mortgages, 10 years for ARMs). This causes higher levels of subordination to build up over time as senior bonds are paid off by prepayments while the subordinate tranches are not.

A graphic illustration of the way the shifting-interest structure would impact the subordinates' principal cash flows is shown in Exhibit 7. Because prepayments are locked out and shifted away from the subordinates for the first five years, the amount of principal paid out is fixed for the first five years across a wide range of prepayment scenarios. Although the principal balance outstanding after the lockout would be affected by changes in prepayment speed, the lockout would greatly dampen the overall average life variability of the bond.

In marked contrast, the impact of changing prepayments is shown on the same average-life, 7-year senior class (see Exhibit 8). Here, principal paydowns change both at the beginning and end of the principal payment win-

Exhibit 7.   Principal Paydowns of a 7-Year Senior Subordinate Tranche

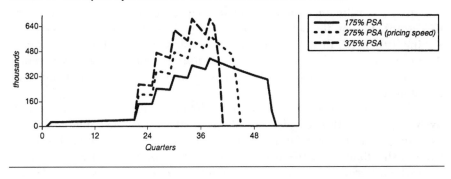

Exhibit 8.   Principal Paydowns of a 7-Year Senior Tranche

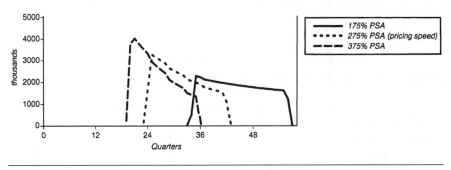

dow. In fact, average-life instability is magnified because of the transfer of all prepayment risk for a period of time.

The side effect of this credit-enhancement technique, which is common to all subordinate pieces, is to reduce significantly their negative convexity (the risk of the duration of a bond changing when it is least desired) and average-life variability. Exhibit 9 shows how the average lives of the two 7-year securities, the senior tranche and the subordinate tranche, compare. The average life of the subordinate tranche at a pricing speed of, for example, 275% PSA would be 7.84 years, about one month shorter than that of the senior tranche. However, in this example, the average life of the subordinate tranche shortens by only about one-half of a year as compared with a shortening of 1.8 years for the senior tranche if prepayments rose to 400% PSA. Similar stability would hold at slower speeds. The subordinate tranche extends by only about one-half of a year as compared to an extension of two years for the senior tranche if prepayments slow to 200% PSA.

A credit-enhancement technique which utilizes both insurance and a senior/subordinate structure is called a *credit certificate*. A standard non-credit tranched subordinate obtains an insurance policy from GE similar to an FSA wrap whereby the subordinate would collect for any credit losses (see Exhibit 10). If GE or an alternative insurer is downgraded, only the subordinate would be affected. The senior bonds respond exactly as a senior tranche in a regular senior/subordinate structure, *i.e.*, they have no additional protection.

The investor should note when evaluating these bonds that the relatively small subordinate (5%–8% of the deal in a single-family, fixed-rate structure) collects for defaults on the entire pool. Because the subordinate collects shortfalls from the insurer, losses act as prepayments, even during the lockout period. Thus, a 1% annual default on collateral with a 6.5% subordinate is equivalent to a 14.4% CPP to the subordinate. Making a speed adjustment for defaults is very important when evaluating these bonds, even when they are in their lockout period.

Exhibit 9. Convexity Characteristics of Senior and Subordinate Tranches

		PSA	100 PSA	150 PSA	200 PSA	275 PSA	350 PSA	400 PSA	500 PSA
Subordinate	Duration	6.46	6.05	5.78	5.51	5.32	5.22	5.05
Tranche	Avg. Life	10.12	9.07	8.44	7.84	7.45	7.25	6.93
Senior	Duration	8.20	7.33	6.54	5.54	5.02	4.58	3.92
Tranche	Avg. Life	15.03	12.24	10.15	7.93	6.91	6.11	5.00

Exhibit 10. Creation of Credit Certificates

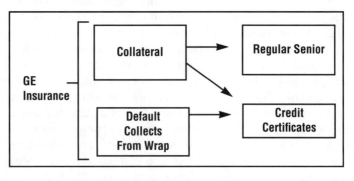

INFLUENCE OF THE RTC: THE REVIVAL OF PASS-FORWARDS AND RESERVE FUNDS

In 1991, the Resolution Trust Corporation began to liquidate the mortgage portfolios of troubled thrifts. Since most of these loans were below market, of sub-standard credit quality, or serviced by too many servicers for accurate reporting, senior bond execution was enhanced by reviving old techniques. The most common of these were pass-forwards and reserve funds. Because the interest only (IO) market for these securities was not developed, selling the IO at market levels was prohibitive. The rating agencies gave little credit for putting the IO in the first-loss position (as a spread account) because at fast prepayments speeds the IO offers little or no protection. One solution to this problem was to use the IO to accelerate the pay-down of the bonds. This tends to mitigate the bonds' sensitivities to changes in prepayments. When prepayments slow, the cash flow derived from the IO increases, offsetting extension; when prepayments increase, the cash flow derived from the IO decreases (see Exhibit 11). The increased stability helped improve execution of the senior bonds.

Also, using interest to pay principal causes overcollateralization because the bonds pay down more quickly than the underlying collateral. As shown in Exhibit 12, the amount of the collateral balance outstanding over time (the solid line) greatly increases relative to the certificate balance outstanding (the dashed line). The difference between the two curves at any time is equal to the excess interest being passed forward. The ratio of the two is shown in the figure on the right. The rating agencies allowed the overcollateralization to replace subordination. In many RTC deals, the IO was used to

Exhibit 11. Sample Pass-Forward Structure

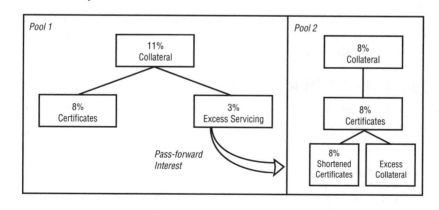

Exhibit 12.   Pass-Forward in RTC 1991—M6 B4

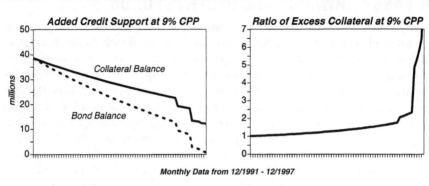

Monthly Data from 12/1991 - 12/1997

pay-down the principal of the subordinates. Once the bonds are retired, the overcollateralization is released to the residual holder.

The RTC deals also helped revive the use of reserve funds. Although reserve funds are typically uneconomical in the efficient single-family market, they were quite necessary in the RTC deals. The market levels required to sell a subordinate in the first-loss position backed by non-generic or high-risk collateral was, like the IO, prohibitive. However, since the RTC was not allowed to own anything with recourse, it utilized reserve funds instead of a retained, first-loss subordinate tranche. These reserves were held by the RTC.

The RTC also played an important role in market development by increasing the number of deals backed by multiple types of collateral. Many RTC deals included fixed and adjustable mortgages as well as single-family, commercial, and multifamily mortgages. Typically a separate reserve fund was required for each collateral grouping dependent on the inherent risk of the collateral.

In most of the RTC structures, the senior cash flows and reserve funds were more or less segregated by collateral groups. However, the subordinates were often used to cross-collateralize from one group to another.[4]

LOWER CREDIT QUALITY MORTGAGES

The success of selling higher risk collateral gave rise to selling non-conforming, non-performing, or delinquent collateral called "A," "B," "C," and "D"

---

4 The rating agencies use a worst-case scenario to determine when cash could be released to the subordinates. Typically cross-collateralization does not make economic sense unless the supporting collateral is at a lower price on average than the collateral being replaced. This is because the rating agencies place minimal value on interest earned by the subordinates.

paper. "A" paper consists of mortgages without delinquencies which would generally conform to agency standards if their loan balances were not too large. "B" and "C" mortgages are made to borrowers with some incriminating mark on their credit history, such as one or a few 30- to 60-day delinquencies. "C" paper may have a few to several 30-day delinquencies or one 90-day delinquency. Borrowers who are constantly delinquent or have a default on their record are classified as "D" paper (see Exhibit 13).

Lower quality paper has the advantage of having more stable prepayment characteristics. Irrespective of rates, these borrowers have a much harder time refinancing. Multiple refinancings spurred by the no point/no fee phenomenon seen in 1993 for higher quality mortgages do not occur. Lower quality borrowers are charged much higher up-front costs in the form of higher points, making a greater change in interest rates necessary before refinancing becomes economical. In addition, these loans often carry prohibitive prepayment penalties (see Exhibit 14).

The additional credit risk inherent in these loans can be offset by the higher interest rate, lower LTV, and more predictable prepayment profile. However, the investor must focus on the strength of the servicer and an accurate assessment of liquidation value rather than the borrower's ability to pay. Appraisals must come from independent sources with quality controls to ensure reliability. An experienced liquidator is of major importance to the amount and timing of liquidation. Typical "B" and "C" loans have LTVs around 65% versus "A" loans at 75%. With accurate valuation, this additional 10% coupled with the higher interest rate should compensate for the higher credit risk. Another factor to consider is the time to foreclosure. The sooner the defaulted property is liquidated, the more valuable it is. California, where the majority of this paper originated, averages 4 months to foreclosure, which is less than the national average of 12 months.

Exhibit 13. Valuation of "B," "C," and "D" Paper

- Accurate liquidation value—appraisals.
- Strength of servicer—workout department.
- Time to foreclosure—national average is 12 months. California is 4, Texas 1.

Exhibit 14. Advantages of "B," "C," and "D" Paper

- More stable prepayments—harder to refinance, higher points, prepayment penalties.
- Lower LTVs—LTVs average 65% versus 75% for "A" paper.
- Higher interest rate.

Familiarity with the reserve funds and more complicated credit-enhancement structures have assisted in the creation of a lower credit quality securitization market. To illustrate, consider BSMSI 93-12, a deal issued by Bear Stearns which included a large percentage of delinquent loans. To facilitate the sale of the subordinate, a reserve fund was added in the first-loss position. The reserve fund was then tranched into four different credit levels, and a buy-back schedule was added which assured some release of cash under the conditions of the schedule. As a result, there was substantial investor participation in a good portion of the reserve fund. Other examples of lower credit quality securitized transactions include EMC 93-L1 and EMC 93-L2, two deals backed exclusively by sub-performing, non-performing, and Real Estate Owned (REO) properties. Sub-performing mortgages are loans that are 3 to 12 payments delinquent with less than 10% equity. REO property includes properties acquired before deal issuance. The net sale proceeds of these properties are passed through to the bondholders.

MONITORING LOW-QUALITY COLLATERAL

Deals that are backed by low-quality mortgages or real property must be evaluated and monitored differently. An investor should be familiar with the unpaid principal balance of the mortgage (UPB), the anticipated net proceeds (ANP), quick-sale brokers' price opinions (BPO), and bond value (BV). The UPB is the outstanding debt owed on the mortgages. ANP for non-performing and REO property is typically assumed to be 85% of BPO. The 15% discount should be sufficient to cover any advances to the servicers and expenses associated with the sale. ANP for sub-performing mortgages is the lesser of UPB and the sum of 10 years of schedule principal and interest. BPO is a drive-by valuation by an independent real estate broker in the community. It is the expected proceeds of a sale which includes assumptions as to the interior of the house and the time involved in marketing. The initial BV is determined by the rating agencies and is assumed to be the maximum amount of bonds the collateral can support given a worst-case scenario. The rating agencies determine a very conservative anticipated net proceeds amount of bonds the collateral can support and a very conservative length of time to receipt of cash flows given a worst-case scenario. This attempts to assure that total cash receipts over the life of the deal will be greater than the amount of bonds issued. Since the rating agencies are more conservative than the expected value, there is built-in overcollateralization. If ANP increases, the amount of overcollateralization increases.

An example of a performance update showing the amount of collateral supporting the bonds outstanding is shown in Exhibit 15, using the assumptions in Exhibit 16.

The unpaid principal balance (UPB) in the first month decreases by the UPB of the liquidated mortgages. Bond value (BV) decreases by the sum of all proceeds less any fees and bond interest. Note that there are no fees assessed in this example. The anticipated net proceeds (ANP) decreases by the sum of the ANP of liquidated mortgages and other proceeds received. The results are shown in Exhibit 15.

Subordinates Pooled Together and Reissued with Various Ratings

Given the increasing sophistication of the market and the successful attempts to securitize lower credit quality collateral, it was only a matter of time before Wall Street began to re-REMIC subordinated pieces (see Exhibit 17). Subordinates from other deals are accumulated in portfolio until there are enough to offer seasoning, liquidity, and diversity. These deals are then tranched into a number of differently rated tranches in an attempt to maximize execution.

While these structures have the added attraction of diversity, the risk is that defaults and loans can sometimes impact securities in unexpected ways

Exhibit 15. Example of a Performance Update

	Unpaid Principal Balance (UPB) ($)	Anticipated Net Proceeds (ANP) ($)	Bond Value (BV) ($)	% BV/ANP
Initial	200,000,000	149,337,000	130,395,000	87.32
Month 1	197,000,000	146,337,000	127,545,000	87.16
Month 2	194,000,000	143,337,000	125,395,000	87.48
Month 3	191,000,000	139,837,000	122,295,000	87.46
Month 4	188,000,000	136,837,000	118,845,000	86.85

Exhibit 16. Assumptions

	Unpaid Principal Balance (UPB) ($)	Proceeds ($)	Anticipated Net Proceeds (ANP) ($)	Other Proceeds Principal ($)	Interest ($)
Month 1	3,000,000	2,700,000	2,100,000	150,000	750,000
Month 2	3,000,000	2,000,000	2,100,000	150,000	750,000
Month 3	3,000,000	2,700,000	2,100,000	400,000	1,000,000
Month 4	3,000,000	3,300,000	2,100,000	150,000	750,000

Exhibit 17.   Compensation of More Senior Tranches When Defaults Occur

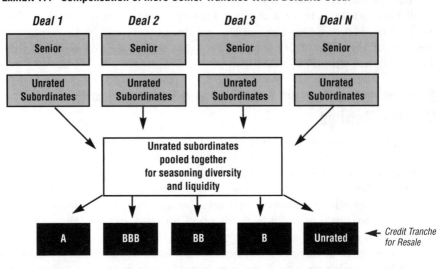

depending on how the deal is structured. One of the most important structural aspects affecting the value of the various subordinate tranches, and one that was initially underestimated by the market, is when and to what extent the more senior tranches are compensated when defaults occur.

When liquidation proceeds are less than the defaulted loan amount, resulting in a loss, different structures typically provide for two ways to compensate the senior securities: (1) only compensate the senior tranches for the lesser of the "senior prepay percent" of the recovered principal[5] or the senior tranche's pro-rata share of the defaulted loan, or (2) pay the senior tranche's pro-rata share of the defaulted loan, even though it may be larger than the amount ultimately recovered. In the first case, when the payoff amount is limited to the lesser of the recovery of the defaulted loan amount, the senior tranche receives only the available cash flows, so the subordinated class's cash flow is undisturbed.

In the second case, however, where the entire loan amount must be paid off up front and the recovery amount is less than the entire defaulted loan amount, the shortfall in cash is diverted from the subordinated classes' interest and principal delaying the cash flows due to the subordinates. If the deal is structured so that the priority of payments is interest-principal-interest-

5 The senior prepay percent equals the senior tranches' percentage share of principal payments plus all prepayments of the subordinates that are allocated to the senior bonds.

principal,[6] then the principal of the first-loss subordinate will be the first to be deferred. If this amount of principal is insufficient, then the *interest* of the first-loss subordinate will be deferred. If this is still insufficient, then the principal of the next lowest tranche will be hit and then its interest, and so on up the credit levels of the structure until the entire cash shortfall is made up to the most senior tranches (see Exhibit 18). If interest as well as principal must be diverted, the interest shortfall to the subordinated classes will be tracked as "deferred interest," payable in subsequent periods before applying cash flow to reduce the principal balances of these classes. Unfortunately, unlike deferred principal balances, deferred interest on many of these deals did not usually accrue interest.[7] In late 1993, one deal that was acutely affected was PruHome Securities 92A. Because this deal was originated in California in 1989 and 1990, the deal was experiencing greater than average losses. In fact, defaults have caused principal and interest to be deferred on subordinates rated as high as A. It is important to note that a cash shortfall is not the same as an actual loss. For example, the A-rated class has experienced interruptions in cash flow, but losses still have not exceeded lower rated classes. If this is the case, there will be sufficient cash to repay deferred interest by the end

Exhibit 18. "I-P-I-P Structure Default Recovery Plan"

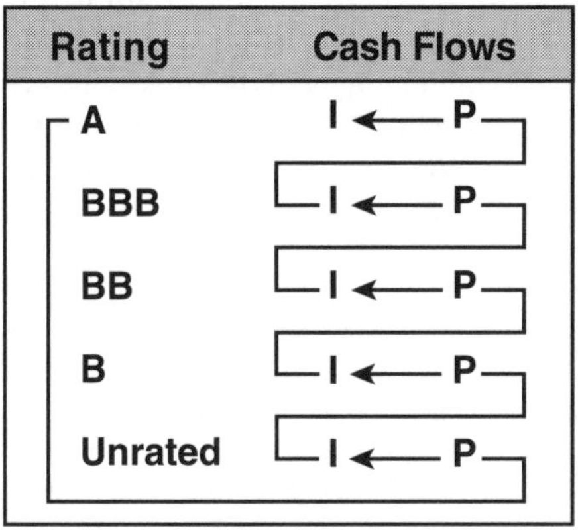

---

6 Also known as I-P-I-P, this means that first interest and then the principal of the highest quality tranche is paid first, followed by the interest and then the principal of the second highest quality tranche, and so on. If there is a default or loss, this order is reversed in terms of which tranches are affected, *i.e.,* the principal of the lowest quality tranches is deferred or lost, then its interest. Next, the principal of the next lowest quality tranche is affected, then its interest, and so on.

7 The prevailing climate suggests a move toward the payment of interest on deferred interest.

of the deal. Thus, even these highly rated tranches could experience a loss in yield even though their subordination levels may be sufficient over time to protect them from any principal losses.

If interest does accrue on interest deferrals each month, then there would be minimal yield loss, only a lag to distribution and a lengthening in the average life of the securities.[8]

VALUATION OF SUBORDINATE SECURITIES

The key to valuing subordinated tranches or securities is to first identify and understand the type of credit-enhancement structure being employed in a deal and then to understand how under that structure various loss and default scenarios will impact the yield (hence value). As a general rule of thumb, the lower the rating of the subordinate tranche, the more differences in structure will tend to impact yield and value. Thus, as an investor reaches for yield by going down in credit quality, the more critical it is for the investor to understand exactly just what type of structure he or she is dealing with. During times when defaults and loss levels are low the investor may not discern the impact of differences in structure; however, as defaults and losses rise, these differences will become quickly apparent to the owner of the subordinate pieces.[9]

The investor should also analyze the quality of the collateral[10] and the underwriting. Although this becomes less important for AA-rated and higher securities because they are so well protected,[11] it is critical for lower rated tranches. As we shall see small changes in defaults can have a large impact on the yield of lower rated tranches. Thus, it is important for the investor to understand the default and loss history of the type of collateral backing the deal and to use these assumptions as a base from which to calculate expected returns.

---

8 Whether the subordinate, not in the first-loss position, ultimately recovers this cash also depends on the amount of credit support remaining.

9 In fact, an unrated piece is generally assumed to lose all principal due. The only question is the timing of losses, and, similar to an interest-only strip, the amount of interest received.

10 For further information regarding the credit quality of different types of collateral, see Brian Lancaster, "An Introduction to Whole Loan Securities," Bear Stearns Mortgage Product Special Report.

11 When an investor is evaluating the credit risk of securities, it is important to use appropriate default scenarios. Thus, if an investor is analyzing higher-rated securities, worst-case default scenarios should be used. If analyzing a lower-rated security, average defaults (and losses) should be assumed. Average and worst-case default scenarios are as follows. Average losses for single-family, fixed-rate, 30-year maturity mortgages are approximately $1/2$ of 1% annually, concentrated in years 2–6, approximately 100% SDA, and 35% severity. This is

SIX COMMON SENIOR/SUBORDINATE SECURITY STRUCTURES

To isolate the impact of different credit-enhancement techniques and default levels on the value of differently rated tranches, yields[12] were calculated under different default assumptions for six structures commonly used in the market (see Exhibit 19). All of the structures are assumed to use the same collateral: net coupon of 7.5%, servicing of .75, a weighted average maturity (WAM) of 357 months, and a pricing speed of 250 PSA. The numbers across the top row show assumed cumulative default percentages spread over years two through six.[13]

Our first structure, "A," shall require that if defaults occur the senior tranche must receive its entire pro-rata share of the defaulted amount as in our example showing the re-REMICing of subordinated tranches; paydown priorities again shall be I-P-I-P, as in our previous example; and overcollateralization may exist, *i.e.*, interest may be converted to principal to pay off a default or loss and the subordinated balance is written down by this amount.

Our "B" structure shall be the same (interest is used to pay senior cash flows) except that no overcollateralization shall exist, *i.e.*, subordinates are written down by principal losses only. Let us now compare the impact of an "A" type structure on the value of subordinate tranches versus that of a "B" structure. Here it is clear that the subordinate tranches fare better under the "B" structure (without overcollateralization) when defaults begin to rise rather than under the "A" structure (with overcollateralization). For example, as shown in the exhibits, when accumulated defaults rise from 0.3% to 1.4% the yield of the unrated or first-loss subordinate tranche plunges from 31.32% to 3.15% for structure A, the structure permitting overcollateralization, as compared with a drop from 31.64% to 10.30% for structure B, the

---

the level that should be focused on when running return analysis. In highly stressed times of depreciating housing prices, such as in Texas during the mid-eighties, losses increased dramatically depending on LTVs. LTVs greater than 90% were running at a 24.1% default rate, and LTVs between 76% and 80% (typical of whole loan pools) reached 8.1%. Assuming 35% severity, these default rates equal losses of 8.4% and 2.9%, respectively. Cumulative defaults can be equated to SDA under a given prepayment speed. Assuming 250 PSA and the Texas default scenario, SDAs would be approximately 1275 and 290, respectively, given the typical collateral outstanding at the time.

12 Negative yields imply loss of initial investment amounts. They can be misleading because they do not accurately reflect timing of the loss. Two bonds with the same dollar amounts of loss can have very different negative yields depending on the timing of the loss. The shorter the time it takes to realize the loss, the greater the negative yield. As the time of the loss approaches infinity, the negative yield approaches zero.

13 The defaults may be converted to loss levels by multiplying by .35, the severity rate assumed.

Exhibit 19. After-Loss Yields

AA-Rated Subordinate Security

Base Yield: 8.88

Structure Type	1.4	2.9	4.3	5.7	8.6	11.4	14.3
A	8.91	8.94	8.94	9.00	8.66	7.28	4.24
B	8.90	8.92	8.93	8.95	8.70	8.01	7.37
C	8.89	8.90	8.91	8.92	8.90	8.29	4.54
D	8.87	8.87	8.86	8.89	8.84	8.08	4.46
E	8.90	8.90	8.91	8.92	8.90	8.17	4.54
F	8.87	8.88	8.87	8.85	8.73	8.65	4.67

Cumulative Default % over Yrs. 2-6

A-Rated Subordinate

Base Yield: 9.13

Structure Type	1.4	2.9	4.3	5.7	7.1	8.6	10.0
A	9.16	9.20	9.03	8.33	6.82	3.96	0.63
B	9.15	9.17	9.06	8.54	8.05	7.59	5.68
C	9.14	9.15	9.16	9.17	7.50	4.10	-0.66
D	9.14	9.15	9.15	9.12	7.59	4.42	-0.08
E	9.14	9.15	9.16	9.17	7.51	4.10	- 0.24
F	9.11	9.08	9.00	9.00	7.89	4.67	0.49

Cumulative Default % over Yrs. 2-6

BBB-Rated Subordinate

Base Yield: 9.48

Structure Type	1.4	2.1	2.9	3.6	4.3	5.0	5.7
A	9.42	9.47	8.78	8.13	6.26	3.85	0.79
B	9.50	9.47	8.97	8.40	8.12	7.89	6.02
C	9.49	9.49	9.51	9.38	6.97	4.08	-0.03
D	9.48	9.48	9.50	9.38	7.07	4.16	0.04
E	9.49	9.48	9.51	9.47	6.97	4.07	-0.03
F	9.42	9.33	9.31	9.30	7.35	4.58	0.99

Cumulative Default % over Yrs. 2-6

BB-Rated Subordinate

Base Yield: 11.73

Structure Type	1.0	1.4	1.9	2.3	2.7	3.1	3.6
A	11.78	11.01	9.83	8.03	5.59	2.42	-2.46
B	11.77	11.23	10.23	9.72	9.34	7.48	5.32
C	11.75	11.76	11.75	9.56	6.52	2.42	-14.92
D	11.74	11.75	11.74	9.72	6.73	2.59	-14.56
E	11.75	11.76	11.75	9.56	6.52	2.42	-14.64
F	11.45	11.32	11.32	9.73	6.90	3.17	-3.82

Cumulative Default % over Yrs. 2-6

B-Rated Subordinate

Base Yield: 13.73

Structure Type	.3	.6	.9	1.1	1.4	1.7	2.0
A	13.75	13.77	12.90	10.83	10.57	5.74	-4.36
B	13.75	13.76	13.06	11.63	10.99	10.64	9.84
C	13.73	13.73	13.74	13.71	12.68	6.67	-9.58
D	13.73	13.73	13.74	13.75	12.92	6.94	-9.07
E	13.73	13.73	13.75	13.71	12.68	6.67	-9.58
F	13.58	13.37	13.09	13.10	12.92	7.56	-11.60

Cumulative Default % over Yrs. 2-6

Exhibit 19. After-Loss Yields *(Continued)*

Base Yield: 40.00		Unrated Subordinate *Cumulative Default % over Yrs. 2-6*						
Structure Type	**.3**	**.6**	**.9**	**1.1**	**1.4**	**1.7**	**2.0**
A	31.32	22.74	15.65	9.92	3.15	0.78	-0.33
B	31.64	24.10	18.19	14.28	10.30	3.83	N/A
C	37.06	33.70	28.67	21.46	13.04	7.20	1.92
D	37.17	33.94	29.60	23.09	15.13	9.40	4.20
E	37.06	33.70	28.67	22.46	13.04	7.20	1.92
F	34.64	30.51	26.41	20.06	10.62	3.74	-1.65

one without overcollateralization. Why? When the subordinates are written down for lost interest (which can then be used to pay off a default of the senior tranche) the subordinates permanently lose the amount by which they were written down.

Where does it go? Eventually it ends up going to the residual holder who receives any excess collateral remaining after the deal is closed. Excess collateral builds in this structure because the extra principal created from the subordinate's balance decreasing by the subordinate's lost interest causes the bonds to be written down faster than the collateral, resulting in leftover collateral which goes to the residual holder. A deal which permits overcollateralization, such as structure "A," clearly favors the residual holder (*i.e.*, the issuer) at the expense of the holder of subordinate securities as defaults rise. Thus, an important question for the subordinate investor to ask is, "Does the balance of the subordinate get written down by lost interest of the more senior bonds, resulting in overcollateralization?"

Now let's see what happens if we create a third structure, "C," where we require that if defaults occur the senior tranche must receive the lesser of the recovered amount or its entire pro-rata share of the defaulted amount. As in case "B," payment priority order shall be I-P-I-P and no overcollateralization shall exist, *i.e.*, the seniors are amortized by scheduled principal, prepayments, and charge-offs for the full amount of the loss. Here the unrated tranche performs better than in "B" because it absorbs fewer losses, *i.e.*, it has to give up less cash to support the senior tranche. This is because its balance is decreasing by normal amortization as well as charge-offs, *i.e.*, it is receiving scheduled principal and prepayments it would not have received in structures "A" or "B." Remember, our senior tranche here is only entitled to the lesser of the recovered amount or its entire pro-rata share of the defaulted amount. In case "B," the senior tranche was entitled to the full defaulted amount.

Because the unrated tranche amortizes faster than under structure "B" as defaults (hence losses) rise, the other subordinates in the deal will have to absorb a higher proportion of charge-offs. For example, when cumulative defaults rise from 1.4% to 1.7% the yield of our B-rated subordinate piece begins to do better (10.64%) as part of a "B"-type structure than it would as part of a "C"-type structure—yield drops to 6.67%, lesser of recovery or entire pro-rata share. The same holds true for the higher BB-rated subordinate where the inferiority of the "C"-type structure shows up when defaults rise from 1.9% to 2.3% (the yield dropping to 9.56% rather than 9.72% if the deal were part of a "B" structure). Thus, under a "C"-type structure, the only bond that performs better is the first-loss subordinate, and the higher the cumulative default rate rises the more the higher-rated subordinates will be affected adversely. Therefore, it is important to ask, "Is the loss to the senior tranche equal to the senior percent (the senior's pro-rata share of cash flows) times the defaulted loan balance, or is it entitled to just the lesser of this amount or the senior prepay percent of recoveries?"

Now let's compare structures "D" and "E." The two structures are nearly identical except for the fact that "D" allows more prepayments to flow through to the mezzanine. Prepayment lockouts are fairly standard, with the exception of directing all subordinate prepayments to the mezzanine for the first seven years or until the current percent of the mezzanine doubles. What's interesting about the difference in outcome between the two structures is that the first-loss tranche in structure "D" (which foregoes more principal) performs better. This is because, at pricing, the mezzanine receives prepayments from the subordinate, making the mezzanines' initial average life shorter and the subordinates' average life longer. For discount securities priced at the same yield, the longer average life returns a lower price. For the same contraction in duration, the yield increases more because of the lower price. Therefore, tranches rated below the AA-rated mezzanine perform better in structure "D" than in structure "E." The mezzanine in structure "D" performs worse because its duration extends more than in structure "E." Although the extension is mitigated by its higher price, this effect is still insufficient to cover the loss of additional prepayments anticipated at pricing.

The final structure we will examine is "F," which, like "B," pays the senior percent of the defaulted loan amount and has no overcollateralization. The twist for structure "F" will be that cash-flow priorities will be I-I-P-P rather than I-P-I-P. As can be discerned by comparing Exhibits 20 and 21, the first-loss, unrated subordinate piece will fare better than under the "B" structure and the higher rated subordinate pieces (or mezzanines) will fare worse. This is because cash flow will be deferred from the principal of the higher rated subordinates *before* the interest of the unrated subordinated is affected. As shown in the preceding exhibits, the yield of the

Exhibit 20. I-P-I-P Structure Default Recovery Pattern

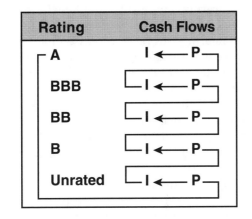

Rating	Cash Flows
A	I ←— P
BBB	I ←— P
BB	I ←— P
B	I ←— P
Unrated	I ←— P

Exhibit 21. I-P-I-P Structure Default Recovery Pattern

Rating	Cash Flows
A	I P
BBB	I P
BB	I P
B	I P
Unrated	I P

unrated subordinate from an "F"-type structure (I-I-P-P) is higher under the various cumulative default levels than under a "B"-type structure (I-P-I-P). At the same cumulative default rates, the yields of our BB subordinate piece are substantially lower than under the "B"-type structure. Thus, as a broad generalization, the first-loss subordinate will tend to do better under an I-I-P-P structure and the higher rated subordinates (or mezzanines) worse.

A couple of other points. When defaults occur early on with an "F"-type structure (I-I-P-P) that is also a shifting-interest or shifting-prepayments[14] structure (which is usually the case), the benefit to the most deeply subordinated tranche is substantial. The reason is that under a shifting-interest structure the unrated first-loss piece is only entitled to scheduled principal payments. All prepayments are going up to the senior tranches. Thus, when defaults occur under an I-I-P-P structure, the unrated tranche has little principal to offer. Most of its cash flow during the lockout period is interest. The principal of other, higher rated subordinates will be hit before the interest of the least rate subordinate is touched.

Subordinates in a second-loss position can also sometimes benefit under the I-I-P-P structure under some low-level default scenarios (hence loss levels). For example, if we compare the yield of our B-rated subordinate under structure "F" between cumulative default rates of 0.9 and 1.4, its yields are higher (13.09% to 12.92%) than if it were part of a "B"-type structure (yields between 13.06% and 10.99%). Although this may seem unusual at first glance, if we look back at the diagram we can see why. Under the I-I-P-P structure, although it is true that the interest of the unrated tranche does not stand before the principal of our B-rated tranche (as it does in the I-P-I-P structure), it is also true that the principal of the higher rated tranche (the BB-rated bond) is being hit before the interest on our B-rated tranche is affected. Thus although the B-rated tranche loses relative to the unrated first-loss piece, it gains at the expense of the higher rated BB-rated piece.

There are a couple of generalizations to note when comparing the structures. Yields are a function of the amount and timing of cash received. When a particular subordinate begins to experience losses, the yield collapses because the security is being written down without receiving cash. The higher the initial price paid for the subordinate, the greater the loss. The loss impact (or the amount of cash received) outweighs the timing issue. Timing is a function of whether a conditional test is triggered, which subordinate triggered the test, and how cash flow is prioritized. Since the subordinates are typically sold at discounts, the sooner the lower priority subordinates get locked out, the greater the principal allocated to the higher priority bonds and the higher their yield. This can be seen, in some cases, by yield increases in the higher priority bonds for a given increase in defaults. In summary, if a particular subordinate is not experiencing losses, the shorter the duration (not necessarily average life) the higher the yield.

The second generalization deals with scheduled payments. Under the default scenarios, the senior bonds never experience a loss. They are paid

---

14 A structure where all collateral prepayments are shifted for a period of time (the lockout) to the senior tranches.

scheduled principal and interest. The total amount of principal never varies but the timing of principal receipts does. The slower the seniors amortize, the more scheduled interest they are due and the more cash flow they "absorb" from other tranches. When the subordinates relinquish less cash initially, as with the lesser of recovery case, the seniors are outstanding longer and ultimately receive more cash.

EVERYTHING YOU SHOULD ALWAYS ASK ABOUT SUBORDINATES BUT MIGHT BE AFRAID TO KNOW

As should now be readily apparent, not all senior/subordinate structures are the same. The investor should always ask how losses and cash are allocated. As a summary of the above structural comparisons, the following discusses some of the most pertinent questions that should be raised before buying a security.

1. Is the loss to the senior equal to the senior percent times the defaulted loan balance or is it the lesser of this amount and senior prepay percent of recoveries?

   When the senior recovery amount is limited to the lesser of recoveries, the first-loss piece performs better. The senior is entitled to less cash flow, and therefore the reduction in the subordinate cash flow is not as severe. Since the subordinate is entitled to more cash flow, balance is retired based on normal amortization versus charge-offs. By retiring the first-loss subordinate faster, less protection remains for the higher rated bonds.

2. Are the interest and principal of each credit level paid or is interest first paid on all credit levels and then principal (*i.e.*, the interest on the subordinates has a higher priority than principal on the seniors)?

   When interest on the subordinates has priority over the senior principal, the subordinate performs better at the expense of the more senior bonds. This only affects the bonds when cash shortfall is greater than the first-loss subordinate principal.

3. Does the balance of the subordinate get written down by lost interest of more senior bonds, thereby resulting in overcollateralization?

   Overcollateralization is worse for the subordinates since this amount is eventually released to the residual holder rather than being returned to the subordinates.

4. Is principal paid to the subordinate limited to outstanding balance, and are losses allocated before principal?

   By allocating losses before principal, losses are concentrated in the lowest priority subordinates. This occurs only in the cross-over periods when the bond retires and therefore has a very small impact on yield. This method of allocation gives more loss to the first-loss subordinate without having to write-down the next loss for the difference.

5. Once the seniors are amortized, does the remaining cash flow pay deferred interest (previously lost interest) or is it released to the subordinates?

Interest, whether deferred or not, always has priority over principal. Lost interest only occurs if the structure did not use the lesser of recoveries and if the cash-flow priorities were interest, principal. If the cash is used to pay deferred interest on higher rated bonds, the lower rated bonds suffer.

6. Is there a principal-only security in the deal, and how is it treated?

POs are typically excluded from default scenarios. When there is discount collateral, there must be a PO to support the bond coupon. Some issuers assume that the discount collateral does not experience losses and concentrate these losses in the premium collateral.

7. What are the conditional tests which lock out the receipt of principal to the subordinate?

There are several tests to determine when the subordinate is entitled to principal. The most common test stops paying prepayment principal to the subordinate if the current subordination level of the subordinate is less than the original amount or if cumulative losses reach a specified percent of senior balance by a specified date. If the lock-out occurs, the subordinate extends in average life, getting less current cash and making the subordinate more vulnerable to future losses. Sometimes these tests also apply to scheduled principal.

8. Does the documentation assume lag to recoveries?

If a lag is assumed and defaults are realized on the defaulted balance plus the amount of interest advanced during the lag, the loss is more severe than in standard deals.

Exhibits 22 and 23 show the answer to these questions for a small sample of deals.

RELATIVE VALUE AMONG SUBORDINATED TRANCHES; BEAR STEARNS TECHNOLOGY

While it is important for the investor to understand the complex interactions of structure on the yields and value of differently rated securities, as shown it can be complex. To help the investor more quickly make the most funda-

Exhibit 22.

Shelf-Series	Question 1	Question 2	Question 3	Question 4
GECAP-9312	Senior Percent* Default balance	IPIP	Over-collateralization	Cash then loss
GECAP-9319	Senior Percent* Default balance	IPIP	No overcollateral	Cash then loss
GECAP-9401	Lesser of Sr Pct* Dflt or Sr Prepay Pct* Recov	IPIP	No overcollateral	Cash then loss
RFC-93S40	Lesser of Sr Pct* Dflt or Sr Prepay Pct* Recov	IPIP	No overcollateral	Loss then cash
RFC-93S45	Lesser of Sr Pct* Dflt or Sr Prepay Pct* Recov	IPIP	No overcollateral	Loss then cash
RFC-93S48	Lesser of Sr Pct* Dflt or Sr Prepay Pct* Recov	IPIP	No overcollateral	Loss then cash
BSMSI-9304	Approximately Sr Pct* Dflt Bal	IIPP	No overcollateral	Cash then loss
BSMSI-9306	Approximately Sr Pct* Dflt Bal	IPIP	Over-collateralization	Cash then loss

Exhibit 23.

Shelf-Series	Question 5	Question 6	Question 7	Question 8
GECAP-9312	Lost interest	No	Standard	12-month lag
GECAP-9319	Lost interest	No	Standard	12-month lag
GECAP-9401	No lost interest	No	Standard	12-month lag
RFC-93S40	No lost interest	Yes	Mezz gets 100% of prepays for 7 yrs or doubling pct.	No lag
RFC-93S45	No lost interest	Yes	Mezz gets 100% of prepays for 7 yrs or doubling pct.	No lag
RFC-93S48	No lost interest	No	Standard	No lag
BSMSI-9304	No lost interest	Yes	Schedule and prepay. Tested	No lag
BSMSI-9306	Lost interest	No	Schedule and prepay. Tested	No lag
PRU	Lost interest		Standard	No lag

mental investment decision—whether the higher yield offered by a lower rated tranche is sufficient compensation versus the lower yield of a higher rated tranche—an analytical system should be used which calculates how high cumulative defaults can mount before the yield of a lower rated tranche collapses to that of a higher rated tranche. By using the default and loss histories of the relevant collateral as a starting point for the default and loss assumptions to input into the model, the investor can then determine whether the extra yield is worth the extra risk. For example, based on the assumptions and subordination sizes, the cumulative default rate of a theoretical pool of collateral can hit 1.6% and the yield of the unrated tranche of our example deal will still be as high as that of the AAA-rated bond (see Exhibit 24). Also, we could show that the yield of the subordinate will hit zero when cumulative defaults hit 2.0%. By comparing these levels with the default histories of the collateral, the investor can then decide whether this is the kind of risk he or she is willing to take.

Default Recovery Analysis—Standard Default Assumption (SDA)

One way to analyze the loss effect on subordinate classes is to value cash flows in different loss/recovery scenarios. Assumptions can be made as to the percent of the pool that will default per year and the applicable recovery rate. This kind of analysis shows the yield sensitivity of the bonds to varying loss scenarios.

One problem with assuming a constant default rate per year regardless of the age of the loan is that it does not take into account the effects of seasoning on a mortgage loan. Specifically, a borrower should be less likely to default the longer he has been living in the home and the more equity he has built up. To correlate age with default rate, the Public Securities Association (PSA) has developed[15] a standard of quoting mortgage default rates simi-

---

Exhibit 24. Cumulative Default Rate Assuming 35% Severity

Rating	When Absorbed by Losses	When Yield of Subordinate Tranche= Yield of AAA Tranche
AA	16.0	9.0
A	10.0	6.4
BBB	5.7	3.8
BB	3.3	2.5
B	1.8	1.6
Unrated	2.0	1.6

---

15 The schedule was derived from input from rating agencies, private mortgage issuers, the expertise of PSA, and historical data. It is hoped that the schedule will help standardize default projections and simplify the comparison of risk between different seasoning deals. It models defaults only and does not consider delinquencies.

lar to the PSA curve for defining prepayment rates called the Standard Default Assumption (SDA) curve.

SDA is an annual percentage schedule that is based on the remaining balance of performing mortgages in a pool. The base schedule assumes that defaults increase by 0.02% monthly for 30 months until they reach 0.6% (see Exhibit 25). Between months 30 and 60 this rate of .6% is held constant. Between months 60 and 120 the rate declines by 0.0095% monthly until it reaches 0.03%. This rate is held constant until maturity. As with PSA, SDA is quoted as a percent of this schedule. For example, 50% SDA would represent each of these default numbers reduced by half; 500% SDA would represent five times the base schedule.

To determine the actual effect on cash flows, assumptions of severity and time between delinquency and liquidation must be determined. Loss severity is the percentage of defaulted loan balance that was not recovered upon liquidation after considering the cost of defaults and advances. It is the actual cash loss stated as a percentage versus the percent of loan balance of a defaulted mortgage over the pool balance. Zero percent loss severity equals 100% recoveries and does not include recovery of unpaid interest.

When evaluating subordinates, prepayments and defaults should be separated. Assuming the PSA standard for defaults, prepayments include voluntary prepayments as well as recoveries from liquidations of foreclosed properties. The conforming mortgage market does not separate prepayments from agency insured losses, and one must therefore be cautious not to overestimate non-conforming prepayments when using the agency prepayment standards

Exhibit 25. Standard Default Assumption (SDA)

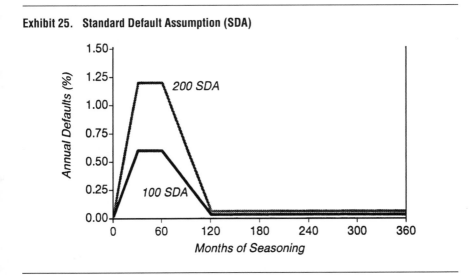

and running SDA. Also, since SDA is based on current performing balances after prepayments (but before scheduled amortization), the faster the prepayment rate the lower the actual dollar amount of defaults. One must be careful not to overestimate defaults under slow prepayment scenarios and not to underestimate defaults under fast prepayment scenarios.

Bear Stearns Credit Model

To help the investor further Bear Stearns is currently working on a credit model which will produce a probability of defaults and estimated recovery rates given a pool of loans, thereby automatically generating a vector of defaults and losses under various rate scenarios. Feeding these vectors into the existing HYDRA system will further simplify the investor's decision-making process.

An initial pass at such a credit model involves being able to differentiate pools of loans on the most basic level.

Using MIDAS, Bear Stearns' proprietary, extensive database of home sale prices across the country, Bear Stearns is able to calculate the current LTV of a pool of loans. This is most valuable for seasoned pools of loans whose geographic locations have gone through marked changes since origination of the loans.[16]

CONCLUSION

The market for credit-enhanced structures has evolved over the last 10 years into a fairly liquid market. The push for more efficient execution combined with growing investor sophistication has led to a variety of new structures and investment opportunities. To correctly exploit them, it is critical that investors understand how these structures work and how they may impact their investments.

---

16 See Bear Stearns Mortgage Product Special Reports, "Home Price Trends: California," Jan. 7, 1994, and "Home Price Trends: California and Illinois," June 29, 1994.

APPENDIX:

DEFAULT CRITERIA: THE DIFFERENT APPROACHES OF THE RATING AGENCIES

The amount of credit enhancement necessary to obtain a given rating is determined by the rating agencies. Nearly all deals are rated by two of four agencies: Standard and Poor's, Moody's, Fitch, or Duff & Phelps. Each rating agency tends to value risk differently. To protect the investor, the issuer is forced to take the highest level of credit enhancement required by two agencies.

However, similarities among the four agencies do exist. *All make a determination as to their expectation for the frequency and timing of defaults as well as the severity of losses.* These are usually based on empirical evidence which analyzes regional demographics and expected economic performance in these areas, loan characteristics, servicing, and underwriting evaluations. Penalties are assigned for high LTVs, high-loan balances, mortgages used for investment purposes, or for second or vacation homes, limited documentation, cash-out refinancings, and other "threatening" characteristics. The differences among the agencies lie in the trigger points,[17] the amount of the penalties, and the severity of the worst-case default scenario. Each distinct rating, from AAA to CCC, has an expected default scenario which is then modified by collateral characteristics. A AAA-rated security must stay intact to a higher default scenario than a CCC-rated one. The integrity of the bond's cash flows must be sustained by the lower level subordinates and/or other credit enhancements in whatever default scenario specified by the relevant rating agency. Therefore, a AAA-rated security might have 10 times the subordinate level of a CCC-rated security.

Similarities among certain structural characteristics also exist. A deal wherein credit enhancement does not grow over time, such as a senior/subordinate structure where the subordinate pays pro-rata, a released spread account,[18] or a reserve fund with a one-time, up-front deposit, requires more up-front enhancement than structures where credit enhancement increases, such as a build-up reserve fund, spread account, or a senior/subordinate with shifting of prepayments.

---

17 Trigger point is a level in each credit-risk category which each agency believes signifies a new level of risk. For example, Standard and Poor's may assign a new level of "penalty" for mortgages of a size greater than the "trigger point" of $400,000, whereas Fitch may assign a different, extra penalty for mortgages in excess of the "trigger point" of $350,000. Each agency has its own schedule of trigger points and penalties for the various credit-risk characteristics described.

18 Such as a spread account which does not accumulate over time but where, after an initial deposit, servicing is "released" or paid out.

Rating agencies believe the most tenuous time for the investor occurs between years 2 and 7. Historical data shows that 50–60% of all defaults occur within the first 5 years for a fixed-rate mortgage. This is because amortization and price appreciation have not had sufficient time to reduce the loan-to-value ratio of the homeowner (*i.e.*, for the homeowner to build up equity). Also at this time the payment history has yet to be established. Credit enhancement levels begin to step-down after 7–10 years depending on the structure and the increase in homeowner equity.

Each rating agency has a unique approach to quantify the credit risk of these factors. The following attempts to describe some of the approaches taken by each rating agency but is not all-encompassing by any means. The investor should always ultimately look to the source.

Fitch

Fitch Investor Services typically uses the mid-1980s Texas default scenario. Texas experienced the most severe decline in real estate values in the post-war period. Fitch believes that the experience of Texas during the mid-1980s is the most relevant for the current mortgage market. Because the experience of Texas is a more recent event, Fitch believes it better represents the character of the typical borrower today—namely, that the borrower has a similar debt-burden or debt-service ratio. Also, loan characteristics such as LTV and weighted average maturity (WAM) are more in line with today's mortgage profiles. Fitch studied 2 million loans between 1981 and 1986 throughout the country while focusing on Texas and found a striking correlation between LTVs and defaults. Cumulative defaults based on the original balance for a given LTV are as shown in Exhibit 26

Default frequency is based on the LTV and specific loan characteristics. Adjustments for limited or alternative documentation range from 1.0 to 1.5 times the original assessment. Cash-out refinancings (which make a loan highly dependent on appraisals) range from 1.1 to 1.25. Second or vacation homes range from 1.1 to 1.25, while ARMs/buydowns range from 1.05 to 1.55. Once default frequency is established, loss severity is determined based on price declines which, in turn, depend on the economic and geographic considerations per region. Fitch analyzed industry diversification, economic interdependence, employment growth, building, and economic trends based

Exhibit 26.

Default	24.1	14.1	6.1	3.3	1.6	0.7
LTV Ratio	>90	81–90	76–80	71–75	61–70	<60

on six regions in the country in order to determine severity. In 1991, Fitch used the loss coverage table shown in Exhibit 27, which may not be too different from what it uses today.

For example, the loss coverage for a BBB from California with a 70–80% LTV would equal 1.2% (.17 × .07). This benchmark would then be adjusted for loan characteristics and performance of the servicer and underwriter. The servicer is important for maintaining the credit quality of the pool. How quickly a foreclosure is processed and how often a successful workout is achieved is very important. The underwriter is responsible for quality control and accurate appraisals.

For A-rated and non-investment-grade paper (lower than BBB), Fitch uses a default model based on 43 regions across the United States recognizing that mortgage performance is more sensitive to the local economy. Additionally, Fitch takes into consideration economic indicators which affect losses.[19] These are unemployment rate, employment growth, personal income growth, population growth, home prices, home sales, and housing starts. Each variable is stressed while taking into consideration the regional diversity of the pool.

Standard and Poor's

Standard & Poor's (S&P) uses the Great Depression era of the 1930s as a worst-case benchmark for foreclosures and loss severity. The Great Depression coupled high unemployment with sharply declining real estate values. S&P understands the differences in United States social and economic culture as well as the differences in loan type (balloon mortgages were popular at the beginning of this century), LTV, and legislation. However, the default experience of Texas in the mid-1980s confirmed S&P's AA loss assumptions. Based on these benchmarks, S&P provides risk assessments for underlying

Exhibit 27. Loss Coverage = Frequency of Foreclosure Times Loss Amount

LTV	AAA	AA	A	BBB	Region	AAA	AA	A	BBB
> 90	0.50	0.35	0.30	0.25	CA	0.32	0.27	0.22	0.17
> 85–90	0.28	0.20	0.16	0.13	No. East	0.37	0.32	0.27	0.22
> 80–85	0.17	0.13	0.11	0.08	SW Cntrl	0.45	0.40	0.35	0.30
> 70–80	0.14	0.11	0.09	0.07	FL,ND,VA	0.34	0.29	0.24	0.19
> 60–70	0.10	0.07	0.05	0.02	So. East	0.40	0.35	0.30	0.25
<= 60	0.08	0.05	0.03	0.02					

---

19 Source: Fitch Mortgage Default Model Regional Summary, January 3, 1994, Fitch Investor Services.

pools and derives credit levels based on these assessments. Since most early securitizations (1970 to early 1980s) were sold as private placements, obtaining performance data is problematic. Based on S&P's database, one of the largest in the industry, Exhibit 28 indicates whole-loan CMO defaults growing as a mortgage pool ages (1993 originations show lower losses than 1986 originations).

S&P also surveyed outstanding losses on residential mortgages and uses this as a measure of a transaction's performance. The analysis resulted in a default curve, similar to the standard default assumption (SDA), with maximum defaults of 13% occurring in years 3–5. By applying this curve to a specific pool, total losses can be forecast. The default curve approach has some shortcomings but generally performs well on average, even though an individual pool may vary significantly. This analysis provides useful information as to the credit protection of subordinated tranches.

S&P's most important determinant of loss is based on economic factors such as a change in housing price, a change in salary, or a change in employment. The next consideration is underwriting. Mortgage payments should be less than 30% of monthly salary. Any loan where payments begin below the fixed-rate equivalent (e.g., GEM, GPM, ARMS, balloons) are subject to greater risk. Income, employment, and down payment should be verified. Solid underwriting helps mitigate errors in economic projections. The last important element in determining loss is credit history. S&P found that LTV mitigates losses but must be below 50% to cover losses in a depression-like scenario. The lower LTV loans with limited documentation of the late 1980s did not deter losses.

In February 1994, S&P published an article concluding that mortgage market fundamentals such as low interest rates, coupled with the improvement in mortgage market information systems, will result in improved credit performance. Two new data sources enabled S&P to re-analyze various default relationships. Accordingly, S&P has revised their loss criteria particularly with 15-year mortgages, jumbo loan balances, seasoned pools, and small pools.

As a benefit to all new loan originations, the lower mortgage rates and the high number of refinancings reduces the debt burden of the individual

---

Exhibit 28. Whole-Loan CMO Issuance ($ Billions)

YEAR	1986	1987	1988	1989	1990	1991	1992	1993
$ Amt.	10.00	10.30	8.90	12.20	16.70	32.20	64.70	42.10
Loss %	0.85	0.99	1.02	0.73	0.58	0.43	0.13	0.03

Source: *S&P Structure Finance*, May 1994

and reduces the lender's carrying costs of foreclosed properties. This has resulted in lower credit requirements, particularly among 15-year paper. Fifteen-year mortgages build equity much faster than comparable 30-year mortgages since more of the payment is applied to principal. Also, because payments are higher for an equal loan balance, 15-year borrowers must have higher income. These benefits, to a lesser degree, are applicable to 20-year mortgages as well. Since these findings are supported by historical data, S&P revised loss severity on shorter-term mortgages.

Using the new market data S&P correlated loan balance and default rates, resulting in new foreclosure frequency adjustment factors. These adjustment factors increase the amount of subordination required. Only loans with balances greater than $400,000 will now be classified as "jumbos" and only these loans will have factors greater than 1.0, regardless of LTV. Loans between $400,001 and $600,000 will have a factor of 1.2 and typically default twice as frequently as loans less than $400,000, loans with balances between $600,001 and $1,000,000 have a 1.6 factor, and loans over $1 million have a multiple of 3.0 and default nearly five times as often as loans with balances less than $400,000. S&P's current adjustments for high LTVs proved adequate.

Seasoned pools have several advantages. A borrower's ability to pay generally increases over time. The loan balance amortizes faster, thereby increasing the borrower's equity, which deters foreclosures. And home prices tend to appreciate over long periods of time. To date, S&P has reduced loss coverage by 25% for loans seasoned 5 to 10 years and 50% for loans seasoned over 10 years. Adjustable-rate loans have improved by half the original percents based on amortization and the willingness of borrowers to make payments.

Pools with less than 300 loans were penalized for possible sampling error assuming that the pool would not be diversified enough to resemble average performance. These numbers were updated for a 99% confidence level normalizing to 300 loans. The updated data reduced the credit enhancement requirements on small pools.

Moody's

Moody's ratings not only incorporate probability of defaults but also include a forward-looking approach which reflects the loss in yield to ultimate losses and addresses nonpayments by the credit-enhancement provider.

Moody's derives a benchmark of subordination levels based on probabilities of default in the "data-rich" single-family, 30-year, fixed-rate, owner-occupied mortgage sector. Millions of loans were statistically analyzed to determine LTV and default correlation. Severity is derived as an expected annual appreciation in home values less a severe loss assumption derived from empirical evidence. Given the frequency of foreclosure and defaults,

Moody's runs a Monte Carlo simulation to assess the effect of a large number of outcomes to determine an expected loss scenario. The change in yield or annual Internal Rate of Return (IRR) of a security due to losses is analyzed and rated. From the benchmark adjustments are made for mortgage characteristics, property characteristics, overall pool characteristics, and servicer quality. Mortgage characteristics include: LTV, type, amortization schedule, coupon, documentation, loan purpose, seasoning, mortgage insurance, and originator quality. Property characteristics include: type, geographic location, and whether the property is owner-occupied. Geographic location determines home value, economic diversity, time to foreclosure, and special hazard. Pool characteristics include: number of loans, concentration, and structure.

Moody's has recently analyzed housing prices[20] through 1993 and showed that loans greater than $203,150 (jumbo loans) have greater price volatility and therefore have a greater loss potential from depreciation. In 1993, homes in the Los Angeles area with values greater than $222,000 depreciated by 22% versus homes between $157,000 and $222,000 depreciating by 14.5%. Moody's believes price volatility will continue and become the dominant force in determining losses, and sees this as a rising credit risk in MBSs.[21]

Duff & Phelps

Similar to Fitch, Duff and Phelps (D&P) focuses on default and loss performance of three million loans throughout the country beginning in 1981 and focuses on Houston in the mid-1980s to resemble severe economic conditions.[22] The credit-enhancement level begins with an analysis of expected loss based on LTV, mortgage type, and property type, further adjusted for pool characteristics, servicer, and underwriter. Based on this data, D&P determined how these features affect losses and determined a housing price index by metropolitan statistic area (MSA), the smallest reliable geographic unit. For each rating, D&P determines an economic scenario which incorporates change in income, change in employment, and change in housing prices. In addition to a nationwide study, D&P analyzed adverse economic conditions in several discrete geographic areas that, if they occurred nationwide, would resemble a moderate recession to a depression-like condition. This enabled D&P to determine to what degree a rating level should sustain losses. A AAA would sustain a depression-like condition, such as in Texas, and a BBB would sustain a recession in a highly industrial concentrated area, such as New York

---

20 "Jumbo Mortgages: Higher Priced Housing Experiences Greater Price Volatility," December 1993, Moody's Investor Services, Structured Finance Special Report.
21 "Moody's Sees Rising Credit Risk in MBS," January 1994, Moody's Investor Services, Structured Finance Special Report.
22 "Rating of Residential MBS," Duff & Phelps Credit Rating Co., 1993.

in the early 1990s. The following are three case studies which assisted D&P in determining their rating requirements.

AAA—Texas by the end of 1986 had 2% of all homes in foreclosure, with Houston suffering the most at a 4% foreclosure rate. Since Texas has a very short time to foreclosure (about one month) D&P believes this is equivalent to more than a 12% nationwide foreclosure rate. Housing prices between September of 1985 and the end of 1988 fell by over 30%. During this time, Houston experienced a 50% decline in oil payroll coupled with an exodus after housing availability grew in anticipation of population growth. For a bond to be rated AAA, it must sustain this kind of severity and a 13% cumulative default rate.

A—According to some data, Boston by May 1992 had 4% of loans in foreclosure with a 14% decrease in median house prices. It appears that construction expanded faster than the local economy could sustain. D&P expects an A-rating to withstand these foreclosure and severity levels without losses. D&P determined a benchmark number of 6.5% in cumulative defaults for an A-rating.

BBB—New York by mid-1992 had 1.3%–2.7% of loans in foreclosure with New Jersey reaching 3.1–5.1%. New York is a specialized case because the financial sector, in 1987, represented 20% of income with only 13% of employment. It is believed that housing prices changed along with the income in this sector. By 1991, employment in the financial markets fell by 10.5%. Home prices between 1988 and 1990 decreased by 13.4% with condominiums/co-ops falling by 33%. This made performance highly dependent on one sector. D&P equates this kind of economy to a BBB rating.

SECTION V

COMMERCIAL
MORTGAGE-BACKED SECURITIES

CHAPTER 25

Commercial Mortgage-Backed Securities

David P. Jacob
Managing Director and
Director of Research
Nomura Securities International, Inc.

Kimbell R. Duncan
Mortgage Securities Product Manager
Nomura International PLC (NIP)

INTRODUCTION

Commercial Mortgage-Backed Securities (CMBS) are receiving greater attention from fixed-income investors as a potential asset class to go along with their allocations to Treasuries, foreign bonds, corporates, residential mortgage-backed securities (MBS), and asset-backed securities (ABS). This new-found focus is not only because of the frantic search for yield in the current, low-yield environment, but because many investors believe the volume and variety of securities available in this market truly have appeal at this time.

CMBS are bonds or other debt instruments collateralized by loans which are secured by commercial real estate. Commercial real estate is income-producing properties that are managed for economic profit. Property types include apartments or other multifamily dwellings, retail centers, hotels, restaurants, hospitals, warehouses, and office buildings.

As of the end of 1992, there was over $1 trillion of commercial mortgages outstanding in the United States, of which less than 3% had been securitized. In comparison, the residential mortgage market had $3.1 trillion outstanding with approximately $1.5 trillion having been securitized. Securitization of commercial mortgages was slow to develop, primarily due to:

- An abundance of alternative sources of capital

- The absence of consistent underwriting standards

- The lack of standard loan documentation

- Poor historical loan performance data

- Excessive leveraging of real estate transactions

Traditional providers of debt capital to the commercial real estate markets include thrifts, banks, and insurance companies, all of which have recently come under regulatory constraints that have reduced their participation in the primary commercial mortgage market. In response, the capital markets are slowly assuming the role of providing much needed funding for commercial real estate transactions.

CMBS issuance has grown dramatically in recent years with the Resolution Trust Corporation (RTC) liquidation of failed-thrift assets. The first RTC multifamily securitization was done in August, 1991 (RTC 91-M1), and the first non-multifamily commercial securitization was completed in February, 1992 (RTC 92-C1). By July 1993, the RTC had securitized close to $14 billion in performing commercial mortgages. This liquidation has forced the markets to confront the issues of securitization. The establishment of underwriting standards, rating criteria, valuation techniques, and more standardized securities structures have paved the way for further growth in commercial mortgage securitization. Issuance of CMBS is expected to grow substantially in the coming years; however, future growth will likely take place in non-RTC transactions since securitization is now viewed by borrowers as a viable means of financing real estate transactions, and asset sales by the RTC should come to completion soon (see Exhibit 1).

The transfer of performing and non-performing loan portfolios, the financing of property acquisitions, and the refinancing of maturing mortgages will contribute to a greater reliance on securitization in coming years. It is estimated that 30% of existing commercial mortgage debt (approximately $300 billion) is expected to refinance in the next 24 months alone. Hence, the CMBS markets will likely experience an explosion in volume as it rushes to meet the substantial demands of the property markets. In just the past year, non-government financing of commercial property in the capital markets has ballooned from approximately $3 billion in 1992 to an estimated $7 billion in 1993. Conservatively, we expect new issue volume to exceed $35 billion per year within the next several years.

The purpose of this chapter is to introduce the commercial mortgage-backed securities markets and to provide investors with a framework for evaluating CMBS. This chapter will concentrate on the securitization of *performing* commercial mortgages since it is our view that future growth of the CMBS markets will be stimulated by the refinancing of maturing loans and the financing of new acquisitions rather than the disposition of non-performing loan portfolios. We begin with an overview of the property markets, followed by a discussion on the major property types which have, thus far, been used as collateral for securitized commercial mortgages. We then give a brief overview of the commercial mortgage markets as a lead-in to securitization. We start our discussion on securitization with the rating process, which has a significant impact on the rest of the securitization process. This is followed by a review of credit-enhancement methods used in the securitization of loans. We then discuss the structuring process with an emphasis on recent structures, and we conclude with a discussion of the relative value of CMBS to other fixed-income securities and relative value within the CMBS markets.

COMMERCIAL PROPERTY MARKETS

Since the late 1980s, the commercial real estate markets have undergone a historic repricing of property assets. A useful source of data regarding the performance of commercial real estate is a series of property indices compiled by

Exhibit 1.   The Growth of CMBS Issuance

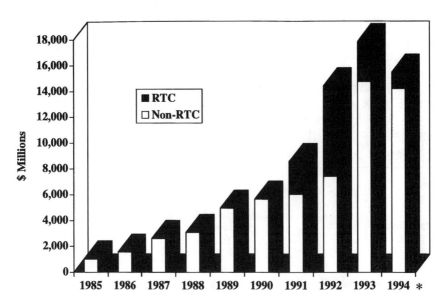

*1994 data as of third quarter

the Frank Russell Company in cooperation with the National Council of Real Estate Investment Fiduciaries (NCREIF) and reported quarterly. The indices represent data collected from members of the NCREIF and are broken down by property type, region, and the components of investment returns (income and appreciation). Using the Russell-NCREIF Appreciation Index as a proxy, the average decline in values for all property types is estimated to be 30% over the past five years (see Exhibit 2). Equitable Real Estate Management estimates in *Emerging Trends in Real Estate: 1994* that there is approximately $1.2 trillion in "institutionally owned" real estate. Assuming a 30% decline in real estate values, institutional real estate portfolios have lost over $350 billion over this time period.

Commercial property values tend to be correlated to the economic conditions of the regions in which they are located and the industries in which they are used. However, declines since the late 1980s have been more severe than would be implied by the recession experienced during this time. There are several fundamental factors that have contributed to this extended correction, including:

- Inflated property values as the result of excessive leveraging of property transactions during the 1980s;

- Technological advances which allow for more mobile professional workforces; and

- Substantial reduction of white-collar employees at large, national corporations.

This deterioration of property values was induced by the collapse of the energy sector in the Southwest during the mid-1980s, followed by a severe contraction of the financial sector later in the decade affecting the Northeast, and, more recently, the downsizing of the defense- and computer-related

---

Exhibit 2.

Asset Class	Average Losses Since 1988 Loss
Multifamily	16%
Office	43%
Retail	20%
Average—All Property Types	30%

industries impacting the West Coast. Because of the largely regional nature of the economic forces that affect the real estate markets, the performance of commercial property can vary widely from region to region. For example, according to the Russell-NCREIF Appreciation Index, for the year ending June 30, 1993, average property values declined by 16.8% on the West Coast compared to only 5.5% in the South.

The recent poor performance of commercial real estate notwithstanding, there are several attributes of the current market environment which point the way to a slow, deliberate recovery throughout the rest of this decade:

- An absence of significant commercial construction

- High returns relative to other investment alternatives

- Lower leverage within real estate transactions

- The emergence of non-traditional sources of capital

- The advent of securitization as a source of funding

Recent evidence suggests that the property markets are beginning to stabilize. For example, the average depreciation of all properties followed in the Russell-NCREIF index declined from 7.3% during the second half of 1992 to 4.1% over the first two quarters of 1993 in spite of localized problems in the California markets. As can be seen in Exhibit 3, write-downs in the South and Midwest in the first half of 1993 were only a fraction of what they were in the second half of 1992. Within the multifamily and retail sectors, the evidence is even more convincing as write-downs in those sectors declined from 2.4% to 0.7% and from 5.5% to 2.0%, respectively, over the same time period.

Further supporting the notion that the property markets are beginning to stabilize is recent performance data on commercial mortgages. The American Council of Life Insurance (ACLI) reports in *Investment Bulletin—No. 1234*, dated August 30, 1993, that commercial mortgage delinquencies dropped from 7.53% during the second quarter of 1992 to 6.35% in the second quarter of 1993 (see Exhibit 4). Moreover, loans in foreclosure had dropped to 2.96% from a peak of 3.50% over the same time period. This improvement in loan performance is even more impressive when one considers that 37% of the universe of loans on which the data is reported are backed by office properties which continued to experience heavy write-downs (the Russell-NCREIF Office Appreciation Index shows write-downs of 16.9% over this time period).

More recently, according to the latest survey of real estate trends by the Federal Depository Insurance Corporation, one-third of the examiners and asset managers cited improvements in their local markets and 58% of those

Exhibit 3.   Depreciation by Region— All Property Types: A Comparison of the Last Two Semesters

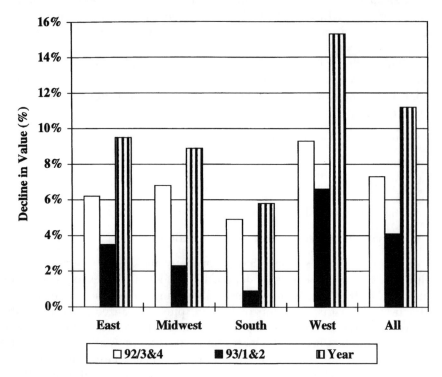

surveyed responded that market conditions were the same as three months ago. This represented the highest percentage since April 1991.

It is our view that the bulk of property value adjustment has already taken place and most commercial property markets are stabilizing. With interest rates near a 20-year historic low at the time of this writing, and a dramatic de-leveraging of property transactions taking place, we anticipate a gradual return to increasing property values during the rest of this decade. Already, in many markets, rents are beginning to increase and vacancy rates are starting to decrease. The increase in cash flows and property values implied by a property market recovery in combination with the currently low leverage of property transactions should encourage debt investors to increase their exposure to the commercial mortgage markets.

Exhibit 4. ACLI Loan Performance Data: Commercial Mortgage Delinquencies and Foreclosures

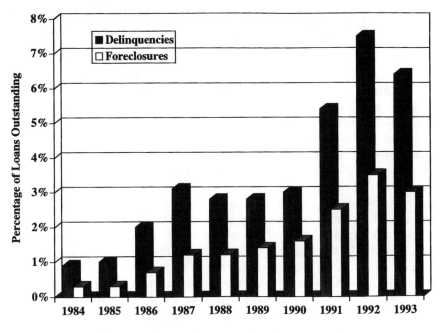

Source: *Investment Bulletin—No. 1234,* American Council of Life Insurance (ACLI).

IMPORTANT PROPERTY TYPES

In the previous section, we discussed recent market trends for the property markets as a whole. In this section we discuss various property types and their current market environment as background for later discussions on risk characteristics of commercial mortgage-backed securities backed by loans on such properties.

Multifamily

Mortgages backed by multifamily properties represent one of the largest sectors of the commercial mortgage market. There are over $300 billion mortgages backed by multifamily properties currently outstanding. For investors already familiar with the residential mortgage market, multifamily mortgages are often their first foray into commercial mortgages. Most are familiar with multifamily properties from everyday experience and are comfortable with the risks of the housing market. While it is true that multifamily mortgages share many of the underlying characteristics of residential mortgages, the primary buffer against loss is the same as with all commercial properties—namely, a property's ability to generate sufficient income to cover debt service.

Another reason for investor comfort with this sector is that there is an agency market for multifamily MBS. For example, from 1988 to 1991, the agencies (GNMA, FNMA, and FHLMC) originated $4.75 billion of multifamily loans, which represented approximately 4% of total originations. In addition, they purchased over $14 billion of loans during the same time period. FNMA and FHLMC have both recently established new programs which allow issuers to swap senior classes from private-label securitizations for guaranteed FNMA or FHLMC certificates. The RTC, as part of the liquidation process of failed thrifts, has also contributed to the securitization of this market. There are 11 multifamily RTC deals outstanding, totaling $4.5 billion as of July 1993. Altogether about 13% of this sector has been securitized. It is anticipated that FNMA and FHLMC will continue to increase their roles in the market by purchasing loans for their own portfolios and by guaranteeing securities backed by multifamily loans. Increasing participation by the agencies should ultimately result in a much greater percentage of the market being securitized.

Multifamily housing starts have been declining since 1986. They accounted for nearly 45% of all housing starts in the early 1970s and nearly 40% in the mid-1980s; however, in 1992, they represented only 14% of total housing starts. However, multifamily housing starts may get a boost from a provision contained in the 1993 budget act that makes permanent a tax credit for the construction and renovation of low-income housing. While this only impacts the construction of low-income multifamily properties, an article in *Business Week* quotes Stanley Duobinis, the director of forecasting for the National Association of Home Builders (NAHB), as saying that this tax credit will be "responsible for all of the increase we see in 1994" in multifamily housing starts.[1]

The minimal amount of new supply has led to a gradual decline in vacancy rates. While statistics from different sources vary, vacancies for multifamily properties currently range from 6% to 7%. This represents the lowest vacancy rate of all property types. However, the decline in vacancies has not been sufficient to stem a decline in average rental rates.

The increased participation of the federal agencies, the fact that multifamily CMBS are SMMEA eligible, and the recent change to a 50% BIS risk weighting on multifamily CMBS for banks and thrifts will lead to mortgage spread tightening in the near term. However, with home affordability having improved in recent years due to declining mortgage rates, there may be some slack in demand for multifamily housing going forward as households opt for home ownership. In the long term, this could result in the deterioration of

---

1 "A Time to Rebuild," *Business Week* (January 10, 1994).

the credit quality of existing CMBS transactions as vacancies increase and a commensurate spread widening. In addition, household formation is declining. "Baby Boomer" household formation is largely complete and, while "Baby-Busters" are entering household formation years (25 to 34 years of age), their demand for housing will be much less than that of the Baby Boomers. On the other hand, an increase in new immigrants will partially offset this decrease in demand, particularly for multifamily housing since most new immigrants have limited resources available for purchasing homes and, consequently, opt for renting.

The performance of multifamily properties is highly sensitive to changes in the economy due to the short-term nature of their leases. Although retail sales continue to increase, employment and consumer confidence have not yet rebounded as strongly.

Nevertheless, the Russell-NCREIF Apartment Index demonstrates that the recent trends are clearly positive for both income and appreciation components of investment returns (Exhibit 5). For the four quarters ending June

Exhibit 5. Russell-NCREIF Apartment Index: Components of Investment Returns

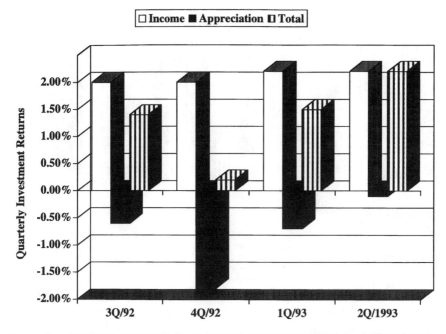

30, 1993, income grew slightly and property value readjustments stabilized to create a more favorable investment market, which has resulted in greater investor comfort with multifamily collateral.

Retail

Retail properties over the last three years have not maintained their values nearly as well as multifamily. According to the Russell-NCREIF Retail Index, (see Exhibit 6) retail property values have declined by 19.7% between 1991–94 and by 7.4% for the four quarters ending June 30, 1993. In 1993, vacancy rates stabilized around 10% and average rental rates have remained unchanged. Performance in the retail sector, however, varies widely by region—the South and the Midwest being the strongest and the West being the weakest.

Shopping centers can be categorized into four types: neighborhood, community, regional, and super-regional. Neighborhood properties serve local clientele, offering service and convenience stores such as drugstores, dry cleaners, banks, *etc.* They are usually built around a supermarket "anchor"

Exhibit 6. Russell-NCREIF Retail Index: Components of Investment Returns

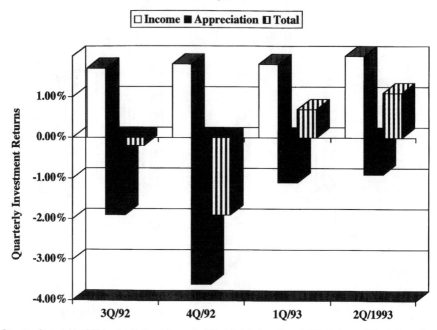

and their sizes are typically between 65,000 and 100,000 square feet. At the other extreme are the super-regionals, which are built around several large department store anchors and range in size from 700,000 square feet to over 1 million square feet. They are typically located near major transportation links and serve large areas encompassing many communities.

Performances of the various retail property types have not been uniform. Historically, super-regionals have done the best; however, more recently, community, shopping centers have done better. Looking forward, neighborhood, community and regional malls will likely experience increased competition from large discount/outlet stores which are gaining in popularity. On the positive side, new construction of retail properties has declined substantially over the last four years and should remain subdued. New construction in 1992 came in at just under 40 million square feet, down from peak of nearly 130 million square feet in the mid-1980s.

Office

The office building sector has suffered severely in this bear market due to overbuilding in the 1980s and the downsizing of corporate America in 1993. According to the Russell-NCREIF Office Index, property values have declined an estimated 48% from the market's peak in 1985 and 16.9% in 1993 alone. Although repricing in the first quarter of 1993 was less severe, a 4.96% decline in the second quarter demonstrates how weak this sector continues to be. We think that there will be further declines before a recovery can begin because vacancy rates remain high and demand for space by financial institutions will continue to contract as a result of an ongoing consolidation of that industry. For example, First City Bancorporation of Texas recently vacated 900,000 square feet in four buildings in the Houston central business district. This contributed to a jump in the Houston vacancy rate to 26.6% in the second quarter from 24.2% in the first quarter. Similarly, in Los Angeles, 700,000 square feet will be vacated as a result of the Bank of America merger with Security Pacific. This should lead to an increase in the vacancy rate, which currently stands at 21%. Furthermore, we think that, if the Clinton health plan is enacted, the need for office space by health insurers will decrease.

When analyzing the current state of the office sector, it is helpful to distinguish between central business district and suburban markets. It is generally assumed that suburban markets should fare better than central business districts in the near term (Exhibit 7). Reasons for companies moving to the suburbs include:

- The decline of inner cities
- Shorter commuting times for employees

Exhibit 7.   Expected Change in Values by Property Type

Asset Class	'92–'93	'93–'94
Office-Downtown	–11%	–4.5%
Office-Suburban	–7.0%	–1.0%
Regional Malls	–3.2%	+0.5%
Retail-Other	–5.4%	–0.6%
Multifamily/Apartments	+3.2%	+4.3%
Hotel	–9.5%	–1.8%

Source: Emerging Trends in Real Estate: 1994. Copyright Equitable Real Estate Investment Management,
          Inc. All rights reserved.

- Technological advances making inter-office communication easier

- Lower operating expenses of suburban offices

However, longer-term prospects for many suburban markets are less certain due to:

- An abundance of developable land

- Less restrictive zoning laws

- Tendency toward smaller, less flexible buildings

- Lack of centralized transportation links

According to Cushman & Wakefield, a national leader in the leasing of office properties, office vacancies in central business districts have dropped to 18.5% in the third quarter of 1993 from 19.6% in the second quarter of 1993—the lowest level in two years. At the same time, suburban vacancy rates have dropped from 20.1% to 18.7%—the lowest level since 1986. However, despite the slight improvement in vacancy rates, effective rents continue to fall.

Many computer-related businesses have chosen to locate in the suburbs, and we believe that the continued consolidation in that industry will cause some suburban markets to lag. For example, over the past several years, IBM vacated 1.7 million square feet of office space in Westchester County, New York, and has announced plans to further reduce space. According to some estimates, the vacancy rate in Westchester County has climbed to approximately 20% from less than 10% in the mid-1980s.

Also, the performance of properties in central business districts relative to those in the suburbs varies widely from city to city. For example, the markets in Atlanta and Washington, D.C., are considered two of the strongest in the nation. However, because of a limited supply of new prime office space on account of strict zoning laws, Washington, D.C., enjoys a stabilizing central business district market while the suburban markets still suffer from abundant supply. On the other hand, Atlanta enjoys a healthy suburban market due to strong job growth and a flight to the suburbs by businesses, while vacancies in the central business district remain high at over 25%.

Not all news is bad for the office sector. New supply of office space will be virtually non-existent over the next several years. Office construction declined to only 23 million square feet in 1992 from its peak of 122 million square feet in 1986 (Exhibit 8) and is expected to fall further in the coming years. The lack of new supply in combination with older buildings becoming obsolete will result in a gradual decrease in vacancy rates and, eventually, an increase in rents for prime space (Class A buildings) in the latter part of this decade.

Hotels

The performance of hotel/hospitality properties is generally more volatile than other property types but the sector is currently showing signs of improving. For example, while delinquencies for the second quarter of 1994 are

---

Exhibit 8.   New Construction of Office Space in U.S.

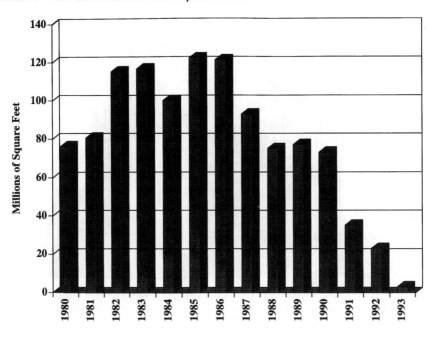

Source: Torto, Wheaton Research and Richard Ellis, Inc.

still high for this sector, they dropped significantly to 10.4% from 15.9% a year earlier (Exhibit 9). According to the Hotel and Motel Brokers of America (HMBA), the average selling price per room in 1992 increased to $18,741 from $18,400 a year earlier. Also, the average room rate for the first half of 1993 was $61.41 per night—2.2% above the average room rate in 1992 and 3.5% above the average room rate for 1991. The average rate of occupancy over this same time period was 62.4%—an improvement of nearly 2% from the same time period in 1992. Demand for hotel space increased in 1992 and early 1993 due to lower travel costs as a result of airfare wars and continued dollar weakness, which has encouraged foreign tourism.

Hotel values are currently below replacement cost and, as a result, very little new supply is expected for the next several years. In 1985, there were over 150,000 hotel rooms built; in 1992, there were under 40,000 new rooms and most of those were in Las Vegas. Looking forward, new supply should continue to shrink due to a lack of development capital. This should result in steadily increasing occupancy rates during the rest of this decade.

Exhibit 9.   ACLI Loan Performance Data—Hotels: Delinquencies & Foreclosures

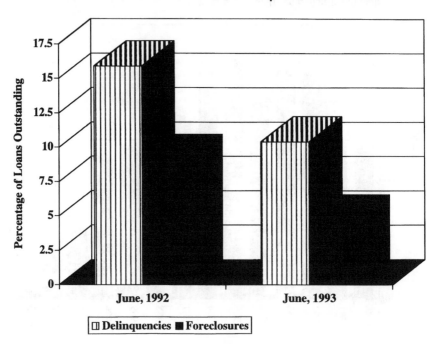

The hotel market can be subdivided into five categories: luxury hotels, upper-market hotels, middle-market hotels, economy motels, and destination resorts. Luxury hotels are those with extensive personalized services; whereas, at the other extreme, economy motels offer limited-service accommodations. Currently, economy and middle-market hotels are the strongest performers due to the increase in cost-consciousness of both business and vacation travelers. The weakest performers are big downtown convention-oriented hotels that are in need of renovation and luxury destination resorts that are burdened by costly overheads.

According to a recent study by Coopers & Lybrand, the U.S. hotel industry is headed toward its first profitable year (1994) in over a decade. Factors contributing to the improving position of this sector are higher revenues due to greater occupancy rates and declining expenses as a result of lower interest costs, declining management fees, and reduced property taxes. This improvement in economic performance should result in greater comfort with hotel collateral by CMBS investors.

COMMERCIAL MORTGAGES

While 1993 witnessed an explosion of equity capital being directed to the real estate markets via REIT IPO's, traditionally real estate has been financed largely with debt—debt represented as much as 85% of the capitalization of many properties. Debt was usually in the form of intermediate-term, fixed-rate loans from thrifts, banks, or insurance companies. The availability of such financing has long been a defining characteristic of the U.S. commercial property markets. However, the availability of financing contracted severely in the early 1990s resulting in the much-publicized "credit crunch."

The concentration of commercial mortgage holdings is quickly changing in response to an increase in regulatory constraints on financial institutions and the development of a liquid commercial mortgage-backed securities market (Exhibit 10). While FASB 115 may encourage some financial institutions to retain commercial mortgage debt in the form of whole loans in order to avoid having to mark-to-market, we believe that the traditional lenders will continue to retreat from lending on commercial real estate directly.

The thrift industry has experienced the largest decline in holdings, estimated at over $100 billion from their mid-1980s peak. Going forward, participation by foreign banks, mutual funds, and pension funds will partially fill the void created from the retrenchment of S&L's, banks, and insurance companies. Securitization and the subsequent development of an efficient commercial mortgage-backed securities market will provide much needed liquidity to the commercial property markets.

Exhibit 10. Holdings of Commercial Mortgages—1992

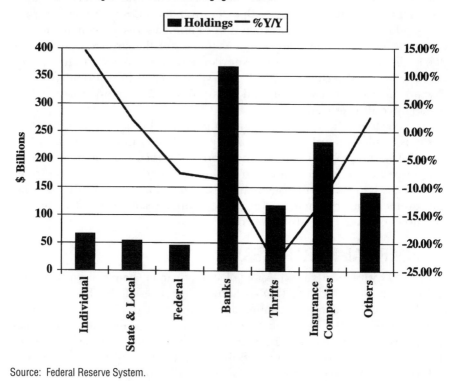

Source: Federal Reserve System.

THE RATING PROCESS

One of the most important financial innovations in the capital markets during the past decade has been the securitization of loans and other receivables. This process involves the transformation of whole loans into securities with attractive investment characteristics such as high credit ratings, enhanced liquidity, and high relative yields. An important element of this process is the utilization of credit enhancement. Before we discuss methods of credit enhancement and the structuring process, we examine the rating process, since the rating agencies exert considerable influence on the rest of the structuring process.

Rating agencies assign ratings on debt and other securitized transactions with regard to the capacity of an issuer to meet its debt obligations. In the view of the rating agencies, a AAA rating for a CMBS issue is equivalent to a AAA rating for a corporate issue as regards the issuer's ability to make payments on its debt. Consequently, the rating agencies have been careful to establish very conservative criteria for rating commercial mortgage-backed securities. In most cases, these rating criteria are the result of in-depth studies of historical loan performance data. In the course of performing such studies, the rating agencies have sought to identify loan characteristics that influence performance and to establish conservative assumptions regarding defaults and losses resulting from foreclosures.

As highlighted earlier, one of the barriers to the development of the commercial mortgage-backed securities market has been the lack of loan performance data. While there are limited sources of commercial loan performance data, a common source used by the rating agencies (notably S&P and Fitch) is the American Council of Life Insurance (ACLI). The ACLI collects data from member life insurance companies and reports delinquency and foreclosure results quarterly. Reporting companies hold about 85% of the total mortgages held by U.S. life insurers. This universe of loans currently represents approximately 18% of the commercial mortgage market in terms of principal outstanding.

The ACLI has collected data on an aggregate basis going back to 1965 and by property type since 1988. Since 1965, delinquencies have ranged

Exhibit 11.   Commercial Mortgage Delinquencies: Quarters Ending June 30, 1965 to 1993

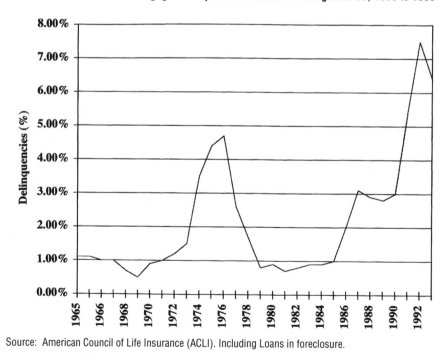

Source: American Council of Life Insurance (ACLI). Including Loans in foreclosure.

from about 0.5% in the late 1960s to a high of 7.53% in the middle of 1992 (Exhibit 11). Cyclical peaks occurred in 1976 and 1992, and cyclical troughs occurred in 1969 and 1981.[2]

The usefulness of this data by itself is limited since it does not provide information regarding either *cumulative* defaults or losses resulting from foreclosures on a static universe of loans which are necessary to develop expectations regarding potential losses on commercial mortgages.

The rating agencies and others have analyzed portfolios of loans to estimate actual cumulative default and loss severity experience. For example, Mark Snyderman of Aldrich, Eastman and Waltch found in a study of a universe of 7,205 loans originated by life insurance companies between 1972 and 1984 that the average cumulative default rate was 12.1% through 1989.[3] In a different study, Fitch Investor Service analyzed a static universe of 1,524 loans ($15.3 billion) originated by major life insurance companies from 1984 to 1987.[4] Through year-end 1991, the average cumulative default rate was 14%. Furthermore, Fitch estimated that, since many loans were restructured rather than foreclosed, the true cumulative default rate was probably closer to 20%. Fitch also estimated that for the remaining life of the loans an additional 10% would default. Thus, they projected total lifetime defaults to be about 30% (conservatively). As a comparison, cumulative default rates for corporate securities rated single–B have been in the range of 30% to 40%.

The Fitch study was performed on a universe of loans that were originated over a very narrow time span. The Snyderman study, on the other hand, highlights the importance of the market environment in which loans are originated (Exhibit 12). For example, loans originated in 1976 and 1977 following a real estate recession during 1974-75 experienced much lower default rates than loans originated during periods of growth. Snyderman hypothesizes that default rates vary according to when loans are originated since underwriting standards change during the course of a real estate cycle. Therefore, the current environment of tightening underwriting standards and lower-leveraged financings should result in the superior future performance of loans originated in recent years; these changes should encourage investors to discount past performance data when projecting future performance.

The Snyderman study also analyzes losses on asset sales resulting from foreclosure. It estimates a loss rate of 32% for those loans originated from 1972 to 1984. Fitch cites loss severity results from several other studies which

---

2 American Council of Life Insurance, "Investment Bulletin No. 1234" (Washington, D.C., August 1993).

3 Mark Snyderman, "Commercial Mortgages: Default Occurence and Estimated Yield Impact," *Journal of Portfolio Management* (Fall 1991).

4 Fitch Investors Service, "Commercial Mortgage Stress Test" (New York, June 1992).

**Exhibit 12.   Lifetime Defaults by Year of Origination: All Property Types—
A Representative Sample**

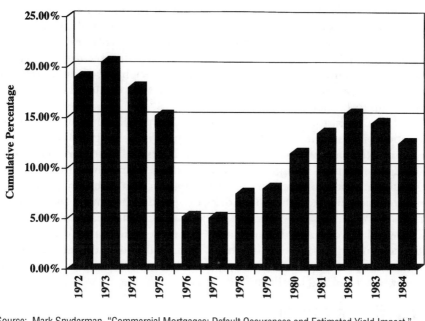

Source: Mark Snyderman, "Commercial Mortgages: Default Occurences and Estimated Yield Impact,"
Journal of Portfolio Management (Fall 1991).

give varying pictures of loss experience. For example, from a study of Midwest life insurance companies' portfolios, they report an average loss severity
of 21% on foreclosed properties. Fitch qualifies those results by noting that
life insurance companies often keep the worst-quality properties on their
books rather than trying to sell them. Thus, loss severity results on this universe tend to be underestimated. On the other extreme, Fitch quotes a Freddie Mac report that maintains that, when the costs of foreclosure are taken
into account, losses averaged 60% on foreclosed multifamily loans. Other
data cited showed losses from 25% to 57.5%.

When rating specific transactions, the rating agencies adjust their expectations of defaults and loss severities to reflect the differences between
the collateral of the transaction being rated and the universe of loans upon
which their studies were performed. For example, S&P utilizes a default
model that incorporates loan characteristics such as interest rate, term, and
property type, which are then used to determine conditional probabilities of
default. Incorporating these expectations, they then require sufficient credit

enhancement such that the securities experience zero losses in scenarios which are defined by some assumed probabilities of default and loss severities on the collateral.

For example, Fitch defines an "A"-level recession scenario as one in which a benchmark universe of loans experiences 30% cumulative defaults. Applying a loss severity of 45%, they expect losses of 13.5% over the life of the loans in such a scenario. Consequently, an "A"-rated security backed by this *benchmark* universe of loans would require sufficient credit enhancement such that it experiences no losses in the event that the collateral experiences losses of up to 13.5%.

Studies of historical loan performance data provide the foundation for the rating process. Such studies are instrumental in helping the rating agencies form expectations regarding potential defaults and losses on commercial mortgages. However, as noted above, they adjust their expectations according to the unique characteristics of each transaction. It is the review of these characteristics and the conclusions drawn regarding the impact such characteristics have on expected losses (and, hence, credit-enhancement levels) about which investors and issuers alike are most concerned. Although the rating agencies differ to some degree in their methodologies, generally each reviews the qualitative and quantitative characteristics of the collateral, the security structure, and legal considerations.

QUALITATIVE REVIEW

Unlike residential mortgages or many asset-backed securities where default behavior can be reasonably modeled to reflect consumer behavior, commercial mortgages are debt instruments that finance businesses. Hence, in their qualitative reviews, the rating agencies concentrate on the characteristics that most influence real estate performance: property types, locations, borrower quality, tenant quality, lease terms, property management, property seasoning, construction quality, insurance coverage, and environmental liability.

Property Type

The risks associated with each property type are obviously very different. Hotels, nursing homes, shopping centers, apartment buildings, office properties, warehouses, *etc.*, are all diverse businesses with different operating margins, cost structures, regulatory constraints, and so on. The fact that these businesses perform differently is borne out by the historical data we have already discussed—the ACLI loan performance data and the Russell-NCREIF property performance indices.[5] Since the timely payment of principal and

---

5 National Council of Real Estate Investment Fiduciaries and Frank Russell Company, "The Russell-NCREIF Estate Performance Report" (Tacoma, Washington, June 1993).

interest on the debt is dependent upon the availability of sufficient income being generated from underlying properties, the rating agencies review the economics for the property type which collateralizes the loans in the same way that they consider the economics of the industry in which a borrowing company belongs when rating a corporate debt transaction.

Multifamily properties, for example, derive most of their income from tenant rents. Since expenses are largely unrelated to levels of occupancy, property managers try to maximize occupancy. Leases usually have terms of one year or less so that projections of revenues are based upon some assumed rate of vacancy in the future. As expected, borrowers and underwriters tend to be more optimistic in their assumptions, whereas the rating agencies look to the demographics and economic prospects of the region in which the property is located when analyzing occupancy assumptions. Expenses consist of management fees, real estate taxes, insurance premiums, repair and maintenance costs, and other miscellaneous costs (*e.g.*, security, landscaping, *etc.*). Multifamily properties benefit from tenant diversity, which protects against economic downturns. Also, apartment tenants are less inclined to demand the latest technological improvements, which might be critical in the office market. In general, multifamily properties are considered to be less risky than most other types (Exhibit 13).

When evaluating securities backed by loans on retail properties, the rating agencies are most concerned with the mix of tenants, the quality of the location, and the economic viability of the tenants' businesses. Unlike apartments where there are many tenants, shopping centers will usually have an anchor tenant who serves as the primary draw to the property and then 10 to 20 specialty stores which serve to diversify the lines of business supporting the property. Income is derived from leases which are usually 3 to 5 years in term. While appearance is very important to shopping center properties, technological obsolescence is not usually a big risk factor. Successful properties generally dominate their local regions, have diverse mixes of tenants, and have good management teams which focus on cost containment and customer service.

Office properties present a different set of operational parameters. Their leases tend to be very long relative to other property types—extending

---

Exhibit 13.   Relative Risk of Major Property Types

Least Risk	Retail
	Multifamily
	Office
Most Risk	Hotel

Source: Standard & Poor's.

as long as 20 years. Consequently, it is important that tenants be contractually responsible for operating expenses (including capital expenses). Also, because of the length of the leases, the credit quality of the tenants becomes a much more important factor in the debt analysis. In many cases, the rating of securities backed by loans on office properties may be tied to the credit rating of the dominant tenant. Although leases will generally extend beyond the maturity of the loans, the rating agencies consider the risk of re-tenanting in the case of tenant default. Office properties need their infrastructures to be kept technologically updated in order to remain competitive and, as a result, the rating agencies may require reserves for future enhancements. Superior office properties are those with quality tenants, state-of-the-art infrastructures, and strong management teams.

Hotels are generally considered to be the most risky type of property. They are clearly different—providing services to short-term guests is a large part of their business operations. Revenues come largely from room rents but meeting rooms, restaurants, and other "extras" contribute significantly to revenues, particularly at luxury hotels. Small increases in occupancy rates or room prices go a long way to improving profitability due to considerable fixed costs. However, unlike apartments, offices, or shopping centers, expenses do increase as occupancy increases; as a result, maximizing occupancy does not always correspond to maximizing long-term profits. Because the performance of hotels depends largely upon the active management of operations, the rating agencies place particular emphasis on the quality of the property management teams. Well-managed properties with competitive positions in their regions present attractive collateral for commercial mortgages.

Location

The local economies in which properties operate can have considerable influence on their performance. The rating agencies study demographic data including population and household formation trends, the dominant types of industry in an area, and even climate to estimate future demand for a particular property type within a local economy. They analyze the impact of infrastructures such as educational facilities, healthcare facilities, recreational attractions, and transportation links. The local political climate is reviewed with emphasis on tax laws, zoning restrictions, and laws governing landlord/tenant rights.

In addition, the rating agencies evaluate existing properties and potential future developments that compete with the underlying properties. The review of competing properties helps them ascertain the supply trends in the local economy for the specific property type. Their analysis will not only focus on the relative value between the underlying properties and competing properties but also the ability of the local economy to support them (*i.e.*, potential supply imbalances).

The rating agencies prefer collateral that is diversified geographically due to the influence that local economies have on the performance of commercial real estate. The value of geographic diversity is demonstrated by the ACLI loan performance data (Exhibit 14), which exhibit very different results across regional economies for loans backed by similar property types. Obviously, the rating agencies penalize single-property transactions for being dominated by one local economy. Transactions with properties distributed among many regional economies are rewarded since this diversity helps insulate the performance of the collateral from a downturn in a particular region. (However, large investors may be able to take advantage of higher yields offered by single-property transactions and manage their risk through portfolio diversification.)

Borrower Quality

Bad character is virtually insurmountable. In transactions with a small number of borrowers, a review of the borrowers' credit histories is performed to

Exhibit 14. ACLI Delinquency Data by Region and Property Type as of June 30, 1993

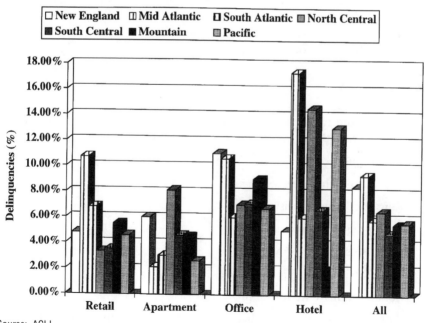

Source: ACLI.

determine the creditworthiness of the borrowers. While CMBS structures are designed to minimize the impact borrowers have on the credit quality of the securities, borrower quality is still an important consideration when projecting future loan performance.

Tenant Quality

Since property income is derived from rents, the ability of tenants to meet their obligations according to their leases is an important consideration in determining the value of most property types. Although "tenant quality" is less applicable to hotels and multifamily properties, the number of rooms/apartments, occupancy rates, and average incomes of the "tenants" are important in determining the quality of these properties. On the other hand, the rating agencies review more closely the tenant profiles of retail and office properties since the number of tenants is usually much smaller and the length of leases much longer. Tenant reviews focus on:

- The number of tenants
- The space occupied by each
- The credit quality of the dominant tenants

In some cases, the rating of CMBS backed by loans on properties with one tenant or a dominant tenant may be tied to the rating of that tenant (particularly in cases when the lease payments of the dominant tenant fully cover the debt service on the loans).

Lease Terms

Cash flow is derived from leases, and property value is derived from cash flow. Hence, the rating agencies review tenant leases to determine the sustainability of cash flows. Important lease terms are:

- Rental rates
- Expiration schedules
- Rent escalation provisions
- Percentage agreements
- Expense payment provisions
- Renewal and cancellation options
- Tenant improvement rent provisions

For properties that have a small number of tenants, particularly retail and office properties, the lease expiration schedules are scrutinized by the rating agencies to determine their impact on cash flows. In addition, the rating agencies will mark-to-market lease terms such that projected cash flows reflect current market rents. As an example, consider the following lease expiration schedule:

Expire Year	# of Leases	% GLA	Cum % GLA	Annual Rent	Market Rent
1994	4	16.73	16.73	$14	$10
1995	7	50.74	67.47	$15	$9
1996	0	0	67.47	N/A	N/A
1997	3	18.14	85.61	$6	$10
Vacant		14.39	100.0	N/A	$10

where GLA is the gross leasable area for the property and rents are expressed in units of dollars per square foot per year. In this example, a significant percentage of leases whose rents are currently above market expire in the first two years. In particular, leases on nearly 51% of the gross leasable area expire in 1995, and the rents on these leases will decline by 40% when renegotiated. In addition, leases whose rents are currently at a discount to market rents will not roll over until 1997. In situations like this, the rating agencies would adjust their income projections to reflect the negative impact of the lease expiration schedule.

The rating agencies and lenders prefer leases that extend beyond the maturity of the loans, whereas borrowers/owners prefer shorter expiration schedules in the anticipation of increasing rents.

When evaluating retail properties, emphasis is placed on the mix of tenants and the economic viability of their businesses. Leases are usually three to five years in duration and may contain percent agreements whereby a portion of rent may be tied to sales, thus making the cash flows on the properties more sensitive to economic conditions. Shopping centers usually have an "anchor" tenant who serves as the draw to the property. The rating agencies pay particular attention to the credit quality of the anchor and the terms of its lease. Renewal options at fixed rent levels are frequently written into leases and are extended at a cost to the landlord. Hence, leases containing such provisions usually carry higher rental rates.

Tenant quality is most important for office properties since these leases tend to be much longer than those of other property types. It is also important that tenants be contractually responsible for operating expenses.

Property Management

Management teams can significantly impact the success of a property. For example, properties that are well managed exhibit less tenant turnover and lower vacancy rates. The rating agencies review the manager's experience, knowledge of the localized markets, and financial resources. They place particular emphasis on the manager's track record for the particular property type represented in the proposed transaction. Also, the rating agencies may require covenants which allow the trustee to replace property management if minimum performance standards are not met or in the case of default.

Property Seasoning

The rating agencies also review the historical performance of the properties—occupancy and cash-flow trends. While historical performance data can be very helpful in projecting future performance of properties, older properties may suffer from the negative effects of aging. For example, properties may become technologically obsolete or may have difficulty competing with newer, more attractive, technologically endowed structures. However, property condition is a better indicator of future performance than age since it reflects a commitment on the part of property owners to long-term viability. In general, some modest seasoning of a property is desirable since the operation of such a building is likely to have stabilized, thereby facilitating the analysis of its financial condition.

Engineering Reports. The rating agencies require issuers to supply independently compiled engineering reports. In particular, they review the age, design, operating systems, and physical appearance of each property. The rating agencies may require issuers to establish reserves against deferred maintenance and/or capital improvements if the engineering reports show the need for repairs. Well-maintained buildings are more likely to exhibit stable future cash flows and remain competitive in future years.

Insurance Coverage. Insurance coverage must be sufficient to protect investors from loss in the case of property damage or interruptions of business resulting from natural disasters, fire, and other types of hazards. The insurers are usually required to maintain a rating of no less than one rating category below the rating of the securities being rated.

Environmental Liability. The rating agencies require environmental reports to be performed on each property. Of particular concern are properties that are, or have been, the site of manufacturing, industrial, or disposal activities. Environmental damage can cause a loss in value and potentially result in substantial clean-up costs. Also, under the laws of certain states, failure to remedy an environmental violation which poses an imminent or substantial endangerment of public health may give rise to a lien on the property which is senior to the lien of an existing mortgage. This would, obviously, affect the value of securities backed by such mortgaged properties.

In addition, it is unclear whether bondholders could potentially be liable for costs related to the clean-up of environmental problems on underlying properties according to current U.S. law. Under the Comprehensive Environmental Response, Compensation and Liability Act of 1980 (CERCLA), a secured lender could be liable as current owner for the cost of environmental clean-up *if it had participated in the management of operations.* Hence, it is possible that, if a lender were to take title to a contaminated property, it could incur liability. In certain circumstances, lenders may choose not to foreclose on contaminated properties to avoid incurring liability for remedial actions.

However, although the risks appear daunting, the rating agencies require thorough environmental reviews to be performed on each property and take the risk of future liability into account when assigning a rating. In fact, if a property is not free of environmental problems, it is not eligible as collateral for a rated transaction unless reserves have been established within the security structure to cover the costs of clean-up.

QUANTITATIVE REVIEW

Whereas qualitative reviews focus on the characteristics of the underlying properties and their impact on property value, quantitative reviews are concerned with the income being generated by the properties and the leverage within the capitalization structures of the properties. More specifically, the rating agencies review the debt service coverage and loan-to-value ratios on each of the loans.

Debt Service

Debt investors are most concerned about the timely payment of principal and interest on their securities. The ultimate source for these cash flows is the net operating income (NOI) of the properties collateralizing the loans. NOI is defined as gross annual revenues less operating expenses before federal income taxes and excluding depreciation. NOI is what is available to meet debt obligations. Properties that cannot generate sufficient cash flow to cover debt payments will default. The rating agencies review the calculation of net operating income and test the revenue and expense components for reasonableness. Prior-year financial statements are used but the rating agencies determine whether the past performance is useful in projecting future potential. They may adjust projected NOI's for special events such that it represents income from stabilized operations. For example, they mark-to-market rents on all leases in projecting income.

An important measure of the creditworthiness of commercial mortgages is the Debt Service Coverage Ratio (DSCR). The DSCR, stated as NOI/Annual

Debt Service, is equal to the NOI from the underlying properties divided by the annual cost of debt service (both principal and interest payments) on the loans. As such, the DSCR measures a borrower's ability to meet periodic debt payments. Therefore, the higher the DSCR, the more creditworthy a loan.

After making adjustments to NOI, the rating agencies require certain minimum DSCRs for various property types in order to achieve specific ratings on securities. Exhibit 15 contains Standard & Poor's indicative minimum DSCRs required for various rating classes on 20-year fixed-rate amortizing securities collateralized by loans on "good" quality properties. The required DSCRs for various property types differ, reflecting the relative riskiness of the underlying businesses.

Minimum required DSCRs are adjusted upward to reflect the results of the rating agencies' reviews of the qualitative characteristics of the collateral, the security structure and the legal documentation. It is therefore possible that two structures backed by the same properties, for example, have different required DSCRs due to one structure introducing more risk than the other.

Exhibit 15. Indicative Minimum DSCRs: S&P

Property Type	Rating	DSCR
Multifamily	AAA	1.75
	AA	1.65
	A	1.50
	BBB	1.40
Office	AAA	2.00
	AA	1.90
	A	1.75
	BBB	1.65
Retail	AAA	1.65
	AA	1.55
	A	1.40
	BBB	1.30
Hotels	AAA	2.70
	AA	2.40
	A	2.10
	BBB	1.80

Source: Standard & Poor's.

Loan-to-Value

Another measure frequently used to indicate the relative safety of collateralized debt is the loan-to-value (LTV) ratio. The LTV is equal to the loan amount divided by the appraised value of the properties, that is Total Loan Amount/Market Value of Property. This is an important measure of the leverage within a transaction and the degree of protection in the event of foreclosure and liquidation. Similar to residential transactions, it quantifies the amount of equity "buffer" in the transaction. Relative to residential mortgages, however, commercial mortgages today tend to be much less leveraged—LTVs below 50% are common. The poor performance of FHLMC's multifamily loan portfolio, as highlighted by the Fitch analysis of loss severities, illustrates the leverage/loss-severity relationship. The lower the LTV, the more creditworthy a loan.

The rating agencies set maximum LTVs for each property type in order to award various ratings. These different LTV levels are meant to correspond to the default rates and the loss severities that the security is designed to withstand (which vary by rating class) since the rate of loss that can be realized on the sale of properties before bondholders experience loss of principal is approximately equal to 1 minus the LTV.

We would like to make several points regarding LTV. First, while the loan amount is known with certainty, estimating the market value of the underlying property is largely subjective. Original cost is obviously not useful. Replacement cost is not used because many properties are valued well below replacement cost in today's market. Recent sale prices of similar properties and actual appraisals are typically used.

The rating agencies determine property values by capitalizing the adjusted net operating income by an assumed market rate of return called the capitalization rate or just the "cap rate." (Herein lies the link between DSCR and LTV. NOI produces debt service coverage *and* NOI determines value.) The cap rate is analogous to the yield of a property and is higher for property types that exhibit greater uncertainty of business operations. Capitalization rates nationally are currently between 8% and 12% for most property types (Exhibit 16).

As the capital markets become a primary source of financing, it is anticipated that capitalization rates become more volatile as they track returns available on financial assets. This will result in greater volatility in property values.

It is important to note that, in the past, appraisals performed by commercial lenders were the result of applying cap rates to NOI projections that incorporated optimistic assumptions regarding future occupancy rates and rent levels. In contrast, the rating agencies determine property values by

---

Exhibit 16. Capitalization Rates by Property Type

Asset Class	Cap Rate
Office—Downtown	10.1%
Office—Suburban	10.7%
Regional Malls	7.9%
Retail/Other	9.6%
Multifamily/Apartment	8.9%

Source: *Emerging Trends in Real Estate: 1994.* Copyright Equitable Real Estate Investment Management, Inc. All rights reserved.

---

applying cap rates to NOI projections assuming current occupancy rates and market rent levels.

If there is a large number of properties, the rating agencies may rely on appraisals performed by one or more independent, accredited Members of the Appraisal Institute (M.A.I.). Such appraisals are usually the result of three approaches to valuation: cost of replacement, recent sales of similar properties, and income valuation. In the event that they rely on third-party appraisals, rating agencies review the methods employed by the appraisers to test for reasonableness and consistency with their own underwriting procedures. In general, however, the rating agencies prefer not to rely on third-party appraisals.

SECURITY STRUCTURE REVIEW

Not all risks associated with commercial mortgages are related to the performance of the underlying properties. The structures of the loans and their interaction with the structure of the securities can introduce the risk that timely payments are not made to investors. The rating agencies review the payment structures of the loans and the securities, the form of credit enhancement being used, the servicer of the loans, and the trustee, for possible introductions of risk.

Payment Structures

Loans on commercial real estate can vary widely with respect to the method of principal repayment and the way in which interest rates are determined. The rating agencies view the risk of various repayment methods differently. Also, they treat floating-rate loans more conservatively than loans carrying fixed rates. They require that the security structure addresses the risks associated with various loan structures.

There are two main repayment mechanisms employed in the commercial mortgage market. Loans can either be fully amortizing to maturity, paying principal and interest each period, or they can pay only interest each period with principal being repaid in one lump sum (balloon) at maturity. Borrowers prefer longer maturity loans with balloon payments and lenders/ investors prefer shorter, amortizing loans. When the collateral underlying the securities are balloon loans, the risk to the investor is greater than when the collateral consists of amortizing loans. This is because there is a risk that the borrower may not be able to refinance his debt in a timely manner at maturity. Hence, with balloon mortgages, the rating agencies are concerned with "extension risk" or the possibility that the borrower does not make the balloon payment on the due date.

Fitch Investor Services has described several approaches that could be used to provide investors with considerable comfort that refinancing will take place before the maturity of securities backed by balloon mortgages. For a single-tranche security structure, where the security and the loans mature at the same time, Fitch suggests that the borrowers should be required to prepare items that lenders require (such as new appraisals, engineering reports, and environmental studies) nine months prior to maturity. Moreover, six months prior to maturity, borrowers should be required to have arranged alternative financing or to have obtained signed sales contracts for the underlying properties. Fitch suggests that, if either requirement is not met, all cash flows, net of scheduled debt service, be used to amortize the debt and, in addition, mortgage rates be increased. These features are called "Demand Notes" and "Rate Step-Ups," respectively. In combination, these requirements provide strong incentive for borrowers to make scheduled balloon payments.

An alternative is to structure the securities so that their final maturity is beyond the maturity of the loans. In this structure, the targeted maturity of the securities is set prior to the final maturity and corresponding to the maturity of the loans. In the event that the borrower does not make the balloon payment on time, the servicer would be required to make advances to the security holders during this tail period in which foreclosure and liquidation takes place.

Also, with balloon mortgages, the expiration schedule of leases has added importance. If a high percentage of leases expire near the maturity of the loan, the refinancing risk of the loan is greater. Hence, the rating agencies prefer to see leases which expire well beyond the maturity of the loans.

Loans which carry floating or adjustable interest rates are more risky since, as interest rates increase, the cost of debt service increases and, therefore, the DSCR drops. In order to achieve high credit ratings on securities backed by these loans, the rating agencies require that loans have caps or that issuers purchase interest-rate caps from an external counterpart with a credit rating no less than one rating class below the rating on the highest-rated security in a transaction. The rating agencies require that minimum DSCR levels are achieved when the interest rates reach their maximum implied by the caps. In cases where the underlying loans have caps, the securities must have corresponding caps. If the underlying loans are uncapped and an issuer has purchased caps, the securities may or may not be capped.

The rating agencies further determine if there is risk introduced by the interaction of the loan structures with the security structures. For example, the rating agencies penalize transactions where interest rates on the collateral are tied to a different index than that which is used to determine the interest rates carried by the securities.

Form of Credit Enhancement

There are several forms of credit enhancement that are used in CMBS securitization. The rating agencies review the impact of credit enhancement on the likelihood that all payments are made in a timely manner. For example, if a third party is the provider of credit enhancement, the rating agencies require that their rating be at least as high as the highest-rated security in the transaction. Or, if credit enhancement is achieved internally, they test to see that payments are made in a timely fashion in the event of delinquencies and may require the establishment of reserves to guarantee the timeliness of payments to security holders.

Servicers

Servicers are responsible for the administration of the mortgage collateral. As such, they perform a number of important functions. They:

- Establish collection and distribution accounts
- Collect and deposit into collection account
  - Payments of principal and interest by the borrowers
  - Any prepayment penalties due
  - Proceeds from liquidation and insurance
  - Any required advances of principal and interest
- Transfer funds from collection account to distribution account
- Make advances from their own funds in the case of delinquencies
- Make advances for taxes, assessments, insurance premiums, *etc.*
- Ensure insurance policies are kept current and in force

- Administer foreclosure proceedings upon default of a loan

- Employ accounting firms to review their performance

By assuring timely payment of principal and interest through foreclosure and liquidation and by scrutinizing the borrowers' performances of their obligations, servicers provide a very important level of protection to investors. Therefore, the rating agencies require that an experienced, well-capitalized servicer is in place. In many cases, a back-up servicer is also required to be appointed from the beginning to insure that a smooth transition can be made if the primary servicer is unable to perform its duties.

Because of the importance of the servicer, the rating agencies conduct a thorough review of both the primary and back-up servicers. They look to see that the historical experience, operations, recovery rates, and financial conditions are of the highest quality. If the servicers are not of the highest quality, the rating agencies may require the issuer to hire a "master" servicer to perform such duties.

Trustee

The trustee holds the mortgage loan documents in trust for the benefit of the security holders. In the event that a servicer fails to make a required advance, the trustee is usually required to do so. On each distribution date, the trustee sends to each investor a statement describing the distribution and the status of the collateral. The trustee or his designated paying agent makes payments from the distribution account to security holders according to the payment rules of the structure. In the event that title to a mortgaged property is acquired through foreclosure, the deed is issued to the trustee on behalf of the security investors and the trustee manages the sale of the properties. The rating agencies review the experience and financial condition of the trustee in the same way they review the servicers.

Legal Considerations

The rating agencies review all relevant legal documentation including trust indentures, pooling and servicing agreements, prospectus supplements or private placement memoranda, and any other agreements with "outside" entities such as interest-rate cap-providers. They establish the status of each lien on the underlying properties. In addition, they review the validity of the proposed structure and the distribution of cash flows as planned by the issuer.

Also, in order to assign a credit rating, the rating agencies require the issuing vehicle to be "bankruptcy remote." A vehicle which meets this requirement and is most often employed in the securitization of commercial mortgages is the Special Purpose Corporation (SPC). In order to qualify as an SPC, an issuer would have to meet specific criteria, including:

- It must not engage in any activity other than owning and managing the pledged collateral;

- It should be restricted from incurring additional debt (except under special circumstances);

- It should be restricted from engaging in a merger, consolidation, or asset transfer with another entity (except under special circumstances); and

- It should have at least one Independent Director.

In addition, the rating agencies require that a transaction be insulated from the insolvency of borrowers, property managers, and others. In general, there may be no liens on the properties senior to the mortgages which collateralize the securities. And, in the case of entities other than the SPC, the rating agencies assume that they go bankrupt to test the ability of the transaction to withstand such events.

While the criteria outlined are generally incorporated in the process of rating all commercial mortgage transactions, the methods of evaluating transactions backed by pools of loans on many properties versus those backed by a loan on a single property are different. With single-property transactions, the rating agencies focus heavily on the economic viability of the property, management, etc. On transactions backed by pools of loans with many properties, the rating agencies may focus on the aggregate loan characteristics if the loans were underwritten using uniform standards and the number of loans is large enough. For example, if there is a large number of properties in a transaction, the rating agencies are unlikely to perform site inspections on each property or to perform their own appraisals. Rather, they emphasize the underwriting criteria of loan originator and inspect a representative sample of the properties. The larger the number of properties in a transaction the more likely the rating agencies will rely on "statistical inference" in quantifying risks.

The rating process is very time-consuming. In fact, it can take as long as six months for a transaction to go through the process from beginning to end. The rating agencies are currently so back-logged that they are turning down transactions simply because they do not have the resources available to rate them. This has resulted recently in many single-rated CMBS issues. However, it is anticipated that the rating agencies will expand their resources dedicated to rating CMBS in 1994–95 in response to an increase in the use of securitization in financing commercial real estate transactions.

In addition, the whole process can be quite subjective since the methodologies employed vary from agency to agency. For example, we discussed how the rating agencies make adjustments to required minimum DSCRs according to the results of their qualitative reviews. If the rating agencies make different qualitative assessments, they will likely differ in their required minimum DSCRs. However, the purpose of the rating agencies is to perform extensive "due diligence" on behalf of investors—the result of which is the classification of securities according to their relative riskiness. In their efforts to classify CMBS consistently with other types of debt securities, the rating agencies have established very conservative rating criteria. It is Nomura's view that because of this conservativeness, CMBS face less risk of future downgrade than similarly rated corporate debt.

S&P published a thorough description of its criteria in *Credit Review*, March 8 1993. Fitch published its default study results and rating criteria in a special release titled *Commercial Mortgage Stress Test*, June 8, 1992. Duff & Phelps has recently updated their guidelines in *The Rating of Commercial Real Estate Securities*, May, 1993. Moody's recently published its rating guidelines in *Commercial Mortgage-Backed Securities: A Review of Moody's Rating Approach*, November 1993.

CREDIT ENHANCEMENT

The rating agencies set minimum DSCRs and maximum LTVs for different rating classifications as a result of their analyses of historical loan performance data, qualitative and quantitative reviews of the collateral, and consideration of the security structure. Usually some form of credit enhancement is necessary in order to achieve these requirements.

For example, if the adjusted NOI from a property backing a loan being securitized is $10 million per year, and the total debt service (including amortization of principal) is $9 million per year, then the DSCR would be 1.11 times. If the rating agencies require a DSCR equal to 1.39 times for the targeted rating, then, in this simplified example, 20% additional credit support would be needed to achieve the desired rating ($1.39 = 1.11 \times 1.25$).

Credit enhancement is the credit support needed in addition to the mortgage collateral to achieve a desired credit rating on the securities. The forms of credit enhancement most often used in the securitization of commercial mortgages are: subordination, overcollateralization, reserve funds, corporate guarantees, and letters of credit. Also, in single-borrower, multiple-property transactions, cross-collateralization and cross-defaulting can further enhance collateral quality.

Subordination

Subordination is the process of sharing the risk of credit losses disproportionately among two or more classes of securities. In its simplest form, the senior/subordinated (or A/B) structure, two classes of securities are collateralized by the pool mortgages with one class providing the credit enhancement for the other. The subordinated class (B-piece or junior class) is in a first-loss position—it absorbs 100% of losses experienced on the collateral until cumulative losses exceed the amount of the subordinated class available to absorb such losses. When delinquencies and defaults occur, cash flows otherwise due to the subordinated class are diverted to the senior class to the extent required to meet its scheduled principal and interest payments. Utilizing subordination, it is possible to create highly rated securities from collateral of all levels of quality.

It is possible to transfer credit losses disproportionately among several classes of securities. This is called credit tranching and is analogous to the tranching of prepayment risk in CMOs and REMICs backed by residential mortgages. Classes are tranched sequentially with respect to loss position—a class does not experience any losses until the classes with more junior positions have been depleted. This is illustrated in Exhibit 17. In this example, class D is the most junior class and provides credit support for classes A, B, and C. Class C is the second most junior class and provides credit support for classes A and B, and so on. There can be any number of credit tranches in a transaction, but the goal of structuring the credit support in this fashion is to minimize the total cost of funds for the issuer. As a result, the issuer's objective is to maximize the size of the higher-rated classes which carry lower yields and minimize the size of the lower-rated classes which carry higher yields. However, the sizes of each class are dictated by the coverage ratios required for a targeted rating.

From the point of view of the investor, credit tranching provides an opportunity to optimize his risk/return profile. Losses are realized first by the equity in the transaction and then by the most junior class of securities. In this way, the most junior class of securities is really in the second loss position. Such classes are popular as more liquid, higher yielding alternatives to equity investments in commercial real estate. Higher-rated classes span the rating spectrum and allow investors to choose the level of credit risk with which they are comfortable.

Overcollateralization

Minimum DSCRs and maximum LTVs can be achieved simply by issuing less debt or, put another way, by posting more collateral. This is analogous to an issuer buying back the subordinated classes from a senior/sub structure, leav-

Exhibit 17.   Credit Tranching

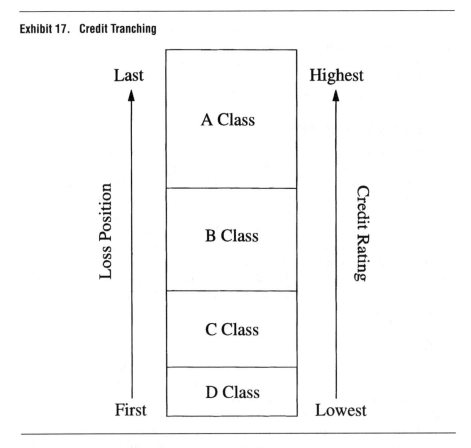

ing only the senior classes to be serviced. Only borrowers that do not need to maximize leverage will opt for this form of credit enhancement. Some Real Estate Investment Trusts (REITs), for example, have used overcollateraliza- tion when issuing debt designed to introduce modest amounts of leverage to their property portfolios.

Reserve Funds

Although subordination is the predominant form of credit enhancement used, many issuers make use of reserve funds either exclusively or in combi- nation with subordination to provide the required level of credit enhance- ment. Reserve funds are usually established with an initial cash deposit from the issuer and may be required to grow over time to some specified mainte- nance level. They are the most liquid form of credit enhancement and are usually in first-loss positions when used in combination with subordination.

The reserve fund balances are usually invested in highly liquid short-term government securities, highly rated commercial paper, and CDs. Because of the relatively low returns available on short-term securities, reserve funds are expensive credit-enhancement alternatives for issuers. However, small reserve funds are frequently established in combination with subordination as a source of liquidity within the credit enhancement structure.

Corporate Guarantees

Guarantees may be provided by the issuer or a third party in an amount equal to the required level of credit enhancement. The guarantor will be obligated to cover losses due to delinquencies and foreclosures up to the amount of the guarantee. A guarantor must have a credit rating at least as high as the highest rated security in the transaction. Corporate guarantees are not used often but when the borrower is a highly rated institution it may find that it can reduce its costs of issuance by guaranteeing the securities. Usually, commercial mortgages are non-recourse loans; that is, they are secured only by properties and their cash flows. In the case of guaranteed transactions, limited recourse is extended to the guarantor, who is usually affiliated in some way with the borrower.

Letters of Credit

A letter of credit (LOC) obligates the provider to cover losses due to delinquencies and foreclosures up to a specified amount. As with corporate guarantees, the provider must be rated at least as highly as the highest rating sought on the securities.

Both corporate guarantees and letters of credit are external sources of credit support. Whereas subordination and reserve funds are set up within the structure of a security and rely solely on the credit quality of the collateral, third-party credit enhancement introduces credit risk not related to the collateral. Subordination is popular with investors since it is not subject to "event risk" or the risk of the downgrading of a third party. However, some investors do prefer LOCs or corporate guarantees because of the "name recognition" of the providers/guarantors.

Cross-Collateralization

For single-issuer, multiple-loan transactions, *cross-collateralization* and *cross-defaulting* may be used to further enhance the credit quality of the securities. Cross-collateralization is a mechanism whereby the properties that collateralize the individual loans are pledged against every loan. In the case that the cash flows from a particular property are not sufficient to meet debt service on its loan, cash flows in excess of debt service from one or more of the other properties in the transaction may be used to meet the debt service of the deficient property. In this way, the NOI of the pool of properties is available to meet the collective debt service on all of the loans. Consequently, an individual loan cannot become delinquent or default as long as there is sufficient cash flow from all of the properties to cover its shortfall.

Cross-defaulting is an extension of cross-collateralization in that any loss on the sale or refinancing of one property can be made up on the sale or refinancing of another. In other words, the net proceeds from the refinancing or sale of all properties within a transaction can be applied to the repayment of principal on every loan. In this way, an investor will not experience loss of principal as long as the net proceeds from the refinancing or sale of the properties are greater than the principal balance of the loans outstanding.

Cross-collateralization and cross-defaulting are powerful credit-enhancement mechanisms possible only within single-borrower, multiple-property transactions.

CMBS STRUCTURES

The interaction among the interests of issuers, investors, and the rating agencies determines CMBS structures and, as a result, they can be quite diverse. However, to date, security structures for CMBS have been relatively simple compared to those found in the residential CMO market. Due to significant call-protection features of commercial mortgages, the structuring process for CMBS is largely related to the allocation of *credit risk*, whereas with residential CMOs, the structuring process focuses predominantly on the allocation of prepayment risk.

We discussed the roles of servicers, trustees, and special purpose corporations in the context of the rating process in the last section. Exhibit 18 demonstrates the interaction of these entities within a CMBS transaction. As we have discussed, servicers and trustees are critical to the debt service process. Servicers interact directly with the borrowers and, consequently, it is important that a servicer has experience with the property type backing a transaction. In some cases, an issuer may choose to employ a "special servicer"—one with considerable experience with the specific property type—to oversee the servicing function. The servicer is usually obligated to make advances in the event that income generated from the properties is temporarily insufficient to meet debt service.

The trustee oversees the flow of funds through the CMBS structure on behalf of the security holders. As part of its duties, the trustee monitors the performance of the servicer and may elect to replace the servicer if certain

Exhibit 18. CMBS Transaction Structure

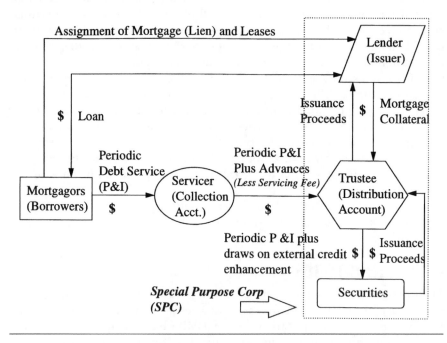

performance standards are not met. The trustee holds the mortgage collateral "in trust" for the security holders and actively manages the distribution of the cash flows collected from the properties. Also, the trustee is responsible for periodic reporting to security holders.

In addition to rules governing the flow of funds through the security structure, most CMBS include covenants that protect investors from the activities of the borrowers. For example, most CMBS include covenants that restrict the ability of the owners to "cherry pick" properties from the collateral (*i.e.,* sell the best properties, leaving the lower quality properties as collateral). There are several forms that such "adverse selection" prohibitions may take, including:

- Owners being required to retire debt equal to 110% to 125% of the balance of the loan on the property being sold

- Resulting DSCRs having to be no lower than before the sale

- Collateral substitution restrictions during non-call periods

In addition, many CMBS include locked-box provisions which give the trustee control over the gross revenues of the properties (Exhibit 19). Accord-

Exhibit 19. Locked-Box Structure

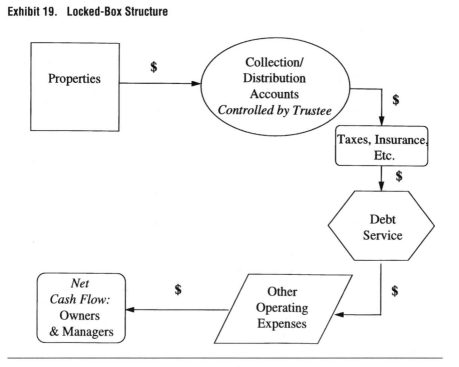

ingly, the trustee is responsible for prioritizing the distribution of cash flows to debt service, taxes, insurance, and other operating expenses. In many cases, management fees are made subordinate to operating expenses and debt service. Owners only have a claim to cash flows net of expenses (including debt service). Consequently, the locked-box structure provides strong incentive for owners and managers to operate the properties with maximum efficiency since they have subordinate claims on income.

In order to protect CMBS investors' liens on the properties, borrowers are prohibited from incurring additional debt (or creating additional liens by other means) on properties pledged as collateral to CMBS. This usually includes the issuance of subordinated debt. (It should be noted that, when subordinated classes are created via credit tranching as a means of credit enhancement, no additional debt or liens on the properties are created.) On the other hand, borrowers are not restricted from issuing debt on other properties not already pledged as collateral to mortgages securitized in CMBS.

While our discussion of the rating process focused on the mortgage collateral, the underlying properties, and the flow of funds through the structure, we now concern ourselves with the forms which the securities can take. These will depend, of course, on the payment characteristics of the loans—terms to maturity, repayment methods, call protection, payment frequency, and interest formulas.

Historically, commercial real estate has been financed with long-term, fixed-rate debt. Even as securitization presents new alternatives for borrowers, most still prefer long terms to maturity and fixed interest rates. On the other hand, because of the current steepness of the yield curve, many borrowers are opting for shorter maturity structures and/or floating-rate structures indexed to short-term interest rates. For example, by reducing the term to maturity from 10 years to 5 years, a borrower currently can save over 50 basis points in annual interest costs.

Everything else being equal, borrowers would like to be able to call their debt at any time without penalty. While such call features are characteristic of residential mortgages, commercial mortgages have historically contained restrictions on prepayments.

Prepayment decisions may be influenced by a variety of economic, geographic, demographic, social, tax, legal, and other factors. In general, if prevailing interest rates fall significantly, debt instruments are more likely to be called. Other factors include the availability of credit for refinancing, changes in tax laws (*e.g.*, changes to depreciation rules), the borrower's net equity position in the property, "due on sale" clauses, and any prepayment penalties or restrictions.

The risk of prepayment has been acutely felt by investors in the corporate debt and residential mortgage markets over the last several years as interest rates have plummeted to their lowest levels in 20 years. Callable securities exhibited substantially lower price appreciation than suggested by their initial durations because, as rates dropped, their durations decreased. As a result, many callable corporate bonds and mortgage-backed securities under, performed investors' return expectations.

Most commercial mortgages, on the other hand, have strong call protection features. Typically, loans are non-prepayable (locked out) for a substantial period of time prior to maturity. In the event of involuntary prepayments during lockout periods or in the event of voluntary prepayments during designated periods, borrowers may be required to pay prepayment penalties which are usually in the form of yield maintenance premiums. Many loan structures combine lockouts and yield maintenance. For example, a loan that has a balloon maturity in seven years may contain a lockout of three years followed by a yield maintenance period of three years and a year without prepayment restrictions. Such call protection features allow commercial mortgages to outperform callable corporate debt and residential mortgages during periods of declining interest rates.

While the calculation of yield maintenance premiums can be quite complicated, they are designed to make investors indifferent to the timing of prepayments. Typically, a yield maintenance premium is equal to the present value of the difference between the interest an investor would earn on the commercial mortgage in the event of no prepayment and what he would earn if the prepaid principal were reinvested at some spread to a Treasury security (or LIBOR in the case of floating-rate loans) with a maturity corresponding to the end of the call-protected period.

For example, suppose a voluntary prepayment of $10 million is made during a yield maintenance period that has 2 years remaining, the loan pays interest monthly at a rate of 8%, and the yield on the 2-year Treasury is 5%. The yield maintenance would be the present value of 24 monthly payments of $18,750 (2.25% × $10 million/12) discounted at annualized rate of 5.75% incorporating a credit spread to Treasuries of 75 basis points. In this case, the yield maintenance premium would be equal to $424,131.

Security structures govern the way that loan payments are distributed to investors. One of the most basic security structures is a fixed-rate pass-through with a single senior class and a single subordinated class. Together they would represent a 100% ownership interest in the underlying commercial mortgages. Principal and interest less any fees (*e.g.*, due the servicer) would be passed-through to the classes according to the percentage each represents of the outstanding balance. The subordination is effected in two ways: first, by the preferential right of the holders of the senior class to receive their distribution before the holders of the subordinate class; second, by the allocation of all realized losses to the subordinated class first. Typically, the order of the distribution of cash flows is as follows: interest to the senior class, principal to the senior class, interest to the junior class, and, finally, principal to the junior class. Realized losses will decrease the percentage amount of the junior class.

As an example, consider the securitization of a $100 million, non-callable, 7-year balloon multifamily loan with a 7.65% coupon, an LTV of 71.4%, and a DSCR of 1.40 times. It might be structured as:

Class	Size	Rating	Coupon	DSCR	LTV
A	$78 million	AA	7.65%	1.80	56%
B	$12 million	BBB	7.65%	1.55	64%
C	$10 million	Non-rated	7.65%		

A slightly more complicated structure would be to strip a portion of the coupon from the senior class (Class A) to create an interest-only class. This would be done to enable senior classes to be priced closer to par (they carry lower yields than the underlying loans due to their enhanced credit quality). For example, in the simple structure considered above, the yield of Class A may be 6.65% thus requiring a coupon strip of 100 basis points to create a par-priced class. The resulting structure would be as follows:

Class	Size	Rating	Coupon	DSCR	LTV
A-1	$78 million	AA	6.65%	1.80**	56%
A-2	$78 million*	AA	1.00%	N/A	N/A
B	$12 million	B	7.65%	1.55	64%
C	$10 million	Non-rated	7.65%		

* Notional amount.   ** Classes A-1 & A-2 combined.

In our view, this coupon strip should trade at a lower yield than the A-1 class for two reasons (assuming the loans are non-callable). First, its duration would be considerably shorter. In this example, the duration of Class A-1 would be 5.44 years compared to 3.24 years for Class A-2. Second, because it has no principal component, it has less risk arising from the balloon payment since all cash flow (with the exception of the final interest payment) has been received prior to the balloon date. Currently, highly call-protected coupon strips trade at higher yields than similarly rated principal-pay classes due to the perception that they exhibit less liquidity.

The next level of complexity would be to credit tranche the loans into several classes spanning the rating spectrum. In this way, issuers can optimize the pricing of risk along the credit curve in the same way that CMO issuers tranche cash flows in time to optimize the pricing of duration along the yield curve. Also, if the loans are amortizing loans or if the loans have long periods of callability, issuers may tranche principal cash flows in time to take advantage of the steep yield curve. As an example consider the following CMBS structure recently used by Nomura to securitize loans on congregate care retirement residences. The collateral consisted of 33 fixed-rate, monthly pay mortgages with an initial aggregate balance of $167.5 million. The loans pay principal monthly according to a 20-year amortization schedule with a final balloon payment due at the end of 8 years. They contain a prepayment lockout for 7 years. Each loan carries an interest rate of 6.85%. The weighted average LTV of all the loans at origination was 79.7% and the weighted average DSCR was 1.22 times. The securities were structured as follows:

Class	Size	Rating	Coupon	DSCR	LTV
A-1	$105.5 million	AAA	6.68%	1.98	50.2%
A-2	$8.4 million	AA	6.68%	1.83	54.2%
A-3	$10.1 million	A	6.68%	1.68	59.0%
B	$10.0 million	BBB	6.68%	1.56	63.8%
C	$10.1 million	BB	6.68%	1.45	68.6%
D	$8.3 million	B	6.68%	1.37	72.6%
E	$15.1 million	Non-rated	6.68%	1.25	79.7%

Principal is allocated sequentially so that Class A-2 receives no principal until Class A-1 is fully retired, Class A-3 receives no principal until Class A-2 is fully retired, and so on. The classes are tranched sequentially even though they are protected from prepayments by the long lockout to take advantage of the steepness of the yield curve. In this case, only the A-1 class receives scheduled amortization since the balloon payment is due before it fully pays down and its average life at issue was approximately 6.5 years. The average life of each of the other classes was 8 years. However, if the borrower makes partial prepayments between the seventh and eighth years, then it is possible that other classes may receive principal before the balloon date.

Credit losses are allocated first to Class E. If losses exceed the coverage provided by Class E, losses are then allocated to Class D; if losses exceed the protection provided by classes D and E, then losses are allocated to Class C; and so on up to Class A-1.

The coupons on the securities have been stripped down to 6.68%. The 17-basis-point spread between the underlying loans and the securities represents servicing and other fees that are paid on an ongoing basis. However, several classes in the transaction were still priced at premiums. We could have stripped a portion of the coupon from each of these to create par-priced classes and interest-only classes. However, due to the presence of a long lockout period, investors were not concerned about high dollar prices and, as such, the execution was superior for premium classes relative to combinations of coupon strips and par-priced classes.

We should emphasize that securitization is not a cheap funding alternative to real estate investors. There are considerable fees incurred in the issuance of securities that are not incurred with other alternatives. For example, typical fees that issuers will incur in a public offering are: rating agency fees ($100,000 per agency), legal costs ($500,000), registration fees ($75,000), printing costs ($50,000), and underwriting fees (1 to 2 percentage points). As a result, smaller issues may be prohibitively expensive, forcing borrowers to consider other alternatives. For this reason, conduits which make loans to many borrowers and issue securities backed by pools of loans are likely to play a major role in the future of commercial mortgage securitization.

The securitization of commercial mortgages is still very new, and security structures to date have been fairly simple. As the CMBS market matures, more complex structures will arise from the efforts of issuers to improve the all-in debt execution provided by securitization. As the market continues to develop, we anticipate the following:

- Greater standardization of security structures

- More sequential-pay structures

- Decreasing subordination levels

- Increasing transaction size

- Application of shifting interest structures

- Equity participations being offered to investors of subordinated classes

VALUATION OF CMBS

Because the CMBS market is young, there are no standard structures or benchmark issues. Also, there are no consistent, publicly available sources of historical yield spreads or relative performance data, which makes it difficult for investors to compare instruments and discern relative value.

Commercial mortgages and CMBS are sometimes viewed as substitutes for corporate bonds. Both markets are large and offer a variety of maturities, call, protection features, and credit risk. A number of factors make CMBS different from corporate bonds:

- CMBS are "structured financings" in which the collateral is secured by properties and their income. The underlying loans are usually non-recourse to the borrower and, as such, credit analysis focuses on the underlying assets; credit analysis of corporate bonds focuses on the credit-worthiness of the borrower.

- The debt service coverage is typically known at the outset of the transaction and is stable, assuming no degradation of the performance of the properties. By contrast, corporate bonds are typically general obligations of the borrowers and debt service coverage is difficult to determine and likely to change in time.

- CMBS typically utilize structural techniques such as subordination to reduce the risk of the underlying businesses to the security holders.

- A CMBS issue is typically insulated from the bankruptcy of each of the parties connected with the transaction. For transactions backed by high-quality properties, it is assumed that downgrade risk is much less than that of corporate bonds.

- The managers of the assets securitizing CMBS must conform to predetermined rules as to how the assets will be managed. Managers of the businesses backing corporate bonds are likely to change strategies in response to changes in the markets in which they operate.

Despite these benefits, it is readily apparent that for comparably rated securities, CMBS trade at much wider yield spreads than corporate bonds

(Exhibit 20). There are several reasons often cited for the difference in offered yield spreads:

- The presence of a "real estate premium"—the result of fearful memories of the recent bear market in real estate and the sub-par performance of poorly structured commercial mortgage transactions from the 1980s;

- The withdrawal from direct lending by some financial institutions due to increased regulatory constraints;

- Investment guidelines of large investor groups that restrict their involvement in new securitized products; and

- The relative illiquidity of CMBS compared to corporate bonds.

Although CMBS spreads have tightened significantly over the last half of this year, we believe that, at current spread levels, CMBS continue to represent better value than corporate bonds. Recently, Marriot International Inc. issued $150 million of a 10-year, non-callable note at +105 over the 10-year Treasury. The notes were rated Baa1 by Moody's and A- by S&P. According to *The Wall Street Journal*, "investors practically crawled over each other" to buy bonds from this deal. A similarly rated hotel-backed CMBS deal would trade at spreads between +275 and +300.

Why do CMBS offer much wider yield spreads even though we believe that the rating agencies are being conservative in their criteria? In our opinion investors are being compensated to participate in a young market that is paying a yield premium to attract new sources of capital. This means that there is opportunity for those that can invest in CMBS and are willing to take the time to learn the characteristics of this young market.

Because investors' opinions diverge as to the future performance of various property types, spread levels for similarly rated securities across various sectors within the CMBS market can differ greatly. In Exhibit 21, we show indicative spreads for a few property types at several points over the second half of

Exhibit 20. CMBS Spreads vs. Corporate Bonds

Rating	CMBS	Corp.
AAA	105	35
AA	135	50
A	180	70
BBB	250	100

Source: Nomura Securities International. Seven-year average lives, strong call protection. Actual spreads can differ greatly from those shown due to differences in security structures.

Exhibit 21. Indicative Spreads by Property Type

Rating	May 1993 Fixed	Floating	August 1993 Fixed	Floating	November 1993 Fixed	Floating
Multifamily						
AAA	115	L+75	105	L+65	90	L+55
AA	150	L+105	140	L+95	115	L+80
A	190	L+165	185	L+160	160	L+135
BBB	280	L+255	255	L+225	220	L+190
Retail						
AAA	130	L+90	120	L+85	105	L+70
AA	165	L+135	150	L+115	130	L+90
A	245	L+220	200	L+175	170	L+145
BBB	330	L+330	280	L+255	235	L+210
Hotels						
AAA	150	L+120	145	L+115	135	L+105
AA	200	L+165	190	L+145	180	L+150
A	265	L+235	235	L+210	230	L+205
BBB	360	L+330	310	L+285	300	L+275
Office						
AAA	150	L+120	145	L+110	125	L+90
AA	200	L+165	190	L+160	145	L+110
A	265	L+240	235	L+205	190	L+165
BBB	360	L+330	310	L+285	265	L+240

Source: Nomura Securities International.

It is important to note that spreads can vary widely from deal to deal based upon various factors including perceived collateral quality, borrower credit history, the number of properties, call protection, etc.

1993. In the multifamily and retail sectors, spreads tightened by 25 to 30 basis points over this time period. Lower-rated securities tightened the most as investors continued to reach for yield in this low interest-rate environment.

However, spreads have tightened much less in the hotel and office sectors. This is partially due to the perception of poor liquidity in these sectors. However, we believe the hotel sector, in particular, is penalized twice for greater uncertainty of business operations of the underlying properties— first, the rating agencies require much higher DSCRs than from other property types in order to achieve the same rating; second, investors require an additional level of protection in terms of higher yield spreads. It is our view that over the next six months spreads in this sector will begin to tighten relative to the other types of properties as investors become familiar with the characteristics of hotel-backed CMBS.

The office sector suffers from investor fears of continued collateral devaluation. Many transactions backed by prime office buildings, on the other hand, have been received very well due to the name recognition of the property or property owners/managers. Going forward, spreads in this sector will become better defined as more transactions backed by pools of loans on good quality office buildings are brought to market.

How can a portfolio manager track and evaluate opportunities in the CMBS market? First, tracking trends in the commercial property markets are important because these will affect spreads for the various CMBS sectors. For example, in the case of the multifamily sector, one should be aware of trends in vacancy rates, rent levels, new construction, *etc.* In our discussion of the various property types, we highlighted several important factors that affect the performance of different property types. Second, in order to be able to evaluate relative value in the securities markets, one needs to keep track of evolving structural standards such as call-protection features, subordination amounts, terms to maturity, *etc.* In addition, one needs to track historical spreads for the various CMBS sectors in order to discern changes in relative value on a historical basis. This can be difficult since CMBS issues can be quite diverse in terms of ratings, structural features, and property types. However, as the market develops, valuation of the various terms will become easier and relative values more discernible.

With respect to evaluating specific CMBS issues, investors should analyze the financials of the properties backing a transaction. Particular emphasis should be placed on the reasonableness of NOI projections, lease schedules, and property valuations. In addition, investors should evaluate the impact of the security structure on value. For example, investors should evaluate the servicer's capabilities for the property type being considered and provisions that impact the way cash flows are distributed to various security classes. Once purchased, investors should monitor updated financial information for the collateral and re-evaluate DSCRs, LTVs, and other measures to see if there is an improvement or deterioration in quality which would cause changes in the market's valuation of the issue. For instance, NOI might improve, causing a better than expected coverage ratio which, in turn, would make the bonds better value. In some cases, ratings may change to reflect changes in quality of the collateral. For example, subordinated classes may be upgraded since, as senior classes pay down, their coverages would improve if there is no deterioration of the collateral.

One approach to relative value analysis is to run various default and loss scenarios and observe their effect on realized yields on the securities. For example, consider again the multiclass structure discussed in the last section:

Class	Face Amount	Rating	Coupon	Zero Loss Yield
A-1	$105.5 million	AAA	6.68%	6.66%
A-2	$8.4 million	AA	6.68%	7.06%
A-3	$10.1 million	A	6.68%	7.46%
B	$10.0 million	BBB	6.68%	8.01%
C	$10.1 million	BB	6.68%	10.61%
D	$8.3 million	B	6.68%	11.50%
E	$15.1 million	Non-rated	6.68%	22.33%

In order to stress these securities, we evaluate the impact of each of the following seven scenarios on realized yields for each class:

1. A total of three properties default, one at the end of each of years three, four, and five

2. 10% of current balance default at the beginning of the second year

3. 10% of current balance default at the beginning of the fifth year

4. 20% of current balance default at the beginning of the second year

5. 20% of current balance default at the beginning of the fourth year

6. 20% of current balance default at the beginning of the sixth year

7. 30% of current balance default at the beginning of the sixth year

In each of the 7 default scenarios we assume a 50% recovery rate at the end of 12 months during which no advances are made to the security holders by the servicer. The following table summarizes the resulting yields for each scenario by class:

Class	Zero Loss Yield	1	2	3	4	5	6	7
A-1	6.66%	6.66	6.66	6.66	6.66	6.66	6.66	6.66
A-2	7.06%	7.06	7.06	7.06	7.06	7.06	7.06	7.06
A-3	7.46%	7.46	7.46	7.46	7.46	7.46	7.46	7.46
B	8.01%	8.01	8.01	8.01	8.01	8.01	8.01	7.16
C	10.61%	10.61	10.61	10.61	9.39	9.79	10.12	9.70
D	11.50%	11.50	11.28	11.50	7.62	9.75	10.58	−5.71
E	22.33%	11.03	7.66	12.45	−156.70	−42.30	−4.38	−10.62

As can be seen in the table, the timing of and amount of defaults have different impacts on the various classes. It is interesting to note that classes A-1 through A-3 experience no reduction yield for all scenarios and that class

B, which carries a BBB rating, experiences a reduction only in scenario 7. The realized yields for class C are not severely impacted in any scenario, and only classes D and E—the most junior classes—experience negative yields for these scenarios. It should be emphasized that we believe that our scenarios are quite onerous since we assume 50% recovery rates after 12 months with no advances being made. (Recall that Fitch found average recovery rates to be better than 60%.)

Another approach that investors should use in assessing relative value is total rate of return analysis. Expected total returns can be calculated, and the amount of spread widening that may be experienced for "break-even" total returns can be used to compare securities. The most difficult aspect of such analysis is estimating the horizon price of the security in question. One way to do this is to estimate what change in NOI would lead to a downgrading (or upgrading) which, in turn, would cause the securities to trade at spreads commensurate with the lower (higher) rating category.

For example, suppose one wants to analyze a AA class from a hotel issue which is trading at 180 basis points over the 7-year Treasury. After reviewing the future prospects of the properties, one projects that there is a 25% chance that the NOI will drop from the original estimate, causing the DSCR to drop from 2.70 to 2.40. Moreover, at a capitalization rate of 9%, the LTV will increase from 58% to 66%. If, due to this deterioration, the rating agencies were to downgrade the security to an A rating, the appropriate spread would go from 180 basis points to 235 basis points. Assuming no change in interest-rate levels, this spread widening would lead to an approximate 2.5% change in price. Offsetting this price depreciation would be the 180 basis points earned over Treasuries plus any price appreciation from the down curve. In this fashion, investors can apply their expectations of various scenarios to come up with expected total rates of return.

In addition, investors could use option pricing theory to price the credit or default option that the lender has extended to the borrower. The security holder can be viewed as having purchased a bond with no credit risk and having sold a default option to the borrower. By assuming that the value of the properties follows some process, one can build a tree of property and loan values with corresponding probabilities. By making the assumption that the borrower will default when the LTV is greater than some threshold (usually 100%), one can solve for the fair value of the default option. In this framework, the default option will be more valuable the higher the initial LTV, the longer the term to maturity, and the more volatile the NOI. The greater the value of the default option, the higher the yield should be for the securities. A comparison between the default-option-adjusted yields and the market yields can be used as a rich-cheap indicator.

Our analysis of the CMBS market suggests that CMBS are attractive relative to other fixed-income instruments. We believe that, as the market matures, investors will begin to emphasize relative value within the sector and, with the development of new tools such as default-option-adjusted yield analysis, greater differentiation between CMBS issues will result. In addition, the market will begin to reflect the different regulatory environments for each sector. For example, the multifamily securities now carry a 50% BIS risk weighting for banks and thrifts. In addition, while most CMBS are not SMMEA eligible, those backed by loans on multifamily or congregate care properties are SMMEA-eligible and, therefore, can be used as collateral for repurchase agreements. These conditions allow multifamily and congregate care CMBS to trade at tighter spreads.

CONCLUSION

We believe that the CMBS market represents an opportunity for investors who are able to evaluate its risks. The spreads at which CMBS currently trade are, in our opinion, in excess of where they should be for their respective ratings. We believe that, at this time, investors are being well compensated for a market that is in its infancy.

The real estate markets are just beginning to stabilize after several years of severe declines. As is usually the case following such a decline, loans are being underwritten using conservative standards. While we are not predicting a major bull market in commercial real estate for the next several years, CMBS investors do not need appreciating property values to do well. CMBS will perform well as long as property values do not decline substantially. We believe property values will slowly trend higher in the coming years.

The CMBS market is growing and investors are beginning to evaluate risks more closely. While there appear to be many specific risks in individual securities (especially single-property transactions), we think that a diversified portfolio of CMBS can significantly outperform a similarly rated corporate bond portfolio. Portfolio managers need to become familiar with this market given the opportunities presented at this time. As investors become more comfortable with this market and as standardization takes hold, liquidity will improve and spreads will tighten. Portfolio managers willing to do the requisite work now will benefit from improved liquidity.

APPENDIX:
NAIC Capital Guidelines

Life insurance companies are required to report in their statutory annual statements reserves held against their investment portfolios. These reserves are broken down into Asset Valuation Reserves (AVR) and Interest Maintenance Reserves (IMR). The AVR are held against assets subject to credit risk, and the IMR are held against assets whose values change in response to changes in interest rates. As such, the AVR is analogous to the risk-based capital guidelines to which banks are subject. The following table is a summary of the indicative reserve factors for each asset category that is used to determine the AVR.

Asset Category	Rating Range	Security Type	Reserve Factor
U.S. Govt.	N/A	Treasuries, GNMA	0%
NAIC1	AAA-A	Agcy. Debs, Corp. Bonds, MBS, ABS, CMBS	0.3%
NAIC2	BBB	" "	1%
NAIC3	BB	" "	4%
NAIC4	B	" "	9%
NAIC5	CCC	" "	20%
NAIC6	Default	" "	30%
Whole Loans*:			
Single/Multifamily Res. Mortgages			0.5%
Guaranteed Municipal Mortgages			0.1%
Other Mortgages (incl. commercial)			3%
Real Estate			10%

*Capital requirements for whole loans may be further adjusted to reflect an individual company's default and loss experience relative to the experience of the industry as a whole.

CHAPTER 26

Quantifying Credit Risk in CMBS

Patrick J. Corcoran, Ph.D.
Vice President
Nomura Securities International, Inc.

Duen-Li Kao
Director
General Motors Investment Management Corporation

INTRODUCTION

Commercial mortgage-backed securities (CMBS) are bonds that are collateralized by commercial mortgage loans. In turn, these commercial mortgage loans are collateralized by underlying real estate property.[1]

Many first-time investors in CMBS were initially persuaded in 1993 by yields that seemed hugely attractive relative to any reasonable calculation of losses. As more and more investors became persuaded that commercial real estate prices had bottomed, spreads narrowed steadily. Today's narrower spreads call for a vehicle for more carefully assessing CMBS fundamentals. At the same time, with real estate prices having, in our view, bottomed in most markets, the analysis must proceed in the context of a fundamentally improved real estate outlook. This chapter attempts to fill this need.

As the emerging market in CMBS develops, assessing the credit experience of these new bonds directly will eventually be possible. At this point in time, however, such a track record is unavailable. Hence, our approach is to assess the track record available in the default experience of the underlying

---

1 Much has been written recently concerning problems of residential mortgage-backed securities and related derivative securities in handling prepayment risk. Residential mortgages of course can be prepaid fully at any time. In contrast, commercial mortgages generally have *very* strong protection against early prepayment. This protection takes the form of absolute prohibitions against prepayment (called lockout) as well as prepayment penalities (so-called yield maintenance provisions). The key point is that the recent problems relating to residential mortgage-backed securities have nothing to do with CMBS.

commercial mortgages. From this record we then infer the likely credit outlook for CMBS.

The first section of the chapter lays out our empirical model. Our model links the delinquency experience of life insurance company loans to the changing prices in the real estate asset markets. To move from a delinquency model to a credit loss model, we need to examine the various credit events in commercial mortgages and the consequent losses. This is the subject of the second section. The third section of the chapter shows how the credit model can be used to project losses for CMBS. The final section brings together the outlook for the real estate markets and the implications for CMBS credit risk. It also looks briefly at some investment strategy implications for the major institutional investors.

THE EMPIRICAL DEFAULT MODEL

It was an early insight of the options literature that a lender/investor in a risky bond could be viewed as owning a Treasury bond plus a short position in a put option to the borrower. In the case of a commercial mortgage, the lender had, in effect, sold the borrower a put option on the underlying property. The borrower could put or sell the underlying real estate property to the lender at a strike price equal to the unpaid loan balance. Interest income over and above the Treasury coupon rate represented the option premium received by the lender for the sale of the underlying put option.

Putting aside transaction costs or other considerations, borrowers would always default on their loans if the property value were to fall below the value of the outstanding loan balance. This is especially the case for commercial mortgages, which are generally non-recourse.[2] The lender has recourse only to the borrower's real estate collateral and not to his other assets. However, in a series of important articles, Kerry Vandell has argued that commercial mortgage borrowers do not exercise the default option "ruthlessly," as described above.[3] Instead, loan defaults are less than ruthless, just as they are for residential mortgages. Vandell's findings heighten the importance of having an empirical default model which captures the actual response of borrowers and lenders to changing real estate markets.

In this options framework, mortgage losses and defaults are negatively related to changing real estate prices. This relationship is shown in Exhibit 1.

---

2 By comparison, in corporate bonds, the options paradigm has proved much more difficult to apply because the underlying "equity" concept is not as well defined. The non-recourse nature of commercial mortgages greatly simplifies the issue in this case.

3 Kerry D. Vandell, "Predicting Commercial Mortgage Foreclosure Experience," *Journal of the American Real Estate and Urban Economics Association* 20 (1992), pp. 55-88, and "Handing Over the Keys: A Perspective on Mortgage Default Research," *Journal of the American Real Estate and Urban Economics Association* 21 (1993), pp. 211-246.

Exhibit 1. Commercial Mortgage Losses, Real Estate Values and LTVs

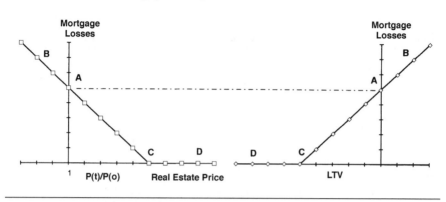

Falling real estate prices, such as occurred from 1988 to 1992, raise loan-to-value (LTV) ratios and, hence, expected losses (position B). Rising real estate prices reduce LTV ratios and eventually drive losses to minimum levels (position C). Beyond this point, further increases in real estate prices (position D) do not materially reduce losses.

The Relationships

In our empirical model, we link American Council on Life Insurance (ACLI) data on loan delinquencies with the Russell-NCREIF Index of property returns and property prices. These data reveal the aggregate linkage between loan performance and real estate prices both by region and major property type beginning in 1988. The loan performance data are available for the nine major census regions. We combined several of these census regions to produce a six-region division that roughly follows the one proposed by Wurtzebach, Hartzell, and Shulman.

For each major sector, we estimated separate statistical relationships to explain loan delinquencies. For example, industrial loan delinquencies in the six regions are negatively related to changes in the price of industrial real estate properties. To capture the price changes for industrial properties we use a national index for industrial property prices and a regional index for commercial property prices. The regional index represents properties of different sectors combined together. We followed the same approach in the other sectors (see Exhibit 2).

As shown there, the coefficients on the real estate price variables reveal a powerful negative relationship between the frequency of delinquent loans and real estate prices. The especially important role of the regional price variable in all the sector equations testifies to the important role of regional

Exhibit 2.   Delinquency Model (Basic)

Sector	Regional Price[a]	Sector Price[b]	Constant	Steady State[d]	R^2	Standard Error	Estimation Period
Apartment	12.61[c]	17.68	33.51	3.22	31.5%	2.11%	1991:Q1
	(4.3)	(2.4)	(5.2)				1993:Q2
Industrial	26.58	2.74	25.83	1.99	63.7%	1.77%	
	(12.8)	(1.7)	(16.2)				1998:Q1
Office	25.88	4.24	33.33	3.21	63.4%	2.19%	to
	(10.1)	(2.5)	(17.3)				1993:Q2
Retail	12.78	9.04	24.27	2.65	66.4%	1.36%	
	(7.7)	(6.4)	(17.7)				

Notes:

a. The regional price variable corresponds to the eight regional "divisions" in the Russell-NCREIF index. These divisional price indices capture price movements for a combination of property types within the region.

b. The sector price indices measure changes in property prices at the national level but specific to the property sector. Thus, the apartment equation focuses on the national apartment index in the Russell-NCREIF database. Since the apartment index has only been available since early 1991, the estimation period for this equation is shorter than for the other equations.

c. Regression coefficiants are numbers in top row. T-statisitics are in second row in parentheses.

d. Since both the regional price variable and the sector price variable measure today's real estate price relative to loan origination, their normalized value corresponding to unchanging price is unity. Thus, if real estate prices do not change, the "steady state" delinquency rate is the sum of the three regression coefficients.

diversification. In the past 20 years the various sub-regions within the U.S. economy have experienced ongoing, rolling recessions with relatively low correlations among these regions. This implies that CMBS investors can achieve a substantial gain from a portfolio that has strong regional diversification.

Looking at delinquency rates for the first quarters of 1990 and 1992 (Exhibit 3) provides a visual sense of the diversity among regions. In the earlier period (top panel), the Mineral Extraction region exhibits the highest loan delinquency rates within each property sector. Two years later (bottom panel), the Mineral Extraction delinquency rates were at the low end for each property type (except apartments).

The sensitivity of loan delinquencies to changing real estate prices can be illustrated graphically (Exhibit 4, left-hand panel). The lines represent the combined impact of both regional and sectoral prices on delinquency rates for large life insurance company loan pools. On the left panel, the intercepts of the lines on the vertical axis represent the "steady state" delinquency rates also shown in Exhibit 2. These delinquency rates correspond to unchanged real estate prices and an initial LTV ratio of 72%. Notice that for these large life insurance company loan pools, an increase in real estate col-

Exhibit 3. Regional and Sector Delinquency Rates

1st Quarter, 1990

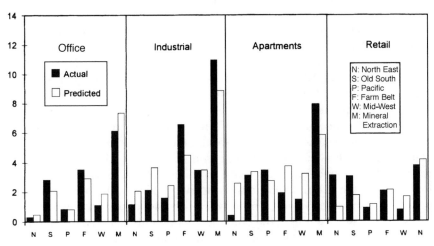

1st Quarter, 1992

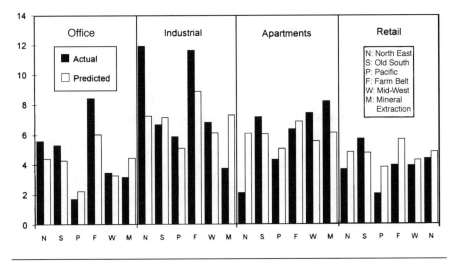

lateral prices of between 8% and 12% is sufficient to reduce projected delinquency rates to zero.

With respect to LTV ratios, an important characteristic of life company portfolios in the 1988-93 period was relatively large dispersion of LTV ratios.

This large dispersion arose because of wide variation in underwriting standards in 1988-89, near the top of the real estate cycle. Moreover, subsequent to 1989, when delinquencies rose sharply, life company lenders "involuntarily" refinanced many poorly performing loans at high LTVs.

Over the period 1988-93, reporting life insurers originated new loans at an average LTV ratio of 72%. This average-life portfolio's LTV is the benchmark from which the impact of changing real estate prices must be computed.

The right-hand panel of Exhibit 4 translates the changing real estate prices into changing LTV ratios. As shown, our results imply that a reduction in LTV ratios from 72% to the mid-60s is sufficient in each sector to reduce expected delinquency rates to zero.

The differences and similarities among the different sectors are also interesting. The retail sector loans have the lowest sensitivity to changing real estate prices, as shown by the flat slope in the retail line. The industrial sector loans also have a moderate flattish slope and, in addition, have the lowest position of any of the delinquency lines in the graph. Finally, the office and apartment sectors show the highest sensitivity (steepest slope) to changing real estate prices. In fact, the position of the office and apartment relationships on the line is virtually identical. This does not mean that office and apartment loans had identical delinquency records in the 1980s. Rather, the office sector was more overbuilt and experienced much larger price declines, pushing office delinquencies much further up the curve than the apartment loan sector.

Other Factors

A number of other factors have an important bearing on the relationship between loan delinquencies and real estate prices. These factors may operate

Exhibit 4. Sector Delinquency Rates, Real Estate Values and LTVs

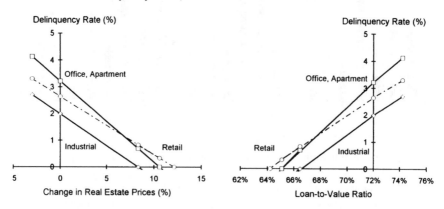

very differently in the future than they did in the 1988-93 period when the model was estimated. Let us consider a number of these factors.

LTV Ratio Dispersion. A rise in the dispersion of the LTV distribution means that more loans are at the high end of the distribution. With the same average LTV, more loans will end up delinquent than in a narrower distribution. In the 1988-93 period, falling real estate prices contributed greatly to high dispersion for LTVs. However, for portfolios of new loans invested in 1994 and flat real estate prices going forward, the LTVs in these portfolios have much lower dispersion.

The Maturity of the Loan Portfolio. The maturity of the life insurer portfolio in the years 1988-93 was approximately 3-1/2 years. This reflected the fact that new loan originations typically had a maturity of about seven years. With a seasoned loan portfolio this translated into existing loans having average maturity of about 3-1/2 years. Moreover, between 1988 and 1993 the maturity of this seasoned portfolio was virtually unchanged. So our data reveal nothing about the impact of changing maturity and loan seasoning on delinquencies.

Our data set does not allow us explicitly to examine the role of amortization—the return of principal on a gradual basis over the life of the loan. Even with unchanging real estate prices, amortization causes a gradual improvement in LTV ratios over time. Hence, delinquencies should also be improving over time. In terms of Exhibit 1, the loan pool "rolls down" the delinquency curve. As shown in Exhibit 5, a 10-year mortgage with an 8% coupon rate can sustain declines in real estate prices over its lifetime ranging from 1.30% per year for a 30-year amortization schedule to 7.25% for a 15-year write-off period and still maintain its original LTV ratio.

In projecting the performance of new loans, it will be important to account for the impact of amortization on the LTV ratio. The vast majority of life company loans are amortizing loans that typically have a 25-year amortization rate. Studies by Mark Snyderman confirm that commercial mortgages

---

Exhibit 5.   Break-Even Changes in Real Estate Prices

| | 10-Year Mortgage Mortgage Coupon Rate (%) | | | | |
Amortization (Years)	6	7	8	9	10
15	−7.96	−7.59	−7.25	−6.91	−6.59
20	−4.29	−3.96	−3.65	−3.36	−3.09
25	−2.66	−2.38	−2.11	−1.88	−1.66
30	−1.77	−1.52	−1.30	−1.11	−0.95

experience positive seasoning.[4,5] Snyderman documented the amount of seasoning that is very close to expectations with a 25-year amortization.

MOVING FROM DELINQUENCY AND FORECLOSURES TO A CREDIT LOSS MODEL

When a borrower misses timely payment of interest or principal on a commercial mortgage, the loan is technically in default or delinquent. In the ACLI statistics delinquent loans are those that are behind in scheduled payments 90 days or more. Once delinquent, a loan can emerge from delinquency in one of two ways. First, the lender may foreclose on the property to settle the debt. Because the borrower has the option to sell the property himself prior to foreclosure, loans settled in the foreclosure process have higher losses. Snyderman's study found a loss severity of 36% for foreclosed loans originated between 1972 and 1986, tracked up to 1991.[6] This means that loss of interest and principal amounted to 36% of the outstanding loan balance.

On the other hand, delinquent loans can also emerge as so-called restructured loans in which the borrower and lender mutually agree to alter the original terms of the loan. The lender might agree to reduce the coupon or to forgive past failures to meet scheduled interest. With restructured loans, the borrower might agree to repay missed interest and principal payments either immediately or over the remaining life of the loan.

Unfortunately we know almost nothing about an important loophole in the rescheduled loans—their loss severity. Of loans that became delinquent in the 1970s and 1980s, as reported by Snyderman, approximately half emerged as restructured loans. The other half emerged as foreclosures. Snyderman's study *assumes* that the loss severity for restructures is 18%, com-

---

4 Mark P. Snyderman, "Commercial Mortgages: Default Occurrence and Estimated Yield Impact," *Journal of Portfolio Management* (Fall 1991), pp. 82-87, and "An Update on Commercial Mortgage Default Costs Using Insurance Regulatory Data," *Real Estate Finance Journal* (Summer 1994).

5 Positive seasoning means improved creditworthiness of loans as they season, or get older. Amortization is the most obvious reason for positive seasoning because it reduces the loan's LTV even with unchanged real estate prices. A second issue is whether mortgage loans with unchanging LTV may change in creditworthiness over time. Our model simulations reported in this chapter assume not, but this is an area for further research. In the corporate bond area, for example, researchers have found negative seasoning for investment-grade bonds and positive seasoning for junk bonds (see Duen-Li Kao, "Illiquid Securities: Issues of Pricing and Performance Measurement," *Financial Analysts Journal* (March/April 1993), pp. 28-35, 77.

6 Snyderman, "An Update on Commercial Mortgage Default Costs Using Insurance Regulatory Data," *op. cit.*

pared to 36% for foreclosures, but provides no evidence to support this assumption.[7]

Using Snyderman's assumption, the *average* delinquent loan will experience a loss severity equal to:

$$(1/2) \times 18\% + (1/2) \times 36\% = 27\%$$

Notice that this is far below the average loss severity on corporate bond defaults, which is generally estimated to be around 60%.[8]

To move from loss severity to the computation of losses, we use the standard formula:

$$\text{Loss} = (\text{Loss Severity}) \times (\text{Delinquency})$$

Suppose our model is projecting a delinquency rate of 1% per year if real estate prices remain at today's levels. In other words, a total of 1% of loans would normally emerge each year either as restructures or foreclosures. Applying the above formula means that the annual loss is $(0.27) \times (1\%)$, or 27 basis points of loss per year.

When this loss severity is used in conjunction with our steady state delinquency rates, the losses seem quite high. For example, the retail sector delinquency rate is 2.65% per year. This means that a pool of retail loans with initial LTV of 72% under the condition of flat real estate prices experiences losses of $(0.27) \times (2.65\%)$, or 71 basis points per year. The question naturally arises: if the prices of the real estate collateral properties are not falling (on average), where do the losses and delinquencies come from? The answer lies in the LTV ratios of loans originated during our model estimation period (1988-93). The unusually high LTV *dispersion* during the period resulted in a relatively large number of high LTV loans with high losses. Because much of this high historical LTV dispersion is irrelevant for projecting loan losses for new loans made today, our model projections tend to be overly pessimistic.

---

7 Our own view is that an 18% loss severity is probably too high for normal real estate markets. An examination of ACLI historical statistics suggests that borrower waiting times in delinquency were much longer in the 1970s and early 1980s than the very difficult 1988-93 period. We feel that lenders dealt with delinquent loans very aggressively in 1988-93 because expected losses were large. (They also had encouragement from the NAIC capital guidelines to do so.) In more normal or favorable real estate markets, prospective losses may have been *negligible*, making patient restructuring the optimal strategy for lenders. Without further empirical study of the matter, however, a strong case cannot be made for Snyderman's assumption or for any other.

8 See Edward I. Altman, "Defaults and Returns in High-Yield Bonds: Analysis Through 1993," Merrill Lynch & Co., 1994, and Moody's Investors Service, *Corporate Bond Defaults and Default Rates: 1970–1993*, Special Report, 1994.

Risk-Neutral Credit Spread

We can use the notion of the risk-neutral credit spread to calculate the impact of the losses computed above on the price of a commercial mortgage whole loan or security. The risk-neutral concept has been discussed by several researchers.[9] Its applications to pricing commercial mortgages and private placements were also reviewed elsewhere.[10] The idea is that a risk-neutral investor should use the Treasury curve to value the cash flow of a risky bond net of expected credit losses. In other words, the discounted value of the nominal cash flow using the risky bond discount rate is equivalent to discounting the net-of-loss cash flow using the Treasury curve. Mathematically, the simplified relationship can be stated as:

Promised Cash Flow / Discount Rate with Credit Risk Spread =

(Promised Cash Flow x Credit Loss Adjustment) / Treasury Discount Rate

whereby *credit loss adjustment* is a function of delinquency rate, relative probability of foreclosure and restructuring, and their respective loss severities.

This concept is useful for figuring the decline in a bond's price or elevation in its up-front yield that is sufficient to just offset anticipated credit losses. Continuing the previous example of calculating loss, suppose that a commercial mortgage carries an 8.5% coupon with a 10-year term and 20-year amortization schedule, while comparable Treasury rate is 7.5% semiannual compounded (s.a.). With the assumptions of delinquency rate of 1% and a credit loss of 27 basis points per year, the "fair or intrinsic" value of credit losses for this mortgage would be $17 per $1000 face value.[11] Note that this analysis focuses only on the losses associated with credit risk. It ignores the values related to the security's illiquid nature (*i.e.*, the value of illiquidity option) and the yield maintenance provisions (*i.e.*, the value of prepayment option).[12]

The credit loss model can also be used to derive the spread required to compensate the possible credit loss. That is, given an assumed delinquency rate and related credit losses, one can calculate the required coupon rate on a mortgage. Using the example above (1% delinquency, a 10-year mortgage with a 20-year amortization, and a 7.5% Treasury rate), an additional yield

---

9   See Jerome S. Fons, "The Default Premium and Corporate Bond Experience," *Journal of Finance* (March 1987), pp. 81-97; Thomas Y. S. Ho, *Strategic Fixed Income Investment* (Homewood, IL: Dow Jones-Irwin, 1990); and Duen-Li Kao, "Valuation: Fair Trading," *Balance Sheet* (Winter 1992/1993), pp. 15-19.

10 See Duen-Li Kao, "Valuation: Fair Trading," and "Illiquid Securities: Issues of Pricing and Performance Measurement Measurement," *op. cit.*

11 The calculation assumes that the bond is held to maturity.

12 For the discussion of implications of these two options, see Patrick J. Corcoran and Duen-Li Kao, "Implications of Asset Illiquidity," in Edward I. Altman and Irwin T. Vanderhoof (eds.), *The Financial Dynamics of the Insurance Industry* (Burr Ridge, IL: Irwin, 1993), pp. 197-211.

spread of 27 basis points (s.a.) would be required to compensate future credit losses for this mortgage traded at par.[13] If the delinquency rate increases to 2% per year, the required credit-loss yield spread would be 53 basis points for a marginal increase of 26 basis points. Note that future periodic cash flows are adjusted by cumulative delinquency rates, which results in a non-linear relationship between price and delinquency rate under the credit loss model. As shown in Exhibit 6, the marginal increase in required credit loss yield spread actually falls as the delinquency rate increases.

Another application of this credit loss model is on deriving implied delinquency rate (*i.e.*, delinquency rate implied by the market quoted mortgage yield).[14] Suppose that a 10-year par-mortgage demands 9.0% coupon amortized over 20 years with similar-term Treasury rate of 7.5% (167 b.p. spread, semiannual compounded), with 50 basis points of this yield spread related to liquidity and prepayment options. With the same assumptions of foreclosure propensity and credit losses as above, we can derive the implied delinquency rate of 4.80% per year. If the future delinquency rate is anticipated to be lower than the implied rate, the mortgage would appear to be cheap.

Exhibit 6.   Relationship between Delinquency Rate and Required Credit Loss Spread

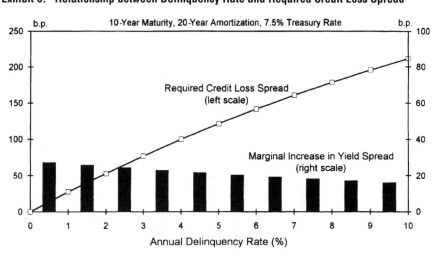

---

13 Since the assumed 20-year amortization rate reduces the LTV in this example, real estate prices must be assumed to decline sufficiently to keep the LTV at a level consistent with 1% delinquency rate. This is also the case in the example in the subsequent paragraph.

14 A similar analytical framework was used to evaluate high-yield bonds in Peter Niculescu, "Breakeven Default Rates," Goldman Sachs Fixed Income Research, November 1990.

ASSESSING LOSSES FOR CMBS

The key point in analyzing losses for CMBS is that they are derived from the underlying whole loans. All cash flows net of underwriting and servicing fees flow through to the bondholders. In a simple pass-through structure, for example, the credit experience of the bonds would simply mirror that of the whole loans.

More commonly, however, credit enhancement is provided to senior bonds through subordination of the claims of junior bondholders. For example, suppose we have a $100 million diversified pool of retail properties with average LTV of 72%. Suppose further that the junior bondholders assume the first 25% of credit loss liability. The situation then looks as shown in Exhibit 7.

From the perspective of the senior bondholders, the 25% subordination of the junior bondholders is equivalent to obtaining additional equity in the underlying real estate properties. This means that the senior bond has a credit outlook equivalent to loans on the underlying properties with 54% LTV.

The junior bonds have loss exposure for the entire $72 million pool of loans. Their position is comparable to the capital or surplus of a bank or insurance company lender. The senior bondholders' position is comparable to that of bank deposits (without deposit insurance) or insurance company policy holders.

Assuming real estate prices have bottomed in most markets, we need to determine the appropriate assumption for an *increase* in real estate prices over the life of the loans. Because the above examples involve negligible risk of credit loss for the senior bondholders, we shall focus our credit analysis on the subordinate bonds.

Before turning to that analysis, we briefly review the real estate outlook to support our assertion that prices have bottomed and will be at least rising modestly in the next several years. In this setting, it is worth noting briefly that the primary issue for senior bondholders in today's real estate environment is not credit risk at all but rather uncertainty in the timing of cash flows. An analysis of this issue is beyond the scope of this chapter.

Exhibit 7. Simple Subordinated Junior/Senior Bond Structure

Whole Loans	CMBS
Commercial Mortgage	Senior Bonds
Loan Pool	($54 Million)
($72 Million)	(Effective LTV = 54%)
LTV = 72%	Subordinate Bonds
	($18 Million)

THE CMBS OUTLOOK AND THE REAL ESTATE OUTLOOK

Our approach to assessing the CMBS credit outlook is derived directly from the real estate market. In the period 1986-93 commercial real estate markets experienced the largest declines since the Great Depression. Over the past year or so, it has become clear even to casual market observers that real estate prices have bottomed in most markets. Moreover, prices have bottomed at levels that are often far below replacement costs. The substantial discounts of real estate asset values to replacement cost essentially preclude new supply in these markets because returns to new development activity are negative.

With real estate prices flat to modestly rising over the next several years, the stage is set for CMBS to perform very strongly. The argument is not that real estate prices will surge dramatically—it is merely that prices have bottomed and will rise modestly.

In this setting, three factors bear positively for CMBS investments:

1. From the perspective of economic theory, a "bottom" for real estate prices is defined in inflation-adjusted terms. Thus, even if prices do not rise subsequently in real terms, nominal real estate prices would keep pace with the general level of inflation. As noted below, a modest rise in real estate prices has a very significant impact on CMBS.

2. The advantage of modestly rising real estate prices for CMBS is that LTVs and associated delinquencies will be trending downward even for a non-amortizing loan. In the case of amortizing loans, however, amortization achieves the same effect even with unchanged real estate prices.

3. From a longer run perspective, real estate prices are expected to rise faster than inflation. With prices so far below replacement cost in so many markets, the resulting absence of new supply will put upward pressure on asset prices. With general inflation running 2% to 3% over the past several years, and allowing for a modest 1% appreciation over and above inflation, a conservative expectation is that real estate prices will rise 3.5% per year.

As noted above, our model projections are likely pessimistic for new loan portfolios because of the high LTV dispersion in the model's estimation period. To explicitly offset part of this bias, a user can make a simple technical adjustment to the model by accounting for a small amount of inflation. In this case, in the example above, a 3.5% inflation rate would actually correspond to a somewhat smaller "true" rate of real estate price appreciation.

CREDIT ANALYSIS FOR SUBORDINATE CMBS

Let us return to our example in Exhibit 7. Against a pool of properties worth $100 million, we have commercial mortgage whole loans of $72 million. Our subordinate bondholders have the $18 million first-loss exposure.

Let us suppose further that the subordinate bonds have a coupon of 10%, a maturity of 10 years, and a triple-B (BBB/Baa) rating and that (for simplicity) the Treasury yield curve is flat at 7.5%. Exhibit 8 looks at risk-neutral credit spreads for three different bonds with different rates of amortization.

First and foremost notice that the net spread in our expected range of increases in real estate prices (at least 3.5% per year) is at or above 200 basis points per year. By comparison, in today's market triple-B corporate bonds exhibit a yield spread about 100 basis points above the 10-year Treasury. Using Altman's 1993 default tables suggests a credit charge of about 37 basis points per year, for a net corporate spread of 63 basis points.[15]

Exhibit 8.   The Impact of Amortization

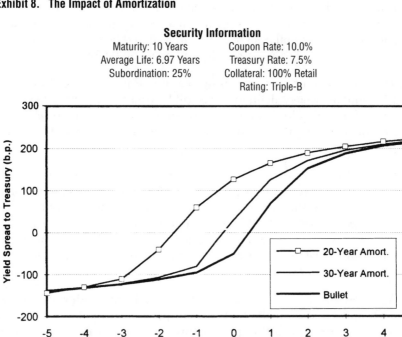

Security Information

Maturity: 10 Years	Coupon Rate: 10.0%
Average Life: 6.97 Years	Treasury Rate: 7.5%
Subordination: 25%	Collateral: 100% Retail
	Rating: Triple-B

---

15 The calculation assumes a 30% recovery price on defaulted, cash-pay subordinated bonds and a 10-year cumulative default rate of 4.8%. Similar to the case of analyzing "B"-class CMBS, the seasoning (negative) effect of triple-B bonds on annual default rates is also considered.

Secondly, the powerful impacts of amortization are evident in adverse scenarios. For example, if real estate prices do not change at all over the life of the bonds, the net spread for the bullet (zero-amortization) is minus 50 basis points. Why is this the case? With no change in real estate prices and no help from amortization, the delinquency rate for the retail loan pool remains at its steady-state level of 2.65% per year. This results in losses of approximately 2.65% × 0.27, or 71 basis points, per year to the loan pool, which are absorbed entirely by the subordinate bondholders. Thus, the debit to the net spread is roughly four times (corresponding to subordination of 25%) 71 basis points, which exceeds the nominal 250-basis-point spread to Treasuries and makes the net spread for the bullet slightly negative.

At zero real estate inflation, the net spread with 30-year amortization is +30 basis points. The spread with 20-year amortization is +120 basis points. Viewed a bit differently, to reduce the net spread with 20-year amortization to −50 basis points, which is the bullet's net spread at zero inflation, the rate of real estate inflation must be reduced about 2% (from zero to −2%). In other words, in this example 20-year amortization is worth 2% of real estate price inflation.

Thirdly, our net spread calculations for the subordinate bond are sensitive to our assumptions about loss severity. Suppose, for example, we used a foreclosure loss severity of 25% (versus 36% in base case) and a restructure loss severity of 10% (versus 18% in base case).[16] The justification would be the favorable point we currently occupy in the real estate cycle with prices having bottomed and no new supply in sight. With zero inflation in real estate prices and no amortization, losses for the whole loans are roughly 47 basis points per year (versus 71 basis points for the base case). The net spread for the subordinate bullet bond in Exhibit 8 is 100 basis points higher at zero inflation. Notice that the assumed differences in the whole-loan loss rate are amplified by a factor of four because the subordination is 25%. If subordination were only 10%, the amplification factor would be 10 times.

Exhibit 9 provides additional detail for the subordinate bond assuming 20-year amortization for the whole-loan pool. The top panel shows that the break-even point to Treasuries occurs when cumulative losses are between 3.5% and 4%. Higher cumulative losses go with lower real estate inflation rates. The bottom panel shows that the subordinate bonds with 20-year amortization are quite robust with respect to assumed real estate price inflation, especially in our expected (3.5%) range.

---

16 This assumption is equivalent to the case discussed in Patrick J. Corcoran, "Assessing the Risks for New Real Estate Loans," *Real Estate Review* (Spring 1994), pp. 10-14, and Patrick J. Corcoran, Dale Fathe-Aazam, and Alberto Perez-Pietri, "The Role of Commercial Mortgages in Fixed Income Investing," *Pension Real Estate Association Quarterly* (January 1994), pp. 26-30.

Exhibit 9.   Sensitivity of "B" Class Yield Spreads

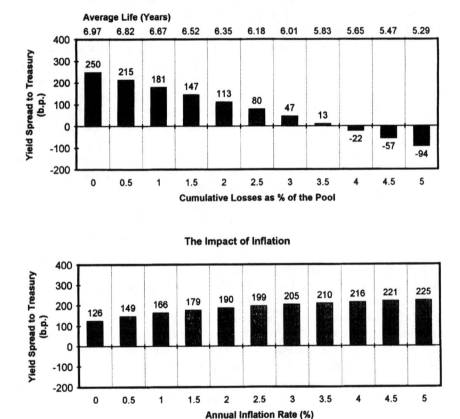

Security Information

Maturity: 10 Years
Average Life: 6.97 Years
Amortization: 20 Years
Subordination: 25%

Coupon Rate: 10.0%
Treasury Rate: 7.5%
Collateral: 100% Retail
Rating: Triple-B

The Impact of the Pool's Losses

The Impact of Inflation

Exhibit 10 examines the sensitivity of the junior bond to the amount of subordination. Recall our base case has 25% subordination. Exhibit 10 contrasts this bond with an alternative bond assumed to bear the same coupon (10%) and lower subordination (10%). The increase in cumulative losses causes the net spread of the junior bond with 10% subordination to decline more rapidly since the same losses are spread over a narrower base.

Exhibit 10.   The Impact of Subordination Percentage

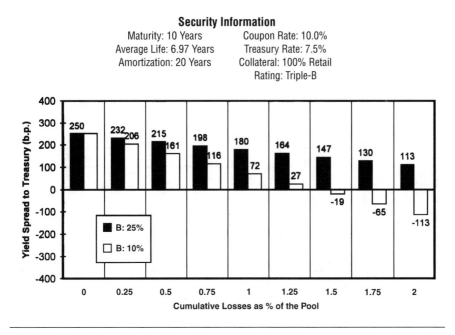

Security Information

Maturity: 10 Years	Coupon Rate: 10.0%
Average Life: 6.97 Years	Treasury Rate: 7.5%
Amortization: 20 Years	Collateral: 100% Retail
	Rating: Triple-B

In practice, the junior bond with 10% subordination would not carry the same coupon as the subordinate bond with 25% subordination. Exhibit 11 carries the analysis a step further. It shows, at a variety of real estate inflation rates, the coupon required on the junior bond with 10% subordination to equate its net spread to that of the junior bond with 25% subordination. For example, in our expected range of at least 3.5% real estate inflation, a coupon about 300 basis points above the 7.5% Treasury rate would equate the net spreads.

Suppose the 10% subordinated bonds were rated double-B (BB/Ba) and traded at a spread of 430 basis points in the market. Since the market spread of this bond exceeds the required coupon spread of 315 basis points (at 3.5% inflation), the 10% subordinated bond looks attractive relative to the junior bond with 25% subordination.[17]

The 10% subordinated bond also looks attractive relative to a comparable corporate bond. The expected net credit loss spread for this CMBS is

---

17 No allowance is taken here for the fact that the bond with lower subordination is a riskier bond since the net spread concept is risk-neutral.

Exhibit 11. Expected Inflation Rates and Required Coupon Spreads

Security Information

Maturity: 10 Years
Average Life: 6.97 Years   Treasury Rate: 7.5%
Amortization: 20 Years   Collateral: 100% Retail
Subordination: 10%

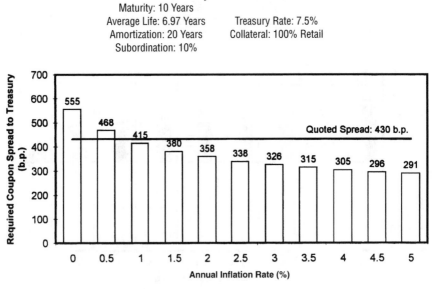

approximately 325 basis points at a 3.5% inflation rate.[18] By comparison, in today's market double-B corporate bonds demand a yield spread about 250 basis points above the 10-year Treasury. Again, Altman's 1993 default tables suggest a credit charge of about 123 basis points per year for a net double-B corporate spread of 127 basis points.[19] The double-B CMBS appears to offer excellent value versus the comparable corporate bond even after adjusting for credit losses. Exhibit 12 summarizes the comparison of CMBS and corporates for double-B and triple-B credit quality.

INVESTMENT STRATEGY IMPLICATIONS

Mutual funds and banks have been the most obvious winners so far in utilizing CMBS to supplement portfolios of fixed-income investments. With CMBS

---

18 The market quoted spread for this 10% subordinated, double-B rated CMBS is 430 basis points. The coupon rate is 115 basis points higher than what is required under a 3.5% inflation scenario (430 basis points minus 315 basis points). This 115 basis points plus the break-even spread of 210 basis points mentioned above result in a net credit loss spread of 325 basis points.

19 The assumptions underlying the calculation are the same as those of triple-B case (see footnote 15) except for the 10-year cumulative default rate of 15.7%.

Exhibit 12.   Comparison of CMBS and Corporates

| | BBB | | BB | |
	CMBS	Corp	CMBS	Corp
Nominal Spread	250	100	430	250
Exp. Credit Loss (1, 2)	−40	−37	−113	−123
Net Credit Spread	210	63	317	127
Recovery	73%	30%	73%	30%
Cumulative Default (3)	2.2%	4.8%	2.3%	15.7%

Note:
(1) Loss calculations consider seasoning effect of default.
(2) Real estate price change: 3.5% per year.
(3) Default statistics for CMBS are pool-level.

trading at excess spreads all along the quality spectrum, managers purchasing CMBS have improved returns and realized important portfolio diversification benefits. The latter benefits arise because real estate risks and corporate bond credit risks are not generally highly correlated.[20]

Pension funds back their liabilities by investing in a wide range of assets. In the real estate arena, however, many plans are invested primarily in direct property ownership. In general, these investments will perform strongly only if real estate rebounds sharply. By contrast, subordinate CMBS priced at today's spreads will do well even in lackluster real estate scenarios. Indeed, in such a setting triple-B or double-B rated CMBS could easily outperform real estate equity.

Insurance companies have historically been investors in both commercial mortgage whole loans and property ownership. In the 1990s, the risk-based capital (RBC) framework promulgated by regulators has severely penalized direct property ownership. In addition, commercial mortgage whole loans require substantially more capital under RBC than CMBS of comparable credit quality. The RBC framework has impacted not only troubled insurers but also solid ones who have been concerned about the "beauty contest" dimension of RBC.

With direct property ownership less viable for insurers, subordinate CMBS allows participation in a strong real estate recovery without severe RBC penalties. This can be done both by purchasing CMBS outright and by issuing CMBS against their own commercial mortgage originations. In the

---

20 See Corcoran, Fathe-Aazam, and Perez-Pietri, "The Role of Commercial Mortgages in Fixed Income Investing," *op. cit.*

latter case, insurers could retain junior bonds issued against their own mortgage loans and sell the senior bonds (same structure as Exhibit 12).

In the same way, insurers can use the emerging CMBS market to deal with troubled loan portfolios. One route is to reduce RBC requirements by shedding the first-loss position and keeping highly rated senior bonds. The other route is to go for repositioning the real estate exposure. The insurer takes cash by selling the senior bonds and keeping the equity-like junior position.

CONCLUSION

This chapter examines the credit outlook for CMBS using a framework which integrates real estate and bond analysis. The use of the risk-neutral credit spread concept allows the user to weigh the losses in any real estate scenario against the up-front yield promised in the bond market. Account is taken of the relative probability of foreclosure and restructure and the respective loss severities. We modeled commercial mortgage delinquencies using data from 1988-93, a period representing the worst commercial real estate markets since the Depression. Combining the results of our model with conservative estimates of loss severities, we established a prudent framework for assessing CMBS credit risk.

In the current market, with real estate prices having bottomed in most regions, the real estate outlook has significantly strengthened relative to a year or two ago. With general inflation in the 2% to 3% range and real estate asset values generally well below replacement cost levels, a conservative benchmark for real estate appreciation going forward is taken to be 3.5% per year.

Under this real estate outlook, senior CMBS (double-A rated or better) involves negligible credit risk with realistic subordination levels and large pools of commercial mortgage whole loans. Furthermore, triple-B and double-B rated subordinate securities offer exceptional values relative to opportunities prevailing in the corporate bond markets.

Investor opportunities to utilize CMBS stem from their "excess spread" relative to corporate. In addition, subordinate CMBS are likely the optimal real estate investment in a slow recovery scenario. In a setting where real estate values and rents are rising slowly, triple-B or double-B-rated CMBS—priced at today's spreads—could easily post total returns exceeding those of equity. For institutional real estate investors, such bonds offer the opportunity for success in a less successful real estate market.

CHAPTER 27

New Ways to Model Default Scenarios for Income Property Loans

William Batts, Jr.
Director, Multifamily Credit Risk
Federal National Mortgage Association

INTRODUCTION

One result of the rapid growth of commercial mortgage-backed securities (CMBS) is increasing attention to (and frustration over) the way that loss expectations for the collateral loans are modeled. The senior/subordinated format is the most popular way to structure transactions involving income property loans. So far, modeling of loss scenarios has been a fairly haphazard activity, usually boiling down to an individual analyst chopping up the losses or placing them in whatever order is desired for the day. Even worse, the loss scenario may be based on nothing more than a misappropriated tid-bit from some other collateral market, like single-family mortgages. There has been no way to model default expectations that depend on and are reflective of the intrinsic characteristics of income property loans.

The income property securities market owes its existence to the development of a mortgage-backed securities market based on single-family loans. However, the income property securities marketplace also finds itself stunted because it has relied too heavily on the single-family securities marketplace for its analytical tools. The primary concern in both markets is the shortening of the life expectancy of securities. However, the single-family mortgage securities market focuses its attention on a shortening due to voluntary prepayment, and this concern has driven nearly all of the analytics and descriptive

---

The opinions expressed in this chapter are those of the author and do not necessarily represent the views of Fannie Mae, or its officers.

language of that arena. In the income property markets, prepayment is at best a secondary concern.

Mortgage defaults are the primary concern of the income property marketplace, not only because lockouts, yield maintenance, and prepayment premiums obviate or provide adequate compensation for early prepayment, but also because defaults are more common and more severe than single-family defaults. Typically, the only way commercial real estate borrowers are allowed to break lockout periods or avoid prepayment premiums is through actual or eminent default, or through an agreed refinancing with the original lender. In short, the concern is not so much that investors will have their principal returned early, but whether the total principal amount due will be returned when principal is returned early. This concern is paramount to investors whose investments' primary structural purpose is loss-absorption. In the income property markets, return of principal much earlier than scheduled (*i.e.,* when yield maintenance is significant or the lockout is in effect) not only signals the possibility of opportunity cost from early principal repayment, but usually entails default and the recognition of actual principal losses as well.

The wholesale absorption of single-family analytics has two negative effects: (1) voluntary prepayment is given more attention than it usually deserves, and (2) when confronting the question of how to model defaults in a securities structure, the commercial MBS market tends to construct default loss scenarios to evolve like prepayment scenarios for single-family loans. The main weakness of such an approach is that there is no way to relate the loss scenario back to characteristics of the pool—the scenarios evolve in such a way that disregards, or provides no basis to judge, whether, for instance, the greatest losses should be expected early or late in the pool's scheduled life, given a certain earnings environment for income properties. Ultimately, this makes it difficult to compare one subordinated investment class to another, because the drivers of loss are so few and so crude, and the roll-out of the loss scenarios is, more often than not, so arbitrary as to be irreplicable by others. This also means that it is difficult to determine the relative safety of "protected" senior classes. Furthermore, loss scenarios are usually concocted in such a way that it is impossible to determine whether the loss scenario itself is credible. The most objectionable of this type of analysis usually starts with the proposition that default is an "involuntary prepayment," and then foists some type of "constant default rate" analysis on the loss expectation.

Refinance risk is also an income property focus, because most conventional commercial mortgage debt is balloon-payment rather than fully amortizing. This also tends to be handled haphazardly in models, yet refinance risk is just as important (at least) as default risks based on other factors. With balloons, *late* return of principal is more of a concern than early return; late return of principal often signals that a property is overleveraged and investor losses are to come. However, refinance risk, even though it is fairly distinct from other kinds of risks, is usually lumped into the overall loss expectations. When refinance risk is not handled as a discrete, identifiable risk in a scenario of default expectations, the loss scenario loses impact—the anticipated source of a loss expectation, whether property operations or interest rates, is almost as important as the amount of the loss expectation itself.

There has been no satisfying or consistently comparable way to get at the "shape" of loss expectancy distributions—to say that a pool's loss expectancy is 7% does not say whether the losses are expected at the beginning, middle, or end of the pool's scheduled life, whether they will be expected mainly from property operations or interest-rate risk, or whether they will be spread out over the life of the pool and over many loans, or are concentrated to one month and to a few loans. This limits a comparison of Pool A to Pool B almost wholly to what loss expectancy percentages are—if they have the same expectancy, then there is very little available to differentiate further between the pools.

The objective of the discussion below is to propose a method for describing the relative risk of income property loan pools in a way that can be useful when those loans comprise part of a security structure. Therefore, the method attempts to reflect both the descriptive features of income property as well as features that are useful in describing securities structures. Furthermore, the method tries to encompass to the two sub-types of the most important causes of early pay-off, default due to net income decline and default due to high refinancing rates.

This chapter describes a *hypothetical sequence of loan default* based on the principles described below. As I will state and imply often throughout this chapter, the method proposed is not for the sake of prediction, but to create a standard of comparison of relative strength.[1] That is, given reliable real estate underwriting information on a loan pool, which loans should we expect to default first, and which ones should we expect to default last? Will the loans in deal no. 1 default more or less easily than the loans in deal no. 2? Even if the expected percentage loss on two pools is the same, are the distributions of the loss amounts comparable? Ultimately, what is the "shape" of the loss expectation given to the pool?

---

1 In this respect, the Default Sequencing Assumption described herein is meant to be no more of a "predictor" than the PSA (Public Securities Association) standard for single-family loan prepayment. The PSA curve is not a predictor; it is a standard of reference—buyers and sellers continue to disagree about whether they expect a pool to run at 50%, 100%, 600%, or whatever percentage of the standard, but they have a common frame of reference in describing prepayment expectations, and, ultimately, in describing and comparing performance. The commercial/multifamily mortgage-backed securities market lacks such a standard.

REVIEW OF PAST DEFAULT MODELING TECHNIQUES

Early on (way back in the 1980s), when investors requested sample loss scenarios for income property loan pools, analysts were easily able to provide a percentage loss expectation for the pool, but creation of loss distributions was always a somewhat more difficult task. Lacking a usable multifamily loan loss "curve," analysts usually crafted scenarios where losses were distributed according to the seven-year single-family loss curve. This appeared to many as a fairly brutal cannibalization of an analytical paradigm from a very different market—something akin to utilizing credit card loss experience to model corporate bond defaults. Its one virtue was that most participants used the same ill-suited tool, even if they themselves recognized its obvious inadequacies, and even if they misapplied the tool inconsistently.

Whether the underlying pool was comprised of fully amortizing loans with a weighted average maturity of 28 years, or balloon loans with a weighted-average maturity of 8 years, the 7-year loss curve did its business in 7 years. This was possible only because loss was treated as a mass separate from the loans that generated the expectation. More specifically, these scenarios display no connection between a given loan's credit characteristics, the expected loan cash flows, and the projections of loss attributed to the loans.

Loss seemed to drop out of the ether in such models. It seemed patently ludicrous to allocate losses on a "curve" unrelated to the characteristics of individual loans.

Another technique utilized for modeling loss expectations is equally woeful. So-called "constant default rates" is a barely altered version of single-family constant prepayment rates, spinning out the loss expectations by reducing the expected loss amount by a certain percentage each year—which also requires a reduction in outstanding pool loan balances by a constant percentage each year. In constant default rate presentations, not only do the periodic loss amounts bear no resemblance to the loss expectations derived for the individual loans, the paid-off balances also bear no resemblance to the loans in the pool. What can be called the "integrity of the loan loss scenario," *i.e.*, keeping scenario losses and paid-off unpaid principal balance (UPB) amounts tied to the specific loans in the pool, is not terribly important in a pool of hundreds or thousands of relatively evenly sized loans, but it is important in a pool of, for example, 50 loans where the largest loan (or expected loss amount) is ten times the size of the smallest.

One technique for constructing loss scenarios provides a useful starting point for discussion—so-called "low-to-high" debt service coverage ratio (DSCR) default scenarios. These scenarios have the virtue of proceeding according to a logical sequence, from the weakest to the strongest loans. The best produced versions of these allocates a predetermined loan loss amount when the loan is assumed to default. Low-to-high scenarios done this way also avoid the mistake of treating the loss as mass separate from the loan.

However, low-to-high scenarios have big weaknesses—the time horizon tends to be the same deal-to-deal (a pool of loans from 1.20 to 1.40 DSCR will default over the same time horizon in the models as a pool of 1.40 to 1.60 DSCR loans); they do not differentiate between, say, a five-year balloon that has a 1.25 DSCR with a 12% loan coupon and another that is otherwise similar but with an 8% coupon and fully amortizing. Ultimately, this renders the results of a low-to-high scenario of limited use in interpreting the scenario and in comparing one transaction to another.

Despite obvious and subtle weaknesses, the low-to-high scenario still provides a useful starting point for creating better scenario analysis. In fact, even the drawbacks of the low-to-high scenario point the way to a more intelligible development of loss scenarios; namely, that scenarios should proceed according to a logical sequence that is generated by and reflective of the loan and its individual loss expectation. Furthermore, the loan default scenario should be sensitive to more of the loan characteristics than simple DSCR and LTV, and it should not produce the same default sequence, over the same time horizon, for loans and pools with widely different features; this makes a meaningful comparison of pools possible. Finally, the source of the losses, whether from operations or from harsh refinance environments, should be identifiable.

RATING AGENCY DEFAULT INCIDENCE AND SEVERITY

The primary aim of the discussion and techniques described below is not to replace the rating agencies' default incidence and severity assumptions, but to supply guarantors, investors, and issuers a common frame of reference in deal-structuring.[2] However, the techniques described below do differ from the rating agencies' approach, and require adjustment if used along with their incidence and severity assumptions. The utility of the "two times" rule to double the loss expectation for balloons, and so-called "hurdle rates" are both denied by the "imputed refinance constant" and "excess refinance risk" methodology employed herein. The "largest loan loss" (as well as any other "static" day-one compositional) approach is not favored over viewing the pool as a set of risks that present themselves at different points in the pool's life.

---

2 The derivation of loss amounts is not the subject of this discussion. Briefly described, the methods for calculating percentage loss expectancy utilize incidence and severity assumptions based on LTV and DSCR. The simplest technique for handling balloon refinance risk is to double the loss percentages if the loan is a balloon. Adjustments based on pool size and composition also figure into the final loss expectation.

DEFINITIONS AND ASSUMPTIONS

There are two types of default risk dealt with in this discussion, broadly characterized as *operational* and *refinance* defaults. Specifically excluded from the discussion are casualty/condemnation and legal/regulatory risks. "Operational default" arises from the inability of the property's operations to generate income sufficient to meet ongoing debt service. This includes both income losses due to increased vacancy or lower rents, as well as expense increases. Operational default therefore refers exclusively to a default before the maturity of the loan, whether ballooning or fully amortizing. "Refinance default," on the other hand, refers exclusively to a default at the maturity of the loan, and represents the inability of the property's operations to generate sufficient income to service the loan balance at maturity, at assumed or then-prevailing interest rates, given minimal underwriting criteria. As such, refinance default refers only to balloon or bullet payment loans.

Admittedly, the operational/refinance risk separation is somewhat artificial, but it is useful in developing a logical construct for default sequencing. In the default sequencing assumption (DSA) described below, a loan may only have an operational or refinance default, but not both. Another way of saying this is that a loan may only default before or at maturity.

There are other assumptions that should be described. This discussion concerns itself only with fixed-rate loans, whether fully amortizing, balloon, or bullet payment. Although the techniques described below can be modified to work for most types of income property loans, the property type primarily considered in this discussion is multifamily.

The Property "Point-of-View"

The first requirement of a default sequencing assumption, then, would be that the ranking of loss possibilities is generated from the individual cash-flow characteristics of the properties supporting the loans, rather than imposed on the pool via some curve. Therefore, any loss amounts should be attributable to individual loans, and the sequence in which losses are accumulated tied both to the relative strength and to the expected cash-flow characteristics of individual loans.[3] To accomplish this, we must approach loss accumulation from the point of view of the property supporting the loan.

What causes a default? In terms of the methodology presented here, a default is a convergence of a property's operating income with its operating expense plus debt service. Although expressed below and throughout the dis-

---

3 This is important not only for sequencing, but necessary for loss expectation calculations to make sense: assuming that all other characteristics are the same, two loans with 1.25 DSCR do not produce the same loss expectation as two loans with a 1.00 DSCR and a 1.50 DSCR.

cussion as a growth in expense, convergence refers either to an increase in expense or a decline in income. For the sake of simplicity, let us assume that the default occurs when this convergence occurs (*i.e.*, that the owner does not "feed" the property[4]). Convergence can be generated by a time series equation, given below:

$$\text{OpInc}\ (1 + y)^n = \text{OpEx}\ (1 + x)^n + \text{Dsvc}$$

where:

OpInc	= property operating income (monthly)
OpExp	= property operating expense (monthly)
Dsvc	= fixed-rate debt service (monthly)
n	= month
x	= the growth rate of OpEx (monthly)
y	= the growth rate of OpInc (monthly)

The convergence month for selected loans is given in Exhibit 1.

By assuming that operating expense increases faster than operating income, we can create a convergence at some month n. The stronger loan is the one whose convergence happens at a higher month n. One notable aspect of

Exhibit 1. Convergence Month for Selected Loans

DSCR:	1.11	1.11	1.11	1.15	1.15	1.15	1.43	1.43	1.43
OpInc:	100	100	100	100	100	100	100	100	100
OpExp:	45	45	45	41	41	41	25	25	25
Dsvc:	45	45	45	45	45	45	45	45	45
x =	.0090	.0090	.0090	.0090	.0090	.0090	.0090	.0090	.0090
y =	.0045	.0030	.0020	.0045	.0030	.0020	.0045	.0030	.0020
Convergence Month	105	53	37	138	75	53	n/a	182	140

---

4 We could, in fact, create a condition for "feeding" the property, *i.e.*, not defaulting immediately at convergence. We could assume, for instance, that a loan that has a 1.15 initial DSCR defaults immediately upon convergence, and that a loan that has an initial DSCR of 1.40 defaults, *e.g.*, six months after convergence. The argument here would be that the owners who have earned significant amounts from a property are more likely to see it through hard times than those who have not (if the hard times are considered temporary). Another reason why, in fact, certain owners do not default immediately when their properties suffer negative income is the fear of tax consequences—successful foreclosure is treated as a sale under the tax code, and if the depreciated basis of a property is lower than the property's acquisition price, an immediately taxable gain has to be recognized by the former owner. Some owners would rather supplement a property's income than be taxed for capital gain. For this discussion, assume that default occurs the month after convergence occurs.

the equation is that loans with different expense ratios (OpExp divided by OpInc) default in different months, even though, for example, the initial debt service and debt service coverage were the same.[5] Two loans that, *ceteris paribus*, have different expense ratios are indeed different—the owner of the one with the lower expense ratio has more certainty about profits from operations. As one would expect, at a certain high coverage—depending on expense ratios—some loans never "converge."

The sequence can be compressed or expanded; by raising the value of x relative to y, convergence occurs sooner; vice versa, by lowering the value of x to y, convergence occurs later, expanding the sequence. The ratio x/y controls the speed of the convergence between property income and expense (below a value 1 there is never a convergence). Even at the same ratio, the actual factors used for x and y can compress or expand the sequence, too—for example, 0.009 and 0.003 produce a different schedule from 0.006 and 0.002.

CONVERGENCE VERSUS COVERAGE

In order to understand how convergence works, a review of basic underwriting concepts is necessary. What does a DSCR of, for example, 1.15 mean? It indicates that income from operations exceeds operating expense and debt service by 15%; 1.15 DSCR represents a pretax profit margin of 13% (.15 divided by 1.15). This would also indicate that a 13% (.15/1.15) reduction in income, through decreases in either occupancy or market rents, would put the property on a break-even basis. A 1.15 DSCR also indicates that roughly 87% (1/1.15) of the property's income is matched by necessary expense, comprised of a fixed component (for this discussion, debt service), and a variable component (operating expense).

The ratio of fixed to variable expenses is where convergence begins to differentiate between all 1.15 DSCR loans. For purposes of this discussion, the term "expense ratio" will refer only to the variable component of the total expenses, *i.e.*, operating expense. Take, for example, Property 1, with a 1.15 DSCR and 60% expense ratio, and Property 2, also having a 1.15 DSCR, but with an expense ratio of 30%. Property 1's 60% expense ratio indicates that 27% of the property's income goes to debt service (1.15 DSCR implies a 13% profit margin). Similarly, Property 2's 30% expense ratio implies 57% of

---

5 One could object to the use of expense ratios to vary "time to default" on a number of grounds, the most obvious being that an operator may keep expenses artificially low by deferring necessary maintenance. There are a number of ways to correct this; we could subtract deferred maintenance from value or add it to loan amount as a lump sum, or "finance" it by adding it to expense or subtracting it from NOI over time. Owners may achieve "below market" expenses by exercising an economy of scale unavailable to the average operator in the respective market. Here we could employ a "market rate" level of expenses.

income goes to debt service. In other words, 27% of Property 1's outflow and 57% of Property 2's outflow is predictable.

It is the variable component of net income that represents the primary risk and opportunity for the owner's profit (= the lender's debt service coverage). For properties with the same loan coverage, a given percentage growth in expenses (OpExp) erodes loan coverage more severely for high-expense-ratio properties than for low-expense-ratio properties. This is shown in Exhibit 2.

Referring to the original assumptions, reduction of each property's operation to a break-even basis (1.00 DSCR), would entail elimination of the 13% profit margin. With no growth in operating income, operating expense would have to grow by the amount of the profit margin to bring the property to a break-even basis (see Exhibit 3).

It would take 5.1% annually compounded growth in expenses to reduce Property 1 to break-even, whereas it would take nearly twice that amount of

Exhibit 2. Comparative Effect of Variable Expense Growth

	Property 1	Property 2
Debt Service Coverage	1.15	1.15
Profit Margin (Excess Coverage/ Total Coverage)	13%	13%
(Variable) Expense Ratio	60%	30%
Remainder: Fixed Expense (Debt Service)	27%	57%
Assume 10% Growth in Operating Expenses:		
(Variable) Expense Ratio	66%	33%
Fixed Expense	27%	57%
Total Expense Ratio	93%	90%
Remainder: Profit Margin	7%	10%
DSCR (1/Total Expense %)	1.075	1.11

Exhibit 3. Break-Even Expense Growth

	Property 1	Property 2
OpExp + Profit (A)	73%	43%
OpExp (B)	60%	30%
Break-Even Exp. Increase (A/B)	122%	143%
Break-Even 5-yr. Compounded Exp. Growth (Yr. 1 = 100)	5.1%	9.4%

expense growth for Property 2 (Property 1 has twice the variable expense ratio of Property 2). When considered from the point of view of income only, the properties are of equal risk—because they have the same amount of coverage, they have the same profit margin. Viewed more broadly and in connection with fixed expense (debt service), the variable expense ratio (OpExp/OpInc) not only refers to operating expenses, but implicitly describes the *variability* of the owner's profit margin and the lender's coverage.[6]

Convergence operates from the variable expense ratio because it can accommodate a view not only of what the profit margin is (*i.e.*, coverage) but also of the profit margin's susceptibility to erosion through both negative events, income loss or expense increase. Coverage limits itself to discussion merely of income loss; convergence, as the name implies, refers more generally to a "squeeze" or elimination of profit through whatever means.

REFINANCE RISK

Given a reasonable set of convergence factors and loan underwriting standards, balloon and bullet payment loans will, in many cases, reach their final payment before the convergence occurs. This provides the opportunity to distinguish refinance risk from operational risk, but also to incorporate balloons and fully amortizing loans within the same sequence. To the extent that the balloon balance comes due before convergence, it can be subjected to a refinance test.

There are a number of ways to calculate refinance risk. One common method is simply to double the loss expectancy for balloons as opposed to fully amortizing loans with the same DSCR/LTV combination. Another common method involves the use of a so-called "hurdle rate." The outstanding principal balance of the loan at the balloon date is assumed to be refinanced at the hurdle rate, usually with an assumed amount of coverage. Given the loan's rate, amortization period, maturity, unpaid principal balance, and current coverage, loans can be tested to see if they clear the hurdle. For loans that do not clear the hurdle, a shortfall can be calculated. The shortfall is the amount by which the unpaid principal balance, at the refinance month, would have to be reduced to be "refinanceable" at the hurdle rate.

One of the problems with hurdle rates is that they tend to be applied in an absolute way. Another way of saying this is that the probability of the rate is always 100%. For example, whether the pool is comprised of loans ballooning in one month as opposed to loans ballooning over a 10-year period, the applicable hurdle rate is typically the same. Furthermore, no "credit" is given for loans that clear the hurdle. Loans that clear a hurdle by 1 basis point are

---

6 Obviously a great number of factors affect the variability of the owner's profit in the "real world," and no substitute for that is provided here.

treated no differently from loans that clear the hurdle by 3 points. Worst of all, the hurdle rate implies that there is zero refinance risk if the loan clears its rate and absolute refinance risk if the loan does not clear it. The hurdle rate methodology also ignores the fact that, by itself, the amount by which a loan clears or fails to clear the hurdle is an indication of the likelihood of a shortfall at refinance.

The argument here is that (1) pool refinance risk cannot be adequately encapsulated by a single number, such as a hurdle rate; (2) that the range of refinance rates supportable by a loan pool is as important as the average; and (3) that refinance risk should be examined on a continuum of possibility that varies at least by rate, and should ultimately scale possibilities based on the time over which loans in a pool must refinance.

A more realistic, fully loaded "disaster rate," if one wanted to create a high enough hurdle, would be around 14% for loans ballooning in the medium or long term (five years or more). However, given the 100% probability of such a rate in the hurdle rate scheme, this would be a "deal-killer" in most contemplated transactions. The fact that not-too-severe hurdle rates (currently, 10% to 11%) are used for most transactions implicitly recognizes the harshness of the 100% probability, and attempts to back away from building a subordinated class around such an assumption. Determining a recourse or subordination amount that would cover the shortfalls from realistic disaster rates, assuming a 100% probability of their occurrence, would render most transactions uneconomic.

We can build a new approach by asking a slightly different question. With hurdle rates the question is, "Can the loan clear the hurdle?" What if we asked instead, "How high a debt service constant can the property support, given today's net operating income and the loan balance to be refinanced at the balloon?" The answer leads us to an *imputed refinance constant*:

$$\frac{\text{Net Operating Income}}{\text{DSCR at Refi}} \div \text{UPB at Refi} = \text{Imputed Refi Constant}$$

where:

Net operating inc ("NOI")	= OpInc – OpExp
DSCR	= Minimum Required Debt Service Coverage Ratio, or NOI/Dsvc
UPB at Refinance	= Loan Balance at Balloon

Obviously, a loan with, say, a 15% imputed refinance constant is, *ceteris paribus,* sturdier than one with a 10.5% constant. But how much sturdier? The hurdle rate method fails to consider this issue—if the property clears the hurdle, then no further test is applied. One way to address the issue of relative refinance risk is to ascribe a probability to the then-prevailing refinance rate exceeding the imputed refinance rate. The "excess" refinance risk, as shown in the probability scale in Exhibit 4, would obviously decline as imputed refinance rates increased. By multiplying the excess probability by a shortfall from a "maximum refinance constant," we could gradate more finely the refinance risk in a pool of loans.[7]

Exhibit 4. Excess Refinance Risk Table

	A	B	A x B
Imputed Refinance Constant	Excess Probability	Refinance Shortfall @ 14.0%	Refinance Risk
9.5%	40.0%	32.14%	12.856%
10.0%	30.0%	28.57%	8.571%
11.0%	10.0%	21.43%	2.143%
13.5%	1.50%	3.57%	0.005%
14.0%	0.05%	0.00%	0.000%
15.0%	0.01%	-7.14%	0.000%

Excess Probability refers to the probability that the constant (for a new, medium-term loan) required to finance the loan's balance at maturity exceeds a given maximum refinance constant, *e.g.*, 14%. Assuming that the required spread-to-Treasury upon refinance is 150 basis points, the excess probability should refer to the chances that the target Treasury exceeds 12.5%.

Refinance Shortfall refers to the percentage of the loan balance at refinance that exceeds the balance that could be serviced (coupon only) at the maximum refinance constant with the original NOI. To calculate refinance shortfall amounts, first divide NOI by a minimum coverage (*e.g.*, $110/1.10 = $100). Divide the NOI figure by the imputed and maximum refinance constants. The difference is the shortfall. For example, if $100 of NOI supports debt at 9.5%, then that would imply roughly $1,053 of principal ($100/.095). At 14%, 100 of NOI would imply roughly $714 of principal (100/.140), a difference of about 32% (1.00 − $714/$1,053).

---

7 The assumptions behind the maximum refinance constant are that, in a "disaster refinance environment," standard underwriting terms do not necessarily apply. For this discussion, it is assumed that refinancing mortgage debt would be pay coupons only. The spread to the relevant Treasury would be, for example, 150 basis points, including servicing. Furthermore, the minimum required coverge might not be "ordinary" minimum levels such as 1.15 or 1.20, but as low as 1.05. In short, the disaster refinance environment should mimic the adjustments that a lender might make to keep a loan that cannot refinance from defaulting.

Another weakness of hurdle rates is that they provide very little idea about the relative overall strength of a given pool in the face of potentially severe refinancing environments. By reviewing such things as minimum and maximum imputed refinance constants and weighted average imputed refinance constants, we could more easily compare the relative strength of one balloon loan pool versus another.

The other important factor in refinance risk is time. There are two aspects about this to note. First, the "Excess Refinance Risk" scale should probably vary with the amount of time remaining until the balloon (that is, depending on the rate environment, an 8.50% loan should have different probabilities depending on whether the balloon occurs 1 year or 10 years from the time of consideration). Second, the scale should be adjusted depending on the spread of balloon maturities (*i.e.,* "maturity spread") within the pool—a pool of 10-year balloons at the same coupon maturing in the same month should treated differently from a pool of loans ballooning over a period from 5 to 15 years.

Addressing the first concern by varying the excess probability scale with a remaining term date is a nice enhancement, but by no means necessary, especially if a relatively small percentage of the pool loan balance matures before, say, five years. The real significance of scaling the excess refinance risk is, once again, to create a standard of comparison and to subdivide identifiable types of risk, which is largely achieved by having a reasonable scale. Generally described, a "reasonable scale" would allocate close to a 100% probability of a higher refinance rate at a certain low constant (say, 5%), and close to 0% probability of a higher refinance rate at certain high constant (say, 14%). The scale should also be more sensitive to changes in the middle range of possibilities (*e.g.,* 8% to 11%) than at the extreme ranges (*e.g.,* 5% to 8%, 11% to 14%). Once again, in this discussion, we are searching for a ruler instead of a crystal ball.

Developing the refinance risk table can be as thoroughgoing as the developer desires (including utilizing a Black-Scholes option pricing model for interest-rate expectations) or it can be fairly simple. A simple method might, for example, take the daily close of the current 5-year Treasury for the last, say, 20 years, and utilize the observations to develop a scale. The scale would indicate the percentage of times the 5-year Treasury, for instance, exceeded a series of yields from say 5% to 13.5%. Whatever method is chosen, the resulting scale should be calibrated against other loss regimes. For example, if the rating agency loss expectation for a 1.25 DSCR, 80% LTV balloon is X%, and the derived excess refinance risk scale indicates a significant multiple or fraction of X%, then one might want to reconsider the scale.

The maximum refinance constant of 14% may also strike some as too low, and it is fair to disagree. However, in developing a maximum refinance constant, an analyst needs to keep in mind a couple of practical realities.

One reality is that almost every note or mortgage specifies a fixed or floating "default rate," that is the coupon to be paid if the borrower defaults or misses a scheduled balloon. If rates are above the default rate, the borrower will simply pay coupons under the existing note, hoping for better rates to come. The other, more basic, reality is that borrowers simply will not borrow long-term at all, if possible, if rates go to certain levels—a high cost of money will reduce the demand for money. Even during the rate environment of 1981–82, very few borrowers would take out a permanent mortgage much above 13%. To assume that they would goes against much practical experience. Furthermore, interest rates, even at 13%, would imply serious devaluation of the old loan balance, and a much changed relationship between rents and expenses. We needn't be too fancy for our own good.

Scaling the probability of refinance shortfalls brings us back to the problem of prediction. Once again, we must keep in mind the intended use of the scale—that is, primarily as a standard of comparison of strength. Intelligent and right-thinking individuals will obviously disagree with the predictive accuracy of the table, and this is what makes markets.

RISK-ADJUSTED MATURITY SCHEDULE (RAMS)

Having derived the convergence sequence for the loans, we may now describe the paydown of the pool in those terms. Take, for example, a loan that converged in month 63. A cash-flow model could produce scheduled principal and interest for the loan, and generate a pay-off of its remaining principal balance at month 63. Let us call this the risk-adjusted maturity schedule (*i.e.*, RAMS) for the loan. Assume a series of loans that converged in months 36, 42, 47, 51, 59, 60, 73, 88, and 103. Utilizing the same method, we could generate a cash-flow schedule that aggregated all of the individual loan cash-flows according to their risk maturity, or convergence.

Many readers are already familiar with weighted average maturity, WAM. We illustrate WAM graphically by creating a distribution based on scheduled principal return. The fulcrum of such a distribution would be its WAM. We could also create such a distribution for risk-weighted average maturity (R-WAM) by generating a risk-adjusted maturity schedule. The fulcrum of the distribution, based on scheduled principal payment until complete loan pay-off at convergence, would be the R-WAM. Theoretically, the risk-weighted average maturity of the pool is always lower than or equal to the scheduled weighted average maturity.

If the loans did not converge at all, the distribution of scheduled and risk maturities would be the same, and the WAM and R-WAM would be the same. If the loans converged, but in the same order as they matured (or if the loans were relatively even in outstanding balances), the scheduled and risk-adjusted maturity distribution for WAM and R-WAM would be the same, but the R-WAM would be to the left of the fulcrum for WAM on the same axis. If the convergence sequence significantly altered the maturity of the loans in the pool (and the loans were of varied outstanding balances), not only could the distribution of scheduled versus risk maturity be considerably different, but the fulcrum could be dramatically shifted to the left on the axis.

From this we may hypothesize. Given an agreed-upon set of convergence variables, if WAM and R-WAM are the same, a pool may be considered more conservatively underwritten than a pool where the R-WAM is lower than the WAM. Furthermore, two pools that have the same WAMs may have very different R-WAMs, based on property expense ratios, loan coverage, and coupons (again, based on the same convergence criteria). The pool with the higher R-WAM may be considered a more conservative risk. However, two pools whose WAMs are the same, and in turn whose R-WAMs are the same as their WAMs, may not be automatically considered equal risks—the assumptions for variables x (especially) and y may not be high enough for the loans to converge.

Although not specifically discussed, there are two types of loans that will not converge: high-coverage fully amortizing loans and balloon loans that reach their maturity before convergence (which does not necessarily imply "high" coverage). These loans may be incorporated into a convergence sequence, as scheduled cash flows. The obvious effect on non-converging loans in the convergence sequence is to limit the difference between WAM and R-WAM.

This also highlights the main weakness of reliance on a R-WAM, and why it has limited use as a description of risk—refinance risk may not be adequately captured.

However, creating a risk-adjusted maturity schedule does achieve a significant advance; we begin to see that pool credit risk is not only a risk based on the composition of the pool at the outset of the pool, but that the composition of the pool, and hence its prospective risks, will change over time. By maturing the loans "from weak to strong" (more or less) we can at least start to get an idea about the comparative "risk horizon" that an investor or guarantor faces in analyzing one pool or another. Therefore, creating a risk-adjusted maturity schedule is not a final step, but a prerequisite to being able to rate the relative riskiness in pools of income property loans.

RISK DISTRIBUTION AND WEIGHTED AVERAGE DOLLAR LOSS EXPECTANCY

We may refine the method utilized in constructing the risk-adjusted maturity schedule to generate an expected loss distribution. Consider converging fully amortizing loans. Instead of generating the remaining principal balance at a convergence month n, we could generate the expected loss amounts (multiplying initial UPB by incidence and severity percentages). This is the risk distribution.

For loans that reach their balloon before they converge, we would generate the excess refinance risk loss amount (based on the then-outstanding UPB) at the balloon month.[8]

Because a loan does not converge does not mean that it does not have a loss expectation when subjected to rating agency criteria. This creates the problem of where to incorporate such losses into a convergence sequence. For non-converging fully amortizing loans, a number of possible techniques may be considered. We could posit the dollar loss expectation up front, but that is counterintuitive, because losses from non-converging loans would be given greater "weight" than the losses from converging loans. If we posited the expected dollar loss at maturity, it also seems counter-intuitive. Consider the situation if we had a pool comprised solely of non-converging fully amortizing loans; the risk of loss, if it were to occur, would occur well before the last payments of the loans. Amortizing the loss according to the loan balance amortization would seem a reasonable approach, except that it has the same problem—the risk is probably past long before the loan balance reaches 0% of the original balance, or even 50%, for that matter, considering that we started with a loan that did not converge (which implies relatively high DSCR, low LTV).

The other problem with amortizing the loss expectation with the loan, in the case of non-converging fully amortizing loans, is that it incorporates losses faster for loans where the risk amortizes faster, the opposite of the desired result. For example, consider two fully amortizing loans with the same outstanding principal amount and maturity, except that Loan A is at 1.15 DSCR (9% coupon) and converges at month n and Loan B is 1.65 DSCR (6% coupon) and does not converge. Amortizing the loss amount with the loans would incorporate Loan B's loss dollars that were amortized before month n a higher present value than the losses attributable to Loan A.

Whenever possible, expected losses attributable to the non-converging loans should not be incorporated into the risk distribution at any point before

---

8 In developing scenarios, a few caveats and hints should be kept in mind. Take, for example, a loss scenario involving converging and non-converging balloon loans. If applying the rating agencies' loss expectancy at convergence, then those losses should be net of the amount attributable to refinance risk. This is because, as stated above, the loans may have operational or refinance risk, but not both. According to the methodology presented here, by virtue of the fact that a loan converged before its balloon, it had higher risk from operations than from potential refinance environments. To apply the rating agency "two times" rule for ballooning loans, for instance, is to add back in the loss that might have been expected at the balloon date—but if the loan converged, this seems hardly necessary.

the losses from the converging loans are fully expended. As stated before, losses from those loans should also not be lumped in at the last payment because the risk is already passed. For now, I would propose incorporating the losses from the non-converging loans, as a lump sum, in month n+1 after the last converging loan converges. Although not a fully satisfactory approach, it makes sense within the model presented here.

Using the technique described above, a risk distribution that allocates the expected loss amounts could be generated. The risk distribution is essentially a derivation of the RAMS, yet may differ from the RAMS, as RAMS may differ from the scheduled cash-flow distribution. This is because a riskier, smaller loan may produce a higher dollar-loss expectation earlier in the transaction than a conservative, larger loan, which may produce a lower dollar-loss later in the transaction. In short, the risk distribution includes loss amounts attributable to refinance risk, and its distribution may differ substantially from the RAMS in its shape. When we calculate the weighted average of the dollar-loss expectancy (WADLE), we may compare that number to the WAM and R-WAM. Although WADLE can never be higher than WAM, it may be higher or lower than R-WAM because of the potential differences between the RAMS and the risk distribution.

RESIDUAL LOSS: IMPLIED ZERO-LOSS LEVEL FOR NON-CONVERGING FULLY AMORTIZING LOANS

The expected losses from non-converging fully amortizing loans comprise what may be considered the "residual risk" of operational default in the pool. This illustrates one of the differences in convergence sequences from loss expectancy—the very choice of variables x and y, given an expense ratio, implies a level of debt service coverage where there is no operational risk attached to the loan, because the loans will not converge, *i.e.*, default. Even though a particular loan may not converge, in accordance with assumptions, such a loan may still have a loss expectancy according to the rating agency criteria.

The level of non-convergence implied by the selection of x and y may be called the "implied zero-loss" or "break-even convergence" level. However, using rates for monthly expense and income growth (x and y, respectively) such as .09% and .03% implies a level of 1.65 DSCR for non-convergence at an expense ratio of 18.3%. A hypothetical rating agency loss expectation for a 1.65 DSCR/40% LTV loan of, say, 1%, would not be captured ordinarily in the convergence sequence, and is therefore a "residual loss."

Keep in mind, however, that the rating agencies' criteria have not been driven by expense ratios, whereas the convergence sequence is quite sensitive to it. As DSCR increases, the range of expense ratios where a loan of a given DSCR would not converge increases, too. Therefore, the convergence sequence isolates the "likelier" targets of possible default within a given DSCR.

THE DEFAULT SEQUENCING ASSUMPTION

The default sequencing assumption, or DSA, is comprised of an x and y variable and a refinance scale (with a maximum refinance constant). Loss expectancy itself, for a given DSCR/LTV combination, is unchanged. If two participants rely on the same loss expectancy criteria and DSA, they should be able to replicate each other's risk-adjusted maturity schedule and risk distribution for a pool of loans.

Manipulating the DSA is simple. Given a set of variables x and y—for instance, .09% and .03%—and a refinance scale with a maximum refinance constant of 14%, we could say that at those values, the risk distribution was created at 100% DSA. To increase or decrease the DSA, we would multiply the variables and divide the imputed refinance constant by the new DSA level; 150% DSA would imply 150% times x and y. In order to adjust imputed refinance constants to the new scale, we would divide the the constant by the DSA multiplier. For example, a loan that had an imputed refinance constant of 14% at 100% DSA, would be subject to the excess refinance risk of a loan with a 9.33% risk (14%/150%) at 150% DSA. The excess refinance risk scale would remain the same, and the imputed refinance constants would be adjusted downward.

The main utility for manipulating the DSA assumption is that recourse and subordination levels can be subjected to tests to see whether the recourse amount is sufficient, and at what particular level of DSA the recourse or subordination amount is exhausted. Furthermore, because recourse and subordination amounts (*i.e.,* loss absorption classes) vary over time—upward through "spread accounts" or downward through distributions based on pool pay-down—the relative sufficiency of the loss absorption class over time and depending on growth or distribution may be measured.

In order to manipulate the loss distribution for the loans, the assumptions have to be modified for *all* of the loans. In other words, if the WADLE for a pool was, for example, 20 years at 100% DSA, then in order to achieve a lower WADLE the analyst would have to increase the DSA assumption until the lower expectancy was met. This way, the loss distribution stays tied to the loan, being both generated by and reflective of the characteristics of the pool. As stated before, imposing loss curves on the loan pool that are not reflective of the characteristics of the loans means that there is no justification for a loss distribution applied to a scenario. This justification is important—if a given pool produces a WADLE of 20 years with an annualized x and y of, say, 9% and 3%, respectively, does a 3.5-year WADLE (7-year final loss) seem justifiable if it takes an annualized x and y of 20% and 10% to achieve it? There is no way to ask such a question without a consistent framework for varying loss distributions; when loss curves are disengaged from loans, the loss scenarios lose context.

CONCLUSION

The techniques described in this chapter are not meant to supplant, or deny the validity of, very much needed statistical work in the multifamily/commercial lending arena. In fact, even the most highly developed state of statistical study that we can envision still leaves the commercial MBS arena without a common language for describing pool performance. Thus, even though constructs such as "covergence sequences" and "imputed refinance constants" may strike some as artificial, that does not deny their usefulness in describing performance: they are not meant to be statistical representations of performance, any more than "100% PSA" is meant to be that in the single-family arena. This discussion is really meant to encourage efforts both in statistical modeling (where would the variables for the constructs come from otherwise?) as well as in creating an analytical language for commercial/multifamily MBS that is independent and robust enough to describe collateral performance for this marketplace.

SECTION VI

VALUATION TECHNIQUES AND
RISK MEASUREMENT

CHAPTER 28

A Comparison of Methods for Analyzing Mortgage-Backed Securities

Andrew S. Davidson
President
Andrew Davidson & Co., Inc.

Robert Kulason
Salomon Brothers

Michael D. Herskovitz
Morgan Stanley

Investors that own or contemplate owning mortgage-backed securities (MBSs) need a method for valuing them. The central issue in all MBS valuation methods is the treatment of prepayment uncertainty. The homeowners' right to prepay their loans introduces a significant degree of uncertainty to the cash flows, and consequently the value, of MBSs.

The relationship between interest rates and MBS prepayment rates directly influences MBS pricing. In a bond market rally prepayment rates rise, reducing the price gains of mortgage-backed securities. In a bear market, however, prepayment rates slow, resulting in increased price losses. This price movement pattern is commonly referred to as "negative convexity".

The dependence of prepayment rates on interest rates affects not only MBS returns but also their interest rate risk. A traditional measure of the price sensitivity of fixed income securities, modified duration, gives the percent change in price caused by a 100 basis point shift in the yield curve. Modified duration is a reasonable price sensitivity measure for

The chapter was written when the authors were at Merrill Lynch, in the Mortgage-Backed Securities Research Department. The authors thank H. Halperin, K. Rogers, J. Van Lang, B. Starr, and N. Perrotis for their assistance. In addition, the authors acknowledge the contribution of L. Murakami.

securities with constant cash flows. It is often inadequate for MBSs, however, because prepayment rates, and consequently cashflows, vary as interest rates change.

The inadequacy of traditional fixed-income analytical tools for valuing MBSs has led to the development of alternative methods. This chapter reviews four approaches to quantifying MBS return and risk characteristics. The methods discussed are: (1) static cash flow yield (SCFY) analysis, (2) total rate of return scenario analysis (SA), (3) option-adjusted spread (OAS) Monte Carlo models, and (4) the refinancing threshold pricing (RTP) model. The first three methods constitute the currently accepted set of valuation techniques. The final method, refinancing threshold pricing, is an approach pioneered at Merrill Lynch.

Multiple approaches to valuing MBSs exist because no single methodology has been shown to explain completely the price performance of these securities. Each of the methods listed has its strengths and weaknesses. SCFY analysis is the simplest approach; however, it ignores a number of factors critical to the valuation of MBSs by assuming constant future interest rates. SA improves on the SCFY methodology by projecting MBS performance in a limited set of interest rate scenarios. OAS Monte Carlo models extend SA by simulating MBS performance over numerous interest rate paths. Critical to the SA and OAS approaches is the manner in which the future interest rate paths are selected and the specification of the relationship between interest rates and MBS prepayment rates. RTP is a binomial option-pricing-based methodology that differs fundamentally from the SA and OAS approaches. RTP directly models the refinancing decision of the individual mortgagor instead of attempting to specify aggregate MBS prepayment rates as a function of interest rates.

The chapter is divided into five sections. One section is devoted to each of the valuation methodologies, and a final section outlines our conclusions and recommendations. Each methodology section contains a description of the technique, the value and risk measures provided, the sensitivity of the results to input parameters, and a summary of the advantages and disadvantages of the approach. Throughout the chapter thirty-year GNMA single family (SF) 8.0%, 9.5%, and 11.0% pass-throughs are used as examples to allow the comparison of results across methodologies. At the time the analyses were conducted, the GNMA 9.5% pass-through was the current coupon. The GNMA 8% and 11% pass-throughs were selected to represent the characteristics of discount and premium MBS, respectively.

STATIC CASH FLOW YIELD

The static cash flow yield (SCFY) is the discount rate that equates the value of future MBS cash flows with their market price. The future cash flows are projected based on the prepayment rate that is anticipated if interest rates remain stable for the life of the security.

SCFY is the basic measure of value in the mortgage market. Its primary advantage is its simplicity; the only required assumption is a prepayment projection. After a prepayment rate has been specified, cash flows can be generated and a yield calculated based on the security's market price. The tradeoff for simplicity is that SCFY analysis ignores a number of factors critical to the valuation of MBSs, including the shape of the yield curve, the distribution and volatility of future interest rates, and the relationship between interest rates and MBS prepayment rates.

Required Assumptions

The only assumption required to compute the SCFY of MBSs is the projected prepayment rate assuming static interest rates. Typically, prepayment projections are made based on the results of a statistical analysis of historical prepayment data, and are generally quoted as conditional prepayment rates (CPR) or percentages of the Public Securities Association (PSA) prepayment model. Investors should be aware that prepayment forecasts based on statistical models imply a confidence interval, which in turn implies a range of possible values for MBS.

Exhibit 1 illustrates the average prepayment forecast and the forecast range for seasoned GNMA pass-throughs made available by thirteen firms through Telerate on March 15, 1988. Using the width of the range as a proxy for forecast uncertainty, it is clear that the level of uncertainty is significant for all coupons and is greatest for premium MBS.

Value Measures

Given a prepayment forecast for an MBS and its market price, its cash flow yield is uniquely determined. *The spread between the MBS static cash flow yield and either its average life or duration-matched Treasury issue has traditionally been used as a measure of value in the mortgage market.*

One way to interpret MBS static cash flow yield spreads to Treasuries is in a historical context. Based on current yield spreads, an evaluation can be made as to whether the mortgage market is historically rich or cheap relative to Treasuries. Further, spread differentials between discounts, currents, and premiums can be compared to determine intra-MBS market relative sector values.

Exhibit 2 shows GNMA MBS yield spreads to the ten-year Treasury bond as a function of the distance of the MBS coupon from the current coupon for selected historical dates.

Premium MBS spreads decline relative to the current coupon spread because the shorter durations of these securities cause them to trade off of

Exhibit 1.   Average Prepayment Forecast and Forecast Range for Seasoned GNMA Pass-Throughs

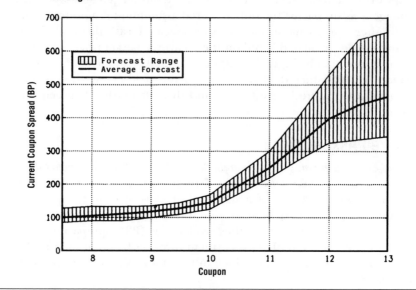

Exhibit 2.   GNMA Yield Spreads to The Ten-Year Treasury Bond for Selected Historical Dates

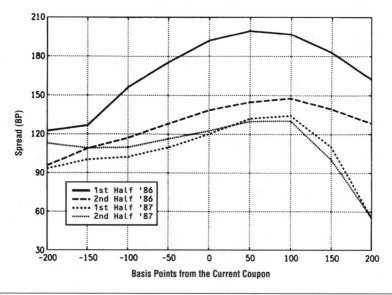

the short end of the yield curve. In order to adjust for the distortion introduced by mismatched durations, Exhibit 3 displays MBS spreads to duration-matched Treasury issues.

Exhibits 2 and 3 demonstrate that MBS spread levels have varied significantly over time. Spread level variation can be related to changes in interest rates and corresponding changes in the option value of mortgage securities. In general, increases in interest rate volatility will raise the value of the short option positions embedded in MBSs, which in turn reduces the prices (widens the spreads) of the securities. Conversely, lower volatility reduces the value of the short option components, thereby increasing the prices (reducing the spreads) of MBSs.

The relationship between spreads and volatility is demonstrated in Exhibit 4, which shows a high degree of correlation between the yield volatility of the ten-year Treasury and the spread between the current coupon GNMA and the ten-year Treasury between January 1985 and January 1988. This is strong evidence that the market uses its assessment of interest rate volatility in pricing MBSs.

In addition to interest rate volatility, SCFY spreads are also affected by the state of the housing market. A robust housing market will generally increase MBS supply, leading to wider MBS yield spreads.

Exhibit 3. GNMA Yield Spreads to Duration-Matched Treasury Issues for Selected Historical Dates

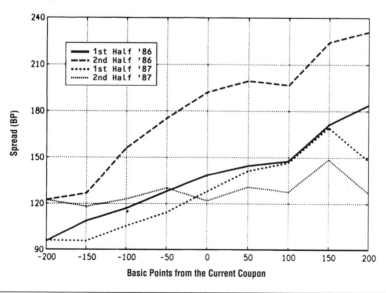

Basic Points from the Current Coupon

Exhibit 4. Yield Volatility of the Ten-Year Treasury Bond and the Spread Between the Current Coupon GNMA and the Ten-Year Treasury Bond

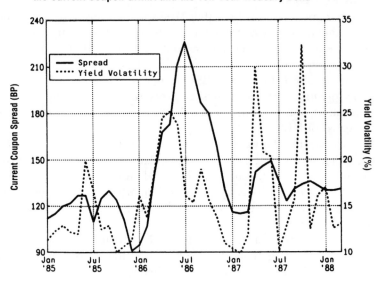

Consequently, an evaluation of MBSs based on SCFY spreads to Treasuries should incorporate current interest rate volatility levels and housing market conditions, and investors' beliefs about the future directions of these factors.

Interest Rate Risk Measures

The weighted average life (WAL) of a MBS is the average time to receipt of the principal of the security. It is used as a measure of the effective maturity of MBS in the place of stated maturity. Stated maturity is a poor measure of effective maturity for MBSs because most principal is amortized or prepaid well before this date. Although an exact relationship between MBS WAL and MBS price sensitivity to interest rates does not exist, it is generally true that the longer the WAL, the greater the interest rate sensitivity. Consequently, WAL can be employed as an indicator of the price risk of MBSs.

Another risk measure that can be obtained from SCFY analysis is Macaulay duration. The Macaulay duration of a security is the present value weighted average time to receipt of its cash flows. For true fixed-income instruments this measure can be shown to be equivalent to the price elasticity of the security with respect to interest rates. However, for MBSs, where cash flows are dependent on interest rates, Macaulay duration is often a poor measure of price sensitivity.

In the sections of this chapter dealing with option-adjusted spread Monte Carlo models and the refinancing threshold pricing model, MBS WALs and Macaulay durations will be compared to effective durations estimated by models that account for the dependence of MBS cash flows on interest rates.

Parameter Sensitivity

Changing the prepayment assumption can materially alter the yield, weighted average life, and duration of MBSs. Exhibit 5 demonstrates this sensitivity, displaying static cash flow yields, weighted average lives, and Macaulay durations for GNMA 8.0%, 9.5%, and 11.0% pass-throughs at constant prices at three different prepayment rates: the minimum, average, and maximum forecasts depicted in Exhibit 1.

As prepayment rates increase, the yield on the discount increases and the yield on the premium decreases. The yield on the current coupon is insensitive to the projected prepayment rate, since it is priced close to par. Weighted average lives and durations for all the pass-throughs decrease with increasing prepayment rates. Because MBS duration depends on the projected prepayment rate, the calculated yield spread to duration-matched Treasuries also depends on this assumption. This is true even for the current coupon, for which the SCFY is nearly independent of the assumed prepayment rate.

Summary

The major attractions of the SCFY methodology are its simplicity and its acceptance by the market as the standard measure of MBS value. The only assumption required is a prepayment projection. After specifying a prepayment rate and generating cash flows, a yield can be calculated based on the security's market price. The tradeoff for simplicity is that by assuming constant future interest rates, the approach ignores a number of factors critical

---

Exhibit 5. Effect of Prepayment Rate Specification on SCFY Risk and Return Measures

GNMA	Price	SCFY(%)			WA (YRS)			Macaulay Duration		
		MIN	AVG	MAX	MIN	AVG	MAX	MIN	AVG	MAX
8.0%	90-20	9.59	9.64	9.79	12.9	12.2	10.6	6.6	6.4	5.8
9.5%	99-10	9.74	9.75	9.75	12.8	10.9	9.2	6.5	5.9	5.3
11.0%	107-00	9.36	9.17	8.97	6.2	5.4	4.7	4.1	3.7	3.4

to the valuation of MBSs, including the shape of the yield curve, the distribution and volatility of future interest rates, and the relationship between interest rates and MBS prepayment rates. Consequently, investors who rely on this methodology must subjectively decide how much spread is required to compensate them for the uncertainty introduced by these factors.

Despite these problems, a historical analysis of SCFY spreads is a useful adjunct to the other valuation methodologies presented in this chapter. In particular, the SCFY approach is most useful for the high premium and deep discount MBSs having cash flows with little sensitivity to interest rates.

SCENARIO ANALYSIS

Scenario analysis (SA) can be used to supplement SCFY analysis by examining the dynamic nature of MBSs. It consists of calculating MBS holding period returns for a variety of possible future interest rate scenarios. For each scenario, cash flows are generated based on coupon, scheduled principal amortization, and prepayments. Cash flows that occur prior to the horizon are reinvested to the end of the holding period. At the horizon, the value of the remaining principal balance is calculated. The rate of growth necessary to equate the initial investment with the sum of the reinvested cash flows and the value of the remaining principal balance at the horizon is the total return for the scenario. The total scenario return is then converted to an annualized rate of return based on the length of the holding period.

Scenario analysis differs from the other approaches presented because it requires the use of a separate valuation model in order to arrive at the security's horizon price. Consequently, it can be employed in conjunction with OAS models or the RTP model to assess the implications of these pricing models for the dynamic performance of MBS in a holding period return context.

A simple but useful alternative horizon pricing model values the MBSs-based on SCFY spreads and projected horizon prepayment rates. The scenario horizon prepayment rate determines MBS WAL at the horizon. A MBS is then priced at a spread to its WAL-matched Treasury issue. Scenario spreads are determined by the SCFY spreads at which the same relative coupon MBS are currently trading. This approach has the advantage of investigating the implications of existing spread relationships on holding period returns. It determines the scenario holding period returns of MBSs assuming current spread relationships are maintained. Using this pricing methodology, SA can be used in conjunction with a historical analysis of SCFY spreads to make assessments of MBS relative sector values. For example, if the expected returns of discount MBSs are inordinately large relative to premium MBSs using this approach, an argument can be made that discount MBS spreads are too large relative to premium MBS spreads. Consequently, discount MBSs would be the better value.

Required Assumptions

Holding Period. The length of the holding period affects the shape of the total rate of return profile. Assuming monotonic parallel yield curve shifts, the effect of the reinvestment rate for interim cash flows will tend to offset the effect of the change in the value of the remaining principal balance at the end of the holding period. Higher interest rates imply greater reinvestment income but lower horizon prices for the remaining principal balance. For short holding periods, the price change of the security will dominate the reinvestment effect; the total scenario rate of return will decrease as interest rates increase. For sufficiently long holding periods, the reinvestment effect will dominate the impact of the horizon price, and total scenario rate of return will increase as interest rates rise.

When employing SA, the conventional practice is to evaluate MBSs based on a one-year holding period. Most investors have an opportunity to rebalance their portfolios at least this often. Further, a one-year holding period limits the effect of the reinvestment rate assumption. A short holding period, however, increases the importance of the horizon pricing model.

Prepayment Rate Function. The specification of the relationship between scenario interest rates and prepayment rates is critical. This relationship defines the embedded option in MBSs, and is what differentiates MBSs from true fixed-income securities. As noted in the SCFY analysis section, the uncertainty of prepayment forecasts for MBSs assuming static interest rates is substantial. The level of difficulty associated with forecasting prepayment rates assuming nonconstant paths of future interest rates is much greater, implying even wider confidence intervals for such projections. Consequently, it is important that investors assess the sensitivity of SA risk and return measures to the prepayment rate function specification.

Interest Rate Distribution and Volatility. The type of interest rate probability distribution and volatility level determine the weights that are assigned to each scenario. This is important when calculating the expected return and the variance of returns across all scenarios. The most popular distributions are the bell-shaped normal and the right-skewed log-normal. Normal implies equal probability of equal absolute changes, while log-normal implies equal probability of equal percentage changes. At low levels of volatility the two assumptions give similar results.

Instead of selecting a probability distribution and a volatility assumption, an investor can subjectively assign probabilities to each of the scenarios. This is feasible only if a small number of scenarios are run.

Generally, the lower the volatility assumption, or for subjective probability distributions, the more heavily weighted the scenarios near the central scenario, the higher the expected return and the lower the variance of returns. The increase in expected return results from the negative convexity of MBSs.

Central Scenario. The interest rate scenarios must be centered on a base case. Two conventional central scenarios are the unchanged market and the implied forward rate scenarios. In the unchanged market scenario, interest rates remain unchanged over the holding period. For the implied forward scenario, interest rates follow paths described by the implied forward rates. Generally, the other scenarios selected assume parallel yield curve shifts about the central scenario. It is also possible to specify scenarios in which yield curve rotations occur. However, the added complexity of specifying such scenarios and assigning probabilities limits their usefulness.

The implied forward scenario is generally considered to be the more theoretically sound central scenario. It also has the advantage of simplifying comparisons between different duration securities; for example, the expected returns on all Treasury bonds are equal under this scenario, independent of maturity.

Horizon Pricing Model. The horizon pricing model is another critical aspect of scenario analysis. It determines the value of the remaining principal balance of MBSs at the horizon. The shorter the horizon, the greater the impact of horizon prices on holding period returns will be.

Number of Scenarios Simulated. The number of scenarios simulated can also affect calculated expected returns and variances of returns. Generally, for MBS pass-throughs these values converge to their asymptotic values when scenarios are run at 50 basis point intervals between -400 and +400 basis point shifts in the yield curve, assuming a one-year horizon.

Reinvestment Rate. The impact of the reinvestment rate is proportional to the length of the holding period. For short holding periods its effect is negligible. Since the standard approach is to assume a one-year holding period, the reinvestment rate assumption is relatively unimportant. If analyses are conducted employing longer holding periods, the sensitivity of the results to this assumption increases.

Value Measures

The expected return is the weighted average of the total rates of return of all the scenarios, where each scenario is weighted by its probability. The scenario weights depend on the assumed level of interest rate volatility and the probability distribution employed.

A more complete value measure is a graph of total returns versus interest rate scenarios (it could also be deemed a risk measure because the dispersion of the returns is evident). This approach has the advantage of visually displaying the dynamic performance characteristics of MBSs. However, comparisons between securities can be difficult, since it is unlikely that one security will completely dominate another.

Interest Rate Risk Measures

One of the most widely used statistical measures of dispersion is variance. The square root of variance is called standard deviation. This measure is particularly useful when dealing with normally distributed data. In this case, approximately 68% of the observations can be expected to lie within one standard deviation of the mean, and 95% within two standard deviations. The greater the variance and standard deviation, the wider the dispersion of scenario returns, and consequently the riskier the security.

Parameter Sensitivity

Exhibit 6 demonstrates the effect of the length of the holding period on the total return profile of a GNMA 9.5% pass-through. As the length of the

Exhibit 6.   Effect of Holding Period on the Total Return Profile of a GNMA 9.5% Pass-Through

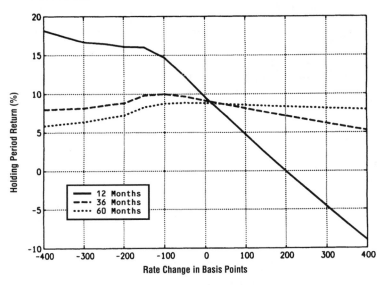

holding period increases, the profile rotates counter-clockwise due to the increasing effect of the reinvestment rate and the reduced impact of the horizon price on scenario returns.

Due to their shorter durations, the corresponding return profiles for premium MBSs would be flatter for the one-year holding period and rotate further counter-clockwise as the length of the holding period increased. Discount MBSs would display the opposite behavior.

Exhibit 7 shows the effect of the specification of the prepayment rate function on the total return profile of a GNMA 11% pass-through. The underlying prepayment model was shifted up and down 15%. A faster prepayment rate specification results in reduced holding period returns in falling interest rate scenarios and increased returns in rising interest rate scenarios, due to the reduction in the duration of MBS cash flows. Current and discount MBSs would behave similarly.

Exhibit 8 displays the effect of interest rate volatility on the expected returns and the standard deviations of returns of GNMA 8%, 9.5%, and 11% pass-throughs, assuming future changes in interest rates are log-normally distributed. The base volatility level was shifted up and down 40%. Increased interest rate volatility results in reduced expected returns and increased standard deviations of returns. The normal distribution would result in slightly higher expected returns, due to its symmetry.

Exhibit 7. Effect of Prepayment Rate Specification on the Total Return Profile of a GNMA 11.0% Pass-Through

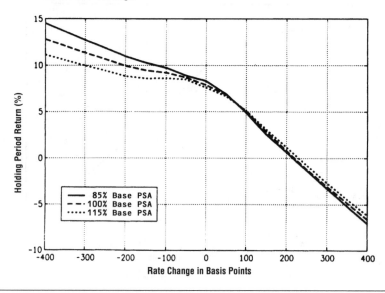

Exhibit 8. Effect of Interest Rate Volatility on SA Risk and Return Measures

	Expected Return (%)			Standard Deviation of Returns (%)		
GNMA	*LOW*	*MID*	*HIGH*	*LOW*	*MID*	*HIGH*
8.0%	8.16	8.01	7.85	3.97	6.30	8.29
9.5%	8.32	7.95	7.47	3.55	5.39	6.88
11.0%	7.43	6.81	6.22	1.75	3.10	4.25

Exhibit 9. Effect of Central Yield Curve Scenario on SA Risk and Return Measures

	Expected Return (%)		Standard Deviation of Returns (%)	
GNMA	*Implied Forward*	*Unchanged Market*	*Implied Forward*	*Unchanged Market*
8.0%	8.01	9.07	6.30	6.41
9.5%	7.95	9.00	5.39	5.50
11.0%	6.81	7.74	3.10	3.15

The expected return of the GNMA 8.0% pass-through displays little sensitivity to interest rate volatility because its embedded prepayment option is far out of the money. The interest rate volatility assumption is more important for current coupon and premium MBS.

Exhibit 9 demonstrates the effect of the central scenario yield curve on the expected returns and the standard deviations of returns for GNMA 8%, 9.5%, and 11% pass-throughs. The implied forward scenario shifts the return profiles downward relative to the unchanged market scenario, and consequently results in lower expected returns. This effect is due to the rising implied forward rates embedded in an upward-sloping yield curve. An inverted yield curve would cause the opposite effect. Although the choice of the central scenario yield curve has a large effect on the absolute levels of MBS expected returns, it has little impact on their relative levels.

Summary

The SA approach extends the SCFY methodology by examining the dynamic nature of MBSs. It can be used in conjunction with other MBS pricing models to assess their implications for the dynamic performance of MBSs in a holding period return context. If the SCFY spread-based pricing approach described in this section is employed, SA investigates the impact of existing spread relationships on MBS holding period returns. This approach can be very useful when used in conjunction with a historical analysis of SCFY spreads. Relative value between MBS market sectors can be evaluated by reviewing existing spread levels in a historical context, and by assessing their impact on MBS expected returns and variances of returns. MBS value relative to other fixed income markets can be evaluated in a similar fashion through a comparison of these values to those calculated for the alternative markets. Further, the historical analysis of SCFY spreads can be used to assess likely future spread movements. This information can in turn be used when evaluating the spread sensitivity of SA results.

Ideally, an investor would like to select the security with the highest expected return and the lowest variance of returns. Usually this is not possible, since it would probably indicate that the security was mispriced. Under normal circumstances, an investor must accept additional risk in order to obtain a higher expected return. SA has the advantage of delineating the available sets of MBS risk/return profiles for specific holding periods.

An additional advantage of SA is that the limited number of scenarios allows the investor to review the assumptions and results of each scenario. A relatively small set of scenarios, however, may not adequately model the effect on value of the complete distribution of future interest rate paths.

OPTION-ADJUSTED SPREADS

In an attempt to improve on the static cash flow yield and scenario analysis measures of MBS value, mortgage market participants have begun to rely on option-adjusted spread (OAS) simulation models. The OAS simulation approach generates numerous interest rate paths that then determine future MBS cash flows. These cash flows are discounted by the simulated interest rates plus the option-adjusted spread. The model solves for the spread that equates the market price to the average simulated price. The simulation approach provides a method for estimating MBS yields and spreads to the Treasury yield curve that are adjusted for the embedded options in these securities. In addition, these models can provide estimates of MBS option cost and effective MBS duration and convexity.[1]

Required Assumptions

Prepayment Rate Function. One of the two critical assumptions in the OAS simulation methodology is the link between interest rates and prepayment rates. If the relationship between interest rates, time, and MBS prepayments

---

1 Michael D. Herskovitz,"Option-Adjusted Spread Analysis for Mortgage-Backed Securities," Chap. 21 in Frank J. Fabozzi (ed.), *The Handbook of Fixed-Income Options*, (Chicago, IL: Probus Publishing, 1989).

is misspecified, the calculated value and risk measures will be biased. The sensitivity of OAS model results to different prepayment function specifications is explored in the parameter sensitivity section.

Interest Rate Diffusion Process. The second critical assumption in the OAS simulation approach is the specification of the interest rate diffusion process. Most models assume that interest rates evolve as a log-normal random walk with a drift that centers the distribution on the implied forward rates. If the yield curve is upward sloping, the implied forward rates will indicate an upward bias to short-term interest rates. This may not reflect investors' rate expectations. However, the use of implied forward rates with the typical positively sloped yield curve builds in the requirement that longer-duration securities must yield more than shorter-duration securities in order to be fairly priced. This is necessary to price noncallable bonds correctly, and is consistent with option pricing theory.

Most models diffuse a single short-term rate. In these models the current MBS coupon, which drives the prepayment function, is assumed to shift deterministically based on the change in the short-term rate. Other models seek to introduce a greater amount of realism into the interest rate process by diffusing both a short- and long-term rate. In this approach the short- and long-term rate changes are less than perfectly correlated, thereby allowing for the possibility of yield curve inversions. The long-term rate is used to drive the prepayment function, while MBS cash flows are discounted back along the short-term rate paths.

Interest Rate Volatility. In addition to specifying an interest rate process, an assumption about interest rate volatility must be made. Higher volatility assumptions increase the dispersion of the simulated interest rate paths. Since MBSs are effectively short a call option, increasing interest rate volatility will increase calculated option cost and decrease option-adjusted spread. The sensitivity of these results to this parameter is discussed in the sensitivity section.

Number of Scenarios Simulated. The reliance of the OAS approach on a set of randomly generated interest rate paths introduces additional uncertainty into the results of these models. The magnitude of the additional uncertainty is inversely proportional to the number of interest rate paths simulated. Consequently, there is a tradeoff between computational efficiency and the confidence intervals of the results.

Averaging Methodology. OAS values are also sensitive to the method used to aggregate the information from the individual interest rate paths. For example, the cash flows for the paths could be averaged first, and then the OAS calculated as the spread that equates this average cash flow vector with the market price of the security. Alternatively, OAS could be defined as the spread that equates the mean of the individual prices for each of the simulated interest rate paths to the market price. Each of these methods will produce different OAS values.

The Merrill Lynch OAS model employs the latter averaging methodology. Under this approach, OAS values can be interpreted as the expected yield spreads of MBSs to Treasuries over the full range of probable interest rate scenarios. The alternative methodology does not fully account for the relationship between scenario interest rates, prepayment rates, and MBS value.

Value Measures

Option-Adjusted Spread. Option-adjusted spread is the primary value measure produced by OAS models. Most models define OAS as the spread that equates the average simulated price to the market price. Implicit in this methodology is the assumption that the fair option-adjusted yield curve for mortgages is a fixed spread over the Treasury yield curve.

When the interest rate diffusion process is centered on the implied forward rates, the OAS has embedded in it the requirement that different duration securities must have different yields in order to be fairly priced. Consequently, OAS values for different duration MBS should be directly comparable.

Option Cost. Spread to Treasury alone may not be a good indicator of MBS relative value. In order to compare various MBSs, the yield spreads should be benchmarked to an appropriate level, namely, the static cash flow yield. The static cash flow yield spread minus the OAS equals the implied option cost.

Interest Rate Risk Measures

Effective Duration and Convexity. By shifting the simulated interest rate paths up and down slightly and holding the OAS fixed, estimates of MBS price sensitivity can be calculated. The average percentage price change can be used to calculate a security's OAS effective duration. OAS effective convexity can be computed by observing the rate of change of the OAS effective duration. These price sensitivity measures can be useful for hedging, since they incorporate the effect of the prepayment option. However, OAS effective durations are measures of price sensitivity, and not of maturity.

OAS Macaulay Duration. A measure of MBS maturity that is adjusted for the prepayment option is the OAS Macaulay duration. This duration measure represents the present value weighted average time to receipt of MBS cash flow averaged across all simulation trials. Exhibit 10 shows the SCFY WAL, SCFY Macaulay duration, OAS Macaulay duration, and OAS effective duration of GNMA 8%, 9.5%, and 11% pass-throughs.

The OAS Macaulay durations of the GNMA 8.0% and 9.5% pass-throughs are shorter than their SCFY Macaulay durations. This result is consistent with expectations. Using the simulation approach, discount and current coupon securities are likely to experience an increase in prepayments relative to the static forecast, as prepayments are near their minimum based on the assumed prepayment model. The OAS effective durations of all the pass-throughs are below their SCFY Macaulay durations, reflecting the negative convexity of MBS. On a relative basis, the OAS effective duration of the GNMA 11.0% pass-through is depressed the most below its SCFY Macaulay duration, while the OAS effective duration of the GNMA 8.0% pass-through is depressed the least.

Parameter Sensitivity

Exhibit 11 demonstrates the effect of the specification of the prepayment rate function on the OAS, option cost, OAS Macaulay duration, and OAS effective duration of GNMA 8%, 9.5%, and 11% pass-throughs. The underlying prepayment model was shifted up and down 15%. A faster prepayment rate specification results in a reduction in both the OAS Macaulay and OAS effective durations of MBSs. A faster prepayment rate specification will

Exhibit 10. A Comparison of SCFY and OAS Risk Measures

GNMA	SCFY WAL (YRS)	SCFY Macaulay Duration	OAS Macaulay Duration	OAS Effective Duration
8.0%	11.5	6.1	5.5	5.8
9.5%	10.5	5.6	4.8	4.1
11.0%	5.8	3.9	3.9	2.3

Exhibit 11. Effect of Prepayment Rate on Specification OAS Risk and Return Measures

	OAS (BP)			Option Cost (BP)			OAS Macaulay Duration			OAS Effective Duration		
GNMA	Low	Mid	High	Low	Mid	High	Low	Mid	High	Low	Mid	High
8.0%	66	79	108	48	35	6	5.8	5.5	5.2	6.0	5.8	5.7
9.5%	51	60	56	67	58	62	5.1	4.8	4.6	4.3	4.1	3.9
11.0%	16	4	-13	102	114	131	4.3	3.9	3.6	2.9	2.3	1.9

generally also increase the OAS of discount MBS and reduce the OAS of premium MBSs.

Exhibit 12 displays the effect of interest rate volatility on the OAS, option cost, OAS Macaulay duration, and OAS effective duration of GNMA 8%, 9.5%, and 11% pass-throughs. The base volatility level was shifted up and down 40%. Increased interest rate volatility results in higher option costs and lower OAS. The OAS effective duration of premium MBSs and discount MBSs is increased and decreased respectively as volatility increases.

Summary

The OAS methodology has a number of advantages over both the SCFY and SA approaches. The large number of simulated future interest rate paths may better model the complete distribution of future rate paths, and improve the statistical significance of the risk and return measures. Further, the risk measures account for the dependence of MBS prepayments on interest rates. If the interest rate diffusion process and the relationship between interest rates and prepayment rates are correctly specified, these price sensitivity measures should be more useful for hedging than their SCFY counterparts.

The major drawback to the OAS approach is that it is basically a black box into which an investor puts assumptions and out of which comes risk and return measures. The prepayment functions and term structure models embedded in OAS models are generally proprietary, precluding the possibility of an investor inspecting these key aspects of the model. Even if the model specifications are available, it may be difficult to evaluate them. This makes it imperative that the investor who employs these models determine their sensitivity to the required assumptions.

Because of the sensitivity of OAS results to model specification and assumptions, these values are difficult to compare on an absolute basis between models. OAS results are best employed as indicators of relative value between similar securities run under identical assumptions using a consistent methodology.

Exhibit 12.   Effect of Interest Rate Volatility on OAS Risk and Return Measures

GNMA	OAS (BP)			Option Cost(BP)			OAS Macaulay Duration			OAS Effective Duration		
	Low	Mid	High	Low	Mid	High	Low	Mid	High	Low	Mid	High
8.0%	104	79	74	10	24	40	5.8	5.5	5.0	6.2	5.8	5.3
9.5%	102	60	24	16	58	94	5.1	4.8	4.4	4.5	4.1	3.7
11.0%	56	4	-41	62	114	160	3.9	3.9	3.7	2.2	2.3	2.5

REFINANCING THRESHOLD PRICING MODEL

The refinancing threshold pricing (RTP) model is a binomial option-pricing-based methodology that differs fundamentally from the SA and OAS approaches. RTP directly models the refinancing decision of the individual mortgagor instead of attempting to specify aggregate MBS prepayment rates as a function of interest rates. This approach is based on three main concepts:

- An options approach is effective in modeling mortgage prepayments, as the mortgagor's ability to prepay the mortgage constitutes an option.

- The costs a mortgagor incurs when refinancing are not paid to the holder of the MBS.

- Mortgagors have different interest rate levels, or thresholds, at which they prepay their mortgages. That is, different homeowners face different levels of refinancing costs.

The concept of heterogeneous mortgagors provides a fundamental and innovative insight into analyzing MBS value and serves as the starting point for the refinancing threshold pricing model. The RTP models the underlying economics of MBSs by focusing on the refinancing decision of the individual mortgagor. These individual refinancing decisions are observed as prepayments. Models that estimate prepayments based on interest rate levels, however, reverse this process. They examine the effect rather than the cause. The RTP provides the potential for robust results and additional insights into MBS valuation because RTP models the underlying process.

The process of valuing a mortgage pool begins with modeling a single mortgage loan. The RTP values individual mortgagor cash flows, given their refinancing costs. This procedure, however, is not repeated for each mortgage in the pool. Instead, the pool is divided into groups of borrowers who share similar refinancing costs. Using market data, the RTP endogenously determines both the costs that mortgagors face, as well as the proportion of the pool in each refinancing cost class. This division into mortgage groups is termed pool composition.[2]

Required Assumptions

Interest Rate Diffusion Process. The first assumption required is the specification of the interest rate diffusion process. A term structure model gener-

---

2 For a more detailed discussion of the RTP approach, refer to *The Refinancing Threshold Pricing Model: An Economic Approach to Valuing MBS,* Merrill Lynch Mortgage-Backed Securities Research, November 1987.

ates a binomial interest rate tree. The rates at the successive branches of the tree, as well as probabilities of interest rates increasing and decreasing, are selected in a manner that is consistent with the observed prices on the current Treasury securities.

The interest rate tree is used by a binomial option pricing model to value each of the endogenously determined refinancing classes in MBSs. When the present value of the mortgagor's cash flows exceeds the remaining principal plus refinancing costs, the mortgage is assumed to be refinanced, and the market value of the mortgage is set equal to the principal amount of the mortgage. Refinancing is not economic when the remaining principal plus refinancing costs is greater than the present value of the cash flows to be paid by the mortgagor.

Interest Rate Volatility. In addition to specifying an interest rate process, an assumption about interest volatility is required. Higher assumed interest rate volatility generally results in a reduction in MBS price due to the increase in the value of the embedded short option position.

Pool Composition. The third required assumption is the pool composition and the associated thresholds. Mortgages in a pool are divided into three classes, according to interest rate sensitivity: very sensitive, moderately sensitive, and not interest rate-sensitive. The degree of interest rate sensitivity depends on the mortgagors' refinancing costs. Mortgagors considered very interest rate-sensitive face low refinancing costs, while mortgagors with less interest rate sensitivity have correspondingly higher refinancing costs. While the pool could be divided into any number of classes, three captures the major implications of heterogeneous borrowers for descriptive purposes.

The model assumes that nonrefinancing prepayments occur at a constant rate over the life of the mortgage pool, and are proportionally drawn from the three refinancing cost classes. At origination, the distribution of mortgagors in refinancing cost classes is assumed to be identical across all pools. This does not imply that each seasoned pool contains an equal number of high, medium, and low interest rate-sensitive borrowers, but rather, the proportion of highly interest rate sensitive individuals in a GNMA 8% pool at origination equals the proportion of highly interest rate-sensitive individuals in a GNMA 10% pool at origination. Over time, the proportions will shift as mortgagors refinance or move. Consequently, one would expect seasoned GNMA 14s to have very few highly and moderately interest-sensitive borrowers remaining in the pool, while seasoned GNMA 7s may have proportions that have not changed much since origination.

After assuming an initial pool distribution, pool composition and refinancing cost levels at origination are determined by recursively comparing market prices with model results until the difference between the two is minimized. These implied pool compositions generally remain stable over time and are consistent with prepayment expectations. Once the value of each of the refinancing classes has been determined, a weighted average is calculated based on the pool composition to determine MBS value.

Value Measures

Price. The RTP directly computes the theoretical price of MBSs. Comparisons between theoretical values and actual market prices may help investors determine MBS relative value.

Implied Spread and Implied Volatility. The term structure model within the RTP model creates a binomial tree of future Treasury rates based on the prices of the current Treasury securities. The RTP model discounts MBS cash flows back through this binomial lattice at the Treasury rate plus some constant spread. This spread reflects the yield premium of MBSs after accounting for the prepayment option held by the mortgagor. The implied spread and volatility are calculated by varying the respective parameter, holding the other constant, and finding the level at which the model price equals the market price. In general, the larger the implied volatility and spread, the cheaper the security.

Interest Rate Risk Measures

By shifting the yield curve up and down slightly, estimates of MBS price sensitivity can be calculated in a manner analogous to that described in the OAS section. In addition, the price sensitivity of MBSs to changes in interest rate volatility can be computed. Exhibit 13 shows the SCFY WAL, SCFY Macaulay duration, RTP effective duration, RTP effective convexity, and RTP dP/dVol[3] of GNMA 8%, 9.5%, and 11% pass-throughs.

Consistent with expectations, the RTP effective durations of the pass-throughs are all below their SCFY Macaulay durations, due to the negative convexity of MBSs. The convexities of the current coupon and premium pass-throughs are negative, whereas that of the discount is slightly positive. The dP/dVol estimates are consistent with the convexity estimates; the more negatively convex a security, the faster its price increases as volatility falls.

Parameter Sensitivity

Exhibit 14 demonstrates the effect of the refinancing cost specification on the RTP price, RTP effective duration, and RTP convexity of GNMA 8%,

---

3 dP/dVol is defined as the price change of MBSs resulting from a 1% reduction in interest rate volatility.

Exhibit 13.   A Comparison of SCFY and RTP Risk Measures

GNMA	SCFY WAL (YRS)	SCFY Macaulay Duration	RTP Effective Duration	RTP Effective Convexity	RTP dP/dVol
8.0%	11.5	6.1	6.0	0.37	-0.02
9.5%	10.2	5.6	5.1	-0.94	0.16
11.0%	5.8	3.9	2.8	-2.48	0.62

Exhibit 14.   Effect of Refinancing Cost Specification on RTP Risk and Return Measures

GNMA	RTP Price			RTP Effective Duration			RTP Duration Convexity		
	Low	Mid	High	Low	Mid	High	Low	Mid	High
8.0%	90-22	90-26	90-27	5.9	6.0	6.1	0.34	0.37	0.38
9.5%	99-00	99-10	99-15	4.8	5.1	5.4	-0.70	-0.94	-0.22
11.0%	105-12	106-29	107-27	0.9	2.8	3.2	-1.57	-2.48	-0.86

Exhibit 15.   Effect of Interest Rate Volatility on RTP Risk and Return Measures

GNMA	RTP Price			RTP Effective Duration			RTP Duration Convexity		
	Low	Mid	High	Low	Mid	High	Low	Mid	High
8.0%	90-22	90-26	90-27	6.1	6.0	5.6	0.53	0.37	-0.01
9.5%	99-15	99-10	98-18	5.4	5.1	4.5	-0.89	-0.94	-0.66
11.0%	107-31	106-29	105-09	3.9	2.8	2.0	-0.89	-2.48	0.57

9.5%, and 11% pass-throughs. Refinancing costs were shifted up and down 25%. Higher refinancing costs reduce the value of the short option position embedded in MBSs, which results in higher model prices. Higher refinancing costs also extend the duration of MBSs due to the reduction in the incentive for mortgagors to prepay their loans.

Exhibit 15 displays the effect of interest rate volatility on the RTP price, RTP effective duration, and RTP effective convexity of GNMA 8%, 9.5%, and 11% pass-throughs. The base volatility level was shifted up and down 40%. Increased interest rate volatility generally results in lower prices and shorter effective durations. The largest effects occur for the current coupon and premium pass-throughs. Discount pass-throughs are less affected by interest rate volatility because their embedded prepayment options are far out of the money.

Summary

As with the OAS approach, the RTP model provides risk and return measures that account for the dependence of MBS prepayments on interest rates. The major attraction of the RTP methodology is its independence from an exogenous prepayment function. By directly modeling the refinancing decision of mortgagors, the method provides the potential for more robust results.

Despite its conceptual relevance, RTP is still essentially a black box into which the investor puts assumptions and out of which comes risk and return measures. The endogenously determined pool compositions are available for inspection, as are the parameters defining the interest rate process. However, it may be difficult for the typical investor to assess the reasonableness of these values. As with the OAS approach, this makes it imperative that the investor assess the sensitivity of RTP results to the required assumptions.

CONCLUSIONS

Multiple approaches to valuing MBSs exist because no single methodology has been shown to explain completely the price performance of these securities. All of the valuation methods discussed in this chapter are useful. However, it is critical that the results of each methodology be assessed in terms of their sensitivity to the specification of, and assumptions required for, each model. Investors should examine not only point estimates of MBS risk and return, but also the confidence intervals associated with these point estimates.

SCFY analysis was the simplest approach reviewed. Although it ignores a number of factors critical to the valuation of MBSs, historical analysis of SCFY spreads is a useful check on the results of other methodologies, and can provide a historical perspective on the MBS market.

SA is a valuable extension of the SCFY approach, examining the dynamic nature of MBSs in a holding period return context. If the spread-based horizon pricing model described in the SA section is used, SA investigates the implications of existing spread relationships for holding period returns. Used in conjunction with a historical analysis of SCFY spreads, this can be an important tool in assessing the relative attractiveness of different MBS coupons.

OAS Monte Carlo models extend SA by simulating MBS performance over a large number of interest rate paths. If the interest rate diffusion process and the relationship between interest rates and prepayment rates are correctly specified, this class of model has the potential to provide MBS risk and return measures superior to those available from SCFY analysis.

The RTP model is a binomial option-pricing-based methodology that differs fundamentally from the OAS approach. RTP directly models the refinancing decision of the individual mortgagor instead of attempting to specify aggregate MBS prepayment rates as a function of interest rates. As with the OAS approach, RTP provides risk and return measures that account for the dependence of MBS prepayments on interest rates. A major attraction of the RTP methodology is that it does not depend on the specification of an exogenous prepayment function. By directly modeling the refinancing decision of mortgagors, RTP provides the potential for more robust results.

The major drawback of both the OAS and RTP approaches is that they are essentially black boxes into which an investor puts assumptions and out of which comes risk and return measures. Even if model specifications are available for inspection, it may be difficult to evaluate them. Consequently, is imperative that investors determine the sensitivity of the results of these models to the assumptions employed. OAS and RTP results should not be used in isolation, but only in conjunction with the results of SCFY analysis and SA. The simpler approaches can be used as checks on the reasonableness of the results of the more sophisticated models.

CHAPTER 29

Introduction to the Option-Adjusted Spread Method

Frank J. Fabozzi, Ph.D., C.F.A.
Editor, Journal of Portfolio Management
and Adjunct Professor of Finance
School of Management, Yale University

Scott F. Richard, D.B.A.
Portfolio Manager
Miller, Anderson & Sherrerd

INTRODUCTION

The traditional approach to the valuation of fixed-income securities is to calculate yield—the yield to maturity, the yield to call for a callable bond, and the cash flow yield for a mortgage-backed security. A superior approach is the option-adjusted spread (OAS) method. Our objective in this chapter is to describe the OAS method. We describe the theoretical foundations of this technique, the input and assumptions that go into the development of an OAS model, and the output of an OAS model, which in addition to the OAS value includes the option-adjusted duration and option-adjusted convexity. In the next chapter, a discussion of the limitations of the OAS model is presented.

STATIC VALUATION

Using OAS to value mortgages is a dynamic technique in that many scenarios for future interest rates are analyzed. Static valuation analyzes only a single interest-rate scenario, usually assuming that the yield curve remains unchanged.

This chapter is adapted from Frank J. Fabozzi and Scott F. Richard, "Valuation of CMOs," Chapter 6 in Frank J. Fabozzi (ed.), *CMO Portfolio Management* (Buckingham, PA: Frank J. Fabozzi Associates, 1994).

One of the standard measures in evaluating any mortgage-backed security is the cash flow yield, or simply "yield." The yield spread is found by spreading the yield to the average life on the interpolated Treasury yield curve. This practice is improper for an amortizing bond even in the absence of interest-rate volatility.

What should be done instead is to calculate what is called the *static spread*. This is the yield spread in a static scenario (*i.e.*, no volatility of interest rates) of the bond over the entire theoretical Treasury spot rate curve, not a single point on the Treasury yield curve. The magnitude of the difference between the traditional yield spread and the static yield spread depends on the steepness of the yield curve: the steeper the curve, the greater the difference between the two values. In a relatively flat interest-rate environment, the difference between the traditional yield spread and the static spread will be small.

There are two ways to compute the static spread. One way is to use today's yield curve to discount future cash flows and keep the mortgage refinancing rate fixed at today's mortgage rate. Since the mortgage refinancing rate is fixed, the investor can usually specify a reasonable prepayment rate for the life of the security. Using this prepayment rate, the bond's future cash flow can be estimated. Use of this approach to calculate the static spread recognizes different prices today of dollars to be delivered at future dates. This results in the proper discounting of cash flows while keeping the mortgage rate fixed. Effectively, today's prices indicate what the future discount rates will be, but the best estimates of future rates are today's rates.

The second way to calculate the static spread allows the mortgage rate to go up the curve as implied by the forward interest rates. This procedure is sometimes called the *zero volatility OAS*. In this case a prepayment model is needed to determine the vector of future prepayment rates implied by the vector of future refinancing rates. A money manager using static spread should determine which approach is used in the calculation.

DYNAMIC VALUATION MODELING

A technique known as simulation is used to value complex securities such as pass-throughs and CMOs. Simulation is used because the monthly cash flows are path-dependent. This means that the cash flows received this month are determined not only by the current and future interest-rate levels, but also by the path that interest rates took to get to the current level.

In the case of pass-throughs, prepayments are path-dependent because this month's prepayment rate depends on whether there have been prior opportunities to refinance since the underlying mortgages were issued. For a CMO, there is an additional source of path dependency: The cash flow to be received this month by a CMO tranche depends on the outstanding balances of the other tranches in the deal. We need the history of prepayments to calculate these balances.

Conceptually, the valuation of pass-through securities using the simulation method is simple. In practice, however, it is very complex. The simulation involves generating a set of cash flows based on simulated future mortgage refinancing rates, which in turn imply simulated prepayment rates.

The typical model that Wall Street firms and commercial vendors use to generate these random interest-rate paths takes as input today's term structure of interest rates and a volatility assumption. The term structure of interest rates is the theoretical spot rate (or zero coupon) curve implied by today's Treasury securities. The volatility assumption determines the dispersion of future interest rates in the simulation. The simulations should be normalized so that the average simulated price of a zero coupon Treasury bond equals today's actual price.

Each OAS model has its own model of the evolution of future interest rates and its own volatility assumptions. Until recently, there have been few significant differences in the interest-rate models of dealer firms and OAS vendors, although their volatility assumptions can be significantly different.

The random paths of interest rates should be generated from an arbitrage-free model of the future term structure of interest rates. By arbitrage-free it is meant that the model replicates today's term structure of interest rates, an input of the model, and that for all future dates there is no possible arbitrage within the model.[1]

The simulation works by generating many scenarios of future interest-rate paths. In each month of the scenario, a monthly interest rate and a mortgage refinancing rate are generated. The monthly interest rates are used to discount the projected cash flows in the scenario. The mortgage refinancing rate is needed to determine the cash flow because it represents the opportunity cost the mortgagor is facing at that time.

If the refinancing rates are high relative to the mortgagor's original coupon rate, the mortgagor will have less incentive to prepay, or even a disincentive (*i.e.*, the homeowner will avoid moving in order to avoid prepaying). If the refinancing rate is low relative to the mortgagor's original coupon rate, the mortgagor has an incentive to refinance.

Prepayments are projected by feeding the refinancing rate and loan characteristics, such as age, into a prepayment model. Given the projected prepayments, the cash flow along an interest-rate path can be determined.

---

1 A risk-neutral, arbitrage-free model of Treasury yields means that at all future dates the price of any long-term bond equals the expected value of rolling short-term bonds to maturity. For more details, see Fischer Black, Emmanuel Derman, and William Toy, "A One-Factor Model of Interest Rates and Its Application to Treasury Bond Options," *Financial Analysts Journal* (January/February 1990), pp. 33–39.

Exhibit 1. Simulated Paths of One-Month Future Interest Rates

Interest-Rate Path Number

Month	1	2	3	...	n	...	N
1	$f_1(1)$	$f_1(2)$	$f_1(3)$	...	$f_1(n)$	...	$f_1(N)$
2	$f_2(1)$	$f_2(2)$	$f_2(3)$	...	$f_2(n)$	...	$f_2(N)$
3	$f_3(1)$	$f_3(2)$	$f_3(3)$	...	$f_3(n)$	...	$f_3(N)$
t	$f_t(1)$	$f_t(2)$	$f_t(3)$	...	$f_t(n)$	...	$f_t(N)$
358	$f_{358}(1)$	$f_{358}(2)$	$f_{358}(3)$	...	$f_{358}(n)$	...	$f_{358}(N)$
359	$f_{359}(1)$	$f_{359}(2)$	$f_{359}(3)$	...	$f_{359}(n)$	...	$f_{359}(N)$
360	$f_{360}(1)$	$f_{360}(2)$	$f_{360}(3)$	...	$f_{360}(n)$	...	$f_{360}(N)$

Notation:
$f_t(n)$ = one-month future interest-rate for month t on path n
N = total number of interest-rate paths

Exhibit 2. Simulated Paths of Mortgage Refinancing Rates

Interest-Rate Path Number

Month	1	2	3	...	n	...	N
1	$r_1(1)$	$r_1(2)$	$r_1(3)$	...	$r_1(n)$	...	$r_1(N)$
2	$r_2(1)$	$r_2(2)$	$r_2(3)$	...	$r_2(n)$	...	$r_2(N)$
3	$r_3(1)$	$r_3(2)$	$r_3(3)$	...	$r_3(n)$	...	$r_3(N)$
t	$r_t(1)$	$r_t(2)$	$r_t(3)$	...	$r_t(n)$	...	$r_t(N)$
358	$r_{358}(1)$	$r_{358}(2)$	$r_{358}(3)$	...	$r_{358}(n)$	...	$r_{358}(N)$
359	$r_{359}(1)$	$r_{359}(2)$	$r_{359}(3)$	...	$r_{359}(n)$	...	$r_{359}(N)$
360	$r_{360}(1)$	$r_{360}(2)$	$r_{360}(3)$	...	$r_{360}(n)$	...	$r_{360}(N)$

Notation:
$r_t(n)$ = mortgage refinancing rate for month t on path n
N = total number of interest-rate paths

To make this more concrete, consider a newly issued mortgage pass-through security with a maturity of 360 months. Exhibit 1 shows N simulated interest-rate path scenarios. Each scenario consists of a path of 360 simulated one-month future interest rates. Just how many paths should be generated is explained later. Exhibit 2 shows the paths of simulated mortgage refinancing rates corresponding to the scenarios shown in Exhibit 1. Assuming these mortgage refinancing rates, the cash flow for each scenario path is shown in Exhibit 3.

Exhibit 3. Simulated Cash Flow on Each of the Interest-Rate Paths

	Interest-Rate-Path Number						
Month	1	2	3	...	n	...	N
1	$C_1(1)$	$C_1(2)$	$C_1(3)$	...	$C_1(n)$	...	$C_1(N)$
2	$C_2(1)$	$C_2(2)$	$C_2(3)$	...	$C_2(n)$	...	$C_2(N)$
3	$C_3(1)$	$C_3(2)$	$C_3(3)$	...	$C_3(n)$	...	$C_3(N)$
t	$C_t(1)$	$C_t(2)$	$C_t(3)$	...	$C_t(n)$	...	$C_t(N)$
358	$C_{358}(1)$	$C_{358}(2)$	$C_{358}(3)$	...	$C_{358}(n)$	...	$C_{358}(N)$
359	$C_{359}(1)$	$C_{359}(2)$	$C_{359}(3)$	...	$C_{359}(n)$	...	$C_{359}(N)$
360	$C_{360}(1)$	$C_{360}(2)$	$C_{360}(3)$	...	$C_{360}(n)$	...	$C_{360}(N)$

Notation:
$C_t(n)$ = cash flow for month t on path n
N   = total number of interest-rate paths

Calculating the Present Value for a Scenario Interest-Rate Path

Given the cash flow on an interest-rate path, its present value can be calculated.[2] The discount rate for determining the present value is the simulated spot rate for each month on the interest-rate path plus an appropriate spread. The spot rate on a path can be determined from the simulated future monthly rates. The relationship that holds between the simulated spot rate for month T on path n and the simulated future one-month rates is:

$$z_T(n) = \{[1 + f_1(n)][1 + f_2(n)] \dots [1 + f_{2T}(n)]\}^{1/T} - 1$$

where

$z_T(n)$ = simulated spot rate for month T on path n
$f_j(n)$ = simulated future one-month rate for month j on path n

Consequently, the interest-rate path for the simulated future one-month rates can be converted to the interest-rate path for the simulated monthly spot rates, as shown in Exhibit 4.

Therefore, the present value of the cash flow for month T on interest rate path n discounted at the simulated spot rate for month T plus some spread is:

---

2 In the next chapter, Robert Kopprash refers to this present value as the path and spread-specific price (or PASS price).

$$PV[C_T(n)] = \frac{C_T(n)}{[1 + z_T(n) + K]^{1/T}}$$

where

$PV[C_T(n)]$ = present value of cash flow for month T on path n
$C_T(n)$ = cash flow for month T on path n
$z_T(n)$ = spot rate for month T on path n
K = spread

The present value for path n is the sum of the present value of the cash flow for each month on path n. That is,

$$PV[Path(n)] = PV[C_1(n)] + PV[C_2(n)] + \ldots + PV[C_{360}(n)]$$

where $PV[Path(n)]$ is the present value of interest-rate path n.

CALCULATION OF OAS

The option-adjusted spread is the spread, K, that when added to all the spot rates on all interest-rate paths will make the average present value of the paths equal to the observed market price (plus accrued interest). Mathematically, OAS is the spread K that will satisfy the following condition:

$$\text{Market Price} = \frac{PV[Path\ (1)] + PV[Path\ (2)] + \ldots + PV[Path\ (N)]}{N}$$

where N is the number of interest-rate paths.

This procedure for valuing a pass-through is also followed for a CMO tranche. The cash flow for each month on each interest-rate path is found

Exhibit 4. Simulated Paths of Monthly Spot Rates

Interest-Rate Path Number

Month	1	2	3	...	n	...	N
1	$z_1(1)$	$z_1(2)$	$z_1(3)$	...	$z_1(n)$	...	$z_1(N)$
2	$z_2(1)$	$z_2(2)$	$z_2(3)$	...	$z_2(n)$	...	$z_2(N)$
3	$z_3(1)$	$z_3(2)$	$z_3(3)$	...	$z_3(n)$	...	$z_3(N)$
t	$z_t(1)$	$z_t(2)$	$z_t(3)$	...	$z_t(n)$	...	$z_t(N)$
358	$z_{358}(1)$	$z_{358}(2)$	$z_{358}(3)$	...	$z_{358}(n)$	...	$z_{358}(N)$
359	$z_{359}(1)$	$z_{359}(2)$	$z_{359}(3)$	...	$z_{359}(n)$	...	$z_{359}(N)$
360	$z_{360}(1)$	$z_{360}(2)$	$z_{360}(3)$	...	$z_{360}(n)$	...	$z_{360}(N)$

Notation:
$z_t(n)$ = spot rate for month t on path n
N = total number of interest-rate paths

according to the principal repayment and interest distribution rules of the deal. In order to do this, a CMO structuring model is needed. In any analysis of CMOs, one of the major stumbling blocks is getting a good CMO structuring model.

In the creation of CMO tranches, some of the tranches wind up more sensitive to prepayment risk and interest-rate risk than the collateral, while some of them are much less sensitive. The objective of the money manager is to figure out how the OAS of the collateral, or, equivalently, the value of the collateral, gets transmitted to the CMO tranches. More specifically, the objective is to find out where the value goes and where the risk goes so that the money manager can identify the tranches with low risk and high value: the ones he or she wants to buy.

Selecting the Number of Interest-Rate Paths

Let's now address the question of the number of scenario paths or repetitions, N, needed to value a mortgage-backed security. A typical OAS run will be done for 256 to 1,024 interest-rate paths. The scenarios generated using the simulation method look very realistic, and furthermore reproduce today's Treasury curve. By employing this technique, the money manager is effectively saying that Treasuries are fairly priced today and that the objective is to determine whether a mortgage-backed security is rich or cheap relative to Treasuries.

The number of interest-rate paths determines how "good" the estimate is, not relative to the truth but relative to the OAS model used. The more paths, the more average spread tends to settle down. It is a statistical sampling problem.

Most OAS models employ some form of *variance reduction* to cut down on the number of sample paths necessary to get a good statistical sample.[3] Variance reduction techniques allow us to obtain price estimates within a tick. By this we mean that if the OAS model is used to generate more scenarios, price estimates from the model will not change by more than a tick. So, for example, if 1,024 paths are used to obtain the estimated price for a tranche, there is little more information to be had from the OAS model by generating more than that number of paths. (For some very sensitive CMO tranches, more paths may be needed to estimate prices within one tick.)

INTERPRETATION OF THE OAS

The procedure for determining the OAS is straightforward, although time-consuming. The next question, then, is how to interpret the OAS. Basically,

---

3 For a discussion of variance reduction, see Phelim P. Boyle, "Options: A Monte Carlo Approach," *Journal of Financial Economics* 4 (1977), pp. 323–338.

the OAS is used to reconcile value with market price. On the left-hand side of the last equation is the market's statement: the price of a mortgage-backed security or derivative. The average present value over all the paths on the right-hand side of the equation is the model's output, which we refer to as value.

What a money manager seeks to do is to buy securities whose value is greater than their price. A valuation model such as the one described above allows a money manager to estimate the value of a security, which at this point would be sufficient to determine whether to buy a security. That is, the money manager can say that this bond is 1 point cheap or 2 points cheap, and so on. The model does not stop here, however. Instead, it converts the divergence between price and value into a yield spread measure, as most market participants find it more convenient to think about yield spread than about price differences.

The OAS was developed as a measure of the yield spread that can be used to reconcile dollar differences between value and price. But what is it a "spread" over? In describing the model above, we can see that the OAS is measuring the average spread over the Treasury spot rate curve, not the Treasury yield curve. It is an average spread because the OAS is found by averaging over the interest-rate paths for the possible spot rate curves.

OPTION COST

The implied cost of the option embedded in any mortgage-backed security can be obtained by calculating the difference between the OAS at the assumed volatility of interest rates and the static spread. That is,

Option cost = Static spread − Option-adjusted spread

The reason that the option cost is measured in this way is as follows. In an environment of no interest-rate changes, the investor would earn the static spread. When future interest rates are uncertain, the spread is less, however, because of the homeowner's option to prepay; the OAS reflects the spread after adjusting for this option. Therefore, the option cost is the difference between the spread that would be earned in a static interest-rate environment (the static spread) and the spread after adjusting for the homeowner's option.

OTHER PRODUCTS OF THE OAS MODEL

Other products of the valuation model are the distribution of the present values on the interest-rate paths, option-adjusted duration, option-adjusted convexity, and simulated average life. Illustrations of the distributions for the path values for various CMO tranches are given in the next chapter.

Option-Adjusted Duration

In general, duration measures the price sensitivity of a bond to a small change in interest rates. Duration can be interpreted as the approximate percentage change in price for a 100-basis-point parallel shift in the yield curve. For example, if a bond's duration is 4, this means a 100-basis-point decrease in interest rates will result in a price increase of approximately 4%. A 50-basis-point increase in yields will decrease the price by approximately 2%. The smaller the change in basis points, the better the approximated change in price will be.

The duration for any security can be approximated as follows:

$$Duration = \frac{V_- - V_+}{2V_0 \, (\Delta y)}$$

where

V_- = price if yield is decreased by x basis points
V_+ = price if yield is increased by x basis points
V_0 = initial price (per \$100 of par value)
Δy = x basis points (in decimal point form)

The standard measure of duration is modified duration. The limitation of modified duration is that it assumes that if interest rates change, the cash flow does not change. Thus, while modified duration is fine for option-free securities such as Treasury bonds, it is inappropriate for mortgage-backed securities, because projected cash flows change as interest rates and prepayments change. When prices in the duration formula are calculated assuming that the cash flow changes when interest rates change, the resulting duration is called *effective duration.*

Effective duration can be computed using an OAS model as follows. First the bond's OAS is found using the current term structure of interest rates. Next the bond is repriced holding OAS constant, but shifting the term structure. Two shifts are used; in one yields are increased, and in the second they are decreased. This produces two average present values: one when interest rates are increased, and one when interest rates are decreased. These average total present values can be viewed as the theoretical prices under small interest-rate changes. Effective duration calculated in this way is often referred to as *option-adjusted duration* or *OAS duration.*

The assumption in using modified or effective duration to project the percentage price change is that all interest rates change by the same number of basis points; that is, there is a parallel shift in the yield curve. If the term structure does not change by a parallel shift, then effective duration will not correctly predict the change in a bond's price.

Option-Adjusted Convexity

The convexity measure of a security is the approximate change in price that is not explained by duration. Basically, convexity is the rate of change of the dollar duration of a security.

The convexity of any bond can be approximated using the formula:

$$\frac{V_+ + V_- - 2(V_0)}{V_0 \, (\Delta y)^2}$$

When the prices used in this formula assume that the cash flows do not change when yields change, the resulting convexity is a good approximation of the standard convexity for an option-free bond. When the prices used in the formula are derived by changing the cash flows (by changing prepayment rates) when yields change, the resulting convexity is called *effective convexity*. Once again, when an OAS model is used to obtain the prices, the resulting value is referred to as the *option-adjusted convexity* or *OAS convexity*.

Simulated Average Life

The average life reported in an OAS model is the average of the average lives along the interest-rate paths. That is, for each interest-rate path, there is an average life. The average of these average lives is the average life reported in an OAS model.

Additional information is conveyed by the distribution of the average life. The greater the range and standard deviation of the average life, the more the uncertainty about the tranche's average life.

ILLUSTRATION[4]

We use a simple CMO deal to show how the tranches and collateral can be analyzed using the OAS methodology. The plain vanilla sequential-pay CMO bond structure in our illustration is FNMA 89-97. A diagram of the principal allocation structure is given in Exhibit 5. The structure includes five tranches, A, B, C, D, and Z, and a residual class. Tranche Z is an accrual bond, and tranche D class is an IOette. The focus of our analysis is on tranches A, B, C, and Z.

The top panel of Exhibit 6 shows the OAS and the option cost for the collateral and the four classes in the CMO structure. The OAS for the collateral is 70 basis points. Since the option cost is 45 basis points, the static spread is 115 basis points (70 basis points plus 45 basis points). The weighted-average OAS of all the classes (including the residual) is equal to the OAS of the collateral.

---

4 For additional illustrations, see Fabozzi and Richard, "Valuation of CMOs," pp. 88–100.

Exhibit 5. Diagram of Principal Allocation Structure for FNMA 89-97

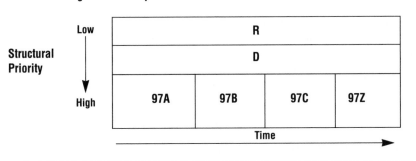

At the time this analysis was performed, April 27, 1990, the Treasury yield curve was not steep. As we noted earlier, in such a yield curve environment the static spread will not differ significantly from the traditionally computed yield spread. Thus, for the four tranches shown in Exhibit 6, the static spread is 52 for A, 87 for B, 95 for C, and 124 for Z.

Notice that the classes did not share the OAS equally. The same is true for the option cost. The value tended to go toward the longer bonds, something that occurs in the typical deal. Both the static spread and the option cost increase as the maturity increases. The only tranches where there appears to be a bit of a bargain are B and C. A money manager contemplating the purchase of one of these middle tranches can see that C offers a higher OAS than B and appears to bear less of the risk, as measured by the option cost. The problem money managers may face is that they might not be able to go out as long as the C tranche because of duration, maturity, or average-life constraints.

Now let's look at modeling risk. Examination of the sensitivity of the tranches to changes in prepayments and interest-rate volatility will help us to understand the interaction of the tranches in the structure and who is bearing the risk.

We begin with prepayments. Specifically, we keep the same interest-rate paths as those used to get the OAS in the base case (the top panel of Exhibit 6), but reduce the prepayment rate on each interest-rate path to 80% of the projected rate.

As can be seen in the second panel of Exhibit 6, slowing down prepayments does not change the OAS for the collateral or its price at all. This is because the collateral is trading close to par. Tranches created by this collateral do not behave the same way, however. The exhibit reports two results of the sensitivity analysis. First, it indicates the change in the OAS. Second, it indicates the change in the price, holding the OAS constant at the base case.

Exhibit 6.   OAS Analysis of FNMA 89-97 Classes A, B, C, and Z (As of 4/27/90)

Base Case (assumes 12% interest-rate volatility)

	OAS (in basis points)	Option Cost (in basis points)
Collateral	70	45
Class		
A	23	29
B	46	41
C	59	36
Z	74	50

Prepayments at 80% and 120% of Prepayment Model
(assumes 12% interest-rate volatility)

	New OAS (in basis points)		Change in Price per $100 par (holding OAS constant)	
	80%	120%	80%	120%
Collateral	70	71	$0.00	$0.04
Class				
A	8	40	−0.43	0.48
B	31	65	−0.86	1.10
C	53	73	−0.41	0.95
Z	72	93	−0.28	2.70

Interest-Rate Volatility of 8% and 16%

	New OAS (in basis points)		Change in Price per $100 par (holding OAS constant)	
	8%	16%	8%	16%
Collateral	92	46	$1.03	−$1.01
Class				
A	38	5	0.42	−0.51
B	67	21	1.22	−1.45
C	77	39	1.22	−1.36
Z	99	50	3.55	−3.41

To see how a money manager can use the information in the second panel, consider tranche A. At 80% of the prepayment speed, the OAS for this class declines from 23 basis points to 8 basis points. If the OAS is held constant, the panel indicates that the buyer of tranche A would lose $0.43 per $100 par value.

Notice that for all the tranches reported in Exhibit 6 there is a loss. How could all four tranches lose if prepayments are slowed down and the collateral does not lose value? This is because tranche D and the residual (R), which are not reported in the exhibit, got all the benefit of that slowdown. Notice that tranche Z is actually fairly well protected, so it does not lose much value as a result of the slowdown of prepayments. Tranche A by contrast is severely affected.

Also shown in the second panel of the exhibit is the second part of our experiment to test the sensitivity of prepayments: the prepayment rate is assumed to be 120% of the base case. Once again, as the collateral is trading at close to par, its price does not move very much, about four cents per $100 of par value. In fact, because the collateral is trading slightly below par, the speeding up of prepayments will make the collateral look slightly better as the OAS increases by 1 basis point.

Now look at the four tranches. They all benefitted. The results reported in the exhibit indicate that a money manager who is willing to go out to the long end of the curve, such as tranche Z, would realize most of the benefits of that speedup of prepayments. Since the four tranches benefitted and the benefit to the collateral was minor, that means tranche D, the IOette, and the residual were adversely affected. In general, IO types of tranches will be adversely affected by a speedup.

Now let's look at the sensitivity to the interest-rate volatility assumption, 12% in the base case. Two experiments are performed: reducing the volatility assumption to 8% and increasing it to 16%. These results are reported in the third panel of Exhibit 6.

Reducing the volatility to 8% increases the dollar price of the collateral by $1 and increases the OAS from 70 in the base case to 92. This $1 increase in the price of the collateral is not equally distributed, however, among the four tranches. Most of the increase in value is realized by the longer tranches. The OAS gain for each of the tranches follows more or less the OAS durations of those tranches. This makes sense, because the longer the duration, the greater the risk, and when volatility declines, the reward is greater for the accepted risk.

At the higher level of assumed interest-rate volatility of 16%, the collateral is severely affected. The collateral's loss is distributed among the tranches in the expected manner: the longer the duration, the greater the loss. In this case tranche D and the residual are less affected.

Using the OAS methodology, a fair conclusion that can be made about this simple plain vanilla structure is: what you see is what you get. The only surprise in this structure seems to be tranches B and C. In general, however, a money manager willing to extend duration gets paid for that risk.

SUMMARY

The valuation model described in this chapter is a sophisticated analytical tool available to analyze mortgage-backed securities. The product of this valuation model is the option-adjusted spread. The results of this model should be stress-tested for modeling risk: alternative prepayment and volatility assumptions.

OAS analysis helps the money manager to understand where the risks are in a CMO deal and to identify which tranches are cheap, rich, and fairly priced. Compared to a sophisticated analytical tool such as OAS analysis, traditional static analysis can lead to very different conclusions about the relative value of the tranches in a deal. This may lead a money manager to buy the expensive tranches and miss the opportunity to invest in cheap tranches.

CHAPTER 30

A Further Look at Option-Adjusted Spread Analysis

Robert W. Kopprasch, Ph.D., C.F.A.
Senior Vice President
Alliance Capital Management, L.P. New York

Researchers have outlined the basic advantages of option-adjusted spread (OAS) methodology, as well as a number of its shortcomings.[1] I believe there are even more fundamental problems with OAS. Before discussing them, I provide a brief review of OAS's good points, as well as the basic methodology.

BACKGROUND

Option-adjusted spread analysis is generally accepted as the "state of the art" in analyzing complicated securities, especially those with uncertain cash flows. It is certainly preferable to comparing securities on the basis of their yields to maturity, a practice common not very long ago. It also offers theoretical advantages over scenario analysis, although an argument will be made later that scenario analysis offers some practical advantages and more insight to the portfolio manager.

---

* Reprinted and expanded, with permission, from *Financial Analysts Journal,* May/June 1994. (The original title, "Option-Adjusted Spread Analysis: Going Down the Wrong Path?") Copyright 1994. The Association for Investment Management and Research, Charlottesville, VA. All rights reserved. The author thanks Martin Leibowitz for his helpful comments.

1 David Babbel and Stavros Zenios, "Pitfalls in the Analysis of Option-Adjusted Spreads," *Financial Analysts Journal,* July/August 1992. The authors note the following pitfalls: (1) OAS is model-dependent, (2) embedded model assumptions are often chosen for convenience rather than "their ability to capture the richness of reality," (3) the OAS is an averaged number, averaged across paths and through time, (4) adding a fixed number of basis points to all rates results in subtle changes to the properties of the distribution, (5) OAS ignores some of the options, such as the default option, (6) there are some abuses in practice, such as using different volatilities for different types of bonds, (7) ranking securities by OAS has some of the same problems as ranking them by yield to maturity.

OAS is the theoretically preferred approach for several reasons. OAS analyzes a security over a large number of interest rate paths, both favorable and unfavorable. If these paths are representative of future possibilities, OAS appears to provide a summary of almost all possible scenarios. Furthermore, in OAS methodology, the interest rate paths are "calibrated" to the current yield curve, eliminating any bias in the selection of scenarios that might occur in scenario analyses.[2] The OAS approach recognizes the security's cash flows along each path, and hence incorporates the optionality of cash flows into the analysis.

There are nevertheless problems in the implementation and especially the interpretation of OAS, which can result in a distorted picture of the behavior of securities and portfolios. As a result, it should never be relied upon as the sole measure of the value of either securities or portfolios.

Basic Description of OAS

In the OAS approach, a series of future interest rate paths (each equally likely) is generated according to a strict set of constraints. This can involve various levels of complexity. The interest rates can be generated by a single-factor model (short rates only) or by multifactor models that simultaneously model several points on the yield curve through time. Volatility can be assumed constant across time, or can be made a function of time (or rate level or maturity). Rates can conform to several possible distributions and can be constrained from reaching severe extremes.

The security is then modeled along each rate path, and an appropriate set of cash flows (for every point along the path) is determined. For non-callable securities, this is a trivial exercise, but for mortgage-backed securities and corporates with option features, some algorithm is required to determine what the level of prepayments will be, or whether the bond will be called, put, *etc.* This process is repeated for every possible interest rate path.

Along each path, the cash flows are discounted at the Treasury rates plus a spread to determine the theoretical "price" of the security. Let us call this "price" the "path and spread-specific price," or PASS price. The OAS process generates a series of PASS prices, one for each path at a given spread. If the average of the PASS prices equals the security's actual price, the spread that was used is, by definition, the option-adjusted spread. If the average price does not equal the security's price, another spread must be chosen, new PASS prices determined and averaged, and so on, until the OAS is found.

---

2 That is, the rates for any given "node" are centered around the forward rate for that time period. In addition, the structure of rates is chosen to be "arbitrage-free."

Exhibit 1.   Discount Rates = Treasury Rates + OAS "Trial" Spread

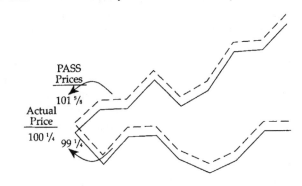

Exhibit 2.   Many Rate Paths

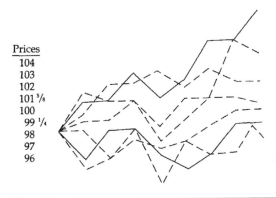

Exhibit 1 shows two stylized paths of short-term Treasury rates that might result from the interest rate modeling process. The dashed lines illustrate how these rates are modified in the iterative search process to determine the OAS. In this figure, the two paths generate the prices shown at the particular trial spread. Exhibit 2 expands Exhibit 1 to show those two rate paths in the larger context of many rate paths and calculated present values. All the prices shown on the left (and the many hundreds more that can't be shown on this diagram) are averaged for comparison with the current price.

This description should make one thing clear: it is extremely unlikely that a security will actually earn its calculated OAS. In fact, depending upon the particular path of rates that actually occurs, the security may wildly outperform or underperform Treasuries, thus realizing either a very high or even a negative spread, regardless of its calculated OAS.[3]

The architects of the various OAS models that abound on Wall Street never intended the OAS to be viewed as a "yield takeout" over Treasuries. Because it's the result of an averaging process, OAS represents a summary of what the future may hold, not a promise. Nevertheless, numerous investors all across the sophistication spectrum have misinterpreted the output as some sort of spread that's locked in to their portfolios after purchase. Some institutions have memos in their files documenting the "profit" on a purchase as the difference between the OAS and the funding spread above Treasuries.

ONE LIFE, ONE PATH

Suppose for a moment that your OAS model can generate interest rates with such uncanny foresight that one of them (you don't know which one) is guaranteed to match actual rates precisely. While such "accuracy" is no doubt desirable (we obviously wouldn't want a model that guarantees that none of its paths will actually occur), it does not necessarily improve the investment selection process.

Now suppose the model produces an OAS of 100 basis points, and that this is considered very attractive based on the security's maturity, quality, liquidity, *etc.* The security could nevertheless prove to be a very poor investment. Suppose the actual path is one for which the OAS model produces a PASS price well below today's price (one of the lower prices in Exhibit 2). With 100% foresight, one would not pay the market price for the security, but only the lower, calculated PASS price, after discounting the security's cash flows at the known Treasury rate path plus 100 basis points (or some lower, "certainty-equivalent" spread).

Unfortunately, an investor relying on OAS analysis would base the investment in the security on the average PASS price, not the specific price from the underperforming path. Certainly, no one expects to be able to predict the future, but even when OAS analysis incorporates the actual future, it does not necessarily improve decision making.

Perhaps the greatest shortcoming of most OAS decision making (aside from the technical details of the models) is the fact that the distribution of PASS prices is not usually provided. This distribution would be of immense value to portfolio managers as a guide to the risk of the security. If PASS prices were tightly concentrated, the current security price would be considered fair

---

3 The OAS methodology described above is based on an average of prices. There are several reasons for this, ranging from technical preference to convenience. The approach could also use average spread instead of average price. In this approach, each path would be evaluated to determine its spread, given today's price, and then the spreads would be averaged.

for a wide range of ultimate paths. Extreme outliers could be examined to determine the paths that generated them, warning managers about the dangerous scenarios. This kind of knowledge would be even more useful in the portfolio context. Asymmetries in return, naturally useful to the portfolio manager, would also be discernible from the distribution pattern of prices. The ability to "reverse trace" returns to the scenarios that generated them is important to portfolio managers and is one of the reasons that scenario analysis is so useful.

The Weather Forecast

It is extremely difficult to measure the effectiveness of an OAS model objectively. After all, the calculated OAS is based on possibly thousands of paths, whereas the actual return on the security is based on one. This is not unlike the local weather forecast. If the forecast calls for 20% chance of rain, how do we measure its accuracy? At any given spot, it either rains or it doesn't; that is, the *ex post* "probability" is either 100% or 0%. If it doesn't rain, was the forecast wrong? If it does rain, does that imply that the probability of rain should have been higher?

What exactly do OAS models measure? They do not actually value an option in the usual sense of option valuation. Instead, they provide an actuarially determined yield effect. This is not meant as a criticism: the models were developed for situations in which the options were so complex or interrelated that simpler models could not provide meaningful results. Unfortunately, the interpretation of OAS often implies that the approach does provide a specific option value, which can be subtracted from the security's yield to provide an option-free "true" spread. If this were so, the OAS might represent the true credit spread of the security. But investors exact a price for uncertainty, and the uncertainty of the option-burdened security should cause it to trade at a higher spread.

This brings up another question: what does spread mean in this context? The uncertain life of the instrument, attributable to its features, makes difficult any comparison of its option-adjusted spread with that of another security. If there is a term structure of OAS, and different maturities (or, more likely, different effective durations) provide different spreads, to what should this spread be compared?[4]

Measurement is further complicated because OAS is a very dynamic value, responding to changes in the level and shape of the yield curve, volatility, prepayments, credit spreads, liquidity, *etc.* And as a "life" measure, based on all of a security's cash flows, OAS may not be able to tell us much about total returns over some shorter horizon. Over the short run at least, returns can be very directional, and an appropriate benchmark may be hard to determine.

---

4. See Babbel and Zenios, "Pitfalls," *op. cit.*

The returns on an interest-only strip with a duration of –25, for example, could be compared with the returns of a similar-duration Treasury portfolio. But what has a duration of –25? We would need to combine a short position with cash to achieve the negative duration. For a $10 million position, we could perhaps short $20 million of 30-year Treasuries, or roughly $35 million of the 10-year, *etc.* Further complicating the task is the fact that other OAS models might calculate an option-adjusted duration of –10, or even –5! The lack of an objective, unambiguous benchmark makes OAS performance measurement more an art than a science.[5]

Average OAS or Portfolio OAS?

The OAS of a portfolio is usually calculated as the weighted average of the OASs of the component securities. This introduces several problems, depending upon why the investor wants to know the average spread. if the investor simply wants to know the daily contribution to return at the current time, this weighting is correct, in the same way that a market-weighted yield provides that information. For other uses, however, this weighting may be incorrect.

When an investor wants an average yield that approximates a portfolio's internal rate of return, the yields must be weighted by both durations and market weights. When the investor wants the average option-adjusted spread to provide the analogous information for spread, he would use the same duration and market weightings.

Even if the proper weightings are used, the OAS calculation is still fraught with traps for investors. Aside from all the modeling problems and the averaging problems, the individual securities may vary dramatically from one another along any given path. Or, possibly worse, they may not!

Consider a two-asset portfolio with equal amounts invested in each security. Suppose that each has an individual OAS of 100 basis points, but each performs much better along certain paths than others. If the securities are highly correlated, they will tend to perform well together along certain paths and poorly together along other paths. Thus, the portfolio returns (along any path) will tend to look like the individual security returns for those same paths. The OAS of the portfolio will be 100 basis points, but the spreads of the portfolio will vary widely across different paths.[6]

---

5 See, however, "The Predictive Power of OASs: An Out-of-Sample Test," *Mortgage Market Review,* August 22, 1991, and Lucchesi, Ochmann, and Smith, "Another Look at Option Adjusted Spreads," *Federal Home Loan Bank of Dallas Quarterly,* Summer 1989.

6 This "spread" refers to the spread over (or under) Treasuries that the security actually provides, based on today's price and the specific path of rates. While returns will naturally vary based on the direction of interest rates, the spread could be reasonably constant or could exhibit wide variations across paths.

If the securities do not act together, a diversification effect occurs, and the worst portfolio performance will not be as bad as the worst individual security performance. This is fairly obvious; the point is, the standard weighted portfolio OAS will still be 100 basis points (although the "true" OAS may be very different), and will completely mask the true performance profile of the portfolio.

The situation is even more complicated when the individual securities have very asymmetric PASS price profiles, which is very likely with mortgage derivatives and other event-driven security types. If the two (negatively correlated) securities provide performance home runs along a few different paths (for example, the high-rate paths for one and the low-rate paths for the other), but mediocre performance along the others (the less extreme rate movements), the portfolio performance profile could look like a bathtub—high spread returns at each end of the path spectrum and mediocre (or even negative) performance along the middle paths. The "expected" spread of 100 basis points would almost never be earned; the investor would most likely have mediocre returns, unless a home run scenario unfolded.

Given sufficient computer power and memory, one can correctly calculate portfolio OAS by following the same algorithm for the portfolio as for individual securities. Along any given path, the cash flows for each individual security are determined and then summed together at each node in the interest rate path. These combined portfolio cash flows are then discounted at the trial spread to determine the portfolio PASS value for the path and spread. This process is repeated for all paths. Then the total portfolio values are averaged to determine if they match today's actual portfolio value. If the average value matches the actual, then the spread is the portfolio OAS; otherwise, another spread will have to be chosen and the discounting repeated.

If portfolio OAS is calculated as described above, and if portfolio managers are given the distribution of portfolio PASS values at the OAS (as suggested above for individual securities), the information will be meaningful. Any diversification effects will be embedded in the distribution. High correlation of securities will result in a wider distribution of portfolio values than low correlation.

A wide distribution suggests that the realized spread of the portfolio (along the path that ultimately occurs) is likely to vary significantly from the calculated OAS. A perfectly diversified and hedged portfolio would be concentrated at only one value. Such information will certainly be of interest to the portfolio manager.

MORTGAGE-BACKED SECURITIES

Mortgage-backed securities (MBS) seem to be particularly appropriate subjects for OAS analysis because of the complexity of their cash flows and the fact that the flows are path-dependent. In practice, however, most MBS OAS models have one particular flaw: the flows are determined by a prepayment model that is deterministic at each node, instead of probabilistic. While a prepayment model is obviously needed to generate the flows, specifying the exact flow rather than sampling from the possible outcomes makes the OAS insensitive to possible real-life variations in prepayments.

Investors will often run an OAS at several multiples of a prepayment model. For example, the cash flows may be generated at 100% of the model and then rerun at 90% and 110% to determine sensitivity.[7] This measures the sensitivity of the OAS to consistent misestimation of the prepayments, but not to the random fluctuations around the model's predictions.

A better approach, but one that requires more computing power, would be to use a probabilistic model and increase the number of runs through the paths in order to capture the distribution of possible prepayments at each node. This "double stochastic" approach will be more accurate in capturing the reality of variable rates and prepayments.

Event-Driven Securities

Certain MBS derivative securities, such as jump-Z tranches of a collateralized mortgage obligation (CMO), present special problems for the OAS model.[8] Jump-Z bonds are support bonds that provide a cushion to the planned amortization classes (PACs) in the CMO. However, under certain circumstances, such as when average or recent prepayment rates exceed a certain level, the jump-Z will suddenly jump in front of the other classes in terms of principal-payment priority. The actual level at which the trigger is set is somewhat arbitrary.[9]

The problem for the model is that the performance of the security depends critically on whether the event occurs or not; the prepayment model within the OAS model must be absolutely correct to capture the true nature of the security. Of course, the same event that triggers the jump-Z will also affect the PACs in the CMO, so even the "safer" tranches have substantial model risk.

There are now a whole variety of event-driven securities outside of the mortgage market, from step-up coupon bonds to various options and complicated swaps. The events that affect these instruments are not necessarily related directly to the interest rate path, either—there may be a change in

---

7 Note that this refers to a multiple of particular rate- and path-dependent model, and does not refer to 90% and 110% PSA.

8 Actually, they present problems in the interpretation of the output of the model. The model will handle the "event" however it is programmed to handle it.

9 In fact, the trigger need not be related to prepayments at all; it could be tied to some Treasury rate reaching a particular level.

credit rating or some other exogenous variable.[10] The OAS model cannot capture the effects of events that are not dependent on the interest rate process. For example, a downgrading may not be completely independent of the interest rate level, but it probably cannot be modeled as a function of the rate path. Downgrading differs from prepayments in this; the primary determinant for prepayments is the level and path of rates, so the OAS approach can model the effects of prepayments, even if not perfectly.

The modeling process is made all the more difficult when multiple currencies are involved. Consider a yen-based investor attempting to determine the yen-based OAS of an investment in U.S. corporate or mortgage-backed securities. Not only must the interest rate paths in yen have all the desirable qualities of the single-currency model, but for each possible change in rates in the host currency, the potential changes in the dollar must be modeled. Then a prepayment model must be layered onto the dollar interest-rate paths.[11]

SCENARIO ANALYSIS TODAY

Scenario analysis is more sophisticated today than the up-and-down parallel shifts assumed only a few years ago. Now it is possible to change the shape of the yield curve and quickly incorporate many of the resulting effects. For the manager whose portfolio may be sensitive to such changes, discovering which scenarios are particularly dangerous, and quantifying the effects, is a very useful exercise. Checking the returns on a variety of scenarios can lend support or provide an early warning. Rather than losing all the information in a black box, the mortgage manager can control everything from the prepayment vector to the exact timing of the change.

Corporate managers can incorporate beliefs about the likely levels of rates that will induce a call and can factor in the timing of the call as well. Although none of the managers' scenarios may accurately reflect the future, together they provide better information than an OAS model. This is not meant as a criticism of the OAS approach, which is intended to summarize all the available information in a single value description. Such a distilled measure obviously cannot provide all the information that exhaustive scenario analysis can. And the scenario approach has its own costs in computer time and personal effort (as well as its own biases in scenario selection).

In the case of CMOs, scenario analysis allows the portfolio manager to specify both the terminal yield curve and the prepayment experience.

---

10 For example, a dealer could create a "home team" tranche that jumps if a particular team makes it to the Super Bowl or Final Four.

11 Alternatively, the dollar-based interest rate paths generate the associated cash flows, which are then discounted by a yen-based rate, which is somehow modeled to the dollar rate paths.

Prepayments can be varied to see the point at which particular tranches start to behave erratically.

There is, however, a catch to the use of scenario analysis as an alternative to OAS analysis. Scenario analysis requires some assumption about the terminal price or yield spread of the security in question. For mortgage-backed securities, or any security with an option component, a traditional yield spread doesn't make sense because the duration of the security varies; hence the point on the yield curve from which the spread must be measured is unknown. Many investors rely on a constant OAS as the pricing spread, which presupposes some correctness and appropriateness in the measurement of the OAS in the first place.

IMPROVING OAS ANALYSIS
Using the "PASS Price" Distribution

A variety of useful information can be obtained from the distribution of PASS prices. To demonstrate this, a series of distributions are provided below for a variety of CMO tranche types.[12] Two aspects of each distribution should be examined: the symmetry (or lack of it) and the "width" or variability across paths. Note the relationship between the width of the distribution and the average life. Note that the x-axis scale has been reset for each chart to show detail, so the charts should not be visually compared to each other. In the first three charts, the x-axis values represent actual price points, and in subsequent charts they represent the lower bound of ranges. One hundred paths were used to generate the PASS prices; the paths used GAT's "Linear Path Space" approach to path generation to minimize the number of paths needed to efficiently sample from the entire range of potential paths.

Exhibit 3 is the price distribution for FHLMC 1251J, a VADM (very accurately determined maturity) tranche. Note that over 91% of the PASS prices occupy a tight price band (less than $1/2$ point). Note also the symmetry of the distribution. Exhibit 4 shows the price distribution for a short PAC. This tranche has an extremely tight and basically symmetric distribution. Again, 91% of the probability is concentrated in three prices, within a range of .65 points. The high/low spread of the entire distribution is only 4 points. The price distribution for a slightly longer PAC is shown in Exhibit 5. It has a symmetric distribution, and 60% of the probability is concentrated within a $1/4$-point range, but it takes a range of 5 points to cover the central 85% of the probability.

Exhibit 6 shows the price distribution for a 6-year WAL PAC. The distribution is symmetric with almost 80% concentrated in the five central price

---

12 Distributions were generated and provided by Global Advanced Technology based on June 1994 levels.

Exhibit 3. Price Distribution for FHLMC1J-VADM

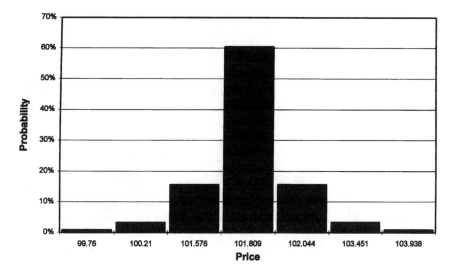

Weighted average life = 1.27 years.

Exhibit 4. Price Distribution for FHLMC 1314HA–PAC

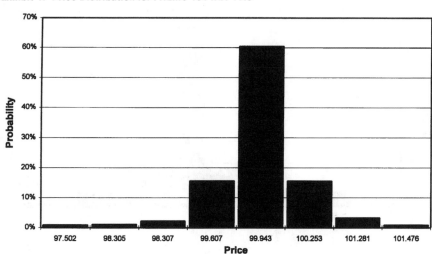

Weighted average life = 1.59 years.

Exhibit 5.   Price Distribution for FHLMC 1466PE–PAC1

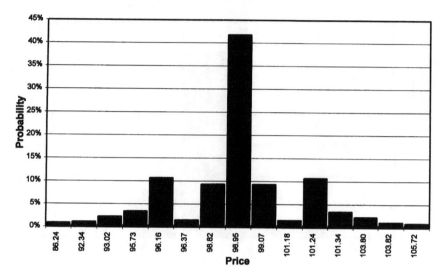

Weighted average life = 2.82 years.

Exhibit 6.   Price Distribution for FHLMC 1411G–PAC1

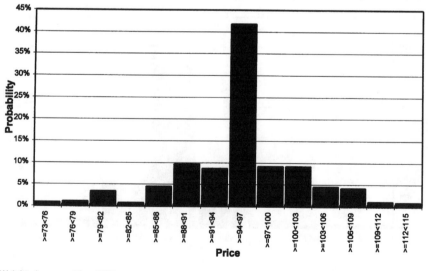

Weighted average life = 6.06 years.

"buckets." However, these span a price range of almost 15 points, significantly wider than the shorter PAC in Exhibit 5.

The price distribution for the non-PAC sequential tranche shown in Exhibit 7 has a distribution that's not too asymmetric. It appears to be a reasonably well-structured security. The five central price ranges encompass 67% of probability. To cover 90% of the probability requires a price range of 83-110. As the WAL of these examples increases, so does the price response across paths.

Exhibits 8 and 9 report some obviously asymmetric securities. The asymmetry normally arises from some type of option characteristic of the tranche. Exhibit 8 shows the price distribution for a long 10-year CMT floater. The majority of its price distribution is near par. The five near-par ranges account for 83% of the probability. But there is a long tail to the left which arises from rising rates and the effect of the 10.5% cap. Exhibit 9 reports the price distribution of a principal-only tranche. The results indicate asymmetry in the opposite direction, with several paths providing a value nearly double the starting price. In this case, it is the low rate paths which cause more rapid prepayments and a faster accretion of the discount.

The TAC inverse floater's price distribution shown in Exhibit 10 is amazingly similar to FH 1554 KA shown in Exhibit 9. This is not too surprising, as inverse floaters are often viewed as an inverse coupon stream attached to a PO. This tranche has a coupon cap of 1.105%, so it is nearly all PO, with very little coupon stream. Therefore, it displays a PO-like price distribution. The PAC-IO tranche price distribution is shown in Exhibit 11 has 96% of the probability concentrated in a 7-point range, indicating that it is a well structured PAC. However, the remaining probability is distributed over a wide range of prices, from 35 to 51, so there are some remote low-rate paths which clearly hurt this bond.

Additional Suggestions for Improving OAS Analysis

The rapid acceptance of OAS as an analytical tool is remarkable in light of its complexity. It provides a good example of how a sophisticated model can work its way into the mainstream, where its limitations are not completely understood.[13]

Several enhancements would eliminate some of the ambiguity of OAS results. First, uncertain events along the interest rate paths, such as bond

---

13 In April 1994, a large ($1.6 billion) hedge fund that invested heavily in mortgage derivatives was forced to liquidate, having lost all its capital. The portfolio was intended to be market-neutral, with an advertised return of 15% to 18%. Because of the portfolio's complexity, the managers presumably relied on OAS models to measure security attractiveness and volatility. The abrupt collapse of the inverse floater market, culminating in the collapse of the fund, vividly demonstrates the limitations of the models.

Exhibit 7.   Price Distribution for FHLMC 1364N–Sequential

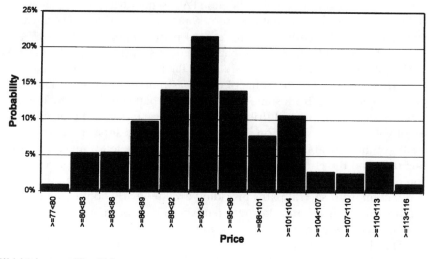

Weighted average life = 10.6 years.

Exhibit 8.   Price Distribution for FHLMC 1208D–Floater

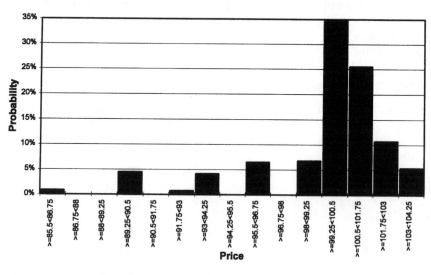

Weighted average life = 12.3 years. Cap = 10.5%. Floor = 0%.

Exhibit 9. Price Distribution for FHLMC 1554KA–Principal Only

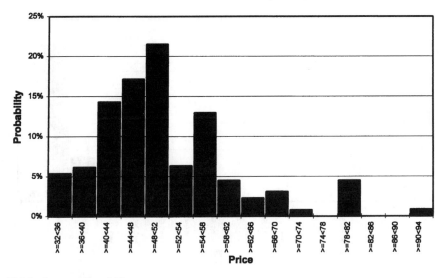

Weighted average life = 8.99 years.

Exhibit 10. Price Distribution for FHLMC 1415–TAC Inverse Floater

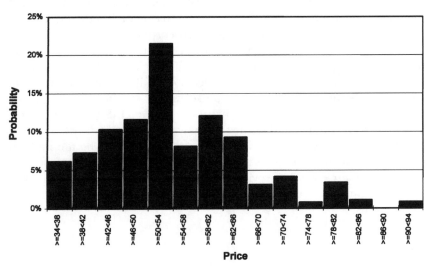

Weighted average life = 11.05 years. Coupon = 21.97% − 2.45 × LIBOR1. Cap = 1.105%.

Exhibit 11. Price Distribution for FHLMC 1480X–PAC 10

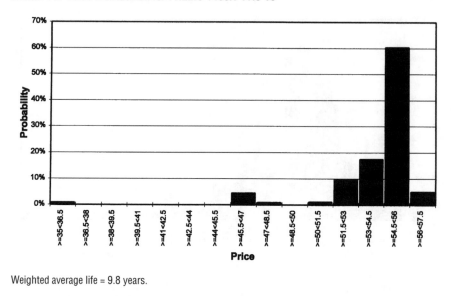

Weighted average life = 9.8 years.

---

calls or prepayments, should be treated as uncertain events, with probabilistic models used in repeated trials along the paths.

Second, while OAS models are usually run several times to estimate option adjusted duration, sensitivities to prepayment levels and volatility should also be provided. More sophisticated corporate bond models could also measure sensitivity to call risk as affected by changes in corporate tax rates, management's desired "efficiency" in refinancing, and so on.

Third, portfolio OAS should be calculated as if the portfolio were one security; that is, the cash flows from all securities should be aggregated to each node prior to discounting, so that the resulting OAS (with all its other problems) can be interpreted in the same way as a single-security OAS.

One particularly useful area of future research would be the measurement of performance of high-OAS portfolios versus their lower-OAS counterparts. This research would provide more information on the usefulness of the OAS (estimated over the entire life of the security) to managers with short horizons.

CHAPTER 31

Consistent, Fair and Robust Methods of Valuing Mortgage Securities

R. Blaine Roberts, Ph.D.
Senior Managing Director
Financial Analytics and Structured Transactions Group
Bear Stearns & Co., Inc.

David Sykes, Ph.D.
Principal Director of Taxable Fixed-Income Research
Alex. Brown & Sons, Inc.

Michael L. Winchell
Senior Managing Director
Risk Management Group
Bear Stearns & Co., Inc.

Over the past decade, mortgage market participants have spent vast sums of money to develop the financial engineering technology in place today. This technology enabled arbitrageurs to slice and dice the cash flows of mortgage pass-throughs in very complex ways, and to allocate across derivative securities, in various degrees, the imbedded call option we know as prepayment. This made the task of assessing the fair value of a mortgage security all the more difficult; determining the fair value of simple pass-throughs alone was difficult enough in 1986. As a result, mortgage investors also have spent heavily to build mortgage pricing models.

In spite of these efforts, many portfolio managers and traders argue that the pricing of mortgage securities remains more art than science, more dependent on market savvy and experience than on prepayment algorithms and contingent cash flow models. To some degree, they are correct. Though state-of-the-art bond valuation models claim to price correctly all securities with contingent cash flows, the results generated by such models do not always mesh with our intuitions about relative value and expected price performance, and for good reason.

Indeed, mortgage valuation models have become more robust. State-contingent cash flow models are crucial to the valuation of securities with cash flows that are dependent on the level of interest rates. The most common of these models is the one-factor stochastic model known as the option-adjusted spread (OAS) model. But as demonstrated below, the relative value of a mortgage security also depends on the impact of nondeterministic factors on cash flows. When factors outside the realm of the model affect the present value of a security, a premium must be earned by the investor. In the context of the one-factor model, nondeterministic prepayment uncertainty must be compensated by additional option-adjusted spread. Only by recognizing the impact of nondeterministic cash flows on value can portfolio managers determine when one mortgage security is cheap relative to another mortgage security. But such fair value determination need not remain an art.

In this chapter we present a definition of fixed-income securities that results in logical benchmarks to test all bond valuation models, and that provides clear insight into the fair value of a mortgage pass-through or derivative, or any other fixed-income security. We present the OAS model as an example of a technique that is quite necessary in the valuation of mortgage securities, but also discuss the limitations of the model when applied to mortgage securities. We demonstrate that under standard, simplifying assumptions, securities having cash flows that are *solely* determined by the level of interest rates should have a zero OAS. We then investigate the impact of the nondeterministic factors on mortgage cash flows. This analysis dispels an erroneous notion that all mortgage securities should earn the same option-adjusted spread.

We believe that the OAS model satisfies the minimum requirements for a bond valuation model. It could be better. We can take point with its assumptions. But we cannot replace it with something that does not satisfy simple benchmarks. OAS cannot be expected to price securities completely when some returns of cash flows are not determined by the rate process on which the model is based. But it doesn't mean we are rudderless, or that the OAS framework is useless.

BENCHMARKS FOR VALUATION MODELS

Without any reliance on a specific stochastic process or any form of expectations hypothesis, preferred habitat theory, or the like, much can be derived from the assumptions of no risk-free arbitrage and no transaction costs. The arbitrage-free pricing principle states that the market will value securities so that whenever a portfolio can be created that matches exactly in every scenario the future values of a given bond, then that portfolio will cost exactly the same as the bond itself. Risk-free arbitrage should not be possible by borrowing or lending at the riskless rate. Investors should not be able to combine fairly priced derivatives in such a way as to generate arbitrage profits; that is, the value of the whole must equal the sum of the parts.

We hold that the arbitrage-free pricing principle provides the minimal requirements for all bond valuation models. These are consistency, fairness, and robustness. A model that adheres to arbitrage-free valuation will price securities fairly. A model that produces values reflective of market conditions is consistent. A model that prices securities fairly and consistently in all states of the world is robust.

The assumption of no risk-free arbitrage also leads to the simple axiom that a pure floater is always worth par. That is a powerful axiom. It allows us to draw a direct relation between the value of a certain cash flow, the default-free payment of principal, and the value of an instrument with completely uncertain but deterministic cash flows, the interest payments of a pure floater, and permits the analysis of some financial components, typically but not always embedded within bonds, having option characteristics. As a result, we can establish benchmarks to test the consistency, fairness, and robustness of bond valuation models.

The Zero-Coupon Yield Curve, the Term Structure

Traditionally, the valuation of fixed-income securities begins with a benchmark of certainty, Treasury securities that have no default risk and no cash flow uncertainty. Assuming no transaction costs and the existence of Treasury securities for every future period in which other securities are to be valued, one can derive the *theoretical* Treasury zero-coupon yield curve, which, if there is no arbitrage, must equal the *actual* Treasury zero yield curve.

Given a default-free term structure, then all bonds with fixed cash flows can be priced easily. This applies whether the world is one of certainty or uncertainty; bonds with *certain cash flows* can be valued given only the no-default yield curve. It is only for securities with *uncertain cash flows* that more is required. Bonds with uncertain cash flows have embedded optional components that need to be priced. However, we need not rely on stochastic models to determine relative value relations among such components, only logic. And any stochastic model we use to determine absolute prices should generate results that are consistent with such logic.

This is not to say that the yield curve is not affected by the degree of uncertainty or randomness of future rates; it is. But the yield curve embodies the valuation of this volatility for bonds with certain cash flows. Thus, *given a yield curve*, a change in volatility will not change the value of fixed cash flow securities. It is another issue as to whether and how a change in volatility affects the yield curve.

The Riskless Short-Term Lending Rate

Determining relative value among alternative investments can be much more difficult when the properties of the instruments vary markedly. How much return should be given up for call protection? How much should we discount a floater when it reaches its cap? Specifically, what is the price of risk? To know this, we must first define a riskless security.

In the context of fixed-income securities, the riskless security is one that returns all principal on demand and without risk of default, and that pays the prevailing riskless rate on the outstanding balance as long as the debt is outstanding. The riskless security has no default risk and no liquidity risk. Because it has no interest rate risk, it is a *pure floater*. If the investor's opportunity cost of lending is always equal to the risk-free rate, and borrowing and lending can be done without transaction costs, then liquidity is not a concern; the term to maturity of any pure floater free of default risk is irrelevant. By simple extension, the timing or amount of principal redemption is not relevant either.

Options on the Riskless Rate

Ignoring credit and liquidity risk, one way to determine the relative value of any financial instrument is to describe, as much as possible, all bond cash flows as a function of the riskless rate. If we can arbitrarily nominate cash flows as principal and interest, then the definition of interest can be expanded to include a payment made on a collection of options written with respect to the level of the riskless rate. Interest rate swaps are explicitly viewed in this manner when the payer of fixed, and also the receiver of floating, is described as being long an interest rate cap and short an interest rate floor, and when those instruments are seen to be, in turn, a collection of individual options on the riskless rate in each payment period.

Options are agreements that specify a payment under certain market conditions (states of the world). An option on the riskless rate would specify a payment, at expiration, given a level of the riskless rate.

Using this perspective, the interest cash flows of a wide variety of fixed-income securities can be described in a manner that highlights the differences and similarities among the instruments using a common yardstick. If two securities represent a collection of identical options, then they should be valued identically.

Describing a Fixed-Rate Note

As an example, consider a simple, three-year U.S. government fixed-rate note paying 10% interest. For ease of presentation, suppose interest is paid annually. We can decompose each interest payment into three separate options on the riskless rate, or the stream of interest payments as a combination of cap and floor agreements. The noteholder is entitled to receive, in every period in which principal is outstanding: (1) the riskless rate, and (2) the difference of 10% minus the riskless rate whenever the riskless rate is *less than* 10%. But the noteholder also gives up (3) the difference of the riskless rate and 10% whenever the riskless rate *exceeds* 10%. While this may seem to be a complex way to describe a 10% interest payment, the approach offers insight into the valuation of fixed-income securities, a way to link the pricing of caps, floors, swaps, floaters, inverse floaters, and fixed-rate securities.

In fact, we present below a set of derivative securities and financial instruments for analysis, all created from the fixed-rate three-year note. To determine whether a contingent cash flow model consistently values the properties of these securities, it is essential to determine which properties or elements are common among the set of securities. The logical relations that describe the common elements of the three-year note and its derivatives form a benchmark against which any bond valuation model should be measured.

Using Options to Define Debt

Defining debt instruments in terms of options on the riskless rate leads to better assessment of relative value of financial instruments and the ability to use one security to hedge another.

A set of financial instruments can be defined as follows:

r is the riskless rate

c is a strike rate for the option on the riskless rate

$F(c)$ is the value of an interest rate floor that receives $c - r$ if $c > r$

$C(c)$ is the value of an interest rate cap that receives $r - c$ if $r > c$

$C(0)$ is the value of an interest rate cap that receives r for all levels of r

P is the value of the lump sum principal paid at maturity

B is the value of a fixed-rate note with coupon c

α is the decimal share of the principal payment for a floater security

FL is the value of a floater with a cap c/α, derived from B

INV is the value of an inverse floater that is a companion to FL

S is the value of an interest rate swap paying r and receiving fixed-rate c

IO is the value of a fixed-rate interest-only strip

The three-year fixed-rate note pays a fixed-rate c regardless of the level of r. If there is no arbitrage, then

$$B = P + C(0) + F(c) - C(c)$$

From this we can derive a floater from the fixed-rate note. Interest will be paid equal to the riskless rate multiplied by the outstanding amount of principal allocated to the floater, subject to a cap. Principal is paid when the three-year note matures. If the floater can claim all the available interest in a given period, the cap strike rate is a function of the principal allocated to the floater:

$$FL = \alpha P + \alpha C(0) - \alpha C(c/\alpha)$$

The inverse floater receives all excess interest, and gets its share of principal paid at maturity as well. The inverse floater is long the interest rate cap that the floater is short:

$$INV = [1 - \alpha]P + [1 - \alpha]C(0) + F(c) - C(c) + \alpha C(c/\alpha)$$

An interest rate swap agreement, in which the investor receives a fixed-rate of c and pays the floating rate, for a period of three years, can also be described:

$$S = F(c) - C(c)$$

Defining Relative Performance and Hedging

Under the assumption of no arbitrage, the value of a pure floater is always par because the security always earns the riskless rate r for every level of r. In other words, the value of a *pure floater* is constant for any change in r. For this to be the case, it must be that if the value of the principal zero changes, the value of $C(0)$ always changes, in an equal but offsetting amount.

$$pure\ FL = P + C(0) \equiv 1$$

$$\Delta\ pure\ FL = \Delta P + \Delta C(0) = 0$$

$$\Delta P = -\Delta C(0)$$

As the pure floater is always par, the value of the fixed-rate note is:

$$B = 1 + F(c) - C(c)$$

Thus, if the fixed-rate note is also at par, then:

$$F(c) = C(c),\ S = 0,\ \text{and}\ C(0) = IO(c)$$

Given that the financial instruments are related as previously defined, and given that the value of a pure floater is constant, we can state that the change in value of these instruments is a function of the change in the value of the options, as follows:

$$\Delta B = \Delta F(c) - \Delta C(c)$$

$$\Delta S = \Delta F(c) - \Delta C(c)$$

$$\Delta FL = -\Delta \alpha C(c/\alpha)$$

$$\Delta INV = \Delta F(c) - \Delta C(c) + \Delta \alpha C(c/\alpha)$$

$$\Delta INV = \Delta [1 - \alpha]P + \Delta \alpha F(c/\alpha)$$

$$\Delta IO = -\Delta P + \Delta S$$

Most of these price performance statements are commonly accepted. For example, swap market participants have always shown that the change in the value of the swap equals the change in the value of the fixed-rate note. The change in price of a floater should be a direct result of the change in the value of the cap. The change in the value of the inverse is equal to the change in the value of the fixed-rate note plus the change in the cap value. The change in the value of an IO is equal to the negative of the change in the value of the PO plus the change in the value of the swap struck at c. The value of the zero strike cap and the value of an IO of the par bond are always equal.

Not defined directly is the value of any cap or floor other than $C(0)$. While we can define one cap or floor in terms of another, such as:

$$\Delta \alpha F(c/\alpha) = \Delta [1 - \alpha]C(0) + \Delta F(c) - \Delta C(c) + \Delta \alpha C(c/\alpha)$$

it is difficult to define any cap or floor without reference to other caps and floors.

Using the Methodology to Sharpen Intuition

We can use this approach to answer some intriguing relative value questions:

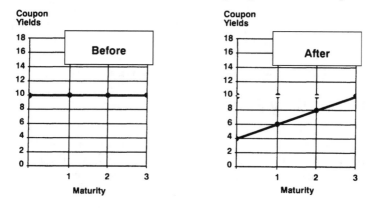

What would happen to the value of a three-year 10% interest rate cap agreement after the yield curve steepens?

The intuitive response is that the 10% cap would have less value if the one-year rate were 6%. However, recall that the value of the fixed-rate note is given by the equation: *fixed-rate note* = $P + C(0) + F(c) - C(c)$. The pure floater is worth par. The fixed-rate note is still worth par. That means the value of *[F(c) - C(c)]* is unchanged, and any change in $F(c)$ will be equal to the change in $C(c)$. There is not enough information to prove $C(c)$ went up or down, but if $C(0)$ is worth more, it would seem to follow that $C(c)$ is also worth more.

What would happen to the value of a three-year 10% interest rate floor agreement after the yield curve steepens?

The intuitive response is that the 10% floor is worth more. From the foregoing analysis of $C(c)$ in the second case, any change in the value of $C(c)$ must be matched by the change in $F(c)$. If the value of the floor is higher when short rates decline, so too is the value of the cap. At this point, it seems our intuition about the cap was wrong and our intuition about the floor was right. It is certain, however, that either both the floor and cap are worth more or they are both worth less.

What would happen to the value of the inverse floater after the yield curve steepens?

Suppose that the floater is structured to receive 80% of the principal (α = 0.8) so that the inverse floater has a 4:1 leverage ratio; that is, the inverse floater's coupon rate increases 4% for every 1% decrease in the riskless rate. With short-term rates dropping to 6% from 10%, the floater coupon would decline to 6% from 10%, and the inverse floater coupon would jump to 26% from 10%.

Intuition says that the inverse floater is worth more now. However, remember that the change in the value of the floater must be the negative of the change in the value of the cap, $\alpha C(c/\alpha)$. Intuition also says the cap with a 12.5% strike is worth less. If the value of the cap is less, then the floater is worth more.

But if the floater is worth more and the fixed-rate note is still par, then the inverse is worth less! Because $\Delta INV = \Delta F(c) - \Delta C(c) + \Delta \alpha C(c/\alpha)$ and $\Delta B = \Delta F(c) - \Delta C(c) = 0$, if not for $\alpha C(c/\alpha)$, the value of the inverse would be unchanged. Here too we seem to have conflicting intuitions.

The Monotonicity Postulate

To resolve the apparent conflict regarding relative value, it is necessary to postulate a relation among caps of various strikes, and likewise floors.

Without resorting to any form of expectations hypothesis and without specifying a particular, parametric stochastic process, we can go further in pricing options by the monotonicity postulate.

Proposition: If any particular interest rate cap increases in value, then all caps with the same notional amortization structure and a higher strike cannot decrease in value. If any interest rate floor increases in value, then all floors with the same notional amortization structure and a lower strike cannot decrease in value.

$$\Delta\ C(c) > 0 \text{ implies } \Delta\ C(c') \geq 0 \text{ for all } c' > c$$

$$\Delta\ F(c) > 0 \text{ implies } \Delta\ F(c') \geq 0 \text{ for all } c' < c$$

Because $C(c')$ is a subset of $C(c)$ if $c' > c$, and $F(c')$ is a subset of $F(c)$ for $c' < c$, it follows that $C(c) \geq C(c')$, and $F(c) \geq F(c')$ in the foregoing statements, but it is not necessarily the case that $\Delta\ C(c) > \Delta\ C(c')$ for $c' > c$.

What would be the change in the value of the interest rate cap agreements $C(0)$, $C(c)$, and $C(c/\alpha)$?

After short rates drop, the yield on the three-year zero-coupon principal would be greater than 10%, approximately 10.28%, because it must be created by being long a three-year 10% fixed-rate note and short the "more expensive" earlier maturing zero-coupon payments. After the decline in short rates, P would be worth 0.58% less. If we hold that a pure floater equals $P + C(0)$ and is always equal to par, if P is worth less, then $C(0)$ is worth 0.58% more.

Given the postulate of monotonicity, if the value of $C(0)$ increases, so too must the values of $C(c)$ and $C(c/\alpha)$ increase, even though by reference to the short-term rate alone, they are more "out-of-the-money." We also know that the change in the value of the inverse floater is positive, and equal to $\Delta \alpha C(c/\alpha)$.

Generalization and Extension

It is a straightforward extension to define the fixed-rate note and components to be collections of period-specific cash flows and to value each period independently. Thus, for example, $C(c)$ becomes $C(c,t)$, which is an interest rate option that receives any positive value of $c - r$ for period t only. Then, the value of an interest rate cap agreement with maturity T is the sum of the values of the period-specific options.

This extension allows one to derive relations between securities with different maturities. For example, securities or agreements with maturities of T and $T + 1$ differ in value only by the single-period values of period T.

The approach is not limited to securities that pay a certain amount of principal on a single and certain maturity date. The analysis can easily be extended such that P is the value of the principal paid as $a(r,t)$, where $a(r,t)$ is an amortization function that depends on r, the riskless rate, and time, t. $A(t)$ is the sum of all prior amounts amortized. Usually $A(T) = 1$; the security is fully amortized by the maturity date T.

$F(c)$ and $C(c)$ now receive interest based on $[1\text{-}A(t)]$, the unamortized amount. This is a relatively generalized formulation where $a(r,t)$ could be determined by a set schedule such as the scheduled principal payment of a fixed-rate, level pay mortgage, or by the exercise of a call option by the issuer.

All the relations derived in the previous section for the fixed-rate note and its derivatives still hold. In particular, we still have:

$$B = P + C(0) + F(c) - C(c)$$

and

$$P + C(0) \equiv 1$$

What is lost is that P can no longer be priced solely by referencing the no-default Treasury yield curve for fixed cash flow securities if $a(r,t)$ depends on the stochastic riskless rate at future times. Thus, one needs a reference market or benchmark set of securities as a replacement, or needs to use a specific stochastic process, or both.

Incorporating Observable Futures, Forwards, and Options Markets

The value of a callable bond, Bc, can be related to that of a noncallable bond, B, and the value of a call option, $OCt(k)$, exercisable at t at a strike price of k:

$$B_c = B - OC(k_t)$$

$$B_c = P + C(0) + F(c) - C(c) - OC_t(k)$$

If k is par, because $P + C(0)$ is par, the value of the call option at expiration is:

$$OC_t(k) = max\ [F_t(c) - C_t(c),\ 0]$$

Prior to time t, the call option will have a value greater than or equal to the value of a noncallable forward swap commencing at t because the range of values of the swap $F_t(c) - C_t(c)$ is a subset of the range of values of $OC_t(k)$. The value of the option at expiration is equal to all of the possible positive values of the swap and greater than all of the negative values of the swap.

As above, we may go further in bounding the price response of a callable bond without reference to term structure theories or any specific random process by appealing to a more general monotonicity postulate. In line with the postulate stated above, it would be natural to assume that if a current swap increases in value, $\Delta F(c) - \Delta C(c) > 0$, forward swaps at the same strike would not decrease in value, $\Delta F_t(c) - \Delta C_t(c) \geq 0$; and further, that the value of the call option would not decrease in value, $\Delta\ OC_t(k) \geq 0$. This produces relations among noncallable bonds, current swaps, forward swaps, call options, and, thus, callable bonds.

THE NECESSITY OF VALUING SECURITIES UNDER CONDITIONS OF UNCERTAINTY

The simplest valuation model for fixed-income securities, including mortgages, is one where the world never changes. In this world, all bonds have the same coupon rates and all would be priced at par. This is far from observed markets.

In the mid-1970s, yield was introduced on Wall Street for bond valuation. A simple yield model is one where the world has changed, but it is presumed that it will never change again. The current yield curve is flat, but there exist other bonds with coupons different from the current yield curve. All bonds are priced to have the same yield as the current yield curve. This simple model for valuation must be rejected.

The next level of sophistication still assumes a world of certainty. In this model, the world may have changed in the past and will change in the future, but that change is certain and determinant from the yield curve. Bonds have different coupons and are priced so that the yield of each cash flow equals the yield of the corresponding Treasury zero security. Options trade at their intrinsic value at expiration appropriately discounted back to the present. Options out-of-the-money have no value; there is no time premium. This model is also inconsistent with observed markets.

A bond-pricing model commonly in use today is the spread-to-the-average-life model. In this framework, the world is uncertain and changing, but uncertainty is not modeled explicitly. Securities trade to a constant spread to the riskless Treasury of the same average life, or in a somewhat more sophisticated variation (but still in the same category), at a constant spread to the Treasury with the same duration.

This model must also be rejected on the basis of fairness. Consider the previous example where the yield curve changes from flat at 10% to upwardly sloping, with a 6% one-year, 8% two-year, and 10% three-year. Fairness requires that the three-year zero-coupon bond's spread to the three-year coupon bond increase from zero to twenty-eight basis points, even though both the three-year zero and the three-year coupon bond have the same average life.

Using duration-matched spreads makes little difference. In the case of the flat yield curve, the durations, as conventionally measured, of the coupon bond and the zero are 2.49 and 2.73, respectively. Once the short-term rates drop, the duration of the coupon bond is unchanged, and the duration of the zero declines to just 2.72. On a duration-matched basis, the error in fair pricing is virtually the same as it would be using the average life.

Thus, the principles of consistency, robustness, and fairness require the broad use of a model that explicitly takes into account the stochastic nature of financial markets. Not to do so invites substantial mispricing and consequent losses when arbitrageurs enter the market. Yield models are not robust. *There is no correct yield for an option.*

THE OPTION-ADJUSTED SPREAD MODEL

Logic alone will not provide us with fair, *absolute* prices for each of the above financial instruments. For that we need a model that explicitly values interest rate uncertainty.

Models will differ in the underlying assumptions and approaches. What is most important is that the model meet the minimal requirements of fairness and consistency, and the usefulness of the benchmarks in assessing a particular model should be apparent.

The OAS model, as presented here, is a robust, fair, and consistent bond valuation model that satisfies all of the benchmarks for valuation models set forth above. Default-free bonds with cash flows that are entirely determined by r, the risk-free interest rate, will be fairly priced at a zero OAS. So too will the components and derivatives be fairly priced at a zero OAS. This is demonstrated below. However, the OAS model values only interest rate uncertainty. When other factors affect the cash flows of a security, these conclusions do not hold.

Over the last decade, the inherent value associated with interest rate uncertainty or volatility has received increasing recognition from the fixed-income markets. This is reflected in the explosive growth of option or option-like instruments whose future cash flows are a function of interest rates, either directly (*e.g.*, caps, floors) or indirectly (option on a fixed-rate bond). Moreover, it is increasingly recognized that all fixed-income products display varying degrees of option-like properties such as convexity, and to this extent their value is affected by interest rate uncertainty.

One-Factor Model

This has caused sophisticated market participants to move away from naive static valuation techniques that ignore volatility and the shape of the yield curve, toward more sophisticated term structure-based stochastic models that are capable of quantifying the value of volatility. One of the more straightforward stochastic, term structure models is the one-factor model of the riskless rate, r. This framework is the foundation for a variety of pricing models, ranging from the mortgage-backed securities' OAS model, to models for pricing American options on fixed-rate bonds, interest rate swaps, and the like.

The one-factor approach models uncertainty as follows. Assume the shape of the term structure depends only on r, the riskless rate. While we know the level of the riskless rate today, we do not know its level at any future time period, $r(t)$. However, suppose that proportional changes in r from one period to the next are normally distributed with a known mean value and standard deviation. The standard deviation (volatility) represents uncertain percentage changes in $r(t)$, which for convenience we assume is constant in each time period, and the mean (drift) represents certain expected percentage changes that may vary across time periods.[1]

This single-factor process becomes a valuation model when the arbitrage-free pricing principle is invoked as the economic rationale behind the pricing process. In other words, we can derive the market's assessment of the value of uncertainty from two components: an observation of the current term structure and an assumption about the volatility of the riskless rate through time.

Implied Forward Rates

Coupled with the arbitrage-free pricing principle, the one-factor model has its simplest incarnation in a world of certainty (no volatility), where it takes the form of the familiar implied forward rate, naive expectations hypothesis. Under certainty, arbitrage considerations imply that the rate of return to holding a default-free bond of any maturity M until it matures must equal the rate of return on cash invested over the same time period earning only the riskless rate. Otherwise, we could earn arbitrage profits by borrowing funds at the riskless rate and investing in the bond, or by short selling the bond and investing the proceeds at the riskless rate, depending on the relation between the bond yield and the riskless rate.

To illustrate, consider the flat term structure shown in Exhibit 1, where the yields on all zero-coupon bonds of various maturity equal 10%. For convenience, lending at the riskless rate is described as an investment in successive one-period bonds, with the term of a riskless period defined to be one year.

If volatility is known to be zero, then by definition the future values of r are known with certainty. The arbitrage-free condition implies that the path

---

1 While the OAS technique can seem very complex, at its core is a simple assumption. The methodology is based on the assumption that there is a known volatility of the riskless rate and there is embedded in the pricing of, for example, Treasury securities, the market's valuation of that volatility. The value of volatility, plus the market's implied expectation of future levels of the riskless rate, combine to specify the mean of the distribution of possible changes in riskless rates.

We can always take point with an assumption, argue that the model could be better, or that it doesn't accurately reflect reality. What is necessary is that if we reject one model in favor of another, that the chosen model still meet very basic criteria, that it satisfy the benchmarks we have outlined in this presentation.

Exhibit 1. Value of Three Successive Zero-Coupon Bonds, Constant Discount Rate

Bond Maturity	Bond Yield	Bond Price	Value of a Series of One Period Bonds
1	10.00%	90.9090 =	$\dfrac{100}{(1+0.10)}$
2	10.00%	82.6446 =	$\dfrac{100}{(1+0.10)\times(1+0.10)}$

Exhibit 2. Value of a Two-Period Zero-Coupon Bond, Rate Varies Over Time

Rate Path	Period 1	Period 2	Value of Two Year	Value of a Series of One Period Bonds
Higher	10.00%	12.00%	81.1688 =	$\dfrac{100}{(1+0.10)\times(1+0.12)}$
Flat	10.00%	10.00%	82.6446 =	$\dfrac{100}{(1+0.10)\times(1+0.10)}$

---

of r must be a constant at 10%. If the riskless rate were higher at 12%, one could reap an arbitrage profit by selling a two-year bond at 82.6446 against a sequence of one-year bonds (lending at the riskless rate) at a total cost of 81.1688, for an arbitrage profit of 1.4758. Conversely, if the riskless rate were lower at 8%, one could earn profits without risk by selling the sequence of one-year bonds (borrowing at the riskless rate) worth 84.1751 and investing in the two-year bond at a price of 82.6446, for a gain of 1.5305. No arbitrage would be available if the one-period rate were 10% in each period, exactly as expected. Exhibit 2 illustrates this.

Using the arbitrage-free pricing principle, *a given term structure, and the assumption of no volatility,* we can derive the market's expectations of the riskless rate in the future, or, as it is generally known, the *implied forward rate.*

Adding Uncertainty to the Framework

The basic tenet under certainty is that in each time period, the rate of return on every default-free bond must equal the prevailing riskless rate. Extending this to valuation in an uncertain world, it is generally referred to as the local expectations hypothesis, which entails pricing on the basis of expected values: the *expected* rate of return on every default-free bond must equal the riskless rate. The approach is as follows. Assume the observed term structure prices reflect the market's risk attitude and valuation of rate uncertainty. Then "tune" the drift term in the riskless rate process so that the model generates expected prices for the term structure bonds that match the observed market prices of those bonds. Thus, the arbitrage-free pricing principle and the assumption that risk assessment is embodied in the term structure allows us to value on the simple basis of *expected* values without assuming that the market is necessarily risk-neutral. That is, this approach does not imply that the market actually expects all default-free bonds to earn the riskless rate; rather, by incorporating the value of uncertainty into the model's drift term, this approach enables us to price *as if* this were the case. Thus, in addition to market expectations about the future values of the short rate, the drift term captures the market price of risk. Moreover, under uncertainty it is generally not possible to determine what portion of the drift term represents risk valuation versus expectations; furthermore, it is not generally necessary.

In practice, there are two methods commonly used to generate the potential future values of *r*. The rates can be regarded as either a binomial branching lattice or as a set of independent paths. Both methods will effectively replicate the same underlying stochastic model of the term structure. The decision to use a particular model is driven by the relation of a particular security's cash flows to interest rates; it does not pertain per se to the fundamental issues of how best to model the term structure under uncertainty.

Given the set of financial instruments presented earlier, and the relations among them that form the benchmarks for valuation models, the following examples demonstrate the fairness, consistency, and robustness of the OAS framework for securities having cash flows entirely determined by the prevailing level of the riskless rate.

For convenience, we will use a simple binomial lattice to demonstrate the consistency and fairness of the OAS model. We assume that in any given future period, the prevailing riskless rate can be either higher or lower than it was in the prior period, with equal likelihood.[2] Given a "flat" term structure under 15% volatility, the potential paths of *r* are shown in Exhibit 3.

Benchmarking the OAS Model

To benchmark the OAS model, we price the components of a bond and its derivatives using the simple lattice presented above. To do this, we present the cash flows of each instrument given each potential level of *r*, and subse-

---

2 The interest rates shown in the exhibit are generated by the formula

$$r_1 = 10\% \times e^{\mu \pm 0.15}, \text{ and } r_2 = r_1 e^{\mu \pm 0.15}.$$

They are rounded for presentation purposes. The rate process is "tuned" to the term structure presented in Exhibit 3 by solving for a μ in each time period so that the term structure bonds are correctly priced.

Exhibit 3.   Potential Levels of Riskless Rate Assuming 15% Volatility

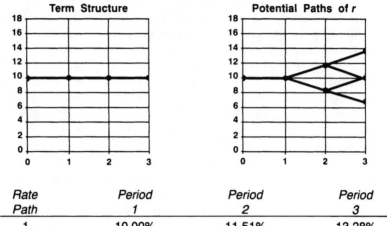

Rate Path	Period 1	Period 2	Period 3
1	10.00%	11.51%	13.28%
2	10.00%	11.51%	9.84%
3	10.00%	8.53%	9.84%
4	10.00%	8.53%	7.29%

quently calculate the expected present value of those cash flows using the prevailing rate.

Exhibit 4 shows the expected present value of the default-free, three-year fixed-rate bond paying interest annually at a 10% coupon rate, and all principal at maturity. The face value of the bond will be 100. While the cash flows are certain each period, the value of the cash flows is not. However, the expected present value of the bond is par; it is the average of the bond values given the four possible paths of the riskless rate over time.

To see how the present value of the security is determined for any specific rate path, recall that each cash flow is discounted using the rates prevailing from its payment date back to today along the path. The present value of the fixed-rate bond's cash flows for Path 1 are shown in Exhibit 5.

Exhibits 6 and 7 show the expected value of a 10% interest rate cap agreement and the expected value of a 10% interest rate floor agreement, respectively. Recall that the cap returns a cash flow only when the riskless rate exceeds 10%; the floor only returns a cash flow when the riskless rate is below 10%.

As specified by the benchmarks, the cap and floor should have equal value when the fixed-rate bond is valued at par.

Exhibit 4. Expected Present Value of a 10% Fixed-Rate Bond

Path	Rate	Cash Flow	Rate	Cash Flow	Rate	Cash Flow		Present Value
1	10.00%	10.00	11.51%	10.00	13.28%	110.00	=	96.4066
2	10.00%	10.00	11.51%	10.00	9.84%	110.00	=	98.8874
3	10.00%	10.00	8.53%	10.00	9.84%	110.00	=	101.3561
4	10.00%	10.00	8.53%	10.00	7.29%	110.00	=	103.3499

Expected Present Value of 10% Fixed-Rate Bond =   100.0000

Exhibit 5. Present Value of a Fixed-Rate Bond's Cash Flows Given a Rate Path

Period	Cash Flow	Present Value		
1	10.00	9.0909	=	$\dfrac{10}{(1 + 0.10)}$
2	10.00	8.1525	=	$\dfrac{10}{(1 + 0.10) \times (1 + 0.1151)}$
3	110.00	79.1633	=	$\dfrac{110}{(1 + 0.10) \times (1 + 0.1151) \times (1 + 0.1328)}$
Total Present Value		96.4066		

Exhibit 6. Expected Present Value of a 10% Interest Rate Cap Agreement

Path	Rate	Cash Flow	Rate	Cash Flow	Rate	Cash Flow		Present Value
1	10.00%	0.00	11.51%	1.51	13.28%	3.28	=	3.5934
2	10.00%	0.00	11.51%	1.51	9.84%	0.00	=	1.2327
3	10.00%	0.00	8.53%	0.00	9.84%	0.00	=	0.0000
4	10.00%	0.00	8.53%	0.00	7.29%	0.00	=	0.0000

Expected Present Value of 10% Interest Rate Cap Agreement   =   1.2065

Exhibit 8 demonstrates that the value of a pure floater is par, as it should be. Exhibits 9 and 10 show the expected value of the floater's two components.

Two derivatives of the fixed-rate bond are the floater and the inverse floater, created by dynamically allocating the interest cash flow of the fixed-rate

Exhibit 7. Expected Present Value of a 10% Interest Rate Floor Agreement

Path	Rate	Cash Flow	Rate	Cash Flow	Rate	Cash Flow		Present Value
1	10.00%	0.00	11.51%	0.00	13.28%	0.00	=	0.0000
2	10.00%	0.00	11.51%	0.00	9.84%	0.16	=	0.1201
3	10.00%	0.00	8.53%	1.47	9.84%	0.16	=	1.3561
4	10.00%	0.00	8.53%	1.47	7.29%	2.71	=	3.3499
Expected Present Value of 10% Interest Rate Floor Agreement							=	1.2065

Exhibit 8. Expected Present Value of a Pure Floater

Path	Rate	Cash Flow	Rate	Cash Flow	Rate	Cash Flow		Present Value
1	10.00%	10.00	11.51%	11.51	13.28%	113.28	=	100.0000
2	10.00%	10.00	11.51%	11.51	9.84%	109.84	=	100.0000
3	10.00%	10.00	8.53%	8.53	9.84%	109.84	=	100.0000
4	10.00%	10.00	8.53%	8.53	7.29%	107.29	=	100.0000
Expected Present Value of Pure Floater							=	100.0000

Exhibit 9. Expected Present Value of the Principal Payment

Path	Rate	Cash Flow	Rate	Cash Flow	Rate	Cash Flow		Present Value
1	10.00%	0.00	11.51%	0.00	13.28%	100.00	=	71.9667
2	10.00%	0.00	11.51%	0.00	9.84%	100.00	=	74.2219
3	10.00%	0.00	8.53%	0.00	9.84%	100.00	=	76.2624
4	10.00%	0.00	8.53%	0.00	7.29%	100.00	=	78.0749
Expected Present Value of Principal Paid at Maturity							=	75.1315

bond given levels of r, and assigning a portion of the principal to each derivative. Given 80 floater bonds derived from 100 of the fixed-rate bonds, and 20 inverse floater bonds, the cash flows and expected present values would be as shown in Exhibits 11 and 12.

Note that the floater and inverse floater present values add up to the collateral, and that the difference between the two securities' value and par (20 and 80, respectively), is given by the value of the 12.50% cap. The floater

Exhibit 10. Expected Present Value of Pure Floater Interest, a 0% Cap Agreement

Path	Rate	Cash Flow	Rate	Cash Flow	Rate	Cash Flow		Present Value
1	10.00%	10.00	11.51%	11.51	13.28%	13.28	=	28.0333
2	10.00%	10.00	11.51%	11.51	9.84%	9.84	=	25.7781
3	10.00%	10.00	8.53%	8.53	9.84%	9.84	=	23.7376
4	10.00%	10.00	8.53%	8.53	7.29%	7.29	=	21.9251
		Expected Present Value of Principal Paid at Maturity					=	24.8685

Exhibit 11. Expected Present Value of a Floater Having a 12.50% Interest Cap—80.00 Face Amount

Path	Rate	Cash Flow	Rate	Cash Flow	Rate	Cash Flow		Present Value
1	10.00%	8.00	11.51%	9.21	13.28%	90.00	=	79.5508
2	10.00%	8.00	11.51%	9.21	9.84%	87.87	=	80.0000
3	10.00%	8.00	8.53%	6.82	9.84%	87.87	=	80.0000
4	10.00%	8.00	8.53%	6.82	7.29%	85.83	=	80.0000
		Expected Present Value of Floater Having a 12.50% Rate Cap					=	79.8877

Exhibit 12. Expected Present Value of an Inverse Floater—20.00 Face Amount

Path	Rate	Cash Flow	Rate	Cash Flow	Rate	Cash Flow		Present Value
1	10.00%	2.00	11.51%	0.79	13.28%	20.00	=	16.8558
2	10.00%	2.00	11.51%	0.79	9.84%	22.13	=	18.8874
3	10.00%	2.00	8.53%	3.18	9.84%	22.13	=	21.3561
4	10.00%	2.00	8.53%	3.18	7.29%	24.17	=	23.3499
		Expected Present Value of an Inverse Floater					=	20.1123

is short the cap, the inverse floater is long the cap. The value of the cap is presented in Exhibit 13.

Exhibit 14 shows the impact of a call option on the value of a fixed-rate bond. In this example, the issuer has the right to exercise a call option, and is assumed to do so when it is economical. The entire bond is callable.

Exhibit 13.   Expected Present Value of a 12.50% Interest Rate Cap Agreement, 80.00 Notional Amount

Path	Rate	Cash Flow	Rate	Cash Flow	Rate	Cash Flow		Present Value
1	10.00%	0.00	11.51%	0.00	13.28%	0.62	=	0.4492
2	10.00%	0.00	11.51%	0.00	9.84%	0.00	=	0.0000
3	10.00%	0.00	8.53%	0.00	9.84%	0.00	=	0.0000
4	10.00%	0.00	8.53%	0.00	7.29%	0.00	=	0.0000

Expected Present Value of 10% Interest Rate Cap Agreement = 0.1123

Exhibit 14.   Expected Present Value of a Callable, 10% Fixed-Rate Bond

Path	Rate	Cash Flow	Rate	Cash Flow	Rate	Cash Flow	Present Value
1	10.00%	10.00	11.51%	10.00	13.28%	110.00 =	96.4066
2	10.00%	10.00	11.51%	10.00	9.84%	110.00 =	98.8874
3	10.00%	10.00	8.53%	110.00	9.84%	0.00 =	101.2327
4	10.00%	10.00	8.53%	110.00	7.29%	0.00 =	101.2327

Expected Present Value of a Callable, 10% Fixed-Rate Bond = 99.4399

Exhibit 15 shows the cash flows and expected present value of an amortizing, partially callable, 10% fixed-rate bond. Similar indexed sinking fund bonds have been issued in the fixed-income market. Among the various financial instruments presented, this bond is the one most like a mortgage security. The difference is that the call feature of these bonds, unlike the typical mortgage security, is *completely* determined by the interest rate process. There are no prepayments due to death or divorce, no lock-in effect, and no "burnout." Interest and principal components of the total cash flow are separately presented.

Note that this 10% fixed-rate coupon bond has a price that is at a discount to par, and at a discount to the noncallable 10% fixed-rate bond. Like a completely callable bond, this discount reflects the value of the call(s) implicit in the amortization scheme. Like a mortgage, this bond's paydown schedule varies inversely with the level of interest rates. Because the bond will pay down more rapidly as interest rates fall, the investor's ability to participate in any market rally is reduced. This compresses the value of the bond,

Exhibit 15. Expected Present Value of an Amortizing, Partially Callable, 10% Fixed-Rate Bond

Path	Rate	Int.	Prin.	Rate	Int.	Prin	Rate	Int.	Prin.	Present Value
1	10.00%	10.00	10.00	11.51%	9.00	1.80	13.28%	8.82	88.20 =	96.8085
2	10.00%	10.00	10.00	11.51%	9.00	1.80	9.84%	8.82	88.20 =	98.9965
3	10.00%	10.00	10.00	8.53%	9.00	89.10	9.84%	0.09	0.90 =	101.1106
4	10.00%	10.00	10.00	8.53%	9.00	89.10	7.29%	0.09	0.90 =	101.1285

Expected Present Value of an Amortizing, Partially Callable Bond   =   99.5110

as illustrated by the compressed price appreciation associated with paths three and four, relative to the performance of a noncallable bond. Note as well the higher present value of the amortizing bond in paths one and two relative to the noncallable bond. (See Exhibit 4.) This is the result of the early redemption of principal in an environment in which prevailing rates exceed the coupon rate.

Valuing to a Zero Option-Adjusted Spread

The above values were all discounted across the rate paths at the riskless rates themselves, with no spread (OAS) added or subtracted. That is, all the above securities were priced to a zero OAS. The reason goes back to the basic arbitrage arguments underlying the option pricing methodology. In particular, if a security's cash flows and/or amortization are a certain function of interest rates, then at the start of any single time period it is possible to create a portfolio of term structure bonds that, at the end of the time period, will have the same future value as this security for every possible value of the short-term rate. Thus the security must cost the same at the start of the time period as the portfolio of Treasuries. Since any portfolio of Treasuries has a zero OAS, it follows that the security itself must have a zero OAS. Intuitively, the idea is that as long as we can exactly recreate the performance of an arbitrary security with a portfolio of Treasuries, then the value of the portfolio and the security must be the same at the start of the hedging period.

This can be shown to be the case for all of the financial instruments presented so far. Any one of them can be recreated by a portfolio of the zero-coupon Treasury securities given by the term structure.

For example, consider the case of the three-period interest rate cap agreement struck at 10%. While on the surface this may appear to be a difficult candidate to replicate with a Treasury portfolio, it is actually quite natural. In fact, it is perfectly analogous to the original Black-Scholes arbitrage-free pricing methodology, wherein a portfolio containing the underlying stock and short-term debt is constructed to replicate the performance of a call option on the stock.

To the extent that short-term rates over time are tied to the term structure, the cap is in effect an option on the term structure. Thus we should be able to replicate the performance of the cap by analogously constructing a portfolio containing an appropriate combination of an underlying term structure bond and short-term debt.

In the case of the simple example presented above, it is not difficult to calculate that the 10% cap can be replicated in the first period by lending 99.20177 for one period and shorting 107.6621 of the two-period bond. If we calculate the price of this portfolio we get:

	Face Amount	Price		Cost
One-Period Bond	99.20177	0.909090	=	90.183426
Two-Period Bond	-107.66207	0.826446	=	-88.976887
				1.206539

The cost of this portfolio is exactly the same as the cap valued above at zero OAS. Clearly, any valuation of the cap to a nonzero spread would create an arbitrage between the cap and the market for term structure bonds. At the end of the first period, the value of the short-term rate for the second period becomes known. At this time, the hedge is rebalanced so as to hedge out the risk for the second period, and so on for the remainder of the future periods.

RELATIVE VALUATION WHEN CASH FLOWS ARE NOT DETERMINISTIC

Callable Bonds When Option Exercise Is Inefficient

In the case of mortgage-backed securities, the exercise of borrower call options is *not* solely a deterministic function of interest rates, but rather a function of various demographic factors and borrowers' financial status. Such conditions can constrain an otherwise economic exercise of the call option, or induce a noneconomic exercise of the option. Furthermore, in the case of conventional mortgages, lenders can exercise put options that generally can be construed as optimal from a financial standpoint, but are restricted to circumstances when the home is sold.

These factors introduce elements that are not determined by the prevailing rate of interest. Even so, the relations that we have derived above for deterministic bonds, their components and derivatives, must also hold for mortgage-backed securities and their components and derivatives. These include floaters, inverse floaters, PAC, companion, interest- and principal-only securities, and the like.

When the one-factor pricing model is applied to the valuation of mortgage product, principal prepayments are made a function of the stochastic rate process. In other words, principal prepayments are treated as completely deterministic with respect to interest rates. As a result, a future prepayment is *known*, within the context of the model, given the prevailing rate of interest. The effects on prepayments of other factors, such as economic growth, housing inflation, month of the year, and age of the loan as a proxy for demographic influences, are typically assumed to be certain and fixed in the model.

We would not expect a model that uses the prevailing interest rate as the only random variable to provide a meaningful fair value for IBM stock. Nor should we expect such a model accurately to value death, divorce, and the "lock-in" effect. Of course, mortgage market participants recognize the limitations of prepayment algorithms; historical experience of specific pools and trusts consistently reveals such limitations.

Confronted with the positive OAS on GNMA pass-through securities, which are free of default risk, the spread must be compensation for prepayment uncertainty. While some analysts point out that an OAS could also be compensation for the increased operational costs of investing in a monthly pay security, and for a lack of liquidity, the impact of these factors in today's mortgage market must be minimal.

Why Different Mortgage Products Should Have Different Option-Adjusted Spreads

When evaluating the vast array of mortgage products, an implicit assumption often used in the marketplace is that fairly priced mortgage securities would have the *same* OAS. This, in general, is not correct.

When a security's return is affected by nondeterministic cash flows, its fair price, in the context of the OAS model, must be such that the investor is compensated for that uncertainty. It follows, then, that the more deterministic are the cash flows of a particular mortgage security, the lower the option-adjusted spread. Thus, wide range, narrow window PAC bonds should have relatively low option-adjusted spreads, and companion/support tranches should have relatively high option-adjusted spreads. To the degree that the value of a bond's cash flows is unaffected by nondeterministic aspect of prepayments, so too should the bond have a lower option-adjusted spread. Thus, high cap floaters should have low spreads, and inverse floaters should have high spreads.

Put another way, just as fairly valued securities with embedded options can have different yields, so too can fairly valued mortgage securities have different option-adjusted spreads.

A Pure Floater with Nondeterministic Amortization

Consider a simple example. Suppose that we created two REMIC tranches using a fixed-rate GNMA pass-through security as the underlying collateral. The two tranches are a floater and an inverse floater, both indexed to the one-month Treasury bill rate. The floater is structured with a very high cap, perhaps as high as 50%. Such a floater might be considered a close approximation to a default-free mortgage floater, a *pure* floater. Just as we argued that the *maturity* of a pure floater is irrelevant, that it would always be worth par, so too might we argue that the *amortization* of a pure floater is irrelevant. We do not need to model prepayments or consider in any way how much principal will be outstanding in any period. As long as the security pays the prevailing rate of interest, it will be worth par. It will also have, in the standard OAS framework, a zero option-adjusted spread.

Fairness requires that the value of the floater and the inverse floater add up to the value of the GNMA collateral. Thus, if the collateral is priced in the market to yield a positive OAS, then the dollar value of that discount giving rise the positive OAS of the collateral must be completely embodied in the inverse floater. It can be shown that the OAS on the inverse is approximately equal to the OAS on the collateral multiplied by the ratio of the market value of the collateral to the value of the inverse floater at a zero OAS. As a rough approximation, the relative OAS of the inverse will be equal to the leverage ratio times the collateral OAS.

Explicitly Valuing Prepayment Uncertainty—Pricing to an Option and Prepayment-Uncertainty Adjusted Spread

In the preceding pages we found that logic alone can be used to provide approximate relative values for interest rate uncertainty, but cannot provide fair, absolute prices without modeling that uncertainty. The same is true for prepayment uncertainty. The statistical error of empirically based prepayment models *can* be explicitly incorporated into the OAS framework. To satisfy the benchmarks for stochastic models, this random error must be "tuned" to a set of securities in a way similar to that in which the random interest rate process is "tuned" to the Treasury curve.

This will result in the market's implied price of prepayment uncertainty over time. Then, as this prepayment uncertainty is allocated disproportionately to derivatives, they will be priced to meet the benchmarks of fairness, consistency, and robustness.

We propose such a model be termed an Option and Prepayment Uncertainty Adjusted Spread (OPAS) model. Within this framework, fairly priced mortgage securities will have the same OPAS, but in general, different OAS values, just as fairly priced deterministic securities can have the same OAS, but different yields.

CHAPTER 32

Towards a New Approach
to Measuring Mortgage Duration

Bennett W. Golub, Ph.D.
Partner
BlackRock Financial Management

INTRODUCTION

Measuring the duration of mortgage-backed securities has been one of the most challenging analytical problems faced by investors in recent years. Reasonable measures of mortgage durations are critical to fixed-income investors given the growing size of the mortgage market and the volatility of monthly mortgage total rate of returns (TRRs). In Exhibit 1, a histogram of GNMA 8.5 monthly TRR's shows a standard deviation of 130 basis points (bps). Considering that mortgage pass-throughs are amongst the least volatile part of a mortgage universe populated by IOs, POs, support bonds, and inverse floaters, the need for viable risk management techniques should be apparent.

A tremendous amount of effort has been devoted to developing various mortgage risk management techniques with varying degrees of success. However, given current approaches, even with good duration estimates,[1] mortgage returns will exhibit a significant amount of unpredictability, as seen in Exhibit 2. For GNMA's, monthly residuals have a standard deviation of 68 bps! Thus, consistent portfolio management requires continual evaluation of the accuracy of approaches relative to new analytical developments and to changes in mortgage market behavior.

In this chapter, some of the different approaches to solving this problem are reviewed and some possible future directions are explored. First, existing approaches to mortgage durations are reviewed. Then, promising

---

1 "Good" estimates are defined later in this chapter.

Exhibit 1.   Distribution of Monthly Total Returns for GNMA 8.5 (4/90–4/93)

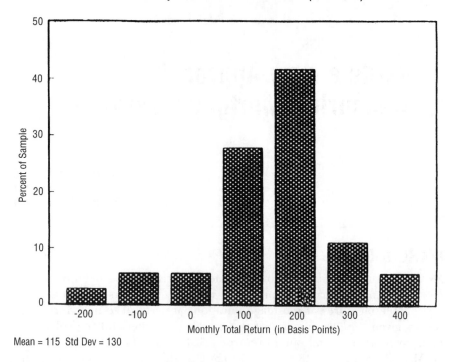

Mean = 115 Std Dev = 130

new directions are briefly discussed. Finally, implications for fixed income investors are drawn.

EXISTING APPROACHES TO MORTGAGE DURATIONS

As almost all fixed-income professionals know, Macaulay is recognized as the first person who thought about explicitly measuring the price risk of a portfolio of bonds. His measure, known as the duration of a bond, is now referred to as the Macaulay duration (or adjusted or unmodified duration). Macaulay's simple formula calculates the time-weighted present value of a bond's cash flows. It measures the change in the value of a bond as the discount factor changes 1% (*i.e.*, 1 + r), meaning that if the yield of a bond with a Macaulay duration of 10 and currently yielding 10% rose 1.1% to 11.1%, its price would drop 10%.

Exhibit 2.   Distribution of Residuals from Coupon Curve Duration Model for GNMA 8.5 (4/90-4/93)

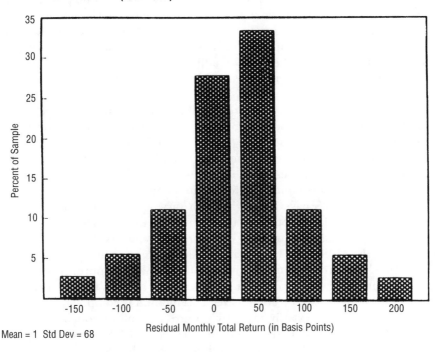

Mean = 1   Std Dev = 68

Residual Monthly Total Return (in Basis Points)

Modified Duration

Most practitioners prefer to think about the price risk of bonds directly in terms of changes in yields (*i.e.*, changes in r, not 1 + r).[2] Thus, when most people talk about duration, they are talking about modified duration (in units of years). This requires a small modification to Macauley's formula. Whichever methodology is chosen to compute a duration (see below and Exhibit 3), the results are almost always interpreted as meaning that a bond with a (modified) "duration" of 10 years would be expected to drop in price 10% if the yield of the bond rose 1%.

For MBS, modified duration is usually computed using an assumed prepayment rate. The prepayment assumption reduces the modified duration

2 Robert Kopprasch, "Understanding Duration and Convexity," Chapter 5 in Frank J. Fabozzi and Irving Pollack (eds.), *The Handbook of Fixed Income Securities* (Homewood, IL: Dow Jones-Irwin, 1987).

that would be computed assuming 30 years of level payments. For example, on 10/4/93, a 30-year FHLMC Gold 7 would have been projected to have a modified duration of 4.78 years. The same FHLMC Gold 7, if no prepayments were assumed, would have had a modified duration of 10.13 years! As shown in Exhibit 3, the modified durations of FHLMC Gold's drop dramatically as their coupons increase until the cash flows projected by the prepayment model "burn out." Thus, the lowest modified duration of 1.64 years is found for FHLMC Gold 9s. The modified durations then increase somewhat for 9.5s and 10s.

As is also well known, standard modified duration formulas are not as useful for bonds with embedded options. Macaulay's formulas don't apply when the value of the bond changes because of both changes in the time value of money and changes in the amount and timing of the bond's cash flows in response to changes in interest rates.

To deal with this limitation, four general approaches for determining the duration of MBS have been tried with varying degrees of success. The first approach (and the approach most akin to the spirit of modified durations) is to generate base, up, and down present values (say plus and minus 50 b.p.) of the MBSs cash flows using different prepayment speeds and discount rates. The prepayment rate used would be the one appropriate for the assumed interest-rate environment. Given these present values, a *percent of price* (POP) *duration* can be computed.[3] This method is computationally simple, but does not necessarily properly capture the full optionality of MBSs and CMOs. Clever CMO structurers quickly learned how to create bonds which had radically different risk profiles outside the modest interest-rate shifts used to compute POP durations. POP durations can also be biased to be a little long relative to observed price performance because they implicitly assume that MBS have constant yield spreads as interest rates change. The same 30-year FHLMC Gold 7 would have a POP duration of 2.79 years. As

---

Exhibit 3.   Alternative Measures of Mortgage Duration

Prices as of 10/4/93

Mortgage Type	Coupon	WAM	Price	Nominal Yield	OAS	Up 50bp Change In OAS	Down 50bp Change In OAS	Modified Duration	POP Duration	OAD	Implied Duration	CCD
FGOLD	6.50%	355	101-17	6.29%	48	-7	18	6.33	4.68	5.14	2.18	3.79
FGOLD	7.00%	350	102-30	6.43%	66	-18	26	5.85	2.79	4.26	3.70	2.37
FGOLD	7.50%	359	103-31	6.49%	92	-26	-15	4.78	1.83	3.96	2.68	1.62
FGOLD	8.00%	343	104-20	5.91%	77	15	-28	3.85	0.42	2.13	1.52	1.02
FGOLD	8.50%	336	105-01	5.15%	49	28	35	2.32	0.19	1.20	0.73	1.67
FGOLD	9.00%	335	106-12	5.43%	84	-35	14	1.64	0.65	1.52	0.61	2.64
FGOLD	9.50%	325	107-27	5.56%	98	-14	3	1.93	1.06	1.67	0.34	3.10
FGOLD	10.00%	323	109-23	5.58%	101	-3	33	2.14	1.48	1.80	-0.04	2.56

---

3 Blaine Roberts of Bear Stearns coined the term POP.

seen in Exhibit 3, the POP durations decline very rapidly with increasing coupon until "burnout" occurs. In all cases, they are markedly lower than the modified duration for their respective coupons.

Option-Adjusted Durations

Option-adjusted durations (OADs) were developed to eliminate the first disadvantage of POP durations by explicitly modelling the embedded options in a bond and simulating their expected behavior in different interest-rate environments. In the mortgage market, OADs are typically inferred from Monte-Carlo type models which actually subject MBSs to a large number of different interest-rate paths.[4] First, an option-adjusted spread (OAS) must be computed. In each of many (*i.e.*, 500-1,000) scenarios, a prepayment model is used to project future cash flows. Given these cash flows and discount rates, different spreads can be tested to see what current price they imply. The OAS is the single discounting spread over the appropriate future interest rates of each scenario which is consistent with the current market price of the MBS. Given the OAS, two other yield curves are created, up and down, say 50 b.p. of parallel shifts. For each of these yield curves, another set of scenarios (*i.e.*, interest-rate paths and cash flows) is created and then discounted using the OAS. These option-adjusted values (OAVs) are then taken to be estimates of the price of the MBS in the up and down yield curve cases. The OAD (and option-adjusted convexity) are then computed using these OAVs and the current market price.

As seen in Exhibit 3, our FHLMC Gold 7 would have had an OAD of 4.26 years. The OADs decline as coupon increases until the 9's. The OADs are longer than the POP durations but shorter than the modified durations for all coupons.

The advantages of OADs are that:

(i) they explicitly model the embedded options so they are ideal for structured securities like CMOs (where all other methods fail);

(ii) they do not require price histories that may not exist or do not reflect current market conditions;

(iii) they lend themselves to other types of scenario analyses (such as non-parallel yield curve shifts); and

(iv) at least until recently, they were relatively accurate predictors of future price sensitivity.

The disadvantages of OADs are that:

---

4 David Jacob and Alden Toevs, "An Analysis of the New Valuation, Duration and Convexity Models for Mortgage-Backed Securities" (New York: Morgan Stanley, January 1987).

(i) they are computationally difficult and time-consuming to calculate,

(ii) they are extremely sensitive to the prepayment model used (which are themselves often inaccurate), and

(iii) recently they have tended to be longer than actual market prices and performance would justify.

Implied Durations

A totally different approach to calculating duration, usually called *implied durations*, uses actual historical price data to statistically estimate the price sensitivity to interest rates *actually exhibited* by MBSs.[5] Regressions are generally run with historical percentage change in prices as the dependent variable and changes in the appropriate Treasury yield as the independent variable. The coefficient of the change in Treasury yield is the implied duration.

Our FHLMC Gold7s would have had an implied duration of 3.7 years measured over the last six months. It is difficult to determine a consistent pattern of the implied durations shown in Exhibit 3 with respect to both the coupon of the MBS and the other duration measures.

The advantages of implied durations are that:

(i) these estimates of interest-rate risk do not rely upon any theoretical formulas or analytical assumptions;

(ii) they are very simple to compute; and

(iii) all they require are some reasonably accurate price series.

The disadvantages of implied durations are that:

(i) good price data is not always available, either because of thin markets or because investors often purchase and then hold fixed-income securities directly purchased from the primary market;

(ii) without imposing some information about the structure of the options embedded in a bond, an implied duration may significantly differ from the actual prospective price risk of the bond;

(iii) price history may lag current market conditions, especially after there has been a sharp and sustained shock to interest rates; and

(iv) spread volatility can cloud the impact of interest rates on changes in bond prices.

---

5 See Paul DeRosa, Laurie Goodman, and Mike Zazzarino, "Duration Estimates of Mortgage-Backed Securities," *Journal of Portfolio Management* (Winter 1993), pp. 32–38.

Coupon Curve Durations

Coupon curve durations (CCDs) represent yet another completely different approach to measuring duration.[6] They are perhaps the simplest durations to calculate. All they require is the coupon curve of prices for similar MBS. Roughly speaking, if interest rates decrease 50 b.p., the market price of a GNMA 7 should rally to the current price of a GNMA 7.5. Similarly, if rates rise 50 b.p., the price of a GNMA 7 should decline to the current price of a GNMA 6.5. Thus, the CCD (and coupon curve convexity) for similarly aged MBS can be determined.

Our FHLMC Gold 7 had a CCD of 2.37 years. The CCDs in Exhibit 3 are shorter for the lower coupon MBS than the OAD's but longer for the higher coupons.

The advantages of CCDs are that:

(i) they are simple;

(ii) based upon BFM's testing, they are relatively accurate; and

(iii) they reflect the market's current expectations.

The disadvantages of CCDs are that:

(i) they can only be applied to fairly generic MBS which are well priced (technically speaking, they only makes sense for MBS with similar WAMs); and

(ii) the approach cannot be extended to CMOs since no two tranches can be easily compared to each other.

Historical Stability

These methods diverge at a fixed point in time as shown in Exhibit 3. As shown in Exhibit 4, the relationship between these different approaches to measuring duration has itself been quite volatile. OADs and CCDs closely tracked each other from 4/90 through 10/91, with CCDs generally being slightly lower. CCDs then began to fall rather dramatically. At one point in the Fall of 1993, the CCD was over two years shorter than the OAD. Implied durations, which appear in Exhibit 4 after 2/92, tended to run between the OAD and CCD.

---

6 The only published reference to CCDs found by the author is Douglas Breeden, "Risk, Return, and Hedging of Fixed-Rate Mortgages," *Journal of Fixed Income* (September 1991). He called them "roll-up, roll-down elasticities" and performed analyses of the accuracy of the approach over the sample period 1/79–12/90. An adaption and update of that article appears as Chapter 36 in this book.

Exhibit 4.   Durations for GNMA 8.5s

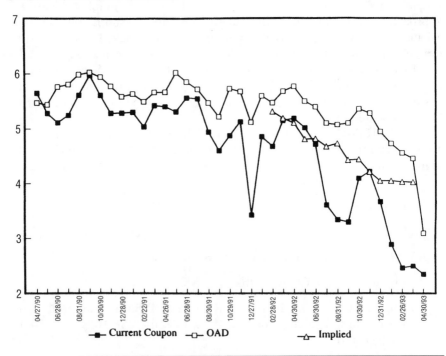

FUTURE APPROACHES TO MORTGAGE DURATIONS

Since all the above approaches have both advantages and disadvantages, investors continue to search for a better way. A better way will be accurate, easy, extensible to new issues or to securities which are difficult to price, and reflective of current conditions in the marketplace.

Currently, at least three alternative approaches to estimating mortgage durations are being explored by practitioners: (1) market-implied corrections to existing prepayment models,[7] (2) market-implied prepayment models, and (3) estimation of the relationships between OAS and the characteristics of an MBS in different interest-rate scenarios.[8] Unfortunately, it is unrealistic to assume that an approach that solves all the problems of existing methods will be easy.

---

7 Richard Klotz and A. Shapiro, "Dealing with Streamlined Refinanced: A New Implied Prepayment Model" (New York: Merrill Lynch 1994).

8 Ravi Sobti, "What Is the 'Correct' Duration for MBS?" (New York: Donaldson, Lukfin & Jenrette 1994).

Market-Implied Corrections

Empirical tests tell us that the CCDs are quite accurate when they are available. Suppose we could somehow adjust our prepayment model so that it better fits the CCDs when run through the simulation model used to compute OADs? If this could be done, the model would be better calibrated so that it would properly predict the duration for generic MBS and, therefore, do a better job of predicting the duration of CMOs. This calibration would be similar in spirit to the procedures currently used to make sure that callable bond models correctly reprice Treasury bonds.

Market-Implied Prepayment Models

If we take the above market-implied corrections approach to its logical extreme, the entire prepayment function might be implied from the marketplace. Other than imposing a basic structure on the "market-implied prepayment model" that would include reasonably stable elements such as seasonality, non-interest-rate sensitive prepayments, a flexible "S-curve" structure for refinancings, and a plausibly shaped burnout function, market prices could tell us what the market is assuming about future prepayments. With this approach, it might not even be necessary to worry about "spreads" because cash flows could be valued based upon their underlying credit. Assuming that decent market prices are available for a range of coupons and WAMs, there should be adequate information available to infer the implied prepayment model.

Estimation of OAS Functions

A less radical approach to improving OADs might be to try to somehow estimate a relationship between OAS and interest rates for a given security. Traditional OAD calculations assume that OAS remains constant in the up and down cases. This is often inconsistent with the marketplace. In October 1993, OAS increased with pass-through coupon, then fell, and then rose again. Exhibit 3 shows the OAS changes implied by the current market prices in the up 50 b.p. and down 50 b.p. cases for each coupon. In November 1994, the pattern reversed with OASs falling with coupon and then rising with the high coupons.

Moreover, while this approach might be workable for pass-throughs, it would require quite a bit of subtlety to be extensible to CMOs. Since CCDs can already be computed for pass-throughs, this approach will make sense only if a reasonable method can be found to extend it to CMOs.

IMPLICATIONS FOR INVESTORS

Given this saga of mortgage durations, how should investors respond to the above strengths and weaknesses of existing approaches and new future directions? Is the problem unsolvable or are more sophisticated solutions within reach that will better tame mortgage risk? The prudent answer is for investors and investment managers to proceed forward cautiously with an active program of reconciling predicted performance with actual performance. Even the best methods will be imperfect and subject to future revision.

Efforts are underway to implement these concepts to create newer and better tools for managing these risks. Keeping pace with changes in the mortgage market will be critical to achieving portfolio objectives. Investors today know a tremendous amount about mortgages securities and continue to improve their techniques. Going forward, actual performance versus projected performance needs to be carefully monitored so that large discrepancies can be quickly identified and portfolios restructured in a timely fashion.

CHAPTER 33

Duration and Convexity Drift of CMOs

David P. Jacob
Managing Director and Director of Research
Nomura Securities International, Inc.

Sean Gallop
Vice President
Nomura Securities International, Inc.

Duration and convexity are the standard measures of the price sensitivity of fixed-income instruments. They are used to compare the relative risk of bonds and portfolios, and help investors look for relative value by enabling them to classify bonds with similar risk profiles. Total rate of return managers often use duration to position their portfolios relative to the major bond indices, and asset/liability managers use these measures to control risk by matching the duration and convexity characteristics of their assets to those of their liabilities.

Duration and convexity are, of course, only summary measures of a security's sensitivity to instantaneous changes in interest rates. They do not provide insight into how a bond's characteristics will change over time. It is important, however, for both the asset/liability manager and the total rate of return manager to know in advance how a security's characteristics can evolve.

For example, an insurance company might use duration and convexity to set up a portfolio of mortgage-backed securities or corporate bonds to back its GIC portfolio. The insurer would like to remain matched so as to minimize the need to rebalance, which would result in increased transaction costs and potential negative impact on surplus. However, simply being matched at the onset does not insure that the book remains matched. In fact, unless the manager perfectly matches the cash flows of the assets and liabilities at the beginning for all future interest rate environments, the duration of the assets and liabilities will inevitably drift apart. The question is how much and how quickly will this drift or mismatch arise. Knowing this beforehand is important for proper management. As we will see, for CMOs, the evolution of the characteristics are sometimes not so obvious.

Alternatively, consider the case of the total rate of return manager who matches the duration, and, perhaps, the convexity of his portfolio with that of some index, and attempts to outperform the index by loading up with bonds that appear to offer substantial up-front yield. If, at the end of the performance measurement period, the price sensitivity characteristics of these bonds have changed substantially (for example, their duration has increased and they are more negatively convex) the market will likely price these bonds at wider spreads, and thus hurt the performance of these securities. For Treasury securities and noncallable corporates this is not a problem, since the duration of bonds with periodic, noninterest-sensitive cash flows, for the most part decline in a well defined and predictable manner as time passes. As a result, experienced portfolio managers either intuitively know or can readily calculate how the duration and convexity of these types of bonds change as time passes.

Unlike Treasuries, however, mortgage-backed securities (MBSs) and their derivatives can exhibit very different, and at first, often nonintuitive price sensitivity characteristics at the performance horizon. Moreover, for many MBSs, the horizon characteristics will be a function of not just the ending interest rate environment, but of what occurs during the holding period as well. For the asset/liability manager, this could necessitate unexpected portfolio rebalancing, and for the total rate of return manager, inferior performance under certain scenarios. For MBSs, the degree to which price sensitivity characteristics improve or deteriorate over time is determined by such factors as prepayment assumptions, yield curve shapes and levels, and liquidity, and for CMOs, structural considerations.

The major conclusion reached in this chapter is that using current price sensitivity characteristics such as duration and convexity as a basis for estimating performance or anticipating the cash flow characteristics of MBSs can be misleading. Investors must assess the current performance characteristics as well as how these characteristics change over time. They should not rely on their intuition derived from traditional bonds. We believe that by using an analytic framework that anticipates a security's horizon characteristics, the investor can more readily distinguish between bonds that appear to offer good value from ones that actually do.

REVIEW OF DURATION AND CONVEXITY FOR TREASURIES

Before discussing the unusual evolution of the duration and convexity of CMO bonds, we first quickly review this evolution for an ordinary Treasury note.

Consider the 7.75 of 2/15/01 which, on 4/3/91, was offered at 98-2 to yield 8.036%. Its modified duration was computed to be 6.701 years. One year forward, assuming the same yield, its duration is 6.232 years. In fact, for a 100-basis point shift up or down in the horizon yield, the duration will vary by no more than 0.12 years. Similar stability would be computed for the convexity. Thus, an asset/liability manager can readily tell how this bond's price sensitivity characteristics change, and therefore anticipate the potential drift between the duration of this bond and that of a liability payment due 6.7 years. Similarly, a manager interested in computing horizon returns can do so easily because he knows that the bond at the horizon will be one year shorter in maturity and roughly half a year shorter in duration. Thus, the horizon price can be computed using an appropriate yield.

EVOLUTION OF DURATION AND CONVEXITY FOR CMOs

Consider instead the bonds shown in Exhibit 1, which were selected from a recently issued CMO. In this FNMA deal the collateral was 9.5%, and the pricing speed was 165 PSA. Exhibit 1 contains the usual information supplied to the portfolio manager by a dealer, or which might have been obtained from an information service.

Both bonds are planned amortization classes (PAC bonds) with average lives (at the pricing speed of 165) of approximately three years. As a result, they are priced at spreads off the three-year Treasury. The first bond is a standard three-year PAC bond, whereas the second is a level 2 PAC, since its average life is protected for a tighter range of PSA and its principal amortization is junior to that of the first bond. The second column shows the spread off the three-year Treasury. The next two columns show the first and last principal payment dates. The following column shows the PSA bands for which the average life is constant. The primary PAC is protected from 90 PSA to 380 PSA, whereas the level 2 PAC is only protected from 140 PSA to 250 PSA. Since the collateral to date has been prepaying at 125 PSA, we show the average life at some speeds below the original pricing speed of 165 PSA. The last three columns in Exhibit 1 show that even at the slower speeds, the average lives remain the same for the first bond. This is because 105 PSA and 125 PSA are still within its PAC band. However, the average life of the second

Exhibit 1. Three-Year PAC Bonds

| | | | | | Avg. Life @ PSA | | |
	Spread	First Pay	Last Pay	PAC Band	105	125	165
PAC	66bp/3yr	7/15/92	6/15/93	90-380	2.8	2.8	2.8
PAC	120bp/3yr	4/15/91	9/15/04	140-250	7.6	4.6	3.1

bond, at 125 PSA, extends to 4.6 years and, at 105 PSA, it extends to 7.6 years. Since these slower speeds are outside the lower band, the extension in average life is expected.

Most managers stop at this point and try to decide whether or not the extra fifty-four basis points provided by the level 2 PAC is sufficient to compensate them for the potential adverse average life variability (*i.e.*, negative convexity). We will return to this point later. At this juncture we would like to analyze what happens to the average life, and the average life sensitivity as time passes.

Exhibit 2 describes how this evolution takes place for the simplest scenario. The exhibit shows the expected average life and sensitivity for each bond at pricing as well as one year forward and two years forward. The first row repeats the numbers from Exhibit 1. For example, at pricing the 3-year PAC has a 2.8 year average life at each of the three PSA speeds listed. In the second row we show the average life and how it varies at the end of the first year, assuming that for the first year the collateral paid at 125 PSA and thereafter at 105, 125, or 165 PSA. For the 3-year PAC, we see that after one year has passed the average life has shrunk by 1 year from 2.8 years to 1.8 years. This is as expected, since, as indicated in Exhibit 1, principal does not begin paying until 7/15/92. Moreover, even if from the end of the first year forward the speed changes up to 165 PSA or down to 105 PSA, the expected average life would still be 1.8 years.

However, the level 2 PAC paints a different picture. As before, the second row shows the average life and how it varies one year out, assuming that during the first year the collateral pays at a 125 PSA. The surprising result is

Exhibit 2. Evolution of Average Life and Average Life Sensitivity

	3-Year PAC		
	PSA		
	105	*125*	*165*
Current	2.8	2.8	2.8
1 Year Forward	1.8	1.8	1.8
2 Years Forward	0.8	0.8	0.8

	Level 2 PAC		
	PSA		
	105	*125*	*165*
Current	7.6	4.6	3.1
1 Year Forward	8.9	5.2	3.1
2 Years Forward	9.5	5.7	3.3

that not only does the average life increase from 4.6 years to 5.2 years, but the sensitivity increases as well. Now, the average life can increase by 3.7 years if speeds decrease to 105 PSA, and can decrease by 2.1 years if speeds increase to 165 PSA. The third row shows the situation two years out assuming 125 PSA for the first two years. The average life and average life sensitivity continue to increase. Since higher prepayment speeds are usually associated with lower interest rates, this security has not only increased in duration as time has passed, it has also become more negatively convex!

Exhibit 3 shows how the average life evolves for each of the bonds for their entire lives for level 105, 125, and 165 PSA scenarios. For example, from the graph in the foreground one can see how the average life under a 105 PSA scenario first increases and then decreases for the level 2 PAC, whereas for the primary PAC, the decline is linear.

Before we examine why such behavior occurs, we note that this example demonstrates how unexpectedly average life can change given a very simple tranche from a very simple deal under a very simple scenario. One can expect even more dramatic effects as the complexity of the deal and realism of the analysis increase. For example, it is entirely possible to find a bond, which for two different scenarios, has two radically different durations and convexities.

As an example, consider a support bond from another recent deal. This deal contains a Z bond[1] that jumps in front of the support bond if the speed on the FNMA 9.0% collateral exceeds the pricing speed of 155 PSA. The first row of Exhibit 4 shows the average life at pricing for speeds ranging from 90 PSA to 200 PSA. Since this bond is a support and is thus junior to the PACs in the deal, its expected average life at pricing declines from 9.5 years to 3.0 years as speeds increase from 90 PSA to 155 PSA. At 165 PSA, its average life extends a bit because the Z bond jumps in front of it. As prepayments occur at still higher speeds such as 200 PSA, the average life resumes its decline. This is because ultimately the higher speed offsets the fact that the Z bond gets paid first. The other rows show, at several points in the future, the average life assuming that prior to that time the speed was 125 PSA. In the second column of Exhibit 4, we see that if the speed stays at 125 PSA, the average life declines at the end of the first year to 4.2 years, and to 4.1 years by the end of 5 years. The next to the last column shows that if the speed stays at 125 PSA for five years and then jumps to and remains at 165 PSA, the average life declines only from 4.9 years to 4.0 years. This is because the Z bond's balance accretes for the first five years, so that when it does jump it has a greater impact than if it had jumped immediately. As a result, the effect of the jump offsets the higher speeds.

---

1 A Z bond is one that accrues rather than pays its interest until other bonds in the deal have been retired. A jump-Z is one that, based on some event, stops accruing and begins paying interest and principal.

Exhibit 3.

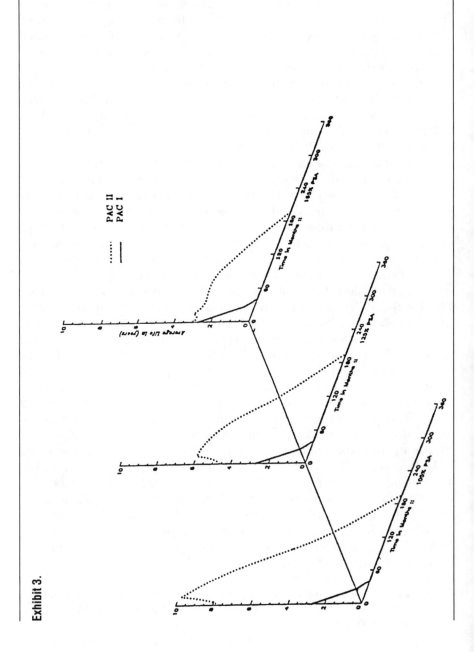

Exhibit 4. Evolution of Average Life

		PSA			
	90	125	155	165	200
Current	9.5	4.9	3.0	3.5	2.5
1 Year Forward	8.8	4.2	2.3	2.8	1.8
5 Years Forward	8.4	4.1	2.2	4.0	2.2
5 Years Forward	12.6	8.2	4.7	4.0	2.2
(with spike to 165 PSA for 1 month)					

Now suppose, instead of these relatively simple scenarios shown in the first three rows of Exhibit 4, the speed starts at 125 PSA, remains there for five years, then jumps for one month to 165 PSA, and finally returns to either 90, 125, 155, 165, or 200 PSA. The expected average life at that point becomes 12.6, 8.2, 4.7, 4.0, or 2.2 years, respectively. It is incredible that this one-month jump could cause this bond's horizon average life and average life sensitivity to be so radically different from that at the beginning or from that five years out, where there was no one-month spike to 165 PSA. Most analyses ignore the horizon characteristics, particularly for complicated scenarios. All the investor is likely to have seen would be the initial average life table and/or price/yield table, neither of which inform him of the possibility of this behavior, let alone explaining why it could happen.

IMPLICATIONS FOR PERFORMANCE AND RISK MANAGEMENT

Given that the price sensitivity of a bond affects the spread at which it trades, one can imagine that the implications for performance and risk management can be substantial. Price sensitivity characteristics of a bond affect the spread at which it trades. Typically, for the same average life, spreads widen as negative convexity increases. Also, everything else equal, the greater the average life, the wider the spread. Exhibit 5 shows recent generic CMO spreads for PAC bonds, TAC bonds, Vanilla bonds, and level 2 PACs at increasing average lives, and the Treasury yield curve as of mid-May 1991. One can see that, in general, the bonds that are the shortest and have the most protection, such as the two-year PACs, trade at the tightest spreads, and the longer, more negatively convex bonds, such as the twenty-year level 2 PACs trade at the widest spreads.

Consider again the first example, in which we compare a three-year PAC with a three-year level 2 PAC. In Exhibit 6 we show some of the pricing

Exhibit 5. Generic CMO Spreads

	2yr	3yr	4yr	5yr	7yr	10yr	20yr
PAC	59	66	76	84	87	93	105
TAC	95	104	108	110	113	116	130
Vanilla	98	106	111	114	116	120	134
Level 2 PAC	110	120	124	130	134	139	143
Treasury Yields	6.84	7.15	7.36	7.75	7.98	8.11	8.20

Exhibit 6. Yield/Average Life at PSA 3-Year PAC Bonds

	Price	Coupon	Yield/Average Life @PSA			OAS	Dur.	Conv.
			105	125	165			
3yr Primary PAC	103-14	9.375	7.82/2.8	7.82/2.8	7.82/2.8	62	2.5	7
3yr Level 2 PAC	102-12	9.500	9.14/7.6	8.69/4.6	8.35/3.1	52	2.7	-69

information on these bonds. Investors must decide between the prepayment protection of the level 1 tranche and the extra yield of the level 2. From an OAS standpoint, in this case, the primary PAC looks like the slightly better value. However, since there are many assumptions that go into an OAS evaluation, and OAS does not give a complete picture of prospective performance, most managers will want to perform a total return analysis. While this deal was priced at 165 PSA, we feel that a 125 PSA makes more sense given the consistently slow prepayment history to date.

In order to compute the expected total return for a year, we need to compute the terminal prices, but, as we have seen, yield spreads, which determine prices, are a function of the average life and sensitivity of the security.

Consider first the regular three-year PAC. At the end of 1-year, we found in Exhibit 2 that this bond's average life moved from 2.8 years to 1.8 years. The difference between the two-year and three-year Treasury is negative thirty-one basis points, and the difference between the two-year and three-year PACs is negative seven basis points. No adjustment is made for change in quality, since the bond remains well protected at the horizon. In total, the horizon yield of 7.44% is thirty-eight basis points tighter than the starting yield of 7.82%. This results in an ending price of 102-21, which translates into a total return of 8.54%.

Now consider the level 2 PAC. At the end of the first year, its average life has risen from 4.6 years to 5.2 years, assuming a 125 PSA. The difference between the four-year and the five-year Treasury is thirty-nine basis points (*this bond has rolled up the yield curve*), and the difference between four-year and five-year level 2 PACs is six basis points. As we noted previously in Exhibit 2, not only has this bond got longer, but its quality has deteriorated, since its average life is more adversely sensitive (*i.e.*, it extends when speeds slow down/rates rise, and contracts when speeds increase/rates fall). As a result we will penalize this bond by an additional four basis points.[2] Thus, the horizon yield is forty-nine basis points greater than at the original yield. The computed terminal price is 101-00, which produces a total return of 7.44%. These results are summarized in Exhibit 7.

The total return of the primary PAC (8.54%) is considerably higher than its yield of 7.82% at a 125 PSA. On the other hand, the level 2 PAC's total return of 7.44% is not only lower than its expected yield of 8.69%, but it is also lower than the expected yield of the primary PAC.

In Exhibit 8 we show the one-year returns for the two bonds for the base case, assuming shifts of 100 basis points up and down, where, as before, we have made adjustments to the horizon spread where appropriate. The level 2 PAC underperforms the primary PAC in all three scenarios. Since the level 2 PAC was initially more negatively convex than the primary PAC, it is not surprising that its relative performance suffers as rates move up or down.

Exhibit 7. Performance Results

	Initial Price	Yield @ 125 PSA	Spread Adjustment Treasury	CMO	Quality	Total	Horizon Price	1 Year Total Return
3yr Primary PAC	103-14	7.82	-31	-7	0	-38	102-21	8.54
3yr Level 2 PAC	102-12	8.69	+39	+6	+4	+49	101-00	7.44

Exhibit 8. 1 Year Total Returns

	Shift in Rates, Basis Points		
	-100	0	+100
Primary PAC	10.07	8.54	7.03
Level 2 PAC	9.07	7.44	3.07
PSA	165	125	105

---

2 For the purposes of this chapter, we arbitrarily used a penalty of four basic points. To be more precise, one needs to look more closely at break-even returns at the market assessment of the value of the additional negative convexity.

This is particularly true in the +100 basis points scenario, because the average life of the level 2 PAC extends considerably. What is unusual in this example is that even in the no-change-in-rates scenario, the level 2 PAC performs so poorly. This occurs because again the bond's performance characteristics have weakened over the holding period.

Of course, one could debate the various spread adjustments used in this example, but the notion that the terminal characteristics of a bond are important in analyzing performance is indisputable. While we chose a straightforward PAC structure to demonstrate the effect on performance, this impact will be still greater for more complicated bonds under more realistic scenarios.

Although the initial OAS differential provides a hint of the prospective performance profile, it is not sufficient to quantify the scenario analysis. Some analysts perform what is known as constant OAS total returns. In this framework the ending price in each scenario is computed by adding the initial OAS to the horizon yield curve in each scenario, and then computing the expected discounted value of projected cash flows. This analysis skirts the issue of the security's ending characteristics, because the methodology directly incorporates the terminal sensitivity of the cash flow. We believe that this type of analysis is a good start, and is far better than computing returns based on constant yield spread analysis. Nevertheless, it is still deficient, because the market tends to price instruments with different durations and convexities at different OAS levels. The difference is sometimes market-directional. For example, when the market is bullish, the demand for interest-only strips (IOs) from mortgage securities declines. While the decline may be justified, it is often dramatic and the OAS for IOs widen greatly during the initial stages of a bullish environment, as the durations become more negative.

Another reason why constant OAS total return is insufficient for the practitioner is because the analysis does not provide insight into the reasons for unusual performance patterns. In order for the investor to be able to distinguish between genuinely attractive opportunities and ones that only appear as such, he needs to know what causes the behavior and how to anticipate it.

The starting point for analyzing these bonds, as with any, should be a thorough understanding of the cash flows. Exhibit 9 shows the monthly principal payments for the primary PAC and the level 2 PAC that were discussed in the first example. The three diagrams show the monthly principal payments for level 105 PSA, 125 PSA, and 165 PSA scenarios. In each diagram the horizontal axis represents time in months, and the vertical axis represents the principal payment in millions of dollars. The dark set of flows are from the primary PAC. The combination of the separate diagrams when read laterally shows that the "shape" of the PAC cash flow is invariant to changes in prepayment.

Exhibit 9.

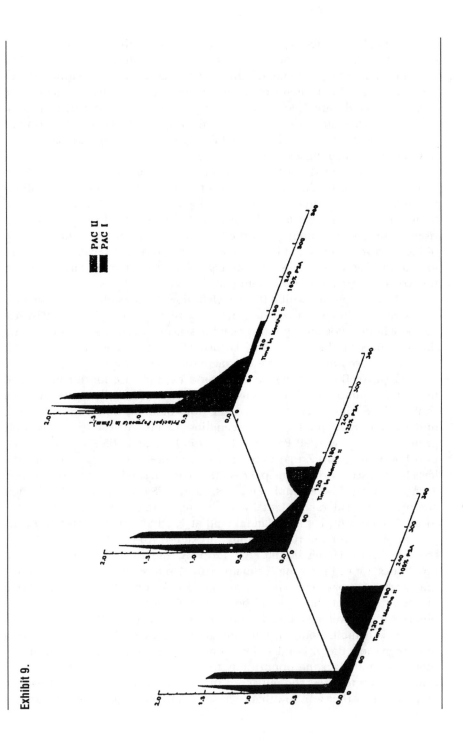

The lightly shaded region shows the paydown of the level 2 PAC. Under each of the scenarios, we see a significant paydown in principal in the first year, and then it begins to tail off. In the 105 PSA scenario the principal paydown is initially high, then drops, and finally begins to pick up toward the end of the bond's life. Looking at this picture, it is no wonder that the average life increases after the first year. The early payments—from a vantage point of time 0—reduce the expected average life. After they are paid down, however, the remaining average life is longer.

The extreme case of this would be a portfolio consisting of two zero coupon bonds of similar balances but different maturity. One zero matures in one year, and the other in ten years. The initial average life of this portfolio is 5.5 years. One year later, however, the average life of the portfolio has risen to nine years assuming that the investor does not reinvest the proceeds of his short zero. Indeed, it is true that the investor could rebalance his portfolio at the end of a year. Such a strategy, however, generates larger transaction costs and greater reinvestment risk.

The diagrams in Exhibit 9 make clear how it is possible that the average life increases. However, these diagrams only represent simple, level PSA scenarios. They do not show how average life sensitivity can vary. In order to do this, one needs to be able to project forward the cash flows for varying PSA scenarios. As we will show, this is crucial in the next example.

The cash flow patterns of the second example are more complicated because the jump Z leads to highly path-dependent cash flow patterns. As a result, it is very important to analyze the flows of all the bonds in such a deal under a variety of nonlevel PSA scenarios. Exhibit 10 shows the monthly principal cash flow at 90 PSA, 125 PSA, 155 PSA, and 165 PSA for the support bond and jump Z that were discussed in the second example. For the level 90 PSA scenario, a principal cash flow pattern similar to that of the level 2 PAC from the first example emerges. At 125 PSA, the principal cash flow compresses considerably. Mentally combining these two diagrams allows one to understand why, if the collateral paid at 125 PSA for five years and then paid at 90 PSA for the rest of its life, it extends from 4.9 years to 8.2 years (see Exhibit 4). Under the 90 PSA, 125 PSA, and 155 PSA scenarios, the Z bond does not begin paying for many years. However, recall that the Z bond jumps when prepayments rise above 155 PSA. As a result, the jump Z bond moves in front of the support bond, thereby causing the extension one observes in the average life table of this deal at pricing.

This exhibit, however, tells only a small part of the story, since, with level scenarios, the Z bond either jumps in the beginning or not, and is therefore, not given the opportunity to have its balance increase via accretion. In order to assess the impact of this, consider Exhibit 11. In these diagrams we show the cash flow that corresponds to the scenarios in the last row

Exhibit 10.

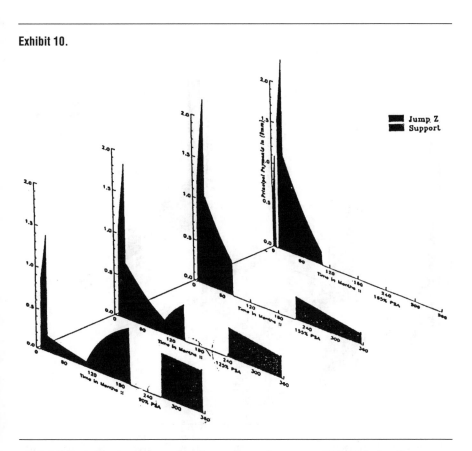

of Exhibit 4. In that scenario, the collateral pays at 125 PSA for five years, then spurts to 165 PSA for one month (recall that this causes the Z bond to jump), and then pays at either 90 PSA, 125 PSA, 155 PSA, or 165 PSA. This one month of 165 PSA causes the principal cash flows of the support bond to split apart. In the 90 PSA scenario there is a 90-month hiatus during which the support bond receives no principal. It is for this reason that the average life after 5 years extends from 4.9 years at pricing to 12.6 years in this scenario. We feel that these diagrams are invaluable for understanding, and, therefore, anticipating the nature of the bonds under consideration.

CONCLUSION

CMO tranches have cash flow patterns which often do not resemble those of more intuitive fixed-income securities. Moreover, the cash flow is not static. It is interest-sensitive and path-dependent. Therefore, as time passes and interest rates and prepayment scenarios unfold, some bond classes undergo radical

Exhibit 11.

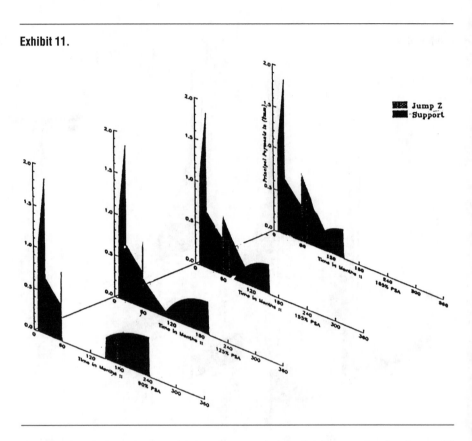

changes in their price sensitivity characteristics. Pricing at the horizon will reflect these altered sensitivities. For the total return account, this can have significant impact on performance. In order to discern value and anticipate the potential decline in quality, the manager should analyze the cash flow carefully. The asset/liability manager must assess the impact of a CMO's changing cash flow on the exposure of his book.

Clearly, some investor several years from now will be holding the bonds that are created today. Duration and convexity do not tell the whole story, since they are summary instantaneous measures. In order to understand how a bond's characteristics can change, investors need to analyze the performance of their securities and picture their cash flows.

CHAPTER 34

Understanding Inverse Floater Pricing

Michael L. Winchell
Senior Managing Director
Risk Management Group
Bear Stearns & Co., Inc.

Michael Levine
Vice President
Mortgage Trading
Bear Stearns & Co., Inc.

THE COMMON MISTAKE

Many investors mistakenly expect the price of an inverse floater to increase with a decline in short-term rates. In fact, the major impact on the price of inverse floaters comes from changes in long-term rates, since so many inverse floaters are created out of long average life, fixed-rate cash flows.

Inverse floaters are characterized by a coupon rate designed to reset inversely with changes in an index, most often that of a short-term rate such as LIBOR. Some inverse floaters have coupon rates that change four, five, or six times as much as the change in the rate index, a multiplicative effect often described as the coupon leverage of the inverse floater. For an inverse floater with high coupon leverage, any drop in the short-term rates causes a large increase in its coupon rate, and thus a sharp increase in the income to the investor in the payment period. It is not surprising, therefore, that many investors expect a drop in short-term rates to cause a price increase in the inverse floater.

However, the expectation that changes in short-term rates have a great impact on the price of inverse floaters does not recognize the direct relation between inverse floaters and the fixed-rate bonds from which they are derived.

Inverse floaters are almost always carved out of an underlying fixed-rate tranche, in conjunction with the creation of a floating-rate tranche. It may be difficult to "see" the fixed-rate tranche behind a floater and its inverse, but it is there nonetheless.

Since the floater and its inverse constitute the entire underlying fixed-rate bond when combined, there must be a "conservation" of market value. A simple observation is that the typical floater remains priced near par given changes in both short- and long-term yields. Its market value remains more or less constant. Thus, any change in the market value of an inverse floater must be primarily the result of a change in the value of the underlying fixed-rate bond, and any change in the market price of the underlying fixed-rate bond must cause a change in the value of the inverse floater. To determine the correct price of an inverse floater, or its price change, the investor should determine the price or price change of the underlying fixed-rate bond, or that of a similar bond in the marketplace.

VIEWING THE INVERSE FLOATER AS A LEVERAGED PURCHASE OF THE FIXED-RATE BOND

Many investors misprice inverse floaters in the secondary market because they fail to recognize the similarity between the cash flows of an inverse floater and the cash flows generated by financing, at a floating rate, a fixed-rate bond similar to the underlying fixed-rate bond. The cash flows of an inverse floater resemble the cash flows available if the investor had purchased the underlying fixed-rate bond from which the inverse was derived, and then financed most of the purchase at the short-term rate used as the index for the floater and the inverse.

If an investor were willing to buy a fixed-rate bond and finance it at short-term rates, then the inverse floater represents a similar opportunity to earn a net interest margin in a steep yield curve environment.

Purchasing an inverse floater may offer a few advantages over purchasing a fixed-rate tranche that is financed at short-term rates. The inverse floater contains an embedded, amortizing, and prepay-sensitive cap on the funding costs, the result of which is that the net interest will never be negative. In addition, funding for the life of the fixed-rate bonds is made secure through the issuance of a floater tranche, perhaps at a lower cost than would be available to the investor otherwise, without concern for any future margin calls. Finally, traditional interest rate cap and funding agreements are subject to the risk of counterparty nonperformance. The REMIC/CMO trust eliminates performance risk. Thus, the investor who desires to earn the net interest margin of long-term assets funded at short-term rates can do this economically through the purchase of an inverse floater, and in a more secure fashion.

THE PARALLEL BETWEEN INVERSE FLOATER RESIDUALS AND INVERSE FLOATER TRANCHES

To see how the inverse floater relates to its underlying fixed-rate bond, consider the many early CMO deals in which only a floater tranche was issued. Pools of fixed-rate mortgage collateral were placed in trust. A single floating-rate tranche was issued by the trust, and the proceeds from the sale of the floater were used to pay for the collateral. From the trust's perspective, a floating-rate liability was issued to *finance* the purchase of fixed-rate mortgage assets, and the liability will amortize with the fixed-rate assets.

In these simple deals, the inverse floater cash flows remain as the *residual* of the CMO deal. The residual holder is entitled to the *net interest margin* between the coupon rate of the collateral, and the coupon rate on the floater. In other words, the inverse floater residual receives any interest left over after having paid the financing cost (*given by the floater coupon rate*) of the fixed-rate pools held by the trust. And as the principal of the assets is paid down, an equal amount of the liabilities is paid down.

Thus, the value of the residual represents the difference in value between the assets, fixed-rate mortgage pools, and the liability, a floating-rate tranche. The fact that inverse floater *tranches* are carved from fixed-rate companion bonds or PAC bonds or plain vanilla bonds does not change the fundamental relation between the inverse and its "collateral."

Inverse floater tranches, just like inverse floating-rate residuals, offer the investor the opportunity to buy both sides of a "balance sheet." On the asset side, the inverse floater represents the underlying fixed-rate bonds. On the liability side, the inverse floater represents a short-term financing arrangement for the assets.

HOW RISKY IS THE INTEREST RATE MISMATCH BUILT INTO AN INVERSE FLOATER?

The allure of inverse floaters is the ability to profit from a steep yield curve through leverage and a significant interest margin. The greater the leverage available to the investor, the higher the potential return on capital, and, accordingly, the greater the risk. Thus, the purchase of an inverse floater in many ways resembles the leveraged funding of long-term mortgage assets at short-term rates that had been the bread-and-butter trade of the thrift industry a decade ago.

What differentiates the inverse floater from the strategy formerly employed by many thrifts is that the inverse floater buyer obtains an amortizing and prepay-sensitive cap on the financing rate (*through the cap on the floater*), and locks in access to funding over the term of the underlying fixed-rate bond, and need not reserve capital for potential margin calls. Neither of these two benefits were readily available to thrifts then, nor are these safety features readily available in the mortgage market today, outside of the inverse floater.

An interest rate cap is an option that pays the investor if the reference rate rises above a strike rate. Without a cap, the investor funding a long average life, fixed-rate asset at short-term rates can be faced with *negative* net interest margin, or in other words, interest expense greater than interest income. Inverse floaters have embedded interest rate caps. Coupon rates can never go below 0%, and some are structured with caps that limit coupon declines at relatively high coupon levels.

This is not to say that the buyer of fixed-rate bonds cannot also buy a cap to provide insurance for a financing arrangement. But consider that, if available, the purchase of an amortizing and prepay-sensitive interest rate cap entails counterparty risk. And the financing arrangement itself presents the potential for losses due to counterparty nonperformance. For instance, if the market value of fixed-rate bonds increases during the term of a repurchase agreement, the investor is exposed to the financier's failure to deliver the assets at the expiration of the agreement. Consequently, inverse floaters provide some advantage over a simple strategy of short-funding long-term fixed-rate assets.

A SIMPLE METHOD TO VALUE INVERSE FLOATERS

A simple technique to arrive at fair value is to ascertain the value on two pieces of the puzzle, and arrive at the third by addition or subtraction.

To value the inverse floater tranche, one need only calculate the total market value of the underlying fixed-rate bond from which it is derived, and then subtract the total market value of the floater that accords the inverse both its cap and its leverage.

Assuming a floater always remains priced at par, all of the change in value of an inverse floater tranche must be the result of a change in the value of the underlying fixed-rate bonds.

Therefore, if $50 million in inverse floaters are derived from $100 million in underlying fixed-rate bonds, and if the floater remains priced at par, the price change of the inverse floaters will be *twice* the price change of the underlying fixed-rate bonds. If only $20 million in inverse floaters are derived from $100 million in the underlying fixed-rate bonds, then given no change in the floater price, the inverse will change in price *five* times more than the underlying fixed-rate tranche.

Floaters, however, do not always remain at par, because the value of embedded interest rate caps often changes. The spread over LIBOR offered by the floater may at times be more than enough compensation for the short cap position, and at other other times, not enough. However, we can still rely on this relatively simple approach to the valuation of inverse floaters because we can continue to use the market price of the floater as a starting point, even if that price isn't par.

HOW THE LEVEL OF THE SHORT-TERM RATE AFFECTS THE VALUE OF INVERSE FLOATERS THROUGH THE CAP

In a steep yield curve environment, a reasonably creditworthy buyer of a five-year Treasury note could probably finance 98% to 99% of the proceeds at a monthly or overnight rate well below the yield of the five-year note. The steeper the curve, the higher the spread and the greater the income.

We would not, however, expect the price of the five-year note to change with the level of overnight repo rates, even though the net interest margin between the assets and the funding costs increases. We expect the price of the five-year note to change only when five-year yields change.

So too is it with inverse floaters. We should expect a change in the price of an inverse floater when market conditions (*yields and prepayment assumptions, for example*) cause a change in price of the underlying bond and similar bonds.

Where the level of short-term rates correctly enters into the valuation process for inverse floaters is through the evaluation of the cap on financing provided by the cap on the floater. This embedded interest rate cap has a value that is commonly determined by reference to the implied forward rate curve, and, since the interest rate cap agreement is an option agreement, by the volatility of short-term rates.

Fixed-income analysts often refer to the *implied forward rate curve* when inverse floaters are analyzed to describe how the coupon rate of the security is expected to change through time. In essence, the market's expectation of future short-term rates are defined by the shape of the yield curve. To explain a steep yield curve, for instance, it must be the case that investors are willing to accept the low yields of short-term securities today because they expect rates to rise in the future.

The implied forward curve is derived in such a way as to make the continuous rollover of an investment at the short-term rate for five years, for example, equivalent to the realized compound yield (total return) of a five-year note. The most common implied forward rate curve used by the market is a Eurobond curve. Some of the curve is derived directly from the Eurodollar futures market, the rest from the swap curve, or swap spreads and the Treasury curve extrapolated for thirty years.

To properly value the cap embedded in the inverse floater properly, one needs the implied forward rate curve and an estimate regarding rate volatility to value the cap. One could use these parameters within an option pricing method such as the option-adjusted spread (OAS) model. However, this supposes we "know" what the right OAS for an inverse floater is.

As an alternative to an OAS model, the investor can approximate the market value of the cap by pricing nonprepay-sensitive, amortizing, over-the-counter caps. To do this, the investor could choose upper and lower bounds for the range of expected prepayments and specify a number of other prepayment estimates. The investor would price different amortizing cap agreements, each based on the outstanding balance of the floater at various prepayment assumptions, but all having a strike rate given by the cap on the floater. The investor would then calculate an average price for the embedded mortgage security interest rate cap, given a weight for each of the prices of the over-the-counter cap agreements.

Note that we use the amortization of the floater to determine the total market value of the cap agreements outstanding. This is because the floater, as the financing arrangement, defines the number of caps available.

WHAT DOES A YIELD SENSITIVITY MATRIX REVEAL?

Yield, as an internal rate of return, assumes the investors put up a certain amount of cash today to receive cash flows in the future. Yield measures the rate of return on a fully paid investment over the life of the security, ignoring reinvested cash flows.

The typical yield sensitivity matrix of an inverse floating-rate tranche or of an inverse floating-rate residual essentially reveals the rate of return generated by fixed-rate bonds that have been financed by the issuance of floating-rate debt. As in any financing of fixed-income assets, the total return depends on the ultimate net interest margin. As in any mortgage financing, the total return can be affected by the rate of prepayment.

The cash flows of a financed purchase of fixed-rate bonds could be expressed as a rate of return on capital assuming various levels of financing rates. We could examine the "yield" of any fixed-rate bond in this fashion.

An Example Comparing an Inverse Floater to the Financing of the Underlying Fixed-Rate Bond

Below we show the similarity between a yield sensitivity matrix for a LIBOR inverse floater tranche carved from a REMIC PAC tranche to the return on equity of the same PAC tranche financed at LIBOR.

Consider the PAC tranche shown in Exhibit 1, similar to many available in the mortgage market priced at 100.10604 to yield 8.09%. The tranche is backed by new FNMA 9.00% MBS pass-throughs.

Before we calculate the returns of a leveraged purchase of the PAC tranche, examine the alternative. Instead of issuing the PAC tranche above, a

Exhibit 1. Fixed-Rate PAC Tranche

Coupon Rate	7.9750%	
Maturity Date	06-25-21	
Projected Average Life	7.95 years	
Prepay Assumption	165% PSA	
PAC Range	90% to 250% PSA	
Face Amount	42,108,000	
Price	100.10604	

PSA	50%	165%	300%
Average Life	10.21	7.95	7.12
Yield	8.09%	8.09%	8.09%

floating-rate tranche and an inverse floating-rate tranche could have been issued using LIBOR as the index rate to reset the coupon on each. The cash flows that would otherwise be paid to the PAC tranche are instead divided between the floater and the inverse floater.

The first step in the process is to carve out a floater tranche. Suppose we want to issue a floating-rate tranche priced at par. Market conditions require that a monthly floater, having this type of amortization schedule and average life, pay forty basis points over one-month LIBOR, and be subject to a coupon rate cap no lower than 10.75%. If we want to issue the maximum amount of floater bonds to achieve the greatest leverage, we will allocate the principal between the floater and the inverse in such a way as to exhaust all available interest from the underlying fixed-rate cash flows at the level of LIBOR at which the floater caps out. This results in a floater tranche face amount of $31,238,260.

The inverse floater is allocated the remaining principal, and both tranches return principal pro rata. The face amount of the inverse floater is $10,869,740.

Assume the level of one-month LIBOR equals 5.6375% on the pricing date. The descriptions of the two tranches that could have been issued, along with the familiar yield sensitivity tables, are shown in Exhibits 2 and 3. The floating-rate tranche now provides built-in financing at forty basis points over LIBOR, capped at 10.750%, with matched amortization and no counterparty credit risk. We can think of the forty-basis-point spread over LIBOR as the market's current evaluation of the embedded interest rate cap.

The inverse floating-rate tranche benefits from the leverage provided by the floater tranche. That is, the investor is able to capture the net interest margin of approximately $42 million in fixed-rate PAC bonds financed at LIBOR +40 basis points, with a cap at a cost of $10,914,390.

Exhibit 2. LIBOR Floating Rate PAC Tranche

Initial Coupon Rate	6.0875%
Coupon Rate Cap	10.750%
Maturity Date	06-25-21
Projected Average Life	7.95 years
Prepay Assumption	165% PSA
PAC Range	90% to 250% PSA
Face Amount	31,238,260
Price	100.0000

PSA	50%	165%	300%	
Average Life	10.21	7.95	7.12	LIBOR
Yield	5.79%	5.79%	5.79%	*5.3125*
Yield	8.84%	8.84%	8.83%	*8.3125*
Yield	10.93%	10.92%	10.92%	*11.3125*
Yield	10.93%	10.92%	10.92%	*14.3125*

Exhibit 3. LIBOR Inverse Floating-Rate Tranche

Initial Coupon Rate	7.9750%
Coupon Rate Cap	29.750%
Maturity Date	06-25-21
Projected Average Life	7.95 years
Prepay Assumption	165% PSA
PAC Range	90% to 250% PSA
Face Amount	10,869,740
Price	100.410773

PSA	50%	165%	300%	
Average Life	10.21	7.95	7.12	LIBOR
Yield	14.82%	14.81%	14.81%	*5.3125*
Yield	5.96%	5.96%	5.97%	*8.3125*
Yield	0.07%	0.09%	0.10%	*11.3125*
Yield	0.07%	0.09%	0.10%	*14.3125*

The structure shown in Exhibit 3 represents the opportunity to buy a leveraged position in the underlying fixed-rate PAC tranche through the inverse floater. The investor could execute a similar strategy by financing the PAC tranche directly. What differs is the financing rate, the presence of a prepay-sensitive interest rate cap, and the absence of counterparty credit risk and margin calls.

Exhibits 4, 5, and 6 display the return on capital of financing the underlying PAC tranche given similar leverage that is, similar capital invested. In the first example (see Exhibit 4), no cap is purchased, as is evident from the negative returns given high LIBOR levels. In the second example (see Exhibit 5), a cap is purchased that amortizes coincident with the outstanding balance of the PAC tranche at the pricing prepayment assumption of 165% PSA. The third example, shown in Exhibit 6, reveals the returns if a cap is purchased to provide protection on a balance equivalent to 50% PSA. Just as is the case for an inverse floater, the rate of return is a function of the level of LIBOR (*assumed to be constant at the indicated rate over the life of the financing arrangement*) and the prepayments that occur.

Exhibit 4. Short-Term Financing of a Fixed-Rate PAC Tranche, No Interest Rate Cap Agreement

	Interest Rate Cap Strike	None
	Interest Rate Cap Cost	None
	Financing Rate	LIBOR Flat
	Total Capital Invested	$10,914,390
	Initial Amount Financed	$31,238,261

PSA	50%	165%	300%	LIBOR
R.O.E.	16.04%	16.03%	16.02%	5.3125
R.O.E.	7.14%	7.14%	7.15%	8.3125
R.O.E.	-1.53%	-1.50%	-1.49%	11.3125
R.O.E.	-9.93%	-9.89%	-9.87%	14.3125

Exhibit 5. Short-Term Financing of a Fixed-Rate PAC Tranche, Interest Rate Cap Agreement Matched at 165% PSA

	Interest Rate Cap Strike	10.750%
	Interest Rate Cap Cost	$440,675
	Financing Rate	LIBOR Flat
	Total Capital Invested	$11,355,065
	Initial Amount Financed	$31,238,261

PSA	50%	165%	300%	LIBOR
R.O.E.	15.22%	15.11%	15.04%	5.3125
R.O.E.	6.58%	6.47%	6.42%	8.3125
R.O.E.	-0.67%	-0.40%	-0.26%	11.3125
R.O.E.	-2.78%	-0.40%	0.69%	14.3125

Exhibit 6. Short-Term Financing of a Fixed-Rate PAC Tranche, Interest Rate Cap Agreement Matched at 50% PSA

Interest Rate Cap Strike	10.750%
Interest Rate Cap Cost	$718,480
Financing Rate	LIBOR Flat
Total Capital Invested	$11,632,870
Initial Amount Financed	$31,238,261

PSA	50%	165%	300%	LIBOR
R.O.E.	14.73%	14.55%	14.46%	*5.3125*
R.O.E.	6.24%	6.07%	5.97%	*8.3125*
R.O.E.	-0.55%	-0.26%	-0.11%	*11.3125*
R.O.E.	-0.55%	1.86%	-2.93%	*14.3125*

In the three financing arrangements presented in Exhibits 4, 5, and 6, the market value of the PAC tranche is assumed constant over the term to maturity. Accordingly, there would be no margin calls that would require additional capital.

The embedded cap of the inverse floater distinguishes the two strategies most. The investor in an inverse floater pays for the cap in the spread over LIBOR paid on the floater. This may be more or less than the direct cost of an interest rate cap agreement, and, in addition, the investor must weigh the risk of counterparty performance. Consider too, that many floaters and inverse floaters are carved out of fixed-rate REMIC tranches having average lives of fifteen years or longer. Although an amortizing, prepay-sensitive cap of such a long term might be available in the market, many investors are unwilling to accept potential performance risk for such a long time span.

SUMMARY

Investors need to compare the relative cost of financing a fixed-rate tranche directly to the implied financing rate of the inverse floater, taking into consideration the relative value of the interest rate cap embedded in the inverse floater, the secure nature of the funding agreement, and the absence of margin calls.

Investors must recognize that the value of inverse floaters depends both on the value of the underlying fixed-rate cash flows and on the value of the floater that provides the inverse with its leverage and its cap. Short-term rates will only impact the value of an inverse floater to the extent they affect the floater and its cap, or the underlying fixed-rate cash flows. Otherwise, the value of an inverse floater and its price movements can be compared to that of the underlying fixed-rate tranche.

SECTION VII

HEDGING STRATEGIES

CHAPTER 35

Hedging Interest-Rate Risks with Futures, Swaps and Options

Michael J. Giarla
Chief Operating Officer, Smith Breeden Associates, Inc.
President, Smith Breeden Family of Mutual Funds

This chapter presents a general approach to constructing hedges of inter-est-rate risks for financial institutions such as savings and loans, commercial banks, and investment banks. The chapter is written at an introductory level that is intended for students, financial officers, regulators, accountants, and members of boards of directors who have not had a large exposure to futures and options hedging. Yet, despite the relatively modest quantitative level of the chapter, almost all of the major concepts of hedging are illustrated in the context of realistic hedging problems. A large amount of data is provided, so that readers may also do their own analysis of mortgage hedges on both a "micro" (security specific) and "macro" (portfolio) level.

For financial intermediaries such as savings and loans and banks, hedging may be described as an attempt to protect the market values of their assets and liabilities from the effects of changes in interest rates. The basic concepts of hedging can be most effectively described by focusing on particular numerical examples. Therefore, the discussion of hedging found in this chapter will be structured around the experiences of one savings and loan association—First Savings and Loan Association.

The chapter is organized as follows. The first section presents background historical data on interest rates, mortgage prepayment rates, Treasury bond and Eurodollar futures prices, and mortgage prices. Interest-rate futures markets are introduced, along with options on futures, interest-rate caps and floors, and interest-rate swaps. The second section presents the concepts of duration and price elasticity and illustrates these concepts for bonds and mortgages with various coupon rates. The third section presents a calculation of a mark-to-market "liquidation value" for an entire firm and illustrates historical changes in this value for First Savings and Loan. This section also shows how to systematically examine interest-rate risk for an institution for many potential changes in interest rates. How to construct an appropriately sized macro hedge for the institution with futures and/or interest rate swaps is shown in the fourth section. It also illustrates the risks involved in not changing the hedge position as time passes and as interest rates change. The fifth section shows how the hedge consisting of futures and swaps can be significantly improved with option positions. The final section concludes the chapter and lists some of the relevant hedging issues that were not examined.

FUTURES, OPTIONS, AND SWAPS: HISTORICAL DATA
Interest-Rates and Mortgage Prepayments

Since it is useful to refer to recent changes in interest rates, Exhibit 1 gives semiannually compounded yields to maturity on Treasury bills and bonds of various maturities for January 31, 1979, to June 30, 1994. In the late 1970s the United States' economy was facing its second major oil shock of the decade, a high rate of inflation, a low level of economic growth, and a declining dollar. On January 31, 1979, the 3-month Treasury bill rate was 9.60% and the 10-year Treasury note rate was 9.12%. By September 31, 1979, the 3-month and 10-year Treasury rates had risen to 10.16% and 9.21%, respectively.

In October 1979, the Federal Reserve changed its operating procedure from targeting the Federal funds rate to targeting a measure of the money supply. This change resulted in considerably more interest-rate volatility, especially in short-term rates, during the next several years. By April 30, 1980, the 3-month Treasury rate increased 482 basis points to 14.98% and the 10-year Treasury rate increased 339 basis points to 12.60%. The slope of the yield curve also inverted substantially more from September 1979 to April 1980, going from a -95 basis point spread between 10-year and 3-month Treasury rates to a spread of -238 basis points.

In the second quarter of 1980, shortly after the establishment of credit controls by the Carter Administration, a brief, but sharp, two-quarter recession began and interest rates, especially short-term rates, dropped dramatically. By August 31, 1980, after substantial easing by the Federal Reserve in the spring and early summer, the 3-month Treasury rate stood at 8.89% (down 609 basis points from April 1980) and the 10-year Treasury rate was 10.62% (down 198 basis points in the 4-month period). The yield curve went from being substantially inverted (-238 basis point spread) to significantly upward sloping (173 basis point spread).

Exhibit 1.   Coupon Treasury Yield Curves 1979–94

	3 Mo	6 Mo	1 Yr	2 Yr	5 Yr	7 Yr	10 Yr	20 Yr	30 Yr	Slope 10-Yr minus 3-Mo
Jan 31 79	9.60	10.08	10.55	9.95	9.28	9.20	9.12	8.96	8.93	-0.48
Feb 29 79	9.61	9.93	10.12	9.60	8.94	8.93	8.92	8.84	8.80	-0.69
Mar 31 79	9.79	10.09	10.35	9.85	9.25	9.19	9.06	9.09	9.05	-0.73
Apr 30 79	9.77	10.05	10.14	9.68	9.18	9.10	9.08	9.01	8.98	-0.69
May 31 79	9.90	9.99	10.37	9.87	9.29	9.30	9.32	9.21	9.19	-0.58
Jun 30 79	9.89	10.03	9.87	9.53	9.01	9.00	9.04	9.05	9.06	-0.85
Jul 31 79	9.25	9.47	9.34	8.94	8.67	8.71	8.76	8.78	8.81	-0.49
Aug 31 79	9.48	9.82	9.68	9.26	8.86	8.96	8.97	8.91	8.95	-0.51
Sep 30 79	10.16	10.42	10.35	9.79	9.32	9.26	9.21	9.06	9.06	-0.95
Oct 31 79	10.44	10.79	10.78	10.05	9.46	9.45	9.42	9.29	9.23	-1.02
Nov 30 79	12.66	13.06	12.90	12.05	11.12	10.91	10.78	10.54	10.22	-1.88
Dec 31 79	11.95	12.32	11.98	11.35	10.45	10.44	10.36	10.08	10.06	-1.59
Jan 31 80	12.53	12.73	11.89	11.21	10.35	10.31	10.31	10.00	10.08	-2.22
Feb 29 80	12.54	12.79	12.32	11.73	11.09	11.15	11.11	11.11	11.08	-1.43
Mar 31 80	14.62	15.17	15.27	14.59	13.48	12.98	12.68	12.27	12.15	-1.94
Apr 30 80	14.98	15.98	15.68	14.57	13.25	12.58	12.60	12.40	12.27	-2.38
May 31 80	10.60	11.13	11.14	10.73	10.73	10.68	10.73	10.81	10.87	0.13
Jun 30 80	7.99	8.43	8.78	9.15	9.68	9.97	10.19	10.31	10.33	2.20
Jul 31 80	8.18	8.35	8.42	8.92	9.46	9.82	9.98	10.01	9.94	1.80
Aug 31 80	8.89	9.16	9.26	9.63	10.08	10.33	10.62	10.68	10.60	1.73
Sep 30 80	10.23	10.91	11.09	11.31	11.58	11.54	11.49	11.33	11.25	1.26
Oct 31 80	11.89	12.31	12.24	12.01	11.81	11.84	11.83	11.83	11.70	-0.06
Nov 30 80	13.29	13.83	13.67	13.08	12.55	12.44	12.38	12.30	12.20	-0.91
Dec 31 80	15.22	15.56	15.04	14.10	13.08	12.60	12.67	12.30	12.28	-2.55
Jan 31 81	15.02	14.96	13.97	13.01	12.57	12.47	12.43	11.96	11.94	-2.59
Feb 29 81	15.27	14.70	13.92	13.26	12.73	12.65	12.64	12.40	12.23	-2.63
Mar 31 81	15.11	15.23	14.74	14.07	13.89	13.53	13.41	13.15	12.95	-1.70
Apr 30 81	13.00	12.93	13.01	13.14	13.33	13.21	13.10	12.89	12.61	0.10
May 31 81	15.62	15.44	15.33	14.79	14.38	14.27	14.13	13.88	13.65	-1.49
Jun 30 81	15.54	14.94	14.46	14.15	13.74	13.49	13.29	13.10	13.10	-2.25
Jul 31 81	15.08	15.21	14.96	14.65	14.25	14.05	13.84	13.64	13.30	-1.24
Aug 31 81	15.60	16.17	16.10	15.77	15.27	14.97	14.72	14.26	13.93	-0.88
Sep 30 81	16.46	17.35	17.13	16.68	16.07	15.72	15.38	15.12	14.74	-1.08
Oct 31 81	15.15	16.25	16.64	16.69	16.18	16.04	15.76	15.58	15.20	0.61
Nov 30 81	13.32	14.01	14.32	14.50	14.74	14.72	14.64	14.69	14.34	1.32
Dec 31 81	10.94	11.79	12.13	12.64	12.96	13.47	13.27	13.58	13.03	2.33
Jan 31 82	11.54	12.88	13.31	13.60	13.89	14.12	13.93	14.05	13.61	2.39
Feb 29 82	13.11	13.78	14.05	14.17	14.09	14.24	14.19	14.17	13.88	1.08
Mar 31 82	13.04	14.12	14.29	14.41	14.11	14.07	13.99	14.05	13.80	0.95
Apr 30 82	13.90	14.27	14.29	14.45	14.30	14.36	14.17	13.86	13.66	0.27
May 31 82	12.96	13.59	13.71	13.95	13.74	13.84	13.81	13.55	13.35	0.85
Jun 30 82	11.97	12.52	12.93	13.57	13.78	13.81	13.69	13.63	13.38	1.72

Exhibit 1. *Continued*

	3 Mo	6 Mo	1 Yr	2 Yr	5 Yr	7 Yr	10 Yr	20 Yr	30 Yr	Slope 10-Yr minus 3-Mo
Jul 31 82	13.32	14.07	14.32	14.55	14.51	14.52	14.32	14.06	13.84	1.00
Aug 31 82	10.12	11.51	12.07	13.15	13.55	13.72	13.63	13.61	13.40	3.51
Sep 30 82	8.66	10.20	11.10	11.94	12.72	12.86	12.77	12.55	12.47	4.11
Oct 31 82	7.79	9.22	10.24	11.23	11.68	11.66	11.93	11.58	11.74	4.14
Nov 30 82	8.15	8.84	9.19	9.83	10.53	10.61	11.05	10.75	10.97	2.90
Dec 31 82	8.51	9.00	9.31	9.92	10.47	10.77	10.69	10.98	10.94	2.18
Jan 31 83	8.13	8.40	8.66	9.46	10.21	10.27	10.31	10.65	10.64	2.18
Feb 29 83	8.36	8.68	8.92	9.59	10.44	10.67	10.75	11.08	11.18	2.39
Mar 31 83	8.15	8.38	8.61	9.40	9.92	10.14	10.24	10.62	10.68	2.09
Apr 30 83	8.95	9.20	9.31	9.86	10.42	10.51	10.59	10.82	10.85	1.64
May 31 83	8.30	8.52	8.70	9.28	9.91	10.07	10.18	10.47	10.50	1.88
Jun 30 83	8.91	9.23	9.46	10.09	10.49	10.77	10.79	11.10	11.13	1.88
Jul 31 83	9.04	9.38	9.60	10.23	10.80	10.85	10.89	11.15	11.13	1.85
Aug 31 83	9.58	10.07	10.49	11.02	11.68	11.73	11.80	11.98	11.91	2.22
Sep 30 83	9.56	10.10	10.47	11.10	11.71	11.88	11.92	12.03	11.96	2.36
Oct 31 83	9.00	9.36	9.77	10.48	11.15	11.34	11.39	11.60	11.46	2.39
Nov 30 83	8.81	9.28	9.74	10.58	11.35	11.58	11.71	11.92	11.80	2.90
Dec 31 83	9.17	9.56	9.91	10.61	11.40	11.51	11.58	11.77	11.64	2.41
Jan 31 84	9.20	9.50	9.80	10.56	11.33	11.47	11.65	11.80	11.76	2.45
Feb 29 84	9.46	9.88	10.16	10.97	11.70	11.86	12.02	12.17	12.14	2.56
Mar 31 84	10.12	10.52	10.78	11.55	12.27	12.38	12.50	12.53	12.51	2.38
Apr 30 84	10.07	10.56	11.05	11.85	12.52	12.66	12.80	12.86	12.85	2.73
May 31 84	10.10	11.27	12.09	12.92	13.70	13.80	13.91	13.78	13.81	3.81
Jun 30 84	10.28	11.40	12.23	13.15	13.71	13.75	13.82	13.73	13.62	3.54
Jul 31 84	10.68	11.28	11.75	12.57	12.83	12.88	12.93	12.97	12.86	2.25
Aug 31 84	11.01	11.44	11.84	12.50	12.80	12.82	12.85	12.67	12.49	1.84
Sep 30 84	10.58	11.08	11.32	12.00	12.46	12.47	12.49	12.34	12.26	1.91
Oct 31 84	9.34	9.84	10.21	11.05	11.49	11.59	11.68	11.65	11.53	2.34
Nov 30 84	8.71	9.16	9.55	10.43	11.14	11.55	11.57	11.68	11.56	2.86
Dec 31 84	8.04	8.49	9.18	9.93	11.10	11.45	11.50	11.67	11.57	3.46
Jan 31 85	8.13	8.55	9.04	9.86	10.77	11.05	11.15	11.27	11.17	3.02
Feb 28 85	8.78	9.31	9.67	10.61	11.52	11.83	11.90	12.06	11.96	3.12
Mar 31 85	8.42	9.03	9.45	10.37	11.28	11.59	11.64	11.84	11.63	3.22
Apr 30 85	7.96	8.26	9.07	9.87	10.88	11.27	11.38	11.66	11.56	3.42
May 31 85	7.32	7.59	8.16	8.93	9.84	10.11	10.26	10.67	10.57	2.94
Jun 30 85	7.15	7.39	7.65	8.62	9.66	10.14	10.15	10.55	10.59	3.00
Jul 31 85	7.53	7.80	8.10	9.00	9.93	10.36	10.52	10.84	10.66	2.99
Aug 31 85	7.29	7.66	8.00	8.93	9.75	10.15	10.26	10.64	10.46	2.97
Sep 30 85	7.29	7.59	7.95	8.86	9.73	10.12	10.29	10.74	10.56	3.00
Oct 31 85	7.43	7.68	7.93	8.68	9.47	9.84	9.99	10.46	10.30	2.56
Nov 30 85	7.39	7.61	7.83	8.47	9.08	9.45	9.58	10.05	9.84	2.19
Dec 31 85	7.26	7.43	7.59	7.98	8.50	8.87	9.01	9.50	9.27	1.75

Exhibit 1. *Continued*

	3 Mo	6 Mo	1 Yr	2 Yr	5 Yr	7 Yr	10 Yr	20 Yr	30 Yr	Slope 10-Yr minus 3-Mo
Jan 31 86	7.20	7.40	7.57	7.97	8.52	8.87	9.06	9.46	9.32	1.86
Feb 28 86	7.24	7.36	7.43	7.71	7.93	8.04	8.14	8.35	8.28	0.90
Mar 31 86	6.53	6.50	6.70	6.90	7.19	7.23	7.35	7.47	7.45	0.82
Apr 30 86	6.27	6.40	6.51	6.80	7.12	7.20	7.35	7.51	7.47	1.08
May 31 86	6.51	6.72	6.90	7.38	7.85	8.04	8.07	8.41	7.77	1.56
Jun 30 86	6.15	6.21	6.41	6.80	7.22	7.30	7.34	7.80	7.24	1.19
Jul 31 86	5.92	6.02	6.14	6.52	6.97	7.17	7.28	7.85	7.43	1.36
Aug 31 86	5.29	5.37	5.54	5.94	6.42	6.72	6.93	7.51	7.20	1.64
Sep 30 86	5.31	5.59	5.80	6.32	6.95	7.26	7.44	7.96	7.61	2.13
Oct 31 86	5.29	5.43	5.69	6.21	6.74	7.09	7.32	7.83	7.61	2.03
Nov 30 86	5.52	5.61	5.73	6.18	6.68	6.99	7.15	7.70	7.42	1.63
Dec 31 86	5.80	5.84	5.92	6.32	6.80	7.08	7.23	7.78	7.48	1.43
Jan 31 87	5.74	5.82	5.91	6.32	6.70	6.98	7.17	7.69	7.47	1.43
Feb 28 87	5.58	5.65	5.86	6.30	6.70	6.96	7.16	7.62	7.46	1.58
Mar 31 87	5.88	6.10	6.22	6.64	7.10	7.38	7.57	7.96	7.92	1.69
Apr 30 87	5.55	6.16	6.51	7.30	7.78	8.01	8.17	8.53	8.43	2.62
May 31 87	5.82	6.42	6.80	7.66	8.13	8.31	8.46	8.74	8.63	2.64
Jun 30 87	5.86	6.12	6.65	7.45	8.00	8.23	8.37	8.68	8.50	2.51
Jul 31 87	6.22	6.41	6.83	7.60	8.20	8.46	8.65	8.98	8.89	2.43
Aug 31 87	6.41	6.61	7.16	7.92	8.54	8.78	8.96	9.23	9.15	2.55
Sep 30 87	6.77	7.13	7.74	8.53	9.16	9.41	9.58	9.84	9.74	2.81
Oct 31 87	5.40	6.16	6.70	7.56	8.30	8.67	8.92	9.09	9.06	3.52
Nov 30 87	5.40	6.42	7.00	7.72	8.45	8.78	8.98	9.19	9.09	3.58
Dec 31 87	5.84	6.44	7.07	7.75	8.39	8.63	8.86	9.05	8.98	3.02
Jan 31 88	5.79	6.29	6.62	7.18	7.75	8.04	8.25	8.48	8.41	2.46
Feb 29 88	5.76	6.01	6.57	7.09	7.62	7.91	8.12	8.41	8.32	2.36
Mar 31 88	5.99	6.48	6.94	7.55	8.18	8.49	8.69	8.94	8.89	2.70
Apr 30 88	6.15	6.65	7.09	7.71	8.33	8.65	8.89	9.09	9.11	2.74
May 31 88	6.59	7.14	7.56	8.12	8.68	8.95	9.14	9.31	9.23	2.55
Jun 30 88	6.74	7.02	7.43	7.96	8.39	8.65	8.80	8.99	8.85	2.06
Jul 31 88	7.15	7.47	7.86	9.32	8.69	8.94	9.09	9.24	9.19	1.94
Aug 31 88	7.50	7.87	8.25	8.66	8.94	9.11	9.23	9.27	9.31	1.73
Sep 30 88	7.47	7.83	8.11	8.41	8.58	8.73	8.83	8.96	8.96	1.36
Oct 31 88	7.59	7.86	8.04	8.18	8.35	8.51	8.63	8.71	8.74	1.04
Nov 30 88	8.07	8.39	8.58	8.79	8.90	8.99	9.04	9.07	9.06	0.97
Dec 31 88	8.36	8.61	9.01	9.13	9.13	9.20	9.13	9.08	8.99	0.77
Jan 31 89	8.64	8.88	9.00	9.09	9.04	9.03	8.99	8.90	8.84	0.35
Feb 28 89	8.96	9.17	9.34	9.43	9.38	9.35	9.27	9.23	9.09	0.31
Mar 31 89	9.18	9.49	9.57	9.64	9.46	9.36	9.27	9.18	9.09	0.09
Apr 30 89	8.79	9.04	9.19	9.28	9.12	9.10	9.08	9.02	8.96	0.29
May 31 89	8.90	8.83	8.84	8.80	8.64	8.62	8.61	8.65	8.60	-0.29

Exhibit 1. *Continued*

	3 Mo	6 Mo	1 Yr	2 Yr	5 Yr	7 Yr	10 Yr	20 Yr	30 Yr	Slope 10-Yr minus 3-Mo
Jun 30 89	8.24	8.13	8.09	8.03	8.00	8.08	8.08	8.13	8.03	-0.16
Jul 31 89	8.06	7.83	7.62	7.42	7.45	7.57	7.72	7.90	7.86	-0.34
Aug 31 89	8.15	8.20	8.27	8.37	8.26	8.28	8.25	8.32	8.19	0.10
Sep 30 89	8.15	8.29	8.45	8.44	8.33	8.35	8.28	8.36	8.23	0.13
Oct 31 89	8.03	7.99	7.89	7.86	7.84	7.90	7.90	8.00	7.90	-0.13
Nov 30 89	7.80	7.76	7.69	7.73	7.72	7.81	7.83	7.98	7.89	0.03
Dec 31 89	7.82	7.99	7.75	7.83	7.84	7.96	7.91	8.08	7.97	0.09
Jan 31 90	7.99	8.11	8.06	8.25	8.32	8.37	8.40	8.58	8.45	0.41
Feb 28 90	8.02	8.13	8.10	8.40	8.45	8.53	8.50	8.60	8.53	0.48
Mar 31 90	8.03	8.22	8.32	8.61	8.64	8.69	8.63	8.76	8.62	0.60
Apr 30 90	8.02	8.39	8.54	8.93	9.02	9.04	9.02	9.11	8.99	1.00
May 31 90	8.01	8.15	8.21	8.47	8.56	8.63	8.59	8.70	8.58	0.58
Jun 30 90	7.98	8.00	8.03	8.21	8.35	8.45	8.41	8.51	8.41	0.43
Jul 31 90	7.72	7.69	7.70	7.87	8.11	8.27	8.34	8.48	8.41	0.62
Aug 31 90	7.60	7.74	7.75	8.06	8.51	8.75	8.85	9.01	8.99	1.25
Sep 30 90	7.35	7.52	7.66	7.98	8.46	8.70	8.81	9.05	8.94	1.46
Oct 31 90	7.33	7.46	7.42	7.76	8.24	8.50	8.65	8.74	8.78	1.32
Nov 30 90	7.24	7.36	7.30	7.52	7.91	8.16	8.25	8.28	8.39	1.01
Dec 31 90	6.63	6.74	6.80	7.13	7.64	7.98	8.06	8.03	8.24	1.43
Jan 31 91	6.37	6.47	6.49	7.04	7.61	7.87	8.01	8.12	8.20	1.64
Feb 28 91	6.22	6.35	6.43	7.08	7.69	7.90	8.04	8.17	8.21	1.82
Mar 28 91	5.86	6.04	6.24	7.01	7.73	7.95	8.05	8.17	8.24	2.19
Apr 30 91	5.68	5.81	6.01	6.75	7.61	7.87	8.01	8.16	8.18	2.33
May 31 91	5.67	5.91	6.14	6.67	7.69	7.91	8.05	8.30	8.27	2.38
Jun 28 91	5.67	5.91	6.29	6.89	7.89	8.12	8.23	8.39	8.42	2.56
Jul 31 91	5.66	5.88	6.13	6.76	7.73	8.00	8.15	8.32	8.34	2.49
Aug 30 91	5.46	5.56	5.71	6.33	7.34	7.66	7.81	7.99	8.06	2.35
Sep 30 91	5.24	5.30	5.38	5.96	6.90	7.23	7.44	7.73	7.80	2.20
Oct 31 91	4.95	5.02	5.07	5.69	6.74	7.14	7.46	7.86	7.91	2.51
Nov 31 91	4.45	4.56	4.66	5.37	6.48	6.96	7.37	7.85	7.94	2.92
Dec 31 91	3.93	3.99	4.07	4.75	5.92	6.35	6.70	7.26	7.40	2.77
Jan 31 92	3.92	4.04	4.19	5.08	6.43	6.88	7.27	7.72	7.76	3.35
Feb 28 92	4.01	4.12	4.29	5.23	6.55	6.91	7.25	7.72	7.74	3.24
Mar 31 92	4.13	4.30	4.49	5.58	6.92	7.21	7.53	7.97	7.96	3.46
Apr 30 92	3.76	3.95	4.30	5.43	6.88	7.22	7.57	8.06	8.03	3.81
May 29 92	3.77	3.94	4.23	5.17	6.61	6.98	7.33	7.79	7.83	3.56
Jun 30 92	3.65	3.76	4.05	4.81	6.27	6.71	7.12	7.69	7.78	3.47
Jul 31 92	3.27	3.66	3.61	4.38	5.82	6.26	6.71	7.36	7.46	3.44
Aug 31 92	3.22	3.34	3.46	4.12	5.57	6.13	6.61	7.23	7.41	3.39
Sep 30 92	2.73	2.90	3.04	3.78	5.31	5.88	6.35	7.10	7.38	3.62
Oct 30 92	3.00	3.28	3.52	4.37	5.88	6.35	6.79	7.47	7.63	3.79

Exhibit 1. *Continued*

	3 Mo	6 Mo	1 Yr	2 Yr	5 Yr	7 Yr	10 Yr	20 Yr	30 Yr	Slope 10-Yr minus 3-Mo
Nov 30 92	3.33	3.58	3.81	4.79	6.22	6.59	6.93	7.47	7.60	3.60
Dec 31 92	3.14	3.37	3.57	4.54	6.03	6.42	6.70	7.23	7.40	3.56
Jan 29 93	2.97	3.18	3.35	4.14	5.54	5.96	6.35	7.02	7.20	3.38
Feb 26 93	3.00	3.13	3.28	3.90	5.20	5.65	6.03	6.66	6.90	3.03
Mar 31 93	2.96	3.08	3.28	3.94	5.23	5.68	6.02	6.64	6.92	3.06
Apr 30 93	2.95	3.05	3.26	3.79	5.11	5.59	6.02	6.70	6.93	3.07
May 28 93	3.12	3.31	3.62	4.24	5.38	5.77	6.15	6.77	6.98	3.03
Jun 30 93	3.07	3.20	3.43	3.99	5.04	5.49	5.77	6.31	6.67	2.70
Jul 30 93	3.09	3.27	3.52	4.12	5.14	5.60	5.80	6.21	6.56	2.71
Aug 31 93	3.06	3.21	3.37	3.84	4.78	5.17	5.44	5.85	6.09	2.38
Sep 30 93	2.98	3.11	3.36	3.86	4.76	5.13	5.37	5.77	6.02	2.39
Oct 29 93	3.10	3.27	3.44	3.97	4.84	5.21	5.42	5.75	5.97	2.32
Nov 30 93	3.20	3.39	3.62	4.22	5.16	5.55	5.82	6.15	6.30	2.62
Dec 31 93	3.04	3.29	3.57	4.23	5.19	5.60	5.79	6.09	6.34	2.75
Jan 31 94	3.03	3.24	3.51	4.12	5.02	5.43	5.65	5.99	6.24	2.62
Feb 38 94	3.42	3.69	3.99	4.66	5.59	5.93	6.13	6.46	6.66	2.71
Mar 31 94	3.56	3.93	4.43	5.18	6.23	6.56	6.75	6.98	7.09	3.19
Apr 29 94	3.95	4.43	5.08	5.74	6.65	6.94	7.05	7.19	7.32	3.10
May 31 94	4.24	4.83	5.34	5.98	6.76	6.99	7.15	7.34	7.42	2.91
Jun 30 94	4.21	4.80	5.49	6.16	6.95	7.21	7.32	7.49	7.62	3.11

Following the brief recession, interest rates again rose substantially and remained at very high levels throughout the remainder of 1980 and most of 1981. By June 30, 1981, 3-month Treasury rates reached 15.54% (up 665 basis points in 10 months) and 10-year rates stood at 13.29% (up 267 basis points). The yield curve had again inverted, with the slope changing by 398 basis points to -225 basis points.

Interest rates fell somewhat during the subsequent recession, which lasted until late 1982 although both long-term and short-term Treasury rates remained at double-digit levels during most of the period. In early July 1982, amid the turmoil created by the impending Third World debt crisis, the shakiness of the United States' banking system (Penn Square Bank had just failed), and a still slumping domestic economy (the unemployment rate would soon reach 10%), Federal Reserve policy became more lenient and rates again fell rapidly. By the end of December 1982, 3-month Treasury rates had fallen to 8.51% (down 481 basis points) and 10-year rates fell to 10.69% (down 363 basis points from July 31 levels).

From late 1982 until early 1984 interest rates remained fairly stable, especially by comparison to the mid-1979 to mid-1982 period. On January 31, 1984, the 3-month Treasury rate was 9.20% and the 10-year Treasury was 11.65%. Four months later, in May 1984, Continental Illinois' problems came to a head and interest rates on 3-month and 10-year Treasuries went to 10.10% (up 90 basis points) and 13.91% (up 226 basis points), respectively. From those levels, interest rates fell dramatically during the remainder of 1984, during 1985, and during the first eight months of 1986. At the end of August 1986, the 3-month rate was 5.29% (down 481 basis points from May 1984) and the 10-year rate was 6.93% (down 698 basis points). Both the level and the degree of upward slope of the term structure changed incredibly in that 2-year period from May 1984 to August 1986. From August 1986 to September 1987 interest rates reversed their downward course, increasing by 148 basis points on 3-month Treasury bills and by 265 basis points on 10-year Treasury notes.

The stock market crash of October 1987 caused a general "flight to quality" reaction by investors and led the Federal Reserve to increase liquidity in the financial system. These actions resulted in an immediate decline in market yields on Treasury securities as well as a significant steepening of the Treasury yield curve (from a difference of 281 basis points between the 10-year and 3-month Treasury rates on September 30, 1987, to a difference of 352 basis points on October 31, 1987).

From October 1987 to April 1989 long-term Treasury rates were remarkably stable while short-term Treasury rates steadily increased. During this period, the 3-month rate increased by 339 basis points (to 8.79%) while the 10-year rate increased by only 16 basis points (to 9.08%), resulting in a very flat term structure. Interest rates generally fell throughout the remainder of 1989, with this period being characterized by very flat and often inverted Treasury yield curves.

During late 1989 and 1990, amid recognition that the United States' economy was slowing and entering a recession, the Federal Reserve embarked on a policy of easier money and credit. As a result, interest rates generally declined with short-term rates falling more than long-term rates, again resulting in a steeper yield curve. Even after the three-quarter-long recession ended (after the first quarter of 1991), the U.S. economy grew at a very slow rate for several quarters. With an environment of slow economic growth and low inflation the federal-funds rate fell from 7% in early 1991 to 3% by December 1992. The Treasury yield curve went from being essentially flat at 8% at the end of 1989 to its steepest slope since the early 1980s as short-term rates fell sharply. A powerful bond market rally soon followed, leading to the lowest long-term Treasury rates (and mortgage rates) in more than 20 years. By the autumn of 1993, long-term government bonds yielded less than 5.8%, substantially lower than the 9% rates of late 1990 and almost inconceivable in the early 1980s, when long-term Treasury bond and mortgage rates were often greater than 12%.

In the first half of 1994, as faster than expected economic growth was accompanied by increasing fears of inflation, the Federal Reserve raised interest rates four times. Interest rates abruptly reversed their downward course of the previous two years and began the fastest increase since 1984. In less than one year, both short- and long-term Treasury rates increased more than two full percentage points. The general movements in the level of Treasury rates, as well as changes in the slope of the term structure during the 1979–94 period, are more easily seen in the time series of 10-year and 3-month Treasury rates found in Exhibit 2.

As interest rates decrease, prepayment rates on mortgages increase. Additionally, prepayment rates are positively related to the strength of the economy, particularly to housing starts. Exhibit 3 shows how prepayment rates changed dramatically during the 1984–94 period. As interest rates fell sharply from May 1984 to August 1986, prepayment rates on GNMA 13s increased from 6% to 52% annually. At the same time, prepayment rates on lower coupon GNMA 8s moved from 3.5% to 9.4%. Not surprisingly, people with lower rates on their fixed-rate mortgages are less inclined to pay them off early. When fixed-rate mortgage rates reached their 20-year lows in 1993, annualized prepayment rates on GNMA 8s increased from 7.6% in February to 30.9% in December. Prepayment rates on GNMA 9s went from 13.7% to 48.3% during this same 11-month period. Such rapid changes in the prepayment characteristics of mortgages makes them particularly challenging financial instruments to hedge effectively.

Exhibit 2.

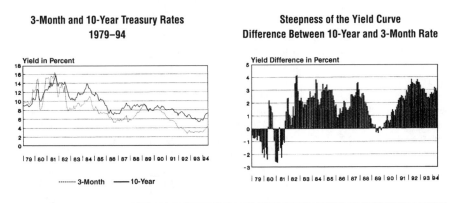

3-Month and 10-Year Treasury Rates
1979–94

Steepness of the Yield Curve
Difference Between 10-Year and 3-Month Rate

Exhibit 3. GNMAs: Annualized Percentage Paydowns from Prepayments

Month	7.00	8.00	9.00	10.00	11.00	12.00	13.00	14.00	15.00	30-Year Fixed Mortgage Rate %	Avg Refinancing Rate Prior Three Months
Jan 84	NA	2.4	2.1	2.0	2.4	1.0	3.9	8.1	14.9	12.82	12.98
Feb 84	NA	2.2	2.2	1.9	2.4	1.1	3.9	8.8	16.5	13.00	12.96
Mar 84	NA	2.7	2.5	2.5	3.0	1.1	5.2	11.5	18.7	13.52	13.11
Apr 84	NA	3.1	2.5	2.4	3.1	1.3	5.5	13.0	19.2	13.78	13.43
May 84	NA	3.5	2.8	2.2	3.1	1.5	6.0	13.7	21.0	14.90	14.06
Jun 84	NA	3.0	2.5	2.1	2.8	1.4	4.7	11.8	16.6	14.67	14.45
Jul 84	NA	2.8	2.2	1.8	2.5	1.2	4.2	9.1	15.1	14.19	14.58
Aug 84	NA	2.3	2.3	1.9	2.7	1.5	4.0	9.6	14.1	14.08	14.31
Sep 84	NA	1.8	1.8	1.5	2.0	1.3	3.4	7.8	10.5	13.70	13.99
Oct 84	NA	2.2	2.1	2.0	2.8	1.6	3.6	7.0	12.1	13.11	13.63
Nov 84	NA	2.1	1.7	1.3	2.2	1.7	3.5	6.8	11.2	12.74	13.18
Dec 84	NA	2.1	1.8	2.2	2.6	1.9	3.2	7.5	11.8	12.74	12.86
Jan 85	NA	2.4	2.2	1.9	3.0	3.1	6.8	10.8	17.4	12.53	12.67
Feb 85	NA	2.3	2.1	2.2	2.7	2.9	5.9	11.8	18.1	13.13	12.80
Mar 85	NA	2.9	2.5	2.2	3.6	3.9	7.2	15.7	22.3	12.84	12.83
Apr 85	NA	3.5	3.0	2.5	3.6	4.9	9.3	18.8	26.7	12.68	12.88
May 85	NA	3.5	2.9	3.1	3.9	4.5	9.1	17.0	26.9	11.59	12.37
Jun 85	NA	3.6	3.2	2.5	3.7	5.5	9.3	18.2	24.1	11.37	11.88
Jul 85	NA	4.3	3.8	3.4	4.9	6.4	13.0	23.6	28.5	11.76	11.57
Aug 85	NA	5.1	4.4	3.9	5.7	8.5	19.7	40.8	35.1	11.60	11.57
Sep 85	NA	4.7	4.1	3.5	5.4	8.6	19.7	38.3	35.8	11.61	11.65
Oct 85	NA	5.1	4.4	4.4	5.6	8.9	18.7	37.1	37.5	11.38	11.53
Nov 85	NA	4.0	3.5	3.2	4.8	6.9	15.6	24.6	24.4	10.77	11.25
Dec 85	NA	4.4	3.9	4.4	4.8	8.0	18.1	32.2	31.1	10.09	10.74
Jan 86	NA	3.8	3.8	3.8	5.5	7.9	18.3	28.0	26.2	10.26	10.37
Feb 86	NA	3.7	3.6	4.3	5.1	13.0	25.9	31.3	25.9	9.50	9.94
Mar 86	NA	4.8	4.6	4.3	9.4	23.4	39.7	45.6	40.4	9.29	9.68
Apr 86	NA	5.6	5.5	7.0	10.9	27.6	44.4	53.5	41.0	9.17	9.32
May 86	NA	6.5	6.2	6.1	15.3	36.2	46.6	57.5	43.7	10.01	9.49
Jun 86	NA	7.8	7.6	8.2	17.6	37.8	45.7	52.1	41.5	9.87	9.68
Jul 86	6.3	8.9	9.0	9.4	19.7	43.3	49.7	52.9	45.2	9.75	9.87
Aug 86	5.4	9.4	9.0	9.3	21.3	46.0	52.1	58.5	46.2	9.07	9.56
Sep 86	5.8	9.4	9.0	9.2	23.0	47.3	51.3	54.9	45.7	9.38	9.40
Oct 86	6.6	9.4	9.2	10.0	23.6	45.3	50.4	53.4	44.2	9.15	9.20
Nov 86	4.1	8.1	8.0	8.9	20.8	38.7	40.1	40.9	34.1	8.47	9.00
Dec 86	6.2	9.1	9.2	10.3	23.3	40.7	43.9	47.2	40.0	8.77	8.79
Jan 87	4.2	6.8	7.4	9.4	21.5	36.1	40.7	45.5	37.4	8.50	8.58
Feb 87	3.8	6.7	7.1	12.0	24.7	36.2	35.1	35.1	29.0	8.45	8.57
Mar 87	3.9	8.4	9.1	17.1	34.5	44.4	42.7	39.9	33.9	8.69	8.54
Apr 87	4.1	9.8	11.2	18.4	37.4	44.7	40.9	38.5	31.2	9.78	8.97
May 87	3.2	5.5	3.3	8.5	27.5	40.5	40.8	42.5	34.0	10.07	9.51

Exhibit 3. *Continued*

Month	7.00	8.00	9.00	10.00	11.00	12.00	13.00	14.00	15.00	30-Year Fixed Mortgage Rate %	Avg Refinancing Rate Prior Three Months
Jun 87	3.7	6.8	4.6	8.1	21.7	36.6	39.9	38.5	35.8	9.85	9.90
Jul 87	3.6	4.8	3.3	6.6	17.7	30.8	36.9	39.7	35.6	9.85	9.92
Aug 87	2.6	3.7	3.0	5.5	13.4	24.6	29.9	30.7	29.1	10.04	9.91
Sep 87	2.6	4.9	3.6	5.4	11.8	23.1	29.4	27.2	29.1	10.70	10.19
Oct 87	2.4	3.4	2.8	4.6	10.6	19.6	24.5	23.7	24.6	10.36	10.36
Nov 87	2.3	2.8	2.3	3.8	8.7	15.8	20.1	22.0	19.9	10.12	10.39
Dec 87	2.3	6.3	3.2	4.4	9.5	18.2	24.0	23.2	23.9	10.11	10.19
Jan 88	1.7	2.3	2.1	3.4	7.7	15.1	18.6	16.2	16.5	9.50	9.91
Feb 88	2.1	2.6	2.3	4.0	8.2	16.5	19.6	21.7	18.8	9.43	9.68
Mar 88	2.6	4.2	3.8	5.4	13.0	23.6	25.1	25.8	23.4	9.76	9.56
Apr 88	2.9	3.7	3.9	5.7	16.3	26.2	27.7	26.8	21.4	9.94	9.70
May 88	2.3	4.1	4.4	6.4	17.2	28.3	28.2	27.4	23.8	10.20	9.96
Jun 88	2.1	5.8	5.1	7.2	16.3	27.4	29.1	28.0	24.6	9.83	9.99
Jul 88	2.8	4.1	4.5	6.5	13.6	22.3	24.9	22.4	21.3	10.15	10.06
Aug 88	2.6	4.5	4.7	7.0	15.4	25.5	27.0	26.9	26.9	10.24	10.07
Sep 88	2.6	5.2	4.6	5.3	12.8	20.1	21.8	20.6	20.6	9.91	10.10
Oct 88	3.0	3.8	4.3	6.8	11.9	19.0	19.7	18.5	18.9	9.62	9.92
Nov 88	2.0	3.9	3.9	5.9	11.0	17.9	20.0	20.5	19.6	10.05	9.86
Dec 88	1.9	4.8	4.5	4.5	12.5	18.7	20.1	17.8	19.6	10.48	10.05
Jan 89	1.4	3.2	3.9	6.0	9.7	16.1	16.4	17.0	16.7	10.25	10.26
Feb 89	2.3	2.9	3.2	4.8	8.4	14.8	17.3	16.2	16.7	10.57	10.43
Mar 89	2.9	4.4	4.4	4.5	10.1	16.9	19.4	17.9	18.4	10.81	10.54
Apr 89	1.5	3.5	4.4	6.1	9.3	15.2	18.6	22.2	22.6	10.58	10.65
May 89	2.1	4.0	4.7	7.8	10.3	16.1	20.4	25.6	22.0	10.09	10.49
Jun 89	2.1	4.8	4.8	5.0	11.1	15.9	18.7	25.6	23.0	9.70	10.12
Jul 89	2.9	4.1	5.0	8.5	11.7	15.6	16.7	21.7	21.3	9.33	9.70
Aug 89	2.5	6.9	6.0	8.9	15.3	20.4	19.6	24.8	23.2	9.90	9.64
Sep 89	3.4	4.7	5.6	6.0	15.1	20.3	19.7	17.9	19.3	9.88	9.70
Oct 89	2.8	4.7	5.3	5.3	16.4	24.0	22.1	22.7	22.4	9.47	9.75
Nov 89	2.3	4.8	5.2	7.4	14.9	20.2	20.5	17.3	18.0	9.42	9.59
Dec 89	2.1	6.4	6.6	8.2	12.1	20.3	16.3	19.9	18.2	9.45	9.44
Jan 90	3.7	5.7	6.3	6.8	11.7	19.4	16.2	13.6	15.6	9.78	9.54
Feb 90	3.1	5.1	5.7	6.4	9.6	16.6	11.8	11.0	13.4	9.89	9.70
Mar 90	3.3	6.4	6.7	7.6	11.3	19.6	15.7	13.8	17.1	9.97	9.88
Apr 90	2.3	6.5	6.8	6.9	10.9	18.4	16.0	16.0	15.1	10.33	10.06
May 90	3.1	6.8	7.7	8.4	11.1	17.0	17.6	16.3	16.7	9.84	10.04
Jun 90	2.3	6.7	7.3	7.9	10.5	16.6	14.1	14.2	16.2	9.67	9.94
Jul 90	3.5	6.9	7.7	8.6	10.2	16.2	15.0	15.0	15.2	9.45	9.65
Aug 90	3.4	7.5	7.7	8.7	11.3	18.3	15.0	16.6	18.0	9.80	9.64
Sep 90	2.2	6.4	6.2	6.6	9.1	14.8	10.6	14.3	14.1	9.78	9.67
Oct 90	2.5	6.6	6.6	7.6	9.8	16.1	14.6	19.1	16.7	9.76	9.77

The GNMA Mortgage Coupon columns (7.00, 8.00, 9.00, 10.00, 11.00, 12.00, 13.00, 14.00, 15.00) fall under the spanning header "GNMA Mortgage Coupon."

Exhibit 3. *Continued*

Month	\multicolumn{9}{c}{GNMA Mortgage Coupon}	30-Year Fixed Mortgage Rate %	Avg Refinancing Rate Prior Three Months
	7.00	8.00	9.00	10.00	11.00	12.00	13.00	14.00	15.00		
Nov 90	3.0	5.7	5.8	6.0	8.5	13.1	12.8	16.7	13.8	9.49	9.67
Dec 90	3.8	5.5	5.7	5.5	7.9	13.2	12.3	14.7	14.2	9.27	9.50
Jan 91	2.9	5.1	5.5	5.6	8.5	14.4	12.7	16.9	13.5	9.12	9.51
Feb 91	2.9	5.1	5.2	5.8	9.6	15.4	13.4	13.7	12.1	9.08	9.29
Mar 91	2.6	5.8	6.2	8.2	13.9	19.7	14.6	17.4	15.6	9.08	9.16
Apr 91	3.5	7.4	7.9	10.0	19.4	26.0	20.0	19.4	19.2	9.03	9.12
May 91	4.5	8.0	8.8	10.5	20.8	28.3	19.0	21.1	18.7	8.99	9.06
Jun 91	3.1	7.9	8.5	9.7	17.5	23.7	18.1	17.0	16.9	9.19	9.03
Jul 91	4.2	7.9	8.4	10.4	18.9	25.2	20.7	19.3	19.1	8.99	9.07
Aug 91	3.9	7.7	8.2	10.5	17.3	22.4	21.7	19.8	20.0	8.72	9.06
Sep 91	3.3	6.7	7.1	9.0	15.5	17.8	16.9	15.1	16.0	8.41	8.97
Oct 91	3.9	7.7	8.3	12.4	19.3	21.8	19.9	14.2	17.8	8.21	8.71
Nov 91	3.4	7.2	7.9	14.4	20.9	23.4	18.8	19.1	17.2	8.22	8.45
Dec 91	4.4	7.9	8.8	17.7	25.3	25.0	19.7	20.0	14.8	7.55	8.28
Jan 92	4.3	7.6	9.1	20.4	25.6	25.3	19.5	19.1	15.8	8.21	7.99
Feb 92	3.5	8.1	9.6	24.7	28.3	26.6	21.0	16.3	15.6	8.08	7.99
Mar 92	3.8	10.7	14.0	29.7	37.9	37.2	27.0	22.4	20.4	8.40	7.95
Apr 92	4.1	10.6	13.6	29.5	37.5	34.8	28.4	27.1	21.2	8.30	8.23
May 92	2.7	9.8	11.8	23.7	31.4	30.6	24.0	20.8	22.5	8.02	8.26
Jun 92	3.3	10.1	12.0	20.8	27.8	29.6	25.3	20.4	20.3	7.84	8.24
Jul 92	3.5	9.9	11.4	19.2	25.5	25.7	22.4	22.0	19.6	7.53	8.05
Aug 92	3.5	9.7	12.3	20.3	23.2	23.8	18.6	19.5	20.3	7.34	7.80
Sep 92	3.1	10.8	14.7	25.9	26.3	26.1	19.6	18.0	19.5	7.27	7.57
Oct 92	2.4	11.3	17.2	29.1	30.1	28.6	20.8	21.6	18.8	7.76	7.38
Nov 92	2.5	11.5	17.1	29.9	28.6	28.1	22.9	20.4	17.9	7.83	7.46
Dec 92	4.8	12.1	17.8	27.0	28.0	25.1	18.8	15.4	13.9	7.55	7.62
Jan 93	2.3	8.1	14.9	24.9	26.2	23.5	19.4	14.9	18.1	7.19	7.71
Feb 93	4.6	7.6	13.7	22.9	23.3	22.0	19.3	24.4	16.7	6.94	7.52
Mar 93	4.9	10.4	22.4	30.0	27.7	25.6	23.1	18.5	17.9	6.92	7.23
Apr 93	4.0	13.3	33.9	37.2	32.0	28.5	23.5	21.6	18.4	6.90	7.02
May 93	4.1	14.5	36.3	37.3	30.9	27.2	20.2	17.0	20.9	6.98	6.92
Jun 93	6.7	16.9	38.6	41.2	36.0	30.8	24.5	23.5	22.5	6.63	6.93
Jul 93	7.7	15.8	35.6	38.4	33.4	28.1	23.4	28.2	22.8	6.61	6.84
Sep 93	6.1	20.6	38.7	38.5	35.3	30.3	25.5	28.2	19.7	6.28	6.50
Oct 93	6.8	24.6	41.0	39.9	34.8	30.1	22.1	20.7	22.0	6.35	6.39
Nov 93	6.6	29.4	45.0	42.6	37.1	32.8	27.7	20.2	23.3	6.78	6.30
Dec 93	6.4	30.9	48.3	47.7	41.9	36.5	31.0	28.4	22.6	6.67	6.47
Jan 94	4.2	20.8	36.9	39.0	36.0	32.9	25.6	26.6	20.8	6.45	6.60
Feb 94	6.0	18.0	33.7	38.0	33.3	32.7	27.7	22.3	21.7	6.93	6.63
Mar 94	7.8	21.5	40.0	46.0	43.9	42.7	36.5	32.2	30.5	7.74	6.68
Apr 94	5.9	16.8	30.9	41.2	39.9	40.2	33.6	26.6	29.1	8.04	7.04

Exhibit 3. *Continued*

Month	7.00	8.00	9.00	10.00	GNMA Mortgage Coupon 11.00	12.00	13.00	14.00	15.00	30-Year Fixed Mortgage Rate %	Avg Refinancing Rate Prior Three Months
May 94	4.6	13.3	22.6	34.7	37.5	39.8	34.2	33.8	28.4	8.10	7.57
Jun 94	4.9	12.3	17.5	27.5	30.5	31.1	27.0	25.8	21.7	8.29	7.96

The top panel of Exhibit 4 displays the typical relationship between prepayments on fixed-rate mortgages and the average market refinancing rate on alternative mortgages. When refinancing rates are higher than a borrower's mortgage rate, he has little financial incentive to refinance. Not unexpectedly, the prepayment "curve" for GNMA 13% mortgage-backed securities (backed by mortgages with fixed interest rates of approximately 13.5%) is very flat for refinancing rates higher than 13%. Prepayments are at a fairly low level (4% to 5%) and do not change very much as mortgage rates rise further.

When refinancing rates fall, however, to levels 1% to 1.5% below the rate on borrowers' existing mortgages, a significant refinancing incentive exists, leading to dramatically higher levels of prepayments. Note the steep slope of the prepayment curve as refinancing rates fall to levels between 1.5% and 3.5% below borrowers' mortgage rates. At some point, at very low levels of market mortgage rates relative to the rate on borrowers' existing loans, prepayments increase much more slowly, usually peaking near the 50% (annualized) level.

The bottom panel of Exhibit 4 displays an interesting prepayment phenomenon most commonly referred to as *prepayment burnout* or *premium burnout*. Since a pool of mortgages represents a heterogeneous mix of individual borrowers, not every borrower in the pool will have the same financial incentive to prepay at any given time. Some people may be less financially sophisticated than others. Some may view refinancing as a nuisance and assign it a higher cost than others (perhaps valuing their time more than others). Some borrowers, whose property values or incomes have fallen, may find it difficult to qualify for a new loan. Borrowers whose loan size is small relative to their annual incomes may be less motivated to refinance than those whose monthly mortgage payments consume a higher percentage of their incomes.

Whatever the reason, it is clear that different borrowers face differing costs of refinancing. When a pool of mortgages encounters its first period of significant refinancing incentive (for GNMA 13s such a period existed in 1986 and 1987), prepayments usually reach a very high level as those borrowers who are more apt to prepay do so. After a period of time, the remaining borrowers represented in the pool are those who have (on average) a lower propensity to prepay. As a result the pool is said to experience prepayment

Exhibit 4.   Prepayments Are a Function of Interest Rates

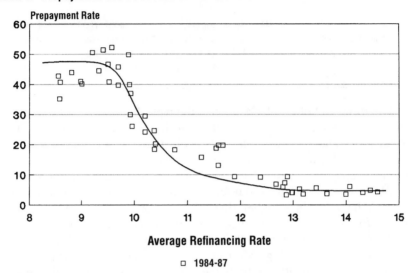

Average Refinancing Rate

□ 1984-87

An Example of Prepayment Burnout

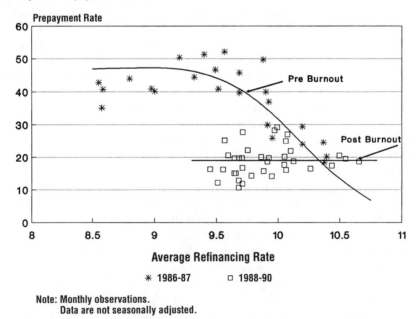

Average Refinancing Rate

✳ 1986-87   □ 1988-90

Note: Monthly observations.
      Data are not seasonally adjusted.

burnout as prepayment rates reach a much lower, stable level. The pool's prepayment rate is now much less sensitive to changes in refinancing rates than it was prior to the "burnout" period.

As the bottom panel of Exhibit 4 displays, during the 1988 to 1990 period GNMA 13 prepayment rates were very stable at around 20% (annualized) in spite of the fact that refinancing rates (between 9.5% and 10.5%) were significantly lower than the 13.5% coupon rates on the underlying mortgages. Note how much faster the GNMA 13s prepaid during the 1986 and 1987 period for similar levels of refinancing rates. Also note that during the 1986–87 period, GNMA 13 prepayment rates were much more sensitive to changes in refinancing rates, increasing from 20% to 50% (annualized) as refinancing rates fell from 10.5% to 9.5%. When mortgage rates reached 20-year lows (6.3%) in 1993 (providing a second major period of refinancing incentive for GNMA 13s), prepayments on GNMA 13s increased only to the upper 20% (annualized) level, far slower than the 50% level reached in 1986 when mortgage rates were above 9%. At this point, GNMA 9s (with coupon rates a full four percentage points lower than GNMA 13s) were prepaying more than twice as fast as the GNMA 13s.

Interest rates, mortgage coupon rates, the health of the economy, the age of a mortgage (seasoning), the time of the year (seasonality), and past refinancing incentives (burnout) all play important roles in determining the level of prepayments on fixed-rate mortgages. Investors and mortgage lenders should understand the relationships between prepayments and these key variables in order to assess the potential risks and returns of their mortgage portfolios.

Futures Contracts and Prices*

Interest-rate futures contracts are actively traded for 4 instruments: (1) 20-year Treasury bonds, (2) 91-one-day Eurodollar time deposits, (3) 91-day Treasury bills, and (4) 10-year Treasury notes. By far the most liquid markets are the 20-year Treasury bond (or T-bonds) and the 91-day Eurodollar (or Euros) markets. End-of-month futures prices for T-bonds and Euros for the 1984–94 period are given in Exhibit 5.

As an example of the terms of a futures contract, let us examine the T-bond contract in more detail. The 20-year Treasury bond futures contract is an agreement between a buyer (the *long*) and a seller (the *short*) to trade a long-term Treasury bond at a future date (the *maturity date*) at a price that is set today. Contracts are traded for only four maturity dates per year—March,

---

*This subsection contains basic institutional material on futures contracts. The next three subsections do the same for options on futures, interest rate swaps, and interest rate caps and floors, respectively. Readers familiar with these instruments should proceed to the next section.

Exhibit 5.

20-Year Treasury Bond Futures Prices

End of	Near Ct Yield	Near	2nd	3rd	4th
Jan 84	11.84%	70.81	70.22	69.66	69.16
Feb 84	12.19%	68.84	68.22	67.72	67.25
Mar 84*	12.69%	66.22	65.66	65.16	64.72
Apr 84	12.99%	64.69	64.13	63.69	63.31
May 84	13.97%	60.16	59.47	58.97	58.59
Jun 84*	14.09%	59.63	59.00	58.56	58.22
Jul 84	13.03%	64.50	63.88	63.41	63.03
Aug 84	12.77%	65.81	65.16	64.63	64.19
Sep 84*	12.49%	67.22	66.63	66.16	65.75
Oct 84	11.85%	70.78	70.03	69.44	68.91
Nov 84	11.70%	71.63	70.91	70.31	69.78
Dec 84*	11.80%	71.06	70.34	69.72	69.19
Jan 85	11.44%	73.19	72.09	71.28	70.59
Feb 85	12.19%	68.88	67.88	67.09	66.47
Mar 85*	12.03%	69.72	68.78	67.97	67.22
Apr 85	11.85%	70.75	69.72	68.81	68.00
May 85	10.78%	77.34	76.41	75.47	74.63
Jun 85*	10.83%	77.06	76.06	75.09	74.16
Jul 85	11.12%	75.19	74.13	73.16	72.28
Aug 85	10.82%	77.13	76.03	75.00	74.06
Sep 85*	11.08%	75.59	74.47	73.44	72.47
Oct 85	10.61%	78.53	77.19	76.03	74.97
Nov 85	10.16%	81.66	80.50	79.47	78.53
Dec 85*	9.69%	85.22	84.25	83.38	82.63
Jan 86	9.64%	85.16	84.09	83.13	82.28
Feb 86	8.55%	94.81	94.00	93.31	92.72
Mar 86*	7.77%	102.31	101.63	101.00	100.44
Apr 86	7.92%	100.75	100.00	99.19	98.41
May 86	8.65%	93.88	93.09	92.34	91.56
Jun 86*	8.04%	99.56	98.75	97.97	97.19
Jul 86	8.22%	97.81	97.00	96.16	95.31
Aug 86	7.76%	102.41	101.72	100.81	99.91
Sep 86*	8.36%	96.56	95.66	94.66	93.75
Oct 86	8.20%	98.09	97.19	96.19	95.22
Nov 86	8.03%	99.72	98.75	97.78	96.81
Dec 86*	8.19%	98.19	97.19	96.19	95.19
Jan 87	8.03%	99.69	98.78	97.88	97.00
Feb 87	7.86%	101.44	100.44	99.50	98.59
Mar 87*	8.16%	98.47	97.44	96.44	95.50
Apr 87	8.74%	93.06	92.09	91.22	90.41

91-Day Eurodollar Prices

End of	Near Ct Yield	Near	2nd	3rd	4th
Jan 84	10.04%	89.96	89.58	89.24	88.94
Feb 84	10.29%	89.71	89.19	88.81	88.50
Mar 84*	11.28%	88.72	88.25	87.88	87.59
Apr 84	11.46%	88.54	87.96	87.51	87.13
May 84	11.97%	88.03	86.49	85.70	85.28
Jun 84*	13.13%	86.87	86.05	85.61	85.30
Jul 84	12.03%	87.97	87.50	87.11	86.82
Aug 84	11.92%	88.08	87.62	87.27	86.99
Sep 84*	11.56%	88.44	88.14	87.82	87.54
Oct 84	10.32%	89.68	89.28	88.87	88.49
Nov 84	9.46%	90.54	89.93	89.47	89.07
Dec 84*	9.52%	90.48	89.88	89.38	88.95
Jan 85	8.93%	91.07	90.57	90.03	89.57
Feb 85	9.69%	90.31	89.45	88.86	88.44
Mar 85*	9.77%	90.23	89.59	89.16	88.79
Apr 85	8.95%	91.05	90.29	89.75	89.31
May 85	7.76%	92.24	91.70	91.22	90.81
Jun 85*	7.93%	92.07	91.58	91.15	90.79
Jul 85	8.36%	91.64	91.15	90.71	90.31
Aug 85	8.14%	91.86	91.52	91.12	90.72
Sep 85*	8.23%	91.77	91.38	90.97	90.60
Oct 85	7.95%	92.05	91.83	91.46	91.09
Nov 85	8.03%	91.97	92.00	91.82	91.53
Dec 85*	7.75%	92.25	92.13	91.92	91.66
Jan 86	7.88%	92.12	92.02	91.84	91.61
Feb 86	7.76%	92.24	92.39	92.36	92.19
Mar 86*	6.97%	93.03	93.06	92.96	92.80
Apr 86	6.75%	93.25	93.26	93.13	92.90
May 86	7.07%	92.93	92.84	92.67	92.41
Jun 86*	6.55%	93.45	93.35	93.14	92.84
Jul 86	6.43%	93.57	93.58	93.48	93.28
Aug 86	5.71%	94.29	94.36	94.27	94.08
Sep 86*	5.99%	94.01	93.89	93.66	94.31
Oct 86	5.89%	94.11	94.10	93.91	93.61
Nov 86	6.03%	93.97	94.07	94.01	93.82
Dec 86*	6.11%	93.89	93.86	93.76	93.57
Jan 87	6.31%	93.69	93.77	93.74	93.62
Feb 87	6.42%	93.58	93.67	93.66	93.57
Mar 87*	6.65%	93.35	93.33	93.28	93.16
Apr 87	7.39%	92.61	92.31	92.12	91.95

Exhibit 5. *Continued*

| 20-Year Treasury Bond Futures Prices | | | | | 91-Day Eurodollar Prices | | | | |
| | Near Ct | Maturity of Contract | | | | Near Ct | Maturity of Contract | | |
End of	Yield	Near	2nd	3rd	4th	End of	Yield	Near	2nd	3rd	4th
May 87	8.85%	92.06	91.06	90.16	89.31	May 87	7.26%	92.74	92.18	91.87	91.65
Jun 87*	8.92%	91.50	90.56	89.69	88.84	Jun 87*	7.42%	92.58	92.31	92.09	91.89
Jul 87	9.15%	89.50	88.50	87.56	86.69	July 87	7.29%	92.71	92.31	92.01	91.76
Aug 87	9.40%	87.50	86.53	85.63	84.78	Aug 87	7.29%	92.71	92.07	91.73	91.46
Sep 87*	10.16%	871.69	80.88	80.06	79.34	Sep 87*	8.60%	91.40	91.02	90.74	90.53
Oct 87	9.39%	87.56	86.59	85.78	85.06	Oct 87	7.58%	92.42	92.22	91.74	91.38
Nov 87	9.38%	87.66	86.75	85.88	85.09	Nov 87	7.68%	92.32	92.33	92.03	91.69
Dec 87*	9.34%	87.97	86.94	86.06	85.25	Dec 87*	7.56%	92.44	92.20	91.86	91.52
Jan 88	8.65%	93.91	92.94	92.06	91.25	Jan 88	7.04%	92.96	92.76	92.47	92.19
Feb 88	8.56%	94.66	93.63	92.66	91.78	Feb 88	6.87%	93.13	93.00	92.75	92.47
Mar 88*	9.09%	90.06	89.03	88.06	87.19	Mar 88*	7.28%	92.72	92.42	92.13	91.87
Apr 88	9.35%	87.91	86.94	86.06	85.28	Apr 88	7.59%	92.41	92.03	91.76	91.56
May 88	9.61%	85.81	84.91	84.03	83.22	May 88	7.77%	92.23	91.69	91.36	91.16
Jun 88*	9.24%	88.75	87.88	87.06	86.28	Jun 88*	7.96%	92.04	91.70	91.52	91.36
Jul 88	9.62%	85.75	85.03	84.38	83.75	Jul 88	8.48%	91.52	91.19	91.14	90.99
Aug 88	9.58%	86.06	85.50	84.94	84.38	Aug 88	8.67%	91.33	90.81	90.86	90.69
Sep 88*	9.24%	88.75	88.25	87.75	87.28	Sep 88*	8.78%	91.22	91.33	91.19	91.02
Oct 88	8.93%	91.41	90.84	90.31	89.84	Oct 88	8.59%	91.41	91.58	91.51	91.37
Nov 88	9.28%	88.47	88.09	87.72	87.41	Nov 88	9.15%	90.85	91.03	90.99	90.98
Dec 88*	9.20%	89.13	88.81	88.56	88.34	Dec 88*	9.38%	90.62	90.56	90.53	90.35
Jan 89	9.00%	90.81	90.63	90.47	90.38	Jan 89	9.54%	90.46	90.43	90.45	90.35
Feb 89	9.32%	88.09	88.19	88.19	88.19	Feb 89	10.27%	89.73	89.47	89.51	89.64
Mar 89*	9.29%	88.41	88.50	88.56	88.59	Mar 89*	10.71%	89.29	89.13	89.04	89.39
Apr 89	9.07%	90.19	90.09	90.00	89.94	Apr 89	9.85%	90.15	90.25	90.21	90.40
May 89	8.74%	93.06	93.00	92.91	92.78	May 89	9.46%	90.54	90.91	90.94	91.00
Jun 89*	8.21%	97.94	97.78	97.56	97.34	Jun 89*	8.53%	91.47	91.66	91.79	91.69
Jul 89	8.03%	99.75	99.56	99.25	98.91	Jul 89	8.21%	91.79	92.21	92.33	92.24
Aug 89	8.39%	96.25	96.22	96.03	95.78	Aug 89	8.89%	91.11	91.30	91.50	91.33
Sep 89*	8.43%	95.84	95.78	95.59	95.38	Sep 89*	8.95%	91.05	91.29	91.39	91.33
Oct 89	8.07%	99.34	99.31	99.09	98.84	Oct 89	8.37%	91.63	92.02	92.00	91.88
Nov 89	8.05%	99.47	99.47	99.25	98.94	Nov 89	8.37%	91.63	92.21	92.31	92.21
Dec 89*	8.14%	98.66	98.53	98.31	98.03	Dec 89*	8.02%	91.98	92.16	92.15	91.92
Jan 90	8.61%	94.25	94.06	93.91	93.72	Jan 90	8.35%	91.65	91.60	91.50	91.27
Feb 90	8.71%	93.31	93.19	93.03	92.84	Feb 90	8.37%	91.63	91.59	91.49	91.30
Mar 90*	8.88%	91.88	91.72	91.56	91.44	Mar 90*	8.69%	91.31	91.19	91.02	90.96
Apr 90	9.24%	88.81	88.63	88.47	88.31	Apr 90	8.81%	91.19	90.92	90.71	90.61
May 90	8.76%	92.91	92.72	92.47	92.28	May 90	8.40%	91.60	91.58	91.47	91.33
Jun 90*	8.60%	94.34	94.03	93.78	93.53	Jun 90*	8.16%	91.84	91.82	91.79	91.64
Jul 90	8.56%	94.69	94.38	94.09	93.81	Jul 90	7.89%	92.11	92.21	92.24	92.09
Aug 90	9.20%	89.16	88.81	88.44	88.06	Aug 90	8.01%	91.99	92.08	92.01	91.86

Exhibit 5. *Continued*

20-Year Treasury Bond Futures Prices						91-Day Eurodollar Prices				
	Near Ct	Maturity of Contract					Near Ct	Maturity of Contract		
End of	Yield	Near	2nd	3rd	4th	End of	Yield	Near	2nd	3rd	4th
Sep 90*	9.17%	89.38	88.97	88.59	88.25	Sep 90*	8.06%	91.94	91.99	91.88	91.65
Oct 90	8.97%	91.09	90.69	90.25	89.84	Oct 90	7.89%	92.11	92.32	92.26	92.08
Nov 90	8.54%	94.91	94.56	94.19	93.78	Nov 90	8.22%	91.78	92.30	92.47	92.44
Dec 90*	8.45%	95.72	95.28	94.84	94.13	Dec 90*	7.20%	92.80	92.89	92.78	92.47
Jan 91	8.38%	96.31	95.78	95.25	94.72	Jan 91	7.06%	92.94	93.00	92.85	92.55
Feb 91	8.40%	96.16	95.53	94.94	94.38	Feb 91	6.87%	93.13	93.26	93.06	92.66
Mar 91	8.42%	95.95	94.78	94.16	93.63	Mar 91	6.52%	93.48	93.21	92.71	92.51
Apr 91	8.37%	96.41	95.63	94.91	94.28	Apr 91	6.08%	93.92	93.66	93.15	92.83
May 91	8.44%	95.75	94.97	94.22	93.59	May 91	6.09%	93.91	93.65	93.20	93.04
Jun 91	8.68%	93.63	92.91	92.28	91.725	Jun 91	6.41%	93.59	93.02	92.91	92.51
Jul 91	8.54%	94.84	94.09	93.95	92.81	Jul 91	6.14%	93.86	93.44	93.39	92.93
Aug 91	8.20%	98.06	97.25	96.53	95.81	Aug 91	5.72%	94.28	93.98	94.00	93.71
Sep 91	8.00%	100.00	99.22	98.41	97.66	Sep 91	5.65%	94.35	94.46	94.29	93.94
Oct 91	8.02%	99.81	98.94	98.00	97.13	Oct 91	5.25%	94.75	94.87	94.66	94.37
Nov 91	8.03%	99.75	98.81	97.84	96.84	Nov 91	4.95%	95.05	95.27	95.14	94.88
Dec 91	7.54%	104.75	103.69	102.69	101.75	Dec 91	4.04%	95.96	95.85	95.64	95.16
Jan 92	7.90%	101.03	99.91	98.88	97.94	Jan 92	4.18%	95.82	95.60	95.23	94.56
Feb 92	7.86%	101.41	100.31	99.28	98.31	Feb 92	4.21%	95.79	95.59	95.26	94.63
Mar 92*	8.13%	98.72	97.69	96.75	95.91	Mar 92*	4.53%	95.47	95.07	94.28	94.01
Apr 92	8.19%	98.13	97.00	95.94	95.03	Apr 92	4.15%	95.85	95.43	94.70	94.47
May 92	7.92%	100.81	99.72	98.63	97.66	May 92	4.02%	95.98	95.71	95.09	94.96
Jun 92*	7.93%	100.66	99.50	98.47	97.41	Jun 92*	3.93%	96.07	95.59	95.49	95.09
Jul 92	7.53%	104.84	103.69	102.56	101.47	Jul 92	3.52%	96.48	96.09	95.99	95.65
Aug 92	7.50%	105.16	103.97	102.81	101.66	Aug 92	3.46%	96.54	96.37	96.34	96.05
Sep 92*	7.46%	105.56	104.41	103.03	101.84	Sep 92*	3.14%	96.86	96.81	96.53	96.18
Oct 92	7.73%	102.75	101.53	100.28	99.13	Oct 92	3.67%	96.33	96.34	95.91	95.46
Nov 92	7.69%	103.16	101.97	100.81	99.69	Nov 92	3.99%	96.01	96.04	95.56	95.07
Dec 92*	7.55%	104.66	103.47	102.34	101.28	Dec 92*	3.64%	96.36	95.93	95.52	94.89
Jan 93	7.31%	107.19	105.94	104.72	103.53	Jan 93	3.31%	96.69	96.49	96.17	95.63
Feb 93	6.98%	110.88	109.63	108.38	107.19	Feb 93	3.23%	96.77	96.65	96.45	96.07
Mar 93*	7.10%	109.53	108.31	107.19	106.16	Mar 93*	3.32%	96.68	96.48	96.06	95.89
Apr 93	7.03%	110.50	109.25	108.03	106.88	Apr 93	3.23%	96.77	96.64	96.25	96.14
May 93	7.02%	110.44	109.16	107.97	106.88	May 93	3.39%	96.61	96.40	95.87	95.74
Jun 93*	6.72%	113.94	112.72	111.59	110.53	Jun 93*	3.43%	96.57	96.19	96.10	95.82
Jul 93	6.59%	115.50	114.31	113.22	112.22	Jul 93	3.34%	96.66	96.23	96.11	95.82
Aug 93	6.26%	119.69	118.41	117.19	116.09	Aug 93	3.25%	96.75	96.45	96.41	96.20
Sep 93*	6.35%	118.53	117.31	116.25	115.25	Sep 93*	3.49%	96.51	96.47	96.26	96.03
Oct 93	6.32%	118.97	117.84	116.84	115.84	Oct 93	3.52%	96.48	96.47	96.26	96.03
Nov 93	6.54%	116.19	114.91	113.84	112.91	Nov 93	3.48%	96.52	96.42	96.15	95.85
Dec 93*	6.68%	114.50	113.44	112.47	112.16	Dec 93*	3.51%	96.49	96.15	95.84	95.43

Exhibit 5. *Continued*

20-Year Treasury Bond Futures Prices										
	Near Ct	Maturity of Contract					Near Ct	Maturity of Contract		
End of	Yield	Near	2nd	3rd	4th	End of	Yield	Near	2nd	3rd	4th

20-Year Treasury Bond Futures Prices					91-Day Eurodollar Prices					
End of	Yield	Near	2nd	3rd	4th	End of	Yield	Near	2nd	3rd	4th
Jan 94	6.46%	117.16	116.06	115.06	114.63	Jan 94	3.36%	96.64	96.35	96.04	95.67
Feb 94	6.85%	112.41	111.34	110.47	109.94	Feb 94	3.78%	96.22	95.84	95.53	95.14
Mar 94*	7.40%	106.25	105.34	104.75	104.06	Mar 94*	4.36%	95.64	95.15	94.67	94.41
Apr 94	7.56%	104.50	103.53	102.91	102.28	Apr 94	4.73%	95.27	94.64	94.14	93.87
May 94	7.65%	103.56	102.63	101.97	101.38	May 94	4.74%	95.26	94.59	93.99	93.74
Jun 94*	7.88%	101.22	100.47	99.78	99.16	Jun 94*	5.36%	94.64	93.95	93.66	93.36

*Old near contract expired. All contracts move one colum left (nearer maturity).

June, September, and December. However, there are typically 10 or 11 different contract maturities being traded at any point in time, covering quarterly futures maturities up to 2.5 to 2.75 years out from the present time.

For convenience in pricing and in computing yields, it is assumed that the bond delivered will have 20 years to maturity at delivery and have an 8% coupon rate. However, in actuality the seller has certain options on the time to maturity of the bond delivered, on its coupon rate, and on the date during the delivery month when delivery actually occurs. In particular, the seller may deliver any long-term U.S. government Treasury bond that is not callable for at least 15 years from the futures maturity date. Of course, bonds that pay higher coupons are more valuable, so the futures invoice price is multiplied upon delivery by an "adjustment factor" that reflects the coupon and maturity of the bonds actually delivered. The adjustment factor is the present value (per $1 par) of the bond's cash flows using a discount rate of 8%. In determining which bond to deliver, the seller computes the price received (from the futures price and the adjustment factors) and the costs (from cash market prices) of all bonds eligible for delivery, then chooses the bond that is "cheapest to deliver," *i.e.*, the bond that maximizes profits for the seller. The advantage of this delivery procedure is that many bonds are eligible for delivery, which eliminates the possibility of someone buying all deliverable bonds and preventing delivery—a *short squeeze*. Additionally, the seller may choose the day during the delivery month upon which to make a delivery.

Most (about 97%) futures contracts do *not* result in delivery, since buyer and seller offset their positions by opposite trades (buyer sells and seller buys back) prior to the first day of the delivery month. However, the possibility of delivery makes the value of the futures contract reflect the provisions of delivery. Thus, since the seller has valuable options on the deliverable bond's coupon and maturity, as well as on the date of delivery, the price of a bond futures contract must be lower than a corresponding cash bond (without options). With these options and delivery risks, one might wonder whether or not the 20-year Treasury bond futures contract's price moves closely with 20-year bond prices. To check this, actual Treasury bond futures prices for the contract nearest maturity were used to find the yield on a 20-year, 8% bond. The results are in the first column of Exhibit 5, corresponding to the prices in column 2. These yields were then regressed on the 20-year cash bond yields in Exhibit 1 (for the 1984 to 1994 period), with the following statistical results:

Bond Futures Rate = 0.53% + 0.965 [20-year Treasury Coupon Rate]
(t=5.0)   (t=176.6)

R-squared = .996   Correlation = .998

Standard Error of Residual = .10%.

Futures Yield minus 20-year Cash Yield:

Range: 2 basis points to 59 basis points

(Avg = 23 basis points)

Thus, despite the seller's options on delivery, the Treasury bond futures contract has a correlation of .998 with the 20-year Treasury rate. This is reassuring, and shows that, for our purposes, little is lost in viewing a long or short position in T-bond futures as being synonymous with a long or short position in 20-year Treasury bonds.

Futures contracts specify a standardized quantity to be delivered per contract. For example, 20-year Treasury bond futures and 10-year Treasury notes both have a standard delivery amount of $100,000 par. In contrast, the 91-day Eurodollar contract and the 91-day Treasury bill contract require delivery of $1,000,000 par. The reason for this difference in par amounts is that the price volatilities of the 91-day instruments are much smaller per dollar of par than for the 10-year and 20-year instruments (which have much longer durations). Futures contracts' quantities are set large enough so that typical daily gains and losses of a single contract are economically meaningful and of somewhat similar sizes in all markets. The typical daily gain or loss on one futures contract is usually $300 – $1,000, with good-faith margin deposits required that are about four times the typical daily move ($1,200 - $4,000).

Price quotes in Treasury bond and Treasury note futures are expressed as percents of par. Thus, given a standard quantity of $100,000 par, the T-bond futures price of 117.16% on January 31, 1994, (from Exhibit 5) represents a value of $117,160 for the T-bond contract. If one T-bond contract was sold short on January 31, 1994, at a 117.16% price and bought back (offset) on February 28, 1994, at a price of 112.41% par, the gain would have been $4,750 ($117,160 - $112,410). Of course, when rates fall, bond prices rise, and a short loses. To see this, note that one might have sold short the near T-bond contract on July 31, 1993, at 115.50% par and bought back on August 31, 1994, at 119.69% par, for a loss of $4,190 per contract. In T-bonds and T-notes, one price *point* is 1% of $100,000, or $1,000.

In 91-day Eurodollars and 91-day Treasury bill contracts, typical price quotes are not really prices, but indexes. From Exhibit 5, the price index for the near Eurodollar futures contract was 96.64 on January 31, 1994. This means that each contract is for $1 million of 91-day Eurodollars at a contractual price that represents an annualized yield to maturity of 3.36% (100 – 96.64), quarterly compounded. Thus, the decrease in Eurodollar futures prices to an index of 94.64 on June 30, 1994, represents a rise in 91-day Eurodollar rates (91-day LIBOR) to 5.36% (100 – 94.64). Every point on the Eurodollar futures index represents a 1% increase in the annual interest rate on 91-day Euros. Since that 1% higher rate is applied to a par amount of $1,000,000 for one quarter of a year to maturity, the change in value of a Eurodollar futures contract for a one point move is: .01 x $1,000,000 x ($1/4$) = $2,500 per contract.

Exhibit 6 summarizes what the futures prices, contract values, and gains and losses are for interest rates from 4% to 20% for the major interest-rate futures contracts—20-year T-bonds, 10-year T-notes, 91-day T-bills, and 91-day Eurodollars. For hedgers in interest-rate futures, this table provides critical information. For example, if interest rates are 7%, the typical dollar move in T-bond futures is $11,557 per contract for a 1% rate move, which is more than four times the $2,500 move in Eurodollars. However, with rates at 13%, the move in T-bonds drops to only $4,951 for a 1% rate change, which is only two times the $2,500 move in Eurodollars. In either case, note that $100,000 par in 20-year bonds moves significantly more in value than does $1,000,000 par in 91-day Eurodollars. Setting up or evaluating a hedge requires a thorough knowledge of these futures gains and losses that occur for various rate moves. In my hedging experience, a focus on the par amounts of these contracts, rather than on the dollar gains and losses for 1% rate moves, is probably the most consistent major error made by regulators and board members in critiquing hedging programs. The duration discussion of the next subsection will explain why the bond contract's movements get smaller as rates increase. Also, the third section of this chapter shows how to calculate correct sizes for futures hedge positions, using the "Average Move" data of Exhibit 6.

Call and Put Options on Futures

A *call option* is an option (your choice) to buy a fixed quantity of a certain *underlying asset* at a fixed exercise price, any time prior to the expiration date of the option. The most liquid interest rate options traded are options

Exhibit 6.   Interest Rate Futures Prices and Dollar Moves

20-Year Treasury Bond Futures

Interest Rate	Futures Price	Contract Value	Move if Rates Up	Average Move
4.00%	154.71	$154,711	$17,057	
5.00%	137.65	$137,654	$14,539	$15,798
6.00%	123.11	$123,115	$12,437	$13,488
7.00%	110.68	$110,678	$10,678	$11,557
8.00%	100.00	$100,000	$9,201	$9,939
9.00%	90.80	$90,799	$7,958	$8,580
10.00%	82.84	$82,841	$6,910	$7,434
11.00%	75.93	$75,931	$6,023	$6,467
12.00%	69.91	$69,907	$5,271	$5,647
13.00%	64.64	$64,636	$4,631	$4,951
14.00%	60.00	$60,005	$4,085	$4,358
15.00%	55.92	$55,920	$3,618	$3,852
16.00%	52.30	$52,302	$3,217	$3,417
17.00%	49.08	$49,085	$2,871	$3,044
18.00%	46.21	$46,213	$2,573	$2,722
19.00%	43.64	$43,640	$2,314	$2,444
20.00%	41.33	$41,326		

10-Year Treasury Note Futures

Interest Rate	Futures Price	Contract Value	Move if Rates Up	Average Move
4.00%	132.70	$132,703	$9,319	
5.00%	123.38	$123,384	$8,506	$8,913
6.00%	114.88	$114,877	$7,771	$8,139
7.00%	107.11	$107,106	$7,106	$7,439
8.00%	100.00	$100,000	$6,504	$6,805
9.00%	93.50	$93,496	$5,958	$6,231
10.00%	87.54	$87,538	$5,463	$5,711
11.00%	82.07	$82,074	$5,014	$5,239
12.00%	77.06	$77,060	$4,606	$4,810
13.00%	72.45	$72,454	$4,236	$4,421
14.00%	68.22	$68,218	$3,899	$4,067
15.00%	64.32	$64,319	$3,592	$3,745
16.00%	60.73	$60,727	$3,312	$3,452
17.00%	57.41	$57,415	$3,058	$3,185
18.00%	54.36	$54,357	$2,825	$2,942
19.00%	51.53	$51,532	$2,613	$2,719
20.00%	48.92	$48,919		

91-Day Eurodollar Futures Contract and 91-Day Treasury Bill Futures Contract

Interest Rate	Futures Price	Contract Value	Move if Rates Up	Average Move
4.00%	96.00	$990,000	$2,500	
5.00%	95.00	$987,500	$2,500	$2,500
6.00%	94.00	$985,000	$2,500	$2,500
7.00%	93.00	$982,500	$2,500	$2,500
8.00%	92.00	$980,000	$2,500	$2,500
9.00%	91.00	$977,500	$2,500	$2,500
10.00%	90.00	$975,000	$2,500	$2,500
11.00%	89.00	$972,500	$2,500	$2,500
12.00%	88.00	$970,000	$2,500	$2,500
13.00%	87.00	$967,500	$2,500	$2,500
14.00%	86.00	$965,000	$2,500	$2,500
15.00%	85.00	$962,500	$2,500	$2,500
16.00%	84.00	$960,000	$2,500	$2,500
17.00%	83.00	$957,500	$2,500	$2,500
18.00%	82.00	$955,000	$2,500	$2,500
19.00%	81.00	$952,500	$2,500	$2,500
20.00%	80.00	$950,000		

on 20-year Treasury bond futures contracts and options on Eurodollar futures. For example, on June 30, 1994, for $1,500 (1 and $32/64\%$, according to *The Wall Street Journal*) one could purchase a call option on the September 1994 Treasury bond futures contract with an exercise price of 102% par, *i.e.*, $102,000. (The standard quantity for the option is the same par amount as the T-bond futures contract, $100,000.) At the time, the September futures contract was selling for 101.22. Although this is an option to buy the September 1994 futures contract, the option expires in the middle of the month prior to the futures expiration—in this case on August 20, 1994.

Consider the possible values of that option on the last moment before it expires on August 20, 1994. If the September futures price is 100 at that time, the option to buy at 102 is worthless—you would rather buy in the market for 100 than exercise your option and buy at 102. However, if the September futures contract is at 105, the option to buy at 102 is worth 3 points, or $3,000 (3% × $100,000). Better yet, if the September futures contract is at 115 on August 20, 1994, the option to buy at 102 is worth 13 points, or $13,000. Thus, the worst that the buyer of a call can do is to let the option expire worthless, losing the $1,500 paid for the option. Yet the potential gains are essentially unlimited, depending only on how high the underlying asset's price might go.

One reason that this option is so cheap is that if the September futures contract stays at 101.22, then this option to buy at 102 becomes worthless. Thus, the September futures must move up 0.78 points before the option is worth anything at expiration. An option like this is said to be *out-of-the-money*, in that the underlying asset's price must move favorably for it to be worth anything. An option to buy the September futures at an exercise price of 100 is *in-the-money*, in that it is worth 1.22 points ($1,220) if exercised immediately. However, the market price of this 100 option is 2 and $36/64\%$ ($2,563), so traders were paying an extra 1 and $22/64\%$ for the prospect of a large increase in bond prices between June 30 and August 20.

A *put option* is an option (your choice) to sell a fixed quantity of a certain underlying asset at a fixed exercise price any time prior to the expiration date of the option. For example, on June 30, 1994, for $1,344 (1 + $22/64\%$), one could purchase a put option on September 1994 Treasury bond futures, with an exercise price of 100% par, *i.e.*, $100,000. Other than being an option to sell, rather than to buy, the terms are identical to the corresponding call option. If one can sell for a higher price without the option, then the option is useless. Thus, at expiration (August 20, 1994), the put's value will be zero if the September T-bond futures is greater than 100. If the September futures is less than 100, then one should exercise the option to sell at 100, prior to its expiration.

Letting F be the futures price at expiration and letting X be the exercise price on the option, call and put payoffs may be described mathematically by:

Call Payoff at Expiration = maximum $[0, F - X]$
Put Payoff at Expiration = maximum $[0, X - F]$

Exhibit 7 presents in tabular form the payoffs on August 20, 1994, from (1) a long position in September futures, (2) a short position in September futures, (3) a call option on September futures with an exercise price of 102, and (4) a put option on September futures with an exercise price of 100. Entry prices for September futures positions are 101.22% par ($101,220), the call costs $1,500, and the put costs $1,344. Exhibit 7 shows several things. First, market prices are such that there is no free lunch: all of these investments have their good and bad points. Secondly, both long and short futures positions have very symmetric payoffs, while options have very asymmetric payoffs. Both call and put options have the potential for very large gains, while their losses are limited. However, if market prices do not move much, both the call and the put expire worthless, resulting in a net total loss of the price paid (while futures lose nothing). Finally, it bears emphasizing that there is no option aspect in a futures contract, in that losses are *not* limited in any useful way. Futures and options payoffs are very different.

Interest-Rate Swaps

Consider a typical bank that receives short-term deposits (that roll over at market rates) and lends the funds to a corporation at a rate that is fixed for five years. The bank gets hurt if interest rates rise, and it has a negative gross spread if the cost of the deposits exceeds its lending rate. On the other hand,

Exhibit 7. Options and Futures Payoffs (% Par)

September 1994 Futures Price on Aug. 20, 1994		Profit on Long Future	Profit on Short Future	Profit on Call Option X = 102		Profit on Put Option X = 100	
% Par	Ct. Value			Gross	Net	Gross	Net
85%	$85,000	($16,219)	$16,219	$0	($1,500)	$15,000	$13,656
90%	$90,000	($11,219)	$11,219	$0	($1,500)	$10,000	$8,656
95%	$95,000	($6,219)	$6,219	$0	($1,500)	$5,000	$3,656
100%	$100,000	($1,219)	$1,219	$0	($1,500)	$0	($1,344)
105%	$105,000	$3,781	($3,781)	$3,000	$1,500	$0	($1,344)
110%	$110,000	$8,781	($8,781)	$8,000	$6,500	$0	($1,344)
115%	$115,000	$13,781	($13,781)	$13,000	$11,500	$0	($1,344)

if rates fall, the bank's profit margin widens, assuming that the borrower cannot easily or cheaply prepay the loan. A typical interest-rate swap is used by a financial institution or corporation to protect against such fluctuations in profitability due to interest rate movements.

With a typical interest-rate swap, the bank pays another institution (the "counterparty") interest at a fixed rate semiannually on a stated principal balance (the "notional principal") throughout the term of the swap. In exchange, the counterparty pays the bank semiannually (simultaneously) interest on the same notional principal, but at a floating rate. The floating rate might be based on three-month or six-month LIBOR, Treasury bill rates, the prime rate, or commercial paper rates. Of course, the floating-rate index specified affects the fixed rate that the bank has to pay. For example, since LIBOR exceeds Treasury bill rates, one has to pay a higher fixed rate to receive LIBOR rather than a T-bill rate.

The fixed rate paid is usually quoted as the current Treasury rate for a maturity equal to the term of the swap, plus a swap spread that varies with the short-term rate chosen. For example, on a 5-year LIBOR swap on June 30, 1994, the fixed rate paid was set at approximately 30 basis points over the 5-year Treasury rate of 6.95% (Exhibit 1), for a total of 7.25%. In exchange, the fixed-rate payer received 6-month LIBOR, adjusted semiannually (9 times) during the 5-year period. The initial six-month LIBOR of 5.25% is fixed for the floating rate payer's first 6 months of the swap.

The hedging aspects of an interest-rate swap are fairly easy to see. If rates jump up dramatically, the bank's cost of funds will jump, but will probably be approximately covered by increased interest received on the swap. On the other hand, if rates fall dramatically, the bank's cost of funds should fall similarly, but its swap income will also fall. The hedge may well be imperfect: the bank's cost of funds may not move perfectly with LIBOR. For example, there may be lags in cost of funds changes. Still, over periods of a year or more, most of those adjustments are fully made, and the swap should reduce risk well, particularly with very large rate moves. Exhibits 8 and 9 show how this five-year swap can be used to effectively turn long-term loans into short-term loans or, alternatively, turn short-term funding into long-term funding.

Consider the potential capital gains and losses on the swap after it has been initiated, but prior to its maturity. One pays a fixed rate for a fixed term, much like issuing (or shorting) a fixed-rate bond. One receives a fixed rate for the first 6 months, then the rate floats with market rates. Thus, the capital gains and losses on the swap are much like those of a short 5-year bond position plus a long 6-month fixed-rate CD. Just like a short Treasury bond futures position, the swap wins when rates increase more than expected and loses when rates fall more than expected. Thus, interest-rate swaps are viewed in this chapter as alternatives to short futures hedge positions, with much of the

---

Exhibit 8. Interest-Rate Swaps Turn Long-Term Loans into Short-Term Loans

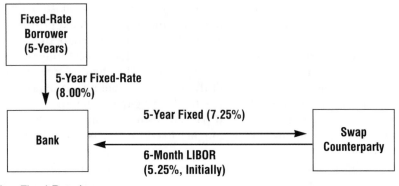

5-Year Fixed-Rate Loan +
5-Year Pay-Fixed/Receive-Floating Swap =
5-Year Floating-Rate Loan

In the first semi-annual period, the bank receives 8.00% - 7.25% + 5.25% = 6.00%

In the subsequent periods, the bank receives 6-month LIBOR + 8.00% - 7.25% = 6-month LIBOR + 0.75%.

Thus, the net position is a floating-rate loan at 6-month LIBOR + 0.75%

---

interest-rate risk analysis being virtually identical for the two. Credit risks, transaction costs, market liquidity, accounting treatment, and relative pricing usually determine whether an institution hedges more with swaps or futures at any point in time.

Aside from being an excellent risk reduction tool, interest-rate swaps also allow an institution to borrow and lend at maturities where it has a comparative advantage, thereby maximizing economic profits. Exhibit 10 uses a simple example to illustrate this concept.

Suppose a bank manager wishing to take a minimal amount of interest-rate risk has a choice of only 6-month loans, 3-year loans, 6-month borrowings, and 3-year borrowings. Note from Exhibit 10 that by funding each potential loan with borrowings with identical maturities (matched funding), the manager can earn a 25 basis point spread and is indifferent between the 6-month and the 3-year pairs of assets and liabilities.

The bank, however, has a comparative advantage in long-term lending and short-term borrowing. For example, 6-month liabilities are obtainable at

Exhibit 9.   Interest Rate Swaps Turn Short-Term Funding into Long-Term Funding

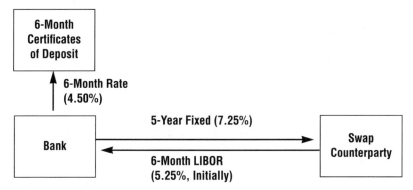

For the first 6 months, the bank pays 4.50% − 5.25% + 7.25% = 6.50%.

In subsequent periods, the bank pays CD rate − 6-month LIBOR + 7.25%.

If the spread between 6-month LIBOR and the 6-month CD rate stays the same, the bank pays 6.50% for five years.

If LIBOR rises relative to the CD rate, then the net cost will be less than 6.50%, and vice versa.

25 basis points under 6-month LIBOR, while 3-year liabilities cost an amount (6.78%) equal to the fixed interest rate on a 3-year swap (6.48% plus the swap spread of 0.30%), roughly equivalent to a 3-year LIBOR rate. The bank, therefore, can fund more cheaply to the LIBOR curve with its short-term borrowings.

On the asset side of the balance sheet, the bank can lend 3-year money at an effective rate of LIBOR plus 25 basis points (7.03% vs. 6.78%) but can only earn LIBOR on its 6-month loans. The bank's comparative advantage in long-term loans is demonstrated by this 25 basis point spread to LIBOR.

Exhibit 10 shows how by entering into an interest-rate swap in which it pays a fixed rate for 3 years and receives 6-month LIBOR, coupled with making 3-year loans and funding these loans with 6-month borrowings, the bank can earn a 50 basis point spread with minimal interest-rate risk. The interest rate swap has not only corrected the maturity mismatch of the bank's assets and liabilities, it has also allowed the bank to borrow and invest at maturities where it has comparative advantages, thus enabling the bank to be a more profitable and effective financial intermediary.

Exhibit 10.

Bank manager is faced with the following choices of assets and liabilities:

| | Asset | Liability | |
Maturity	Yield	Yield	Spread
6 months	5.25%	5.00%	0.25%
3 years	7.03%	6.78%	0.25%

Assume manager can:

Roll 6-month asset at 6-month LIBOR for at least 3 years.
Roll 6-month liability at 6-month LIBOR minus 25 basis points for at least 3 years.

Market Interest Rates:

| | Treasury | | Interest Rate |
Maturity	Yield	LIBOR	Swap Spread
6 months	4.80%	5.25%	
1 year	5.49%	5.75%	
2 years	6.16%		0.25%
3 years	6.48%		0.30%

Which assets and liabilities should the manager choose?

If the manager chooses any pair of matched assets and liabilities, he will earn a spread of 25 basis points.

However, if he chooses the 3-year asset, the 6-month liability, and an interest rate swap (pay fixed for 3 years, receive 6-month LIBOR), he receives a wider spread:

Fix Payments		**Floating Payments**	
Asset Yield:	7.03%	Liability Cost:	LIBOR - 0.25%
Swap Payment:	-6.78%	Swap Payment:	LIBOR
Fixed Net:	0.25%	Floating Net:	0.25%

Net Spread	
Fixed Net:	0.25%
Floating Net:	0.25%
	0.50%

Swap (risk management) allowed the manager to borrow and invest at maturities where he had a comparative advantage (widest asset and tightest liability spread to the LIBOR curve) and could earn a higher net spread.

NOTE: All rates shown have been converted to bond-equivalent, semi-annual compounded rates.

Interest-Rate Caps and Floors

Interest-rate caps and floors are series of options on short-term interest rates where each successive option's time to maturity (known as the reset date) is greater by a fixed-length time interval (usually three months). The options in a specific cap or floor usually have identical strike rates. Caps and floors are traded for a large number of short-term interest rates, a similar set of interest rates for which interest rate swaps are available. Most often, however, caps and floors are based on 1-, 3-, or 6-month LIBOR. The contract usually contains a specific notional amount (as does an interest-rate swap) or (less often) a notional amount which varies with time.

Caps and floors protect the buyer from adverse movements in the underlying interest rate. Since a cap is a series of put options on a short-term interest rate, an increase in rates (with corresponding price decreases) makes the puts more valuable. Thus, caps protect the owner against rising rates and floors, which are series of call options, benefit the owner when interest rates fall (and prices rise).

As with most options, the purchaser of a cap or floor usually pays the price (premium) for the contract at the time of purchase. In return for the premium the cap writer is obligated to pay the holder of the cap an amount equal to the greater of zero or the short-term spot rate in the market minus the strike rate on the cap times the notional amount of the cap at each reset date (maturity of each successive option in the cap). Similarly, the writer of a floor must pay its holder an amount equal to the greater of zero and the difference between the strike rate and the short-term spot rate on the floor's notional principal amount at each reset date.

Exhibit 11 displays how the payments work for a cap and a floor. For both contracts the strike rate is assumed to be 6% and the index rate is 3-month LIBOR. The cap and floor have a stated term of 3 years and thus contain 11 options, the first expiring in 3 months, the last in 33 months. Payments are made in *arrears*, meaning that a payment will be made 3 months following each reset date, bringing the last payment date to 36 months from inception of the contract. Most caps and floors are designed to pay in arrears. The purchaser of a cap or a floor must be careful to check on the characteristics of the option before purchase, since a lack of contract standardization exists.

Caps and floors are not traded on an exchange. On the contrary, the market for these options is an over-the-counter (OTC) market. The cap or floor holder is exposed to the credit risk of the option writer to the extent that he is owed payments on the option or in the event that he wishes to sell the option. Thus, as with interest-rate swaps, counterparty credit risk is an important consideration when one is looking to purchase a cap or a floor.

Exhibit 11.   Cap and Floor Cash Flows

Assumptions:
Short-term Index Rate: 3-month LIBOR
Strike Rate: 6.0%
Notional Principal: $10 million
Term: 3 Years
Frequency of Reset: 3 Months
Cap Price: 2.98% * Notional Amount
Floor Price: 0.95% * Notional Amount
Payments: in arrears

CAP CASH FLOWS
Cap Premium ($298,000) at Purchase

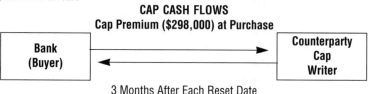

3 Months After Each Reset Date

Maximum of zero and 3 months' interest on $10 million at rate of 3-month LIBOR at reset date minus 6%. If 3-month LIBOR at reset is less than 6%, payment is zero. If LIBOR is, say, 10%, payment is equal to 3 months' interest on $10 million at a rate of 4% (10%–6%) or approximately $100,000.

CAP CASH FLOWS
Floor Premium ($95,000) at Purchase

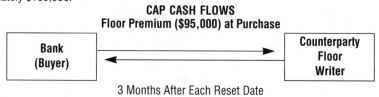

3 Months After Each Reset Date

Maximum of zero and 3 months' interest on $10 million at rate of 6% minus 3-month LIBOR at the reset date. If 3-month LIBOR at reset is greater than 6%, payment is zero. If LIBOR is, say 4%, payment is equal to 3 months' interest on $10 million at a rate of 2% (6%–4%) or approximately $50,000.

Cap and floor prices (premiums) are quoted as a percentage of the contract's notional amount. Exhibit 12 displays quoted prices for (the purchase of) caps and floors on June 30, 1994. For example, a three-year, 6% cap with a notional principal amount of $10 million would cost $298,000 (2.98% of $10 million). Notice that cap and floor prices display the characteristics one would expect of options. For both caps and floors, prices increase as the time to maturity increases, holding the strike rate constant. For caps, which are puts, increasing the strike rate makes the security less valuable. For floors, which contain a series of calls, increasing the strike rate makes the security more valuable.

Exhibit 12.   Cap and Floor Prices June 30, 1994

A. 3-Month LIBOR Caps

Strike Rate

Maturity	5.00%	6.00%	7.00%	8.00%	9.00%
1 year	0.79	0.34	0.16	0.07	—
2 years	2.63	1.47	0.79	0.40	0.21
3 years	4.79	2.98	1.79	1.07	0.62
4 years	7.07	4.65	2.98	1.89	1.18
5 years	9.38	6.39	4.28	2.83	1.86
7 years	13.67	9.69	6.80	4.75	3.30
10 years	19.13	14.15	10.34	7.55	5.47

B. 3-Month LIBOR Floors

Strike Rate

Maturity	5.00%	6.00%	7.00%	8.00%	9.00%
1 year	0.04	0.31	0.84	1.50	2.22
2 years	0.14	0.63	1.59	2.86	4.30
3 years	0.24	0.95	2.27	4.03	6.09
4 years	0.35	1.26	2.89	5.09	7.68
5 years	0.48	1.57	3.49	6.07	9.14
7 years	0.76	2.19	4.63	7.89	11.78
10 years	3.09	3.09	6.19	10.30	15.19

NOTE: Prices are expressed as a percentage of an option's underlying notional amount.
3-month LIBOR on 6/30/94 was 4.875%.

Compared to short-term, exchange-traded options, caps and floors have several major advantages, but also possess some major disadvantages. Exchange-traded options on futures are much more liquid than caps and floors and are thus more apt to be used the more frequently one anticipates trading these options. In addition, the safety of the exchange provides comfort to the purchaser of options in contrast to the buyer of a cap or floor who is subject to the credit risk of his counterparty for the remaining life (or holding period) of the option.

In spite of these disadvantages, caps and floors have become widely used hedges by financial institutions. The popularity of caps and floors largely stems from the fact that these contracts are a source of long-term options and that the underlying LIBOR index is more highly correlated with the interest rates on financial institutions' assets and liabilities than Treasury rates. Since the options embedded in mortgages and other assets and liabilities of financial institutions are long-term in nature, a better hedge may often be obtained using caps and floors than by using short-term, exchange-traded options on futures. These advantages and the growing liquidity of the cap and floor market have made these options contracts a valuable and widely used risk management tool for financial institutions.

PRICE ELASTICITY, DURATION, AND CONVEXITY

To understand gains and losses on bonds that occur as interest rates move, it is important to understand the duration or *price elasticity* of an asset or liability. Quite simply, the price elasticity of an asset or liability is the percentage change in its market value that occurs for a 1% or 100 basis points move in interest rates. Thus, if a 10-year bond has a price elasticity of (minus) 6%, then its price will move up by about 6% if rates move down 100 basis points, and its price moves down by about 6% if rates increase 100 basis points. Obviously, a bond with a price elasticity of 6% is more sensitive to interest rates than a bond with an elasticity of 1%.

The sensitivity of the market value of a *firm* to interest rates is dependent upon the price elasticities of its assets and liabilities. Consider a simple example of a brand-new bank that has $5 million in net worth, $95 million of money market deposit accounts (MMDAs) that reprice daily, and $100 million of 10-year fixed-rate bonds. Since the liabilities reprice daily, their rates are always fair rates and their market values are always equal to their book or par amounts. Thus, the liabilities have a price elasticity of zero. Exhibit 13 gives the market values of this firm's assets and liabilities for the current case and for scenarios 1% lower rates and 1% higher rates. (Keep in mind that these are small moves relative to what has happened to market interest rates during the last decade.)

From Exhibit 13, one can see that a new and very solid firm with a true 5% capital/assets ratio goes to a $-1 million true net value of its assets and liabilities with only a 1% move up in rates. Just that 1% rate move is sufficient to make the firm unable to pay off its depositors if it had to liquidate its assets. To prevent this possible failure, the firm might wish to hedge its interest-rate risk with interest-rate futures, swaps or options.

Exhibit 13. Example of Price Elasticity and Market Value Risk

	Par Amount	Price Elasticity	Market Value if: Rates Down 1%	Rates Up 1%
Assets:				
10-year fixed rate bonds	$100 mln	.06	$106 mln	$94 mln
Liabilities:				
Money market deposit accounts	$95 mln	.00	$95 mln	$95 mln
Net Worth (market)	$5 mln		$11 mln	$-1 mln

This firm wins or loses (net) $6 million dollars for every 1% rate move. If one has to choose a single, simple measure that indicates the net interest rate risk of the firm, this *value sensitivity to a 1% rate move* should be it. To compute the value sensitivity of the firm, one has to estimate the price elasticities of each of the firm's assets and liabilities, and then a computation similar to the one shown in Exhibit 13 can be made. Subsequent sections of this chapter will examine these types of risk in much more detail.

Duration, expressed in years, simply measures the weighted average time until cash flow payment for the financial instrument. *Modified duration* equals duration divided by one plus the interest rate. The reason that the duration computation is useful for interest-rate risk management is that it can be shown mathematically and in practice that, for standard-fixed rate bonds (not mortgages), modified duration is equal to price elasticity, which is the best measure of interest-rate risk.

Exhibit 14 gives an example of how to calculate duration for two bonds— a 10-year and a 5-year bond, both with 7% coupons and par of $100. The current fair interest rate is assumed to be 7%. Note that the bond with the longer time to maturity has the larger duration and price elasticity, but not proportionally so. As can be seen, modified duration predicts the price elasticity very well for both bonds. The 5-year bond has a modified duration of 4.10 years and the price elasticity (expressed as the average percentage price change for a 100 basis point increase and decrease in interest rates) is 4.10%. The 10-year bond's modified duration is 7.02 years, and the price elasticity is 7.04%.

Duration was derived by Macaulay long ago as an approximation to price elasticity, using an assumption that the cash flows of the investment are fixed and independent of interest rates. Unfortunately for this derivation, with fixed-rate mortgages the entire principal can typically be prepaid at any time, thereby changing the cash flows for the remaining 20 to 30 years of the mortgage. Thus, duration approximations to price sensitivity just do not work well for mortgages. The following actual data illustrate this point.

Exhibit 15 gives cash prices for GNMA insured fixed-rate mortgages for each month-end during the 1984–94 period for mortgage coupons from 6% to 15%. All of these price quotes are percents of par, so a price of 75 represents a mortgage with a rate below current rates selling at a 25% discount from par. Similarly, a price of 108 indicates a mortgage with a higher coupon than currently issued mortgages that is selling for an 8% premium. Typically, the higher the mortgage coupon, the more valuable the mortgage, since the mortgage payments are higher for higher coupons. The prices in Exhibit 15 reveal that mortgages increased in price from 1984 to 1986, and from 1991 to 1993 as interest rates declined substantially. However, as interest rates increased during 1987, mortgage prices generally fell, at least for lower coupon

Exhibit 14. Duration, Modified Duration and Price Elasticity

Example: Rates start at 7% with bonds priced at par. Rates change to either 6% or 8%. At 6% the 10-year is worth $107.36 and the 5-year price is $104.21. At 8% the price of the 10-year is $93.29 and the 5-year bond's price is $96.01.

Definitions:

Duration	=	Weighted average of years when cash flows received using PV fractions as weights.
Modified Duration	=	Duration divided by 1 + R, where R is the current annual market interest rate.
Price Elasticity	=	Percentage change in price expressed per 1% (100 bp) rate change.

10-Year Bond

Year	Discount Factor At: 6%	7%	8%	Cash Flow	Present Value at: 6%	7%	8%	PV/Total @7%	PV/Total x Years
1	0.943	0.935	0.926	7	$6.60	$6.54	$6.48	0.07	0.07
2	0.890	0.873	0.857	7	6.23	6.11	6.00	0.06	0.12
3	0.840	0.816	0.794	7	5.88	5.71	5.56	0.06	0.17
4	0.792	0.763	0.735	7	5.54	5.34	5.15	0.05	0.21
5	0.747	0.713	0.681	7	5.23	4.99	4.76	0.05	0.25
6	0.705	0.666	0.630	7	4.93	4.66	4.41	0.05	0.28
7	0.665	0.623	0.583	7	4.66	4.36	4.08	0.04	0.31
8	0.627	0.582	0.540	7	4.39	4.07	3.78	0.04	0.33
9	0.592	0.544	0.500	7	4.14	3.81	3.50	0.04	0.34
10	0.558	0.508	0.463	107	59.75	54.39	49.56	0.54	5.44
					$107.36	$100.00	$93.29	1.00	7.52

Duration	=		7.52 Years
Modified Duration	=	7.52/1.07 =	7.02 Years
Price Elasticity	=	.5*[(107.36-100.0)+(100.0-93.29)]/100.0 =	7.04%

5-Year Bond

Cash Flow	Present Value at: 6%	7%	8%	PV/Total @7%	PV/Total x Years
7	$6.60	$6.54	$6.48	0.07	0.07
7	6.23	6.11	6.00	0.06	0.12
7	5.88	5.71	5.56	0.06	0.17
7	5.54	5.34	5.15	0.05	0.21
107	79.96	76.29	72.82	0.76	3.81
	$104.21	$100.00	$96.01	1.00	4.39

Duration	=		4.39 Years
Modified Duration	=	4.39/1.07 =	4.10 Years
Price Elasticity	=	.5*[(104.21-100.0)+(100.0-96.01)]/100.0 =	4.10%

NOTES: For very small rate movements Price Elasticity converges to Modified Duration. This relationship can be proven by taking the derivative of the bond price with respect to the bond's yield and expressing the result as a percentage (in absolute value) of the bond's price.

For regular bonds, duration and price elasticity increase as rates fall and decrease as rates rise. For mortgages, the opposite is true, as mortgage pre-payments increase when rates fall, thereby shortening durations. As discussed in the text, the above duration calculation should not be used for mort-

Exhibit 15. GNMA Cash Mortgage Prices

End of Month	Futures Prices (Near Contract)		Mortgage Coupon Rate										Approx. Par Mortgage	Bond Futures Yield
	T-Bond	Euro	6.0	7.0	8.0	9.0	10.0	11.0	12.0	13.0	14.0	15.0		
Jan 84	70.81	89.96	NA	NA	76.88	81.38	86.78	92.44	NA	102.63	106.50	108.75	12.50	11.84%
Feb 84	68.84	89.71	NA	NA	75.00	79.63	85.31	90.88	NA	102.63	106.06	108.13	12.75	12.19%
Mar 84	66.22	88.72	NA	NA	72.75	77.25	82.63	88.50	NA	99.13	106.13	107.63	13.25	12.69%
Apr 84	64.69	88.54	NA	NA	71.25	75.94	81.19	86.94	NA	97.94	102.50	105.38	13.50	12.99%
May 84	60.16	88.03	NA	NA	66.38	70.38	75.38	81.38	NA	92.19	97.38	101.38	14.50	13.97%
Jun 84	59.63	86.87	NA	NA	66.63	70.63	75.63	81.13	NA	92.31	98.06	101.75	14.50	14.09%
Jul 84	64.50	87.97	NA	NA	71.00	75.00	80.00	85.13	NA	96.00	101.47	104.41	13.75	13.03%
Aug 84	65.81	88.08	NA	NA	70.63	74.63	80.13	85.63	NA	96.38	101.50	104.44	13.75	12.77%
Sep 84	67.22	88.44	NA	NA	72.00	76.38	81.50	87.38	NA	98.00	102.13	105.50	13.50	12.49%
Oct 84	70.78	89.68	NA	NA	75.25	79.75	85.13	90.75	NA	100.25	104.00	106.50	13.00	11.85%
Nov 84	71.63	90.54	NA	NA	76.45	81.63	87.38	93.13	NA	101.63	104.88	107.88	12.50	11.70%
Dec 84	71.06	90.48	NA	NA	76.88	81.63	86.88	92.88	97.75	102.00	106.00	108.81	12.50	11.80%
Jan 85	73.19	91.07	NA	NA	78.25	82.88	88.38	94.38	98.75	102.88	106.63	109.13	12.25	11.44%
Feb 85	68.88	90.31	NA	NA	74.88	79.38	84.38	90.13	95.06	100.19	104.50	108.31	13.00	12.19%
Mar 85	69.72	90.23	NA	NA	76.44	80.69	85.94	91.56	96.53	101.53	106.53	109.13	12.50	12.03%
Apr 85	70.75	91.05	NA	NA	77.44	81.75	86.88	92.63	97.44	102.44	106.63	109.13	12.50	11.85%
May 85	77.34	92.24	NA	NA	83.06	87.63	93.00	98.00	101.88	105.50	108.75	110.69	11.50	10.78%
Jun 85	77.06	92.07	NA	NA	83.56	88.31	94.06	99.13	102.75	106.13	108.50	111.88	11.25	10.83%
Jul 85	75.19	91.64	NA	NA	82.19	86.63	92.00	97.00	101.69	105.75	109.13	112.25	11.50	11.12%
Aug 85	77.13	91.86	NA	NA	83.19	87.81	93.00	98.19	102.50	106.50	109.50	112.81	11.50	10.82%
Sep 85	75.59	91.77	NA	NA	83.63	88.06	93.19	97.88	102.56	106.56	109.50	111.50	11.50	11.08%
Oct 85	78.53	92.05	NA	NA	85.63	90.13	95.19	99.63	104.00	107.84	110.00	111.63	11.00	10.61%
Nov 85	81.66	91.97	NA	NA	87.78	92.31	97.38	101.94	106.19	108.56	110.31	112.00	10.50	10.16%
Dec 85	85.22	92.25	NA	NA	91.31	96.25	101.38	104.81	107.13	108.19	109.44	112.13	9.75	9.69%
Jan 86	85.16	92.12	NA	NA	90.25	95.00	100.28	104.19	106.84	108.56	110.25	113.13	10.00	9.64%

Exhibit 15. *Continued*

End of Month	Futures Prices (Near Contract)		Mortgage Coupon Rate										Approx. Par Mortgage	Bond Futures Yield
	T-Bond	Euro	6.0	7.0	8.0	9.0	10.0	11.0	12.0	13.0	14.0	15.0		
Feb 86	94.81	92.24	NA	NA	95.00	99.13	103.25	105.88	107.09	108.16	109.78	112.63	9.25	8.55%
Mar 86	102.31	93.03	NA	NA	95.81	100.19	104.38	106.75	107.88	108.19	110.25	114.00	9.00	7.77%
Apr 86	100.75	93.25	NA	NA	95.88	100.00	104.38	107.31	107.31	107.44	109.75	114.25	9.00	7.92%
May 86	93.88	92.93	NA	NA	91.25	95.44	101.38	104.94	105.63	106.50	109.38	114.38	9.75	8.65%
Jun 86	99.56	93.45	NA	NA	93.69	97.13	102.19	105.38	105.75	106.44	107.06	114.31	9.50	8.04%
Jul 86	97.81	93.57	NA	NA	95.25	97.88	103.44	106.44	106.94	107.44	110.00	112.00	9.25	8.22%
Aug 86	102.41	94.29	NA	NA	97.25	100.38	104.88	106.84	107.38	107.50	109.75	113.00	9.00	7.76%
Sep 86	96.56	94.01	NA	NA	95.38	98.63	104.25	107.13	107.81	108.38	109.06	113.88	9.25	8.36%
Oct86	98.09	94.11	NA	NA	96.38	99.69	105.13	107.50	107.75	108.75	109.72	114.00	9.00	8.20%
Nov 86	99.72	93.97	NA	NA	98.56	102.06	106.88	107.59	107.69	108.53	109.66	114.00	8.50	8.03%
Dec 86	98.19	93.89	NA	NA	98.13	101.56	106.38	107.69	108.09	109.00	109.66	114.00	8.50	8.19%
Jan 87	99.69	93.69	NA	NA	99.13	102.88	106.94	107.69	108.13	109.31	110.56	114.00	8.25	8.03%
Feb 87	101.44	93.58	NA	NA	99.00	103.38	107.56	107.94	108.50	109.50	111.00	114.00	8.25	7.86%
Mar 87	98.47	93.35	NA	NA	97.19	102.09	106.63	107.81	108.94	110.00	112.25	115.00	8.50	8.16%
Apr 87	93.06	92.61	NA	NA	92.88	97.38	102.00	105.38	107.38	109.50	112.00	114.00	9.50	8.74%
May 87	92.06	92.74	NA	NA	92.06	96.00	100.38	104.44	107.44	109.75	112.00	114.00	10.00	8.85%
Jun 87	91.50	92.58	NA	NA	93.06	96.75	101.50	105.94	108.75	110.88	113.13	115.00	9.75	8.92%
Jul 87	89.50	92.71	NA	NA	92.31	96.81	101.88	106.00	108.69	110.50	112.88	114.88	10.00	9.15%
Aug 87	87.50	92.71	NA	NA	90.88	95.19	100.03	105.13	108.56	110.75	112.56	114.75	10.00	9.40%
Sep 87	81.69	91.40	NA	NA	88.63	92.53	96.75	101.69	106.63	110.00	112.50	114.50	10.75	10.16%
Oct 87	87.56	92.42	NA	NA	90.41	94.72	99.19	103.31	106.94	109.56	111.94	114.56	10.25	9.39%
Nov 87	87.66	92.32	NA	NA	90.97	95.22	99.56	104.75	108.22	109.78	111.84	114.53	10.25	9.38%
Dec 87	87.97	92.44	NA	NA	91.44	95.56	100.06	104.38	107.81	109.75	111.75	114.31	10.00	9.34%
Jan 88	93.91	92.96	NA	NA	95.00	99.13	102.81	107.13	109.66	111.63	113.25	115.13	9.50	8.65%
Feb 88	94.66	93.13	NA	NA	95.13	99.38	103.44	107.31	109.69	111.94	113.50	115.25	9.50	8.56%

Exhibit 15. *Continued*

End of Month	Futures Prices (Near Contract)		Mortgage Coupon Rate										Approx. Par Mortgage	Bond Futures Yield
	T-Bond	Euro	6.0	7.0	8.0	9.0	10.0	11.0	12.0	13.0	14.0	15.0		
Mar 88	90.09	92.72	NA	NA	92.50	97.00	101.5	106.44	109.31	112.38	113.13	115.13	9.75	9.09%
Apr 88	87.91	92.41	NA	NA	91.81	96.38	100.69	105.28	108.84	111.31	113.31	113.31	10.00	9.35%
May 88	85.81	92.23	NA	NA	90.00	94.00	99.50	104.25	108.75	111.25	113.34	112.53	10.25	9.61%
Jun 88	88.75	92.04	NA	NA	92.59	96.84	101.09	106.06	109.59	112.09	113.72	114.06	9.75	9.24%
Jul 88	86.19	91.52	NA	NA	91.22	95.13	100.25	105.00	108.59	111.56	113.28	113.47	10.00	9.62%
Aug 88	86.06	91.33	NA	NA	90.66	94.44	99.75	104.03	107.75	110.69	113.22	113.16	10.25	9.58%
Sep 88	88.75	91.22	NA	NA	92.59	96.44	101.34	105.13	108.56	110.31	113.25	113.06	9.75	9.24%
Oct 88	91.41	91.41	NA	NA	94.72	98.28	102.81	105.81	109.22	110.81	113.28	112.66	9.50	8.93%
Nov 88	88.47	90.82	NA	NA	91.88	95.56	100.69	104.00	108.16	110.25	112.56	111.94	10.00	9.28%
Dec 88	89.13	90.62	NA	NA	91.13	94.44	99.38	102.88	107.03	109.28	111.81	111.19	10.25	9.20%
Jan 89	90.81	90.46	NA	NA	92.00	95.38	100.13	103.13	107.41	109.53	111.66	112.47	10.00	9.00%
Feb 89	88.09	89.73	NA	NA	90.38	93.88	98.56	101.94	106.53	108.97	111.28	112.09	10.50	9.32%
Mar 89	88.41	89.29	NA	NA	89.50	93.81	97.88	101.41	105.84	109.06	111.28	112.09	10.50	9.29%
Apr 89	90.19	90.15	NA	NA	90.19	94.63	98.75	102.03	107.28	110.72	113.47	113.47	10.50	9.07%
May 89	93.06	90.54	NA	NA	92.56	96.81	100.78	103.22	108.09	111.13	113.41	113.41	10.00	8.74%
Jun 89	97.94	91.47	NA	NA	94.81	98.44	102.38	104.53	109.00	111.59	113.66	113.66	9.50	8.21%
Jul 89	99.75	91.79	NA	NA	96.72	100.31	103.38	105.22	109.94	112.94	114.34	114.34	9.00	8.03%
Aug 89	96.25	91.11	NA	NA	93.75	98.13	101.19	104.22	108.91	112.47	113.81	113.81	9.75	8.39%
Sep 89	95.84	91.05	NA	NA	93.63	97.94	102.59	103.59	108.13	111.63	113.13	113.13	9.50	8.43%
Oct 89	99.34	91.63	NA	NA	95.66	99.75	103.13	104.50	108.53	111.84	113.44	113.44	9.25	8.07%
Nov 89	99.47	91.63	NA	NA	94.69	99.88	103.13	105.69	108.63	110.69	112.75	112.75	9.25	8.05%
Dec 89	98.66	91.98	NA	NA	95.63	99.56	103.00	105.88	109.00	110.88	112.75	115.44	9.25	8.14%
Jan 90	94.25	91.65	NA	NA	93.09	97.59	101.69	104.78	108.19	109.88	111.44	113.94	9.75	8.61%
Feb 90	93.31	91.63	NA	NA	93.38	97.38	101.69	104.41	108.03	109.75	111.69	114.53	9.75	8.71%
Mar 90	91.88	91.31	NA	NA	93.00	97.06	101.25	104.13	107.50	109.38	111.28	114.09	9.75	8.88%

Exhibit 15. *Continued*

End of Month	Futures Prices (Near Contract)		Mortgage Coupon Rate										Approx. Par Mortgage	Bond Futures Yield
	T-Bond	Euro	6.0	7.0	8.0	9.0	10.0	11.0	12.0	13.0	14.0	15.0		
Apr 90	88.81	91.19	NA	NA	90.44	94.81	99.53	103.13	107.19	109.53	111.09	113.56	10.25	9.24%
May 90	92.91	91.60	NA	NA	93.44	97.50	101.91	104.50	107.91	110.50	112.34	115.09	9.75	8.76%
Jun 90	94.34	91.84	NA	NA	94.44	98.47	102.69	105.22	108.06	110.44	112.47	115.25	9.25	8.60%
Jul 90	94.69	92.11	NA	NA	95.13	99.44	103.56	106.44	109.44	111.72	113.84	116.72	9.25	8.56%
Aug 90	89.16	91.99	NA	NA	92.69	97.06	101.88	105.53	109.25	111.69	113.41	116.06	9.75	9.20%
Sep 90	89.38	91.94	NA	NA	93.50	98.03	101.94	105.44	109.13	111.47	113.13	115.75	9.50	9.17%
Oct 90	91.09	92.34	NA	NA	94.06	98.34	102.06	105.53	109.66	111.63	113.38	116.13	9.50	8.97%
Nov 90	94.91	91.78	NA	NA	95.50	100.03	103.69	106.63	110.63	112.63	115.06	118.00	9.00	8.54%
Dec 90	95.72	92.80	NA	NA	96.34	100.63	102.38	106.78	111.19	113.81	115.81	118.78	9.00	8.45%
Jan 91	96.31	92.94	NA	91.09	96.94	101.25	104.75	107.53	111.63	113.84	115.75	118.78	8.75	8.38%
Feb 91	96.16	93.13	NA	93.59	96.90	101.00	104.44	107.31	111.38	113.16	116.34	119.56	8.75	8.40%
Mar 91	95.47	93.48	NA	91.03	96.50	100.97	104.50	107.47	111.56	113.38	116.53	119.72	8.75	8.42%
Apr 91	96.41	93.92	NA	91.53	97.13	101.31	105.00	107.75	111.94	113.81	116.94	120.16	8.75	8.37%
May 91	95.75	93.91	NA	91.22	97.16	101.31	104.75	107.97	112.50	114.34	117.53	120.78	8.75	8.44%
Jun 91	92.94	93.59	NA	90.63	96.03	100.47	104.41	108.03	112.81	114.75	117.84	121.13	9.00	8.68%
Jul 91	94.84	93.86	NA	91.47	97.25	101.63	105.56	108.78	113.44	115.19	118.38	121.63	8.50	8.54%
Aug 91	98.06	94.28	NA	93.66	99.06	102.91	106.31	109.22	113.53	115.19	118.28	121.72	8.25	8.20%
Sep 91	100.00	94.35	NA	95.09	100.09	103.84	107.38	110.28	114.38	115.97	119.19	122.69	8.00	8.00%
Oct 91	99.81	94.75	NA	96.13	101.06	104.69	108.13	110.88	114.53	116.34	119.63	123.13	7.75	8.02%
Nov 91	99.75	95.05	NA	94.75	101.44	105.00	108.00	111.66	114.94	116.38	119.53	123.03	7.75	8.03%
Dec 91	104.75	95.96	NA	97.72	103.69	106.56	108.63	111.91	116.13	119.75	122.66	126.25	7.50	7.54%
Jan 92	101.03	95.82	NA	95.38	99.69	104.90	107.44	111.38	115.13	117.13	119.13	121.13	8.00	7.90%
Feb 92	101.41	95.79	NA	94.16	100.13	104.88	107.81	111.25	115.25	118.41	121.25	124.81	8.00	7.86%
Mar 92	98.72	95.47	NA	91.88	98.38	103.56	107.13	110.88	115.75	118.44	121.22	124.75	8.25	8.13%
Apr 92	98.13	95.85	NA	92.00	98.63	103.81	107.50	110.88	115.88	118.84	121.66	125.03	8.25	8.19%
May 92	100.81	95.98	NA	94.78	100.13	105.23	108.63	111.13	115.00	117.41	120.25	123.56	8.00	7.92%

Exhibit 15. *Continued*

End of Month	Futures Prices (Near Contract)		Mortgage Coupon Rate										Approx. Par Mortgage	Bond Futures Yield
	T-Bond	Euro	6.0	7.0	8.0	9.0	10.0	11.0	12.0	13.0	14.0	15.0		
Jun 92	100.66	96.07	NA	94.78	101.25	106.25	109.06	111.63	116.13	119.59	122.50	125.88	7.75	7.93%
Jul 92	104.84	96.48	NA	97.44	102.63	106.31	108.38	111.38	116.00	121.66	125.06	128.94	7.50	7.53%
Aug 92	105.16	96.54	NA	98.22	103.47	107.00	109.50	112.19	116.00	119.81	122.72	129.03	7.25	7.50%
Sep 92	105.56	96.86	NA	97.63	103.75	107.25	109.63	112.50	116.88	120.56	123.47	126.84	7.50	7.46%
Oct 92	102.75	96.33	NA	95.75	101.50	105.75	109.25	112.38	116.25	117.22	120.22	123.50	7.75	7.73%
Nov 92	103.16	96.01	NA	95.50	101.31	105.88	109.38	112.50	116.38	117.41	120.44	123.78	7.75	7.69%
Dec 92	104.66	96.36	NA	96.88	102.69	106.56	109.44	112.63	116.50	117.34	120.38	123.69	7.50	7.55%
Jan 93	107.19	96.69	95.47	99.06	104.19	108.25	109.66	112.50	115.84	117.28	120.28	123.63	7.00	7.31%
Feb 93	110.88	96.77	97.09	101.00	104.94	107.56	110.16	112.63	116.03	117.47	120.50	123.84	6.75	6.98%
Mar 93	109.53	96.68	96.66	100.38	105.00	107.66	110.03	113.16	115.94	117.38	120.09	123.06	7.00	7.10%
Apr 93	110.16	96.79	93.63	100.44	105.06	107.56	110.25	113.00	116.63	117.31	120.06	123.06	7.00	7.03%
May 93	110.44	96.61	93.22	99.97	105.13	107.66	110.63	113.63	116.88	118.31	121.06	124.09	7.00	7.02%
Jun 93	113.94	96.57	96.03	102.06	106.09	108.06	110.66	113.66	116.41	117.97	120.69	123.66	6.75	6.72%
Jul 93	115.50	96.66	95.94	102.06	106.31	108.13	110.88	113.50	116.75	119.06	120.91	124.06	6.75	6.59%
Aug 93	119.69	96.75	99.00	103.50	106.25	107.38	110.25	113.50	116.75	117.84	120.66	123.78	6.25	6.26%
Sep 93	118.53	96.51	98.88	103.00	105.50	106.88	110.38	113.50	116.75	118.03	120.69	123.63	6.25	6.35%
Oct 93	118.75	96.48	98.75	103.00	105.44	106.56	109.75	113.50	116.75	117.91	120.44	123.25	6.25	6.32%
Nov 93	115.50	96.51	95.97	101.13	104.69	106.31	109.69	113.91	116.88	118.13	120.63	123.38	6.75	6.54%
Dec 93	114.50	96.49	96.44	101.63	105.31	106.94	110.19	113.50	116.75	118.44	120.94	123.72	6.75	6.68%
Jan 94	117.16	96.64	97.59	102.72	105.72	106.91	110.41	113.94	116.91	118.16	120.66	123.38	6.50	6.46%
Feb 94	112.41	96.22	94.38	100.28	104.88	106.88	110.25	113.84	116.19	118.09	120.53	123.22	7.00	6.85%
Mar 94	106.25	95.64	88.81	95.34	100.91	104.91	108.63	113.41	115.75	117.44	119.88	122.56	8.00	7.40%
Apr 94	104.50	95.27	87.09	93.66	99.50	103.75	107.66	113.38	116.22	118.47	121.00	123.78	8.00	7.56%
May 94	103.56	95.26	87.03	93.56	99.44	103.66	106.84	111.41	113.91	115.31	117.84	120.56	8.00	7.65%
Jun 94	101.22	94.64	85.19	92.06	98.38	103.34	107.28	111.19	113.19	115.47	118.03	120.81	8.25	7.88%

mortgages. During the 1988–90 period mortgage prices were considerably less volatile than they were during the 1984–87 time period.

Standard calculations of duration for these mortgages, as in Exhibit 14, result in modified durations of five to six years. This implies that a 1% increase or decrease in interest rates should move mortgage prices by 5% to 6% in the opposite direction. For the 600 basis points decrease in rates from May 1984 to August 1986, standard duration methods predict mortgage price increases of 30% to 36%. In fact, GNMA 8s increased from 66.38 to 97.25, an increase of 46.5%, substantially more than predicted! GNMA 11s increased about as expected, from 81.38 to 106.84, or 31.3%. GNMA 13s increased significantly less than standard duration projects—going from 92.19 to 107.50, an increase of only 16.6%.

Exhibit 16 illustrates much more clearly what happens to price elasticities for mortgages and bonds as interest rates change. Exhibit 16 was constructed by choosing 9 months of actual mortgage and bond prices from the complete set of data in Exhibit 15. The months chosen are months with 20-year Treasury bond futures rates near 6, 7, 8, 9, 10, 11, 12, 13, and 14%. Thus, they span the entire range of interest rates covered during the

Exhibit 16. Price Elasticities for T-Bond Futures and GNMA Mortgages

Month End	Rate	Rate Change	20-Year Treasury Bond Futures Price	Elastic	GNMA 9s Price	Elastic	GNMA 11s Price	Elastic	GNMA 13s Price	Elastic
Aug 93	6.26%		$119.69		$107.38		$113.50		$117.84	
		0.59%		-10.31%		-0.79%		0.51%		0.36%
Feb 94	6.85%		$112.41		$106.88		$113.84		$118.09	
		1.15%		-9.60%		-2.47%		-2.72%		-1.56%
Sep 91	8.00%		$100.00		$103.84		$110.28		$115.97	
		1.20%		-9.03%		-5.44%		-3.59%		-3.08%
Aug 90	9.20%		$89.16		$97.06		$105.53		$111.69	
		0.96%		-8.76%		-5.10%		-3.54%		-2.92%
Nov 85	10.16%		$81.66		$92.31		$101.94		$108.56	
		0.96%		-8.25%		-6.41%		-5.05%		-2.70%
Jul 85	11.12%		$75.19		$86.63		$97.00		$105.75	
		0.91%		-7.99%		-7.53%		-6.16%		-4.39%
Mar 85	12.03%		$69.72		$80.69		$91.56		$101.53	
		0.96%		-7.52%		-6.13%		-5.26%		-3.68%
Apr 84	12.99%		$64.69		$75.94		$86.94		$97.94	
		0.98%		-7.15%		-7.47%		-6.53%		-5.99%
May 84	13.97%		$60.16		$70.38		$81.38		$92.19	

1984–94 period. From these data, price elasticities are computed at each interest-rate level for Treasury bond futures and for GNMA 9s, 11s, and 13s, respectively.

Several features of "the market's" price elasticities are evident from Exhibit 16. First, Treasury bond futures elasticities are larger (negative) when rates are low than when rates are high. This means that Treasury bond futures prices rise at an increasing rate as rates decline. This phenomenon can also be seen from the dollar moves in Exhibit 6 for T-bond futures. Alternatively, as rates increase, T-bond prices fall by smaller and smaller amounts. The reason for this is explained by duration analysis. As rates increase, the present values of distant cash flows become smaller fractions of the bond's value, resulting in a smaller duration for the bond. As rates decrease, distant cash flows are a larger fraction of bond value, thereby increasing the bond's duration.

The change in duration as rates change is called *convexity*. Changes of the type shown by T-bond futures are evidence of positive convexity. All else held constant, positive convexity is a good thing if you are long the bond and bad if you are short the bond. Note that as rates move, longs win increasingly large amounts as rates fall, and they lose smaller and smaller amounts as rates increase—a very nice situation indeed! Since the long's gains are the short's losses in futures markets, shorts see increasingly large losses as rates fall, and diminishing incremental profits as rates rise. Thus, the short effectively has negative convexity, or *concavity*, which is bad.

Price elasticities on mortgages change much more than do those on T-bonds. When rates are low, mortgages have small price elasticities; when rates increase, price elasticities increase and mortgage prices fall by larger amounts. Thus, mortgages have adverse changes in elasticities for their owners; *i.e.*, negative convexity. Mortgage holders can win only small amounts, but they can lose much larger amounts. This is surely one reason why mortgage rates appear high in relation to Treasury rates, since mortgage investors must be compensated to be induced to take on this negative convexity.

Mortgages have negative convexity because of the prepayment option that borrowers possess. Since borrowers can always pay off their mortgages at 100% (par), mortgage prices cannot exceed par by much. (Since there are points and other costs involved in refinancing with another mortgage, mortgage prices can exceed par by 2% to 5%, and many borrowers will not prepay.) The likelihood of massive prepayments when rates fall sharply (verified in Exhibit 3) means that mortgage prices must increase at a slower and slower rate as interest rates decrease and send mortgage prices above par. In Exhibit 16, the GNMA 11s are the classic illustration of this prepayment option effect. When prices are below par, the GNMA 11s have a price elasticity of about 6%, but the elasticity drops to 3.5% at prices between 102 and 104, and drops further to approximately zero at prices above 113.

The GNMA 13s illustrate the same type of effect, but a closer look at Exhibit 15 reveals an unusual phenomenon. As T-bond rates increased from about 8% (in April 1986) to 9% (in June 1987) GNMA 13s actually increased in price (from $107.44 to $110.88). This presumably occurred as investors thought that the likely dramatic reduction in prepayments would offset the higher discount rate for the mortgages' cash flows. Thus, the price elasticity actually had the opposite sign of a standard elasticity at that time. Exhibit 16 displays a similar response (lower prices) to decreasing rates by GNMA 11s and GNMA 13s between August 1993, and February 1994.

Many institutions buy GNMA mortgages and hedge them by shorting Treasury bond futures or by financing at long-term fixed rates. This hedging strategy typically reduces interest-rate risk substantially. More precisely, the risk is changed from a prediction of where the level of interest rates is going to one of where mortgage rates are going relative to Treasury rates. This latter risk is the "basis risk" of a hedge of mortgages with Treasury bond futures. The basis is the difference between cash and futures prices. In this mortgage hedge, the relevant cash price is a mortgage price, whereas the futures hedge is in T-bonds. Thus, basis risk here is the risk that mortgage rates will increase relative to Treasury rates, thereby decreasing the market values of mortgages relative to Treasury bonds.

The year 1986 exhibited an amazing example of basis risk. Referring to Exhibit 15, put yourself in the position of an owner of GNMA 12s on December 31, 1985. Your hedge in Treasury bonds is a short position, since all data to that point indicated that mortgage prices fall as interest rates increase. In the first six months of 1986, interest rates fall sharply, with T-bond futures prices increasing from 85.22 to 99.56, resulting in losses of more than $14,000 per contract shorted. That is not in itself a bad thing, as long as the other side of the hedge (the GNMA 12s) increases in value to compensate. Instead, the GNMA 12s actually decrease in value from 107.13 to 105.75. Both sides of the hedge have lost—an impossible situation! These losses showed up in investment banks' income statements during the second quarter of 1986, since they held many mortgages hedged with futures. (Similar losses would have appeared in savings and loans' income statements, if they had marked to market.)

In the second half of 1986, the poor hedge situation occurred again. Bond prices fell, so the short hedge profited. When the short hedge profits, one expects to see cash market losses, but the GNMA 12s increased in value. Thus, both sides of the hedge won in the latter half of 1986. The net result for the entire year of 1986 is that bond futures increased by 13 points, whereas the GNMA 12s increased by about 1 point—just the usual positive correlation of bonds and mortgages! The risks shown by these unpredictable movements of mortgage prices relative to T-bond prices are extreme forms of basis risk. No hedge is perfect—some basis risk always remains.

Exhibits 17 and 18 display this basis risk for current coupon mortgage securities for the 1984–94 period. At each month-end the approximate yield on mortgages priced at par is compared to the yield on 7-year Treasury notes. The 7-year Treasury was chosen as the benchmark for comparison because it is the T-note whose price elasticity is most similar to that of current coupon mortgages. The difference between the yield on the mortgages and the yield on seven-year Treasury notes provides an estimate of the "basis"–the yield spread between mortgages and Treasury securities with similar risk characteristics. As Exhibits 17 and 18 show, the basis was always positive during the 1984–94 period (meaning the mortgages yielded more than comparable Treasury securities), but this spread was hardly constant. At the beginning of 1984, the spread between mortgages and Treasuries was approximately 1.5%. This spread stayed fairly stable until early April 1986, when mortgage prepayments surged as long-term rates fell in tandem with oil price declines. The spread reached its widest level in July 1986 at 2.66%. This increase in the mortgage/Treasury basis largely explains why mortgage investors hedged with Treasury-based instruments lost money during most of 1986.

Exhibit 17. Mortgage and Treasury Yields, 1984–94

End of Month	FNMA Par Yield	7-Year Treasury Yield	FNMA Par Yield Minus 7-Year Treasury Yield
Jan-84	13.00	11.47	1.53
Feb-84	13.19	11.86	1.33
Mar-84	13.73	12.38	1.35
Apr-84	14.00	12.66	1.34
May-84	15.17	13.80	1.37
Jun-84	14.93	13.75	1.18
Jul-84	14.43	12.88	1.55
Aug-84	14.31	12.82	1.49
Sep-84	13.92	12.47	1.45
Oct-84	13.30	11.59	1.71
Nov-84	12.92	11.55	1.37
Dec-84	12.92	11.45	1.47
Jan-85	12.70	11.05	1.65
Feb-85	13.32	11.83	1.49
Mar-85	13.02	11.59	1.43
Apr-85	12.85	11.27	1.58
May-85	11.72	10.11	1.61
Jun-85	11.49	10.14	1.35
Jul-85	11.90	10.36	1.54
Aug-85	11.73	10.15	1.58
Sep-85	11.74	10.12	1.62

Exhibit 17. *Continued*

End of Month	FNMA Par Yield	7-Year Treasury Yield	FNMA Par Yield Minus 7-Year Treasury Yield
Oct-85	11.50	9.84	1.66
Nov-85	10.87	9.45	1.42
Dec-85	10.17	8.87	1.30
Jan-86	10.35	8.87	1.48
Feb-86	9.57	8.04	1.53
Mar-86	9.36	7.23	2.13
Apr-86	9.23	7.20	2.03
May-86	10.09	8.04	2.05
Jun-86	9.95	7.30	2.65
Jul-86	9.83	7.17	2.66 (H)
Aug-86	9.13	6.72	2.41
Sep-86	9.45	7.26	2.19
Oct-86	9.22	7.09	2.13
Nov-86	8.52	6.99	1.53
Dec-86	8.83	7.08	1.75
Jan-87	8.55	6.98	1.57
Feb-87	8.50	6.96	1.54
Mar-87	8.74	7.38	1.36
Apr-87	9.85	8.01	1.84
May-87	10.15	8.31	1.84
Jun-87	9.93	8.23	1.70
Jul-87	9.93	8.46	1.47
Aug-87	10.12	8.78	1.34
Sep-87	10.80	9.41	1.39
Oct-87	10.45	8.67	1.78
Nov-87	10.20	8.78	1.42
Dec-87	10.19	8.63	1.56
Jan-88	9.57	8.04	1.53
Feb-88	9.50	7.91	1.59
Mar-88	9.83	8.49	1.34
Apr-88	10.02	8.65	1.37
May-88	10.29	8.95	1.34
Jun-88	9.90	8.65	1.25
Jul-88	10.23	8.94	1.29
Aug-88	10.32	9.11	1.21
Sep-88	9.99	8.73	1.26
Oct-88	9.69	8.51	1.18
Nov-88	10.13	8.99	1.14
Dec-88	10.56	9.20	1.36
Jan-89	10.33	9.03	1.30

Exhibit 17. *Continued*

End of Month	FNMA Par Yield	7-Year Treasury Yield	FNMA Par Yield Minus 7-Year Treasury Yield
Feb-89	10.66	9.35	1.31
Mar-89	10.90	9.36	1.54
Apr-89	10.67	9.10	1.57
May-89	10.17	8.62	1.55
Jun-89	9.77	8.08	1.69
Jul-89	9.40	7.57	1.83
Aug-89	9.97	8.28	1.69
Sep-89	9.95	8.35	1.60
Oct-89	9.53	7.90	1.63
Nov-89	9.49	7.81	1.68
Dec-89	9.51	7.96	1.55
Jan-90	9.85	8.37	1.48
Feb-90	9.96	8.53	1.43
Mar-90	10.04	8.69	1.35
Apr-90	10.41	9.04	1.37
May-90	9.91	8.63	1.28
Jun-90	9.74	8.45	1.29
Jul-90	9.52	8.27	1.25
Aug-90	9.87	8.75	1.12
Sep-90	9.85	8.70	1.15
Oct-90	9.84	8.50	1.34
Nov-90	9.56	8.16	1.40
Dec-90	9.33	7.98	1.35
Jan-91	9.18	7.87	1.31
Feb-91	9.14	7.90	1.24
Mar-91	9.14	7.95	1.19
Apr-91	9.09	7.87	1.22
May-91	9.05	7.91	1.14
Jun-91	9.25	8.12	1.13
Jul-91	9.05	8.00	1.05
Aug-91	8.77	7.66	1.11
Sep-91	8.46	7.23	1.23
Oct-91	8.26	7.14	1.12
Nov-91	8.27	6.96	1.31
Dec-91	7.59	6.35	1.24
Jan-92	8.26	6.88	1.38
Feb-92	8.13	6.91	1.22
Mar-92	8.45	7.21	1.24
Apr-92	8.35	7.22	1.13
May-92	8.07	6.98	1.09

Exhibit 17. *Continued*

End of Month	FNMA Par Yield	7-Year Treasury Yield	FNMA Par Yield Minus 7-Year Treasury Yield
Jun-92	7.89	6.71	1.18
Jul-92	7.57	6.26	1.31
Aug-92	7.38	6.13	1.25
Sep-92	7.31	5.88	1.43
Oct-92	7.81	6.35	1.46
Nov-92	7.87	6.59	1.28
Dec-92	7.59	6.42	1.17
Jan-93	7.23	5.96	1.27
Feb-93	6.97	5.65	1.32
Mar-93	6.95	5.68	1.27
Apr-93	6.92	5.59	1.33
May-93	7.00	5.77	1.23
Jun-93	6.64	5.49	1.15
Jul-93	6.62	5.60	1.02 (L)
Aug-93	6.30	5.17	1.13
Sep-93	6.32	5.13	1.19
Oct-93	6.39	5.21	1.18
Nov-93	6.83	5.55	1.28
Dec-93	6.72	5.60	1.12
Jan-94	6.46	5.43	1.03
Feb-94	6.97	5.93	1.04
Mar-94	7.79	6.56	1.23
Apr-94	8.00	6.94	1.06
May-94	8.16	6.99	1.17
Jun-94	8.35	7.21	1.14

Standard Deviations: (in percent, monthly data)	FNMA Par Yield	7-Year Treasury Yield	FNMA Par Yield Minus 7-Yr Treasury
Levels	1.96	1.91	0.30
Changes	0.38	0.39	0.17

Correlations FNMA Par Yield vs. 7-Year Treasury Yield:
Levels	0.989
Changes	0.906

NOTE: All rates are expressed as bond-equivalent yields.

As discussed earlier, when the basis widens (an increase in the mortgage/Treasury yield spread) an investor who owns mortgages and hedges with Treasuries will experience either a loss or at least less profits than

Exhibit 18.   Basis Risk Between Mortgages and Treasuries

FNMA PAR YIELD vs. 7-YEAR TREASURY YIELD
Monthly, 1984–94

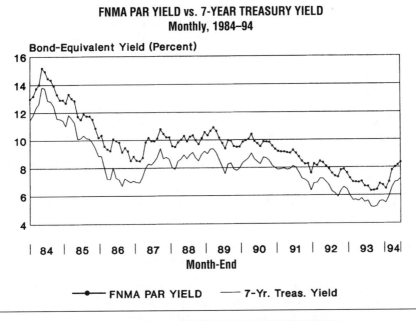

FNMA PAR YIELD MINUS 7-YEAR TREASURY YIELD
Monthly, 1984–94

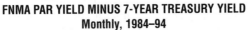

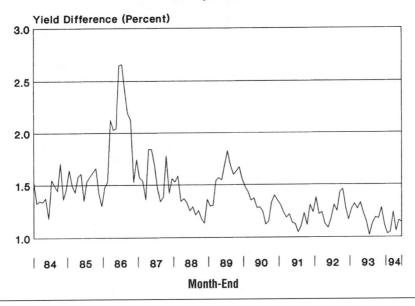

expected. As described above, in 1986 many mortgage investors who hedged with Treasury securities suffered losses during the period due to widening yield spreads of mortgages relative to Treasuries.

Late in 1986, the spread began to decline and it has continued to trend downward since 1987. This spread narrowing has been caused by 5 major factors:

1. Increased demand for mortgage-backed securities for use in collateralized mortgage obligations (CMOs).

2. A general increase in the number and characteristics of mortgage-backed securities' investors.

3. Increased investor sophistication and understanding of the prepayment behavior of mortgages.

4. Lower interest-rate volatility, making the prepayment option less valuable to the borrower.

5. Risk-based capital requirements for financial institutions which established low capital requirements for mortgages relative to other asset types.

When the basis tightens, a hedger will usually experience larger than expected profits. This is especially true of those savvy investors who purchased mortgages in 1986, hedged the interest-rate risk of these securities, and held onto their mortgages until at least late 1986 or early 1987.

Exhibits 17 and 18 also display the beneficial risk-reducing effects of hedging. Hedging reduced the risk to an investor in mortgages from the fluctuations in the nominal level of mortgage interest rates (high of 15.17%, low of 6.30%) to the fluctuations in the yield spread between mortgages and Treasuries (high of 2.66%, low of 1.02%). Note the high correlation between the yields of current coupon mortgages and seven-year Treasury notes during the 1984–94 period (.989 for rate levels and .906 for monthly rate changes). These correlations indicate that such Treasury securities would have been an effective hedge of current coupon mortgages during this time period. Further evidence of hedge effectiveness is the fact that the standard deviations (the most common measure of financial risk) of monthly mortgage rate levels and changes (1.96% and 0.38%, respectively), representing unhedged mortgage portfolio risk, were significantly higher than the standard deviations of levels and changes in the mortgage/Treasury yield spread (0.30% and 0.17%, respectively), representing the risk of portfolios of current coupon mortgages hedged with seven-year Treasury notes (and similar to the risk of mortgage portfolios hedged with seven-year interest-rate swaps).

Clearly, classic duration measures are very useful for standard bonds, but may be very misleading for mortgages. However, Wall Street now essentially defines the *effective duration* of a mortgage by its price elasticity. For the sake of simplicity of language, this chapter will use the terms *duration* and *elasticity* interchangeably to mean the percentage change in the market value of a financial instrument for a 100 basis point (1%) change in the level of interest rates. Thus, the description might be duration, but the relevant calculation is elasticity.

Given these elements of futures, options, swaps, caps, floors, mortgages, duration, convexity, and elasticity, we are now ready to examine the interest-rate risk for a typical firm and to construct hedges for it.

LIQUIDATION VALUE AND INTEREST RATE RISK FOR A FIRM

Liquidation Value

The first step in evaluating the financial condition and interest-rate risk of an institution involves calculating the market value of the firm's assets and liabilities. Since the main objective of a hedging program is to protect the firm against changes in its market value caused by changes in interest rates, the market value (not the book value) of the firm and its component parts must be calculated. The terms *market value* and *liquidation value* will be used interchangeably in the following discussion. The liquidation value may be thought of as being that amount of money which would be left over if the firm sold its assets and repurchased its liabilities at current market prices.

The condensed balance sheet of First Savings and Loan Association is found in Exhibit 19. On June 30, 1994, the date of the analysis, the institution had assets totalling $1.85 billion and a book net worth of $112.2 million (6% of assets). Exhibit 19 lists the book value, the average term to maturity or repricing, the actual interest rate, the current fair rate on those assets and liabilities, the price elasticity or modified duration, and the market value of each of the major balance sheet categories of the Association. The market value of each item is calculated by discounting its associated cash flows using the current market discount rate as determined by the purchase price of like assets or the issue rate on new liabilities.

In the case of First Savings, since interest rates have increased during the nine months prior to the date of the analysis (June 30, 1994), many of the balance sheet items have market values which are significantly different from their stated book values. For example, the Association owns $677 million of fixed-rate conventional mortgages. Since the average coupon rate on these mortgages is lower than the current market rate for conventional mortgages, the market value of these assets is less than the stated book value. Exhibit 19 indicates that the market value of the firm's fixed-rate mortgages is $667.3 million, or $9.7 million less than the stated book value ($677 million).

Exhibit 19. First Savings and Loan Association—Condensed Balance Sheet and Liquidation Value

June 30, 1994

	Book Value (Mil) (1)	Avg Term (Years) (2)	Avg Rate (%) (3)	Current Fair Rate (4)	Rate Change (5)	Elast or Mod. Duration (6)	Gain/Loss From Book (Mil) (7)	Market Value (Mil) (8)
Assets								
Liquidity Investments	105.8	0.1	4.45%	4.45%	0.00%	0.1%	0.0	105.8
Adjustable Rate Mortgages	1,008.8	0.8	6.24%	6.28%	0.04%	1.9%	-0.7	1,008.1
Fixed Rate Mortgages	677.0	28.3	7.90%	8.29%	0.39%	3.7%	-9.7	667.3
Commercial & Consumer Loans	60.8	0.7	9.25%	9.75%	0.50%	0.6%	-0.2	60.6
Total Assets	1,852.5	10.8	6.84%	7.02%	0.18%	2.4%	(10.7)	1,841.8
Liabilities								
Money Market Accounts	103.8	0.0	4.05%	4.05%	0.00%	0.0%	0.0	103.8
FHLB Advances	74.1	2.8	6.75%	6.46%	-0.29%	2.5%	0.5	73.6
Fixed Rate Deposits	1562.5	0.8	3.30%	3.78%	0.48%	0.8%	5.7	1,556.8
Total Liabilities	1,740.4	1.2	8.43%	7.54%	-0.89%	1.1%	6.2	1,734.2
Net Worth	112.1						-4.5	107.6
Non-Balance Sheet Items:								
Interest Rate Swap (750 m/n notional)	0	3.5	7.33%	7.10%	-0.23%	3.0%	-4.9	- 4.9
Liquidation Value	112.1 +						-9.4	= 102.7

Similar market value losses (below book value) are characteristic of most of the other asset categories, as well. For instance, the market value of the Association's commercial and consumer loan portfolio is $0.7 million less than its stated book value. An asset or liability's market value gain is approximately equal to the product of three items: (1) its price elasticity, (2) the rate change since purchase, and (3) the amount. For example, there are $60.8 million of consumer and commercial loans. Multiplying the unfavorable rate increase of 0.5% since origination by the elasticity of 0.6 results in a 0.3% capital loss on $60.8 million—a $0.2 million loss.

In spite of original terms to maturity of 30 years, the adjustable-rate mortgages show a smaller loss (in both absolute and percentage terms) than the fixed-rate mortgages. This phenomenon is quite easy to explain. There is an average of 9 months to repricing, as indicated by an "average term" of .8 years. Since the adjustable-rate mortgages reprice quickly, the interest rate charged on these assets is brought back into line with the market only a short time after the level of market interest rates changes. Once interest rates change, these adjustable-rate assets earn either sub-market or higher-than-market rates for a much shorter period of time than do the Association's fixed-rate assets. The shorter the time period to repricing or maturity, the smaller (in percentage terms) is the effect of a given change in the level of interest rates on the market value of any financial asset or liability.

Adjustable-rate mortgages are not without interest-rate risk, however, as indicated by elasticities of 1.9% shown in Exhibit 19. Adjustable-rate mortgage loans have limits (caps) that restrict the amount by which the coupon rate adjusts to market rate increases during any period (typically one year) or during the life of the mortgage. These caps make the adjustable-rate mortgages act more like fixed-rate mortgages (more interest-rate risk) when rates increase by a large amount in a short period of time.

Since First Savings' short-term liquidity investments reprice (on average) every 30 days, the corresponding price elasticity or duration is small (.1), indicating that a 100 basis point decrease in interest rates will result in only a .1% increase in the value of these assets. Conversely, the fixed-rate mortgages of the Association have a market value sensitivity to a 100 basis point interest-rate change of approximately 3.7% (duration of 3.7 years). The average elasticity of the firm's assets, taken as a group, is approximately 2.4%. The elasticities of fixed-rate mortgages are significantly less than their stated terms to maturity because of the anticipated prepayments on these securities, as discussed in the previous section.

A brief look at the liability portion of the balance sheet indicates that the Association is paying below-market interest rates on its FHLB advances and fixed-rate deposits. Since the Association is paying a rate which is lower than the rate at which new liabilities could currently be issued (at par), First Savings has a market value gain on these liabilities. The rate on Money Market Deposit Accounts (MMDAs) adjusts almost instantaneously to changes in market interest rates. Since the speed of adjustment is so rapid on these instruments, changes in market interest rates have virtually no effect on the value of MMDAs. For this reason, MMDAs are shown in Exhibit 19 as having equivalent market and book values and a duration of zero (negligible sensitivity to interest-rate changes).

The Association's interest-rate swaps are agreements by the firm to pay to counterparties an average, fixed-rate of 7.33%, semi-annually compounded, and to receive from the counterparty a floating rate (3-month LIBOR) every 3 months. The interest-rate swap effectively "converts" $750 million of three-month liabilities into $750 million of 3.5-year borrowings. The swaps were entered into during prior periods at then fair market rates for liabilities with corresponding maturities. Because market rates have generally fallen since the inception of these interest-rate swaps, the Association will be paying a higher-than-market rate (unless interest rates rise) over the remaining life of the swaps. As shown in Exhibit 19, marking the swaps to market indicates a $4.9 million loss. Note that the book value of the swaps is shown as zero because no money changes hands when a swap is entered into.

The liquidation value of the Association is now easily computed by adding the market value adjustments (from book value) of all financial assets and liabilities to the book net worth. As shown in Exhibit 19, First Savings' liquidation value stood at $102.7 million as of June 30, 1994, which is $9.4 million under its book value. It is this market or liquidation value that we wish to protect from changes in interest rates.

Of course, the liquidation value computation in Exhibit 19 can and should be done each month. As interest rates change and as the firm's composition of assets, liabilities, and swaps changes, the liquidation value of the firm will change. Like most financial institutions, the composition of First Savings' assets and liabilities does not change much from month to month. Therefore, before First Savings hedged with interest-rate swaps, the dominant factor that changed the firm's liquidation value in the short run was the level of interest rates. Exhibit 20 shows the liquidation value of First Savings monthly from January 31, 1984, through June 30, 1994. The firm's value on January 31, 1984, was negative. When interest rates rose in early 1984, the firm sank rapidly. Then, in late 1984, the firm began to recover as interest rates fell. As rates fell further in 1985 and in 1986, First Savings recovered and finally went into the black in liquidation value.

In early 1986, after again becoming solvent on a liquidation value basis, First Savings decided to hedge most of its interest-rate risk. Notice from Exhibit 20 how stable the firm's liquidation value became after April 1986. Exhibit 20 also displays how First Savings' liquidation value grew steadily during the 1986–94 period in spite of significant fluctuations in market interest rates.

Exhibit 20.   First Savings Liquidation Value vs. Market Interest Rates 1984–94

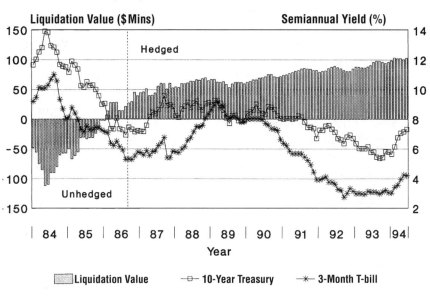

| Liquidation Value | ─⊟─ 10-Year Treasury | ─*─ 3-Month T-bill |

Interest-Rate Risk

Now that the value of the firm and its component parts have been calculated, it is necessary to assess what the exact interest-rate risks of the firm are at the date of the analysis, June 30, 1994. More specifically, how much money does the Association lose if rates increase by 1%, 2%, 3%, or 4%? How much does it win for decreases in rates that range from 1% to 4%? The discussion of duration in the previous section briefly touched upon this for the case of 1% moves up and down in rates.

Looking at the elasticity column in Exhibit 19 again, we can see that the average elasticity of First Savings' assets is 2.4%, yet the average elasticity of its liabilities is only 1.1% (not including its interest-rate swaps). If the interest-rate sensitivities of a firm's assets and liabilities are approximately equal, the firm is not subject to much risk from small parallel shifts in the term structure of interest rates. However, First Savings has a portfolio which is characteristic of many financial institutions—longer duration assets (mainly fixed-rate mortgages) funded primarily by shorter duration sources of funds (CDs). Therefore, if interest rates rose, First Savings' assets would decline in value by more than the gain on its liabilities.

In order to more easily demonstrate the fact that First Savings is exposed to changes in interest rates, it is useful to calculate the market values of the firm and its component parts under different interest-rate scenarios. Exhibit 21 presents the estimated value of each asset and liability category for parallel shifts in the Treasury yield curve of between minus 4% and plus 4% (in increments of 100 basis points).

The line in Exhibit 21 labelled "Change in Economic Net Worth (Unhedged)" gives the net market value gain or loss that First Savings' balance sheet (not including its interest-rate swaps) would incur from changes in interest rates ranging from 4% higher to 4% lower than base rates on June 30, 1994. This range of interest rates covers 10-year Treasury rates between 3.32% and 11.32%. The value of the firm's assets and liabilities would increase by $65.8 million (from $107.6 million to $173.2 million) if rates drop by 4%. If rates increase by 4% the value of the firm's assets and liabilities drops by $152.4 million (from $107.6 million to $-44.8 million). Without any hedging the economic value of the firm would go to zero with about a 3% increase in interest rates (to 10.32% on the 10-year T-note). For a 1% movement in interest rates in either direction, the unhedged First Savings would see its value change by approximately $31 million or 29% of its book net worth. Clearly, this firm would have very significant interest-rate risk relative to its net worth if it did not hedge.

First Savings' interest-rate swaps reduce the firm's interest-rate risk substantially, especially for small movements in interest rates. The bottom line in Exhibit 21 shows the changes in First Savings' liquidation value that would result from changes in market interest rates. Note the firm's value changes by an average of $8.3 million for a rate move of plus or minus 1%. This average change in value is only one fourth of the change in value of the firm without its interest-rate swaps. Thus, the interest-rate swaps have reduced the interest-rate risk of the firm's value (at the margin) by approximately 75%. Despite this achievement the firm is still subject to some interest-rate risk as it loses value when rates rise and gains somewhat when rates fall. The firm's value falls substantially for large rate movements in either direction (reflecting the customer options inherent in its assets and liabilities) but the firm's value does not go negative if rates increase or decrease by as much as 4% from current levels.

To identify very easily which assets and liabilities have the greatest dollar interest-rate sensitivities for First Savings, the market values of each of the asset categories are graphed versus interest-rate changes in Exhibit 22, and the liabilities and interest-rate swaps are graphed in Exhibit 23. The liquidation value is plotted in Exhibit 24, as are the assets', the liabilities', and the swaps' sensitivities. Exhibit 22 reveals that the fixed-rate mortgages have market values that are very interest-rate-sensitive. The liquidity investments and First Savings' consumer and commercial loans have market values that are not very rate-sensitive. The adjustable-rate mortgages (ARMs) fall in between on a percentage basis but comprise the majority of the firm's assets. These numbers square with

Exhibit 21. First Savings and Loan Association—Analysis of Interest Rate Sensitivity

June 30, 1994

Market Values of Assets and Liabilities At Various Interest Rates

Rate Change From Base:	-4%	-3%	-2%	-1%	0%	1%	2%	3%	4%
10-Year Interest Rate	3.32%	4.32%	5.32%	6.32%	7.32%	8.32%	9.32%	10.32%	11.32%
T-Bond Futures Price	156.95%	139.56%	124.74%	112.07%	101.22%	91.83%	83.74%	76.71%	70.59%
Assets									
Liquidity Investments	105.4	105.5	105.6	105.7	105.8	105.7	105.6	105.5	105.4
Adjustable Rate Mortgages	1062.5	1052.4	1040.6	1026.0	1008.1	987.1	962.6	935.4	906.1
Fixed-Rate Mortgages	733.8	724.9	711.2	691.3	667.3	641.5	615.5	590.3	566.3
Commercial & Consumer Loans	62.2	61.8	61.4	61.0	60.6	60.3	59.9	59.6	59.3
Total Assets	1963.9	1944.6	1918.8	1884.0	1841.8	1794.5	1743.6	1690.8	1637.1
Liabilities									
Money Market Accounts	103.8	103.8	103.8	103.8	103.8	103.8	103.8	103.8	103.8
FHLB Advances	81.4	79.4	77.4	75.5	73.6	71.8	70.0	68.4	66.7
Fixed-Rate Deposits	1605.5	1593.0	1580.7	1568.7	1556.8	1545.2	1532.8	1522.4	1511.4
Total Liabilities	1790.7	1776.2	1761.8	1747.9	1734.2	1720.7	1706.6	1694.6	1681.9
Net Worth (Economic – Unhedged)	173.2	168.4	157.0	136.1	107.6	73.8	37.0	-3.8	-44.8
Change in Economic Net Worth (Unhedged)	65.6	60.8	49.4	28.5	0.0	-33.8	-70.6	-111.4	-152.4
Non-Balance Sheet Items:									
Interest-Rate Swap	-104.3	-77.8	-52.5	-28.2	-4.9	17.5	38.9	59.5	79.2
Liquidation Value (Hedged)	69.0	90.6	104.5	107.9	102.7	91.3	75.9	55.7	34.4
Change in Liq. Value (Hedged)	-33.8	-12.1	1.8	5.2	0.0	-11.5	-26.8	-47.0	-68.3

Exhibit 22.   First Savings and Loan Association: Interest-Rate Sensitivities of Assets

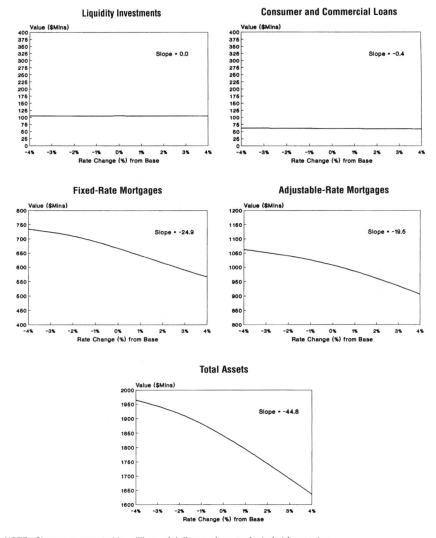

NOTE: Slopes are reported in millions of dollars and are evaluated at base rates.

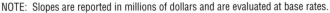

the duration and price elasticity analysis of the previous section. Similarly, the fixed-rate deposits, fixed-rate FHLB advances, and fixed-rate interest-rate swaps have somewhat rate-sensitive market values, whereas the MMDAs have values that are not sensitive to changes in interest rates.

Exhibit 23.   First Savings and Loan Association: Interest-Rate Sensitivities of Liabilities and Swaps

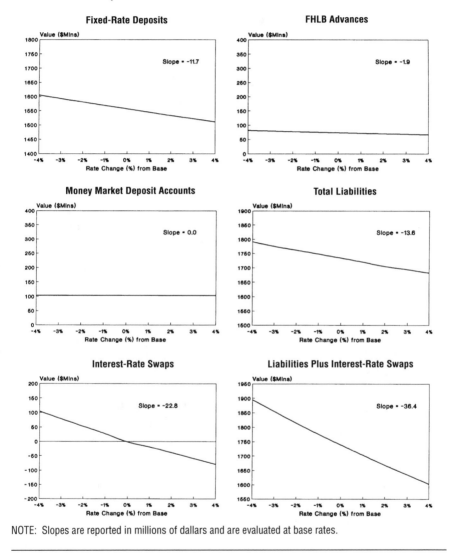

NOTE: Slopes are reported in millions of dollars and are evaluated at base rates.

The amount of rate sensitivity of the combined liabilities' and swaps' values is not as large as the assets' rate sensitivities, so the liquidation value has a rate sensitivity that is in the same direction as the assets (note Exhibit 24). For example, with a 4% rate increase the assets lose $204.7 million of

Exhibit 24. First Savings and Loan Association
Current Portfolio (Aggregate) Liquidation Value

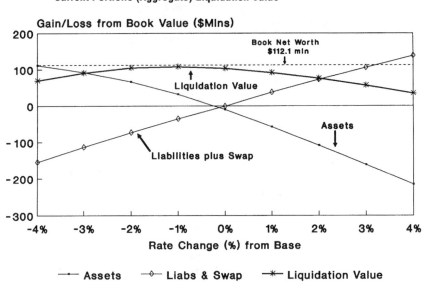

Gain/Loss from Book Value ($Mlns)

—•— Assets   —◇— Liabs & Swap   —✳— Liquidation Value

NOTE: Liquidation Value is sum of Book Net Worth, Loss on Assets and Swaps, and Gain on Liabilities

market value, whereas the liabilities beneficially drop in value by $52.3 million and the interest-rate swaps gain back 84.1 million. The net result is a decrease in liquidation value of $68.3 million (- 204.7 + 52.3 + 84.1 = - 68.3) from the base case.

The graphs in Exhibits 22-24 apply to First Savings position on June 30, 1994. They are based upon current (June 30, 1994) rates, current assets, liabilities, and swaps. They are the relevant graphs for current (June 1994) decision making. However, they do not really give an historical perspective of the interest-rate risk of the institution. Exhibit 20 showed the historical fluctuations in the liquidation value of the institution, prior to June 30, 1994. Exhibit 25 shows the interest-rate sensitivity for 1% rate moves that First Savings has had monthly in the past 10 years.

The firm's interest-rate sensitivity gap has narrowed over the past 10 years for 3 reasons. First, as rates fell, the mortgages held by First Savings prepaid more quickly, thereby shortening their durations and reducing their interest-rate sensitivities. Second, beginning in early 1986, First Savings entered into a number of interest-rate swaps. Third, the firm began to fund some of its assets with longer-term FHLB advances. This longer-term funding source more closely matched the interest-rate risk of First Savings' mortgage

Exhibit 25.   First Savings and Loan Association Value Sensitivity to Rates 1984–94

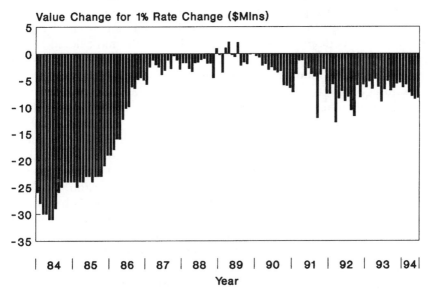

assets than did its short-term deposit liabilities. This significantly closed the gap between the rate sensitivities of assets and liabilities. The interest-rate swaps and FHLB advances help to protect the firm by having gains when rates are high, which is just when the assets are losing.

HEDGING WITH FUTURES AND SWAPS: CORRELATION STATISTICS

Referring again to Exhibit 21, First Savings and Loan currently (June 30, 1994) has a liquidation value of $102.7 million, which reflects gains and losses on assets, liabilities, and interest-rate swaps. If rates increase by 1%, First Savings' liquidation value falls to $91.3 million. If rates decrease by 1%, the liquidation value increases to $107.9 million. Averaging the up ($5.2 million) and down ($11.5 million) movements in liquidation value, First Savings wins or loses about $8.3 million when interest rates move by 1%. The specific hedge employed should be designed to provide a gain when rates are up, which is when the firm needs the gain, because of its low "cash value"—the firm's net value excluding any hedges that are utilized. The firm should expect to have a loss on the hedge when rates are down, since the firm is well-off then, with a high cash value. In the absence of any such hedging program, First Savings' long-run profit margin would be tenuous, at best.

Now that the direction and magnitude of the interest-rate risk have been identified, the next step in the analysis is to select the *instruments* which will comprise the hedging position and to determine the *sizes* of the hedging positions necessary to adequately protect the institution from changes in interest rates. As discussed earlier in this chapter, the most liquid interest-rate futures markets are those for 20-year Treasury bonds (T-bonds) and those for 91-day Eurodollar time deposits (Euros). Since these (of the available futures contracts) allow us to separately hedge long-term and short-term interest rate fluctuations, we will consider hedging only in T-bonds and Euros at the present time.

The direction and size of a futures hedge are both easy to compute and to understand. All financial officers, board members, and regulators should be able to do at least the following simple analysis and calculation. Short positions in these Treasury bond and Eurodollar futures contracts are the appropriate positions, because the hedge must be designed to benefit First Savings when the rest of its portfolio loses value—*i.e.*, when interest rates increase. When interest rates increase, bond prices fall and the short wins. Conversely, the short futures position loses money when interest rates fall and the firm has economic gains. The number of contracts is chosen so as to equate the futures gains or losses with the "cash" losses or gains under the different interest-rate scenarios. The total futures gain or loss is the product of the number of futures contracts held times the gain or loss per contract. Thus, to have futures gains and losses balance cash gains and losses for a 1% change in rates, one need only solve the following equation:

$$
\begin{array}{cccc}
\text{Futures Gain} & \text{Number of} & \text{Gain/Contract} & \text{Change in Present} \\
\text{for 1\% Rate} \ = & \text{Contracts} \ \times & \text{of Short for 1\%} \ = - & \text{Value of Firm for} \\
\text{Change} & \text{Held Short} & \text{Rate Change} & \text{a 1\% Rate Change}
\end{array}
$$

Solving:

$$
\begin{array}{c}
\text{Number of} \\
\text{Contracts} \\
\text{Held Short}
\end{array}
\ = \
\dfrac{-\ \begin{array}{c}\text{Change in PV of Firm for}\\ \text{1\% Rate Change}\end{array}}{\begin{array}{c}\text{Gain/Contract of Short for}\\ \text{1\% Rate Change}\end{array}}
$$

To find the number of contracts to be held to give the correctly offsetting futures move, one must know how much is gained or lost in T-bonds and Euros if rates move by 1%. A table of these dollar moves at different rates is given in Exhibit 6, covering 20-year Treasury bond futures, 10-year Treasury notes, 91-day Treasury bills, and 91-day Eurodollars. On June 30, 1994, the near Treasury bond futures price was 101.22, implying a yield near 7.88%. From Exhibit 6, a short T-bond futures contract at that rate level wins about $9,390 if rates increase to 8.88% and loses about $10,850 if rates fall to 6.88%. The average dollar move for a T-bond contract is $10,120 for a 1% rate move. In contrast, a Eurodollar time deposit contract wins or loses only $2,500 for a 1% rate move. Thus, if short and long rates move in parallel by 1%, the T-bond contract will generate more than four times ($10,120/ $2,500) as much dollar gain or loss as will the Euro contract, despite having a par amount that is only one tenth the Euro's amount.

Given that the firm gains or loses on average about $8.3 million for a 1% rate move and given that one T-bond futures contract gains or loses about $10,120 at the same time, one can compute the approximate number of T-bond futures contracts that need to be held with the above formula:

$$\text{Number of Contracts Held Short} = \frac{-\$ -8,300,000}{\$10,120} = 820 \text{ contracts short}$$

With this position, if rates move up 1%, the 820 T-bonds short will each gain $9,390, for a total of $7.7 million, which offsets a significant portion of the cash (non-futures) loss that occurs. If rates fall, due to the "convexity" of T-bond prices, a slightly larger loss occurs: 820 × $10,850 = $8.9 million. If Euros were used in the hedge instead of T-bonds, the correct number of Euro futures contracts would be $8,300,000/$2,500 = 3,320 contracts short. The number of Euro contracts that must be held is about 4 times the number of T-bond contracts, since each Euro moves only about one fourth as much as one T-bond (again assuming parallel shifts of short and long rates).

Banks and savings and loans must report their futures positions to their regulators. Note the difference in the par amounts reported with Eurodollar and Treasury bond hedges that have *the same average dollar moves*. With T-bonds, only 820 contracts are held short, each with a par amount of $100,000, for a total par amount of 820 × $100,000 = $82.0 million. This does not seem to be an unreasonable futures position for a $1.8 billion institution, so it usually raises no regulatory concern. However, if the institution hedges with Eurodollars, the par amount is $1 million per contract times 3,320 contracts, a total par shorted of $3.32 billion. Having a futures position with a par amount well over the amount of assets of the institution raises many red flags for bank examiners. Yet the position is correctly balanced, so it is appropriate. Of course, the difference is that the price elasticity (modified duration) of 20-year T-bonds is about 10% (10 years), whereas the elasticity for 91-day Eurodollars is only about $1/40$ that amount, at 0.25%. Thus, almost 40 times the par in T-bonds must be held in Eurodollars for an equivalent hedge. To prevent poor analysis, the regulatory focus must be on dollar moves of the position for 1% rate moves, rather than on par amounts. Unfortunately, a focus on par amounts has led to many embarrassingly incorrect statements made by examiners about hedging programs.

If the term structure always had parallel shifts, it would not matter whether the futures hedge was done with T-bonds or with Euros, as long as the correct number of contracts was held for the market used. However, as can be seen in Exhibit 1, the term structure does not always move in parallel fashion. For example, comparing June 1985 rates to January 1986 rates, one sees that the 3-month T-bill rate increased by 5 basis points, whereas the 20-year rate decreased by 109 basis points. If First Savings' cash position moved mostly with short-term rates and 820 T-bond futures contracts were shorted as a futures hedge, then the firm would not have gained on its cash position, but would have lost about $10,000 per contract on its futures (about $8.2 million in futures losses).

The risk that the cash position will move somewhat differently than the hedge position is the basis risk described in the second section. Exhibit 26 gives a good illustration of basis risk versus interest-rate risk using the liquidation value history of First Savings. The top panel (also shown in Exhibit 20) shows the relationship between First Savings' liquidation value and market interest rates. Notice that there was a strong (negative) relationship between the firm's value and the level of interest rates until the firm began hedging in early 1986. Since the firm began hedging, there appears to be little relationship between changes in the firm's value and market interest rates.

The bottom panel displays the relationship between the firm's value and the interest spread between par coupon mortgages and comparable Treasury notes. In the early (unhedged) period there is little relationship between the mortgage/Treasury yield spread (the basis) and the firm's liquidation value. During the hedged period (after April 1986), the firm's value is significantly affected by changes in the basis. For example, when mortgage spreads to Treasury widened during mid-1986, the firm's value fell. As the basis narrowed in late 1986 and early 1987, the firm's value rose accordingly.

As these graphs clearly display, First Savings reduced its overall interest-rate risk from that of its unhedged period (where month-to-month changes in the firm's value were largely determined by changes in the level of market interest rates) to that of the later "hedged" period (where changes in the firm's value were largely determined by changes in the yield spread between mortgages and Treasury securities). As Exhibits 17 and 18 have already shown, the basis risk is considerably smaller than the risk of going unhedged. By shorting contracts for the hedge which are most highly correlated with the cash position, this basis risk is minimized, but it is never eliminated. That is why hedging is correctly called "speculation in the basis." The good news is

Exhibit 26a. First Savings and Loan Association: Liquidation Value vs. Short and Long Rates

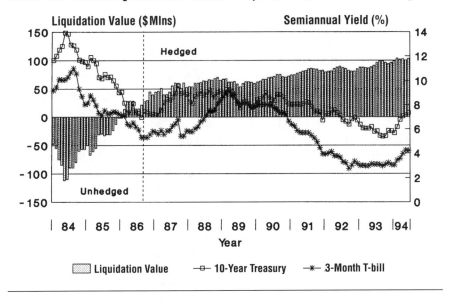

Exhibit 26b. First Savings and Loan Association: Liquidation Value vs. Mortgage Spread

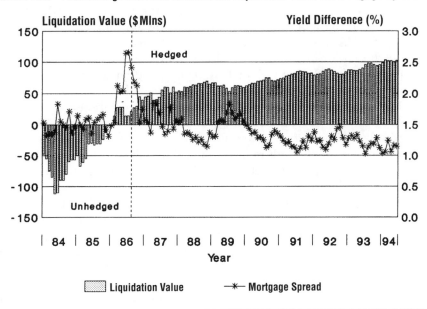

that the correlations between interest-rate futures and cash market bond values are usually quite high, and the basis risk is considerably smaller than the risk of going unhedged.

Exhibits 27 and 28 present means, standard deviations, and correlations for GNMA mortgage prices for coupons from 8% to 15% and for the near Treasury bond and Eurodollar futures contracts. The data used is that of Exhibit 15, which was obtained primarily from Salomon Brothers. Exhibit 27 calculates statistics for price levels and their correlations, whereas Exhibit 28 calculates statistics for monthly changes in those same price levels. Both sets of tables have value and present much the same story, but statisticians usually prefer to focus on Exhibit 28—the data on monthly price changes (as those monthly changes are more nearly serially uncorrelated). Since interest rates fell sharply during this period, particularly in late 1985 and early 1986, mortgage prices should and did behave differently later in the sample. For this reason, the data sample was divided into two major subperiods: the 1984–85 subperiod (high rates) and the 1986-94 subperiod (low rates). The 1986–87 subperiod is also highlighted in order to display the unusual behavior of mortgage prices during this period. All statistics are presented for the entire sample period, as well as for each of the subperiods.

Focusing on Exhibit 27, the standard deviations show that long- and short-term futures prices were more volatile in 1986–94 than in 1984–85. Mortgage prices were generally less volatile in the 1986–94 period, just as would be expected when rates are low and mortgage prices "cap out" above par due to large prepayments. For example, the volatility of GNMA 10s dropped from 6.54% of par to 3.76% of par—the most dramatic change. In contrast, GNMA 13s were already significantly above par, so their price volatility did not drop as much. GNMA 8s, with an average price of only 97 (compared to the 104.6 of GNMA 10s), had a less dramatic change in price volatility than the GNMA 10s.

Looking at the correlation matrices for the entire period in Exhibits 27 and 28, one sees that all of the mortgages have significant, positive correlations with both T-bond futures and with Eurodollar futures. Using price levels, correlations with T-bonds ranged from .84 for GNMA 14s and GNMA 15s to .97 for GNMA 8s, and correlations with Eurodollars ranged from .87 for GNMA 10s to .92 for GNMA 15s.

For the entire sample period, correlations for monthly price changes are lower than for price levels, ranging from .34 to .83 with T-bonds and from .35 to .69 for Eurodollars. Again, these correlations are statistically significant, but their values clearly indicate the presence of basis risk. Higher coupon securities have higher prepayments and lower price elasticities, so one expects them to be more highly correlated with short-term rates than with long-term rates. This occurs during most of the subperiods shown, as higher coupon

Exhibit 27. Means, Standard Deviations and Correlations Using Price Levels

A. Bond and Mortgage Prices: Means and Standard Deviations

Variable	Entire Period 1/84–6/94		First Subperiod 1984–85		Second Subperiod 1/86–6/94		Third Subperiod 1986–87	
	Mean	Std Dev'n	Mean	Std Dev'n	Mean	Std Dev'n	Mean	Std Dev'n
BondFut	92.90	13.19	71.32	6.23	97.98	8.38	94.47	5.88
Eurofut	92.94	2.36	90.23	1.60	93.58	2.04	93.06	0.73
GNMA 8	93.20	9.23	77.45	6.35	96.90	4.86	94.20	3.05
GNMA 9	97.14	8.85	81.92	6.51	100.73	4.40	98.15	2.91
GNMA 10	101.29	8.14	87.20	6.54	104.61	3.76	102.89	2.85
GNMA 11	104.93	7.32	92.56	6.09	107.84	3.60	105.92	1.58
GNMA 13	110.94	5.98	101.80	4.59	113.09	3.87	108.92	1.22
GNMA 14	113.52	5.64	105.67	3.57	115.37	4.28	110.78	1.46
GNMA 15	116.06	5.89	108.38	3.21	117.87	4.83	114.05	0.71

B. Correlation Matrix—Entire Period: 1/84–6/94

	BondFut	Eurofut	GNMA 8	GNMA 9	GNMA 10	GNMA 11	GNMA 13	GNMA 14	GNMA 15
BondFut	1.000								
Eurofut	0.870	1.000							
GNMA 8	0.974	0.882	1.000						
GNMA 9	0.959	0.875	0.996	1.000					
GNMA 10	0.953	0.866	0.993	0.997	1.000				
GNMA 11	0.946	0.890	0.987	0.990	0.993	1.000			
GNMA 13	0.884	0.871	0.937	0.942	0.929	0.948	1.000		
GNMA 14	0.849	0.873	0.896	0.899	0.879	0.905	0.986	1.000	
GNMA 15	0.849	0.924	0.888	0.890	0.869	0.894	0.954	0.973	1.000

Exhibit 27. Continued

C. Correlation Matrix—First Subperiod: 1984–85

	BondFut	Eurofut	GNMA 8	GNMA 9	GNMA 10	GNMA 11	GNMA 13	GNMA 14	GNMA 15
BondFut	1.000	0.935	0.992	0.993	0.993	0.992	0.960	0.911	0.920
Eurofut	0.935	1.000	0.941	0.943	0.945	0.958	0.956	0.928	0.951
GNMA 8	0.992	0.941	1.000	1.000	0.998	0.994	0.968	0.927	0.935
GNMA 9	0.993	0.943	1.000	1.000	0.999	0.996	0.970	0.929	0.937
GNMA 10	0.993	0.945	0.998	0.999	1.000	0.998	0.974	0.932	0.940
GNMA 11	0.992	0.958	0.994	0.996	0.998	1.000	0.981	0.944	0.952
GNMA 13	0.960	0.956	0.968	0.970	0.974	0.981	1.000	0.980	0.978
GNMA 14	0.911	0.928	0.927	0.929	0.932	0.944	0.980	1.000	0.986
GNMA 15	0.920	0.951	0.935	0.937	0.940	0.952	0.978	0.986	1.000

D. Correlation Matrix—Second Subperiod: 1/86–6/94

	BondFut	Eurofut	GNMA 8	GNMA 9	GNMA 10	GNMA 11	GNMA 13	GNMA 14	GNMA 15
BondFut	1.000	0.835	0.942	0.902	0.906	0.872	0.688	0.665	0.715
Eurofut	0.835	1.000	0.919	0.924	0.935	0.963	0.806	0.794	0.882
GNMA 8	0.942	0.919	1.000	0.985	0.980	0.953	0.819	0.802	0.851
GNMA 9	0.902	0.924	0.985	1.000	0.988	0.959	0.842	0.827	0.880
GNMA 10	0.906	0.935	0.980	0.988	1.000	0.966	0.796	0.781	0.849
GNMA 11	0.872	0.963	0.953	0.959	0.966	1.000	0.859	0.846	0.898
GNMA 13	0.688	0.806	0.819	0.842	0.796	0.859	1.000	0.993	0.951
GNMA 14	0.665	0.794	0.802	0.827	0.781	0.846	0.993	1.000	0.955
GNMA 15	0.715	0.882	0.851	0.880	0.849	0.898	0.951	0.955	1.000

Exhibit 27. *Continued*

E. Correlation Matrix—Third Subperiod: 1986–87

	BondFut	Eurofut	GNMA 8	GNMA 9	GNMA 10	GNMA 11	GNMA 13	GNMA 14	GNMA 15
BondFut	1.000	0.843	0.898	0.871	0.886	0.860	-0.532	-0.602	-0.287
Eurofut	0.843	1.000	0.832	0.765	0.832	0.839	-0.405	-0.568	-0.228
GNMA 8	0.898	0.832	1.000	0.984	0.981	0.931	-0.249	-0.423	-0.261
GNMA 9	0.871	0.765	0.984	1.000	0.984	0.929	-0.184	-0.350	-0.185
GNMA 10	0.886	0.832	0.981	0.984	1.000	0.959	-0.257	-0.423	-0.213
GNMA 11	0.860	0.839	0.931	0.929	0.959	1.000	-0.200	-0.366	-0.149
GNMA 13	-0.532	-0.405	-0.249	-0.184	-0.257	-0.200	1.000	0.899	0.537
GNMA 14	-0.602	-0.568	-0.423	-0.350	-0.423	-0.366	0.899	1.000	0.482
GNMA 15	-0.287	-0.228	-0.261	-0.185	-0.213	-0.149	0.537	0.482	1.000

Exhibit 28.   Means, Standard Deviations and Correlations Using Price Changes

A. Bond and Mortgage Price Changes: Means and Standard Deviations

Variable	Entire Period 1/84–6/94		First Subperiod 1984–85		Second Subperiod 1/86–6/94		Third Subperiod 1986–87	
	Mean	Std Dev'n	Mean	Std Dev'n	Mean	Std Dev'n	Mean	Std Dev'n
BondFut	0.24	3.00	0.63	2.76	0.16	3.05	0.11	4.17
Eurofut	0.04	0.46	0.10	0.64	0.02	0.40	0.01	0.47
GNMA 8	0.17	1.85	0.63	2.40	0.07	1.69	0.01	2.08
GNMA 9	0.18	1.77	0.65	2.55	0.07	1.52	-0.03	2.08
GNMA 10	0.16	1.64	0.63	2.68	0.06	1.27	-0.05	1.79
GNMA 11	0.15	1.39	0.54	2.53	0.06	0.93	-0.02	1.26
GNMA 13	0.10	1.22	0.24	2.00	0.07	0.95	0.07	0.53
GNMA 14	0.09	1.22	0.13	1.78	0.08	1.05	0.10	0.93
GNMA 15	0.10	1.23	0.15	1.33	0.09	1.20	0.09	0.74

B. Correlation Matrix—Entire Period: 1/84–6/94

	BondFut	Eurofut	GNMA 8	GNMA 9	GNMA 10	GNMA 11	GNMA 13	GNMA 14	GNMA 15
BondFut	1.000	0.679	0.872	0.829	0.751	0.668	0.418	0.342	0.397
Eurofut	0.679	1.000	0.691	0.671	0.646	0.662	0.518	0.353	0.361
GNMA 8	0.872	0.691	1.000	0.963	0.898	0.816	0.583	0.487	0.481
GNMA 9	0.829	0.671	0.963	1.000	0.945	0.877	0.575	0.451	0.430
GNMA 10	0.751	0.646	0.898	0.945	1.000	0.924	0.583	0.453	0.413
GNMA 11	0.668	0.662	0.816	0.877	0.924	1.000	0.678	0.516	0.462
GNMA 13	0.418	0.518	0.583	0.575	0.583	0.678	1.000	0.855	0.753
GNMA 14	0.342	0.353	0.487	0.451	0.453	0.516	0.855	1.000	0.753
GNMA 15	0.397	0.361	0.481	0.430	0.413	0.462	0.753	0.753	1.000

Exhibit 28.   *Continued*

C. Correlation Matrix—First Subperiod: 1984–85

	BondFut	Eurofut	GNMA 8	GNMA 9	GNMA 10	GNMA 11	GNMA 13	GNMA 14	GNMA 15
BondFut	1.000	0.787	0.959	0.956	0.956	0.960	0.830	0.681	0.705
Eurofut	0.787	1.000	0.763	0.763	0.768	0.790	0.735	0.508	0.533
GNMA 8	0.959	0.763	1.000	0.997	0.992	0.981	0.876	0.755	0.768
GNMA 9	0.956	0.763	0.997	1.000	0.995	0.986	0.879	0.740	0.772
GNMA 10	0.956	0.768	0.992	0.995	1.000	0.992	0.882	0.734	0.765
GNMA 11	0.960	0.790	0.981	0.986	0.992	1.000	0.900	0.755	0.792
GNMA 13	0.830	0.735	0.876	0.879	0.882	0.900	1.000	0.843	0.852
GNMA 14	0.681	0.508	0.755	0.740	0.734	0.755	0.843	1.000	0.912
GNMA 15	0.705	0.533	0.768	0.772	0.765	0.792	0.852	0.912	1.000

D. Correlation Matrix—Second Subperiod: 1/86–6/94

	BondFut	Eurofut	GNMA 8	GNMA 9	GNMA 10	GNMA 11	GNMA 13	GNMA 14	GNMA 15
BondFut	1.000	0.670	0.868	0.827	0.746	0.653	0.283	0.242	0.328
Eurofut	0.670	1.000	0.653	0.613	0.560	0.579	0.357	0.258	0.298
GNMA 8	0.868	0.653	1.000	0.949	0.860	0.747	0.401	0.348	0.385
GNMA 9	0.827	0.613	0.949	1.000	0.914	0.813	0.336	0.270	0.298
GNMA 10	0.746	0.560	0.860	0.914	1.000	0.849	0.281	0.236	0.259
GNMA 11	0.653	0.579	0.747	0.813	0.849	1.000	0.404	0.306	0.317
GNMA 13	0.283	0.357	0.401	0.336	0.281	0.404	1.000	0.874	0.755
GNMA 14	0.242	0.258	0.348	0.270	0.236	0.306	0.874	1.000	0.706
GNMA 15	0.328	0.298	0.385	0.298	0.259	0.317	0.755	0.706	1.000

Exhibit 28. Continued

E. Correlation Matrix—Third Subperiod: 1986–87

	BondFut	Eurofut	GNMA 8	GNMA 9	GNMA 10	GNMA 11	GNMA 13	GNMA 14	GNMA 15
BondFut	1.000	0.732	0.861	0.869	0.799	0.672	-0.099	-0.164	0.151
Eurofut	0.732	1.000	0.599	0.640	0.698	0.698	0.076	-0.155	0.212
GNMA 8	0.861	0.599	1.000	0.979	0.922	0.785	0.189	-0.077	-0.051
GNMA 9	0.869	0.640	0.979	1.000	0.960	0.808	0.177	0.000	0.051
GNMA 10	0.799	0.698	0.922	0.960	1.000	0.892	0.247	0.078	0.082
GNMA 11	0.672	0.698	0.785	0.808	0.892	1.000	0.437	0.124	0.121
GNMA 13	-0.009	0.076	0.189	0.177	0.247	0.437	1.000	0.545	0.109
GNMA 14	-0.164	-0.155	-0.007	0.000	0.078	0.124	0.545	1.000	-0.205
GNMA 15	0.151	0.212	-0.051	0.051	0.082	0.121	0.109	-0.205	1.000

securities are more highly correlated with Eurodollar futures than with T-bond futures, while the reverse is true for low-coupon discount securities.

As was discussed earlier in this chapter (Exhibit 15), 1986 was a very unusual year for mortgage price movements relative to Treasury bond prices. In the first half of the year, bond prices rose dramatically (from 85 to 99), while mortgages with coupons above 12% actually fell in price. In the second half of the year, this pattern reversed as high-coupon mortgages increased in price while T-bond futures fell. These unprecedented moves clearly show a negative correlation of high-coupon mortgages with T-bonds during 1986. These negative correlations show up in the subperiod correlation matrices for the 1986–87 subperiod, and show up as reduced correlations of high-coupon mortgages with T-bonds for the entire sample. In the first subperiod when rates were high (1984–85), all mortgage coupons examined had correlations with T-bonds in excess of .9 and coupons below 11 had correlations over .99. Even in the difficult 1986–87 subperiod, correlations are quite good (the lowest being .86) for mortgages with coupons up to 2% to 3% over the par coupons. But the correlations on super-high coupon mortgages (with coupons more than 3% over par) were not reliable and were often negative. While researchers can understand why very high coupon mortgages can have negative price elasticities, most would be uncomfortable long-hedging them, with the assumption of negative price elasticities. Suffice it to say that very high coupon mortgages are difficult to hedge. However, that worry is mitigated by the fact that there is relatively little price volatility in them to hedge.

Let us use these correlation statistics to determine which contracts to short for First Savings' hedge. From the graphs of Exhibits 22-24, we see that the major liquidation value risk is generated by interest-rate risk of the fixed-rate mortgages that the firm holds. Thus, movements in liquidation value are likely to be quite closely related to mortgage rate movements. Assuming that these mortgage values are closely related to the GNMA 8 prices in Exhibit 15, the best hedge is found by looking at various futures' correlations with those GNMA 8 prices. Using price levels, the 3-month Eurodollar price has a correlation with GNMA 8s of .88 and the 20-year T-bond contract has a correlation with GNMA 8s of .97. Using price changes, the correlations of Euros and T-bonds with GNMA 8s are .69 and .87, respectively. Thus, if one had to choose one of those markets for the hedge, the 20-year T-bond futures would be chosen for its highest correlation with the GNMA 8s.

If more futures markets and bond maturities were examined, one would see that GNMA 8s have the highest correlation with 7- to 10-year T-notes, for which the futures market is not as liquid as the futures market for T-bonds. However, since (with a smooth term structure) 10-year rates are much like a weighted average of 3-month rates and 20-year rates, the best correlation with First Savings' liquidation value is obtained with a mix of

3-month Eurodollar futures and 20-year T-bond futures, with most of the weight placed on the T-bonds. An attempt to find the exact composition of the best hedge is beyond the scope of this chapter; it would involve taking account of the changing durations of both the mortgages and the T-bonds as rates change. As shown earlier in this chapter, as rates fall the durations of T-bonds lengthen, whereas the durations of GNMA 8s shorten due to higher prepayment rates on the underlying mortgages. Thus, the optimal hedge needs to be periodically rebalanced, as is illustrated in the next section.

Exhibit 29 displays the results of a hedge consisting of a short position of 1,660 91-day Eurodollar futures contracts and 411 20-year T-bond futures contracts. For a parallel rate increase of 1%, the portfolio will make about $8.0 million (1660 x $2,500 + 411 x $9,390), which significantly reduces the cash losses and is similar to the sensitivities of the "all T-bonds" and "all Euros" positions calculated earlier. The graph displayed in Exhibit 29 contains 3 elements: (1) the June 30, 1994, liquidation value curve (hedged with swaps only) from Exhibit 24, (2) the futures gains and losses curve for this proposed position, and (3) the combined result of the liquidation value hedged with swaps and futures. Note the behavior of the 3 curves at the base level and plus or minus 1%. The liquidation value (without futures) falls rapidly as interest

**Exhibit 29.   First Savings and Loan Association
Liquidation Value Hedged with Swaps and Futures**

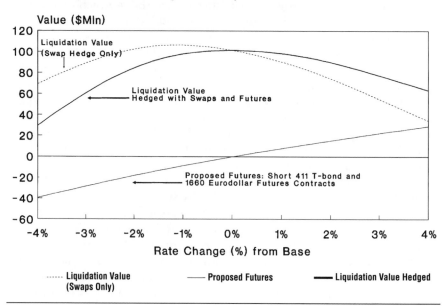

rates increase from base levels and increases slightly as rates decrease. The futures hedge profits increase as rates decrease. The combined effect of futures gains and cash losses result in a fairly stable hedged value for the firm (between $99.3 and $102.7 million) for interest-rate moves of 1% or less from base. Also note that the liquidation value falls by a small but equal amount for rate moves of plus or minus 1% from base. Thus, First Savings is in a position of neutrality with respect to the direction of interest rates, whereas before hedging with futures the firm clearly benefitted from (and was betting on) a decline in the level of market interest rates.

In studying Exhibit 29, one sees that while interest-rate swaps and futures do a very good job of stabilizing the liquidation value of the firm for small rate moves, the precision of the hedge "falls off in the tails." That is, for large interest-rate moves in either direction, the hedged liquidation value ultimately falls. The fact that the institution is significantly hurt by large interest-rate moves in either direction is graphically displayed by the curved (concave or "negatively convex") shape of the hedged liquidation value line in Exhibit 29. When interest rates rise the rate of prepayment on the Association's mortgages decreases, rate increases on the firm's adjustable-rate mortgages are limited by caps, and the value of these mortgages falls faster than does the value of the institution's liabilities and the futures contracts and swaps employed as a hedge. At very low levels of interest rates the rate of prepayment on First Savings' mortgages increases dramatically and the value of these mortgages rises at a slower rate than does the value of the liabilities and hedges. The Association's exposure to large interest-rate moves can be hedged with options which are examined in the next section.

HEDGING WITH OPTIONS

Most fixed-rate mortgage loans are written with options that are valuable to the borrower. Most commonly, the borrower has an option to prepay all or part of the mortgage at his discretion without penalty. When the mortgage was originally issued, the lender should have received compensation in the form of fees or a higher interest rate to offset the value of the option. Similarly, the owner of a fixed-rate mortgage-backed security is short a call option, i.e., he has written a call option to the borrower on the present value of the mortgage payments.

The higher the level of prevailing mortgage rates relative to a borrower's mortgage rate, the lower the value of his prepayment option, since he is less likely to refinance his mortgage. Conversely, the firm which owns a fixed-rate mortgage asset can expect that the level of prepayments (exercise of the options) on the security will increase as market rates decrease. Since the value of a prepayment option will increase as interest rate levels decrease, the Association will suffer a loss unless the change in the value of the prepayment option is hedged. The caps embedded in adjustable-rate mortgages are, similarly, valuable options (caps) which the lender has granted the borrower. These options protect the borrower (and hurt the lender) when market interest rates rise.

As interest rates change, the sensitivities of assets, liabilities, and hedging instruments may change by different amounts, leaving the firm in a situation of having to periodically rebalance the hedge. Consider Exhibit 29, which shows that the hedge is initially duration matched, but as interest-rate levels change, the hedge loses in both directions. When rates rise, the values of mortgages fall faster than the values of the institution's liabilities and hedges (the rate of prepayments decreases and the mortgages' durations lengthen). When rates fall, prepayments accelerate and the values of the mortgages rise at slower rates than do the values of both the liabilities and swap and futures hedges. This effect reflects changes in the value of the option component of the Association's fixed-rate mortgages. A hedge that initially matches the interest-rate sensitivity of the assets with the sensitivity of the liabilities plus hedges (as was done with the futures hedge described above) will not necessarily be balanced after a change in interest rates has occurred.

One can choose to counteract this problem by rebalancing the hedge periodically. Rebalancing the hedge position entails costs (including transactions costs) which are akin to the cost of buying options and which increase with the volatility of interest rates and the frequency of rebalancing. With the development of, and liquidity present in, the markets for options such as LIBOR caps and floors, options on T-bond, and options on Eurodollar futures, it is feasible and often desirable to use these options markets to create more accurate hedge positions which protect the Association against changes in the value of the prepayment option. Since short-term rates sometimes move differently from long-term rates, options on long-term and short-term rates should play an important role in improving hedging precision.

Exhibit 30 (which has three graphs) displays First Savings' proposed options position (Exhibit 30b) which would complement its swaps and short futures position and complete its hedge. It is necessary to buy out-of-the-money puts (caps) and calls (floors) to create an options position with the (convex) shape exactly opposite to the (concave) shape of the graph of the liquidation value hedged only with swaps and futures (Exhibit 30a). Exhibit 30c graphs the new hedged value of the firm for different interest-rate scenarios. Note that the inclusion of options in the hedge has eliminated the decline in Association value for large interest-rate movements. In fact, the estimated hedged liquidation value for a 400 basis point increase in rates is $91.2 million. This compares to - $152.4 million if unhedged and $63.6 million hedged with swaps and futures only. (See Exhibit 31.)

Exhibit 30a. First Savings and Loan Association: Liquidation Value Hedged with Swaps and Futures Only

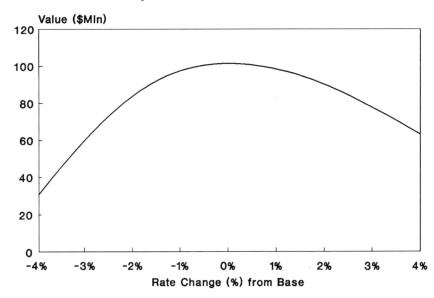

As the previous section describing interest-rate caps and floors indicated, these securities are a source of long-term options (unlike exchange-traded options on futures). As a result, caps and floors are often better hedges of the long-term options (prepayment options and rate caps) embedded in financial institutions' portfolios than are options on futures contracts. In practice, an institution's management may wish to design a hedge containing both short-term (more liquid) and long-term options, especially if hedge rebalancing occurs frequently. The costs of alternative options positions, in relation to their associated benefits, should always be carefully considered.

In summary, by using futures and options as hedging instruments, the net sensitivity of First Savings to changes in interest rates is reduced dramatically. In fact, even for extreme movements in rates (down 400 basis points and up 400 basis points), the resulting exposure represents significantly less than 1% of assets and less than 10% of the firm's net worth. For 300 basis point moves, the exposure is only 0.5% of assets and 7% of the institution's net worth. The hedge is well-balanced throughout a wide range of interest-rate moves as the result of utilizing options contracts. Similar results can be attained by dynamically adjusting the futures hedge position, but the costs may be higher and the firm would be exposed to changes in the volatilities of interest rates.

Exhibit 30b.   First Savings and Loan Association: Proposed Options

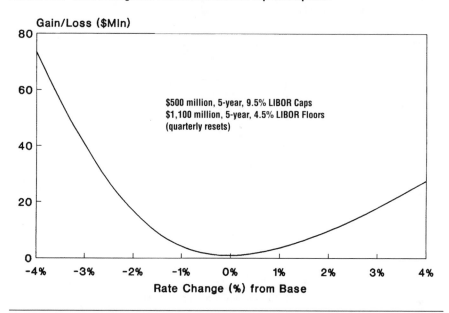

Gain/Loss ($Mln)

$500 million, 5-year, 9.5% LIBOR Caps
$1,100 million, 5-year, 4.5% LIBOR Floors
(quarterly resets)

Rate Change (%) from Base

After a cursory examination of the graph found in Exhibit 30c, one may conclude that First Savings' options hedging strategy stochastically dominates the alternative strategy of not hedging with options. Since Exhibits 30 and 31 indicate that First Savings' liquidation value, after hedging with options, is everywhere (for all possible interest-rate moves) greater than or equal to the firm's liquidation value without options, one could draw the conclusion that the options hedging strategy is superior in all instances. Certainly this conclusion must not be correct, since we have seen from an earlier section of this chapter that options do not provide the investor with a proverbial "free lunch."

The key to understanding this apparent paradox lies in the fact that the graph shown in Exhibit 30c demonstrates only the effect of *instantaneous* movements in interest rates on the liquidation value of First Savings. At the "split second" that the options are purchased, First Savings' liquidation value is the same (ignoring transactions costs) as it was before it purchased the options. Therefore, the liquidation value lines of Exhibit 30c are tangent to each other at "base" levels of interest rates. In reality, as time passes, these liquidation value curves drift upward and downward as the firm earns income.

Hedging strategies change not only a firm's liquidation value for sudden changes in interest rates; they also alter the rate at which the liquidation value "drifts" by changing a firm's income pattern over time, making it more

Exhibit 30c.   First Savings and Loan Association: Effect of Proposed Hedge

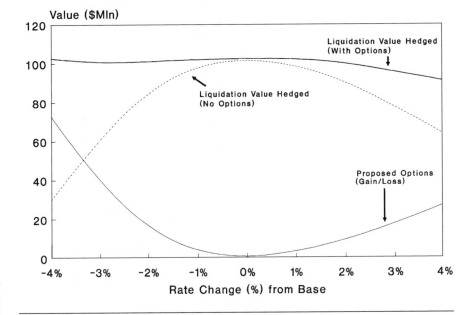

**Exhibit 31.   First Savings and Loan Association
Liquidation Value Hedged with Swaps, Futures and Options**

	($ Millions)								
Rate Change from Base	-4%	-3%	-2%	-1%	0%	1%	2%	3%	4%
Liquidation Value Hedged With Swaps	69.0	90.6	104.5	107.9	102.7	91.3	75.9	55.7	34.4
Total Gain/Loss on Futures	-39.5	-28.2	-18.0	-8.6	0.0	8.0	15.5	22.5	29.2
Liquidation Value Hedged with Swaps and Futures	29.5	62.4	86.6	99.3	102.7	99.3	91.4	78.2	63.6
Gain/Loss on $500 Mln, 5-Yr, 9.5% LIBOR Caps	-7.4	-6.9	-5.7	-3.5	0.0	5.1	11.9	20.5	30.7
Gain/Loss on $1,100 Mln, 5-Yr, 4.5% LIBOR Floors	80.6	44.5	20.2	6.3	0.0	-1.8	-2.6	-2.9	-3.1
Total Gain/Loss on Caps and Floors	73.3	37.7	14.5	2.8	0.0	3.3	9.3	17.5	27.6
Liquidation Value Hedged with Swaps, Futures, & Options	102.7	100.1	101.1	102.1	102.7	102.5	100.7	95.8	91.2

stable. In this example, First Savings must begin to amortize the cost of the options ($2.2 million per year) immediately after their purchase. Obviously, if interest rates do not move very much, First Savings' options will expire worthless and the firm would have been better off (in retrospect) by not hedging. If interest rates move substantially, causing large gains on the options, First Savings will have been better off by hedging with options. There also exist scenarios for moderate movements in interest rates where the firm would be neither better nor worse off by purchasing options than by not purchasing options.

First Savings' hedging strategy reduces risk in the sense that the firm's liquidation value and income are expected to be less volatile as a result. Of course, only one of the infinite number of possible interest-rate scenarios will become reality and First Savings may, in retrospect, have been better off if it had not purchased options in the first place. Since First Savings' management is risk-averse and does not have the ability to predict changes in interest rates, it chooses to hedge with options, thereby trading off the ability to earn slightly higher earnings (and liquidation value) during periods of less volatile interest rates for much improved earnings and value in the event of significant interest rate changes.

When thought about in this context, hedging with options may be considered akin to purchasing an insurance policy against adverse movements in interest rates. When purchasing insurance, the policyholder does not know what will eventually happen but is concerned that under certain circumstances he will incur significant losses. The policyholder is willing to give up some current income (the policy premium) for the payoffs that he will receive if these adverse circumstances come to be realized. Just as the purchaser of insurance does not know if he will be better or worse off until the date his policy expires or pays off, the management of First Savings does not know if it would have been better off (by hedging with options) until its options have expired or have been exercised. However, the policyholder, the management, and the shareholders of First Savings are more comfortable knowing that the chances of large—and potentially catastrophic—losses have been eliminated.

With any well-constructed hedge, it should always be possible to identify futures contracts with particular assets and liabilities. This view of hedging is termed *micro hedging*, as opposed to the *macro hedging* perspective which looks at the interest-rate risks of the entire Association. Indeed, for regulatory and accounting purposes, the identification of futures contracts as micro hedges is necessary. After a little thought, it should be clear that the same steps which were described and followed for First Savings on a "macro" level can also be carried out for any subset of its assets or liabilities.

When hedging mortgages without the use of options, if is often necessary to add more hedges when rates increase and subtract some when rates fall. This is necessary since one is hedging the prepayment option—essentially by recreating that option with a dynamic trading strategy. It can be shown that the cumulative gains and losses on cash positions in GNMA mortgage-backed securities have correlations in excess of .95 with Treasury bond futures hedge gains and losses in spite of a difficult hedging environment in 1986. In Chapter 36, "Risk, Return, and Hedging of Fixed-Rate Mortgages", Douglas T. Breeden provides an excellent treatment of mortgage hedging issues including the dynamic nature of mortgage elasticities and the risks and returns from specific mortgage coupons on a both a hedged and an unhedged basis.

Thus, despite the demonstrated basis risk, the hedges of mortgages are very effective over large interest-rate swings. If one makes the case that the basis risk is so large as to vitiate the usefulness of futures, then one is simply not looking carefully at the data. The volatilities of the hedged positions are much, much smaller than the volatilities of unhedged positions.

It should be pointed out that it is possible to micro hedge some assets and liabilities without hedging others, thereby making the firm actually *more* risky than without the hedge. By examining *all* assets and liabilities, the possibility of a risk-increasing set of micro hedges can be eliminated. Thus, a requirement that all hedges be identified as micro hedges is one that any good hedging program should be able to meet. However, it is not true that any hedging program that can be viewed as a set of micro hedges is "safe" or "appropriate" or even "risk-reducing." Complete asset and liability analysis, such as the one presented in the last two sections for First Savings, is necessary in order to obtain an assurance that the hedge is really risk-reducing.

CONCLUSION

This chapter presented an integrated approach to the assessment and hedging of interest-rate risk. The chapter started with the basics of futures, options, interest-rate swaps, and mortgages and proceeded to more complex hedging analysis. Issues of duration and price elasticities for mortgages were examined, although more remains to be done. Changes in mortgage elasticities were documented using data from 1984–94—a time of very volatile interest rates. The difficulties of hedging mortgages and the basis risks of hedging them with futures were dramatically illustrated.

Within the chapter are graphs that give a relatively complete, elementary presentation of risk analysis and of the construction of futures and option hedges. The chapter can be read ignoring the statistics to obtain this graphic presentation (particularly with the First Savings example). Still, many investors, regulators, and portfolio managers are significantly beyond this elementary understanding, so the statistical data and results are available.

A great amount of data on Treasury rates, futures prices, mortgage prices, and prepayments was presented, so that readers may pursue the many interesting questions that were not addressed in the chapter. Some of the significant issues not examined are: (1) optimal hedge portfolios of futures contracts, balancing both T-bonds and Eurodollar contracts with various maturities; (2) costs of option protection and the returns achieved with option-hedging strategies; (3) performance of interest-rate swaps as hedges; and (4) optimal dynamic hedging strategies. Daily data and portfolio rebalancing would also be interesting and would probably improve some of the hedge performance aspects, but at some transaction cost. These issues are beyond the scope of this chapter.

CHAPTER 36

Risk, Return and Hedging of Fixed-Rate Mortgages

Douglas T. Breeden, Ph.D.
President and Chairman of the Board
Smith Breeden Associates, Inc.
and Research Professor of Finance
Fuqua School of Business, Duke University*

INTRODUCTION

The risk, return and hedging aspects of mortgages are more complicated than most fixed-income securities, because mortgages give the borrower the option to prepay the loan at par at any time during the life of the loan. Our understanding of risk, return, pricing and hedging of securities with options has been propelled by the seminal work of Black and Scholes and the literature that has built upon that work[1]. Unfortunately, but interestingly, mortgages are much more complicated option-like securities than those dealt with by Black and Scholes. For example, Black and Scholes assumed (1) that interest rates were constant, (2) that the option was "European" in that it could only be exercised on the final maturity date, (3) that the exercise price was known and fixed, and (4) that the returns on the underlying asset were normally distributed. Of course, the volatility of interest rates is the reason the prepayment option in a mortgage has value and is of interest. Furthermore, it may well be optimal for different people to exercise their prepayment options at different times, particularly as they have different effective costs of exercising their

---

* This research project began with my work with Michael Giarla that was published as Chapter 37 in the second edition of *The Handbook of Mortgage-Backed Securities* ("Hedging Interest-Rate Risks with Futures, Swaps, and Options"). I wish to gratefully acknowledge the help of Michael Giarla, Campbell Harvey, Timothy Rowe and especially my research assistants, Michelle Rodgerson and Kathryn Waseleski.

1 Fischer, Black and Myron S. Scholes, "The Pricing of Options and Corporate Liabilities," *Journal of Political Economy* 81, (May-June 1973): 637-659.

options. Finally, the underlying asset for the prepayment option is a bond, which certainly does not have normally distributed returns.

In this chapter, mortgages are viewed as far too complicated to value precisely and rigorously, even with the Black-Scholes model and the many improvements developed in subsequent years. Given this view, the goal here is much more limited and data oriented. Data on interest rates, prepayment rates, and mortgage prices are used to develop risk and return properties and hedging methods that reflect the information in market prices. Assuming that market prices reflect the information of very well-informed investors, mortgage prices for different coupons should reflect some of the most up-to-date values and models of the complicated prepayment options. This chapter, uses both the cross-section of mortgage prices by coupon and the time series of prices and prepayment rates to develop risk and return estimates and hedging strategies. As the chapter shows, many of the risk functions inferred empirically do have characteristics expected from the option pricing theory of Black and Scholes.

MORTGAGE PAYMENTS AND THE PREPAYMENT OPTION

Consider a borrower who takes out a standard, 30-year, fixed-rate mortgage for $100,000 to buy a house worth $125,000. One can calculate that the mortgage must have level monthly payments of $952.32 to amortize the loan and reflect an annual interest rate of 11%, compounded monthly. As this is a fixed-rate, fixed-payment loan, if market rates increase to 12%, the present value of the borrower's fixed payments declines to $92,583. A smaller debt is good for the borrower, which reflects the now below-market rate of 11%. On the other hand, if rates decrease to 10%, the borrower's present value of payments increases to $108,518, reflecting the fact that the borrower's loan is now above the current market rate. Exhibit 1 shows the entire schedule of payments and their present values for three different mortgages with 9%, 11%, and 13% rates, respectively, discounted at current market rates from 7% to 18%.

A typical fixed-rate mortgage provides the borrower with the option to pay off the mortgage at the unpaid outstanding balance ($100,000 initially), usually with no prepayment penalty. Continuing with the 11% fixed-rate mortgage example, if rates decrease to 10% the borrower's same monthly payments would amortize a new loan for $108,518, which could be obtained from another bank to pay off the old loan. By prepaying, the borrower pockets $8,518 in present value (8.52 "points" or % of par), less any refinancing costs not included in the rate (usually assumed to be 2-5 points). The gross amounts of the refinancing gains from prepaying mortgages with 9%, 11%, and 13% coupons are also in Exhibit 1. From the table, the gains from refinancing and prepayment can be quite large, as, for example, a 13% mortgage refinanced at 9% results in a $37,481 gain per $100,000 of loan balance, less refinancing costs.

Exhibit 1. Value of the Option to Prepay

Borrower's Fixed Mortgage Rate

100,000 Loan
Monthly Loan Payment:

Current Mortgage Rate	20-Year TBond Yield	TBond Futures Price	9.00% $804.62			11.00% $952.32			13.00% $1,106.20		
			PV (Payment)	Prepayment Profit	TBond Call *X=105.14 Q=0.84	PV (Payment)	Prepayment Profit	TBond Call X=86.68 Q=0.99	PV (Payment)	Prepayment Profit	TBond Call X=72.82 Q=1.16
7.00%	5.50%	130.10	120,941	20.94	20.94	143,141	43.14	43.14	166,270	66.27	66.27
8.00%	6.50%	116.66	109,657	9.66	9.66	129,786	29.79	29.79	150,757	50.76	50.72
9.00%	7.50%	105.14	100,000	0.00	0.00	118,357	18.36	18.34	137,481	37.48	37.39
10.00%	8.50%	95.23	91,687	0.00	0.00	108,518	8.52	8.50	126,052	26.05	25.93
11.00%	9.50%	86.68	84,490	0.00	0.00	100,000	0.00	0.00	116,158	16.16	16.03
12.00%	10.50%	79.27	78,224	0.00	0.00	92,583	0.00	0.00	107,543	7.54	7.46
13.00%	11.50%	72.82	72,738	0.00	0.00	86,090	0.00	0.00	100,000	0.00	0.00
14.00%	12.50%	67.19	67,908	0.00	0.00	80,374	0.00	0.00	93,360	0.00	0.00
15.00%	13.50%	62.25	63,634	0.00	0.00	75,316	0.00	0.00	87,485	0.00	0.00
16.00%	14.50%	57.90	59,834	0.00	0.00	70,818	0.00	0.00	82,260	0.00	0.00

*X=exercise price
Q=quantity of call options purchased.

Looking at Exhibit 1's column of "Prepayment Profits" for the 11% mortgage, one can see that they are equal to a call option on the present value of the mortgage's fixed cash flows without prepayments, with an exercise price of par. The call option is "in the money" if rates have fallen below the fixed mortgage rate, and many models assume that the mortgage will be refinanced and prepaid. Thus, in theory, whenever the current market mortgage rate is below the fixed coupon rate (or far enough below to offset refinancing costs), the bank or mortgage investor will be paid off and receive $100,000 (or 100% par). If rates have risen above the mortgage's fixed rate, then the borrower is assumed to keep the mortgage outstanding, resulting in values below par for the bank or mortgage investor. Thus, from the mortgage investor's point of view, the prepayment option is "Heads (rates up) I lose, as my bond falls in value" and "Tails (rates down) I don't win, as the mortgage is prepaid at par." This asymmetric situation (called "negative convexity" from its payoff graph's curvature) is not attractive unless one is compensated for this option risk. Insured mortgage investors are compensated by a positive spread of about 1.25% above Treasury rates of comparable duration.

A mortgage investor's theoretical payoff pattern is shown in Exhibits 2 and 3. The investor's profits are identical to buying a straight, long-term, fixed-rate bond that cannot be prepaid (which has interest-rate risk) and shorting a call option on that bond to the borrower. Alternatively, and equivalently through the "put and call parity" relationship, the investor's position has the risk of investing in riskless, short-term Treasury bills and having written a put option on the long-term, fixed-rate bond having the level payments promised on the mortgage. If rates decrease, the investor receives a certain amount (called at par), whereas if rates increase the mortgage remains outstanding (put to the investor) at a loss in market value. The values of prepayment options on mortgages with different coupons are very similar to Treasury bond options with different exercise prices (see Exhibit 1). For example, the prepayment option on a 9%, 30-year mortgage has similar payoffs to those of 0.84 call options on 20-year T-bond futures with an exercise price of 105.14. Similarly, the payoffs on the prepayment options of 11% and 13% mortgages are like those of 0.99 and 1.16 T-bond options with exercise prices of 86.68 and 72.82, respectively.

As simple as this analysis is, we will see that it is remarkably useful in understanding hedging and pricing for fixed-rate mortgages. To hedge these risks, we create offsetting positions through dynamic trading strategies or option purchases. As noted, a mortgage may be viewed either as long a bond and short a call, or just short a put. Thus, to hedge a mortgage security, one can either (1) short a straight bond and purchase or dynamically create a call option or (2) purchase or dynamically create a put option. Whether or not a mortgage is properly priced depends upon whether or not

Exhibit 2A.   Mortgage = Bond – Call Option

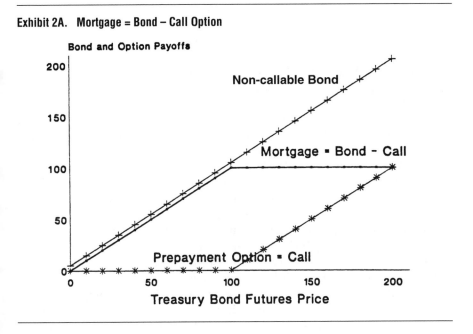

Exhibit 2B.   Mortgage = Riskless Bills – Put Option

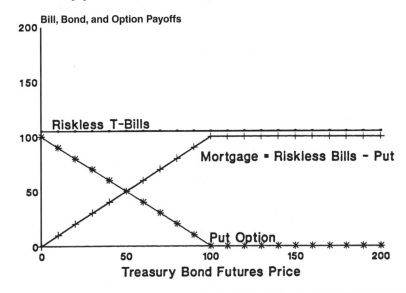

the interest rate-spread between the mortgage's yield and that on comparable-risk, noncallable-bonds is too large or too small in relation to the costs of option purchases or the costs of option creation.

INTEREST RATE VOLATILITY AND THE MORTGAGE-TREASURY YIELD SPREAD

Most data sets on mortgage-backed securities (MBS) start in the mid-1980s, as that is when the MBS market grew most rapidly and when data availability was improved considerably. Early work on hedging MBS was done by Breeden and Giarla, which used data for the 3-1/2 year period from 1984 to mid-1987[2]. For this study, data for the 13-year period from December 31, 1977 to December 31, 1990 were collected. This gives much more power to examine effects of recession (1980, 1981-82), rate volatility (1979-82), and burnout effects on mortgage prepayments, pricing, and hedging (1988-90). Price data were obtained from *The Wall Street Journal* for the entire period, and prepayment data were obtained from Salomon Brothers monthly from 1983-90 and from Drexel, Burnham, Lambert data annually from 1978-82. The price data from *The Wall Street Journal* are known to contain several errors, so the data were carefully checked by examining the time series of price changes for the various coupons, as well as the time series of price spreads across coupons. Apparent errors in the data were corrected prior to the analysis. As the prices examined were for MBS guaranteed by the Government National Mortgage Association (GNMA), which has a "full faith and credit" guarantee of the U.S. Government, credit risk is not a serious issue and is ignored throughout the chapter.

Interest-rate volatility increased dramatically in 1979 when the Federal Reserve changed its monetary policy. Exhibit 3 shows the levels of both short-term and long-term interest rates from the end of 1977 to mid-1991. Both short-term (3-month) and long-term (10-year) rates exceeded 15% in 1981 and then dropped to as low as 5% and 7%, respectively. These huge interest-rate movements caused correspondingly huge price movements in mortgages, Treasury bonds, and futures prices. In addition to changes in the general level of rates, note also that the slope of the yield curve changed quite significantly during the period examined. It was significantly downward sloping in 1979, turning to steeply upward sloping in 1983-84, to downward-sloping in 1989, and back to a sharp upward slope in 1991. As McConnell and Singh have shown, the slope of the yield curve has significant implications for prepayment rates on adjustable-rate mortgages (ARMs) versus fixed-rate

---

2 Douglas T. Breeden and Michael J. Giarla, "Hedging Interest-Rate Risks with Futures, Swaps, and Options," in *The Handbook of Mortgage-Backed Securities,* 2nd edition, Frank J. Fabozzi, ed., (Chicago, IL: Probus Publishing Co., 1987).

Exhibit 3.   3-Month and 10-Year Treasury Rates, December 1977 to May 1991

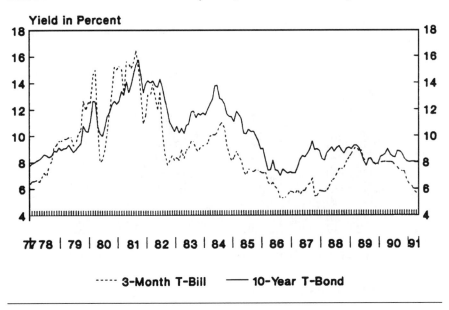

----- **3-Month T-Bill**   ——— **10-Year T-Bond**

mortgages[3]. It is plausible that the slope of the yield curve also affects prepayments on fixed-rate mortgages.

Exhibit 4 shows the spread in yields between current market rates for par GNMA mortgage securities and 7-year Treasury securities, which have similar price elasticity. As this compares spreads of securities with similar credit risks (none) and similar interest-rate risks, the spread's fluctuations should primarily reflect the value of the prepayment option described in the previous section. The borrower's prepayment option has greater value in times of greater rate volatility, and lenders and investors should require greater spreads of promised mortgage yields over Treasury yields at those times. As interest-rate volatility was greatest from 1979 to 1982 and in late 1985 to 1986, it is comforting that Exhibit 5 shows that mortgage-Treasury spreads were widest during those periods. Prior to late 1979 and from 1987-90, rate volatility was comparatively low, which made the borrower's prepayment option less valuable and the equilibrium mortgage-Treasury spread low. Thus, the general pattern of movements is broadly consistent with Section II's simple prepayment option analysis.

3 John J. McConnell, and Manoj K. Singh, "Prepayments and the Valuation of Adjustable-Rate Mortgage-Backed Securities," *Journal of Fixed Income* 1, (June 1991): 21-35.

Exhibit 4. Mortgage = Bond – Call Option

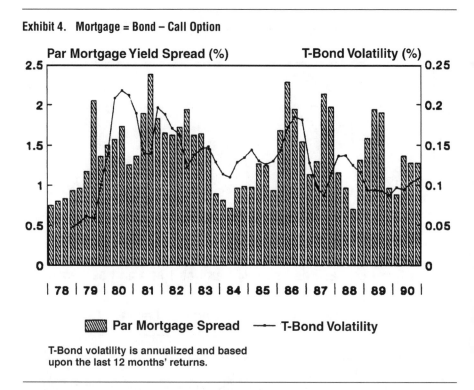

Par Mortgage Yield Spread (%)   T-Bond Volatility (%)

|▨ Par Mortgage Spread   —•— T-Bond Volatility

T-Bond volatility is annualized and based
upon the last 12 months' returns.

PREPAYMENT DATA AND ANALYSIS

Responding to these changing interest-rate and macroeconomic environments, prepayment rates changed dramatically during the 1978-90 period.
Prepayment rates on fixed-rate mortgages respond primarily to the following
factors: (1) the mortgage's coupon rate in relation to current refinancing
opportunities, (2) the age of the mortgage, (3) the season of the year, (4) the
degree of burnout, and (5) the growth/recession state of the macroeconomy.

The effects of the major variables on prepayments are as follows. First,
higher coupon mortgages should have higher prepayment rates, as Exhibit 1
showed that their profit from prepayments is larger. Secondly, few people
refinance immediately after they enter into a mortgage loan. As the mortgage ages, people become more mobile and more inclined to refinance,
which leads to increases in prepayment rates. After about 2 years, FHA mortality series show that prepayments on par mortgages flatten out at about an
annual prepayment rate of 6% and the mortgages are viewed as well-seasoned. Next, mobility and prepayments are related to weather for home-
building and school year timing, both of which lead to increases in prepay-

ments during the summer and decreases during the winter. Richard and Roll showed that the longer mortgage rates have been below the mortgage's coupon rate and it has been optimal to refinance, the more the composition of the pool's borrowers changes towards those who, for a variety of reasons, tend to be less inclined to refinance[4]. The slowing of the prepayment rate of a pool of mortgages as the quick payers depart is called the burnout effect. Finally, economic growth affects job mobility and, therefore, prepayment rates, as mortgages are often prepaid when the borrower moves to another location. Slower economic growth leads to less mobility and slower prepayments. The exhibits to follow illustrate all of these effects.

Exhibit 5 shows the annualized percentage paydowns from prepayments quarterly from 1978 to 1990 for GNMAs with coupons from 8% to 15%. Note that these prepayment rates are for mortgages with fixed maturities, so the time series reflect mortgages that are aging. In contrast to FNMA and FHLMC mortgage-backed securities, all of the mortgages underlying a GNMA MBS have initial maturities of 30 years, so one can be assured that a GNMA MBS of this 30-year type that matures in 2010 was issued in 1980. Also note that no data exists for high coupon mortgages prior to 1980, as rates had never before been high enough for those high coupon MBS to be issued! From Exhibit 5, one sees the aging effect from examining mortgages with coupons of 10% or higher, which were recently issued. Immediately after the mortgages were issued, prepayment rates were very low (usually <1%). Then, despite the very high interest rates of 1981-82, prepayment rates increased on these new mortgages, while the prepayments of seasoned discounts such as GNMA 8s and 9s slowed due to the very high interest rates.

The general sensitivity of prepayments to interest-rate movements is also easy to see. When rates were high in 1981-82, prepayments were low. When rates dropped sharply in 1985-86, prepayment rates accelerated dramatically from the 5%-10% range to as high as 45% on high coupons. Subsequent to that 1986-87 period of very rapid prepayments, the burnout effect described became apparent. Despite the fact that interest rates generally remained low in the 1988-90 period, prepayment rates on high coupon mortgages dropped by half or more. The expected seasonal pattern of prepayments is shown in Exhibit 6 with prepayments lowest in the winter and highest in summer.

A problem with examining the risks of investments in mortgage-backed securities is that the volatile movements in interest rates often dominate the effects of variables other than interest rates and lead to apparent non-stationarities in the relationships. For example, when GNMA 13s sold for a discount to par in 1981-82, it was not optimal to prepay them. However, during most of

---

4 Scott F. Richard, and Richard Roll, "Prepayments on Fixed-Rate Mortgage-Backed Securities," *Journal of Portfolio Management* 15, (Spring 1989): 73-82.

Exhibit 5. GNMA Annualized Paydowns from Prepayments, Quarterly 1978–90

Date	Par Mtg. Yield (%)	3-Month Treasury (%)	10-Year Treasury (%)	Slope 10-Yr-3-M (%)	TBond Futures	Mortgage Coupon Annualized Percentage Paydown							
						8%	9%	10%	11%	12%	13%	14%	15%
33178	8.73	6.65	8.12	1.47	95.94	6.4	6.7						
63078	9.33	7.21	8.59	1.38	93.00	6.4	6.7						
93078	9.32	8.07	8.50	0.43	93.31	6.4	6.7						
123178	10.13	9.60	9.12	-0.48	90.34	6.4	6.7						
33179	10.06	9.77	9.08	-0.69	90.19	7.1	2.2	0.1					
63079	9.88	9.25	8.76	-0.49	91.81	7.1	2.2	0.1					
93079	11.50	10.44	9.42	-1.02	87.78	7.1	2.2	0.1					
123179	11.67	12.53	10.31	-2.22	82.19	7.1	2.2	0.1	0.8				
33180	14.08	14.98	12.60	-2.38	67.94	3.4	2.2	0.7	0.8				
63080	11.39	8.18	9.98	1.80	81.19	3.4	2.2	0.7	0.8				
93080	13.57	11.89	11.83	-0.06	70.69	3.4	2.2	0.7	0.8				
123180	13.72	15.02	12.43	-2.59	71.38	3.4	2.2	0.7	0.8				
33181	14.57	13.00	13.10	0.10	67.06	1.4	1.3	1.2	1.4		0.7		
63081	15.94	15.08	13.84	-1.24	64.38	1.4	1.3	1.2	1.4		0.7		
93081	18.42	15.15	15.76	0.61	56.00	1.4	1.3	1.2	1.4		0.7		
123181	15.95	11.54	13.93	2.39	61.91	1.4	1.3	1.2	1.4		0.7		
33182	16.01	13.90	14.17	0.27	61.94	1.1	1.1	1.3	1.9		2.6	2.3	4.2
63082	16.14	13.32	14.32	1.00	60.69	1.1	1.1	1.3	1.9		2.6	2.3	4.2
93082	13.38	7.79	11.93	4.14	71.06	1.1	1.1	1.3	1.9		2.6	2.3	4.2
123182	12.21	8.13	10.31	2.18	76.63	1.3	1.6	1.5	2.1	0.4	3.5	4.2	19.8
33183	12.13	8.95	10.59	1.64	75.97	2.3	3.5	2.0	3.1	0.7	5.8	16.4	46.4
63083	12.49	9.04	10.89	1.85	74.44	3.3	5.2	2.7	4.0	1.1	9.1	22.3	35.7
93083	12.79	9.00	11.39	2.39	72.72	3.7	5.8	3.0	4.4	1.8	8.4	15.6	21.0
123183	12.69	9.26	11.76	2.50	70.03	2.8	4.4	2.4	3.6	1.7	7.4	12.3	19.9
33184	13.20	9.98	12.43	2.45	66.22	2.6	2.5	2.9	3.7	3.1	7.8	11.6	22.1
63084	14.52	10.26	13.83	3.57	59.63	3.5	2.8	3.2	4.3	4.1	8.9	16.1	19.8
93084	13.46	10.58	12.40	1.82	67.22	2.5	2.3	2.5	3.4	3.8	7.1	11.5	12.7

Exhibit 5. *Continued*

Date	Par Mtg. Yield (%)	3-Month Treasury (%)	10-Year Treasury (%)	Slope 10-Yr-3-M (%)	TBond Futures	Mortgage Coupon Annualized Percentage Paydown							
						8%	9%	10%	11%	12%	13%	14%	15%
123184	12.45	8.08	11.45	3.37	71.06	2.3	2.0	2.4	3.3	3.6	6.6	9.5	14.3
33185	12.65	8.44	11.63	3.19	69.72	2.5	2.3	2.5	3.4	4.0	7.6	13.4	22.3
63085	11.40	7.01	10.15	3.14	77.06	3.5	3.0	3.1	4.2	5.7	9.6	17.9	24.0
93085	11.41	7.27	10.33	3.06	75.59	4.7	4.1	4.2	6.0	9.1	16.1	31.8	35.8
123185	9.76	7.24	8.98	1.74	85.22	4.7	4.6	4.3	5.7	9.6	17.1	30.7	30.8
33186	9.00	6.51	7.38	0.87	102.31	4.4	5.1	4.4	7.2	16.2	25.0	34.8	39.8
63086	9.58	6.13	7.42	1.29	99.56	7.3	7.3	7.0	14.7	38.1	41.0	50.4	41.5
93086	9.24	5.31	7.49	2.18	95.56	10.0	9.7	10.3	21.2	49.3	47.2	51.9	46.7
123186	8.61	5.79	7.25	1.46	98.19	9.6	9.0	10.4	21.9	43.3	41.8	45.2	37.5
33187	8.53	5.95	7.62	1.67	98.47	7.7	8.0	12.2	24.4	41.2	36.1	37.2	33.4
63087	9.75	6.22	8.65	2.43	91.50	10.6	10.2	16.1	29.4	42.9	35.6	40.6	37.5
93087	10.80	5.40	8.92	3.52	81.69	8.5	8.8	10.6	16.7	27.4	27.8	31.7	29.2
123187	10.01	5.79	8.25	2.46	87.97	6.4	7.2	8.0	11.2	18.8	19.1	22.3	22.4
33188	9.80	6.15	8.89	2.74	90.09	5.3	5.9	6.5	9.9	19.7	17.2	22.6	24.3
63088	9.90	7.15	9.09	1.94	88.75	7.9	8.5	10.6	15.3	27.5	24.9	29.0	26.2
93088	9.90	8.36	9.13	0.77	88.75	8.1	7.6	9.9	12.9	21.2	21.3	24.3	21.2
123188	10.34	8.64	8.99	0.35	89.13	6.8	7.9	8.3	10.7	18.8	17.0	21.6	19.6
33189	10.69	8.79	9.08	0.29	88.41	5.3	5.5	6.4	8.2	15.6	14.7	22.0	21.2
63089	9.51	8.06	7.72	-0.34	97.94	5.9	6.6	7.4	8.9	15.6	16.6	22.0	20.0
93089	9.80	8.03	7.90	-0.13	95.84	7.1	6.3	9.1	11.6	19.1	16.1	20.4	20.7
123189	9.33	7.99	8.40	0.41	98.66	6.4	7.1	8.6	12.7	20.6	17.0	20.2	18.5
33190	9.92	8.02	9.02	1.00	91.88	5.7	6.2	6.9	10.9	18.2	14.6		17.8
63090	9.63	7.72	8.34	0.62	94.34	6.7	7.3	7.7	10.8	17.3	15.9		16.6
93090	9.77	7.33	8.65	1.32	89.38	6.9	7.2	8.0	10.2	16.4	13.5		13.5
123190	9.14	6.37	8.01	1.64	95.72	5.9	6.0	6.4	8.7	13.8	13.1		13.8

Source: 1979–1982 Drexel Burnham Lambert (Annual), 1983–1990 Salomon Brothers (monthly).
Prices and rates are end of quarter. Prepayment rates are averages for the quarter.

Exhibit 6. GNMA Seasonal Prepayment Multipliers, 1983–90

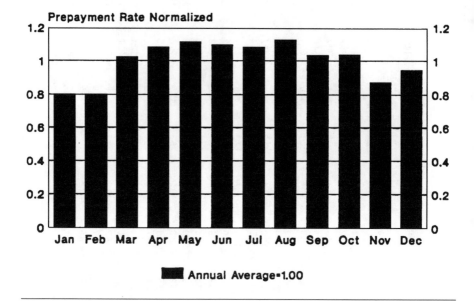

Annual Average=1.00

the remaining period they were premiums and it was optimal to prepay. As will be shown in the next sections, mortgage price volatilities should be and are very different in those different circumstances. A simple transformation of the data that will be often used in this chapter (as it generally works very well) is to examine data series for investment strategies sorted by a given spread of the mortgage's coupon minus the coupon of the current par mortgage. Thus, instead of examining the prepayment rates, risks, and returns of GNMA 13s, we often will look at those series for the changing (but well-defined) set of mortgages that have coupons that are, say, 2% to 3% above the current par mortgage rate, *i.e.*, "premium mortgages." This transformation mitigates the interest-rate effect and allows a better examination of other effects.

Exhibit 7 shows annual averages of prepayment rates for securities sorted by their spreads to the par mortgage rate. The higher prepayment rates of high coupons are apparent from examining this table, as is the burnout effect. In Exhibit 7, the annual growth rate of GNP, the number of housing starts, and the national unemployment rate are all displayed as indicators of macroeconomic performance and mobility. The recession periods of mid-1980 and late-1981 through 1982 have very low prepayment rates, even on seasoned discounts sorted so as to approximately hold interest rates constant. This shows the expected macroeconomic effect. Studies that start

Exhibit 7. Average Annual GNMA Prepayments by Coupon—Par Mortgage Rate

The coupon range columns are grouped under **Discounts** (−4.99/−4.00 through −0.49/0.00) and **Premiums** (0.50/0.99 through 5.00/5.99). Values are "Annualized Paydown from Prepayments (%)".

Year	Avg. Par Mtg. (%)	House Starts (000)	GNP Growth (%)	Unemp (%)	−4.99/−4.00	−3.99/−3.00	−2.99/−2.00	−1.99/−1.00	−0.99/−0.50	−0.49/0.00	0.00/0.49	0.50/0.99	1.00/1.49	1.50/1.99	2.00/2.49	2.50/2.99	3.00/3.99	4.00/4.99	5.00/5.99
1978	9.14	2,020	5.3	6.1					8.0	8.9	6.7								
1979	10.65	1,745	2.5	5.8			3.9	7.7	1.0	0.3									
1980	12.98	1,292	−0.2	7.1		1.7	1.2	4.1	2.1	3.2	2.5	3.7	3.2	4.8	4.8				
1981	15.71	1,084	1.9	7.6	1.3	1.2	1.3	1.1	0.4	1.4	0.3								
1982	14.77	1,062	−2.5	9.7	1.5	2.4	2.4	1.2	3.4	2.1	3.4	3.5		4.8	4.2	12.0			
1983	12.52	1,703	3.6	9.6	3.7	3.6	2.2	2.7	3.9	4.5	7.1	10.3		19.8	18.9	40.7	37.3		
1984	13.27	1,750	6.8	7.5	2.5	2.7	3.2	3.4	7.2	6.9	11.2	10.2	12.7	15.7	15.9	16.0			
1985	11.64	1,742	3.4	7.2			3.4	4.9	4.1	5.4	6.5	8.6	11.1	14.0	18.8	25.1	26.3	26.8	30.8
1986	9.21	1,805	2.7	7.0				3.7	8.0	8.0	7.7	8.0	10.4	15.6	23.6	31.7	37.4	41.6	40.5
1987	9.50	1,621	3.4	6.2					8.6	9.9	12.1	16.0	18.6	23.6	28.8	27.2	30.2	32.3	34.1
1988	9.84	1,488	4.5	5.5				7.2	8.0	8.3	10.0	10.9	14.1	17.7	17.8	20.7	21.0	22.3	21.9
1989	9.84	1,376	2.5	5.3				6.5	6.8	7.5	8.2	9.7	11.8	13.2	15.3	18.2	17.6	19.9	19.7
1990	9.67	1,193	1.0	5.5				6.5	6.8	7.0	7.6	9.2	10.4	12.0	15.2	14.4	14.8	15.5	15.0
Averages																			
1978–82		1,441	1.4	7.3	1.4	1.8	2.2	3.4	3.0	3.2	3.2	3.6	3.2	4.8	4.5	12.0			
1983–87		1,724	4.0	7.5	3.1	3.2	2.9	4.0	6.3	6.9	8.9	10.6	13.2	17.7	21.2	28.1	32.8	33.6	35.1
1988–90		1,352	2.7	5.4				6.7	7.2	7.6	8.6	9.9	12.1	14.3	16.1	17.7	17.8	19.2	18.8
1978–90		1,529	2.7	6.9	2.3	2.3	2.5	4.5	5.2	5.6	6.9	9.0	11.5	14.1	16.3	22.9	26.4	26.4	27.0

*GMP Growth is in real terms.
Economic data are all from the U.S. Department of Commerce.

with data from the mid-1980s often cannot detect this effect, as their tests have little power due to the consistency of growth from 1983-90. Studies that use older data that cover recessions typically find a strong macroeconomic effect, particularly related to housing starts.

Exhibit 8 graphs the relationship of prepayment rates by degree of premium or discount for the entire time period of 1978-90. Prepayments form an "S-curve" as they flatten out at both ends of the graph. For very high premiums, it is optimal for most people to refinance and prepay and they are probably doing so with as much haste as ever, whether the rate saving is 3% or 5%. For deep discounts, it is not optimal for most borrowers to prepay, and they are probably minimizing prepayments. Still, there is always a base level of prepayments due to forced house sales, nuisance mortgage balance levels, refinancing against higher collateral values and fiscally conservative borrowers who simply wish to reduce debt. Most of these effects are relatively insensitive to rates and form the flat base of minimal core prepayments.

Exhibits 9A, 9B, 9C show average prepayment rate curves for three sub-periods that were chosen to illustrate the major effects. The first subperiod, 1978-82 has many new mortgages originated when rates surged from 9% to 16% during the period. Prepayments are generally low during this subperiod

Exhibit 8. GNMA Prepayment Rates vs. Coupon-Par Average, 1978–90

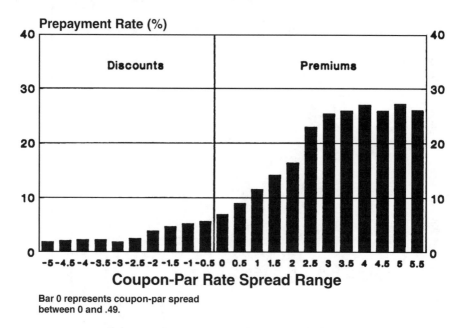

Bar 0 represents coupon-par spread
between 0 and .49.

due to the lack of seasoning (aging) of these mortgages. During the 1983-87 period, these same mortgages become well-seasoned and the expected S-curve of prepayments is quite dramatic. Following those rapid paydowns, prepayment rates slow in the 1988-90 period due to burnout effects. Exhibit 10 displays clearly the change in the prepayment function for GNMA 13s pre- and post-burnout.

MORTGAGE PRICE CURVES

In this section, historical mortgage prices are presented and analyzed. End-of-month bid price data were collected and analyzed from *The Wall Street Journal* for all coupons, including half coupons. Exhibit 11 presents end-of-quarter prices (expressed as a percent of par) for mortgages with coupons ranging from 8% to 15%.

A number of observations can be made from Exhibit 12. First, as interest rates increased from the 7.5% level at the end of 1977 to over 15% in September 1981, 20-year Treasury bond futures prices dropped as expected from 99% to 56% of par. Prices for GNMA 8s dropped from 97 to 56 over the same period, moving very much in step with T-bond futures. From September

Exhibit 9A.   GNMA Prepayment Rates vs. Coupon-Par Average, 1978–82

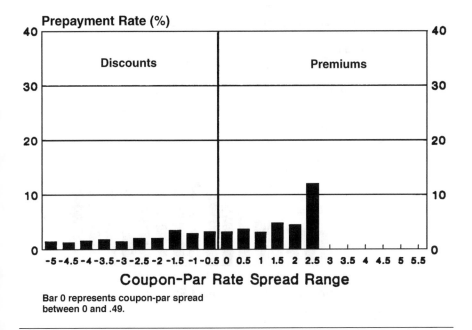

Coupon-Par Rate Spread Range

Bar 0 represents coupon-par spread
between 0 and .49.

Exhibit 9B.   GNMA Prepayment Rates vs. Coupon-Par Average, 1983–87

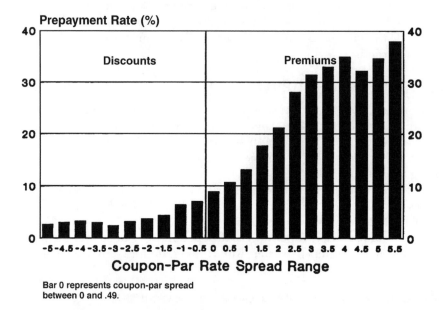

Coupon–Par Rate Spread Range

Bar 0 represents coupon-par spread
between 0 and .49.

Exhibit 9C.   GNMA Prepayment Rates vs. Coupon-Par Average, 1988–90

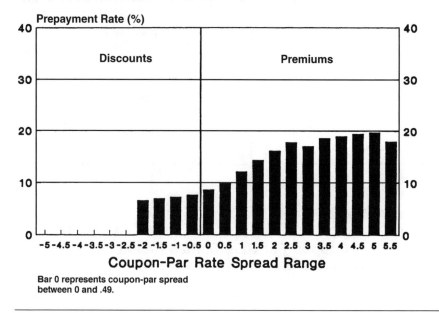

Coupon–Par Rate Spread Range

Bar 0 represents coupon-par spread
between 0 and .49.

Exhibit 10.   Prepayment Burnout of GNMA 13s

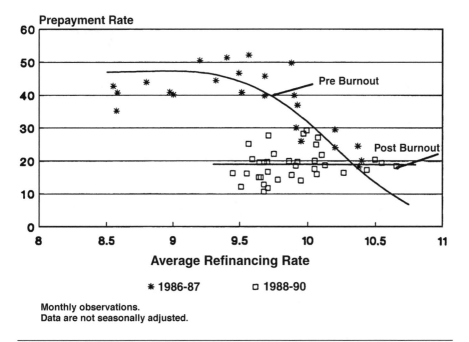

Average Refinancing Rate

✱ 1986-87   ❑ 1988-90

Monthly observations.
Data are not seasonally adjusted.

1981 to December 1990, rates fell back to the 8% level, the near bond futures price increased to 96 and GNMA 8s increased to 94. As shown earlier in this chapter, a mortgage is like a fixed-rate bond less a call option. As bond prices fell, the call option for GNMA 8s became almost worthless, so the GNMA 8's price behavior should be very similar to that of long-term T-bonds. Looking across different coupons, one sees that all mortgage prices move up and down generally with T-bond futures prices and opposite movements in interest rates, reflecting their fixed rates.

To see the effect of the prepayment option, examine the movements of GNMA 13 prices in relation to T-bond futures prices. In contrast to the GNMA 8s which were always discounts, the GNMA 13s sold for discounts to par in 1981, 1982, and 1984, but sold for premiums during all other years (when mortgage rates were below 13%). As interest rates increased from March 1981 to September 1981, T-bond futures dropped 11 points from 67 to 56 and GNMA 13s dropped 14 points from 92 to 78. From then until the end of 1982, T-bond futures increased by 20 points to 76 and GNMA 13s increased by 25 points to 103. Thus, during this period of high rates and discount prices, GNMA 13s were just as volatile as T-bond futures. However, as interest rates continued to drop from December 1982 to December 1986, and T-bond

Exhibit 11. GNMA Fixed-Rate Mortgage Prices

| Date | Market Yields, Spreads, and Futures Prices | | | | | | GNMA Prices by Mortgage Coupon | | | | | | | |
	Par Mtg. Yield	7-Year Treasury	Par Mtg. Treasury	3-Month Libor	TED Spread	T-Bond Futures	8%	9%	10%	11%	12%	13%	14%	15%
123177	8.50%	7.61%	0.89%	7.31%	1.03%	99.50	96.88	103.44						
33178	8.73	7.98	0.75	7.56	0.91	95.94	94.66	101.75						
63078	9.33	8.53	0.80	8.75	1.54	93.00	91.50	98.00						
93078	9.32	8.49	0.83	9.56	1.49	93.31	92.34	98.16						
123178	10.13	9.20	0.93	11.81	2.21	90.34	89.75	94.56						
33179	10.06	9.10	0.96	10.69	0.92	90.19	89.75	94.72						
63079	9.88	8.71	1.17	10.69	1.44	91.81	91.13	95.53						
93079	11.50	9.45	2.05	12.88	2.44	87.78	86.00	90.44						
123179	11.67	10.31	1.36	14.56	2.03	82.19	81.56	85.69	90.31	96.13				
33180	14.08	12.58	1.50	20.00	5.02	67.94	70.78	74.34	78.38	83.75				
63080	11.39	9.82	1.57	9.69	1.51	81.19	84.44	88.84	93.81	98.59				
93080	13.57	11.84	1.73	13.75	1.86	70.69	74.94	77.69	82.19	86.94				
123180	13.72	12.47	1.25	17.75	2.73	71.38	72.16	75.81	80.38	85.97				
33181	14.57	13.21	1.36	14.94	1.94	67.06	68.75	72.25	77.00	81.75		91.94		
63081	15.94	14.05	1.89	17.69	2.61	64.38	64.69	67.56	72.06	76.78		86.84	91.31	
93081	18.42	16.04	2.38	17.75	2.60	56.00	56.06	59.75	64.13	68.56		78.00	82.06	
123181	15.95	14.12	1.83	13.80	2.26	61.91	62.25	66.34	71.03	76.38		86.53	91.91	96.09
33182	16.01	14.36	1.65	15.30	1.40	61.94	62.75	67.25	71.72	76.75		86.84	91.56	95.06
63082	16.14	14.52	1.62	15.95	2.63	60.69	63.13	67.19	71.53	76.69		86.19	90.63	94.75
93082	13.38	11.66	1.72	11.05	3.26	71.06	73.63	78.25	82.91	88.59		98.63	101.47	104.22
123182	12.21	10.27	1.94	9.31	1.18	76.63	78.72	83.72	88.78	94.28		103.38	105.69	107.50
33183	12.13	10.51	1.62	9.63	0.68	75.97	80.16	85.13	89.53	94.53		103.34	105.47	105.91
63083	12.49	10.85	1.64	9.75	0.71	74.44	77.81	82.78	87.75	92.66		102.31	105.16	106.41
93083	12.79	11.34	1.45	9.56	0.56	72.72	76.69	81.09	86.06	91.06		101.03	105.13	107.41
123183	12.69	11.80	0.89	9.94	0.68	70.03	75.31	80.13	85.41	90.91	96.50	101.47	105.44	107.94
33184	13.20	12.39	0.81	10.81	0.83	66.22	72.63	77.28	82.47	88.22	93.84	98.97	104.16	107.44
63084	14.52	13.81	0.71	12.13	1.87	59.63	66.66	70.69	75.63	81.13	86.81	92.34	98.00	101.84
93084	13.46	12.50	0.96	11.50	0.92	67.22	72.16	76.66	81.41	87.50	93.12	98.16	102.41	105.53
123184	12.45	11.47	0.98	8.75	0.67	71.06	76.97	81.72	87.13	93.25	98.16	101.97	106.03	108.81
33185	12.65	11.68	0.97	9.06	0.62	69.72	76.63	80.81	85.94	91.56	96.56	101.63	106.25	108.69

Exhibit 11. Continued

| | Market Yields, Spreads, and Futures Prices | | | | | | GNMA Prices by Mortgage Coupon | | | | | | | |
| | Par Mtg. | 7-Year | Par Mtg. | 3-Month | TED | T-Bond | | | | | | | | |
Date	Yield	Treasury	Treasury	Libor	Spread	Futures	8%	9%	10%	11%	12%	13%	14%	15%
63085	11.40	10.14	1.26	7.81	0.80	77.06	83.50	88.28	94.03	98.75	102.16	106.13	108.97	112.41
93085	11.41	10.17	1.24	8.06	0.79	75.59	83.88	88.28	93.16	97.88	102.88	106.84	109.63	111.69
123185	9.76	8.83	0.93	8.00	0.76	85.22	91.22	96.09	101.31	104.81	107.44	108.25	109.59	112.03
33186	9.00	7.32	1.68	7.44	0.93	102.31	95.72	100.00	104.22	106.91	108.25	108.34	108.81	114.06
63086	9.58	7.30	2.28	6.88	0.75	99.56	93.69	97.28	102.19	105.25	105.78	106.56	107.28	114.25
93086	9.24	7.30	1.94	6.13	0.82	96.56	95.41	98.72	104.28	107.25	107.91	108.47	109.06	113.44
123186	8.61	7.07	1.54	6.38	0.59	98.19	98.22	101.63	106.53	107.75	108.13	109.13	110.06	114.31
33187	8.53	7.40	1.13	6.63	0.68	98.47	97.31	102.31	106.69	107.84	108.91	110.06	112.53	115.00
63087	9.75	8.46	1.29	7.25	1.03	91.50	91.00	96.09	101.31	105.88	108.72	111.34	113.03	115.00
93087	10.80	8.67	2.13	8.31	2.91	81.69	83.78	89.38	95.41	101.19	106.38	109.44	112.00	114.00
123187	10.01	8.04	1.97	7.44	1.65	87.97	88.16	94.00	99.97	104.56	108.00	109.78	112.00	114.00
33188	9.80	8.65	1.15	6.94	0.79	90.09	89.31	95.97	101.00	107.91	110.13	111.94	114.13	115.00
63088	9.90	8.94	0.96	7.94	0.79	88.75	89.00	94.88	100.56	105.97	109.47	112.00	113.75	115.50
93088	9.90	9.20	0.70	8.75	0.39	88.75	89.13	94.94	100.53	105.19	108.25	110.31	113.41	114.63
123188	10.34	9.03	1.31	9.38	0.74	89.13	87.44	93.03	98.31	103.06	105.88	108.38	111.81	112.56
33189	10.69	9.11	1.58	10.31	1.52	88.41	86.25	91.59	96.72	101.25	104.25	107.91	110.69	111.22
63089	9.51	7.57	1.94	9.31	1.25	97.94	93.16	97.81	102.09	105.50	108.44	110.16	110.75	111.00
93089	9.80	7.90	1.90	9.19	1.16	95.84	92.13	96.69	100.94	104.47	108.84	110.69	111.25	111.38
123189	9.33	8.37	0.96	8.38	0.39	98.66	94.25	98.63	102.78	105.72	108.84	109.38	111.94	112.31
33190	9.92	9.04	0.88	8.50	0.48	91.88	90.66	95.69	100.38	104.06	107.50	111.00		
63090	9.63	8.27	1.36	8.38	0.66	94.34	92.13	97.09	101.72	105.13	108.13	111.94		
93090	9.77	8.50	1.27	8.31	0.98	93.38	90.63	96.06	101.22	105.25	109.13	111.94		
123190	9.14	7.87	1.27	7.63	1.26	95.72	94.38	99.41	103.56	106.94	111.50	113.50	115.03	116.53

Bid, % Par

Price data from *The Wall Street Journal*.

The TED Spread is 3-month LIBOR minus the 3-month T-bill yield.

Yield for 3-month LIBOR and 3-month T-bill from Salomon.

Exhibit 12.   SNMA Fixed Rate Mortgage Prices

| | Market Yields, Spreads and Future Prices | | | | | | GNMA Prices By Mortgage Coupon | | | | | | | |
Date	Par Mtg. Yield	7-Year Treasury	Par Mtg. Treasury	3-Month Libor	TED Spread	TBond Futures	8%	9%	10%	11%	12%	13%	14%	15%
123177	8.50%	7.61%	0.89%	7.31%	1.03%	99.50	96.88	103.44						
33178	8.73	7.98	0.75	7.56	0.91	95.94	94.66	101.75						
63078	9.33	8.53	0.80	8.75	1.54	93.00	91.50	98.00						
93078	9.32	8.49	0.83	9.56	1.49	93.31	92.34	98.16						
123178	10.13	9.20	0.93	11.81	2.21	90.34	89.75	94.56						
33179	10.06	9.10	0.96	10.69	0.92	90.19	89.75	94.72						
63079	9.88	8.71	1.17	10.69	1.44	91.81	91.13	95.53						
93079	11.50	9.45	2.05	12.88	2.44	87.78	86.00	90.44						
123179	11.67	10.31	1.36	14.56	2.03	82.19	81.56	85.69	90.31	96.13				
33180	14.08	12.58	1.50	20.00	5.02	67.94	70.78	74.34	78.38	83.75				
63080	11.39	9.82	1.57	9.69	1.51	81.19	84.44	88.84	93.81	98.59				
93080	13.57	11.84	1.73	13.75	1.86	70.69	74.94	77.69	82.19	86.94				
123180	13.72	12.47	1.25	17.75	2.73	71.38	72.16	75.81	80.38	85.97				
33181	14.57	13.21	1.36	14.94	1.94	67.06	68.75	72.25	77.00	81.75		91.94		
63081	15.94	14.05	1.89	17.69	2.61	64.38	64.69	67.56	72.06	76.78		86.84	91.31	
93081	18.42	16.04	2.38	17.75	2.60	56.00	56.06	59.75	64.13	68.56		78.00	82.06	
123181	15.95	14.12	1.83	13.80	2.26	61.91	62.25	66.34	71.03	76.38		86.53	91.91	96.09
33182	16.01	14.36	1.65	15.30	1.40	61.94	62.75	67.25	71.72	76.75		86.84	91.56	95.06
63082	16.14	14.52	1.62	15.95	2.63	60.69	63.13	67.19	71.53	76.69		86.19	90.63	94.75
93082	13.38	11.66	1.72	11.05	3.26	71.06	73.63	78.25	82.91	88.59		98.63	101.47	104.22
123182	12.21	10.27	1.94	9.31	1.18	76.63	78.72	83.72	88.78	94.28		103.38	105.69	107.50
33183	12.13	10.51	1.62	9.63	0.68	75.97	80.16	85.13	89.53	94.53		103.34	105.47	105.91
63083	12.49	10.85	1.64	9.75	0.71	74.44	77.81	82.78	87.75	92.66		102.31	105.13	106.41
93083	12.79	11.34	1.45	9.56	0.56	72.72	76.69	81.09	86.06	91.06		101.03	105.13	107.41
123183	12.69	11.80	0.89	9.94	0.68	70.03	75.31	80.13	85.41	90.91	95.50	101.47	105.44	107.94
33184	13.20	12.39	0.81	10.81	0.83	66.22	72.63	77.28	82.47	88.22	93.84	98.97	104.16	107.44
63084	14.52	13.81	0.71	12.13	1.87	59.63	66.66	70.69	75.63	81.13	86.81	92.34	98.00	101.84
93084	13.46	12.50	0.96	11.50	0.92	67.22	72.16	76.66	81.41	87.50	93.12	98.16	102.41	105.53
123184	12.45	11.47	0.98	8.75	0.67	71.06	76.97	81.72	87.13	93.25	98.16	101.97	106.03	108.81
33185	12.65	11.68	0.97	9.06	0.62	69.72	76.63	80.81	85.94	91.56	96.56	101.63	106.25	108.69

Exhibit 12. Continued

Market Yields, Spreads and Future Prices / GNMA Prices By Mortgage Coupon

Date	Par Mtg. Yield	7-Year Treasury	Par Mtg. Treasury	3-Month Libor	TED Spread	TBond Futures	8%	9%	10%	11%	12%	13%	14%	15%
63085	11.40	10.14	1.26	7.81	0.80	77.06	83.50	88.28	94.03	98.75	102.16	106.13	108.97	112.41
93085	11.41	10.17	1.24	8.06	0.79	75.59	83.88	88.28	93.16	97.88	102.88	106.84	109.63	111.69
123185	9.76	8.83	0.93	8.00	0.76	85.22	91.22	96.09	101.31	104.81	107.44	108.25	109.59	112.03
33186	9.00	7.32	1.68	7.44	0.93	102.31	95.72	100.00	104.22	106.91	108.25	108.34	108.81	114.06
63086	9.58	7.30	2.28	6.88	0.75	99.56	93.69	97.28	102.19	105.25	105.78	106.56	107.28	114.25
93086	9.24	7.30	1.94	6.13	0.82	96.56	95.41	98.72	104.28	107.25	107.91	108.47	109.06	113.44
123186	8.61	7.07	1.54	6.38	0.59	98.19	98.22	101.63	106.53	107.75	108.13	109.13	110.06	114.31
33187	8.53	7.40	1.13	6.63	0.68	98.47	97.31	102.19	106.69	107.84	108.91	110.06	112.53	115.00
63087	9.75	8.46	1.29	7.25	1.03	91.50	91.00	96.09	101.31	105.88	108.72	111.34	113.03	115.00
93087	10.80	8.67	2.13	8.31	2.91	81.69	83.78	89.38	95.41	101.19	106.38	109.44	112.00	114.00
123187	10.01	8.04	1.97	7.44	1.65	87.97	88.16	94.00	99.97	104.56	108.00	109.78	112.00	114.00
33188	9.80	8.65	1.15	6.94	0.79	90.09	89.31	95.97	101.00	107.91	110.13	111.94	114.13	115.00
63088	9.90	8.94	0.96	7.94	0.79	88.75	89.00	94.88	100.56	105.97	109.47	112.00	113.75	115.50
93088	9.90	9.20	0.70	8.75	0.39	88.75	89.13	94.94	100.53	105.19	108.25	110.31	113.41	114.63
123188	10.34	9.03	1.31	9.38	0.74	89.13	87.44	93.03	98.31	103.06	105.88	108.38	111.81	112.56
33189	10.69	9.11	1.58	10.31	1.52	88.41	86.25	91.59	96.72	101.25	104.25	107.91	110.69	111.22
63089	9.51	7.57	1.94	9.31	1.25	97.94	93.16	97.81	102.09	105.50	108.44	110.50	110.75	111.00
93089	9.80	7.90	1.90	9.19	1.16	95.84	92.13	96.69	100.94	104.47	108.84	110.16	111.25	111.38
123189	9.33	8.37	0.96	8.38	0.39	98.66	94.25	98.63	102.78	105.72	108.84	110.69	111.94	112.31
33190	9.92	9.04	0.88	8.50	0.48	91.88	90.66	95.69	100.38	104.06	107.50	109.38		
63090	9.63	8.27	1.36	8.38	0.66	94.34	92.13	97.09	101.72	105.13	108.13	111.00		
93090	9.77	8.50	1.27	8.31	0.98	89.38	90.63	96.06	101.22	105.25	109.13	111.94	115.03	
123190	9.14	7.87	1.27	7.63	1.26	95.72	94.38	99.41	103.56	106.94	111.50	113.50		116.53

Bid, % Par

Price data from *The Wall Street Journal.*

The TED Spread is 3-month LIBOR minus the 3-month T-bill yield.

Yield for 3-month LIBOR and 3-month T-bill from Salomon.

futures rose by 22 points from 76 to 98, GNMA 13s only increased by 6 points to 109. The reason for this limiting of price increases is the surge in GNMA 13 prepayments shown in Exhibit 5 from 3% annually in 1982 to over 40% annually in late 1986. From Exhibit 1, given no prepayments and a current mortgage rate of 9%, the value of the GNMA 13 would exceed 137% of par. The rapid prepayments that occurred in 1986 caused the GNMA 13s to sell for 109 rather than the 137 price that would have occurred with no prepayments. Not all borrowers prepay as soon as refinancing rates appear attractive, so mortgages do sell at prices significantly above par, "capping out" at about 110-115 from the data of Exhibit 2 and 11. Theoretical pricing models that derive mortgage prices that never significantly exceed par due to optimal prepayments are not very realistic.

Exhibits 14, 15, 16, 17 give historical relationships of GNMA 9s, 11s, 13s, and 15s to Treasury bond futures prices. The fits are statistically quite significant, with the high coupon 15s having the least precise fit, *i.e.*, the greatest "basis risk." The curvature (negative convexity) predicted by the option analysis of Exhibit 2A is increasingly evident in the graph sequence as one moves to the high coupon GNMA 11s, 13s, and 15s. As Exhibit 1 illustrated, these mortgages are effectively short call options on T-bond futures with different exercise prices. As these calls become in-the-money, the mortgage's price gains are substantially limited by significantly increased prepayments. The shapes of these curves are as anticipated earlier in this chapter in that they resemble curves for riskless investments less put options with various exercise prices.

RISK ANALYSIS WITH IMPLIED MORTGAGE PRICE ELASTICITIES

This section shows that the cross-section of mortgage prices for different coupons can be used to find "implied price elasticities" or modified durations for mortgages. These implied price elasticities are shown in the following section to be useful as measures of risk and for the construction of hedges.

First, consider what an appropriate risk measure for a mortgage investment should be. For straight bonds, modified duration is extremely useful because of its close theoretical and practical relationship to price volatility. Unfortunately, for mortgages the standard calculation of modified duration is usually an incorrect and misleading measure of price sensitivity. This statement applies both to duration computed using scheduled cash flows without prepayments, as well as calculations with expected cash flows based on a current forecast of future prepayment rates. The problem is caused by the fact that the duration of cash flows change systematically with interest rates as borrowers use the prepayment option to their benefit.

Exhibit 14.   GNMA 9 Prices vs. T-Bond Futures, Monthly, December 1977–December 1990

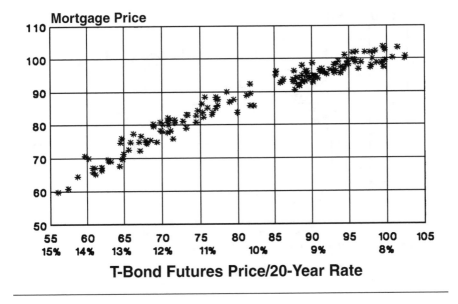

Exhibit 15.   GNMA 11 Prices vs. T-Bond Futures, Montly, October 1979–December 1990

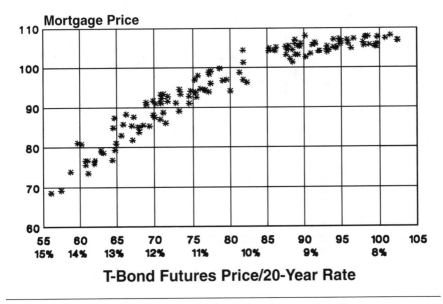

Exhibit 16.   GNMA 13 Prices vs. T-Bond Futures, Monthly, February 1981–December 1990

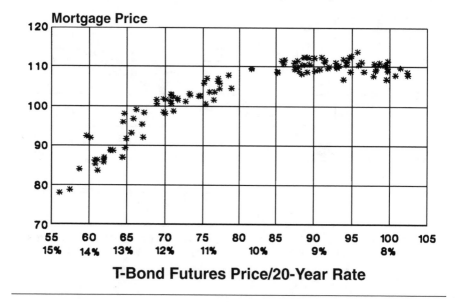

T-Bond Futures Price/20-Year Rate

Exhibit 17.   GNMA 15 Pirces vs. T-Bond Futures, Monthly, October 1981–December 1990

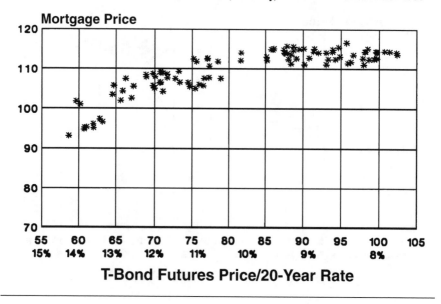

T-Bond Futures Price/20-Year Rate

To see the potential error in using duration calculations for price volatility, consider the case of a high coupon mortgage security before it has been burned out, such as GNMA 13s at the middle of 1985. The prepayment rate at that time was about 10-15% annually. As the par mortgage rate was near 11.5%, the 13s were premiums by 1.5%. Looking at Figure 12's S-curve of the prepayment function at that time, one sees that mortgages in this premium range have the most sensitivity of prepayments to movements in interest rates. Duration computed at that time based upon-cash flow forecasts would be in the 4-5 year range. The standard risk management usage of duration would infer that this mortgage moves 4% to 5% for 100-basis-point moves up or down in rates. During the subsequent year (June 1985 to June 1986) the par mortgage rate dropped by almost 200 basis points, so the duration-based estimate is that the GNMA 13 would increase in price by approximately 8% from 106 to 114. In actuality, the price only increased by 0.5% to 106.56.

Why did the GNMA 13s increase in price by such a small amount as rates plummeted and prepayments accelerated sharply to the 40% level? Increased prepayments cause capital losses on paydowns of premiums which largely offset the price benefit from discounting cash flows at 200-basis-point lower rates. Was this predictable, given the drop in rates by 200 basis points? Although the extent of the prepayment increase was not easily predicted, rational models would all have had some significant sensitivity of premium mortgages' prepayments to rate moves. By using a prepayment *function* rather than a point estimate, one recognizes that, for premium securities, price moves upward are limited by prepayment increases. Similarly for premiums, price moves downward are also limited by reduced prepayments as rates increase. Thus, premiums have shorter "effective durations" and price elasticities due to the systematic prepayment effect. For discount mortgages, the same type of analysis gives the result that effective durations should be greater than standard computations, as price moves upward on discounts are enhanced by the capital gains of increased prepayments caused by lower rates.

Market participants are now well aware of the effects of changing prepayments on price volatility, although not many were in mid-1985. As we see from the example, correctly understanding the prepayment function and its price effect can be more important than interest-rate moves in the prices of premium securities. One method for using market prices to capture that effect is to use the following "roll-up, roll-down" approach (which can be justified as an approximation, given the homogeneity of option prices in the ratio of the underlying asset's price to the exercise price). This approach simply estimates what the value of a GNMA 13 will be if rates decrease by 1% by the current market price of the GNMA 14. As rates decrease by 1%, a GNMA 13 that has a coupon 1.5% over the old par mortgage rate will then have a 2.5% premium to the new rate. However, the GNMA 14s have premium of

2.5% over the old par rate. The price of the GNMA 14s presumably reflects the market's prepayment forecast for 2.5% premium securities, as well as its valuation of that option. Using the price of the 14s takes advantage of some of the market's knowledge. Correspondingly, for a 1% increase in rates, the GNMA 13 becomes an 0.5% premium, to which the price of GNMA 12s currently correspond.

Using the roll-up, roll-down approach on June 30, 1985, gives a price elasticity of 2.7% for the GNMA 13s if rates move down by 1%, and a price elasticity of 3.9% if rates move up by 1%. This is consistent with the adversely asymmetric payoff pattern (negative convexity) anticipated due to the prepayment option. In December 1985, after rates had dropped sharply and prepayments had begun to accelerate, the GNMA 13 roll-up, roll-down elasticities were reduced to 1.2% and 0.8% as the market began to painfully feel the prepayment option's shortening of effective durations. Using these "implied price elasticities" from market prices would have given much better volatility predictions in the subsequent year than would standard duration calculations.

Exhibits 13A–13C give the monthly time series of implied elasticities based upon the price spreads of GNMA 9s and 8s, 11s and 10s, and 13s and 12s, respectively. Generally, these implied elasticities behave in sensible ways. In each graph, elasticities decrease as interest rates fall and bond prices increase, since prepayments increase and effective durations shorten. Furthermore,

Exhibit 18.   Implied Elasticities: GNMA 9 & 8 Prices, Monthly, Dec. 1977–Dec. 1990

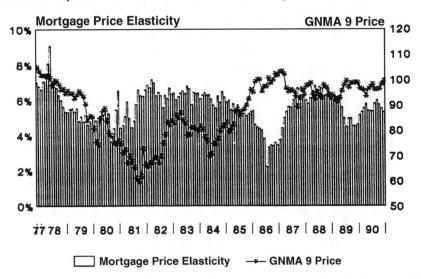

Exhibit 19.   Implied Elasticities: GNMA 11 & 10 Prices, Monthly, Oct. 1979–Dec. 1990

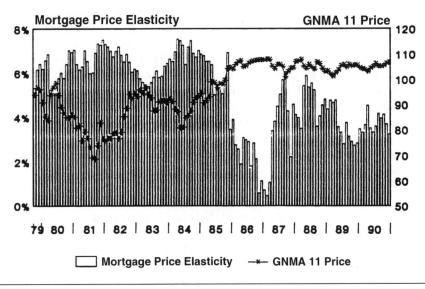

Exhibit 20.   Implied Elasticities: GNMA 13 & 12.5 Prices, Monthly, Feb. 1981–Dec. 1990

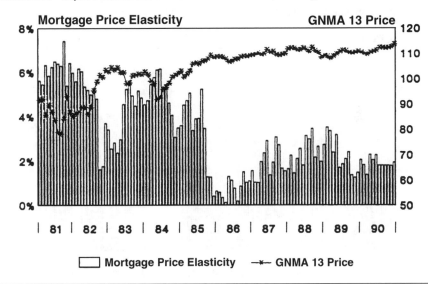

comparing the elasticities across graphs, one sees that implied elasticities for high coupons (premiums) are smaller than for low coupons (discounts). Certainly, that pattern of risk estimates is validated by subsequent price volatility, as is shown in the next sections. Implied price elasticities are very useful in assessing subsequent price risk.

The non-stationarities of mortgage price risks are striking in the implied price elasticity graphs of Figures 13A-13C. Seeing these, it just is not sensible to treat GNMA 13s or other coupons as if they have a well-defined, stationary risk profile that is valid for long periods of time. The risks of these depend very much upon the level of interest rates, which affects whether the mortgage is a premium or a discount security, as well as the speed of prepayments. To develop a much more stationary risk profile for fixed-rate mortgage investments, the transformation is made to trading strategies that invest in mortgages with constant spreads to the par coupon. Thus, instead of considering a buy-and-hold strategy with GNMA 13s, consider a strategy of adjusting each month to always hold the mortgage coupon that is, say, 1.5% over the par coupon. As rates increase (decrease), higher (lower) coupon mortgages are bought. Exhibit 14 shows the time series of elasticities from these trading strategies, and Figures 15A-15C present the results graphically.

Exhibits 15A-15C show that these strategies give much more stationary risk profiles than investing in constant coupon mortgages. Exhibit 15A shows that the implied elasticities for investing in GNMAs with discounts of 1% or

Exhibit 22. Implied Elasticities for GNMA Discounts, Coupon-Par: < –1%

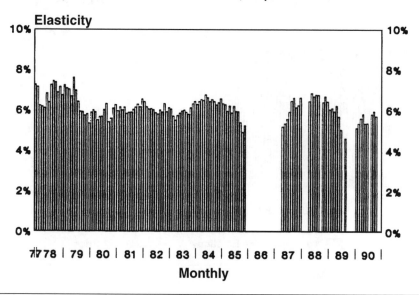

Exhibit 23.   Implied Elasticities for GNMA Premiums, Coupon-Par: +1% to +2%

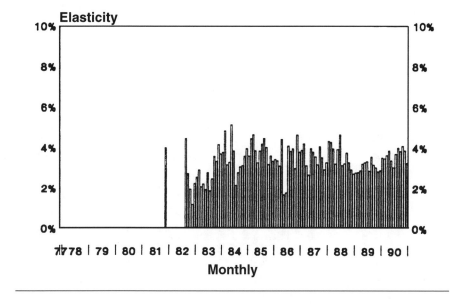

Exhibit 24.   Implied Elasticities GNMA High Premiums, Coupon-Par: > +3%

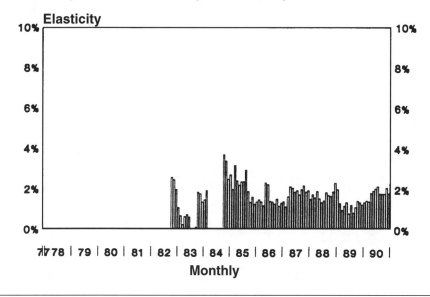

Exhibit 21. Summary of Elasticities

		Monthly Cross-Sectional Simple Averages						12-Month Moving Averages					
Date	Par Mtg. Yield	Discount <-1%	Discount 0% to -1%	Premium 0% to +1%	Premium 1% to 2%	Premium 2% to 3%	Premium >3%	Discount <-1%	Discount -1% to 0%	Premium 0% to 1%	Premium 1% to 2%	Premium 2% to 3%	Premium 3% to 4%
123177	8.50	7.2%	6.9%	6.8%									
33178	8.73	6.2%	7.6%	7.5%									
63078	9.33	6.4%	7.3%										
93078	9.32	7.4%	6.3%										
123178	10.13	6.7%						6.8%	7.0%	7.7%			
33179	10.06	7.0%						6.9%	6.6%	8.6%			
63079	9.88	7.0%	5.1%					7.1%	6.0%				
93079	11.50	5.9%						6.8%	5.6%				
123179	11.67	5.3%	6.4%					6.5%	5.7%				
33180	14.08	5.9%						6.2%	5.8%				
63080	11.39	5.7%	5.1%					5.8%	5.6%				
93080	13.57	5.4%						5.8%	5.7%				
123180	13.72	6.3%						5.9%	5.1%				
33181	14.57	6.0%						5.9%	5.1%				
63081	15.94	5.9%						6.0%					
93081	18.42	6.1%						6.0%					
123181	15.95	6.6%	4.6%	4.3%				6.1%	4.8%	4.2%	4.0%		
33182	16.01	6.0%	5.2%					6.1%	4.8%	4.2%	4.0%		
63082	16.14	5.9%	4.8%					6.1%	4.7%	4.5%	4.0%		
93082	13.38	5.9%	5.5%	3.7%	2.7%	4.3%		6.1%	4.7%	4.4%	3.7%	4.3%	
123182	12.21	6.1%	4.4%	5.3%	2.2%	1.7%	2.0%	6.1%	4.7%	4.3%	2.5%	2.7%	2.3%
33183	12.13	5.5%	4.8%	5.3%	2.0%	0.4%	0.2%	5.9%	4.7%	4.5%	2.5%	2.1%	1.5%
63083	12.49	6.0%	4.9%	5.4%	2.8%	1.2%	0.6%	5.9%	4.8%	4.6%	2.4%	1.9%	1.2%
93083	12.79	5.8%	5.5%	4.9%	3.6%	2.2%	0.1%	5.9%	5.0%	4.7%	2.3%	1.6%	1.1%
123183	12.69	6.4%	5.7%	4.9%	3.7%	2.4%	1.4%	5.9%	5.2%	5.0%	2.8%	1.6%	0.9%
33184	13.20	6.5%	5.6%	5.2%	3.2%	3.8%		6.1%	5.4%	5.0%	3.1%	1.9%	1.2%
63084	14.52	6.6%	6.2%	3.9%	3.8%			6.3%	5.7%	4.8%	3.6%	2.3%	1.4%

Exhibit 21. *Continued*

Date	Par Mtg. Yield	Discount <-1%	Monthly Cross-Sectional Simple Averages						12-Month Moving Averages				
			Discount 0% to -1%	Premium 0% to +1%	Premium 1% to 2%	Premium 2% to 3%	Premium >3%	Discount <-1%	Discount -1% to 0%	Premium 0% to 1%	Premium 1% to 2%	Premium 2% to 3%	Premium 3% to 4%
93084	13.46	6.4%	5.5%	4.1%	3.1%	4.0%		6.4%	5.6%	4.8%	3.6%	3.0%	1.7%
123184	12.45	6.6%	5.2%	4.8%	3.9%	2.6%	2.5%	6.5%	5.5%	4.6%	3.5%	3.3%	2.6%
33185	12.65	5.9%	5.6%	4.7%	4.6%	2.3%	3.2%	6.4%	5.4%	4.5%	3.6%	3.2%	2.9%
63085	11.40	6.2%	5.0%	3.2%	3.8%	2.7%	2.4%	6.3%	5.1%	4.4%	3.5%	2.9%	2.7%
93085	11.41	5.4%	5.1%	5.2%	4.0%	2.6%	1.9%	6.1%	5.1%	4.3%	3.9%	2.5%	2.6%
123185	9.76		5.2%	5.6%	3.3%	1.6%	1.3%	5.8%	5.2%	4.6%	3.9%	2.3%	2.2%
33186	9.00		4.5%	4.9%	3.1%	1.3%	1.4%	5.7%	5.0%	4.7%	3.6%	2.1%	1.9%
63086	9.58		4.3%	5.2%	1.8%	0.4%	2.2%	5.5%	5.1%	5.0%	3.4%	1.7%	1.8%
93086	9.24		2.8%	5.4%	3.9%	0.6%	1.3%	5.1%	4.6%	5.1%	3.3%	1.3%	1.5%
123186	8.61		2.7%	3.5%	3.8%	0.6%	1.3%		3.9%	4.9%	3.4%	1.0%	1.5%
33187	8.53		5.2%	5.0%	3.1%	1.0%	1.6%		3.7%	4.7%	3.5%	0.8%	1.5%
63087	9.75	5.6%	5.5%	5.3%	3.8%	2.2%	1.9%	5.4%	4.0%	4.7%	3.7%	1.2%	1.5%
93087	10.80	6.6%	6.2%	6.1%	4.1%	2.8%	2.0%	5.8%	5.1%	4.9%	3.6%	1.6%	1.7%
123187	10.01	6.6%	6.3%	5.4%	3.3%	1.9%	1.9%	6.0%	5.9%	5.3%	3.5%	2.0%	1.8%
33188	9.24		5.9%	6.0%	3.9%	2.0%	1.6%	6.0%	6.0%	5.6%	3.6%	2.3%	1.9%
63088	9.90	6.7%	6.3%	5.8%	4.6%	2.7%	1.4%	6.4%	6.2%	5.7%	3.7%	2.4%	1.8%
93088	9.39		6.3%	5.8%	3.7%	2.3%	1.7%	6.5%	6.2%	5.6%	3.7%	2.5%	1.7%
123188	10.34	6.4%	5.6%	5.0%	2.7%	2.2%	2.3%	6.6%	6.1%	5.5%	3.6%	2.5%	1.7%
33189	10.69	5.9%	5.4%	4.7%	2.9%	3.5%	1.0%	6.4%	5.9%	5.3%	3.3%	2.7%	1.7%
63089	9.51	5.0%	4.7%	4.3%	3.3%	2.2%	0.8%	6.2%	5.6%	5.0%	3.1%	2.7%	1.5%
93089	9.30		5.2%	4.4%	3.2%	2.6%	1.1%	5.9%	5.3%	4.6%	3.1%	2.7%	1.4%
123189	9.33		4.5%	4.2%	2.9%	2.9%	1.3%	5.6%	4.9%	4.4%	3.0%	2.9%	1.2%
33190	9.92	5.6%	5.3%	4.7%	3.6%	2.7%	1.4%	5.4%	4.9%	4.4%	3.2%	2.7%	1.2%
63090	9.63	5.4%	5.1%	4.7%	3.0%	3.0%	2.0%	5.3%	4.9%	4.4%	3.3%	2.9%	1.4%
93090	9.77	5.9%	5.6%	5.3%	3.8%	3.6%	1.8%	5.5%	5.1%	4.7%	3.4%	3.0%	1.6%
123190	9.14		5.2%	4.3%	3.3%	4.2%	1.8%	5.5%	5.3%	4.8%	3.6%	3.2%	1.8%
Averages		6.1%	5.37%	4.99%	3.37%	2.32%	1.58%	6.06%	5.29%	4.95%	3.40%	2.34%	1.72%

more from the par coupon are quite stable for the 13-year period at approximately 6%. Exhibit 15B shows that buying coupons 1% to 2% over par gives a relatively stable elasticity of 3.5%, and Figure 10C shows that 3% or greater premium investments have relatively stable elasticities near 1.5-2%. Thus, a stable risk strategy in fixed-rate mortgages can be constructed, but requires dynamic adjustment of the portfolio's coupon mix.

DYNAMIC HEDGING STRATEGIES

This section presents the results of simulated, dynamic hedging strategies for mortgages. The simulations are of hedges that are dynamically adjusted using the implied elasticities from mortgage prices. For every month from January 1978 to December 1990, implied elasticities were computed for adjacent mortgage coupons. These elasticities were sorted by their spreads to the par mortgage coupon as in Exhibit 14, typically with two coupons being averaged in each bucket, *e.g.*, 11.0s and 11.5s. To reduce the impact of price reporting errors on the results, the monthly elasticities for the last 12 months were averaged for each 1% coupon bucket and used in the construction of the hedges. A separate dynamic hedging simulation was run for each mortgage coupon. For each coupon, every month its spread to the par coupon was computed and its elasticity was estimated from the functions of Exhibit 14. Based upon that elasticity and the current elasticity of the near 20-year Treasury bond futures, the hedge position was computed, as well as its gain or loss during the next month. Adding the mortgage's coupon income, its gain or loss on principal paid down, and any capital gain or loss due to price changes gives the total profit for the month, from which the rate of return was computed.

The performances of the hedges can be seen in several ways. First, the hedges will be examined graphically with three different perspectives, following which the statistical data are examined. Exhibit 16 graphs the cumulative total return on GNMA 9s, which were available for the entire period of 1979-90 (losing 1 year to the moving average development of the elasticity function). Graphs for the other coupons are very similar and are not shown. The pattern in all graphs shows that the hedging was successful, in that the return is more stable. However, the hedge gives a lower return than being unhedged, as interest rates generally fell during the simulation periods.

The hedges' fluctuations due to basis risks are more apparent if the dominant uptrend is removed by examining excess returns. As most financing of mortgage securities is done in repurchase agreements ("repos") at rates near or below 3-month LIBOR, excess returns over LIBOR were computed for each mortgage coupon. Exhibits 17A and 17B are representative of these results. GNMA 8s and 9s, which were discounts in most of the period, generally earned a sub-LIBOR hedged return, whereas premiums such as

Exhibit 25.   Cumulative Investment Performance GNMA 9s Value of $1 Unhedged and Hedged

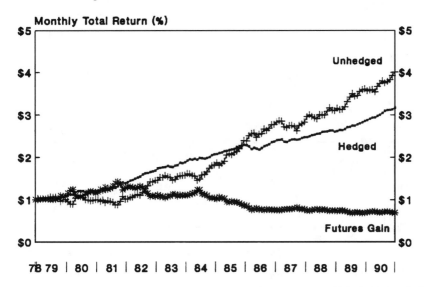

GNMA 13s and GNMA 15s earned hedged returns in excess of LIBOR. In both Figures 12A and 12B, the reflection of futures gains and losses with cash gains and losses is apparent. With a hedge, when the cash profit is up, the futures hedge profit is down, and vice versa. The "Net Hedged" return is much more stable than either futures or cash returns, and stays nearer the zero excess return line. As these returns are hedged to betas near zero, the equilibrium excess returns to the hedging strategies should on average be near zero.

Exhibits 18A and 18B clearly show the hedge effectiveness, as they give scatter plots of monthly and cumulative cash gains and losses versus corresponding futures gains and losses. The graphs for other coupons look quite similar to 13A and 13B. Futures gains and losses of the hedges are approximately "equal but opposite," as the slopes are near 1.00. Comparing Exhibits 28 and 29, one sees the more precise fit over time as many monthly gain and loss fluctuations in the basis cancel out.

Another interesting way to view hedged returns is to graph their monthly gains and losses on the same scale as the unhedged returns. The hedged returns should show less volatility. Exhibits 19A and 19B show these graphs for GNMA 9s and 13s, respectively. These figures show clearly the lower volatility of hedged monthly returns during the volatile interest-rate

Exhibit 26.   Cumulative Investment Performance GNMA 9 Return in Excess of LIBOR

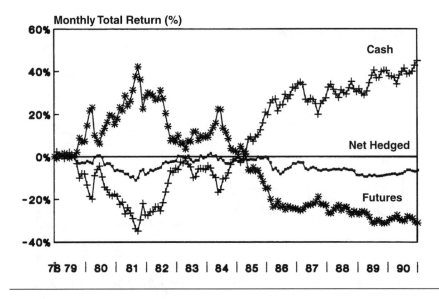

Exhibit 27.   Cumulative Investment Performance GNMA 13 Return in Excess of LIBOR

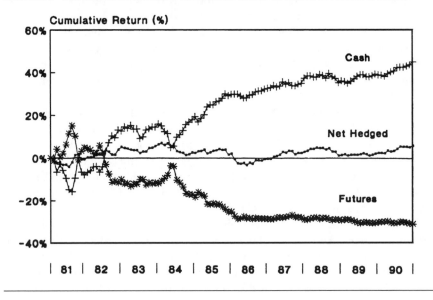

Exhibit 28.   Monthly Hedge Performance, GNMA 13s Hedged with T-Bond Futures

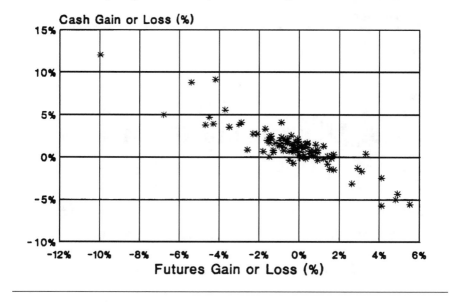

Exhibit 29.   Cumulative Hedge Performance, GNMA 13s Hedged wtih T-Bond Futures

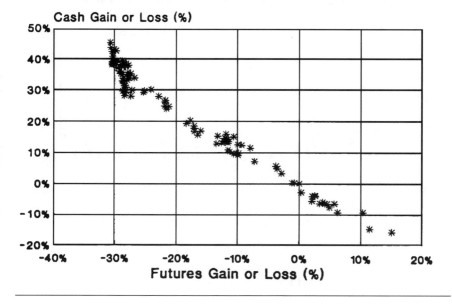

Exhibit 30.   Futures Hedge Performance, GNMA 9 Total Return Hedged vs. Unhedged

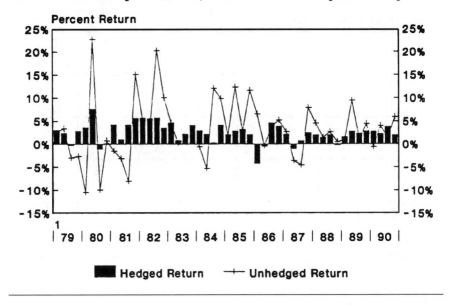

Exhibit 31.   Futures Hedge Performance, GNMA 13 Total Return Hedged vs. Unhedged

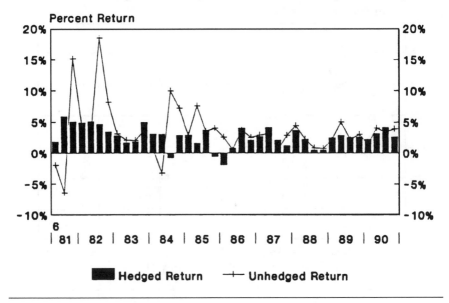

period of 1979-86. In the more recent period of relatively low interest rate volatility, the more volatile GNMA 9s show reduced volatility from hedging, but the GNMA 13s do not. During this recent period of lower rates, the GNMA 13s have sold for high premiums and have relatively little price volatility. As a result, the basis risk of the hedge is so great that the hedge effects little reduction in volatility. Thus, Exhibits 19A and 19B presage the different statistical results for the subperiods analyzed in the next section.

The most interesting features of these mortgage hedges are the dynamic option creation aspects. As shown earlier in this chapter, mortgages should have negative convexity due to the written prepayment options. Price graphs presented earlier verified the presence of the expected curvature. Hedges for mortgages essentially are creating put options, as mortgage risks are analogous to those of written puts. Exhibit 20 graphs the hedge elasticities for GNMA 13s versus Treasury bond prices. These elasticities summarize the dynamic trading strategy for GNMA 13s. When bond prices are high, elasticities (risks), and hedge positions are low. When bond prices are low, prepayments slow and the bond has a high elasticity and requires a large hedge position. Thus, the hedge sells short large amounts of T-bond futures at low prices and buys some of them back as prices increase (and rates fall). The similarities to theoretical delta hedging curves of the option pricing literature are striking. This is the same type of trading strategy for creating a put option, as it should be. Graphs for other coupons trace out portions of that curve, with the portion depending upon whether the security was primarily a premium or a discount. GNMA 13s were both above and below par, so they trace out the entire curve.

Another expected option-like feature is demonstrated in Exhibit 21. This plots the actual cumulative hedge profit versus Treasury bond futures prices. As the hedge creates a put option, the payoffs should be similar to the payoffs on a put option. Again, the dynamic hedge gives the expected payoff pattern, as the payoffs created have positive convexity that is a hedge for the negative convexity of the prepayment option. Graphs not shown of these cumulative payoffs for other coupons also resemble put options, with the strike prices varying with the mortgage's coupon, as expected.

Another important aspect of mortgage hedging and pricing is illustrated in Figure 16, as the curve drifts to the left as time passes. This is normal and is due to the "whipsaw loss" or "option creation cost" present in any dynamic option replication. Whipsaw losses are incurred when the option creation strategy involves buying more contracts at higher prices and selling at lower prices, as put and call option creation strategies do. With that dynamic trading strategy, an increase in price followed by a return to the previous price results in a net loss due to buying high and selling low, which is a whipsaw loss. As time passes, whipsaw losses accumu-

Exhibit 32. Dynamic Mortgage Hedges, GNMA 13 Elasticities vs. T-Bond Futures

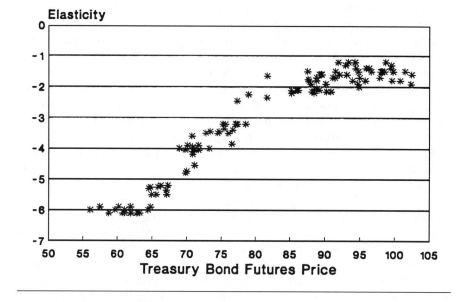

Exhibit 33. Dynamic Mortgage Hedges, GNMA 13 Cumulative Hedge Gains vs. T-Bonds

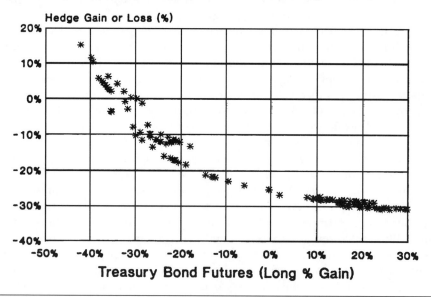

late. They are the implicit costs of option creation, as one cannot create options for zero cost.

Estimates of the option creation costs are important in mortgage pricing, as they differ by coupon, are economically significant, and are the most complex part of a modern "option-adjusted spread" analysis. The extent of the loss is related more to the volatility of the trading position than to the general scale of it (which relates to the mortgage's elasticity). Thus, the whipsaw cost for a coupon is found by comparing its dynamic hedging returns to those of a constant hedge with the same average elasticity. As that average elasticity is only known ex post, it could be viewed as one that assumes "perfect foresight." As the perfect foresight elasticity has the same overall interest-rate exposure as the actual dynamic hedge, the difference in average return will be the loss due to the dynamic hedge adjustments about the average elasticity.

Whipsaw costs were estimated for each mortgage coupon for two major subperiods for which there was a meaningful amount of data by coupon, 1982-86 and 1987-90. Exhibit 22 shows the annualized excess returns of the perfect foresight hedges over those of the dynamic hedging strategies. The amounts range from lows of 10-25 basis points for deep discounts and very high premiums to 130-170 basis points for coupons between par and 3% premiums to par. As the amount of dynamic hedge adjustment can be seen from Exhibit 14 (and Exhibit 20) to be greatest for coupons in that low premium range, the general shape of the whipsaw curve is sensible. In terms of the usual option pricing nomenclature, whipsaw is caused by changes in the "delta hedge ratio." Changes in delta are sometimes called "gammas," which are shown by Cox and Rubinstein to be greatest for options that are "at the money."[5] Low premium mortgages are mortgages whose prepayment options are "at-the-money" for many borrowers, as there are some costs to refinancing. Note that whipsaw costs were lower in the more recent period of low volatility of interest rates, as expected. The general levels of whipsaw costs by coupon, in Exhibit 22, are of the same general magnitudes (but somewhat higher for the low premiums) as those assumed by many research firms today.

STATISTICAL ANALYSIS OF MORTGAGE RISKS, RETURNS, AND HEDGES

This section presents a statistical analysis of the returns on mortgages from 1979 to 1990 (both hedged and unhedged) and compares them to Treasury returns of comparable duration, as well as to returns of major bond and

---

5 John C. Cox, and Mark Rubinstein, *Options Markets*, (Englewood Cliffs, NJ: Prentice-Hall, 1985), Chapter 5.

Exhibit 34.   GNMA Mortgage Option Creation Costs, Sorted by Coupon-Par

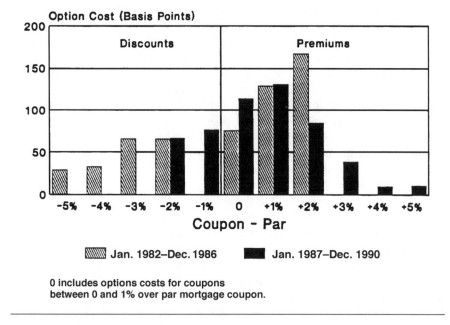

Option Cost (Basis Points)

Coupon - Par

▨ Jan. 1982–Dec. 1986   ■ Jan. 1987–Dec. 1990

**0 includes options costs for coupons
between 0 and 1% over par mortgage coupon.**

stock indices. Betas are presented for mortgages relative to the Salomon Brothers Mortgage Index, to 20-year Treasury bond futures, and to Standard and Poor's 500 stock price index.

Unfortunately, data are not available for all mortgage coupons for the entire period (see Exhibit 11). GNMA 10s and 11s were only introduced in late 1979, after the surge in interest rates generated originations of those higher rate mortgages. GNMA 13s, 14s, and 15s were introduced at various times during 1981; prior to that time mortgage interest rates had never been that high. An oddity is the fact that rates jumped so quickly in 1981 and 1982 that GNMA 12s were not issued in large enough amounts to be quoted in *The Wall Street Journal* until the end of 1983. Finally, GNMA 14s and 15s had prepaid so much that their prices became of extremely poor quality and *The Wall Street Journal* stopped quoting them in March, 1990. Given this ragged data set, the analysis is done for three subperiods: calendar years 1979-81, 1982-86, and 1987-90. The first and second subperiods had generally very high and volatile rates, whereas the more recent subperiod had lower rates and lower rate volatility.

Exhibit 23 gives for each of the subperiods the means and standard deviations of monthly returns for both hedged and unhedged on all GNMA coupons from 8% to 15%. For comparison purposes, Ibbotson Associates' series of "Intermediate-Term Government Bonds" and "Long-Term Government Bonds" were also analyzed, as they represent total returns on benchmark 5-year and 20-year government bonds. Additionally, returns for the Salomon Brothers Mortgage Index, Standard and Poor's 500 stock price index, the Shearson Lehman Government/Corporate Index, 3-month Treasury bills, and 3-month LIBOR are also shown.

During the 1979–81 period, average mortgage returns unhedged and other long-term bonds were lower than those on Treasury bills, as rates increased significantly during the period. Hedged returns on mortgages were much higher than unhedged returns, as the hedges provided protection for the fall in rates. Comparing standard deviations across subperiods, we see that the 1979–81 period had the highest volatility of returns and rates. The ranking of returns was reversed as rates fell in the 1982–86 and 1987–90 periods. In both of those periods, hedge losses reduced the returns on mortgages. However, in both 1982–86 and 1987–90, the hedged returns on mortgages exceeded those of Treasury bills. Unhedged returns in mortgages were similar to those of comparable duration Treasuries in the 1982–86 period and exceeded them in the 1987–90 period.

Next, let us examine Exhibit 23 for the effectiveness of the dynamic hedging strategies in reducing risk. For GNMA 8s, 9s, 10s, and 11s, in all subperiods, the dynamically hedged returns were of substantially lower volatility than the unhedged returns. For the high coupons, hedges were very effective in reducing risk in the 1982–86 period when rates were high and there was great rate volatility. In the 1987–90 period, the dynamic hedges were not helpful in reducing the risks of high coupons. Their primary risks then were prepayment basis risks that were independent of (or very non-linear in) interest rates. During 1987–90, elasticities for the high coupons were very small, so mortgage investors were aware of the limited usefulness of interest-rate hedges for them.

In an alternative analysis of dynamic hedging, Exhibit 24 shows the results of regressions of unhedged mortgage returns on the dynamic futures hedge returns. These results are compared to those for similar regressions on Treasury bond futures percentage (excess) returns for a long position. Both of these regressions benefit from being able to fit the slope ex post. This is an advantage over the actual dynamic hedges, as they only used data available at the times the hedges are placed. There are two interesting analyses with Exhibit 24. First, the slopes in the dynamic futures hedge regressions should be approximately 1.00. They are for the discounts, but are less than that for the high coupons, particularly during the 1987–90 period. As futures hedge positions are chosen in advance, the mortgages' negative convexities will make the hedges seem too large ex post when rates decline. This is at least a partial explanation for the slopes being less than 1.00 in the last two subperiods and greater than 1.00 in the first subperiod. The slopes for the Treasury bond futures regressions give the estimated interest-rate elasticities of the mortgages divided by the elasticity of the 20-year Treasury bond contract. In each period, those estimates sensibly decline in each period for the higher coupons.

The second comparison from Exhibit 24 is more subtle, but of significant interest, as it displays the hedging advantage of dynamic adjustments. The period of greatest rate volatility for which there were many coupons is the second subperiod, 1982–86. For mortgages hedged with a fixed slope (estimated ex post) in T-bond futures, the R-squareds range from 0.78 to 0.38. Note that the dynamic mortgages are constructed from the same Treasury bond futures returns, but with dynamically changing hedge ratios. The dynamic adjustments improve the R-squareds to a range of 0.84 to 0.52. For the high coupon mortgages, which went through significant changes in elasticities during that period, the improvement in hedge correlation is especially large. Thus, in times of great rate volatility, dynamic hedging strategies significantly improve hedge correlation. In times of low rate volatility (e.g., 1987–90), the dynamic hedging strategy does not improve upon a static hedging strategy. The results of the same regression equations are also shown in Exhibit 23 for the longest time period for which coupons from 8% to 15% were continuously available, November 1981 to March 1990. They show even more clearly the higher correlations of the dynamic hedging strategies than those of the static hedging strategies with the same hedge instrument.

Finally, Exhibit 24 shows the "betas," or return sensitivities, of mortgage returns on different coupons to movements in the Salomon Brothers Mortgage Index and to Standard and Poor's 500 stock price index. As the Salomon index includes these mortgages, it is not surprising to see very strong relationships there. Furthermore, the higher betas for discounts than for premiums make intuitive sense and are consistent with the elasticity analyses. What is more interesting is that the GNMA 8s and 9s have had recent increases in betas. This is partly because the index also includes premiums, which have had reduced elasticities as rates have fallen, and partly due to the growing weight on FNMA and FHLMC mortgage securities, which have lower elasticities.

The mortgage index regressions of Exhibit 24 and the Treasury bond futures regressions of Exhibit 23 give bond market betas for mortgages. Betas relative to the stock market are in the second panel of Exhibit 24. Stock market betas for mortgages move much like other bonds' betas move across the subperiods. During the 1979–81 period and the 1982–86 period, these betas are significantly positive in the 0.20 to 0.40 range, consistent with other studies. These occurred because interest rates increased when the stock market went down in the recessions of 1980 and 1981–82, and rates decreased when the stock market increased during the growth years from late 1982 through 1986. In the 1987–90 period, the stock market did well, while rates were relatively stable, leading to betas that were insignificantly different from zero.

CONCLUSION

This chapter has examined risks, returns, and hedging for fixed-rate mortgages. The paper presented the theoretical reasons for negative convexity of mortgages and showed that the data support the theory. A method for using the market's implied price elasticities for risk analysis and hedging was explored in detail. The method was found to be successful in constructing hedges of these very complicated securities. The dynamic nature of the hedging strategies was shown to generate whipsaw losses that are due to the replication of the prepayment option. Estimates of the whipsaw losses were computed and are very reasonable in size and in pattern relative to those used by current mortgage researchers.

Returns on mortgages were examined for both hedged and unhedged positions. The average levels of returns exceeded Treasury returns of comparable durations. However, in hedging simulations, it was found that some hedged returns exceeded LIBOR financing costs and some did not. The evidence presented here appears to be consistent with returns on mortgages in aggregate that are commensurate with their risks. However, the methods for estimating "whipsaw" option replication costs and implied price elasticities for mortgages with changing risks should help investors in their attempts to identify relative value in the mortgage markets.

CHAPTER 37

Options on Mortgage-Backed Securities

William A. Barr
Vice President
Fuji Securities Inc.

INTRODUCTION

Over-the-counter (OTC) options on mortgage-backed securities (MBSs) are a well developed, long established market. Sophisticated mortgage bankers use the market to hedge their pipeline, which is subject to fallout risk. Investors in MBSs enhance their returns by writing covered calls and puts on their mortgage portfolios. Market making in mortgage options is one of the services major dealers in MBSs offer their customers. With options on mortgages being a significant part of the general MBS market, understanding some of the unique features of this options market is important.

This chapter will discuss the conventions of the mortgage options market, the differences between Treasury options and mortgage options, the influence of prepayments on mortgage options, mortgage pipeline hedging, and split fee options. The chapter will conclude with two comments on mortgage options as a return enhancing tool for portfolio managers.

MARKET CONVENTIONS: OTC OPTIONS ON MORTGAGE-BACKED SECURITIES

Options require specification of five items: (1) the underlying security, (2) the strike price, (3) the expiration date, (4) whether the option is a put or call, and (5) whether the option is American or European. Below are the conventions the OTC mortgage options market uses to specify these items.

This chapter was written when Mr. Barr was Associate Director of the Mortgage Department at Bear Stearns & Co., Inc.

1. The underlying security is a TBA (the pools to be announced) MBS (GNMA, FNMA, FHLMC). The delivery month must also be specified for that security. The mortgage market prices forward delivery. If a mortgage option is exercised, the underlying mortgage must be delivered in the month specified by the option agreement. The option is valued using the price associated with the underlying security's delivery month.

2. The strike price is usually quoted as a price difference to the underlying price of the delivery month. For example, a dealer bidding at the money calls would set a strike price that is the bid price of the underlying security. A dealer offering a one point out of the money call would set a strike price one point above the security's offer price. Finally, a dealer bidding a one and one-half point out of the money put would set the strike one and one-half points down from the offer side of the market. Of course, a customer can ask a dealer to bid or offer an option with a specific strike.

3. Expiration dates for OTC mortgage options are also known as notification dates. Expiration/notification dates can be any business day prior to one week before delivery; the week before delivery allows time for inventory adjustments and allocations. Mortgage bankers seem to prefer expiration dates two weeks prior to the mortgage delivery date. The dealer community trades with expiration dates one week prior to mortgage delivery. If a customer does not specify the expiration date, then the option is priced to the same date as is the dealer convention, that is, one week prior to mortgage delivery.

4. The option must be a put or call.

5. The American or European designation of the option is not relevant. The dealer convention is that mortgage options are always European. The delivery of the underlying mortgage security and the delivery of the mortgage if the option is exercised are on the same date, and therefore there is virtually no carry component in the option value that could induce an early exercise.

DIFFERENCES BETWEEN TREASURY OPTIONS, OTC AND EXCHANGE-TRADED, AND OTC MORTGAGE OPTIONS

The primary difference between mortgage options and Treasury options is the underlying securities. To choose between one and the other is to take a position in the relative pricing of mortgages versus Treasuries. Also, depending on the maturity of the Treasury underlying the option, there could be yield curve risk as well. (Mortgage options versus options on a ten-year Treasury note would entail mortgage/Treasury pricing risk and little yield curve risk. Mortgage options versus options on a thirty-year Treasury bond or two-year Treasury note would include yield curve risk.) To choose between options on mortgages and options on Treasuries is therefore to make a market sector position decision.

INSTITUTIONAL DIFFERENCES BETWEEN EXCHANGE-TRADED TREASURY OPTIONS AND OTC MORTGAGE OPTIONS

The institutional distinction between the OTC mortgage options and OTC Treasury options markets is nominal. However, the institutional difference between the OTC options market and the exchange-traded options market is great. What are the differences between these two markets? Should positions ever be taken in exchange-traded Treasury options for institutional reasons when a position in mortgage options is preferred? The seven most important differences are as follows:

1. *Underlying security*: A Treasury futures contract is the underlying instrument for the exchange-traded option. A specific MBS is the underlying security of an OTC mortgage option. Since an exchange-traded option is in lieu of a mortgage option, there is relative price risk of the futures contract to the mortgage market. In particular, the price risk of a position in exchange-traded options incorporates cash/futures relative price risk, potential yield curve risk, and mortgage/Treasury relative price risk. There is no relative price risk associated with mortgage options, since the underlying security is a mortgage.

2. *Strikes*: There is only a set number of strikes to choose from in the exchange-traded options market. With OTC mortgage options, the customer can choose any strike. There is no restriction on the strike of an OTC mortgage option.

3. *Expiration dates*: There is only a set number of expiration dates to choose from in the exchange-traded options market. The expiration dates are one day a month, and the months with expirations dates are the current month and March, June, September, and December. With OTC mortgage options, the customer can choose any expiration date up to one week prior to the mortgage delivery date. There is no restriction on the expiration date of an OTC mortgage option.

4. *Option liquidity*: With exchange-traded options the bid/ask spread is 3/64ths for front month expiration dates and 6/64ths to 10/64ths for back month expiration dates. Generally, $100 million par amount

(thousand contracts) can trade at these prices. The bid/ask spread for mortgage options across the dealer market for front month expiration dates is 3/64th to 5/64ths (often, the option price market is locked, with the only distinction being the strike). For back month options the bid/ask spread is 4/64ths to 8/64ths. Exactly as with the exchange-traded options, $100 million par amount can trade at these prices. The option bid/ask spreads in both markets incorporate the price spread in the underlying security, and therefore are comparable. There is no liquidity lost in trading OTC mortgage options.

5. *Pricing information*: Pricing information is readily available from price vendors for exchange-traded options. This information can be supplied real-time. For OTC mortgage options, access to pricing information requires calling dealers for quotes. With a pricing service, price information is more readily available for exchange-traded options than for OTC mortgage options. Without a price service, there is no difference between OTC mortgage options and exchange traded options in the accessibility of price information.

6. *Commissions*: There are commissions associated with trading exchange-traded options. The prices quoted in the market are gross prices and not net commissions paid. In the OTC mortgage market, the prices quoted are net. There are no additional fees paid with an OTC mortgage option trade.

7. *Credit*: When buying options at an exchange, the contraparty credit exposure is with the exchange's clearing corporation. There is also credit exposure to the clearing member with whom the option position is held. The credit exposure of an OTC mortgage option is with the dealer from whom the option is bought.

There is no reason to position exchange-traded Treasury options when the preferred trade position is mortgage options. The only significant institutional distinction between OTC mortgage options and exchange-traded options is with respect to credit exposure. If the OTC option is purchased from a well capitalized dealer, this distinction is nominal. The decision to position in OTC mortgage options versus exchange-traded options should be purely an economic one.

THE IMPACT OF PREPAYMENTS ON MORTGAGE OPTION PRICING

Mortgage option pricing is effected by the underlying mortgage's prepayment expectations. In particular, the faster the expected prepayment speeds of an option's underlying MBS, the lower the implied volatility used to value the option.

Prepayment of principal is a characteristic of MBSs. The prepayment of principal will shorten the life/maturity of a MBS. Modified duration is determined in part by the maturity of a security. With MBSs, it is estimated using the best guess of the mortgage's future prepayments.

When yields change, the change in a security's price is a function of the security's modified duration. The larger the modified duration, the greater a security's price change for a given change in yields. Price volatility is therefore a function of modified duration.

Prepayment speeds determine the maturity of a MBS, maturity determines the security's modified duration, and modified duration determines price volatility. Therefore, prepayments and the market's best estimates of future prepayment speeds influence the price volatility of a MBS. Since expected volatility is a fundamental part of option pricing and positioning, estimates of future mortgage prepayment speeds significantly influence option prices.

The likelihood of prepayment speeds being high or low is in part a function of alternative financing opportunities in the mortgage market. If an existing MBS has a high coupon relative to the current market mortgage origination rates (the price of the security would be above par), then the prepayment speed is expected to be high. If an existing MBS has a low coupon relative to the current market mortgage origination rates (the price of the security would be below par), then the prepayment speed is expected to be low. Therefore, MBSs priced above par have shorter expected maturities, shorter modified durations, and lower price volatilities (given equal yield volatilities) than MBSs priced below par.

The impact of prepayment speeds on option pricing is significant. The higher the coupon of the MBS, the lower the option-implied price volatility. Exhibit 1 is a list of at-the-money options prices and implied price volatilities

Exhibit 1. At-the-Money Option Prices for GNMA Securities, Trade Date March 25,1991

Coupon	May Price	Implied Volatility	Option Price	Expiration Date
8.00	94:03	5.78	0:24	5/07
9.50	96:25	5:48	0:23+	5/07
9.00	99:14	5.07	0:22	5/07
10.00	103:75	4.01	0:19+	5/13
10.50	105:15	3.20	0:15+	5/13
11.00	107:10	2.59	0:13	5/13

for GNMA securities expiring in May 1991. One can see how the implied volatilities fall as the coupons increase.

Also, for MBSs that are priced in the market near par and above, the strike price of an option will affect an option's implied price volatility. For these securities, out-of-the-money puts (and in-the-money calls) will have higher implied price volatilities than out-of-the-money calls (and in-the-money puts). Currently (April 11, 1991), the options market values strikes that are different from at the money with a change in implied price volatility of 0.3% per point. For options with strikes below at the money, implied volatility increases 0.3% per point compared with the at-the-money implied volatility. For options with strikes above at the money, implied volatility decreases 0.3% per point. (For example, if at-the-money options are valued at 5.0% implied price volatility, then two-point out-of-the-money puts would be valued at 5.6% implied price volatility. One-point out-of-the-money calls would be valued at 4.7% implied price volatility.)

The fact that the strike price influences the implied volatility of an option for current and premium priced MBSs is not surprising. Existing prepayment expectations are embedded in at-the-money options. For out-of-the-money options, not only are existing prepayment expectations accounted for in the option pricing, the change in prepayment expectations if the option moved closer to being at the money is also incorporated (*i.e.*, the market price of the underlying security moved toward the strike price). If, for example, a MBS is priced at 99:00, and a call option on the MBS with a 102:00 strike is priced, then the implied volatility to price the option would incorporate both the prepayment expectations currently in the market with the 99:00 price and the expected prepayment speeds consistent with a 102:00 price level.

To summarize, prepayments influence option pricing in two ways. First, across MBSs, the higher the price of a MBS is, the faster its expected prepayment speed will be; the faster expected prepayment speeds are, the lower the implied price volatility used to value options on that MBS will be. Second, with a particular MBS, the higher (lower) the strike relative to at the money is, the lower (higher) the implied price volatility used to value the option will be. This option pricing adjustment is due to changes with expected prepayment speeds associated with the market moving to a price level that would make the strike at the money.

HEDGING THE OPTION EMBEDDED IN THE MORTGAGE PIPELINE

The management of mortgage pipeline risk is one of the primary determinants of a mortgage banker's profitability. The key to managing this risk efficiently and effectively is to understand that a major component of this risk is option risk. A mortgage banker who issues a commitment letter or who guarantees a firm rate when accepting a mortgage application has sold a put option to the potential borrower. After a commitment is made, the homeowner has the right but not the obligation to "take out the loan," that is, the option to sell or to put the mortgage loan to the mortgage banker. If rates fall or the home sale falls through, the homeowner may decide not to take out the mortgage. Thus, the mortgage pipeline manager has effectively sold a mortgage put option to the potential homeowner.

Managing the mortgage pipeline's implicit put option is critical to successful mortgage banking. In the following, pipeline risk is described and its put option component identified. Next, two ways to hedge the option embedded in mortgage origination are discussed. Finally, the way to choose between the two hedging methods is suggested.

Pipeline Risk-Price Risk and Fallout Risk

Price risk: Mortgage pipeline price risk arises from the difference between the terms of the borrower's mortgage loan and the terms available in the market where the loan is sold, that is, the price paid and the price received (sold) for the mortgage. The longer the period between the time a commitment is made to a borrower and the time the mortgage is sold in the market, the greater the price risk.

Mortgage bankers can deal with this risk by selling and delivering mortgage loans as soon as they are originated. Mortgages, though, are costly to sell in small lots; better execution is obtained if the mortgages are grouped and sold in fairly large amounts. To group the mortgages into large amounts, the mortgage banker has to hold mortgages in inventory, and waiting to accumulate large amounts of mortgages in inventory exposes the mortgage banker to changing interest rates. Selling mortgages for future delivery is a way to hedge inventory risk while accumulating large blocks. However, the availability of future inventory to be delivered against the forward sale must be known with certainty. Selling forward against mortgage commitments subject to fallout can leave the mortgage banker short if the mortgages do not close. How does the mortgage banker hedge commitments subject to fallout risk? Hedging the fallout risk is hedging the option component of mortgage origination.

Fallout risk: Fallout risk arises from the fact that the borrower can choose to close or not to close after the mortgage banker has made a mortgage loan commitment. Falling interest rates with cheaper alternative mortgage financing will cause closings on mortgage commitments to decrease. On the other hand, if mortgage rates rise, commitments with "locked-in rates" will have a high likelihood of closing, since alternative financing is more expensive. Rates up, the mortgage banker owns inventory; rates down, the mortgage banker is flat inventory. From the mortgage banker's viewpoint, he is in a lose/neutral situation. The fallout risk profile is exactly the same as the risk profile of a short put option.

Managing Fallout Risk: Two Alternatives

The solution to the fallout risk problem is to acquire a position that offsets the risk profile of commitments subject to fallout risk. There are two ways to acquire such a position: using OTC mortgage options or self-hedging.

Hedging with options: OTC mortgage put options generate the same but opposite risk profile of the commitment fallout risk. Therefore, buying put options is one solution to the fallout risk problem. When interest rates go up, the owner of the put is short the MBS underlying the put. When interest rates go down, the put owner has no position in the put's underlying MBS. The mortgage banker has a win/neutral position that offsets the lose/neutral position of the fallout subject mortgage commitments.

What are the costs and benefits of owning put options? The cost is the price paid for the option—this fee is lost if the option is held to expiration. The benefit is that the price risk of the pipeline subject to fallout is known for certain and with at-the-money puts eliminated.

Self-hedging: How does a mortgage banker deal with the lose/neutral characteristics of the mortgage origination fallout risk without using options? If the mortgage banker does nothing and sells only forward pipeline that will certainly close, he then is faced with the lose/neutral position for interest rates going up or down. When interest rates go up, he will experience a loss as he becomes long inventory that was subject to fallout risk but is not yet sold. When interest rates come down, he loses nothing, since he never sold inventory forward that subsequently fell out. Alternatively, the mortgage banker could create a neutral/lose situation for interest rates up or down. He creates this scenario by selling all commitments forward, including commitments subject to fallout risk. If interest rates go up, he loses nothing, since the mortgages that are subject to fallout risk close and are delivered against the forward sells. On the other hand, if interest rates go down, then the mortgage banker experiences fallout, and ends up being short with the forward sells that were against the pipeline subject to fallout. The mortgage banker is betting on interest rates if he follows either course of action.

To self-hedge and not bet on interest rates, the mortgage banker can sell forward a "50%" hedge against the pipeline subject to fallout risk. The 50% hedge ensures that he is only exposed to half his fallout risk. If interest rates go up and all the pipeline subject to fallout close, the mortgage banker is long only half the inventory subject to fallout risk. If interest rates come down and none of the fallout pipeline closes, the mortgage banker is only short half the inventory subject to fallout risk. The mortgage banker loses in both scenarios, but the losses are less than if he either does nothing or if he sells all his commitments and is wrong.

What are the benefits and costs of self-hedging? The benefit is that there is no fee. Unlike a put option, where a fee is paid to own the right to sell mortgages, there is no fee paid for self-hedging. The cost of self-hedging is the unlimited loss potential that is embedded in the hedge position. If interest rates rise or fall dramatically (such as in April 1987 and October 1987), the losses from hedging only 50% of the pipeline subject to fallout can be substantial. Also, since the loses are potential at the time the self-hedge is implemented, the uncertainty associated with a self-hedging program is a source of anxiety, and this anxiety could also be considered a cost of self-hedging.

How to Choose between Hedging with Options and Self-Hedging

The mortgage banker must compare the costs and benefits of the two hedging methods in the context of his future outlook on interest rate changes.

- Hedging with Options

    Cost: The fee
    Benefit: No price risk and no anxiety.

- Self–Hedging

    Cost: Unlimited price risk and the associated anxiety.
    Benefit: No fee

Hedging with at-the-money put options is the more cost-effective hedge if, by the option's expiration date, the market price of the MBS underlying the option is expected to move more than twice the option fee. Self-hedging is the more cost-effective hedging method if the market price of the MBS is expected to change less than twice the amount of the option fee. The mortgage banker must decide how much MBS prices will move over the term of the option, and compare that movement with the option price. The mortgage banker must also decide on the value of anxiety associated with the unlimited loss potential of self-hedging.

No matter which hedging method is chosen, there is a cost to hedging. The best result the mortgage banker can achieve is zero cost (which results from self-hedging with no subsequent price movement, and buying back the hedge at the original sell price). The cost of the implicit put that is a part of mortgage origination cannot be escaped. The mortgage banker can only minimize that cost by choosing the best hedging strategy.

SPLIT FEE OPTIONS

A split fee option is an option on an option. Split fee options are a commonly sold instrument in the OTC mortgage options market. The customers generally are mortgage bankers, who purchase them as an alternative to purchasing traditional OTC mortgage options when hedging their pipeline risk. Split fee options are also know as compound options, and calls on puts, or calls on calls.

This discussion will describe the characteristics of split fee options and give a framework for deciding whether or not to position them relative to traditional option positions.

Traditional options require five characteristics to be specified: a strike, an expiration date, an underlying security, whether the option is a put or call, and whether the option is American or European. With traditional options, the option owner will decide on the expiration date whether or not to exercise the option. There is only one decision for the option owner after the option is purchased.

Split fee options require the above five characteristics and two more, a second fee and a second fee expiration date (the window date). A fee is paid today for the split fee option. Then, on the window date the split fee option owner decides whether or not to pay the second fee. If the second fee is not paid, the option becomes void; if the second fee is paid, the option continues to be valid. Then the option owner must decide on the expiration date whether or not to exercise the option. With split fee options there are potentially two decisions to make after the option is purchased.

With traditional options, the purchaser will specify the option characteristics and then ask what is the fee or price for the option. With split fee options, the purchaser will specify the five items of a traditional option, and then will specify the fee that will be paid today for the split fee option, and the window date. The purchaser then asks what will be the second fee payable on the window date. The second fee is the decision variable with split fee options.

How is the second fee affected by the variables unique to split fee options and by implied volatility? The variables unique to split fee options are the window date and the amount that is set for the first fee (*i.e.*, the fee paid today). The window date can be any day between today and the expiration date; the first fee can be any amount. How does changing the window date and first fee affect the second fee? Do different levels of implied volatility affect the sensitivities of the window date and first fee?

Exhibits 2, 3, and 4 compare a split fee pricing with a traditional option, and show the sensitivities of the second fee to the first fee, window date, and implied volatility. The price of a traditional option is also shown.

Exhibit 2. Fee Comparison: Split Fee Option to Corresponding Traditional Option

	Total Fee	First Fee	Second Fee
Traditional	1:04+	—	—
Split Fee Option Window			
3/28/91	1:09	0:16	0:25
4/26/91	1:17	0:16	1:01
5/28/91	1:29+	0:16	1:13+

Trade date:	February 26, 1991
Strike and underlying price:	97:17
Implied volatility:	5.5%
Expiration date:	June 11, 1991
European Put	

Exhibit 3. Second Fee Sensitivity to Implied Volatilities and First Fee

First Fee	Implied Volatilities		
	4.5	5.5	6.5
0:04	1:12	1:26	2:08+
0:08	0:30+	1:10	1:22+
0:12	0:22	1:00	1:11
0:16	0:16	0:25	1:02+
0:20	0:10+	0:18+	0:27+
0:24	0:06	0:13+	0:21+

Trade date:	February 26, 1991
Underlying security	GNMA 8.50 June
Strike and underlying price:	97:17
Expiration date:	June 11, 1991
Window date:	March 28, 1991
European Put	

Exhibit 4.   Second Fee Sensitivities to the Window Date

First Fee	3/28/91	Window Date 4/26/91	5/28/91
0:04	1:26	2:18	3:11+
0:08	1:10	1:27	2:14+
0:12	1:00	1:12	1:27+
0:16	0:25	1:01	1:13+
0:20	0:18+	0:24	1:01
0:24	0:13+	0:16+	0:23

Trade date: February 26, 1991
Underlying security   GNMA 8.50 June
Strike and underlying price: 97:17
Expiration date: June 11, 1991
European Put

The split fee option is on a GNMA 8.5 to be delivered if exercised on the regular PSA settlement date in June 1991. The date on which the split fee option is evaluated (trade date) is February 26, 1991. The strike price is at the money, which is 97:17. The expiration date is June 11, 1991. The split fee option is a put and is European. The window dates for the second fee are March 28, 1991, April 26, 1991, and May 28, 1991.

Exhibit 2 shows that the sum of the first and second fees is always greater than the fee of the traditional option. This relationship will hold for all window dates and for all combinations of first and second fees where the first fee is less than the fee of the corresponding traditional option.

Exhibit 3 shows the relationship of the first fee to the second fee for the split fee option with a March 28, 1991 window date. The first observation to be made from the exhibit is that the higher the first fee is, the lower the second fee will be. The second observation is that this relationship between fees is not linear. For a 32nd change ($312.50/million par amount) in the first fee, changes in the second fee vary depending on the initial level of the first fee. For a set change in the first fee, the smaller the initial level of the first fee, the larger is the change in the second fee. The third observation is that the higher the implied volatility, the higher is the second fee, and this relationship is linear.

Exhibit 4 shows the relationship of the second fee to the window date. The three window dates are March 28th, April 26th, and May 28th. The relationship between the window and the second fee is not linear. The days between March 28th and April 26th are cheaper in terms of the second fee than the days between April 26th and May 28th.

To summarize the sensitivities, the higher the implied volatility is, the higher the second fee will be. The lower the first fee, the higher the second fee, which will increase at a geometric rate. And finally, the farther into the future the window date is, the higher the second fee will be, which again will increase at a geometric rate.

Mortgage bankers use split fee options to attempt to reduce the fees they pay for their pipeline hedging. Instead of buying traditional options to cover their pipeline subject to fallout, the mortgage banker will purchase split fee options. The first fee of the split fee is less than the fee of the traditional option, and therefore initially the cost of hedging the pipeline is less than it would be using traditional options.

Now, if one of two events happen by the window date, the mortgage banker will be better off with owning split fees than if he bought traditional options. First, the mortgage banker will benefit from split fee options if, by the window date, the amount of pipeline subject to fallout is reduced from original estimates. By purchasing split fee options, the mortgage banker reduces the cost of his insurance by not paying traditional options fees for pipeline hedging he subsequently did not need. Second, if implied volatility falls, the cost of the identical option in the market could be cheaper than the second fee. The mortgage banker, instead of paying the second fee, could replace the split fee with the same option more cheaply from the market. If the implied volatility fell enough, the combination of the first fee and the price of replacing the option on the window date from the market could be less than the initial traditional option fee.

The cost of a split fee is the additional price that is paid over and above the price of the identical put that is a traditional option when combining the first and second fees. If the mortgage banker finally decides to exercise the second fee, he would have been better off purchasing the traditional option.

MORTGAGE OPTIONS TO ENHANCE PORTFOLIO RETURNS

Options as a return-enhancing device is a frequently discussed topic. Therefore, only two points will be mentioned concerning mortgage options for enhancing returns.

First, total return investors attempt to capture all the potential value that can be generated from a collateral investment. With securities, returns are generated from coupon income, price appreciation, financing specials, and price volatility. To capture the value derived from price volatility, the total return investor must be involved with options. Investors can enhance returns by both buying and selling options; choosing which to do and when is the difficult part. When the investor does not think interest rates will change significantly over a time period, selling options over the same time period will increase returns by the amount of the option fee less any price movement. On the other hand, when the investor expects interest rates to change significantly, options are a way of creating leverage to benefit from the price move while limiting risk. Without participating in options, the total return investor is leaving a major contributor of value out of his collection of investment tools.

Second, the mortgage options market is unique among short-dated options markets. For other options markets, the net sum of long and short option positions in the investor and dealer community is zero. For every option long in the investment community there is an option short. With these options no net value is created or lost in the investment community; only the price risk of the underlying security has been redistributed.

Mortgage options are different. Homebuyers receive from mortgage bankers puts as a part of the mortgage origination process. Mortgage bankers in turn buy puts from the dealer community to hedge the home-owner put position they are short. The dealers either stay short options or purchase options from mortgage investors. Unlike in other security markets, the investor and dealer community is net short options, with homebuyers net long options. To induce the investment community to accept the net short option position, homebuyers must pay a price for purchasing and taking away their options. By supplying a service to the consuming public, returns to the investment community from being short options on mortgages are probably higher than being short options on other securities, where the net investment community position is zero.

CONCLUSION

Over-the-counter mortgage options are an integral part of the market for MBSs. Mortgage bankers need to look at the mortgage options market to determine the value of the option embedded in their mortgage pipeline, and to hedge that pipeline. Investors in MBSs can use options to enhance the returns on their mortgage portfolios. Knowledge of the mortgage options market is important to achieve these goals.

SECTION VIII

ACCOUNTING AND TAX
CONSIDERATIONS

CHAPTER 38

FAS 115 and MBS Portfolio Management

Brian Lancaster
Managing Director
Bear Stearns & Co., Inc.

Ken Spindel
Managing Director
Bear Stearns & Co., Inc.

Andrew Taddei
Managing Director
Bear Stearns & Co., Inc.

INTRODUCTION

The implementation of FAS 115 has changed forever the way a major part of the fixed income investor universe values and selects securities. Particularly for mortgage-backed securities portfolios, scenario analysis becomes more important than ever. This rigorous analysis is required on each of the security, portfolio and balance sheet levels to different extents. In this chapter, we review the most important concepts, strategies and technologies for implementing FAS 115 initially and for operating under the standard on an ongoing basis.

REVIEW AND ANALYSIS

While previous accounting guidance (like FAS 60 for insurers) made reference to a held-to-maturity standard, reporting practice had resulted in a held-to-foreseeable future or held-for-long-term standard. The FFIEC Policy

The authors would like to thank Jeff Hingst for his efforts in running portfolio analytics for this chapter.

Statement on Securities Activities (for banks and savings associations) permits securities to be carried at amortized cost only when the institution has the positive intent and ability to hold for long-term investment purposes. This poorly defined standard has allowed institutions to manage investment portfolios as long as there were reasons for these transactions other than taking gains or picking up yield.

Infrequent transactions carried out in the context of a prudent overall business plan—one that did not result in a pattern of recognizing gains while leaving underwater securities in portfolio—would be accepted. Words like long-term, infrequent, and pattern were not defined, allowing significant flexibility to manage portfolios. Determination of whether an institution was engaging in investment, held-for-sale, or trading activity was very much left to auditor and examiner discretion. As such, thorough documentation of economic motivations and rigorous analyses supporting transactions have generally been required. They have allowed financial managers to justify actively managing their balance sheets through securities activities in portfolios ostensibly held for long-term investment purposes.

FAS 115 removes the flexibility granted by poorly defined standards. It moves to a definitive held-to-maturity (HTM) requirement for securities to be held at amortized cost, forcing a much larger portion of securities portfolios to a market value reporting standard. In addition to requiring managers to have a positive intent and ability to hold securities to maturity, it removes the ability of managers to utilize securities held at amortized cost for most of the reasons they have been held by financial institutions historically. That is, even if a positive intent and an ability to hold to maturity exists, securities an institution anticipates selling in response to: changes in interest rates and related prepayment risk, asset/liability management needs, liquidity needs, changes in availability of or yield on alternative investments, changes in funding sources or foreign currency risk, *etc.*, would not be eligible to be placed in the held-to-maturity portfolio.

Any securities not classified as HTM or trading are considered available-for-sale (AFS) securities. The AFS category replaces the held-for-sale category. AFS securities are marked-to-market with unrealized gains and losses reported as a separate component of shareholders equity (tax effected). There is no earnings impact. Securities in the old held-for-sale category were carried at the lower of cost or market value with an earnings impact (no earnings impact for insurance companies). The definition of trading securities remains essentially unchanged. These securities are marked-to-market with unrealized gains and losses included in earnings.

The securities reporting classifications are summarized in Exhibit 1.

Exhibit 1. Securities Reporting Classifications as per FAS 115

- **Held-to-Maturity Securities** are measured at amortized cost. A positive intention and ability to hold to maturity is required. Securities that an institution intends to hold only for an indefinite period, such as those it anticipates selling in response to the following items, should not be classified as held-to-maturity:
  - Changes in interest rates and related prepayment risk
  - Liquidity needs (for example due to deposit withdrawals or increased loan demand)
  - Changes in availability of or yield on alternative investments
  - Changes in funding sources and terms
  - Changes in foreign currency risk

- **Trading Securities** are bought and held principally for purpose of selling in near term. Reflect active and frequent buying and selling with the objective of generating profits from short-term price movements. Include MBS held-for-sale in conjunction with mortgage banking activities, as described in FAS 65. Measured at fair value with unrealized holding gains and losses are included in earnings.

- **Available-for-Sale Securities** are investments not classified as trading or held-to-maturity securities. Measured at fair value with unrealized holding gains and losses reported as a net amount in a separate component of shareholders equity until realized.

CLASSIFICATION

How should an institution classify its securities? Remember there is no one right answer! While FAS 115 moves to a held-to-maturity standard, classifications are still based on management's intent. After considering differences in balance sheet composition, regional economics and resulting real estate values and loan demand, portfolio size relative to the balance sheet, portfolio composition, capital posture, operating philosophy, past portfolio activity, and finally, management's intent, we find that there are as many approaches to implementing FAS 115 as there are institutions.

There are no set percentages of how much of a portfolio should go into one category or another. Nor are there any standards mandating that certain securities be classified one way or another. The entire process is institution specific. For example, one manager might place a newly created, less liquid, "cheap" (because of its lesser liquidity) mortgage security, such as a 20-year pass-through, in a held-to-maturity account because he intends only to enjoy the higher yield and not sell the security. Another manager might place the bond in an available-for-sale account intending to sell the security if its spread tightens as the market becomes more liquid.

Any cursory attempt to classify securities based solely on security characteristics, institution size, or target percentages perceived to be acceptable to auditors or examiners may result in classifications that limit future flexibility to actively manage the balance sheet. There is no substitute for an evaluation of management's intent. As such, we recommend that managers convert the requirements of FAS 115 into a set of questions and ask those questions for each security (or group of securities with similar characteristics) in portfolio, as well as evaluate past uses and management practices for similar securities. Why did I buy this security? How have I managed similar positions in the last few years? Given the current characteristics of the instrument, do I have the positive intent and ability to hold to maturity? Do I anticipate selling in response to changes in interest rates and related prepayment risk, *etc.*?

Once an institution has evaluated its intent with respect to each security and established a first pass at classifying securities, it must now reevaluate these classifications on a portfolio basis. The process may be iterative. Is the yield profile on the held-to-maturity securities portfolio acceptable? Will this portfolio provide me with the core earnings levels I need to cover liability costs when rates are up 100, 200, 300 basis points or more? In different rate scenarios, can I live with the average life profile when it no longer relates to corresponding liabilities? How does this affect my ability to hold to maturity? Do I have enough securities in available-for-sale to provide me with sufficient flexibility to manage my balance sheet for asset/liability purposes? Is there enough in this portfolio to provide me with ample liquidity to meet deposit withdrawals in times of disintermediation or to fund loans in periods of high loan demand? Given my AFS classifications, do the capital ratios fall below targeted levels in plausible rate changes? How about in what management believes to be the most likely rate change scenario? If so, the classifications have to be "fine tuned"—the iterative process. The most basic of these questions for classifying securities are summarized in Exhibit 2.

FAS 115 REPORTING SYSTEMS AND TECHNOLOGY

To help the investor answer these questions easily, firms can incorporate complete FAS 115 reporting systems into their portfolio valuation systems. We recommend a system that is straightforward, yet flexible and would work as follows: 1) it should be able to produce a sample portfolio showing how the

---

Exhibit 2. Classification of Securities

- **Is the yield profile of the HTM portfolio acceptable?**
  - Most important for premium/discount holdings
- **Is the impact to capital from market value changes in the AFS account acceptable?**
  - Deposit insurance premiums, prompt corrective action
- **How will average life profile affect my ability to hold to maturity?**
  - IRR component classifications

---

market value, purchase yields, average lives, total returns, durations, and convexities of each of the securities and the portfolios will change under various rising and falling rate scenarios (see Exhibit 3 for an example FAS 115 report); 2) a useful system should then be able to rank these securities based on a wide variety of investor criteria, such as most volatile to least volatile and *vice versa*, largest unrealized capital gains to smallest gains, *etc.*, thereby allowing the investor to easily segregate groups of securities in various accounts; 3) then, most importantly, summary tables showing how key valuation measures, such as total assets, core capital, leverage ratios, purchase yields, and market values are affected depending on the strategy used to classify different securities should be available. Exhibits 4-7 provide summary information on a $179 million portfolio used as an example in this section.

Let's assume a manager has this $179 million portfolio of securities and his goal is to establish a $40 million AFS portfolio to provide flexibility for potential liquidity needs. Additionally, since the institution is capital-constrained, the portfolio manager would classify the securities with an eye toward bolstering base case capital ratios while limiting their volatility in changing rate scenarios. To do so, he wants to classify those securities with the greatest gains in his available-for-sale portfolio and the rest in the held-to-maturity. His portfolio would be entered, and the Bear Stearns reporting system would first rank his securities from the ones with the greatest current unrealized gains to those with the least. To decide how much to place in the available-for-sale portfolio, the manager could then place varying amounts of the securities with the biggest unrealized gains in the available-for-sale category, and let the system quickly calculate the impact on his portfolio yields, total assets (including the mark-to-market effect), core capital (including the tax affected mark-to-market effect), and leverage ratios. In Exhibit 5, he examines the extreme case of placing $40 million of those securities with the greatest gains in the available-for-sale category, the rest in held-to-maturity. As shown in Exhibit 5, if we compare this strategy with his current situation (see entry under "None" in *FAS 115 Leverage Summary* – Exhibit 4), the system calculates that he will improve his leverage ratio from 5.85% to 6.08% in the base case, a gain of 23 basis points.[1] If he is dissatisfied with the outcome, the system could search for other solutions until an optimal solution is solved for, subject to any imposed constraints.

Bear Stearns' new FAS 115 reporting system is also useful because it allows the investor to see, in one unified report, the impact of an investment decision based not only on yield (for HTM) or total return (for trading), but

---

1 While the scenario impacts on the leverage ratio are considered in this chapter for illustrative purposes, banks and savings associations operate under tandem constraints of leverage and risk-based capital (with an interest rate risk component to capital soon to come). A thorough analysis should include an evaluation of the impact of alternative strategies on each of these capital requirements.

Exhibit 3. FAS 115 Report

Bond (Sorted by Ascending MV Chg. $M In Scenario +300)

		-100	Unch.	+100	+200	+300
FHLMC-1611 Y4	*MV Chg. ($M)*	**210.06**		**-224.76**	**-461.26**	**-694.82**
Cpn.:	5.250%	*MV Chg. (%)*	4.21		-4.50	-9.24	-13.93
Curr. Face:	5,000M	*Purchase Yield (%)*	5.47	5.47	5.47	5.47	5.47
Book Price:	99.1800	*Average Life (yrs.)*	4.34	4.34	4.34	4.34	4.38
Book Gain:	13.50M	*PSA (%)*	386	223	148	112	93
Maturity:	01/15/16	*CPP (%)*	18.42	11.22	7.59	5.81	4.83
Mkt. Value:	4,989.28M	*Duration*	3.768	4.357	4.879	5.210	5.334
Mkt. Price:	99.4500	*Convexity*	-0.383	-0.124	-0.143	0.056	0.157
		12-Mos. ROR (%)	9.48	6.39	2.98	-1.05	-5.46
FHLMC-1552 Y5	*MV Chg. ($M)*	**188.64**		**-215.75**	**-446.34**	**-677.20**
Cpn.:	5.500%	*MV Chg. (%)*	3.75		-4.29	-8.87	-13.46
Curr. Face:	5,000M	*Purchase Yield (%)*	5.49	5.50	5.50	5.50	5.50
Book Price:	100.0200	*Average Life (yrs.)*	3.36	4.09	4.09	4.09	4.20
Book Gain:	14.00M	*PSA (%)*	391	228	152	115	95
Maturity:	2/15/14	*CPP (%)*	19.16	11.75	7.95	6.07	5.03
Mkt. Value:	5,032.58M	*Duration*	3.041	4.059	4.677	5.040	5.225
Mkt. Price:	100.3000	*Convexity*	-0.776	-0.237	-0.167	0.032	0.173
		12-Mos. ROR (%)	8.96	6.42	3.27	-0.57	-4.85
FNMA-93167 Y4	*MV Chg. ($M)*	**112.41**		**-127.84**	**-263.88**	**-399.86**
Cpn.:	5.500%	*MV Chg. (%)*	3.70		-4.21	-8.69	-13.17
Curr. Face:	3,000.00M	*Purchase Yield (%)*	5.18	5.24	5.24	5.24	5.24
Book Price:	100.8200	*Average Life (yrs.)*	3.39	4.17	4.17	4.17	4.21
Book Gain:	1.80M	*PSA (%)*	380	223	148	113	94
Maturity:	04/25/14	*CPP (%)*	18.82	11.54	7.82	5.99	4.98
Mkt. Value:	3,036.94M	*Duration*	2.946	4.008	4.570	4.924	5.082
Mkt. Price:	100.8800	*Convexity*	-0.865	-0.216	-0.154	0.027	0.134
		12-Mos. ROR (%)	8.73	6.21	3.10	-0.60	-4.74
FNMA-086642	*MV Chg. ($M)*	**8.87**		**-11.14**	**-27.69**	**-53.33**
Cpn.:	5.282%	*MV Chg. (%)*	0.30		-0.38	-0.95	-1.82
Curr. Face:	2,893.67M	*Purchase Yield (%)*	3.70	4.42	5.43	6.44	7.45
Book Price:	101.9700	*Average Life (yrs.)*	2.17	2.60	3.07	3.65	4.34
Book Gain:	-34.43M	*PSA (%)*	598	454	431	407	380
Maturity:	05/01/29	*CPP (%)*	30.45	23.93	22.87	21.71	20.39
Mkt. Value:	2,925.95M	*Duration*	0.432	0.306	0.468	0.724	1.008
Mkt. Price:	100.7800	*Convexity*	0.193	-0.070	-0.095	-0.201	-0.110
		12-Mos. ROR (%)	4.35	4.74	5.36	5.83	6.05

(continued)

Exhibit 3. *Continued*

Bond (Sorted by Ascending MV Chg. $M In Scenario +300)

		-100	Unch.	+100	+200	+300
FHLMC-160026	*MV Chg. ($M)*	**2.27**		**-2.36**	**-4.73**	**-7.08**
Cpn.: 8.000%	*MV Chg. (%)*	2.86		-2.97	-5.96	-8.91
Curr. Face: 76.61M	*Purchase Yield (%)*	7.77	7.79	7.80	7.82	7.83
Book Price: 100.0000	*Average Life (yrs.)*	3.36	3.59	3.80	3.99	4.14
Book Gain: 2.44M	*PSA (%)*	317	285	258	236	219
Maturity: 09/01/07	*CPP (%)*	19.03	17.09	15.47	14.14	13.15
Mkt. Value: 79.45M	*Duration*	2.689	2.921	3.080	3.162	3.190
Mkt. Price: 103.1900	*Convexity*	-0.109	-0.028	-0.015	0.037	0.071
	12-Mos. ROR (%)	8.61	6.81	4.81	2.65	0.43
FHLMC-1449 F2	*MV Chg. ($M)*	**0.37**		**-0.32**	**-0.63**	**-0.93**
Cpn.: 4.822%	*MV Chg. (%)*	0.02		-0.02	-0.04	-0.06
Curr. Face: 1,574.13M	*Purchase Yield (%)*	7.50	7.43	7.48	7.83	8.21
Book Price: 99.2500	*Average Life (yrs.)*	0.18	0.23	0.35	0.57	3.37
Book Gain: 9.44M	*PSA (%)*	684	493	347	259	211
Maturity: 12/15/07	*CPP (%)*	36.12	26.63	18.94	14.28	11.66
Mkt. Value: 1,576.63M	*Duration*	0.022	0.021	0.020	0.019	0.019
Mkt. Price: 99.8500	*Convexity*	-0.008	0.004	0.000	0.000	0.001
	12-Mos. ROR (%)	3.97	4.82	5.69	6.54	6.54
Portfolio Wtd. Avg.	*MV Chg. (%)*	2.96		-3.30	-6.83	-10.39
	Purchase Yield (%)	5.32	5.45	5.62	5.82	6.02
	Average Life (yrs.)	3.18	3.58	3.65	3.76	4.19
	Duration	2.547	3.146	3.558	3.817	3.936
	Convexity	-0.453	-0.151	-0.130	-0.007	0.093
	12-Mos. ROR (%)	7.87	5.96	3.73	1.02	-2.09
Portfolio Totals	*MV Change ($MM)*	**0.52**		**-0.58**	**-1.20**	**-1.83**
Book Gain: 6.75M	*MV + Accr. ($MM)*	18.16	17.64	17.06	16.44	15.81

also on book yield (income) and price performance, as would be reported in the AFS account using some of the most sophisticated valuation techniques currently available. Prior to FAS 115, most securities holdings of depository institutions were reported at amortized cost and were available for ongoing management of the institution as long as there was no indication of gains trading demonstrated by this portfolio activity. Under FAS 115, all flexibility from securities holdings must come from that subset of securities in the AFS category.[2] Management must be much more conscious of the price performance

---

2 Remember, securities sales in response to liquidity needs, asset liability management requirements or to changes in interest rates are not permitted from the HTM account.

Exhibit 4.   XYZ Savings Bank
FAS 115 Leverage Summary

				Leverage Ratio		
Available-for-Sale Strategy		**-100**	**Base**	**+100**	**+200**	**+300**
None		5.85%	5.85%	5.85%	5.85%	5.85%
Capital Enhancement:	$40MM	6.11%	6.08%	6.01%	5.89%	5.75%
Entire Portfolio:	$179MM	6.37%	6.16%	5.87%	5.51%	5.09%
Highest $ Volatility:	$40MM	5.93%	5.87%	5.77%	5.65%	5.50%
Lowest $ Volatility:	$40MM	5.94%	5.93%	5.91%	5.89%	5.85%

			Projected Book Yield		
Corresponding					
Held-to-Maturity Portfolio	**-100**	**Base**	**+100**	**+200**	**+300**
None	5.35%	5.60%	5.81%	6.00%	6.17%
Capital Enhancement Strategy	5.12%	5.32%	5.50%	5.66%	5.80%
Highest $ Volatility Strategy	5.44%	5.67%	5.87%	6.05%	6.21%
Lowest $ Volatility Strategy	5.28%	5.55%	5.78%	5.98%	6.15%

ASSUMPTIONS:
- Leverage ratio based on changes in fixed income portfolio only
- Results shown are based on an effective tax rate of 39.5% provided by XYZ
- Base leverage ratio calculation = equity capital - (goodwill and other intangibles) / average assets - (goodwill and other intangibles)
- Base capital: 28,080M   Base assets: 480,000M
- Gross pretax capital adjustment for base scenario:
  Capital enhancement $2000M
  Portfolio in AFS: $2767M
  Highest $ volatility: $ 136M
- $ Volatility calculated in +300 scenario

of securities in the AFS portfolio and how total rate of return and market value measures capture this performance.

When considering the purchase of new securities which will be placed in the AFS account, total rate of return[3] is an extremely useful measure of a security's economic value over a specific holding period and should be used. From an economic perspective, it allows the investor to make a better purchase decision than yield or market value measures. However, under FAS

---

3 Total rate of return has not been very widely used historically by financial institutions. Therefore, results may be surprising. The total rate of return of a security equals the value of a security realized over a specific time period. It includes the income, return of principal, and reinvestment of the cash flows received as well as the difference between the mark-to-market price at the end of the time period and the purchase price at the beginning of the time period expressed as a percentage of the beginning market value (purchase price multiplied by the outstanding face amount at purchase).

Exhibit 5.   XYZ Savings Bank FAS 115 Summary Capital Enhancement Strategy

	-100	Base	+100	+200	+300
MV Change %	0.744	0.000	-1.545	-4.018	-7.168
Purchase Yield	6.181	6.583	6.944	7.240	7.488
Average Life	2.121	2.645	3.259	3.880	4.514
Total Return	4.482	4.879	4.831	3.757	1.626
MV Change $(000)	*303*	*0*	*-629*	*-1635*	*-2916*

	-100	Base	+100	+200	+300
Total Assets ± Mark-To-Market Effect	482,303	482,000	481,371	480,365	479,084
Core Capital + Tax Effected Mark-To-Market	29,473	29,290	28,909	28,301	27,526
Leverage Ratio	*6.11%*	*6.08%*	*6.01%*	*5.89%*	*5.75%*

ASSUMPTIONS: • Core capital and total assets as of 9/30/93 provided by XYZ
• Results shown are based on an effective tax rate of 39.5%, provided by XYZ
• Capital and leverage ratio based on changes in fixed income portfolio only
• Base leverage ratio calculation = equity cap - (goodwill and other intangibles) / average assets - (goodwill and other intangibles)
• Approximately $40MM of securities with the greatest unrealized gain in the base case are classified as available-for-sale

115, total rate of return will not correctly measure the impact to income over mark-to-market periods as total return considers mark-to-market gains and losses as going to income. FAS 115 only accounts for these unrealized gains and losses as an impact to capital until the security is actually sold. In addition, when a security is already on the books at a price which is different from the market, total return will not measure the components of income and capital impact as FAS 115 requires. (Later in this chapter, an analysis showing how both total return and market value measures should be considered in developing appropriate strategies under FAS 115 is presented.)

Importance of an FAS 115 Report

While this kind of FAS 115 report is a useful tool to help institutions classify securities, it is also a key piece of documentation. Under FAS 115, auditor and examiner discretion still plays a large part—especially for initial implementation. Institutions will be required to support and justify portfolio classifications to the satisfaction of auditors and examiners. As a result, documentation is critical. Individual portfolio transactions were documented in the past to demonstrate that activity was consistent with an intent and ability to hold for long-term purposes. Similarly, implementation of FAS 115 should be viewed as one large transaction carrying the single most important documentation burden of any securities transaction. An FAS 115 report will not only help management evaluate intent, but will help institutions support their classifications by providing concise, comprehensive information on performance characteristics of securities on an individual and portfolio basis.

When evaluating whether AFS instruments provide required liquidity, a cash flow analysis of loans as well as securities should be performed under a variety of scenarios including a change in interest rates of more than 100 basis points. Cash-flow analysis of the securities portfolio will provide additional documentation to support securities classifications. This analysis is particularly useful to support HTM classifications when examiners question whether management might need to sell HTM securities for liquidity purposes.

Failure to Evaluate Management's Intent Often Leads to Pitfalls

The most useful aspect of any FAS 115 reporting system is an ability to quickly highlight the benefits and pitfalls of some of the more common strategies that may appear reasonable at first glance. Often, only vigorous analytics can help identify weaknesses.

One of the common strategies investors are implementing could lead to a "volatility trap." These investors are putting high-volatility securities in the held-to-maturity account (HTM), locking away the volatility, and all low-volatility securities in the available-for-sale account (AFS), to provide liquidity while limiting fluctuations of capital ratios. This approach, while seeming reasonable at first, can result in a lower yielding, underwater held-to-maturity portfolio in a rising rate environment. As shown in Exhibit 6, our portfolio manager's leverage ratio improves again as in the capital enhancement strategy, in this case from 5.85% to 5.93% (compare entry under "None" with "Lowest $ Volatility" scenario in Exhibit 4) and remains in a stable range between 5.85% and 5.94% whether rates rise or fall. However, the projected book yield of the held-to-maturity portfolio falls from 5.60% to 5.55% in the base case and remains below the original book yield whether rates rise or fall. This strategy can also be problematic as the resulting HTM portfolio may have a profile similar to a portfolio resulting from gains trading as it is described by regulators. Such cursory classifications will be criticized by examiners and will additionally result in the inability to manage the most volatile positions—"pruning losers," as most portfolio managers would need flexibility to do.

Another trap investors could fall into is "the liquidity trap." Take the extreme example of a portfolio manager who has had a high level of activity over time and does not believe he now can justify holding any securities to

Exhibit 6.   XYZ Savings Bank FAS 115 Summary Low $ Volatility Securities

	-100	Base	+100	+200	+300
MV Change %	0.223	0.000	-0.386	-0.931	-1.654
Purchase Yield	5.587	5.784	5.958	6.114	6.240
Average Life	0.805	0.945	1.082	1.220	1.363
Total Return	2.965	3.824	4.499	4.819	5.104
MV Change $(000)	*91*	*0*	*-158*	*-381*	*-677*

	-100	Base	+100	+200	+300
Total Assets ± Mark-to-Market Effect	480,810	480,719	480,561	480,338	480,042
Core Capital + Tax Effected Mark-to-Market	28,570	28,515	28,419	28,284	28,105
Leverage Ratio 5.94%		*5.94%*	*5.93%*	*5.91%*	*5.89%*	*5.85%*

ASSUMPTIONS:
- Core capital and total assets as of 9/30/93 provided by XYZ
- Results shown are based on an effective tax rate of 39.5%, provided by XYZ
- Capital and leverage ratio based on changes in fixed income portfolio only
- Base leverage ratio calculation = equity cap - (goodwill and other intangibles) / average assets - (goodwill and other intangibles)
- Approximately $40MM of lowest $ volatility securities in the +300 scenario are classified as available-for-sale

maturity, so all securities are classified in the AFS account. Certain institutions can successfully operate with this "maximum balance sheet flexibility" posture—those with high capital levels and/or low-volatility portfolios or small securities portfolios relative to balance sheet size. However, most institutions placing all securities in the AFS portfolio would need to manage the volatility of capital ratios by limiting this AFS portfolio to very short average life and adjustable/floating-rate products. Such positions will squeeze earnings and result in competitive disadvantages on the liability side, loan pricing, and policy underwriting. Although past portfolio activity influences this portfolio manager's classifications, he can respond more appropriately by identifying a change of intent that is brought about by the new standard and arrive at more balanced classifications.

The flip side of the liquidity trap is to place all securities in the HTM account. In this case, an institution places all securities in the HTM account because it has not sold any securities for a long period of time and does not anticipate selling any in the near future. As with the liquidity trap, some institutions may be able to operate under this strategy, but they will be few. This is the strategy of least balance sheet flexibility. Just because sales were not necessary in the recent past or unanticipated in the future does not mean the institution does not need balance sheet flexibility. For this reason (and to avoid confrontations with auditors or examiners), institutions should place some amount of securities in the AFS portfolio to provide flexibility.

During the course of our discussions, we have seen an increasing number of institutions arriving at very reasonable compromises to these traps. For example, one reasonable strategy that is becoming increasingly common is for investors to go to the first few highest volatility positions in the Bear Stearns report and earmark them for the AFS account because they would have to be managed most actively (see Exhibit 7). As part of this strategy, investors would also place some of the lowest volatility positions in the HTM account—floaters, for example. The case is made that the only securities that really have a long-term place on the balance sheet are those that would provide the institution with sensitivity to changing rates—for a typical liability sensitive institution. As shown below for this portfolio, this strategy boosts the book yield of the HTM portfolio under a variety of rate changes. However, it also adds volatility to the institution's leverage ratio because of the need to mark-to-market high dollar volatility securities (see Exhibit 4). While every institution is different and each will arrive at different classifications, these easily identified traps can be avoided by all.

Exhibit 7.   XYZ Savings Bank FAS 115 Summary High $ Volatility Securities

	-100	Base	+100	+200	+300
MV Change %	1.510	0.000	-2.052	-4.820	-8.071
Purchase Yield	5.019	5.349	5.632	5.860	6.048
Average Life	2.450	2.934	3.409	3.830	4.240
Total Return	5.686	5.261	4.552	3.066	0.752
MV Change $(000)	*590*	*0*	*-801*	*-1881*	*-3151*

	-100	Base	+100	+200	+300
Total Assets ± Mark-to-Market Effect	480,726	480,136	479,335	478,255	476,985
Core Capital + Tax Effected Mark-to-Market	28,519	28,162	27,678	27,024	26,256
Leverage Ratio	*5.93%*	*5.87%*	*5.77%*	*5.65%*	*5.50%*

ASSUMPTIONS: • Core capital and total assets as of 9/30/93 provided by XYZ
              • Results shown are based on effective tax rate of 39.5%, provided by XYZ
              • Capital and leverage ratio based on changes in fixed income portfolio only
              • Base leverage ratio calculation = equity cap - (goodwill and other intangibles) / average assets - (goodwill and other intangibles)
              • Approximately $40MM of highest $ volatility securities in the +300 scenario are classified as available-for-sale

INVESTMENT STRATEGIES

While many FAS 115 portfolio strategies exist, it is important to remember that no single strategy works for every institution. We provide below some common strategies that have been successfully utilized in many permutations.

Stop Loss Methodology

The available-for-sale portfolio may be managed using a stop loss methodoloy—just like an equities portfolio. However, the investor should be careful not to set stop loss levels too close to the market or the activity level may be high enough to raise concerns that the institution is engaging in trading activity in the AFS portfolio. If auditors/examiners reclassify securities as trading, the unrealized gains or losses would flow through earnings.

While FAS 115 requires that sales or transfers from the held-to-maturity account (HTM) be rare or immaterial, transfers from the AFS account to the HTM account are permitted. The ability to make these transfers may be used selectively, in conjunction with the stop loss methodology—but only in moderation. Otherwise, the HTM portfolio that would result would look much like that resulting from gains trading.

Barbell Strategy

Investors who are considering the purchase of securities for the available-for-sale portfolio may want to consider the benefits of a barbell strategy, *i.e,*. purchasing two securities, one short and one long duration security—the average duration of which equals that of a single security. *Ceteris paribus*, a barbell of securities will usually outperform a single same duration security on a total rate of return basis as rates rise and fall or as the yield curve flattens. This is generally true because barbells have more positive convexity[4] (or less negative convexity, as in the case of mortgage securities) than a single security of the same duration. Thus, as rates rise or fall, the barbell's returns are magnified in a rally and protected in a back-up. This is illustrated in Exhibit 8, where we compare the total rates of return of a single, current coupon security, 30-year FNMA 6s, and a barbell consisting of 90% of a 10-year PAC (FNMA 9361K) and 10% of a 1-year broken PAC Z (FNMA 8972-Z). As the exhibit shows, the barbell combination is duration matched with the pass-through; however, as rates rise or fall, we pick up more return than in the base case. This trade is

---

4 Convexity is the rate of change of duration for a 100 basis points move in rates. It is a useful attribute because it causes a security's duration to shorten as rates rise and to increase as rates fall, thereby magnifying gains in a rally and mitigating losses in a back-up.

Exhibit 8.   Total Rate of Return (Annualized 6-Mo. Horizon) for a Barbell Strategy

		Price	Yield	Dur.	-100	-50	Flat	+50	+100
BUY	90% FNMA 93-61 K	102:20	6.43	6.91	19.06	13.44	6.87	0.30	-6.33
	10-Yr. PAC								
	10% FNMA 89-72 Z	101:14	4.75	0.61	3.99	4.34	4.54	4.63	4.07
	1-Yr. Busted PACZ								
Combination			6.26	6.27	17.53	12.52	6.63	0.74	-5.28
SELL	100% FNMA 6.0s	98:19	6.26	6.24	16.75	12.06	6.44	0.37	-5.83
Total Return Pick-Up			*0*	*+.03*	*+78*	*+45*	*+19*	*+37*	*+55*

particularly attractive because we do not give up yield. Usually the market "charges" for the extra convexity offered by a barbell through a yield give-up. Because this bond barbell combination is so cheap we can pick up convexity without giving up yield.

Barbell/Segmentation Strategy

Although the expected economic benefit of the above barbell strategy is captured by a total return analysis indicating that the investor is making a wise economic decision, under FAS 115 the investor must consider how the purchase and the designation of the securities in a AFS or HTM will impact market value. Under FAS 115, the benefit of the barbell strategy can be enhanced by segmenting the barbell, placing the short duration leg in the available-for-sale account, and placing the long duration bond in the held-to-maturity account. By implementing this strategy, the investor can help stabilize the impact of rate changes on the market value, capital, and hence, leverage ratios of an institution. For example, assume an institution has $10 million to invest and knows it may need some, but not all, of this cash to fund loans over the next six months. The institution could purchase $10 million of a 3.4-year PAC which has an effective duration of 3.538, placing $6 million in the available-for-sale account and $4 million in the held-to-maturity account. Or it could create and purchase a barbell consisting of $6 million of a 1.6-year PAC, placing it in the available-for-sale account, and $4 million of 30-year GNMA 6s, placing them in the held-to-maturity account. By taking this tack, the investor could reduce the change in market value when rates rise and fall from a volatile range of a $660.3 million decline to a $207.1 million gain, to a more stable change of a $32.3 million gain and a $289.7 million decline (see Exhibits 9 and 10). The impact on capital would, of course, be correspondingly stabilized as well.

This type of segmented strategy could be particularly important for institutions, such as insurance companies, that need longer duration assets to

Exhibit 9.   XYZ Savings Bank FAS 115 Summary
Bullet Strategy $10MM Effective Duration = 3.538

Effective Duration: 3.538 Available-for-Sale: $6MM	-100	Base	+100	+200	+300
MV Change %	3.451	0.000	-3.653	-7.375	-11.003
Purchase Yield	4.916	4.916	4.916	4.916	4.915
Average Life	3.444	3.444	3.444	3.453	3.652
Total Return	8.025	5.731	3.132	.204	-2.830
MV Change $(000)	*207.1*	*0*	*-219.2*	*-442.5*	*-660.3*
Impact On Capital	*125.3*	*0*	*-132.6*	*-267.7*	*-399.5*

Effective Duration: 3.538 Held-to-Maturity: $4MM	-100	Base	+100	+200	+300
Projected Purchase Yield	4.916	4.916	4.916	4.916	4.915
Average Life	3.444	3.444	3.444	3.453	3.652

Effective Duration: 3.538 Total Portfolio: $10MM	-100	Base	+100	+200	+300
Average Life	3.444	3.444	3.444	3.453	3.652
Purchase Yield	4.916	4.916	4.916	4.916	4.915

ASSUMPTIONS: • Portfolio proxied with $10MM 3.4-yr. PAC—FFIEC eligible
                     • Assumed XYZ effective tax rate of 39.50%

match their liabilities. In the given example (see Exhibits 11 and 12), the investor needed assets with a duration of 5.457. The added stability in market value and capital impact provided by the segmented strategy is even greater than in our first shorter duration example. In this case, the impact on the insurance companies capital stabilizes from a volatile range of 163.4 to -482.5, to 19.5 to -171.2. *Remember, however, that this strategy must be done in moderation, or the institution could end up in the volatility trap with underwater, low-yielding securities locked in its held-to-maturity account in a rising rate environment.* Next, we explain how to mitigate the impact of the volatility trap by using off-balance sheet interest rate swaps.

Off-Balance Sheet Interest Rate Swaps

Swaps can help an investor manage the price sensitivity of a security in the held-to-maturity account without selling it. To mitigate the liquidity trap, the investor can arrange an off-balance sheet interest rate swap against the longer duration cash security classified in the held-to-maturity portfolio, transforming it into a synthetic shorter duration instrument. For example, let us

Exhibit 10.   XYZ Savings Bank FAS 115 Summary
Barbell Strategy $10MM Effective Duration = 3.538

Effective Duration:	0.984					
Available-for-Sale:	$6MM	-100	Base	+100	+200	+300
MV Change %		.525	0.000	-1.452	-3.056	-4.714
Purchase Yield		3.751	4.135	4.204	4.204	4.204
Average Life		1.274	1.638	1.726	1.726	1.726
Total Return		3.174	4.245	3.964	3.348	2.665
MV Change $(000)		32.3	0	-89.2	-187.8	-289.7
Impact On Capital		19.5	0	-54.0	-113.6	-175.3

Effective Duration:	7.444					
Held-to-Maturity:	$4MM	-100	Base	+100	+200	+300
Projected Purchase Yield		6.186	6.161	6.151	6.147	6.145
Average Life		7.778	11.065	13.018	14.124	14.757

Effective Duration:	3.538					
Total Portfolio:	$10MM	-100	Base	+100	+200	+300
Average Life		3.846	5.366	6.191	6.628	6.879
Purchase Yield		4.714	4.936	4.974	4.972	4.971

ASSUMPTIONS: • Portfolio proxied with $6MM 1.6-yr. PAC and $4MM GNMA 6.00
• Assumed XYZ effective tax rate of 39.50%

assume the longer duration security in the held-to-maturity portfolio is a 5-year Treasury security owned at par with a $1 million face amount, as shown in Exhibit 13. The investor could swap the fixed-rate cash flows generated by the Treasury for cash flows that float along with LIBOR. In the example, the investor would receive the 9.25% fixed-rate coupon cash flows of the Treasury security and pay a swap dealer the current yield on the 9.25s of 1998 fixed rate based on a $1 million notional amount of principal for five years. In exchange the investor would receive from the swap dealer 1-month LIBOR less 25 basis points,[5] thereby creating, in effect, a synthetic floater paying 1-month LIBOR plus 400 basis points. By converting the security into a synthetic floater, the price sensitivity or duration of the combination would be greatly diminished.

It is important to note that the swap must be executed against a security classified in the held-to-maturity portfolio, so that it may receive the desired

---

5 In this example, the swap dealer would pay 1-month LIBOR less 25 basis points, because the swap rate prevailing at the time of this analysis was "pay 5.25% fixed and receive 1-month LIBOR floating."

Exhibit 11. XYZ Insurance Company FAS 115 Summary
Bullet Strategy $10MM Effective Duration = 5.457

Effective Duration:	5.457					
Available-for-Sale:	$6MM	-100	Base	+100	+200	+300
MV Change %		5.424	0.000	-5.538	-10.907	-16.019
Purchase Yield		5.663	5.663	5.663	5.662	5.655
Average Life		5.940	5.944	5.944	5.968	6.472
Total Return		10.834	6.489	1.807	-3.065	-7.894
MV Change $(000)		270.1	0	-275.7	-543.1	*-797.6*
Impact On Capital		163.4	0	-166.8	-328.6	*-482.5*

Effective Duration:	5.457					
Held-to-Maturity:	$4MM	-100	Base	+100	+200	+300
Projected Purchase Yield		5.663	5.663	5.663	5.662	5.655
Average Life		5.940	5.944	5.944	5.968	6.472

Effective Duration :	5.457					
Total Portfolio:	$10MM	-100	Base	+100	+200	+300
Average Life		5.940	5.944	5.944	5.968	6.472
Purchase Yield		5.663	5.663	5.663	5.662	5.655

ASSUMPTIONS: • Portfolio proxied with $10MM 5.9-year PAC
• Assumed XYZ effective tax rate of 39.50%

hedge accounting treatment. That is, it would not have to be marked to market. If swaps are executed against an asset in the available-for-sale account, then they must be marked-to-market.[6]

Off-Balance Sheet CMO Swaps

CMO swaps offer investors similar possibilities if mortgage securities are held in the held-to-maturity portfolio. CMO swaps are similar to regular interest swaps, except that the notional amount of principal outstanding would amortize at different rates depending on mortgage prepayment speeds. Because of this feature, CMO swaps can be used to effectively transform the cash flows generated by a mortgage security as prepayments change.

For example, an investor with an existing CMO floater, such as FNMA 93231-FA (see Exhibit 14) in the held-to-maturity account, could combine it

---

6 At the time of this writing, the FASB is preparing a draft on accounting for hedging transactions, and current treatment may change. Nevertheless, even under current guidance, accounting treatment of swaps has varied from one audit firm to another. Investors should consult their own auditors to determine appropriate treatment for swaps.

Exhibit 12.   XYZ Insurance Company FAS 115 Summary
Barbell Strategy $10MM Effective Duration = 5.453

Effective Duration:	0.998					
Available-for-Sale:	$6MM	-100	Base	+100	+200	+300
MV Change %		.538	0.000	-1.467	-3.074	-4.733
Purchase Yield		3.753	4.136	4.204	4.204	4.204
Average Life		1.276	1.639	1.726	1.726	1.726
Total Return		3.190	4.253	3.962	3.346	2.662
MV Change $(000)		*32.2*	*0*	*-87.7*	*-183.7*	*-282.9*
Impact On Capital		*19.5*	*0*	*-53.1*	*-111.1*	*-171.2*
Effective Duration:	11.998					
Held-to-Maturity:	$4MM	-100	Base	+100	+200	+300
Projected Purchase Yield		6.375	6.665	6.790	6.808	6.808
Average Life		5.464	9.210	13.031	13.753	13.753
Effective Duration:	5.453					
Total Portfolio:	$10MM	-100	Base	+100	+200	+300
Average Life		2.972	4.705	6.304	6.597	6.597
Purchase Yield		4.815	5.160	5.251	5.259	5.259

ASSUMPTIONS: • Portfolio proxied with $6MM 1.6-yr. PAC and $4MM 9.2-yr. Z Bond
                • Assumed XYZ effective tax rate of 39.50%

Exhibit 13.

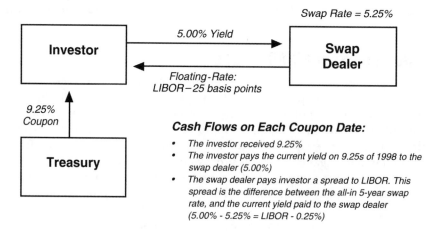

Cash Flows on Each Coupon Date:

• The investor received 9.25%
• The investor pays the current yield on 9.25s of 1998 to the swap dealer (5.00%)
• The swap dealer pays investor a spread to LIBOR. This spread is the difference between the all-in 5-year swap rate, and the current yield paid to the swap dealer (5.00% - 5.25% = LIBOR - 0.25%)

Exhibit 14.   Synthetic CMO Plain Vanilla

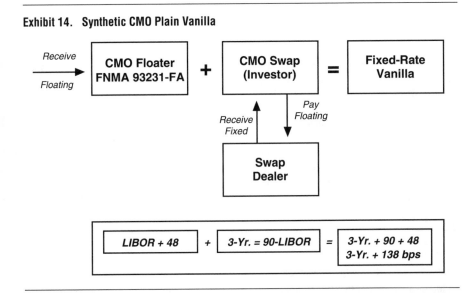

with a CMO swap to create a higher yielding, shorter stated final maturity, plain vanilla security. In the case illustrated, the investor would receive LIBOR + 48 basis points from the CMO floater, pay the swap dealer LIBOR, and receive the 3-year Treasury plus 90 basis points, for a net spread of the 3-year Treasury plus 138 basis points. Because the CMO floater was in the held-to-maturity portfolio, the CMO swap and the synthetic combination would receive hedge accounting treatment and could be held at cost.

Because FNMA 93231-FA has a 3-year average life at pricing and is backed by dwarf 6s, so too does our CMO swap. In fact, as shown in Exhibit 15, the average life profile of the CMO swap is designed so that it will match that of the FNMA 93231-FA. In fact, just about any type of cash flows can be created with a CMO swap. The investor merely specifies the average life, final maturity, coupon, *etc.*, as well as the reference group of collateral as in this case dwarf 6s. Actual prepayments of the reference group of collateral determine the prepayment rate at which the notional principal outstanding will amortize. The reference group may be as specific as a pool or one coupon over a range of WAMs.

For further details on how CMO swaps work and their preferential capital requirements for banks and thrifts, see Exhibit 16.

Exhibit 15. Average Life Profile

				% PSA				
Prepayment	100	160	200	250	300	400	500	600
CMO Swap	7.91	5.07	3.99	4.31	4.42	2.05	1.70	1.50
FNMA 93231-FA	7.91	5.07	3.99	4.31	4.42	2.05	1.70	1.50

Security	Type	Collateral	Settle.	Prepay Speed	Cap	Avg. Life	Price	Yield
FNMA 93231-FA	Floater	FNMA 6s 15-yr.	12/30/93	200	8.00%	3.99	99:28	LIBOR + 48
CMO Swap	Swap	FNMA 6s 15-yr.	12/30/93	200	—	3.99		Fixed: 3-yr. + 99 Floating: (LIBOR)

Exhibit 16. A CMO Swap Transaction

A CMO swap is similar to a traditional interest rate swap but with an amortizing notional face.
- An exchange between two parties of fixed or floating interest payments
- Payments are calculated from a notional face
- The notional face will amortize based upon prepayments experienced on a specifically identified mortgage pool or a group of reference collateral (*i.e.*, GNMA 9s WAM 2021–2022)

Advantages of CMO Swaps over Securities
- *Enhanced yields versus CMO securities*
- *Flexibility in structuring*

The CMO Swap is used as a substitute for a financed fixed-rate security:

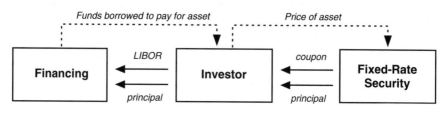

(continued)

Exhibit 16. *Continued*

Bank/Thrift Capital Advantage of CMO Swap (Current Price $103) vs. Cash Security

	$100 Purchase of Agency CMO	$100 Notional Amount CMO Swap
Risk-Based Capital Weighting	20%	50%[1]
Fully-Phased-in Capital Requirement	8%	8%
On-Balance Sheet Credit Exposure	$100	Potential Exposure[2] 0.5% x Notional =$0.05/$100 Notional Current Exposure Mark-to-Mkt. value x Notional =$3.0/$100 Notional
Risk-Based Capital Requirement	$100 x 20% x 8% = **$1.60/$100 Principal Amt.**	= ($0.50 + $3.0) x 50% x 8% = **$0.14/$100 Notional Amt.**

1 This is the highest risk weighting for swaps, regardless of counterparty.
2 Potential exposure = $0 if there is less than 1 year to maturity or if swap is single currency floating to floating.
3 This is the replacement cost of the swap; equals $0 at inception.

- Shorter final maturities
- Stable PAC bands
- Choice of settlement dates
- Longer amortization lockouts
- Higher floater caps
- Higher leverage and shorter average life inverses
- *Flexibility in choice of reference collateral*
- *Potentially preferable regulatory and accounting treatment*
- *Financing advantages*
- *Large transactions possible*

Disadvantages of CMO Swaps
- *Perceived liquidity*
  - Dependent on structures
- *Credit risk*
  - Mitigated with two-way collateralization
- *Minimum size requirement*

CMO Swap Strategies
- **Substitutes for financed fixed-rate securities**
  - Receive fixed on a CMO swap
- **Substitutes for fixed-rate securities purchased with cash**
  - Buy a floater; fix its coupon with CMO swap

(continued)

Exhibit 16. *Continued*

- Buy a perpetual; fix its coupon with a CMO swap
- Rollover CDs; fix their coupons with a CMO swap
- **Substitutes for financed inverse floaters**
  - Receive fixed on several CMO swaps; buy caps
- **Substitutes for inverse floaters purchased with cash**
  - Buy a fixed-rate security; buy caps; receive fixed on several CMO swaps
  - Buy a floater; buy caps; receive fixed on several CMO swaps
- **Substitutes for IO inverse**
  - Buy a cap; receive fixed on a high-coupon CMO swap

Limited Liquidity Securities Strategy

Investors should not put highly liquid securities in the held-to-maturity account, since they would be paying a premium (higher price, lower spread) for liquidity that will be of no, or little, use to them. For example, private placements, 20-year securities, relocation mortgage securities, GNMA IIs, $1/4$ coupon pass-throughs, odd-lot pass-throughs, and selected off-the-run Treasuries all typically trade at cheaper prices because of their lesser liquidity (see Exhibits 17 and 18). These would all make excellent candidates for the held-to-maturity account. Investors may want to put some less liquid, newer securities that

Exhibit 17.   Liquidity Differentials

	12/17/1993		01/04/1994	
	Yield	Spread/ Treasury	Yield	Spread/ Treasury
10-Year UST				
On-the-Run	5.78	0/10-yr.	6.69	0/10-yr.
Off-the-Run (Dur.-Matched)	5.95	17/10-yr.	6.85	16.7/10-yr.
Agency Conv. 30-Year				
Current Coupon	6.57	93/10-yr.	7.50	75/11.4-yr.
Current +150 basis points	6.46	166/4.5-yr.	7.15	125/5.2-yr.
GNMA 30-Year 7.00				
GNSF	6.68	112/7.5-yr.	7.50	82/11-yr.
GNMA II	6.73	116/8.3-yr.	7.59	91/11-yr.
Agency Conv. 30-Year				
8.00	6.75	168/4.73-yr.	7.44	75/7.85-yr.
8.25	6.68	190/3.82-yr.	7.69	139/7.88-yr.
8.50	6.47	169/3.67-yr.	7.18	124/5.28-yr.

Exhibit 18.   Oddlot Price Differentials January Settlement – Bid Side as of 1/10/94

	Current Face Size			
	50M	**225M**	**350M**	**500M**
GNMA 6.50 30-Year	-8/32	-4/32	-2/32	0
GNMA 9.00 30-Year	-1 16/32	-6/32	-4/32	-2/32
FNMA 6.50 30-Year	-8/32	-4/32	-2/32	0
FNMA 9.00 30-Year	-1 16/32	-6/32	-4/32	-2/32
15-Year Gold 6.00	-8/32	-4/32	-2/32	0
FNMA ARM 4.50%	-1 4/32	-16/32	-16/32	-12/32

have the potential of becoming more liquid as issuance picks-up in the available-for-sale account, with the expectation that they will sell the security when its liquidity premium diminishes and its spread tightens.

SUMMARY

FAS 115 will have a major impact on the investment strategies and reporting of much of the investor universe, particularly those involved in the mortgage-backed security market. A more comprehensive evaluation of management's intent is required and analytical tools must be utilized more extensively. It behooves the savvy investor to take time to understand the concepts, strategies, and relevant technologies reviewed in this chapter so he can create optimal portfolios, not only on an economic basis but from the perspective of FAS 115 reporting requirements.

CHAPTER 39

Federal Income Tax Treatment of Mortgage-Backed Securities

James M. Peaslee
Partner
Cleary, Gottlieb, Steen & Hamilton

David Z. Nirenberg
Counsel
Weil, Gotshal & Manges *

I. DISTINGUISHING CHARACTERISTICS OF MORTGAGE-BACKED SECURITIES

The subject of this chapter is the U.S. federal income taxation of mortgage-backed securities.[1] The enactment of the Tax Reform Act of 1986 (TRA 1986) was a watershed event in this area. TRA 1986 gave birth to a new scheme for taxing pools of mortgages that qualify as *real estate mortgage investment conduits* or *REMICs* and the holders of REMIC securities. The legislation also changed the treatment of discount on non-REMIC mortgage-backed securities to take account of the unusual payment characteristics of those securities. The REMIC rules have had the effect of increasing greatly the variety of mortgage-backed securities that are routinely issued to include many that would have been considered fanciful in 1986.

This chapter is concerned primarily with mortgage-backed securities that are supported exclusively (or almost so) by (1) payments made on a fixed pool

---

* © James M. Peaslee and David Z. Nirenberg, 1995.

1 The discussion in this chapter is current through January 1, 1995 and is, of course, subject to change through subsequent legislation, administrative actions, or judicial decisions. A more complete discussion of the topic, complete with citations to, and reprints of, primary source materials may be found in J. Peaslee & D. Nirenberg, Federal Income Taxation of Mortgage-Backed Securities (rev. ed., 1994, Probus Publishing) (hereinafter "Peaslee & Nirenberg"). This book includes a more complete description of questions raised in structuring issuances of mortgage-backed securities (including a discussion of entity classification issues and the qualification tests for REMICs).

of mortgages, or (2) payments made on a fixed pool of mortgages together with earnings from the reinvestment of those payments over a short period (generally not more than six months).[2] Typically, these securities have two payment features that distinguish them economically from conventional publicly held debt obligations: their principal amount (if any) is payable in installments and they are subject to mandatory calls to the extent the mortgages that fund them are prepaid.

Some mortgage-backed securities are further distinguishable from conventional, callable bonds by the fact that their value is attributable largely or entirely to rights to a fixed or variable share of the interest on mortgages. These securities are issued at a very high premium over their principal amount (which may be zero). Because the unamortized premium is forfeited if the securities are prepaid, holders of such securities may experience a zero or negative rate of return, even in the absence of defaults. The highly contingent nature of these securities poses a problem for any system that seeks to measure periodic income and loss.

In terms of tax attributes, mortgage-backed securities may differ from conventional debt instruments in two other respects. First, in the hands of institutional investors, mortgage-backed securities may qualify for certain tax benefits associated with investments in real property mortgages. Second, certain types of mortgage-backed securities are treated for tax purposes as ownership interests in the underlying mortgages rather than as equity or debt of the issuing entity. This "look-through" feature raises a host of tax issues.

The federal income tax questions peculiar to mortgage-backed securities relate primarily to the features described above, the legal structures that are used in transforming whole mortgages into non-REMIC mortgage-backed securities and the REMIC rules.

This chapter addresses only federal tax issues. Readers are cautioned that while the state or local income or franchise tax consequences of issuing, investing in, or sponsoring mortgage-backed securities often mirror the federal consequences, there can be material differences.[3]

II. TYPES OF MORTGAGE-BACKED SECURITIES
A. Introduction

The principal types of mortgage-backed securities currently available are pass-through certificates, pay-through bonds, equity interests in issuers of

---

2 Thus, debt obligations that are secured by mortgages, but have payment terms unrelated to those of the mortgage collateral, are not addressed.

3 Many states have adopted whole or partial tax exemptions for entities that qualify as REMICs under federal law. A list of these exemptions may be found in Peaslee & Nirenberg, *supra*, n.1., Appendix B.

pay-through bonds, and REMIC interests. REMIC interests are either *regular interests* (which from a tax perspective resemble pay-through bonds) or *residual interests* (which from a tax perspective resemble equity interests in issuers of pay-through bonds that are taxed as partnerships).

These securities have two common features: first, they can be used, alone or in combination, to repackage whole mortgages in a manner that increases their attractiveness as investments, and second, the issuers of the securities generally are not subject to tax on the income from the underlying mortgages as it passes through their hands to investors.

It would not be economical to issue a mortgage-backed security unless it were possible to eliminate all material incremental taxes on the issuer. Thus, it is not ordinarily feasible to issue mortgage-backed securities in the form of stock of a corporation. The income from mortgages held by the corporation would bear the full weight of the corporate income tax because no offsetting deductions would be allowed in computing the corporation's taxable income for dividends paid on the stock.

The various types of mortgage-backed securities that are currently available address the problem of the issuer-level taxes in different ways. Pass-through certificates are generally issued by a *grantor trust*, which is not considered to be a taxable entity; indeed, for almost all federal income tax purposes, the trust is simply ignored. Issuers of pay-through bonds, or the owners of such issuers, are generally subject to income tax on the taxable income from the mortgages supporting the bonds (which is gross income less deductions), but the burden of that tax typically is small because of the interest deductions allowed for interest on the bonds. A REMIC is exempt from tax by statute (except for certain penalty taxes).

The ability of a non-REMIC issuer of pay-through bonds to avoid an issuer-level income tax changed dramatically at the beginning of 1992, when special tax rules governing *taxable mortgage pools* or *TMPs* became effective. These rules automatically classify as a corporation any trust, partnership, or other entity if at least 80 percent of its assets are debt obligations, more than half of those obligations are real estate mortgages, and the entity issues two or more classes of pay-through bonds with different maturities. A TMP is, with limited exceptions, subject to corporate tax on its taxable income and cannot join in a consolidated return with other corporations. In most, although not all cases, it would be economically infeasible for an entity to issue pay-through bonds if it would as a result become a TMP. The TMP rules were enacted as an adjunct to the 1986 REMIC legislation to ensure that, after a five-year transition period, REMICs (which are subject to certain tax avoidance rules) would be the exclusive means of issuing multiple-class mortgage-backed securities without an issuer-level tax.[4]

---

4 TMPs are more fully discussed in Peaslee & Nirenberg, *supra*, n.1., Chapter 3, Part D.

Sections B through E of this part describe more fully pass-through certificates, pay-through bonds, equity interests in issuers of pay-through bonds, and REMIC interests. Although REMIC interests may take the form of pass-through certificates, pay-through bonds, or equity interests, except where otherwise indicated, these terms will be used in this chapter to refer only to securities not subject to the REMIC rules.

Ordinarily, the mortgages underlying mortgage-backed securities are not in default when the securities are issued, and either are expected to produce only modest default losses or are guaranteed or insured against loss by third parties. The discussion in Parts B through E below relates only to securities of this type.[5]

Most of the mortgage-backed securities that are issued today take the form of pass-through certificates or REMIC interests. Nonetheless, a discussion of pay-through bonds, and equity interests in issuers of such bonds, continues to be relevant for three principal reasons. First, REMICs were patterned after (and designed to improve on) pre-1992 owner trusts that issued pay-through bonds. Some knowledge of these predecessor securities is helpful in understanding the REMIC rules. Second, entities holding mortgages and issuing pay-through bonds may not be TMPs, either because they issue only a single class of debt, or because the mortgages are financially troubled. (The TMP rules contain an exception for entities formed to liquidate distressed loans.) Last, techniques developed in the mortgage area are being used to finance automobile loans and other non-mortgage receivables. While issuers without real property mortgages cannot take advantage of the REMIC rules, they also are not TMPs.[6]

Section F of this Part considers another type of trust security that takes the form of a pass-through certificate but has the economic characteristics of debt of the issuing trust. These securities will be referred to as *pass-through debt certificates.* They have been issued almost exclusively by trusts holding automobile loans or credit card or other non-mortgage receivables, but in special cases the structure could have applications for mortgages. Moreover, the tax analysis of the certificates provides an interesting contrast to the analysis of more conventional types of asset-backed securities.

---

5 Issues arising in the securitization of financially troubled mortgages are discussed in Peaslee & Nirenberg, *supra,* n.1.

6 A bill was introduced in Congress in 1993 that would create a new vehicle for issuing securities backed by non-mortgage receivables. See H.R. 2065 (introduced May 11, 1993) (providing for the creation of Financial Asset Securitization Investment Trusts, or FASITs). See also American Bar Association, Tax Section, Committee on Financial Transactions, "Legislative Proposal to Expand the REMIC Provisions of the Code to Include Non-mortgage Assets," 46 *Tax Law Review* 299 (Spring 1991). Further, certain municipal bond dealers have proposed the establishment of a new vehicle, a *Tax Exempt Municipal Investment Conduit (TEMIC).* See "Draft of TEMIC Legislation Available," 94 *Tax Notes Today* 4-64 (January 6, 1994).

B. Pass-Through Certificates

1. General Description

In their most common form, pass-through certificates are issued by a trust or custodial arrangement that holds a fixed pool of mortgages. The mortgages may bear interest at a fixed or adjustable rate. The arrangement is created by a sponsor that transfers the mortgages to the trust against receipt of the certificates and then, typically, sells all or a portion of the certificates to investors. The certificates evidence ownership by the holders of specified interests in the assets of the trust.

To avoid an entity-level tax, the trust must be classified as a trust for tax purposes and not as an association taxable as a corporation. Trust classification can be achieved only if the trust has, with a limited exception, a single class of ownership interests and the power under the trust agreement to change the composition of the mortgage pool or otherwise to reinvest mortgage payments is severely restricted. (The exception to the single-class-of-ownership requirement allows stripped certificates and senior and subordinated certificates, as described below.)[7]

Given these tax constraints, pass-through certificates are generally issued in a single class, with each holder having a pro rata interest in the mortgage pool. Thus, if 1,000 such certificates are issued, each would represent a right to $1/_{1,000}$ of each payment of principal and interest on each mortgage in the pool. Mortgage payments received by the trustee are passed through to certificate holders, generally monthly in parallel with the receipt of mortgage payments by the trust. The distributions are reduced by fees for mortgage servicing, pool administration, and any applicable guarantees or pool insurance. These fees generally are fixed in advance over the life of the pool so that certificate holders can be guaranteed a specified "pass-through rate" of interest on the principal balance of the certificates, representing the earnings on the mortgages after deduction of such fees. Depending on the mortgages in the pool and the fees charged, the pass-through rate may be fixed or variable.[8]

A trust that issues pass-through certificates and is classified as a trust is taxed under the grantor trust rules set forth in section 671.[9] Consequently, for

---

7 For a more detailed discussion of the requirements for classification of a trust as a grantor trust see Peaslee & Nirenberg, *supra*, n.1, at Chapter 3. The Treasury regulations that prevent multiple-class trusts from being classified as trusts are known colloquially as the "Sears regulations."

8 The pass-through rate will always represent economically a weighted average of the interest rates (net of fees) on the mortgages. Thus, the pass-through rate will be a fixed number only if the interest rate on each mortgage, net of the fees payable out of such interest, is the same for all mortgages held by the trust and constant over time.

9 Unless otherwise specified, references herein to sections are to the Internal Revenue Code of 1986 (the "Code").

federal income tax purposes, the trust is effectively ignored and certificate holders are recognized as the owners of the mortgages held by the trust.

One consequence of disregarding the separate existence of a pass-through trust is that certificate holders who report taxable income under a cash method of accounting (which is true of virtually all holders who are individuals) must report income for tax purposes based on the timing of receipts of mortgage payments by the trust, *not* on the timing of distributions made to them by the trust. The trustee is viewed as an agent collecting mortgage payments on the certificate holders' behalf. While certificate holders are obliged to include in income the gross amount of interest on the mortgages, they are allowed deductions (subject to special limitations in the case of individuals) for mortgage servicing and other expenses paid out of such interest, again on the theory that those amounts are paid on their behalf. An individual certificate holder's deductions for servicing and other expenses may be limited under section 67, which provides that an individual is allowed certain, miscellaneous, itemized deductions (including deductions for investment expenses) only to the extent that the aggregate amount of such deductions exceeds 2 percent of the individual's adjusted gross income. In addition, an individual is subject to an alternative minimum tax (*AMT*) at graduated rates up to 28 percent of alternative minimum taxable income (*AMTI*) if such tax exceeds the individual's regular federal income tax liability. No deduction is allowed for investment expenses in computing an individual's AMTI.

Because pass-through certificate holders are treated as owning the assets of the issuing trust certain special rules that apply to loans to individuals (see, *e.g.*, Part III.E.1. and footnote 21) and real estate loans held by certain institutional investors (see Part V) would apply to the certificates.

2. Stripped Pass-Through Certificates

Pass-through certificates may also represent, instead of a pro rata share of all payments on the underlying mortgages, a right to a fixed percentage of the principal payments and a different fixed percentage of the interest payments.[10] Such pass-through certificates are often referred to as *stripped mortgage-backed securities* or *stripped pass-through certificates*. They are generally sold when there is a divergence of views regarding anticipated prepayment rates. The principal component of a mortgage, viewed in isolation without interest, is more valuable the earlier it is repaid. On the other hand, interest ceases when principal is repaid, so that the interest component of a mortgage, standing alone without principal, is more valuable the later the date on which principal is

---

10 In general, these percentages must be set at the time of issuance of the certificates and may not be changed subsequently. Otherwise, the trust issuing the certificates would be considered an association taxable as a corporation and would be subject to an entity-level tax.

repaid. Thus, by varying the mix between principal and interest, the effect of prepayments on a class of pass-through certificates can be changed.

The earliest stripped pass-through certificates that were publicly available *reduced* the effect on investors of changes in prepayment speeds by transforming discount or premium mortgages into par securities. To illustrate this type of transaction, suppose that a thrift institution holds a pool of mortgages bearing interest at a rate of 10 percent (net of servicing) at a time when the current market rate of interest for pass-through certificates is 8 percent. If the thrift believes that investors will assume a higher prepayment rate, and thus would be willing to pay a smaller premium for a pro rata interest in the mortgages than the thrift thinks is appropriate, the thrift could keep the premium, and insulate investors from the risk of a reduction in yield resulting from prepayments by retaining a right to $1/5$ of each interest payment on the mortgages and selling pass-through certificates at par with an 8 percent pass-through rate.[11] Similarly, if the thrift held discount mortgages and wished to sell pass-through certificates at par based on those mortgages, it could accomplish its objective by allocating to the certificates all of the interest payments but only a fraction of the principal payments.

Stripped pass-through certificates have also been created that *increase* the effect on *all* investors of variations in prepayment speeds by creating greater discounts and premiums than are inherent in the underlying mortgages. At the extreme, there is a complete separation in the ownership of rights to interest and principal. In a typical transaction, mortgages are transferred to a trust in exchange for two classes of certificates. One class (referred to as *PO Strips*) represents the right to receive 100 percent of each principal payment on the mortgages. The other class (*IO Strips*) represents the right to receive 100 percent of each interest payment. PO Strips, which are similar to zero coupon bonds payable in installments, are issued at a substantial discount and are purchased by investors who expect a high rate of prepayments compared with the market as a whole, or who wish to hedge against a risk of loss from declining interest rates. (Declining interest rates generally increase prepayments and thus increase the value of PO Strips.) IO Strips, which are issued with what amounts to an infinite premium, are purchased by investors who expect a low rate of prepayments or who wish to hedge against a risk of loss from rising interest rates.

---

11 Sometimes, rather than retaining a portion of interest on the loans, the sponsor charges a fee for servicing the mortgage loans (an "excess servicing" fee) that has the same effect. Excess servicing is typically characterized as an ownership interest in the mortgages for federal income tax purposes.

3. Senior/Subordinated Pass-Through Certificates

Pass-through certificates typically provide for some type of credit support that protects investors from defaults or delinquencies in payments on the underlying mortgages. The credit support may take the form of a guarantee, insurance policy, or other agreement by the sponsor or a third party to replace defaulted or delinquent payments or purchase defaulted or delinquent loans. Credit support can also be provided in whole or in part by creating senior and subordinated classes of pass-through certificates. Mortgage defaults or delinquencies are charged first against distributions that otherwise would be made on the subordinated class until they are exhausted, thereby protecting the senior class. Additional credit support may be provided through a reserve fund that is funded initially either with cash provided by the sponsor or with monies diverted from the subordinated class during the early years of the pool. It is common practice to require that any reserve fund be held outside of the trust as security for a limited recourse guarantee of the mortgages, to avoid possible classification of the trust as an association taxable as a corporation. For the same reason, it was also common practice before 1992 to restrict the transfer of subordinated certificates by the trust sponsor. This concern was eliminated by an IRS ruling.

C. Pay-Through Bonds

Unlike pass-through certificates, which represent an ownership interest in mortgages, a pay-through bond is a debt obligation of a legal entity that is collateralized by mortgages (or interests in mortgages). A holder is considered to own the bond, but not an interest in the underlying mortgages, in the same way that the holder of a public utility bond, for example, would be considered the owner of the bond but not of the power generating station that secures it. Although the payment terms of a pay-through bond and of the underlying mortgage collateral are not identical, the relationship between them may be quite close. In most cases, the mortgages, and earnings from the reinvestment of mortgage payments over a short period, are expected to be the sole funding source for payments on the bonds, and mortgage prepayments are "paid through," in whole or in part, to bondholders in the form of mandatory calls on the bonds.

A *collateralized mortgage obligation (CMO)* is a type of pay-through bond which is divided into classes. As described further below, these classes typically have different maturities and payment priorities. Most often, CMOs are issued by a special purpose entity organized by a sponsor. The entity is typically an owner trust or corporation, although a partnership or possibly even a limited liability company could be used. As further described below, owner trusts and other non-corporate issuers of pay-through bonds may be classified as corporations for tax purposes under the TMP rules if they issue bonds after 1991.

Where the issuer is an owner trust, the trust is established pursuant to a trust agreement between the sponsor and an independent trustee, acting as *owner trustee*. The owner trustee is usually a commercial bank. In most transactions, the sponsor initially transfers a nominal amount of cash to the owner trustee against the receipt of certificates representing the equity or ownership interest in the owner trust. When the CMOs are issued, the mortgage collateral is transferred to the owner trustee in exchange for the net proceeds of the CMOs plus any additional cash equity contribution that may be made to the owner trust, either by the sponsor or by other investors in exchange for new ownership certificates. The sponsor may retain its certificates or sell all or a portion of them to others. The owner trustee pledges the mortgage collateral to another commercial bank acting as *bond trustee* on behalf of the holders of the CMOs under a bond indenture. Over the life of the CMOs, the bond trustee collects payments on the collateral, reinvests those payments over a short period, makes payments on the CMOs, pays expenses, and remits any excess to the owner trustee, which distributes such excess (after paying or providing for expenses) to the owners of the equity of the owner trust. Equity interests in issuers of pay-through bonds are discussed further below.

If the issuer of CMOs is not an owner trust, the structure is substantially the same, with the issuer and the owners of its equity replacing the owner trustee and the beneficiaries of the trust. The federal income tax treatment of the holders of CMOs is not generally affected by whether the issuer is classified as a corporation, trust, or partnership.

CMOs are a more recent innovation than pass-through certificates. They are similar to pass-through certificates in that they are funded primarily out of payments received on a fixed pool of mortgages or interests in mortgages and, as a group, closely resemble those mortgages or interests in terms of the timing and amounts of payments. Unlike pass-through certificates, however, CMOs are typically divided into classes that have different maturities and different priorities for the receipt of principal, and, in some cases, interest. Most often, there are "fast-pay" and "slow-pay" classes. Thus, all principal payments (including prepayments) may be made first to the class having the earliest stated maturity date until it is retired, then to the class with the next earliest maturity date until it is retired, and so on. Alternatively, principal payments may be allocated among classes to ensure, to the extent possible, that designated classes receive principal payments according to a fixed schedule. Under that arrangement, the greater stability in the timing of payments on the designated classes (often called *planned amortization class* or *PAC bonds*) would be balanced by greater variability in the timing of payments on the remaining classes (often called *support classes*). Payment priorities may also change (either temporarily or permanently) based on the occurrence of some triggering event (such as interest rates reaching a certain level). Classes of this type are known colloquially as *non-sticky jump classes* (where changes in priorities are temporary) and *sticky jump classes* (where changes are permanent). Another common feature of CMOs is an *interest accrual* or *compound interest class* that receives no interest or principal payments until all prior classes have been fully retired. Until that time, the interest that accrues on an interest accrual class is added to its principal balance and a corresponding amount is paid as additional principal on prior classes. When CMOs were first issued, there was typically only one interest accrual class which was the class with the latest stated maturity date. It supported all prior classes. Because the different classes of CMOs were typically denominated by letters indicating payment priority, accrual bonds became known as *Z bonds*. More recently, issues of CMOs have included classes of Z bonds that are inserted between other classes of bonds with shorter and longer terms, and accrual classes that support (colloquially, are local to) only certain, designated prior classes.

Three other differences between CMOs and pass-through certificates are worth noting. First, CMOs may bear interest at a floating rate (a rate that varies directly, or in some cases inversely, with an index of market rates of interest, such as LIBOR), even though interest is paid on the mortgage collateral at a fixed rate. Second, CMOs generally provide for quarterly payments, with the issuer being responsible for reinvesting monthly receipts on the mortgages until the next CMO payment date. Finally, CMOs are usually callable at the option of the issuer at a time when a material amount of CMOs remain outstanding, so that the issuer can potentially benefit from increases in the value of the collateral by selling the collateral and retiring the CMOs.

Tax considerations dictated the original choice of pay-through bonds over pass-through certificates as the vehicle for creating mortgage-backed securities with different maturities or a floating interest rate not related to the mortgage collateral. If a typical non-REMIC pass-through trust issued multiple classes of pass-through certificates (that is, ownership interests in the trust) having either of these features, then it is likely that the trust would be classified as an association taxable as a corporation and the certificates would be treated as stock. As a result, the trust would be subject to corporate income tax on the gross income from the mortgages it holds with no deduction for "dividends" paid to certificate holders. An issuer of pay-through bonds, or its owners, may also be subject to corporate income tax on the taxable income of the issuer. However, because pay-through bonds are recognized for tax purposes to be debt of the issuer, deductions are allowed for interest on the bonds.

The status of pay-through bonds as debt obligations of the issuer rather than ownership interests in the underlying mortgages has other tax consequences. For example, holders are taxed based on the payments they are entitled to receive on the bonds rather than on the payments received by the issuer on the underlying mortgages.

D. Equity Interests in Issuers of Pay-Through Bonds

It will be helpful to consider separately the economic and tax-related features of equity interests in issuers of pay-through bonds.

1. Economic Features

Where an issuer of debt has assets that produce uncertain cash flows and debt with a fixed payment schedule, substantial equity is needed to fill in the gap and provide assurance to creditors that they will be paid. By contrast, virtually no equity would be needed by an issuer of pay-through bonds to protect bond holders if the bonds provided for payments matching in the aggregate the payments (including prepayments) to be made on the underlying mortgages, and that collateral was essentially risk-free from a credit standpoint (for example, because it benefits from a GNMA, FNMA, or FHLMC guarantee). A dollar-for-dollar matching of payments on assets and liabilities could be achieved without giving the bonds "equity features" since the underlying assets are themselves debt instruments.

Unfortunately, the most efficient economic result is not generally achievable for tax reasons. An issuer that was a pure conduit would run a material risk of losing deductions for interest it pays on its bonds, on the ground that the bonds should be recharacterized for tax purposes as disguised ownership interests in the issuer or in a separate corporation holding the collateral.

Although there are no hard and fast rules and opinions differ, most tax counsel would consider the following combination of factors sufficient to conclude that a typical issue of CMOs backed by GNMA, FNMA, or FHLMC pass-through certificates will be recognized to be debt for tax purposes: (1) the regular interval between payments on the bonds is not less than three months and monthly mortgage payments are reinvested until needed to make payments on the bonds in money market instruments earning interest at a current market rate at the time they are purchased; (2) the issuer has a right to call the bonds at a price of 100% of their principal amount when the total outstanding principal amount of bonds has been reduced to approximately 20% of the original aggregate principal amount of all bonds; and (3) the cash payments available to be distributed to the equity owners, determined based on reasonable assumptions as to reinvestment rates, expenses, and mortgage prepayments, have a present value at the time of issuance of the bonds, calculated using as the discount rate the highest initial yield of any class of bonds, of between one and two percent of the aggregate issue price of all of the bonds. If these tests are met, tax counsel typically would not insist on any minimum initial balance sheet equity or rights to substitute mortgage collateral.

An issuer that has these features will produce some surplus cash that is available for distribution on the equity interests. The cash would be attributable to the spreads between the rates of interest on the mortgages and on one or more classes of bonds, reinvestment income that exceeds the amounts assumed in sizing the issue of bonds, gain resulting from the exercise of rights to call the bonds, and any excess of budgeted over actual administrative expenses.

2. Tax Features

The taxes imposed with respect to an equity interest in an issuer of pay-through bonds will depend on the amount and timing of the issuer's taxable income, the tax classification of the issuer (whether it is a corporation, partnership, or trust) and the circumstances of the equity owners.

Any equity interest can be expected to generate taxable income equaling the economic income from the investment based on the actual or anticipated cash distributions thereon. Issuers of pay-through bonds may also produce taxable income that is non-economic in the sense that it will always be reversed through subsequent losses. Such income, which is commonly referred to as *phantom income*, generally arises when pay-through bonds are divided into different classes with staggered maturities, and the longer-term classes have higher yields than the shorter-term classes. Phantom income is discussed in greater detail in Part IV.E.

If the issuer of an equity interest is classified for tax purposes as a partnership or trust, then it is not itself subject to tax; instead, its taxable income is allocated among the equity owners in accordance with their respective interests. Such income is taxable to them regardless of the cash distributions they receive. The ultimate tax burden depends on the circumstances of the owners (*e.g.*, whether they have offsetting losses or tax credits).

The result is quite different where an issuer is a corporation (or classified as a corporation). A corporation is subject to the corporate income tax on its taxable income. Unless a corporation is a member of an affiliated group of corporations filing a consolidated return, losses or credits of shareholders cannot be used to reduce the corporation's tax bill. A corporation can join in a federal consolidated return with other corporations only if other group members own at least 80 percent of its stock, measured by voting power and value (but disregarding certain non-voting, non-participating preferred stock). However, TMPs must file separate returns. In the absence of tax consolidation, earnings of a corporation are potentially subject to a second layer of taxation when they are distributed to shareholders. The additional shareholder taxes would be reduced by the dividends received deduction in the case of distributions made to corporations. They may also be reduced by tax losses or credits available to the shareholders.

E. REMICs

As the prior discussion indicates, a grantor trust cannot issue pass-through certificates that are divided into multiple classes with staggered maturities. Also, pay-through bonds cannot be created that provide for payments, in the aggregate, that precisely mirror the payments on a fixed pool of mortgage collateral. Thus, certain securities that are attractive economically cannot be issued as either pass-through certificates or pay-through bonds, because they have a class structure inconsistent with the grantor trust rules and match the underlying mortgages too closely to be recognized for tax purposes as debt. Moreover, even if a security could be issued as a pay-through bond, compared with an ownership interest in mortgages, debt often has financial accounting disadvantages (the need to show the debt on someone's balance sheet) and tax disadvantages for certain institutional investors (the debt is not considered a real property loan). Finally, holders of equity interests in issuers of pay-through bonds may realize phantom income.

To address some of these concerns, TRA 1986 enacted the REMIC rules (sections 860A through 860G). These rules treat a pool of mortgages that meets certain requirements (relating to, among other things, the composition of its assets and the payment terms of the securities issued) as a REMIC if an appropriate election is made, and state how the REMIC and the holders of interests therein will be taxed.[12]

The REMIC rules are applied to a pool of mortgages and related securities based on their functional characteristics, without regard to legal form. Thus, a REMIC may be a state law trust, corporation, partnership, or simply a segregated pool of mortgages that is not a separate legal entity. Similarly, REMIC interests may be evidenced by ownership certificates, debt instruments, stock, partnership interests, or a contractual right to receive payments. The functional approach of the REMIC rules allows the state law legal form of a REMIC and the interests therein to be structured to best achieve financial accounting and other non-tax objectives.

By statute, a REMIC is not subject to an entity-level tax (except for certain penalty taxes). Instead, the income from its assets is allocated among the holders of REMIC interests. All of the interests in a REMIC must be either

---

12 The discussion below in the text provides only a brief overview of the REMIC rules, which are described in detail in Peaslee & Nirenberg, *supra*, n.1, at Chapters 4–5.

regular interests or *residual interests*, as those terms are defined in the REMIC rules. There is no required number of classes of regular interests. By contrast, a REMIC must have one (and only one) class of residual interests. In general, regular interests resemble conventional debt in that they must have a specified principal amount, and interest thereon (if any) must be based on a fixed or floating rate. A regular interest may also entitle the holder to a non-varying "specified portion" of the interest payments on underlying mortgages, with or without some additional claim to principal. There are no similar limitations on the economic characteristics of residual interests. Credit losses may be allocated in any way that is desired among different classes of REMIC interests. Further, a REMIC can hold assets in a credit or expense reserve fund.

The income of a REMIC is allocated among the different classes of interests as follows. The income of holders of each class of regular interests is determined as if those interests were debt of the REMIC. The holders of the residual interest are allocated all income of the REMIC, determined as if it were a taxable entity but reduced by the interest deductions that would be allowed to the REMIC if the regular interests were debt.

The allocation of income among REMIC interests is similar to the allocation that would be made if the REMIC were an owner trust taxed as a partnership and the regular interests and residual interests were pay-through bonds and equity interests in the trust, respectively. However, there are important differences between REMICs and owner trusts. First, as previously noted, there is no requirement that a REMIC or REMIC interests take any particular legal form. Second, the characterization of regular interests as debt of a REMIC follows directly from the statute, and there is no requirement that a REMIC have any minimum equity value or that the payments on regular interests and the underlying mortgages be mismatched. In addition, for purposes of determining the taxation of the sponsor of a REMIC and the status of regular interests as real property loans in the hands of institutional holders, regular interests are treated as ownership interests in the underlying mortgages rather than as debt.

While the REMIC rules represent a significant step forward in the tax law governing mortgage-backed securities, they are not the answer to every prayer. The REMIC rules were created primarily to permit the issuance of multiple class pass-through certificates. They achieve that goal, but do little more. The REMIC rules do not, for example, offer much relief from the restrictions on management powers that apply to grantor trusts. The permitted activities of a REMIC are limited, in much the same manner as a grantor trust, to holding a fixed pool of mortgages and distributing payments currently to investors. Indeed, in some respects (particularly in disposing of assets), a REMIC has even less freedom of action than a grantor trust. Another significant problem with the taxation of non-REMIC mortgage-backed securities—the phantom income that is recognized by issuers, or the owners of issuers, of certain pay-through bonds—also is not resolved by the REMIC rules. Indeed, they make it *worse*. Where a REMIC issues multiple classes of regular interests with staggered maturities, phantom income is realized by residual interest holders in much the same manner as if they held equity interests in an owner trust and the regular interests were pay-through bonds. However, the REMIC residual holders must contend with certain anti-tax avoidance rules that do not apply to owner trusts. As explained in the introduction to this Part II, the TMP rules were adopted largely to prevent taxpayers from choosing owner trusts over REMICs in order to achieve more favorable treatment of holders of equity interests.

F. Pass-Through Certificates Taxable as Debt

1. Description of Structure

Ordinarily, non-REMIC trusts issue one of two types of interests: pass-through certificates that are treated for tax purposes as ownership interests in the assets of the trust, or debt instruments that are recognized for those purposes to be debt of the trust. Trusts formed to hold automobile, credit card, and other non-mortgage receivables have issued to investors a third type of interest that takes the *form* of a pass-through certificate but represents *economically* debt of the issuing trust. These certificates are referred to here as *pass-through debt certificates*. Pass-through debt certificates are cast as ownership interests notwithstanding their economic similarity to debt so the sponsor can characterize the sale of the certificates as a sale of trust assets rather than a borrowing for financial accounting or other, non-tax purposes.

In a typical transaction, the payments due on pass-through debt certificates are not tied directly to payments made on any identified fixed pool of receivables,[13] and the trust is not fully protected against the risk of delinquencies and defaults on the receivables it holds. Sometimes, floating rate pass-through certificates are issued that are backed by fixed rate receivables. The trust is able to make required payments on the certificates despite the mismatching of receipts and payments and delinquency or default losses because the amount of certificates it issues is significantly smaller than the amount of trust assets. In other words, there is, to use a debt term, substantial overcollateralization. The residual interest in the trust (that is, the right to all assets remaining after making payments on the certificates) is retained by the trust sponsor.

---

13 To bridge gaps between the timing of receipts and payments, the trust may have a right to reinvest payments until they are needed to make payments on the certificates. In addition, the trust sponsor may have the right to add new receivables to the trust or to substitute new receivables for old ones.

2. Tax Analysis

The federal income tax analysis of pass-through debt certificates is somewhat complex. In most transactions, it is very clear that the certificates are debt (either of the issuing trust or of the sponsor) except in name. Where that is true, the certificates should be taxed as debt (and not as ownership interests in the trust), at least if the certificates are consistently treated as debt for tax purposes by the trust and the holders of interests in the trust. Nonetheless, in some cases this conclusion is open to potential challenge by the Internal Revenue Service on the ground that the parties to a transaction should be bound by their choice of form.

If in a particular case pass-through debt certificates were characterized for tax purposes as ownership interests in the issuing trust, the trust would not be classified as a trust (because it would have multiple ownership classes). Instead, it would be classified either as an association taxable as a corporation or as a partnership, depending on the terms of the trust and its interests. In the transactions where issuers are not able to conclude with a high degree of confidence that the debt characterization of the pass-through debt certificates will withstand challenge, steps are taken to ensure that if the debt argument fails, the trust will be classified as a partnership so that the trust itself will not be subject to tax.

As a partnership, the trust itself would not be subject to tax. Instead, the sponsor and certificate holders would be treated as partners and would be required to include in income their distributive shares of the income of the trust. It is likely that each certificate holder's share would approximately equal the interest income such holder would have reported had the certificates been classified as debt. As a result, most U.S. investors would not be significantly affected if pass-through debt certificates were characterized as partnership interests. However, because of the special rules that apply to such investors, certificate holders that are non-U.S. persons, pension plans, or other tax-exempt organizations, and possibly certain financial institutions, may have a strong desire to avoid such a characterization.

3. Application to Mortgages

Except as described in the next paragraph, the tax structure described above has not been widely used by trusts that hold real property mortgages (as opposed to automobile or credit card receivables) for several reasons. First, since the beginning of 1987, such a trust potentially could qualify as a REMIC. If the REMIC rules applied, the pass-through debt certificates would be considered regular interests in the REMIC. Thus, the principal tax objectives of sponsors of pass-through debt certificates (avoidance of a tax on the issuing trust and treatment of the certificates as debt) would be achieved with certainty under the REMIC rules. Second, if the REMIC rules did not apply, the risks that a sponsor would be required to assume (in terms of a mismatching between payments on the mortgages and on the certificates) in order to establish that pass-through debt certificates are economically debt of the issuing trust are likely to be more significant for mortgages than for other consumer receivables, because mortgages have longer maturities and, ordinarily, less predictable payment patterns. Third, the steps required to make available a partnership backup argument could represent an additional economic cost. Finally, the availability of a partnership backup argument would be constrained by the TMP rules, which can be applied under an anti-avoidance rule to an entity that does not borrow but has outstanding equity classes resembling debt.

Despite these considerations, mortgage-backed securities resembling pass-through debt certificates have been issued in so-called "kitchen sink" transactions. These transactions are unusual in that neither the REMIC rules nor the TMP rules apply. Typically, a trust acquires existing agency-backed interest-only and principal-only pass-through certificates or REMIC regular interests. The trust issues two classes of beneficial ownership certificates: a senior floating rate class (F) that bears interest at a spread over an interest rate index (generally LIBOR), and a residual class (R). All cash is distributed on the F class until it is retired, after which distributions are made on the R class. Because of contingencies affecting payments of principal, the F class may not meet the definition of a REMIC regular interest. For that reason, the trust does not make a REMIC election. The trust is structured, in much the same way as a trust issuing pass-through debt certificates, so that it is classified as a partnership rather than an association taxable as a corporation. The trust is not a TMP because it does not have debt classes with multiple maturities.

From an economic standpoint, the F class bears a strong resemblance to debt of the trust. Nonetheless, the argument for overcoming the form of the F class as an ownership interest is somewhat weaker here than in typical transactions where pass-through debt certificates are issued, because the trust assets consist of a fixed pool of mortgage-backed securities, the timing of payments on the F class is tied to the timing of receipts on those assets, and the F class is subject to some risk of nonpayment because of factors other than mortgagor defaults. For that reason, the F certificates are typically sold on the basis that they will be characterized as partnership interests for tax purposes, but with disclosure that they may be recharacterized as debt.

III. TAXATION OF HOLDERS OF MORTGAGE-BACKED SECURITIES TAXABLE AS DEBT

A. Introduction

As Part II indicates, from the perspective of investors, mortgage-backed securities can be divided into three groups: those taxable as debt; REMIC residual interests and equity interests in owner trusts that are not TMPs, which generally are taxed based on the net income of the REMIC or trust, respectively; and equity interests in TMPs which are treated as stock in a corporation. Part III discusses the taxation of holders of mortgage-backed securities taxable as debt.

The following categories of mortgage-backed securities are taxable as debt:

- REMIC regular interests, which the Code deems to be debt obligations of the issuing REMIC, regardless of their legal form;

- pass-through certificates, which are considered ownership interests in the underlying mortgages; and

- CMOs and other pay-through bonds, which are debt obligations of the entity that issues them.[14]

References in this Part to mortgage-backed securities should be understood to be references to one of these three types of securities. Also, except where otherwise indicated, references to debt instruments or obligations, or bonds, include REMIC regular interests.

In applying the tax rules for debt instruments to a pass-through certificate, it should be kept in mind that such a certificate is not generally considered a single security for tax purposes, but instead represents an ownership interest in each of the mortgages held by the issuing trust. Technically, the holder of a pass-through certificate should calculate income or loss for each mortgage separately by allocating among the mortgages, in proportion to their respective fair market values, the price paid for the certificate and the price received on resale. Such an allocation is rarely necessary in practice, however, because in most instances the tax results obtained by viewing the mortgages alternatively in isolation or as a single, aggregated debt instrument would be the same. For convenience, and except where otherwise noted, the discussion in this Part of mortgage-backed securities assumes the security is in all cases a debt obligation of one debtor (either an interest in a single mortgage or a single pay-through bond).

The mortgage-backed securities considered in this Part generally are subject to the Code rules governing conventional debt instruments. Thus, for example, stated interest on such a security generally is taxable as ordinary income as such interest accrues, for an accrual method taxpayer, or when it is received, for a cash method taxpayer. Assuming the security is purchased at its principal amount, principal payments represent a nontaxable return of the investor's capital regardless of when principal is paid. Upon sale of the secu-

---

14 The list also includes pass-through debt certificates, assuming they are recognized to be debt of the issuing trust.

rity, gain or loss is recognized in an amount equal to the difference between the net proceeds of such sale and the seller's *adjusted basis* in the security (generally, the seller's cost for the security, increased by amounts included in income and reduced by losses and payments received). With limited exceptions, any such gains or losses are treated as capital gains or losses if the security is held as a *capital asset*, which generally would be the case unless the holder is a dealer in securities. Capital gain is long-term if the security has been held at the time of sale for more than one year. A preferential tax rate applies to long-term capital gain income earned by high-income individuals (although not to capital gains of corporations). An amount paid as accrued interest upon sale of a mortgage-backed security between interest payment dates is treated by the seller as an interest payment and may be used by the purchaser to offset the interest received on the next interest payment date.[15]

The tax treatment of a mortgage-backed security is more complex if the security was purchased at a price different from its principal amount, that is, at a discount or a premium. If a mortgage-backed security is purchased at a discount and the full principal amount is eventually paid, the excess of the principal amount over the cost of the security represents additional income. A question then arises as to the proper timing of recognition of that income and its character as ordinary income or capital gain. The purchase of a security at a premium raises similar concerns. These questions are addressed in the remainder of this Part.

B. Overview of Taxation of Discount and Premium

The traditional approach to the tax treatment of a debt instrument deals separately with three sources of income—stated or coupon interest, original

---

15 Two exceptions to these rules apply to REMIC regular interests, but they are likely to have little, if any, practical significance for most investors. First, income from REMIC regular interests must always be reported under an accrual method even if the holder is otherwise a cash method taxpayer. Second, gain recognized by an investor on a sale of a REMIC regular interest that otherwise would be capital gain will be treated as ordinary income to the extent such gain does not exceed the excess of (1) the income that would have been reported by the investor if it had reported income as it accrued based on a yield to the investor equal to 110% of the "applicable Federal rate" (generally, an average yield of U.S. Treasury obligations of different ranges of maturities published monthly by the Service) in effect for the month in which the interest was acquired by the investor, over (2) the ordinary income previously reported by the investor. The legislative history of the 110% rule indicates that it was intended to prevent the underaccrual of original issue discount because of the failure to take account of mortgage prepayments. Another special rule of minor significance relates to regular interests in "single-class REMICs" (a defined term which includes certain multiple-class REMICs) held by individuals and certain pass-through entities. Such holders are required to include in income, and are treated as paying, an allocable share of the REMIC's investment expenses.

issue discount, and market discount—and one item of expense (or offset to interest)—bond premium. Stated interest was discussed above; discount and premium are considered here.

In general, *original issue discount* (or *OID*) is discount at which a debt obligation was sold to investors in connection with its original issuance, and *market discount* is discount that arises from decreases in the market value of a debt obligation following its issuance. The technical definition of OID is somewhat complicated and includes not only discount at which an obligation is issued below its principal amount but also stated interest that is not paid currently over the life of the obligation. The most important difference, in terms of tax consequences, between OID and market discount is that, in general, OID is includible in income by the holder of a discount obligation as the discount accrues under a constant yield method, whereas (absent certain taxpayer elections) market discount is taxable only when principal payments are received or the obligation sold. In January of 1994, the Service issued extensive final regulations interpreting the OID rules of the Code, which will sometimes be referred to as the *OID regulations.*

There is a fundamental difference between REMIC regular interests and pay-through bonds, on the one hand, and pass-through certificates, on the other hand, which affects the status of discount as OID. Regular interests and pay-through bonds are considered obligations in their own right for tax purposes, so that any discount at which they are issued is generally OID (even if such discount can be traced to market discount on underlying mortgages). By contrast, pass-through certificates are treated as ownership interests in, rather than debt of, the issuing trust. As a result, OID will exist for those certificates only if the mortgages held by the trust have OID (which is rare for residential mortgages) or the bond stripping rules discussed below apply.

Although (absent a holder election) the Code does not require market discount on a debt instrument to be included in income by the holder as it accrues, it nonetheless provides a number of special rules governing market discount. Gain on the sale of a debt instrument is treated as ordinary income (which is interest income for most purposes) to the extent that it does not exceed the market discount that has accrued thereon and not yet been included in income. In the case of debt instruments that have some OID, accruals of market discount are generally proportionate to accruals of OID. A principal payment on a debt instrument generally must be included in income by the holder, as a payment of accrued market discount, to the extent it does not exceed the portion of the market discount on the entire instrument that has accrued during the period the holder owned the instrument and not yet been included in income. As a result, where the holder of a debt instrument receives principal payments at least annually that equal or exceed accruals of market discount, such discount effectively will be included in income as it accrues. Deductions for interest on debt incurred (or continued) to finance market discount bonds are deferred to prevent the generation of losses attributable to the current deductibility of interest and the deferral of market discount income.

Prior to 1986, there was considerable uncertainty as to how mortgage prepayments should be taken into account in accruing OID. TRA 1986 addressed the point by enacting section 1272(a)(6). This section requires OID to be accrued on REMIC regular interests and pay-through bonds based on changes in the present value of the instrument. Present values are calculated (1) by taking account of actual mortgage prepayments that have already occurred and projecting the rate at which future prepayments will occur using an assumed prepayment rate, and (2) using the original yield to maturity as the discount rate. This accrual method (which we refer to as the PAC method for reasons explained below) does not by its terms apply to pass-through certificates except when they are held by a REMIC.

The special Code rules governing OID and market discount do not apply to *de minimis* amounts of discount on a debt instrument. In general, such discount is recognized by the holder ratably as principal payments are received and is characterized as gain from the retirement of the instrument.

The distinction between OID and market discount is blurred by the "bond stripping" rules of section 1286. These rules apply when rights to principal and interest on a debt obligation are held separately or in different proportions and play a significant role in the taxation of certain pass-through certificates. If rights to payments on a debt obligation qualify as stripped bonds, then, with certain exceptions, all income from the holding of those rights (both stated interest and discount) is subject to taxation under the OID rules.

With respect to *de minimis* discount, or discount on a pass-through certificate or other obligation that is not subject to the PAC method, a further distinction in determining the tax treatment of discount is whether the debtor is an individual, corporation, or other legal entity. Gain realized upon the receipt of a payment of principal on the obligation of an individual that is treated as gain from retirement of the obligation (and not as OID or accrued market discount) is *always* ordinary income, whereas gain from the retirement of an obligation of a corporation or other legal entity may be capital gain if the obligation is held as a capital asset.

Unlike discount, all premium on a given debt instrument is treated alike. Premium on a debt instrument that is held for investment can be amortized if an election is made by the holder under section 171. Amortized premium will offset interest income to the extent thereof and otherwise will be allowed as a deduction. Premium is amortized under a constant-yield method that is similar to the method used in calculating accruals of OID.

The discussion of discount in this Part assumes that the mortgage-backed securities in question have an original term to maturity of more than one year. A different tax regime, which is of little relevance in the mortgage area, applies to discount on short-term obligations.

C. Original Issue Discount

This Part explains how the OID rules apply to REMIC regular interests and pay-through bonds. Specifically, the discussion will define OID, describe how accruals of OID are calculated under the PAC method, illustrate the method with an example, and describe special rules for debt instruments with variable or contingent interest. Unless otherwise stated, it is assumed that interest on a debt obligation accrues at a fixed rate. Pass-through certificates are addressed in Part D.

1. OID Defined

Original issue discount is defined as the excess of the stated redemption price at maturity of an obligation over its issue price. However, if the amount of discount as so defined is less than a *de minimis* amount (generally $1/4$ of one percent of the stated redemption price at maturity times the number of complete years to maturity), then the amount of OID is considered to be zero. The *stated redemption price at maturity* is not limited to the principal amount, but also includes all payments of stated interest other than *qualified stated interest payments*. A qualified stated interest payment is any one of a series of payments equal to the product of the outstanding principal balance and a single, fixed rate (appropriately adjusted for the length of time between payments) that is payable unconditionally at least annually during the entire term of the obligation (variable rates are discussed below). Thus, interest is not qualified stated interest (and is includible in OID) to the extent it is payable during any year at a rate higher than the lowest rate at which interest is payable during any year over the life of the instrument. For example, all interest on an interest accrual or compound interest bond (which provides for the complete deferral of interest for at least one year) is includible in OID. A portion of the interest on a bond with a payment lag (that is, a lag between the end of the period over which interest accrues and the date on which such interest is paid) may be includible in OID if the bond has more than *de minimis* OID.

Under the OID regulations, the issue price of each debt instrument in an issue issued for money is the first price at which a substantial amount of the debt instruments is sold to investors.

Accrued interest with which a debt instrument is issued is generally included in both the issue price and stated redemption price at maturity of the instrument. However, if the first interest payment is made within one year of the issue date and at least equals the amount of pre-issuance accrued interest, then such interest may be directly offset against such accrued interest (with the result that both amounts may be disregarded in OID calculations).

2. OID Accruals Under the PAC Method

An investor who purchases a pay-through bond having OID at a yield to maturity not less than the yield to maturity at which it was initially offered must include in income, for each taxable year in which the investor holds the bond, the portion of the OID that is considered to accrue in such year (regardless of whether the investor otherwise reports income under a cash or accrual method of tax accounting). As explained in more detail below, the portion of the OID on a bond that is considered to accrue in any period generally equals the amount by which the value of the bond would increase during such period if it continued at all times to have a yield to maturity equal to its yield to maturity at the time of issuance, calculated based on its issue price. This method of accruing OID is known as the *constant yield, compound interest,* or *scientific* method. It gives effect to the compounding of interest by including accrued but unpaid OID in the base to which the yield to maturity of the bond is applied in calculating future accruals of such discount.

The yield to an investor of a debt obligation purchased at a discount below its principal amount is greater the shorter the life of the obligation. In the case of most pay-through bonds, it is highly probable that principal will be prepaid to some degree. The possibility of prepayments raises two related issues: first, whether OID should be accrued based on a yield that is calculated assuming that prepayments will occur at some reasonable rate; and second, how income is to be adjusted to account for differences between the assumed prepayment rate (a zero rate or a reasonable estimate) and the actual prepayment rate. Prior to the enactment of TRA 1986, there were no certain answers to these questions. TRA 1986 clarified that, in the case of a pay-through bond issued after December 31, 1986, (1) the yield that is used in calculating accruals of OID will be determined based on a reasonable assumption (the Prepayment Assumption) as to the rate at which the underlying mortgages will be prepaid, and, if earnings on temporary investments would affect the timing of payments on the bond, the rate of those earnings; (2) income will be adjusted in each taxable year (whether or not principal payments are made on the bond in that year) to reflect the economic gain or loss for that year (calculated based on changes in present values assuming a constant yield) resulting from past and present differences between actual prepayment experience and the Prepayment Assumption, but assuming that future prepayments on remaining mortgages will conform to the Prepayment Assumption; and (3) in general, those adjustments will increase or decrease interest income and not be treated as capital gain or loss. The method for calculating accruals of OID introduced by TRA 1986 will be referred to as the *prepayment assumption catch-up method,* or *PAC method* for short.

In general, the Prepayment Assumption for any issue of bonds corresponds to the prepayment rate assumed in pricing the initial offering of the bonds and is stated in the offering materials for the bonds. Once determined, the Prepayment Assumption will not change to reflect changes in prepayment rates occurring after the issuance of the bonds. The Prepayment Assumption relates to a pool of mortgages and not to classes of bonds. Accordingly, for any pool of mortgages, the same assumption must be used with respect to each class of bonds that is affected by the performance of that pool. Once determined, the Prepayment Assumption will not change to reflect changes in expectations of future prepayment rates. However, the PAC method does take actual prepayment experience into account.

A bondholder is required to include in gross income in each taxable year the sum of the *daily portions* of OID for each day during the taxable year on which it holds the bond. For an investor who purchased the bond in the initial offering at the issue price, two steps are needed to determine the daily portions of OID. First, a calculation is made of the portion of the OID that is allocable to each *accrual period* during the term of the bond. For a bond that provides for payments at fixed intervals over its life except for a short initial or final period, the accrual periods are generally the periods that end on each payment date and begin on the day after the immediate preceding payment date (or in the case of the first such period, begin on the issue date). Second, the portion of the OID attributed to each accrual period is allocated ratably to each day during the period to determine the daily portion of OID for that day.

Under the PAC method, the amount of OID on a bond that is attributed to each accrual period is the *excess* of:

- the sum of the present value, as of the end of the accrual period, of all of the payments, if any, to be made on the bond in future periods and the amount of any payments made on the bond during the accrual period that are includible in its stated redemption price at maturity, over

- the adjusted issue price of the bond at the beginning of such period.

The present value of the future payments on the bond would be calculated for this purpose (1) assuming that the mortgages underlying the bond will be prepaid in future periods in accordance with the Prepayment Assumption (but taking account of the actual prepayments that have occurred to date) and (2) using a discount rate equal to the *yield to maturity* of the bond.

The yield to maturity of the bond is the discount rate, assuming compounding at the end of each accrual period, that causes the present value of all future payments on the bond to equal its issue price on the issue date, calculated assuming that the bond will be prepaid in all periods in accordance with the Prepayment Assumption. The *adjusted issue price* of a bond at the beginning of an accrual period equals its issue price, increased by the aggregate amount of OID on the bond attributed to all prior accrual periods, if any, and decreased by the amount of any payments made on the bond in prior periods that were includible in its stated redemption price at maturity. Thus, the adjusted issue price represents an initial purchaser's remaining capital investment in the bond, adjusted for the amount of OID that has been earned and included in income for tax purposes but not yet paid. Special rules apply to initial short accrual periods.

The method of calculating daily accruals of OID outlined above applies to any investor that purchases a pay-through bond at a price equal to or less than its adjusted issue price at the time of purchase. Where the purchase price exceeds the adjusted issue price, the holder is allowed to offset that excess amount *(acquisition premium)* against the daily portions of OID. In particular, each daily portion is reduced by a fixed fraction. The numerator of the fraction is the acquisition premium and the denominator is the sum of the daily portions (determined without regard to any acquisition premium adjustment) for all days on or after the purchase date through the maturity date of the bond. Thus, if the acquisition premium for any bondholder represents 25% of the aggregate amount of OID that remains to be accrued after the purchase date, the amount of OID that would otherwise be required to be included in the holder's income for any day would be reduced by 25%. An investor that buys an OID bond at a premium (*i.e.*, a price exceeding its remaining stated redemption price at maturity) is not required to include any OID in income.

If prepayments on mortgages backing a discount bond are slower than assumed, it may be possible for the PAC formula to produce an amount for an accrual period that is negative. The TRA 1986 legislative history states that in such an event the amount of OID allocable to the period would be treated as zero and the computation of OID for the next accrual period (and presumably for successive periods until the formula produced a positive amount of OID) would be made by treating the first accrual period and the later ones as a single accrual period. Although the language is not entirely clear it appears to mean only that no deduction for negative amounts of OID will be allowed, and the adjusted issue price at the beginning of each accrual period (determined under normal rules) will be increased by any negative amounts of OID for prior periods for which no deduction was allowed.[16]

---

16 For a discussion of negative accruals of OID in the context of prepayment losses on interest only (or other high coupon) REMIC regular interests, see Peaslee & Nirenberg, *supra*, n.1, Chapter 6, Part G.1.

3. Example

It will help in explaining the PAC method to apply it to a concrete example. For the sake of simplicity, the example assumes an obligation that pays interest currently at a fixed rate and provides for a single payment of principal. The extension of the method to obligations that provide for payments of principal in installments is straightforward, although the computations can rapidly become burdensome. We will begin by assuming no anticipated or actual prepayments.

Consider a pay-through bond having a principal amount of $1,000 that was issued at a price of $770.60 on April 1, 1994, bears interest at an annual rate of 8%, payable on April 1 and October 1, and matures on April 1, 2004. Principal is required to be paid prior to maturity out of principal prepayments on the mortgage collateral. The bond has OID of $229.40. Suppose initially that the Prepayment Assumption is that no mortgage will be prepaid, and that, under that assumption, the entire $1,000 will be paid at maturity. Given that assumption, the semiannual yield to maturity of the bond, based on compounding at the end of each accrual period, is 6%.[17] The OID allocable to the first accrual period ending October 1, 1994, is $6.24. This represents the *excess* of:

- the sum of (1) the present value as of October 1, 1994 of the future payments to be made on the bond, calculated using a discount rate equal to the yield to maturity of the bond and assuming, in accordance with the Prepayment Assumption, no future prepayments ($776.84), and (2) the principal payments made on the bond in the accrual period, which are the only payments includible in its stated redemption price at maturity ($0), over

- the adjusted issue price at the beginning of the accrual period, which for the first accrual period equals the issue price of $770.60.

The corresponding amount for the second accrual period ending April 1, 1995 is $6.61 [($783.45 + $0) − $776.84]. If the initial holder of the bond reports income based on the calendar year, the holder would include in income for 1994 the sum of all daily portions for the first accrual period ending October 1, 1994 ($6.24) and the sum of the daily portions for the days in the second accrual period which are on or prior to December 31, 1994. Using a 30-days-per-month/360-days-per-year convention, the second accrual period consists of 180 days, of which 90 are on or prior to December 31, 1994. Thus, the sum of the daily portions of OID for the days in the second accrual period

---

17 In other words, the present value of all interest and principal payments on the bond, calculated using a discount rate for each semiannual period of 6%, equals the $770.60 purchase price.

that are on or prior to December 31, 1994 is $90/_{180}$ times $6.61, or (rounding up) $3.31. The total amount of OID includible in income by such holder in 1994 is therefore $9.55 ($6.24 + $3.31). The adjusted issue prices for the bond are plotted as line *a* in Exhibit 1.

It has been assumed so far that the pay-through bond is not expected to be, and is not in fact, prepaid. However, the PAC method accommodates both expected and actual prepayments. Expected prepayments are taken into account by assuming that the mortgages underlying the bond will prepay according to the Prepayment Assumption, both initially in calculating the yield to maturity and over time in determining the present value of future payments. Actual prepayment experience affects the amount and timing of the current payments and expected future payments that enter into the PAC formula.

To illustrate the consequences of different prepayment expectations, suppose that the Prepayment Assumption is changed and that under the new assumption the entire $1,000 principal amount of the bond will be paid four years prior to maturity on April 1, 2000. Given that assumption, the semi-annual yield of the bond would increase from 6% to 6.87%. Using that yield

Exhibit 1. Adjusted Issue Prices of Bond Under Different Prepayment Assumptions

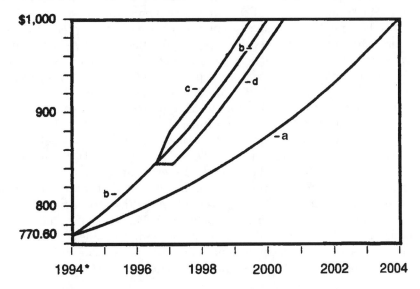

* The adjusted issue price plotted above each year is the adjusted issue price for April 1 of that year.
From *The Federal Income Taxation of Mortgage-Backed Securities, Revised Edition*, by James M. Peaslee and David Z. Nirenberg, (Chicago: Probus Publishing Co. 1994), 239. Reprinted with permission.

in the formula set forth earlier,[18] and assuming that prepayments occur in accordance with the Prepayment Assumption, the amounts of OID allocable to the first two accrual periods would increase from $6.24 and $6.61, calculated above, to $12.92 [($783.52 + $0) − $770.60] and $13.82 [($797.34 + $0) − $783.52]. The adjusted issue prices of the bond based on the new Prepayment Assumption are shown as line b in Exhibit 1.

To illustrate the case where prepayments are received at a faster than expected pace, suppose that prepayments on the bond described in the immediately preceding paragraph conform to the Prepayment Assumption until October 1, 1997, but because of greater than expected prepayments between October 2, 1997 and April 1, 1998, the bond is fully retired on April 1, 1998. In that event, the adjusted issue price on October 1, 1997 would equal $881.99, the present value at that time of all future payments on the bond, calculated assuming a $1,000 payment of principal on April 1, 2000. Under the PAC formula, the amount of OID allocable to the accrual period ending April 1, 1998 would equal $118.01, which is the excess of the payments received during the accrual period that are includible in the stated redemption price at maturity, or $1,000, plus the present value of all future payments ($0, because the bond is fully retired at the end of the period) over $881.99. Thus, the OID that otherwise would be included in income over two years and six months (October 1, 1997 through April 1, 2000) is allocated instead to the accrual period ending April 1, 1998 because of the earlier than expected prepayments.

The PAC method also takes account of changes in the expected timing of future payments determined by applying the Prepayment Assumption to actual mortgage principal balances. Return once more to the bond described in the second preceding paragraph. If prepayments follow the Prepayment Assumption until October 1, 1996, the adjusted issue price of the bond at that time would be $844.73, the present value of the future payments on the bond based on a $1,000 payment of principal on April 1, 2000. If mortgage prepayments continued to track the Prepayment Assumption throughout the next accrual period ending April 1, 1997, the amount of OID that would be allocated to that period would be $18.01. However, suppose instead that during that accrual period, mortgage prepayments are, alternatively, faster or slower than anticipated. As a result, it is determined (by applying the Prepayment Assumption to the mortgages held by the issuer at the end of the accrual period) that the $1,000 principal amount will be paid six months earlier, in the case of the faster prepayments, or six months later, in the case of the slower prepayments, than originally anticipated. Moving the expected

---

18 The OID regulations require yield, when expressed as a percentage, to be calculated with at least two-decimal-place accuracy. A greater number of significant digits was used in the example, with the results being rounded to the nearest cent.

retirement date forward (or back) increases (or decreases) the present value of the future payments on the bond as of April 1, 1997 from $862.74 to $881.99 (or $844.73), and thus increases (or decreases) the amount of OID allocated under the PAC method to the accrual period ending April 1, 1997 to $37.26 (or $0), respectively.

The effect of the two six-month changes in expected retirement dates on the adjusted issue prices for the bond is shown graphically in Exhibit 1. Lines *c* and *d* show adjusted issue prices giving effect to the faster or slower prepayments, respectively, during the accrual period ending April 1, 1997 (assuming that there are no deviations from the Prepayment Assumption in subsequent periods). The effect of the difference in prepayments on the amount of OID allocated to the accrual period ending April 1, 1997 is represented by the vertical distance between line *b* and line *c* or *d*, as the case may be, on that date.

The examples just discussed involve a bond that provides for only a single payment of principal. In most cases, however, pay-through bonds provide for payments of principal in installments. The only difference that this change would cause in applying the PAC method is that the amount included in the formula for payments that are included in the stated redemption price at maturity would be positive for each accrual period during which some principal amount is paid.

4. Variable Rates

REMIC regular interests are allowed to pay interest at a variable rate, to the extent provided in regulations. The REMIC regulations allow a wide range of variable rates based on interest rate indices or a weighted average of the rates on the underlying mortgages. Combinations of different indexed, weighted average, or fixed rates are also allowed. Further, a REMIC regular interest can pay interest equal to a specified portion of the interest payments on one or more qualified mortgages bearing interest at a variable rate.

The OID regulations divide variable rate debt instruments into two groups: *variable rate debt instruments* or *VRDIs* and *contingent payment debt instruments*. Different substantive rules apply to each type of obligation. The definition of VRDI is tailored to the needs of the OID rules and is not the same as the definition of permitted variable-rate regular interests. The VRDI definition is both narrower and broader in some respects. Under current law, many variable-rate regular interests would fall into the contingent payment category.

The OID rules are applied to a VRDI by converting the variable interest payments into equivalent, fixed-interest payments and then applying the general OID rules to the resulting fixed-rate instrument. Qualified stated interest or OID allocable to an accrual period is adjusted if the actual interest for the period differs from the assumed fixed-interest amount. The adjustment increases or decreases qualified stated interest if the fixed interest for the period is qualified stated interest and the adjustment is reflected in the amount actually paid during the period. Otherwise, the adjustment increases or decreases OID for the accrual period.

As of this writing, the tax rules governing contingent payment debt instruments are in a state of flux. Although a set of proposed tax rules exist, they are flawed, are widely expected never to be adopted as final regulations, and to a growing extent are given little weight as a source of guidance on the tax treatment of contingent debt securities. In practice, the principles of the VRDI rules are applied to all types of variable-rate REMIC regular interests, and also generally to variable-rate non-REMIC pay-through bonds if the variation in rates is based on changes in market interest rates, even where those rules do not technically apply.

One major payment contingency affecting most mortgage-backed securities is, of course, uncertainty as to the timing of mortgage prepayments. The PAC method takes direct aim at this problem, and, accordingly, will most likely be considered to preempt any more general contingent payment rules that may be adopted as a means of dealing with prepayments. The PAC method can easily be combined with the principles of the VRDI rules. Those rules account for OID as if it were earned with respect to a hypothetical, fixed-rate debt instrument, and income on that instrument can be calculated under the PAC method in the normal way.

A REMIC regular interest can bear interest at a rate equal to a weighted average of the interest rates on qualified mortgages held by the REMIC (provided those mortgages themselves bear interest at a fixed or variable rate permitted under the REMIC rules). In a case where mortgages bear interest at different fixed rates, then the rate payable in each period will depend on the relative principal balances of the mortgages taken into account in the average. The Prepayment Assumption can be used to predict the relative balances of individual mortgages in future periods and hence the average rate. Once uncertainty as to future payments has been eliminated, the PAC method can be applied. If the loans included in the weighted average include one or more variable-rate loans, then the principles of the VRDI rules could be applied to address the variable-rate contingency.

D. Pass-Through Certificates

The degree to which the OID rules will influence the taxation of a pass-through certificate depends primarily on whether the stripped bond rules of section 1286 apply. If they do, then the OID rules will play a central role. On the other hand, OID is unlikely to be present in pass-through certificates that do not fall within that section, except in cases in which the underlying mortgages provide for negative amortization or have teaser rates (initial below market rates) that reflect unusually large discounts below market rates. The two types of pass-through certificates are considered next, beginning with those subject to the stripped bond rules.

1. Pass-Through Certificates Subject to the Stripped Bond Rules

Definition of Stripped Bond or Coupon. Section 1286 contains special rules governing the taxation of stripped bonds and stripped coupons. A *stripped bond* is a bond issued with coupons (which, for this purpose, include any rights to receive stated interest), where there is a separation in ownership between the bond and any coupons that have not yet come due. A *stripped coupon* is a coupon relating to a stripped bond. The tax treatment of stripped bonds and stripped coupons is generally the same, and the term *stripped bond* will be used in this discussion to refer to both.

The classic example of a bond-stripping transaction is a sale by the owner of a whole bond of unmatured interest coupons to one investor and rights to principal to a second investor. (Alternatively, the seller could sell only the coupons or the rights to principal and retain the remaining interests in the bond.) IO and PO Strips represent the extension of this transaction pattern to mortgage-backed securities.

Subject to two important exceptions described in the next paragraph, the bond-stripping rules also extend to situations in which there is some but not complete separation in the ownership of rights to principal and interest. One common example is the transaction described above in which a mortgage originator holding discount or premium mortgages creates pass-through certificates that can be sold at par by retaining a share of interest payments (in the case of the premium mortgages) or a share of principal payments (in the case of the discount mortgages). Where mortgages have a range of interest rates, rights to interest payments exceeding the lowest common rate may also be retained in order to provide a single pass-through rate for investors. The retention of a partial ownership interest in mortgage interest payments is often achieved mechanically by charging excess servicing. The IRS has ruled that excess servicing (defined as a right to payments for servicing that exceed compensation at a market rate) is treated for tax purposes as an ownership interest in mortgage interest payments.

Section 1286 does not apply to investors purchasing an interest in a stripped mortgage (one from which some interest coupons have been removed) in two cases: (1) where the stripped mortgage would be considered to have no OID under the general OID *de minimis* rule if, *immediately after* the separation in ownership of the interest strip, the stripped mortgage was newly issued at an issue price equal to the price at which it is sold to investors; and (2) where the amount of interest that has been stripped from the mortgage (including excess servicing but not including reasonable servicing compensation) does not exceed 100 basis points per annum (without regard to whether the stripped mortgage would have OID if it were newly issued). Whether these exceptions apply to a stripped mortgage in the hands of any investor depends on the nature of the original stripping transaction and not on the price paid for the stripped mortgage by the investor. The first of the two rules has the practical effect of nullifying section 1286 for investors purchasing pass-through certificates from which some interest has been stripped, if those certificates were not sold immediately following the stripping transaction at a discount below their principal amount that exceeded $\frac{1}{6}$ of 1 percent of the aggregate principal amount of the mortgages multiplied by their remaining weighted-average life (calculated assuming no prepayments and by rounding partial years to zero).

The consequences of recombining all of the stripped interests in a single debt instrument are not clear. It appears, however, that section 1286 would continue to apply to those interests in the hands of any person who has held any of them as a stripped bond, but would not apply to a new investor who purchases all of the stripped interests together.

Treatment of Stripped Bonds. Subject to the exceptions described in the last section, section 1286 generally transforms the discount at which a stripped bond is purchased into OID. Specifically, section 1286(a) provides that if a person purchases a stripped bond, then, for purposes of applying the OID rules of the Code, the stripped bond will be treated, while held by that person, as a bond originally issued on the purchase date having OID equal to the excess of the stated redemption price at maturity of the stripped bond over its purchase price. However, no amount is treated as OID if that excess amount is less than a *de minimis* amount (determined by applying the general OID definition as if the stripped bond were a newly issued debt obligation with an issue price equal to the purchase price). Where a stripped bond is considered to be purchased with more than a *de minimis* amount of OID, then under the OID rules of the Code, the holder will be required to include such OID in income in each taxable year as it accrues. In calculating accruals of OID, all payments on a debt instrument of a single borrower should be aggregated and treated as a single stripped bond with a single yield to maturity. It is not clear if rights to stated interest payments included in a stripped bond would be treated as qualified stated interest where they would be so treated if the stripped bond were a newly issued bond, or whether they would instead be included automatically in OID, but this issue does not have much practical significance.

A significant issue that arises in calculating accruals of OID with respect to pass-through certificates that are stripped bonds is whether the PAC method applies (and, if so, what Prepayment Assumption is used). As a technical matter, the PAC method does not apply, because a pass-through certificate (other than one held by a REMIC) is not the type of security to which the method applies. Nevertheless, many issuers, for purposes of information reporting, and many investors, calculate income as if that method did apply, generally based on a Prepayment Assumption determined at the time of issuance of the certificates. Alternatively, an investor might be able to use a Prepayment Assumption based on expectations as of the date on which it purchased its certificates. Because the PAC method is based on the prepayment experience of a pool of mortgages, it would make sense if that method is applied to treat all mortgages underlying a pass-through certificate as a single debt instrument with a single yield.

If the PAC method does not apply to pass-through certificates that are stripped bonds, then income should be computed under a method that is similar to the PAC method except that the Prepayment Assumption used in calculating the yield to maturity and present values would be an assumption that no future mortgage prepayments will occur, and income or loss that results when a mortgage is prepaid (calculated, generally, in a manner similar to the PAC method by comparing the amount received, if any, as a result of the prepayment with the present value of the payments that would have been received if the mortgage loan had not been prepaid) would be income or loss from retirement of the mortgage loan and not an adjustment to OID. Any such income or loss would be ordinary income or loss if the mortgage loans are obligations of individuals, and generally would be capital gain or loss if they are obligations of corporations, partnerships, or other legal entities and the pass-through certificates are held as capital assets. Deductions for losses would not be curbed by the PAC method limitation on deductions for negative OID.

2. Pass-Through Certificates that Are Not Stripped Bonds

OID is not likely to be encountered in a pass-through certificate to which the stripped bond rules do not apply unless, as discussed below, interest payments on the underlying mortgages are scheduled to increase over time. The exchange of such pass-through certificates for mortgages is not treated as the creation of a new debt security for tax purposes. Accordingly, the existence or lack of OID is not affected by the price at which the certificates were originally sold. Rather, it is necessary to apply the OID definition to the original loan between the mortgagor and the mortgage originator, giving effect to the price at which the loan was originated.

In the case of a fixed-rate residential mortgage originated after March 1, 1984, some portion of the stated interest payments may be includible in OID if the amount unconditionally payable as interest in each year, expressed as a percentage of the outstanding principal balance of the loan, is stepped up or down over the term of the loan. For example, such a mortgage generally will be considered to have OID, even if it was originated at par, if it provides for negative amortization of principal or, subject to a special *de minimis* rule for interest holidays and teaser rates, bears interest payable at fixed rates that are scheduled to increase over the life of the loan. The general effect of applying the OID rules to loans with these features will be to require holders (1) of a negative amortization loan to include stated interest in income as it accrues, and (2) of a loan that bears interest at increasing rates to include interest in income as it accrues based on the yield to maturity of the loan (that is, a yield representing a blend of the stated interest rates).

An adjustable-rate residential mortgage typically would be a VRDI. Accordingly, the OID rules generally should be applied by treating the mortgage as if it provided for fixed interest payments equal to the interest that would be paid if the applicable interest-rate index were frozen at its value on the date of origination of the mortgage, with adjustments then being made in each month for differences between the assumed and actual interest rates. Under that approach, subject to the special *de minimis* rule for interest holidays and teaser rates, stated interest would be included in whole or in part in OID if the mortgage provides for a scheduled increase in interest payments not dependent on a change in the index. Also, if over the life of an adjustable-rate mortgage, the index increases and accrued interest is not paid currently because of a payment cap, the unpaid interest would be includible in income as it accrues under the VRDI rules.

If a mortgage is considered to have been issued with OID, an investor's interest therein most likely would be taxable under a method similar to the PAC method, except that the Prepayment Assumption used in calculating yield and present values would be an assumption that no prepayments will occur, and any gain from a prepayment would be treated as gain from retirement of the mortgage loan, not as an adjustment to OID.

E. Market Discount

1. Overview

Any discount at which an obligation is purchased below its principal amount (if the obligation has no OID) or below its adjusted issue price (if the instrument does have OID) is considered to be market discount. The treatment of market discount was significantly altered by The Tax Reform Act of 1984 ("TRA 1984") and TRA 1986.

Prior to the enactment of TRA 1984, market discount on a mortgage-backed security was generally allocated among all principal payments in proportion to their amounts, regardless of when they were due. The discount was included in income as principal payments were received or when the security was sold. Thus, if an obligation having an outstanding principal amount of $1,000 was purchased by an investor for $750, the investor would report 25% of each principal payment as income when the payment was received while it held the obligation. Such income was ordinary income (although not interest income) if the obligation was the debt of an individual; otherwise, it was generally capital gain, assuming the obligation was held as a capital asset. Given the same assumption, gain realized upon sale of the obligation was always capital gain. Such gain would reflect any market discount allocated to the principal of the obligation that remained unpaid at the time of the sale, because the seller's adjusted basis for purposes of computing gain would equal the portion of the initial purchase price, reflecting the market discount, that was allocated to such unpaid principal.

TRA 1984 and TRA 1986 did not change the rule of prior law that permits market discount on an obligation to be deferred until the obligation is disposed of or principal thereon is paid. However, TRA 1986 introduced a rule for allocating discount among principal payments that can significantly increase the amount of market discount income that is recognized when a principal payment is made. For an obligation that provides for partial principal payments in each accrual period, which describes many mortgage-backed securities, this change can have the effect of substantially eliminating the difference between OID and market discount in terms of the timing of the inclusion of such discount in income.

As a result of TRA 1984, market discount income reported by the holder of an obligation is treated as ordinary interest income for most tax purposes to the extent of the portion of the discount that accrued while the holder held the obligation. TRA 1984 also provided rules to ensure that accrued market discount will not be exempted from tax under certain nonrecognition provisions in the Code. Finally, another TRA 1984 amendment defers deductions for all or a portion of the tax losses that otherwise might be generated by borrowing at market rates to finance low-coupon market discount obligations, claiming current deductions for interest expense on the borrowing and deferring the inclusion in income of the market discount until the obligation is disposed of or repaid. These special market discount rules do not apply to an obligation that has a fixed maturity date not exceeding one year from issuance.[19]

---

19 TRA 1984 also offers investors an election, in section 1278(b), to treat market discount as OID. Market discount obligations affected by the election are not subject to the income conversion and loss deferral rules described in the text.

2. Detailed Discussion

TRA 1984 added to the Code section 1276, which provides that gain from a sale or other disposition of an obligation acquired with *market discount*[20] will be treated as ordinary income (generally as interest income) to the extent the gain does not exceed the portion of the market discount that is considered to have accrued from the acquisition date to the time of the sale or other disposition. Subject to certain exceptions, such income is recognized notwithstanding other non-recognition rules in the Code. Similarly, the stripping of a market discount obligation is considered a disposition that triggers the recognition of accrued market discount.

Discount that otherwise would be market discount is not treated as market discount for purposes of sections 1276 through 1278 if it is less than a *de minimis* amount. Any such *de minimis* discount is included in income ratably as principal payments are received, and is characterized as gain from retirement of the debt instrument.

TRA 1986 introduced a new rule for determining the amount of market discount income that is recognized when a partial principal payment is made. The rule, found in section 1276(a)(3), states that a partial principal payment on an obligation will be included in gross income as ordinary income to the extent of the accrued market discount on the obligation. In other words, the market discount that must be included in income when a principal payment is received is not, as under prior law, simply the portion of the remaining market discount that is allocable to the principal paid (for example, half of such discount if half of the principal balance is paid), but instead is generally the lesser of the amount of the payment and the amount of market discount that has accrued (but not yet been included in income) on the obligation as a whole. As discussed below, special rules govern the treatment of prepayments. If principal payments are made in each year at least equal to the market discount that accrues in that year, then the new rule effectively requires market discount to be included in income as it accrues.

For a non-REMIC pass-through certificate, it appears that the rule for partial principal payments would be applied separately to each of the underlying mortgages rather than to the certificates as a whole, so that principal payments received on one mortgage would not result in the recognition of accrued market discount on other mortgages. On the other hand, a REMIC regular interest would be treated as a single obligation for this purpose, even if it takes the form of a pass-through certificate.

---

20 *Market discount* is defined in section 1278(a)(2) as the excess of the stated redemption price at maturity of an obligation over its basis immediately after its acquisition by the taxpayer. However, for an obligation having OID, the stated redemption price at maturity is replaced by the adjusted issue price.

Subject to the discussion in the next paragraph, market discount is considered to accrue on an obligation under a straight-line method unless the holder elects, on an obligation-by-obligation basis, to use a constant yield method. If the election is made, accrued market discount for any period equals the portion of such discount that would have been included in the holder's income during that period as accrued OID if the obligation had been issued on the date on which it was purchased by the holder and the market discount had been OID. Sophisticated investors are likely to make a constant yield election for all of their market discount bonds, because the election slows the rate at which market discount accrues.

TRA 1986 authorized the Treasury to issue regulations to determine the amount of accrued market discount with respect to an obligation on which principal is payable in installments. The legislative history states that until these regulations are issued, holders of such obligations may elect to accrue market discount either in the same manner as OID or (1) in the case of debt obligations that have OID, in proportion to the accrual of OID, or (2) for debt obligations that have no OID, in proportion to payments of stated interest. For an obligation that would be subject to the PAC method for accruing OID if the instrument had such discount (which would include any pay-through bond issued after December 31, 1986), the same Prepayment Assumption that would be used in accruing OID will be used in accruing market discount, regardless of which of the foregoing methods is used. Issuers of obligations subject to the PAC method are required to report information necessary to calculate accruals of market discount.

If accruals of market discount are calculated under a method similar to the PAC method, then actual prepayments would be reflected automatically in the calculation of accrued discount. The treatment of prepayments on a debt instrument is less clear where the PAC method does not apply (for example, in the case of pass-through certificates that are not stripped bonds). In such a case, the rate of accrual of market discount should be calculated disregarding the possibility of optional prepayments. If and when a loan is prepaid *in full*, the holder would recognize gain from retirement of the instrument. That gain would be treated as ordinary income to the extent it does not exceed the accrued market discount on the instrument that has not previously been included in income. Any remaining gain would have the same character as if the special market discount rules did not apply (see Part E.1).

Where a debt instrument is prepaid *in part*, it is necessary to address three questions. First, is the amount of prepaid principal that is treated as a payment of accrued market discount limited to the accrued market discount attributable to the portion of the instrument that is prepaid? Second, is the holder required to recognize any portion of the unaccrued market discount on the obligation? Finally, if accrued and unaccrued market discount are included in income only to the extent they are allocated to the portion of the instrument that is prepaid, how is that allocation to be made?

The treatment of partial prepayments in the OID regulations gives some indication of the current views of the Service on these points. The OID regulations contain a payment-ordering rule that generally treats a payment on a debt instrument first, as a payment of accrued OID and, second, as a payment of principal. This rule does not apply, however, to a *pro-rata prepayment* (defined as a prepayment that results in a substantially pro-rata reduction of each payment remaining to be paid on the instrument). A pro-rata prepayment is treated instead as a payment in retirement of a portion of the instrument, resulting in the same amount of gain or loss as if the retired portion of the instrument were a separate instrument that was retired in full. All tax attributes of the instrument (adjusted issue price, the holder's basis, and accrued but unpaid OID), determined immediately before the prepayment, are allocated between the retired and remaining portions of the instrument based on their principal amounts.

While the OID regulations make no mention of section 1276, presumably the same principles would apply in determining the effect of a prepayment on market discount. Thus, in the case of a pro-rata prepayment of a market discount bond, the holder would allocate its tax basis, adjusted issue price and accrued market discount pro-rata between the retired and remaining portions of the bond, and treat the prepayment as if it were a prepayment in full of the retired portion of the bond. Any other prepayment would be treated in the same manner as a scheduled payment (first, as a payment of accrued OID and, second, as a payment of accrued market discount, in each case on the obligation as a whole, third, as a return of basis that reduces the adjusted issue price dollar-for-dollar but not below zero, and, fourth, as gain from retirement of the debt instrument). Thus, the prepayment would not trigger the recognition of any unaccrued market discount except to the extent basis has been reduced to zero. Although a non-pro-rata prepayment would increase the instrument's yield (calculated based on the adjusted issue price and future payments), there is no rule that adjusts the yield used in calculating future accruals of market discount under the constant yield method (where it applies). In general, holders of residential mortgages would prefer the rule for non-pro-rata prepayments over the rule for pro-rata prepayments. Remaining market discount on those mortgages is more likely to be unaccrued than accrued because accrued market discount must be included in income as scheduled principal payments are received.

The preamble to the OID regulations states that partial retirement treatment is restricted to pro-rata prepayments because that type of prepayment is common and the extension of the rule to non-pro-rata prepayments would be unduly complex. These statements were apparently made without the mortgage markets in mind. Almost invariably, partial prepayments on residential mortgages are not pro-rata prepayments but are credited against the last payments due. As a result, under the principles of the OID regulations, full and partial prepayment in the same amount will have different consequences for investors. However, information necessary to distinguish the two types of prepayments is not ordinarily reported to holders of pass-through certificates, so that even a well meaning investor would be unable to treat the two differently. Under these circumstances, holders are likely to make the simplifying assumption that all prepayments are prepayments in full.

TRA 1984 also added section 1277 to the Code, which requires the deferral of tax losses that otherwise would result from financing an investment in market discount obligations with debt that bears interest at a current market rate.

Section 1277 states that "net direct interest expense" with respect to a market discount obligation shall be allowed as a deduction in any taxable year only to the extent such expense exceeds the market discount that accrues during the days in such year on which the taxpayer held the obligation. The rate of accrual of market discount is determined under the rules of section 1276 described earlier (including the election to use a constant yield method). Net direct interest expense is the excess of the interest paid or accrued during the taxable year on debt incurred, or continued, to purchase, or carry, the market discount obligation over the aggregate amount of interest on the obligation (including OID) includible in gross income for the taxable year by the holder. The "incurred or continued to purchase or carry" standard used to link a borrowing with an investment in market discount obligations is amorphous and yet familiar, having been used for many years under section 265 in determining whether investments in tax-exempt bonds are debt financed. A special interest expense allocation rule applies to banks and thrifts.

The deductions for net direct interest expense on a market discount obligation that are disallowed under section 1277 are allowed (subject to other limitations that may apply to deductions for interest expense) (1) when the market discount obligation is disposed of in a taxable transaction, or (2) if the taxpayer so elects, prior to such a disposition to the extent necessary to offset any net interest income on the obligation (the excess of the interest income over interest expense on related borrowings) recognized in years subsequent to a year in which the deductions were disallowed.

The policy underlying section 1277 is that deductions for apparent losses resulting from a leveraged investment in a market discount obligation should be deferred, if and to the extent the losses are offset economically by the accrual of market discount, until the accrued market discount is included in income. Thus, if an investor borrows at 12% to finance the purchase of an 8% mortgage that has a yield, taking account of market discount, of 11%, the investor's economic loss is only 1%, the amount by which the rate of interest paid on the borrowing exceeds the yield on the mortgage. Obviously, income and expense would be mismatched if a deduction were allowed for the apparent additional 3 percentage-point loss before the corresponding amount of accrued market discount income is recognized.

F. Premium

Section 171 generally allows the holder of a debt instrument purchased at a premium (unless the holder is a dealer in securities) to elect to amortize such premium over the period from the date of purchase to the maturity date of the instrument (or, if it results in less rapid amortization of the premium, over the period to an earlier call date). For this purpose, premium is determined with reference to the basis of a debt instrument and the "amount payable on maturity" or, if it results in smaller amortizable bond premium for the period to an earlier call date, the "amount payable on earlier call date." Amortized premium is allocated among the interest payments on a debt instrument and, to the extent so allocated, is applied against and reduces those payments. Any amount not so allocated is allowed as a deduction.

Section 171 was significantly amended by TRA 1986, effective for debt instruments issued after September 27, 1985. Under the amended section, premium is amortized under a constant yield method. In applying that method, prepayments should be accounted for under a method similar to the PAC method, at least in the case of a debt instrument issued after December 31, 1986 to which the PAC method would apply if such instrument had been issued at a discount.[21]

Premium on a debt instrument that is not amortized under section 171 is allocated among the principal payments to be made on the instrument and is allowed as a loss deduction when those payments are made. Such a loss would be an ordinary loss for an obligation of an individual (or a partnership or trust if the obligation was issued prior to July 2, 1982) and otherwise would be a capital loss, provided the obligation is held as a capital asset.

---

21 For a debt instrument issued on or before September 27, 1985, an investor may elect to amortize premium under section 171 only if the instrument was issued by a corporation or a government or political subdivision thereof. If the election is made, premium is amortized under the method of amortizing bond premium that the holder regularly employs, provided such method is reasonable, and otherwise under a straight-line method.

In determining whether premium may be amortized on a pass-through certificate evidencing an interest in mortgages, the date of origination of the mortgages would determine whether the new or old version of section 171 applies. Thus, an election could be made under section 171 to amortize premium on a pass-through certificate backed by residential mortgages that are obligations of individuals only to the extent the mortgages were originated after September 27, 1985.

IV. TAXATION OF HOLDERS OF EQUITY INTERESTS IN OWNER TRUSTS AND REMIC RESIDUAL INTERESTS

A. Introduction

Part IV discusses the federal income taxation of holders of (1) equity interests in owner trusts that are not TMPs and (2) REMIC residual interests. The tax characteristics that are common to both types of securities are considered first, followed by a review of special considerations applicable to owner trusts and special considerations applicable to REMIC residual interests. The section concludes with a discussion of phantom income. Except as otherwise indicated, in Part IV the term "owner trust" means an owner trust that is not a TMP, the term "conduit issuer" means an owner trust or a REMIC, the term "equity interest" means an equity interest in a conduit issuer, and the terms "bond" and "CMO" include REMIC regular interests. Because, absent special circumstances, it is unlikely that a mortgage-backed security will be intentionally structured as an equity interest in a TMP, the taxation of TMPs, and holders of equity interests in TMPs, is not addressed.[22]

B. Common Tax Characteristics

Conduit issuers are generally not subject to tax. Instead, each holder of an equity interest is required to include in income its share of the taxable income (or loss) of the related conduit issuer allocable to that holder without regard to the distributions made by the issuer. In computing taxable income, the conduit issuer would have income from the mortgage collateral, the reinvestment of mortgage payments, and any reserve fund investments, and would be allowed deductions for interest (including OID), retirement premiums on the bonds it issues, and operating expenses. In any period, the deductions allowed for bond interest (net of any premium received by the issuer) generally would equal the income that would be reported by original holders of the bonds if they bought the bonds on the issue date at the issue price (for bond issues having more than one class, computed on a class-by-class basis), except that the OID *de minimis* rule would be ignored. A conduit issuer that retires a bond for an amount less than its adjusted issue price generally would have ordinary cancellation of indebtedness income equal to the difference. It may be possible to offset that income against the basis of assets or other tax attributes if the issuer is insolvent.

C. Special Considerations Applicable to Owner Trusts

As discussed above, an owner trust may be classified either as a grantor trust or as a partnership. A major difference between grantor trusts and partnerships is

---

22 For a discussion, see Peaslee & Nirenberg, *supra*, n.l., Chapter 8.

that a grantor trust is essentially ignored for federal income tax purposes, whereas a partnership is recognized as an entity for some tax purposes. Thus, if an owner trust is classified as a grantor trust, each holder of an equity interest therein would be treated as if the holder purchased and owned directly a share of the assets of the trust, subject to its share of the indebtedness of the trust. Accordingly, each holder would have an initial tax basis in its share of the trust's assets equal to the cost of its equity interest plus its share of the aggregate adjusted issue price of the bonds at the time of purchase of the equity interest. In addition, the holder's income would be computed under its own method of accounting, and the holder would make any applicable tax elections, for example, to amortize bond premium on the mortgage collateral. If the holder sold an interest in the owner trust, it would be considered to sell an interest in the underlying mortgages. Accordingly, as discussed further below, if the holder was a thrift institution or bank, any resulting gain or loss would be ordinary income or loss. Cash distributions from a grantor trust are not taxable.

By contrast, if an owner trust is classified as a partnership, taxable income would be computed, and in general elections made, at the partnership (or owner trust) level, using the partnership's accounting method (which almost always would be an accrual method). Each holder of an equity interest would report its share of the partnership's taxable income in the holder's taxable year in which the taxable year of the partnership ends. In most cases, the taxable year of the partnership would be the calendar year. Each partner would be considered to own an interest in the partnership (as contrasted with a direct interest in partnership assets). The partnership interest would have an initial basis in the hands of the partner equal to its original cost (the cash purchase price, or the basis of property exchanged for such interest in a tax-free exchange), plus the partner's share of partnership liabilities. Over time, such basis would be increased by the partner's share of partnership income and contributions, and decreased by the partner's share of losses and distributions (treating as distributions any reductions in the partnership's liabilities). The amount of the partnership's liabilities in respect of the bonds would equal the bonds' aggregate adjusted issue price, as described above.

Unlike a grantor trust, a partnership is considered to have its own basis in its assets (inside basis). While initially the inside basis of an owner trust that is classified as a partnership would equal the sum of the holders' bases in their equity interests (outside basis), a discrepancy could develop if (1) equity interests were sold at a gain or loss and (2) the sale did not result in (and is not followed by) a termination of the partnership under section 708. Under section 708, a partnership is considered to be terminated and reformed if 50% or more of the total interest in partnership income and capital is sold or exchanged within a 12-month period. Any discrepancy between inside and outside bases following a sale of a partnership interest at a gain (or loss) could result in overtaxation (or undertaxation) of the purchasing partner. The partnership could eliminate or mitigate the problem by making an election under section 754 to adjust the basis of its assets for purposes of computing the taxable income of the purchasing partner.

If an owner trust is classified as a partnership, then gain or loss from the sale of an equity interest may be capital gain or loss, even though in the case of a thrift institution or bank, a sale of a direct ownership interest in the mortgages held by the trust automatically would be ordinary income or loss. Such gain or loss would be computed by comparing the seller's adjusted basis in its partnership interest with the amount realized in the sale (which would include the seller's share of the trust's liabilities). Distributions of cash by a partnership to a partner are not taxable unless they exceed the partner's basis in its partnership interest, in which case the excess is treated as gain from sale of that interest. Gain from this source would be rare in the case of an owner trust because an equity owner's basis in its equity interest would include its share of the trust's liability for the bonds.

A pension plan, charity, individual retirement account, or other tax-exempt organization that is subject to tax on its unrelated business taxable income (UBTI) under section 512 will be taxable on substantially all of its income from an equity interest in an owner trust, regardless of whether the trust is classified as a grantor trust or partnership.

D. Special Considerations Applicable to REMICs

From a tax perspective, a REMIC resembles a partnership more than a grantor trust. Income or loss is computed at the level of the REMIC and is then allocated among the holders of residual interests as ordinary income or loss. Specifically, taxable income or loss of the REMIC is computed for each calendar quarter, and each holder of a residual interest is considered to earn, on each day it holds such interest, that day's ratable share of the REMIC's taxable income or loss for the quarter. Neither the Code nor the legislative history indicates how a REMIC should allocate its taxable income for a year among different calendar quarters. Hopefully, some flexibility will be allowed in choosing an allocation method.

In general, the taxable income of a REMIC is determined in the same manner as in the case of an individual. However, there are five statutory exceptions to this rule. First, a REMIC must use an accrual method of accounting. Second, regular interests, if not otherwise debt instruments, are treated as indebtedness of the REMIC, so that, among other consequences, interest thereon is deductible. Third, market discount on any qualified mortgage or other debt instrument held by the REMIC is includible in income as if such discount were OID (and the obligation were issued on the date on which it is acquired by the REMIC). Fourth, items of income, gain, loss, or deduction allocable to a prohibited transaction are disregarded. Finally, deductions for net operating loss carryovers or carrybacks are not allowed. Certain other minor adjustments are also found in the REMIC regulations. They treat all gain or loss from the disposition of an asset as ordinary, and allow deductions for ordinary and necessary operating expenses, interest, and bad debts without regard to certain limitations that apply to individual taxpayers.

The deductions allowed to a REMIC for interest or other income on a regular interest should match inclusions in income by an original holder who acquires the interest at its issue price. Thus, the discussion above of the timing of income recognition by holders of regular interests is also relevant in determining the taxable income of a REMIC. Indeed, these issues may be more significant for the REMIC than for regular interest holders because of the special anti-tax avoidance rules (discussed in Part E) applicable to residual interests. There is no counterpart to these rules for regular interests. One timing issue that is particularly significant in determining a REMIC's taxable income is whether deductions are allowed to holders (and there is a corresponding inclusion in income by the REMIC) for negative amounts determined under the PAC method with respect to high-coupon regular interests.

A REMIC does not recognize gain or loss on the issuance of regular or residual interests in exchange for cash or other property. If a REMIC distributes property in kind with respect to a regular or residual interest, *gain* is recognized by the REMIC in the same manner as if it had sold such property to the distributee at its fair market value, and the basis of the property to the distributee is that same amount.

In order to calculate the taxable income of a REMIC, it is necessary to determine the REMIC's basis in its assets. In general terms, the REMIC's aggregate basis in its assets at the time it is formed equals the aggregate issue price of all REMIC interests (both regular interests and residual interests). Although there is no clear guidance on the point, that aggregate basis presumably would be allocated first to cash and cash equivalents held by the REMIC, and then among the other assets of the REMIC in proportion to their fair market values.

The most significant assets of a REMIC are the qualified mortgages that it holds. Income from holding those mortgages is determined under the rules discussed above, except that a REMIC must include discount in income as it accrues under the PAC method, in the same manner as if the mortgages had been issued on the date on which they were acquired by the REMIC with an issue price equal to their initial basis to the REMIC. A REMIC that sells or disposes of qualified mortgages recognizes gain or loss determined under general tax principles.

No Code provision permits or requires adjustments to be made to a REMIC's basis in its assets to reflect subsequent purchases of residual interests at a price greater or less than the seller's adjusted basis. The legislative history of TRA 1986 indicates that it "may be appropriate" to make such adjustments, but leaves the issue unresolved. The REMIC regulations do not address the point.

Under section 67, an individual is allowed to deduct investment expenses (other than interest) only to the extent they exceed 2% of his adjusted gross income. Also, investment expenses are not deductible in calculating AMTI, the tax base for the alternative minimum tax. In the case of investment expenses of a REMIC, these rules are applied at the investor rather than REMIC level. Specifically, a REMIC must allocate its investment expenses among certain holders of REMIC interests (referred to as "pass-through interest holders"). Pass-through interest holders are required to include the amount of allocated expenses in income and are allowed an offsetting deduction if and only if the deduction would have been allowed had they incurred the expenses directly (in other words, for individuals, the 2% limitation applies and the expenses are not deductible in calculating AMTI). A pass-through interest holder is defined generally as an individual (other than certain non-resident aliens), trust or estate, or certain pass-through entities, including another REMIC, but not including a REIT or pension plan. Beneficial rather than record ownership is taken into account in determining whether an interest is held by a pass-through interest holder.

Ordinarily, a REMIC's investment expenses are allocated pro-rata among all residual interests (although only pass-through interest holders are required to take the allocated amount into account in determining their tax liability). However, in the case of a *single-class REMIC*, a portion of the REMIC's investment expenses must also be allocated to each class of regular interests. In particular, a single-class REMIC must allocate its investment expenses for any calendar quarter ratably to the days in the quarter and then among the regular and residual interests outstanding on any day in proportion to the income accruing on those interests for that day. A single-class REMIC is defined as any REMIC that would be classified as a grantor trust in the absence of a REMIC election, including any multiple class trust that falls within the exceptions in the Sears regulations for trusts with stripped, or senior and subordinated, pass-through certificates. Because of the requirement to allocate investment expenses, it will be necessary for a REMIC to determine whether any "excess servicing" with respect to the mortgages it holds (or in which it owns an interest) is truly servicing (and thus an investment expense of the REMIC) or is instead an ownership interest in the mortgages retained by the servicer (and thus not such an investment expense). Similarly, where a REMIC's qualified mortgages are pass-through certificates, the REMIC will need to determine whether any excess servicing charged with respect to the mortgages underlying the certificates is truly servicing or an ownership interest in the mortgages.

In the case of a REMIC that is not a single-class REMIC, as indicated above, all investment expenses are allocated pro-rata among individual holders of the residual interest. Because the value of the residual typically is small compared with the REMIC's assets and expenses, the requirement to include those expenses in income without a full, offsetting deduction (or any deduction in calculating AMTI) can produce seriously adverse consequences for individual holders that are out of all proportion to the value of their investments.

Special rules apply to the portion of the income from a residual interest that is an *excess inclusion*. With limited exceptions, excess inclusions are *always* subject to tax, even in the hands of tax-exempt investors. The excess inclusion rules were adopted primarily to ensure taxation of phantom income and are discussed further in that context below. Income from residual interests that is not an excess inclusion should be exempt from tax in the hands of pension plans and other tax-exempt entities that are taxable only on UBTI to the same extent as, for example, income from a partial ownership interest in mortgages (that is, residual interests should not be considered debt-financed merely because the regular interests are considered debt obligations of the REMIC for some tax purposes).

A REMIC will have a net loss for any calendar quarter in which its deductions exceed its gross income. Such a loss may not be carried over or back to other periods by the REMIC, but instead is allocated among the current holders of the residual interest in the same manner as taxable income. However, the portion of a net loss that is allocable to the holder of a residual interest will not be deductible by the holder to the extent it exceeds the holder's adjusted basis in such interest at the end of the quarter (or at the time of disposition of such interest, if earlier), determined before taking account of such loss. Such adjusted basis would generally equal the cost of the interest to the holder, increased by any amount the holder has previously reported as income from such interest, and decreased (but not below zero) by any losses it has deducted and any distributions it has received. The holder's basis does not include any amount on account of the REMIC's liabilities. Any loss that is not currently deductible by reason of the basis limitation may be carried forward indefinitely and deducted from the holder's share of the REMIC's taxable income in later periods, but otherwise cannot be used.

If a residual interest is sold, the seller will recognize gain or (except as described below) loss equal to the difference between its adjusted basis in such interest and the amount realized in the sale. Such gain or loss generally will be capital gain or loss if the residual interest is held as a capital asset, except that if the holder is a bank or thrift, the gain or loss will always be ordinary. If the seller acquires (or enters into a contract or option to acquire) any residual interest in a REMIC, any equity interest in an owner trust or any interest in a taxable mortgage pool that is comparable to a residual interest in a REMIC, during the period beginning six months before, and ending six months after, the date of the sale, then the sale will be treated as a "wash sale" subject to section 1091. Any loss realized in a wash sale is not currently deductible, but instead increases the seller's adjusted basis in the newly acquired interest.

Distributions on a REMIC residual interest are treated as a non-taxable return of capital to the extent of the holder's basis in its interest. Distributions in excess of basis are treated as gain from the sale of the residual interest.

E. Phantom Income

1. General

If a conduit issuer purchased a pool of mortgages and financed the purchase entirely with borrowed funds, and the debt service on the borrowings exactly matched the payments received on the mortgages, then the issuer would have no economic gain or loss from the transaction (assuming the mortgages are held to maturity and all payments are used to repay the borrowings). Given the lack of *economic* profit or loss, it might be expected that the interest or discount income on the assets and deductions in respect of the borrowings would exactly match for tax purposes as well, resulting in no *taxable* income or loss for the issuer. While that result would hold true over the entire life of the transaction, it may not be true in any particular year. The issuer may be required to report positive amounts of taxable income in some taxable years that are offset by matching losses in other periods. Non-economic taxable income and losses of this type are generally referred to as *phantom income* and *phantom losses*.

In a typical offering of multiple-class sequential-pay bonds by a conduit issuer, some phantom income will be realized in the early years after the issuance of the bonds, followed by a corresponding amount of phantom losses in subsequent years. The cause is a difference in the distribution over time of the yields that are used in calculating mortgage income and bond deductions. In particular, interest deductions are calculated separately for each class of bonds, based on the yield to maturity of that class. Thus, the aggregate deductions allowed in any year will be determined by reference to the weighted average yield to maturity of all classes of bonds outstanding in that year. With a rising yield curve, the yield to maturity is lower for shorter maturity classes of bonds than for longer dated classes. As a result, the weighted average yield to maturity of outstanding bonds increases over time as bonds are retired. By contrast, the yield to maturity of the mortgages remains constant, because they are not divided into sequential pay classes. The combination of income based on a fixed yield and deductions based on an escalating yield produces the pattern of phantom income and losses previously described.

Where REMIC securities are issued using two tiers of REMICs, phantom income resulting from yield curve effects is realized only by the upper-tier REMIC (and is allocated to the residual interest in that REMIC).[23] The reason is that, in determining the taxable income of the two REMICs, the lower-tier regular interests held by the upper-tier REMIC are aggregated and treated as a single class of debt obligations with a single yield.

Phantom income can be illustrated with a simple example. Consider a conduit issuer that purchases at par a mortgage that bears interest at a rate of 10%, payable annually, and provides for two principal payments of $500 each, due one year and two years after the date of purchase, respectively. At the time of such purchase, the conduit issuer issues two bonds, each of which provides for a single principal payment of $500 at maturity. The first bond is issued at par, matures at the end of one year, and bears 8% interest, payable at maturity. The second bond bears 10% interest, payable annually, matures at the end of two years, and is issued at a price of $491.44 to yield 11%. For simplicity, bond issuance and administrative costs are ignored. The conduit issuer is required to invest $8.56 of equity to finance the purchase of the mortgage and in exchange receives a cash distribution of $10 at the end of the first year and nothing thereafter, as shown in Exhibit 2.

The taxable income, economic income, and phantom income and loss realized by the conduit issuer in each of the two years that the bonds are outstanding are shown in Exhibit 3. The equity has received its entire economic return at the end of the first year. The loss of $4.50 in the second year is a phantom loss that offsets the same amount of phantom income in the first year.

Another way to describe the phantom income problem is that the owner of an equity interest is not permitted to amortize the cost of its interest directly against the cash distributions the owner expects to receive, as would be possible, for example, if the right to those distributions were treated for tax purposes as a debt obligation of the conduit issuer. Instead, the owner must recover its investment over the life of the underlying mortgages. Thus, as shown in Exhibit 3, although the equity interest in the conduit issuer becomes worthless following the distribution of the $10 payment at the end of the first year, the equity investor is permitted to treat as a return of capital in that year only $4.06 (the excess of the $10 distribution over taxable income of $5.94) rather than the full $8.56 cost of the equity interest.

Another, less significant, source of phantom income for non-REMIC issuers that does not relate to the sequential-pay nature of bonds arises from the rule that requires holders of pass-through certificates to report income based on the timing of receipt of payments on the underlying mortgages

---

23 For a discussion of two-tier REMICs, see Peaslee & Nirenberg, *supra*, n.1., Chapter 4, Part C.7.

Exhibit 2. Mortgage and Bond Payments

	Years from Bond Issuance		
	0	**1**	**2**
Mortgage Payments	($1,000.00)	$600	$550
Bond 1 Payments	500.00	(540)	—
Bond 2 Payments	491.44	(50)	(550)
Funds Available to Conduit Issuer	(8.56)	10	—

Exhibit 3. Income and Loss of the Conduit Issuer

	First Bond Year	Second Bond Year
Mortgage Income (10% of principal balance)	$100.00	$50.00
Deduction on Bond 1 (8% of principal balance)	(40.00)	—
Deduction on Bond 2 ($50 plus original issue discount of $4.06 in first year and $4.50 in second year)	(54.06)	(54.50)
Taxable Income (Loss) (mortgage income minus bond deductions)	5.94	(4.50)
Economic Income ($10 minus $8.56)	1.44	—
Phantom Income (Loss) (taxable income minus economic income)	4.50	(4.50)

rather than the timing of distributions on the certificates (which lags the receipt of mortgage payments). Even where there is a close matching between the payments and aggregate income on pass-through certificates and the payments and deductions on bonds, there can be an acceleration of income and subsequent loss because the period over which income is reported on the certificates (from the date of acquisition of the certificates until mortgage principal is received) is shorter than the period for accruing deductions on the bonds.

It is not clear whether the same result arises when a REMIC holds a pass-through certificate. A REMIC is required to report market discount income on qualified mortgages (including pass-through certificates) under the PAC method as such discount accrues. Under the PAC method, discount accrues based on a prepayment assumption that is applied to the entire underlying pool. Because individual mortgages lose their tax identity under this approach, many REMICs calculate income from pass-through certificates based on the distributions made on the certificates, as if they were pay-through bonds.

2. Acceleration of Net Remaining Phantom Losses through Sales of Equity Interests

When an equity interest is sold, the seller generally recognizes gain or loss equal to the difference between the amount realized in the sale and its adjusted basis in the interest. If the seller has recognized a net amount of phantom income, that amount would have increased the adjusted basis of the interest but not its value. As a result, the gain that otherwise would be realized from the sale would be decreased, or the loss would be increased, by the net amount of phantom income. Stated differently, the corresponding amount of future phantom losses that otherwise would be recognized over time generally would be accelerated into the taxable year of the sale. However, if the sale produces a net loss, this tax advantage may not be achieved for two reasons. First, for most investors other than banks, thrifts, and securities dealers, loss from the sale of an equity interest would be a capital loss that can be offset only against capital gain. Second, loss from the sale of a REMIC residual interest may be deferred under the special REMIC "wash sale" rule discussed in Part D., above.

3. Special Rules for REMICs; Excess Inclusions and Negative Value Residual Interests

Overview. Phantom income realized by a REMIC is taxable to the holders of the residual interest. However, unlike equity interests in owner trusts, there is no tax requirement that a REMIC residual interest have any minimum economic value. In addition, because phantom income is not economic income, a residual interest could produce substantial phantom income without having any economic value. Accordingly, absent special rules, the tax on phantom income associated with residual interests could be avoided easily by reducing the economic value of those interests to a nominal sum and transferring them (and the related tax liability) to investors that are tax-exempt, or are not currently paying federal income tax (for example, because they have unrelated losses).

To frustrate such tax avoidance, a portion of the income from a residual interest, referred to as an *excess inclusion*, is, with an exception discussed below for certain thrift institutions, subject to federal income taxation in all events. Thus, an excess inclusion with respect to a residual interest (1) may not, except as described below, be offset by any unrelated losses or loss carryovers of the owner of such interest; (2) will be treated as UBTI if the owner is a pension plan or other organization that is subject to tax only on its UBTI; (3) is not eligible for any exemption from, or reduction in the rate of, withholding tax if the owner is a foreign investor; and (4) may not be offset with an increased deduction for variable contract reserves if the owner is a life insurance company. Any tax resulting from these rules can, however, be offset with otherwise available credits.

The rule that prevents the use of unrelated losses to offset excess inclusion income does not prevent the holder of a residual interest from using losses from a disposition of the residual interest to offset excess inclusion income, provided the holder's taxable income from other sources is at least as great as its excess inclusion income. For example, if in a given taxable year, the holder has excess inclusion income of $100 and also realizes a loss of $100 from the sale of the residual interest which (apart from the excess inclusion rules) is currently deductible, then the holder's taxable income would not increase because of ownership of the residual interest, provided the holder's taxable income, disregarding the residual interest, is at least $100. In a case where a residual interest is held by a partnership or S corporation, the prohibition on offsetting losses might apply at both the entity and owner levels, although there seems to be no authority addressing the point.

If the holder of a residual interest is a corporation that is part of a group of corporations that files a consolidated federal income tax return, the entire group is ordinarily treated as one taxpayer in applying the excess inclusion rules. However, thrifts are subject to a special regime (discussed below).

The tax on excess inclusion income could potentially be avoided by transferring residual interests to holders that do not pay taxes because they are governmental entities, have no assets, or are located outside of the United States. Special measures exist to prevent the avoidance of tax through transfers of this type.

The next six sections address various topics relating to excess inclusions: the definition of the term; the exemption for thrifts from the limitation on the use of losses; special rules for REITs, RICs, and other pass-through entities; surrogate taxes that are imposed in lieu of taxes on governmental holders of residual interests; rules disregarding tax-motivated transfers of residual interests; and flaws in the existing excess inclusion rules (which have the effect of overstating phantom income).

The effectiveness of the battery of rules aimed at ensuring taxation of excess inclusion income is evidenced by the fact that residual interests are often economic liabilities (*i.e.*, have negative value), because the tax burden on the holder exceeds the value of any right to receive distributions.[24]

Definition of Excess Inclusion. In general terms, the excess inclusion with respect to a residual interest equals the excess of the income from the holding of the interest over the income that would have accrued on the interest if it had earned income at all times from its issuance at a constant, compounded rate equal to 120% of a long-term U.S. Treasury borrowing rate. More precisely, in any calendar quarter, the excess inclusion is the excess, if any, of (1) the taxable income of the REMIC allocated to the holder, over (2) the sum of the *daily accruals* for all days during the quarter on which the holder owns the residual interest. The daily accruals are determined by allocating to each day in the calendar quarter its ratable portion of the product of the *adjusted issue price* (defined below) of the residual interest at the beginning of the calendar quarter and 120% of the *Federal long-term rate* (defined below) in effect at the time the residual interest was issued. The adjusted issue price at the beginning of any calendar quarter equals the issue price of the residual interest, increased by the sum of the daily accruals for all prior quarters and the amount of any contributions made to the REMIC with respect to the residual interest after the startup day, and decreased (but not below zero) by the aggregate amount of payments made on the residual interest in all prior quarters. The Federal long-term rate is an average of current yields on Treasury obligations with a remaining term greater than nine years, computed and published monthly by the Service.

As an exception to the general rule just described, the Treasury has authority to issue regulations treating *all* income from the holding of a REMIC residual interest as an excess inclusion if the interest does not have *significant value.* The legislative history of TRA 1986 indicates that these regulations may be retroactive in "appropriate cases," but in any event will not apply where the value of the residual interest is at least 2% of the combined value of all REMIC interests. The current REMIC regulations do not implement the significant value rule. Whether it is ever implemented is likely to be of limited importance because the formula for calculating excess inclusions already is linked (through the definition of daily accruals) to the issue price of a residual interest. Thus, if a residual interest has a nominal value, the daily accruals would be close to zero and virtually all of the income from the interest would be an excess inclusion without regard to the significant value rule.

---

24 For a discussion of certain issues raised by negative value residuals, see Peaslee & Nirenberg, *supra*, n.1., Chapter 7, Part E.4.h.

Thrift Exception. Certain thrift institutions are exempt from the rule (discussed above) prohibiting excess inclusions from being offset with unrelated losses. The exemption applies, however, only to residual interests that have significant value. A residual interest meets this test if (1) the aggregate issue price of the residual interests in the REMIC is at least 2% of the aggregate issue price of all regular and residual interests in the REMIC, and (2) the anticipated weighted average life of the residual interest is at least 20% of the anticipated weighted average life of the REMIC. The second part of the test prevents the 2% test from being met during only a short initial period, after which capital invested in the residual interest is withdrawn.

As indicated above, if a group of corporations files a consolidated return, the group generally is treated as one taxpayer for purposes of applying the excess inclusion rules. However, the thrift exception is applied separately to each thrift that is a member of such a group. As a result, losses of a thrift generally cannot be offset against excess inclusions realized by other group members (including other thrifts) in a consolidated return. Similarly, losses of other group members generally cannot offset any excess inclusions of a thrift that exceed the losses of that thrift (determined without regard to the excess inclusions). The only exception to this rule is that a thrift and a *qualified subsidiary* are combined and treated as a single thrift (so that losses of one can offset excess inclusions of the other). A corporation is a qualified subsidiary for this purpose if (1) all of its stock, and substantially all of its indebtedness, is held directly by the thrift, and (2) it is organized and operated exclusively in connection with the organization and operation of one or more REMICs. Thus, a qualified subsidiary apparently cannot issue non-REMIC pay-through bonds or purchase interests in REMICs in the secondary market.

Pass-Through Entities. Normally, the taxable income of an entity that holds residual interests cannot be less than the excess inclusions that it realizes from those interests. How does this rule apply to real estate investment trusts (*REITs*) and regulated investment companies (*RICs*)? These two types of entities are generally subject to a corporate tax on their taxable income, but they are allowed deductions in determining such income for dividends paid to shareholders. Can excess inclusion income be offset with a dividends paid deduction?

The answer is "yes." REITs and RICs are taxable on "real estate investment trust taxable income" (defined in section 857(b)(2)) and "investment company taxable income" (defined in section 852(b)(2)), respectively. These special brands of income are calculated by making adjustments to the "taxable income" of the REIT or RIC. One of these adjustments is the dividends paid deduction. Thus, a requirement that "taxable income" not be less than the amount of excess inclusions would not prevent the use of that deduction to eliminate the tax base of a REIT or RIC.

On the other hand, the fact that a REIT or RIC can avoid tax on its excess inclusion income does not import that the tainted character of such income disappears. Instead, the taint is shifted to the shareholders of the REIT or RIC. In the case of REITs, section 860E(d) authorizes regulations to be issued that would (1) allocate among the shareholders of a REIT the excess of the REIT's aggregate excess inclusions over REIT taxable income (as defined in section 857(b)(2), excluding any net capital gain), and (2) treat any amount so allocated to a shareholder as if it were an excess inclusion from a residual interest held by such shareholder. Similar rules apply to RICs, bank common trust funds, and certain cooperative organizations that are taxed under part 1 of subchapter T of the Code. No regulations have been issued under this grant of authority. Although pass-through entities generally can escape tax on excess inclusion income allocated to investors, as described in the next section, a pass-through entity in which interests are owned by certain governmental entities may be taxed on excess inclusions allocated to those entities.

Surrogate Taxes on Excess Inclusions Allocable to Certain Governmental Entities. Although every effort has been made to ensure that excess inclusions will be subject to tax under the Code, certain organizations that are exempt from all taxes under the Code could potentially hold residual interests without paying tax on excess inclusions. The REMIC rules refer to such a holder as a *disqualified organization.* The principal example of a disqualified organization is a governmental entity.

A number of measures have been adopted to prevent tax on excess inclusions from being avoided through the ownership of residual interests by disqualified organizations. An entity cannot qualify as a REMIC unless it adopts reasonable arrangements designed to ensure that residual interests are not held by such organizations. In addition, if a disqualified organization (1) holds a residual interest despite such arrangements, or (2) becomes an indirect owner of such an interest through a pass-through entity, then a tax is imposed on someone else as a substitute for the tax on excess inclusions that would have been paid by the disqualified organization if it had been a taxpayer. In the first of these two situations, the "surrogate tax" is imposed on the person that transferred the residual interest to the disqualified organization. In the second, the pass-through entity is taxed. The sections which follow describe in more detail the operation of the surrogate taxes on transfers and pass-through entities.

Transfer tax. A tax is imposed on transfers of REMIC residual interests to disqualified organizations. The tax is generally imposed on the transferor. However, if the transfer is made through an agent for a disqualified organization (for example, a securities firm buying as a broker for a disqualified organization), then the tax is imposed on the agent rather than on the transferor, apparently even if the transferor is aware of the transferee's identity.

A transferor or agent can protect itself from any possible liability for the tax by obtaining a statement from the transferee stating under penalties of perjury that the transferee is not a disqualified organization. Although section 860E(c)(4) refers to an "affidavit," a formal, notarized document is not required; a statement indicating that it is made under penalties of perjury will suffice. Further, because disqualified organizations do not have social security numbers (as distinguished from employer identification numbers), in the case of a transfer to an individual the transferee's statement may simply provide a social security number and recite under penalties of perjury that the number is that of the transferee. The affidavit will not be effective, however, if the transferor or agent, as the case may be, has actual knowledge, as of the time of the transfer, that the affidavit is false. Transferors of residual interests and persons buying such interests on behalf of others often obtain such affidavits as a matter of course.

If the tax applies to a transfer of a residual interest, it is calculated by multiplying the highest marginal federal corporate income tax rate by an amount equal to the present value of the total anticipated excess inclusions on such interest for periods after the transfer. Anticipated excess inclusions are determined using the same Prepayment Assumption that applies in accruing OID under the PAC method, and present values are computed using the applicable Federal rate as the discount rate. Where a tax is imposed on a transfer of a residual interest to a disqualified organization, the issuing REMIC is required, within 60 days after request, to provide the information necessary for computing the tax to the person required to pay the tax and to the Service. The REMIC may charge the taxpayer (but not the Service) a reasonable fee for providing the information.

The Service has authority to waive the tax on any transfer of a residual interest if, within a reasonable time after discovery that the transfer was subject to tax, steps are taken so that the interest is no longer held by the disqualified organization and the Service is paid a surrogate tax equal to the product of the highest marginal corporate tax rate and the amount of excess inclusions that accrued on the residual interest while it was held by the disqualified organization.

Tax on pass-through entities. A tax is imposed on any pass-through entity (as defined below) if a disqualified organization is the *record* holder of an interest in the entity. A pass-through entity may rely on a statement from a record holder made under penalties of perjury to establish that it is not a disqualified organization if the entity does not know that the statement is false. The tax equals the highest marginal federal corporate income tax rate multiplied by the amount of excess inclusions allocable to the interest in the entity held of record by the disqualified organization. No tax is imposed on a pass-through entity if interests in the entity are owned beneficially by a disqualified organization, provided the disqualified organization is not the record holder. In these circumstances, the nominee is treated as the pass-through entity (as described in the next paragraph) and is subject to the tax.

A *pass-through entity* is defined as any RIC, REIT, bank common trust fund, partnership, trust, or estate. The term also includes cooperative organizations taxed under part 1 of subchapter T of the Code. The definition does not include corporations taxed under subchapter S, presumably because the definition of an S corporation would not allow a disqualified organization to be a stockholder. Except as provided in regulations, a person holding an interest in a pass-through entity as a nominee for another person is treated with respect to that interest as a pass-through entity (and the other person is treated as a record holder of an interest in the deemed pass-through entity represented by the nominee arrangement).

To illustrate how the tax operates, suppose that a REIT holds a REMIC residual interest and a broker holds stock in the REIT as a nominee for a disqualified person. In that event, the broker and not the REIT would be subject to tax on the portion of the excess inclusions of the REIT that is allocable to the interests in the REIT held for the disqualified organization through the broker.

Any tax imposed on a pass-through entity is deductible from the entity's ordinary gross income. Further, a REIT or a RIC is permitted to charge against dividends paid to a disqualified organization the tax expense arising out of its ownership of stock without causing dividends paid by the REIT or RIC to be preferential within the meaning of section 562(c) (which disallows the dividends paid deduction for preferential dividends). A REIT should be able to prohibit record ownership of its stock by a disqualified organization without running afoul of the tax requirement that it have transferable shares.

Certain Tax-Motivated Transfers Disregarded. The panoply of measures described above for ensuring the payment of tax on excess inclusion income has two potential gaps: First, a residual interest could be transferred to a U.S. person that is subject to U.S. taxes but has no assets or otherwise does not intend to pay taxes that are due. Second, a residual interest could be transferred to a foreign person that, as a practical matter, will not pay U.S. taxes unless the taxes are withheld, in circumstances where the distributions on the residual interest from which tax may be withheld are less than the current tax liability.

The REMIC regulations fill in these gaps by disregarding certain transfers of residual interests where the collection of tax from the transferee is doubtful. The effect of disregarding a transfer of a residual interest is that the transferor continues to be liable for the tax on income, including excess inclusions, from the interest. Where a residual interest is newly issued to a person other than the REMIC sponsor, the REMIC sponsor is treated as the transferor.

As described in the next two sections, different standards apply in disregarding transfers depending on whether the transferee is a U.S. or non-U.S. person.

Transfers to U.S. persons. The regulations disregard the transfer of any "non-economic" residual interest (described below) to a U.S. person if a significant purpose of the transfer is to impede the assessment or collection of tax. Such a purpose exists if the transferor either knew or should have known (had "improper knowledge") that the transferee would be unwilling or unable to pay the taxes due on its share of the taxable income of the REMIC.

Under a safe harbor rule, a taxpayer is presumed not to have improper knowledge if:

- the transferor conducts, at the time of the transfer, a reasonable investigation of the financial condition of the transferee and, as a result of the investigation, finds that the transferee historically paid its debts as they came due and found no significant evidence to indicate that the transferee will not continue to do so, and

- the transferee represents to the transferor that it understands that as a holder of the residual interest, it may incur tax liabilities in excess of any cash flows on the residual interest and that the transferee intends to pay taxes associated with holding the residual interest as they become due.

It is not clear why the rule is only a presumption. If there are factors indicating that the transferee will not pay taxes that become due, those factors should be taken into account in determining whether the transferor made a reasonable investigation and the proper findings, and not prevent the safe harbor from applying if its terms are met. Otherwise, the rule would be worthless.

The regulations do not explain how extensive an investigation must be in order to be reasonable. Only a fairly cursory investigation should be required where the transferee is known to conduct substantial activities other than holding residual interests, and there are no obvious signs of financial distress. Needless to say, conducting an investigation will be more difficult for transferees that are privately held companies than for an SEC reporting company.

A residual interest is considered to be non-economic for this purpose unless *at the time of the transfer:*

- the present value of the expected future distributions thereon at least equals the product of the present value of anticipated excess inclusions and the highest marginal corporate income tax rate for the year of the transfer, and

- the transferor reasonably expects that, for each anticipated excess inclusion, the transferee will receive distributions from the REMIC at or after the time taxes accrue on the anticipated excess inclusion in an amount sufficient to satisfy the accrued taxes.

A non-economic residual interest includes not only interests that have a nominal fair market value at the time of the transfer, but also interests that have substantial values but may receive distributions in advance of realizing excess inclusion income. There is no requirement that distributions sufficient to pay taxes on excess inclusions be made within any particular period following the accrual of such income, although delays in the timing of distributions will reduce their present value. Because the determination of whether a residual interest is non-economic is made at the time of transfer, a residual interest that is economic for part of its life can become non-economic (and thus have restricted transferability) at a later time.

Transfers to foreign investors. As further discussed below, a foreign investor holding a residual interest generally is subject to a 30% withholding tax on excess inclusion income. Under current law, the tax is imposed on excess inclusions not as the income accrues, but only when distributions are made on the residual interests. The REMIC regulations prevent this rule from being abused by disregarding any transfer to a foreign person of a residual interest that has "tax avoidance potential." A "foreign person" should include anyone who may be subject to U.S. withholding tax. A residual interest has tax avoidance potential unless, *at the time of the transfer*, the transferor reasonably expects that, for each excess inclusion, the REMIC will distribute to the transferee residual interest holder an amount that will equal at least 30% of the excess inclusion, and such amount will be distributed at or after the time at which the excess inclusion accrues and not later than the close of the calendar year following the calendar year of accrual.

If a residual interest is transferred to a foreign person, a transfer of the residual interest by that person to a U.S. person will be disregarded (so that taxes will continue to be withheld on distributions) if the effect of the transfer would be to allow the transferor to avoid the withholding taxes on excess inclusions. Thus, it is not possible to avoid the taxes on excess inclusions by having a foreign person hold a residual interest while excess inclusions accrue and then transferring it to a U.S. person before the related cash distributions are made.

Negative Value Residual Interests. Residual interests often have negative fair market values, because the tax cost of the associated phantom income exceeds the value of any right to receive distributions. In such a case, an owner would need to pay another party to take over its ownership position.

Although there are no authorities addressing the point, the party receiving such a payment should be required to include it in income as an ordinary item.[25]

V. SPECIAL RULES FOR CERTAIN INSTITUTIONAL INVESTORS

This Part discusses special tax rules that apply to certain categories of institutions investing in mortgage-backed securities. These institutions are thrifts, banks, REITs, pension plans, and other tax-exempt organizations, life insurance companies, and securities dealers. This Part does not attempt to address comprehensively the complex tax rules governing these types of organizations.

A. Thrift Assets, REIT Assets and Income Tests

Thrifts are subject to a tax-related assets test. In particular, a thrift is allowed deductions for additions to bad debt reserves calculated under the percentage-of-taxable-income method, and qualifies for certain other tax benefits available to the thrift industry, only if at least 60% of its assets are assets listed in section 7701(a)(19)(C). The list includes, among other assets, loans "secured by an interest in [residential] real property" (but generally not loans secured by commercial real property). In addition, more favorable bad debt reserve rules may apply to loans held by thrifts if those loans are "qualifying real property loans" within the meaning of section 593(d). The treatment of pay-through bonds, pass-through certificates, and REMIC interests under these provisions is discussed below.

An assets test also applies to REITs. An entity qualifies as a REIT only if at least 75% of its assets are *real estate assets* (including interests in mortgages on real property), U.S. Government securities, cash items, or cash. In addition, a REIT must derive at least 75% of its gross income from real estate related sources, including "interest on obligations secured by mortgages on real property or on interests in real property" and gain from the sale or other disposition of those obligations (assuming they are not held in a dealer capacity).

In general, pay-through bonds do not qualify as real property loans for purposes of the thrift and REIT tests because they are not directly secured by real property (but only by debt instruments that are so secured). With the

---

25 For a more complete discussion of this point, see Peaslee & Nirenberg, *supra*, n.1., Chapter 7, Part E.4.h.

possible exception of IO Strips held by thrifts, pass-through certificates are considered qualifying thrift and REIT assets to the extent the issuing trust holds such assets, because the holders of such certificates are treated for tax purposes as the owners of the trust's assets under the grantor trust rules.

In any calendar quarter, both regular interests and residual interests in REMICs are qualifying assets for thrifts and REITs, and the income on such interests qualifies for the REIT 75% income test, in the same proportion that the assets and income of the REMIC are qualifying assets and income. However, if 95% or more of the assets of the REMIC are qualifying assets during a calendar quarter, then the regular and residual interests will be considered qualifying assets, and the income on such interests will qualify for the REIT 75% income test in their entirety for that quarter. If one REMIC owns regular interests in a second REMIC, then the 95% test generally is applied separately to each. However, if the REMICs are part of a "tiered structure," the 95% test is applied only once to both REMICs, treating them as if they were a single REMIC. Two REMICs are considered "tiered" if it was contemplated when both REMICs were formed that some or all of the regular interests of one REMIC would be held by the other REMIC. The amount of a residual interest that may be counted as a qualifying asset is either the adjusted basis or value of the interest, not the adjusted basis or value of the underlying assets of the REMIC.

A REIT that owns an equity interest in an owner trust is considered to own qualifying assets to the extent that the trust holds such assets, provided the trust is classified as a trust or partnership for tax purposes. The same would hold true for a thrift investor if the owner trust is a grantor trust. The result is less certain for thrift investors, however, if the owner trust is classified as a partnership for tax purposes.

B. Tax-Exempt Organizations

Qualified pension plans, charitable institutions, individual retirement accounts, and certain other entities that are otherwise exempt from federal income taxation are nonetheless subject to tax on their unrelated business taxable income. UBTI generally does not include interest or dividend income or gain from the sale of investment property unless such income is derived from property that is debt-financed. Thus, income from pass-through certificates, pay-through bonds, REMIC regular interests, and equity interest in TMPs would not be considered UBTI unless the security is itself debt-financed. On the other hand, all or substantially all of the income from an equity interest in an owner trust that is classified as a grantor trust or partnership would be UBTI even if the equity interest itself is not debt-financed. In the case of a REMIC residual interest, any amount of income that is an "excess inclusion" is deemed to be UBTI in the hands of an investor that is subject to tax on UBTI. Other income from a residual interest should not be UBTI unless the interest is itself debt-financed. Special considerations apply to pass-through debt certificates (or more generally to securities that resemble debt but may be considered partnership interests for tax purposes).

C. Life Insurance Companies

The general Code rules pertaining to the accrual of discount on debt securities do not apply to life insurance companies. Under section 811(b), life insurance companies generally are required to take original issue discount into account under the method they regularly employ in maintaining their books, if such a method is reasonable. A life insurance company that realizes excess inclusion income from a REMIC residual interest may not offset such income through an increased deduction for variable contract reserves.

D. Ordinary Income Treatment for Debt Instruments Held by Banks and Thrifts

Under section 582(c), certain banks and thrift institutions are required to report gain or loss from the sale of an "evidence of indebtedness" as ordinary income or loss. Pass-through certificates, pay-through bonds, and both regular and residual interests in REMICs are considered evidences of indebtedness for this purpose. It is unclear whether section 582(c) would apply to a financial institution's indirect interest in debt instruments held by an owner trust taxed as a partnership.

A bank may be considered a dealer in securities and, thus, may be subject to the rules described immediately below.

Securities Dealers

Special rules apply to dealers in securities. As described below, the law in this area was changed significantly in 1993 by the enactment of section 475, which expands the definition of dealer and requires dealers to account for income from securities under a mark to market method.

Traditionally, a dealer has been defined as a merchant in securities who, in the ordinary course of business, buys securities for resale to customers with an expectation of earning a profit that is attributable to merchandising efforts. A dealer is distinguished from a trader who seeks to profit from a short-term rise in value not attributable to such marketing efforts or an investor holding property for the production of income. A bank or thrift that originates mortgages for resale may be a dealer under the traditional definition. For purposes of applying the rules governing securities dealers, a "security" would include most of the conventional types of mortgage-backed securities.

The consequences of being a securities dealer include the following: (1) gain or loss with respect to a security held in a dealer capacity is ordinary income (unless, in the case of loss, the security was identified as held for investment), and gain from the sale of a security held for investment is ordinary income unless the security was identified as held for investment; (2) the wash sale rules do not apply to sales of securities by a dealer in the ordinary course of its business; and (3) under section 475, gain or loss is accounted for by marking securities to market (unless, generally, the securities are held for investment, are debt instruments acquired or originated in the ordinary course of business and not held for sale, or are hedges of assets or liabilities not subject to the mark to market regime, and are timely identified as such).

Section 475 was added to the Code by the Revenue Reconciliation Act of 1993. Before the advent of this section, a dealer could, for tax purposes, inventory securities held in a dealer capacity and value unsold inventory at cost, market value, or the lower of cost or market. In addition to eliminating methods of inventory valuation based to any extent on cost, section 475 extends the mark to market requirement to securities that are not held in a traditional dealer capacity. Thus, acting as a dealer with respect to any securities can have consequences for the treatment of securities held in a non-dealer capacity. Section 475 also adopts an expanded definition of "dealer." A dealer is defined as any person who (1) regularly purchases securities from, or sells securities to, customers in the ordinary course of business, or (2) regularly offers to enter into swaps or other derivative transactions with customers in the ordinary course of business. The first part of this definition may treat as a dealer any person who regularly buys or originates loans and sells them, even if, in effecting the sales, that person is not acting as a traditional merchant.

The mark to market rules of section 475 do not apply to REMIC residual interests that, *when acquired,* have "negative value." Specifically, under regulations, a residual interest is not considered to be a "security" for purposes of this section in the hands of any taxpayer if, as of the date the taxpayer acquires the interest, it has negative value, measured under a formula. A residual interest has negative value if the present value of the anticipated tax liabilities associated with holding the interest exceeds the sum of (1) the present value of the expected future distributions on the interest and (2) the present value of the anticipated tax savings associated with holding the interest as the REMIC generates losses. Once it is determined that a residual interest is a security, its value for purposes of applying section 475 should be its actual market value (whether positive or negative).

VI. TAXATION OF SPONSORS

Previous Parts of this chapter concentrated on the taxation of issuers and investors. This Part looks at sponsors. For any issue of securities backed by a pool of mortgages, the term *sponsor* is used here broadly to refer to any person who (1) owned an interest in those mortgages before the securities were issued and (2) immediately after issuance of the securities, holds (at least temporarily) some or all of the securities or another interest in the securities' issuer. The tax treatment of a sponsor may be affected by many factors. Therefore, this discussion in Part VI is intended only as a general summary of the most likely tax results in a number of common situations.

The tax consequences to a sponsor of the issuance and sale of mortgage-backed securities depend primarily on (1) whether the transaction is treated for tax purposes as a financing or sale, and (2) if it is a sale, the proportion of the property held by the sponsor that is considered to be sold. Pledging an asset as security for a loan is not ordinarily considered a taxable disposition of the asset. On the other hand, if the asset (or an interest therein) is sold, the seller recognizes gain or loss equal to the difference between the amount realized in the sale and its adjusted basis in the property sold.

As the discussion below explains, these basic tax principles apply in different ways to sponsors of pass-through certificates, pay-through bonds, and REMIC interests.

Before turning to the different types of mortgage-backed securities, it is worth taking note of special considerations that apply to a sponsor that is also a servicer and receives *excess servicing* (a servicing fee in excess of reasonable compensation for the services performed). In 1991, the Service issued a ruling holding that excess servicing must be treated as an ownership interest in the related mortgages (or, more technically, as a stripped coupon within the meaning of section 1286). As a result, such a sponsor must allocate some part of its basis in the mortgages it sells to excess servicing, thereby increasing its gain (or reducing its loss) from the sale. References in this section to ownership interests in mortgages, or pass-through certificates evidencing such ownership interests, should be understood to include excess servicing.

A. Pass-Through Certificates

The tax treatment of sponsors of pass-through certificates is for the most part straightforward. The exchange of mortgages for *all* of the pass-through certificates issued by a grantor trust is not a taxable event. When the sponsor sells some or all of those certificates, however, it is treated as selling an interest in the underlying mortgages and recognizes gain or loss accordingly. The gain or loss equals the difference between the amount realized in the sale and the portion of its aggregate adjusted basis in the mortgages that is allocated to the certificates sold (which would be a pro-rata portion if there is only one class of ownership interests in the trust).

B. Through Bonds

Two steps may be involved in issuing pay-through bonds: (1) the issuance of the bonds for cash and (2) the transfer of all or a portion of the mortgage collateral by a sponsor to the issuer in exchange for cash and/or other consideration. The issuance of the bonds is not considered a sale of the collateral and is not otherwise a taxable event. The tax treatment of the transfer of the mortgages to the issuer is quite complex and would depend on at least three factors, the first two of which are related: (1) whether for tax purposes the transfer is treated as a sale, or is instead viewed as an exchange of mortgages for an equity interest in the issuer, (2) the extent to which equity interests in the issuer are owned by the sponsor rather than unrelated investors, and (3) whether the issuer is, for tax purposes, a grantor trust, partnership, or corporation.

In very general terms, if the issuer is an owner trust that is classified as a grantor trust, then the sponsor would recognize gain or loss as a result of the transfer of mortgages to the issuer only if equity interests in the issuer are owned by persons other than the sponsor, and then only to the extent that the sponsor would recognize gain or loss if it transferred directly to those other persons an interest in the mortgages corresponding to the equity interest they own.

If the issuer is classified as a partnership, gain from a sale of the mortgages to the partnership would be recognized, but loss would not be recognized if the sponsor owns more than 50% of the equity interests in the issuer. No gain or loss would be recognized upon an exchange of mortgages for an equity interest.

Finally, if the issuer is a corporation, gain or loss from a sale of mortgages to the issuer by the sponsor generally would be recognized. However, if the sponsor is a corporation that files a consolidated federal income tax return with the issuer, then any such gain or loss would be deferred. Moreover, even if the sponsor and the issuer do not file a consolidated return, loss would be deferred, or in some cases shifted to the issuer, if the sponsor and the issuer are part of the same "controlled group" (a group of corporations tied together through more than 50% stock ownership links). If the mortgages are exchanged for stock (or stock and cash) upon formation of the issuer, loss would not be recognized in the exchange. Gain may be recognized in an amount not exceeding the amount of cash received, but any such gain would be deferred to the same extent as gain from a sale. The transferor may also recognize interest income up to the amount of accrued market discount on the mortgages not previously included in income.

Regardless of the tax status of the issuer or whether gain or loss was recognized upon transfer of the mortgages to the issuer, if the sponsor sells some or all of its equity interest in the issuer to unrelated investors, it will recognize gain or loss in that sale equal to the difference between the amount realized and its adjusted basis in the portion of the equity interest that is sold.

C. REMICs

With a limited exception, a sponsor that transfers mortgages to a REMIC in exchange for regular and residual interests, either directly or through intermediaries, does not recognize gain or loss in the exchange. The aggregate adjusted basis of the property transferred (increased by the REMIC's organizational expenses) is allocated among the REMIC interests received in proportion to their respective fair market values on the pricing date or, if none, the startup day. Each time the sponsor sells an interest in the REMIC (whether a regular interest or a residual interest), it recognizes gain or loss equal to the excess of the amount realized (net of syndication expenses) over its basis in that interest. The tax consequences to the sponsor would be the same if the REMIC, instead of issuing regular and residual interests to the sponsor in exchange for mortgages, issued those interests to the sponsor or unrelated investors for cash and used that cash to purchase the mortgages from the sponsor. The alternative transaction would be characterized for tax purposes as a contribution of the mortgages by the sponsor to the REMIC in exchange for all interests in the REMIC, followed by a sale by the sponsor for cash of those interests which it does not retain.

As this discussion suggests, the major difference in tax consequences for a sponsor of pay-through bonds of making or not making a REMIC election relates to the portion of the sponsor's overall economic gain or loss (represented by the difference between the sum of the fair market values of the bonds and equity interests in the issuer and the sponsor's basis in the mortgages) that is recognized at the time of the bond offering and upon sale of equity interests in the issuer. If no election is made, the sponsor would not recognize any portion of such gain or loss at the time of the bond sale, but would recognize a portion of such gain or loss each time an equity interest is sold, corresponding to the portion of the equity interest that is sold. By contrast, if a REMIC election is made, the sponsor would recognize a portion of such gain or loss equal to the portion of *all* interests in the issuer (equity and bonds) that is sold, as those interests are sold. Thus, for example, if the bonds represent 95% of the value of all REMIC interests, 95% of such gain or loss would be recognized when the bonds are sold. Of course, the recognition of gain or loss is only one of a number of factors influencing the decision whether to make a REMIC election.

The tax consequences for a sponsor of the creation and sale of pass-through certificates would be substantially the same whether or not a REMIC election is made.

A REMIC interest that is issued in exchange for mortgages or other property generally is taxed as if it had been issued at a price equal to its initial fair market value. Under section 860F(b)(1), the income of the sponsor from holding any REMIC interest is adjusted to take account of any difference between its issue price and initial basis in the hands of the sponsor. In particular, that difference is required to be included in income if the issue price is higher, or is allowed as a deduction if the issue price is lower, (1) in the case of a regular interest, as if that difference were original issue discount or bond premium, respectively, or (2) in the case of a residual interest, ratably over the anticipated weighted average life of the REMIC.

APPENDIX

Lakhbir S. Hayre, DPhil.
Director of Mortgage Research
Salomon Brothers

Cyrus Mohebbi, Ph.D.
Managing Director
Market Group
Prudential Securities Inc.

MORTGAGE MATHEMATICS
Mortgage Cash Flow without Prepayments

Monthly Payment. For a level-payment mortgage, the constant monthly payment is

$$M_n = \frac{B_0 \left(\dfrac{G}{1200}\right)\left(1 + \dfrac{G}{1200}\right)^N}{\left[\left(1 + \dfrac{G}{1200}\right)^N - 1\right]}$$

where

M_n = Monthly payment for month n;
B_0 = Original balance;
G = Gross coupon rate (%);
N = Original term in months (e.g., 360).

Remaining Balance. The remaining balance after n months is

$$B_n = \frac{B_0 \left[\left(1 + \dfrac{G}{1200}\right)^N - \left(1 + \dfrac{G}{1200}\right)^n\right]}{\left[\left(1 + \dfrac{G}{1200}\right)^N - 1\right]}$$

where B_n = Remaining balance at the end of month n.

Principal Payment. The amount of principal paid in month n is given by

$$P_n = \frac{B_0 \left(\dfrac{G}{1200}\right)\left(1 + \dfrac{G}{1200}\right)^{n-1}}{\left[\left(1 + \dfrac{G}{1200}\right)^N - 1\right]}$$

where P_n = Principal paid in month n.

Interest Payment. The amount of interest paid in month n can be written as

$$I_n = \frac{B_0 \left(\dfrac{G}{1200}\right)\left[\left(1 + \dfrac{G}{1200}\right)^N - \left(1 + \dfrac{G}{1200}\right)^{n-1}\right]}{\left[\left(1 + \dfrac{G}{1200}\right)^N - 1\right]} = B_{n-1}\left(\dfrac{G}{1200}\right)$$

where I_n = Interest paid in month n.
It should be noted that

$$G = S + C$$

where S = Service fee (%)
and C = Security coupon rate (%),

$$\text{so } \textit{Servicing Amount} = \left(\frac{S}{C + S}\right) I_n.$$

Therefore, the cash flow to the security holder in month n is given by

$$CF_n = P_n + I_n - \textit{Servicing Amount} = P_n + \left(\frac{C}{C + S}\right) I_n$$

Prepayment Measuring Conventions

For a given pool of mortgages, let
B_n = Remaining principal balance per dollar of mortgage at the end of month n if there are no prepayments.

C_n = Pool factor (*i.e.*, actual remaining principal balance per dollar of mortgage) at the end of month n.

Let $Q_n = C_n/B_n$. If one thinks of the pool as consisting of a very large number of $1 mortgages, each of which can terminate separately, then Q_n represents the percentages of mortgages still remaining at the end of month n. Then

Percentage of initial balance has been prepaid = $1 - Q_n$.

For month n, the single monthly mortality, or *SMM*, stated as a decimal, is given by

SMM = Proportion of $1 mortgages outstanding at the beginning of the month that are prepaid during the month

$$\frac{Q_{n-1} - Q_n}{Q_{n-1}} = 1 - \frac{Q_n}{Q_{n-1}}$$

For the period from month m to month n, the constant SMM rate that is equivalent to the actual prepayments experienced is given by

$$(1 - SMM)^{n-m} = \frac{Q_n}{Q_m},$$

i.e.,

$$SMM = 1 - \left(\frac{Q_n}{Q_m}\right)^{\frac{1}{n-m}}$$

The conditional prepayment rate, or CPR (also expressed as a decimal), is the SMM expressed as an annual rate, and is given by

$$1 - CPR = (1 - SMM)^{12},$$

$$CPR = 1 - (1 - SMM)^{12}.$$

i.e.,

Inverting,

$$SMM = 1 - (1 - CPR)^{\frac{1}{12}}.$$

Percentage of PSA. If a mortgage prepays at a rate of 100% PSA, then the CPR for the month when the mortgage is n months old is

$$CPR = 6\% \times \frac{n}{30} \qquad \text{if } n \le 30$$

$$= 6\% \qquad \text{if } n > 30$$

$$= 6\% \times Min\left(1, \frac{n}{30}\right) \qquad \text{for any } n.$$

For a general prepayment rate of $x\%$ PSA, for age n,

$$CPR = 6\% \times \frac{x}{100} \times \frac{n}{30} \qquad \text{if } n \le 30$$

$$= 6\% \times \frac{x}{100} \qquad \text{if } n > 30$$

$$= 6\% \times \frac{x}{100} \times Min\left(1, \frac{n}{30}\right) \qquad \text{for any } n.$$

Conversely, if a mortgage of age n months prepays at a given CPR, the PSA rate for that month is given by

$$\% \text{ of } PSA = CPR \times \frac{100}{6} \times \frac{30}{n} \qquad \text{if } n \le 30$$

$$= CPR \times \frac{100}{6} \qquad \text{if } n > 30$$

$$= CPR \times \frac{100}{6} \times Max\left(1, \frac{30}{n}\right) \qquad \text{for any } n.$$

Mortgage Cash Flow with Prepayments

Let $\hat{M}_n$, $\hat{P}_n$, $\hat{I}_n$, and $\hat{B}_n$ denote the actual monthly scheduled payment, scheduled principal, interest and remaining (end-of-month) balance for month n. Let SMM_n be the prepayment rate in month n, stated as a decimal, and let

$$Q_n = (1 - SMM_n)(1 - SMM_{n-1}) \ldots (1 - SMM_1).$$

The *total monthly payment* in month n is given by

$$\hat{M}_n = \frac{\hat{B}_{n-1}\left(\dfrac{G}{1200}\right)\left(1 + \dfrac{G}{1200}\right)^{N-n+1}}{\left[(1 + \dfrac{G}{1200})^{N-n+1} - 1\right]} = M_n Q_{n-1}.$$

The *scheduled principal* portion of this payment is given by

$$\hat{P}_n = \frac{\hat{B}_{n-1}\left(\dfrac{G}{1200}\right)}{\left[\left(1 + \dfrac{G}{1200}\right)^{N-n+1} - 1\right]} = P_n Q_{n-1}.$$

The *interest* portion is given by

$$\hat{I}_n = \hat{B}_{n-1}\left(\frac{G}{1200}\right) = I_n Q_{n-1}.$$

The *unscheduled principal payment* in month n is written as

$$PR_n = (\hat{B}_{n-1} - \hat{P}_n)\, SMM_n.$$

The *remaining balance* is given by

$$\hat{B}_n = \hat{B}_{n-1} - \hat{P}_n - PR_n = B_n Q_n.$$

The total cash flow to the investor is

$$\hat{CF}_n = \hat{P} + PR_n + \left(\frac{C}{C + S}\right)\hat{I}_n.$$

Average Life

Average life assigns weights to principal paydowns according to their arrival dates.

$$\text{Average Life (in years)} = \frac{1}{12} \sum_{t=1}^{N} \frac{(t + \alpha - 1)(Principal_t)}{\sum_{t=1}^{N} Principal_t}$$

where

$$
\begin{aligned}
t &= \text{Time subscript, } t = 1, \ldots N. \\
Principal_t &= \text{Principal arriving at time } t. \\
N &= \text{Number of months until last principal cash flow comes in.} \\
\alpha &= \text{Days between settlement date and first cash flow date,} \\
&\quad \text{divided by 30 } (i.e., \text{ the fraction of a month between settle-} \\
&\quad \text{ment date and first cash flow date).}
\end{aligned}
$$

Macaulay Duration

Duration assigns time weights to the present values of all cash flows.

$$\text{Macaulay Duration (in years)} = \frac{1}{12} \sum_{t=1}^{N} \frac{\dfrac{(t + \alpha - 1) C(t)}{(1 + r/1200)^{t + \alpha - 1}}}{\sum_{t=1}^{N} \dfrac{C(t)}{(1 + r/1200)^{t + \alpha - 1}}}$$

where

$$
\begin{aligned}
C(t) &= \text{Cash flow at time } t. \\
r &= \text{Cash flow yield of mortgage (\%).}
\end{aligned}
$$

Cash Flow Yield

To obtain the cash flow yield, the present value of the security's cash flows on the settlement date is equated to its initial price P plus its accrued interest I.

$$P + I = \sum_{t=1}^{N} \frac{C(t)}{(1 + r/1200)^{t + \alpha - 1}}.$$

This equation is solved iteratively for r. The solution is called the *mortgage yield*.

Bond-Equivalent Yield

The interest on a mortgage security is compounded monthly, whereas the interest on bonds such as Treasuries and corporates is compounded semiannually. The compounding frequency is reflected in the yield of a security. Therefore, to make mortgage yields and bond yields comparable, the yield of a mortgage is normally converted to a bond-equivalent yield, *i.e.*, a yield based on semiannual compounding of the mortgage's interest payments.

A yield based on monthly compounding can be converted to a bond-equivalent yield and vice versa as follows:

r = Mortgage yield based on monthly compounding (%).

y = Bond-equivalent yield (%).

$$y = 200 \left[\left(1 + \frac{r}{1200} \right)^6 - 1 \right],$$

$$r = 1200 \left[\left(1 + \frac{y}{200} \right)^{1/6} - 1 \right].$$

Total Return

$$y_h = \begin{array}{c} \text{Total return} \\ \text{over a holding period } h \\ \text{(percent)} \end{array} = \frac{\begin{array}{c} \text{Sales} \\ \text{proceeds} \\ \text{paid} \end{array} - \begin{array}{c} \text{Total} \\ \text{price} \\ \end{array} + \begin{array}{c} \text{Total net cash flow} \\ \text{received during} \\ \text{the holding period} \end{array} + \begin{array}{c} \text{Total reinvestment} \\ \text{income during} \\ \text{the holding period} \end{array}}{\text{Total price paid}} \times 100 \,.$$

The bond-equivalent total return rate y_{BE} is given by

$$\left(1 + \frac{Y_h}{100} \right)^{12/h} = \left(1 + \frac{y_{BE}}{200} \right)^2 \,.$$

Modified Duration

Modified duration is given by

$$Modified\ Duration = \frac{Macaulay\ Duration}{1 + y/200}$$

where y = Bond-equivalent yield (%).

Index

J-K

L